ISC Exams 2026

All in One®

Chemistry

Class 12

Simplified Theory

Topic & Chapter Exercises

Exam Pattern Questions

Specimen & Sample Papers

Authors
Saleha Parvez

Co-Authors
Vandana

arihant
SUCCESS AND NOTHING LESS

arihant
SUCCESS AND NOTHING LESS

ARIHANT PRAKASHAN
(School Division Series)

卐 ADMINISTRATIVE & PRODUCTION OFFICES
Regd. Office
'Ramchhaya' 4577/15, Agarwal Road, Darya Ganj, New Delhi -110002
Tele: 011- 47630600, 43518550; Fax: 011- 23280316
卐 *Head Office*
Kalindi, TP Nagar, Meerut (UP) - 250002, Tel: 0121-7156203, 7156204

卐 SALES & SUPPORT OFFICES
Agra, Ahmedabad, Bengaluru, Bareilly, Chennai, Delhi, Guwahati, Hyderabad, Jaipur, Jhansi, Kolkata, Lucknow, Nagpur & Pune.

PO No : TXT-XX-XXXXXXX-X-XX

Published By Arihant Publications (India) Ltd.

For further information about the books published by Arihant, log on to www.arihantbooks.com or e-mail at info@arihantbooks.com
Follow us on

卐 PRICE ₹490.00

PRODUCTION TEAM

Publishing Managers
Mahendra Singh Rawat & Keshav Mohan

Cover Designer
Salman Shaikh

Inner Designer
Ankit Tyagi

Project Head
Akansha Tomar

Page Layouting
Sanjay Yadav

Proof Reader
Sarthak

Index *cum* Study Planner

One Book- Endless Features

to Help you Succeed

In this Chapter

At the start of each chapter, all the chapter topics have been listed, so that students may know what they are going to study.

CHAPTER 01

Solutions

In our daily life, we usually come across the substances which are mixtures of two or more pure substances. Solution is one of the most important classes of mixtures which is homogeneous in composition and properties.

- Solutions, Terms Expressing Concentration of Solutions
- Solubility
- Vapour Pressure of Liquid Solutions
- Colligative Properties and Determination of Molar Mass

Complete Theory in Each Chapter

To make the students understand the chapter completely, each chapter has been divided into Individual Topics and each topic has detailed theory, supported by examples, well labelled diagrams, tables etc.

TOPIC 01 **Solutions, Terms Expressing Concentration of Solutions**

(i) A solution is a homogeneous mixture of two or more substances whose composition can be varied within certain limits. Here, homogeneous mixture means that its composition and properties are uniform throughout the mixture. In such a mixture, the component that is present in the largest quantity is known as **solvent**.

(ii) The one or more components present in the solution other than the solvent are called **solute**.

(iii) The physical state in which solution exists is determined by the state of solvent.

Types of solutions

On the basis of solvent, the solution may be of the following types:

(i) **Aqueous Solution** When solute is dissolved in water, it is known as aqueous solution, e.g. ethanol in water.

(ii) **Non-aqueous Solution** When solute is dissolved in a solvent other than water, it is known as non-aqueous solution, e.g. iodine in alcohol (tincture of iodine).

Solved Examples

To explain the application of concept, Solved Examples have been given in between the theory. These examples have been solved in Step-by-Step manner, so that students can learn the problem solving process completely.

Example 1 Calculate the mass percentage of benzene (C_6H_6) and carbon tetrachloride (CCl_4), if 22 g of benzene is dissolved in 122 g of CCl_4. **NCERT Intext**

Sol. Mass of solution = Mass of benzene + Mass of carbon tetrachloride

$$= (22 + 122) \text{g} = 144 \text{ g}$$

$$\text{Mass \% of benzene} = \frac{\text{Mass of benzene}}{\text{Mass of solution}} \times 100$$

$$= \frac{22}{144} \times 100 = 15.28\%$$

$$\text{Mass \% of } CCl_4 = \frac{\text{Mass of } CCl_4}{\text{Mass of solution}} \times 100$$

$$= \frac{122}{144} \times 100 = 84.72\%$$

One Book- Endless Features
to Help you Succeed

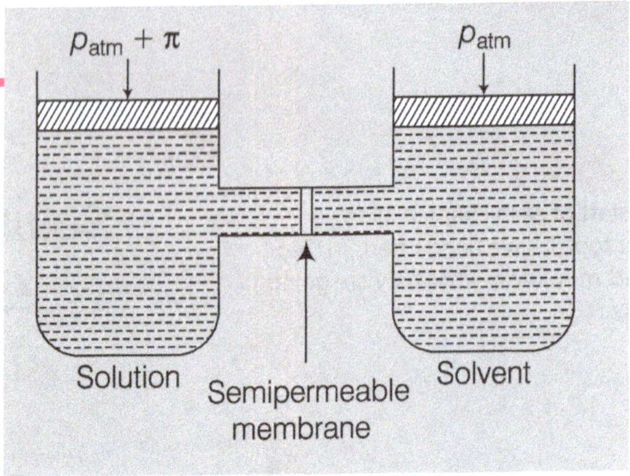

Illustrative Figures

To make the concepts completely visible, illustrative diagrams have been given at various place.

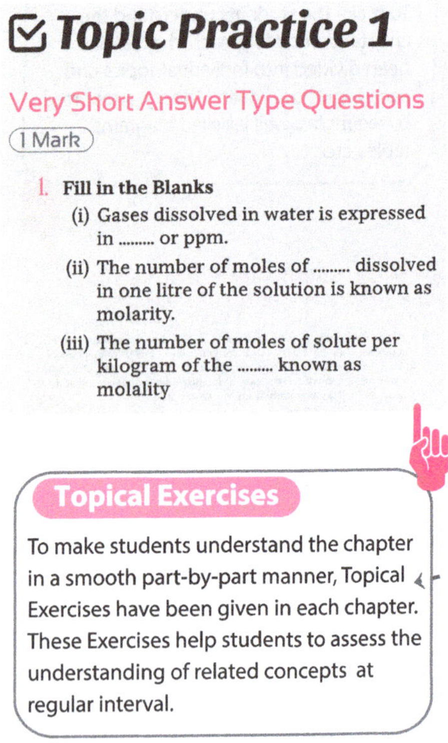
Topic Practice 1

Very Short Answer Type Questions

1 Mark

1. **Fill in the Blanks**
   (i) Gases dissolved in water is expressed in .... or ppm.
   (ii) The number of moles of .... dissolved in one litre of the solution is known as molarity.
   (iii) The number of moles of solute per kilogram of the .... known as molality

Topical Exercises

To make students understand the chapter in a smooth part-by-part manner, Topical Exercises have been given in each chapter. These Exercises help students to assess the understanding of related concepts at regular interval.

Chapter Summary

Summary of chapter given at the end of each chapter helps to revise the chapter quickly at the time of examination or routine school tests.

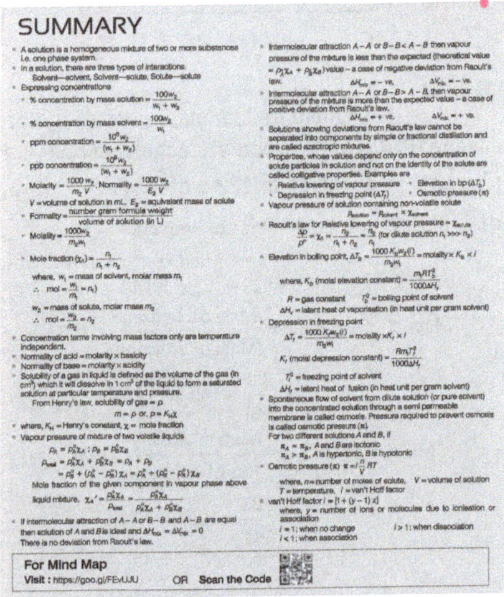
SUMMARY

For Mind Map
Visit : https://goo.gl/FEvUJU OR Scan the Code

One Book- Endless Features

to Help you Succeed

Chapter Practice

The students can check their understanding of the chapter through Chapter Practice given at the end of each chapter.

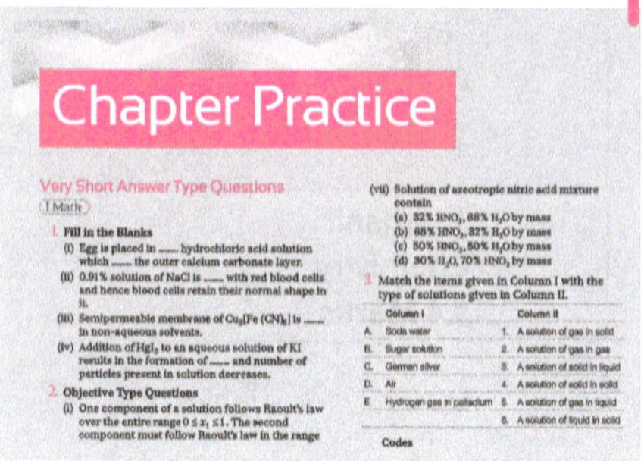

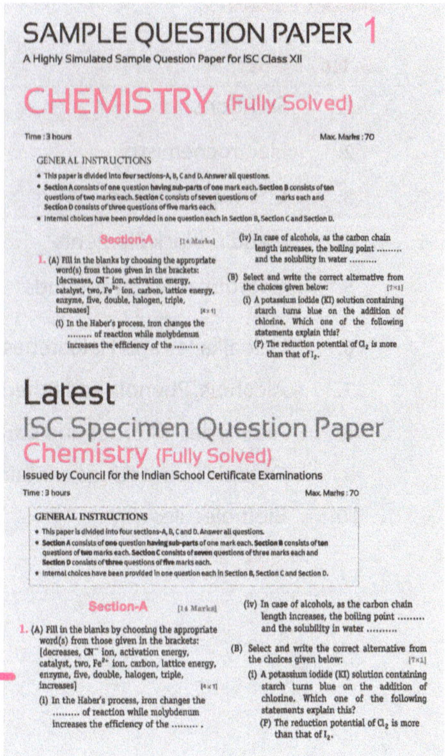

Sample Question Papers & Latest ISC Specimen Paper

Chapterwise study is not the only feature of this book, after the Chapterwise Study it has a supplement of **3 Sample Question Papers** and **Latest ISC Specimen Paper.**

Latest Course *Structure*

There will be two papers in the subject.

Paper I	Theory : 3 Hours	70 Marks
Paper II	Practical : 3 Hours	15 Marks
	Project Work	10 Marks
	Practical File	5 Marks

PAPER THEORY — 70 Marks

S. No.	UNIT	TOTAL WEIGHTAGE
1.	Solutions	Physical Chemistry **25 Marks**
2.	Electrochemistry	
3.	Chemical Kinetics	
4.	*d* and *f* -Block Elements	Inorganic Chemistry **14 Marks**
5.	Coordination Compounds	
6.	Haloalkanes and Haloarenes	Organic Chemistry **31 Marks**
7.	Alcohols, Phenols and Ethers	
8.	Aldehydes, Ketones and Carboxylic Acids	
9.	Organic Compounds containing Nitrogen	
10.	Biomolecules	
	TOTAL	**70 Marks**

1. SOLUTIONS

Study of concentration of solutions of solids in liquids, liquid in liquid, solubility of gases in liquids, solid solutions, Colligative properties - Raoult's law of relative lowering of vapour pressure (1st & 2nd), elevation of boiling point, depression of freezing point, osmotic pressure. Use of colligative properties in determining molecular masses of solutes, abnormal molecular mass association and dissociation, van't Hoff factor.

Normality, molality, molarity, mole fraction, ppm, as measures of concentration. Definition of the above with examples. Simple problems based on the above.

(i) Solubility of gases in liquids – Henry's Law, simple numericals based on the above.

(ii) Raoult's Law for volatile solutes and non volatile solutes, ideal solution, non-ideal solution. Azeotropic mixtures – definition, types, graphical representation, fractional distillation with examples.

(iii) Colligative properties – definition and examples, and its use in determination of molecular mass.

(a) Relative lowering of vapour pressure: Definition and mathematical expression of Raoult's Law. Determination of relative molecular mass by measurement of lowering of vapour pressure.

(b) Depression in freezing point: molal depression constant (cryoscopic constant) – definition and mathematical expression (derivation included).

(c) Elevation in boiling point method: molal elevation constant (ebullioscopic constant) definition and mathematical expression (derivation included).

(d) Osmotic pressure: definition and explanation. Natural and chemical semipermeable membranes, reverse osmosis, isotonic, hypotonic and hypertonic solutions. Comparison between diffusion and osmosis. Application of osmotic pressure in the determination of relative molecular mass.
van't Hoff- Boyle's Law, van't Hoff – Charles' Law, van't Hoff - Avogadro's law.

(e) Abnormal molecular mass: Dissociation and Association with suitable examples.

(f) van't Hoff factor for the electrolytes which dissociate and the molecules which associate in solution. Modification of the formula of colligative 178 *properties based on van't Hoff factor. Simple problems. Calculation of degree of dissociation and association. Experimental details not required.*

Numerical problems based on all the above methods. Experimental details not required.

2. ELECTROCHEMISTRY

Electrolytic and electrochemical cells. Redox reactions in electrochemical cells. Electromotive Force (emf) of a cell, standard electrode potential, Nernst equation and its application to chemical cells. Relation between Gibb's energy change and emf of a cell.

Conductance in electrolytic solutions, specific, equivalent and molar conductivity, variations of conductivity with concentration, graphs; Kohlrausch's Law of electrolysis and Faraday's Laws of electrolysis. Dry cell and lead accumulator, fuel cells, corrosion.

(i) Electrochemical cells: introduction, redox reactions (principle of oxidation and reduction in a cell).

(ii) Galvanic cells - introduction; representation, principle – oxidation reduction. Mechanism of production of electric current in a galvanic cell.

(iii) Measurement of potential. Single electrode potentials. Standard hydrogen electrode (E^o) - definition, preparation, application and limitations.

Standard electrode potential - Measurement of standard electrode potential of Zn^{++} / Zn , Cu^{++} / Cu, *half cell (using standard hydrogen electrode).*

Cell notation – representation. Factors affecting electrode potential with explanation - main emphasis on the temperature, concentration and nature of the electrode.

(iv) Electrochemical series. Its explanation on the basis of standard reduction potential. Prediction of the feasibility of a reaction.

(v) Nernst equation and correlation with the free energy of the reaction with suitable examples.

Prediction of spontaneity of a reaction based on the cell emf.

Numericals on standard electrode potential of half-cells, cell emf, relationship between free energy and equilibrium constant, standard electrode potential and free energy.

(vi) Comparison of metallic conductance and electrolytic conductance. Relationship between conductance and resistance. Specific resistance and specific conductance.

Cell constant: Calculation of cell constant. Meaning of equivalent conductance. Meaning of molar conductance. General relationship between specific conductance, molar conductance and equivalent conductance (units and graphs).

Units, numericals. Molar conductance of a weak electrolyte at a given concentration and at infinite dilution. Kohlrausch's Law – definition, applications and numericals.

(vii) *Faraday's laws of Electrolysis. Faraday's First Law of electrolysis. Statement, mathematical form. Simple problems. Faraday's Second Law of electrolysis: Statement, mathematical form. Simple problems. Relation between Faraday, Avogadro's number and charge on an electron. $F = N_A e$ should be given (no details of Millikan's experiment are required).*

(viii) *Batteries: Primary and Secondary Cells: Leclanche cell, mercury cell, Lead storage battery and fuel cell – structure, reactions and uses.*

(ix) *Corrosion: Concept, mechanism of electrochemical reaction, factors affecting it and its prevention.*

3. CHEMICAL KINETICS

Meaning of Chemical Kinetics – slow and fast reactions. Rate of a reaction - average and instantaneous rate (graphical representation). Factors affecting rate of reaction: surface area, nature of reactants, concentration, temperature, catalyst and radiation. Order and molecularity of a reaction, rate law and specific rate constant. Integrated rate equations and half-life (only for zero and first order reactions), concept of collision theory (elementary idea, no mathematical treatment). Concept of threshold and activation energy, Arrhenius equation.

(i) *Meaning of chemical kinetics, Scope and importance of Kinetics of the reaction, slow and fast reactions – explanation in terms of bonds.*

(ii) *Rate of Reaction: definition, representation of rate of reaction in terms of reactants and products, determination of rate of reactions graphically, instantaneous and average rate of reaction. Factors affecting rate of reaction.*

(iii) *Law of mass Action: statement and meaning of active mass. Explanation with an example – general reactions.*

(iv) *Effect of concentration of reactants on the rate of a reaction: Qualitative treatment, based on the law of mass action, statement of rate law, General rate equation – Rate = k(concentration of the reactant)$_n$, where k is rate constant and n is the order of the reaction, relationship between the rate of the reaction with rate constant with respect to various reactants.*

(v) *Order of a reaction: meaning, relation between order and stoichiometric coefficients in balanced equations, order as an experimental quantity, rate equation for zero order reaction and its unit, mathematical derivation of rate equation for first order reaction, characteristics of first order reaction – rate constant is independent of the initial concentration, units to be derived, definition of half-life period, derivation of expression of half-life period from first order rate equation.*

Problems based on first order rate equation and half-life period.

(vi) *Molecularity of the reaction: Meaning – physical picture, relation between order, molecularity and the rate of a reaction, Differences between order and molecularity of a reaction.*

(vii) *The concept of energy: Exothermic and endothermic reactions, concept of energy barrier, threshold and activation energy, formation of activated complex, effect of catalyst on activation energy and reaction rate.*

(viii) *Collision theory: Condition for a chemical change – close contact, particles should collide. Collisions to be effective – optimum energy and proper orientation during collision. Energy barrier built-up when the collision is about to take place, Activated complex formation, difference in energy of the reactant and the product – exothermic and endothermic reactions with proper graphs and labelling.*

(ix) *Mechanism of the reaction: meaning of elementary reaction, meaning of complex and overall reaction, explanation of the mechanism of the reaction, slowest step of the reaction. Relationship between the rate expression, order of reactants and products at the rate-determining step, units of rate constant – explanation with suitable examples.*

(x) *Effect of temperature on the rate constant of a reaction: Arrhenius equation –$K=Ae^{Ea/RT}$, meaning of the symbols of Arrhenius equation, related graph, evaluation of E_a and A from the graph, meaning of slope of the graph, conversion from exponential to log form of the equation, relationship between the increase in temperature and the number of collisions. Numerical based on Arrhenius equation.*

4. *d* and *f*-BLOCK ELEMENTS

Position in the periodic table, occurrence, electronic configuration and characteristics of transition metals, general trends in properties of the 3*d*-series of transition metals - metallic character, ionisation enthalpy, oxidation states, ionic radii, colour of ions, catalytic property, magnetic properties, interstitial compounds, alloy formation, preparation and properties of $K_2Cr_2O_7$ and $KMnO_4$.

Lanthanoids and actinoids

(i) *d-Block: 3d, 4d and 5d series Study in terms of metallic character, atomic and ionic radii, ionisation enthalpy, oxidisation states, variable valency, formation of coloured compounds, formation of complexes, alloy formation.*

(ii) *f-Block: 4f and 5f series: Electronic configuration, atomic and ionic radii, oxidisation states, formation of coloured compounds, formation of complexes, alloy formation. Lanthanoid contraction and its consequences. Chemical reactivity – with oxygen, hydrogen, halogen, sulphur, nitrogen, carbon and water. Actinoids - oxidation states and comparison with lanthanoids.*

(iii) *Potassium permanganate: structure, shape, equation of extraction from pyrolusite ore, its oxidising nature in acidic, basic and neutral medium, use in redox titration. Oxidising nature in acidic* [$FeSO_4$, $(COOH)_2.2H_2O$, KI], *basic* (KI) *and neutral* (H_2S) *mediums to be done.*

(iv) *Potassium dichromate: structure, shape, equation of extraction from chromite ore and its use in titration. Oxidising nature in acidic, basic and neutral medium, use in redox titration. Interconversion of chromate and dichromate ion (effect of* pH*).*

5. COORDINATION COMPOUNDS

Concept of complexes, definition of ligands, coordination number, oxidation number. IUPAC nomenclature of mononuclear coordination compounds. Isomerism (structural and stereo). Bonding, Werner's theory, VBT and CFT. Colour, magnetic properties and shapes. Importance of coordination compounds (in qualitative analysis, extraction of metals and biological system).

(i) *Definition of coordination compounds / complex compounds, differences with a double salt, study of ligands – mono-, bi-, tri- , tetra-, penta-, hexa- and polydentate, chelating ligands, definition of coordination number, its calculation for a complex coordination sphere, study of oxidation state of an element in a complex, its calculation, IUPAC rules of nomenclature of coordination compounds.*

(ii) *Isomerism – structural, stereo types and examples.*

(iii) *Valence bond theory of coordination compounds – examples of formation of inner orbital and outer orbital complexes (high and low spin, octahedral, tetrahedral and square planar), prediction of magnetic character.*

(iv) *Crystal field theory – crystal field splitting in tetra and octahedral systems. Explanation of colour and magnetic character.*

(v) *Stability of coordination compounds (explain stability on the basis of magnitude of K) as mentioned above.*

(vi) *Importance and uses.*

6. HALOALKANES AND HALOARENES

Haloalkanes: General formula, nomenclature and classification. Nature of C–*X* bond, physical and chemical properties, mechanism of substitution reactions, optical rotation.

Haloarenes: Basic idea, nature of C–*X* bond, substitution reactions (directive influence of halogen in monosubstituted compounds only).

Uses and environmental effects of - dichloromethane, trichloromethane, tetrachloromethane, iodoform, freons & DDT.

Nature of C-X bond

Naming the halogen derivatives of alkanes by using common system and IUPAC system for mono, di and tri-halo derivatives.

Preparation of haloalkanes from:

Alkane and halogen, Alkene and hydrogen halide, Alcohols with PX_3, PCl_5 *and* $SOCl_2$ *, Halide exchange method (Finkelstein and Swarts), Silver salt of fatty acids (Hunsdiecker).*

Physical properties: *state, melting point, boiling point and solubility.*

Chemical properties: *nucleophilic substitution reactions* (S_N1, S_N2 *mechanism in terms of primary, secondary and tertiary halides). Reaction with: sodium hydroxide, water, sodium iodide, ammonia, primary amine, secondary amine, potassium cyanide, silver cyanide, potassium nitrite, silver nitrite, silver salt of fatty acid and lithium-aluminium hydride.*

Elimination reaction (Saytzeff's rule) / β-elimination. Reaction with metals: sodium and magnesium (Wurtz's reaction, Grignard's reagent preparation). Chloroform and iodoform: preparation and properties. Structure of freons. Preparation of haloarenes by Sandmeyer's and Gattermann's reaction, by electrophilic substitution.

Physical properties: *State, melting point, boiling point and solubility.*

Chemical properties:

Electrophilic substitution (chlorination nitration and sulphonation) with mechanism, Nucleophilic substitution (replacement of chlorine with -OH, -NH_2*) with mechanism, Reduction to benzene, Wurtz-Fittig reaction, Fittig reaction, Addition reaction with magnesium (formation of Grignard reagent), Structure of DDT.*

7. ALCOHOLS, PHENOLS AND ETHERS

Alcohols: Classification, general formula, structure and nomenclature. Methods of preparation, physical and chemical properties (of primary alcohols only), identification of primary, secondary and tertiary alcohols, mechanism of dehydration, uses with special reference to methanol and ethanol.

(i) *Classification into monohydric, dihydric and polyhydric alcohols, general formulae, structure and nomenclature of alcohols. Difference between primary, secondary and tertiary alcohols in terms of structure, physical properties and chemical properties.*

(ii) *Methods of preparation:*

Hydration of Alkenes – direct hydration, indirect hydration, hydroboration oxidation, From Grignard's reagent, Hydrolysis of alkyl halides, Reduction of carbonyl compounds, From primary amines.

Manufacture of methanol by Bosch process and ethanol by fermentation of carbohydrates, chemical equations required (only outline of the method of manufacture, detail not required).

Properties:

Acidic nature of alcohols:, Reaction with sodium, Esterification with mechanism, Reaction with hydrogen halides.

Reaction with PCl_3, PCl_5, *and* $SOCl_2$, *Reaction with acid chlorides and acid anhydrides, Oxidation, Dehydration with mechanism.*

Uses of alcohols.

(iii) *Conversion of one alcohol into another.*

(iv) *Distinction between primary, secondary and tertiary alcohols by Lucas' test.*

Phenols: Classification and nomenclature. Methods of preparation, physical and chemical properties, acidic nature of phenol, electrophilic substitution reactions, uses of phenols.

Preparation of phenol from diazonium salt, chlorobenzene (Dow's process) and from benzene sulphonic acid. Manufacture from Cumene.

Physical properties: state and solubility.

Chemical properties:

Acidic character of phenol, Reaction with sodium hydroxide, Reaction with sodium, Reaction with zinc, Reaction with acetyl chloride and acetic anhydride, Reaction with phosphorus penta chloride, Bromination, nitration and sulphonation (Electrophilic substitution reactions), Kolbe's reaction (formation of salicylic acid), Reimer – Tiemann reaction, Test for phenol – $FeCl_3$ *test, azo dye test.*

Aliphatic Ethers: General formula, structure and nomenclature. Methods of preparation, physical and chemical properties, uses.

Ethers: structure of ethereal group. Preparation from alcohol (Williamson's synthesis).

Physical properties: state, miscibility.

Chemical properties:

Reaction with chlorine, Oxidation (peroxide formation), Reaction with HI, *Reaction with* PCl_5.

Aryl Ethers

Physical properties – state and solubility.

Chemical properties – preparation of anisole (Williamson's synthesis), electrophilic substitution (halogenation, nitration and Friedel-Crafts reaction.) Uses of ether.

8. ALDEHYDES, KETONES AND CARBOXYLIC ACIDS

Aldehydes and Ketones : Nomenclature, structure of methods of preparation of aldehydes and ketones, physical and chemical properties, mechanism of nucleophilic addition, reactivity of alpha hydrogen in aldehydes and uses.

Preparation: *From alcohol, From alkenes (ozonolysis), From alkynes (hydration), From acid chlorides (Rosenmund's reduction, reaction with dialkyl cadmium), From calcium salt of carboxylic acids, From nitriles (Stephen reaction, Grignard's reagent), From esters.*

Physical properties – state and boiling point.

Chemical properties: *Nucleophilic addition reactions with mechanism (ammonia and its derivatives,* HCN, $NaHSO_3$ *and Grignard's reagent), Oxidation reactions, iodoform reaction, Reduction: reduction to alcohol and alkanes (Clemmensen's reduction, Wolff-Kishner reduction, red phosphorus and* HI*), Base catalysed reactions (with mechanism): Aldol condensation, cross Aldol condensation, Cannizzaro's reaction.*

Tests: *difference between formaldehyde and acetaldehyde; aldehydes and ketones.*

Uses of aldehydes and ketones.

Aromatic aldehyde (Benzaldehyde)

Lab preparation from toluene by oxidation with chromyl chloride.

Physical properties: *state and stability.*

Chemical properties: *Oxidation and reduction, Nucleophilic addition reaction (hydrogen cyanide and sodium bisulphite), Reactions with ammonia and its derivatives (hydroxyl amine, hydrazine and phenyl hydrazine), Reaction with phosphorus pentachloride, Cannizzaro reaction, Benzoin condensation, Perkin's reaction, Electrophilic substitution - halogenation, nitration and sulphonation.*

Test: *distinction between aromatic and aliphatic aldehydes.*

Uses of benzaldehyde.

Carboxylic Acids: Classification, general formula and structure of carboxylic group. Nomenclature, acidic nature, methods of preparation, physical and chemical properties and uses.

Classification of mono and di carboxylic acids with examples.

Preparation of aliphatic and aromatic carboxylic acid:

From alcohols, aldehydes, From nitriles, From Grignard's reagent.

Physical properties: state, boiling point and solubility.

Chemical properties:

Acidic character: (aliphatic, aromatic carboxylic acids with the effect of substituents on the acidic character – to be dealt with in detail), Reaction with active metals, alkalies, carbonates and bicarbonates, Formation of acid derivatives.

Decarboxylation (chemical and Kolbe's electrolytic reaction), HVZ reactions, Substitution of benzene ring (meta directive effect of carboxylic acid group) nitration and sulphonation.

Tests for acids: formic acid, acetic acid and benzoic acid.

Uses of formic acid, acetic acid and benzoic acid.

9. ORGANIC COMPOUNDS CONTAINING NITROGEN

Aliphatic amines: General formula and, classification of amines. Structure of the amino group, nomenclature. Methods of preparation, physical and chemical properties, uses, identification of primary, secondary and tertiary amines.

Amines

Nomenclature, classification with examples, structure, general formula.

Methods of preparation:

From alcohol, From alkyl halide, From cyanide, From amide (Hofmann's degradation), From nitro compounds, Gabriel phthalimide synthesis.

Physical properties: comparison between primary, secondary and tertiary amines in terms of – state, solubility, boiling point (hydrogen bonding), comparison with alcohols.

Chemical properties:

Basic character of amines – comparison between primary, secondary and tertiary alkyl amines/ ammonia/ aniline. Effect of substituents on the basic strength of aniline, Alkylation and acylation with mechanism, Reaction with nitrous acid, Carbylamine reaction.

Distinction between primary, secondary and tertiary amines (Hinsberg's Test).

Aniline

Preparation reduction of nitrobenzene.

Physical properties – state, solubility and boiling point.

Chemical properties:

Reaction with HCl and H_2SO_4, Acetylation, alkylation, Benzoylation, Carbylamine reaction, Diazotisation, Electrophilic substitution (bromination, nitration and sulphonation)

Tests for aniline.

Uses of aniline.

Cyanides and Isocyanides

Methods of preparation:

Cyanides:

From alkyl halide, From amide, Isocyanides, From alkyl halide, From primary amines

Diazonium salts: Preparation, chemical reactions and importance in synthetic organic chemistry.

Preparation from aniline;

Properties: Sandmeyer's reaction, Gattermann reaction and Balz – Scheimann reaction, replacement of diazo group by –H, –OH,–NO_2, coupling reaction with phenol and aniline.

10. BIOMOLECULES

Carbohydrates – Definition, classification (aldoses and ketoses), monosaccahrides (glucose and fructose), D-L configuration oligosaccharides (sucrose, lactose, maltose), polysaccharides (starch, cellulose, glycogen); Importance of carbohydrates.

Carbohydrates: definition, classification - mono (aldose, ketose), oligo (di, tri, tetra saccharides) and polysaccharides with examples: reducing sugars and non reducing sugars – examples and uses.

Establishment of structures for glucose and fructose (open and cyclic).heating with HI, reaction with hydroxylamine, bromine water, acetic anhydride, nitric acid and phenyl hydrazine.

Test for glucose and fructose (bromine water test with equation).

Disaccharides – structures of sucrose, maltose and lactose (glycosidic linkage).

Polysaccharides – starch, cellulose, glycogen.

Proteins – structural units of proteins. Basic idea of - amino acids, peptide bond, polypeptides, proteins, structure of proteins - primary, secondary, tertiary structure and quaternary structures (qualitative idea only), denaturation of proteins. Enzymes, hormones - elementary idea only.

Proteins: Amino acids – general structure, classification and zwitter ion formation. Isoelectric point. Classification of proteins on the basis of molecular shape; primary, secondary, tertiary and quaternary, structures of proteins, denaturation of proteins. (Definitions only. Details and diagrams are not required).

Vitamins - Classification and functions.

Vitamins A, B, C, D, E and K: classification (fat soluble and water soluble), deficiency diseases. (Chemical names and structures are not required).

Nucleic Acids - DNA and RNA.

Nucleic acids: basic unit – purine and pyrimidine, DNA – structure (double helical), RNA (No chemical structure required). Differences between DNA and RNA.

List of
Important Topics
from each chapter

On the basis of analysis of last 8 years' board examination papers, we have identified important topics from each chapter.

Chapter 1: Solutions

- Ideal Solution
  (Average Marks in last 8 years ; 2025 - 3 Marks, 2023 - 1 Mark)
- Colligative Properties and Relative Molecular Mass of Non-volatile Substance
  (Average marks in last 8 years; 2025 -11 Marks, 2024 - 9 Marks, 2023 - 7 Marks, 2020 - 10 Marks, 2019 - 9 Marks, 2018 - 9 Marks)

Chapter 2: Electrochemistry

- Faraday's Law of Electrolysis
  (Average Marks in last 8 years, 2025 -2 Marks, 2024 - 2 Marks, 2023 - 2 Marks, 2019 - 2 Marks)
- Electrochemical Cells, Galvanic Cell
  (Average Marks in last 8 years; 2025 -5 Marks, 2024 - 1 Mark, 2023 - 1 Mark, 2018 - 1 Mark)
- Electrode Potential and Nernst equation
  (Average Marks in last 8 years; 2025 -3 Marks, 2024 - 5 Marks, 2023 - 5 Marks, 2020 - 3 Marks, 2019 - 4 Marks, 2018 - 5 Marks)
- Conductance of Electrolytic Solution
  (Average Marks in last 8 years; 2025 -1 Mark, 2024 - 6 Marks, 2023 - 3 Marks; 2019 - 4 Marks)

Chapter 3: Chemical Kinetics

- Rate of Reaction Order
  (Average Marks in last 8 years; 2025 -8 Marks, 2024 - 1 Mark, 2019 - 2 Marks; 2018 - 2 Marks)
- Integrated Rate of Equation and Half-life
  (Average Marks in last 8 years; 2024 - 4 Marks, 2023 - 4 Marks, 2019 - 5 Marks, 2018 - 2 Marks)
- Activation Energy and Catalysis
  (Average Marks in last 8 years; 2024 - 2 Marks, 2023 - 4 Marks, 2020 - 4 Marks, 2019 - 1 Mark, 2018 - 3 Marks)

Chapter 4: *d* and *f* Block Elements

- Chemistry of Transition Elements
  (Average Marks in last 8 years; 2025 -4 Marks, 2024 - 5 Marks, 2023-4 Marks, 2020 - 4 Marks, 2019 - 4 Marks, 2018 - 4 Marks)
- Inner Transition Elements Chemistry
  (Average Marks in last 8 years; 2025 -1 Mark, 2024 - 1 Mark, 2023 - 1 Mark, 2019 - 1 Mark, 2018 - 3 Marks)
- Compounds $KMnO_4$ and $K_2Cr_2O_7$
  (Average Marks in last 8 years; 2025 -2 Marks, 2024 - 1 Mark, 2023 - 2 Marks, 2020 - 1 Mark, 2019 - 3 Marks, 2018 - 3 Marks)

Chapter 5: Coordination Compounds

- Oxidation State and IUPAC Name
  (Average Marks in last 8 years; 2024 - 2 Marks, 2023 - 2 Marks, 2020 - 3 Marks, 2019 - 4 Marks 2018 - 3 Marks)
- Ligand and Coordination Number
  (Average Marks in last 8 years; 2025 -1 Mark, 2024 - 2 Marks, 2023 - 2 Marks)
- Isomerism
  (Average Mark in last 8 years; 2025 -2 Marks, 2024 - 3 Marks, 2023 - 3 Marks, 2020 - 3 Marks, 2018 - 2 Marks)
- VBT, Hybridisation and Magnetic Behaviour
  (Average Marks in last 8 years; 2025 -1 Mark, 2020 - 5 Marks, 2018 - 1 Mark)

Chapter 6: Haloalkane and Haloarenes

- Haloalkanes - Preparation
  (Average Marks in last 8 years; 2025 - 2 Marks, 2023 - 3 Marks, 2020 - 1 Mark)
- Properties of Haloalkanes and Haloarenes
  (Average Marks in last 8 years; 2025 - 3.5 Marks, 2024 - 3 Marks, 2023 - 1 Mark, 2020 - 1 Mark, 2019 - 2 Marks, 2018 - 1 Mark)
- Crystal Field Theory
  (Average Marks in last 8 years; 2025 - 3 Marks)

Chapter 7: Alcohols, Phenols and Ethers

- Alcohols
  (Average Marks in last 8 years; 2025 - 3 Marks, 2024 - 9 Marks, 2023 - 4 Marks, 2020 - 4 Marks, 2019 - 2 Marks, 2018 - 2 Marks)
- Phenols
  (Average Marks in last 8 years; 2025 - 5 Marks, 2024 - 2 Marks, 2023 - 3 Marks, 2020 - 2 Marks, 2019 - 3 Marks)

- Ethers
  (Average Marks in last 8 years; 2025 - 1 Mark, 2024 - 2 Marks, 2023 - 2 Marks, 2020 - 2 Marks, 2018 - 2 Marks)

Chapter 8: Aldehydes, Ketones and Carboxylic Acids

- Aldehydes
  (Average Marks in last 8 years; 2025 - 2 Marks, 2024 - 6 Marks, 2023 - 5 Marks, 2020 - 2 Marks, 2019 - 4 Marks, 2018 - 2 Marks)
- Ketones
  (Average Marks in last 8 years; 2025 - 1 Mark, 2024 - 3 Marks, 2023 - 2 Marks, 2020 - 4 Marks, 2019 - 4 Marks, 2018 - 3 Marks)
- Test for Identification
  (Average Marks in last 8 years; 2024 - 2 Marks, 2019 - 1 Mark, 2018 - 1 Mark)
- Carboxylic Acid
  (Average Marks in last 8 years; 2025 - 5 Marks, 2024 - 2 Marks, 2023 - 3 Marks, 2020 - 4 Marks, 2019 - 4 Marks, 2018 - 4 Marks, 2017 - 4 Marks)

Chapter 9: Organic Compounds containing Nitrogen

- Amines
  (Average Marks in last 8 years; 2025 - 4.5 Marks, 2024 - 4 Marks, 2023 - 7 Marks, 2020 - 5 Marks, 2019 - 2 Marks, 2018 - 3 Marks)

Chapter 10: Biomolecules

- Carbohydrates
  (Average Marks in last 8 years; 2025 - 2 Marks, 2024 - 2 Marks, 2023 - 1 Mark, 2020 - 1 Mark)
- Proteins and Amino Acid
  (Average Marks in last 8 years; 2025 - 1 Mark, 2024 - 1 Marks, 2023 - 2 Marks, 2020 - 1 Mark, 2018 - 1 Mark)
- Vitamins
  (Average Marks in last 8 years; 2025 - 1 Mark, 2024 - 1 Marks, 2023 - 1 Mark, 2019 - 2 Marks, 2018 - 2 Marks.

CHAPTER

01

Solutions

In our daily life, we usually come across the substances which are mixtures of two or more pure substances. Solution is one of the most important classes of mixtures which is homogeneous in composition and properties.

- Solutions, Terms Expressing Concentration of Solutions
- Solubility
- Vapour Pressure of Liquid Solutions
- Colligative Properties and Determination of Molar Mass

TOPIC 01 Solutions, Terms Expressing Concentration of Solutions

(i) A solution is a homogeneous mixture of two or more substances whose composition can be varied within certain limits. Here, homogeneous mixture means that its composition and properties are uniform throughout the mixture. In such a mixture, the component that is present in the largest quantity is known as **solvent**.

(ii) The one or more components present in the solution other than the solvent are called **solute.**

(iii) The physical state in which solution exists is determined by the state of solvent.

Types of solutions

On the basis of solvent, the solution may be of the following types:

(i) **Aqueous Solution** When solute is dissolved in water, it is known as aqueous solution, e.g. ethanol in water.

(ii) **Non-aqueous Solution** When solute is dissolved in a solvent other than water, it is known as non-aqueous solution, e.g. iodine in alcohol (tincture of iodine).

(iii) **Saturated Solution** Those solution in which no more solute can be dissolved at the same temperature and pressure, is known as saturated solution.

(iv) **Unsaturated Solution** An unsaturated solution is one in which more solute can be dissolved without changing the temperature.

On the basis of number of components, the solution may be of the following types:

(i) **Binary Solution** The solution which contains two components is called binary solution, e.g. salt solution.

(ii) **Ternary Solution** The solution which contains three components either two solvents and one solute or one solvent and two solutes is called ternary solutions, e.g. salt, sugar and water solution.

(iii) The naming (binary, ternary, quaternary) goes on as the number of components increases. In this chapter, we will focus on binary solutions only.

On the basis of physical state of components, solution can be broadly divided into three types. Their further subdivisions and examples are tabulated below :

Types of solutions	Solute	Solvent	Examples
Solid solutions	Gas	Solid	Hydrogen in palladium.
	Liquid	Solid	Mercury with sodium forming an amalgam.
	Solid	Solid	Alloys like bronze and many others.
Liquid solutions	Gas	Liquid	Oxygen in water, aerated drinks, carbon dioxide in water.
	Liquid	Liquid	Alcoholic beverages are basically solutions of ethanol in water.
	Solid	Liquid	Sucrose (table sugar) or salt in water.
Gaseous solutions	Gas	Gas	Air which is mostly mixture of nitrogen and oxygen gases.
	Liquid	Gas	Chloroform mixed with nitrogen gas, humidity in air.
	Solid	Gas	Camphor in nitrogen gas, dust or smoke.

Methods of Expressing Concentration of Solutions

Composition of a solution can be described by expressing its concentration. The concentration of a solution may be defined as the amount of solute present in the given quantity of the solution. There are several methods by which we can describe the concentration of the solution:

1. Mass Percentage (w/w)

The mass percentage of a solute in a given solution is the mass of the solute in gm per 100 g of the solution.

Mass % of a solute

$$= \frac{\text{Mass of the solute in the solution}}{\text{Total mass of the solution}} \times 100$$

Let, w_B be the mass of solute (B) and w_A be the mass of solvent (A), then

$$\text{Mass percentage} = \frac{w_B}{w_A + w_B} \times 100$$

e.g. A 10% glucose solution in water means that 10 g of glucose is dissolved in 90 g of water resulting in a 100 g of solution.

Example 1 Calculate the mass percentage of benzene (C_6H_6) and carbon tetrachloride (CCl_4), if 22 g of benzene is dissolved in 122 g of CCl_4. **NCERT Intext**

Sol. Mass of solution = Mass of benzene + Mass of carbon tetrachloride

$= (22 + 122)\text{g} = 144 \text{ g}$

$$\text{Mass \% of benzene} = \frac{\text{Mass of benzene}}{\text{Mass of solution}} \times 100$$

$$= \frac{22}{144} \times 100 = 15.28\%$$

$$\text{Mass \% of } CCl_4 = \frac{\text{Mass of } CCl_4}{\text{Mass of solution}} \times 100$$

$$= \frac{122}{144} \times 100 = 84.72\%$$

2. Volume Percentage (V/V)

The volume percentage is the volume of the solute dissolved per 100 mL of the solution.

Volume % of a solute

$$= \frac{\text{Volume of the solute}}{\text{Total volume of solution}} \times 100$$

Solutions containing liquids are commonly expressed in volume percentage, e.g. 100 mL of 35% (V/V) solution of ethylene glycol contains 35 mL of ethylene glycol and 65 mL of water.

Example 2 What amount of water is required to make 10% ethanol in water solution using 10 mL of pure ethanol?

Sol. Given, volume of pure ethanol = 10 mL

volume% of ethanol = 10%

Total amount of solution = ?

$$\text{Volume \% of ethanol} = \frac{\text{Volume of ethanol}}{\text{Total volume of solution}} \times 100$$

or $$10 = \frac{10}{\text{Total volume of solution}} \times 100$$

$\Rightarrow$ Total volume of solution = 100 mL

Thus, the amount of water used = 100 − amount of ethanol

= 100 − 10 = 90 mL

3. Mass by Volume Percentage (w/V)

It is the mass of solute dissolved in 100 mL of the solution.

$$\text{Mass by volume \%} = \frac{\text{Mass of solute}}{\text{Total volume of solution}} \times 100$$

e.g. A 10% solution of sodium chloride (w/V) means that 10 g of sodium chloride is dissolved in 100 mL of solution.

This unit is commonly used in medicines and pharmacy.

4. Parts Per Million (ppm)

When a solute is present in trace quantities, the concentration is expressed in parts per million (ppm). It is defined as the quantities of the solute in grams present in 10^6 gm of the solution.

$$\text{ppm} = \frac{\text{Mass of solute}}{\text{Mass of solution}} \times 10^6$$

Concentration in parts per million can also be expressed as mass to mass, volume to volume and mass to volume. e.g.

(i) The concentration of pollutants in water or atmosphere is often expressed in terms of $\mu g\ mL^{-1}$ or ppm.

(ii) Gases dissolved in water is expressed in $mg\ kg^{-1}$ or ppm.

Example 3 If 1 L of a solution contains 5 mL of a certain disinfectant then express this concentration in ppm.

Sol. Amount of disinfectant $= 5\ mL = 5 \times 10^{-3}$ L

Amount of solution = 1 L

$$\text{Then, ppm} = \frac{\text{Amount of disinfectant}}{\text{Amount of solution}} \times 10^6$$

$$= \frac{5 \times 10^{-3}}{1} \times 10^6 = 5 \times 10^3 \text{ ppm}$$

5. Mole Fraction (χ)

It is the ratio of number of moles of one component to the total number of moles of all the components present in the solution. Commonly used symbol for mole fraction is χ.

(i) **Mole Fraction of a Component**

$$= \frac{\text{Number of moles of the component}}{\text{Total number of moles of all the components}}$$

(ii) **Mole Fraction of Solute**

$$\chi_{(\text{solute})} = \frac{n_{(\text{solute})}}{n_{(\text{solute})} + n_{(\text{solvent})}}$$

(iii) **Mole Fraction of Solvent**

$$\chi_{(\text{solvent})} = \frac{n_{(\text{solvent})}}{n_{(\text{solute})} + n_{(\text{solvent})}}$$

where, n_{solute} and n_{solvent} are the number of moles of solute and solvent respectively.

Example 4 Calculate the mole fraction of benzene in solution containing 30% by mass in carbon tetrachloride. **NCERT Intext**

Sol. For 100 g of solution, mass of benzene in the solution = 30 g

[As, benzene in CCl_4 = 30%]

$\therefore$ Mass of carbon tetrachloride = (100 − 30) g = 70 g

Molar mass of benzene

$(C_6H_6) = 12 \times 6 + 1 \times 6 = 78\ g\ mol^{-1}$

Molar mass of $CCl_4 = 12 + 4 \times 35.5$

$= 154\ g\ mol^{-1}$

$$\therefore \text{Number of moles of benzene} = \frac{\text{Mass of benzene}}{\text{Molar mass of benzene}}$$

$$= \frac{30\ g}{78\ g\ mol^{-1}} = 0.385 \text{ mol}$$

$$\text{Number of moles of } CCl_4 = \frac{\text{Mass of } CCl_4}{\text{Molar mass of } CCl_4}$$

$$= \frac{70\ g}{154\ g\ mol^{-1}} = 0.455 \text{ mol}$$

$$\text{Mole fraction of benzene } (\chi_1) = \frac{\text{Moles of benzene}}{\text{Total moles in the solution}}$$

$$= \frac{0.385}{0.385 + 0.455}$$

$$= \frac{0.385}{0.84} = 0.458$$

And mole fraction of $CCl_4\ (\chi_2) = 1 - 0.458$

$= 0.542$ (as $\chi_1 + \chi_2 = 1$)

6. Molarity (*M*)

It is defined as the number of moles of solute dissolved in one litre of the solution.

$$\text{Molarity} = \frac{\text{Number of moles of solute}}{\text{Volume of solution (in litre)}}$$

(i) **Molarity of Solution after Dilution** If molarity and volume of solution are changed from M_1, V_1 to M_2, V_2 then

$$M_1V_1 = M_2V_2 \qquad \text{(Molarity equation)}$$

If n_1 moles of reactant '1' react with n_2 moles of reactant '2' then

$$\frac{M_1V_1}{n_1} = \frac{M_2V_2}{n_2}$$

(ii) **Molarity of Solution after Mixing** If two solutions of the same solute are mixed then molarity of the resulting solution,

$$M = \frac{M_1V_1 + M_2V_2}{V_1 + V_2}$$

Volume of water added to get a solution of molarity M_2 from V_1 mL of molarity M_1 is

$$V_2 - V_1 = \left(\frac{M_1 - M_2}{M_2}\right)V_1$$

Note Molarity is a volume dependent entity. Therefore, it varies with temperature due to change in volume of solution.

Unit of molarity = g - mol/L

e.g. 0.25 mol L^{-1} (or 0.25 M) solution of NaOH means that 0.25 mol (or 10 g) of NaOH has been dissolved in one litre (or one cubic decimetre).

Example 5 Calculate the molarity of each of the following solutions.

(i) 30 g of $Co(NO_3)_2 \cdot 6H_2O$ in 4.3 L of solution.

(ii) 30 mL of 0.5 M H_2SO_4 diluted to 500 mL. **NCERT Intext**

Sol. (i) Molecular mass of $Co(NO_3)_2 \cdot 6H_2O$

$$= 58.7 + 2\times(14 + 3\times 16) + 6\times(2\times 1 + 16)$$
$$= 58.7 + 124 + 108 = 290.7 \text{ g mol}^{-1}$$

Number of moles of $Co(NO_3)_2 \cdot 6H_2O$

$$= \frac{\text{Mass of solute}}{\text{Molecular mass}} = \frac{30}{290.7} = 0.103 \text{ mol}$$

$$\text{Molarity of solution} = \frac{\text{Number of moles of solute}}{\text{Volume of solution (L)}}$$

$$= \frac{0.103}{4.3} = 0.024 \text{ M}$$

(ii) (a) **First method**

$\because$ 1000 mL of 0.5 M H_2SO_4 will contain $H_2SO_4 = 0.5$ mol

$\therefore$ 30 mL of 0.5 M H_2SO_4 will contain H_2SO_4

$$= \frac{0.5}{1000} \times 30 = 0.015 \text{ mol}$$

$$\text{Molarity of solution} = \frac{\text{Number of moles of solute}}{\text{Volume of solution (L)}}$$

$$= \frac{0.015}{0.500} = 0.03 \text{ M}$$

(b) **Second method**

$$M_1V_1 = M_2V_2$$
$$0.5 \times 30 = M_2 \times 500$$
$$M_2 = 0.03\text{M}$$

7. Normality (N)

It is the number of gram equivalents of the solute dissolved in one litre of the solution at a certain temperature.

$$\text{Normality } (N) = \frac{\text{Number of gram equivalents of solute}}{\text{Volume of solution (L)}}$$

Normality (N)

$$= \frac{\text{Number of gram equivalents of solute} \times 1000}{\text{Volume of solution (mL)}}$$

[where, gram equivalents of solute

$$= \frac{\text{Mass of solute in grams } (w)}{\text{Equivalent weight } (E) \text{ of solute}}\Bigg]$$

Thus, $\text{Normality } (N) = \dfrac{w \times 1000}{E \times V(\text{mL})}$ g eq. dm^{-3}

(where, w is mass of solute.) ($1 dm^3 = 1 L$)

Unit of normality = g equiv · litre^{-1}

e.g. 0.25 g eq. L^{-1} (or 0.25 N) solution of KOH means that 0.25g eq. or mol of KOH has been dissolved in one litre.

(i) **Normality of Solution after Dilution** If normality and volume of solution are changed from N_1, V_1 to N_2, V_2 then $N_1V_1 = N_2V_2$ (Normality equation) If n_1 moles of reactant '1' react with n_2 moles of reactant '2', then

$$\frac{N_1V_1}{n_1} = \frac{N_2V_2}{n_2}$$

(ii) **Normality of Solution after Mixing** If two solutions of the same solute are mixed then normality of the resulting solution,

$$N = \frac{N_1V_1 + N_2V_2}{V_1 + V_2}$$

Volume of water added to get a solution of normality N_2 from V_1 mL of normality N_1 is

$$V_2 - V_1 = \left(\frac{N_1 - N_2}{N_2}\right)V_1$$

Like molarity, normality is also a volume dependent entity. Therefore, it changes with temperature.

When a solution is diluted x times, its normality also decreased by x times.

Example 6 Calculate the mass of H_2SO_4 present in 500 cm^3 of a seminormal solution.

Sol. According to the normality relation, $w = \dfrac{N \times E \times V}{1000}$

In the present case, $N = \dfrac{1}{2}$ (solution is seminormal)

$$E = \frac{\text{Molecular mass}}{\text{Basicity}} = \frac{98}{2} = 49 \; V = 250 \text{ cm}^3$$

$$\therefore \quad w = \frac{\frac{1}{2} \times 49 \times 500}{1000} = 12.25 \text{ g}$$

Hence, the given solution contains 12.25 g of H_2SO_4.

Note A one N solution is called a normal solution and consists of one gram-equivalent of a substance dissolved per litre of the solution. Some common terms which is used as follows:

N = normal, $N/10$ = decinormal,
$N/100$ = centinormal,
$N/2$ = seminormal etc.

8. Molality (m)

It is defined as the number of moles of solute per kilogram of the solvent.

$$\text{Molality} = \frac{\text{Moles of solute}}{\text{Mass of solvent (in kg)}}$$

Since, molality is a volume independent entity. Therefore, it is independent of temperature.

Unit of molality = mol kg^{-1}

e.g. 1.00 mol kg^{-1} (or 1.00 m) solution of KCl means that 1 mole (74.5 g) of KCl is dissolved in 1 kg of water.

Example 7 If the density of some lake water is 1.25 g mL^{-1} and it contains 92 g of Na^+ ions per kg of water. Calculate the molality of Na^+ ions in the lake.

Sol. Number of moles in 92 g of Na^+ ions

$$= \frac{\text{Mass}}{\text{Molecular mass}} = \frac{92}{23} = 4 \text{ mol}$$

$$\text{Molality of } Na^+ \text{ ions} = \frac{\text{Number of moles}}{\text{Mass of solvent (kg)}}$$

$$= \frac{4}{1} = 4 \text{ mol kg}^{-1}$$

Relations between Concentration Terms

Different relations between concentration terms are as given below.

(i) **Relation between normality and percentage of solute**

$$N = \frac{x \times d \times 10}{E}$$

where, x = % of the solute by mass

d = density of solution in g/mL

E = equivalent mass of solute

(ii) **Relation between normality and strength in g/L**

$$\text{Normality } (N) = \frac{\text{Mass of solute (in g)}}{\text{Equivalent weight} \times \text{volume (in L)}}$$

$$= \frac{\text{Strength in g / L}}{\text{Equivalent weight}}$$

(iii) **Relation between normality and molarity**

$$\text{Normality} = \frac{\text{Number of g - equivalents of solute}}{\text{Volume of solution (in L)}}$$

and,

$$\text{Molarity} = \frac{\text{Number of moles of solute}}{\text{Volume of solution (in L)}}$$

$$\therefore \frac{\text{Normality}}{\text{Molarity}} = \frac{\text{Number of g - equivalent of solute}}{\text{Number of moles of solute}}$$

$$= \frac{\text{Molecular weight}}{\text{Equivalent weight}}$$

(iv) **Relation between molarity and strength in g/L**

$$\text{Molarity } (M) = \frac{\text{Weight of solute (in g)}}{\text{Molecular weight of solute} \times \text{volume of solution (in L)}}$$

$$\text{Molarity } (M) = \frac{\text{Strength in g / L}}{\text{Molecular weight of solute}}$$

(v) **Relation between molarity (M) and mole fraction of the solute (χ)**

$$\chi = \frac{MM_1}{M(M_1 - M_2) + 1000\, d}$$

where, d = density of the solution in g mL^{-1}

M_1 = molar mass of solvent

M_2 = molar mass of solute

M = molarity of solution

(vi) **Relation between molality (m) and molarity (M)**

$$\text{Molality } (m) = \frac{M}{d - MM_2}$$

(If d in kg/L and M_2 in kg/mol)

$$\text{Molality } (m) = \frac{M}{1000d - MM_2} \times 1000$$

(If d in g/L and M_2 in g/mol)

$$\text{Molarity } (M) = \frac{m \times d}{1 + \dfrac{m \times M_2}{1000}}$$

where, M_2 = molar mass of the solute

d = density of the solution

(vii) **Relation between molality (m) and mole fraction of the solute (χ)**

$$\chi = \frac{mM_1}{1000 + mM_1}$$

where, M_1 = molecular mass of the solvent

Note ⇒ Normality × equivalent weight

= Molarity × molecular weight

For an acid : $\dfrac{\text{Molecular weight}}{\text{Equivalent weight}}$ = Basicity

∴ Normality of an acid = Molarity × basicity

For a base : $\dfrac{\text{Molecular weight}}{\text{Equivalent weight}}$ = Acidity

∴ Normality of a base = Molarity × acidity

Topic Practice 1

Very Short Answer Type Questions

1 Mark

1. **Fill in the Blanks**
   (i) Gases dissolved in water is expressed in .... or ppm.
   (ii) The number of moles of .... dissolved in one litre of the solution is known as molarity.
   (iii) The number of moles of solute per kilogram of the .... known as molality.

2. **Objective Type Questions**
   (i) Which of the following statements is not correct about homogeneous mixtures?
   (a) These have uniform composition throughout the mixture
   (b) These show same physical properties throughout the mixture
   (c) These have same chemical properties throughout the mixture
   (d) These always contain a solute and a solvent

   (ii) Solvent is the component of a solution
   (a) which is present in large excess
   (b) which is responsible for the chemical properties of solution
   (c) which determines the physical state of solution
   (d) Both (a) and (c)

   (iii) Consider the solution of ethanol. In this
   (a) ethanol is dissolved in water
   (b) the components are in same phase
   (c) ethanol is present in excess
   (d) Both (a) and (b)

   (iv) Complete the following statement by selecting the correct alternative from the given choices of the following terms used for denoting concentration of a solution, the one which does not get affected by temperature, is
   (a) molarity
   (b) molality
   (c) normality
   (d) formality

3. Match the terms given in Column I with statements given in Column II.

Column I	Column II
A. Mass percentage	1. $\frac{\text{Number of moles of the solute component}}{\text{Volume of solution in litre}}$
B. Volume percentage	2. $\frac{\text{Number of moles of a component}}{\text{Total number of moles of all the components}}$
C. Mole fraction	3. $\frac{\text{Volume of the solute component in solution}}{\text{Total volume of solution}} \times 100$
D. Molality	4. $\frac{\text{Mass of the solute component in solution}}{\text{Total mass of the solution}} \times 100$
E. Molarity	5. $\frac{\text{Number of moles of the solute components}}{\text{Mass of solvent in kilogram}}$

4. Correct the following statement.
   "Molality of a solution depends on temperature".

5. Give an example of a solid solution in which the solute is a gas. **NCERT**

6. Calculate the mass percentage of aspirin ($C_9H_8O_4$) in acetonitrile (CH_3CN), when 6.5 g of $C_9H_8O_4$ is dissolved in 450 g of CH_3CN. **NCERT**

7. State the main advantage of molality over molarity as the unit of concentration.

Short Answer Type I Questions

2 Marks

8. 46 g of ethyl alcohol is dissolved in 18 g of water. Calculate the mole fraction of ethyl alcohol. (Atomic weight of C = 12, O = 16, H = 1) **ISC 2011**

9. If the molality of an aqueous solution of cane sugar is 0.4445, what is the mole fraction of cane sugar? **ISC 2008**

10. Calculate the mole fraction of water in a sodium hydroxide solution which has 80 g of NaOH and 54 g of H_2O. (Molar masses of Na = 23, O = 16, H = 1) **ISC 2005**

11. Calculate the amount of benzoic acid (C_6H_5COOH) required for preparing 250 mL of 0.15 M solution in methanol. **NCERT**

12. Calculate the mass of urea (NH_2CONH_2) required in making 2.5 kg of 0.25 molal aqueous solution. **NCERT Intext**

Short Answer Type II Questions

3 Marks

13. Define the term solution. How many types of solutions are formed? Write briefly about each type with an example. NCERT

14. Concentrated nitric acid used in the laboratory work is 68% nitric acid by mass in aqueous solution. What should be the molarity of such a sample of the acid, if the density of the solution is 1.504 g mL^{-1}? NCERT

15. Calculate (i) molality (ii) molarity and (iii) mole fraction of KI if the density of 20% (mass/mass) aqueous KI is 1.202 g mL^{-1}. NCERT

16. A solution of glucose in water is labelled as 10% w/w. What would be the molality and mole fraction of each component in the solution?
If the density of the solution is 1.2 g mL^{-1}, then what shall be the molarity of the solution? NCERT

17. (i) Define the following terms:
(a) molarity (b) molality NCERT
(ii) What is the molality of a urea solution in which 0.0100 g of urea $[(NH_2)_2CO]$ is added to 0.3000 dm^3 of water at STP?

Long Answer Type Questions

5 Marks

18. (i) A sample of drinking water was found to be severely contaminated with chloroform ($CHCl_3$), supposed to be carcinogen. The level of contamination was 15 ppm (by mass).
(a) Express this in per cent by mass.
(b) Determine the molality of chloroform in the water sample. NCERT
(ii) An antifreeze solution is prepared from 222.6 g of ethylene glycol ($C_2H_6O_2$) and 200 g of water. Calculate the molality of the solution. If the density of the solution is 1.072 g mL^{-1}, then what shall be the molarity of the solution? NCERT

19. How many mL of 0.1 M HCl are required to react completely with 1 g mixture of Na_2CO_3 and $NaHCO_3$ containing equimolar amounts of both? NCERT

Hints & Solutions

1. (i) mg kg^{-1} (ii) Solute (iii) Solvent
2. (i) d, (ii) d, (iii) d, (iv) b
3. A – 4, B – 3, C – 2, D – 5, E – 1
4. The correct statement is as follows:
"Molarity of a solution depends on temperature".
5. Solution of hydrogen (solute) in palladium (solvent).
6. Mass percentage of aspirin $= \dfrac{\text{Mass of aspirin}}{\text{Total mass of solution}}$

$$= \frac{6.5 \text{ g}}{(450 + 6.5) \text{ g}} = 1.424\%$$

7. Molality does not change with change in temperature while molarity decreases with rise in temperature.
8. Given, mass of ethyl alcohol $(w) = 46$ g,
Mass of water $(W) = 18$ g
We know that, molecular weight of ethyl alcohol (C_2H_5OH)

$$= 2 \times 12 + 5 \times 1 + 16 + 1$$
$$= 46 \text{ g/mol}$$

Number of moles of ethyl alcohol in 46 g

$$= \frac{\text{Given mass of ethyl alcohol}}{\text{Molar mass of ethyl alcohol}} = \frac{46}{46} = 1 \text{ mol}$$

Molecular weight of water

$$(H_2O) = 2 \times 1 + 16 = 18 \text{ g/mol}$$

Number of moles of water in 18 g $= \dfrac{18}{18} = 1$ mol

∴ Mole fraction of ethyl alcohol

$$= \frac{n_{C_2H_5OH}}{n_{C_2H_5OH} + n_{H_2O}} = \frac{1}{1+1} = \frac{1}{2} = 0.5$$

9. Given, molality of cane sugar solution = 0.4445 mol/kg
That means, number of moles (n) of cane sugar present in 1 kg of water = 0.4445
We know that, number of moles of water,

$$= \frac{1000}{18} = 55.5555$$

(∵ Density of water = 1000 kg / m^3 = 1 g / cm^3, molecular weight of H_2O = 18 g mol^{-1})

Thus, molarity $= \dfrac{\text{number of moles of water}}{\text{volume (L)}}$

$$= \frac{1000/18}{1} = 55.5555 \text{ M}$$

Mole fraction of cane sugar $= \dfrac{n_{\text{Solute}}}{n_{\text{Solute}} + N_{\text{Solvent}}} = \dfrac{n}{n+N}$

$$= \frac{0.4445}{0.4445 + 55.5555} = \frac{0.4445}{56} = 0.0079$$

10. Molecular mass of NaOH $= 23 + 16 + 1 = 40\ \text{g mol}^{-1}$

Number of moles of NaOH in 80 g (n)

$$= \frac{\text{Mass of NaOH}}{\text{Molecular mass of NaOH}} = \frac{80}{40} = 2\ \text{mol}$$

Molecular mass of water $= 2 + 16 = 18\ \text{g mol}^{-1}$

Number of moles of water in 54 g, $(N) = \frac{54}{18} = 3\ \text{mol}$

Total number of moles in solution

$= n + N = 2 + 3 = 5\ \text{mol}$

Mole fraction of water in solution

$$= \frac{\text{Number of moles of water}}{\text{Total number of moles present in solution}}$$

$$= \frac{N}{n+N} = \frac{3}{5} = 0.6$$

11. 0.15 M solution means 0.15 mole of benzoic acid are present in 1 L or 1000 mL of solution.

Molar mass of benzoic acid (C_6H_5COOH)

$= 6\times 12 + 5\times 1 + 1\times 12 + 2\times 16 + 1 = 122\ \text{g mol}^{-1}$

$\because$ 1 mole of benzoic acid $= 122\ \text{g}$

$\therefore$ 0.15 mole of benzoic acid $= 0.15\times 122 = 18.3\ \text{g}$ (1)

$\because$ 0.15 mole are present in 1000 mL of solution.

So, 1000 mL of solution contains benzoic acid = 18.3 g

$\therefore$ 250 mL of solution contains benzoic acid

$$= \frac{18.3\times 250}{1000} = 4.575\ \text{g}$$ (1)

12. Since, the molal aqueous solution of urea is 0.25 m.

$\therefore$ Moles of urea = 0.25 mol

Mass of solvent (water) = 1 kg = 1000 g

Molar mass of urea (NH_2CONH_2)

$= 14 + 2 + 12 + 16 + 14 + 2$

$= 60\ \text{g mol}^{-1}$

$\therefore$ 0.25 mole of urea $= 0.25\ \text{mol}\times 60\ \text{g mol}^{-1} = 15\ \text{g}$ (1/2)

Total mass of solution $= 1000\ \text{g} + 15\ \text{g} = 1015\ \text{g} = 1.015\ \text{kg}$

Thus, 1.015 kg of solution contains urea = 15 g (1/2)

$\therefore$ 2.5 kg of solution will require urea

$$= \frac{15\ \text{g}}{1.015\ \text{kg}}\times 2.5\ \text{kg} = 37\ \text{g}$$ (1)

13. Refer to text on pages 1 and 2. (Solution and type of solution)

14. 68% nitric acid by mass means that

Mass of nitric acid = 68 g

and Mass of solution = 100 g

Molar mass of $HNO_3 = 1 + 14 + 3\times 16 = 63\ \text{g mol}^{-1}$

$\therefore$ Number of moles of 68 g $HNO_3 = \frac{68}{63}\ \text{mol} = 1.079\ \text{mol}$ (1)

$\because$ Density of solution $= 1.504\ \text{g mL}^{-1}$

$\therefore$ Volume of solution $= \frac{100}{1.504}\ \text{mL} = 66.5\ \text{mL} = 0.0665\ \text{L}$ (1)

Thus, the molarity of the solution

$$= \frac{\text{Moles of the solute}}{\text{Volume of solution (in L)}} = \frac{1.079}{0.0665}\ \text{M}$$

$= 16.23\ \text{M}$ (1)

15.

Key Idea

- As density and mass % is given, so find the mass of solute and solvent (as x% solution contains x g solute in $(100 - x)$ g solvent).
- Find the volume of the solution, using the relation
  $$\text{Volume} = \frac{\text{Mass}}{\text{Density}}$$
- Recall the formulae of molality, molarity and mole fraction to calculate them.

(i) **Molality** (m)

Weight of KI in 100 g of water = 20 g

Weight of water in the solution

$= (100 - 20)\ \text{g} = 80\ \text{g} = 0.08\ \text{kg}$

Molar mass of KI $= 39 + 127 = 166\ \text{g mol}^{-1}$

Molality of the solution

$$(m) = \frac{\text{Number of moles of KI}}{\text{Mass of water (in kg)}} = \frac{(20\ \text{g})/(166\ \text{g mol}^{-1})}{(0.08\ \text{kg})}$$

$= 1.506\ \text{mol kg}^{-1} = 1.506\ \text{m}$ (1)

(ii) **Molarity** (M)

Weight of the solution = 100 g

Density of the solution $= 1.202\ \text{g mL}^{-1}$

$$\text{Volume of the solution} = \frac{\text{Weight of solution}}{\text{Density}}$$

$$= \frac{(100\ \text{g})}{(1.202\ \text{g mL}^{-1})} = 83.19\ \text{mL} = 0.083\ \text{L}$$

Molarity of the solution (M)

$$= \frac{\text{Number of gram moles of KI}}{\text{Volume of solution in litres}} = \frac{(20\ \text{g})/(166\ \text{g mol}^{-1})}{(0.083\ \text{L})}$$

$= 1.45\ \text{mol L}^{-1} = 1.45\ \text{M}$ (1)

(iii) **Mole fraction of KI**

Number of moles of KI,

$$n_{KI} = \frac{\text{Mass of KI}}{\text{Molar mass of KI}} = \frac{20\ \text{g}}{166\ \text{g mol}^{-1}} = 0.12\ \text{mol}$$

Number of moles of water

$$n_{H_2O} = \frac{\text{Mass of water}}{\text{Molar mass of water}} = \frac{80\ \text{g}}{18\ \text{g mol}^{-1}} = 4.44\ \text{mol}$$

Mole fraction of KI

$$\chi_{KI} = \frac{n_{KI}}{n_{KI} + n_{H_2O}} = \frac{(0.12\ \text{mol})}{(0.12 + 4.44)\ \text{mol}} = \frac{0.12}{4.56} = 0.0263$$ (1)

16. 10 g glucose is present in 100 g solution, i.e. there is 90 g of water = 0.090 kg of water

Number of moles of 10 g glucose $= \frac{10}{180}\ \text{mol} = 0.0555\ \text{mol}$

Number of moles of 90 g $H_2O = \frac{90}{18} = 5$ mol

Molality of glucose $= \frac{0.0555 \text{ mol}}{0.090 \text{ kg}} = 0.617$ m (1)

Mole fraction of glucose, $\chi_{\text{glucose}} = \frac{0.0555}{5 + 0.0555} = 0.01$

$\chi_{(H_2O)} = 1 - 0.01 = 0.99$ (1)

$\because$ The density of solution = 1.2 g mL^{-1} (Given)

$\therefore$ Volume of 100 g solution $= \frac{100}{1.2}$ mL

$= 83.33$ mL $= 0.08333$ L

Thus, molarity $= \frac{0.0555 \text{ mol}}{0.08333 \text{ L}} = 0.67$ M (1)

17. (i) (a) Refer to text on pages 3-4 (Molarity).

(b) Refer to text on page 5 (Molality). (1)

(ii) Given that, mass of urea = 0.010 g

Molar mass of urea

$[(NH_2)_2CO] = 2 \times 14 + 4 \times 1 + 12 + 16 = 60$ g mol^{-1}

$\therefore$ Moles of urea $= \frac{0.010}{60}$ mol

Water at STP $= 0.3\ dm^{-3} = 0.3$ kg

[As, density = 1 g cm^{-3} = 1 kg dm^{-3}] (1)

$$\text{Molality} = \frac{\text{Moles of solute}}{\text{Mass of solvent (kg)}}$$

$$= \frac{0.010}{60 \times 0.3} = 5.55 \times 10^{-4} \text{ m}$$ (1)

18. (i) (a) 15 ppm means 15 parts in million (10^6) parts by mass in the solution.

Therefore, % by mass $= \frac{15}{10^6} \times 100$

$= 15 \times 10^{-4} = 1.5 \times 10^{-3}\%$ (1)

(b) Taking 15 g chloroform in 10^6 g of the solution, mass of solvent $\approx 10^6$ g

Molar mass of $CHCl_3 = 12 + 1 + 3 \times 35.5$

$= 119.5$ g mol^{-1}

$$\therefore \text{Molality} = \frac{\text{Mass of } CHCl_3 / \text{Molar mass}}{\text{Mass of water (in kg)}}$$

$$= \frac{15/119.5}{10^6} \times 1000$$

$= 1.25 \times 10^{-4}$ m (1)

(ii) Mass of ethylene glycol = 222.6 g

Molar mass of ethylene glycol ($C_2H_6O_2$)

$= (12 \times 2) + (1 \times 6) + (16 \times 2) = 24 + 6 + 32 = 62$ g mol^{-1}

Mass of water = 200 g = 0.2 kg

$$\text{Molality } (m) = \frac{\text{Mass of ethylene glycol / Molar mass}}{\text{Mass of solvent in kg}}$$

$$= \frac{(222.6 \text{ g}) / (62 \text{ g mol}^{-1})}{0.2 \text{ kg}}$$

$= 17.95$ mol kg^{-1} = 17.95 m (1)

Density of the solution = 1.072 g mL^{-1}

Mass of solution = Mass of solute + Mass of solvent

= 222.6 g + 200 g = 422.6 g

$$\text{Volume} = \frac{\text{Mass}}{\text{Density}} = \frac{422.6 \text{ g}}{1.072 \text{ g mL}^{-1}} = 394.2 \text{ mL}$$ (1)

$$\text{Molarity } (M) = \frac{\text{Mass of ethylene glycol / Molar mass}}{\text{Volume in litres}}$$

$$= \frac{(222.6 \text{ g}) / (62 \text{ g mol}^{-1})}{0.3942 \text{ L}}$$

$= 9.10$ mol L^{-1} = 9.10 M (1)

19. Suppose, amount of Na_2CO_3 present in the mixture = x g

$\therefore$ $NaHCO_3$ present in the mixture $= (1 - x)$ g

Molar mass of $Na_2CO_3 = 2 \times 23 + 12 + 3 \times 16 = 106$ g mol^{-1}

Molar mass of $NaHCO_3 = 23 + 1 + 12 + 3 \times 16 = 84$ g mol^{-1}

$\therefore$ Moles of Na_2CO_3 in x g $= \frac{x}{106}$ and

moles of $NaHCO_3$ in $(1 - x)$ g $= \frac{1 - x}{84}$ (1)

As mixture contains equimolar amounts of the two,

$$\therefore \quad \frac{x}{106} = \frac{1 - x}{84}$$

or $106 - 106x = 84x$ or $x = \frac{106}{190}$ g $= 0.558$ g (1/2)

Thus, number of moles of $Na_2CO_3 = \frac{0.558}{106} = 0.00526$ mol (1/2)

and number of moles of

$$NaHCO_3 = \frac{1 - 0.558}{84} = \frac{0.442}{84} = 0.00526 \text{ mol}$$ (1/2)

Again by reactions,

$Na_2CO_3 + 2HCl \longrightarrow 2NaCl + H_2O + CO_2 \uparrow$

$NaHCO_3 + HCl \longrightarrow NaCl + H_2O + CO_2 \uparrow$ (1/2)

$\because$ 1 mole of Na_2CO_3 requires HCl = 2 mol

$\therefore$ 0.00526 mole of Na_2CO_3 requires HCl

$= 0.00526 \times 2$ mol $= 0.01052$ mol (1/2)

$\because$ 1 mole of $NaHCO_3$ requires HCl = 1 mol

$\therefore$ 0.00526 mole of $NaHCO_3$ requires HCl = 0.00526 mol (1/2)

$\therefore$ Total HCl required = (0.01052 + 0.00526) mol

= 0.01578 mol

Again, 0.1 mole of 0.1 M HCl is present in 1000 mL of HCl.

$\therefore$ 0.01578 mole of 0.1 M HCl will be present in HCl

$$= \frac{1000}{0.1} \times 0.01578 = 157.8 \text{ mL}$$ (1)

TOPIC 02 Solubility

Solubility of a substance is its maximum amount that can be dissolved in a specified amount of solvent at a specified temperature. It depends upon the nature of solute and solvent as well as temperature and pressure.

Let us consider the effect of these factors in solution of a solid or gas in a liquid.

Solubility of a Gas in a Liquid

The solubility of any gas in a particular liquid is the volume of the gas (in cubic centimetre, cc) that can be dissolved in unit volume (1cc) of the liquid to form the saturated solution at certain temperature and under a pressure of one atmosphere.

Factors Affecting the Solubility of a Gas in a Liquid

These are as follows:

(i) **Nature of gas** (solute) **and liquid** (solvent) The solubility of different gases in the same solvent varies, e.g. gases like hydrogen, oxygen, nitrogen and helium, etc., dissolve in water to a small extent whereas the gases like NH_3, HCl, SO_2, etc., are highly soluble in water.

(ii) **Effect of temperature** The solubility of a gas decreases with increase in temperature. This is because when a gaseous solution is heated, the molecular motion of gaseous particles increases, as a result some molecules escape out of the solution.

(iii) **Effect of pressure** The solubility of a gas increases with increase in pressure.

Henry's Law

Henry was the first one to give a quantitative relation between pressure and solubility of a gas in a solvent which is called Henry's law. It states that at a constant temperature, the solubility of a gas in a liquid is directly proportional to the pressure of the gas present in equilibrium with liquid (above the surface of liquid or solution).

The most common forms of Henry's law states that, the partial pressure of the gas in vapour phase (p) is proportional to the mole fraction of the gas (χ) in the solution. It is expressed as:

$$p \propto \chi \quad \text{or} \quad \boxed{p = K_H \cdot \chi} \qquad \text{...(i)}$$

where, K_H is called **Henry's law constant.** Hence, $K_H = \frac{1}{K'}$

Graphical Representation to Validate Henry's Law

If we draw a graph between the partial pressure of the gas against the mole fraction of the gas in solution at a given temperature, then a straight line passing through the origin is obtained as shown in the figure given below.

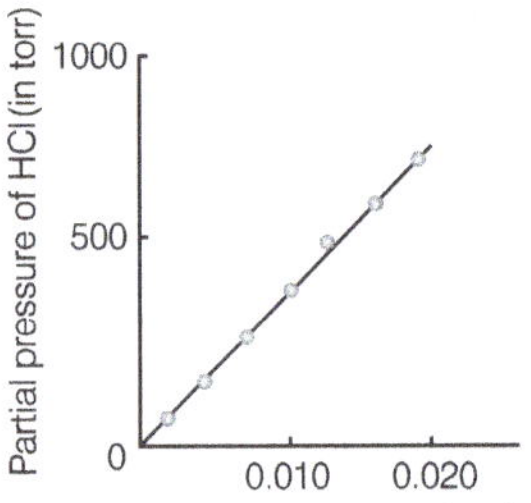

Experimental results for the solubility of HCl gas in cyclohexane at 293 K. The slope of the line is the Henry's law

Henry's law is applied to each gas which is independent of the presence of other gases.

Note Different gases have different K_H values at the same temperature which suggests that K_H is a function of the nature of the gas.

Example 1 H_2S, a toxic gas with rotten egg like smell, is used for qualitative analysis. If the solubility of H_2S in water at STP is 0.195 m, calculate Henry's law constant. **NCERT Intext**

Sol. Solubility of H_2S gas = 0.195 m, i.e. 0.195 moles in 1 kg of the solvent (water)

$\because$ Number of moles of H_2O in 1 kg of the solvent (water)

$$= \frac{1000 \text{ g}}{18 \text{ g mol}^{-1}} = 55.55 \text{ mol}$$

$\therefore$ Mole fraction of H_2S gas in the solution

$$(\chi) = \frac{0.195}{0.195 + 55.55} = \frac{0.195}{55.745} = 0.0035$$

Pressure at STP = 0.987 bar

According to Henry's law, $p_{H_2S} = K_H \times \chi_{H_2S}$

or $$K_H = \frac{p_{H_2S}}{\chi_{H_2S}} = \frac{0.987 \text{ bar}}{0.0035} = 282 \text{ bar}$$

Limitations of Henry's Law

It is applicable only when

(i) the pressure of the gas is not too high and temperature is not too low.

(ii) the gas should not undergo any chemical change.

(iii) the gas should not undergo association or dissociation in the solution.

Example 2 At same temperature, H_2 is more soluble in water than He. Which of them has higher value of K_H and why?

Sol. He has higher value of K_H because if the gas has more solubility, its K_H value will be low.

Applications of Henry's Law

Henry's law finds several applications in industries. It also explains many biological phenomenon.

These are as follows:

(i) **In the Production of Carbonated Beverages** To increase the solubility of CO_2 in soft drinks and soda water, the bottle is sealed under high pressure.

(ii) **In Deep Sea Diving** Scuba divers (deep-sea divers) breath air at high pressure under water. Increased pressure increases the solubility of atmospheric gases (like nitrogen) in blood. When divers come towards surface, the pressure gradually decreases resulting in the release of dissolved gases from blood. This leads to the formation of bubbles of nitrogen in the blood, which blocks capillaries and gives rise to an ailment called **bends or decompression sickness.**

To avoid bends, as well as the toxic effects of high concentrations of nitrogen in the blood, the tanks used by scuba divers are filled with air diluted with helium (11.7% helium, 56.2% nitrogen and 32.1% oxygen).

(iii) **For People Living at High Altitudes or Climbers** At high altitudes, the partial pressure of oxygen is less than that at the ground level. This leads to low concentration of oxygen in the blood and tissues of people living at high altitudes or climbers. Consequently, they feel weak both physically and mentally. These are the symptoms of a medical condition known as **anoxia.**

Topic Practice 2

Very Short Answer Type Questions

(1 Mark)

1. Fill in the Blanks

(i) An ....solution is one in which more solute can be dissolved without changing the temperatrue.

(ii) The solubility of a gas .... with increase in temperature.

(iii) According to Henry's law at a constant temperature, the solubility of a gas in a liquid is............proportional to the partial pressure of the gas present-above the surface of liquid or solution.

2. Objective Type Questions

(i) The solubility of a gas varies directly with pressure of the gas is based upon **ISC 2008**

(a) Raoult's law
(b) Henry's law
(c) Nernst distribution law
(d) None of the above

(ii) What happens to the solubility of substance with rise in temperature, if the dissolution process is endothermic?

(a) Increases
(b) Decreases
(c) Increases or decreases, depending upon the nature of substance
(d) No effect of temperature on solubility

(iii) 15 g of sucrose is dissolved in 50 mL of water and some pressure is applied on the surface of solution formed. It will result in

(a) increased solubility
(b) decreased solubility
(c) slight increase in solubility
(d) no effect on solubility

(iv) Which of the following statements is true about Henry's law?

(a) The solubility of solid in a liquid is directly proportional to the partial pressure of the solid present above the surface of liquid or solution
(b) The solubility of a gas in a liquid is directly proportional to the partial pressure of the gas present above the surface of liquid or solution
(c) The solubility of a liquid in gas is directly proportional to the partial pressure of liquid present above the surface of gas
(d) The solubility of a gas in solid is directly proportional to the partial pressure of gas present above the surface of solid

3. Match the following Henry's law constant values for gases in water at 298 K.

Column I		Column II	
A.	Argon	(i)	1.83×10^{-5}
B.	CO_2	(ii)	0.413
C.	Formaldehyde	(iii)	40.3
D.	Methane	(iv)	0.611
E.	Vinyl chloride	(v)	1.67

Codes

	A	B	C	D	E		A	B	C	D	E
(a)	(iii)	(iv)	(ii)	(i)	(iv)	(b)	(iii)	(i)	(v)	(ii)	(iv)
(c)	(iii)	(v)	(i)	(ii)	(iv)	(d)	(iii)	(ii)	(v)	(iii)	(iv)

4. Why do gases always tend to be less soluble in liquid as the temperature is raised? **NCERT**

5. Aquatic animals are more comfortable in cold water than in warm water? **ISC 2018**

Short Answer Type I Questions

(2 Marks)

6. Why does soda water fizz when the bottle is opened? Name the law that explains this phenomenon. **ISC 2014**

7. State Henry's law. What is the effect of temperature on the solubility of a gas in a liquid?

8. What is the significance of Henry's law constant K_H? **NCERT Exemplar**

Short Answer Type II Questions

(3 Marks)

9. The air is a mixture of a number of gases. The major components are oxygen and nitrogen with approximate proportion of 20% and 79% by volume at 298 K, respectively. The water is in equilibrium with air at a pressure of 10 atm. At 298 K, if the Henry's law constant for oxygen and nitrogen are 3.30×10^7 mm Hg and 6.51×10^7 mm Hg respectively, calculate the composition of these gases in water. **NCERT**

10. The partial pressure of ethane over a saturated solution containing 6.56×10^{-3} g of ethane is 1 bar. If the solution were to contain 5.0×10^{-2} g of ethane, then what will be the partial pressure of the gas? **NCERT**

Long Answer Type Questions

(5 Marks)

11. Henry's law constant for CO_2 in water is 1.67×10^8 Pa at 298 K. Calculate the quantity of CO_2 in 500 mL of soda water when packed under 2.5 atm CO_2 pressure at 298 K.

12. (i) Henry's law constant for the molality of methane in benzene at 298 K is 4.27×10^5 mm of Hg. Calculate the solubility of methane in benzene at 298 K under 760 mm of Hg.

(ii) The solubility of $Ba(OH)_2 \cdot 8H_2O$ in water is 5.6 g per 100 g of water at 288 K. Calculate the molality of hydroxide ion in saturated solution of $Ba(OH)_2 \cdot 8H_2O$ at that temperature.

(iii) Mention some important applications of Henry's law. **NCERT**

Hints & Solutions

1. (i) unsaturated (ii) decreases (iii) directly

2. (i) Henry's law (ii) Increases

(iii) No effect on solubility

(iv) The solubility of a gas in a liquid is directly proportional to the partial pressure of the gas present above the surface of liquid or solution.

3. (c) A– (3), B–(5), C–(1), D–(2), E–(4)

4. As dissolution of gas in liquid is an exothermic process (Gas + Solvent $\rightleftharpoons$ Solution + Heat). So, on increasing the temperature, equilibrium shifts towards the backward direction.

5. Oxygen is present in dissolved state in water. As per Henry's law when temperature rises, solubility of a gas decreases in solvent, it means solubility of oxygen in warm water is less than cold water. This makes aquatic species respirate comfortably in cold water.

6. Soda water is prepared by dissolving CO_2 in water under a pressure of 5 to 10 atm. The bottle is tightly capped to prevent the escape of CO_2. When the bottle is opened the pressure reduced and most of the dissolved CO_2 gas escapes from the solution in the form of fizz or effervescence. This phenomenon is based upon **Henry's law of solubility of gases**. This law states that, 'at constant temperature, the solubility of gas in a liquid is directly proportional to the pressure of the gas.'

7. Refer to Page 10 (Henry's law)

Effect of temperature Solubility of gases decreases with increase in temperature.

8. According to Henry's law, $p \propto x \Rightarrow p = K_H \chi$. Higher the value of Henry's law constant (K_H), the lower is the solubility of the gas in a liquid. Thus, the solubility of a gas in the given liquid can be increased by increasing pressure.

9. Given that, total pressure of air in equilibrium with water = 10 atm

As air contains 20% oxygen and 79% nitrogen by volume.

∴ Partial pressure of oxygen

$$(p_{O_2}) = \frac{20}{100} \times 10 \text{ atm} \Rightarrow 2 \text{ atm} = 2 \times 760 \text{ mm Hg}$$

$$= 1520 \text{ mm Hg} \quad \textbf{(1/2)}$$

Partial pressure of nitrogen, $(p_{N_2}) = \frac{79}{100} \times 10$ atm

$$= 7.9 \text{ atm} = 7.9 \times 760 \text{ mm Hg} = 6004 \text{ mm Hg} \quad \textbf{(1/2)}$$

Given that, $K_H(O_2) = 3.30 \times 10^7$ mm Hg

$K_H(N_2) = 6.51 \times 10^7$ mm Hg

According to Henry's law,

$$p_{O_2} = K_H \times \chi_{O_2}$$

or $$\chi_{O_2} = \frac{p_{O_2}}{K_H} = \frac{1520 \text{ mm Hg}}{3.30 \times 10^7 \text{ mm Hg}} = 4.61 \times 10^{-5}$$ (1)

$$p_{N_2} = K_H \times \chi_{N_2}$$

or $$\chi_{N_2} = \frac{p_{N_2}}{K_H} = \frac{6004 \text{ mm Hg}}{6.51 \times 10^7 \text{ mm Hg}} = 9.22 \times 10^{-5}$$ (1)

10. According to Henry's law,

$$m \propto p$$

$$m = Kp$$

$$6.56 \times 10^{-3} \text{ g} = K \times 1 \text{ bar}$$

$$K = 6.56 \times 10^{-3} \text{ g bar}^{-1}$$ (1½)

Again, when $m' = 5.00 \times 10^{-2}$ g, $p' = ?$

$$m' = K \times p'$$

$$5.00 \times 10^{-2} \text{ g} = 6.56 \times 10^{-3} \text{ g bar}^{-1} \times p'$$

$$p' = \frac{5.00 \times 10^{-2}}{6.56 \times 10^{-3}} = 7.62 \text{ bar}$$ (1½)

11.

> **Key Idea** To calculate the mass of CO_2 dissolved, calculate the mole fraction of CO_2 by using Henry's law,
>
> $p = K_H \times \chi$ or $\chi = \frac{p}{K_H}$
>
> Then, calculate the number of moles and finally the mass.

Step **I** Calculation of number of moles of CO_2

According to Henry's law,

$$\text{Mole fraction of } CO_2\ (\chi_{CO_2}) = \frac{\text{Partial pressure of } CO_2}{K_H \text{ for } CO_2}$$

$$K_H = 1.67 \times 10^8 \text{ Pa} = \frac{(1 \text{ atm})}{(101325 \text{ Pa})} \times (1.67 \times 10^8 \text{ Pa})$$

$$= 1.648 \times 10^3 \text{ atm}$$ (1)

$$\chi_{CO_2} = \frac{2.5 \text{ atm}}{(1.648 \times 10^3 \text{ atm})} = 1.52 \times 10^{-3}$$ (1)

$$n_{H_2O} = \frac{(500 \text{ g})}{(18 \text{ g mol}^{-1})} = 27.78 \text{ mol}$$ (1)

$$\chi_{CO_2} = \frac{n_{CO_2}}{n_{CO_2} + n_{H_2O}} = \frac{n_{CO_2}}{n_{H_2O}} = \frac{n_{CO_2}}{(27.78 \text{ mol})}$$

$$n_{CO_2} = \chi_{CO_2} \times (27.78 \text{ mol})$$

$$= (1.52 \times 10^{-3}) \times (27.78 \text{ mol}) = 0.0422 \text{ mol}$$ (1)

Note n_{CO_2} is considered negligible due to its low solubility in water.

Step **II** Calculation of mass of dissolved CO_2 in water

Mass of CO_2

= Number of moles of CO_2 ×Molar mass of CO_2

$= (0.0422 \text{ mol}) \times (44 \text{ g mol}^{-1}) = 1.857$ g (1)

12. (i) According to Henry's law, $p = K_H \cdot \chi$

So, $$\chi = \frac{p}{K_H} = \frac{760}{4.27 \times 10^5} = 1.78 \times 10^{-3}$$

or the mole fraction of methane in benzene is 1.78×10^{-3}. (1)

(ii) Molar mass of $Ba(OH)_2 \cdot 8H_2O = 137 + 2 \times 17 + 8 \times 18$

$= 315 \text{ g mol}^{-1}$

∵ 100 g water has 5.6 g of $Ba(OH)_2 \cdot 8H_2O$

∴ 1000 g water will have $Ba(OH)_2 \cdot 8H_2O = 56$ g

Number of moles of

$$Ba(OH)_2 \cdot 8H_2O = \frac{56}{315} = 0.178 \text{ mol}$$

Thus, molality of $Ba(OH)_2 = 0.178$ m (1)

$$Ba(OH)_2 \longrightarrow Ba^{2+} + 2OH^-$$

Molality of OH^- ions = 2 × molality of $Ba(OH)_2$

$= 2 \times 0.178 = 0.356$ m (1)

(iii) Refer to text on page 11 (Applications of Henry's law). (2)

TOPIC 03 Vapour Pressure of Liquid Solutions

Vapour Pressure

The maximum pressure exerted by the vapour of a liquid at a particular temperature in a state of dynamic equilibrium is known as **vapour pressure** of the liquid at that temperature.

The vapour pressure of a liquid depends on the following factors :

(i) **Nature of liquid** Liquids having strong intermolecular forces possess lower vapour pressure at a given temperature.

(ii) **Temperature** Vapour pressure increases with increase in temperature.

(iii) **Presence of impurities** The presence of non-volatile impurities lowers the vapour pressure while that of volatile impurities raises the vapour pressure of a liquid.

Raoult's Law

For Solution Containing Volatile Solutes

This law states that "at a given temperature, for a solution of volatile liquids, the partial vapour pressure of each component of the solution is directly proportional to its mole fraction present in solution".

Let us consider that two volatile liquids 1 and 2 have mole fractions as χ_1 and χ_2, respectively. If p_1 and p_2 are the vapour pressures of these components in the solution, respectively, at same temperature then according to Raoult's law,

For component 1, $p_1 \propto \chi_1$ or $p_1 = p_1^\circ \chi_1$

Similarly, for component 2, $p_2 = p_2^\circ \chi_2$

According to Dalton's law of partial pressure, the total pressure (p_{total}) over the solution phase in the container will be sum of the partial pressures of the components of the solution and is given as

$$p_{total} = p_1 + p_2$$

So, $$p_{total} = p_1^\circ \chi_1 + p_2^\circ \chi_2$$

As we know, $\chi_1 + \chi_2 = 1$ or $\chi_1 = 1 - \chi_2$,

Then, $$p = p_1^\circ (1 - \chi_2) + p_2^\circ \chi_2$$

$$p = p_1^\circ + (p_2^\circ - p_1^\circ)\chi_2$$

Graphical Representation of Raoult's Law

A plot of p_1 and p_2 *versus* the mole fractions χ_1 and χ_2 for a solution gives a linear plot as shown in the figure below :

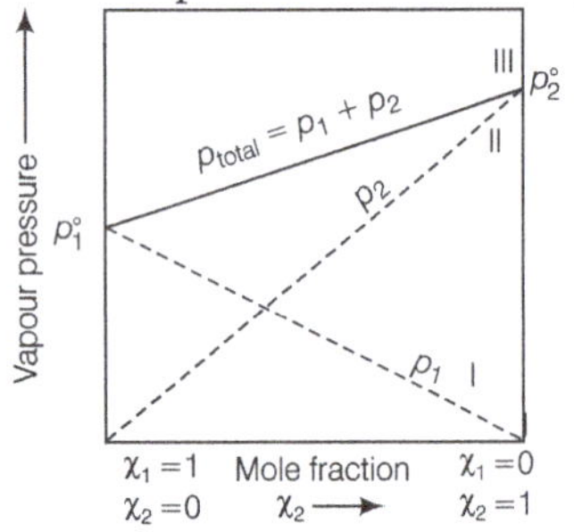

Plot of vapour pressure and mole fraction of an ideal solution at constant temperature

In the above figure, the dashed lines I and II represent the partial pressure of the components. (It can be seen from the plot that p_1 and p_2 are directly proportional to χ_1 and χ_2, respectively.) These lines (I and II) pass through the points for which χ_1 and χ_2 are equal to unity. The total vapour pressure is given by line marked III in the figure.

The plot (line III) of p_{total} *versus* χ_2 is a straight line as shown in figure. Assuming that $p_1^\circ < p_2^\circ$ i.e. component 1 is less volatile than component 2, then the minimum value of p_{total} is p_1° and the maximum value is p_2°.

The composition of vapour phase in equilibrium with the solution can be determined by the partial pressures of the components. If y_1 and y_2 are the mole fractions of the components 1 and 2 respectively in the vapour phase then, using Dalton's law of partial pressure;

$$p_1 = y_1 p_{total}; \quad p_2 = y_2 p_{total}$$

In general, for a solution containing a number of volatile components (liquids), for any component i,

$$p_i = y_i \cdot p_{total}$$

Raoult's Law as a Special Case of Henry's Law

According to Raoult's law, the vapour pressure of a volatile component in a given solution is given by

$$p_i = \chi_i p_i^\circ$$

If in the solution of a gas in a liquid, the volatile component exists as a gas then, according to Henry's law, $p = K_H \chi$, i.e. partial pressure of the volatile component (gas) is directly proportional to the mole fraction of that component (gas) in the solution.

Therefore, Raoult's and Henry's laws become identical except that their proportionality constants (K_H-Henry's constant and p_i° constant for Raoult's law) are different. Therefore, Raoult's law becomes a special case of Henry's law in which K_H becomes equal to p_i°.

Example 1 The vapour pressure of ethyl alcohol at 298 K is 20 mm of Hg. Its mole fraction in a solution with methyl alcohol is 0.40. What is its vapour pressure in solution if the mixture obeys Raoult's law?

Sol. According to Raoult's law, $p_A = p_A^\circ \chi_A$

Vapour pressure of pure ethyl alcohol (p_A°) = 20 mm of Hg

Mole fraction of ethyl alcohol (χ_A) = 0.40

Vapour pressure of ethyl alcohol in solution (p_A) = $20 \times 0.40 = 8$ mm of Hg

Example 2 The vapour pressures of pure liquids *A* and *B* are 450 and 700 mm of Hg at 350 K, respectively. Find out the composition of the liquid mixture, if total vapour pressure is 600 mm of Hg. Also, find the composition of the vapour phase. **NCERT Intext**

Sol. Given, $p_A^\circ = 450$ mm of Hg, $p_B^\circ = 700$ mm of Hg

$p_{total} = 600$ mm of Hg

According to Raoult's law,

$$p_A = \chi_A \times p_A^\circ \; ; \; p_B = \chi_B \times p_B^\circ \Rightarrow (1 - \chi_A)\, p_B^\circ$$

$$p_{total} = p_A + p_B = \chi_A p_A^\circ + (1 - \chi_A)\, p_B^\circ$$

$$= p_B^\circ + (p_A^\circ - p_B^\circ)\chi_A$$

On substituting the values, we get

$$600 = 700 + (450 - 700)\chi_A$$

or $$250\chi_A = 100 \text{ or } \chi_A = \frac{100}{250} = 0.40$$

Thus, composition of the liquid mixture will be

Mole fraction of $A(\chi_A) = 0.40$

Mole fraction of $B(\chi_B) = 1 - 0.40 = 0.60$

$\therefore \quad p_A = \chi_A \times p_A^\circ$

$= 0.40 \times 450$ mm of Hg $= 180$ mm of Hg

$p_B = \chi_B \times p_B^\circ = 0.60 \times 700$ mm of Hg $= 420$ mm of Hg

Thus, in vapour phase, mole fraction of A

$$= \frac{p_A}{p_A + p_B} = \frac{180}{180 + 420} = 0.30$$

Mole fraction of $B = 1 - 0.30 = 0.70$

For Solutions Containing Non-volatile Solutes

Raoult's law may be stated as the relative lowering of vapour pressure of a volatile solvent due to dissolution of a non-volatile solute in it, is equal to the mole fraction of the solute.

i.e. $$\frac{p^\circ - p}{p^\circ} = \chi_{\text{solute}} = \frac{n}{n+N}$$

where, $\frac{p^\circ - p}{p}$ = Relative lowering of of vapour pressure

n = Number of moles of solute, N = Number of moles of solvent, χ_{solute} = Mole fraction of solute

This is another form of **Raoult's law.**

Ideal and Non-ideal Solutions

The binary liquid-liquid solutions can be divided into ideal and non-ideal solutions on the basis of Raoult's law.

Ideal Solutions

The solutions which obey Raoult's law over the entire range of concentration are known as ideal solutions.

The characteristic properties of these solutions are :

(i) The enthalpy of mixing the pure components to form the solution is zero, i.e. $\Delta_{\text{mix}} H = 0$.

(ii) The volume of mixing is also zero, i.e. $\Delta_{\text{mix}} V = 0$.

The above two properties mean that no heat is absorbed or evolved when the components are mixed.

Also the volume of the solution is equal to the sum of volumes of the two components.

Examples of this type of solutions are :

(i) n-hexane + n-heptane

(ii) Bromoethane + chloroethane

(iii) Benzene + toluene

(iv) Chlorobenzene + bromobenzene

Non-Ideal Solutions

When a solution does not obey Raoult's law over the entire range of concentration, it is called non-ideal solution.

The characteristic properties of such solutions are :

(i) The enthalpy of mixing of pure components to form the solution is not zero. It may have a positive or negative value. i.e. $\Delta_{\text{mix}} H \neq 0$

(ii) The volume of mixing is also not zero. Volume may increase or decrease after mixing. i.e. $\Delta_{\text{mix}} V \neq 0$.

The vapour pressures of these solutions are either higher or lower than that predicted by Raoult's law.

If it is higher, then the solution exhibits **positive deviation** and if it is lower, then it exhibits **negative deviation** from Raoult's law. The plots of vapour pressure as a function of mole fractions for such solutions are shown in the figures given below :

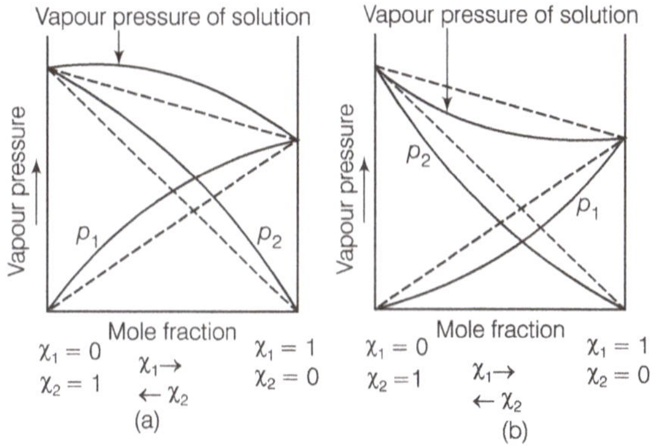

The vapour pressures of two component systems as a function of composition
(a) a solution that shows positive deviation from Raoult's law and
(b) a solution that shows negative deviation from Raoult's law

In case of positive deviation from, the intermolecular interactions, i.e. A—B interactions are weaker than in pure components, i.e. A—A or B—B.

Examples of this type of solutions are :

(i) Carbon disulphide + acetone

(ii) Ethanol + cyclohexane

(iii) Acetone + benzene

In case of **negative deviation** from ideal behaviour intermolecular interactions, i.e. A—B interactions are stronger than those between A—A or B—B.

This decreases the escaping tendency of molecules of A or B component and consequently, the vapour pressure decreases resulting in negative deviation from Raoult's law [Fig. (b)].

Examples of this type of solutions are:

(i) Chloroform + diethyl ether

(ii) Phenol + aniline (iii) Water + nitric acid

Difference between solutions having positive deviation from ideal behaviour and the solutions having negative deviation from ideal behaviour are given in the table below:

Solutions having positive deviation from ideal behaviour	Solutions having negative deviation from ideal behaviour
The intermolecular interactions, i.e. $A — B$ interactions are weaker than in pure components, i.e. between $A—A$ or $B—B$.	The intermolecular interactions, i.e. $A — B$ interactions are stronger than in pure components, i.e. between $A — A$ or $B — B$.
$p_1 > p_1^\circ \chi_1$ and $p_2 > p_2^\circ \chi_2$	$p_1 < p_1^\circ \chi_1$ and $p_2 < p_2^\circ \chi_2$
$\Delta_{mix}H$ = positive (endothermic)	$\Delta_{mix}H$ = negative (exothermic)
$\Delta_{mix}V$ = positive	$\Delta_{mix}V$ = negative
Heating increases solubility.	Heating decreases solubility.

Depending upon the extent of deviation from Raoult's law, a new category of binary mixtures, known as azeotropes, is formed. It is discussed below.

Azeotropic Mixtures

The solutions of completely miscible liquids, which boils at constant temperature and can distilled over without any change in composition are called **azeotropes** or **azeotropic mixtures.**

The solutions which shows large negative deviation from Raoult's law, form **maximum boiling azeotropes** and the solutions which shows large positive deviation from Raoult's law, form **minimum boiling azeotropes.**

(i) **Minimum boiling azeotropes** are formed by those liquid pairs which show positive deviation from ideal behaviour. Such azeotropes have boiling points lower than either of the components, e.g. C_2H_5OH (95.57%) $+H_2O$ (4.43%) (by mass).

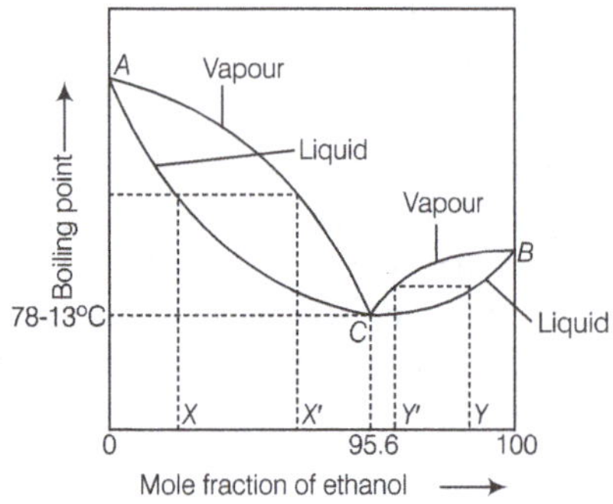

B.P-Composition graph for alcohol-water system

(ii) **Maximum boiling azeotropes** are formed by those liquid pairs, which show negative deviation from ideal behaviour.

Such azeotropes have boiling points higher than either of the components. e.g. H_2O (20.22)% +HCl (79.78%) by mass.

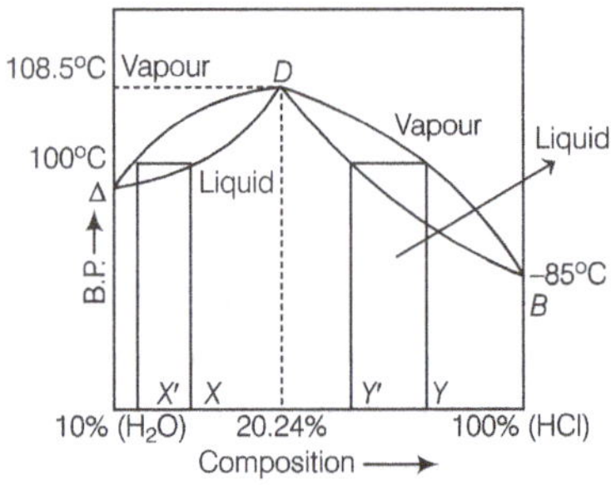

B.P – Composition graph for HCl-H_2O system

Fractional Distillation

For the separation of two liquids which have nearly equal boiling points, i.e. their boiling points are within the limit of 10 K to 15 K (For example, acetone 329 K and methyl alcohol 338 K), the process of simple distillation cannot be used as vapours of both the liquids will be formed simultaneously and thus, the distillate will also contain both of them.

In such case, the distillation is done with the help of specially **designed fractionating columns.** Such a distillation is called fractional distillation. A mixture of acetone and methyl alcohol is separated by this process.

Topic Practice 3

Very Short Answer Type Questions

1 Mark

1. Fill in the Blanks

(i) Solution which strictly obey .... law are called .... solutions. **ISC 2012**

(ii) The .... pressure of an aqueous solution of 0.1 M cane sugar is .... than that of pure water.

(iii) The solution which shows large .... deviation from Raoult's law, form maximum boiling azeotropes. **ISC 2010**

(iv) In case of negative deviation from Raoult's law; intermolecular interactions, i.e. $A—B$ interactions are .... than those between $A—A$ or $B—B$.

2. **Objective Type Questions**

(i) p_A and p_B are the vapour pressure of pure liquid components A and B respectively of an ideal binary solution. If x_A represents the mole fraction of component A, the total pressure of the solution will be

(a) $p_A + x_A(p_B - p_A)$ (b) $p_A + x_A(p_A - p_B)$
(c) $p_B + x_A(p_B - p_A)$ (d) $p_B + x_A(p_A - p_B)$

(ii) The total pressure (p_{total}) over the solution phase in the container will be the sum of the partial pressures of the components of the solution. This statement to belongs

(a) Raoult's law (b) Henry's law
(c) Dalton's law of partial pressures
(d) All of the above

(iii) Which one of the following is not correct for an ideal solution?

(a) It must obey Raoult's law (b) $\Delta H = 0$
(c) $\Delta V = 0$ (d) ΔH or $\Delta V \neq 0$

(iv) Which of the following statements is/are true for an ideal solution?

(a) No heat is absorbed or evolved when the compponents are mixed
(b) Volume of solution = sum of volume of two component
(c) Intermolecular attraction forces between A—A or B—B components are equal to that of A—B.
(d) All of the above

3. Match the items of Column I with Column II.

Column I (Intermolecular interaction)	Column II (Example)
A. A—B > A—A or B—B interaction	(i) Hexane and heptane
B. $\Delta V_{mix} = 0$	(ii) Chloroform and acetone
C. $\Delta V_{mix} < 0$	(iii) Chlorobenzene and bromobenzene
D. Follows Raoult's law in all conditions of T and p.	(iv) Water and nitric acid

Codes

	A	B	C	D
(a)	(i, iii)	(i, iii)	(iii, iv)	(i, ii)
(b)	(ii, iv)	(i, iii)	(ii, iv)	(i, iv)
(c)	(iii, iv)	(i, iii)	(ii, iii)	(i, ii)
(d)	(i, ii, iii)	(i, ii, iii),	(iv, i, ii)	(ii, i, iii)

4. Define the term ideal solution.

5. What role does the molecular interaction play in solution of alcohol and water? **NCERT**

6. How is the vapour pressure of a solvent affected when a non-volatile solute is dissolved in it?

Short Answer Type I Questions

2 Marks

7. Why is the vapour pressure of a solution of glucose in water lower than that of water? **NCERT Exemplar**

Or

If a table spoon of sugar is added to water, then what happens to vapour pressure of water?

8. What is the similarity between Raoult's and Henry's laws?

9. What is the mass of a non-volatile solute (molar mass 60g mol^{-1}) that needs to be dissolved in 100 g of water in order to decrease the vapour pressure of water by 25%? What will be the molality of the solution? **ISC 2010**

10. (i) Gas (A) is more soluble in water than gas (B) at the same temperature. Which one of the two gases will have the higher value of K_H (Henry's constant) and why?

(ii) In non-ideal solution, what type of deviation shows the formation of maximum boiling azeotropes?

11. What type of deviation is shown by a mixture of ethanol and acetone? Give reason.

12. On mixing liquid X and liquid Y, volume of the resulting solution decreases. What type of deviation from Raoult's law is shown by the resulting solution? What change in temperature would you observe after mixing liquids X and Y?

13. Define azeotropes. What type of azeotrope is formed by the positive deviation from Raoult's law? Give an example.

Short Answer Type II Questions

3 Marks

14. Amongst the following compounds, identify which are insoluble, partially soluble and highly soluble in water?

(i) Phenol (ii) Toluene
(iii) Formic acid (iv) Ethylene glycol
(v) Chloroform (vi) Pentanol **NCERT**

15. Suggest the most important type of intermolecular interaction in the following pairs.

(i) n-hexane and n-octane
(ii) I_2 and CCl_4

(iii) $NaClO_4$ and water
(iv) Methanol and acetone
(v) Acetonitrile (CH_3CN) and acetone (C_3H_6O)
(vi) Water and alcohol **NCERT**

16. The vapour pressure of pure liquids *A* and *B* at 400K are 450 and 700 mmHg respectively. Find out the composition of liquid mixture if total vapour pressure at this temperature is 600 mmHg.

17. 100 g of liquid *A* (molar mass 140 g mol^{-1}) was dissolved in 1000 g of liquid *B* (molar mass 180 g mol^{-1}). The vapour pressure of pure liquid *B* was found to be 500 torr. Calculate the vapour pressure of pure liquid *A* and its vapour pressure in the solution, if the total vapour pressure of the solution is 475 torr. **NCERT**

18. Benzene and toluene form ideal solution over the entire range of composition. The vapour pressures of pure benzene and toluene at 300 K are 50.71 mm of Hg and 32.06 mm of Hg, respectively. Calculate the mole fraction of benzene in the vapour phase, if 80 g of benzene is mixed with 100 g of toluene. **NCERT**

19. At 25°C the vapour pressures of benzene (C_6H_6) and toluene (C_7H_8) are 93.4 torr and 26.9 torr, respectively. A solution is made by mixing 35.0 g of benzene and 65.0 g of toluene. At what applied pressure, in torr, will this solution boil at 25°C ?

20. At some temperature, the vapour pressure of pure C_6H_6 is 0.256 bar and that of pure $C_6H_5CH_3$ (toluene) is 0.0925 bar. If the mole fraction of toluene in solution is 0.6.

Then,
(i) what will be the total pressure of the solution?
(ii) what will be the mole fraction of each component in vapour phase?

Long Answer Type Questions

5 Marks

21. What is meant by positive and negative deviations from Raoult's law and how is the sign of $\Delta_{mix}H$ related to positive and negative deviations from Raoult's law? **NCERT**

22. (i) Two liquids *A* and *B* boil at 155°C and 190°C, respectively. Which of them has a higher vapour pressure at 80°C?
(ii) Heptane and octane form ideal solution. At 373 K, the vapour pressures of the two liquid components are 105.2 kPa and 46.8 kPa, respectively. What will be the vapour pressure of a mixture of 26.0 g of heptane and 35.0 g of octane? **NCERT**
(iii) The vapour pressure of water is 12.3 kPa at 300 K. Calculate the vapour pressure of one molal solution of non-volatile, non-ionic solute in water. **NCERT**

23. Vapour pressure of pure acetone and chloroform at 328 K are 741.8 mm of Hg and 632.8 mm of Hg, respectively. Assuming that they form ideal solution over the entire range of composition, plot p_{total}, $p_{chloroform}$ and $p_{acetone}$ as a function of $\chi_{acetone}$. The experimental data observed for different compositions of mixture is

$100 \times \chi_{acetone}$	0	11.8	23.4	36.0	50.8	58.2	64.5	72.1
$p_{acetone}$/ mm of Hg	0	54.9	110.1	202.4	322.7	405.9	454.1	521.1
$p_{chloroform}$/ mm of Hg	632.8	548.1	469.4	359.7	257.7	193.6	161.2	120.7

Plot this data also on the same graph paper. Indicate whether it has positive deviation or negative deviation from the ideal solution. **NCERT**

24. A solution is prepared by dissolving 2.0 g of sucrose and 2.0 g of urea in 100 g of water at 298 K. Calculate the vapour pressure of the solution, if the vapour pressure of pure water at 298 K is 23.56 torr. (Molecular weight of urea = 60 and sucrose = 342) **ISC 2006**

Hints & Solutions

1. (i) Raoult's law, ideal (ii) vapour, less
(iii) negative (iv) stronger

2. (i) → (d) (ii) → (a) (iii) → (d) (iv) → (d)

3. (b) A (ii, iv), B (i, iii), C (ii, iv), D (i, iv)

4. The solutions which obey Raoult's law over the entire range of concentration are known as ideal solutions. e.g., (i) chlorobenzene and *n*-octane, solution of *n*- heptane and *n*-octane. (1)

5. There is strong hydrogen bonding in alcohol molecules as well as water molecules. On mixing these solutions, the molecular interactions are weakened. Hence, they show positive deviations from ideal behaviour. Therefore, the solution will have higher vapour pressure and lower boiling point than that of water and alcohol.

6. When a non-volatile solute is added to a solvent, its vapour pressure decreases because some of the surface sites are occupied by solute molecules. Thus, less space is available for the solvent molecule to vaporise.

7. In the solution, the surface has both solute and solvent molecules, so the fraction of the surface covered by solvent molecules gets reduced. Hence, the number of solvent molecules escaping from the surface is reduced, resulting in lowering the vapour pressure.
Thus, the vapour pressure of the solution of glucose in water is lower than that of pure water. (2)

8. **Similarity between Raoult's and Henry's laws** Both the laws are applied to volatile component in solution. (1)
Both the laws state that the vapour pressure of one component is proportional to the mole fraction of that component. (1)

9. The expression for Raoult's law for the solution containing non-volatile solute is

$$\frac{\Delta p}{p^\circ} = \frac{p^\circ - p}{p^\circ} = \frac{n}{n+N} = \frac{w/m}{w/m + W/M}$$

where, p° = vapour pressure of pure solvent
p = partial vapour pressure
n = number of moles of solute
N = number of moles of solvent
w = weight of solute
m = molar mass of solute
W = weight of solvent
M = molar mass of solvent

Molar mass of solvent
Given, $\Delta p = 25\%$ (atm)
i.e. $p^\circ = 100$ (atm),
$m = 60$, $W = 100$ g,
$M = 18$ (for water),
$w = ?$

$$\frac{25}{100} = \frac{w/60}{w/60 + 100/18} \Rightarrow \frac{1}{4} = \frac{w/60}{\frac{18w + 60 \times 100}{18 \times 60}}$$

$\Rightarrow \quad w = 111.11$ g

Mass of solute required is 111.11 g.
Now, Molality (m)

$$= \frac{\text{Number of moles of solute}}{\text{Mass of solvent in kg}}$$

$$= \frac{111.11/60}{100/1000} = 18.518$$

Hence, molality of the solution is 18.518 mol kg^{-1}.

10. Solubility is inversely proportional to K_H, i.e. Henry's constant of the gas.
(i) Greater the value of K_H, lower is the solubility of the gas. As gas (A) is more soluble in water than gas (B) at the same temperature, hence the gas (A) has lower value of K_H. In other words, gas (B) has higher value of K_H than gas (A) at the same temperature. (1)
(ii) In non-ideal solutions, the solutions that show large negative deviation from Raoult's law form maximum boiling azeotropes. e.g. Mixture of nitric acid and water. (1)

11. A mixture of ethanol and acetone shows positive deviation because in this case, A—B interactions are weaker than A—A and B—B interactions. Due to this, vapour pressure increases which results in positive deviation. (2)

12. **Hint** It is an example of negative deviation. Since, $\Delta_{mix} V$ is negative hence $\Delta_{mix} H$ is also negative and temperature rises. Refer to text on page 15 (Non-ideal solutions). (2)

13. Refer to text on page 16 (Azeotropic mixture). (2)

14. (i) **Phenol** Partially soluble (Reason: Phenol has polar —OH group and non-polar —C_6H_5 group).
(ii) **Toluene** Insoluble (Reason: Toluene is non-polar, water is polar.)
(iii) **Formic acid** Highly soluble (Reason : Hydrogen bonding).
(iv) **Ethylene glycol** Highly soluble (Reason : Hydrogen bonding).
(v) **Chloroform** Insoluble (Reason: H-bonds are formed although polarity is present).
(vi) **Pentanol** Partially soluble (Reason: —OH group is polar but long hydrocarbon part is non-polar).
$\left(6 \times \frac{1}{2} = 3\right)$

15. (i) Since, both are non-polar. Hence, intermolecular interactions between them are **London dispersion forces.**
(ii) Same as (i).
(iii) Since, $NaClO_4$ gives Na^+ and ClO_4^- ions in the solution while water is a polar molecule. Hence, intermolecular interactions between them will be **ion-dipole interactions**.
(iv) Both are polar, they form intermolecular H-bonds with each other.
(v) As both are polar molecules. Hence, intermolecular interactions between them will be **dipole-dipole** interactions.
(vi) Same as (iv). $\left(6 \times \frac{1}{2} = 3\right)$

16. Refer to Example 2 on pages 14 and 15.
[**Ans** In liquid mixture, $\chi_A = 0.40$; $\chi_B = 0.60$]

17. Number of moles of liquid A (solute)

$$= \frac{100 \text{ g}}{140 \text{ g mol}^{-1}} = \frac{5}{7} \text{ mol}$$

Number of moles of liquid

$$B = \frac{1000 \text{ g}}{180 \text{ g mol}^{-1}} = \frac{50}{9} \text{ mol}$$

∴ Mole fraction of A in the solution (χ_A)

$$= \frac{5/7}{5/7 + 50/9} = \frac{5/7}{395/63} = \frac{5}{7} \times \frac{63}{395} = \frac{45}{395} = 0.114$$ (1/2)

$\therefore$ Mole fraction of B in the solution (χ_B)

$= 1 - 0.114 = 0.886$ (1/2)

Also, given

$$p_B^\circ = 500 \text{ torr}$$

According to Raoult's law,

$$p_A = \chi_A p_A^\circ = 0.114 \times p_A^\circ \quad (1)$$

$$p_B = \chi_B p_B^\circ = 0.886 \times 500 = 443 \text{ torr}$$

$$p_{\text{total}} = p_A + p_B$$

or $475 = 0.114 p_A^\circ + 443$

or $p_A^\circ = \dfrac{475 - 443}{0.114} = 280.7$ torr (1)

Substituting the value of p_A° in Eq. (i), we get

$$p_A = 0.114 \times 280.7 \text{ torr} = 32 \text{ torr} \quad (1)$$

18. Molar mass of benzene $(C_6H_6) = 78 \text{ g mol}^{-1}$

Molar mass of toluene $(C_7H_8) = 92 \text{ g mol}^{-1}$

$n_{C_6H_6}$ (number of moles of benzene)

$$= \frac{80 \text{ g}}{78 \text{ g mol}^{-1}} = 1.026 \text{ mol}$$

$n_{C_7H_8}$ (number of moles of toluene)

$$= \frac{100 \text{ g}}{92 \text{ g mol}^{-1}} = 1.087 \text{ mol}$$

Mole fraction of benzene,

$$\chi_{C_6H_6} = \frac{1.026 \text{ mol}}{(1.026 + 1.087) \text{ mol}} = 0.486 \quad (1/2)$$

Mole fraction of toluene

$$\chi_{C_7H_8} = 1 - 0.486 = 0.514 \quad (1/2)$$

Applying Raoult's law,

Partial vapour pressure of benzene in solution

$$p_{C_6H_6} = p^\circ_{C_6H_6} \times \chi_{C_6H_6} = (50.71 \text{ mm of Hg}) \times (0.486)$$

$= 24.65$ mm of Hg (1/2)

Partial vapour pressure of toluene in solution

$$p_{C_7H_8} = p^\circ_{C_7H_8} \times \chi_{C_7H_8} = 32.06 \text{ mm of Hg} \times 0.514$$

$= 16.48$ mm of Hg (1/2)

Total vapour pressure of solution

$p = 24.65$ mm of Hg $+ 16.48$ mm of Hg

$= 41.13$ mm of Hg

Mole fraction of benzene in vapour phase

$$= \frac{\chi_{C_6H_6} \times p^\circ_{C_6H_6}}{p_{\text{total}}} = \frac{0.486 \times 50.71}{41.13} = 0.6 \quad (1)$$

19. This solution of benzene and toluene will boil at 25°C when the pressure above the solution is equal to the sum of the vapour pressures of benzene and toluene in the solution.

Partial vapour pressure of benzene, $p^\circ_{C_6H_6} = 93.4$ torr

Partial vapour pressure of toluene,

$$p^\circ_{C_6H_5CH_3} = 26.9 \text{ torr}$$

Given mass of $C_6H_6 = 35$ g and mass of $C_6H_5CH_3 = 65$ g

Molar mass of $C_6H_6 = 12 \times 6 + 1 \times 6$

$= 72 + 6 = 78 \text{ g mol}^{-1}$

Therefore, the number of moles of C_6H_6,

$$n_{C_6H_6} = \frac{35}{78} = 0.449 \quad (1/2)$$

Molar mass of $C_6H_5CH_3 = 12 \times 6 + 1 \times 5 + 12 + 1 \times 3$

$= 92 \text{ g mol}^{-1}$

Therefore, the number of moles of $C_6H_5CH_3$,

$$n_{C_6H_5CH_3} = \frac{65}{92} = 0.707 \quad (1/2)$$

Now, the mole fractions of C_6H_6 and $C_6H_5CH_3$ are

$$\chi_{C_6H_6} = \frac{n_{C_6H_6}}{n_{C_6H_6} + n_{C_6H_5CH_3}} = \frac{0.449}{0.449 + 0.707} = \frac{0.449}{1.156} = 0.388 \quad (1/2)$$

$$\chi_{C_6H_5CH_3} = \frac{n_{C_6H_5CH_3}}{n_{C_6H_5CH_3} + n_{C_6H_6}} = \frac{0.707}{0.707 + 0.449}$$

$$= \frac{0.707}{1.156} = 0.612 \quad (1/2)$$

Therefore, vapour pressure of C_6H_6 and $C_6H_5CH_3$ are

$$p_{C_6H_6} = p^\circ_{C_6H_6} \times \chi_{C_6H_6}$$

$= 93.4 \times 0.388 = 36.24$ torr

$$p_{C_6H_5CH_3} = p^\circ_{C_6H_5CH_3} \times \chi_{C_6H_5CH_3}$$

$= 26.9 \times 0.612 = 16.46$ torr

Total vapour pressure of the solution,

$$p_{\text{total}} = p_{C_6H_6} + p_{C_6H_5CH_3}$$

$= 36.24 + 16.46 = 52.7$ torr (1)

20. (i) According to Raoult's law,

For toluene, $p_1 = p_1^\circ \times \chi_1$

$p_1^\circ = 0.0925$ bar

and $\chi_1 = 0.6$

Then, $p_1 = 0.0925 \times 0.6 = 0.0555$ bar (1/2)

For benzene, $p_2 = p_2^\circ \times \chi_2$

Mole fraction of benzene,

$$\chi_2 = 1 - \chi_1 = 1 - 0.6 = 0.4$$

and $p_2^\circ = 0.256$ bar

Then, $p_2 = 0.256 \times 0.4 = 0.1024$ bar (1/2)

Total vapour pressure of solution,

$$p_{\text{total}} = p_1 + p_2$$

$= 0.0555 + 0.1024 = 0.158$ bar (1)

(ii) Mole fraction of toluene in vapour phase

$$y_1 = \frac{p_1}{p_{\text{total}}} = \frac{0.0555}{0.158} = 0.351 \quad (1/2)$$

Mole fraction of benzene in vapour phase

$$y_2 = \frac{p_2}{p_{\text{total}}} = \frac{0.1024}{0.158} = 0.648 \quad (1/2)$$

21. Refer to text on pages 15 and 16 (Non-ideal solutions) (5)

22. (i) As A boils at low temperature as compared to B. Hence, A is more volatile, thus it has higher vapour pressure. (1)

(ii) Given that, $p^{\circ}_{\text{heptane}} = 105.2$ kPa,

$$p^{\circ}_{\text{octane}} = 46.8 \text{ kPa}$$

Molar mass of heptane $(C_7H_{16}) = 100 \text{ g mol}^{-1}$

(As $C_7H_{16} = 7 \times 12 + 16 = 84 + 16 = 100$)

Molar mass of octane $(C_8H_{18}) = 114 \text{ g mol}^{-1}$

(As $C_8H_{18} = 8 \times 12 + 18 = 96 + 18 = 114$)

Number of moles of 26.0 g heptane

$$= \frac{26.0 \text{ g}}{100 \text{ g mol}^{-1}} = 0.26 \text{ mol}$$

Number of moles of 35.0 g octane

$$= \frac{35.0 \text{ g}}{114 \text{ g mol}^{-1}} = 0.31 \text{ mol}$$

$$\chi_{\text{heptane}} = \frac{0.26 \text{ g}}{0.26 + 0.31} = 0.456 \quad (1/2)$$

$$\chi_{\text{octane}} = 1 - 0.456 = 0.544 \quad (1/2)$$

$$p_{\text{heptane}} = 0.456 \times 105.2 \text{ kPa} = 47.97 \text{ kPa}$$

$$p_{\text{octane}} = 0.544 \times 46.8 \text{ kPa} = 25.46 \text{ kPa}$$

$$p_{\text{total}} = 47.97 + 25.46 = 73.43 \text{ kPa} \quad (1)$$

(iii) As solution is 1 molal, it means that 1 mole of solute is dissolved in 1000 g of solvent (water).

No. of moles of solute $= 1$ mol, $p^{\circ}_{\text{solvent}} = 12.3$ kPa

No. of moles of water $= \frac{1000}{18} = 55.55$ mol

Total moles $= 56.55$ mol

Mole fraction of water $\chi_{H_2O} = \frac{n_1(\text{solvent})}{n_1 + n_2(\text{solution})} = \frac{55.55}{56.55}$ (1)

$$p_{\text{solution}} = p^{\circ}_{\text{solvent}} \times \chi_{H_2O}$$

$$p_{\text{solution}} = 12.3 \times \frac{55.55}{56.55} = 12.08 \text{ kPa} \quad (1)$$

23.

χ_{acetone}	0.0	0.118	0.234	0.360	0.508	0.582	0.645	0.721
p_{acetone} /mm of Hg	0	54.9	110.1	202.4	322.7	405.9	454.1	521.1
$p_{\text{chloroform}}$ /mm of Hg	632.8	548.1	469.4	359.7	257.7	193.6	161.2	120.7
p_{total}	632.8	603.1	579.7	562.4	580.9	600.0	615.9	642.5

(2½)

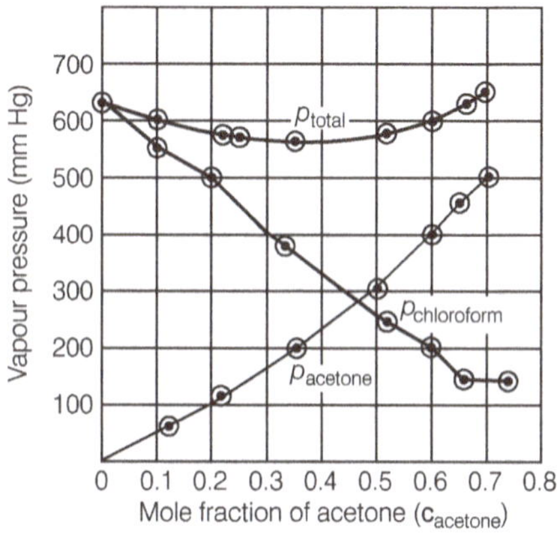

(2½)

As the plot for p_{total} dips downwards, hence the solution shows negative deviation from Raoult's law. (1)

24. According to Raoult's law,

$$\frac{\Delta p}{p^{\circ}} = \frac{p^{\circ} - p}{p^{\circ}} = \frac{n}{n + N}$$

$$= \frac{w/m}{w/m + W/M}$$

where, p° = vapour pressure of pure solvent

p = partial vapour pressure

n = number of moles of solute

N = number of moles of solvent

w = weight of solute

m = molar mass of solute

W = weight of solvent

Given that, $p^{\circ} = 23.56$ torr

Number of moles of solute (n),

= Number of moles of sucrose + Number of moles of urea

$$= \frac{w_s}{m_s} + \frac{w_u}{m_u}$$

$$n = \frac{2}{342} + \frac{2}{60}$$

Number of moles of solvent (water),

$$N = \frac{100}{18}$$

$$\therefore \frac{23.56 - p}{23.56} = \frac{\frac{2}{342} + \frac{2}{60}}{\frac{2}{342} + \frac{2}{60} + \frac{100}{18}}$$

$$= 0.007$$

$$23.56 - p = 0.007 \times 23.56$$

$$= 0.165$$

$$p = 23.56 - 0.165$$

$$= 23.395\text{s torr}$$

Hence, the vapour pressure of the solution is 23.395 torr.

TOPIC 04 Colligative Properties and Determination of Molar Mass

Colligative Properties

The properties of solutions which depend only on the number of solute particles irrespective of their nature, relative to the total number of particles present in the solution, are called colligative properties.

There are four important colligative properties :

(i) Relative lowering of vapour pressure
(ii) Elevation in boiling point
(iii) Depression in freezing point
(iv) Osmosis and osmotic pressure

Relative Lowering of Vapour Pressure

On adding non-volatile solute to a solvent, the vapour pressure of the solution decreases. Lowering of vapour pressure depends only on the concentration of the solute particles and it is independent of their identity.

Let χ_1 is the mole fraction of pure solvent, χ_2 is the mole fraction of solute, p_1° is the vapour pressure of pure solvent and p is that of solution.

Since, solute is non-volatile, so the vapour pressure of the solution (p_1) will be only due to the solvent. Thus, according to **Raoult's law**,

$$p_1 = p_1^\circ \chi_1 \text{ or } p \Rightarrow p_1 = p_1^\circ \chi_1$$

This, equation establishes a relation between vapour pressure of the solution, mole fraction and vapour pressure of the solvent. Since, χ_1 is always less than 1, hence, vapour pressure of the solution p will always be less than the vapour pressure of pure solvent (p_1°).

So, lowering in vapour pressure of solvent is given as

$$\Delta p_1 = p_1^\circ - p_1 = p_1^\circ - p_1^\circ \chi_1 = p_1^\circ (1 - \chi_1)$$

But $\quad \chi_1 = 1 - \chi_2 \quad \text{or} \quad \chi_2 = 1 - \chi_1$

So, $\quad \Delta p_1 = p_1^\circ \chi_2$

or $\quad \chi_2 = \dfrac{\Delta p_1}{p_1^\circ} = \dfrac{p_1^\circ - p_1}{p_1^\circ}$

So, **relative lowering in vapour pressure of an ideal solution containing the non-volatile solute is equal to the mole fraction of the solute at a given temperature.**

In a solution containing several non-volatile solutes, the lowering of the vapour pressure depends on the sum of the mole fraction of different solutes.

Determination of Molar Mass of Solute

To express the lowering of vapour pressure in terms of molar mass, let W_1, W_2 are the masses and M_1 and M_2 are the molar masses of the solvent and solute respectively.

As, we know that $\quad \chi_2 = \dfrac{n_2}{n_1 + n_2}$

where, n_1 and n_2 are the number of moles of solvent and solute, respectively.

Since, $\quad \chi_2 = \dfrac{W_2 / M_2}{\dfrac{W_1}{M_1} + \dfrac{W_2}{M_2}}$

But for dilute solutions, $\dfrac{W_2}{M_2} << \dfrac{W_1}{M_1}$

or $\quad n_2 << n_1$

So, $\quad \dfrac{W_1}{M_1} + \dfrac{W_2}{M_2} \approx \dfrac{W_1}{M_1} \quad \text{or} \quad \chi_2 = \dfrac{W_2/M_2}{W_1/M_1}$

So, $\quad \dfrac{p_1^\circ - p_1}{p_1^\circ} = \dfrac{W_2 M_1}{W_1 M_2}$

or $\quad \dfrac{p_1^\circ - p_1}{p_1^\circ} = \dfrac{n_2}{n_1}$

So, molar mass of solute can be determined by

$$\boxed{M_2 = \dfrac{W_2 M_1}{W_1 \left(\dfrac{p_1^\circ - p_1}{p_1^\circ} \right)}}$$

Example 1 An aqueous solution of 2% non-volatile solute exerts a pressure of 1.004 bar at the normal boiling point of the solvent. What is the molar mass of the solute? **NCERT**

Key Idea Addition of non-volatile solute in a solution results in relative lowering of vapour pressure. For dilute solution, molar mass of solute can be determined by using the formula,

$$M_2 = \dfrac{W_2 M_1}{W_1 \left(\dfrac{p_1^\circ - p_1}{p_1^\circ} \right)}$$

Sol. Vapour pressure of pure water at the boiling point

$(p_1^\circ) = 1 \text{ atm} = 1.013 \text{ bar}$

Vapour pressure of solution $(p) = 1.004$ bar (Given)

2% non-volatile solute means

Mass of solute $(W_2) = 2\text{ g}$

Mass of solution $= 100\text{ g}$

$\therefore$ Mass of solvent$(W_1) = 98\text{ g}$

Applying Raoult's law for dilute solution, as n_2 (moles of solute) is very small in comparison to n_1 (moles of solvent).

$\therefore$ n_2 can be neglected from denominator.

Lowering in vapour pressure,

$$\frac{p_1^\circ - p}{p_1^\circ} = \frac{n_2}{n_1 + n_2} \approx \frac{n_2}{n_1} = \frac{W_2 / M_2}{W_1 / M_1} = \frac{W_2}{M_2} \times \frac{M_1}{W_1}$$

$$\frac{(1.013 - 1.004)}{1.013 \text{ bar}} = \frac{2\text{ g}}{M_2} \times \frac{18 \text{ g mol}^{-1}}{98 \text{ g}}$$

or $$M_2 = \frac{2 \times 18}{98} \times \frac{1.013}{0.009} \text{ g mol}^{-1} = 41.35 \text{ g mol}^{-1}$$

Note Relative lowering in vapour pressure is a colligative property while vapour pressure and lowering in vapour pressure are not.

Elevation in Boiling Point (Ebullioscopy)

The boiling point of a liquid is that temperature at which its vapour pressure becomes equal to the atmospheric pressure. Generally, the vapour pressure of liquid increases with increase of temperature but vapour pressure of the solvent decreases in the presence of non-volatile solute.

This difference in the boiling points of the solution (T_b) and pure solvent (T_b°) is called as **elevation in boiling point** (ΔT_b). Elevation in boiling point depends on the number of solute molecules rather than their nature.

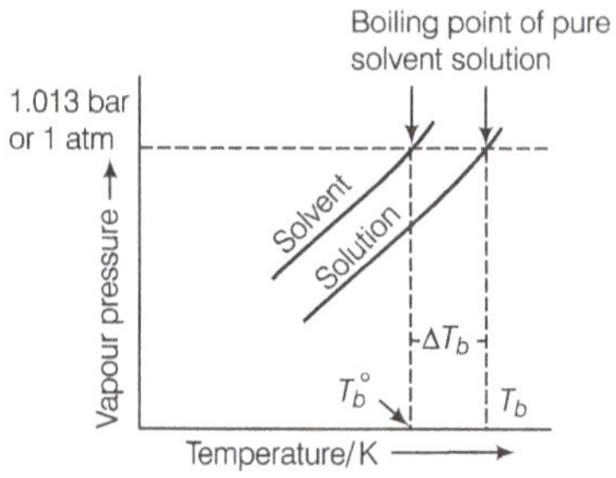

The vapour pressure curve for solution lies below the curve for pure water. The figure shows that ΔT_b denotes the elevation in boiling point of a solvent in solution

The given figure depicts the variation of vapour pressure of the pure solvent and solution as a function of temperature.

Elevation in boiling point is given by $\Delta T_b = T_b - T_b^\circ$

Experiments have shown that for dilute solution, the elevation in boiling point is directly proportional to the molal concentration of the solute in a solution (m).

Thus, $\Delta T_b \propto m$ or $\Delta T_b = K_b m$

where, m (molality) is the number of moles of solute dissolved in 1 kg of solvent and K_b is the constant of proportionality, called **molal boiling point elevation constant** or **ebullioscopic constant**. The unit of K_b is K kg mol^{-1}.

If $m = 1$ molal

Then, $\Delta T_b = K_b$

Thus, molal boiling point elevation constant, K_b is defined as the elevation in boiling point for 1 molal solution, i.e. a solution containing 1 g mole of solute dissolved in 1000 g of the solvent.

Determination of Molar Mass of Solute

If W_2 gram of solute of molar mass M_2 is dissolved in W_1 gram of solvent, then molality, m of the solution is given as:

$$\text{Molality } (m) = \frac{\text{Moles of solute } (n_2) \times 1000}{\text{Weight of solvent } (W_1) \text{ (in gram)}}$$

where, n_2 is the number of moles of solute.

$$\text{Moles of solute } (n_2) = \frac{W_2}{M_2}$$

Thus, $$m = \frac{W_2 \times 1000}{M_2 \times W_1}$$

But $\Delta T_b = K_b m$

So, we get $$\Delta T_b = \frac{K_b \times W_2 \times 1000}{M_2 \times W_1}$$

Therefore, $$\boxed{M_2 = \frac{K_b \times W_2 \times 1000}{\Delta T_b \times W_1}}$$

This expression is used to determine the molar mass of solute.

Example 2 Boiling point of water at 750 mm of Hg is 99.63°C. How much sucrose is to be added to 500 g of water such that it boils at 100°C ?
[K_b for water is 0.52 K kg mol^{-1}] **NCERT Intext**

(i) Since, boiling point is changing, apply the formula for elevation in boiling point, $\Delta T_b = K_b \cdot m$

(ii) $m = \dfrac{W_B}{M_B \cdot W_A}$ (in kg)

So, $\Delta T_b = \dfrac{K_b \cdot W_B}{M_B \times W_A}$ or $W_B = \dfrac{\Delta T_b \times M_B \times W_A}{K_b}$

(iii) Find ΔT_b as $\Delta T_b = T_b = T_b - T_b^\circ$

T_b = Boiling point of solution

T_b° = Boiling point of pure solvent

Sol. Mass of water $(W_A) = 500 \text{ g} = 0.5 \text{ kg}$

Elevation in boiling point

$(\Delta T_b) = 100^\circ \text{C} - 99.63^\circ \text{C} = 0.37^\circ \text{C} = 0.37 \text{ K}$

Molal elevation constant $(K_b) = 0.52 \text{ K kg mol}^{-1}$

Molar mass of sucrose $(C_{12}H_{22}O_{11})$

$(M_B) = (12 \times 12) + (22 \times 1) + (16 \times 11) = 342 \text{ g mol}^{-1}$

$$W_B = \frac{M_B \times \Delta T_b \times W_A}{K_b}$$

$$= \frac{(342 \text{ g mol}^{-1}) \times (0.37 \text{ K}) \times (0.5 \text{ kg})}{(0.52 \text{ K kg mol}^{-1})} = 121.7 \text{ g}$$

Depression in Freezing Point (Cryoscopy)

The freezing point is that temperature at which the solid and the liquid states of the substance have the same vapour pressure. When a non-volatile solute is added to a solvent, the freezing point of thus formed solution is always lower than that of pure solvent as the vapour pressure of the solvent decreases in the presence of non-volatile solute. This difference in the freezing point is known as depression in freezing point.

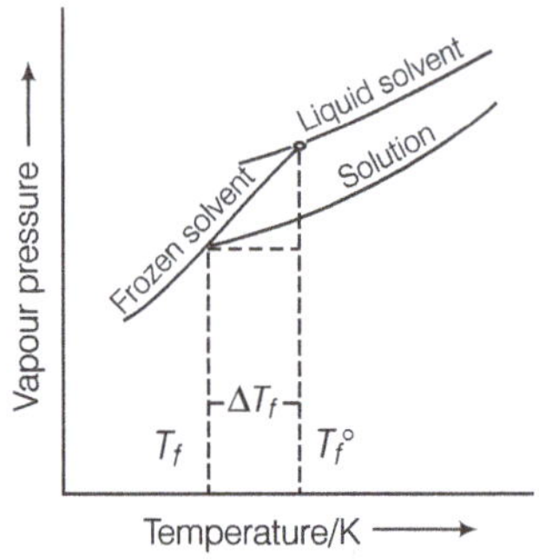

Figure showing ΔT_f, depression in freezing point of a solvent in a solution

If T_f° is the freezing point temperature (in kelvin) of pure solvent and T_f is the freezing point temperature (in kelvin) of the solution when non-volatile solute is dissolved in it then, depression in freezing point (ΔT_f) is given by

$$\Delta T_f = T_f^\circ - T_f$$

For dilute solutions, $\Delta T_f \propto m$

or $$\boxed{\Delta T_f = K_f m}$$

where, m is the molal concentration (or molality) of the solution and K_f is the proportionality constant, which depends on the nature of the solvent is known as **molal freezing point depression constant** or **molal depression constant** or **cryoscopic constant**. The unit of K_f is K kg mol^{-1}. If $m = 1$ molal, then $\Delta T_f = K_f$

Thus, molal freezing point depression constant is defined as the depression in freezing point for 1 molal solution, i.e. a solution containing 1g mole of solute dissolved in 1000 g of solvent.

Note Elevation in boiling point and depression in freezing point are colligative properties while boiling and freezing points are not.

Determination of Molar Mass of Solute

Similar to elevation in boiling point,

$$\Delta T_f = \frac{K_f \times W_2 \times 1000}{W_1 \times M_2}$$

or $$\boxed{M_2 = \frac{K_f \times W_2 \times 1000}{\Delta T_f \times W_1}}$$

This expression is used to determine the molar mass of solute.

Applications of Depression in Freezing Point

(i) **In Making Antifreeze Solutions** The running of a car in sub-zero weather even when the radiator is full of water (which freezes below 273 K) has been possible due to fact that depression in freezing point of water takes place when appropriate amount of suitable solute (usually ethylene glycol) called antifreeze is dissolved in the water.

(ii) **In Melting of Ice on the Roads** In winter season common salt (NaCl) or anhydrous $CaCl_2$ is spread on the roads to melt ice.This is because freezing mixture of ice and salt has a very low freezing point of –21°C and that of $CaCl_2$-ice mixture of –55°C. Thus, as long as the temperature of the surrounding is above these temperatures, the mixtrue does not freeze and ice keeps on melting.

Example 3 A 5% solution (by mass) of cane sugar in water has freezing point of 271 K. Calculate the freezing point of a 5% glucose in water, if freezing point of pure water is 273.15 K. **NCERT**

Key Idea Freezing point of pure water is 273.15 K (0°C) and that of given solution is 271 K, i.e. we have depression in freezing point.So,

(i) Apply the formula of depression in freezing point for cane sugar.

(ii) Similarly, find the depression in freezing point for glucose.

(iii) Compare the two equations to find the freezing point of glucose.

Sol. **For cane sugar solution**

$$\text{Molality of sugar solution} = \frac{W_2}{M_2} \times \frac{1000}{W_1}$$

Here, $W_2 = 5\text{ g}$, $M_2 = 342\text{ g mol}^{-1}$ (sugar), $W_1 = 95\text{ g}$

$$\text{Molality } (m) = \frac{5}{342} \times \frac{1000}{95} = 0.154\text{ m}$$

ΔT_f for sugar solution $= 273.15 - 271 = 2.15$ K

$$\Delta T_f = K_f \times m$$

$$\therefore \quad K_f = \frac{2.15}{0.154}$$

For glucose solution

Here, $W_2 = 5\text{ g}$, $m_2 = 180\text{ g mol}^{-1}$ (glucose),

$W_1 = 95\text{ g}$

$$\text{Molality of glucose solution} = \frac{5}{180} \times \frac{1000}{95} = 0.2924\text{ m}$$

$$\Delta T_f = K_f m$$

$$\therefore \quad \Delta T_f\text{ (glucose)} = \frac{2.15}{0.154} \times 0.2924 = 4.08$$

$\therefore$ Freezing point of glucose solution $= 273.15 - 4.08$
$= 269.07$ K

Osmosis and Osmotic Pressure

The phenomenon of the flow of solvent molecules through a semipermeable membrane from pure solvent to the solution is known as **osmosis.**

Semipermeable Membranes

These membranes appear to be continuous sheets or films, yet they contain a network of submicroscopic holes or pores. It allows solvent molecules like water to pass through their holes but binds the passage for molecules of solute like salt.

Types of Semipermeable Membrane

Vegetable membranes and animal membranes are **natural semipermeable membranes** while copper ferrocyanide, silicates of iron, cobalt and nickel are **chemical semipermeable membranes.**

If semipermeable membrane is placed between the pure solvent and solution as shown in the figure given below, the solvent molecules will flow through the membrane from pure solvent to the solution.

Importance of Osmosis

The biological importance of osmosis are given below :

(i) A raw mango placed in concentrated salt solution loses water *via* osmosis and shrivel into pickle.

(ii) Wilted flowers revive when placed in fresh water through osmosis.

(iii) A carrot that has become limp because of water loss into the atmosphere can be placed into the water making it firm once again through osmosis.

(iv) Through osmosis, blood cell collapse due to loss of water when placed in water containing more than 0.9% (mass/volume) salt solution.

(v) People taking a lot of salt or salty food experience water retention in tissue cells and intercellular spaces because of osmosis. This results in puffiness or swelling is called **edema.**

(vi) Water movement from soil into plant roots and subsequently into upper portion of the plant is partly due to osmosis.

(vii) The preservation of meat by salting and of fruits by adding sugar protects against bacterial action. Through the process of osmosis, a bacterium on salted meat or sugared fruits loses water, shrivels and dies.

Difference between Osmosis and Diffusion

(i) Diffusion is intermixing of molecules or ion etc resulting from the random thermal agitation thus, there is no restriction to motion of any kind of particles while in osmosis only solvent molecules flow.

(ii) Osmosis takes place through a semipermeable membrane while for diffusion, it is not required.

(iii) A homogeneous mixture is obtained as a result of diffusion. On the other hand no mixing is possible in osmosis.

(iv) Diffusion cannot be prevented while osmosis can be stopped by applying pressure to the solution.

Osmotic Pressure (π)

The osmotic pressure of a solution is the excess pressure that must be applied to a solution to prevent osmosis, i.e. to stop the passage of solvent molecules through a semipermeable membrane into the solution. It is a colligative property as it depends upon the number of solute molecules and not on their nature.

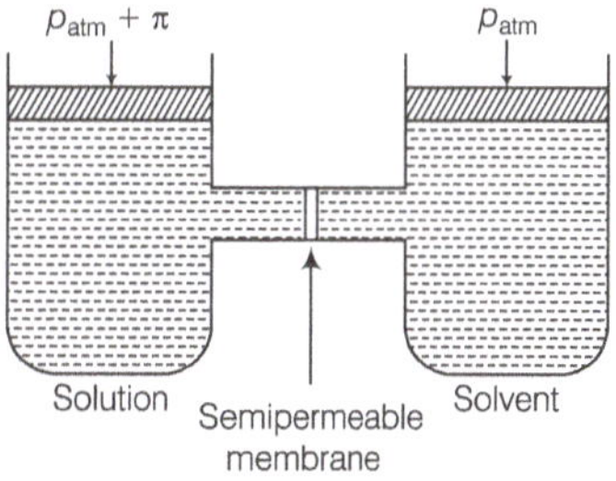

The excess pressure equal to the osmotic pressure must be applied on the solution side to prevent osmosis

Laws of Osmotic Pressure

van't Hoff established that the solute particles present in a solution behave exactly like the molecules of a gas. He found that the ordinary laws obeyed by gases are also obeyed by dilute solutions and these are called **laws of osmotic pressure.**

(i) **Boyle's-van't Hoff Law** states that the osmotic pressure (π) of a solution is directly proportional to its concentration (C), when the temperatue is kept constant.

Let, π be the osmotic pressure and C be the concentration of a dilute solution, then

$$\pi \propto C \quad \text{(at constant temperature)}$$

or

$$\pi \propto \frac{1}{V}$$

(where, V is the volume containing one mole of the solute when concentration of solution is expressed in mol/L).

Caution point The osmotic pressure of a solution containing 1 mole of solute particle per litre (1 M) at 0°C is 22.4 atm.

(ii) **Charles'-van't-Hoff Law** According to which the osmotic pressure of dilute solution is directly proportional to its absolute temperature (T), when the concentration of solution is kept constant.

$$\pi \propto T \quad \text{(at constant concentration)}$$

(where, T is a absolute temperature)

(iii) **Avogadro's van't Hoff Law** states that equal volumes of dilute solutions of different solutes, having the same temperature and osmotic pressure contain equal number of molecules, i.e. isotonic solutions at a given temperature have same molar concentration.

$$\boxed{\pi \propto n}$$

(where, n is the number of moles of solute in V litres of a solution at temperature T)

(iv) **General Equation for Dilute Solutions** It is obtained by combining the above three laws

Mathematically it is shown as,

$$\pi V = nRT \text{ or } \pi = CRT$$

If R is in L atm $mol^{-1}K^{-1}$, π will be in atmosphere. If R is in J $mol^{-1}K^{-1}$, π will be in pascal or Nm^{-2}.

The value of R is taken to be 0.0821 L atm K^{-1} mol^{-1} when π is expressed in atmosphere, V in litres and T in Kelvin. This equation is termed as **van't-Hoff equation.**

Application of Osmotic Pressure in the Determination of Relative Molecular Mass of a Solute

Since, osmotic pressure is directly proportional to the concentration (C) of the solution at a given temperature (T)

$$\pi \propto C \Rightarrow \pi = CRT = \frac{w_2}{m_2}\frac{RT}{V}$$

On the basis of above formula, we can calculate molecular mass of solute as, $m_2 = \dfrac{w_2 RT}{V\pi}$

where, m_2 = molecular mass of solute

w_2 = mass of solute

V = volume of solution (in litre)

π = osmotic pressure

Advantages of Osmotic Pressure Measurement

(i) Osmotic pressure measurements are made at room temperature. Thus, this method can be used for substances like proteins, polymers, etc. without damaging them.

(ii) The magnitude of osmotic pressure is very large even in dilute solution. So, it can be maeasured with greater accuracy.

Example 4 Calculate the osmotic pressure (in pascals) exerted by a solution prepared by dissolving 1.0 g of polymer (molar mass 185000) in 450 mL of water at 37°C. **NCERT Intext**

Sol. From the relation,

$$\pi = CRT = \frac{n}{V}RT,$$

we can find the value of π.

Mass of polymer = 1.0 g

Here, number of moles of solute dissolved (n)

$$= \frac{1.0 \text{ g}}{185000 \text{ g mol}^{-1}} = \frac{1}{185000} \text{ mol}$$

$$V = 450 \text{ mL} = 0.450 \text{ L}$$

$$T = 37°\text{C} = 37 + 273 = 310 \text{ K}$$

$$R = 8.314 \text{ kPa L K}^{-1} \text{ mol}^{-1}$$

$$= 8.314 \times 10^3 \text{ Pa L K}^{-1}\text{mol}^{-1}$$

Substituting these values, we get

$$\pi = \frac{1}{185000}\text{mol} \times \frac{1}{0.45 \text{ L}} \times 8.314 \times 10^3 \text{ Pa L K}^{-1}\text{mol}^{-1} \times 310 \text{K}$$

$$= 30.96 \text{ Pa}$$

Types of Solutions on the Basis of Osmotic Pressure

There are three types of solutions on the basis of concentration and hence the applied osmotic pressure:

(i) **Isotonic Solution** or (**Iso-osmotic Solution**) Two solutions having same osmotic pressure at a given temperature are called isotonic solutions. There is no osmosis between these two solutions as they have same molar concentration.

(ii) **Hypertonic Solution** A solution having more osmotic pressure than the other solution is called hypertonic solution.

(iii) **Hypotonic Solution** A solution having less osmotic pressure than the other solution is called hypotonic solution.

Reverse Osmosis and Water Purification

The direction of osmosis can be reversed, if a pressure larger than the osmotic pressure is applied to the solution side. Now, the pure solvent flows out of the solution through semipermeable membrane. This phenomenon is called reverse osmosis. This method is used in desalination to get salt free-water from sea water as shown in the figure.

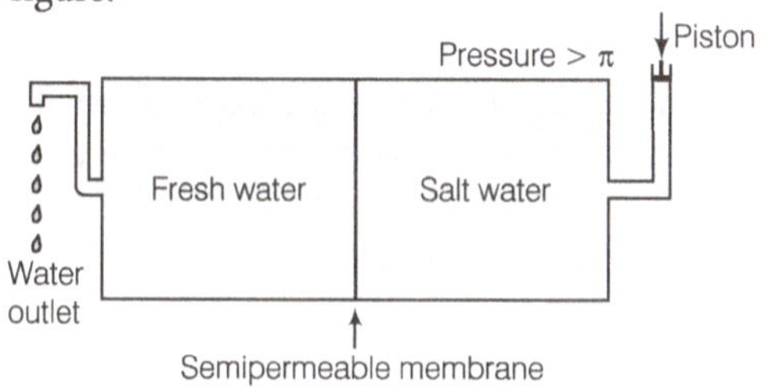

Reverse osmosis occurs when a pressure larger than the osmotic pressure is applied on the more concentrated solution side

When a pressure higher than the osmotic pressure of the sea water is applied, pure water passes through the semipermeable membrane leaving dissolved salt ions and other impurities behind. The pressure required for the reverse osmosis is quite high. Variety of polymer membrane is available for this purpose. The most commonly used semipermeable membrane is that of cellulose acetate. This method of purification is boon for the regions where fresh water is scarcely available.

Abnormal Molecular Mass

For the substances undergoing association, dissociation, etc., in the solution, experimentally observed molecular mass determined from colligative properties is different from the normal value as expected from its chemical formula. This observed molecular mass is known as **abnormal molecular mass.**

e.g. Ionic compounds when dissolved in water dissociates into cations and anions, e.g. one mole of KCl (74.5g) in water dissociates into K^+ and Cl^- ions. While the molecules of few organic compounds like acetic acid or benzoic acid dimerise in benzene due to H-bonding.

The molecular association of a solute in solution leads to a observed molar mass higher than normal molar mass of solute while molecular dissociation of a observed solute leads to a molar mass which is less than the normal value of the molar mass of the solute.

Note Larger the value of molecular mass of the solute, smaller the observed value of colligative properties, i.e. relative lowering of vapour pressure, elevation in boiling point (ΔT_b), depression of freezing point (ΔT_f) and osmotic pressure (π).

van't Hoff Factor (i)

In 1880, van't Hoff introduced a factor i, known as van't Hoff factor to account for the extent of dissociation or association. It is defined as the ratio of the experimental value of the colligative property to the calculated value of the colligative property.

$$i = \frac{\text{Normal (calculated) molar mass}}{\text{Observed (abnormal) molar mass}}$$

$$= \frac{\text{Observed colligative property}}{\text{Calculated colligative property}}$$

$$\text{Colligative property} \propto \frac{1}{\text{Molar mass}}$$

van't Hoff factor can be applied in case of dissociation and association as follows

(i) **In Case of Dissociation** When substance is an electrolyte, the number of particles increases in solution and the colligative property increases accordingly. Suppose 1 molecule of solute A dissociates to give n ions and α is the degree of dissociation.

	A	$\rightleftharpoons n B$
Initially	1 mol	0
After dissociation	$(1 - \alpha)$ mol	$n\alpha$

Total number of moles present in solution

$$= (1 - \alpha) + n\alpha = 1 + (n - 1)\,\alpha$$

van't Hoff factor, $i = 1 + (n - 1)$

$$\alpha > 1 \text{ if } n \geq 2$$

and $$\alpha = \frac{(i - 1)}{(n - 1)}$$

(ii) **In case of association** When substance undergoes association, the number of particles decreases in solution and consequently the value of colligative property decreases.

e.g. molecules of acetic acid dimerise in benzene due to hydrogen bonding.

$$2CH_3COOH \rightleftharpoons (CH_3COOH)_2$$

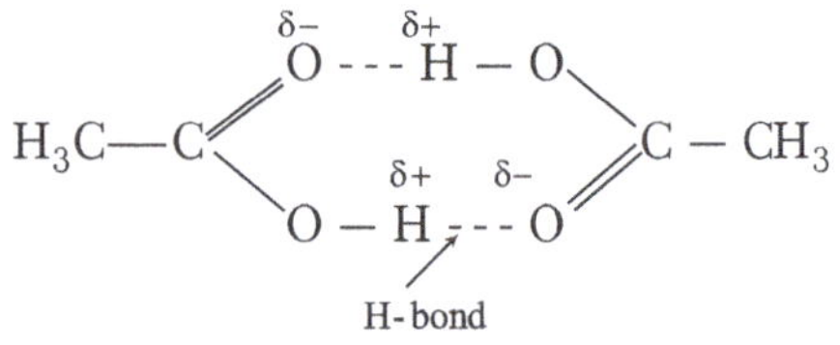

Suppose n molecules associate to form one giant molecule and α is the degree of association.

	nA $\rightleftharpoons$	$(A)_n$
Initially	1 mol	0
At equilibrium	$(1-\alpha)$ mol	$\frac{\alpha}{n}$

Total number of moles in solution

$$=(1-\alpha)+\frac{\alpha}{n}=1+\left(\frac{1}{n}-1\right)\alpha$$

$$\text{van't Hoff factor (i)} = 1+\left(\frac{1}{n}-1\right)$$

$$\alpha<1 \text{ if } n \geq 2 \text{ and } \quad \alpha=\frac{(i-1)}{\frac{1}{n}-1}$$

Modified forms of Colligative Properties

Due to inclusion of van't Hoff factor, the modified forms of colligative properties are:

Relative lowering of vapour pressure, $\frac{\Delta p}{p^\circ}=i\chi_2$

or $$\frac{p_1^\circ - p_1}{p_1^\circ}=i\cdot\frac{n_2}{n_1}$$

Elevation in boiling point, $\Delta T_b = iK_b m$

Depression in freezing point, $\Delta T_f = iK_f m$

Osmotic pressure, $\pi = iCRT$ or $\frac{in_2RT}{V}$

Example 5 Determine the amount of $CaCl_2$ ($i=2.47$) dissolved in 2.5 L of water such that its osmotic pressure is 0.75 atm at 27°C. **NCERT**

> **Key idea** First calculate the moles of $CaCl_2$ by applying van't Hoff equation, $\pi = iCRT$ and $C=\frac{n_B}{V}$
> Then, calculate the amount of $CaCl_2$ by multiplying the moles with molar mass.

Sol From, $\pi = iCRT = i\frac{n}{V}RT$

or $$n=\frac{\pi\times V}{i\times R\times T}$$

Here, $\pi = 0.75$ atm; $V = 2.5$ L, $i = 2.47$;

$T = 300$ K $\quad (\because 27+273)$;

$R = 0.0821 \text{ L atm K}^{-1}\text{mol}^{-1}$

$$\Rightarrow \quad n=\frac{0.75 \text{ atm}\times 2.5 \text{ L}}{2.47\times 0.0821 \text{ L atm K}^{-1}\text{mol}^{-1}\times 300 \text{ K}}$$
$$= 0.0308 \text{ mol}$$

Molar mass of $CaCl_2 = 40 + 2\times 35.5$
$= 111 \text{ g mol}^{-1}$

$\therefore$ Amount of $CaCl_2$ dissolved $= n\times M$
$= 0.0308\times 111 \text{ g} = 3.42$ g

Example 6 A 0.5% aqueous solution of KCl was found to be freeze at −0.24°C. Calculate the van't Hoff factor and degree of dissociation of the solute at this concentration.

(K_f for water = 1.86 K kg mol^{-1}).

Sol. Given, $K_f = 1.86 \text{K kg mol}^{-1}$, $W_2 = 0.5$ g, $W_1 = 100$ g,

$\Delta T_f = 0.24°C$

$$\text{Observed molecular mass of KCl} = \frac{1000\times K_f\times W_2}{\Delta T_f\times W_1}$$

$$=\frac{1000\times 1.86\times 0.5}{0.24\times 100}=38.75 \text{ g mol}^{-1}$$

Normal molecular mass of KCl $= 38.75 + 35.5 = 74.25 \text{ g mol}^{-1}$

$$\text{van't Hoff factor} = \frac{\text{Normal molecular mass}}{\text{Observed molecular mass}}$$

$$i=\frac{74.25}{38.75}=1.92$$

$$\underset{(1-\alpha)}{KCl} \rightleftharpoons \underset{\alpha}{K^+} + \underset{\alpha}{Cl^-}$$

Total number of particles $= 1-\alpha+\alpha+\alpha = 1+\alpha$

$i = 1+\alpha$ or $1.92 = 1+\alpha$

So, $\alpha = 1.92 - 1 = 0.92$, i.e. 92% dissociated.

Topic Practice 4

Very Short Answer Type Questions

1 Mark

1. Fill in the Blanks

(i) The ...... of the boiling point of solvent by the addition of a non-volatile solute is .... proportional to the molality of the solution. **ISC 2009**

(ii) The elevation of boiling point of 0.5 M K_2SO_4 solution is .... that of 0.5 M urea solution. The elevation of boiling point of 0.5 M KCl solution is ...... that of 0.5 M K_2SO_4 solution. **ISC 2019**

(iii) The properties of solutions, which depends only on the number of .... particles irrespective of their nature, relative to the total number of particles present in the .... are called colligative properties.

(iv) People taking a lot of salt or salty food experience water retention in tissue cells and ...... spaces.

(v) The van't Hoff factor of acetic acid solution is ...... than one and the value of normal colligative property is ...... than the observed colligative property of this solution. **ISC 2014**

2. Objective Type Questions

(i) For a dilute solution containing 2.5 g of a non-volatile, non-electrolyte solute in 100 g of water, the elevation in boiling point at 1 atm pressure is 2°C. Assuming concentration of solute is much lower than the concentration of solvent, the vapour pressure (mm of Hg) of the solution is ($K_b = 0.76$ K kg mol^{-1})

(a) 724 (b) 740
(c) 736 (d) 718

(ii) An equimolar solution of non-volatile solutes *A* and *B*, shows a depression in freezing point in the ratio of 2:1. If *A* remains in its normal state in the solution, the state of *B* in the solution will be **ISC 2024**

(a) normal (b) hydrolysed
(c) associated (d) dissociated

(iii) An aqueous solution of urea freezes at −0.186°C, K_f for water = 1.86 K kg mol^{-1}, K_b for water = 0.512 K kg mol^{-1}. The boiling point of urea solution will be **ISC 2018**

(a) 373.065 K (b) 373.186 K
(c) 373.512 K (d) 373.0512 K

(iv) Out of the following solutions, the one having the highest boiling point will be **ISC 2011**

(a) 0.1 M NaCl
(b) 0.1 M $BaCl_2$
(c) 0.1 M KNO_3
(d) 0.1 M $K_4[Fe(CN)_6]$

(v) The molal freezing point constant of water is 1.86 K kg mol^{-1}. Therefore, the freezing point of 0.1 M NaCl solution in water is expected to be **ISC 2015**

(a) −1.86°C (b) −0.372°C
(c) −0.186°C (d) +0.372°C

(vi) The molecular weight of sodium chloride determined by measuring the osmotic pressure of its aqueous solution is **ISC 2009**

(a) double the theoretical value
(b) same as the theoretical value
(c) half the theoretical value
(d) three times the theoretical value

(vii) For a dissociated solute in solution, the value of van't Hoff factor is

(a) zero (b) one
(c) greater than one (d) less than one

3. Correct the following statement by changing the underlined part of the sentence.
Water boils below 100°C by the addition of NaCl. **ISC 2008**

4. Match the laws given in Column I with expressions given in Column II.

Column I		Column II	
A.	Raoult's law	1.	$\Delta T_f = K_f m$
B.	Henry's law	2.	$\pi = CRT$
C.	Elevation in boiling point	3.	$p = x_1 p_1^\circ + x_2 p_2^\circ$
D.	Depression in freezing point	4.	$\Delta T_b = K_b m$
E.	Osmotic pressure	5.	$p = K_H \cdot x$

Codes

	A	B	C	D	E		A	B	C	D	E
(a)	3	5	4	1	2	(b)	1	2	3	5	4
(c)	2	3	5	4	1	(d)	5	4	1	2	3

5. Explain boiling point elevation constant for a solvent.

Or

Define molal elevation constant, K_b.

6. What are the units of molal depression constant? **ISC 2014**

7. Define cryoscopic constant. **ISC 2013**

8. A solution X is prepared by dissolving 3 moles of glucose in one litre of water and a solution Y is prepared by dissolving 1.5 moles of sodium chloride in one litre of water. Will the osmotic pressure of X be higher, lower or equal to that of Y?

Give a reason for your answer. **ISC 2012**

Short Answer Type I Questions

(2 Marks)

9. A solution is prepared by dissolving 9.25 g of non-volatile solute in 450 mL of water. It has an osmotic pressure of 350 mm of Hg at 27°C. Assuming the solute is non-electrolyte, determine its molecular mass.

($R = 0.0821$ L atm $K^{-1}mol^{-1}$) **ISC 2019**

10. Calculate the mass of ascorbic acid (molecular mass = 176 g/mol) that should be dissolved in 155 g of acetic to cause a depression of freezing point by 1.15 K. Assume that ascorbic acid does not dissociate or associate in the solution.

(K_f for acetic acid = 3.9 K kg/mol) **ISC 2023**

11. List any four factors on which the colligative properties of a solution depend.

12. Calculate the mass of a non-volatile solute (molar mass 40 g mol^{-1}) which should be dissolved in 114 g of octane to reduce its vapour pressure to 80%. **NCERT**

13. Vapour pressure of water at 293 K is 17.535 mm of Hg. Calculate the vapour pressure of water at 293 K when 25 g of glucose is dissolved in 450 g of water. **NCERT**

14. A 2 molal solution of sodium chloride in water causes an elevation in the boiling point of water by 1.88 K. What is the value of van't Hoff factor? What does it signify?

(K_b = 0.52 K kg mol^{-1}) **ISC 2014**

15. Explain, why on addition of 1 mole of NaCl to 1 L of water, the boiling point of water increases, while addition of 1 mole of methyl alcohol to 1 L of water decreases its boiling point? **NCERT Exemplar**

16. 18 g of glucose, $C_6H_{12}O_6$ (molar mass = 180 g mol^{-1}) is dissolved in 1 kg of water in a sauce pan. At what temperature will this solution boil?

(K_b for water = 0.52 K kg mol^{-1}, boiling point of pure water = 373.15 K).

17. Arrange the depression in freezing point of water observed for the same molar concentrations of acetic acid, trichloroacetic acid and trifluoroacetic acid. Explain this order as well. **NCERT**

18. The freezing point of a solution containing 0.3 g of acetic acid in 30 g of benzene is lowered by 0.45 K. Calculate the van't Hoff factor. (Atomic weight of C = 12, H = 1, O = 16, K_f for benzene = 5.12 K kg mol^{-1}) **ISC 2013**

19. Calculate the boiling point of urea solution when 6 g of urea is dissolved in 200 g of water.

(K_b for water = 0.52 K kg mol^{-1}, boiling point of pure water = 373 K, mol. wt. of urea = 60) **ISC 2019**

20. A solution of urea in water has a boiling point of 100.18°C. Calculate the freezing point of the solution.

(K_f for water is 1.86 K kg mol^{-1} and

K_b for water is 0.512 K kg mol^{-1}) **ISC 2012**

21. Calculate the freezing point of a solution containing 60 g of glucose

(Molar mass = 180 g mol^{-1}) in 250 g of water.

(K_f of water = 1.86 Kkg mol^{-1})

22. When 0.4 g of oxalic acid is dissolved in 40g of benzene, the freezing point of the solution is lowered by 0.45 K. Calculate the degree of association of acetic acid. Acetic acid forms dimer when dissolved in benzene.

(K_f for benzene = 5.12 K kg mol^{-1}, at. wt. C = 12, H = 1, O = 16) **ISC 2019**

23. How does sprinkling of salt help in clearing the snow covered roads in hilly areas? Explain the phenomenon involved in the process. **NCERT Exemplar**

24. Calculate the mass of compound (molar mass = 256 g mol^{-1}) to be dissolved in 75 g of benzene to lower its freezing point by 0.48 K.

(K_f = 5.12 K kg mol^{-1})

25. Given reasons for the following:

(i) Measurement of osmotic pressure method is preferred for the determination of molar masses of macromolecules such as proteins and polymers.

(ii) Elevation of boiling point of 1 M KCl solution is nearly double than that of 1 M sugar solution.

26. Determine the osmotic pressure of a solution prepared by dissolving 25 mg of K_2SO_4 in 2 L of water at 25°C, assuming that it is completely dissociated. **NCERT**

27. The osmotic pressure of blood at 37°C is 8.21 atm. How much glucose in grams should be used per litre of aqueous solution for an intravenous injection so that it is isotonic with blood ? (Molecular wt. of glucose = 180 g/mol) **ISC 2023**

28. If 200 cm^3 of an aqueous solution of protein contains 1.26 g of protein, the osmotic pressure of the solution at 300 K is found to be 2.57×10^{-3} atm.

    Calculate the molar mass of protein.

    ($R = 0.0821$ L atm K^{-1} mol^{-1}) **ISC 2024**

29. At 300 K, 36 g of glucose present in a litre of its solution has an osmotic pressure of 4.98 bar. If the osmotic pressure of the solution is 1.52 bar at the same temperature, what would be its concentration? **NCERT**

30. When kept in water, raisin swells in size. Name and explain the phenomenon involved with the help of a diagram. Give three applications of the phenomenon. **NCERT Exemplar**

31. Define the following terms:
    (i) Abnormal molar mass
    (ii) van't Hoff factor

Short Answer Type II Questions

3 Marks

32. At 25°C, the saturated vapour pressure of water is 3.165 kPa (23.75 mm of Hg). Find the saturated vapour pressure of a 5% aqueous solution of urea (carbamide) at the same temperature. (Molar mass of urea = 60.05 g mol^{-1}).

33. A solution is prepared by dissolving 10 g of non-volatile solute in 200 g of water. It has a vapour pressure of 31.84 mm Hg at 308 K. Calculate the molar mass of the solute. (Vapour pressure of pure water at 308 K = 32 mm of Hg)

34. Vapour pressure of pure water at 298 K is 23.8 mm of Hg. 50 g of urea (NH_2CONH_2) is dissolved in 850 g of water. Calculate the vapour pressure of water for this solution and its relative lowering. **NCERT Intext**

35. What will be the vapour pressure of a solution containing 5 moles of sucrose ($C_{12}H_{22}O_{11}$) in 1 kg of water, if the vapour pressure of pure water is 4.57 mm of Hg? (C = 12, H = 1, O = 16) **ISC 2014**

36. Calculate the boiling point of solution when 4 g of $MgSO_4$ (M = 120 g mol^{-1}) was dissolved in 100 g of water assuming $MgSO_4$ undergoes complete ionisation.
    (K_b for water = 0.52 K kg mol^{-1})

37. Ethylene glycol is used as an antifreeze agent. Calculate the amount of ethylene glycol to be added to 4 kg of water to prevent it from freezing at −6° C.(K_f for H_2O = 1.85 K mol^{-1}kg) **ISC 2013**

38. Calculate the mass of ascorbic acid (vitamin C, $C_6H_8O_6$) to be dissolved in 75 g of acetic acid to lower its melting point by 1.5°C. (K_f for acetic acid = 3.9 K kg mol^{-1}). **NCERT Intext**

39. Two elements A and B form compounds having molecular formula AB_2 and AB_4. When dissolved in 20 g of benzene (C_6H_6), 1 g of AB_2 lowers the freezing point by 2.3 K whereas 1.0 g of AB_4 lowers it by 1.3 K. The molal depression constant for benzene is 5.1 K kg mol^{-1}. Calculate atomic masses of A and B. **NCERT**

40. An aqueous solution containing 12.48 g of barium chloride ($BaCl_2$) in 1000 g of water, boils at 100.0832°C. Calculate the degree of dissociation of barium chloride.
    (K_b for water = 0.52 kg mol^{-1}, atomic weight Ba= 137, Cl=35.5) **ISC 2018**

41. 3.9 g of benzoic acid dissolved in 49 g of benzene shows a depression in freezing point of 1.62 K. Calculate the van't Hoff factor and predict the nature of solute (associated or dissociated).
    (Given : Molar mass of benzoic acid = 122 g mol^{-1}, K_f for benzene = 4.9 K kg mol^{-1})

42. The freezing point of benzene decreases by 0.45°C when 0.2 g of acetic acid is added to 20 g of benzene. If acetic acid associates to form a dimer in benzene, then what will be the percentage association of acetic acid in benzene? (K_f for benzene = 5.12 K kg mol^{-1})

43. When 2 g of benzoic acid is dissolved in 25 g benzene, it shows a depression in freezing point equal to 1.62 K. Molal depression constant (K_f) of benzene is 4.9 K kg mol^{-1} and molecular

weight of benzoic acid = 122 g/mol. What will be the percentage association of the benzoic acid ?

(Benzoic acid forms dimer when dissolved in benzene). **ISC 2023**

44. An aqueous solution containing 12.50 g of barium chloride in 1000 g of water boils at 373.0834 K. Calculate the degree of dissociation of barium chloride.

[Given K_b for $H_2O = 0.52$ K kg mol^{-1}; molecular mass of $BaCl_2 = 208.34$ g mol^{-1}] **ISC 2024**

45. The freezing point of a solution containing 5.85 g of NaCl in 100 g of water is $-3.348°$C. Calculate van't Hoff factor '*i*' for this solution. What will be the experimental molecular weight of NaCl? [3]

(K_f for water = 1.86 K kg mol^{-1}, atomic weight of Na = 23, Cl = 35.5) **ISC 2018**

Long Answer Type Questions

5 Marks

46. A solution containing 30 g of a non-volatile solute exactly in 90 g of water has a vapour pressure of 2.8 kPa at 298 K. Further, 18 g of water is then added to the solution and the new vapour pressure becomes 2.9 kPa at 298 K. Calculate

(i) molar mass of the solute.

(ii) vapour pressure of water at 298 K. **NCERT**

47. Calculate the depression in the freezing point of water when 10 g of $CH_3CH_2CHClCOOH$ is added to 250 g of water. $K_a = 1.4 \times 10^{-3}$, $K_f = 1.86$ K kg mol^{-1}. **NCERT**

48. 19.5 g of CH_2FCOOH is dissolved in 500 g of water. The depression in the freezing point of water observed is 1.0°C. Calculate the van't Hoff factor and dissociation constant of fluoroacetic acid. (K_f for water is 1.86 K kg mol^{-1}) **NCERT**

49. (i) An aqueous solution of a non-volatile solute freezes at 272.4 K, while pure water freezes at 273.0 K. Determine the following :

(Given, $K_f = 1.86$ K kg mol^{-1}, $K_b = 0.512$ K kg mol^{-1} and vapour pressure of water at 298 K = 23.756 mm of Hg)

(a) The molality of solution.

(b) Boiling point of solution.

(c) The lowering of vapour pressure of water at 298 K.

(ii) A solution containing 1.23 g of calcium nitrate in 10 g of water, boils at 100-975°C at 760 mm of Hg.

Calculate the van't Hoff factor for the salt at this concentration.

(K_b for water = 0.52 K kg mol^{-1}, molecular weight of calcium nitrate = 164 g mol^{-1}) **ISC 2020**

50. (i) A solution containing 0.5 g of KCl dissolves in 100 g of water and freezes at $-0.24°$C. Calculate the degree of dissociation of the salt. (K_f for water = 1.86°C).
(Atomic weights of K = 39, Cl = 35.5)

(ii) If 1.71 g of sugar (molar mass = 342) are dissolved in 500 mL of an aqueous solution at 300 K, what will be its osmotic pressure?

(iii) 0.70 g of an organic compound when dissolved in 32 g of acetone produces an elevation of 0.25°C in the boiling point. Calculate the molecular mass of organic compound.

(K_b for acetone = 1.72 K kg mol^{-1}) **ISC 2015**

51. (i) Determine the freezing point of a solution containing 0.625 g of glucose ($C_6H_{12}O_6$) dissolved in 102.8 g of water.

(Freezing point of water = 273 K, K_f for water = 1.87 K kg mol^{-1}, (at. wt. of C = 12, H = 1, O = 16)

(ii) A 0.15 M aqueous solution of KCl exerts an osmotic pressure of 6.8 atm at 310 K. Calculate the degree of dissociation of KCl.

($R = 0.0821$ L atm K^{-1}mol^{-1}).

(iii) A solution containing 8.44 g of sucrose in 100 g of water has a vapour pressure 4.56 mm of Hg at 273K. If the vapour pressure of pure water is 4.58 mm of Hg at the same temperature, calculate the molecular weight of sucrose. **ISC 2017**

52. (i) The elevation in boiling point when 0.30 g of acetic acid is dissolved in 100 g of benzene is 0.0633°C. Calculate the molecular weight of acetic acid from this data.

What conclusion can you draw about the molecular state of the solute in the solution?

(Given K_b for benzene = 2.53 K kg mol^{-1}, at. wt. of C = 12, H = 1, 0 = 16).

(ii) Determine the osmotic pressure of a solution prepared by dissolving 0.025 g of K_2SO_4 in 2 litres of water at 25°C, assuming that K_2SO_4 is completely dissociated. ($R = 0.0821$ L atm K^{-1} mol^{-1}, mol. wt. of K_2SO_4 = 174 g mol^{-1}) **ISC 2020**

53. (i) A 10% aqueous solution of cane sugar (mol.wt. = 342) is isotonic with 1.754% aqueous solution of urea. Find the molecular mass of urea.

(ii) The molecular weight of an organic compound is 58 g mol^{-1}. What will be the boiling point of a solution containing 48 g of the solute in 1200 g of water?
[K_b for water = 0.513°C kg mol^{-1}; boiling point of water =100°C]

(iii) What will be the value of van't Hoff factor (i) of benzoic acid, if it dimerises in aqueous solution? How will the experimental molecular weight vary as compared to the normal molecular weight? **ISC 2016**

Hints & Solutions

1. (i) elevation, directly (ii) More than, less than
(iii) solute, solution (iv) intercellular
(v) less, more

2. (i) a, (ii) (d), (iii) d, (iv) d, (v) d, (vi) c, (vii) c

3. The correct statement is as follows:

Water boils above 100°C by the addition of NaCl. It is because, NaCl is a strong electrolyte and it dissociates into 2 ions ($\overset{+}{Na}$ and $\overset{-}{Cl}$).

Therefore, its van't Hoff value is 2 and the elevation of boiling point ΔT_b, is proportional to i.

4. (a) A–3, B–5, C–4, D–1, E–2

5. We know that, $\Delta T_b = K_b m$

If $m = 1$, then $\Delta T_b = K_b$. Thus, boiling point elevation constant is equal to the elevation in boiling point, when 1 mole of a solute is dissolved in 1 kg of solvent. It is also called Ebullioscopic constant.

6. The units of molal depression constant are K kg mol^{-1}.

7. It is the depression in freezing point produced on dissolving one mole of a substance in 1000 g or 1 kg of the solvent.

8. Osmotic pressure of the two solutions X and Y will be same.

Osmotic pressure is a colligative property which depends on the number of particles present in solution. Since, glucose is non-electrolyte.

∴ Value of van't Hoff factor i for glucose $= 1$ and $n = 3$ moles

Value of van't Hoff factor i for NaCl = 2 and $n = 1.5$ moles

Now for glucose, osmotic pressure, $\pi = \dfrac{inRT}{V}$

[Here, volume (V) of water = 1000 mL]

$$= 1 \times 3\,RT/1000 = 3\,RT/1000$$

For NaCl, osmotic pressure, $\pi = \dfrac{inRT}{V}$

$$= 2 \times 1.5\,RT/1000 = 3RT/1000$$

So, π is same for both the solutions.

9. Given,

Mass of non-volatile solute $(w_B) = 9.25$ g

Volume of water $(V_A) = 450$ mL

Osmotic - pressure $(\pi) = \dfrac{350}{760} = 0.46$ atm

Temperature $(T) = 27 + 273 = 300$ K

Gas constant $(R) = 0.0821$ L atm $K^{-1} mol^{-1}$

Now,

$$\because \quad \pi = CRT = \frac{w_B \times 1000 \times RT}{M_B \times V}$$

∴ M_B [molecular mass of non-volatile solute]

$$= \frac{w_B \times 1000 \times R \times T}{V \times \pi}$$

or, $$M_B = \frac{w_B \times 1000 \times R \times T}{V \times \pi}$$

or, $$= \frac{9.25\text{ g} \times 1000 \times 0.0821\text{ L atm K}^{-1}\text{ mol}^{-1} \times 300\text{ K}}{450\text{ mL} \times 0.46\text{ atm}}$$

$$M_B = \frac{227827.5}{20.7} = 1100.6\text{ g mol}^{-1}$$

Hence, molecular mass of non - volatile solute $= 1100.6$ g mol^{-1}

10. w_1, mass of acetic acid $= 155$ g

M_2, molecular mass of $(C_6H_8O_6) = 176$ g/mol

Depression in freezing point = 1.15 K

We know,

$$\Delta T_f = \frac{k_f \times 1000 \times w_2}{M_2 \times w_1}$$

$$1.15 = \frac{3.9 \times 1000 \times w_2}{176 \times 155}$$

$$w_2 = \frac{176 \times 155 \times 1.15}{3.9 \times 1000} = 8.04\text{ g}$$

11. (i) Number of particles of solute
(ii) Association or dissociation of solute
(iii) Concentration of solution
(iv) Temperature $\left(4 \times \frac{1}{2} = 2\right)$

12. Here, $p = 80\%$ of $p_1^\circ = 0.80 p_1^\circ$

Number of moles of solute $(n_2) = \dfrac{W_2}{40}$ mol

Number of moles of solvent (octane)

$$n_1 = \frac{114\text{ g}}{114\text{ g mol}^{-1}} = 1\text{ mol}$$

($\therefore$ As molar mass of $C_8H_{18} = 114\text{ g mol}^{-1}$)

Now, $\frac{p_1^\circ - p}{p_1^\circ} = \chi_2 = \frac{n_2}{(n_1 + n_2)}$ (1)

$\therefore \quad \frac{p_1^\circ - 0.80p_1^\circ}{p_1^\circ} = \frac{(W_2/40)}{(W_2/40 + 1)}$

$$0.2\left(\frac{W_2}{40} + 1\right) = \frac{W_2}{40}$$

or $\quad \frac{0.8W_2}{40} = 0.2$

or $\quad W_2 = 10\text{ g}$ (1)

13. Here, $p^\circ = 17.535$ mm of Hg, $W_2 = 25$ g,

$W_1 = 450$ g

For solute (glucose, $C_6H_{12}O_6$), $M_2 = 180\text{ g mol}^{-1}$

For solvent (H_2O), $M_1 = 18\text{ g mol}^{-1}$

According to Raoult's law,

$$\frac{p_1^\circ - p_1}{p_1^\circ} = \frac{n_2}{n_1 + n_2}$$

or $\quad \frac{p_1^\circ - p_1}{p_1^\circ} = \frac{n_2}{n_1} = \frac{W_2/M_2}{W_1/M_1}$

($\because$ for dilute solution $n_2 >>> n_1$)(1)

or $\quad \frac{17.535 - p_1}{17.535} = \frac{W_2 M_1}{W_1 M_2}$

$$\frac{17.535 - p_1}{17.535} = \frac{25 \times 18}{450 \times 180} = \frac{25}{4500} = 0.00556$$

or $\quad = 17.535 - p_1 = 0.09749$

$p_1 = 17.4375$ mm of Hg ≈ 17.44 mm of Hg (1)

14. Given molality, $m = 2$

Elevation in boiling point, $\Delta T_b =$,
van't Hoff factor, $i = ?$,

$K_b = 0.52\text{ K kg mol}^{-1}$

we know that, $\Delta T_b = i\, K_b\, m$

van't Hoff factor, $i = \Delta T_b / K_b \times m = \frac{1.88}{0.52 \times 2} = 1.807$

Since, value of van't Hoff factor is greater than one, it signifies that solute undergoes dissociation.

15. NaCl is a non-volatile solute. So, its addition to water lowers the vapour pressure of water. Hence, boiling point of water (solution) increases. Whereas methyl alcohol is more volatile than water. So, its addition to water increases the total vapour pressure of the solution. It results in decrease in boiling point of water.

16. Given,

W_a = weight of H_2O (solvent) = 1 kg

W_b = weight of $C_6H_{12}O_6$ (glucose, solute) = 18 g

$T_b^\circ = 373.15$ K

$K_b = 0.52\text{ K kg mol}^{-1}$

M_b = molar mass of solute (glucose) = 180 g mol^{-1}

$$\Delta T_b = \frac{K_b \times 1000 \times W_b}{M_b \times W_a}$$

$$= \frac{(0.52\text{ K kg mol}^{-1}) \times 1000 \times 18\text{ g}}{(180\text{ g mol}^{-1}) \times 1000\text{ g}}$$

$$= \frac{9360}{180000} = 0.052\text{ K}$$ (1)

As we know that,

$$\Delta T_b = T_b - T_b^\circ$$

$$0.052 = T_b - 373.15$$

$$T_b = 373.15 + 0.052 = 373.202\text{ K}$$

≈ 373.20 K (approx.) (1)

17. The depression in freezing point is in the order:

Acetic acid < trichloroacetic acid < trifluoroacetic acid

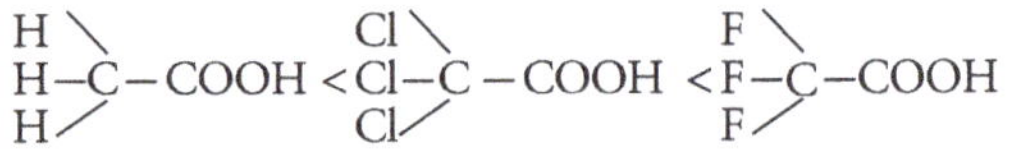
(1)

Fluorine has the highest electron withdrawing inductive effect, so trifluoroacetic acid is the strongest acid and acetic acid is the weakest acid. Therefore, trifluoroacetic acid ionises to the greater extent and acetic acid ionises to the minimum extent. Greater the number of ions produced, greater is the depression in freezing point. (1)

18. Given, amount of acetic acid (w) = 0.3 g,

Given, amount of benzene (W) = 30 g,

Depression in freezing point, $\Delta T_f = 0.45$

$K_f = 5.12\text{ K kg mol}^{-1}$

We know that, $\Delta T_f = iK_f\, m$

(where, m is molality and i represents van't Hoff factor)

Molality, $m = \frac{w \times 1000}{M' \times W} = \frac{0.3 \times 1000}{60 \times 30}$

$= 0.166 \approx 0.17$

[as molar mass of acetic acid (CH_3COOH)

$M' = 2 \times 12 + 4 \times 1 + 2 \times 16 = 60\text{ g mol}^{-1}$]

Now, $\quad i = \frac{\Delta T_f}{K_f \times m} = \frac{0.45}{5.12 \times 0.17} = 0.517$

19. Given,

Mass of solute (urea), i.e. $w_B = 6$ g

Mass of water (solvent), i.e. $w_A = 200$ g

Molar mass of urea, $M_B = 60\text{ g mol}^{-1}$

K_f for water = $0.52\text{ K kg mol}^{-1}$

Boiling point (b.p) of pure water = 373 K

$\because \Delta T_b$ (elevation in b.p) $= K_f \times \frac{w_B}{M_B} \times \frac{1000}{w_A}$

$$\Delta T_b = \frac{0.52\text{K kg mol}^{-1} \times 6 \text{ g} \times 1000}{60 \text{ g mol}^{-1} \times 200 \text{ g}} = 0\cdot26°\text{K}$$

20. (i) First we will calculate the molality (m) of the solution, by using the formula, $\Delta T_b = K_b \times m$.

(ii) Then we will find out the depression of freezing point using molality of solution, using the formula, $\Delta T_f = K_f \times m$ and then calculate the freezing point of solution by

$$\Delta T_f = T_f' - T_f^{\circ}.$$

Calculation of molality (m) of the solution

Given, boiling point of solution

$= 100.18 + 273 = 373.18$ K

Boiling point of water $= 100 + 273 = 373$

$\therefore$ Elevation in boiling point,

$$\Delta T_b = 373.18 \text{ K} - 373 \text{ K} = 0.18 \text{ K}$$

We know that, $\Delta T_b = K_b \times m$

$$\therefore \text{Molality, } m = \frac{\Delta T_b}{K_b} = \frac{0.18}{0.512} = 0.351 \text{ mol kg}^{-1}$$

(as $K_b = 0.512$ K kg mol^{-1})

Calculation of freezing point

We know that ,

$$\Delta T_f = K_f \times m$$
$$= 1.86 \times 0.351 = 0.652\text{K (as } K_f = 1.86 \text{ K kg mol}^{-1})$$

$$T_f = T_f' - \Delta T_f = 273 \text{ K} - 0.652 \text{ K} = 272.34 \text{ K}$$

(as freezing point of water $= 0°\text{C} = 273$ K)

$$T_f = -\,0.652\,°\text{C}$$

21. Molality of solution,

$$m = \frac{w_2}{M_2} \times \frac{1000}{w_1} \quad \text{...(i)}$$

where, w_2 weight of glucose $= 60$ g

M_2 molar mass of glucose $= 180$ g

w_1 weight of solvent (water) $= 250$ g

Putting value in Eq. (i)

$$= \frac{60\text{g}}{180\text{g}} \times \frac{1000\text{g}}{250\text{g}}$$

Molality $m = 1.33$ (1)

Now, $\Delta T_f = K_f m$, $K_f = 1.86$ K kg mol^{-1}

$$\Delta T_f = 1.86 \text{ K kg mol}^{-1} \times 1.33 \text{ m}$$
$$\Delta T_f = 2.47 \text{ K}$$

Freezing point of pure water $= 273.15$ K

$\therefore$ freezing point of solution $= (273.15 - 2.47)$ K

$= 270.68$ K

22. Given,

Mass of oxalic acid $= 0.4$ g (w_B)

Mass of benzene $= 40$ g(w_A)

K_f for benzene $= 5.12$ K kg mol^{-1}

Molar mass of oxalic acid $[C_2O_4H_2] = 90$ g mol^{-1}

$(2\times12 + 4\times16 + 2\times1)$, i.e. (M_B)

ΔT_f (lowering in freezing point) $= 0.45$ K

$$\text{Now, } \Delta T_f = i \times K_f \times \frac{w_B}{M_B} \times \frac{1000}{w_A}$$

$$i = \frac{\Delta T_f \times M_B \times w_A}{K_f \times w_B \times 1000}$$

$$i = \frac{0.45 \text{ K} \times 90 \text{ g mol}^{-1} \times 40 \text{ g}}{5.12 \text{ K kg mol}^{-1} \times 0.4 \text{ g} \times 1000} = 0.79$$

Also, $i = 1 - \alpha + \frac{\alpha}{2}$ (For association)

where, i = vant' Hoff factor and

α = degree of association.

$$0.79 = 1 - \alpha + \frac{\alpha}{2} = 1 - \alpha\left[1 - \frac{1}{2}\right]$$

$$0.79 = 1 - \frac{\alpha}{2} \Rightarrow \frac{\alpha}{2} = 1 - 0.79 = 0.21$$

$\therefore$ $\alpha = 0.42$ or 42%

23. When salt is spread over snow covered roads, solution of salt and water is formed and as a result, depression in freezing point of water occurs. At the ambient temperature, snow starts melting and it helps in clearing the roads. (2)

24. Given that, $K_f = 5.12$ K kg mol^{-1}

Mass of benzene, $W_1 = 75$ g

Depression in freezing point,

$$\Delta T_f = 0.48 \text{ K}, M_2 = 256 \text{ g mol}^{-1}$$

If W_2 is the mass of compound,

$$\text{Then,} \quad \Delta T_f = \frac{K_f \times W_2 \times 1000}{W_1 \times M_2} \quad (1/2)$$

(where, M_2 is molar mass of compound)

$$\text{or} \quad 0.48 = \frac{5.12 \times W_2 \times 1000}{75 \times 256} \quad (1/2)$$

$$\therefore \quad W_2 = \frac{0.489 \times 75 \times 256}{5.12 \times 1000} = 1.8 \text{ g} \quad (1)$$

25. (i) The osmotic pressure method has the advantage over other methods as pressure measurement is around the room temperature and the molarity of the solution is used instead of molality.

(ii) Elevation in boiling point is directly proportional to 'i'. (i.e. $\Delta T_b \propto i$). Now as given in the question, elevation of boiling point of 1 M KCl solution is nearly double than that of 1 M sugar solution. It is because KCl being ionic, dissociates into K^+ and Cl^- and therefore it's van't Hoff factor, i is 2 whereas for sugar van't Hoff factor is 1 as it does not undergo such a dissociation.

26. K_2SO_4 dissolved $= 25$ mg $= 0.025$ g

Volume of solution $= 2$ L

$$T = 25°\text{C} = 25 + 273 = 298 \text{ K}$$

Molar mass of $K_2SO_4 = 2 \times 39 + 32 + 4 \times 16$
$= 174 \text{ g mol}^{-1}$

As, K_2SO_4 dissociates completely as follows:

$$K_2SO_4 \longrightarrow 2K^+ + SO_4^{2-} \quad (1/2)$$

i.e. ions produced = 3

$\therefore$ $i = 3$

$$\therefore \quad \pi = iCRT = i\frac{n}{V}RT$$
$$= i \times \frac{W}{M} \times \frac{1}{V}RT \quad (1/2)$$
$$= 3 \times \frac{0.025 \text{ g}}{174 \text{ g mol}^{-1}} \times \frac{1}{2 \text{ L}} \times 0.0821 \text{ L atm K}^{-1}\text{mol}^{-1} \times 298 \text{ K}$$
$$= 5.27 \times 10^{-3} \text{ atm} \quad (1)$$

27. Given,

$\pi_{\text{blood}} = 8.21$ atm, $V = 1\text{L}$, $T = 37°\text{C} = 37 + 273 = 310$ K

Blood and glucose are isotonic,

So, both will have same osmotic pressure,

We know,

$$\pi V = nRT$$
$$n = \frac{\pi V}{RT}$$
$$n = \frac{8.21 \times 1.0}{0.0821 \times 310} = \frac{10}{31}$$

Weight of glucose = $n \times$ molecular weight

$$= \frac{10}{31} \times 180 = 58.064 \text{ g} \quad (2)$$

28. Given, Volume of aqueous solution of a protein = 200 cm^3

Amount of protein = 1.26 g

Osmotic pressure, $\pi = 2.57 \times 10^{-3}$ atm

$R = 0.0821 \text{ L atm K}^{-1} \text{mol}^{-1}$ or $T = 300$ K

as $\pi = CRT = \frac{n}{V}RT = \frac{w}{MV}RT$

$$M = \frac{1.26 \times 0.0821 \times 300}{2.57 \times 10^{-3} \times 0.2} = 60.38 \text{ g/mol}^{-1} \quad (2)$$

29. $\pi = CRT = \frac{n}{V}RT = \frac{W_2 \times RT}{M_2 \times V}$

For both solutions, R, T and V are constant.

$\therefore$ In the first case, ($M_2 = 180$ for glucose)

$$4.98 = \frac{36}{180} \times \frac{R \times 300}{V} \quad \text{...(i)}$$

In the second case, $1.52 = \frac{W_2}{M_2 V} \times R \times 300$ ...(ii)

On dividing Eq. (ii) by Eq. (i), we get

$$\frac{W_2}{M_2 V} \text{ or } C = 0.061 \text{ mol L}^{-1} \quad (2)$$

30. This phenomenon is called endoosmosis, i.e. movement of water inside the raisin and shown with the help of diagram as:

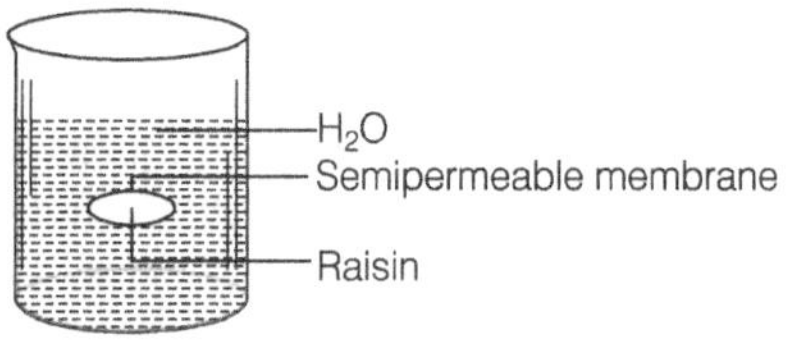

(1)

The process of osmosis is of immense biological as well as industrial importance. It is evident from the following examples:

(i) Movement of water from soil into plant roots and subsequently into upper portion of the plant is partly due to osmosis.

(ii) Preservation of meat against bacterial action by the addition of salt.

(iii) Preservation of fruits against bacterial action by adding sugar. Bacterium in canned fruit loses water through the process of osmosis and become inactive.

(iv) Reverse osmosis is used in desalination of water. (1)

31. Refer to text on pages 27-28 (Abnormal molecular mass and van't Hoff factor i)

32. $\frac{p_1^\circ - p_1}{p_1^\circ} = \chi_2 = \frac{n_2}{n_1}$ [for dilute solution, $n_2 << n_1$]

$$\frac{p_1^\circ - p_1}{p_1^\circ} = \frac{W_2 \times M_1}{M_2 \times W_1} \quad (1)$$

Given, $p_1^\circ = 3.165$ kPa, $W_2 = 5$ g, $W_1 = 95$ g

$M_2 = 60.05 \text{ g mol}^{-1}$, $M_1 = 18 \text{ g mol}^{-1}$

$$\frac{3.165 - p_1}{3.165} = \frac{5 \times 18}{60.05 \times 95} = 0.0158 \quad (1)$$

$$3.165 - p_1 = 0.050 \text{ or } p_1 = 3.115 \text{ kPa} \quad (1)$$

33.
$$\frac{p_1^\circ - p_1}{p_1^\circ} = \frac{n_2}{n_1}$$
$$\frac{p_1^\circ - p_1}{p_1^\circ} = \frac{W_2}{M_2} \times \frac{M_1}{W_1} \quad (1)$$

$p_1^\circ = 31.84$ mmHg

$W_2 = 10$ g, $W_1 = 200$ g

$M_2 = ?$, $M_1 = 18$ g

$$\frac{32 - 31.84}{32} = \frac{10 \times 18}{200 \times M_2}$$

$$M_2 = 180 \text{ g mol}^{-1} \quad (2)$$

Molar mass of solute = 180 g mol^{-1}.

34. Here, $p^\circ = 23.8$ mm of Hg, $W_2 = 50$ g, $W_1 = 850$ g

For solute, urea (NH_2CONH_2), $M_2 = 60 \text{ g mol}^{-1}$

For solvent (H_2O), $M_1 = 18 \text{ g mol}^{-1}$

According to Raoult's law,

$$\frac{p_1^\circ - p_1}{p_1^\circ} = \frac{n_2}{n_1 + n_2}$$

or $$\frac{p_1^\circ - p_1}{p_1^\circ} = \frac{n_2}{n_1} = \frac{W_2/M_2}{W_1/M_1}$$

(for dilute solution, $n_1 + n_2 \simeq n_1$) (1)

or $$1 - \frac{p_1}{p_1^\circ} = \frac{W_2 \times M_1}{W_1 \times M_2}$$

Substituting the values, we get

$$1 - \frac{p_1}{23.8} = \frac{50}{60} \times \frac{18}{850} = \frac{3}{170}$$

$$\frac{p_1}{23.8} = 1 - \frac{3}{170} = \frac{167}{170}$$

$$p_1 = \frac{167 \times 23.8}{170} = \frac{3974.6}{170}$$

$= 23.38$ mm of Hg (1)

Relative lowering of vapour pressure

$$= \frac{p_1^\circ - p_1}{p_1^\circ} = \frac{23.80 - 23.38}{23.80} = \frac{0.42}{23.80} = 0.018$$ (1)

35. Given, number of moles of sucrose $(n) = 5$ mol

Mass of solvent (water) $= 1$ kg

Vapour pressure of pure water $(p^\circ) = 4.57$ mm of Hg

Vapour pressure of solution $(p) = ?$

According to Raoult's law,

$$\frac{p^\circ - p}{p^\circ} = \frac{n}{n+N}$$ (where, N is number of moles of water)

$$\frac{4.57 - p}{4.57} = \frac{5}{5 + 55.5} \quad \left(\text{as } N = \frac{1000}{18} = 55.5 \text{ mol}\right)$$ (1)

$$4.57 - p = \frac{4.57 \times 5}{60.5} = 0.377$$

$\therefore \quad p = 4.57 - 0.377 = 4.193$ mm of Hg (2)

36. Given, weight of solute, $W_2 = 4$ g

weight of solvent, $W_1 = 100$ g

$i = 2$ (as $MgSO_4$ dissociates completely into 2 ions)

$$MgSO_4 \rightleftharpoons Mg^{2+} + SO_4^{2-}$$

$K_b = 0.52$ K kg mol^{-1}, $M_2 = 120$ g mol^{-1} (1)

$\therefore$ The elevation in boiling point of solution,

$$\Delta T_b = \frac{i \times K_b \times W_2 \times 1000}{M_2 \times W_1}$$

where, i = van't Hoff factor, W_2 = weight of solute

W_1 = weight of solvent, M_2 = molar mass of solute

$$\Delta T_b = \frac{2 \times 0.52 \times 4 \times 1000}{120 \times 100} = 0.346 \text{ K}$$ (1)

At boiling point of pure water is 100°C or 373 K.

$$T_b = \Delta T_b + T_b^\circ$$

$\therefore \quad T_b = 373 + 0.346 = 373.346$ K (1)

37. Given, mass of water $(W) = 4$ kg, $K_f = 1.85$ K kg mol^{-1}

$$\Delta T_f = 0 - (-6) = 6°\text{C}$$

(as, freezing point of pure water is 0°C.)

Mass of ethylene glycol $(w) = ?$

Molar mass of ethylene glycol

$(CH_2OH \cdot CH_2OH)$, $M' = 62$ g mol^{-1}

We know that,

$$\Delta T_f = \frac{K_f \times w}{M' \times W \text{ (kg)}}$$

$$\therefore \quad w = \frac{\Delta T_f \times M' \times W(\text{kg})}{K_f} = \frac{6 \times 62 \times 4}{1.85} = 804.32 \text{ g}$$

38. Lowering in melting point $(\Delta T_f) = 1.5°$C

Mass of solvent (CH_3COOH), $W_1 = 75$ g

Molar mass of solvent (CH_3COOH),

$M_1 = 60$ g mol^{-1}

[as $CH_3COOH = 12 + 3 + 12 + 16 + 16 + 1 = 60$]

Molar mass of solute $(C_6H_8O_6)$,

$M_2 = 72 + 8 + 96 = 176$ g mol^{-1}

[as, $C_6H_8O_6 = 6 \times 12 + 8 \times 1 + 6 \times 16 = 176$] (1)

For acetic acid, $K_f = 3.9$ K kg mol^{-1} [Given]

Applying the formula,

$$M_2 = \frac{1000 K_f W_2}{W_1 \Delta T_f}, \text{ we get}$$

$$W_2 = \frac{M_2 \times W_1 \times \Delta T_f}{1000 \times K_f}$$ (1)

$$= \frac{(176 \text{ g mol}^{-1})(75 \text{ g})(1.5 \text{ K})}{(1000)(3.9 \text{ K kg mol}^{-1})} = 5.077 \text{ g}$$ (1)

39. Applying the formula, $M_2 = \dfrac{1000 K_f W_2}{W_1 \times \Delta T_f}$

For AB_2, $M_{AB_2} = \dfrac{1000 \times 5.1 \times 1}{20 \times 2.3} = 110.87$ g mol^{-1} (1/2)

For AB_4, $M_{AB_4} = \dfrac{1000 \times 5.1 \times 1}{20 \times 1.3} = 196.15$ g mol^{-1} (1/2)

Suppose atomic masses of A and B are a and b respectively, then

Molar mass of $AB_2 = a + 2b = 110.87$ g mol^{-1} ...(i)

Molar mass of $AB_4 = a + 4b = 196.15$ g mol^{-1} ...(ii)

On subtracting Eq. (i) from Eq. (ii) gives

$$2b = 85.28$$

Therefore, $b = 42.64$

On substituting the value of b in Eq. (i), we get

$$a + 2 \times 42.64 = 110.87 \quad \text{or} \quad a = 25.59$$

Thus, atomic mass of $A = 25.59$ u,

Atomic mass of $B = 42.64$ u (1+1)

40. Given, $w_2 = 12.48$g, $w_1 = 1000$g,

T_b(solution) $= (100.0832 + 273)$ K $= 373.0832$K

K_b for $H_2O = 0.52$ kg mol^{-1}

and $M_2(BaCl_2) = 208$ g mol^{-1}

$\Delta T_b = T_b - T_b^{\circ} = 373.0832\text{K} - 373\text{K} = 0.0832\text{ K}$ (1)

$$M_2(\text{Observed}) = \frac{K_b \times w_2 \times 1000}{\Delta T_b \times w_1}$$

$$\frac{0.52\text{ kg mol}^{-1} \times 12.48\text{g} \times 1000}{0.0832\text{ K} \times 1000\text{g}}$$

$M_2(\text{Observed}) = 78\text{g mol}^{-1}$ (1)

$$i = \frac{M_2\text{ (Calculated)}}{M_2\text{ (Observed)}} = \frac{208\text{g mol}^{-1}}{78\text{g mol}^{-1}} = 2.67$$

For $BaCl_2$, $m = 3$ as it gives 3 ions on dissociation.

$$\alpha = \frac{i-1}{m-1} = \frac{2.67-1}{3-1} = \frac{1.67}{2} = 0.835,\ \alpha = 83.5\%$$ (1)

41. The given quantities are :

$W_2 = 3.9\text{ g}$, $W_1 = 49\text{ g}$ $\Delta T_f = 1.62\text{ K}$,

$K_f = 4.9\text{ K kg mol}^{-1}$

Apply van't Hoff equation, $\Delta T_f = i K_f \cdot m$

where, i = number of ions

$$\Delta T_f = \frac{i \cdot K_f \times W_2 \times 1000}{M_2 \times W_1}$$ (1)

$$\Rightarrow 1.62\text{ K} = \frac{i \cdot 4.9\text{ K kg mol}^{-1} \times 3.9\text{ g} \times 1000}{122\text{ g mol}^{-1} \times 49\text{ g}}$$

$$i = \frac{1.62 \times 122 \times 49}{4.9 \times 3.9 \times 1000} = 0.51$$ (1)

As the value of $i < 1$ thus, benzoic acid is an associated solute. (1)

42. Let the degree of association of acetic acid (CH_3COOH) in benzene is α, then

$$2CH_3COOH \rightleftharpoons (CH_3COOH)_2$$

Initial moles	1	0
Moles at equilibrium	$1-\alpha$	$\frac{\alpha}{2}$

$\therefore$ Total moles $= 1 - \alpha + \frac{\alpha}{2} = 1 - \frac{\alpha}{2}$ or $i = 1 - \frac{\alpha}{2}$ (1)

Now, depression in freezing point (ΔT_f) is given as

$$\Delta T_f = i K_f m \quad \text{...(i)}$$

where, K_f = molal depression constant or cryoscopic constant.

m = molality

$$\text{Molality} = \frac{\text{number of moles of solute}}{\text{weight of solvent (in kg)}} = \frac{0.2}{60} \times \frac{1000}{20}$$ (1)

Putting the values in Eq. (i)

$$\therefore \quad 0.45 = \left[1 - \frac{\alpha}{2}\right](5.12)\left[\frac{0.2}{60} \times \frac{1000}{20}\right]$$

$$1 - \frac{\alpha}{2} = \frac{0.45 \times 60 \times 20}{5.12 \times 0.2 \times 1000} \Rightarrow 1 - \frac{\alpha}{2} = 0.527$$

$$\Rightarrow \quad \frac{\alpha}{2} = 1 - 0.527$$

$$\therefore \quad \alpha = 0.946$$

Thus, percentage of association = 94.6% (1)

43. Given, $w_{\text{Benzoic acid}} = 2\text{ g}$, $K_f = 4.9\text{ K kg mol}^{-1}$

$w_{\text{Benzene}} = 25\text{ g}$, $\Delta T_f = 1.62\text{ K}$.

Now, $$\Delta T_f = K_f \times \frac{w_{\text{Benzoic acid}} \times 1000}{M_{\text{Benzoic acid}} \times w_{\text{Benzene}}}$$

$$1.62 = \frac{4.9 \times 2\text{ g} \times 1000}{M_{\text{Benzoic}} \times 25\text{ g}}$$

$$M_{\text{Benzoic}} = \frac{4.9 \times 2 \times 1000}{1.62 \times 25} = 241.98\text{ g/mol.}$$

$$2C_6H_5COOH \rightleftharpoons (C_6H_5COOH)_2$$

At $t = 0$	x	0
At $t = t$	$1 - x$	$\frac{x}{2}$

If x is the degree of association, $(1 - x)$ mole of benzoic acid left undissociated and corresponding $\frac{x}{2}$ as associated moles of C_6H_5COOH at equilibrium.

So, total no. of moles of particles at equilibrium

$$= 1 - x + \frac{x}{2} = 1 - \frac{x}{2} = i$$

$$i = \frac{\text{Normal molecular mass}}{\text{Abnormal molecular mass}}$$

$$1 - \frac{x}{2} = \frac{122}{241.98} \Rightarrow \frac{x}{2} = 1 - \frac{122}{241.98}$$

$\Rightarrow \quad x = 0.992$

$\Rightarrow \quad 99.2\ \%$

44. Given, boiling point of water = 373.0834 K

Actual boiling point of water = 373 K

$\therefore \quad \Delta T = 373.0834 - 373 = 0.0834\text{ K}$

Amount of $BaCl_2 = 12.5\text{ g}$

Amount of water = 1000 g

K_b for $H_2O = 0.52\text{ K kg mol}^{-1}$

Molecular mass of $BaCl_2 = 208.34\text{ g mol}^{-1}$.

$$\text{Moles of } BaCl_2 = \frac{12.5}{208.34} = 0.0599 \approx 0.06$$

$$\text{Molality} = \frac{0.06 \times 1000}{1000} = 0.06\text{ mol/kg}$$

Now, $\Delta T_b = K_b \cdot m \cdot i$

$$0.0834 = 0.52 \times 0.06 \times i$$

$$i = \frac{0.0834}{0.52 \times 0.06} = 2.67 \simeq 2.7$$

As, $\underset{1-x}{BaCl_2} \rightleftharpoons \underset{x}{Ba^{2+}} + \underset{2x}{2Cl^-}$

$$i = 1 - x + x + 2x$$

$$2.7 = 1 + 2x \Rightarrow x = \frac{1.7}{2} = 0.85$$

Therefore, degree of dissociation is 85%.

45. Given, $w_2 = 5.85\text{ g}$, $w_1 = 100\text{g}$, $m_1 = 18\text{ g mol}^{-1}$ for H_2O

Depression in freezing point $(\Delta T_f) = T_f^{\circ} - T_f$

$$\Delta T_f = 0°C-(-3.348)°C = 3.348°C = 3.348K \quad (1)$$

$$\therefore M_2 = \frac{1000\times K_f \times w_2}{\Delta T_f \times w_1}$$

$$\therefore M_2 = \frac{1000\times 1.86K \text{ kg mol}^{-1}\times 5.85 \text{ g}}{3.348 \text{ K}\times 100\text{g}} = 32.5 \text{ g mol}^{-1} \quad (1)$$

Calculated molecular mass of NaCl=23+35.5 = 58.5 g mol^{-1}

$$\text{Now, } i = \frac{\text{Calculated molecular mass}}{\text{Observed molecular mass}} = \frac{58.5}{32.5} = 1.8$$

$\therefore$ van't Hoff factor (i) =1.8 (1)

46. (i) Suppose the molar mass of solute = M g mol^{-1}

$$\text{Number of moles of solute } (n_2) = \frac{30}{M} \text{ mol}$$

$$\text{Number of moles of } H_2O\ (n_1) = \frac{90 \text{ g}}{18 \text{ g mol}^{-1}} = 5 \text{ mol}$$

$$p_1 = 2.8 \text{ kPa}$$

$$\frac{p_1^\circ - p_1}{p_1^\circ} = \frac{n_2}{n_1+n_2} \quad (1)$$

$$\frac{p_1^\circ - 2.8}{p_1^\circ} = \frac{30/M}{5+30/M} \text{ or } 1-\frac{2.8}{p_1^\circ} = \frac{30/M}{5+30/M}$$

$$\text{or} \quad \frac{2.8}{p_1^\circ} = 1-\frac{30/M}{5+30/M} = \frac{5}{5+30/M}$$

$$\text{or} \quad \frac{p_1^\circ}{2.8} = \frac{5+30/M}{5} = 1+\frac{6}{M} \quad \text{...(i) (1)}$$

On adding 18 g of water, $n(H_2O)$ =6 mol

($\because 5+1=6$ mol)

Then, $p_1' = 2.9$ kPa

$$\therefore \frac{p_1^\circ - 2.9}{p_1^\circ} = \frac{30/M}{6+30/M} \Rightarrow 1-\frac{2.9}{p_1^\circ} = \frac{30/M}{6+30/M}$$

$$\text{or} \quad \frac{2.9}{p_1^\circ} = 1-\frac{30/M}{6+30/M} = \frac{6}{6+30/M}$$

$$\text{or} \quad \frac{p_1^\circ}{2.9} = \frac{6+30/M}{6} = 1+\frac{5}{M} \quad \text{...(ii) (1)}$$

On dividing Eq. (i) by Eq. (ii), we get

$$\frac{2.9}{2.8} = \frac{1+6/M}{1+5/M}$$

$$\text{or} \quad 2.9\left(1+\frac{5}{M}\right) = 2.8\left(1+\frac{6}{M}\right)$$

$$\text{or} \quad 2.9+\frac{14.5}{M} = 2.8+\frac{16.8}{M}$$

$$\Rightarrow \quad M = 23 \text{ u} \quad (1)$$

(ii) Putting $M=23$ in Eq. (i), we get

$$\frac{p_1^\circ}{2.8} = 1+\frac{6}{23} = \frac{29}{23} \text{ or } p_1^\circ = \frac{29}{23}\times 2.8 = 3.53 \text{ kPa} \quad (1)$$

47. Molar mass of $CH_3CH_2CHClCOOH$

$= 15+14+13+35.5+45 = 122.5$ g mol^{-1}

Number of moles of 10 g of $CH_3CH_2CHClCOOH$,

$$n_2 = \frac{10}{122.5} \text{ mol} = 8.16\times 10^{-2} \text{ mol}$$

$\therefore$ Molality of the solution (m)

$$= \frac{W_2\times 1000}{M_2\times W_1} = \frac{n_2\times 1000}{W_1}$$

$$= \frac{8.16\times 10^{-2} \text{ mol}}{250 \text{ g}} \times 1000 \text{ g kg}^{-1}$$

$$= 0.3264 \text{ mol kg}^{-1} \quad (1)$$

or $C = 0.3264$ mol kg^{-1}

If α is the degree of dissociation for $CH_3CH_2CHClCOOH$, then

$$CH_3CH_2CHClCOOH \rightleftharpoons CH_3CH_2CHClCOO^- + H^+$$

Initial conc.	C mol L^{-1}	0	0
At equilibrium	$C(1-\alpha)$	$C\alpha$	$C\alpha$

$$\therefore \quad K_a = \frac{C\alpha\cdot C\alpha}{C(1-\alpha)} \approx C\alpha^2 \quad (1)$$

$$\text{or} \quad \alpha = \sqrt{\frac{K_a}{C}} = \sqrt{\frac{1.4\times 10^{-3}}{0.3264}} = 0.065 \quad (1)$$

To calculate van't Hoff factor

$$CH_3CH_2CHClCOOH \rightleftharpoons CH_3CH_2CHClCOO^- + H^+$$

Initial moles	1	0	0
Moles at equilibrium	$(1-\alpha)$	α	α

Total moles $= 1-\alpha+\alpha+\alpha = 1+\alpha$

$$i = \frac{1+\alpha}{1} = 1+\alpha = 1+0.065 = 1.065 \quad (1)$$

Therefore, $\Delta T_f = iK_f m = 1.065\times 1.86\times 0.3264 = 0.65°$ (1)

48. Here, $W_2 = 19.5$ g, $W_1 = 500$ g,

$$K_f = 1.86 \text{ K kg mol}^{-1}, (\Delta T_f)_{obs} = 1.0°C$$

$$\therefore M_2(\text{observed}) = \frac{1000 K_f W_2}{W_1 \Delta T_f}$$

$$= \frac{(1000)(1.86 \text{ K kg mol}^{-1})(19.5 \text{ g})}{(500 \text{ g})(1.0 \text{ K})} = 72.54 \text{ g mol}^{-1} \quad (1)$$

M_2 (calculated) for CH_2FCOOH

$= 14+19+45 = 78$ g mol^{-1}

$$\text{van't Hoff factor } (i) = \frac{(M_2)_{cal}}{(M_2)_{obs}} = \frac{78}{72.54} = 1.0753 \quad (1)$$

Suppose degree of dissociation at the given concentration is α. Then,

$$CH_2FCOOH \rightleftharpoons CH_2FCOO^- + H^+$$

Initial moles	C mol L^{-1}	0	0
Moles at equilibrium	$C(1-\alpha)$	$C\alpha$	$C\alpha$

Total moles $= C(1-\alpha)+C\alpha+C\alpha = C(1+\alpha)$

$\therefore \; i = \dfrac{C(1+\alpha)}{C} = 1 + \alpha$

or $\quad \alpha = i - 1 = 1.0753 - 1 = 0.0753$ (1)

$$K_a = \frac{[CH_2FCOO]^- \, [H]^+}{[CH_2FCOOH]} = \frac{C\alpha \cdot C\alpha}{C(1-\alpha)} = \frac{C\alpha^2}{1-\alpha}$$ (1)

Taking volume of the solution as 500 mL,

$$C = \frac{n}{V} = \frac{W_2}{M_{2(cal)}} \times \frac{1}{V} = \frac{19.5}{78} \times \frac{1}{500} \times 1000 = 0.5 \text{ M}$$

$$\therefore \quad K_a = \frac{C\alpha^2}{1-\alpha} = \frac{(0.5)\,(0.0753)^2}{1-0.0753} = 3.07 \times 10^{-3}$$ (1)

49. (i) (a) Given : $T_f = 272.4$ K

$T_f^\circ = 273.0$ K

$K_f = 1.86$ K kg mol^{-1}

$K_b = 0.512$ K kg mol^{-1}

Vapour pressure of water at 298 K = 23.756 mm Hg

$m = ?$

As we know, $\Delta T_f = K_f \times m$

$\therefore \quad 0.6 = 1.86 \times m$

or $\quad m = \dfrac{0.6}{1.86}$ (1)

Thus, molality of solution = 0.323 molar

(b) T_b (Boiling point of solution) = ?

we know , $\dfrac{\Delta T_f}{\Delta T_b} = \dfrac{K_f}{K_b}$

$\therefore \quad \dfrac{0.6}{\Delta T_b} = \dfrac{1.86}{0.512} \Rightarrow \Delta T_b = \dfrac{0.6 \times 0.152}{1.86} = 0.17$ K

Also, $\quad \Delta T_b = T_b - T_b^\circ \Rightarrow 0.17 = T_b - 273$

$\therefore \quad 0.17 + 273 = T_b$

$273.17 \text{ K} = T_b$ (1)

$\therefore$ Boiling point of solution is 273.17 K.

(c) Lowering of vapour pressure at 298 K = ?

we know, $\dfrac{p^\circ - p}{p^\circ} = \dfrac{(760 - 23.756) \text{ mm Hg}}{760 \text{ mm Hg}}$

$\therefore \quad \dfrac{p^\circ - p}{p^\circ} = 0.969$ (1)

(ii) Given, mass of calcium nitrate = 1.23 g

Mass of water = 10 g

T_b for solution = 100.975° C

K_b for water = 0.52 K kg mol^{-1}

Molecular weight of calcium nitrate = 164 g mol^{-1}

As we know,

$$\Delta T_b = i \times K_b \times m \Rightarrow \Delta T_b = i \times K_b \times \frac{W_B}{M_B} \times \frac{1000}{W_A}$$

$$100.975 - 100^\circ\text{C} = i \times 0.52 \times \frac{1.23}{164} \times \frac{1000}{10}$$

or $\quad 0.975 = i \times 0.52 \times 0.75$

$\therefore \quad i = 2.5$ (2)

50. (i) Given, Weight of KCl (solute) = 0.5 g

Weight of solvent (water) = 100 g

Depression in freezing point (ΔT_f) = 0.24°C

$K_f = 1.86$°C

Molecular mass of KCl = 39 + 35.5 = 74.5 g mol^{-1} (1)

From depression in freezing point

$$\Delta T_f = i \times K_f \times m$$

$$0.24^\circ\text{C} = i \times 1.86^\circ\text{C} \times \frac{0.5}{74.5} \times \frac{1000}{100} \Rightarrow i = 1.92$$

For KCl, $\quad i = 1 + \alpha$

(where α is the degree of dissociation)

$\alpha = 1.92 - 1 \Rightarrow \alpha = .92$ or 92% (1)

(ii) Given, Weight of sugar = 1.71 g

Molar mass of sugar = 34.2 g mol^{-1}

Volume of solvent = 500 mL

Temperature = 300 K (1)

Osmotic pressure, $\pi = CRT$

$$C = \frac{1.71}{342} \times \frac{1000}{500}$$

$\pi = 0.01 \times 0.0821$ L atm/Kelvin/mol $\times 300$K (1)

$C = 0.01$ mol/L, $\pi = 0.2463$ atm

(iii) Given, $\Delta T_b = 0.25°$, or 0.25 K

$\Rightarrow \quad \Delta T_b = K_b \times m$

$$0.25 = 1.72 \times \frac{0.70}{\text{molecular weight}} \times \frac{1000}{32 \text{ g}}$$

Molecular weight = 150.5 g

51. (i) Given, Freezing point of water = 273 K (1)

Weight of solute (glucose), $w = 0.625$ g

Weight of solvent, $W = 102.8$ g

Molecular weight of solute, $m = (C_6H_{12}O_6)$

$= 12 \times 6 + 1 \times 12 + 16 \times 6$

$= 180$ g mol^{-1} (1)

K_f for water = 1.87 K kg mol^{-1}

For glucose as solute, $i = 1$

$$\therefore \quad \Delta T_f = \frac{1000 \times K_f \times w}{m \times W}$$

$$= \frac{1000 \times 1.87 \times 0.625}{180 \times 102.8} = 0.063 \text{ K}$$

$\therefore$ Freezing point of solution = $T_f + \Delta T_f$

(where, T_f is freezing point of water = 0°C = 273 K)

= 273 + 0.063 = 273.063 K (1)

(ii) Osmotic pressure (π) = CRT

Given, $C = 0.15$ M, $R = 0.0821$ L atm K^{-1} mol^{-1}

$T = 310$ K

$\therefore \; \pi = CRT = 0.15 \text{ M} \times 0.0821 \text{ L atm K}^{-1} \text{ mol}^{-1} \times 310 \text{ K}$

= 3.82 atm (1)

Observed π = 6.8 atm

$\therefore$ van't Hoff factor,

$$i = \frac{\text{Observed magnitude of } \pi}{\text{Normal magnitude of } \pi} = \frac{6.8}{3.82} = 1.78$$

Chapter Practice

Very Short Answer Type Questions

1 Mark

1. **Fill in the Blanks**
   (i) Egg is placed in .... hydrochloric acid solution which .... the outer calcium carbonate layer.
   (ii) 0.91% solution of NaCl is .... with red blood cells and hence blood cells retain their normal shape in it.
   (iii) Semipermeable membrane of $Cu_2[Fe(CN)_6]$ is .... in non-aqueous solvents.
   (iv) Addition of HgI_2 to an aqueous solution of KI results in the formation of .... and number of particles present in solution decreases.

2. **Objective Type Questions**
   (i) One component of a solution follows Raoult's law over the entire range $0 \le x_1 \le 1$. The second component must follow Raoult's law in the range when x_2 is
   (a) close to zero (b) close to 1
   (c) $0 \le x_2 \le 0.5$ (d) $0 \le x_2 \le 1$
   (ii) If two substances A and B have $p^\circ_A : p^\circ_B = 1:2$ and mole fraction in solution $= 1:2$, then mole fraction of A in vapours is
   (a) 0.33 (b) 0.25 (c) 0.52 (d) 0.2
   (iii) Which of the following has least freezing point?
   (a) 1% sucrose (b) 1% NaCl
   (c) 1% $CaCl_2$ (d) 1% glucose
   (iv) Which of the following would exert maximum osmotic pressure?
   (a) Decinormal aluminium sulphate
   (b) Decinormal barium chloride
   (c) Decinormal sodium chloride
   (d) A solution obtained by mixing equal volumes of (b) and (c)
   (v) The van't Hoff factor of $BaCl_2$ at 0.01 M concentration is 1.98. The percentage of dissociation of $BaCl_2$ at this concentration is
   (a) 49 (b) 69 (c) 89 (d) 98
   (vi) The solution that forms maximum boiling azeotrope is
   (a) carbon disulphide – acetone
   (b) benzene – toluene
   (c) acetone – chloroform
   (d) *n*-hexane – *n*-heptane
   (vii) Solution of azeotropic nitric acid mixture contain
   (a) 32% HNO_3, 68% H_2O by mass
   (b) 68% HNO_3, 32% H_2O by mass
   (c) 50% HNO_3, 50% H_2O by mass
   (d) 30% H_2O, 70% HNO_3 by mass

3. Match the items given in Column I with the type of solutions given in Column II.

	Column I		Column II
A.	Soda water	1.	A solution of gas in solid
B.	Sugar solution	2.	A solution of gas in gas
C.	German silver	3.	A solution of solid in liquid
D.	Air	4.	A solution of solid in solid
E.	Hydrogen gas in palladium	5.	A solution of gas in liquid
		6.	A solution of liquid in solid

Codes

	A	B	C	D	E
(a)	1	2	4	5	3
(b)	2	3	1	4	5
(c)	5	4	3	1	2
(d)	5	3	4	2	1

4. What do you mean by parts per million?
5. Will the molality of a solution at 50°C be same, less or more than molarity at 25°C?
6. What is the molality of NH_3 in a solution containing 0.85g of NH_3 in 100 mL of a liquid of density 0.85g cm^{-3}?
7. What is the density of 3.60 M sulphuric acid, which is 29% H_2SO_4 by mass?
8. What is the sum of mole fractions of all the components in a three component system?
9. Give an example of solid solution in which the solute is a gas.
10. What happens to vapour pressure of water if a table spoon of sugar is added to it?
11. How much urea should be dissolved in 50 g of water, so that its vapour pressure at room temperature is reduced by 25%?

12. Why the vapour pressure of the solution is found to be less than that of the solvent?
13. What type of liquids form ideal solutions?
14. Give two basic differences between ideal and non-ideal solutions.
15. Why cannot we separate an azeotropic mixture by distillation?
16. *A* and *B* liquids on mixing produced a warm solution.Which type of deviation is this and why?
17. Why is osmotic pressure considered as a colligative property?
18. A person suffering from high blood pressure should consume less common salt. Give reason.
19. What possible value of '*i*' will it have, if solute molecules undergo association in solution?
20. What would be the value of van't Hoff factor for a dilute solution of Na_2SO_4 in water?
21. Between 2M glucose solution and 1M glucose solution, which one has a lower freezing point?
22. Are equimolar solutions of sodium chloride and urea isotonic? Give reason.

Assertion-Reason

Directions (Q. Nos. 23-27) In the following questions. an Assertion (A) is followed by a corresponding Reason (R). Use the following keys to choose the appropriate answer.

(a) Both (A) and (R) are correct, (R) is the correct explanation of (A).
(b) Both (A) and (R) are correct, (R) is not the correct explanation of (A).
(c) (A) is correct; (R) is incorrect.
(d) (A) is incorrect; (R) is correct.

23. **Assertion** (A) When NaCl is added to water, a depression in freezing point is observed.

Reason (R) The lowering of vapour pressure of a solution causes depression in the freezing point.

24. **Assertion** (A) Aquatic species are more comfortable in cold water rather than in warm water.

Reason (R) Different gases have different K_H values at the same temperature.

25. **Assertion** (A) Cryoscopic constant depends on nature of solvent.

Reason (R) Cryoscopic constant is a universal constant.

26. **Assertion** (A) The vapour pressure of 0.1M sugar solution is less than that of 0.1M potassium chloride solution.

Reason (R) Lowering of vapour pressure is directly proportional to the number of species present in the solution.

27. **Assertion** (A) Osmotic pressure is a colligative property. CBSE 2021 (Term I)

Reason (R) Osmotic pressure of a solution depends on the molar concentration of solute at any temperature, *T*.

Case-Study

28. The concentration of a solute is very important in studying chemical reactions because it determines how often molecules collide in solution and thus indirectly determine the rate of reactions and the conditions at equilibrium.

There are several ways to express the amount of solute present in a solution. The concentration of a solution is a measure of the amount of solute that has been dissolved in a given amount of solvent or solution. Concentration can be expressed in terms of molarity, molality parts per million, mass percentage, volume percentage, etc.

Answers the following questions given below

(i) If 0.1M $AgNO_3$ and 0.1 M NaCl solutions are mixed in same volume, then what will be the concentration of nitrate ions?

(ii) What would be the concentration of 100 mL solution in which 6.02×10^{20} molecules of urea are present?

(iii) Name any two concentration terms which are independent of the temperature.

29. The spontaneous flow of solvent molecules from solvent side to solution side or from a region of lower concentration to a region of higher concentration through a semipermeable membrane is called osmosis. It is different from that of diffussion, where the movement is in reverse direction.

The minimum pressure that has to be exerted/ applied on the solution to prevent the entry of solvent into solution through semipermeable membrane is called osmotic pressure.

This concept is used in desalination of sea water. The growth of plants depends mainly on the phenomenon of osmosis. Two solutions having same osmotic pressure are called **isotonic**. Osmotic pressure is a colligative property. Molecular mass of a solute can be determined from the osmotic pressure measurements. Osmotic pressure is represented by π.

Also, $\pi V = nRT$.

When there are two solutions and if one of the solutions is of lower osmotic pressure, it is called **hypotonic** and the other is called **hypertonic** with respect to other. The osmotic pressure can be experimentally measured by using Berkeley Hartley method.

Answers the following questions given below

(i) Are equimolar solutions of sodium chloride and urea isotonic?

(ii) What is the Berkeley-Hartley method and name the semipermeable membrane used in this method?

(iii) What happens if red blood cells are removed from the body and placed in pure water?

Short Answer Type I Questions

(2 Marks)

30. Which out of molality, molarity and mole fraction of a solution will remain unchanged and why?

31. A solution obtained by mixing 300 g of 25% and 400 g of 40% solution by mass. Calculate the mass % of the resulting solution.

32. Calculate the molality of K_2CO_3 solution which is formed by dissolving 2.5 g of it in 1 L of solution. Density of solution is 0.85 g mL^{-1}.

33. Distinguish between the terms molality and molarity. Under what conditions are the molarity and molality of a solution nearly the same?

34. How many grams of concentrated nitric acid solution should be used to prepare 250 mL of 2.0 M HNO_3? (The concentrated acid is 70% HNO_3)

35. K_H value for Ar(g), CO_2(g), HCHO(g) and CH_4(g) are 40.39, 1.67, 1.83×10^{-5} and 0.413 respectively. Arrange these gases in the order of their increasing solubility and giving suitable reason.

36. Why the solubility of Glauber's salt ($Na_2SO_4 \cdot 10H_2O$) first increases upto 32.4°C and then decreases?

37. Consider the solute-solvent interactions and arrange the following compounds in the order of increasing solubility in ethanol with suitable explanations.
NaCl, cycloheptane, H_2O, CH_3COCH_3

38. At 80°C, the vapour pressure of a pure liquid A is 520 mm of Hg and that of pure liquid B is 1000 mm of Hg. If a mixture of A and B boils at 80°C and 1 atm pressure, then what is the amount of A in the mixture?

39. What type of liquids form non-ideal solutions?

40. Why constant boiling mixtures behave like a single component when subjected to distillation?

41. Write four differences between solutions having positive deviation and solutions having negative deviations from Raoult's law.

42. Explain why the boiling point of a solvent is increased on dissolving a non-volatile solute into it?

43. A solution prepared by dissolving 1.25 g of oil of winter green (methyl salicylate) in 99 g of benzene has a boiling point of 80.31°C and K_b for benzene is 2.53 K kg mol^{-1}. Find molar mass of the solute. (Boiling point of benzene = 80°C).

44. Calculate the freezing point of an aqueous solution containing 10.50 g of $MgBr_2$ in 200 g of water (molar mass of $MgBr_2$ = 184 g, K_f for water =1.86 K kg mol^{-1}).

45. What is the advantage of using osmotic pressure as compared to other colligative properties for the determination of molar masses of solutes in solutions?

46. Define the following terms:
(i) Isotonic solutions
(ii) Hypertonic solutions
(iii) Hypotonic solutions

47. What is the value of van't Hoff factor for 0.1M ideal solution?

48. An electrolyte AB is 50% ionised in aqueous solution. Calculate the freezing point of 1 molal aqueous solution.

49. A storage battery contains a solution of H_2SO_4, 38% by weight. At this concentration, van't Hoff factor is 2.50. At what temperature, will the battery contents freeze?

50. Four solutions of K_2SO_4 with the concentration 0.1 M, 0.01M, 0.001M and 0.0001M are available. For which concentration, there is maximum value of van't Hoff factor?

Short Answer Type II Questions

3 Marks

51. State the law correlating the pressure of a gas and its solubility in a liquid. State an application of this law.

52. At what partial pressure, oxygen will have a solubility of 0.05 g L^{-1} in water at 293 K? [Henry's constant (K_H) for O_2 in water at 293 K is 34.86 k bar. Assume the density of the solution to be same as that of the solvent.]

53. The solubility of pure nitrogen gas at 25°C and 1 atm is 6.8×10^{-4} mol L^{-1}. What is the concentration of nitrogen dissolved in water under atmospheric condition? The partial pressure of nitrogen gas in the atmosphere is 0.78 atm.

54. Write three differences between ideal and non-ideal solutions.

55. Explain with example the concept of minimum boiling azeotropes and maximum boiling azeotropes.

56. (i) Define molality in terms of elevation in boiling point.
(ii) Derive the relation between elevation in boiling point and the molecular mass of a non-volatile solute.

57. A 5% solution (by mass) of cane sugar in water has a freezing point of 271 K. Calculate the freezing point of 5% (by mass) solution of glucose in water. The freezing point of pure water is 273.15 K. (Molar mass of cane sugar = 342 g mol^{-1} and molar mass of glucose = 180 g mol^{-1})

58. Explain, how the measurement of depression in freezing point can be used for the determination of molecular masses of non-volatile solutes?

59. Discuss biological and industrial importance of osmosis.

60. (i) If the membrane used for the determination of osmotic pressure is slightly torn, how will it influence the measured value of osmotic pressure?
(ii) The boiling point of benzene is 353.23 K. When 1.80 g of a non-volatile solute was dissolved in 90 g of benzene, the boiling point is raised to be 354.11 K. Calculate the molar mass of the solute.
(K_b for benzene is 2.53 K kg mol^{-1})

61. (i) Why does the use of pressure cooker reduce cooking time?
(ii) How does van't Hoff factor helps in the determination of degree of association or dissociation of a solute in solution?

62. (i) When dehydrated fruits and vegetables are placed in water, they slowly swell and return to their original shape. Why? What is the effect of temperature on this process? Explain.
(ii) Prove that relative lowering in vapour pressure of a liquid on addition of non-volatile solute is a colligative property.

63. Calculate the freezing point depression expected for 0.0711 m aqueous solution of Na_2SO_4. If this solution actually freezes at 0.320°C, what would be the value of van't Hoff factor? (K_f for water is 1.86°C kg mol^{-1})

64. What mass of NaCl must be dissolved in 65.0 g of water to lower the freezing point of water by 7.50°C? The freezing point depression constant (K_f) for water is 1.86°C/m. Assume van't Hoff factor for NaCl is 1.87.
(Molar mass of NaCl = 58.5 g mol^{-1}).

Long Answer Type Questions

5 Marks

65. (i) Why does a solution of chloroform and acetone show negative deviation from Raoult's law?
(ii) State how the vapour pressure of a solvent is affected, when a non-volatile solute is dissolved in it?
(iii) A solution of glucose ($C_6H_{12}O_6$) in water is labelled as 10% by weight. What would be the molality of the solution? (Molar mass of glucose = 180 g mol^{-1})

66. (i) Two liquids *X* and *Y* boil at 100°C and 120°C respectively. Which of them has higher vapour pressure at 50°C and why?
(ii) Calculate the boiling point of a solution prepared by adding 15.00 g of NaCl to 250 g water. (K_b for water = 0.512 K kg mol^{-1}; molar mass of NaCl = 58.44g)

(iii) Calculate the lowering of vapour pressure for 0.1 m aqueous solution of non-electrolyte at 75°C. ($\Delta H = 9.720$ K cal mol^{-1}, $p_2 = 742.96$ torr)

67. (i) What is van't Hoff factor?

(ii) What possible values can it have if the solute molecules undergo dissociation?

(iii) An aqueous solution containing 12.48 g of barium chloride in 1.0 kg of water boils at 373.0832 K. Calculate the degree of dissociation of barium chloride.

(Given, K_b for $H_2O = 0.52$ K m^{-1}; molar mass of $BaCl_2 = 208.34$ g mol^{-1}).

Answers

1 (i) dilute, dissolves (ii) isotonic

(iii) soluble (iv) K_2HgI_4

2 (i) d, (ii) d, (iii) c, (iv) a, (v) a, (vi) c, (vii) b

3 A → (5) B → (3) C → (4) D → (2) E → (1)

4 When a solute is present in trace quantities, the concentration is expressed in parts per million (ppm).

$$\text{ppm} = \frac{\text{Number of parts of the component}}{\text{Total number of parts of all components of the solutions}} \times 100$$

5 Molarity decreases with increase in temperature, hence, less at 50°C while, molality remains constant.

6 $\text{Molality} = \frac{\text{Moles of solute}}{\text{Mass of solvent (in kg)}}$ [**Ans** 0.597 m]

7 $\text{Molarity} = \frac{\text{Number of moles of solute}}{\text{Volume of solution (in litre)}}$ [**Ans** 1.22 g /mL]

8 For a given solution, sum of all the mole fraction is unity, i.e.,

$x_1 + x_2 + x_3 + ... x_i = 1$

9 Hydrogen gas in palladium.

10 Vapour pressure decreases, due to the addition non-volatile solute.

11 **Hint** Use the equation $\frac{p^\circ_1 - p_1}{p^\circ_1} = \frac{w_1 \times M_1}{w_2 \times M_2}$ [**Ans** 41.62 g]

12 In case of solid-liquid solution, the surface has both solute and solvent molecules; thereby the fraction of the surface covered by the solvent molecules gets reduced and thus decrease in vapour pressure occurs.

13 The solutions which obey Raoult's low over the entire range of concentration are known as ideal solutions.

14 (i) Ideal solutions obey's Raoult law while non-ideal solutions do not obey the Raoult's law.

(ii) $\Delta_{mix}H$ and $\Delta_{mix}V = 0$ (ideal solution)

$\Delta_{mix}H$ and $\Delta_{mix}V \neq 0$ (non-ideal solution)

15 Azeotropic mixtures have the same composition in liquid and vapour phase and boil at constant temperature, hence it is not possible to separate the components by fractional distillation.

16 On mixing *A* and *B* produced a warm solution, which means heat is evolved, i.e., exothermic. In case of negative deviation $\Delta H_{mix} < 0$, i.e. heat is evolved due to the formation of stronger bonds.

17 Osmotic pressure is a colligative property as it depends upon the number of solute molecules and not on their nature.

18 People taking a lot of salt or salty food experience water retention in tissue cells and inter cellular spaces because of osmosis.

19 In association, observed molar mass being more than the normal, so *i* has a value less than one ($i < 1$).

20 $Na_2SO_4 \rightleftharpoons 2Na^+ + SO_4^{2-}$ $(\therefore i = 3)$

21 **Hint** Higher the concentration, lower is the freezing point.

22 Two solution having same osmotic pressure at a given temperature are called isotonic solutions.

$$\pi = iCRT \begin{pmatrix} i \text{ for NaCl} = 2 \\ i \text{ for urea} = 1 \end{pmatrix}$$

As NaCl and urea have different values of *i* and therefore, they are not isotonic solutions.

23. (*a*) Both (A) and (R) are correct and (R) is the correct explanation of (A). Actually lowering of vapour pressure is observed due to intermolecular interaction of solvent-solute particles.

24. (*b*) Aquatic species are more comfortable in cold water rather than in warm water because the solubility of gases decreases with increase of temperature.

25. (*c*) (A) is correct but (R) is incorrect.

The value of cryoscopic constant depends on the nature of the solvent.

Hence, it is not a universal constant.

26. (*d*) Lowering of vapour pressure is directly proportional to the number of species present in solution. Sugar is a non-electrolyte, however KCl is an electrolyte and dissociates in solution to give particles.

Hence, there is greater lowering in vapour pressure in case of KCl. Hence, the vapour pressure of 0.1M sugar solution is more than that of 0.1 M potassium chloride solution.

Thus, (A) is incorrect but (R) is correct.

27. (*a*) Both (A) and (R) are correct and (R) is the correct explanation of (A).

Osmotic pressure is a colligative property as it depends upon number of mole of solutes.

28. (i) (*a*) Molarity (concentration) of nitrate ions

$$= \frac{\text{Number of moles of nitrate ions}}{\text{Total volume (in L)}}$$

$$\Rightarrow \frac{0.1V}{V+V} = \frac{0.1}{2} = 0.05 \text{ M}$$

(ii) Given, number of molecules of urea $= 6.02 \times 10^{20}$

Number of moles

= Number of molecules of urea/Avogadro's number

$$\therefore \text{ Number of moles} = \frac{6.02 \times 10^{20}}{6.02 \times 10^{23}}$$

$$= 1 \times 10^{-3} \text{ mol}$$

Volume of the solution $= 100 \text{ mL} = \frac{100}{1000} = 0.1 \text{ L}$

Concentration of urea solution (in mol L^{-1})

$$= \frac{1 \times 10^{-3}}{0.1} = 1 \times 10^{-2} \text{ mol L}^{-1}$$

$$= 0.01 \text{mol/L or M}$$

(iii) Molality and mole fraction both do not change with temperature.

29. (i) Equimolar solutions of sodium chloride and urea are not isotonic because they do not have same osmotic pressure due to different van't Hoff factor.

(ii) Berkeley-Hartley method is used to measure the osmotic pressure of the liquid solution.

The semipermeable membrane used in Berkeley-Hartley method is $Cu_2[Fe(CN)_6]$.

(iii) If the red blood cells are removed from the body and placed in pure water, then the pressure inside the cell increases.

30 Molality (amount of moles per 1kg of the solvent, mol/kg) and mole fraction (mol/mol) will remain constant since they are independent of volume of the solution which changes with temperature.

31 [**Ans** 6.65%]

32 **Hint** Consider mass number as atomic number. [**Ans** 0.02 m]

33 Molarity is defined as the number of moles of solute per one litre of the solution while molality is defined as the number of moles of solute per kilogram of solvent.

Because the density of water at 25°C is around 1kg/L thus molality is approximately equal to molarity for dilute aqueous solutions at this temperatures.

34 [**Ans** 45 g]

35 **Hint** Ar < CO_2 < CH_4 < HCHO

36 **Hint** With rise in temperature, it loses water of crystallisation.

37 **Ans** NaCl < H_2O < CH_3COCH_3 < Cyclopentane

38 [**Ans** Mole per cent of $A = 50\%$]

39 Refer to text on pages 15 and 16 (Topic-3, Non-ideal solutions)

40 Distillation process is based on the difference of boiling point among the different components of a mixture. All the components of constant boiling mixture, boil at the same temperature and thus, they behave as a single components and the components cannot be separated out.

41 Refer to table given at page 16 (Topic 3, Non-ideal solutions).

42 **Hint** Non-volatile solute decreases vapour pressure of a solution. Refer to text on page 23 (Topic-4, Elevation in boiling point) (Ebullioscopy).

43 [**Ans** 152.11×10^3 g mol^{-1}]

44 [**Ans** –0.146° C]

45 Refer to text on page 26 (Topic-4, Application of osmotic pressure in the determination of relative molecular mass of a solute).

46 Refer to text on page 27 (Topic-4, Types of solutions on the basis of osmotic pressure).

47 **Hint** Consider no dissociation or dissociation [**Ans** = 1]

48 [**Ans.** –2.79°C]

49 [**Ans** 29.06°C]

50 **Hint** Higher the concentration, lower is the value of van't Hoff factor.

51 Refer to text on page 10 (Topic-2, Henry's law).

52 **Hint** $p = K_H \chi$ [**Ans** 1.834 bar]

53 [**Ans** 5.3×10^{-4}m]

54 Refer to text on pages 15-16. (Topic-3, Ideal and non-ideal solutions).

55 Refer to text on page 16 (Topic-3, Azeotropic mixtures).

56 For (i) and (ii) Refer to text on page 23 (Topic-4, Elevation in boiling point) (Ebullioscopy).

57 [**Ans** 269.065 K]

58 Refer to text on page 24 (Topic-4, Depression in freezing point)(Cryoscopy).

59 Refer to text on pages 25-27 (Topic-4, Importance of osmosis, reverse or osmosis and water purification).

60 (i) Solvent will diffuse into solution and concentration of solute will decrease. Therefore, measured value of osmotic pressure will be lower. (1)

(ii) (**Ans.** 57.5 g mol^{-1}) (2)

61 (i) A pressure cooker uses the pressure to keep the water in the liquid form even though it is far above the boiling point and hence the temperature is far above 100°C. Because the pressure build up inside causes higher cooking temperatures thus reducing cooking times.

(ii) Refer to text on page 27-28 (Topic-4, van't Hoff factor (*i*)).

62 (i) The cell walls of the fruits and vegetables act as semipermeable membrane. When they are dried, concentration inside become higher. By placing in water, the process of osmosis takes place. So, they swell and return to their original form.

(ii) Refer to text on page 22 (Topic 4, Relative lowering of vapour pressure).

63 [**Ans** 0.397°C, 2.42]

64 [**Ans** 28.678 g]

65 (i) Refer to text on page 15 (Topic-3, Non-ideal solutions).

(ii) Refer to text on pages 13-14 (Topic-3, Raoult's law).

(iii) **Ans.** 0.617 m

66 (i) The boiling point is the temperature at which vapour pressure becomes equal to atmospheric pressure. Secondly boiling point and vapour pressure are opposite to each other.

Thus, tendency to vaporise is more for X because its boiling point is low. So, larger amount of vapour will form over surface at low temperature for X than Y.

(ii) [**Ans.** 373.53K]

67 (i) Refer to text on pages 27-28 (Topic-4, van't Hoff factor).

(ii) Refer to text on pages 27-28 (Topic-4, van't Hoff factor).

(iii) [**Ans.** 83.33%]

RELATED ONLINE VIDEOS

Visit : https://youtu.be/XHl3oxFRzJQ
OR **Scan the Code**

Visit : https://youtu.be/YnnS1RqgEv8
OR **Scan the Code**

Visit : https://youtu.be/VVP5RpSUN50
OR **Scan the Code**

Visit : https://youtu.be/QRYT-QfPBK4
OR **Scan the Code**

CHAPTER

02

Electrochemistry

Electrochemistry is a branch of chemistry that deals with the study of relationship between electron flow and redox reaction. We can say that electrochemistry is related with electrical conductance in a solution and associated chemical changes. As these chemical changes involves production or consumption of electricity, hence these are called as **electrochemical changes**. The device inside which these changes are carried out are known as cells. These cells have commercial importance in our daily life.

- Electrochemical Cells
- Conductivity of Electrolytic Solution and Its Measurements
- Electrolytic Cells and Electrolysis
- Electrochemical Cells in Action

TOPIC 01 Electrochemical Cells

An electrochemical cell is a device in which chemical energy of the redox reaction is converted into electrical energy while electrolytic cell do the reverse.

$$\text{Chemical energy} \underset{\text{Electrolytic cell}}{\overset{\text{Electrochemical cell}}{\rightleftharpoons}} \text{Electrical energy}$$

Batteries and fuel cells convert chemical energy into electrical energy and are used in various instruments and devices. The reactions carried out electrochemically can be energy efficient and less polluting. Therefore, study of electrochemistry is important for creating new technologies that are eco-friendly.

Note A chemical reaction in which electrons are lost by one substance and gained by another is called **redox reaction**. In redox reaction, transfer of electrons generate electric current.

Galvanic Cell

A device which can generate electricity by means of a chemical reaction is called an electrochemical cell. It converts chemical energy into electrical energy. A galvanic cell generates electric current on account of a redox reaction occurring in it.

An example of this type of device is Daniell cell.

> **Salt Bridge**
>
> It is a U-shaped glass tube containing electrolytes (KCl, KNO_3, NH_4Cl, etc.) mixed in some kind of gel (like gelatine or agar-agar). It plays an important role in working of electrochemical cell as it:
>
> - completes the circuit
> - maintains the electrical neutrality of solutions in each of the respective half-cells.
>
> Salt bridge added in Daniell cell was as an improvement of original galvanic cell. In original cell, electricity flow stops after some time as positive charge accumulates at oxidation half-cell and negative at reduction half-cell which balance the redox free energy and hence, stops the redox reaction. But when salt bridge is present, it provides anions and cations to respective half-cells thus, maintaining the neutrality of both the half-cells.

Daniell Cell

It consists of zinc rod dipped in zinc sulphate solution and a copper rod in copper sulphate solution. These two solutions are connected by an electric circuit and a salt bridge as shown in the figure.

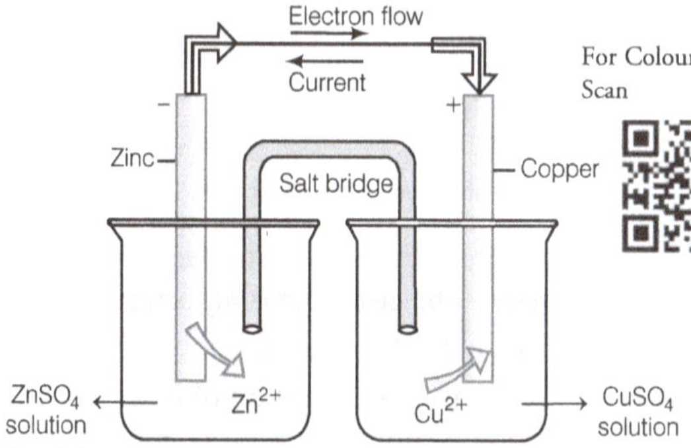

For Colour Fig. Scan

Daniell cell having Zn and Cu electrodes dipping in the solutions of their respective salts

Working Procedure (Mechanism of Production of Electric Current)

In this cell, an electrode is dipped into the solution of its own salt. This combination is called a half-cell or redox couple. In a half-cell, either a reduction or an oxidation reaction occurs. Oxidation occurs at **anode** whereas, reduction occurs at the **cathode**.

The two half-cell reactions in a Daniell cell are :

(a) $Cu^{2+}(aq) + 2e^- \rightarrow Cu(s)$ (reduction half reaction)

(b) $Zn(s) \rightarrow Zn^{2+}(aq) + 2e^-$ (oxidation half reaction)

(i) The copper electrode may be called as the reduction half-cell and the zinc electrode, the oxidation half-cell.

The overall redox reaction occurs as :

$$Cu^{2+}(aq) + Zn(s) \longrightarrow Cu(s) + Zn^{2+}(aq)$$

(ii) The two half-cells are connected by a metallic wire through a voltmeter and a switch, externally. The electrolyte of the two half-cells are connected internally through a salt bridge. Sometimes, both the electrodes are dipped in the same electrolyte solution and in such cases, we do not require a salt bridge.

(iii) An electrical potential energy of 1.1 V is generated from the Daniell cell, when the concentration of Zn^{2+} and Cu^{2+} ions is 1 mol dm^{-3}. If an external opposite potential is applied to the galvanic cell and increased slowly, we find that the reaction continues to take place till the opposing voltage reaches the value of 1.1 V, the reaction stops altogether and no current flows through the cell.

Any further increase in the external potential, again starts the reaction but in opposite direction. It now functions as an **electrolytic cell**, a device for using electrical energy to carried out non-spontaneous chemical reactions. Hence, an electrochemical cell can behave like an electrolytic cell, when $E_{ext} > E_{cell}$.

Functioning of Daniell Cell in Presence of External Voltage

Following three cases are possible when E_{ext} is applied :

Case I **When the external potential is lower than 1.1V.** Under this condition, electrons flow from Zn rod to Cu rod. Hence, current flows from Cu to Zn. Zinc dissolves at anode and copper deposits at cathode.

Case II **When the external potential is equal to 1.1V.** Chemical reactions in the cell stop and there is no flow of electrons or current.

Case III **When the external potential is more than 1.1V.** The reactions get reversed and so, the polarity of the electrodes. This cell is then called an **electrolytic cell.** Now, electrons flow from Cu to Zn and current flows from Zn to Cu. Zinc is deposited at the zinc electrode and copper dissolves at copper electrode.

Some Important Terms Related to Cell

1. Electrode Potential

At each electrode-electrolyte interface, metal ions in the solution have a tendency to leave the electrolyte and deposit on the electrode, trying to make it positively charged. Similarly, at the metal electrode, the metal atoms lose electrons, making the electrode negatively charged and metal ions formed go to the electrolyte. As a result of this, a separation of charge occurs at the electrode. Depending on the net charge at the equilibrium, the electrode may be positively or negatively charged with respect to the solution. In this way, a potential difference develops between the electrode and the electrolyte. This is called the **electrode potential**.

Factors Affecting the Magnitude of Electrode Potential

(i) **Nature of Metal or Electrode** More active metals like Zn have a strong tendency to lose electrons and hence, has high electrode potential. On the other hand, Cu being less active has lower tendency to lose electrons and hence, has lower electrode potential.

(ii) **Concentration of Metal Ions in Solution** As the concentration of metal ions in solution increases, the electrode potential decreases and *vice-versa.*

(iii) The change in the temperature of the solution also changes the electrode potential.

2. Standard Electrode Potential

The electrode potential under the conditions of unit concentration (1M) (i.e. the concentrations of all the species involved in a half-cell is unity) at 1atm pressure and 25°C (298 K) of all the species in the half-cell is called the **standard electrode potential**. According to the IUPAC convention, standard reduction potential of a cell is now called the standard electrode potential. The value of the oxidation potential of the same cell reaction will be the same with the reversed sign.

3. Cell Potential

In Daniell or galvanic cell, the anode is the negative electrode and the cathode is the positive electrode. So, there exists a potential difference between the two electrodes. The potential difference between the two half-cells is called the **cell potential** and is measured in volts (V). It is the difference between standard reduction potential of cathode and standard reduction potential of anode.

$$E^\circ_{cell} = E^\circ_{cathode} - E^\circ_{anode}$$

When switch is in the on position, the flow of electrons is from negative electrode to the positive electrode and the direction of current flow is opposite to that of electron flow.

Measurement of Standard Electrode Potential

(i) In order to compute the emf of a cell, we have to apply the relationship

$$E_{cell} = E_{right} - E_{left}$$

However, individual cell emf cannot be measured. It is the potential difference between the two electrodes that is measurable in a circuit by a voltmeter.

(ii) Therefore, in order to measure the half-cell potential, the other half-cell in this set up has to be assigned an arbitrary value. This is done by assigning a potential of zero called a **Standard Hydrogen Electrode** (SHE). Therefore, the potential difference recorded in the voltmeter in a cell circuit, one half-cell of which is the standard hydrogen electrode, is attributed to the other electrode.

The SHE is represented as: $Pt(s)\,|\,H_2(g)\,|\,H^+(aq)$

in which the reaction occurs as

$$H^+(aq) + e^- \longrightarrow \frac{1}{2}H_2(g)$$

and is assigned a zero potential at all temperatures. The construction of the SHE is shown in the figure below:

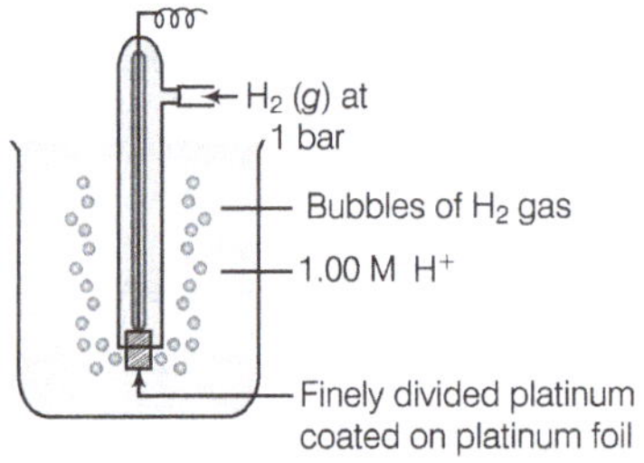

Standard Hydrogen Electrode (SHE)

(iii) SHE consists of a platinum electrode coated with platinum black. The electrode is dipped in solution of 1M H^+ ions and pure H_2 gas is bubbled through it at 1 bar pressure. The concentration of both the reduced and oxidised forms of hydrogen is maintained at unity.

(iv) At 298K, the emf is measured by combining the SHE of the anode with another half-cell of the cathode, resulting into the standard reduction potential of the other half-cell (cathode). In this manner, half-cell potentials are measured.

(v) EMF of the cell $= E^\circ_{cell} = E^\circ_R - E^\circ_L$

As E°_L for SHE is zero, $E^\circ = E^\circ_R - 0 = E^\circ_R$

The superscript degree (°) indicates standard conditions.

Electromotive Force (emf) of a Cell

It is the potential difference, when no current is drawn through the cell. It is measured in volts (V).

EMF = Reduction potential of cathode − Reduction potential of anode

It depends upon the following factors :

(i) Nature of metal and its ions

(ii) Concentrations of electrolytes used

(iii) Temperature

Cell Representation

While representing the galvanic cell, the anode is written on the left and the cathode on the right. A vertical line separates the metal from the metal ion (electrolyte solution) and a double vertical line indicates a salt bridge connecting the two half-cells (two electrolytes). The state of the metal and the solution is written with the concentration of the electrolyte in parenthesis.

$$E_{cell} = E_{right\ (cathode)} - E_{left\ (anode)}$$

Let us consider an example to understand the concept.

Step I. Write the chemical reaction

Cell reaction

$$Cu(s) + 2Ag^+(aq) \longrightarrow Cu^{2+}(aq) + 2Ag(s)$$

Step II. Split the reaction into two half-cell reactions.

Half-cell reactions

At cathode (reduction) :

$$2Ag^+(aq) + 2e^- \longrightarrow 2Ag(s)$$

At anode (oxidation)

$$Cu(s) \longrightarrow Cu^{2+}(aq) + 2e^-$$

Step III. Represent the complete reaction according to the conversion discussed above.

$$Cu(s)\,|\,Cu^{2+}(aq)\,||\,Ag^+(aq)\,|\,Ag(s).$$

The EMF of the cell can be represented as

$$E_{cell} = E_{right} - E_{left}$$

For cell reaction;

$$Cu(s) + 2Ag^+(aq) \longrightarrow Cu^{2+}(aq) + 2Ag(s)$$

$$E_{cell} = E_{Ag^+/Ag} - E_{Cu^{2+}/Cu}$$

Example 1 (i) Formulate the electrochemical cell representing the reaction,

$$2Cr(s) + 3Fe^{2+}(aq) \longrightarrow 2Cr^{3+}(aq) + 3Fe\ (s)$$

(ii) Calculate E°_{cell}

[Given, $E^\circ_{Cr^{3+}/Cr} = -0.74$ V, $E^\circ_{Fe^{2+}/Fe} = -0.44$ V]

Sol. (i) Representation of the given cell,

$$Cr(s)\ |\ Cr^{3+}(aq)\,||\,Fe^{2+}(aq)\,|\,Fe(s)$$

(ii) $E^\circ_{cell} = E^\circ_{right} - E^\circ_{left}$

As, $E^\circ_{Cr^{3+}/Cr} = -0.74$ V ; $E^\circ_{Fe^{2+}/Fe}$ -0.44 V

$= -0.44 - (-0.74) = -0.44 + 0.74 = 0.30$ V

Calculation of EMF of the Cell

If we take the example of Daniell cell,

(i) The measured emf of the cell,

$$Pt(s)|H_2(g, 1\,bar)|H^+(aq, 1M)||Cu^{2+}(aq, 1M)|Cu(s)$$

and the value for the standard electrode potential of the half-cell reaction,

$Cu^{2+}(aq) + 2e^- \longrightarrow Cu(s)$ is equal to 0.34 V.

(ii) Similarly, the measured emf of the cell,

$$Pt(s)|H_2(g, 1bar)|H^+(aq, 1M)||Zn^{2+}(aq, 1M)|Zn(s)$$

and the value for the standard electrode potential of the half-cell reaction,

$Zn^{2+}(aq) + 2e^- \longrightarrow Zn(s)$ is equal to -0.76V.

(iii) The positive value of the standard electrode potential in the first case indicates that Cu^{2+} ions get reduced more easily than H^+ ions. In other words, we can say that hydrogen gas can reduce copper ion under the standard conditions. Thus, Cu does not dissolve in HCl. In nitric acid, copper is oxidised by nitrate ion and not by hydrogen ion.

(iv) The negative value of the standard electrode potential in the second case indicates that H^+ions can oxidise zinc. In other words, we can say that zinc ions can reduce hydrogen ions.

(v) Taking sign convention, the half-cell reactions for the Daniell cell can be written as:

$$Zn(s) \longrightarrow Zn^{2+}(aq) + 2e^- \quad \text{(at left electrode)}$$

$$Cu^{2+}(aq) + 2e^- \longrightarrow Cu(s) \quad \text{(at right electrode)}$$

The overall cell reaction can be written as:

$$Zn(s) + Cu^{2+}(aq) \longrightarrow Zn^{2+}(aq) + Cu(s)$$

EMF of the cell $= E^\circ_{cell} = E^\circ_R - E^\circ_L$

$= 0.34\ V - (-0.76)V = 1.10V$

Difference between Potential Difference and EMF

S.No.	Potential difference	EMF
1.	It is the difference between the electrode potentials of the two electrode under any condition.	It is the potential difference between the two electrodes of the cell when no current is flowing in the circuit (i.e. in an open circuit).
2.	It is less than the maximum voltage obtained from the cell (i.e. EMF of the cell).	It is the maximum voltage obtained from the cell.
3.	It is measured by a simple voltmeter.	It is measured by potentiometeric method only so that the EMF sent by the potentiometric source is equal and opposite to that of the cell and there is no net current flowing in the circuit. It cannot be measured by voltmeter which draws current.
4.	It is not responsible for the flow of steady current in the circuit.	It is responsible for the flow of steady current in the circuit.

Note Some metals like platinum or gold are used as inert electrodes. They do not participate in the reaction but provide their surface for oxidation or reduction reactions and for the conduction of electrons, e.g.

Pt is used in hydrogen electrode : $Pt(s)|H_2(g)|H^+(aq)$ with half-cell reaction, $H^+(aq) + e^- \longrightarrow \frac{1}{2}H_2(g)$

Bromine electrode : $Pt(s)|Br_2(aq)|Br^-(aq)$ with half-cell reaction, $\frac{1}{2}Br_2(aq) + e^- \longrightarrow Br^-(aq)$

Electrochemical Series and Its Applications

The arrangement of various standard half-cells in the order of their decreasing values of standard reduction potentials is called electrochemical series.

Standard Electrode Potentials at 298K
(Electrochemical series)

Increasing strength of oxidising agent (↑ upward); Increasing strength of reducing agent (↓ downward)

Reaction (oxidised form + $ne^- \longrightarrow$ reduced form)

Oxidised form	Reduced form	E° / V
$F_2(g) + 2e^-$	$\longrightarrow 2F^-$	2.87
$Co^{3+} + e^-$	$\longrightarrow Co^{2+}$	1.81
$H_2O_2 + 2H^+ + 2e^-$	$\longrightarrow 2H_2O$	1.78
$MnO_4^- + 8H^+ + 5e^-$	$\longrightarrow Mn^{2+} + 4H_2O$	1.51
$Au^{3+} + 3e^-$	$\longrightarrow Au(s)$	1.40
$Cl_2(g) + 2e^-$	$\longrightarrow 2Cl^-$	1.36
$Cr_2O_7^{2-} + 14H^+ + 6e^-$	$\longrightarrow 2Cr^{3+} + 7H_2O$	1.33
$O_2(g) + 4H^+ + 4e^-$	$\longrightarrow 2H_2O$	1.23
$MnO_2(s) + 4H^+ + 2e^-$	$\longrightarrow Mn^{2+} + 2H_2O$	1.23
$Br_2 + 2e^-$	$\longrightarrow 2Br^-$	1.09
$NO_3^- + 4H^+ + 3e^-$	$\longrightarrow NO(g) + 2H_2O$	0.97
$2Hg^{2+} + 2e^-$	$\longrightarrow Hg_2^{2+}$	0.92
$Ag^+ + e^-$	$\longrightarrow Ag(s)$	0.80
$Fe^{3+} + e^-$	$\longrightarrow Fe^{2+}$	0.77
$O_2(g) + 2H^+ + 2e^-$	$\longrightarrow H_2O_2$	0.68
$I_2 + 2e^-$	$\longrightarrow 2I^-$	0.54
$Cu^+ + e^-$	$\longrightarrow Cu(s)$	0.52
$Cu^{2+} + 2e^-$	$\longrightarrow Cu(s)$	0.34
$AgCl(s) + e^-$	$\longrightarrow Ag(s) + Cl^-$	0.22
$AgBr(s) + e^-$	$\longrightarrow Ag(s) + Br^-$	0.10
$2H^+ + 2e^-$	$\longrightarrow H_2(g)$	0.00
$Pb^{2+} + 2e^-$	$\longrightarrow Pb(s)$	−0.13
$Sn^{2+} + 2e^-$	$\longrightarrow Sn(s)$	−0.14
$Ni^{2+} + 2e^-$	$\longrightarrow Ni(s)$	−0.25
$Fe^{2+} + 2e^-$	$\longrightarrow Fe(s)$	−0.44
$Cr^{3+} + 3e^-$	$\longrightarrow Cr(s)$	−0.74
$Zn^{2+} + 2e^-$	$\longrightarrow Zn(s)$	−0.76
$2H_2O + 2e^-$	$\longrightarrow H_2(g) + 2OH^-(aq)$	−0.83
$Al^{3+} + 3e^-$	$\longrightarrow Al(s)$	−1.66
$Mg^{2+} + 2e^-$	$\longrightarrow Mg(s)$	−2.36
$Na^+ + e^-$	$\longrightarrow Na(s)$	−2.71
$Ca^{2+} + 2e^-$	$\longrightarrow Ca(s)$	−2.87
$K^+ + e^-$	$\longrightarrow K(s)$	−2.93
$Li^+ + e^-$	$\longrightarrow Li(s)$	−3.05

Note (i) Negative E° means that the redox couple is stronger reducing agent than H^+ / H_2, e.g. Zn^{2+}/Zn (−0.76).
(ii) Positive E° means that the redox couple is a weaker reducing agent than H^+ / H_2, e.g. Ag^+/Ag (+ 0.80).

Characteristics of Electrochemical Series

(i) The negative sign of standard reduction potential (SRP) indicates that the electrode when joined with standard hydrogen electrode (SHE) behaves as anode ion, oxidation occur at that electrode. Similarly, positive sign of SRP indicates that behaviour of electrode as cathode when joined with SHE.

(ii) The above findings indicate that elements which are better reducing agents than hydrogen, get their place above hydrogen in this series (such elements have negative value of SRP) while elements which are better oxidising agents than hydrogen, get their place below the hydrogen in this series (such elements have (+) ve value of their SRP).

(iii) Elements which get oxidised easily are good reducing agent or metals and elements which get reduced easily are good oxidising agent or non-metals.

Applications of Electrochemical Series

(i) **For Comparing the Reactivity of Metals** A metal with lower SRP can have the ability to displace metal with higher SRP from their solutions. Second thing, the reactivity of metal decreases from top to bottom in electrochemical series, i.e. metals higher in the series are more active than metals lying lower in the series.

(ii) **For Comparing the Oxidising and Reducing behaviour of elements** Oxidising nature decreases from top to bottom and reducing behaviour increases in the same pattern in electrochemical series.

(iii) **For the Calculation of emf of the Cell** The formula is used to calculate emf as

$$E^\circ_{cell} = E^\circ_{cathode} - E^\circ_{anode}$$

(iv) **For Predicting the Thermal Stability of Metallic Oxide** The thermal stability of the metal oxide depends on its electropositive nature. As the electropositivity decreases from top to bottom, the thermal stability of the oxide also decreases from top to bottom.

The oxides of metals with high positive reduction potential is not stable towards heat. The metal which come below copper form unstable oxides, i.e. these are decomposed on heating.

(v) **For Predicting the Product of Electrolysis** When two or more types of ions (positive and negative) are present in solution, the ion which is stronger oxidising agent out of the given cations and the ion which is stronger reducing agent out of the given anion will liberated (or discharged) first at cathode and anode respectively.

(vi) **For Protecting the Metal from Corrosion** It is done through
- plating the metal with a thin layer of a less easily oxidised metal.
- allowing a protective film over it such as metal oxide.
- galvanisation in which steel is coated with zinc (a more active metal).

(vii) **For Predicting the Feasibility of a Reaction** A redox reaction is feasible only if the species with high SRP is reduced (accepts the electrons) and the species with lower SRP is oxidised (loses the electrons).

(viii) **In the Extraction of Metal** (displacement reactions) A more electropositive metal can displace a less electropositive metal from its salt solution. This principle can be applied in the extraction of less electropositive metal like Au, Ag etc.

Nernst Equation

The equation which gives the relation between electrode potential, temperature and concentration of metal ions is called Nernst equation.

Nernst Equation for Electrode Potential

The standard potentials are always measured under standard conditions, i.e. when the pressure of a gas is 1 atm, concentration of ions is 1 mol dm^{-3} and the temperature is 298 K. However, practically standard conditions are hardly achieved or used.

According to Nernst, the electrode reaction is

$$M^{n+}(aq) + ne^- \longrightarrow M(s)$$

The electrode potential measured against standard hydrogen electrode, can be written as:

$$\boxed{E_{(M^{n+}/M)} = E^\circ_{(M^{n+}/M)} - \frac{RT}{nF}\ln\frac{[M]}{[M^{n+}]}}$$

This is known as the **Nernst equation.**

For pure solids, $[M] = 1$

$$E_{(M^{n+}/M)} = E^\circ_{(M^{n+}/M)} - \frac{RT}{nF}\ln\frac{1}{[M^{n+}]} \quad \ldots\text{(i)}$$

Here, $E^\circ_{(M^{n+}/M)}$ is the standard reduction potential of the electrode, R is the universal gas constant having value 8.314 $JK^{-1}mol^{-1}$, n is the number of electrons involved in the reaction, T is the temperature in K, $[M^{n+}]$ is the concentration of the metal ion M^{n+}, and F is the Faraday constant whose value is 96500 C mol^{-1} (approx.).

Using logarithm to the base 10 value, Eq. (i) becomes,

$$E = E^\circ_{(M^{2+}/M)} - \frac{2.303RT}{nF}\log\frac{1}{[M^{n+}]}$$

At $T = 298$ K, and putting values of all constants, we get,

$$\boxed{E = E^\circ_{(M^{n+}/M)} - \frac{0.059}{n}\log\frac{1}{[M^{n+}]}}$$

Nernst Equation for emf of a Cell

For the cathode of Daniell cell, the emf is

$$E_{(Cu^{2+}/Cu)} = E^\circ_{(Cu^{2+}/Cu)} - \frac{RT}{2F}\ln\frac{1}{[Cu^{2+}(aq)]}$$

For the anode of Daniell cell, the emf is

$$E_{(Zn^{2+}/Zn)} = E^\circ_{(Zn^{2+}/Zn)} - \frac{RT}{2F}\ln\frac{1}{[Zn^{2+}(aq)]}$$

The cell potential of the Daniell cell is given by

$$E_{cell} = E_{(Cu^{2+}/Cu)} - E_{(Zn^{2+}/Zn)}$$

$$= \left[E^\circ_{(Cu^{2+}/Cu)} - \frac{RT}{2F}\ln\frac{1}{[Cu^{2+}(aq)]}\right] - \left[E^\circ_{(Zn^{2+}/Zn)} + \frac{RT}{2F}\ln\frac{1}{[Zn^{2+}(aq)]}\right]$$

$$E_{cell} = E^\circ_{(Cu^{2+}/Cu)} - E^\circ_{(Zn^{2+}/Zn)} - \frac{RT}{2F}\left[\ln\frac{1}{[Cu^{2+}(aq)]} - \ln\frac{1}{[Zn^{2+}(aq)]}\right]$$

$$E_{cell} = E^\circ_{cell} - \frac{RT}{2F}\ln\frac{[Zn^{2+}]}{[Cu^{2+}]}$$

At $T = 298$ K,

$$\boxed{E_{cell} = E^\circ_{cell} - \frac{0.059}{2}\log\frac{[Zn^{2+}]}{[Cu^{2+}]}}$$

According to the above equation,

- E_{cell} is directly dependent upon concentration of Cu^{2+} and inversely dependent upon the concentration of Zn^{2+} ions.
- E_{cell} decreases as temperature decreases and number of electrons involved in the reaction increases.

For a general electrochemical reaction of the type,

$$aA + bB \xrightarrow{ne^-} cC + dD$$

The Nernst equation can be written as:

$$\boxed{E_{cell} = E^\circ_{cell} - \frac{RT}{nF} \ln Q}$$

$$\Rightarrow \quad E_{cell} = E^\circ_{cell} - \frac{RT}{nF} \ln \frac{[C]^c[D]^d}{[A]^a[B]^b}$$

At $T = 298$ K,

$$E_{cell} = E^\circ_{cell} - \frac{0.0591}{n} \log \frac{[C]^c[D]^d}{[A]^a[B]^b}$$

Example 2 Calculate emf of the following cell at 25 °C.

$$Fe|Fe^{2+}(0.001M)||H^+(0.01M)|H_2(g)\ (1bar)|Pt(s)$$

$$E^\circ_{(Fe^{2+}/Fe)} = -0.44\text{ V};\ E^\circ_{(H^+/H_2)} = 0.00\text{V}$$

Sol. For the given cell representation, the cell reaction will be

$$Fe(s) + 2H^+(aq) \longrightarrow Fe^{2+}(aq) + H_2(g)$$

The standard emf of the cell will be,

$$E^\circ_{cell} = E^\circ_{H^+/H_2} - E^\circ_{Fe^{2+}/Fe},$$

$$E^\circ_{cell} = 0 - (-0.44) = 0.44\text{ V}$$

The Nernst equation for the cell reaction at 25°C,

$$E_{cell} = E^\circ_{cell} - \frac{0.0591}{n} \log \frac{[Fe^{2+}]}{[H^+]^2}$$

$$= 0.44 - \frac{0.0591}{2} \log \frac{[0.001]}{[0.01]^2}$$

$$= 0.44 - 0.02955\ (\log 10)$$

$$= 0.44 - 0.02955\ (1) \qquad [\because \log 10 = 1]$$

$$= 0.41045\text{V} = 0.41\text{ V}$$

Equilibrium Constant from Nernst Equation

In Daniell cell, the following reaction takes place

$$Zn(s) + Cu^{2+}(aq) \longrightarrow Zn^{2+}(aq) + Cu(s)$$

As the time passes, the reaction proceeds. The concentration of Zn^{2+} keeps on increasing and the concentration of Cu^{2+} keeps on decreasing. At the same time, voltage of the cell on the voltmeter keeps on decreasing. After sometime, there is no change in the concentration of Cu^{2+} and Zn^{2+} ions and at that time, voltmeter gives zero reading.

At equilibrium, when there is no current in the circuit, a Daniell cell shows zero potential in the voltmeter.

$$\text{Therefore, } E_{cell} = 0 = E^\circ_{cell} - \frac{2.303\,RT}{2F} \log \frac{[Zn^{2+}]}{[Cu^{2+}]}$$

$$\text{or} \quad E^\circ_{cell} = \frac{2.303\,RT}{2F} \log \frac{[Zn^{2+}]}{[Cu^{2+}]}$$

At equilibrium, for the above reaction

$$\frac{[Zn^{2+}]}{[Cu^{2+}]} = K_C$$

Therefore, at 298 K, the above equation can be written as:

$$E^\circ_{cell} = \frac{0.0591}{2} \log K_C = 1.1\text{V}$$

Which gives the K_C value as:

$$\log K_C = \frac{(1.1\text{ V} \times 2)}{0.059\text{ V}} = 37.288$$

$$K_C = 2 \times 10^{37} \text{ at 298 K}$$

Such a high value of K_C shows that the reaction has proceeded almost to the completion before attainment of equilibrium condition.

Hence, the value of K_C determines the extent of cell reaction. In general, at equilibrium

$$\boxed{E^\circ_{cell} = \frac{2.303\,RT}{nF} \log K_C}$$

Thus, the above equation gives a relationship between equilibrium constant of the reaction and standard potential of the cell in which that reaction takes place. Thus, equilibrium constant of the reaction is difficult to measure otherwise, can be calculated from the corresponding E° value of the cell.

Concentration Cells

Two electrodes of the same metal dipped separately into two solutions of the same electrolyte having different concentrations and the solutions are connected through salt bridge, such cells are known as concentration cells, e.g. copper ion concentration cell.

$$Cu\,|\,Cu^{2+}\ (C_1)\,||\,Cu^{2+}\ (C_2)\,|\,Cu$$

$$E_{cell} = \frac{0.0591}{n} \log \frac{C_2}{C_1}, \text{ where } C_2 > C_1 \text{ and } E^\circ_{cell} = 0$$

The electrode placed in high concentration electrolyte acts as cathode and that placed in low concentration electrolyte acts as anode.

Example 3 Calculate the equilibrium constant for the reaction.

$$Fe(s) + Cd^{2+}(aq) \rightleftharpoons Fe^{2+}(aq) + Cd(s)$$

[Given, $E^\circ_{Cd^{2+}/Cd} = -0.40V$, $E^\circ_{Fe^{2+}/Fe} = -0.44$ V]

> **Key Idea**
> (i) First, find E°_{cell} by using formula,
> $E^\circ_{cell} = E^\circ_{right} - E^\circ_{left}$ or $E^\circ_{cathode} - E^\circ_{anode}$
> (ii) Find $\log K_C$ by using formula,
> $E^\circ_{cell} = \frac{0.0591}{n} \log K_C$
> (iii) Find K_C using antilog table.

Sol. $E^\circ_{cell} = E^\circ_{cathode} - E^\circ_{anode}$

$= -0.40 - (-0.44)$

$= -0.40 + 0.44 = 0.04$ V

$E^\circ_{cell} = \frac{0.059}{n} \log K_C$

$E^\circ_{cell} = \frac{0.059}{2} \log K_C = 0.04$ V

or $\log K_C = \frac{2 \times 0.04}{0.059} = 1.356$

$K_C = \text{antilog } 1.356 = 22.70$

Electrochemical Cell and Gibbs Energy of the Reaction

When a cell reaction takes place, electrical energy is produced. Thus, electrical work done by the cell results in corresponding decrease in the free energy of the cell. Electrical work done in one second is equal to the electrical potential multiplied by total charge passed.

To obtain maximum work from a galvanic cell, charge has to be passed reversibly.

The reversible work done by a galvanic cell is equal to the decrease in its Gibbs energy. Let nF is the amount of charge passed, E is the emf of the cell and $\Delta_r G$ is the Gibbs energy of the reaction, then

$$\Delta_r G = -nFE_{cell}$$

Under standard conditions (i.e. when molar concentration of all reacting species is unity at 298 K), the emf of a cell is related to the Gibbs free energy as:

$$\Delta_r G^\circ = -nFE^\circ_{cell}$$

where, n is the number of electrons involved in the reaction and F is the Faraday's constant.

The relation between cell potential (E°_{cell}), free energy (ΔG°) and equilibrium constant is given by

or $\boxed{\Delta_r G^\circ = -2.303\, RT \log K_C}$

as $\Delta G^\circ = -nFE^\circ_{cell}$ and $E^\circ_{cell} = \frac{2.303RT}{nF} \log K_C$

E_{cell} is an intensive property but ΔG is an extensive thermodynamic property whose value depends on n. Thus, if we write the reaction,

$$Zn(s) + Cu^{2+}(aq) \longrightarrow Zn^{2+}(aq) + Cu(s),$$

$$\Delta_r G = -2FE_{cell}$$

But when we write the reaction,

$$2Zn(s) + 2Cu^{2+}(aq) \longrightarrow 2Zn^{2+}(aq) + 2Cu(s),$$

$$\Delta_r G = -4FE_{cell}$$

If the concentration of all the reacting species is unity, then $E_{cell} = E^\circ_{cell}$

and we have $\Delta_r G^\circ = -nFE^\circ_{cell}$

E°_{cell} measurement can give us the value of thermodynamic quantity, $\Delta_r G^\circ$, standard Gibbs energy of the reaction which later help in the calculation of equilibrium constant by the equation, $\Delta_r G^\circ = -RT \ln K$.

> **IMPORTANT POINT**
> At the stage of chemical equilibrium in the cell, $E_{cell} = 0$
> $\Delta_r G = -nFE_{cell} = -nF \times 0 = 0$
> The reaction is feasible only, when
> E_{cell} = positive or $\Delta_r G$ = negative.

Example 4 The standard electrode potential (E°) for Daniell cell is +1.1 V. Calculate, the ΔG° for the reaction.

$$Zn(s) + Cu^{2+}(aq) \longrightarrow Zn^{2+}(aq) + Cu(s)$$

$$(1 \text{ F} = 96500 \text{ C mol}^{-1})$$

Sol. $Zn(s) + Cu^{2+}(aq) \longrightarrow Zn^{2+}(aq) + Cu(s)$

$E^\circ = +1.1$ V, $\Delta G^\circ = ?$

$1F = 96500$ C mol^{-1}, $n = 2$

$\Delta G^\circ = -nFE^\circ_{cell} = -2 \times 96500 \times 1.1$

$= -212300$ J mol^{-1}

Example 5 Calculate the cell emf and $\Delta_r G^\circ$ for the cell reaction at 25° C.

$$Zn(s) \mid Zn^{2+}(0.1M) \parallel Cd^{2+}(0.01M) \mid Cd(s)$$

[Given, $E^\circ_{Zn^{2+}/Zn} = -0.763$ V,
$E^\circ_{Cd^{2+}/Cd} = -0.403$ V
$1F = 96500$ C mol^{-1},
$R = 8.314$ JK^{-1}mol^{-1}]

Find $E^\circ_{cell} = E^\circ_{cathode} - E^\circ_{anode}$ then, $\Delta_r G^\circ$ by using formula, $\Delta_r G^\circ = -nFE^\circ_{cell}$.

Sol. $E°_{cell} = E°_{right} - E°_{left}$

$= -0.403 - (-0.763) = 0.36$ V

$$E_{cell} = E°_{cell} - \frac{0.059}{n} \log \frac{[Zn^{2+}(aq)]}{[Cd^{2+}(aq)]}$$

$$E_{cell} = 0.36 - \frac{0.059}{2} \log \frac{0.1}{0.01} \qquad [n = 2]$$

$$E_{cell} = 0.36 - 0.0295 \log 10 = 0.36 - 0.0295 \times 1 = 0.3305 \text{ V}$$

$$\Delta_r G° = -nFE°_{cell} = -2 \times 96500 \times 0.36$$

$$= -69480 \text{ J mol}^{-1} = -69.48 \text{ kJ mol}^{-1}$$

Topic Practice 1

Very Short Answer Type Questions

1 Mark

1. Fill in the Blanks

(i) An electrochemical cell converts ...... energy to ...... energy. **ISC 2014**

(ii) A galvanic cell converts .... energy into ....energy. **ISC 2018**

(iii) In galvanic cell, electrons flow from ...... to ...... through the connecting wires. **ISC 2013**

(iv) Copper displaces ....from its solution because it has .... reduction potential. **ISC 2002**

(v) Nernst equation is used for ...... cell. **ISC 2012**

2. Objective Type Questions

(i) Which one of the following statements is true for the galvanic cell ? **ISC 2023**

(a) Electrons flow from copper electrode to zinc electrode.

(b) Current flows from zinc electrode to copper electrode.

(c) Cations move towards copper electrode.

(d) Cations move towards zinc electrode.

(ii) For a spontaneous reaction $\Delta G°$ and $E°$ cell will be respectively **ISC 2017**

(a) − ve and + ve (b) + ve and − ve

(c) + ve and + ve (d) − ve and − ve

(iii) The cell reaction is spontaneous or feasible when emf of the cell is. **ISC 2019**

(a) negative

(b) positive

(c) zero

(d) either positive or negative

(iv) When zinc granule is dipped into copper sulphate solution, copper is precipitated because **ISC 2011**

(a) both, copper and zinc have a positive reduction potential

(b) reduction potential of copper is higher than that of zinc

(c) reduction potential of zinc is higher than that of copper

(d) both, zinc and copper have a negative reduction potential

(v) The standard electrode potentials of four elements *A*, *B*, *C* and *D* are − 3.05, 1.66, −0.40 and 0.80 V, respectively. The highest chemical reactivity will be shown by **ISC 2006**

(a) *A* (b) *B*

(c) *C* (d) *D*

(vi) If the standard electrode potential of an electrode is greater than zero then

(a) its oxidised form is more stable as compared to hydrogen gas

(b) its reduced form is more stable as compared to hydrogen gas

(c) its reduced form is less stable as compared to hydrogen gas

(d) All of the above

3. Match the following Columns and choose the correct option using the codes given below:

Column I	Column II
A. $Zn + Cu^{2+} \longrightarrow Cu + Zn^{2+}$	(i) Cathode half reaction is $Cu^{2+} + 2e^- \rightarrow Cu$
B. $Mg + Cu^{2+} \longrightarrow Cu + Mg^{2+}$	(ii) Electrons flows from metal to Cu side.
C. $2Ag^+ + Cu \longrightarrow Cu^{2+} + 2Ag$	(iii) $E°_{anode} < E°_{cathode}$
D. $H_2 + Cu^{2+} \longrightarrow H^+ + Cu$	(iv) Hydrogen electrode is used

Codes

	A	B	C	D
(a)	(i),(ii),(iii)	(i),(ii),(iii)	(iii)	(i),(iii),(iv)
(b)	(i),(ii),(iii)	(iii)	(ii)	(i)
(c)	(i),(iii)	(iii),(ii)	(ii)	(i),(iii)
(d)	(iii),(ii)	(i),(ii)	(i),(ii),(iv)	(i),(iii)

4. Arrange the following metals in the order in which they displace each other from the solution of their salts.

Al, Cu, Fe, Mg and Zn **NCERT**

5. If a reaction has an equilibrium constant $K < 1$, then $E°$ is positive or negative? What is the value of K, when $E° = 0$ V ?

6. What happens, when a nickel rod is dipped into a copper sulphate solution? Justify your answer. ($E^{\circ}_{Ni^{2+}/Ni} = -0.25$V and $E^{\circ}_{Cu^{2+}/Cu} = +0.34$V). **ISC 2014**

7. What is standard hydrogen electrode? **ISC 2014**

8. Two metallic elements A and B have the following standard potentials:
$A = 0.40$V, $B = 0.80$V, what would you expect, if element A was added to an aqueous salt solution of element B? Give a reason for your answer. **ISC 2013**

9. Arrange Ag, Cr and Hg metals in the increasing order of reducing power.
Given, $E^{\circ}_{Ag^{+}/Ag} = +0.80$ V,
$E^{\circ}_{Cr^{3+}/Cr} = -0.74$ V and $E^{\circ}_{Hg^{2+}/Hg} = +0.79$ V **ISC 2013**

10. The reduction potential of a metal X is -0.76 V while that of Y is -2.38 V. Which of the two metals is a stronger reducing agent? Give a reason for your answer. **ISC 2010**

11. Will nickel displace copper from a 1 M solution of copper sulphate? Justify your answer.
($E^{\circ}_{Ni^{2+}/Ni} = -0.25$ V, $E^{\circ}_{Cu^{2+}/Cu} = +0.34$ V). **ISC 2010**

12. Correct the following statement:
Copper displaces both zinc and silver from their solutions.

13. Under what condition,
$E_{cell} = 0$ or $\Delta G = 0$? **NCERT Exemplar**

Short Answer Type I Questions

2 Marks

14. What is an electrochemical series? How is it useful in predicting whether a metal can liberate hydrogen from acid or not?

15. Given the standard electrode potentials,
$K^{+} / K = -2.93$ V, $Ag^{+} / Ag = 0.80$ V
$Hg^{2+} / Hg = 0.79$ V, $Mg^{2+} / Mg = -2.37$ V,
$Cr^{3+} / Cr = -0.74$ V
Arrange these metals in their increasing order of reducing power. **NCERT**

16. Calculate the potential of hydrogen electrode in contact with a solution whose pH is 10. **NCERT Intext**

17. Calculate the maximum possible electrical work that can be obtained from a galvanic cell under standard conditions at 298 K **ISC 2024**

$$Zn|\underset{(aq)}{Zn^{2+}}||\underset{(aq)}{Ag^{+}}|Ag$$

Given $E^{\circ}_{(Zn^{2+}/Zn)} = -0.76$ V; $E^{\circ}_{Ag^{+}/Ag} = +0.80$ V

18. Calculate the emf $\Delta G°$ for the cell reaction at 25°C.
$Zn(s)|\underset{(0.1\,M)}{Zn^{2+}(aq)^{2+}}||\underset{(0.01\,M)}{Cd^{2+}(aq)}|Cd(s)$
Given, $E^{\circ}_{Zn^{2+}/Zn} = -0.763$ and $E^{\circ}_{Cd^{2+}/Cd} = -0.403$ V **ISC 2018**

19. Calculate the emf and ΔG for the given cell at 25°C:
$Cr(s)|Cr^{3+}(0.1\,M)||\,dFe^{2+}(0.01M)|Fe(s)$
Given, $E^{\circ}_{Cr^{3+}/Cr} = -\;0.74$ V, $E^{\circ}_{Fe^{3+}/Fe} = -0.44$ V
(1 F = 96500 C, $R = 8.314$ JK^{-1} mol^{-1}) **ISC 2020**

20. Calculate the emf of the following cell reaction at 298 K:
$$Mg(g) + Cu^{2+}\ (0.0001\ M) \longrightarrow Mg^{2+}(0.001\ M) + Cu(s)$$
The standard potential ($E°$) of the cell is 2.71 V. **ISC 2015**

21. Calculate the emf of the following cell at 298 K. **ISC 2023**
$Cu|Cu^{2+}(0.025M)||Ag^{+}(0.005M)|Ag$
Given : $E^{\circ}_{Cu^{2+}/Cu} = 0.34$ V; $E^{\circ}_{Ag^{+}/Ag} = 0.80$ V.
1 Faraday = 96500 C mol^{-1}

22. Mention any two factors affecting the electrode potential of a metal. **ISC 2009**

Short Answer Type II Questions

3 Marks

23. Write the Nernst equation for the cell reaction in the Daniell cell. How will the E_{cell} be affected when concentration of Zn^{2+} ions is increased? **NCERT Exemplar**

24. For the cell,

$Zn|Zn^{2+}(\alpha = 1) \| Cu^{2+}(\alpha = 1)|Cu$

Given, that $E^\circ_{Zn/Zn^{2+}} = -0.76\,V$,

$E^\circ_{Cu^{2+}/Cu} = +0.339\,V$

(i) Write the cell reaction.

(ii) Calculate the emf and free energy change at 298 K involved in the cell.

(Faraday's constant = 96500 C) **ISC 2017, 2005**

25. Calculate the value of E_{cell} at 298 K for the following cell :

$Al|Al^{3+}(0.01\,M)\|Sn^{2+}(0.015\,M)|Sn$

Given; $E^\circ_{Al^{3+}/Al} = -1.66\,V$ and

$E^\circ_{Sn^{2+}/Sn} = -0.14\,V$ **ISC 2013**

26. Calculate the maximum work that can be obtained from the given electrochemical cell constructed with two metals *M* and *N*.

$(E^\circ_{M^{2+}/M} = -0.76\,V, E^\circ_{N^{2+}/N} = +0.34\,V)$

The cell reaction is

$M + N^{2+} \longrightarrow M^{2+} + N$ **ISC 2012**

27. For the following cell, calculate the emf.

$Al|Al^{3+}(0.01\,M)\|Fe^{2+}(0.02\,M)|Fe$

Given, $E^\circ_{Al^{3+}/Al} = -1.66\,V$,

$E^\circ_{Fe^{2+}/Fe} = -0.44\,V$ **ISC 2009**

28. Calculate the emf and ΔG for the cell reaction at 298 K.

$Mg_{(s)}|Mg^{2+}_{(0.1M)}\|Cu^{2+}_{(0.01M)}|Cu_{(s)}$

Given, $E^\circ_{cell} = 2.71\,V$, $1F = 96,500\,C$ **ISC 2019**

29. In the button cells, widely used in watches and other devices, the following reaction takes place

$$Zn(s) + Ag_2O(s) + H_2O(l) \longrightarrow Zn^{2+}(aq) + 2Ag(s) + 2OH^-(aq)$$

Determine E° and ΔG° for the reaction.

(Given, $E^\circ_{Ag^+/Ag} = +0.80\,V$, $E^\circ_{Zn^{2+}/Zn} = -0.76\,V$) **NCERT**

30. The cell in which the following reaction occurs,

$2Fe^{3+}(aq) + 2I^-(aq) \longrightarrow 2Fe^{2+}(aq) + I_2(s)$

has $E^\circ_{cell} = 0.236\,V$ at 298 K, calculate the standard Gibbs energy and the equilibrium constant of the cell reaction. **NCERT Intext**

Long Answer Type Questions

5 Marks

31. Study the diagram given below that represents Cu-Ag electrochemical cell and answer the questions that follow.

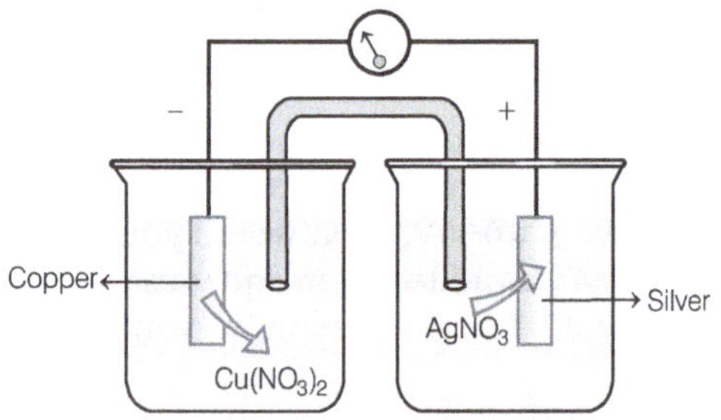

Given, $E^\circ_{(Cu^{2+}/Cu)} = 0.337\,V$; $E^\circ_{(Ag^+/Ag)} = 0.799\,V$

(i) Write the cell reaction for the above cell.

(ii) Calculate the standard emf of the cell.

(iii) It the concentration of $[Cu^{2+}]$ is 0.1 M and E_{cell} is 0.422 V, at 25°C, calculate the concentration of $[Ag^+]$

(iv) Calculate ΔG for the cell. **ISC 2024**

32. Depict the galvanic cell in which the reaction

$Zn(s) + 2Ag^+(aq) \longrightarrow Zn^{2+}(aq) + 2Ag(s)$

takes place.

Further show

(i) which of the above electrode is negatively charged?

(ii) the carriers of the current in the cell.

(iii) an individual reaction at each electrode. **NCERT**

33. Using the standard electrode potentials, predict if the reaction between the following is feasible.

(i) $Fe^{3+}(aq)$ and $I^-(aq)$ (ii) $Ag^+(aq)$ and $Cu(s)$

(iii) $Fe^{3+}(aq)$ and $Br^-(aq)$ (iv) $Ag(s)$ and $Fe^{3+}(aq)$

(v) $Br_2(aq)$ and $Fe^{2+}(aq)$

Given standard electrode potentials,

$E^\circ_{1/2\,I_2, I^-} = 0.541\,V$, $E^\circ_{Cu^{2+}, Cu} = 0.34\,V$,

$E^\circ_{1/2\,Br_2, Br^-} = 1.09\,V$, $E^\circ_{Ag^+, Ag} = 0.80\,V$

$E^\circ_{Fe^{3+}, Fe^{2+}} = 0.77\,V$ **NCERT**

34. Calculate the standard cell potentials of galvanic cell in which the following reactions take place:

(i) $2Cr(s) + 3Cd^{2+}(aq) \longrightarrow 2Cr^{3+}(aq) + 3Cd$

(ii) $Fe^{2+}(aq) + Ag^+(aq) \longrightarrow Fe^{3+}(aq) + Ag(s)$

Calculate the $\Delta_r G^\circ$ and equilibrium constant for these reactions. **NCERT**

Hints & Solutions

1. (i) chemical, electrical (ii) chemical, electrical
(iii) anode, cathode (iv) silver, lower
(v) electrochemical

2. (i) (a) In Galvanic cell, cations move towards Cu (cathode) and accumulated as metal.
(ii) → (a)
(iii) (b) Free energy, i.e. ΔG° must be negative for a cell reaction to be spontaneous or feasible and

$$\Delta G^\circ = -nF E^\circ_{cell} = (-) \text{ ve}$$

where, n = number of electrons
F = charge in Faraday
E° = emf of the cell

Therefore, E°_{cell}, i.e. emf of the cell must be positive and (b) is the correct option.
(iv) → (b)
(v) → (a)
(vi) → (b)

3. (a) A-(i),(ii),(iii); B-(i),(ii),(iii); C-(iii); D-(i),(iii),(iv)

4. The order in which the metals displace each other from their salts solution is Mg, Al, Zn, Fe, Cu.

5. $E^\circ = \frac{0.0591}{n} \log K$

If $K < 1$ (say 0.01), then $E^\circ = \frac{0.0591}{n} \log 0.01 = \frac{-2 \times 0.0591}{n}$

E° is thus negative.
If $E^\circ = 0$V, then $K = 1$

6. Since, the standard electrode potential of Ni is less than that of Cu, it is above Cu in the series and possesses greater reducing power.
So, nickel can displace copper from copper sulphate solution.

$$Cu^{2+}(aq) + Ni(s) \longrightarrow Ni^{2+}(aq) + Cu(s)$$

7. **Standard Hydrogen Electrode** (SHE) is an electrode in which H_2 gas at one atmospheric pressure is passed through a solution of H^+ ions of 1M concentration at 25°C placed in contact with Pt foil. This electrode is also called **Normal Hydrogen Electrode** (NHE). Its potential is taken as zero.

8. Standard potential of $A < B$. Hence, A has more reducing power than B. So, when A is added to an aqueous salt solution of B, B will form precipitate and A will form the salt, displacing B from its salt solution.

9. Since, the standard potential values are in the order of

$$E^\circ_{Cr^{3+}/Cr}(-0.74\text{ V}) < E^\circ_{Hg^{2+}/Hg}(0.79\text{V}) < E^\circ_{Ag^+/Ag}(0.80\text{V})$$

i.e. they are arranged in the increasing order to gain electrons. To lose electron or to act as reducing agent, the order will be reverse,

i.e. $E^\circ_{Ag^+/Ag} < E^\circ_{Hg^{2+}/Hg} < E^\circ_{Cr^{3+}/Cr}$

10. Reduction potential of X (−0.76 V) > Y (−2.38 V).
Strong reducing agents have a large negative value.
Hence, metal Y is a stronger reducing agent than metal X.

11. Refer to answer no. 6

12. Zinc displaces both copper and silver from their solutions.

Or

Copper displaces only silver from the solution not zinc.
The reduction potential of three elements is in the order Zn < Cu < Ag. Hence, zinc is most reactive.

13. At the stage of chemical equilibrium in the cell.

14. The arrangement of various standard half-cells in the order of their decreasing values of standard reduction potentials is called **electrochemical series.**
In the electrochemical series, metals that are placed above hydrogen are reactive metals and these reacts with acids like HCl (dil.), H_2SO_4 (dil.) to produce salt and hydrogen gas and have, placed below hydrogen.

$$\text{Metal + Dil. acid} \longrightarrow \text{Salt + Hydrogen}$$

e.g. $\underset{\text{Zinc}}{Zn(s)} + \underset{\text{(Dil.)}}{2HCl(aq)} \longrightarrow \underset{\text{Zinc chloride}}{ZnCl_2(aq)} + \underset{\text{Hydrogen gas}}{H_2(g)\uparrow}$

Metals like Cu, Hg, Ag, Au, are less reactive and these do not react with acid to liberate hydrogen gas and hence, placed below hydrogen.

15. The lower the reduction potential, the higher is the reducing power.

$$Ag < Hg < Cr < Mg < K \quad (2)$$

16. For hydrogen electrode,

$$H^+ + e^- \longrightarrow \frac{1}{2}H_2$$

Applying Nernst equation,

$$E_{(H^+/1/2H_2)} = E^\circ_{(H^+/1/2H_2)} - \frac{0.0591}{n} \log \frac{1}{[H^+]} \quad (1)$$

$$= 0 - \frac{0.0591}{1} \log \frac{1}{(10^{-10})}$$

($\because$ pH = 10, $[H^+] = 10^{-10}$M)

$$= 0 - \frac{0.0591}{1} \times (10 \log 10) = -0.591 \text{ V}$$

Thus, $E_{(H^+/1/2H_2)} = -0.591$ V (1)

17. Given, $E^\circ_{(Zn^{2+}/Zn)} = -0.76$ V

$E^\circ_{(Ag^+/Ag)} = 0.80$ V

$E^\circ_{cell} = 0.8 - (-0.76) = 1.56$ V

$W_{electrical} = -nFE^\circ_{cell} = -2 \times 96500 \times [1.56]$
$= -301{,}080$ J $= -301.1$ kJ

18. The cell reaction is

$$Zn(s) + Cd^{2+}(aq) \rightarrow Cd(s) + Zn^{2+}(aq)$$

E° of the cell is given by

$$E^\circ_{cell} = E^\circ_{right} - E^\circ_{left} = -0.403 - (-0.763) = 0.36 \text{ V}$$

Applying Nernst equation to the cell reaction

$$E_{cell} = E^\circ_{cell} - \frac{0.059}{n}\log\frac{[Zn^{2+}(aq)]}{[Cd^{2+}(aq)]},$$

$$E_{cell} = 0.36 - \frac{0.059}{2}\log\frac{0.1}{0.01} \qquad [\because n = 2]$$

$$E_{cell} = 0.36 - 0.0295\log 10 = 0.36 - 0.0295 \times 1 = 0.3305 \text{ V}$$

Now,

$$\Delta_r G^\circ = -nFE^\circ_{cell} = -2 \times 96500 \times 0.33 = -63690 \text{ J mol}^{-1}$$
$$= -63.69 \text{ kJ mol}^{-1}$$

19. Refer to page no. 57 (Similar to example 5).

[**Ans.** $E_{cell} = 0.290$ V, $\Delta G = -167.91$ kJ mol^{-1}]

20. $Mg(s) + Cu^{2+}(0.0001M) \longrightarrow Mg^{2+}(0.001M) + Cu(s)$

Standard electrode potential = 2.71 V

$$E = E^\circ_{cell} - \frac{0.0591}{n}\log\frac{[Mg^{2+}]}{[Cu^{2+}]}$$

$$E = 2.71 - \frac{0.0591}{2}\log\frac{0.001}{0.0001} = 2.71 - \frac{0.0591}{2}\log 10$$

$$E = 2.71 - 0.02955 = 2.68 \text{ V}$$

21. $Cu + 2Ag^+ \longrightarrow Cu^{2+} + 2Ag(s)$

$$E^\circ_{cell} = E^\circ_{cathode} - E^\circ_{anode} = 0.80 - 0.34 = 0.46 \text{ V}$$

Applying the Nernst equation,

$$E = E^\circ - \frac{0.059}{2}\log\frac{[Cu^{2+}]}{[Ag^+]^2}$$

$$= 0.46 - \frac{0.059}{2}\log\frac{[0.025]}{[0.005]^2}$$

$$\Rightarrow \quad 0.46 - 0.0295\log\frac{0.025}{0.025 \times 10^{-3}}$$

$$\Rightarrow \quad 0.46 - 0.0295 \times 3\log 10 = 0.46 - 0.0885 = 0.3715 \text{ V}$$

22. Two factors affecting electrode potential of a metal.

(i) **Position of the metal in electrochemical series** More reactive the metal, greater is the tendency to lose electrons and hence, lower is the value of reduction potential of the metal. Thus, act as a strong reducing agent.

(ii) **Concentration of metal ions in the solution** Dependence of the electrode potential of a metal on concentration of the electrolyte is given by Nernst equation. For the electrode reaction,

$$M^{n+}(aq) + ne^- \longrightarrow M(s)$$

$$E_{M^{n+}/M} = E^\circ_{M^{n+}/M} + \frac{2.303RT}{nF}\log\frac{[M^{n+}(aq)]}{[M(s)]}$$

23. $Zn(s) + Cu^{2+}(aq) \longrightarrow Zn^{2+}(aq) + Cu(s)$

$$E_{cell} = E^\circ_{cell} - \frac{0.0591}{2}\log\left[\frac{Zn^{2+}}{Cu^{2+}}\right]$$

According to this equation, E_{cell} decreases when concentration of Zn^{2+} ions is increased. (3)

24. **Key idea** Electrical energy or the maximum work is the measure of EMF of cell.

$$W_{max} = nFE^\circ_{cell}$$

According to thermodynamics, free energy change (ΔG°) is equal to maximum work.

Hence, $-W_{max} = \Delta G^\circ = -nFE^\circ_{cell}$

(i) Cell reaction

$$Zn(s) + Cu^{2+}(aq) \longrightarrow Cu(s) + Zn^{2+}(aq)$$

i.e. At cathode

$$Cu^{2+}(aq) + 2e^- \longrightarrow Cu(s);\ E^\circ_{Cu^{2+}/Cu} = 0.339 \text{ V}$$

At anode

$$Zn(s) \longrightarrow Zn^{2+}(aq) + 2e^-;\ E^\circ_{Zn/Zn^{2+}} = 0.761 \text{ V}$$

(ii) $E^\circ_{cell} = E^\circ_{cathode} - E^\circ_{anode}$

Given, $E^\circ_{Zn,\,Zn^{2+}} = +0.761$ V

$E_{Cu^{2+},Cu} = +0.339$ V

$E^\circ_{Zn^{2+},\,Zn} = -0.761$

Hence, $E^\circ_{cell} = E^\circ_{Cu^{2+}/Cu} - E^\circ_{Zn^{2+}/Zn}$

$= 0.339 - (-0.761) = 1.1$ V

Putting the value of E° in $\Delta G^\circ = -nFE^\circ$

where, $n = 2$, $F = 96500$ C

$\Delta G^\circ = -2 \times 96500 \times$

$= -212.3$ kJ

25. Given, $E^\circ_{Al^{3+}/Al} = -1.66$ V

and $E^\circ_{Sn^{2+}/Sn} = -0.14$ V

At anode, $Al(s) \longrightarrow Al^{3+}(aq) + 3e^-$ $\times 2$

At cathode, $Sn^{2+}(aq) + 2e^{-1} \longrightarrow Sn(s)$ $\times 3$

Hence, $n = 6$

$$E^\circ_{cell} = E^\circ_{cathode} - E^\circ_{anode} = -0.14 - (-1.66)$$
$$= -0.14 + 1.66 = 1.52 \text{ V}$$

$$E_{cell} = E^\circ_{cell} - \frac{0.059}{n}\log\frac{[Al^{3+}]^2}{[Sn^{2+}]^3}$$

$$= 1.52 - \frac{0.059}{6}\log\frac{(0.01)^2}{(0.015)^3} = 1.52 - \frac{0.059}{6} \times 1.47$$

$$= 1.52 - 0.0144 = 1.5055 \text{ V}$$

26. EMF of the cell is a measure of the maximum useful work that can be obtained under standard conditions.

$$W_{max} = -nFE^{\circ}_{cell}$$

where, n = number of moles of electrons transferred,
F = one Faraday, E°_{cell} = EMF of the cell in standard state.

Given, $E^{\circ}_{M^{2+}/M} = -0.76$ V

$E^{\circ}_{N^{2+}/N} = +0.34$ V

So, $n = 2$

$$E^{\circ}_{cell} = E^{\circ}_{cathode} - E^{\circ}_{anode}$$
$$= 0.34 - (-0.76) = 1.1 \text{ V}$$
$$W_{max} = -nFE^{\circ}_{cell},$$
$$= -2 \times 96500 \times 1.1 \quad (1F = 96500 \text{ C})$$
$$= -212300 \text{ J} = -212.3 \text{ kJ}$$

27. Given, $E^{\circ}_{Al^{3+}/Al} = -1.66$ V

$E^{\circ}_{Fe^{2+}/Fe} = -0.44$ V

For the cell,

At cathode, $[Fe^{2+}(aq) + 2e^- \longrightarrow Fe(s)] \times 3,$

$E^{\circ}_{Fe^{2+}/Fe} = -0.44$ V

At anode, $[Al(s) \longrightarrow Al^{3+}(aq) + 3e^-] \times 2,$

$E^{\circ}_{Al/Al^{3+}} = -1.66$ V

Overall cell reaction is

$$3Fe^{2+}(aq) + 2Al(s) \longrightarrow 3Fe(s) + 2Al^{3+}(aq)$$

Hence, $n = 6$

According to Nernst equation,

$$E_{cell} = E^{\circ}_{cell} - \frac{0.0591}{n} \log_{10} \frac{[\text{Product}]}{[\text{Reactant}]}$$
$$= E^{\circ}_{cell} - \frac{0.0591}{6} \log \frac{[Al^{3+}]^2}{[Fe^{2+}]^3}$$

$$E^{\circ}_{cell} = E^{\circ}_{cathode} - E^{\circ}_{anode}$$
$$= -0.44 - (-1.66)$$
$$= -0.44 + 1.66 = 1.22$$

Given, $[Al^{3+}] = 0.01$ M, $[Fe^{2+}] = 0.02$M

$$E_{cell} = 1.22 - \frac{0.0591}{6} \log \frac{(0.01)^2}{(0.02)^3} = 1.209 \text{ V}$$

28. $\Delta G^{\circ} = -nFE^{\circ}_{cell}$

where, n = no. of electrons participate = 2

Given, $E^{\circ}_{cell} = 2 \cdot 71$ V = emf of cell

F = charge = 96500 C

$\therefore \Delta G = -2 \times 96500 \times 2 \cdot 71 = -523030 \text{J mol}^{-1}$

$-\Delta G = -523.030$ kJ/mol

Hence, $\Delta G = -523.030$ kJ/mol

Now, $E_{cell} = E^{\circ}_{cell} - \frac{0.0591}{n} \log \frac{[Mg^{2+}]}{Cu^{2+}}$

$$= 2.71 - \frac{0.0591}{2} \log \frac{[0.1]}{[0.01]}$$
$$= 2.71 - 0.02955 = 2.68045$$

$\therefore$ Emf of cell = 2.68045

29. Since, $E^{\circ}_{Ag^+/Ag} > E^{\circ}_{Zn^{2+}/Zn}$, the zinc electrode is the anode. The half-cell reactions are as follows :

At anode $\quad Zn(s) \longrightarrow Zn^{2+}(aq) + 2e^-$

At cathode $\quad Ag(aq) + e^- \longrightarrow Ag(s)$

Overall cell reaction is

$$Zn(s) + 2Ag^+(aq) \longrightarrow Zn^{2+}(aq) + 2Ag(s) \quad (1)$$
$$E^{\circ}_{cell} = E^{\circ}_{cathode} - E^{\circ}_{anode}$$
$$= 0.80 \text{ V} - (-0.76) \text{ V} = 1.56 \text{ V} \quad (1)$$
$$\Delta G^{\circ} = -nFE^{\circ}_{cell}$$
$$= -2 \times 96500 \text{ C mol}^{-1} \times 1.56 \text{ V}$$
$$= -301080 \text{ J mol}^{-1} = -301.08 \text{ kJ mol}^{-1} \quad (1)$$

30. Two half-reactions for the given redox reaction may be written as:

$$2Fe^{3+}(aq) + 2e^- \longrightarrow 2Fe^{2+}(aq)$$
$$2I^- \longrightarrow I_2 + 2e^-$$

2 moles of electrons are involved in the reaction, so $n = 2$.

$$\Delta_r G^{\circ} = -nFE^{\circ}_{cell} \quad (1)$$
$$= -(2) \times (96500 \text{ C mol}^{-1}) \times (0.236 \text{ V})$$
$$= -45548 \text{ C V} = -45548 \text{ J}$$
$$\Delta_r G^{\circ} = -45.55 \text{ kJ} \quad (1)$$
$$\log K_C = -\frac{\Delta G^{\circ}}{2.303 RT}$$
$$= -\frac{(-45.55 \text{ kJ})}{2.303 \times (8.314 \times 10^{-3} \text{kJ K}^{-1}) \times (298 \text{ K})}$$
$$= 7.983$$
$$K_C = \text{antilog}(7.983) = 9.616 \times 10^7 \quad (1)$$

31. (i) The cell reaction for the given cell

$2Ag^+(aq) + 2e^- \longrightarrow 2Ag(s)$ [Reduction half- cell]

$Cu(s) \longrightarrow Cu^{2+}(aq) + 2e^-$[Oxidation half- cell]

Overall reaction is given as

$2Ag^+(aq) + Cu(s) \longrightarrow 2Ag(s) + Cu^{2+}(aq)$

(ii) Standard emf of the cell, i.e. $E^{\circ}_{Cell} = E_{Cathode} - E_{Anode}$

$$= E^{\circ}_{Ag^+/Ag} - E_{Cu^{2+}/Cu}$$
$$= (0.799 - 0.337) \text{V}$$
$$E^{\circ}_{cell} = 0.462 \text{ V}$$

(iii) Given, concentration of Cu^{2+}, i.e. $[Cu^{2+}] = 0.1$ M

$E_{cell} = 0.422$V

$T = 25$°C

Concentration of Ag^+, i.e. $[Ag^+]$=?

As, we know that,

$$E_{cell} = E^\circ_{cell} - \frac{0.059}{2}\log\frac{[Cu^{2+}]}{[Ag^+]^2}$$

$$0.422 = 0.462 - \frac{0.059}{2}\log\frac{[0.1]}{[Ag^+]^2}$$

$$= 0.462 - 0.0295\,[\log[0.1] - \log\,[Ag^+]^2]$$

$$= 0.462 - 0.0295\log[0.1] + 0.0295\times 2\log[Ag^+]$$

$$= 0.462 + 0.0295 + 0.059\log[Ag^+]$$

$$= 0.4915 + 0.0591\log[Ag^+]$$

$$-0.0695 = 0.059\log[Ag^+]$$

$$-1.178 = \log[Ag^+]$$

$$[Ag^+] = 0.066\,M$$

(iv) $\Delta G^\circ = -nFE^\circ_{cell} = -2\times 96500\times 0.462$

$= -89166\ J\ mol^{-1}$

$= -89.166\ kJ\ mol^{-1}$

32. **Key idea** Anode is negative electrode and cathode is positive electrode. Anode is always the site of oxidation and cathode is the site of reduction. In a galvanic cell, anode half-cell is written on the left and cathode half-cell on right. Salt bridge is represented as parallel lines ||.

The galvanic cell for the reaction is represened as :

$$Zn(s)|Zn^{2+}(aq)||2Ag^+(aq)|2Ag(s)$$

(i) Zinc electrode (anode) is negatively charged.

(ii) Electrons and ions.

(iii) At anode, $Zn(s) \xrightarrow{\text{Oxidation}} Zn^{2+}(aq) + 2e^-$

At cathode, $2Ag^+(aq) + 2e^- \xrightarrow{\text{Reduction}} 2Ag(s)$

33. The reaction will be feasible, if emf of the cell reaction is positive.

(i) $Fe^{3+}(aq) + I^-(aq) \longrightarrow Fe^{2+}(aq) + \frac{1}{2}I_2$

$E^\circ_{cell} = E^\circ_{Fe^{3+}/Fe^{2+}} - E^\circ_{1/2\,I_2/I^-} = 0.77 - 0.54$

$= 0.23$ V (feasible) (1)

(ii) $2Ag^+(aq) + Cu(s) \longrightarrow 2Ag(s) + Cu^{2+}(aq)$

$E^\circ_{cell} = E^\circ_{Ag^+/Ag} - E^\circ_{Cu^{2+}/Cu}$

$= 0.80 - 0.34 = 0.46$ V (feasible) (1)

(iii) $Fe^{3+}(aq) + Br^-(aq) \longrightarrow Fe^{2+}(aq) + \frac{1}{2}Br_2$

$E^\circ_{cell} = E^\circ_{Fe^{3+}/Fe^{2+}} - E^\circ_{1/2\,Br_2/Br^-}$

$= 0.77 - 1.09 = -0.32$ V (not feasible) (1)

(iv) $Ag(s) + Fe^{3+}(aq) \longrightarrow Ag^+(aq) + Fe^{2+}(aq)$

$E^\circ_{cell} = E^\circ_{Fe^{3+}/Fe^{2+}} - E^\circ_{Ag^+/Ag} = 0.77 - 0.80$

$= -0.03$ V (not feasible) (1)

(v) $\frac{1}{2}Br_2(aq) + Fe^{2+}(aq) \longrightarrow Br^-(aq) + Fe^{3+}(aq)$

$E^\circ_{cell} = E^\circ_{1/2\,Br_2/Br^-} - E^\circ_{Fe^{3+}/Fe^{2+}}$

$= 1.09 - 0.77 = 0.32$ V (feasible) (1)

34. **Key idea** Calculate (i) E°_{cell} from $E^\circ_{cathode}$ and E°_{anode} as $E^\circ_{cell} = E^\circ_{cathode} - E^\circ_{anode}$

(i) $\Delta_r G^\circ$ by using the formula, $\Delta G^\circ = -nFE^\circ_{cell}$

(ii) K_C by using the formula $\Delta_r G^\circ = -2.303RT\log K_C$.

For both reactions.

(i) Given, $E^\circ_{Cr^{3+}/Cr} = -0.74$ V; $E^\circ_{Cd^{2+}/Cd} = -0.40$ V

(a) Calculation of standard cell potential (E°)

$E^\circ_{cell} = E^\circ_{cathode} - E^\circ_{anode}$

$= (-0.40) - (-0.74) = +0.34$ V

$E^\circ_{cell} = +0.34$ V

(b) Calculation of $\Delta_r G^\circ$

$\Delta_r G^\circ = -nFE^\circ_{cell}$

$= -(6\ mol)\times(96500\ C\ mol^{-1})\times(0.34\ V)$

$= -196860$ C V $= -196860$ J

$= -196.86$ kJ

$\Delta_r G^\circ = -196.86$ kJ

(c) Calculation of equilibrium constant (K_C)

$\Delta_r G^\circ = -2.303\,RT\log K_C$

$$\log K_C = \frac{-\Delta_r G^\circ}{2.303\,RT}$$

$$= -\frac{(-196860\ J)}{2.303\times(8.314\ JK^{-1})\times(298K)} = 34.501$$

K_C = Antilog (34.501) = 3.17×10^{34}

$K_C = 3.17\times 10^{34}$

(ii) Given, $E^\circ_{(Ag^+/Ag)} = 0.80$ V; $E^\circ_{(Fe^{3+}/Fe^{2+})} = 0.77$ V

(a) Calculation of standard cell potential (E°)

$E^\circ_{cell} = E^\circ_{cathode} - E^\circ_{anode} = (0.80) - (0.77)$ V $= 0.03$ V

$E^\circ_{cell} = +0.03$ V

(b) Calculation of $\Delta_r G^\circ$

$\Delta_r G^\circ = -nFE^\circ_{cell}$

$= -(1\ mol)\times(96500\ C\ mol^{-1})\times(0.03V)$

$= -2895$ CV $= -2895$ J $= -2.985$ kJ

$\Delta_r G^\circ = -2.895$ kJ

(c) Calculation of equilibrium constant (K_C)

$\Delta_r G^\circ = 2.303\,RT\log K_C$

$$\log K_C = \frac{\Delta_r G^\circ}{2.303\,RT}$$

$$= -\frac{(-2895\ J)}{2.303\times(8.314\ JK^{-1})\times(298\ K)} = 0.5074$$

K_C = Antilog (0.5074) = 3.22

$K_C = 3.22$

TOPIC 02 Conductivity of Electrolytic Solutions

Conductance of Electrolytic Solutions

Before introducing the concept of conductance of electricity through electrolytic solutions, we must revise few terms related to conductance of electricity which we have studied in physics.

1. Resistance

It is defined as the hindrance provided by a conductor in the passage of current. Every substance offers resistance to the flow of electricity to a small or large extent. A substance which offers greater resistance will allow less electricity to flow through it.

The electrical resistance, R of any object is directly proportional to its length, l and inversely proportional to its area of cross-section, A. Thus,

$$R \propto \frac{l}{A} \quad \text{or} \quad R = \rho \frac{l}{A}$$

Here, ρ is **resistivity** (specific resistance) of the object.

2. Resistivity

It is defined as the resistance offered by a substance of 1m length with area of cross-section equal to $1\,m^2$.

Thus, resistivity $(\rho) = R\frac{A}{l}$

Units of resistivity $= \text{ohm} \times \frac{cm^2}{cm}$

$= \text{ohm cm or } \Omega \text{ cm or } \Omega \text{ m in SI unit.}$

It can be seen that

$$1\,\Omega m = 100\,\Omega cm$$

or $$1\,\Omega cm = 0.01\,\Omega m$$

IUPAC recommends the term resistivity over specific resistance.

3. Conductance

The ease with which current flows through a conductor is known as its conductance (G). It is the inverse of resistance. Therefore, resistance and conductance are related with each other as :

$$G = \frac{1}{R}$$

Thus, $$\frac{1}{R} = \frac{1}{\rho} \times \frac{1}{l/A} = \frac{1}{\rho} \cdot \frac{A}{l}$$

Substituting $\frac{1}{R}$ by G and $\frac{1}{\rho}$ by κ, we have the equation as:

$$G = \kappa \frac{A}{l}$$

The SI unit of conductance (G) is Siemens (S). It can be also written as $\text{ohm}^{-1} (\Omega^{-1})$ or mho.

4. Specific Conductivity

The inverse of resistivity is called conductivity, (κ) also known as the specific conductance or conductivity. It can be defined as the conductance of a solution of 1m length with area of cross-section equal to $1\,m^2$.

i.e. $G = \kappa$ (when, $l = 1$ m and $A = 1m^2$)

$$\kappa = \frac{1}{\rho}$$

Units of conductivity $(\kappa) = \frac{1}{\text{ohm} \cdot \text{cm}} = \text{ohm}^{-1}\text{cm}^{-1}$

or $\Omega^{-1}\ \text{cm}^{-1}$

In SI units, l is expressed in m, area of cross-section in m^2 so that the unit of conductivity is $S\ cm^{-1}$.

(The SI unit of conductivity is $S\ m^{-1}$ but quite often, κ is expressed in $S\ cm^{-1}$. $1S\ cm^{-1} = 100\ S\ m^{-1}$)

The magnitude of conduction depends upon the nature of the material. It also depends upon the temperature and pressure at which the measurements are made. Materials are classified into conductors, insulators and semiconductors. It depends on the magnitude of their conductivity.

5. Equivalent Conductivity (Λ_{eq})

Equivalent conductivity (Λ_{eq}) of an electrolytic solution at dilution V_{eq} is the conductance of an solution containing one gram equivalent of the electrolyte dissolved in V_{eq} cm^3 of the solution. Λ_{eq} is related to the specific conductivity, κ as $\Lambda_{eq} = \kappa \times V_{eq}$

where, V_{eq} is the volume of the solution (in cm^3) containing one garm equivalent of the electrolyte.

The units of Λ_{eq} are $\text{ohm}^{-1}\ cm^2 eq^{-1}$ or $S\ cm^2 eq^{-1}$.

The equivalent conductivity and specific conductivity are related by following expression

$$\Lambda = \Lambda_{eq} \times V \text{(in mL)}$$

where, V = volume of solution containing 1 gram equivalent of electrolyte. If the concentration of the electrolyte is C gram equivalents per litre, then volume of the solution containing 1 gram equivalent will be $1/C$ times or $1000/C$ mL.

Thus,

$$\boxed{\Lambda_{eq} = \kappa \times \frac{1000}{C}}$$

where,

C = concentration of solution expressed in g equiv L^{-1}.

6. Molar Conductivity

Molar conductivity of a solution is the conductance of solution containing one mole of electrolyte, kept between two electrodes having unit length between them and large cross-sectional area, so as to contain the electrolyte.

In other words, molar conductivity is the conductance of the electrolytic solution kept between the electrodes of a conductivity cell at unit distance but having area of cross-section large enough to accommodate sufficient volume of solution that contains one mole of the electrolyte. It is denoted by Λ_m.

The molar conductivity and specific conductivity are related by the following expression,

$$\Lambda_m = \frac{\kappa}{C}$$

If κ is expressed in $\Omega^{-1}m^{-1}$ or $S\,m^{-1}$ unit and the concentration, C in mol m^{-3}, then the unit of Λ_m will be $\Omega^{-1}m^2mol^{-1}$ or $S\,m^2\,mol^{-1}$.

$$\Lambda_m = \frac{\kappa \times 1000}{M}$$

where, M is the molarity of the electrolytic solution.

$$1\ Sm^2mol^{-1} = 10^4\ Scm^2mol^{-1}$$

or, $$1\ Scm^2mol^{-1} = 10^{-4}\ Sm^2mol^{-1}$$

Also, the equivalent conductance and molar conductance are related by the following expression, $\Lambda_{eq} = \Lambda_m / Z$, where Z = number of individual charges that are carried by the ions of electrolyte.

7. Cell Constant (*)

Specific conductance is the reciprocal of specific resistance, i.e. $\kappa = \frac{1}{\rho}$

and $\rho = \frac{RA}{l} \Rightarrow \kappa = \frac{1}{RA/l} = \frac{1}{R}\left(\frac{l}{A}\right)$

$$\kappa = C\left(\frac{l}{A}\right)$$

where, C = Conductance of the cell

l = Distance of separation of two electrodes

A = Area of cross-section of two electrodes.

The quantity $\left(\frac{l}{A}\right)$ is called cell constant and is expressed in cm^{-1}. Knowing the value of cell constant and conductance of the solution, the specific conductance can be calculated as given below:

Specific conductance = conductance × cell constant

i.e. $$\kappa = \frac{1}{R} \times \frac{l}{A}$$

Different Types of Materials

(i) **Conductors** The substance which have very large conductivity are known as conductors, e.g. metals and their alloys, certain non-metals like carbon-black, graphite and some organic polymers are electronically conducting.

(ii) **Metallic Conductors** In metallic conductors, the flow of electricity takes place due to the flow of electrons only, i.e. no flow of matter. Thus, the matter does not decompose. Due to the vibration of Kernels, the electrical conduction decreases with decrease in temperature.

(iii) **Electrolytic Conductors** In electrolytic conductors, the flow of electricity takes place due to the flow of charge, i.e. matter decomposes into ions. The electrical conduction increases with increase of temperature due to increase in dissociation.

Comparison of Metallic and Electrolytic Conduction

S.N.	Metallic Conduction	Electrolytic Conduction
1.	Electric current flows due to the movement of electrons.	Electric current flows due to the movement of ions.
2.	No chemical change occurs.	Ions are oxidised or reduced at the electrodes.
3.	If does not involve the transfer of any matter.	It involves transfer of matter in the form of ions.
4.	Resistance increases with increase in temperature.	Resistance decreases with increase in temperature.
5.	Faraday's law is not followed.	Faraday law is followed.

(iv) Insulators The substances which have very low conductivity are known as insulators, e.g. glass, ceramics, etc.

(v) **Semiconductors** The substances which have conductivity between conductors and insulators are known as semiconductors, e.g. silicon, doped silicon and gallium arsenide.

(vi) **Superconductors** The substances which have zero resistivity or infinite conductivity, are known as superconductors, e.g. metals and their alloys at very low temperatures (0 to 15 K). Now a days, a number of ceramic materials and mixed oxides show superconductivity at temperatures as high as 150 K.

Example 1 The electrical resistance of a column of 0.05 M NaOH solution of diameter 1 cm and length 50 cm is $5.55 \times 10^3\ \Omega$. Calculate its resistivity, conductivity and molar conductivity.

> (i) Calculate area from radius by using, $A = \pi r^2$
> (ii) Calculate resistivity from the formula, $\rho = \frac{RA}{l}$
> (iii) Calculate conductivity (κ) from resistivity as $\kappa = 1/\rho$
> (iv) Calculate molar conductivity, Λ_m by using the formula
> $$\Lambda_m = \frac{\kappa \times 1000}{M}$$

Sol. Area, $A = \pi r^2 = 3.14 \times \left(\frac{1}{2}\right)^2 \text{cm}^2 = 0.785 \text{ cm}^2$

$$\text{Resistivity, } \rho = \frac{RA}{l} = \frac{5.55 \times 10^3 \Omega \times 0.785 \text{ cm}^2}{50 \text{ cm}} = 87.135\, \Omega \text{ cm}$$

$$\text{Conductivity, } \kappa = \frac{1}{\rho} = \frac{1}{87.135} \Omega^{-1} \text{ cm}^{-1}$$

$$= 0.01148\ \Omega^{-1}\text{cm}^{-1} = 1.148 \times 10^{-2} \text{ S cm}^{-1}$$

Molar conductivity,

$$\Lambda_m = \frac{\kappa \times 1000}{M} = \frac{1.148 \times 10^{-2} \times 1000}{0.05}$$

$$= 229.6 \text{ S cm}^2 \text{ mol}^{-1}$$

Variation of Conductivities with Concentration

Conductivity or specific conductivity always decreases with decrease in concentration (i.e. with dilution) of both the strong and weak electrolytes. This is due to the fact that the number of ions that carry current in a unit volume of solution always decreases with decrease in concentration.

The conductivity of a solution is the conductance of a unit volume of the solution, kept between two platinum electrodes with unit area of cross-section and at a distance of unit length. The molar conductivity is the conductance of that volume of the solution which contains one mole of the electrolyte. Conductivity is expressed as, $G = \frac{\kappa A}{l} = \kappa$ (both A and l are unity in their appropriate units in m or cm) while molar conductivity is expressed as $\Lambda_m = \kappa V$

It is because $\Lambda_m = \frac{\kappa A}{l}$

$\because \quad l = 1$ and $A = V$

[volume containing 1 mole of electrolyte]

Equivalent conductivity of a solution of an electrolyte increases with decrease in concentration.

Molar conductivity increases with decrease in concentration (i.e. with dilution). This is because the total volume V of solution containing one mole of electrolyte increases.

Note When the concentration approaches zero, the molar conductivity reaches a limiting value, known as **limiting molar conductivity** and is denoted as Λ_m°.

Variation in Λ_m with Concentration

(For Strong and Weak Electrolytes)

1. For Strong Electrolytes

Practically strong electrolytes completely dissociate at all concentrations. For strong electrolytes, Λ_m increases slowly with dilution. This can be represented by equation, **Debye-Huckel-Onsager equation.**

$$\Lambda_m = \Lambda_m^\circ - A\sqrt{C}$$

If we plot Λ_m against $\sqrt{C}$, we get a straight line with slope as '$-A$' and intercept as 'Λ_m°'. The value of constant A depends upon the type of electrolyte. i.e. the charges on the cation and anion produced on the dissociation of electrolyte in the solution.

Thus, $NaCl, CaCl_2, MgSO_4$ are known as 1-1, 2-1 and 2-2 electrolytes, respectively. All electrolytes of a particular type have the same value of A.

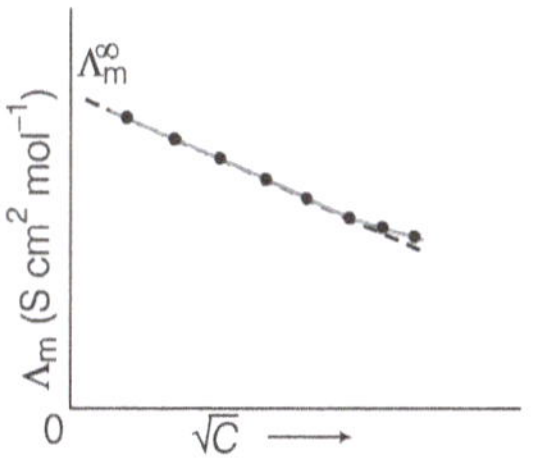

Variation of Λ_m with $\sqrt{C}$ for KCl (strong electrolyte)

2. For Weak Electrolytes

The electrolytes which do not ionise completely in aqueous as well as in molten state are called weak electrolytes, e.g. H_2CO_3, CH_3COOH, etc. A weak electrolyte (like acetic acid) is not completely dissociated at all concentrations. With dilution, the degree of dissociation increases, resulting in increase in the number of ions. In case of weak electrolytes, the Λ°_m value increases steeply with dilution, especially in the low concentration region.

In this region, the graph of weak electrolytes in a plot of Λ_m against $\sqrt{C}$ becomes parallel to the Y-axis. So, the limiting molar conductivity of a weak electrolyte cannot be determined by extrapolation of the plot. At infinite dilution ($C \rightarrow$ zero) electrolyte dissociates completely ($\alpha = 1$), but at such low concentration the conductivity of the solution is so low that it cannot be measured accurately. It is rather determined by applying the Kohlrausch law of independent migration of ions.

Through Kohlrausch law, we can determined Λ°_m values of weak electrolyte (discussed later in this chapter).

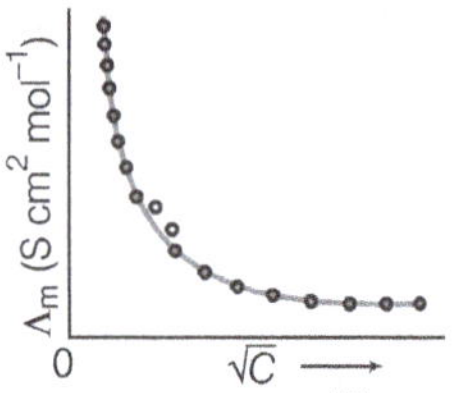

Variation of Λ_m with $\sqrt{C}$ for weak electrolyte (CH_3COOH).

> **Degree of Dissociation**
>
> The ratio of molar conductivity (Λ_m) at a specific concentration (C) to the molar conductivity at infinite dilution, i.e. limiting molar conductivity, Λ°_m is known as degree of dissociation.
>
> At any concentration C, if α is the degree of dissociation, then for a weak electrolyte, $\alpha = \dfrac{\Lambda_m}{\Lambda^\circ_m}$
>
> Since, for a weak electrolyte,
>
> $$K_a = \frac{C\alpha^2}{(1-\alpha)} = \frac{C\Lambda_m^2}{(\Lambda^\circ_m)^2\left(1-\dfrac{\Lambda_m}{\Lambda^\circ_m}\right)} = \frac{C\Lambda_m^2}{\Lambda^\circ_m(\Lambda^\circ_m - \Lambda_m)}$$

Kohlrausch Law

Kohlrausch examined Λ°_m values for a number of strong electrolytes and found that for a pair of electrolytes with the same negative ion but differing only in the positive ion, the difference between the Λ°_m values is constant.

e.g.

$$\Lambda^\circ_{m(KCl)} - \Lambda^\circ_{m(NaCl)} = \Lambda^\circ_{m(KBr)} - \Lambda^\circ_{m(NaBr)}$$
$$= \Lambda^\circ_{m(KI)} - \Lambda^\circ_{m(NaI)}$$
$$= 23.4\,\Omega^{-1}cm^2mol^{-1}\ (Scm^2mol^{-1})$$

Similarly, with a common cation, the difference between Λ°_m values is also found constant.

$$\Lambda^\circ_{m(KBr)} - \Lambda^\circ_{m(KCl)} = \Lambda^\circ_{m(NaBr)} - \Lambda^\circ_{m(NaCl)}$$
$$= 1.8\,\Omega^{-1}cm^2mol^{-1} \qquad (Scm^2mol^{-1})$$

The above observation led to formulate the **Kohlrausch law of independent migration of ions.**

It states that "limiting molar conductivity of an electrolyte is the sum of the individual contributions of the cation and the anion of the electrolyte".

e.g. $\Lambda^\circ_{m\,(NaCl)} = \lambda^\circ_{Na^+} + \lambda^\circ_{Cl^-}$

where, $\Lambda^\circ_{m(NaCl)}$ is the molar conductivity of NaCl and $\lambda^\circ_{Na^+}$ and $\lambda^\circ_{Cl^-}$ are limiting molar conductivity of sodium and chloride ions respectively.

In general, if an electrolyte produces ν_+ cations and ν_- anions, the above equation becomes

$$\Lambda^\circ_m = \nu_+\lambda^\circ_+ + \nu_-\lambda^\circ_-$$

Applications of Kohlrausch Law

Some important applications of Kohlrausch law are as follows:

(i) The molar conductivity of weak electrolytes at infinite dilution can be calculated by using Kohlrausch's law.

(ii) Degree of dissociation of weak electrolyte (like acetic acid) at a given concentration can be calculated.

(iii) Knowing the degree of dissociation (α), the dissociation constant (K) of the weak electrolyte at a given concentration of the solution, can be calculated.

(iv) Solubility of sparingly soluble salts can be calculated as solubility

$$= \frac{\kappa \times 1000}{\Lambda^\circ_m}\ (mol/L)$$

Example 2 Calculate Λ°_m for acetic acid,

Given that, $\Lambda^\circ_{m\,(HCl)} = 426\ S\,cm^2\,mol^{-1}$

$\Lambda^\circ_{m\,(NaCl)} = 126\ S\,cm^2\,mol^{-1}$

$\Lambda^\circ_{m\,(CH_3COONa)} = 91\ S\,cm^2\,mol^{-1}$

Sol. $\Lambda^{\circ}_{m\ (CH_3COOH)} = \Lambda^{\circ}_{H^+} + \Lambda^{\circ}_{CH_3COO^-}$

$= \Lambda^{\circ}_{H^+} + \Lambda^{\circ}_{Cl^-} + \Lambda^{\circ}_{CH_3COO^-} + \Lambda^{\circ}_{Na^+} - \Lambda^{\circ}_{Cl^-} - \Lambda^{\circ}_{Na^+}$

$= \Lambda^{\circ}_{m\ (HCl)} + \Lambda^{\circ}_{m\ (CH_3COONa)} - \Lambda^{\circ}_{m\ (NaCl)}$

$=(426 + 91 - 126)\ S\ cm^2\ mol^{-1}$

$= 391\ S\ cm^2\ mol^{-1}$

Example 3 Conductivity of 0.00241 M acetic acid solution is $7.896 \times 10^{-5} S\ cm^{-1}$.
Calculate its molar conductivity in this solution. If Λ°_m for acetic acid be 390.5 S $cm^2\ mol^{-1}$, what would be its dissociation constant? **NCERT**

(i) First, find molar conductivity using the formula,

$$\Lambda^C_m = \frac{\kappa \times 1000}{C}.$$

(ii) Then, find degree of dissociation (α) and dissociation constant (K_a) by using formula,

$$\alpha = \frac{\Lambda^C_m}{\Lambda^{\circ}_m} \text{ and } K_a = \frac{C\alpha^2}{1-\alpha}, \text{ respectively.}$$

Sol. Given, $\kappa = 7.896 \times 10^{-5}\ S\ cm^{-1}$,

$\Lambda^{\circ}_{m\ (CH_3COOH)} = 390.5\ S\ cm^2\ mol^{-1}$

and Molarity (M) = 0.00241 M

Molar conductivity, $\Lambda^C_m = \frac{\kappa \times 1000}{\text{Molarity}}$

$$= \frac{7.896 \times 10^{-5} S\ cm^{-1} \times 1000}{0.00241\ M\ (mol\ cm^{-3})}$$

$$\Lambda^C_m = 32.76\ S\ cm^2\ mol^{-1}$$

Degree of dissociation,

$$\alpha = \frac{\Lambda^C_m}{\Lambda^{\circ}_m} = \frac{32.76}{390.5}$$

$$= 8.4 \times 10^{-2}$$

For dissociation constant of acetic acid, CH_3COOH

$$CH_3COOH \rightleftharpoons CH_3COO^- + H^+$$

	CH_3COOH	CH_3COO^-	H^+
Initial conc.	C	0	0
After time t,	$C - C\alpha$	$C\alpha$	$C\alpha$

Dissociation constant,

$$K_a = \frac{[CH_3COO^-][H^+]}{[CH_3COOH]} = \frac{C\alpha^2}{1-\alpha}$$

$$K_a = \frac{0.00241\ (8.4 \times 10^{-2})^2}{(1 - 0.084)}$$

$$= 1.86 \times 10^{-5}$$

Topic Practice 2

Very Short Answer Type Questions

(1 Mark)

1. Fill in the Blanks

(i) The unit of conductance is .... and that of specific conductance is .... **ISC 2016**

(ii) Equivalent conductivity is the conducting power of all the ions furnished by one .... of an electrolyte present in a definite .... of the solution. **ISC 2020**

(iii) The molar conductance of a solution ... with dilution, while its specific conductance ... with dilution. **ISC 2014**

(iv) As concentration of an electrolytic solution increases, its ... conductance increases but ... conductance decreases. **ISC 2003**

(v) The degree of dissociation of a weak electrolyte is ... proportional to the ... of its molar concentration. **ISC 2006**

(vi) Kohlrausch's law is related to ... . **ISC 2014**

2. Objective Type Questions

(i) The unit of equivalent conductance is

(a) $ohm^{-1}\ cm^2\ equiv^{-1}$ (b) $ohm^{-1}\ cm^2\ g^{-1}$
(c) $ohm\ cm^2\ equiv^{-1}$ (d) $ohm^{-1}mol^{-1}$ **ISC 2010**

(ii) Select the incorrect statement.

(a) SI units of resistance is $kg\ m^2/s^3A^2$
(b) Wheat stone bridge is used to measure resistance as well as resistivity
(c) Resistance = resistivity, when $l = 1$ m and $A = 1\ m^2$
(d) Inverse of resistance is called specific conductance

(iii) The correct statement about conductivity is

(a) it is the inverse of resistivity
(b) its SI unit is Sm^{-1}
(c) it is equal to conductance, when $\frac{l}{A} = 1m^{-1}$
(d) All of the above

(iv) What happens to the composition of metallic conductor when electron enters at one end and go out through other end?

(a) There will be change in metallic conductor
(b) Metallic conductor remain unchanged

(c) There will be change in metallic conductor only in the presence of applied pressure
(d) Metallic conductor will behave as insulator

(v) Correct the following statement:
For a strong electrolyte, the plot of equivalent conductance *versus* concentration of the solution is a straight line. **ISC 2002**

(vi) Correct the following statement:
On dilution of a solution, its equivalent and specific conductance increases. **ISC 2001**

3. Match the following Column I (expressions) with Column II and choose the correct option using the codes given below:

	Column I		Column II
A.	$\rho l / A$	(i)	Conductivity
B.	$1/R$	(ii)	Conductance
C.	RA/l	(iii)	Resistance
D.	$1/\rho$	(iv)	Resistivity

Codes

	A	B	C	D		A	B	C	D
(a)	(iii)	(iv)	(ii)	(i)	(b)	(iii)	(ii)	(iv)	(i)
(c)	(iv)	(iii)	(i)	(ii)	(d)	(iv)	(i)	(iii)	(ii)

4. Specific conductivity of 0.20 M solution of KCl at 298 K is 0.025 S cm^{-1}. Calculate its molar conductivity. **ISC 2017**

5. Give a reason for the following:
Specific conductance decreases with dilution whereas equivalent conductance increases with dilution. **ISC 2007**

6. Why alternating current is used for measuring resistance of an electrolytic solution? **NCERT Exemplar**

7. Define the equivalent conductivity. **ISC 2018**

Short Answer Type I Questions

2 Marks

8. Define molar conductance of a solution. State its unit. How is it related to the specific conductance of a solution? **ISC 2013**

9. The conductivity of 0.2 M KCl solution is 3×10^{-2} $^{-1}$ $^{-1}$. Calculate its molar conductance.

10. A solution of 0.1 N KCl offers a resistance of 245 Ω. Calculate the specific conductance and the equivalent conductance of the solution if the cell constant is $^{-1}$. **ISC 2010**

11. Calculate the equivalent conductivity of 1 M H_2SO_4 whose specific conductivity is 26×10^{-2} ohm^{-1} cm^{-1}. **ISC 2006**

12. The resistance of a conductivity cell containing 0.001 M KCl solution at 298 K is 1500 Ω. What is the cell constant, if the conductivity of 0.001 M KCl solution at 298 K is 0.146×10^{-3} S cm^{-1}?

Short Answer Type II Questions

3 Marks

13. 0.05 NaOH solution offered a resistance of 31.6 Ω in a conductivity cell at 298 K. If the cell constant of the cell is 0.367 cm^{-1}, calculate the molar conductivity of the NaOH solution. **ISC 2014**

14. Calculate the degree of dissociation (α) of acetic acid, if its molar conductivity (Λ_m) is 39.05 S cm^2 mol^{-1}. **ISC 2020**
(Given, $\lambda^\circ_{(H^+)}$ = 349.6 S $cm^2 mol^{-1}$ and $\lambda^\circ_{(CH_3COO^-)}$ = 40.95 S cm^2 mol^{-1})

15. State Kohlrausch's law and give its mathematical expression mentioning the terms involved in it. **ISC 2010**

16. A conductivity cell has a cell constant of 0.5 cm^{-1}. This cell when filled with 0.01 sodium chloride solution has a resistance of 384 Ω at 25°C. Calculate the equivalent conductivity of 0.01 M sodium chloride at 25°C. **ISC 2000**

17. The specific conductivity of a solution containing 5g of anhydrous $BaCl_2$ (molecular weight = 208) in 1000 cm^3 of a solution is found to be 0.0058 ohm^{-1} cm^{-1}. Calculate the molar and equivalent conductivity of the solution. **NCERT Intext**

18. The specific conductance of 2.5×10^{-4} M formic acid is 5.25×10^{-5} $ohm^{-1} cm^{-1}$. Calculate its molar conductivity and degree of dissociation.
Given $\lambda^\circ_{(H^+)}$ = 349.5 $ohm^{-1} cm^2 mol^{-1}$ and
$\lambda^\circ_{(HCOO^-)}$ = 50.5 $ohm^{-1} cm^2 mol^{-1}$ **ISC 2023**

19. Calculate Λ°_m for $BaCl_2$ and $Al_2(SO_4)_3$ from the following data. **ISC 2024**
For Λ°_m Ba^{2+} = 127.2 S cm^2 mol^{-1},
Λ°_m Al^{3+} = 189 S cm^2 mol^{-1}

$\Lambda^{\circ}_{m} Cl^- = 76.3 \text{ S cm}^2 \text{ mol}^{-1}$,

$\Lambda^{\circ}_{m} SO_4^{2-} = 160 \text{ S cm}^2 \text{ mol}^{-1}$

20. A 0.05 M NH_4OH solution offers the resistance of 50 Ω to a conductivity cell at 298 K. If the cell constant is 0.50 cm^{-1} and molar conductance of NH_4OH at infinite dilution is 471.4 $\Omega^{-1} cm^2 mol^{-1}$. Calculate:
   (i) Specific conductance
   (ii) Molar conductance
   (iii) Degree of dissociation **ISC 2016**

21. A 0.05 M NH_4OH solution offers the resistance of 30.8 ohms to a conductivity cell at 298 K. If the cell constant is 0.343 cm^{-1} and molar conductance of NH_4OH at infinite dilution is 471.4 S cm^2 mol^{-1}, calculate the following.
   (1) Specific conductance
   (2) Molar conductance
   (3) Degree of dissociation **ISC 2024**

Long Answer Type Questions

5 Marks

22. Define conductivity and molar conductivity for the solution of an electrolyte. Discuss their variation with concentration. **NCERT**

23. (i) Define the following terms:
   (a) Specific conductance
   (b) Kohlrausch's law
   (ii) The resistance of a conductivity cell containing 0.001 M KCl solution at 298 K is 1500 ohm. What is the cell constant and molar conductivity of 0.001 M KCl solution, if the conductivity of this solution is $0.146 \times 10^{-3} \text{ohm}^{-1}\text{cm}^{-1}$ at 298 K?

24. The resistance of a conductivity cell with 0.1 M KCl solution is 200 ohm. When the same cell is filled with 0.02 M NaCl solution, the resistance is 1100 ohm. If the conductivity of 0.1 M KCl solution is 0.0129 $\text{ohm}^{-1}\text{cm}^{-1}$, calculate the cell constant and molar conductivity of 0.02M NaCl solution.

The emf (E°_{cell}) of the following reaction is 0.89 V.

$$3Sn^{4+} + Cr \longrightarrow 3Sn^{2-} + 2Cr^{3-}$$

Calculate the value of ΔG° for the reaction. Predict whether the above reaction will be spontaneous or not. **ISC 2023**

Hints & Solutions

1. (i) $\Omega^{-1}, \Omega^{-1}cm^{-1}$
   (ii) gram equivalent, volume
   (iii) increases, decreases
   (iv) specific, equivalent
   (v) inversely, square root
   (vi) infinite dilution

2. (i)→(a), (ii)→(d), (iii)→(d), (iv)→(b)
   (v) For a strong electrolyte, the plot of equivalent conductance *versus* square root of the concentration of the solution is a straight line.
   (vi) On dilution of solution, its equivalent and molar conductivity increases.

3. (b) A→ (iii), B→ (ii), C→ (iv), D → (i)

4. Given, Specific conductivity (κ) = 0.025 S cm^{-1}
   Concentration (C) = 0.20 M
   Now, molar conductivity $(\Lambda_m) = \frac{1000}{C} \times \kappa$
   $$= \frac{1000}{0.2} \times 0.025 = 125 \text{ Scm}^2\text{mol}^{-1}$$

5. Specific conductance depends on number of ions per unit volume. On dilution, number of ions will decrease per unit volume. Hence, specific conductance of the solution will decrease.

   Equivalent conductance is the product of specific conductivity and volume of the solution containing one gram equivalent of the electrolyte.

   As the decreasing value of specific conductivity is more than compensated by the increasing value of V, so the value of Λ increases with dilution.

6. Alternating current is used in electrolysis, so that concentration of ions in the solution remains constant and exact value of resistance is measured.

7. **Equivalent conductivity** of a solution is defined as the conductance of all the ions produced from one gram equivalent of the electrolyte dissolved in V_{eq} cm^3 of the solution when the distance between the electrodes is one cm and the area of electrodes is so large that the whole of the solution is contained between them. It is represented by Λ_{eq}.

8. The conductance of that volume of solution which contains one mole of the solute and is placed between two parallel electrode of 1 cm distance apart and having sufficient area to hold the whole of the solution is called its **molar conductance**.

   It is denoted by Λ. If the concentration of a solution is C mol/L, then volume of the solution containing 1 mole of the electrolyte will be $1/C$ L or $1000/C$ cc. Hence, Λ and κ can be related as $\Lambda = \frac{1000}{C} \times \kappa$, where κ is specific conductance. Its units are $ohm^{-1}\ cm^2\ mol^{-1}$ in CGS and $ohm^{-1}\ m^2\ mol^{-1}$ in SI system.

9. We know that molar conductance and conductivity of a solution are related as

$$\Lambda_m = \frac{1000}{C} \times \kappa$$

where, Λ_m is molar conductance, C = concentration and Λ_{sp} is specific conductance or conductivity of a solution.

Given, $C = 0.2$ M, $\Lambda_{sp} = 3 \times 10^{-2}\ \Omega^{-1}\ cm^{-1}$

Putting value,

$$\Lambda = \frac{1000}{0.2} \times 3 \times 10^{-2}$$

$$= \frac{30}{0.2} = 1.5 \times 10^2\ \Omega^{-1}\ cm^2\ mol^{-1}$$

10. $G^*(= R \times \kappa)$ is known as cell constant,

$$\kappa = \frac{l}{RA}$$

where, l = length, A is cross-sectional area and R = resistance

Given, $R = 245\Omega$,

Cell constant = 0.571 cm^{-1}

Hence, specific conductance, $K = G^*/R$

$$\kappa = \frac{0.571}{245} = 0.00233\ \Omega^{-1}\ cm^{-1} = 2.33 \times 10^{-3}\ \Omega^{-1} cm^{-1}$$

Equivalent conductance, $\Lambda_{eq} = \frac{1000}{C} \times \kappa$

Concentration, $C = 0.1$ N

$$\Lambda_{eq} = \frac{1000}{0.1} \times 2.33 \times 10^{-3} = 23.3\ \Omega^{-1}\ cm^2\ equiv^{-1}$$

11. Equivalent conductivity, $\Lambda_{eq} = \frac{1000}{C} \times \kappa$

Given, concentration C = 1M,

specific conductance, $\kappa = 26 \times 10^{-2}\ \Omega^{-1}\ cm^{-1}$

Equivalent conductance,

$$\Lambda = \frac{1000}{1 \times 2} \times 26 \times 10^{-2} = 130\ S\ cm^2\ equiv^{-1}$$

12. Given, conductivity, $\kappa = 0.146 \times 10^{-3}\ S\ cm^{-1}$

Resistance, $R = 1500\ \Omega$

∴ Cell constant $= \kappa \times R$ (1)

$= 0.146 \times 10^{-3} \times 1500$

$= 0.219\ cm^{-1}$ (1)

13. Molar conductivity $\Lambda_m = \frac{1000}{C} \times \kappa$

where, κ = specific conductivity

$$\kappa = \frac{l}{RA} = \frac{\text{cell constant } (G^*)}{R}$$

Given, concentration, $C = 0.05$ M,

resistance $R = 31.6\ \Omega$

Cell constant = 0.367 cm^{-1}

$$\Lambda_m = \frac{1000}{C} \times \kappa = \frac{1000}{C} \times \frac{G^*}{R}$$

$$\Lambda_m = \frac{1000}{0.05} \times \frac{0.367}{31.6} = 232.278\ \Omega^{-1}\ cm^2\ mol^{-1}$$

14. Refer to page no. 69 (Similar to example 3).

[**Ans.** $\alpha = 0.099$]

15. Each ion makes a certain definite contribution to the total molar conductivity of an electrolyte at infinite dilution, irrespective of the nature of the other ion of the electrolyte, which led to a generalised 'Kohlrausch's law'.

'This law states that the molar conductance of an electrolyte at infinite dilution is equal to the sum of the molar conductance of the two ions (cations and anions).'

$$\Lambda^\infty = \Lambda_+^\infty + \Lambda_-^\infty$$

where, Λ_+^∞ and Λ_-^∞ are the ionic conductivities of the cation and anion, respectively.

If an electrolyte furnishes more than one cation and anion then, according to Kohlrausch's law,

$$\Lambda_m^\infty (A_m B_n) = m\Lambda_A^\infty + n\Lambda_B^\infty$$

where, m and n are the number of cations and anions per formula unit of electrolyte. Λ_A^∞ and Λ_B^∞ are the ionic conductivities of the ions A and B.

16.

> **Key idea** $\Lambda_{eq} = \frac{1000}{C} \times \kappa$,
>
> where, Λ_{eq} = equivalent conductance,
> κ = specific conductance,
>
> C is concentration in gram equivalent per unit volume.
>
> $$\kappa = \frac{\text{Cell constant } (G^*)}{\text{Resistance } (R)}$$

Given, cell constant = 0.5 cm^{-1},

Concentration, $C = 0.01$ M, $R = 384\ \Omega$

Equivalent conductance,

$$\Lambda_{eq} = \frac{1000}{0.01} \times \kappa$$

$$\Lambda_{eq} = \frac{1000}{0.01} \times \frac{G^*}{R} = \frac{1000}{0.01} \times \frac{0.5}{384}$$

(For NaCl, 0.01 M = 0.01 N)

$$= 130.2\ \Omega^{-1}\ cm^2\ equiv^{-1}$$

17. Conductivity $(\kappa) = 0.0058\ ohm^{-1}\ cm^{-1}$

Molar mass of $BaCl_2$ = 208 g mol^{-1}

As 5 g of $BaCl_2$ is present in 1000 cm^3 of the solution.

$$\therefore \text{Molar concentration } (C) = \frac{1}{208} \times \frac{5}{1000} \times 1000\ mol\ L^{-1}$$

$$= 0.0240\ mol\ L^{-1}$$

$$\therefore \text{Molar conductivity, } \Lambda_m = \frac{\kappa \times 1000}{M}$$

$$= \frac{0.0058\ ohm^{-1} cm^{-1} \times 1000\ cm^3 L^{-1}}{0.0240\ mol\ L^{-1}}$$

$$= 241.67\ ohm^{-1} cm^2 mol^{-1}$$

In $BaCl_2$, equivalent weight

$$= \frac{\text{molecular weight}}{2} = \frac{208}{2} = 104$$

∴ Concentration of solution in gram equivalent per litre

$$= \frac{1}{104} \times \frac{1}{200} \times 1000 = 0.0480$$

∴Equivalent conductivity, $\Lambda_{eq} = \frac{\kappa \times 1000}{N}$

$$= \frac{0.0058 \text{ ohm}^{-1}\text{cm}^{-1} \times 1000 \text{ cm}^3\text{L}^{-1}}{0.0480 \text{ g eqL}^{-1}}$$

$$= 120.83 \text{ ohm}^{-1}\text{cm}^2\text{eq}^{-1}$$

18. $\Lambda_m = \frac{\kappa \times 1000}{C} (\Omega^{-1}\text{cm}^{-1} = S)$

$$= \frac{5.25 \times 10^{-5}\Omega^{-1}\text{cm}^{-1} \times 1000}{2.5 \times 10^{-4} \text{mol cm}^{-3}} = 210 \text{ S cm}^2 \text{ mol}^{-1}$$

$$\Lambda^\circ_{(HCOOH)} = \Lambda^\circ_{(HCOO^-)} + \Lambda^\circ_{H^+}$$

$$= 50.5 + 349.5 = 400 \text{ S cm}^2 \text{ mol}^{-1}$$

$$\alpha = \frac{\Lambda_m}{\Lambda^\circ_m} = \frac{210}{400} = 0.52 \text{ or } 52\%$$

19. Given, $\Lambda^\circ_m Ba^{2+} = 127.2 \text{ S cm}^2 \text{ mol}^{-1}$

$$\Lambda^\circ_m Al^{3+} = 189 \text{ S cm}^2 \text{ mol}^{-1}$$

$$\Lambda^\circ_m Cl = 76.3 \text{ S cm}^2 \text{ mol}^{-1}$$

$$\Lambda^\circ_m SO_4^{2-} = 160 \text{ S cm}^2 \text{ mol}^{-1}$$

$$\Lambda^\circ_m BaCl_2 = \Lambda^\circ_m Ba^{2+} + 2\Lambda^\circ_m Cl^-$$

$$= 127.2 + 2 \times 76.3 = 127.2 + 152.6$$

$$= 279.8 \text{ S cm}^2 \text{ mol}^{-1}$$

$$\Lambda^\circ_m Al_2(SO_4)_3 = 2\Lambda^\circ_m Al^{3+} + 3\Lambda^\circ_m SO_4^{2-}$$

$$= 2 \times 189 + 3 \times 160 = 858 \text{ S cm}^2 \text{ mol}^{-1}$$

20. Given, $R = 50\ \Omega$, concentration = 0.05 M

Cell constant, $G = 0.50 \text{ cm}^{-1}$,

Molar conductance at infinite dilution,
$\Lambda^\infty = 471.4\ \Omega^{-1} \text{ cm}^2 \text{ mol}^{-1}$

(i) Specific conductance = G/R

$$\kappa = \frac{0.5}{50} = 0.01\ \Omega^{-1} \text{ cm}^{-1}$$

(ii) Molar conductance, $\Lambda_m = \frac{1000 \times \kappa}{\text{molarity}}$

$$= \frac{1000 \times 0.01\ \Omega^{-1} \text{ cm}^{-1}}{0.05 \text{ mol cm}^{-3}}$$

$$= 200\ \Omega^{-1} \text{ cm}^2 \text{ mol}^{-1}$$

(iii) Degree of dissociation $(\alpha) = \frac{\Lambda_m}{\Lambda^\infty_m}$

$$= \frac{200\Omega^{-1} \text{ cm}^2\text{mol}^{-1}}{471.4\Omega^{-1} \text{ cm}^2 \text{ mol}^{-1}} = 0.42$$

21. Given, concentration of NH_4OH solution = 0.05 M

Resistance = 30.8 ohm

Temperature = 298 K

Cell constant $(G^*) = \frac{l}{A} = 0.343 \text{ cm}^{-1}$

Molar conductance Λ^∞_m of NH_4OH at infinite dilution

$$= 471.4 \text{ S cm}^2 \text{ mol}^{-1}$$

(1) **Specific conductance** $= \frac{1}{\rho} = \frac{1}{R} \times \frac{l}{A}$

$$= \frac{1}{30.8 \text{ (ohm)}} \times 0.343 \text{ cm}^{-1}$$

$$= 0.01113 \text{ ohm}^{-1} \text{ cm}^{-1}$$

(2) **Molar conductance**, $\Lambda^c_m = \frac{\kappa \times 1000}{\text{Molarity}}$

$$= \frac{0.01113 \times 1000}{0.05} \approx 222 \text{ S cm}^2\text{mol}^{-1}$$

(3) **Degree of dissociation** $\alpha = \frac{\Lambda^c_m}{\Lambda^\infty_m} = \frac{222.6}{471.4} = 0.472$

22. Refer to text on pages 65, 66 and 67. (Conductivities and variation of conductivities with concentration)

23. (i)(a) **Specific conductance** : It is also known as conductivity and represented by symbol κ called 'kappa'.

The specific conductance can be defined as the conductance of a solution of 1cm length with area of cross section equal to 1cm^2. i.e.

$$G_{\text{(conductance)}} = \text{kappa}$$

where, $(l = 1\text{cm and } A = 1\text{cm}^2)$

or, $$G = \kappa(\text{kappa}).\frac{A}{l}$$

or, $$\kappa = G.\frac{l}{A}$$

Note $\frac{l}{A}$ is known as cell constant.

(b) **Kohlarush's Law** The law state that "the limiting equivalent (or molar) conductivity or equivalent (or molar) conductivity at infinite dilution is the sum of the equivalent or molar conductivities of cations and anions," NaCl, if conductivity of Na^+ and Cl^- ions is λ°_c and λ°_a then

$$\Lambda^\circ_{eq \text{ (Sum)}} \text{ or } \Lambda^\circ_m = \lambda^\circ_c + \lambda^\circ_a$$

(ii) Given, concentration (C) of KCl solution = 0.001 M.

resistance (R) of 0.001 M KCl = 1500 Ω.

Conductivity (K) at 298 K of KCl solution

$$= 0.146 \times 10^{-3}\Omega^{-1}\text{cm}^{-1}$$

Also,

$$\because \quad \kappa(\text{Kappa}) = \frac{1}{R} \times \frac{l}{a}$$

where, $\frac{l}{a}$ = cell constant

$\therefore \quad \frac{l}{a} = \kappa(\text{Kappa}) \times R$

$= 0.146 \times 10^{-3} \times 1500$

Cell constant = $219 \times 10^{-3} \text{cm}^{-1}$

and $\wedge_m$ (molar conductivity) $= \frac{\kappa \times 1000}{C}$

$= \frac{0.146 \times 10^{-3} \times 1000}{0.001}$

Hence, = 146 S $\text{cm}^2\text{mol}^{-1}$

Cell constant = $219 \times 10^{-3} \text{ cm}^{-1}$

Molar conductivity = 146 S $\text{cm}^2 \text{ mol}^{-1}$

24. For 0.1 M KCl solution,

$\kappa = 0.0129 \Omega^{-1}\text{cm}^{-1}$

Conductivity, $\kappa = \frac{G}{R}$ (G = Cell constant)

$0.0129 = \frac{G}{200}$

$\Rightarrow \quad G = 200 \times 0.0129 = 2.58 \text{ cm}^{-1}$

Given that, the conductivity cell is same for both solutions, hence the conductivity and cell constant for the solution will be same.

So, for 0.02 M NaCl solution, $G = 2.58 \text{ cm}^{-1}$

and the molar conductivity will be

$\Lambda_m = \frac{\kappa \times 1000}{C}$

$= \frac{0.0129 \times 1000}{0.02}$

$= 645 \Omega^{-1}\text{cm}^2\text{mol}^{-1}$

At cathode, $(Sn^{4+} + 2e^- \longrightarrow Sn^{2+}) \times 3$

At anode,

$(Cr \longrightarrow Cr^{3+} + 3e^-) \times 2$

$3Sn^{4+} + 2Cr + 6e^- \longrightarrow 3Sn^{2+} + 2Cr^{3+} + 6e^-$

So, $\quad n = 6$

Given, $E^\circ_{\text{cell}} = 0.89$ V

By the equation $\Delta G^\circ = -nFE^\circ_{\text{cell}}$

$= -6 \times 96500 \times 0.89 = -515.3$ kJ

The above reaction will be spontaneous as the value of ΔG° is $-$ive.

TOPIC 03 Electrolytic Cells and Electrolysis

Electrolysis

It is the process by which an electrolyte in molten state or in aqueous solution conducts an electric current and gets decomposed into its constituent ions that move towards the oppositely charged electrodes.

Faraday's Laws of Electrolysis

The **quantitative aspect of electrolysis** was studied extensively by Michael Faraday and his laws of electrolysis are known as Faraday's laws of electrolysis.

1. Faraday's First Law

It states that "the amount of chemical reaction occurring at any electrode by passing current is directly proportional to the quantity of electricity passed through the electrolyte (in solution or in molten state)".

Thus, w g of the substance gets deposited on passing Q coulomb of electricity.

$$w \propto Q$$

or $\quad w = ZQw = Z \times it \quad (\because Q = it)$

where, Q = quantity of electricity, i = current (in A), t = time (in s), Z = constant of proportionality called electrochemical equivalent. It is defined as the amount of the substance deposited when 1 A of current is passed for 1 sec (1 C of charge is passed). Its unit is g C^{-1}.

2. Faraday's Second Law

It states that "when the same quantity of electricity is passed through different electrolytes, the amounts of different substances formed are directly proportional to their equivalent weights (i.e. atomic mass of the metal divided by the number of electrons required to reduce a cation of the metal)".

$$\frac{w_1}{E_1} = \frac{w_2}{E_2} = \frac{w_3}{E_3} = \ldots$$

where, w is the mass of substance and E is its equivalent weight.

Faraday's Constant

The amount of electricity (or charge) required for oxidation or reduction depends on the stoichiometry of the electrode reaction e.g.

$$Ag^+(aq) + e^- \longrightarrow Ag(s)$$

One mole of the electron is required for the reduction of one mole of silver ions. The charge on an electron is 1.602×10^{-19} C.
Therefore, the charge on one mole of electrons is
$N_A \times 1 \times 1.6021 \times 10^{-19}$ C

$$= 6.02 \times 10^{23} \text{mol}^{-1} \times 1.6021 \times 10^{-19} \text{C}$$

Charge = 96487 C $\text{mol}^{-1} \approx$ 96500 C mol^{-1}.

This quantity of electricity is called Faraday's constant and is represented by the symbol F.

Note Combining Faraday's laws, we get, $Z = \frac{E}{F} = \frac{W}{Q}$.

Relation between Faraday's Constant (F), Avogadro's Number N_0 (or N_A) and Charge on an Electron

$$e^- = \frac{F}{N_A}$$

Since, $F = 96500$ C, $N_A = 6.023 \times 10^{23}$ mol^{-1}

$$\therefore \quad e^- = \frac{F}{N_A} = \frac{96500 \text{ C mol}^{-1}}{6.023 \times 10^{23} \text{mol}^{-1}} = 1.6 \times 10^{-19} \text{C}$$

Charge on an ion is given by the following formula:

$$\text{Charge on an ion} = \frac{nF}{N_A}$$

where, n = valency of an ion

Example 1 An aqueous solution of copper sulphate, $CuSO_4$ was electrolysed between platinum electrodes using a current of 0.1287 A for 50 min.
[Given atomic mass of Cu = 63.5 g mol^{-1}]

(*i*) Write the cathodic reaction.
(*ii*) Calculate
  (*a*) electric charge passed during electrolysis.
  (*b*) mass of copper deposited at the cathode.
  [Given, 1F = 96500 C mol^{-1}]

(i) Cathode is the site of reduction.
(ii) Use $Q = it$, to find the amount of charge passed and $m = Zit = \frac{\text{Equivalent weight} \times it}{96500}$, to find the mass of copper deposited.

Sol. Given that,

$$t = 50 \times 60 = 3000 \text{ s}, i = 0.1287 \text{A}$$

(i) $Cu^{2+} + 2e^- \longrightarrow Cu(s)$

(ii) (a) $Q = it = 0.1287 \times 3000 = 386.1$ C

(b) $m = Z \times i \times t = \frac{\text{Eq. wt.}}{96500} \times i \times t$

$$= \frac{63.5}{2 \times 96500} \times 386.1 = 0.127 \text{ g}$$

Some Important Examples of Electrolysis

1. Electrolysis of Molten Sodium Chloride

It produces sodium metal at the cathode and chlorine gas at the anode. This happens according to the following reactions :

At cathode $Na^+(aq) + e^- \longrightarrow Na(s)$

At anode $2Cl^-(aq) \longrightarrow Cl_2(g) + 2e^-$

2. Electrolysis of Aqueous Solution of Sodium Chloride (Brine)

It is more complicated. Since, the solution is in water, so there are two dissociation reactions producing four different ions.

$$NaCl \longrightarrow Na^+ + Cl^-$$
$$H_2O \longrightarrow H^+ + OH^-$$

At cathode, there are two possible reactions:

$$Na^+(aq) + e^- \longrightarrow Na(s); \quad E^\circ_{cell} = -2.71 \text{ V}$$

$$H^+(aq) + e^- \longrightarrow \frac{1}{2}H_2(g); \quad E^\circ_{cell} = 0.00 \text{ V}$$

The reaction with the higher value of E° is preferred. Thus, the reaction at the cathode during electrolysis is

$$H^+(aq) + e^- \longrightarrow \frac{1}{2}H_2(g) \quad \text{...(i)}$$

But $H^+(aq)$ is produced by the dissociation of H_2O,

i.e. $H_2O(l) \longrightarrow H^+(aq) + OH^-(aq)$ ...(ii)

Therefore, net reaction at the cathode are the sum of Eqs. (i) and (ii).

$$H_2O(l) + e^- \longrightarrow \frac{1}{2}H_2(g) + OH^- \quad \text{...(iii)}$$

At anode, possible oxidation reactions are:

$$Cl^-(aq) \longrightarrow \frac{1}{2}Cl_2(g) + e^-, \; E^\circ_{cell} = 1.36 \text{ V}$$

$$OH^- \longrightarrow \frac{1}{2}H_2O + \frac{1}{4}O_2 + e^- \quad \text{...(iv)}$$

or, $2H_2O(l) \longrightarrow O_2(g) + 4H^+(aq) + 4e^-$,

$E^\circ_{cell} = 1.23$ V ...(v)

Reaction (v) is the sum of reaction (ii) and reaction (iv). The reaction with the lower value of $E°$ is preferred at the anode. Thus, we expect oxidation of water to take place at the anode. However, due to the oxygen overpotential, liberation of chlorine gas is preferred. Hence,

At cathode

$$H_2O\,(l) + e^- \longrightarrow \frac{1}{2}H_2(g) + OH^-(aq)$$

At anode $$Cl^-(aq) \longrightarrow \frac{1}{2}Cl_2\,(g) + e^-$$

Net reaction

$$NaCl\,(aq) + H_2O\,(l) \longrightarrow Na^+\,(aq) + OH^-(aq) + \frac{1}{2}H_2(g) + \frac{1}{2}Cl_2\,(g)$$

3. Electrolysis of Brine Using, Hg as a Cathode

At cathode $$Na^+ + e^- \longrightarrow Na$$

$$Na + Hg \longrightarrow Na\text{—}Hg$$

$$2Na\text{-}Hg + 2H_2O \longrightarrow 2NaOH + Hg + H_2(g)$$

At anode

$$Cl^-\,(aq) \longrightarrow \frac{1}{2}Cl_2(g) + e^-;\ E°_{cell} = 1.36\,V$$

$$2H_2O(l) \longrightarrow O_2\,(g) + 4H^+\,(aq) + 4e^-;\quad E°_{cell} = 1.23\,V$$

The reaction with lower value of $E°$ should be preferred but due to overvoltage of oxygen, Cl_2 gas is discharged at anode.

4. During Electrolysis of Sulphuric Acid

The following reactions are possible:

At anode

(i) $$2H_2O(l) \longrightarrow O_2(g) + 4H^+(aq) + 4e^-;$$

$$E°_{cell} = +1.23\,V$$

(ii) $$2SO_4^{2-}(aq) \longrightarrow S_2O_8^{2-}\,(aq) + 2e^-;$$

$$E°_{cell} = 1.96\,V$$

For dilute sulphuric acid, reaction (i) is preferred but at higher concentration of H_2SO_4, reaction (ii) is preferred.

At cathode $$H^+ + e^- \longrightarrow \frac{1}{2}H_2(g);\ E°_{cell} = 0.00V$$

Topic Practice 3

Very Short Answer Type Questions

(1 Mark)

1. **Fill in the Blanks**
   (i) The cell which converts electrical energy to chemical energy are called ....
   (ii) Chemical reactions and the process which take place in a electrolytic cell is called ....
   (iii) According to Faraday's law, one gram equivalent of ion is liberated by .... **ISC 2002**

2. **Objective Type Questions**
   (i) Electrochemical equivalent is the amount of substance which gets deposited from its solution on passing electrical charge equal to **ISC 2016**
   (a) 96,500 C (b) 1 C
   (c) 60 C (d) 965 C
   (ii) The quantity of electricity required to deposit 1.15 g of sodium from molten NaCl (Na = 23, Cl = 35.5) is **ISC 2012**
   (a) 1F (b) 0.5 F (c) 0.05 F (d) 1.5 F
   (iii) The number of Faraday's required to reduce one mole of Cu^{2+} to metallic copper is **ISC 2009**
   (a) one (b) two (c) three (d) four
   (iv) The number of Faradays which will be required to reduce 4 g equivalents of Cu^{2+} to Cu metal is **ISC 2005**
   (a) 1 (b) 2 (c) 3 (d) 4
   (v) A current liberates 0.50 g of hydrogen in 2 h. The weight of copper (atomic weight =63.5) deposited at the same time by the same current through copper sulphate solution is **ISC 2014**
   (a) 63.5 g (b) 31.8 g (c) 15.9 g (d) 15.5 g

3. Match the following Column 1 with column II and choose the correct option using the codes given below:

	Column I		Column II
A.	Faraday's first law	(i)	$\frac{W_1}{E_1} = \frac{W_2}{E_2}$
B.	Faraday's second law	(ii)	$W \propto Q$
C.	Faraday's constant	(iii)	$i \times t$
D.	Q	(iv)	96500 C mol^{-1}

Codes

	A	B	C	D		A	B	C	D
(a)	(ii)	(i)	iv)	(iii)	(b)	(i)	(ii)	(iii)	(iv)
(c)	(ii)	(i)	iii)	(iv)	(d)	(iii)	(i)	(ii)	(iv)

4. How much charge is required for the reduction of 1 mole of Cu^{2+} to Cu? **NCERT**

5. Calculate the mass of Ag deposited at cathode when a current of 2A was passed through a solution of $AgNO_3$ for 15 min. **ISC 2019**
(Given : Molar mass of Ag = 108 g mol^{-1}, 1F = 96500 C mol^{-1}).

6. Calculate the time taken to deposit 1.27 g of copper at cathode when a current of 2 ampere is passed through the solution of $CuSO_4$.
(Atomic weight of Cu = 63.5 g mol^{-1}) **ISC 2023**

7. When acidulated water (dil. H_2SO_4) is electrolysed, will the pH of the solution be affected? Justify your answer. **NCERT Exemplar**

8. Name the law or principle to which the following observations confirm:
When 9650 Coulombs of electricity is passed through a solution of copper sulphate, 3 .175 g of copper is deposited on the cathode (At.wt. of Cu = 63.5). **ISC 2017**

9. Calculate the number of Coulombs required to deposit 5.4g of Al, when the electrode reaction is
$$Al^{3+} + 3e^- \longrightarrow Al$$
[Atomic weight of Al = 27 g/mol] **ISC 2016**

10. How many hours does it take to reduce 3 moles of Fe^{3+} to Fe^{2+} with 2.0 A current intensity? **ISC 2016**

11. Name the law or principle confirmed by the following observation.
When 96500 C of electricity is passed through acidulated water, 5.6 L of oxygen at STP is liberated at the anode. **ISC 2013**

Short Answer Type I Questions

(2 Marks)

12. What is the amount of charge required to carry out the conversion of 1 mole of Al^{3+} ions to Al according to the following reaction,
$$Al^{3+} + 3e^- \longrightarrow Al$$
Or How much charge is required for the reduction of 1 mole of Al^{3+} to Al? **NCERT**

13. If a current of 0.5 A flows through a metallic wire for 2 h, then how many electrons would flow through the wire? **NCERT Intext**

14. How much charge is required for the following reduction: 1 mole of MnO_4^- to Mn^{2+}? **NCERT**

15. How much electricity in terms of Faraday is required to produce
(i) 20.0 g of Ca from molten $CaCl_2$?
(ii) 40.0 g of Al from molten Al_2O_3? **NCERT**

16. (i) State Faraday's first law of electrolysis.
(ii) How many electrons will flow when a current of 5 A is passed through a solution for 200 s? **ISC 2011**

17. A current of 10 A is passed for 80 min and 27 s through a cell containing dilute sulphuric acid.
(i) How many moles of oxygen gas will be liberated at the anode?
(ii) Calculate the amount of zinc deposited at the cathode when another cell containing $ZnSO_4$ solution is connected in series (Atomic weight of Zn = 65). **ISC 2007**

Short Answer Type II Questions

(3 Marks)

18. How much electricity is required in Coulomb for the oxidation of
(i) 1 mole of H_2O to O_2?
(ii) 1 mole of FeO to Fe_2O_3? **NCERT**

19. A solution of $Ni(NO_3)_2$ is electrolysed between platinum electrodes, using a current of 5 A for 20 min. What mass of Ni is deposited at the cathode? **NCERT**

20. 0.3605 g of a metal is deposited on the electrode by passing 1.2 A of current for 15 min through a salt solution. The atomic weight of the metal is 96. What is the valency of metal. **ISC 2014**

21. A current of 4 A is passed through a molten solution for 45 min. 2.977 g of metal is deposited. Calculate the charge carried by the metal cation if its atomic mass is 106.4 g/mol. **ISC 2002**

22. In the diagram of the electrolytic cell given below, *A*, *B* and *C* are connected in series having electrolytes of $ZnSO_4$, $AgNO_3$ and $CuSO_4$ respectively. A steady current of 1.5 A was passed until 1.45 g of Ag was deposited at the cathode of cell *B*.

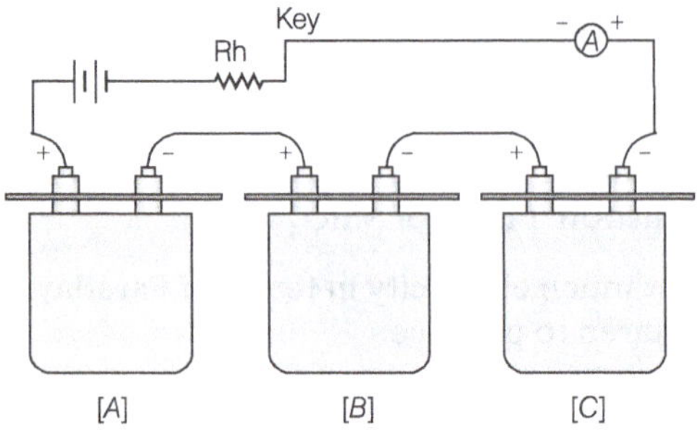

(Atomic mass of Ag = 108, Cu = 63.5, Zn = 65.3)

Answer the following questions.

(i) How long did the current flow?

(ii) What weight of Cu and Zn was deposited at cathode? **ISC 2024**

Long Answer Type Questions

5 Marks

23. Three electrolytic cells *A*, *B* and *C* containing solutions of zinc sulphate, silver nitrate and copper sulphate, respectively are connected in series. A steady current of 1.5 A was passed through them until 1.45 g of silver deposited at the cathode of cell *B*. How long did the current flow? What mass of copper and zinc were deposited in the concerned cells?

(Atomic mass of Ag = 108, Zn = 65.4, Cu = 63.5)

NCERT

Hints & Solutions

1. (i) Electrolytic cell
(ii) electrolysis
(iii) 96500 C

2. (i)→a, (ii)→c, (iii)→b, (iv)→d, (v)→b

3. (a) A→(ii), B→(i), C→(iv), D→(iii)

4. $Cu^{2+} + 2e^- \longrightarrow Cu(s)$

Charge required for the reduction of 1 mole of Cu^{2+}

$= 2F = 2 \times 96500$ C

$= 193000$ C

5. Given, current $(I) = 2$ A

Time $(t) = 15$ min

Quantity of electricity passed will be

$Q = It = 2 \times 15 \times 60 = 1800$ C **(1)**

Electrolysis of $AgNO_3$

$$Ag^+ + e^- \longrightarrow Ag(s)$$

(Atomic mass of Ag = 108 g mol^{-1})

As, 108 g of Ag has 96500 C

$\therefore$ 1800 C will deposit $= \dfrac{108 \times 1800}{96500}$ g of Ag

$= 2014$ g of Ag **(1)**

6. Reaction taking place is

$$Cu^{2+} + 2e^- \longrightarrow Cu \quad (n = 2)$$

By Faraday's first law,

$$W = ZQ = Zit$$

where, W = amount deposit

i = current

t = time

$$Z = \frac{\text{atomic weight}}{\text{no. of } e^- \times F}$$

So, we get

$$1.27 = \frac{63.5 \times 2 \times t}{2 \times 96500}$$

$$t = \frac{2 \times 96500 \times 1.27}{63.5 \times 2}$$

7. pH of the solution depends upon the concentration of H^+ ions present in solution. Thus, pH of the solution will not be affected as (H^+) remains constant.

During electrolysis of acidulated water, following reactions take place:

At anode $2H_2O \longrightarrow O_2 + 4H^+ + 4e^-$

At cathode $4H^+ + 4e^- \longrightarrow 2H_2$

8. Faraday's first law of electrolysis is confirmed from the given statement which states that 'the amount of substance deposited at a particular electrode as a result of electrolysis is directly proportional to the quantity of electricity passed'.

9. $Al^{3+} + 3e^- \longrightarrow Al$

For 27g (1mol) of Al required = 3×96500 C

$\therefore$ 1 g of Al required $= \dfrac{3 \times 96500}{27}$ C

$\therefore$ 5.4 g of Al required $= \dfrac{3 \times 96500}{27} \times 5.4 = 57900$ C

Thus, the number of Coulombs required to deposit 5.4 g of Al is = 57900 C.

10. Given, current = 2 A

Number of moles of iron = 3 moles

From number of moles, weight of iron = 168 g

From Faraday's equation,

$$w = zIt$$

$$t = \frac{168 \times 96500}{56 \times 2 \times 3600}$$

$\Rightarrow$ $t = 40.2$ h

11. Faraday's first law of electrolysis is confirmed from the given statement which states that 'the amount of substance deposited at a particular electrode as a result of electrolysis is directly proportional to the quantity of electricity passed'.

12. The number of electrons involved in the reaction is three.

Therefore, the amount of electricity required for one mole of Al^{3+} ions
$= 3F$ or $3 \times 96500\,C = 289500C$ (2)

13. Here, current $i = 0.5$ A, time $t = 2$ h

Quantity of charge (Q) passed = Current (i) × Time (t)
$= (0.5\text{ A}) \times (2 \times 60 \times 60\text{ s})$
$= 3600\text{ A s} = 3600\text{ C}$ (1)

Again, $Q = ne^-$

where, n = number of electrons, e^- = charge on electron

$$\therefore \quad n = \frac{Q}{e^-} = \frac{3600C}{1.6 \times 10^{-19}C}$$
$$= 2250 \times 10^{19}$$

Thus, number of electrons $= 2.250 \times 10^{22}$ (1)

14. The charge on manganese is + 7 in MnO_4^-. The chemical reaction involved is

$$Mn^{7+} + 5e^- \longrightarrow Mn^{2+}$$ (1)

Therefore, to convert 1 mole of MnO_4^- to Mn^{2+} ions, 5F of electricity is required. The amount of charge is therefore, $5 \times 96500\,C = 482500\,C$. (1)

15. (i) Electrode reaction : $Ca^{2+}(aq) + \underset{2F}{2e^-} \longrightarrow \underset{40g}{Ca(s)}$

To produce 40 g of Ca from molten $CaCl_2$, electricity required $= 2F$

To produce 20 g Ca from $CaCl_2$, electricity required $= 1F$ (1)

(ii) Electrode reaction :

$$Al_2O_3(l) + \underset{6F}{6e^-} \longrightarrow \underset{\substack{(2 \times 27) \\ = 54g}}{2Al} + 3O^{2-}$$

To produce 54 g Al from molten Al_2O_3, electricity required = 6F

To produce 40 g Al from molten Al_2O_3, electricity required $= \frac{(6F) \times (40g)}{(54g)} = 4.44$ F **(1)**

16. (i) **Faraday's First Law of Electrolysis** The amount of chemical deposition at the particular electrodes from an electrolytic solution is directly proportional to the charge passed through the electrolytic solution.

$w \propto Q$ or $w \propto it$ or $w = Zit$

where, Z is a constant known as electrochemical equivalent of the given substance, i is current, t is time, w is the amount of substance and Q is charge.

(ii) Given, current, $i = 5$A and time, $t = 200$ s

Amount of charge $Q = it$ (from Faraday's first law)

$= 5 \times 200 = 1000$ C

$\because$ 96500 C of electric charge is carried by 6.0×10^{23} electrons.

$\therefore$ 1000 C of electric charge is carried by

$$\frac{6.0 \times 10^{23}}{96500} \times 1000 = \frac{6000 \times 10^{23}}{96500}$$
$$= 6.217 \times 10^{21}\text{ electrons}$$

17. According to Faraday's first law of electrolysis,

$$w = Z.\,it = \frac{E}{96500}it$$

(i) Given, current, $i = 10$ A

$t = 80$ min 27 s $= 80 \times 60 + 27$ s $= 4827$ s

Equivalent weight, E for oxygen $= 8$

Weight of O_2 liberated $= \frac{8 \times 10 \times 4827}{96500} = 4$g

Moles of oxygen $= \frac{\text{Weight}}{\text{Molecular weight}}$

(Molecular weight of O_2 = 16 × 2 = 32)

$$= \frac{4}{32} = 0.125\text{ moles of } O_2$$

(ii) **According to Faraday's second law of electrolysis,** When the same quantity of electricity is passed through the solutions of different electrolytes connected in series, the masses of the substances liberated (or deposited) at the electrodes are directly proportional to their equivalent masses.

i.e. $$\frac{\text{Mass of } O_2}{\text{Mass of Zn}} = \frac{\text{Equivalent weight of } O_2}{\text{Equivalent weight of Zn}}$$

Let x be the amount of Zn deposited

$$\therefore \quad \frac{4}{x} = \frac{8}{65/2} \quad \text{(equivalent weight of Zn = 65 / 2)}$$

$$x = 4 \times \frac{65}{2 \times 8} = 16.25\text{ g}$$

18. (i) $H_2O \longrightarrow 2H^+ + \frac{1}{2}O_2 + 2e^-$ (1/2)

$\therefore$ The electricity required for the oxidation of 1 mole of H_2O is 2 F $= 2 \times 96500\,C = 193000\,C = 1.93 \times 10^5\,C$ (1)

(ii) $$FeO \longrightarrow \frac{1}{2}Fe_2O_3$$

i.e. $$\underset{1\text{ mol}}{Fe^{2+}} \longrightarrow Fe^{3+} + \underset{1F}{e^-}$$ (1/2)

$\therefore$ The electricity required is 1 F $= 1 \times 96500$ C
$= 96500$ C (1)

19. Here, current = 5A, time = 20 min

Quantity of electricity passed will be

$$Q = it = 5\text{ A} \times 20 \times 60\text{ s} = 6000\text{ C}$$ (1)

Electrolysis of $Ni(NO_3)_2$ gives

$Ni^{2+} + 2e^- \longrightarrow Ni$ (Atomic mass of Ni = 58.7) (1)

Therefore, electricity required for 1 mole, i.e. 58.7 g Ni is 2F = 2 × 96500 C

$\because$ 2 × 96500 C deposit Ni = 58.7 g

$\therefore$ 6000 C will deposit Ni $= \frac{58.7 \times 6000}{2 \times 96500}$ g = 1.825 g **(1)**

20. $w = Zit = \frac{E}{96500} \times it$ (according to Faraday's first law)

Given, amount of metal, $w = 0.3605$ g

Current, $i = 1.2$ A, time, $t = 15$ min $= 15 \times 60$ s

$$0.3605 = \frac{E}{96500} \times 1.2 \times 15 \times 60$$

where, E is equivalent weight of metal

$$E = \frac{0.3605 \times 96500}{1.2 \times 15 \times 60} = 32.211$$

$$E = 32.21$$

$$\text{Equivalent weight} = \frac{\text{Atomic weight}}{\text{Valency}}$$

$$\text{Valency} = \frac{96}{32.21} = 2.98 \cong 3$$

(As atomic weight of metal is 96)

Hence, valency of metal $= 3$

21. **Key idea** According to Faraday's first law,

$$w = Zit = \frac{Eit}{96500}$$

Given, current $i = 4$A,

time $t = 45$ min $= 45 \times 60$ s,

weight of metal, $w = 2.977$ g

$$2.977 = \frac{E \times 4 \times 45 \times 60}{96500}$$

where, E is equivalent weight of metal.

$$E = \frac{96500 \times 2.977}{4 \times 45 \times 60} = 26.6 \text{ g of metal}$$

Equivalent weight of the metal $= 26.60$ g

$$\text{Equivalent weight} = \frac{\text{Atomic weight}}{\text{Valency}}$$

$$\text{Valency} = \frac{106.4}{26.6} = 4$$

Hence, valency of the element $= 4$.

The metal cation can be M^{4+}.

The charge of an electron is 1.6×10^{-19} C.

$$M^{4+} + 4e^- \longrightarrow M$$

Charge of 4 electrons $= 1.6 \times 10^{-19} \times 4$

(As $Q = ne^-$ where, n is the number of electrons)

$= 6.4 \times 10^{-19}$ C

22. (i) Given, Current = 1.5 A

Amount of Ag = 1.45 g

For Cell B Atomic mass of Ag = 108, Cu = 63.5, Zn = 65.3

As $Ag^+ + e^- \rightleftharpoons Ag$ (at cathode)

1 mole of Ag is deposited by 96500 C

1.45 g of Ag will be deposited by $= \frac{96500 \times 1.45}{108}$

$= 1295.6$ C

Now, $Q = It$

$1295.6 = 1.5 \times t$

$t = 864$ s

(ii) **For Cell** A $Zn^{2+} + 2e^- \longrightarrow Zn$

$\therefore$ 2 moles of electrons (2×96500 C of current) produces 1 mole (65.3 g) of zinc.

$\therefore$ 1295.6 of electricity will deposit $= \frac{65.3}{2 \times 96500} \times 1295.6$

$= 0.438$ g of zinc

For Cell C $Cu^{2+} + 2e^- \longrightarrow Cu$

2 moles of electrons (2×96500 C of current) produces 1 mole (63.5 g) of Cu

1295.6 C of electricity will deposit $= \frac{63.5 \times 1295.6}{2 \times 96500}$

$= 0.426$ g of Cu

23. $\underset{}{Ag^+} + \underset{1F}{e^-} \longrightarrow \underset{1 mol}{Ag}$

$\because$ 108 g of Ag is deposited by 96500 C

$\therefore$ 1.45 g of Ag will be deposited by $= \frac{96500 \times 1.45}{108}$

$= 1295.6$ C (1)

$Q = it$ or 1295.6 C $= 1.5$ A $\times t$

$\therefore$ $t = \frac{1295.6 \text{ C}}{1.5} \Rightarrow t = 863.7$ s (1)

The reaction related to the deposition of copper is

$$Cu^{2+} + 2e^- \longrightarrow \underset{63.5 g}{Cu}$$

$\because$ 2×96500 C electricity deposits 63.5 g of Cu (1/2)

$\therefore$ 1295.6 C electricity will deposit

$= \frac{63.5 \times 1295.6}{2 \times 96500}$ g of Cu, i.e. 0.426 g of Cu. (1)

The reaction related to the deposition of zinc is

$$Zn^{2+} + \underset{2 \times 96500 C}{2e^-} \longrightarrow \underset{65.4 g}{Zn}$$

$\because$ 2×96500 C electricity deposits 65.4 g of Zn. (1/2)

$\therefore$ 1295.6 C electricity will deposit $\frac{65.4 \times 1295.6}{2 \times 96500}$ g of Zn,

i.e. 0.44 g of Zn. (1)

TOPIC 04

Electrochemical Cells in Action

Batteries (Commercial Cells)

A battery (which contains one or more than one electrochemical cell connected in series) or a cell that we use as a source of electrical energy is basically a galvanic cell, which converts the chemical energy of the redox reaction into electrical energy.

For a battery to be of practical use, it should be reasonably light, compact and its voltage should not vary appreciably during its use.There are mainly two types of batteries:

Primary Batteries

A primary battery (non-chargeable battery) is a device in which reactions occur only once and after use (over a period of time), battery becomes dead and cannot be reused. It produces electric current for a period of time and with time when no more chemicals remain available to take part in the reaction, the cell dies.

The most familiar examples of this type of batteries are Leclanche cell and mercury cell.

1. Leclanche Cell (Dry Cell)

It consists of a zinc container which acts as the anode. The cathode is a carbon (graphite) rod surrounded by a mixture of powdered manganese dioxide and carbon. The space between the electrodes is filled with moist paste of ammonium chloride and zinc chloride.

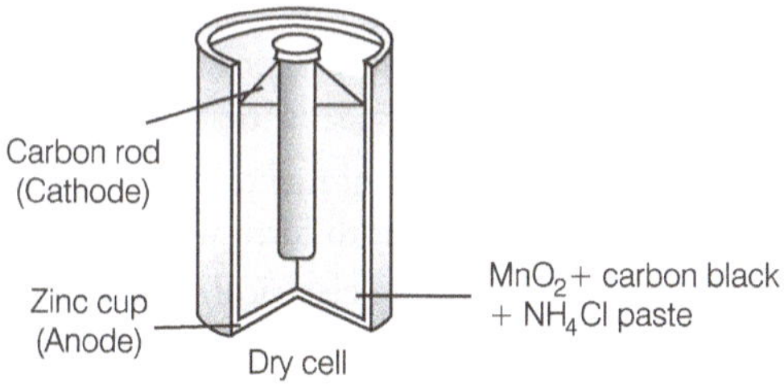

Dry cell

The reactions occurring at the cathode and the anode are:

At anode $Zn(s) \longrightarrow Zn^{2+} + 2e^-$

At cathode $MnO_2 + NH_4^+ + e^- \longrightarrow MnO(OH) + NH_3$

In the reaction at cathode, manganese is reduced from the +4 oxidation state to the +3 state. NH_3 produced in the reaction forms a complex with Zn^{2+} to give $[Zn(NH_3)_4]^{2+}$. The cell has a potential of about 1.5 V.

Use of Leclanche cell It is commonly used in transistors and clocks.

2. Mercury Cell

It consists of zinc-mercury amalgam as anode. The cathode is a paste of mercuric oxide (HgO) and carbon powder. The electrolyte consists of a mixture of KOH and ZnO.

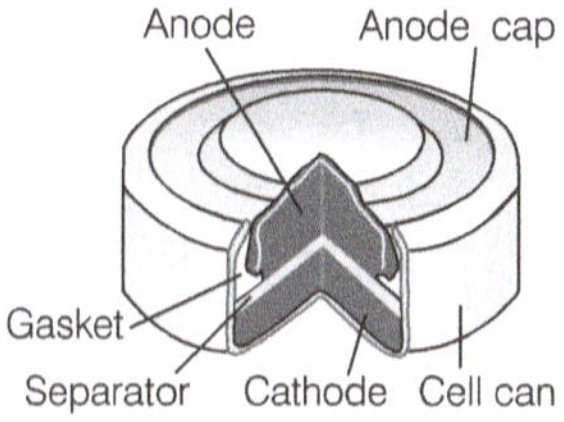

Mercury cell

The reducing agent is zinc and the oxidising agent is mercuric (II) oxide.

The electrode reactions of a mercury cell can be written as:

At anode

$$Zn(Hg) + 2OH^- \longrightarrow ZnO(s) + H_2O + 2e^-$$

At cathode

$$HgO + H_2O + 2e^- \longrightarrow Hg(l) + 2OH^-$$

The overall reaction of the cell is written as:

$$Zn(Hg) + HgO(s) \longrightarrow ZnO(s) + Hg(l)$$

The potential of a mercury cell is approximately 1.35 V. It remains constant as in the overall cell reaction no ions are involved in solution whose concentration can change during the life span of the cell. Thus, it lasts longer.

Use of mercury cell It is suitable for low current devices like hearing aids, watches, etc.

Secondary Batteries

A secondary cell after use can be recharged by passing current through it in the opposite direction so that it can be used again. A good secondary cell can undergo a large number of discharging and charging cycles. Two important secondary batteries — lead storage battery and nickel- cadmium battery are as follows:

1. Lead Storage Battery

It consists of a lead anode and a grid of lead packed with lead dioxide as cathode. A 38% solution of sulphuric acid acts as the electrolyte. When the battery is in use (discharging), the cell reactions are:

At anode : $Pb(s) + SO_4^{2-}(aq) \longrightarrow PbSO_4(s) + 2e^-$

At cathode

$$PbO_2(s) + SO_4^{2-}(aq) + 4H^+(aq) + 2e^- \longrightarrow PbSO_4(s) + 2H_2O(l)$$

The overall reaction of the cell is written as :

$$Pb(s) + PbO_2(s) + 2H_2SO_4(aq) \longrightarrow 2PbSO_4(s) + 2H_2O(l)$$

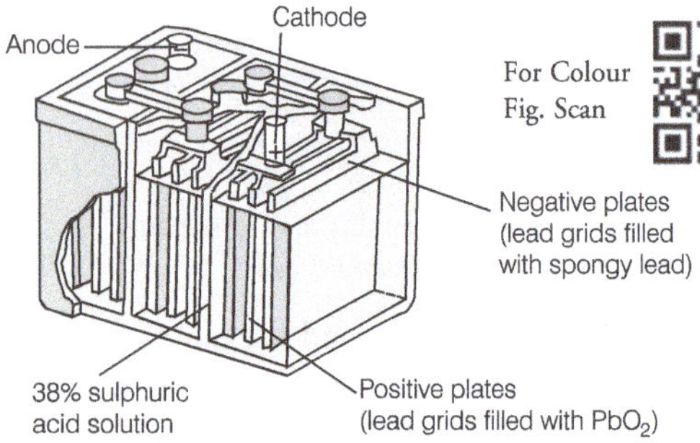

For Colour Fig. Scan

The lead storage battery

During charging, current is passed through the terminals from external source. The reactions are reversed and $PbSO_4(s)$ on anode and cathode is converted into Pb and PbO_2, respectively. **Use of Lead storage Battery** It is commonly used in automobiles and power inverters.

2. Nickel-Cadmium Battery

It consists of a cadmium anode and metal grid containing NiO_2 as cathode. KOH solution is electrolyte. The overall cell reaction of Ni-Cd cell during discharging is

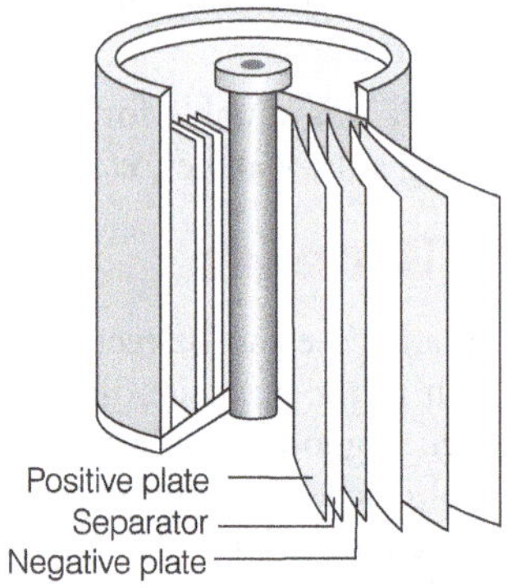

For Colour Fig. Scan

A rechargeable nickel-cadmium cell in a jelly roll arrangement and separated by a layer soaked in moist sodium or potassium hydroxide

Overall reaction

$$Cd(s) + NiO_2(s) + 2H_2O(l) \longrightarrow Cd(OH)_2(s) + Ni(OH)_2(s)$$

At anode $Cd(s) + 2OH^-(aq) \longrightarrow Cd(OH)_2(s) + 2e^-$

At cathode $NiO_2(s) + 2H_2O(l) + 2e^- \longrightarrow Ni(OH)_2(s) + 2OH^-(aq)$

It has longer life than the lead storage cell but more expensive to manufacture.

Fuel Cell

It is a galvanic cell in which chemical energy from combustion of fuels like hydrogen, methane, methanol, etc., is converted into electrical energy. In this type of galvanic cells, reactants are continuously feed to the electrodes, which react to produce electricity and products thus formed are continuously removed from the electrolyte department.

(i) It is highly efficient (70%) method when compared to the efficiency of thermal power plants (40%), that is a major source of pollution.
(ii) High efficiency.
(iii) Pollution free working.
(iv) Continuous supply of energy.

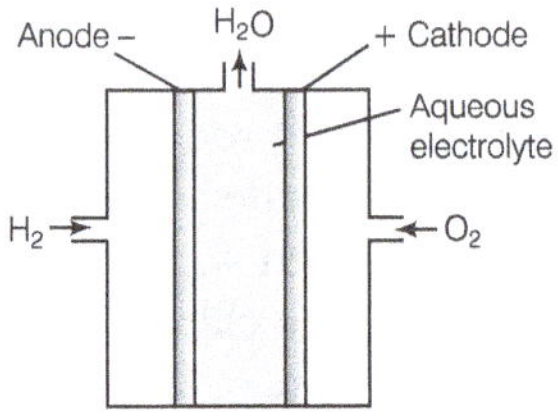

Fuel cell using H_2 and O_2 produces electricity

(v) One of the most successful fuel cells uses the reaction of hydrogen with oxygen to form water.
(vi) It was used for providing electrical power in Apollo space programme. The water vapours produced during the reaction were condensed and added to the drinking water supply for the astronauts.

In the cell, hydrogen and oxygen are bubbled through porous carbon electrodes into concentrated aqueous sodium hydroxide solution. Finely divided platinum or palladium acts as a catalyst. The electrode reactions for the cell are:

At cathode

$$O_2(g) + 2H_2O(l) + 4e^- \longrightarrow 4OH^-(aq)$$

At anode

$$2H_2(g) + 4OH^-(aq) \longrightarrow 4H_2O(l) + 4e^-$$

The overall reaction of the cell is written as:

$$2H_2(g) + O_2(g) \longrightarrow 2H_2O\,(l)$$

This cell runs as long as the reactants are supplied. There have been tremendous progress in the development of new electrode materials, better catalyst and electrolytes for increasing the efficiency of fuel cells.

Uses

These have been used in automobiles on an experimental basis.

Corrosion

It is an electrochemical process in which a metal is oxidised to metal oxide or other salt of the metal by losing electrons to oxygen or other electronegative element and forms a coating on the metal surface. The rusting of iron, tarnishing of silver surface, surface of copper and bronze turning green are some of the examples of corrosion.

Mechanism of Electrochemical Reaction of Corrosion

Rusting (or corrosion) occurs in the presence of water and air. The place of iron object where rusting takes place, acts as anode. This is the place at which oxidation occurs and iron oxide is formed.

Electrons release at anodic spot move through the metal and go to another spot on the metal and reduce oxygen in the presence of H^+ which is believed to be available from H_2CO_3 formed due to dissolution of carbon dioxide from air into water. This spot behaves as the cathode.

The anode and cathode reactions are :

At anode $2Fe(s) \longrightarrow 2Fe^{2+}(aq) + 4e^-$;

$$E^{\ominus}_{(Fe^{2+}/Fe)} = -0.44\ V$$

At cathode $O_2\,(g) + 4H^+(aq) + 4e^- \longrightarrow 2H_2O\,(l)$;

$$E^{\ominus}_{H^+\,|\,O_2\,|\,H_2O} = 1.23\ V$$

The overall reaction of the cell is written as :

$$2Fe(s) + O_2(g) + 4H^+(aq) \longrightarrow 2Fe^{2+}\,(aq) + 2H_2O(l)\,;\quad E^{\ominus}_{(cell)} = 1.67\ V$$

The ferrous ions obtained are further oxidised by atmospheric oxygen to ferric ion which comes out as rust in the form of hydrated ferric oxide ($Fe_2O_3 . xH_2O$) and with further production of H^+ ions.

e.g. corrosion of iron in atmosphere.

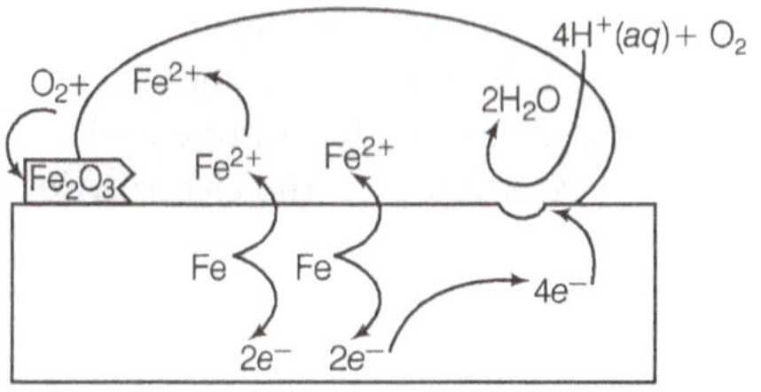

Atmospheric Oxidation

$$2Fe^{2+}(aq) + 2H_2O(l) + \frac{1}{2}O_2(g) \longrightarrow Fe_2O_3(s) + 4H^+(aq)$$

Factors Affecting Corrosion

(i) More the reactivity of metal, the more will be the possibility of the metal getting corroded.

(ii) A rise in temperature (with in reasonable limit) increases the rate of corrosion.

(iii) Presence of CO_2 in natural water increase rusting of iron.

(iv) Presence of impurities help in setting up voltaic cells, which increase the speed of corrosion.

(v) When the iron surface is coated with layers of metal more active than iron, then the rate of corrosion is retarded.

Prevention of Corrosion

Prevention of corrosion is very necessary because enormous damage occurs to buildings, bridges, ships and all other objects made up of metals especially iron.

Some of the methods generally used for prevention of corrosion are:

1. Barrier Protection

It can be achieved by coating the metal surface with paints, oil or grease or by certain chemicals like $FePO_4$ that provides a tough adherent film on the metal surface.

2. Galvanisation

The metal which is most often used for covering iron with more active metal is zinc and the process is called **galvanisation**. The layer of zinc on the surface of iron, when comes in contact with moisture, oxygen and carbon dioxide in air, a protective invisible thin layer of basic zinc carbonate, $ZnCO_3 . Zn(OH)_2$ is formed due to which the galvanised iron sheets lose their lustre and also tends to protect it from further corrosion.

3. Electroplating

The process of coating an inferior metal with a superior metal by electrolysis is known as **electroplating**. The metal to be electroplated is made cathode and the metal to be deposited is made anode in the electrolytic bath containing a solution of a salt of the anodic metal.

On passing the electric current, the metal of the anode dissolves out and is deposited on the cathode, in the form of a thin film.

4. Anodising

Anodising is an electrochemical process that converts the metal surface into a decorative, durable, corrosion-resistant, anodic oxide finish. Aluminium is ideally suited to anodising process.

Topic Practice 4

Objective Type Questions

1. Which one of the following statements is correct regarding the dry cell? **ISC 2024**
   (P) Zinc container acts as an anode in dry cell.
   (Q) Zinc container touches the paste of MnO_2 and carbon.
   (R) Dry cell can be charged easily.
   (S) Graphite rod acts as a cathode in dry cell.
   (a) (P) and (R) (b) (Q) and (R)
   (c) (P) and (S) (d) (Q) and (S)

Very Short Answer Type Questions

(1 Mark)

2. Unlike dry cell, the mercury cell has a constant cell potential throughout its useful life. Why? **NCERT Exemplar**
3. What advantage do the fuel cells have over primary and secondary batteries? **NCERT Exemplar**
4. Define fuel cell.
5. Explain, corrosion of metals. **ISC 2018**

Short Answer Type I Questions

(2 Marks)

6. Write the chemistry of recharging the lead storage battery, highlighting all the materials that are involved during recharging. **NCERT Intext**

Short Answer Type II Questions

(3 Marks)

7. What is corrosion? What are the factors which affect corrosion? CO_2 is always present in natural water. Explain its effect (increases, stops or no effect) on rusting of iron.

Long Answer Type Questions

(5 Marks)

8. Explain how rusting of iron is envisaged as setting up of an electrochemical cell? **NCERT Intext**

Hints & Solutions

1. Among the given statements (P) and (S) are correct while (Q) and (R) are incorrect.
   - Zinc container cannot touch is the paste of MnO_2 and carbon as the space between the electrode is filled with moist paste of ammonium chloride and zinc chloride.
   - Dry cell cannot be charged easily.
2. The potential of mercury cell (~1.35 V) remains constant. As in the overall cell reaction no ions are involved in solution whose concentration can change during the life span of the cell. Thus, it lasts longer.
3. Primary batteries contain a limited amount of reactants and are discharged when the reactants have been consumed. Secondary batteries can be recharged but it takes a long time. Fuel cell run continuously as long as the reactants are supplied to it and products are removed continuously.
4. Refer to text on page 82 (Fuel cell).
5. **Corrosion of Metals**
   It is basically an electrochemical phenomenon in which a metal oxide or other salt of the metal forms a coating on the metal surface, e.g. rusting of iron, in which the following reactions take place:
   Oxidation, at anode $2Fe(s) \longrightarrow 2Fe^{2+}(aq) + 4e^-$
   Reduction, at cathode
   $$O_2(g) + 4H^+(aq) + 4e^- \longrightarrow 2H_2O(l)$$
   The **overall reaction** is
   $$2Fe(s) + O_2(g) + 4H^+(aq) \longrightarrow 2Fe^{2+}(aq) + 2H_2O(l)$$
6. Refer to text on page 82 (Lead storage battery).
7. Refer to text on page 83 (Corrosion).
8. In corrosion, a metal is oxidised by the loss of electrons to oxygen with the formation of oxides. So, an electrochemical cell is set-up, e.g. rusting of iron.
   Refer to text on page 83.

SUMMARY

- Electrochemistry deals with the relationship between electrical and chemical energy.
- Device which converts chemical energy to electrical energy is called electrochemical cell while that in which electrical energy is used to carry out a non-spontaneous reaction, is called electrolytic cell.
- **Electrochemical or voltaic (galvanic) cells** are of a type that produce electricity as a result of chemical reaction.
  For the reaction, $Zn(s) + Cu^{2+}(aq) \rightleftharpoons Cu(s) + Zn^{2+}(aq)$
  Cell representation is given as, $Zn \mid Zn^{2+}(C_1) \| Cu^{2+}(C_2) \mid Cu$
  The SHE is represented as, $Pt(s)|H_2(g)|H^+(aq)$ in which the reaction occurs as, $H^+(aq) + e^- \longrightarrow \frac{1}{2}H_2(g)$
- In **galvanic cell** oxidation occurs at anode and is a –ve plate, reduction occurs at cathode and is a +ve plate.
- Potential difference between the metal and the metal ion in which electrode is dipped, is **electrode potential** (E) in a given state and standard electrode potential ($E°$) in a standard state:
  $E^\circ_{Zn/Zn^{2+}} = E^\circ_{ox}$ (standard oxidation potential of Zn/Zn^{2+})
  $E^\circ_{Cu^{2+}/Cu} = E^\circ_{red}$ (standard reduction potential of Cu^{2+}/Cu)
  $E^\circ_{cell} = E^\circ_{ox} + E^\circ_{red}$. (take $E°$ values according to reaction)
  $E_{cell} = E_{ox} + E_{red}$ or $E^\circ_{cell} = E^\circ_R - E^\circ_L$
  E°_R and E°_L are standard reduction potential.
- In electrochemical series (ECS), E°_{red} values measured *wrt* SHE are arranged in increasing order. Based on ECS, reaction is spontaneous if reducing agent is above oxidising agent.
  Metals lying above hydrogen in ECS will react with dilute acid forming H_2.
  Oxides of Hg and below it in ECS will give metal on heating.
- Nernst equation : $E_{cell} = E^\circ_{cell} - \frac{2.303\,RT}{nF}\log K$
  $E_{cell} = E^\circ_{cell} - \frac{0.0591}{n}\log K$, where K is reaction quotient
  for $Zn + Cu^{2+} \longrightarrow Cu + Zn^{2+}$; $K = \frac{[Zn^{2+}]}{[Cu^{2+}]}$
  (used also if half-cells are given).
- Electrical work, $\Delta G = -nFE$ in a given state
  $\Delta G^\circ = -nFE^\circ$ in a standard state
  $\Delta G^\circ = -2.303\,RT\log K_{eq}$
- $E^\circ_{cell} = \frac{2.303\,RT}{nF}\log K_{eq}$, $E^\circ_{cell} = \frac{0.0591}{n}\log K_{eq}$ at 298 K
- **Conductors** Substances which allows the electric current to flow through it. The conductors may be metallic or electrolytic.
- The power of an electrolyte to conduct electric current is called **conductance** or **conductivity.**
- Conductance is defined as reverse of resistance, which measures the obstruction in the flow of current while conductivity is reciprocal of resistivity.
- Conductance : ohm^{-1} or S (Siemen)
- Specific conductance : $ohm^{-1}\ cm^{-1}$ or $ohm^{-1}\ m^{-1}$ or $S\ m^{-1}$
- Cell constant : cm^{-1} or m^{-1}
- Specific conductance = conductance × cell constant
  Λ_{eq} = equivalent conductance $= \frac{1000 \times \text{specific conductance}}{\text{conc. (normality)}}$
  Λ_m = molar conductance $= \frac{1000 \times \text{specific conductance}}{\text{conc. (molarity)}}$
  Λ_{eq} : $ohm^{-1}\ cm^2\ equiv^{-1}$ or $S\ cm^2\ equiv^{-1}$ or $S\ m^2\ equiv^{-1}$
  Λ_m : $ohm^{-1}\ cm^2\ mol^{-1}$ or $S\ cm^2\ mol^{-1}$ or $S\ m^2\ mol^{-1}$
- Debye-Huckel Onsager equation
  $$\Lambda_m = \Lambda_m^\infty - [A + B\Lambda_m^\infty]\sqrt{C}.$$
  A and B are called Debye-Huckel constants.
- Λ_{eq}^∞ and Λ_m^∞ both increase with decrease in concentration (or increase in dilution) and when $C \to 0$, $\Lambda_{eq} = \Lambda_{eq}^\infty$
  $$\Lambda_m = \Lambda_m^\infty$$
  Λ_{eq}^∞ and Λ_m^∞ are values at infinite dilution such that $C \to 0$
- By Kohlrausch's law, $\Lambda_m^\infty = x\lambda_+^\infty + y\lambda_-^\infty$
- **In electrolytic cell** Oxidation occurs at anode but is +ve plate, reduction occurs at cathode but is –ve plate.
- **Faraday's Laws of Electrolysis**
  First law
  w (amount deposited) $= zit = zC$
  where, z is electrochemical equivalent,
  $$z = \frac{\text{atomic wt.}}{n \times 96500}$$
  i = current (in amp), t = time (in sec.)
  C = Coulombs of electricity, thus 1 F of electricity will deposit 1 g equivalent of metal, i.e., 108 g of Ag, 12 g of Mg and 9 g of Al.
- **Second law** $\frac{\text{wt. of metal } A}{\text{wt. of metal } B} = \frac{\text{eq. wt. of } A}{\text{eq. wt. of } B}$
- Electrolysis of molten NaCl(l) gives sodium at cathode; electrolysis of *aq*. NaCl solution gives NaOH, H_2 at cathode and Cl_2 at anode.
- Electrolysis of sulphuric acid.
  At anode $2H_2O \longrightarrow 4H^+ + O_2 + 4e^-$
  At cathode $H^+ + e^- \longrightarrow \frac{1}{2}H_2(g)$
- The corrosion of metals, such as the rusting of iron, is an electrochemical phenomenon.
- Batteries, which consist of one or more electrochemical cells, are used widely as self-contained power sources, e.g. dry cell, lead storage battery etc.

For Mind Map

Visit : https://goo.gl/Tkq8pS OR **Scan the Code**

Chapter Practice

Very Short Answer Type Questions

1 Mark

1 Fill in the Blanks

(i) SI units of conductance ....

(ii) On dilution as number of ions per cm^3 decreases, conductivity ....

(iii) For a weak electrolyte, there is a very large increase in conductance with dilution especially near infinite .... as number of ions increases.

(iv) Zinc layer is made on Fe-wire to prevent it from........... and a process called ....

2 Objective Type Questions

(i) The incorrect statement about electrochemistry is

(a) the study of generation of electricity by spontaneous chemical reactions

(b) the study of use of electrical energy to bring out a non-spontaneous chemical reaction

(c) reaction based on it is not so efficient and ecofriendly

(d) transmission of sensory signals through cells to brain are of electrochemical origin

(ii) $Zn(s) + Cu^{2+}(aq) \longrightarrow Zn^{2+}(aq) + Cu(s)$

The above redox reaction is used in

(a) Galvanic cell (b) Daniell cell
(c) Voltaic cell (d) All of these

(iii) For the generation of electrode potential of 1.1 V, the ideal concentration of zinc and copper ion (in mol dm^{-3}) in the Galvanic cell is

(a) 1 and 1 (b) 2 and 1
(c) 3 and 2 (d) 4 and 2

(iv) Compound *XA*, *XB*, *XC* are added into separate test tubes containing *A*, *B*, *C* solutions. *XB* react with *A* and *C*. *XA* does not react with any of these. *XC* reacts with *A*.
Which of the following is the correct decreasing order for the oxidation of the anions?

(a) A^-, B^-, C^-

(b) B^-, C^-, A^-

(c) C^-, A^-, B^-

(d) B^-, A^-, C^-

(v) Select the strongest reducing agent from the given electrode potential.

(a) $E^\circ_{Zn^{2+}/Zn}$ (b) $E^\circ_{Cr^{3+}/Cr}$ (c) $E^\circ_{H^+/H_2}$ (d) $E^\circ_{Fe^{3+}/Fe^{2+}}$

3 Match the following Column I with type of electrolyte in Column II and choose the correct option using the codes given below :

	Column I		Column II
A.	NaCl	(i)	2-1 electrolyte
B.	$CaCl_2$	(ii)	2-2 electrolyte
C.	$MgSO_4$	(iii)	1-1 electrolyte

Codes

	A	B	C		A	B	C
(a)	(i)	(iii)	(ii)	(b)	(iii)	(ii)	(i)
(c)	(iii)	(i)	(ii)	(d)	(i)	(ii)	(iii)

4 When does an electrochemical cell behaves like an electrolytic cell?

5 Can absolute electrode potential of an electrode be measured?

6 What does the negative sign in the expression $E^\circ_{Zn^{2+}/Zn} = -0.76$ V mean?

7 List the factors on which molar conductivity of ionic solution depends.

8 List the factors on which conductivity of electrolyte depends.

9 The specific conductivity of a saturated solution of silver chloride is 2.30×10^{-6} S cm^{-1} at 25°C. Calculate the solubility of silver chloride at 25°C. Λ^∞ for Ag^+ and Cl^- ions are 61.9 and 76.3 S cm^2 mol^{-1} respectively.

10 From the values of a Faraday constant (96500 C mol^{-1}) and Avogadro number (6.023×10^{23}), calculate the coulomb charge on an electron.

11 How will the pH of brine (*aq* NaCl solution) be affected when it is electrolysed?

12 What is a primary cell? Give one example.

13 What features of a cell enables practical use of battery?

14 Mention the uses of mercury cell.

15 What is the advantage of nickel-cadmium cell over lead-storage battery?

16 List the advantages of using H_2 -O_2 fuel cell over ordinary cell.

17 Write the Nernst equation for single electrode potential.

18 What is the efficiency of a fuel cell? What is the use of a fuel cell?

19 Suggest a metal that can be used for cathodic protection of iron against rusting.

20 Write the relation between cell potential and equilibrium constant.

21 Why does a cell stops working after sometime?

Assertion-Reason

Directions (Q. Nos. 22-33) In the following questions an Assertion (A) is followed by a corresponding Reason (R). Use the following keys to choose the appropriate answer.

(a) Both (A) and (R) are correct and (R) is the correct explanation of (A).
(b) Both (A) and (R) are correct but (R) is not the correct explanation of (A).
(c) (A) is correct and (R) is incorrect.
(d) (A) is incorrect but (R) is correct.

22. **Assertion** (A) E_{cell} should have positive value for the cell to function.

Reason (R) $E_{anode} < E_{cathode}$

23. **Assertion** (A) 96500 C charge is required for the reduction of one mole of silver ions.

Reason (R) The amount of electricity (or charge) required for oxidation or reduction depends on the stoichiometry of the electrode reaction.

24. **Assertion** (A) Mercury cells give a constant voltage throughout its life.

Reason (R) Electrolyte KOH is not involved in the reaction.

25 **Assertion** If a solution contains both $H^+$and Na^+ ions, the H^+ ions are reduced first at cathode.

Reason Cations with higher $E°$value reduced first at cathode. **ISC 2023**

26 **Assertion:** Specific conductiity of all electrolytes decreases on dilution.

Reason: On dilution, the number of ions per unit volume decreases. **ISC 2024**

Case Study

27 Standard reduction potentials of half-cells are arranged from the highest (positive) value to the lowest (negative) value in a table. More negative the emf value, stronger is the reducing agent. The more positive the emf value, the weaker is the reducing agent as it is compared to H^+/H_2.

As one goes from top to bottom in the table in which electrochemical half-cells are arranged in the order of highest reduction potential to the lowest, the reducing power increases, whereas from the bottom of the table to the top, the oxidising power increases.

(i) The standard reduction potnetials of three metallic cations, *viz* x, y and z are + 0.52, – 3.03 and – 1.18 V respectively. What will the order of reducing capability of the given metals?

(ii) Which is a stronger oxidising agent in aqueous medium, Cr^{2+} or Fe^{2+}?
Given, $E^\circ_{Cr^{2+}/Cr} = -0.91$ V and $E^\circ_{Fe^{2+}/Fe} = -0.44$ V

(iii) Why does zinc react with dilute hydrochloric acid but silver does not?

28 One of the simplest method to prevent corrosion is to prevent the surface of the metallic object to come in contact with atmosphere.

This can be done by applying paint or some chemicals such as bisphenol on the surface of the metal so that the surface does not come in contact with the atmosphere.

The other way is to cover the surface by coating the metal surface with inert metals like zinc, tin, etc. An electrochemical method is to provide a sacrificial electrode of another metal (like Mg, Zn, etc.) which corrodes itself but saves the object.

(i) Can chromium used for coating iron?

(ii) What will happen if the protective layer of tin over an iron pipe is broken at the same place?

(iii) Saline water can cause rusting of iron more quickly than ordinary water. How?

Short Answer Type I Questions

(2 Marks)

29 Write the Nernst equation and emf of the following cell at 298 K.
$Fe(s)|Fe^{2+}(0.001M)||H^{+}(1M)|H_2(g)$ (1 bar) | Pt

30 The potential for the cell below is found to be 0.25 V.
$Pt(s)|H_2(g)|H^{+}(aq), (1 \text{ mol}/L)||Cu^{2+}(aq, C \text{ mol}/L)|Cu(s)$
What is the value of C ?

31 (i) Why does zinc react with dilute sulphuric acid but copper does not?
(ii) Why it is not possible to measure the single electrode potential?

32 The emf of a cell corresponding to the reaction, $Zn(s)+2H^{+}(aq) \longrightarrow Zn^{2+}(0.1\text{ M})+H_2(g, 1\text{atm})$ is 0.28 V at 25°C.
Write the half-cell reactions and calculate the pH of the solution at the hydrogen electrode.
$E^{\circ}_{Zn^{2+}/Zn} = -0.76\text{ V}, E^{\circ}_{H^{+}/H_2} = 0$

33 Find the equilibrium constant for the reaction,
$Cu^{2+} + In^{2+} \rightleftharpoons Cu^{+} + In^{3+}$
Given that, $E_{Cu^{2+}/Cu^{+}} = 0.15$ V,
$E^{\circ}_{In^{2+}/In^{+}} = -0.4\text{ V}, E^{\circ}_{In^{3+}/In} = 0.42\text{ V}$

34 A current of 3.7 A is passed for 6 h between nickel electrodes in 0.5 L of a 20 M solution of $Ni(NO_3)_2$. What will be the molarity of solution at the end of electrolysis?

35 Calculate the emf for the given cell at 25°C.
$Cr|Cr^{3+}(0.1\text{ M})||Fe^{2+}(0.01\text{ M})|Fe$
[Given, $E^{\circ}_{Cr^{3+}/Cr} = -0.74$ V, $E^{\circ}(Fe^{2+}/Fe) = -0.44$ V]

36 Which of the following solutions has larger molar conductance?
(i) 0.08 M solution having conductivity equal to $2.0 \times 10^{-2} \Omega^{-1} cm^{-1}$.
(ii) 0.10 M solution having resistivity equal to $58\ \Omega$ cm.

37 Conductivity of two electrolytic solutions A and B each having a concentration of 0.1 M are 8.5×10^{-2} S cm^{-1} and 4.1×10^{-4} S cm^{-1} respectively. Which among the two offers less resistance to the flow of current ?

38 The Λ°_m values for NaCl and KCl are 126.5 and 149.9 Ω^{-1} cm^2 mol^{-1} respectively. The ionic conductance of Na^{+} at infinite dilution is 50.1 Ω^{-1}cm^2 mol^{-1}. Calculate the ionic conductance at infinite dilution for potassium ion (K^{+}).

39 Calculate the degree of dissociation of acetic acid at 298 K, given that
$\Lambda^{\circ}_{m\,(CH_3COOH)} = 11.7$ S cm^2 mol^{-1}
$\Lambda^{\circ}_{m\,(CH_3COO^{-})} = 40.9$ S cm^2 mol^{-1}
$\Lambda^{\circ}_{m\,(H^{+})} = 349.1$ S cm^2 mol^{-1}

40 A solution of $MgSO_4$ is electrolysed for 20 min with a current of 1.5 A. What mass of magnesium is deposited at the cathode?

41 In the electrolysis of aqueous sodium bromide, there are two possible anodic reactions.
$2H_2O(l) \longrightarrow O_2(g) + 4H^{+}(aq) + 4e^{-}, E^{\circ} = 1.23$ V
$2Br^{-}(aq) \longrightarrow Br_2(g) + 2e^{-}, E^{\circ} = 1.08$ V
Which reaction occurs at anode and why?

42 Explain why electrolysis of aqueous solution of NaCl gives H_2 at cathode and Cl_2 at anode? Write overall reaction.
Given, $E^{\circ}_{Na^{+}/Na} = -2.71$ V, $E^{\circ}_{H_2O/H_2} = -0.83$ V,
$E^{\circ}_{Cl_2/Cl^{-}} = +1.36$ V, $E^{\circ}_{H^{+}/H_2/H_2O} = +1.23$ V

43 What is a nickel-cadmium cell? State its one merit and one demerit over lead storage cell. Write the overall reaction that occurs during discharging of this cell.

44 Give an example of a fuel cell and write the cathode and anode reactions for it.

45 How is galvanisation different from cathodic protection of iron?

46 A lead-storage cell can act both as galvanic and electrolytic cells. Explain.

47 State and explain three methods of prevention of rusting of iron.

Short Answer Type II Questions

(3 Marks)

48 Calculate the standard cell potential at 25°C for the electrochemical cells, $Zn|Zn^{2+}||Cu^{2+}|Cu$, where the reference half-cell is
(i) SHE (ii) Ag/AgCl electrode.

49 Calculate the standard electrode potential of $Ni^{2+}|Ni$ electrode if emf of the cell, $Ni(s)|Ni^{2+}(0.01\ M)||Cu^{2+}(0.1\ M)|Cu(s)$ is 0.059 V. [Given, $E^{\circ}_{Cu^{2+}/Cu} = +0.34$ V]

50 A strip of nickel metal is placed in a 1 molar solution of $Ni(NO_3)_2$ and a strip of silver metal is placed in a one molar solution of $AgNO_3$. An electrochemical cell is created when the two solutions are connected by a salt bridge and the two strips are connected by wires to a voltmeter.

(i) Write the balanced equations for the overall reaction occurring in the cell

(ii) Calculate the cell potential, E, at 25° C for the cell, if the initial concentration of $Ni(NO_3)_2$ is 0.100 molar and the initial concentration of $AgNO_3$ is 1.00 molar.
[$E^{\circ}_{Ni^{2+}/Ni} = -0.25$ V, $E^{\circ}_{Ag^+/Ag} = 0.80$ V, $\log 10^{-1} = -1$]

51 Consider the following cell reaction;
$$2Fe(s) + O_2(g) + 4H^+(aq) \longrightarrow 2Fe^{2+}(aq) + 2H_2O(l);\ E^{\circ} = 1.67\ V$$
and $[Fe^{2+}] = 10^{-3}$ M, $p(O_2) = 0.1$ atm and pH = 3. What is the cell potential at 25°C?

52 Calculate the potential for half-cell containing 0.10 M $K_2Cr_2O_7(aq)$, 0.20 M $Cr^{3+}(aq)$ and 1.0×10^{-4} M $H^+(aq)$.

The half-cell reaction is
$$Cr_2O_7^{2-}(aq) + 14H^+(aq) + 6e^- \longrightarrow 2Cr^{3+}(aq) + 7H_2O(l)$$
and the standard electrode potential is given as $E^{\circ} = 1.33$ V.

53 One half-cell in a voltaic cell is constructed from a silver wire dipped in silver nitrate solution of unknown concentration. The other half-cell consists of a zinc electrode in a 0.10 M solution of $Zn(NO_3)_2$. A voltage of 1.48 V is measured for this cell. Use this information to calculate the concentration of silver nitrate solution.
[Given, $E^{\circ}_{Zn^{2+}/Zn} = -0.763$ V, $E^{\circ}_{Ag^+/Ag} = +0.80$V]

54 Degree of dissociation of pure water is 1.9×10^{-9}. Molar ionic conductances of H^+ ions and OH^- ions at infinite dilution are 200 S $cm^2\ mol^{-1}$ and 350 S $cm^2 mol^{-1}$ respectively. What is the molar conductance of water?

55 The molar conductivity (π_m) of KCl solutions, at different concentration at 298 K, is plotted as shown in the figure given below:

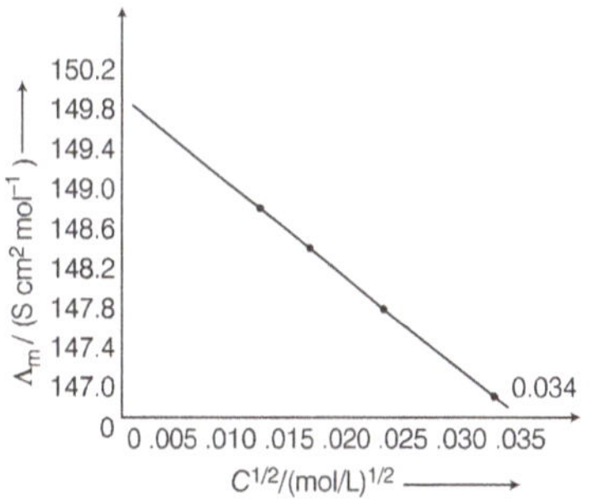

Determine the value of λ°_m and A for KCl.

56 How many molecules of chlorine should be deposited from molten sodium chloride in one minute by a current of 300 mA?

57 Electric current is passed through two cells A and B in series. Cell A contains aqueous solution of Ag_2SO_4 and platinum electrodes. Cell B contains aqueous solution of $CuSO_4$ and copper electrodes. The current is passed till 1.6 g of oxygen is liberated at the anode in cell A. Calculate the quantities of copper and silver deposited at the cathode of the two cells. [Atomic mass O = 16, Cu = 63.5, Ag = 108]

58 How many grams of silver could be plated out on a serving tray by electrolysis of a solution containing silver in +1 oxidation state for a period of 8.0 h at a current of 8.46 A ? What is the area of the tray, if the thickness of the silver plating is 0.00254 cm ? Density of silver is 10.5 g/cm^3.

59 (i) Calculate the strength of the current required to deposit 1.2 g of magnesium from molten $MgCl_2$ in 1 h.
[1 F = 96500 C mol^{-1}, atomic mass of Mg = 24.0]

(ii) An electric current of 0.15 A is passed through 500 mL of 0.15 M copper sulphate solution. How much time is required to deposit all the copper?

60 In the process of electrolysis of CrO_3, the following reaction occurs.
$$CrO_3(aq) + 6H^+ + 6e^- \longrightarrow Cr(s) + 3H_2O$$
Calculate

(i) amount of chromium deposited when 24,000 C of charge passed.

(ii) time required to deposit 1.5 g chromium using 12.5 A current. (Atomic mass of (Cr = 52))

61 Calculate the standard free energy change taking place in H_2-O_2 fuel cell in which the following reactions occur.

(i) $O_2 + 4H^+ + 4e^- \longrightarrow 2H_2O;\ E^{\circ} = 1.229$ V

(ii) $2H_2 \longrightarrow 4H^+ + 4e^-;\ E^{\circ} = 0.000$ V

62 Give the half-cell and net reactions in the following batteries.

(i) Leclanche cell

(ii) Nickel-cadmium battery

(iii) Lithium-manganese dioxide cell

Long Answer Type Questions

5 Marks

63 (i) Calculate the equilibrium constant for the reaction.

$$2Fe^{3+} + 3I^- \rightleftharpoons 2Fe^{2+} + I_3^-$$

The standard reduction potential in acidic condition is 0.78V and 0.54 V, respectively, for Fe^{3+}/Fe^{2+} and I_3^-/I couples.

(ii) From the following molar conductivities at infinite dilution :

Λ°_m for $Ba(OH)_2 = 457.6 \Omega^{-1}cm^2mol^{-1}$

Λ°_m for $BaCl_2 = 240.6 \Omega^{-1}cm^2mol^{-1}$

Λ°_m for $NH_4Cl = 129.8 \Omega^{-1}cm^2mol^{-1}$

Calculate Λ°_m for NH_4OH.

64 Write the Nernst equation and emf of the following cells at 298 K.

(i) $Sn(s)|Sn^{2+}(0.050M)||H^+(0.020M)|H_2(g, 1bar)|Pt(s)$

(ii) $Pt(s)|Br_2(l)|Br^-(0.010M)||H^+(0.030M)|H_2(s, 1bar)|Pt(s)$

65 The following curve is obtained when molar conductivity, Λ_m is plotted against the square root of concentration, $C^{1/2}$ along y and x-axis respectively for the two electrolytes X and Y.

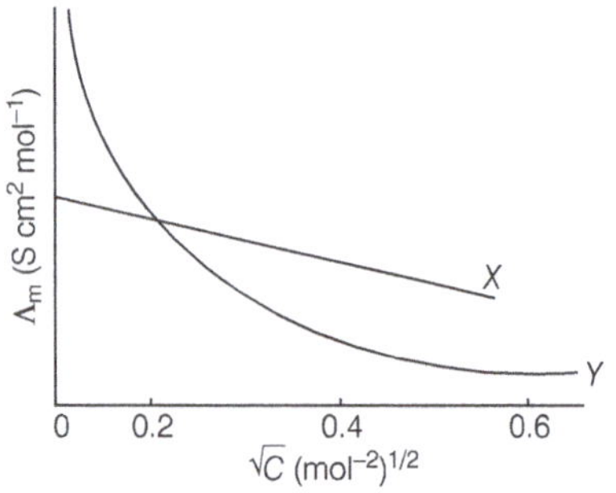

(i) What can you say about the nature of these two electrolytes?

(ii) Account for the increase in Λ_m for the electrolytes X and Y with dilution.

(iii) Determine Λ^∞_m for these electrolytes.

66 Discuss the products obtained in

(i) electrolysis of aqueous solution of brine.

(ii) electrolysis of sulphuric acid.

67 (i) How much time is required for 1.5 g Ag to deposit when 1.50 A current is passed through an electrolytic cell containing $AgNO_3$ solution with inert electrodes?

(ii) A current of 1.70 A is passed through 300.0 mL of 0.160 M solution of $ZnSO_4$ for 230 s with a current efficiency of 90 per cent. Find out the molarity of Zn^{2+} after the deposition of zinc. Assume the volume of the solution to remain constant during electrolysis.

68 (i) Two electrolytic cells containing silver nitrate solution and dilute sulphuric acid were connected in a series. A steady current of 2.5 A was passed through them till 1.078 g of silver was deposited (Ag = 107.8 g/mol)

(a) How much electricity was consumed?

(b) What is the weight of oxygen gas liberated during the reaction?

(ii) How many moles of Hg will be produced by electrolysing 1.0 M $Hg(NO_3)_2$ solution with a current of 2.00 A for 3 hours? [$Hg(NO_3)_2 = 200.6$ g / mol]

69 Iron may be protected from rusting by coating with zinc or tin. By referring to the data given below, explain why zinc protects iron more effectively than tin?

$Zn^{2+} + 2e^- \longrightarrow Zn$; $E° = -0.76$ V

$Fe^{2+} + 2e^- \longrightarrow Fe$; $E° = -0.44$ V

$Sn^{2+} + 2e^- \longrightarrow Sn$; $E° = -0.14$ V

70 (i) Why hydrogen is considered as a fuel resource for future?

(ii) How can we generate energy from hydrogen fuel?

(iii) Why do we need to reduce our usage of carbonaceous fuels?

71 (i) Write the chemistry of discharging the Leclanche cell, highlighting all the materials that are involved during cell reactions. State its use.

(ii) What is the difference between primary and secondary cells? Differentiate using their applications also.

(iii) Prevention of corrosion is of prime importance. Comment.

Answers

1 (i) Siemens (S)
(ii) decreases
(iii) dilution
(iv) rusting, galvanisation

2 (i) →c, (ii) → d, (iii) → a, (iv) → b, (v) → a

3 (c) A → (iii), B → (i), C → (ii)

4 When $E_{ext} > E_{cell}$

5 No.

6 Negative $E°$ means that the redox couple is stronger reducing agent than H^+/H_2.

7 Inter-ionic attraction, polarity of a solvent, viscosity, temperature and concentration.

8 Charge on ions, size of the ions in which they dissociate and concentration of ions.

9 [**Ans.** $S = 1.67 \times 10^{-5}$ mol L^{-1}]

10 $E = \frac{F}{N_A} = \frac{96500 \text{ C mol}^{-1}}{6.022 \times 10^{23} \text{mol}^{-1}} = 1.6 \times 10^{-19} \text{C}$

11 When aqueous NaCl solution is electrolysed, H_2 is liberated at cathode, Cl_2 at anode and NaOH is formed in the solution. Hence, pH of solution will rise.

12 A primary battery or cell is a device in which reactions occurs only once and after use (over a period of time), battery becomes dead and can not be reused, e.g. mercury cell.

13 For a battery to be of practical use it should be resonably light, compact and its voltage should not vary appreciably during its use.

14 **Uses of mercury cell** It is suitable for low current devices like hearing aids, watches, etc.

15 Nickel-cadmium battery has longer life span than the lead storage cell.

16 H_2-O_2 fuel cell run continuously as long as the reactions are supplied to it and products are removed continuously.

17 For $M^{n+}(aq) + ne^- \longrightarrow M(s)$

$$E_{M^{n+}/M} = E°_{M^{n+}/M} - \frac{RT}{nF} \ln \frac{1}{[M^{n+}]}$$

18 Fuel cell is highly efficient (70%) method when compared to the efficiency of thermal power plants (40%) that is a major source of pollution. Fuel cell have been used in automobiles on an experimental basis. H_2 - O_2 fuel cell was used for providing electrical power in Apollo space programme.

19 Cr,Sn or Zn.

20 $E°_{cell} = \frac{2.303\ RT}{nF} \log K_C$.

21 A cell becomes dead after a long time, even if it has not been used because the acidic NH_4Cl corrodes the zinc container.

22 (c) For reaction to be spontaneous, E_{cell} should have a positive value. This is true only when $E_{cathode} > E_{anode}$.

23 (a) Both (A) and (R) are correct and (R) is the correct explanation of (A).

24 (c) Mercury cell gives the constant voltage throughout its life because the overall reaction does not involve any ion in the solution, concentration of which changes during its whole life. Thus, (A) is correct but (R) is incorrect.

25 (a) Both (A) and (R) are correct and (R) is the correct explanation for (A).

When a solution contains both H^+ and Na^+ ions, H^+ ions are reduced first because $E°$ for hydrogen is 0V which is higher than $E°_{(Na^+)}° = -2.71$ V.

26 (a) Both (A) and (R) are correct and (R) is the correct explanation for (A).

27 (i) More the negative value of standard reduction potential, stronger will be the reducing strength (ability).
Hence, the correct order will be $y > z > x$.
(ii) $E°$ for Cr is more negative than that of Fe. Thus, Fe gets reduced and Cr gets oxidised which means Fe is a stronger oxidising agent.
(iii) Zinc lies above hydrogen, whereas silver lies below hydrogen in the electrochemical series. Thus, zinc being more reactive, reacts with dilute hydrochloric acid but silver cannot.

28 (i) Chromium is a corrosion-resistant metal which forms layer on iron.
(ii) Iron will corrode faster than tin as the oxidation potential of iron is more than that of tin.
(iii) The presence of Na^+ and Cl^- ions in saline water increases the conductance of the solution in contact with metal surface.
Consequently this accelerates the formation of Fe^{2+} ions and causes rusting.

29 $E_{cell} = E°_{H^+/H_2} - E°_{Fe^{2+}/Fe}$

$$E_{cell} = E°_{cell} - \frac{0.0591}{n} \log \frac{[Fe^{2+}]}{[H^+]^2}$$

30 [**Ans.** $C = 8.89 \times 10^{-4}$ mol^{-1}]

31 (i) Refer to text on pages 54 and 55.
(Topic-1, Electrochemical series and its applications)
(ii) It is not possible to measure the absolute potential of a single electrode because neither the oxidation nor the reduction reaction can ocear by itself.

32 **Oxidation half cell reaction**

$$Zn(s) \longrightarrow Zn^{2+}(aq) + 2e^-$$

Reduction half cell reaction

$$2H^+_{(aq)} + 2e^- \longrightarrow H_2(g)$$

pH = 8.6

33 [**Ans.** $K = 10^{10}$]

34 [**Ans.** $M = 1.172$ M]

35 Refer to solved example 5 on pages 57 and 58.

36 (i) $\Lambda_m = 250\,\Omega^{-1}\text{cm}^2\text{mol}^{-1}$

(ii) $\Lambda_m = 172.4\,\Omega^{-1}\ \text{cm}^2\text{mol}^{-1}$

Thus, solution (i) has larger molar conductance

37 $\kappa \propto \frac{1}{R}$

Hence, B will offer greater resistance.

38 **Ans.** $\Omega^{\circ}_{\kappa^+} = 73.5\,\Omega^{-1}\ \text{cm}^2\ \text{mol}^{-1}$

39 Refer to solved example 3 on pages 69.

40 Refer to solved example 1 on page 75.

41 Refer to text on pages 75-76 [Topic-3, Some important examples of electrolysis].

42 Refer to text on pages 75-76 [Topic-3, Some important examples of electrolysis].

43 Refer to text on page 82 [Topic-4, N- battery].

44 Refer to text on pages 82-83 [Topic-4, Fuel cell].

45 Refer to text on page 83 [Topic-4, Corrosion].

46 Refer to text on pages 82 [Topic-4, Lead storage battery].

47 Refer to text on page 83 [Topic-4, Corrosion].

48 [**Ans.** (i) 0.76 V, 0.34 V (ii) 0.98 V, 0.12 V]

49 [**Ans.** 0.31 V]

50 (i) $\text{Ni}(s) + 2\text{Ag}^+(aq) \rightarrow \text{Ni}^{2+}(aq) + 2\text{Ag}(s)$

(ii) $E_{\text{cell}} = 1.0795$ V

51 [**Ans.** 1.57 V]

52 [**Ans.** $E_{\text{cell}} = 0.78$ V]

53 [**Ans.** $= 1.24 \times 10^{-2}$ M]

54 [**Ans.** 1.045×10^{-6} S cm^2 mol^{-1}

$A = 87.46\,\Omega^{-1}\ \text{cm}^2\ \text{mol}^{-1}/\text{mol}/\text{L}^{-1}]^{1/2}$

55 [**Ans.** $\lambda^{\circ}_m = 149.8\ \text{S}^{-1}\ \text{cm}^2\ \text{mol}^{-1}$]

For value of A use, $\Lambda_m = \Lambda^{\circ}_m - A\sqrt{C}$

56 [**Ans.** 5.616×10^{19} molecules]

57 [**Ans.** Ag = 21.6 g, Cu = 6.35 g]

58 [**Ans.** : Area of the tray, 1.02×10^4 cm^2]

59 (i) [$i = 1.34$ A]

(ii) $t = 33.687$

60 (i) 2.15 g

(ii) **Hint** [Use $\Rightarrow W = Zit$]

61 [**Ans.** – 474.4 kJ]

62 (i) Refer to text on page 81. (Topic-4 Leclanche cell).

(ii) Refer to text on page 82 (Topic 4, Nickel-cadmium battery).

(iii) **At anode** $\text{Li}(s) \longrightarrow \text{Li}^+ + e^-$

At cathode $\text{MnO}_2(s) + \text{Li}^+ + e^- \longrightarrow \text{LiMnO}_2(s)$

63 (i) [**Hint** $E^{\circ}_{\text{cell}} = \frac{0.0591}{n} \log K$] [**Ans.** $K_{\text{eq}} = 10^8$]

(ii) 283.35 cm^{2}mol^{-1}

64 For (i), (iii) Refer to text on page 55 (Topic-1, Nernst equation).

65 Refer to text on page 67 (Topic 2, Variation of conductivity with concentration).

66 Refer to text on pages 75-76 [Topic-3, Some important examples of electrolysis].

67 (i) Refer to solution 59 (ii).

(ii) [**Ans.** 0.154 M]

68 (i) (a) [**Ans.** 965 C]

(b) [**Ans.** 0.16 g]

(ii) $\text{Hg}^{2+} + 2e^- \longrightarrow \text{Hg}$

Quantity of electricity $= i.t$

$= 2\ \text{A} \times 3 \times 60 \times 60 = 21600$ C

2×96500 C of electricity produce mercury = 1 mol

21600 C of electricity will produce mercury

$= \frac{1}{2 \times 96500} \times 21600 = 0.112$ mol

69 Refer to text on pages 83-84 [Topic-4, Prevention of corrosion].

70 (i), (ii) Refer to text on page 82 [Topic-4, Fuel cell].

(iii) **Hint** Causes pollution

71 (i) Refer to text on page 81 (Primary battery).

(ii) Refer to text on pages 81-82 (Primary and secondary battery).

(iii) Refer to text on pages 83-84 (Prevention of corrosion).

CHAPTER

03

Chemical Kinetics

The word kinetics is derived from the Greek word '*kinesis*' meaning movement. **Chemical kinetics** is the branch of chemistry which deals with the study of the chemical reactions with respect to the reaction rates, the factors affecting the rate of reactions and the mechanism by which the reactions proceed.

- Rate of Chemical Reaction, Rate Equation and Rate Constant
- Molecularity and order of a Chemical Reaction
- Integrated Rate Equations
- Temperature Dependence of the Rate of a Reaction

TOPIC 01 Rate of Chemical Reaction,Rate Equation and Rate Constant

Chemical Reactions

When one or more substances undergo a change which results in the formation of a new product, it is called **chemical reaction.**

On the basis of their speeds, chemical reactions are of three types which are as follows :

(i) **Very Fast Reactions** Some reactions (such as ionic reactions) occur very fast. It is practically impossible to measure the speed of such reactions, e.g. precipitation of AgCl from $AgNO_3$ and NaCl.

(ii) **Very Slow Reactions** Some reactions are very slow and here the speed of reaction is so slow that again it is not possible to measure the speed of such reactions, e.g. rusting of iron in the presence of air and moisture.

(iii) **Moderately Slow Reactions** These type of reactions proceed with a measurable speed at room temperature. Thus, these reactions are utilised in the study of chemical kinetics, e.g. inversion of cane sugar and hydrolysis of starch.

Reason for Difference in Rate of Chemical Reactions

A chemical reactions involve breaking and formation of bonds. Therefore, different bonds require different amount of energy for breaking and different amount of energy is evolved during bond formation. Thus, the rates of different reactions are different. Thus, ionic reactions are instantaneous because no bonds are to be broken in case of these reactions.

On the other hand, molecular reactions are very slow because they require the breaking of strong covalent bonds.

Note Reactions involving ionic species are very fast reactions. Ionic reactions generally occur in 10^{-12} to 10^{-16}s.

Rate of a Chemical Reaction

The speed or the rate of a chemical reaction can be defined as the change in concentration of reactants or products per unit time. It can be expressed in terms of

(i) the rate of decrease in concentration of any one of the reactants, or

(ii) the rate of increase in concentration of any one of the products.

Consider a simple hypothetical reaction, assuming that the volume of the system remains constant such that one mole of the reactant R produces one mole of the product P,

$$R \longrightarrow P$$

If $[R]_1$ and $[P]_1$ are the concentrations of reactant, R and product, P respectively at time t_1 and $[R]_2$ and $[P]_2$ are the concentrations at time t_2, then

$$\Delta t = t_2 - t_1$$

$$\Delta R = [R]_2 - [R]_1 \text{ or } \Delta P = [P]_2 - [P]_1$$

(Here, the square brackets are used to express molar concentration.)

Rate of disappearance of R

$$= \frac{\text{Decrease in concentration of } R}{\text{Time taken}} = -\frac{\Delta[R]}{\Delta t} \quad \ldots\text{(i)}$$

Rate of appearance of P

$$= \frac{\text{Increase in concentration of } P}{\text{Time taken}} = +\frac{\Delta[P]}{\Delta t} \quad \ldots\text{(ii)}$$

Since, $\Delta[R]$ is a negative quantity (as concentration of reactant is decreasing), it is multiplied by –1 to make the rate of the reaction a positive quantity as rate is always a positive quantity.

Note Symbol Δ is used for larger change and symbol 'd' is used for smaller change.

Units of rate of reaction mol $L^{-1}s^{-1}$ or atm s^{-1}.

Average Rate of Reaction

If the rate of appearance of products or disappearance of reactants comprises over a long interval of time then it is expressed as **average rate of reaction**, r_{av}.

$$\therefore \quad r_{av} = -\frac{\Delta[R]}{\Delta t} \quad \ldots\text{(i)}$$

$$= +\frac{\Delta[P]}{\Delta t} \quad \ldots\text{(ii)}$$

Eqs. (i) and (ii) represent the average rate of a reaction (r_{av}), which depends upon the change in concentration of reactants or products and the time taken for that change to occur. e.g.

For the reaction,

$$PCl_5(g) \longrightarrow PCl_3(g) + Cl_2(g)$$

Rate may be expressed as :

$$r_{av} = -\frac{\Delta[PCl_5]}{\Delta t} = \frac{\Delta[PCl_3]}{\Delta t} = \frac{\Delta[Cl_2]}{\Delta t}$$

Instantaneous Rate of Reaction

The concentration of reactants goes on decreasing with time, therefore, the rate of a reaction does not remain constant throughout the reaction process. In other words, rate of a reaction may be expressed at a particular moment of time. Such a reaction rate is called **instantaneous rate of reaction** (r_{inst}). It is expressed as

$$\therefore \quad r_{inst} = -\frac{d[R]}{dt} = \frac{d[P]}{dt}$$

As $\Delta t \rightarrow 0$, Instantaneous rate = Average rate

e.g. For the reaction,

$$2NO(g) + O_2(g) \longrightarrow 2NO_2(g)$$

Rate is given by

$$r_{inst} = \frac{-1}{2}\frac{d[NO]}{dt} = \frac{-d[O_2]}{dt} = \frac{+1}{2}\frac{d[NO_2]}{dt}$$

Graphically Determination of Rate of a Reaction

Rate of a reaction can be determined from the slope of the graph between the concentration of any of the reactants or products and time as given below:

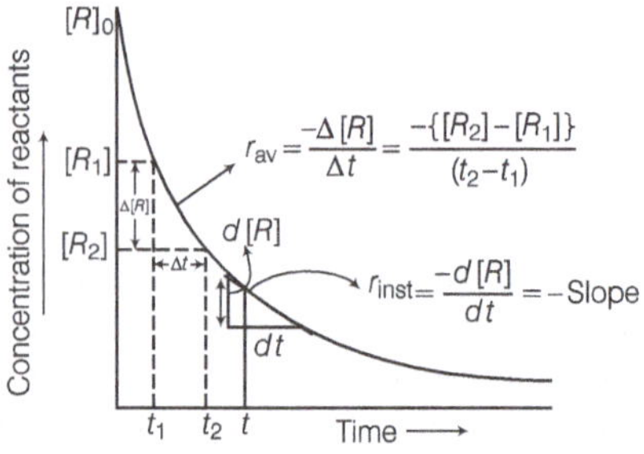

(a)

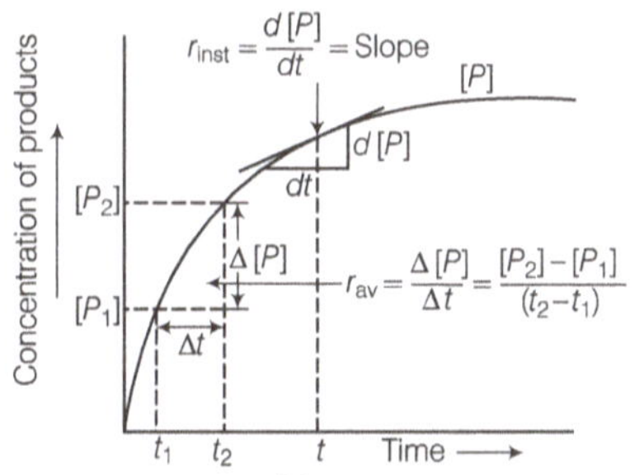

(b)

Determination of instantaneous and average rate of a reaction

e.g. Consider the following reaction,

$$C_4H_9Cl + H_2O \longrightarrow C_4H_9OH + HCl$$

during different intervals of time.

t/s	$[C_4H_9Cl]$/mol L^{-1}
0	0.100
50	0.0905
100	0.0820
150	0.0741
200	0.0671
300	0.0549
400	0.0439
700	0.0210
800	0.017

Its instantaneous rate can be find out by using following graphical method.

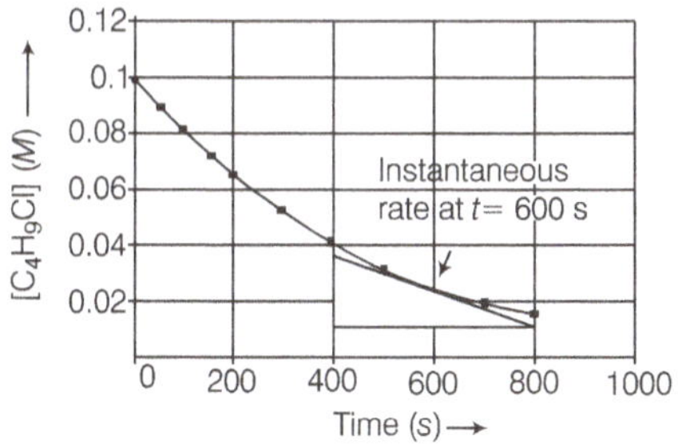

Instantaneous rate of hydrolysis of butyl chloride (C_4H_9Cl)

Determination of instantaneous rate graphically is done by drawing a tangent at time t on either of the curves for concentration of R and P *vs* time t and calculating its slope (figure). If we plot a graph of concentration of butyl chloride as a function of time and if, we draw a tangent that touches the curve at $t = 600$ s, then the slope of this tangent gives the instantaneous rate. In the above example, at $t = 600$ s,

$$r_{inst} = -\frac{d[R]}{dt} = -\left(\frac{0.0165 - 0.037}{(800-400)\,s}\right) \text{mol L}^{-1}$$

$$= 5.12 \times 10^{-5} \text{ mol L}^{-1}\text{s}^{-1}$$

Similarly,

at $t = 250$ s, $r_{inst} = 1.22 \times 10^{-4}$ mol $L^{-1}s^{-1}$

$t = 350$ s, $r_{inst} = 1.0 \times 10^{-4}$ mol $L^{-1}s^{-1}$

$t = 450$ s, $r_{inst} = 6.4 \times 10^{-5}$ mol $L^{-1}s^{-1}$

Example 1 For the reaction, $2A \longrightarrow$ products, the concentration of A decreases from 0.5 mol L^{-1} to 0.4 mol L^{-1} in 10 min. Calculate the rate during the interval. **NCERT Intext**

Sol. Rate of reaction = Rate of disappearance of A

$$= -\frac{1}{2}\frac{\Delta[A]}{\Delta t} = -\frac{1}{2}\frac{(0.4-0.5) \text{ mol L}^{-1}}{10 \text{ min}}$$

$$= 0.005 \text{ mol L}^{-1}\text{min}^{-1}$$

Example 2 For the reaction, $R \longrightarrow P$, the concentration of a reactant changes from 0.03 M to 0.02 M in 25 min. Calculate the average rate of reaction using units of time both in minutes and seconds. **NCERT Intext**

> Average rate of reaction = Rate of change of $[R]$ or $[P]$
> $= \dfrac{\text{Change in concentration of } [R] \text{ or } [P]}{\text{Time taken}}$

Sol. For the reaction, $R \longrightarrow P$

Average rate of reaction

$$= \frac{\text{Change in concentration of reactant/product}}{\text{Time taken}}$$

$$= -\frac{\Delta[R]}{\Delta t} = -\frac{\{[R_2]-[R_1]\}}{t_2 - t_1} = -\frac{(0.02-0.03) \text{ M}}{25 \text{ min}}$$

$$= \frac{0.01 \text{ M}}{25 \text{ min}} = 4 \times 10^{-4} \text{ mol L}^{-1}\text{min}^{-1}$$

Converting unit of time in seconds

$$\frac{4 \times 10^{-4}}{60} \text{mol L}^{-1}\text{s}^{-1} = 6.66 \times 10^{-6} \text{ mol L}^{-1}\text{ s}^{-1}$$

Example 3 The decomposition of N_2O_5 in CCl_4 at 318 K has been studied by monitoring the concentration of N_2O_5 in the solution. Initially the concentration of N_2O_5 is 2.33 mol L^{-1} and after 184 minutes, it is reduced to 2.08 mol L^{-1}. The reaction takes place according to the equation

$$2N_2O_5(g) \longrightarrow 4NO_2(g) + O_2(g)$$

Calculate the average rate of this reaction in terms of hours, minutes and seconds. What is the rate of production of NO_2 during this period? **NCERT Intext**

Sol. Average range $= \frac{1}{2}\left\{-\frac{\Delta[N_2O_5]}{\Delta t}\right\}$

$$= -\frac{1}{2}\left[\frac{(2.08 - 2.33)\ \text{mol L}^{-1}}{184\ \text{min}}\right]$$

$$= 6.79 \times 10^{-4}\ \text{mol L}^{-1}/\text{min}$$

$$= (6.79 \times 10^{-4}\ \text{mol L}^{-1}\ \text{min}^{-1}) \times (60\ \text{min}/1\text{h})$$

$$= 4.07 \times 10^{-2}\ \text{mol L}^{-1}/\text{h}$$

$$= 6.79 \times 10^{-4}\ \text{mol L}^{-1} \times 1\ \text{min}/60\text{s}$$

$$= 1.13 \times 10^{-5}\ \text{mol L}^{-1}\text{s}^{-1}$$

According the given equation,

$$\text{Rate} = \frac{1}{4}\left\{\frac{\Delta[NO_2]}{\Delta t}\right\}$$

$$\frac{\Delta[NO_2]}{\Delta t} = 6.79 \times 10^{-4} \times 4\ \text{mol L}^{-1}\ \text{min}^{-1}$$

$$= 2.72 \times 10^{-3}\ \text{mol L}^{-1}\ \text{min}^{-1}$$

Factors Influencing Rate of a Reaction

Rate of a chemical reaction depends upon the experimental conditions like concentration of one or more reactants (pressure in case of gases), temperature, catalyst and surface area of the reactants.

(i) **Concentration of Reactants** Reactions occur with greater speed when concentration of the reactants is increased. Conversely, reaction rate decreases as the concentrations of the reactants decrease.

(ii) **Temperature** Reaction rates are normally favoured by increase of temperature.

(iii) **Catalyst** A catalyst alters the speed of reaction. It helps to attain the equilibrium quickly. It participates in the reaction without being consumed. (we will discuss in detail later in this chapter.)

(iv) **Surface Area of the Reactants** Smaller the particle size, greater the surface area and faster is the reaction.

(v) **Nature of the Reactants and the Products** Rates of reactions are influenced by the nature of reactants and products. The reactivity of a substance depends on the ease with which the specific bonds are broken or formed. e.g. The oxidation of nitric oxide to nitrogen dioxide takes place considerably faster while oxidation of CO to CO_2 takes place slowly.

(vi) **Presence of Light or Radiation** Rate of reaction increased by the use of certain radiations. The photons of these radiations having frequencies (ν) possess sufficient energies ($E = h\nu$) to break certain bonds in reactants. For, e.g. some reactions do not takes place in the dark rather they require light for their initiations.

e.g. $$H_2 + Cl_2 \xrightarrow{h\nu} 2HCl$$

Such reactions are called "**photochemical reactions**".

Dependence of Rate of a Reaction on the Concentration of Reactants

As we have already discussed that with increase in concentration of reactants, the rate of reaction increases. This shows that there must be a quantitative relation between concentration of reactants and the rate of a reaction.

Law of Mass Action

A generalisation in regard of quantitative dependence of reaction on the concentration of reactants was put forward as law of mass action by chemists **Guldberg** and **Waage** in 1867.

According to this law, at constant temperature, the rate of a chemical reaction is directly proportional to the product of active masses of reacting species, with each active mass term raised to the power equal to the stoichiometric coefficient of that species in the chemical reaction.

e.g. For a general reaction, $aA + bB \longrightarrow \text{Products}$

Rate of reaction $\propto [A]^a\,[B]^b$, where $[A]$ and $[B]$ are active masses of reactants A and B respectively.

Active mass of a substance in the solution or gas phase is equal to its molar concentration.

Unit of active mass : g mol L^{-1}

Rate Equation

Rate of a chemical reaction at a given temperature may depend on the concentration of reactants and products. The representation of rate of reaction in terms of concentration of the reactants is called the **rate law, rate equation** or **rate expression.**

Consider a general reaction,

$$aA + bB \longrightarrow cC + dD$$

where, a, b, c and d are the stoichiometric coefficients of reactants and products.

The rate expression for the above reaction is

$$\text{Rate} \propto [A]^x[B]^y$$

where, exponents x and y are determined experimentally and may or may not be equal to the stoichiometric coefficients (a and b) of the reactants. Above equation can also be written as:

$$\text{Rate} = k[A]^x[B]^y$$

$$-\frac{d[R]}{dt} = k[A]^x[B]^y$$

This form of equation is known as **differential rate equation**, where k is the proportionality constant called **rate constant**. Rate law for a chemical reaction cannot be decided from the balanced chemical equation. i.e. theoretically. It has to be determined experimentally e.g.

$$2NO(g) + O_2(g) \longrightarrow 2NO_2(g), \text{ Rate} = k[NO]^2[O_2]$$

$$CHCl_3 + Cl_2 \longrightarrow CCl_4 + HCl,$$

$$\text{Rate} = k[CHCl_3][Cl_2]^{1/2}$$

In the former reaction, the exponents of the concentration terms are same as their stoichiometric coefficients. On the other hand, in latter reaction, the exponents of the concentration terms are not same as their stoichiometric coefficients.

Rate Constant (Specific Reaction Rate)

From the rate equation, when concentration of all the reactants is unity, then

$$\boxed{\text{Rate} = k}$$

where, k is called the **rate constant.**

Hence, rate constant can be defined as the **rate of chemical reaction** when concentration of each reactant is unity. Thus, the rate constant is also called the **specific rate of reaction.**

Characteristics of Rate Constant

(i) Rate constant is a measure of the rate of reaction. Greater the value of the rate constant, faster is the reaction.

(ii) Each reaction has a definite value of the rate constant at a particular temperature and its value for the same reaction changes with change in temperature.

(iii) Its value does not depend upon the concentrations of the reactants.

(iv) The unit of rate constant depends upon the order of the reaction.

Example 4 The following results have been obtained during the kinetic studies of the reaction,

$$2A + B \longrightarrow C + D.$$

NCERT

Exp.	[A] / mol L^{-1}	[B] / mol L^{-1}	Initial rate of formation of [D] / mol L^{-1} min^{-1}
1.	0.1	0.1	6.0×10^{-3}
2.	0.3	0.2	7.2×10^{-2}
3.	0.3	0.4	2.88×10^{-1}
4.	0.4	0.1	2.40×10^{-2}

Determine the rate law and the rate constant for the reaction.

Sol. Rate law may be expressed as :

$$\text{Rate} = k[A]^x[B]^y$$

$$(\text{Rate})_1 = 6.0 \times 10^{-3} = k(0.1)^x(0.1)^y \quad \text{...(i)}$$

$$(\text{Rate})_2 = 7.2 \times 10^{-2} = k(0.3)^x(0.2)^y \quad \text{...(ii)}$$

$$(\text{Rate})_3 = 2.88 \times 10^{-1} = k(0.3)^x(0.4)^y \quad \text{...(iii)}$$

$$(\text{Rate})_4 = 2.40 \times 10^{-2} = k(0.4)^x(0.1)^y \quad \text{...(iv)}$$

$$\frac{(\text{Rate})_1}{(\text{Rate})_4} = \frac{6.0 \times 10^{-3}}{2.40 \times 10^{-2}} = \frac{k(0.1)^x(0.1)^y}{k(0.4)^x(0.1)^y}$$

or $$\frac{1}{4} = \frac{(0.1)^x}{(0.4)^x} = \left(\frac{1}{4}\right)^x$$

$\therefore$ $x = 1$

$$\frac{(\text{Rate})_2}{(\text{Rate})_3} = \frac{7.2 \times 10^{-2}}{2.88 \times 10^{-1}} = \frac{k(0.3)^x(0.2)^y}{k(0.3)^x(0.4)^y}$$

or $$\frac{1}{4} = \frac{(0.2)^y}{(0.4)^y} = \left(\frac{1}{2}\right)^y$$

$\therefore$ $y = 2$

Now, rate law expression is given by

$$\text{Rate} = k[A][B]^2$$

Rate constant, k can be determined by placing the values of A, B and rate of formation of D. By taking the values from any experiment, say experiment 2.

$$\text{Rate} = k[A][B]^2$$

$$k = \frac{\text{Rate}}{[A][B]^2} = \frac{7.2 \times 10^{-2} \text{ mol L}^{-1}\text{ min}^{-1}}{(0.3 \text{ mol L}^{-1})(0.2 \text{ mol L}^{-1})^2}$$

or $k = 6.0 \text{ mol}^{-2}\text{ L}^2\text{min}^{-1}$

Topic Practice 1

Very Short Answer Type Questions

1 Mark

1. Fill in the Blanks

(i) Rates of reactions are influenced by the nature of .... and ....

(ii) .... the particle size, greater the surface area and .... is the reaction.

(iii) Active mass of a substance in the solution or gas phase is .... to its molar concentration.

(iv) Rate constant is a .... of the rate of reaction.

(v) Rate constant does not depend upon the .... of the reactants.

2. Objective Type Questions

(i) Rate of which of the following reactions can be determined easily?

(a) Rusting of iron in the presence of air and moisture
(b) Hydrolysis of starch
(c) Reaction of silver nitrate with sodium chloride
(d) All of the above

(ii) For the reaction,

$$5Br^- + BrO_3^- + 6H^+ \longrightarrow 3Br_2 + 3H_2O$$

if $-\frac{d[Br^-]}{dt} = k_1[Br^-], -\frac{d[BrO_3^-]}{dt} = k_2[Br^-],$

$\frac{d[Br_2]}{dt} = k_3[Br^-]$ then k_1, k_2 and k_3 are related as :

(a) $k_1 = 5k_2 = 1.66k_3$ (b) $3k_1 = k_2 = 5k_3$
(c) $5k_1 = 3k_2 = k_3$ (d) $k_1 = k_2 = k_3$

(iii) During a chemical reaction with increase in time, rate of a reaction

(a) decreases
(b) increases
(c) remains constant
(d) show irregular trends

(iv) The correct statement among the following is

(a) square brackets in the expression $\Delta[R]$ shows the equivalent concentration
(b) units of rate of reaction are concentration time^{-1}
(c) units of rate in terms of partial pressure is atmosphere L^{-1}
(d) rate at a given time interval is called instantaneous rate

(v) For the reaction,

$$Hg(l) + Cl_2(g) \longrightarrow HgCl_2(s)$$

The rate of reaction is given as :

(a) $\frac{\Delta[HgCl_2]}{\Delta t}$ (b) $-\frac{\Delta[Hg]}{\Delta t}$
(c) $-\frac{\Delta[Cl_2]}{\Delta t}$ (d) Either (a) or (b) or (c)

3. Match the following Columns and choose the correct option using the codes given below:

Column I	Column II
A. Very fast reaction	(i) Rusting of iron in the presence of air and moisture.
B. Very slow reaction	(ii) Precipitation of AgCl from $AgNO_3$ and NaCl.
C. Moderately slow reaction	(iii) Inversion of cane sugar.

Codes

(a) A-(ii), B-(i), C-(iii) (b) A-(i), B-(ii), C-(iii)
(c) A-(iii), B-(ii), C-(i) (d) A-(i), B-(iii), C-(ii)

4. Why does the rate of any reaction generally decreases during the course of the reaction? NCERT Exemplar

5. For the reaction, $2N_2O_5(g) \longrightarrow 4NO_2(g) + O_2(g)$, the rate of formation of $NO_2(g)$ is $2.8 \times 10^{-3} Ms^{-1}$. Calculate the rate of disappearance of $N_2O_5(g)$.

Short Answer Type I Questions

2 Marks

6. How can you determine the rate law of the following reaction? NCERT Exemplar

$$2NO(g) + O_2(g) \longrightarrow 2NO_2(g)$$

7. For the reaction, $2A + B \longrightarrow A_2B$; The rate $= k[A][B]^2$ with $k = 2.0 \times 10^{-6} mol^{-2} L^2 s^{-1}$. Calculate the initial rate of reaction when $[A] = 0.1$ mol L^{-1}, $[B] = 0.2$ mol L^{-1}. Calculate the rate of reaction after $[A]$ is reduced to 0.06 mol L^{-1}. NCERT

8. For the reaction $A + B \rightarrow C + D$, the initial rate for different reactions and initial concentration of reactants are given below: [2]

S.No.	Initial conc.		Initial rate ($mol\ L^{-1}\ s^{-1}$)
	$[A]$ mol L^{-1}	$[B]$ mol L^{-1}	
1	1.0	1.0	2×10^{-3}
2	2.0	1.0	4×10^{-3}
3	4.0	1.0	8×10^{-3}
4	1.0	2.0	2×10^{-3}
5	1.0	4.0	2×10^{-3}

(i) What is the overall order of reaction?
(ii) Write the rate law equation. ISC 2019

Short Answer Type II Questions
(3 Marks)

9. For the reaction, $2NO(g) + Cl_2(g) \longrightarrow 2NOCl(g)$

The following data were collected. All the measurements were taken at 263 K.

Exp. No.	Initial [NO] (M)	Initial $[Cl_2]$ (M)	Initial rate of disappearance of Cl_2 (M/min)
1.	0.15	0.15	0.60
2.	0.15	0.30	1.20
3.	0.30	0.15	2.40
4.	0.25	0.25	?

(i) Write the expression for rate law.
(ii) Calculate the value of rate constant and specify its units.
(iii) What is the initial rate of disappearance of Cl_2 in experiment 4?

Hints & Solutions

1. (i) reactants, products (ii) Smaller, faster
(iii) equal (iv) measure
(v) concentration

2. (i) → (b), (ii) → (a), (iii) → (a), (iv) → (b), (v) →(d)

3. (a) A-(ii), B-(i), C-(iii)

4. The rate of a reaction depends on the concentration of the reactants. As the reaction proceeds to forward direction, concentration of reactant decreases and that of product increases. So, the rate of reaction generally decreases during the course of reaction. (1)

5. For the reaction, $2N_2O_5(g) \longrightarrow 4NO_2(g) + O_2(g)$

Overall rate of reaction is

$$-\frac{1}{2}\frac{d[N_2O_5]}{dt} = +\frac{1}{4}\frac{d[NO_2]}{dt} = +\frac{d[O_2]}{dt}$$

Given, $\frac{d[NO_2]}{dt} = 2.8 \times 10^{-3}\ Ms^{-1}$, $-\frac{d[N_2O_5]}{dt} = ?$

$$\therefore \quad -\frac{1}{2}\frac{d[N_2O_5]}{dt} = \frac{1}{4}\frac{d[NO_2]}{dt}$$

Putting the given values in the above equation, we get

$$\frac{-d[N_2O_5]}{dt} = \frac{1}{4} \times 2 \times 2.8 \times 10^{-3}\ Ms^{-1} = 1.4 \times 10^{-3}\ Ms^{-1}$$ (1)

6. We can determine the rate of this reaction as a function of initial concentrations either by keeping the concentration of one of the reactants constant and changing the concentration of the other reactants or by changing the concentration of both the reactants e.g. for the given reaction,

(i) Keeping $[O_2]$ constant, if the concentration of NO is doubled, rate is found to become four times. This shows that

$$\text{Rate} \propto [NO]^2$$ (1)

(ii) Keeping [NO] constant, if the concentration of $[O_2]$ is doubled, rate is also found to become double. This shows that

$$\text{Rate} \propto [O_2]$$

Hence, overall rate law will be

$\text{Rate} = k[NO]^2[O_2]$

Rate law expression:

$$-\frac{1}{2}\frac{\Delta[NO]}{\Delta t} = \frac{-\Delta[O_2]}{\Delta t} = \frac{1}{2}\frac{\Delta[NO_2]}{\Delta t}$$ (1)

7. (i) *Case* **I** Initial rate $= k[A][B]^2$ (Given)

$= (2.0 \times 10^{-6} mol^{-2} L^2 s^{-1}) \times (0.1\ mol\ L^{-1}) \times (0.2\ mol\ L^{-1})^2$

$= 8.0 \times 10^{-9} mol\ L^{-1} s^{-1}$ (1)

(ii) *Case* **II** Concentration of A at a particular time $= 0.06\ mol\ L^{-1}$

Amount of A reacted $= (0.1 - 0.06) = 0.04\ mol\ L^{-1}$

Amount of B reacted $= \frac{1}{2} \times 0.04\ mol\ L^{-1}$

$= 0.02\ mol\ L^{-1}$

Concentration of B at a particular time

$= (0.2 - 0.02)\ mol\ L^{-1} = 0.18\ mol\ L^{-1}$

Rate $= k[A][B]^2 = (2.0 \times 10^{-6} mol^{-2} L^2 s^{-1}) \times (0.06\ mol\ L^{-1}) \times (0.18\ mol\ L^{-1})^2$

$= 3.89 \times 10^{-9} mol\ L^{-1} s^{-1}$ (1)

8. Rate $= K[A]^a [B]^b$

Where, a = order of A and b = order of B on comparing S.No. (1) and (2), we get

$$\frac{(\text{Rate})_2}{(\text{Rate})_1} = \frac{[A]_2^a [B]_2^b}{[A]_1^a [B]_1^b}$$

$$\frac{4\times 10^{-3}}{2\times 10^{-3}} = \frac{(2)^a (1)^b}{(1)^a (1)^b}$$

$$2 = (2)^a \Rightarrow a = 1$$

$\therefore$ Order of $A = 1$

Similarly, on comparing (1) and (4), we get

$$\frac{(\text{Rate})_4}{(\text{Rate})_1} = \frac{[A]_4^a [B]_4^b}{[A]_1^a [B]_1^b}$$

$$\frac{2\times 10^{-3}}{2\times 10^{-3}} = \frac{(1)^a (2)^b}{(1)^a (1)^b}$$

$$(1) = (1)^a \Rightarrow a = 0$$

$\therefore$ Order of $B = 0$

(i) Therefore, overall order of reaction $= 1 + 0 = 1$,

(ii) and rate law is $r = K[A]$.

9. (i) The rate law for the reaction,

Rate $= k[\text{NO}]^2[\text{Cl}_2]$ (Refer example 4 on page 122 (Rate equation)) (1)

(ii) Rate constant can be calculated by substituting the value of rate, [NO] and $[\text{Cl}_2]$ from any of the experiments.

$$k = \frac{\text{Rate}}{[\text{NO}]^2[\text{Cl}_2]} = \frac{0.60}{(0.15)^2(0.15)} = \frac{0.60}{0.00338}$$

$= 177.51 \text{ mol}^{-2}\text{L}^2\text{min}^{-1}$ (1)

(iii) Let initial rate of disappearance of Cl_2 in experiment 4 is r_4.

$\therefore \quad r_4 = k[\text{NO}]^2[\text{Cl}_2]$

$= 177.51 \times (0.25)^2(0.25)$

$= 2.77$ M/min (1)

TOPIC 02 Molecularity and Order of a Chemical Reaction

Molecularity of a Reaction

The number of reacting species (atoms, ions or molecules) taking part in an elementary reaction, which must collide simultaneously in order to bring about a chemical reaction is called molecularity of the reaction.

e.g.

(i) If a reaction involves the decomposition of only a single species, the molecularity is one and it is called **unimolecular reaction.**

For, e.g. in case of decomposition of NH_4NO_2 and O_2F_2, the molecularity is 1.

$$NH_4NO_2 \longrightarrow N_2 + 2H_2O$$
$$O_2F_2 \longrightarrow O_2 + F_2$$

(ii) The decomposition of HI is a **bimolecular reaction** as it involves the collision of two molecules.

$$2HI\,(g) \longrightarrow H_2\,(g) + I_2\,(g)$$

(iii) The reaction between NO and O_2 is a **trimolecular reaction** as collision of three molecules results into the product.

$$2NO\,(g) + O_2\,(g) \longrightarrow 2NO_2\,(g)$$

Reactions with molecularity greater than three (trimolecular) are rare as probability of more than three molecules colliding simultaneously to form product(s) is very low.

Note Molecularity has no meaning for complex reactions as these reactions are supposed to take place in a sequence of a number of steps. It can be determined only for the elementary reactions.

$$KClO_3 + 6FeSO_4 + 3H_2SO_4 \longrightarrow KCl + 3Fe_2(SO_4)_3 + 3H_2O$$

This reaction seems to be a tenth order reaction but actually it is a second order reaction. This indicates that the reaction takes place in several steps.

Mechanism of a Reaction

A sequence of intermediate steps or all elementary processes proposed to account for the overall stoichiometry of a reaction is called the **mechanism of the reaction.** The simple chemical reactions which occur only in one step are called **elementary reactions** whereas the reactions which occur in two or more steps are called **complex reactions.**

A complex reaction proceeds through a series of elementary reactions. Each elementary reaction has its own molecularity and its own rate. The overall rate of a complex reaction is governed by the rate of slowest elementary step, which is known as **rate determining step.**

Rate Determining (Slow) Step

As discussed above, even a simple looking reaction might have been proceeding through several steps. Out of these steps, the slowest step of the reaction is considered as the rate determining step of the chemical reaction and decides the **overall rate** of the reaction.

Consider the following reaction,

$$2N_2O_5 \longrightarrow 4NO_2 + O_2$$

The rate law for this equation is found to be,

$$\text{Rate of reaction} = k[N_2O_5]$$

If the reaction occur by the collisions of two N_2O_5 molecules as indicated by the balanced equation, it would be a second order reaction as :

$$\text{Rate} = k\,[N_2O_5]^2$$

But observed rate law suggests that it is a first order reaction which implies that the reaction is a complex reaction.

So, it must take place in two steps in such a way that the slowest step should involve only one molecule of N_2O_5.

Step I $N_2O_5 \xrightarrow{\text{Slow}} NO_2 + NO_3$

Step II $N_2O_5 + NO_3 \xrightarrow{\text{Fast}} 3NO_2 + O_2$

The first step, being slow, is the rate determining step. Since, the rate determining step is unimolecular, so it has order one.

The rate of reaction depends not only on the reactants but may also depend upon the substances present as a catalyst. e.g. Decomposition of H_2O_2, which is catalysed by I^- ion in an alkaline medium.

$$2H_2O_2 \xrightarrow[\text{Alkaline medium}]{I^-} 2H_2O + O_2$$

The rate equation for this reaction is found to be,

$$\text{Rate} = \frac{-d[H_2O_2]}{dt} = k[H_2O_2][I^-]$$

This reaction is first order with respect to both H_2O_2 and I^-. Evidences suggest that this reaction takes place in two steps:

Step I $H_2O_2 + I^- \xrightarrow{\text{Slow}} H_2O + IO^-$

Step II $H_2O_2 + IO^- \xrightarrow{\text{Fast}} H_2O + I^- + O_2$

The first step is slow, so it is rate determining step. Species IO^- is called as an **intermediate**, since it is formed during the course of the reaction but not in the overall balanced equation. Hence, rate of formation of the intermediate will determine the rate of this reaction. It is concluded that, order of complex reaction is determined from the slowest step. Molecularity of the slowest step is equal to the order of the overall reaction.

Order of a Reaction

The power to which the concentration terms of a particular reactant in the rate law is raised is called the **order of reaction** with respect to that reactant, while the sum of all the powers to which all the concentration terms in the rate law equation are raised is called overall order of reaction.

For a general reaction,

$$aA + bB \longrightarrow cC + dD, \quad \text{Rate} = k[A]^x[B]^y$$

Here, x and y, calculated experimentally, indicate how sensitive the rate is to the change in concentrations of A and B.

Sum of these exponents, i.e. $x + y$ gives the overall order of a reaction whereas, x and y represent the order with respect to the reactants A and B, respectively.

Order of a reaction can be 0, 1, 2, 3 and even a fraction.

For instance, if rate of any reaction is expressed as:

$$\text{Rate} = k[A]^{1/2}[B]^{3/2}$$

$$\text{Then, order} = x + y = \frac{1}{2} + \frac{3}{2} = 2$$

Hence, reaction is said to be of second order.

The units of rate constants of different orders are different. This can be easily illustrated below:

For a general reaction,

$$aA + bB \longrightarrow cC + dD$$

$$\text{Rate} = k[A]^x[B]^y$$

where, $x + y = n$ = order of the reaction

$$k = \frac{\text{Rate}}{[A]^x[B]^y} = \frac{\text{concentration}}{\text{time}} \times \frac{1}{(\text{concentration})^n}$$

$$= (\text{concentration})^{1-n}\ \text{time}^{-1}$$

(where, $[A] = [B]$)

Considering SI units of concentration, mol L^{-1} and time, s, the unit of $k = (\text{mol}\,L^{-1})^{1-n}\,s^{-1}$.

Thus, the units of k for different order of reaction are given below:

- **For zero order** ($n = 0$) **reaction,**

$$2NH_3 \longrightarrow N_2 + 3H_2$$

$$\text{Unit of } k = \frac{\text{mol L}^{-1}}{\text{s}} \times \frac{1}{(\text{mol L}^{-1})^0} = \text{mol L}^{-1}\text{s}^{-1}$$

- **For first order ($n = 1$) reaction,**

$$N_2O_5 \longrightarrow N_2O_4 + \frac{1}{2}O_2$$

$$\text{Unit of } k = \frac{\text{mol L}^{-1}}{\text{s}} \times \frac{1}{(\text{mol L}^{-1})^1} = \text{s}^{-1}$$

- **For second order ($n = 2$) reaction,**

$$H_2 + I_2 \longrightarrow 2HI$$

$$\text{Unit of } k = \frac{\text{mol L}^{-1}}{\text{s}} \times \frac{1}{(\text{mol L}^{-1})^2} = \text{mol}^{-1}\text{L s}^{-1}$$

- **For nth order reaction,**

$$\text{Unit of } k = \frac{\text{concentration}}{\text{time}} \times \frac{1}{(\text{concentration})^n}$$

$$k = \frac{\text{mol L}^{-1}}{\text{s}} \times \frac{1}{(\text{mol L}^{-1})^n}$$

$$= \frac{1}{\text{s}} \times \frac{1}{(\text{mol L}^{-1})^{n-1}} = (\text{mol L}^{-1})^{1-n}\text{s}^{-1}$$

Note Rate constants of gaseous reactions are expressed in terms of partial pressure instead of concentration.

Units of Rate Constants for Reactions of Different Order

Reaction	Reaction in solutions	Gaseous reactions
Zero order	$\text{mol L}^{-1}\text{s}^{-1}$	atm s^{-1}
First order	s^{-1}	s^{-1}
Second order	$\text{mol}^{-1}\text{L s}^{-1}$	$\text{atm}^{-1}\text{ s}^{-1}$
nth order	$(\text{mol L}^{-1})^{1-n}\text{s}^{-1}$	$(\text{atm})^{1-n}\text{ s}^{-1}$

Example 1 For a reaction, $P \longrightarrow Q$, the rate becomes 8 times when concentration of P is doubled. What is the order of the reaction?

Sol. Let Rate, $r = k[P]^n$ ...(i)

$8r = k[2P]^n$ ...(ii)

On dividing Eq. (ii) by Eq. (i), we get

$$\frac{8r}{r} = \frac{k[2P]^n}{k[P]^n} \text{ or } [2]^3 = [2]^n \text{ or } n = 3$$

Therefore, order of the reaction is 3.

Example 2 From the rate expression for the following reactions, determine their order of reaction and the dimensions of the rate constant. NCERT

(i) $3NO(g) \longrightarrow N_2O(g)$, Rate $= k\,[NO]^2$

(ii) $H_2O_2(aq) + 3I^-(aq) + 2H^+ \longrightarrow 2H_2O(l) + I_3^-$, Rate $= k[H_2O_2]\,[I^-]$

(iii) $CH_3CHO(g) \longrightarrow CH_4(g) + CO(g)$, Rate $= k[CH_3CHO]^{3/2}$

(iv) $C_2H_5Cl(g) \longrightarrow C_2H_4(g) + HCl(g)$, Rate $= k[C_2H_5Cl]$

Sol. (i) Rate $= k\,[NO]^2$,

Order of reaction = 2

Unit (dimension) of rate constant,

$$k = \frac{\text{Rate}}{[NO]^2} = \frac{\text{mol L}^{-1}\text{s}^{-1}}{(\text{mol L}^{-1})^2} = \text{mol}^{-1}\text{L s}^{-1}$$

(ii) Rate $= k\,[H_2O_2]\,[I^-]$, Order of reaction $= 1 + 1 = 2$

$$\text{Unit of } k = \frac{\text{Rate}}{[H_2O_2]\,[I^-]} = \frac{\text{mol L}^{-1}\text{s}^{-1}}{(\text{mol L}^{-1})\,(\text{mol L}^{-1})}$$

$$= \text{mol}^{-1}\text{L s}^{-1}$$

(iii) Rate $= k\,[CH_3CHO]^{3/2}$

Order of reaction $= \frac{3}{2}$

$$\text{Unit of } k = \frac{\text{Rate}}{[CH_3CHO]^{3/2}} = \frac{\text{mol L}^{-1}\text{s}^{-1}}{(\text{mol L}^{-1})^{3/2}}$$

$$= \text{mol}^{-1/2}\text{L}^{1/2}\text{s}^{-1}$$

(iv) Rate $= k\,[C_2H_5Cl]$, Order of reaction = 1

$$\text{Unit of } k = \frac{\text{Rate}}{[C_2H_5Cl]} = \frac{\text{mol L}^{-1}\text{s}^{-1}}{\text{mol L}^{-1}} = \text{s}^{-1}$$

Difference between Molecularity and Order of Reaction

Molecularity and order of a reaction can be distinguish as follows:

S.No.	Molecularity	Order
1.	The number of reacting species which must collide simultaneously in order to carry out a chemical reaction is called molecularity of a reaction.	The sum of powers of the concentrations of the reactants in the rate law expression is called the order of that chemical reaction.
2.	Molecularity is always a whole number value only, i.e.1, 2, 3	Order of reaction may have zero, whole number or fractional values.
3.	Molecularity is a theoretical concept.	Order of reaction is determined experimentally.
4.	Molecularity is applicable to elementary reactions. For complex reactions, it has no meaning.	Order of reaction is applicable to elementary as well as complex reactions.
5.	For simple reactions, molecularity can be obtained from the stoichiometry of the equations.	For simple reactions, order of reaction may or may not be equal to the number of molecules of the reactants as seen from the balanced equation.
6.	Molecularity of a reaction cannot be zero.	Order of a reaction can be zero.

Topic Practice 2

Very Short Answer Type Questions

1 Mark

1. Fill in the Blanks

(i) For a particular reaction, the value of rate constant is $0.05\ s^{-1}$. The reaction is of .... order and will be .... of the initial concentration. ISC 2024

(ii) Order of reaction may have zero, whole number or .... values.

(iii) When the concentration of a reactant of first order reaction is doubled, the rate of reaction becomes .... times, but for a .... order reaction, the rate of reaction remains the same. ISC 2019

(iv) The sum of powers of the concentrations of the reactants in the rate law expression is called the .... of that chemical reaction.

(v) Unit of rate constant for a second order reaction is ....

(vi) For a first order reaction, the unit of rate is .... and that of rate constant is .... ISC 2011

2. Objective Type Questions

(i) The unit of the rate constant of nth order is

(a) $mol^{1-n}\ L^{n-1}\ s^{-1}$ (b) $mol^{n-1}\ L^{1-n}\ s^{-1}$

(c) $mol^{n-1}\ L^{n-1}\ s$ (d) $mol^{n}\ L^{1-n}\ s^{-1}$

(ii) Reaction of chloroform with chlorine is an example of fraction order reaction. Its rate law expression is rate $= k[CHCl_3][Cl_2]^{1/2}$.

If both are assumed in gaseous state and pressure is measured in bar then units of rate and rate constant respectively are

(a) $bar\ min^{-1}$, $bar^2\ min^{-1}$

(b) $bar\ min^{-1}$, $bar^{-1/2}\ min^{-1}$

(c) $bar^{-1/2}$, min^{-1}, $bar^2\ min^{-1}$

(d) $bar\ min^{-1}$, $bar^{1/2}\ min^{-1}$

(iii) The rate law expression for the reaction, $2NO + O_2 \longrightarrow 2NO_2$ is rate $= k[NO]^2[O_2]$.

The unit of rate constant (k) is

(a) $mol\ L^{-1}\ s^{-1}$ (b) s^{-1}

(c) $mol^{-2}\ L^2\ s^{-1}$ (d) $mol\ L^{-1}$

(iv) The reaction between X and Y is first order with respect to X and second order with respect to Y. If the concentration of X is halved and the concentration of Y is doubled, the rate of reaction will be ISC 2008

(a) same as the initial value

(b) three times the initial value

(c) double the initial value

(d) half the initial value

3. Match the following Columns and choose the correct option using the codes given below :

	Column I (Reaction)		Column II (Units of rate constant)
A.	Zero order reaction	(i)	$mol\ L^{-1}\ s^{-1}$
B.	First order reaction	(ii)	s^{-1}
C.	Second order reaction	(iii)	$mol^{-1}\ L\ s^{-1}$

Codes

	A	B	C		A	B	C
(a)	(ii)	(i)	(iii)	(b)	(iii)	(ii)	(i)
(c)	(i)	(ii)	(iii)	(d)	(iii)	(i)	(ii)

4. Identify the order of reaction from each of the following units of rate constant (k). ISC 2017

(i) $mol\ L^{-1}sec^{-1}$ (ii) $mol^{-1}L\ sec^{-1}$

5. What is the order of reaction whose rate constant has the same unit as the rate of reaction? ISC 2016

6. Write the rate equation for the reaction, $2A + B \longrightarrow C$, if the order of the reaction is zero. NCERT Exemplar

7. For a certain reaction, the rate law is, Rate $= k[A][B]^{3/2}$. Can this belongs to an elementary reaction? NCERT Exemplar

Short Answer Type I Questions

2 Marks

8. We can not determine the order of a reaction by taking into consideration the balanced chemical equation? Give reason. NCERT Exemplar

9. (i) Write the rate law expression for the reaction $A + B + C \rightarrow D + E$. If the order of reaction is first, second and zero with respect A, B and C respectively.

(ii) How many times the rate of reaction will increase, if the concentration of A, B and C are doubled in the equation given in (i) above?

10. A reaction is of second order with respect to a reactant. How is the rate of reaction affected, if the concentration of the reactant is

(i) doubled ? (ii) reduced to half ? NCERT

11. The conversion of molecules x to y follows second order kinetics. If concentration of x is increased to three times, how will it affect the rate of formation of y? NCERT Intext

12. What is the difference between order of a reaction and the molecularity of a reaction? ISC 2017, 15

Short answer Type II Questions

3 Marks

13. For the reaction $A + B \rightleftharpoons$ Product, following data was obtained.

Experiment number	Initial concentration of [A] (mol L^{-1})	Initial concentration of [B] (mol L^{-1})	Initial rate (mol L^{-1} min^{-1})
1	0.15	0.15	9.6×10^{-2}
2	0.30	0.15	3.84×10^{-1}
3	0.15	0.30	1.92×10^{-1}
4	0.30	0.30	7.68×10^{-1}

Calculate the following.
(i) The overall order of the reaction.
(ii) The rate law equation.
(iii) The value of rate constant. ISC 2024

14. For the reaction:
$2H_2 + 2NO \rightleftharpoons 2H_2O + N_2$ the following rate data was obtained:

S.No.	[NO], mol L^{-1}	[H_2], mol L^{-1}	Rate : mol, L^{-1} sec^{-1}
1	0.40	0.40	4.6×10^{-3}
2	0.80	0.40	18.4×10^{-3}
3	0.40	0.80	9.2×10^{-3}

Calculate the following :
(i) The overall order of reaction.
(ii) The rate law.
(iii) The value of rate constant (k).

15. The reaction between A and B is of first order with respect to A and zero order with respect to B. Fill in the blanks in the following table.

Exp. No.	[A] /mol L^{-1}	[B] /mol L^{-1}	Initial rate/ mol L^{-1} min^{-1}
1.	0.1	0.1	2.0×10^{-2}
2.	—	0.2	4.0×10^{-2}
3.	0.4	0.4	—
4.	—	0.2	2.0×10^{-2}

NCERT

16 In a reaction between A and B, the initial rate of reaction (r_0) was measured for different initial concentrations of A and B as given below:

A/mol L^{-1}	0.20	0.20	0.40
B/mol L^{-1}	0.30	0.10	0.05
r_0/mol L^{-1} s^{-1}	5.07×10^{-5}	5.07×10^{-5}	1.43×10^{-4}

What is the order of the reaction with respect to A and B? NCERT

17. A study of chemical kinetics of the reaction $A + B \longrightarrow$ products, gave the following data at 25°C.

Experiment	[A]	[B]	$\frac{d(\text{Product})}{dt}$
1.	1.0	0.15	4.20×10^{-6}
2.	2.0	0.15	8.40×10^{-6}
3.	1.0	0.20	5.60×10^{-6}

Find
(i) the order of reaction with respect to A.
(ii) the order of reaction with respect to B.
(iii) the rate law. ISC 2012

18. A reaction is of second order in A and first order in B.
(i) Write the differential rate equation.
(ii) How is the rate affected on increasing the concentration of A three times?
(iii) How is the rate affected when the concentration of both A and B is doubled?

Long Answer Type Question

5 Marks

19. Consider the following reaction,

$$2NO(g) + Cl_2(g) \longrightarrow 2NOCl(g)$$

The rate of reaction becomes doubled when the concentration of Cl_2 is doubled. However, when the concentration of both the reactants are doubled, the rate becomes eight times. What is the order with respect to NO and with respect to reactant chlorine? What is the overall order of reaction?

Hints & Solutions

1. (i) First, independent (ii) fractional (iii) Two, zero
   (iv) order (v) $L\ mol^{-1}s^{-1}$ (vi) $mol\ L^{-1}s^{-1}$, s^{-1}
2. (i)- a, (ii)- b (iii)- c, (iv)- c,
3. (c) A→ (i), B→ (ii), C→ (iii)
4. (i) $mol\ L^{-1}sec^{-1} \rightarrow$ Zero order reaction. (½)
   (ii) $mol^{-1}L\ sec^{-1} \rightarrow$ Second order reaction. (½)
5. In zero order of reaction rate constant and rate of reaction has the same unit, i.e. $mol\ L^{-1}s^{-1}$. (1)
6. The rate equation for the given reaction is rate $= k[A]^0[B]^0 = k$ (1)
7. For an elementary reaction, order of reaction must be equal to the molecularity but molecularity should be integral. For the given rate law, order of reaction comes out to be 5/2 [1 + 3/2]. As molecularity cannot be fractional.
   Therefore, order is not equal to molecularity. Hence, the given rate law does not belong to an elementary reaction. (1)
8. The rate of reaction may not depend upon all the molecules of a reactant present in the balanced chemical equation. Thus, balanced chemical equation often leads to incorrect order or rate law.
   $$5Br^-(aq) + BrO_3^-(aq) + 6H^+(aq) \longrightarrow 3Br_2(aq) + 3H_2O\ (l)$$
   This is actually a fourth order reaction but it seems to be a twelfth order reaction. Actually, the reaction is complex and occurs in several steps. The order of such reaction is determined by the slowest step in the reaction mechanism. (2)
9. (i) The rate law expression for the reaction $A + B + C \longrightarrow D + E$ is $r = k[A][B]^2$.
   Order of reaction is first, second and zero with respect to A, B and C. (1)
   (ii) If the concentration of A, B and C are doubled then rate is given by
   $r_1 = k\,[2A][2B]^2 \quad r_1 = 8k\,[A][B]^2$
   ∴ New rate r_1 is 8 times of previous rate, r. Hence, rate of reaction increases by 8 times. (1)
10. (i) If the concentration of reactant A is doubled, i.e. $[A] = 2a$
    Then, rate $= k\,(2a)^2 = 4\,ka^2$
    Rate of reaction becomes 4 times. (1)
    (ii) When concentration of A is reduced to $\frac{1}{2}$,
    i.e. $[A] = \frac{1}{2}a \Rightarrow$ rate $= k\left(\frac{a}{2}\right)^2 = \frac{1}{4}\,ka^2$
    Rate of reaction becomes 1/4 times, i.e. reduced to one-fourth. (1)
11. For the reaction, $x \rightarrow y$
    Reaction rate, $(r) = k\,[x]^2$ (for 2nd order) ...(i) (1)
    If the concentration of x is increased three times, then
    Reaction rate, $(r') = k\,[3x]^2 = k \times [9x^2]$ ...(ii)
    On dividing Eq. (ii) by Eq. (i), we get
    $$\frac{r'}{r} = \frac{k \times [9x^2]}{k \times [x^2]} = 9$$
    It means that the rate of formation of y will increase by nine times. (2)
12. Refer text on page 102 (Difference between molecularity and order of a reaction). (2)
13. Let, the order w.r.t A and B be α and β respectively.
    Rate law expression may be written as
    $$\text{Rate} = k[A]^\alpha\,[B]^\beta$$
    ∴ $9.6 \times 10^{-2} = k[0.15]^\alpha\,[0.15]^\beta$ ...(i)
    or $3.84 \times 10^{-1} = k[0.3]^\alpha\,[0.15]^\beta$ ...(ii)
    or $1.92 \times 10^{-1} = k[0.15]^\alpha\,[0.3]^\beta$ ...(iii)
    or $7.68 \times 10^{-1} = k[0.3]^\alpha\,[0.3]^\beta$ ...(iv)
    Dividing Eqs. (i) by (ii), we get
    $$\frac{9.6 \times 10^{-2}}{3.84 \times 10^{-1}} = \frac{k[0.15]^\alpha\,[0.15]^\beta}{k[0.3]^\alpha\,[0.15]^\beta}$$
    $$\left[\frac{1}{4}\right] = \left[\frac{1}{2}\right]^\alpha \Rightarrow \left[\frac{1}{2}\right]^2 = \left[\frac{1}{2}\right]^\alpha$$
    ∴ $\alpha = 2$
    Dividing Eqs. (i) by (iii), we get
    $$\frac{9.6 \times 10^{-2}}{1.92 \times 10^{-1}} = \frac{k[0.15]^\alpha\,[0.15]^\beta}{k[0.15]^\alpha\,[0.3]^\beta}$$
    $$\Rightarrow \quad \left[\frac{1}{2}\right]^1 = \left[\frac{1}{2}\right]^\beta \Rightarrow \beta = 1$$
    (i) The overall order of the reaction is 3.
    (ii) Rate law expression.
    $$\text{Rate} = k[A]^2\,[B]^1$$
    (iii) From expression (i) rate constant can be calculated as
    $$9.6 \times 10^{-2} = k[0.15]^2\,[0.15]^1$$
    $$k = \frac{9.6\times10^{-2}\ mol\ L^{-1}\ min^{-1}}{[0.15]^3\,(mol\ L^{-1})^3}$$
    $$= 28.44\ mol^{-2}\ L^2\ min^{-1}$$
14. Given, $2H_2 + 2NO \rightleftharpoons 2H_2O + N_2$
    Let, the given reaction is of order q with respect to H_2 and p with respect to NO.
    The rate of formation H_2O and N_2 can also be written as :
    (a) $4.6 \times 10^{-3} = k\,[A]^p\,[B]^q = k\,[0.4]^p\,[0.4]^q$ ...(i)
    (b) $18.4 \times 10^{-3} = k(0.8)^p\,(0.4)^q$ ...(ii)
    (c) $9.2 \times 10^{-3} = k(0.4)^p\,(0.8)^q$ ...(iii)
    From Eq. (i) and (ii), we get

$$\frac{18.4\times10^{-3}}{4.6\times10^{-3}}=\frac{k(0.8)^p\,(0.4)^q}{k(0.4)^p\,(0.4)^q}\qquad 4=(2)^p\Rightarrow(2)^2=(2)^p$$

Hence, $p = 2$

From Eq. (i) and (iii), we get

$$\frac{9.2\times10^{-3}}{4.6\times10^{-3}}=\frac{k(0.4)^p\,(0.8)^q}{k(0.4)^p\,(0.4)^q}\Rightarrow\quad 2=(2)^q$$

$\therefore\quad q=1$

(i) Overall order of reaction is $(2+1)=3$ (1)

(ii) Rate law equation, $r=k\,[NO]^2\,[H_2]$ (1)

(iii) $r=k\,[H_2]\,[NO]^2$

Rate constant,

$$k=\frac{r}{[H_2]\,[NO]^2}=\frac{4.6\times10^{-3}}{[0.4]\,[0.4]^2}=7.18\times10^{-2}\ \text{mol}^{-2}\text{L}^2\text{s}^{-1}$$ (1)

15. The rate expression, Rate $=k\,[A]^1[B]^0=k\,[A]$

For experiment 1, $[A]=0.1$ mol L^{-1}

So, rate $=2.0\times10^{-2}=k\,[0.1\text{ mol L}^{-1}]$

$$\therefore\quad k=\frac{2.0\times10^{-2}\text{ mol L}^{-1}\text{min}^{-1}}{0.1\text{ mol L}^{-1}}=0.2\text{ min}^{-1}$$

For experiment 2, rate $=k[A]$

$4.0\times10^{-2}\text{mol L}^{-1}\text{min}^{-1}=0.2\text{ min}^{-1}[A]$

$$[A]=\frac{4.0\times10^{-2}\text{mol L}^{-1}\text{min}^{-1}}{0.2\text{ min}^{-1}}=0.2\text{ mol L}^{-1}$$

$[A]=0.2$ mol L^{-1} (1)

For experiment 3, rate $=k\,[A]$

Rate $=0.2\text{ min}^{-1}\times0.4\text{ mol L}^{-1}$

Rate $=8\times10^{-2}\text{mol L}^{-1}\text{min}^{-1}$ (1)

For experiment 4, rate $=k\,[A]$

$$\Rightarrow\ [A]=\frac{\text{Rate}}{k}\Rightarrow[A]=\frac{2.0\times10^{-2}}{0.2}=0.1\text{ mol L}^{-1}$$ (1)

16. Rate law states that rate $=k\,[A]^x[B]^y$

$(\text{Rate})_1=k[0.20]^x[0.30]^y=5.07\times10^{-5}$ ...(i)

$(\text{Rate})_2=k[0.20]^x[0.10]^y=5.07\times10^{-5}$ ...(ii)

$(\text{Rate})_3=k[0.40]^x[0.05]^y=1.43\times10^{-4}$ ...(iii)

On dividing Eq. (i) by Eq. (ii), we get (1)

$$\frac{(\text{Rate})_1}{(\text{Rate})_2}=\frac{k[0.20]^x[0.30]^y}{k[0.20]^x[0.10]^y}=\frac{5.07\times10^{-5}}{5.07\times10^{-5}}=1$$

$$[3]^y=[3]^0$$

$$y=0$$

Now, on dividing Eq. (iii) by Eq. (ii), we get

$$\frac{(\text{Rate})_3}{(\text{Rate})_2}=\frac{k\,(0.40)^x(0.05)^0}{k\,(0.20)^x(0.10)^0}=\frac{1.43\times10^{-4}}{5.07\times10^{-5}}$$

$2.8205=2^x$ (1)

$\log 2.8205=x\log 2$

$$x=\frac{0.4503}{0.3010}=1.5$$

Thus, order of the reaction with respect to A and B are 1.5 and 0, respectively. (1)

17. Rate of reaction $\propto$ [Concentration]^n

where, n is order of reaction.

Given, $A+B\longrightarrow$ Products

Suppose the given reaction is of order p with respect to A and q with respect to B. The rate of formation of product can be written as

$4.20\times10^{-6}=k[1.0]^p\,[0.15]^q$ ...(i)

$8.40\times10^{-6}=k[2.0]^p\,[0.15]^q$ ...(ii)

$5.60\times10^{-6}=k[1.0]^p\,[0.20]^q$ ...(iii)

On dividing Eq. (ii) by Eq. (i), we get

$$\frac{8.40\times10^{-6}}{4.20\times10^{-6}}=\left[\frac{2.0}{1.0}\right]^p\Rightarrow\ (2)^1=2^p$$

$\therefore\quad p=1$

On dividing Eq. (iii) by Eq. (i), we get

$$\frac{5.6\times10^{-6}}{4.2\times10^{-6}}=\left[\frac{0.20}{0.15}\right]^q\Rightarrow\left(\frac{4}{3}\right)^1=\left(\frac{4}{3}\right)^q$$

$\therefore\quad q=1$

Hence,

(i) The order of reaction with respect to A is 1. (1)

(ii) The order of reaction with respect to B is 1. (1)

(iii) The rate law can be written as,

Rate $=k\,[A]\,[B]$ (1)

18. A reaction is second order in A and first order in B.

(i) Differential rate equation,

$$\text{Rate}=-\frac{d[R]}{dt}=k[A]^2[B]$$ (1)

(ii) When the concentration of A is increased three times, i.e. $3A$, then

Rate $=k\,[3A]^2[B]\ =9k[A]^2[B]=9$ (rate)

This shows that rate will increase 9 times to the initial rate. (1)

(iii) When concentration of both A and B is doubled then,

Rate $=k[2A]^2[2B]=8k[A]^2[B]=8$(rate)

This shows that rate will increase 8 times to the initial rate. (1)

19. $2NO(g)+Cl_2(g)\longrightarrow 2NOCl(g)$

Let the rate of reaction be

$r_1=k[NO]^\alpha[Cl_2]^\beta$ ...(i)

$r_2=2r_1=k[NO]^\alpha[2Cl_2]^\beta$ ...(ii)

$r_3=8r_1=k[2NO]^\alpha[2Cl_2]^\beta$ ...(iii)

On dividing Eq. (ii) by Eq. (i), we get

$$\frac{r_2}{r_1}=\frac{2r_1}{r_1}=\frac{k[NO]^{\alpha}\cdot[2Cl_2]^{\beta}}{k[NO]^{\alpha}\cdot[Cl_2]^{\beta}}$$

$$\therefore \quad (2)^1=(2)^{\beta}$$

$$\beta=1 \quad \textbf{(1)}$$

Similarly, on dividing Eq. (iii) by Eq. (i), we get

$$\frac{r_3}{r_1}=\frac{8r_1}{r_1}=\frac{k[2NO]^{\alpha}\cdot[2Cl_2]^{\beta}}{k[NO]^{\alpha}\cdot[Cl_2]^{\beta}}$$

$$8=(2)^{\alpha}\cdot(2)^{\beta}$$

$$8=(2)^{\alpha}\cdot(2)^1\ ;\ 4=(2)^{\alpha}$$

$$(2)^2=(2)^{\alpha}\ ;\ \alpha=2 \quad \textbf{(1)}$$

$$\therefore \quad r=k[NO]^2[Cl_2]^1 \quad \textbf{(1)}$$

As, order with respect to NO = 2

Order with respect to $Cl_2=1$

Overall order of reaction = 2 + 1 = 3. (2)

TOPIC 03 Integrated Rate Equations

The differential rate equation is integrated to get a relation between directly measured experimental data, i.e. concentrations at different time and rate constant.

The integrated rate equations are different for the reactions of different reaction orders.

The integrated equation is used for determining the rate constant of the reaction.

In this topic, we shall determine these equations only for zero and first order chemical reactions.

Zero Order Reactions

The reaction in which rate of the reaction is directly proportional to zero power of the concentration of reactants is called zero order reaction.

Thus, in zero order reaction, the rate does not depend on the concentration of any of the reactants.

Consider the reaction,

$$R \longrightarrow P$$

$$\text{Rate}=-\frac{d[R]}{dt}$$

$$=k[R]^0=k\times 1$$

$$d[R]=-k\,dt$$

On integrating both sides,

$$[R]=-kt+I \quad \ldots(i)$$

where, I is the constant of integration.

Initially, at $t=0$, the concentration of the reactant $R=[R]_0$, where R_0 is the initial concentration of the reactant.

From Eq. (i), we have

$$[R]_0=-k\times 0+I$$

On substituting, $[R]_0=I$ in the Eq.(i) we get

$$[R]=-kt+[R]_0 \quad \ldots(ii)$$

Simplifying Eq. (ii), gives

$$k=\frac{[R]_0-[R]}{t} \quad \ldots(iii)$$

If we plot $[R]$ against t, we get a straight line with slope equal to $-k$ and intercept equal to $[R]_0$ as shown in the below figure.

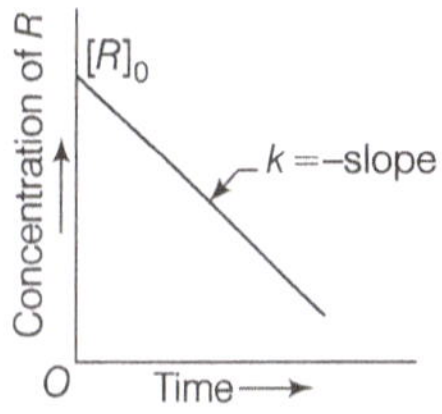

Variation in the concentration vs time plot for a zero order reaction

Also, as the rate is independent of concentration, the plot of rate versus concentration will be straight line parallel to the concentration axis as shown below:

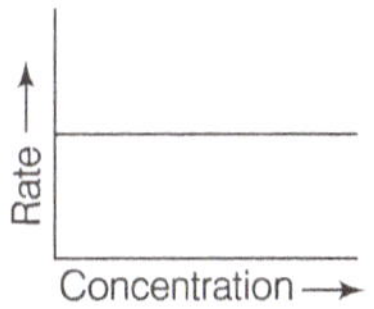

Plot of rate versus concentrations for the reaction of zero order

Examples of the Zero Order Reactions

Zero order reactions are not so common and they occur under special conditions. Some enzyme catalysed reactions and reactions which occur on metal surfaces are few examples of zero order reactions, e.g. decomposition of gaseous ammonia on platinum surface at high temperature and pressure.

$$2NH_3(g) \xrightarrow{1130\text{ K, Pt catalyst}} N_2(g) + 3H_2(g)$$

$$\text{Rate} = k[NH_3]^0 = k$$

Note The decomposition of NH_3 on finely divided platinum surface is of first order when concentration (pressure) of NH_3 is low.

In this reaction, at high pressure, surface of platinum catalyst is saturated with ammonia (gas) molecules. So, a further change in reaction conditions is unable to alter the amount of ammonia on the surface of the catalyst making rate of the reaction independent of its concentration.

First Order Reactions

The reaction in which the rate of the reaction is directly proportional to the first power of the concentration of the reactant, R is called first order reactions.

For the reaction, $R \longrightarrow P$

$$\text{Rate} = -\frac{d[R]}{dt} = k[R] \text{ or } \frac{d[R]}{[R]} = -kdt$$

On integrating the equation, we get

$$\ln[R] = -kt + I \quad \ldots(i)$$

where, I is the constant of integration.

In the beginning when $t = 0$, $R = [R]_0$, where $[R]_0$ is the initial concentration of the reactant.

∴ Eq. (i) can be rewritten as

$$\ln[R]_0 = -k \times 0 + I$$

$$\ln[R]_0 = I$$

On substituting $I = \ln[R]_0$ in the Eq. (i) to get

$$\ln[R] = -kt + \ln[R]_0 \quad \ldots(ii)$$

or

$$\ln\frac{[R]}{[R]_0} = -kt \quad \ldots(iii)$$

or

$$\frac{1}{t}\ln\frac{[R]}{[R]_0} = -k \text{ or } k = \frac{1}{t}\ln\frac{[R]_0}{[R]} \quad \ldots(iv)$$

or

$$k = \frac{2.303}{t}\log\frac{[R]_0}{[R]} \quad \ldots(v)$$

The Eq. (v) is usually written as:

$$\boxed{k = \frac{2.303}{t}\log\frac{a}{(a-x)}}$$

where, a is the initial concentration of reactant, R and $(a-x)$ is the concentration of reactant R, left after time t as x moles of it get changed to products after time t.

i.e. $[R]_0 = a$ and $[R] = (a-x)$

Rate Equation at Time T_1 and T_2

In First Order Reaction

If concentrations of the reactants are measured at time t_1 and t_2.

At time t_1, $\quad \ln[R]_1 = -kt_1 + \ln[R]_0 \quad \ldots(vi)$

At time t_2, $\quad \ln[R]_2 = -kt_2 + \ln[R]_0 \quad \ldots(vii)$

Here, $[R]_1$ and $[R]_2$ are concentrations of the reactants at time t_1 and t_2, respectively.

On subtracting Eq. (vi) from Eq. (vii), we have

$$\ln[R]_1 - \ln[R]_2 = -kt_1 - (-kt_2)$$

or,

$$\ln\frac{[R]_1}{[R]_2} = k(t_2 - t_1)$$

$$k = \frac{1}{t_2 - t_1}\ln\frac{[R]_1}{[R]_2} \quad \ldots(viii)$$

$$k = \frac{2.303}{t_2 - t_1}\log\frac{[R]_1}{[R]_2}$$

Exponential form of Eq. (iii) can be written as:

$$\boxed{[R] = [R]_0 e^{-kt}} \quad \ldots(ix)$$

If we plot ln $[R]$ against t, we get a straight line with slope $= -k$ and intercept equal to $\ln[R]_0$ as shown in figure (a).

The first order rate Eq. (v) can also be written as:

$$\log\frac{[R]_0}{[R]} = \frac{kt}{2.303} \quad \ldots(x)$$

If we plot a graph between $\log[R]_0/[R]$ vs t, we get a straight line with the slope $= k/2.303$ as shown in figure (b).

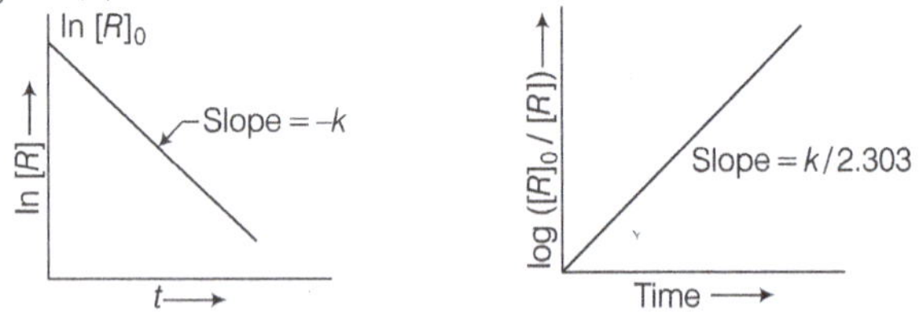

(a) A plot between ln [R] and time (t) for a first order reaction

(b) Plot of $\log[R]_0/[R]$ vs time for a first order reaction

Examples of the First Order Reactions

(i) All natural and artificial radioactive decay of unstable nuclei take place by first order kinetics.

$$^{226}_{88}\text{Ra} \longrightarrow {}^{4}_{2}\text{He} + {}^{222}_{86}\text{Rn}$$

$$\text{Rate} = k\,[\text{Ra}]$$

(ii) Hydrogenation of ethene and decomposition of N_2O_5 and N_2O are more examples of first order reactions.

$$C_2H_4(g) + H_2(g) \rightarrow C_2H_6(g); \quad \text{Rate} = k[C_2H_4]$$

$$N_2O_5(g) \rightarrow N_2O_5(g) + \frac{1}{2}O_2(g); \text{ Rate} = k[N_2O_5]$$

$$N_2O(g) \rightarrow N_2(g) + \frac{1}{2}O_2(g); \text{ Rate} = k[N_2O]$$

Example 1 Consider a certain reaction $A \longrightarrow$ products, with $k = 2.0 \times 10^{-2} s^{-1}$. Calculate the concentration of A remaining after 100 s if the initial concentration of A is 1.0 mol L^{-1}. **NCERT**

Sol. $k = 2.0 \times 10^{-2} s^{-1}$; $[A]_0 = 1.0$ mol L^{-1}; $t = 100$ s

$$k = \frac{2.303}{t} \log \frac{[A]_0}{[A]}$$

Therefore, $2.0 \times 10^{-2} s^{-1} = \frac{2.303}{100 \text{ s}} \log \frac{1.0 \text{ mol L}^{-1}}{[A]}$

$$2.0 \times 10^{-2} s^{-1} = \frac{2.303}{100 \text{ s}} (\log 1 - \log [A])$$

$$2.0 \times 10^{-2} s^{-1} = \frac{2.303}{100 \text{ s}} (0 - \log [A])$$

$$-\log [A] = \frac{2.0 \times 10^{-2} s^{-1} \times 100 \text{ s}}{2.303}$$

or $$[A] = \text{antilog}\left(-\frac{2.0 \times 10^{-2} s^{-1} \times 100 \text{ s}}{2.303}\right)$$

or $$[A] = 0.135 \text{ mol L}^{-1}$$

Pressure Change Method for the Calculation of the Value of Rate Constant

Let us consider a typical first order gas phase reaction,

$$A(g) \longrightarrow B(g) + C(g)$$

Let p_i be the initial pressure of A at time $t = 0$ and p_t be the total pressure at time, t. Integrated rate equation for such a reaction can be derived as :Total pressure, $p_t = p_A + p_B + p_C$ (pressure units) where p_A, p_B and p_C are the partial pressures of A, B and C, respectively.

If x atm be the decrease in pressure of A at time t and one mole each of B and C is being formed, then increase in pressure of B and C will also be x atm each.

	$A(g)$	$\longrightarrow$	$B(g)$	+	$C(g)$
At $t = 0$	p_i atm		0 atm		0 atm
At time t	$(p_i - x)$ atm		x atm		x atm

$$p_t = (p_i - x) + x + x = p_i + x$$

$$x = (p_t - p_i)$$

where, $p_A = p_i - x = p_i - (p_t - p_i) = 2p_i - p_t$

$\because$ $$k = \frac{2.303}{t} \log\left(\frac{p_i}{p_A}\right)$$

$\therefore$ $$\boxed{k = \frac{2.303}{t} \log \frac{p_i}{(2p_i - p_t)}}$$

Example 2 The following data were obtained during the first order thermal decomposition of SO_2Cl_2 at a constant volume,

$$SO_2Cl_2(g) \longrightarrow SO_2(g) + Cl_2(g)$$

Exp. No.	Time/s^{-1}	Total pressure/atm
1.	0	0.5
2.	100	0.6

Calculate the rate of the reaction when total pressure is 0.65 atm. **NCERT**

Sol.

	$SO_2Cl_2(g)$	$\longrightarrow SO_2(g)$	$+ Cl_2(g)$
Initially at $t = 0$	p_i	0	0
After time t	$p_i - p$	p	p

Total pressure after time t, i.e.

$$p_t = p_i - p + p + p = p_i + p$$

$\therefore$ $p = p_t - p_i$

So, $p_{SO_2Cl_2} = p_i - p = p_i - (p_t - p_i)$
$= p_i - p_t + p_i = 2p_i - p_t$

$\because$ $$k = \frac{2.303}{t} \log\left(\frac{p_i}{p_A}\right)$$

$\therefore$ $$k = \frac{2.303}{t} \log \frac{p_i}{(2p_i - p_t)}$$

(a) Calculation of rate constant, k

Given, $p_i = 0.5$ atm; $p_t = 0.6$ atm

$$k = \frac{2.303}{t} \log \frac{p_i}{(2p_i - p_t)} = \frac{2.303}{(100 \text{ s})} \log \frac{0.5 \text{ atm}}{0.4 \text{ atm}}$$

$$= \frac{2.303}{(100 \text{ s})} \log 1.25 = \frac{2.303}{(100 \text{ s})} \times 0.0969 = 2.23 \times 10^{-3} s^{-1}$$

(b) Calculation of reaction rate when total pressure is 0.65 atm

$p_{SO_2Cl_2} = 0.5 - (0.65 - 0.50) = (1 - 0.65) = 0.35$ atm

$k = 2.23 \times 10^{-3} s^{-1}$

Rate $= k \times p_{SO_2Cl_2} = (2.23 \times 10^{-3} s^{-1}) \times (0.35 \text{ atm})$

Rate $= 7.8 \times 10^{-4}$ atm s^{-1}

Half-Life of a Reaction

The time in which the concentration of a reactant is reduced to one-half of its initial concentration is called the half-life of a reaction. It is represented as $t_{1/2}$.

Derivation of Half-Life of a Reaction from Zero Order Rate Equation

For a zero order reaction, $k = \frac{[R]_0 - [R]}{t}$

At $t = t_{1/2}$, $[R] = \frac{1}{2}[R]_0$

The rate constant at $t_{1/2}$ becomes

$$k = \frac{[R]_0 - 1/2[R]_0}{t_{1/2}} \Rightarrow \boxed{t_{1/2} = \frac{[R]_0}{2k}}$$

It is clear that $t_{1/2}$ for a zero order reaction is directly proportional to the initial concentration of the reactants and inversely proportional to the rate constant. The graph of $t_{1/2}$ versus initial concentration of reactant is shown below:

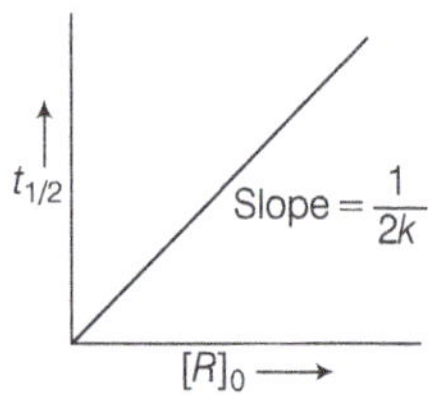

Plot of $t_{1/2}$ vs initial concentration for zero order reaction

Derivation of Half-life of a Reaction from First Order Rate Equation

For the first order reaction,

$$k = \frac{1}{t}\ln\frac{[R]_0}{[R]} \text{ or } k = \frac{2.303}{t}\log\frac{[R]_0}{[R]}$$

At $t_{1/2}$, $[R] = \frac{[R]_0}{2}$

Therefore, $k = \frac{2.303}{t_{1/2}}\log\frac{[R]_0}{[R]_0/2}$

$$\text{or } k = \frac{2.303}{t_{1/2}}\log 2 \text{ or } k = \frac{2.303}{t_{1/2}}\times 0.301$$

or $$\boxed{t_{1/2} = \frac{0.693}{k}}$$

Thus, for first order reaction, $t_{1/2}$ is independent of $[R]_0$ and hence, constant. The graph between the concentration and $t_{1/2}$ of the reaction is shown as follows :

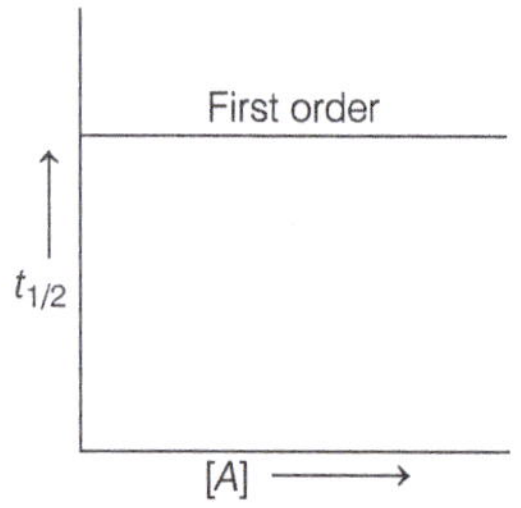

Variation of concentration with $t_{1/2}$ for first order reaction

The half-life of a reaction with nth order is given as:

$$t_{1/2} \propto \frac{1}{[R]_0^{n-1}}$$

Therefore, for zero order reaction, $t_{1/2} \propto [R]_0$. For first order reaction, $t_{1/2}$ is independent of $[R_0]$. For second order reaction $t_{1/2} \propto \frac{1}{[R_0]}$ and so on.

The time required to complete any definite fraction of a first order reaction can be calculated as follows:

(i) **Time Required to Complete One-third of the Reaction**

$[A]_0 = a, [A] = a - a/3 = 2/3a$

$$\therefore\ t_{1/3} = \frac{2.303}{k}\log\frac{a}{2/3a} = \frac{2.303}{k}\log\frac{3}{2}$$

$$t_{1/3} = \frac{2.303}{k}\log\frac{3}{2}$$

(ii) **Time Required to Complete Three-Fourth of the Reaction**

$$[A]_0 = a, [A] = a - \frac{3}{4}a = \frac{1}{4}a$$

$$\therefore t_{3/4} = \frac{2.303}{k}\log\frac{a}{1/4a} = \frac{2.303\log 4}{k}$$

$$t_{3/4} = \frac{2.303\log 4}{k} = 2t_{1/2}$$

Also, $t_{87.5\%} = 3\times t_{1/2}$ and $t_{99.9\%} = 10\times t_{1/2}$

(iii) **Time Required to Complete nth Fraction of the Reaction**

$$[A]_0 = a, [A] = a - \frac{a}{n} = a\left(1-\frac{1}{n}\right)$$

$$\therefore\quad t_{1/n} = \frac{2.303}{k}\log\frac{a}{a\left(1-\frac{1}{n}\right)}$$

or $$t_{1/n} = \frac{2.303}{k}\log\frac{1}{\left(1-\frac{1}{n}\right)}$$

Thus, the time required to complete any definite fraction of a first order reaction is independent of the initial concentration.

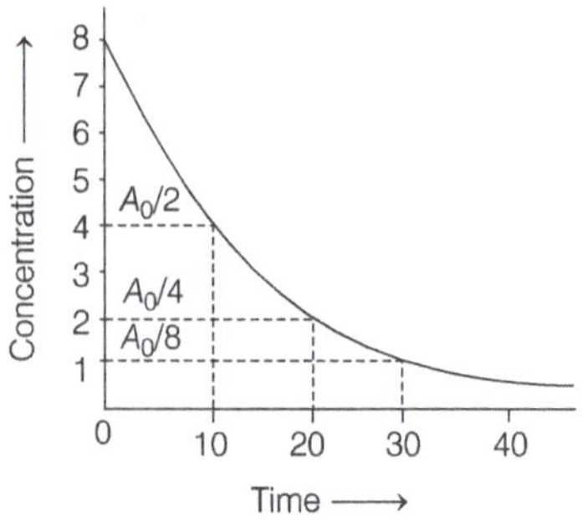

Variation of time with concentration for first order reaction

Amount of substance after first half-life,

$$A_1 = \frac{A_0}{2}$$

After two half-lives $A_2 = \frac{A_0}{4} = \frac{A_0}{2^2}$

After n half-lives $A_n = \frac{A_0}{2^n} = A_0\left(\frac{1}{2}\right)^n$

where, n = number of half-lives

Note k_1^{-1} is called **average life** (T_{av}) of first order reaction.

$$T_{av} = \frac{1}{k_1} = \frac{t_{1/2}}{0.693} = 1.44\,t_{1/2}$$

$$t_{1/4} = \frac{3}{2}t_{1/2}$$

Example 3 The half-life for radioactive decay of ^{14}C is 5730 yr. An archaeological artifact containing wood had only 80% of the ^{14}C found in a living tree. Calculate the age of the sample. **NCERT**

(i) Since, all the radioactive processes follow first order kinetics, rate constant from $t_{1/2}$ can be calculated as :

$k = 0.693/t_{1/2}$

(ii) Then, put the value of k in the expression of first order rate constant to find t.

Sol. $t_{1/2} = \frac{0.693}{k}$ (For first order reaction)

$$\therefore \quad k = \frac{0.693}{t_{1/2}} = \frac{0.693}{5730}\text{yr}^{-1}$$

We know that,

$$t = \frac{2.303}{k}\log\frac{[R]_0}{[R]} = \frac{2.303}{\frac{0.693}{5730}}\log\frac{100}{80} \qquad \left(\text{As, } k = \frac{0.693}{t_{1/2}}\right)$$

$$= \frac{2.303 \times 5730}{0.693}\log\frac{100}{80} = \frac{2.303 \times 5730}{0.693}\log 1.25$$

$$= \frac{2.303 \times 5730}{0.693} \times 0.0969 = 1845 \text{ yr (approx.)}$$

Therefore, the age of the given archaeological artifact containing wood is 1845 yr.

Differential Integrated Rate Laws for the Reactions of Zero and First Order

Order	0	1
Reaction type	$R \rightarrow P$	$R \rightarrow P$
Differential rate law	$d[R]/dt = -k$	$d[R]/dt = -k[R]$
Integrated rate law	$kt = [R]_0 - [R]$	$[R] = [R]_0 e^{-kt}$ or or $kt = \ln\{[R]_0/[R]\}$
Straight line plot	$[R]$ vs t	$\ln [R]$ vs t
Half-life	$[R]_0/2k$	$\ln 2/k$
Units of k	conc. time^{-1} or mol $L^{-1}s^{-1}$	time^{-1} or s^{-1}

Pseudo First Order Reaction

The reactions which are not actually of first order but behave so due to altered conditions are called pseudo first order reactions. In such a chemical reaction between two substances, one reactant is present in large or excess amounts. e.g. When 0.01 mole of ethyl acetate is hydrolysed with 10 moles of water, amounts of the various constituents at the beginning ($t = 0$) and completion (t) of the reaction are mentioned below:

$$CH_3COOC_2H_5 + H_2O \xrightarrow{H^+} CH_3COOH + C_2H_5OH$$

	$CH_3COOC_2H_5$	H_2O	CH_3COOH	C_2H_5OH
$t = 0$	0.01mol	10 mol	0 mol	0 mol
t	0 mol	9.99 mol	0.01mol	0.01mol

The concentration of water is not considered in calculation as its concentration does not get altered much during the course of reaction.

$$\text{Rate} = k'\,[CH_3COOC_2H_5][H_2O] \qquad \text{...(i)}$$

But term $[H_2O]$ can be taken as constant, then Eq. (i) becomes

$$\text{Rate} = k[CH_3COOC_2H_5], \text{ where } k = k'[H_2O]$$

The reaction behaves as first order reaction. Such reactions are pseudo first order reactions. Inversion of cane sugar is another pseudo first order reaction.

$$\underset{\text{Cane sugar}}{C_{12}H_{22}O_{11}} + H_2O \xrightarrow{H^+} \underset{\text{Glucose}}{C_6H_{12}O_6} + \underset{\text{Fructose}}{C_6H_{12}O_6}$$

$$\text{Rate} = k[C_{12}H_{22}O_{11}]$$

Note The pseudo first order reactions are also called pseudo unimolecular reactions.

Example 4 In a pseudo first order hydrolysis of an ester in water, the following results were obtained :

t/s	0	30	60	90
[Ester]/mol L^{-1}	0.55	0.31	0.17	0.085

(i) Calculate the average rate of reaction between the time interval 30 to 60 s.

(ii) Calculate the pseudo first order rate constant for the hydrolysis of an ester. **NCERT**

Sol. (i) Average rate during the interval 30-60 s.

$$\frac{C_2 - C_1}{t_2 - t_1} = \frac{0.31 - 0.17}{60 - 30} = \frac{0.14}{30}\text{ mol}L^{-1}s^{-1}$$

$$= 4.67 \times 10^{-3} \text{ mol } L^{-1} s^{-1}$$

(ii) $k' = \frac{2.303}{t}\log\frac{[A]_0}{[A]}$

Here, $[A]_0 = 0.55, t = 30$

$$k = \frac{2.303}{30}\log\frac{0.55}{0.31} = 1.91 \times 10^{-2}s^{-1}$$

$t = 60\,s,\quad k' = \dfrac{2.303}{60}\log\dfrac{0.55}{0.17} = 1.96\times 10^{-2}s^{-1}$

$t = 90\,s,\quad k' = \dfrac{2.303}{60}\log\dfrac{0.55}{0.085} = 2.07\times 10^{-2}s^{-1}$

$$\text{Average } k' = \frac{1.91 + 1.96 + 2.07}{3}\times 10^{-2}$$
$$= 1.98\times 10^{-2}s^{-1}$$

Topic Practice 3

Very Short Answer Type Questions

(1 Mark)

1. Fill in the Blanks

(i) In first order reaction, change in unit of concentration does not alter the value of ....

(ii) A plot of $\log_{10}[A]$ *vs t* is a .... with a slope equal to ....

(iii) Half-life period of a .... order reaction is .... on the concentration of the reactant. **ISC 2013**

2. Objective Type Questions

(i) For a zero order reaction a graph of concentration (along y-axis) and time (along x-axis) is linear with

(a) a zero intercept and a +ve slope
(b) a zero intercept and a −ve slope
(c) a non-zero intercept and a −ve slope
(d) a non-zero intercept and a +ve slope

(ii) For a first order reaction, the half-life period ($t_{1/2}$) is **ISC 2023**

(a) proportional to the initial concentration
(b) inversely proportional to the initial concentration
(c) proportional to the square root of the initial concentration
(d) independent of the initial concentration

(iii) For a first order reaction, the rate constant for the decomposition of N_2O_5 is $6\times 10^{-4}\ s^{-1}$. The half-life period for the decomposition in seconds is **ISC 2015**

(a) 11.55 (b) 115.5 (c) 1155 (d) 1.155

(iv) 75% of a first order reaction was completed in 32 min. When was 50% of the reaction completed? **ISC 2011**

(a) 24 min (b) 16 min (c) 8 min (d) 4 min

(v) The half-life period of a first order reaction is 20 minutes. The time required the concentration of the reactant to change form 0.16 M to 0.02 M is **ISC 2017**

(a) 80 minutes (b) 60 minutes
(c) 40 minutes (d) 20 minutes

3. Match the terms of Column I with Column II and choose the correct option using the codes given below.

	Column I (Reaction)		Column II (Order of the reactions)
A.	Inversion of cane sugar.	(i)	Zero order reaction
B.	Decomposition of N_2O .	(ii)	First order reaction
C.	Thermal decomposition of HI on gold surface.	(iii)	Pseudo order reaction

Codes

	A	B	C		A	B	C
(a)	(i)	(ii)	(iii)	(b)	(ii)	(iii)	(i)
(c)	(iii)	(ii)	(i)	(d)	(ii)	(i)	(iii)

4. Name the order of reaction which proceeds with a uniform rate throughout. **ISC 2017**

5. Correct the following statements by changing the underlined part of the sentence.
(Do not change the whole sentence.)
<u>The rate constant of a first order reaction</u> is directly proportional to the concentration of the reactant. **ISC 2008, 04**

6. A first order reaction is 50% complete in 30 min at 27°C. Calculate the rate constant of the reaction at 27°C.

7. Time required to decompose SO_2Cl_2 to half of its initial amount is 60 min. If the decomposition is a first order reaction, calculate the rate constant of the reaction. **NCERT**

8. If the half-life period of a first order reaction is 69.3 s. What is the value of its rate constant? **(ISC 2013)**

Short Answer Type I Questions

(2 Marks)

9. A reaction, reactant ⟶ product is represented by (the graph) **NCERT Exemplar**

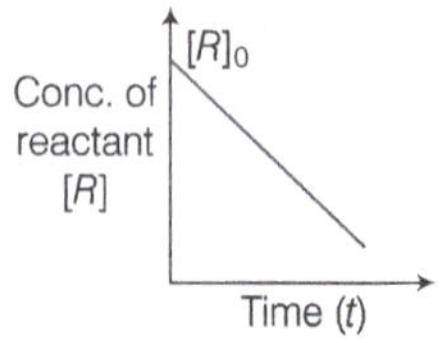

(i) Predict the order of the reaction in this case.

(ii) What does the slope of the graph represent? Write the unit of the represented quantity.

10. The decomposition of NH_3 on platinum surface, $2NH_3(g) \xrightarrow{Pt} N_2(g) + 3H_2(g)$ is a zero order with $k = 2.5 \times 10^{-4}$ mol $L^{-1}s^{-1}$. What are the rates of production of N_2 and H_2? **NCERT**

11. 40% of a first order reaction is completed in 50 minutes. How much time will it take for the completion of 80% of this reaction ? **ISC 2018**

12. Show that for a first order reaction the time required to complete 75% of reaction is about 2 times more than that required to complete 50% of the reaction. **ISC 2019**

13. 25% of a first order reaction is completed in 30 minutes. Calculate the time taken in minutes for the reaction to go to 90% completion. **ISC 2019**

14. In a first order reaction, 10% of the reactant is consumed in 25 min. Calculate
    (i) the half-life period of the reaction.
    (ii) the time required for completing 87.5% of the reaction. **ISC 2016**

15. A substance decomposes by the following first order kinetics. If 50% of the compound is decomposed in 120 min, how long will it take for 90% of the compound to decompose? **ISC 2015**

16. In a first order reaction, 10% of the reactant is consumed in 25 min. Calculate
    (i) half-life of the reaction
    (ii) the time required for completing 17% of the reaction. **ISC 2013**

17. The rate constant for a first order reaction is 60 s^{-1}. How much time will it take to reduce the initial concentration of the reactant to its 1/16th value? **NCERT**

Short Answer Type II Questions

3 Marks

18. Show that the time required for the completion of 75% of a reaction of first order is twice the time required for the completion of 50% of the reaction. **ISC 2010**

19. A first order reaction has a rate constant 1.15×10^{-3} s^{-1}. How long will 5 g of this reactant take to reduce to 3 g? **NCERT**

20. Sucrose decomposes in acid solution into glucose and fructose according to the first order rate law, with $t_{1/2} = 3$ h. What fraction of sample of sucrose remains after 8h? **NCERT**

21. Calculate the half-life of a first order reaction from their rate constants given below:
    (i) 200 s^{-1} (ii) 2 min^{-1} (iii) 4 yr^{-1} **NCERT**

22 20% of first order reaction is completed in five minutes. How much time will the 60% reaction take to complete ? Calculate the half-life period ($t_{1/2}$) for the above reaction. **ISC 2023**

Long Answer Type Questions

5 Marks

23. During nuclear explosion, one of the products is ^{90}Sr with half-life of 28.1 yr. If 1 μ g of ^{90}Sr was absorbed in the bones of a newly born baby instead of calcium, how much of it will remain after 10 yr and 60 yr if it is not lost metabolically? **NCERT**

24. For the decomposition of azoisopropane to hexane and nitrogen at 543 K, the following data is obtained:

t (s)	*p*(mm of Hg)
0	35.0
360	54.0
720	63.0

Calculate the rate constant. **NCERT**

25. The experimental data for the decomposition of

$$N_2O_5, [2N_2O_5 \longrightarrow 4NO_2 + O_2]$$

in gas phase of 318 K are given below : **NCERT**

t/s	$10^{-2} \times [N_2O_5]$ /mol L^{-1}
0	1.63
400	1.36
800	1.14
1200	0.93
1600	0.78
2000	0.64
2400	0.53
2800	0.43
3200	0.35

(i) Plot $[N_2O_5]$ against *t*.
(ii) Find the half-life period for the reaction.
(iii) Draw a graph between log $[N_2O_5]$ and *t*.
(iv) What is the rate law?
(v) Calculate the rate constant.
(vi) Calculate the half-life period from *k* and compare it with (ii).

26. Consider the reaction, $A + B \longrightarrow C + D$
The initial rates for different initial concentrations of the reactants are given below:

	Initial concentration (mol/L)		Initial rate (mol/L-s)
	[A]	[B]	
(a)	1.0	1.0	2.0×10^{-3}
(b)	2.0	1.0	4.0×10^{-3}
(c)	4.0	1.0	8.0×10^{-3}
(d)	1.0	2.0	2.0×10^{-3}
(e)	1.0	4.0	2.0×10^{-3}

(i) What are the order of reaction with respect to *A* and *B*?
(ii) What is the overall order?
(iii) Write the rate law equation.
(iv) Calculate the rate constant.
(v) Suggest a possible mechanism. **ISC 2005**

Hints & Solutions

1. (i) k (rate constant) (ii) straight line, $\frac{-k}{2.303}$
(iii) first, independent
2. (i) → (c), (ii) → (d), (iii) →(c), (iv) → (b), (v) → (b)
3. (c) A→ (iii), B → (ii), C→(i)
4. Zero order reaction **(2)**
5. **The rate of a first order reaction** is directly proportional to the concentration of the reactants.
Rate of a reaction ∝ [Concentration of reactant]^n
where, n = order of reaction.
For first order,
Rate of reaction ∝ [Concentration of reactant]^1 **(1)**
6. For first order reaction, $t_{1/2} = \frac{0.693}{k}$
where, $t_{1/2}$ = half-life period and k = rate constant
As the reaction is 50% completed in 30 min, thus, $t_{1/2} = 30$ min
$$k = \frac{0.693}{t_{1/2}} = \frac{0.693}{30}, \quad k = 0.0231 \text{ min}^{-1}$$ **(1)**
7. Rate constant
$$k = \frac{0.693}{t_{1/2}} = \frac{0.693}{60 \text{ min}} = \frac{0.693}{(60 \times 60) \text{ s}} = 1.925 \times 10^{-4} \text{s}^{-1}$$ **(1)**
8. Half-life period, $t_{1/2} = \frac{0.693}{k}$ for first order reaction
Given, half-life period, $t_{1/2} = 69.3$ s
Rate constant, $k = ?$ **(1)**
$$k = \frac{0.693}{69.3} = 0.01 \text{ s}^{-1}$$

9. (i) The reaction is of zero order. (1)
(ii) Slope of the graph $= -k = \frac{d[R]}{dt}$ (1/2)
The unit of k, for zero order reaction is mol $L^{-1}s^{-1}$. (1/2)

10. $2NH_3(g) \xrightarrow{Pt} N_2(g) + 3H_2(g)$
For zero order reaction, rate = k
$$\therefore \text{ Rate} = -\frac{1}{2}\frac{d[NH_3]}{dt} = +\frac{d[N_2]}{dt}$$
$$= +\frac{1}{3}\frac{d[H_2]}{dt} = 2.5 \times 10^{-4} \text{ mol L}^{-1}\text{s}^{-1}$$ (1)
∴ Rate of production of N_2
$$= \frac{d[N_2]}{dt} = 2.5 \times 10^{-4} \text{ mol L}^{-1}\text{s}^{-1}$$ (1/2)
Rate of production of H_2
$$= \frac{1}{3}\frac{d[H_2]}{dt} = 2.5 \times 10^{-4} \text{ mol L}^{-1}\text{s}^{-1}$$
$$= \frac{d[H_2]}{dt} = 7.5 \times 10^{-4} \text{ mol L}^{-1}\text{s}^{-1}$$ (1/2)

11. For the first order reaction, $k = \frac{2.303}{t} \log \frac{a}{a-x}$
When, $x = \frac{40a}{100} = 0.4a$, $t = 50$ min.
$$\therefore k = \frac{2.303}{50 \text{ min}} \log \frac{a}{a - 0.4a} \text{ or } k = \frac{2.303}{50 \text{ min}} \log \frac{a}{0.6a}$$
$$= 0.010138 \text{ min}^{-1}$$ **(1)**
Now, $t = ?$ when reaction is 80% complete, i.e. $x = 0.8a$
$k = 0.010138 \text{ min}^{-1}$
$$\therefore t = \frac{2.303}{k} \log \frac{a}{a-x} = \frac{2.303}{0.010138 \text{ min}^{-1}} \log \frac{a}{a - 0.8a}$$
$$= \frac{2.303}{0.010138 \text{ min}^{-1}} \log \frac{1}{0.2a} = 158.78 \text{ min}$$ **(1)**

12. Let, initial amount $(a) = 100$
Time required to complete 75% $(t_{75\%}) = t_{75\%}$.
Amount at $t_{75\%}$, i.e $(a-x)_1 = 100 - 75 = 25$.
Amount at $t_{50\%}$, i.e $(a-x)_2 = 100 - 50 = 50$.
Where, time required to complete 50% $= t_{50\%}$.
$$\text{Now, } \frac{t_{75\%}}{t_{50\%}} = \frac{\log\left[\frac{a}{(a-x)_1}\right]}{\log\left[\frac{a}{(a-x)_2}\right]} = \frac{\log\frac{100}{25}}{\log\frac{100}{50}}$$
$$\frac{t_{75\%}}{t_{50\%}} = \frac{\log 4}{\log 2} = \frac{0.6020}{0.3010} = 2$$
Hence, $t_{75\%} = 2 \times t_{50\%}$, i.e. time required to complete 75% of a reaction is about 2 times more than that required to complete 50% of the reaction.

13. Given, time for 25% completion of reaction = 30 minutes

Let, [initial concentration] = 100

Then, $[a-x]$, i.e. at $\underset{\text{Completion}}{25\%}$ $= 100 - 25 = 75$ %

and $t = 30$ minutes

Therefore, $K = \frac{2.303}{t}\log\frac{a}{a-x} = \frac{2.303}{30}\log\frac{100}{75}$

$= 0.0767 \log 1.333 = 0.0767 \times 0.1250$

$= 0.00958$

$K = 0.0096 \text{ min}^{-1}$

∴Time taken to complete 90% of reaction will be

$$t = \frac{2.303}{K}\log\frac{100}{10} = \frac{2.303}{0.0096}\log 10$$

$$= \frac{2.303}{0.0096}\times 1 = 239.89 \approx 240 \text{ min}$$

14. (i) For first order reaction,

Rate constant, $k = \frac{2.303}{t}\log_{10}\frac{[A_0]}{[A]}$

where, t is time, $[A_0]$ is initial concentration and $[A]$ is the concentration of reactant left after the time, 't'.

Given, $t = 25$ min, suppose $[A_0] = 100$

$$[A] = 100 - \left(\frac{10\times 100}{100}\right) = 100 - 10$$

Then, $k = \frac{2.303}{25}\log_{10}\left(\frac{100}{100-10}\right)$ [As $\log 1.11 = 0.0453$]

$$= \frac{2.303}{25}\times 0.0453 = 0.004 \text{ min}^{-1}$$

Now, half-life $t_{1/2} = \frac{0.693}{k} = \frac{0.693}{0.004} = 173.25$ min **(1)**

(ii) Given so, $[A] = 100 - 87.5$,

From the formula of rate constant,

$$k = \frac{2.303}{t}\log_{10}\frac{[A_0]}{[A]}$$

$$0.004 = \frac{2.303}{t}\log_{10}\frac{100}{100-87.5}$$

$t = \frac{2.303}{0.004}\times 0.9030$ [As $\log 8 = 0.9030$]

$t = 519.95$ min **(1)**

15. If $a = 100$, $a - x = 100 - 50 = 50$

For 50% completion of the reaction.

$$t_{50\%} = \frac{2.303}{k}\log\frac{100}{50} \Rightarrow 120 = \frac{2.303}{k}\times 0.3010$$

[As $\log 2 = 0.3010$]

$k = \frac{2.303}{120}\times .3010 \Rightarrow k = .0057$ **(1)**

For 90% completion of the reaction.

If $a = 100$; $a - x = 100 - 90 = 10$

$$t_{90\%} = \frac{2.303}{k}\log\frac{100}{10}$$

$\Rightarrow t_{90\%} = \frac{2.303}{.0057}\times 1$ [As $\log 10 = 1$]

$t_{90\%} = 404$ min

16. (i) Refer to solution 14 (i).

(ii) From the formula of rate constant,

when $[A] = 100 - 17$, we get

$$k = \frac{2.303}{t}\log\frac{[A]_0}{[A]}$$

$$0.004 = \frac{2.303}{t}\log\frac{100}{100-17}$$

$\Rightarrow t = \frac{2.303}{0.004}\times 0.0809$ [As $\log 1.205 = 0.0809$]

$= 46.57$ min **(1)**

17. For first order reaction,

$$t = \frac{2.303}{k}\log\frac{a}{(a-x)} \quad \text{...(i)}$$

Given, $(a-x) = \frac{a}{16}$; $k = 60 \text{ s}^{-1}$

On putting the values in Eq. (i)

$$t = \frac{2.303}{60 \text{ s}^{-1}}\log\frac{a\times 16}{a} = \frac{2.303}{60 \text{ s}^{-1}}\log 16$$

$$= \frac{2.303}{60 \text{ s}^{-1}}\log 2^4 = \frac{2.303}{60 \text{ s}^{-1}}\times 4\log 2 \quad (1)$$

$$= \frac{2.303}{60 \text{ s}^{-1}}\times 4\times 0.3010$$

Time $(t) = 4.62\times 10^{-2}$s (1)

18. For a first order reaction, rate constant $k = \frac{2.303}{t}\log\frac{[A]_0}{[A]}$

where, t is time, $[A]_0$ is initial concentration and $[A]$ is concentration left after time t.

For 75% completion, suppose $[A]_0 = 100$,

then $[A] = 100 - 75 = 25$

$k = \frac{2.303}{t}\log\frac{100}{25} = \frac{1.386}{t}$ [As $\log 4 = 2\log 2 = 2\times 0.3010$]

For 50% completion, $k = \frac{0.693}{t_{1/2}}$ **(1)**

But, for a given reaction, k is constant

$\therefore \frac{1.386}{t} = \frac{0.693}{t_{1/2}} \Rightarrow \frac{t}{t_{1/2}} = \frac{1.386}{0.693} = 2$ **(1)**

or $t = 2t_{1/2}$

So, time (t) required for completion of 75% of a reaction is twice the time required for completion of 50% (half-life) of the reaction. **(1)**

19. For a first order reaction, $t = \frac{2.303}{k}\log\frac{[R]_0}{[R]}$ (1)

$$t = \frac{2.303}{(1.15\times 10^{-3}\text{s}^{-1})}\times\log\frac{(5 \text{ g})}{(3 \text{ g})}$$

$$= \frac{2.303}{(1.15 \times 10^{-3} s^{-1})} (\log 5 - \log 3) \quad (1)$$

$$= \frac{2.303}{(1.15 \times 10^{-3} s^{-1})} (0.6990 - 0.4771)$$

$$= 2.0 \times 10^{3} \times 0.2219 \text{ s} = 443.8 \text{ s}$$

or time = 444 s (1)

20. For first order reactions,

$$k = \frac{0.693}{t_{1/2}} = \frac{0.693}{(3.0 \text{ h})} \quad \text{or} \quad t = \frac{2.303}{k} \log \frac{[A]_0}{[A]} \quad (1)$$

or
$$\log \frac{[A]_0}{[A]} = \frac{k \times t}{2.303}$$

$$\log \frac{[A]_0}{[A]} = \frac{0.693}{3 \text{ h}} \times \frac{8 \text{ h}}{2.303} = 0.8024$$

$$\frac{[A]_0}{[A]} = \text{antilog } 0.8024 = 6.345 \quad (1)$$

$$[A]_0 = 1 \text{ M}; \quad [A] = \frac{[A]_0}{6.345} = \frac{1 \text{ M}}{6.345} = 0.1576 \text{ M}$$

After 8 h, sucrose left = 0.1576 M (1)

21. (i) $t_{1/2} = \frac{0.693}{200 \text{ s}^{-1}} = 0.346 \times 10^{-2} \text{s} = 3.46 \times 10^{-3} \text{s}$ (1)

(ii) $t_{1/2} = \frac{0.693}{2 \text{ min}^{-1}} = 0.346 \text{ min} = 3.46 \times 10^{-1} \text{min}$ (1)

(iii) $t_{1/2} = \frac{0.693}{4 \text{ yr}^{-1}} = 0.173 \text{ yr} = 1.73 \times 10^{-1} \text{yr}$ (1)

22. $t_{20\%} = 5 \text{ min}$

Let $[A]$ be initial concentration $= 100$

After 5 min, $[A] = 100 - 20 = 80$

For Ist order,

$$k = \frac{2.303}{t} \log_{10} \frac{[A]_0}{[A]}$$

$$= \frac{2.303}{5} \log_{10} \frac{100}{80} = 0.0446 \text{ min}^{-1}$$

For 60% completion of reaction, the time will be

$$t = \frac{2.303}{k} \log \frac{[A]_0}{[A]}$$

Here, $[A]_0 = 100$ and $[A] = 100 - 60 = 40$.

So, $t = \frac{2.303}{0.0446} \times \log \frac{100}{40} = \frac{2.303}{0.0446} \log 2.5$

$t = 20.5$ min

$t_{1/2}$ for this reaction is

$$t_{1/2} = \frac{0.693}{k} = \frac{0.693}{0.0446 \text{ min}^{-1}} = 15.538 \text{ min}$$

23. $t_{1/2} = 28.1 \text{ yr}, \; k = \frac{0.693}{t_{1/2}} = \frac{0.693}{28.1} \text{yr}^{-1}$

For first order reaction,

$$t = \frac{2.303}{k} \log \frac{a}{(a-x)}$$

***Case* I** $a = 1 \, \mu\text{g}, \; t = 10 \text{ yr}, \; k = \frac{0.693}{28.1} \text{yr}^{-1}$

$$10 = \frac{2.303}{0.693} \times 28.1 \log \frac{a}{(a-x)} \quad (1/2)$$

$$\log \frac{a}{(a-x)} = \frac{10 \times 0.693}{2.303 \times 28.1} = 0.107$$

$$\frac{a}{(a-x)} = \text{antilog}(0.107) = 1.279 \quad (1)$$

$$(a-x) = \frac{a}{1.279} = \frac{(1 \, \mu\text{g})}{1.279} = 0.7819 \, \mu\text{g}$$

Amount left after 10 yr = 0.7819 μg (1)

***Case* II** $a = 1 \, \mu\text{g}, t = 60 \text{ yr}, \quad k = \frac{0.693}{28.1} \text{yr}^{-1}$

$$60 = \frac{2.303}{0.693/28.1} \times \log \frac{a}{(a-x)} \quad (1/2)$$

$$\log \frac{a}{(a-x)} = \frac{(60 \text{ yr}) \times 0.693 / 28.1 \text{ yr}^{-1}}{2.303} = 0.642$$

$$\frac{a}{(a-x)} = \text{antilog } 0.642 = 4.385 \quad (1)$$

$$(a-x) = \frac{a}{4.385} = \frac{(1 \, \mu\text{g})}{4.385} = 0.2280 \, \mu\text{g}$$

Amount left after 60 yr = 0.2280 μg (1)

24. Let the pressure of azoisopropane decreases by x atm. As 1 mole of azoisopropane decompose to give 1 mole of N_2 and 1 mole of hexane (C_6H_{14}), the pressure of N_2 and hexane increases by x atm.

$$\underset{\text{Azoisopropane}}{(CH_3)_2CHN{=}NCH(CH_3)_2(g)} \longrightarrow N_2(g) + C_6H_{14}(g)$$

At $t = 0$	35.0 atm	0 atm	0 atm
At time, t	$(35.0 - x)$ atm	x atm	x atm (1)

$$p_t = p_{\text{azoisopropane}} + p_{N_2} + p_{C_6H_{14}}$$

$$p_t = 35.0 - x + x + x$$

$$p_t = 35 + x \Rightarrow x = p_t - 35$$

$$\therefore \; p_{\text{azoisopropane}} = 35.0 - (p_t - 35) = 70 - p_t \quad (1)$$

(i) Rate constant after 360 s $= k_1$

At $t = 360$ s, $p_i = 35$ atm, $p_t = 54$ atm

$\therefore \; p_{\text{azoisopropane}} = (70 - 54)$ atm = 16 atm

$\therefore$ Rate constant, k_1

$$= \frac{2.303}{360} \log \frac{35}{16} = \frac{2.303}{360} \log 2.187$$

$$= \frac{2.303 \times 0.33984}{360}$$

$$= 2.17 \times 10^{-3} \text{ s}^{-1} \quad (1)$$

(ii) Rate constant after 720 s, k_2

$p_i = 35$ atm, $p_t = 63.0$ atm

$\therefore \; p_{\text{azoisopropane}} = (70 - 63)$ atm = 7 atm

$\therefore$ Rate constant,

$$k_2 = \frac{2.303}{720} \log \frac{35}{7} = \frac{2.303}{720} \log 5$$

$$= \frac{2.303 \times 0.6990}{720} \quad (1)$$

$$= 2.24 \times 10^{-3}\ s^{-1}$$

Average rate constant,

$$k = \frac{(2.17 + 2.24)}{2} \times 10^{-3} = 2.21 \times 10^{-3}\ s^{-1} \quad (1)$$

25. (i) The plot of $[N_2O_5]$ against time is shown below :

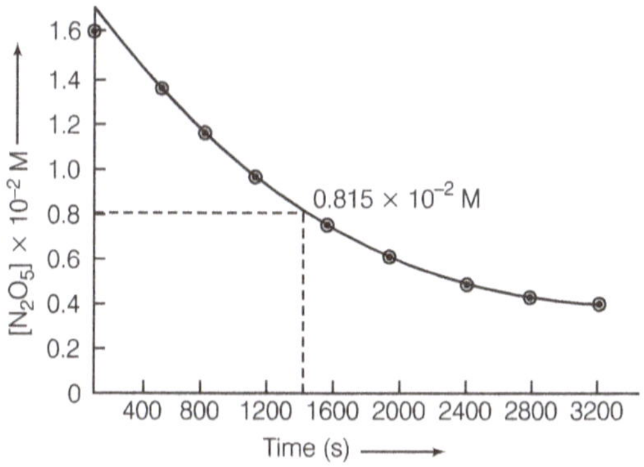

(1)

(ii) Initial concentration [at $t = 0$] of $N_2O_5 = 1.63 \times 10^{-2}$ M

Half of its concentration $= \frac{1.63 \times 10^{-2}}{2} = 0.815 \times 10^{-2}$ M

From, the above graph, the time which corresponds to 0.815×10^{-2} M concentration is 1450 s.

Hence, $t_{1/2} = 1450$ s (1)

(iii)

t/s	$10^{-2} \times [N_2O_5]$ / mol L^{-1}	$\log [N_2O_5]$
0	1.63	− 1.79
400	1.36	− 1.87
800	1.14	− 1.94
1200	0.93	− 2.03
1600	0.78	− 2.11
2000	0.64	− 2.19
2400	0.53	− 2.28
2800	0.43	− 2.37
3200	0.35	− 2.46

The plot of $\log [N_2O_5]$ and time can be represented as :

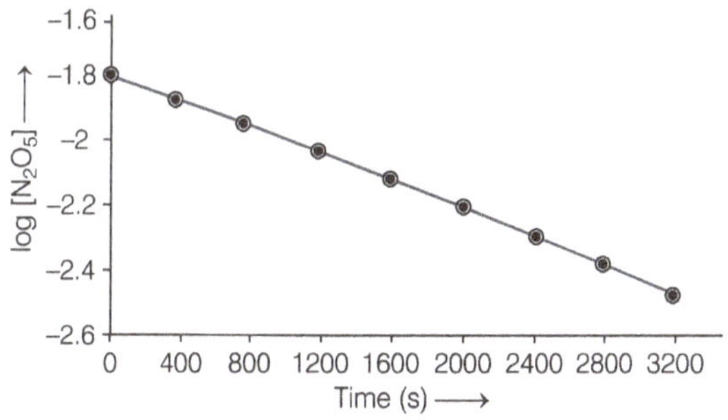

(1)

(iv) As the plot of $\log [N_2O_5]$ *versus* time obtained is a straight line, hence it is a reaction of first order.

$\therefore$ Rate $= k[N_2O_5]$ (1/2)

(v) For first order reaction, the slope of the line

$$= -\frac{k}{2.303} \quad \text{...(i)}$$

$$\therefore \quad \text{Slope} = \frac{-2.46 - (-1.79)}{3200 - 0} = \frac{-0.67}{3200} \quad \text{...(ii)}$$

Equating Eqs. (i) and (ii), we get

$$-\frac{k}{2.303} = \frac{-0.67}{3200}$$

or $k = \frac{0.67 \times 2.303}{3200}$

or $k = 4.82 \times 10^{-4}\ s^{-1}$ (1)

(vi) $t_{1/2} = \frac{0.693}{k} = \frac{0.693}{4.82 \times 10^{-4}\ s^{-1}} = 1438$s

Half-life period ($t_{1/2}$) are calculated from the formula and slope are approximately the same. (1/2)

26. Rate of reaction $\propto$ [concentration]^n , where n is the order of reaction.

Given reaction, $A + B \longrightarrow C + D$

Suppose the given reaction is of order p with respect to A and q with respect to B.

The rate of formation of C and D can also be written as :

(a) $2.0 \times 10^{-3} = k[A]^p[B]^q = k(1)^p(1)^q$ ... (i)

(b) $4.0 \times 10^{-3} = k(2)^p(1)^q$ ... (ii)

(d) $2.0 \times 10^{-3} = k(1)^p(2)^q$ ... (iii)

From Eqs. (i) and (ii), we get

$$\frac{4.0 \times 10^{-3}}{2.0 \times 10^{-3}} = \frac{k(2)^p(1)^q}{k(1)^p(1)^q} \Rightarrow (2)^1 = 2^p$$

Hence, $p = 1$

From Eqs. (i) and (iii), we get

$$\frac{2.0 \times 10^{-3}}{2.0 \times 10^{-3}} = \frac{k(1)^p(2)^q}{k(1)^p(2)^q} \Rightarrow 1 = 2^q \Rightarrow 2^0 = 2^q$$

$q =$

(i) The order of reaction with respect to A is first order, i.e. $r \propto [A]$ and with respect to B is zero order, i.e. $r \propto [B]^0$. (1)

(ii) Overall order is one $(1 + 0 = 1)$. (1)

(iii) Rate law equation is, $r = k[A][B]^0$

where, k is rate constant. (1)

(iv) Since, $r = k[A]$

Then rate constant, $k = \frac{r}{[A]} = \frac{2 \times 10^{-3}}{1.0} = 2 \times 10^{-3}\ s^{-1}$ (1)

(v) Firstly either A or B takes part in the reaction to generate reactive intermediate, which then attacks on other to give the product.

$$A \longrightarrow A^*$$

$$A^* + B \longrightarrow C + D \quad (1)$$

TOPIC 04 Temperature Dependence of the Rate of a Reaction

Most of the chemical reactions are accelerated by increase in temperature. It has been found that **for a chemical reaction with rise in temperature by 10°, the rate constant is nearly doubled.** e.g. In decomposition of N_2O_5, the time taken for half of the original amount to decompose is 12 min at 50°C, 5 h at 25°C and 10 days at 0°C. The effect of temperature is usually expressed in terms of **temperature coefficient** which is the ratio of velocity constant of a reaction at two temperature differing by 10°C.

$$\text{Temperature coefficient} = \frac{k_{(t+10)^\circ C}}{k_{t^\circ C}}$$

In the below figure, the peak of the curve represents the kinetic energy possessed by the maximum fraction of molecules, that is known as **most probable kinetic energy**. Very less number of molecules possess either very low or very high kinetic energy.

Most of the molecules have average or intermediate kinetic energies between the most probable kinetic energy and the lowest kinetic energy.

On raising temperature to (t + 10°C) the maximum of the curve shifts to higher kinetic energy value and the curve spreads to the right such that there is a greater proportion of molecules with much higher energies.

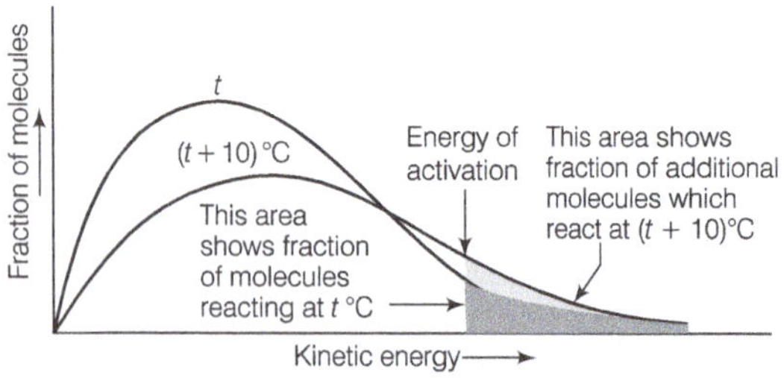

Distribution curve showing temperature dependence of rate of a reaction

However, the total area under the curve must be constant, since total probability must be one at all times. We can determine E_a (activation energy) with the Maxwell Boltzmann distribution curve.

Rise in temperature of the substance increases the fraction of molecules that collides with energies more than E_a.

The graph shows that in the curve at (t + 10)°C the area showing the fraction of reacting molecules having energy equal to or greater than activation energy gets doubled and hence, double the rate of a reaction.

Arrhenius Equation

The temperature dependence of rate of a chemical reaction is expressed by Arrhenius equation,

$$k = Ae^{-E_a/RT}$$

where, A is the Arrhenius factor or the frequency factor, also called **pre-exponential** factor. It is a constant and specific to a particular reaction. R is gas constant and E_a is the activation energy measured in joules/mole ($J\ mol^{-1}$).

Thus, Arrhenius equation is a quantitative relationship between rate constant and temperature.

Note The temperature dependence of the rate of a chemical reaction was first proposed by J.H. van't Hoff but Arrhenius provided its physical justification and interpretation.

Activation Energy

The activation energy can be defined as "The energy that activates passive or non-active molecules after its adsorption or minimum energy in excess to normal energy of molecules, which molecules must possess in order to form product on collision.

The concept of activation energy gives us an idea whether a given reaction is slow or fast at a given temperature. A reaction which has lower activation energy proceed at a faster rate at a given temperature or *vice-versa.*

The differences in activation energy are mainly responsible for observed difference in rates of reactions. The concept of activation energy as applied to chemical reaction can be explained by plotting energy against the progress of reaction as shown in the figure below :

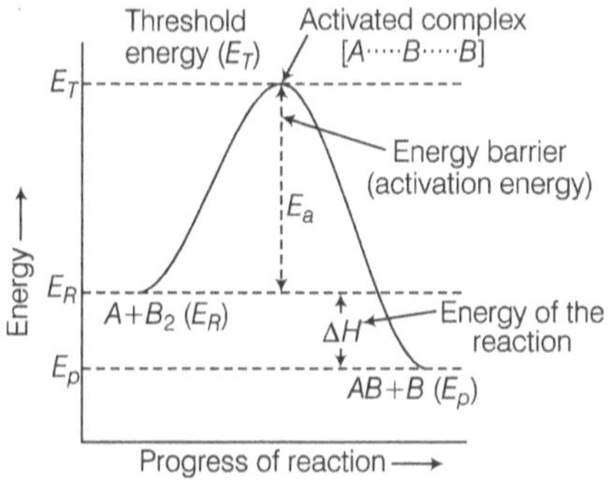

$$E_a = E_T - E_R$$

Note Threshold energy is the minimum energy which the colliding molecules must have for effective collision. Effective collisions are those collisions which lead to the formation of product molecules.

The different plots related to activation energy with progress of reaction are explained below :

(i) **Activated Complex and Progress of a Reaction**

The reactants (having energy equal to E_R) do not convert directly into desired products. The reactants firstly absorb energy equal to the activation energy (E_a) and form activated complex. The activated complex which is formed has a short life-span and hence it splits into products to acquire stable state with a lower energy which is equal to the energy of the products (E_P). The energy of the products (E_p) is less than that of the reactants (E_R).

$$E_a = E_T - E_R,$$
$$\Delta E = E_p - E_R$$

where, ΔE = Energy of the reaction.

If energy released by the dissociation of activated complex is greater than that absorbed for its formation, there is net release of energy [See fig. (a)] and the reaction is said to be **exothermic**. For such reactions,

$$E_p < E_R$$

Hence, $\Delta E = E_p - E_R = -\text{ve}$

On the other hand, if energy absorbed for the formation of activated complex is greater than that released when it dissociates, the net result is absorption of energy [See fig. (b)] and the reaction is said to be **endothermic**. For such reactions,

$$E_p > E_R$$

Hence, $\Delta E = E_p - E_R = +\text{ve},$

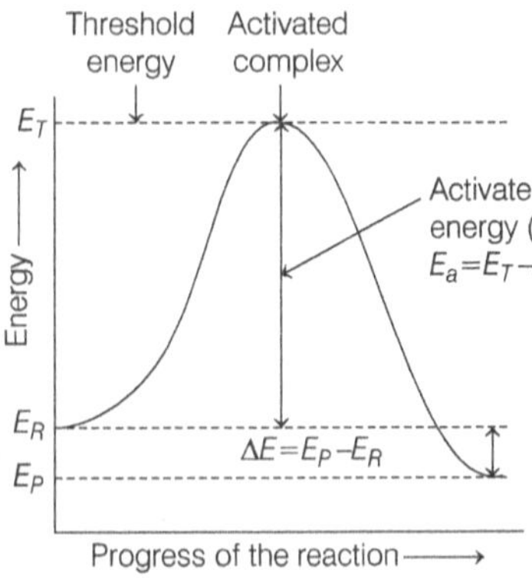

(a) Exothermic reaction (ΔE = −ve)

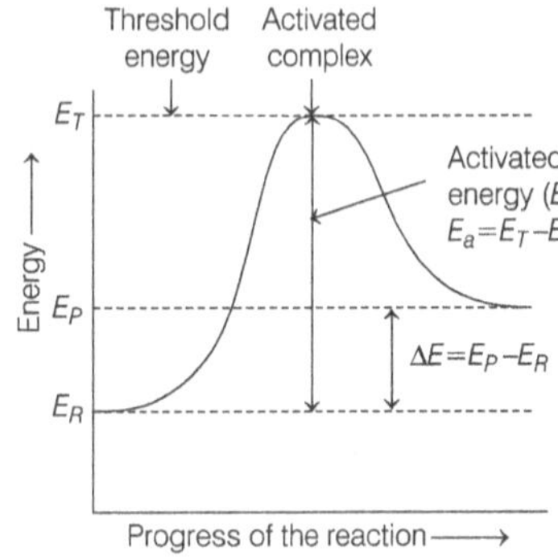

Concept of activated complex

(a) Exothermic reaction (ΔE = −ve)

(b) Endothermic reaction (ΔE = +ve)

(ii) **Activation Energies and Reversible Reactions**

Consider a reversible reaction, $A + B \rightleftharpoons C + D$

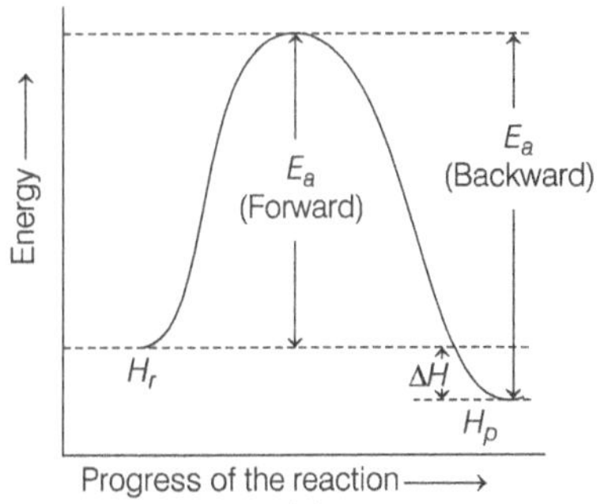

(a)

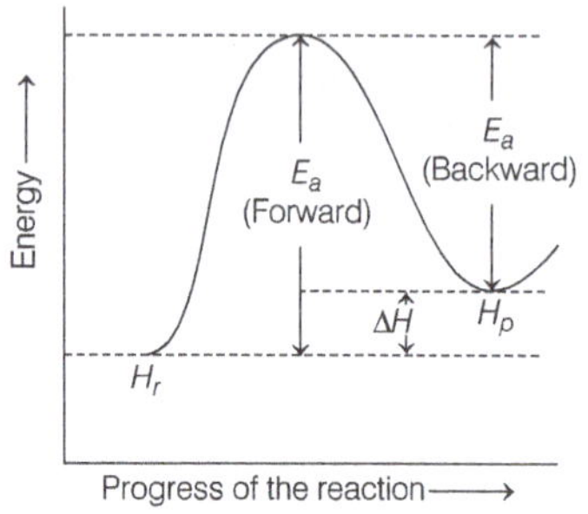

(b)

Activation energies for forward and backward reactions in case of (a) exothermic (ΔH = −ve) and (b) endothermic (ΔH = +ve) reactions

It is clear from the graphs that reactant molecules in the forward reaction and the product molecules in their backward reaction have to pass through the transition state even though the activation energies for the forward, $E_{a\,(\text{forward})}$ and the backward, $E_{a(\text{backward})}$ reactions are different. They are related to ΔH as follows :

$\Delta H = E_a(\text{forward}) - E_a(\text{backward})$

[E_a = Activation energy of a reaction]

- For exothermic reaction ($\Delta H = -$ve)

  (Activation energy for forward reaction)
  < (Activation energy for backward reaction)
- For endothermic reaction ($\Delta H = +$ve)

  (Activation energy for forward reaction)
  > (Activation energy for backward reaction)

Note (i) Different reactions have different rates because their activation energies are different. Lesser the activation energy, faster is the reaction rate.

(ii) Activation energy can never be zero. If $E_a = 0$, then according to Arrhenius equation, $k = A$, i.e. every collision between molecules leads to a chemical reaction. This can never be true.

Calculation of Activation Energy

In Arrhenius equation, $k = Ae^{-E_a/RT}$, the factor $e^{-E_a/RT}$ represents the fraction of molecules that have kinetic energy more than the activation energy (E_a). Thus, it is clear from Arrhenius equation that increasing the temperature or decreasing the activation energy will result in an increase in the rate of the reaction and an exponential increase in the rate constant. The calculation of activation energy carried out by two methods are as follows:

(i) Graphical Method

Taking natural logarithm on both sides, the Arrhenius equation becomes,

$$\ln k = -\frac{E_a}{RT} + \ln A$$

This equation is of the form $y = mx + c$, which is a equation of a straight line. Thus, the plot of ln k *versus* $1/T$ gives a straight line with negative slope which is equal to $-\frac{E_a}{R}$ and intercept of ln A.

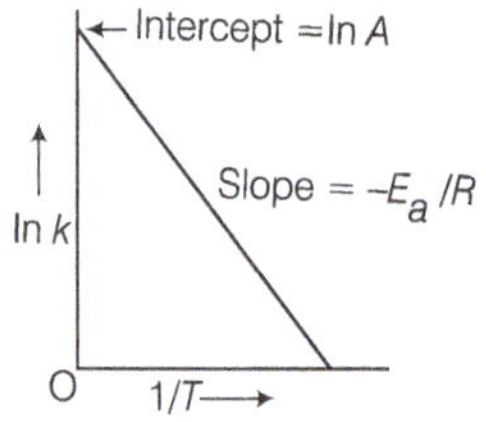

A plot between ln k and 1/T

(ii) Experimental Method

E_a and A can also be determined from the rate constants at two different temperatures.

$$\ln k = -\frac{E_a}{RT} + \ln A \quad \text{or} \quad \log k = -\frac{E_a}{2.303\,RT} + \log A$$

Let k_1 and k_2 be the rate constants at temperatures T_1 and T_2.

Then, $$\log k_1 = -\frac{E_a}{2.303\,RT_1} + \log A \quad \text{...(i)}$$

$$\log k_2 = -\frac{E_a}{2.303\,RT_2} + \log A \quad \text{...(ii)}$$

A = constant for the given reactions.

Subtracting Eq. (i) from Eq. (ii), we have

$$\log k_2 - \log k_1 = \frac{E_a}{2.303\,RT_1} - \frac{E_a}{2.303\,RT_2}$$

$$\log \frac{k_2}{k_1} = \frac{E_a}{2.303\,R}\left[\frac{1}{T_1} - \frac{1}{T_2}\right]$$

$$\boxed{\log \frac{k_2}{k_1} = \frac{E_a}{2.303\,R}\left[\frac{T_2 - T_1}{T_1 T_2}\right]}$$

Example 1 The decomposition of hydrocarbon follows the equation, $k = (4.5 \times 10^{11}\ \text{s}^{-1})\,e^{-28000\,\text{K}/T}$. Calculate E_a. **NCERT**

Sol. According to Arrhenius equation, $k = Ae^{-E_a/RT}$ ...(i)

According to the given data

$$k = (4.5 \times 10^{11}\ \text{s}^{-1})\,e^{-28000\ \text{K/T}} \quad \text{...(ii)}$$

On comparing both equations, we have

$$-\frac{E_a}{RT} = \frac{-28000\ \text{K}}{T}$$

$$E_a = (28000\ \text{K}) \times R = (28000\ \text{K}) \times (8.314\ \text{K}^{-1}\text{J mol}^{-1})$$

$$= 232792\ \text{J mol}^{-1}$$

$$E_a = 232.792\ \text{kJ mol}^{-1}$$

Effect of Catalyst

A **catalyst** is a substance which increases the rate of reaction without itself undergoing any permanent chemical change, e.g. hydrogen and oxygen do not react at room temperature but in the presence of spongy or powder platinum, the reaction occurs vigorously. Similarly, MnO_2 catalyses the following reaction in the order to raise its rate considerably.

$$2KClO_3 \xrightarrow{MnO_2} 2KCl + 3O_2$$

The word catalyst should not be used when the added substances reduces the rate of reaction. In such cases, the substance is called **inhibitor**.

According to **intermediate complex theory**, a catalyst participates in a chemical reaction by forming temporary bonds with the reactants resulting in an intermediate complex formation.

This has a transistory existence and decomposes to yield products and the catalyst.

For a general reaction of the type,

$$A + B \longrightarrow AB$$

Uncatalysed reaction proceeds as:

$$A + B \longrightarrow [A - B] \longrightarrow \underset{\text{Product}}{AB}$$

Catalysed reaction proceeds as:

$$\underset{\text{Reactants}}{A + B +} \underset{\text{Catalyst}}{C} \longrightarrow \underset{\text{Intermediate complex}}{ABC} \longrightarrow \underset{\text{Product}}{A—B} + \underset{\text{Catalyst regenerated}}{C}$$

Since, the catalyst is regenerated after the decomposition of the intermediate so, a small amount of catalyst is enough for a large amount of reactants.

It is believed that the catalyst provides an alternate pathway or reaction mechanism by reducing the activation energy between reactants and products, hence lowering the potential energy barrier as shown in the figure given below.

It is also clear from the Arrhenius equation ($k = Ae^{-E_a/RT}$) that lower the value of E_a faster will be the rate of reaction.

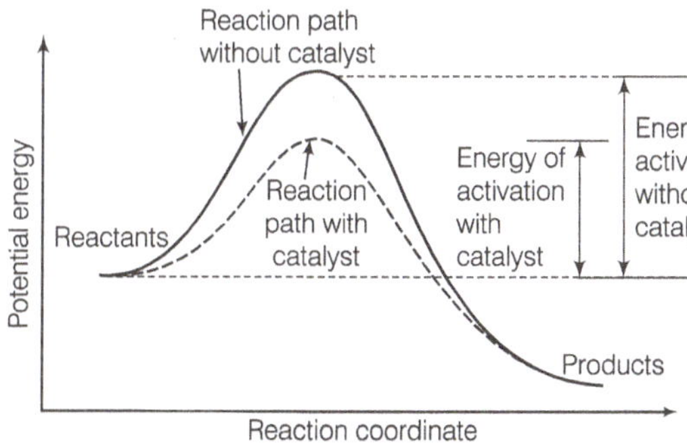

Effect of catalyst on activation energy

Characteristics of a Catalyst

(i) A small amount of the catalyst can catalyse a large amount of reactions.

(ii) A catalyst does not alter Gibbs energy, ΔG of a reaction.

(iii) It does not change the equilibrium constant rather it helps in attaining the equilibrium faster, i.e. it catalyses the forward and backward reactions both to the same extent so that the equilibrium state remains same but is reached earlier.

(iv) A catalyst catalyses the spontaneous reactions but does not catalyse non-spontaneous reactions.

(v) A catalyst is highly specific. They have an ability to direct the reaction to yield a particular product. The reaction with same reactants but different catalyst may yield different products.

(vi) A catalyst never starts a reaction which has no tendency to proceed.

Collision Theory of Chemical Reactions

To explain the effect of temperature on rection rates, collision theory was proposed by Max Trautz and William Lewis in 1916. Collision theory is based on kinetic theory of gases. According to this theory, the reactant molecules are assumed to be hard spheres and reaction is postulated to occur when molecules collide with each other. **The number of collisions per second per unit volume of the reaction mixture is called collision frequency** (Z). E_a is another factor which affects the rate of chemical reactions.

For a bimolecular elementary reactions, $A + B \rightarrow$ Products

Rate of reaction can be expressed as:

$$\text{Rate} = Z_{AB}\, e^{-E_a/RT}$$

where, Z_{AB} is the collision frequency of the reactants A and B and $e^{-E_a/RT}$ is the fraction of molecules with energies equal to or greater than E_a. When Arrhenius equation, $k = Ae^{-E_a/RT}$ is compared to the above equation, A can be related to the **collision frequency** (Z).

Not all the collisions result into product. Collisions in which molecules have sufficient kinetic energy (which is also called **threshold energy**) and proper orientation result into breaking of bond between the reacting species and formation of new bonds to form products. These collisions are referred to as the **effective collisions.**

Note Threshold energy = activation energy + energy possessed by reacting species

On the other hand, collisions with improper orientation make the molecules bounce back leading to the formation of no products.

e.g. Formation of methanol from bromomethane depends upon the orientation of reactant molecules.

$$CH_3Br + OH^- \longrightarrow CH_3OH + Br^-$$

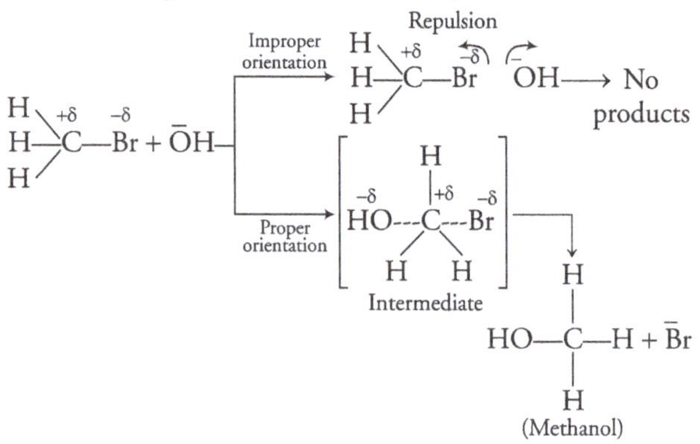

Proper and improper orientations of colliding molecules

When the orientation factor is taken into account, the expression becomes

Reaction rate $= PZ_{AB}\, e^{-E_a/RT}$

where, P is orientation factor or steric factor or probability factor. It takes into account the fact that in a collision, molecules must be properly oriented. Therefore, in collision theory activation energy and proper orientation of the molecules together determine the criteria for an effective collision and thus, the rate of a chemical reaction.

Limitation of Collision Theory

This theory explains the results of a number of reactions but it does not give satisfactory explanation in some cases as it considers atoms/molecules to be hard spheres and ignores their structural aspects.

Topic Practice 4

Very Short Answer Type Questions

(1 Mark)

1. Fill in the Blanks

(i) Activation energy can be determined by .... **ISC 2013**

(ii) Arrhenius equation is related to .... **ISC 2002**

(iii) The activated complex has .... reactant character and partial product character.

(iv) The rate of formation of intermediate will determine the rate of ....

2. Objective Type Questions

(i) The correct increasing order of the time taken for half of the decomposition of N_2O_5 at the temperature 50°C, 0°C and 25°C will be

(a) 50°C < 0°C < 25°C (b) 50°C < 25°C < 0°C
(c) 0°C < 25°C < 50°C (d) 0°C < 50°C < 25°C

(ii) Relationship between threshold energy, activation energy and energy possessed by reacting species is

(a) threshold energy = activation energy + energy possessed by reacting species
(b) threshold energy = activation energy − energy possessed by reacting species
(c) activation energy = threshold energy + energy possessed by reacting species
(d) None of the above

(iii) Arrhenius equation may not be represented as

(a) $\ln \frac{k}{A} = -\frac{E_a}{RT}$
(b) $k = Ae^{-E_a/RT}$
(c) $\log A = \log k + \frac{E_a}{2.303RT}$
(d) $\log k - \left(\frac{E_a}{RT}\right) = A$

(iv) In a plot of $\log k$ vs $1/T$, the slope is **ISC 2012**

(a) $-E_a/2.303$ (b) $E_a/2.303\,R$
(c) $E_a/2.303$ (d) $-E_a/2.303\,R$

(v) What is the activation energy for a reaction, if its rate doubles when the temperature is raised from 20°C to 35°C? ($R = 8.314$ J mol^{-1}K^{-1})

(a) 342 kJ mol^{-1} (b) 269 kJ mol^{-1}
(c) 34.7 kJ mol^{-1} (d) 15.1 kJ mol^{-1}

3. Match the given property in Column I with its related value in Column II.

Rate constant (k) of a reaction is given by

$$\log_{10} k(\text{min}^{-1}) = 5 - \frac{2\times 10^3 k}{T}$$

Column I		Column II
A. Arrhenius constant in (min^{-1})	(i)	1.0
B. Order of reaction	(ii)	2.0
C. Rate of the reaction at initial concentration of 0.2 M at 500 K	(iii)	10^5
D. Energy of activation (in kcal)	(iv)	9.2

Codes

	A	B	C	D
(a)	(iii)	(i)	(ii)	(iv)
(b)	(iii)	(iv)	(ii)	(i)
(c)	(iv)	(i)	(iii)	(ii)
(d)	(iv)	(i)	(ii)	(iii)

4. Oxygen is available in plenty in air yet fuels do not burn by themselves at room temperature. Explain. **NCERT Exemplar**

5. Why in redox titration of $KMnO_4$ *versus* oxalic acid, we heat oxalic acid solution before starting the titration? **NCERT Exemplar**

6. In some case, it is found that a large number of colliding molecules have energy more than threshold energy, yet the reaction is slow. Why? **NCERT Exemplar**

Short Answer Type I Questions

2 Marks

7. Correct the following statement. The rate constant of a reaction increases linearly with increase in temperature. **ISC 2003**

8. What is the effect of temperature on the rate constant of a reaction? How can this effect of temperature on rate constant be represented quantitatively? **NCERT**

9. Draw a graph which is used to calculate the activation energy of a reaction. Give the appropriate expressions used to calculate the activation energy graphically. **ISC 2006**

Short Answer Type II Questions

3 Marks

10. (i) The rate constant of a reaction at 500 K and 700 K are 0.02 s^{-1} and 0.07 s^{-1} respectively. Calculate the value of E_a (activation energy).
(ii) A radioactive substance which emits alpha particle follows first order reaction. The half-life period of this radioactive substance is 30 hours. Calculate the fraction in percent (%) of the radioactive substance which remains after 90 hours. **ISC 2024**

11. The rate of a reaction becomes four times when the temperature changes from 293 K to 313 K. Calculate the energy of the activation (E_a) of the reaction assuming that it does not change with temperature.
$[R = 8.314 \text{ JK}^{-1} \text{ mol}^{-1}, \log 4 = 0.6021]$ **NCERT**

12. The activation energy for the reaction, $2HI(g) \longrightarrow H_2(g) + I_2(g)$ is 209.5 kJ mol^{-1} at 581 K. Calculate the fraction of molecules of reactants having energy equal to or greater than activation energy. **NCERT**

13. First order reaction is 50% completed in 40 minutes at 300 K and in 20 minutes at 320 K. Calculate the activation energy of the reaction. **ISC 2023**

14. The rate of the chemical reaction doubles for an increase of 10 K in absolute temperature from 298 K. Calculate E_a. **NCERT**

Or

The rate of most reactions become double when their temperature is raised from 298 K to 308 K. Calculate their activation energy.
(Given, $R = 8.314 \text{ J mol K}^{-1}$)

15. The rate constant for the decomposition of hydrocarbons is $2.418 \times 10^{-5} s^{-1}$ at 546 K. If the energy of activation is 179.9 kJ mol^{-1}, what will be the value of pre-exponential factor? **NCERT**

Long Answer Type Questions

5 Marks

16. (i) Write the mathematical expression for the variation of rate constant of a reaction with temperature.
(ii) How can you graphically find the activation energy of the reaction from the above expression.
(iii) The slope of the line in the graph of log k (k = rate constant) versus $\frac{1}{T}$ is –5841.
Calculate the activation energy of the reaction. **ISC 2014**

17. The time required for 10% completion of a first order reaction at 298 K is equal to that required for its 25% completion at 308 K. If the value of A is $4 \times 10^{10} s^{-1}$. Calculate k at 318 K and E_a. **NCERT**

18. The rate constant for the decomposition of N_2O_5 at various temperatures is given below.

T/°C	0	20	40	60	80
$10^5 \times K/s^{-1}$	0.0787	1.70	25.7	178	2140

Draw a graph between ln k and $1/T$ and calculate the values of A and E_a. Predict the rate constant at 30°C and 50°C. **NCERT**

Hints & Solutions

1. (i) Arrhenius equation (ii) rate constant
(iii) partial (iv) reaction

2. (i) b, (ii) a, (iii) d, (iv) d (v) c

3. (a) A → (iii), B → (i), C → (ii), D → (iv).

4. The activation energy for the combustion of fuels is very high at room temperature. **(1)**

5. On increasing the temperature, the rate of reaction increases. Thus, on heating the oxalic acid solution before titration, the rate of decolourisation becomes fast and hence, rate of reaction increases. **(1)**

6. It is due to improper orientation of reacting molecules. **(1)**

7. According to Arrhenius equation,

$$k = Ae^{-E_a/RT}$$

The rate constant of a reaction decreases exponentially with increases in temperature. **(2)**

8. Refer to the text on page 118.
[**Hint** On increasing the temperature to 10°C, i.e. $t+10$, the rate of reaction becomes doubled.] (2)

9. According to Arrhenius equation,

$$k = Ae^{-E_a/RT}$$

Taking log on both sides, we get

$$\log k = \log A - \frac{E_a}{2.303RT}$$

Comparing with straight line equation, i.e. $y = mx + c$

where,

$$y = \log k,\ x = \frac{1}{T}$$

$$m(\text{slope}) = -\frac{E_a}{2.303R}$$

Intercept $c = \log A$

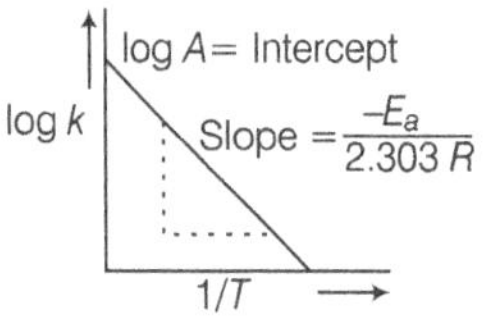

Graph between log k vs $1/T$

After plotting, $\log k$ vs $\frac{1}{T}$ graph,

slope of line will be $-\frac{E_a}{2.303R}$. Knowing the value of the slope and gas constant, the activation energy can be calculated with the help of equation,

$E_a = -2.303R \times \text{slope}$ **(2)**

10. (i) Given, $T_1 = 500$ K, $T_2 = 700$ K

$k_1 = 0.02\ s^{-1}, k_2 = 0.07\ s^{-1}$

We know that,

$$\log\frac{k_2}{k_1} = \frac{E_a}{2.303R}\left(\frac{1}{T_1} - \frac{1}{T_2}\right)$$

$$\log\left(\frac{0.07}{0.02}\right) = \frac{E_a}{2.303 \times 8.314}\left(\frac{1}{500} - \frac{1}{700}\right)$$

$$\log(3.5) = \frac{E_a}{19.15}\left[\frac{200}{350000}\right]$$

$$E_a = \frac{0.54 \times 19.15 \times 350000}{200}$$

$$= 18096.75\ \text{J mol}^{-1}$$

$$= 18.096\ \text{kJ mol}^{-1}$$

(ii) Given, Half-life of radioactive substance = 30 hr = 1800 min

We know that, $t_{1/2} = \frac{0.693}{k}$

$$\Rightarrow \quad k = \frac{0.693}{t_{1/2}} = \frac{0.693}{1800}$$

$$= 0.000385\ \text{min}^{-1}$$

Also for first order reaction,

$$t = \frac{2.303}{k}\log\frac{[N_0]}{[N]}$$

$$90 \times 60 = \frac{2.303}{0.0003.85}\log\frac{[N_0]}{[N]}$$

$$\log\left[\frac{N_0}{N}\right] = \frac{90 \times 60 \times 0.000385}{2.303} = 0.9027$$

$$\frac{N_0}{N} = \text{Antilog}\ [0.9027] = 7.9928$$

11. Given, $T_1 = 293$ K, $T_2 = 313$ K, $k_2/k_1 = 4$,
$R = 8.314\ \text{JK}^{-1}\ \text{mol}^{-1}$, $\log 4 = 0.6021$

We know, $\log\frac{k_2}{k_1} = \frac{E_a}{2.303R}\left[\frac{T_2 - T_1}{T_1T_2}\right]$ (1)

$$\therefore \quad \log 4 = \frac{E_a}{2.303 \times 8.314}\left[\frac{313 - 293}{313 \times 293}\right] \quad (1)$$

$$\Rightarrow \quad 0.6021 = \frac{E_a}{19.147}\left[\frac{20}{91709}\right]$$

$$\Rightarrow \quad E_a = \frac{0.6021 \times 19.147 \times 91709}{20}$$

$$\Rightarrow \quad E_a = 52862.94\ \text{J mol}^{-1} \quad (1)$$

12. For the given reaction, $E_a = 209.5\ \text{kJ mol}^{-1}$
$= 209500\ \text{J mol}^{-1}$

$T = 581$ K,

$R = 8.314\ \text{JK}^{-1}\text{mol}^{-1}$

The fraction of molecules having energy equal to or greater than E_a is

$$x = e^{-E_a/RT} \quad (1)$$

$$\therefore \ln x = -E_a/RT$$

$$\log x = -\frac{E_a}{2.303\ RT}$$

$$= -\frac{209500\ \text{J mol}^{-1}}{2.303 \times 8.314\ \text{JK}^{-1}\ \text{mol}^{-1} \times 581\ \text{K}}$$

$$= -18.8323 \quad (1)$$

$x = \text{antilog}\ (-18.8323)$

$x = 1.471 \times 10^{-19}$ (1)

13. $t_{1/2}$ for first order reaction is given by

$$t_{1/2} = \frac{0.693}{k}$$

$$\text{for 300 K, } k_1 = \frac{0.693}{t_{1/2}} = \frac{0.693}{40}$$

$$\text{for 320 K, } k_2 = \frac{0.693}{t_{1/2}} = \frac{0.693}{20}$$

From Arrhenius equation,

$$\log\left(\frac{k_2}{k_1}\right) = \frac{E_a}{2.303\,R}\left(\frac{1}{T_1} - \frac{1}{T_2}\right)$$

$$\log\left(\frac{40}{20}\right) = \frac{E_a}{2.303 \times 8.314 \text{ J mol}^{-1}\text{K}^{-1}}\left[\frac{1}{300} - \frac{1}{320}\right]$$

$$\log 2 = \frac{E_a}{19.147 \text{ J mol}^{-1}\text{K}^{-1}}\left[\frac{320-300}{300 \times 320}\right]\text{K}$$

$$0.3010 = \frac{E_a}{19.147 \text{ J mol}^{-1}\text{K}^{-1}} \times 0.0002083 \text{ K}$$

$$E_a = 27664 \text{ J/mol}$$

14. According to Arrhenius equation,

$$\log\frac{k_2}{k_1} = \frac{E_a}{2.303R}\left[\frac{1}{T_1} - \frac{1}{T_2}\right] \quad (1)$$

$$\frac{k_2}{k_1} = 2, T_1 = 298 \text{ K}, T_2 = 308 \text{ K}, R = 8.314 \text{ JK}^{-1}\text{ mol}^{-1}$$

$$\log 2 = \frac{E_a}{2.303 \times (8.314 \text{JK}^{-1}\text{mol}^{-1})}\left[\frac{1}{298\text{K}} - \frac{1}{308\text{K}}\right]$$

$$\text{or } 0.3010 = \frac{E_a}{2.303 \times (8.314 \text{J mol}^{-1})} \times \frac{10}{298 \times 308} \quad (1)$$

$$E_a = \frac{0.3010 \times 2.303 \times 8.314 \times 298 \times 308}{10} (\text{J mol}^{-1})$$

$$= 52897.78 \text{J mol}^{-1} = 52.898 \text{ kJ mol}^{-1}$$

Activation energy for the reaction $= 52.898$ kJ mol^{-1} (1)

15. According to Arrhenius equation,

$$\log k = \log A - \frac{E_a}{2.303RT} \quad (1/2)$$

We have, $k = 2.418 \times 10^{-5}\text{s}^{-1}$;

$E_a = 179.9$ kJ mol^{-1}

or 179900 J mol^{-1};

$R = 8.314$ J K^{-1}mol^{-1};

$T = 546$ K

$$\Rightarrow \quad \log A = \log k + \frac{E_a}{2.303RT} \quad (1/2)$$

$$= \log(2.418 \times 10^{-5}\text{s}^{-1}) + \frac{179900 \text{J mol}^{-1}}{2.303 \times (8.314 \text{JK}^{-1}\text{mol}^{-1}) \times 546 \text{ K}}$$

$$\log A = -4.6184 + 17.21 = 12.5916 \quad (1)$$

$$A = \text{antilog } 12.5916 = 3.9 \times 10^{12}\text{s}^{-1} \quad (1)$$

16. (i) Rate constant, k and temperature related to each other by Arrhenius equation,

$$k = Ae^{-E_a/RT}$$

where, k = rate constant

A = pre-exponential factor (frequency or collision factor)

E_a = activation energy, T = temperature (in K)

R = gas constant

(ii) By plotting graph between $\log k$ and $1/T$, we get slope $= -E_a/2.303R$.

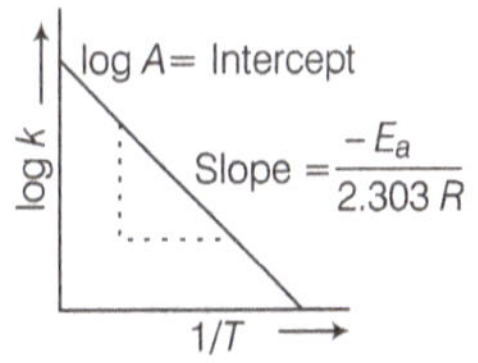

Graph between log k vs 1/T

Thus, by using relation,

Slope $= -\dfrac{E_a}{2.303R}$ activation energy, E_a can be calculated by knowing the value of the slope and gas constant.

(iii) Given, slope $= -5841$

We know that, slope $= -\dfrac{E_a}{2.303R}$

$$\therefore E_a = -2.303 \text{ R} \times \text{slope}$$

$$= -2.303 \times 8.314 \times (-5841)$$

$$= 111838.4 \text{ J / mol}$$

$$E_a = 111.838 \text{ kJ / mol}$$

17. (i) For first order reaction,

$$k = \frac{2.303}{t}\log\frac{[R]_0}{[R]}$$

$$\text{At 298 K, } k_1 = \frac{2.303}{t}\log\frac{100}{90} \quad \text{...(i)} \quad (1/2)$$

$$\text{At 308 K, } k_2 = \frac{2.303}{t}\log\frac{100}{75} \quad \text{...(ii)} \quad (1/2)$$

On dividing Eq. (ii) by Eq. (i),

$$\frac{k_2}{k_1} = \frac{\log(100/75)}{\log(100/90)} = \frac{0.1249}{0.0458} = 2.73 \quad (1)$$

According to Arrhenius equation,

$$\log\frac{k_2}{k_1} = \frac{E_a}{2.303\,R}\left[\frac{T_2 - T_1}{T_1T_2}\right]$$

$$\log 2.73 = \frac{E_a}{2.303\,R}\left[\frac{308-298}{298 \times 308}\right]$$

$$E_a = \frac{\left[0.4361 \times 2.303 \times (8.314 \text{ JK}^{-1}\text{ mol}^{-1}) \times 298 \times 308\right]}{10}$$

$$E_a = 76640 \cdot 27 \text{ J mol}^{-1}$$

$$= 76 \cdot 640 \text{ kJ mol}^{-1} \quad (1)$$

(ii) According to Arrhenius equation,

$$\log k = \log A - \frac{E_a}{2.303\,RT}$$

$$\log k = \log (4 \times 10^{10}) - \frac{76640 \cdot 27\ \text{J mol}^{-1}}{2.303 \times (8.314\ \text{J mol}^{-1}\ \text{K}^{-1}) \times (318\ \text{K})}$$

$$\log k = 10.6021 - 12.5870 = -1.9849$$ **(1)**

$$k = \text{antilog}\,(-1.9849) = 1.035 \times 10^{-2}\ \text{s}^{-1}$$

So, $E_a = 76.640$ kJ mol^{-1}

$$k = 1.035 \times 10^{-2}\ \text{s}^{-1}$$ **(1)**

18. (i) To draw the graph between $\ln k$ *versus* $1/T$, we rewrite the data as follows:

T (K)	$1/T$	$\ln k$
273(0°C)	$0.003663 = 3.66 \times 10^{-3}$	−14.06
293(20°C)	$0.003413 = 3.41 \times 10^{-3}$	−10.98
313(40°C)	$0.003194 = 3.19 \times 10^{-3}$	−8.27
333(60°C)	$0.003003 = 3.00 \times 10^{-3}$	−6.33
353(80°C)	$0.002833 = 2.83 \times 10^{-3}$	−3.85

(2)

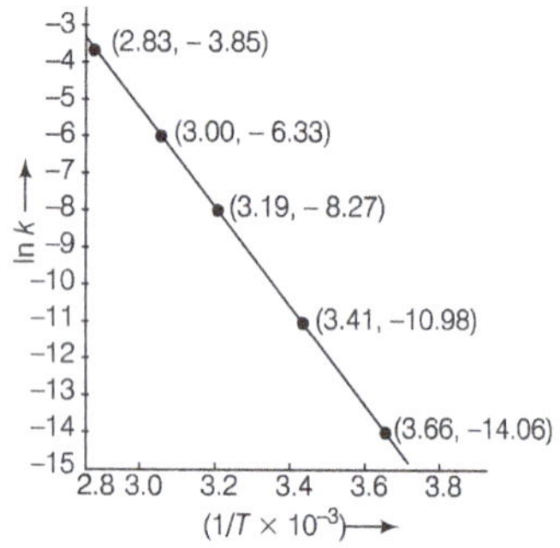

(ii) From the graph, we find the slope

$$\text{Slope} = \frac{-2.4}{0.00047} = \frac{-E_a}{2.303\,R}$$

∴ Activation energy,

$$E_a = \frac{2.4 \times 2.303 \times 8.314\ \text{J mol}^{-1}}{0.00047}$$

$$= 97772\ \text{J mol}^{-1}$$

$$= 97.772\ \text{kJ mol}^{-1}$$

$$\Rightarrow \quad E_a = 97.772\ \text{kJ mol}^{-1}$$ **(1)**

(iii) We know that,

$$\ln k = \ln A + \frac{-E_a}{RT}$$

On comparing it with $y = mx + c$. The equation of line in intercept form,

$$\ln k = \left(-\frac{E_a}{R}\right)\frac{1}{T} + \ln A$$

$\log A$ = value of intercept on Y-axis, i.e. on the $\log k$-axis $= (-1 + 7.2) = 6.2$ $\quad [y_2 - y_1 = -1 - (7.2)]$

Frequency factor, $A = \text{antilog}\ 6.2 = 1585000$

or, $\quad A = 1.585 \times 10^{6}$ collisions s^{-1} **(1)**

(iv) Value of rate constant k can be find by the study of graph.

T(K)	$1/T$	Values of log K from graph	Values of K
303	0.003300	− 4.2	$6.31 \times 10^{-5}\text{s}^{-1}$
323	0.003096	− 2.8	$1.585 \times 10^{-3}\text{s}^{-1}$

(1)

SUMMARY

- The branch of chemistry that deals with the study of the speed or rate of chemical reactions, factors affecting the rates of reaction and the mechanism by which reaction proceed is known as **chemical kinetics.**
- **Rate of reaction** It is the change in the concentration of any one of the reactants or products per unit time. In aqueous reactions, the unit of rate is $molL^{-1}s^{-1}$ while in the case of gaseous reaction, the unit of rate is atm s^{-1}.
- **Instantaneous rate** It is the rate at a particular instant.

  For $R \rightarrow P$, $\quad r_{ins} = -\frac{d\,[R]}{dt} = +\frac{d\,[P]}{dt}$
- **Average rate** It is the rate over a long time interval,

  $$r_{av} = -\frac{\Delta R}{\Delta t} = +\frac{\Delta P}{\Delta t}$$
- For a reaction, $pA \rightarrow qB + rC$

  $$\text{rate} = -\frac{1}{p}\frac{d\,[A]}{dt} = +\frac{1}{q}\frac{d\,[B]}{dt} = +\frac{1}{r}\frac{d\,[C]}{dt}$$

  p, q, r = integer of balanced equation.
- **Rate law** It is the expression of rate in terms of molar concentration of reactants.

  For a reaction, $xA + yB \rightarrow zC$, Rate $= k\,[A]^p\,[B]^q$

  [p and q may or may not be equal to x and y.]
- **Rate constant** (k) It is the rate of chemical reaction when concentration of each reactant is unity. It is also called specific reaction rate. It depends only upon temperature.

  Unit of $k = \left(\frac{\text{mol}}{\text{L}}\right)^{1-n} s^{-1}$ where, [n = order of reaction.]
- **Molecularity of reaction** It shows number of species taking part in an elementary (one step) reaction. It never be equal to zero and always a whole number. It has no meaning in complex reaction (reactions involving more than one steps).
- **Order of reaction** It is the sum of powers of concentration terms in the rate law expression. It is determined experimentally. e.g. Rate $= k[A]^p[B]^q$, Order $= p + q$
- **Zero order reaction** In this reaction, the rate does not depend on the concentration of any of the reactants.

  Rate, $\frac{-d\,[R]}{dt} = k$ or $kt = [R]_0 - [R]$, $t_{1/2}$ (half-life) $= \frac{[R]_0}{2k}$

  Plot of $[R]$ *versus* $[t]$ is a straight line with slope of $-k$ and intercept $[R]_0$.

  First order reaction In this reaction, the rate is proportional to the first power of the concentration of the reactant.

  $$k = \ln\frac{[R]}{[R_0]} = -kt$$

  or, $\quad k = \frac{2.303}{t}\log\frac{a}{(a-x)} \quad$ [a = initial concentration]

  $$t_{1/2} = \frac{\ln 2}{k} = \frac{0.693}{k}$$

  Plot of $\ln[R]_{versus}\,[t]$ is a straight line with slope of $-k$ and intercept of $\ln[R]_0$.

  In terms of pressure, $k = \frac{2.303}{t}\log\frac{p_i}{2p_i - p_t}$
- **Pseudo first order reaction** These reactions are not actually of first order but behave so due to altered conditions. e.g. hydrolysis of ester.
- **Temperature coefficient** The effect of temperature is usually expressed in terms of temperature coefficient. For every 10° rise in temperature, the rate becomes double.
- **Arrhenius equation** The temperature dependence of rate of a chemical reaction is expressed as

  $k = Ae^{-E_a/RT}$ [where, A = pre-exponential factor, R = gas constant, E_a = activation energy]

  $$\log\frac{k_2}{k_1} = \frac{E_a}{2.303R}\left(\frac{T_2 - T_1}{T_1T_2}\right)$$
- **Activation energy** (E_a) It is the energy required by the reactant molecules for effective collision to form products.

  Threshold energy It is the minimum energy which the colliding molecules must have for effective collision.
- **Effect of catalyst** A catalyst increases the rate of reaction by providing a path of lower activation energy. It cannot initiate a reaction, it can only accelerate the rate of reaction. It neither alters free energy change nor enthalpy of the reaction.
- **Collision theory** According to this theory,

  $$\text{rate} = Z_{AB}\,e^{-E_a/RT}$$

  where, Z_{AB} = collision frequency

For Mind Map

Visit : https://goo.gl/k19ZPA OR **Scan the Code**

Chapter Practice

Very Short Answer Type Questions

1 Mark

1 Fill in the Blanks

(i) k^{-1} (k is rate constant in s^{-1}) is called .... and k^{-1}= .... T_{50}.

(ii) For most of the reactions, the rate is .... for every 10°C rise in temperature.

(iii) All radioactive decomposition reactions are ....

2 Objective Type Questions

(i) The rate law for a reaction between the substance P and Q is given by rate $= k[P]^a[Q]^b$. On doubling the concentration of P and reducing the concentration of Q to one-half, the ratio of the new rate to the earlier rate of the reaction will be

(a) $\frac{1}{2^{(a+b)}}$ (b) $2^{(a-b)}$ (c) $(a-b)$ (d) $(a+b)$

(ii) The incorrect statement among the following is

(a) order of reaction is the sum of powers of concentration of the reactants in the rate law expression

(b) elementary reactions are only one step reactions

(c) rate of elementary reactions depends upon the slowest step, i.e. rate determining step of reaction

(d) All of the above

(iii) Which one of the following statements for the order of a reaction is incorrect?

(a) Order is not influenced by stoichiometric coefficient of the reactants

(b) Order of reaction is sum of power of the concentration terms of reactants to express the rate of reaction

(c) Order of reaction is always whole number

(d) Order can be determined only experimentally

(iv) In a first order reaction, reactant concentration 'C' varies with time 't' as

(a) C decreases with $\frac{1}{t}$

(b) $\log C$ decreases with $\frac{1}{t}$

(c) $\frac{1}{C}$ increases linearly with t

(d) $\log C$ decreases linearly with t

(v) For a hypothetical reaction,

$$A \longrightarrow P$$

the rate constant is 0.12 s^{-1}. Which of the following statements is/are correct, if $[R]_0$ is the initial concentration?

(a) $t_{1/2} = \frac{[R]_0}{0.12 \times 12}$ (b) $t_{1/2} = \frac{3}{2(0.12)[R]_0^2}$

(c) $t_{1/2} = \frac{0.693}{0.12}$ (d) $t_{1/2} = \frac{0.693}{0.12 \times 3}$

3 Match the statements given in Column I and Column II and choose the correct option using the given codes below.

	Column I		Column II
A.	Catalyst alters the rate of reaction.	(i)	Cannot be fraction or zero.
B.	Molecularity	(ii)	Proper orientation is not there.
C.	Second half-life of first order reaction.	(iii)	By lowering the activation energy.
D.	$e^{-E_a/RT}$	(iv)	Is same as the first.
E.	Energetically favourable reactions are sometimes slow.	(v)	Total probability is one.
F.	Area under the Maxwell, Boltzmann curve is constant.	(vi)	Refers to the fraction of molecules with energy equal to or greater than activation energy.

Codes

	A	B	C	D	E	F
(a)	(iii)	(i)	(iv)	(vi)	(ii)	(v)
(b)	(iv)	(iii)	(i)	(vi)	(ii)	(v)
(c)	(i)	(iii)	(iv)	(ii)	(iv)	(v)
(d)	(vi)	(ii)	(v)	(iv)	(iii)	(i)

4 Under what conditions, a bimolecular reaction is kinetically first order?

5 For a reaction, $X + H_2O \longrightarrow Y$, rate $\propto [X]$. What is its

(i) molecularity? (ii) order of reaction?

6 In what case order of reaction is equal to the sum of the stoichiometric coefficients of reactants in the balanced chemical equation for a reaction?

7 If the reaction has the rate constant 1.9×10^{-4} atm^{-1}s^{-1} then predict the order of the reaction.

8 If the rate of any reaction is Rate $= k[A]^1[B]^1$ then, what is the order of the reaction?

9 Why does the hydrolysis of ethyl acetate being a bimolecular reaction is said to be a first order reaction?

10 What is the value of rate constant at an extremely high temperature? Is this rate constant feasible?

Assertion-Reason

Directions (Q. Nos. 11-15) In the following questions, an Assertion (A) is followed by a corresponding Reason (R). Use the following keys to choose the appropriate answer.

(a) Both Assertion and Reason are correct, Reason is the correct explanation of Assertion.
(b) Both Assertion and Reason are correct, Reason is not the correct explanation of Assertion.
(c) Assertion is correct; Reason is incorrect.
(d) Assertion is incorrect; Reason is correct.

11. **Assertion** (A) For a zero order reaction the unit of rate constant and rate of reaction are same.
Reason (R) Rate of reaction for zero order reaction is independent of concentration of reactant. CBSE 2023

12. **Assertion** (A) For complex reactions, molecularity and order are not same.
Reason (R) Order of reaction may be zero. All India 2020

13. **Assertion** (A) Hydrolysis of an ester follows first order kinetics. All India 2020
Reason (R) Concentration of water remains nearly constant during the course of the reaction.

14. **Assertion** (A) Reactions of higher order are rare.
Reason (R) The chances of simultaneous multimolecular collision are extremely small.

15. **Assertion** (A) All collisions of reactant molecules lead to product formation.
Reason (R) Only those collisions in which molecules have correct orientation and sufficient kinetic energy lead to compound formation.

Case-Study

16. Chemistry is about change where chemicals with well defined properties are converted into other substances. Scientists and students try to find out the feasibility, extent and rate of the reaction for understanding the chemical reaction.

The rate equation for any chemical reaction is the expression that provides a relationship between the rate of the reaction and reactants participating in the chemical reaction. If the equation is dependent on the concentration of the reacting species, it is called the differential rate equation.

We integrate the differential rate equation to get the relation between concentration at different points and rate constant integrated rate equations were introduced due to the difficulty in determining the rate of the reaction from concentration time graph.

Read the passage and answer the following questions.

(i) The decomposition of nitrogen pentaoxide

$$2N_2O_5(g) \longrightarrow 4NO_2(g) + O_2(g)$$

is a first order reaction. The plot of log $[N_2O_5]$ *vs* time (min) has slope $= 0.01389$. Calculate the rate constant k for the reaction.

(ii) Draw the plot for $t_{1/2}$ *vs* $[A]_0$ for zero order reaction.

(iii) For a first order, how is the rate of reaction is affected if the initial concentration of reactant is tripled.

17. Arrhenius equation for first order reactions are useful for modeling the timing and temperature of petroleum generation from organic rich shales and kerogens at laboratory scales (e.g. per minute), based on pyrolysis 52 peak data is measured at multiple heating rates, and for burial histories occurring over geological time scales (e.g. per millions of years).

First order reactions are accompanied by second order reactions and physical changes impacting the kerogens as they thermally mature, so simple Arrhenius equation first order reaction modeling can only provide an approximation of the complete petroleum generation process. Thermally immature shale and/or kerogen samples yield less complex pyrolysis S2-peaks than thermally mature sample and provide more credible kinetic distributions when modeled at multiple heating rates with the Arrhenius equation.

More credible kinetic fits to the S2-peak pyrolysis data are derived by allowing the activation energy (E) and the frequency factor (A) to vary for each reaction to derive good-fit kinetic distributions than by applying the commonly used assumption that the A value remain constant for the set of parallel reactions included in the distribution.

(i) Give the SI unit for activation energy.

(ii) The plot of $\ln k$ *versus* $\frac{1}{T}$ gives a straight line. What is the value of slope and intercept in this graph ?

(iii) If the activation energy for a reaction is zero and is $1.72 \times 10^5 s^{-1}$ at 300 K. Calculate the rate constant at 310 K.

Short Answer Type I Questions

2 Marks

18 For the reaction, $N_2(g) + 3H_2(g) \longrightarrow 2NH_3(g)$ under certain conditions of temperature and partial pressure of the reactants, the rate of formation of NH_3 is 0.001 $kg\,h^{-1}$. Determine the rate of conversion of H_2 under the same conditions.

19 $A + 2B \longrightarrow 3C + 2D$

The rate of disappearance of B is 0.5×10^{-3} mol L^{-1} s^{-1}. What will be

(i) rate of the reaction?

(ii) rate of change in concentration of A and C ?

20 The rate of a reaction is given by rate $= k[N_2O_5]$. In this equation, what does k stand for? What is meant by elementary step in a reaction?

21 For a reaction $P \rightarrow Q$, the rate becomes 27 times when concentration of P is tripled. What is the order of the reaction?

22 The concentration of R in the reaction; $R \longrightarrow P$; was measured as a function of time and the following data is obtained:

$[R]$ mol L^{-1}	1.0	0.75	0.40	0.10
t (min)	0.0	0.05	0.12	0.18

Determine the order of reaction.

23 The half-life period and initial concentration for a reaction are as given below. What is the order of reaction?

Initial concentration (M)	350	540	158
$t_{1/2}$(hr)	425	275	941

24 A substance disintegrated 87.5% in 45 min. What is its half-life?

25 One-fourth of reaction is completed in 32 min. What is the half-life period of this reaction? How is half-life period related to initial concentration for a second order reaction?

26 The rate constant of a reaction of zero order in A is 3.0×10^{-3} mol L^{-1} s^{-1}. How long will it take for the initial concentration of A to fall from 0.10 M to 0.075 M?

27 The half-life period of a first order reaction is 60 min. What percentage will be left after 120 minutes?

28 For a reaction, $X(g) \longrightarrow Y(g) + Z(g)$ the half-life period is 10 min. In what period of time would the concentration of X be reduced to 10% of original concentration?

29 The rate constant for a first order reaction is 60 s^{-1}. How much time will it take to reduce the concentration of the reactant of 1/10 th of its initial value?

30 If time taken for half of the first order reaction to complete is t_1, whereas that for $3/4^{th}$ of the reaction to complete is t_2. How are t_1 and t_2 related to each other?

31 Find the molecularity of the reaction, $Cl \longrightarrow \frac{1}{2} Cl_2(g)$. Give the potential energy diagram to explain activation energy.

32 State the role of activated complex in a reaction and state its relation with activation energy.

33 (i) Illustrate graphically the effect of catalyst on activation energy.

(ii) Catalysts have no effect on the equilibrium constant, why?

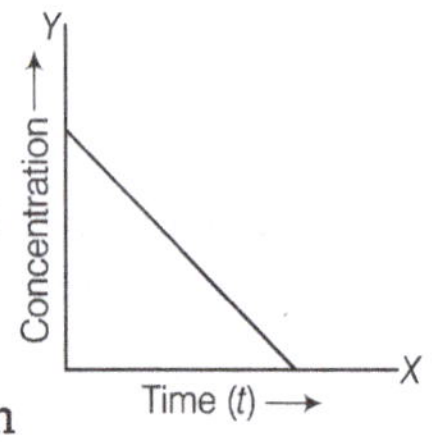

34 The rate of a chemical reaction doubles for every 10°C rise in temperature. If the temperature is raised from 10° to 30°C, what will be the increase in the rate of the reaction?

35 The activation energy of a reaction is 94.14 kJ mol^{-1} and the value of rate constant at 298 K is $18 \times 10^{-5} s^{-1}$. Calculate the frequency factor or pre-exponential factor, A.

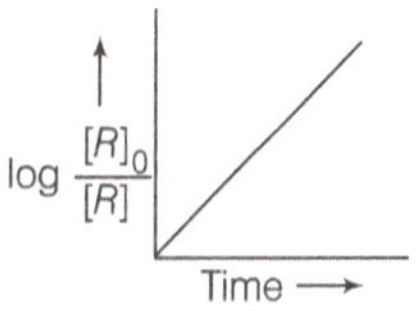

36 For a reaction, the energy of activation is zero. What is the value of rate constant at 300 K, if $k = 1.6 \times 10^{6} s^{-1}$ at 280 K?

37 The data given below is for the reaction,

$$2N_2O_5(g) \longrightarrow 4NO_2(g) + O_2(g)$$

S. No.	N_2O_5 (mol L^{-1})	Rate of disappearance of N_2O_5 (mol $L^{-1}min^{-1}$)
1.	1.13×10^{-2}	34×10^{-5}
2.	0.84×10^{-2}	25×10^{-5}
3.	0.62×10^{-2}	18×10^{-5}

Determine for this reaction,
(i) Order of reaction (ii) Rate law
(iii) Rate constant

Short Answer Type II Questions

(3 Marks)

38 Derive the equation for the rate constant of a first order reaction and show that the time required for the completion of half of the first order reaction is independent of initial concentration.

39 What will be the initial rate of a reaction if its rate constant is $10^{-3} min^{-1}$ and the concentration of reactant is 0.2 mol dm^{-3}? How much of the reactant will be converted into products in 200 min?

40 The decomposition of N_2O_5 according to the equation.

$$2N_2O_5(g) \longrightarrow 4NO_2(g) + O_2(g)$$

is a first order reaction. After 30 min, in a closed vessel, the total pressure is found to be 284.5 mm of Hg and on complete decomposition, the total pressure is 584.5 mm of Hg. Then, find the rate constant of the reaction.

41 Half-life of a first order reaction is 8×10^{4} s. What percentage of the initial reactant will react in 2 h?

42 The rate of first order reaction is 0.04 mol $L^{-1}s^{-1}$ at 10 min and 0.03 mol $L^{-1}s^{-1}$ at 20 min after initiation. Thus, find the half-life of the reaction.

43 The rate constant of a certain reaction is given by:

$$\log k = 6.8 - \frac{213}{T} + 5.7 \log T$$

Calculate E_a at 127°C.

44 The rate of a particular reaction triples when temperature changes from 60°C to 100°C. Calculate the activation energy of the reaction.

45 If the rate constants of a reaction are $1 \times 10^{3} s^{-1}$ and $2 \times 10^{3} s^{-1}$ at 27°C and 37°C, respectively. Calculate the activation energy (E_a) of the reaction.

46 In the Arrhenius equation for a certain reaction, the value of A (frequency factor) and E_a (activation energy) are $4 \times 10^{13} s^{-1}$ and 98.6 kJ mol^{-1}, respectively. If the reaction is of first order, then find that at what temperature will its half-life period be 10 min?

47 The activation energy of a first order reaction is 187.06 kJ mol^{-1} at 750 K and the value of pre-exponential factor, A is $1.97 \times 10^{12} s^{-1}$.
Calculate the rate constant and half-life.
(Given : $e^{-30} = 9.35 \times 10^{-14}$)

48 Two reactions,
(i) $A \longrightarrow$ Products,
(ii) $B \longrightarrow$ Products, follow first order kinetics.

The rate of reaction (i) is doubled when the temperature is raised from 300 K to 310 K. The half-life for this reaction at 310 K is 10 min. At the same temperature, B decomposes twice as fast as A. If the energy of activation for the reaction (ii) is half that of reaction (i), calculate the rate constant of the reaction (ii), at 300 K.

Long Answer Type Questions

(5 Marks)

49 The experimental data for the reaction;

$$2A + B_2 \longrightarrow 2AB; \text{ is}$$

Experiment	$[A]$ M	$[B_2]$ M	Initial rate (mol L^{-1} s^{-1})
1.	0.50	0.5	1.6×10^{-4}
2.	0.50	1.0	3.2×10^{-4}
3.	1.00	1.0	3.2×10^{-4}

Write the most probable rate equation for the reaction giving reason for your answer.

50 Answer the following questions on the basis of the curve given below for a zero order reaction.

$$R \longrightarrow P$$

(i) Find the relation between slope of this line and rate constant.

(ii) If the slope is 2×10^{-4} mol L^{-1} s^{-1} then calculate the rate constant.

51 Consider the reaction, $A \xrightarrow{k} B$. The change in concentration with time t is shown in the graph.

(i) Predict the order of the reaction.

(ii) Derive the expression for the time which is required to complete the reaction.

(iii) Find the slope of the curve.

52 $^{238}_{92}U$ changes to $^{206}_{92}$Pb by successive radioactive decay. A sample of uranium was analysed and found to contain 1.0 g of ^{238}U and 0.1 g of ^{206}Pb had accumulated due to decay of ^{238}U, find out the age of ore. (Half-life of $^{238}U = 4.5 \times 10^9$ years)

53 For the hydrolysis of methyl acetate in aqueous solution, the following results were obtained.

t / s	0	30	60
$[CH_3COCH_3]$/mol L^{-1}	0.60	0.30	0.15

(i) Show that it follows pseudo first order reaction, as the concentration of water remains constant.

(ii) Calculate the average rate of reaction between the time interval 30 to 60 s.
(Given: log 2 = 0.3010, log 4 = 0.6021)

Hints & Solutions

1 (i) Average life time, 1.443
(ii) doubled (iii) First order reactions

2 (i) (b) $2^{(a-b)}$
(ii) (c) rate of complex reactions depends upon the slowest step, i.e. rate determining step of reaction.
(iii) (c) Order of reaction may have zero, fractional or whole number value.
(iv) (d) log C decreases linearly with t.
(v) (c) $t_{1/2} = \dfrac{0.693}{0.12}$

3 (a) A $\rightarrow$ (iii), B $\rightarrow$ (i), C $\rightarrow$ (iv), D $\rightarrow$ (vi), E $\rightarrow$ (ii), F $\rightarrow$ (v)

4 Refer to text on page 111 (Topic-3, Pseudo first order reaction). (1)

5 (i) molecularity = 2 (ii) order = 1 (1)

6 In elementary reactions, molecularity is equal to the order of the reaction. (1)

7 Second order reaction. (1)

8 Second order reaction (1)

9 $CH_3COOC_2H_5 + H_2O \longrightarrow CH_3COOH + C_2H_5OH$
Rate = $k\,[CH_3COOC_2H_5]\,[H_2O]^0$

10 $k = Ae^{-E_a/RT} \Rightarrow k = A$, if $T \rightarrow \infty$
No, this rate is not feasible. (1)

11 (a) For zero order reaction

$$\text{Rate} = k[A]^\circ$$
$$\text{Rate} = k$$

$\therefore$ Both A and R are correct and R is the correct explanation of A.

12 (b) Order of overall reaction is equal to molecularity of slowest step. They are equal for elementary reaction, but for complex reactions, they may be different.
However, order can be zero and fractional but molecularity can not be zero. Thus, both (A) and (R) are correct but (R) is not the correct explanation of (A).

13 (a) Consider the hydrolysis of an ester

$$CH_3COOC_2H_5 + H_2O \longrightarrow CH_3COOH + C_2H_5OH$$
$$\text{Rate} = k[CH_3COOC_2H_5][H_2O]$$

Hydrolysis of an ester follows first order because the concentration of water, $[H_2O]$ remains nearly constant and the change in the concentration of acid will result in very negligible change in the concentration of H^+/OH^- ion during the course of the reaction.
Thus, both (A) and (R) are correct and (R) is the correct explanation of (A).

14 (a) The reactions of higher order are rare because the chances of multimolecular collisions at the same time to give product are very low.
Hence, (A) and (R) are correct and (R) is the correct explanation of (A).

15 (d) Not all collisions of reactant molecules lead to product formation, only effective collisions means molecules which have proper and correct orientation and sufficient kinetic energy during collisions can form product.
Hence, (A) is incorrect and (R) is correct.

16 (i) Slope $= -\dfrac{k}{2.303}$

$$= -2.303 \times \text{slope} = 2.303 \times 0.01389$$
$$= 3.2 \times 10^{-2}\ \text{min}^{-1}$$

(ii)

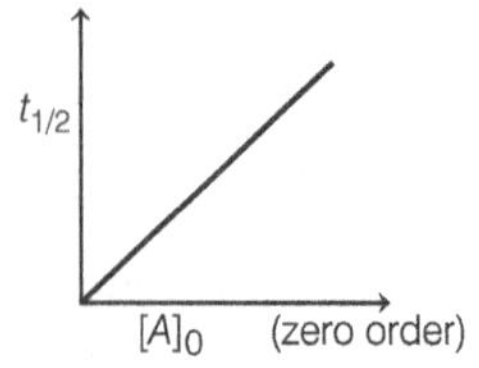

For first order reaction rate $= k[R]^1$

(iii) If the concentration is increased by three times then the rate of the reaction will also increases by three times.

17 (i) J mol^{-1}

(ii)

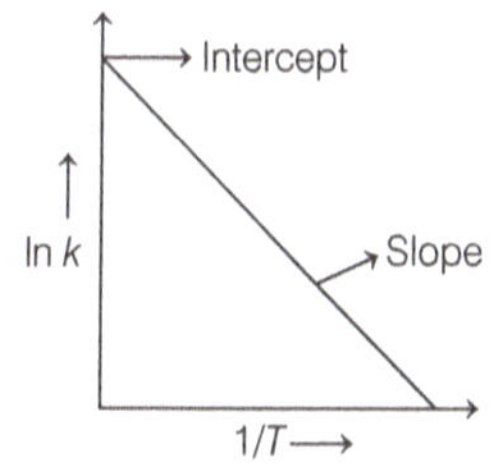

(iii) $E_a = 0 \Rightarrow \log\frac{k_2}{k_1} = 0 \Rightarrow \frac{k_2}{k_1} = 1$

$[\therefore k_2 = k_1 = 1.72\times10^5\,s^{-1}]$

18 Rate $= -\frac{d[N_2]}{dt} = -\frac{1}{3}\frac{d[H_2]}{dt} = \frac{1}{2}\frac{d[NH_3]}{dt}$ [**Ans** 0.0045 kg h^{-1}] (2)

19 Rate $= -\frac{d[A]}{dt} = -\frac{1}{2}\frac{d[B]}{dt} = +\frac{1}{3}\frac{d[C]}{dt} = +\frac{1}{2}\frac{d[D]}{dt}$

(i) Rate of reaction is $0\cdot25\times10^{-3}$ mol L^{-1} s^{-1}. (1)

(ii) Rate of change in concentration of A and C are respectively $0\cdot25\times10^{-3}$ mol L^{-1} s^{-1} and $0\cdot75\times10^{-3}$ mol L^{-1} s^{-1}. (1)

20 k here stands for the proportionality constant known as rate constant. (2)

21 Third order reaction. (2)

22 $k_1 = \frac{[R_0]-[R]_1}{t} \Rightarrow k_1 = \frac{[1\cdot0]-[0\cdot75]}{0\cdot05}$

$k_2 = \frac{[R_0]-[R]_1}{t} \Rightarrow k_2 = \frac{[1\cdot0]-[0\cdot40]}{0\cdot12}$ (1)

23 Second order reaction. [**Ans.** Zero order reaction] (2)

24 Calculate k followed by $t_{1/2}$.

Rate constant, $k = \frac{2.303}{t}\log\frac{a}{a-x}$

Half time $(t_{1/2}) = \frac{0.693}{k}$ [**Ans.** $t_{1/2} = 26$ min] (2)

25 $t_{1/2} = \frac{3}{2}t_{1/2}$ [**Ans.** 21.3 min]

Half life, $t_{1/2} \propto \frac{1}{[R]_0^{n-1}}$ (2)

26 $t = \frac{1}{k}\{[A]_0 - [A]\}$ [**Ans.** $t = 8.33$ s]

27 $k = \frac{0.693}{t_{1/2}},\ t = \frac{2.303}{k}\log\frac{[A]_0}{[A]}$ [**Ans.** 25%] (2)

28 $t_{1/2} = \frac{0.693}{k},\ t = \frac{2.303}{k}\log\frac{a}{a-x}$ [**Ans.** 33 min] (2)

29 Use the equation,

$t = \frac{2.303}{k}\log\frac{a}{a-x}$ [**Ans.** $t = 3.8\times10^{-2}$ s] (2)

30 $t_{3/4} : t_{1/2} = 2$ (2)

31 Refer to text on page 100 (Topic-2, Molecularity of a reaction) and text on page 118 (Topic 4, Arrhenius equation). (2)

32 Refer to text on page 118 (Topic-4, Arrhenius equation)(2)

33 Refer to text on page 121 (Topic-4, Effect of catalyst). (2)

34 3 times. (2)

35 According to Arrhenius equation,

$\log k = \log A - \frac{E_a}{2.303RT}$

We have, $k = 18\times10^{-5}\,s^{-1}$, $E_a = 94.14$ kJ mol^{-1},

$T = 298$ K, $R = 8.314$ JK^{-1} mol^{-1}

$\log A = \log k + \frac{E_a}{2.303RT} = \log(18\times10^{-5}\,s^{-1})$

$+ \frac{94140\ J\,mol^{-1}}{2.303\times(8.314\,JK^{-1}\,mol^{-1})\times 298\,K}$

$\log A = -3.744 + 16.5 = 12.756$

$A = \text{antilog}\,(12.756) = 5.7\times10^{12}\,s^{-1}$ (2)

36 $\log\frac{k_2}{k_1} = -\frac{E_a}{2.303R}\left[\frac{1}{T_2} - \frac{1}{T_1}\right] \therefore\ k_2 = k_1$ (2)

37 (i) Second order reaction. (ii) Rate $= [N_2O_5]^2$

(iii) $3\times10^{-2}\,mol^{-1}Ls^{-1}$ (2)

38 Refer to text on page page 132 (Topic-3, First order. reaction) and on page 133 (Topic-3, Half-life of a reaction). (3)

39 (i) Initial rate of reaction $= 10^{-3}\times0\cdot2$ mol dm^{-3} min^{-1}

$\Rightarrow 0\cdot2\times10^{-3}$ mol $dm^{-3}min^{-1}$ (1)

(ii) Use, $k = \frac{2.303}{t}\log\frac{a}{a-x} \Rightarrow 10^{-3} = \frac{2.303}{12\times10^3 s}\log\frac{0.2}{a-x}$

$\log\frac{0.2}{a-x} = 5.210 \Rightarrow 0.2 = 1.62181\times10^5\,(a-x)$

$a - x = 1.23\times10^{-6}$ (2)

40 Use, $k = \frac{2.303}{t}\log\frac{p_i}{2p_i - p_t}$

Refer to Example 2 on page 109.

(Topic-3, Pressure change method for the calculation of the value of rate constant). (3)

41 $t_{1/2} = 8\times10^4 s \Rightarrow k = \frac{0.693}{t_{1/2}} = \frac{0.693}{8\times10^4} = 8.66\times10^{-6}$

Then, use $k = \frac{2.303}{t}\log\frac{a}{a-x}$ (3)

42 $k = \frac{2.303}{t}\log\frac{a}{a-x} \Rightarrow k = \frac{2.303}{600\,s}\log\frac{0.04}{0.03} \Rightarrow k = 4.8\times10^{-4}$

$t_{1/2} = \frac{0.693}{k} = \frac{0.693}{4.8\times10^{-4}} = 1.44\times10^3 s$ (3)

43 Compare the given equation by, $\log k = \log A - \frac{E_a}{2.303RT}$

and then calculate E_a [**Ans.** $4\cdot07$ kJ mol^{-1}] (3)

44 Refer to solution 14 on page 125 (Topic-4). (3)

45 Given, $k_1 = 1\times10^3 s^{-1}$, $k_2 = 2\times10^3 s^{-1}$

$T_1 = 300$ K. $T_2 = 310$ K, $R = 8.314\, JK^{-1} mol^{-1}$

$$\log\frac{k_2}{k_1} = -\frac{E_a}{2.303R}\left[\frac{1}{T_2} - \frac{1}{T_1}\right]$$ [**Ans.** 53·60 kJ/mol] (3)

46 $A = 4\times10^{13} s^{-1}$, $E_a = 98.6$ kJ mol^{-1}

$$\log k = \log A - \frac{E_a}{2.303RT}$$

$$\log k = \log(4\times10^{13}) - \frac{98600}{2.303\times8.314\times T}$$ (1)

Now, $t_{1/2} = \frac{0.693}{k}$ [For first order reaction]

$$k = \frac{0.693}{600s} = 1.155\times10^{-3} s^{-1}$$ (1)

$$\therefore \log(1.155\times10^{-3}) = \log(4\times10^{13}) - \frac{98600}{2.303\times8.314\times T}$$

$$2.93 = \frac{13.60 - 5149.6}{T} \Rightarrow T = 311.53 \text{ K}$$ (1)

47 $$\log k = \log A - \frac{E_a}{2.303RT}$$

$$\log k = \log(1.97\times10^{12}) - \frac{187060}{2.303\times8.314\times750}$$

$\log k = 12.30 - 13.026 \Rightarrow \log k = -0.726$

$k = 0.188 \Rightarrow t_{1/2} = \frac{0.693}{k} = \frac{0.693}{0.188} = 3.686$ (3)

48 $$\log\frac{k_2}{k_1} = -\frac{E_a}{2.303R}\left[\frac{1}{T_2} - \frac{1}{T_1}\right]$$

$$\log 2 = -\frac{E_a}{2.303\times8.314}\left[\frac{1}{310} - \frac{1}{300}\right]$$

$E_a = 53944\cdot4$ J/mol $\Rightarrow \log k_2 = \log A - \frac{Ea}{2\cdot303RT}$

$$\therefore \log 0.0693 = \log A - \frac{26972\cdot2}{2\cdot303\times8\cdot314\times310} \Rightarrow \log A = 3\cdot38$$ (1)

Now, $\log k_1 = \log 3.38 - \frac{53944\cdot4}{2\cdot303\times8\cdot314\times300}$

$\Rightarrow k_1 = 9\cdot77\times10^{-7}$ min^{-1} (1)

49 Refer to Example 4 on pages 96 and 97 (Topic-1, Rate equation and rate constant). (5)

50 (i) Refer to text on page 107 (Topic-3, Zero order reaction).

(ii) $k = -2\times10^{-4}$ mol $L^{-1}s^{-1}$ (5)

51 (i) First order reaction

(ii) Refer to text on page 108 (Topic-3, First order reaction).

(iii) Slope $= k / 2.303$ (5)

52 Refer to Example 3 on page 111 (Topic-3, Half-life of a reaction).[**Ans** 7.099×10^8 years] (5)

53 (i) Refer to text on page 111 (Topic-3, Pseudo first order reaction).

(ii) Refer to Example 4 on pages 111 and 112. (Topic-3, Pseudo first order reaction). (5)

RELATED ONLINE VIDEOS

Visit : https://youtu.be/DbEecMtO6aY
OR **Scan the Code**

Visit : https://youtu.be/m8S2nKFGHxs
OR **Scan the Code**

Visit : https://youtu.be/CgWo7da74wE
OR **Scan the Code**

CHAPTER

04

d-and f-Block Elements

The elements positioned between *s*-block (group 1 and 2) and *p*-block (group 13-18) elements are classified as *d*-block and *f*-block elements, based on the electronic configurations. The *d*-block elements are situated from groups 3 to 12 and are also called **transition elements** because of their position in the periodic table in between the *s*-block and *p*-block elements.

The *f*-block elements are present in group 3 (periods 6 and 7) only and are also called **inner-transition elements**. The *f*-block elements are further classified as lanthanides (lying in 6th period) and actinides (lying in 7th period).

TOPIC 01 Transtion Elements and Their Properties

d-Block Elements

The elements which have incompletely filled *d*-orbitals in their ground state or in any of oxidation state are called ***d*-block elements** (transition elements).

The presence of partly filled *d*-or *f*-orbitals in their atoms sets the study of the transition elements and their compounds apart from that of the main group elements. Various precious metals like silver, gold and platinum, and industrially important metals like iron, copper and titanium form part of the transition metals.

Position of d-Block Elements in the Periodic Table

The *d*-block occupies the large middle section situated between *s*-and *p*-blocks in the periodic table. The name 'transition' given to the elements of *d*-block is only because of their position between *s*-and *p*-block elements.

The *d*-orbitals of the penultimate energy level in their atoms receive electrons giving rise to the three rows of the transition metals, i.e. $3d$, $4d$ and $5d$. The fourth row of $6d$ is still incomplete.

(i) **First transition series** or **$3d$- series** Scandium ($_{21}$Sc) to Zinc ($_{30}$Zn).

(ii) **Second transition series** or **$4d$-series** Yttrium ($_{39}$Y) to Cadmium ($_{48}$Cd).

(iii) **Third transition series** or **5*d*-series** Lanthanum ($_{57}$La) to Mercury ($_{80}$Hg).
Excluding $_{58}$Ce to $_{71}$Lu.

(iv) **Fourth transition series** or **6*d*-series** Actinium ($_{89}$Ac) to Copernicium ($_{112}$Cn) excluding $_{90}$Th to $_{103}$Lr.

Ouccurrence

d-block elements are present as oxides, hydroxides and carbonates in low oxidation-state, these are basic in nature. Halides and other salts of *d*-block elements are generally stable in water.

Major ores of some of the transition metals are as follows :

(i) (Ti) → as TiO_2 (Rutile)
(ii) (V) → as $PbCl_2.Pb_3(VO_4)_2$ (Vanaditie)
(iii) (Cr) → as $FeCrO_4$ (Chromite)
(iv) (Mn) → as MnO_2 (Pyrolusite)
(v) (Fe) → Fe_2O_3 (Haematite), $FeCO_3$ (siderite)
(vi) (Co) → $CoAs_2$ (Sumalite)
(vii) (Ni) → as $NiMgSiO_4O_{10}(OH)_8$ (Laterites)
(viii) (Cu) → as $CuFeS_2$ (Copper pyrites),
(ix) $CuCO_3.(OH)_2$ (Malachite).

Electronic Configuration of the *d*-Block Elements

General electronic configuration of transition metals is $(n-1)\,d^{1\text{-}10}\,ns^{1\text{-}2}$, where n is the outermost shell which may have one or two electrons, whereas $(n-1)$ stands for the inner *d*-orbitals which may have one to ten electrons.

Exception

(i) Some of the exceptions are observed in electronic configuration due to very little energy difference between $(n-1)d$ and ns orbitals such as

$$\text{Cr}: 3d^5, 4s^1 \text{ instead of } 3d^4, 4s^2$$

$$\text{Cu}: 3d^{10}, 4s^1 \text{ instead of } 3d^9, 4s^2$$

(ii) These anomalous configuration is because of half-filled configuration in Cr and completely filled configuration in Cu which are more stable. Though Cu atom has completely filled *d*-orbital but still considered as a transition element because Cu in its II oxidation state shows $4d^9$ configuration.

Outer electronic configuration of transition elements (Ground State) **1st series**

	Sc	Ti	V	Cr	Mn	Fe	Co	Ni	Cu	Zn
Z	21	22	23	24	25	26	27	28	29	30
4s	2	2	2	1	2	2	2	2	1	2
3*d*	1	2	3	5	5	6	7	8	10	10

2nd series

	Y	Zr	Nb	Mo	Tc	Ru	Rh	Pd	Ag	Cd
Z	39	40	41	42	43	44	45	46	47	48
5s	2	2	1	1	1	1	1	0	1	2
4*d*	1	2	4	5	5	7	8	10	10	10

3rd series

	La	Hf	Ta	W	Re	Os	Ir	Pt	Au	Hg
Z	57	72	73	74	75	76	77	78	79	80
6s	2	2	2	2	2	2	2	1	1	2
5*d*	1	2	3	4	5	6	7	9	10	10

4th series

	Ac	Rf	Db	Sg	Bh	Hs	Mt	Ds	Rg	Cn
Z	89	104	105	106	107	108	109	110	111	112
7s	2	2	2	2	2	2	2	2	1	2
6*d*	1	2	3	4	5	6	7	8	10	10

General Properties of the Transition Elements (*d*-Block)

1. Metallic Character

(i) Transition elements display typical metallic properties such as high tensile strength, ductility, malleability, high thermal and electrical conductivity and metallic lustre. With the exceptions of Zn, Cd, Hg and Mn, they have one or more typical metallic structures at normal temperatures.

(ii) They are very much hard and have very low volatility except Zn, Cd and Hg.

(iii) They have high melting and boiling points. The high melting point of these metals is due to the involvement of greater number of electrons from $(n-1)d$ in addition to the *ns*-electrons in the interatomic metallic bonding.

(iv) In any row, the melting points of these metals rise to a maximum at d^5 and fall regularly with the increase in atomic number except Mn and Tc.

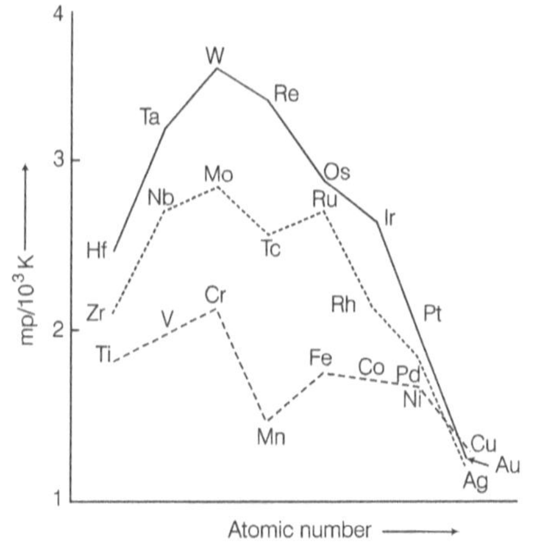

Trends in melting points of transition elements

2. Atomic and Ionic Radii

Atomic/ionic size is expressed in terms of radii. Atomic and ionic radii decrease with increase in atomic number.

Atomic and ionic radii of transition elements period first decreases till the middle, becomes almost constant and then increase towards the end of periods. Atomic and ionic radii increase while going down the group. However, variation within a series is quite small. This is because the new electron enters a *d*-orbital each time the nuclear charge increases by unity. Due to poor shielding of *d*-electrons, attractive forces increase between the nucleus and valence electrons and hence size decreases.

(i) However, at the end of the series, size of elements increases due to the increase in the magnitude of repulsive forces between electrons.

(ii) On comparing atomic sizes we obtained the following graph :

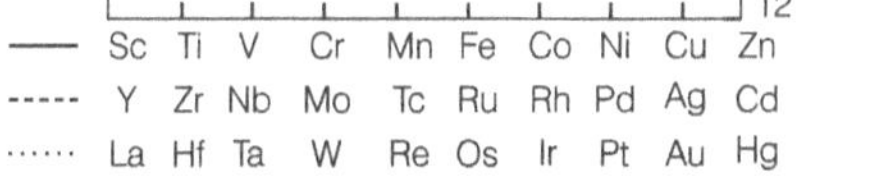

Trends in atomic radii of transition elements

(iii) As it is clear from the above figure that there is an increase in the curve from the first (3*d*) to the second (4*d*) series of the elements but the radii of the third (5*d*) series are virtually the same.

(iv) As a result, density of transition metals increases from left to right in a period because atomic radius decreases and atomic mass increases.

Note Lanthanoid contraction is a special characteristic of lanthanoids as they occupy the same position in periodic table. Due to this contraction, the second and third *d* series exhibit similar radii, e.g. Zr (160 pm) and Hf (159 pm) have similar physical and chemical properties.

3. Enthalpy of Atomisation

Energy required to convert metallic crystal into individual atom is known as enthalpy of atomisation. The transition metals have high enthalpy of atomisation because of strong interatomic interaction due to unpaired electrons. It first increases, reaches to the maximum in the middle of each series and then decreases. *d*-block elements have higher enthalpies of atomisation.

4. Ionisation Enthalpies (IE)

(i) Ionisation enthalpy is generally high for each series of transition elements due to small size of atoms. For a particular transition series, ionisation enthalpy increases generally on moving from left to right in a period.

(ii) The variation in ionisation enthalpy within the *d*-block is small due to the screening effect and attractive force acting together.

(iii) First ionisation energy $(IE)_1$ of 5*d*-elements are higher than those of the 3*d* and 4*d*-elements. This is due to greater effective nuclear charge acting on outer valence electrons because of the weak shielding of the nucleus by 4*f*-electrons. The ionisation energies of the 3*d*- and 4*d*-elements are irregular.

(iv) Ionisation of first two electrons from an atom of a transition element will take place with the removal of *s*-electrons in preference to the *d*-electron.

(v) In 3*d*-series, first four members show little difference in values and last four are also fairly close. Zn shows quite high value due to extra stability of completely filled orbitals. The high values of IE_3 for Cu, Ni and Zn explain why they show a maximum oxidation state of +2.

(vi) IE_2 of the first transition series increases almost regularly with increase in atomic number. However, the value for Cr and Cu are sufficiently higher than those of their neighbours. This is due to their stable electronic configurations.

5. Variable Valency and Oxidation States

(i) Transition metals show a great variety of oxidation states in their compounds (variable valency) except the first and the last element.

This is because of the fact that the difference in the energy of $(n-1)$ d-electrons and ns-electrons is small which implies that electrons from both energy levels can take part in bonding.

Oxidation states of the first row transition metals
(The most common ones are typed in bold)

Sc	Ti	V	Cr	Mn	Fe	Co	Ni	Cu	Zn
+2	+2	+2	+2	**+2**	**+2**	**+2**	**+2**	+1	**+2**
+3	+3	+3	**+3**	+3	**+3**	**+3**	+3	**+2**	
	+4	+4	+4	+4	+4	+4	+4		
		+5	+5	+5	+5				
			+6	+6	+6				
				+7					

(ii) **For 3*d*-series** In 3d-series, the most common oxidation state among all the elements is +2 except Sc (Sc = +3). Oxidation states first increases from Sc to Mn due to increase in number of unpaired electrons and then decreases because pairing takes place. Fe and Ni show zero oxidation state in metal carbonyls.

(iii) The elements which give the greatest number of oxidation states occur in or near the middle of the series. e.g., Mn has oxidation states from +2 to +7.

(iv) Transition elements in their low oxidation states usually form ionic compounds. In higher oxidation states, compounds are normally covalent.

(v) **Stability of higher oxidation states** increases in a group from top to bottom due to increase in the distance from the outermost shell, e.g. in group 6, Mo (VI) and W (VI) are found to be more stable than Cr (VI). That's why, Cr (VI) in the form of dichromate is a strong oxidising agent, whereas MoO_3 and WO_3 are not.

(vi) Low oxidation states are found if a complex compound has ligands capable of π-acceptor character and σ-bonding, e.g. $Ni(CO)_4$ and $Fe(CO)_5$, the oxidation state of nickel and iron is zero in the presence of CO as ligand.

Note The oxidation state of a metal in a solvent depends on the nature of the solvent, e.g. Cu^+ is unstable in aqueous solution and undergo disproportionation reaction.

(vii) Transition metals show their highest oxidation states with fluorine and oxygen because F and O are small in size and the most electronegative elements. 3d transition metals form stable halides.

(viii) Oxygen stabilises the highest oxidation state in the oxides more than fluorine (highest fluoride of Mn is MnF_4 whereas highest oxide is Mn_2O_7) due to the ability of oxygen to form multiple bonds with the metal atoms, e.g. in the covalent oxide Mn_2O_7, each Mn is tetrahedrally surrounded by oxygen including a Mn—O—Mn bridge.

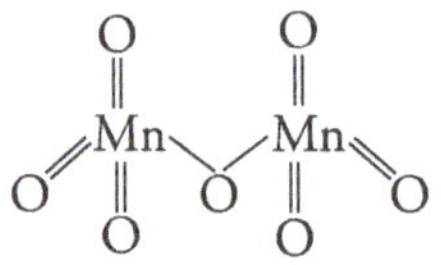

Example 1 What may be the stable oxidation state of the transition element with the following d-electron configuration in the ground state of their atoms : $3d^3, 3d^5, 3d^8$ and $3d^4$? **NCERT**

Sol. Stable oxidation states :

$3d^3$: Vanadium (General electronic configuration $3d^3 4s^2$) : oxidation states +2, +3, +4 and +5.

$3d^5$: Chromium(General electronic configuration $3d^5 4s^1$): oxidation states +3, +4 and +6.

$3d^5$: Manganese (General electronic configuration $3d^5 4s^2$): oxidation states +2, +4, +6, +7.

$3d^8$: Nickel (General electronic configuration $3d^8 4s^2$) : oxidation states +2, +4.

$3d^4$: Such configuration does not exist in ground state.

6. Magnetic Properties

(i) On applying a magnetic field to substances, two types of magnetic behaviour are observed as **diamagnetism** and **paramagnetism**. Most of the transition metals have one or more unpaired electron. So, they are paramagnetic in nature.

(ii) Paramagnetism arises due to the rotation of electron (spin motion) around the axis and revolution around the nucleus (orbital motion) as the number of unpaired electrons increases, paramagnetism increases.

(iii) Those transition elements which have paired electrons are **diamagnetic**. A paramagnetic substance is characterised by its magnetic moment which is calculated by 'spin only' formula. i.e.

$$\mu = \sqrt{n(n+2)} \text{ BM}$$

where, n is the number of unpaired electrons and BM is Bohr magneton, the unit of magnetic moment.

(iv) Magnetic moment increases with the increasing number of unpaired electrons. Substances which are attracted very strongly by a magnetic field and their domains are aligned in one direction are called **ferromagnetic substances**, e.g. Fe, Co, Ni. In fact, ferromagnetism is an extreme form of paramagnetism.

Example 2 Calculate the magnetic moment of a divalent ion in aqueous solution, $[Fe(H_2O)_6]^{2+}$, if atomic number of Fe is 26.

Sol. Magnetic moment $(\mu) = \sqrt{n(n+2)}$ BM

Atomic number of $Fe = 26 = [Ar]3d^6 4s^2$

$$Fe^{2+} = [Ar]3d^6 4s^0 = \boxed{\uparrow\downarrow}\boxed{\uparrow}\boxed{\uparrow}\boxed{\uparrow}\boxed{\uparrow}$$

So, $\mu = \sqrt{n(n+2)}$

$= \sqrt{4(4+2)} = \sqrt{24} = 4.89$ BM

7. Formation of Coloured Ions

(i) When an unpaired electron from a lower energy *d*-orbital is excited to a higher energy *d*-orbital, the energy of excitation corresponds to the frequency of light absorbed. This frequency generally lies in the visible region. This type of transition is known as *d*-*d* transition.

(ii) The colour observed corresponds to the complementary colour of the light absorbed. The frequency of light absorbed is determined by the nature of the ligand. Thus, most of the compounds of transition metals are coloured due to *d*-*d* transition. Transition metal ions having d^0 or d^{10} configuration are colourless.

Note Few compounds in which transition metal has d^0 configuration, may also exhibit colour due to charge transfer. e.g. CrO_3 has d^0 configuration of Cr and shows orange colour due to charge transfer.

8. Formation of Complex Compounds

(i) Complex compounds are those compounds in which the metal ions bind a number of anions or neutral molecules, giving characteristic properties to the complexes.

(ii) The transition metals form a large number of complex compounds due to the comparatively smaller size of the metal ions, their high charge density and vacant *d*-orbitals for bond formation.

9. Catalytic Properties

(i) Many transition metals and their compounds are used as catalyst. Particularily many oxides act as good catalysts. Their catalytic activity is due to their ability to adopt multiple oxidation states and to form complexes.

(ii) Transition metals because of their variable valencies sometimes form unstable intermediate compounds and provide a new path with lower activation energy for the reaction, e.g. V_2O_5 (contact process), finely divided iron (in Haber's process) and nickel (in catalytic hydrogenation).

(iii) In some cases, transition metals provide a suitable surface for the reaction to take place. The reactants are adsorbed on the surface of the catalyst. This weakens the bonds between atoms in the reactant molecules.

10. Formation of Interstitial Compounds

(i) Interstitial compounds are those which are formed when small atoms such as H, C, N etc. are trapped inside the interstitial space of crystal lattices of metals.

(ii) They are generally non-stoichiometric and are neither typically ionic nor covalent, e.g. Mn_4N, TiC, Fe_3H, $TiH_{1.7}$, $VH_{0.56}$, etc.

(iii) The formulas quoted do not correspond to any normal oxidation state of the metal. These compounds are hard (some borides approach diamond in hardness, chemically inert, metallic conductor and have high melting point than those of pure metals.

11. Alloy Formation

(i) An alloy is a blend of metals prepared by mixing the components. An alloy is a homeogeneous solid solution.

(ii) Atoms of transition metal due to similar sizes, can easily take place in the crystal lattice of another metal in the molten state and are miscible with each other forming alloys. These are generally hard, resistant to corrosion and have high melting point.

Topic Practice 1

Very Short Answer Type Questions

(1 Mark)

1. **Fill in the Blanks.**

(i) The outermost electronic configuration of Cu is............ .

(ii) The most common oxidation state for the elements of 3*d*-series is ....

(iii) The transition metals show.........'*A*'.........character because of the presence of unpaired electrons and Cu^+ is.........'*B*'.........because its electronic configuration is $[Ar]3d^{10}$. **ISC 2015**

In the above sentence '*A*' and '*B*' are

(a) paramagnetic, diamagnetic
(b) noble, paramagnetic
(c) noble, diamagnetic
(d) diamagnetic, paramagnetic

(iv) The magnetic moment for an ion having d^5 configuration is .... B.M.

(v) Zinc oxide is reduced by .... at 1673K to form zinc and .... **ISC 2020**

2. Objective Type Questions

(i) Transition metal with low oxidation number will act as
(a) an oxidising agent (b) a base
(c) an acid (d) None of these

(ii) The spin only magnetic moment of Mn^{4+} ion is nearly
(a) 3 BM (b) 6 BM
(c) 4 BM (d) 5 BM

(iii) Which one of the following oxides is ionic?
(a) MnO (b) MnO_2
(c) Mn_2O_2 (d) CrO_3

(iv) Which one of the following compounds is diamagnetic and colourless ? **ISC 2024**
(a) $K_2Cr_2O_7$ (b) $ZnSO_4$
(c) $KMnO_4$ (d) $Cr_2(SO_4)_3$

3. Match metals ions in Column I with their magnetic moment (in BM) in Column II and select the correct codes given below.

	Column I		Column II
A.	Cr^{3+}	(i)	$\sqrt{35}$
B.	Fe^{2+}	(ii)	$\sqrt{24}$
C.	Ni^{2+}	(iii)	$\sqrt{15}$
D	Mn^{2+}	(iv)	$\sqrt{8}$

Codes

	A	B	C	D		A	B	C	D
(a)	(i)	(iii)	(ii)	(iv)	(b)	(ii)	(i)	(iv)	(iii)
(c)	(iii)	(ii)	(iv)	(i)	(d)	(iv)	(iii)	(i)	(ii)

4. Silver atom has completely filled *d*-orbitals ($4d^{10}$) in its ground state. How can you say that it is a transition element? **NCERT**

5. What is the electronic configuration of chromium atom (Z=24)?

6. The second and third rows of transition elements resemble each other much more than they resemble the first row. Why? **NCERT Exemplar**

7. In the series Sc (Z = 21) to Zn (Z = 30), the enthalpy of atomisation of zinc is lowest, i.e. 126 kJ mol^{-1}. Why? **NCERT**

8. Which transition metal of the 3*d*-series exhibits the largest number of oxidation states and why? **NCERT**

9. Why are Mn^{2+} compounds more stable than Fe^{2+} towards oxidation to their +3 state? **NCERT**

10. Why is the highest oxidation state of a metal exhibited in its oxide or fluoride only? **NCERT**

11. Explain, why Cu^+ is diamagnetic but Cu^{2+} paramagnetic (Z = 29)? **ISC 2013**

12. Give reason, Zn^{2+} salts are white but Cu^{2+} salts blue in colour. **ISC 2014, 2013, 2010**

Short Answer Type I Questions (2 Marks)

13. What are interstitial compounds?

14. Write down the electronic configuration of
(i) Cr^{3+} (ii) Cu^+ (iii) Co^{2+} (iv) Mn^{2+} **NCERT**

15. In a given transition series, there is no significant changes in the atomic radii of elements with increase in atomic number. Explain why? **ISC 2011**

16. Explain briefly how +2 oxidation state becomes more and more stable in the first half of the first row transition elements with increasing atomic number? **NCERT**

Or Compare the stability of +2 oxidation state for the elements of the first transition series. **NCERT**

17. Explain, why oxidation states of transition elements first increases from Sc to Mn and then decreases?

18. Explain why Cu^+ ion is not stable in aqueous solution? **NCERT**

Or Explain why Cu (I) ion is not known in aqueous solution?

19. Which metal in the first series of transition metals exhibit +1 oxidation state most frequently and why? **NCERT**

20. Predict which of the following will be coloured in aqueous solution?
Ti^{3+}, V^{3+}, Cu^+, Sc^{3+}, Mn^{2+}, Fe^{3+} and Co^{2+}. Give reasons for each. **NCERT**

21. State a reason for each of the following. **ISC 2023**
(i) $La(OH)_3$ is more basic than $Lu(OH)_3$.
(ii) Transition elements and their compounds act as catalyst.

22. Give a reason for the following. **ISC 2023**
(i) Cu^{+2} salts are paramagnetic, while Cu^+ salts are diamagnetic.

(ii) Mn^{+2} compounds are more stable than Fe^{+2} compounds.

23. (i) Why is Mn^{+2} ion more stable the Fe^{+2} ion? **ISC 2024**

(Atomic number of Mn = 25 and Fe = 26)

(ii) Trivalent lanthanoid ions such as La^{3+} $(Z = 57)$ and Lu^{+3} $(Z = 71)$ do not show any colour in their solution. Give a reaction.

24. Explain the following observations:

(i) Copper atom has completely filled *d* orbitals $(3d^{10})$ in its ground state, yet it is regarded as a transition element.

(ii) Cr^{2+} is a stronger reducing agent than Fe^{2+} in aqueous solutions.

25. Give a reason for each of the following. **ISC 2024**

(i) Zinc, cadmium and mercury are considered as *d*-block elements but not regarded as transition elements.

(ii) Transition metals possess a great tendency to form complex compounds.

26. Account for each of the following. **ISC 2024**

(i) Zirconium (Zr) and Hafnium (Hf) are difficult to separate.

(ii) Salts of cupric (Cu^{2+}) ion are coloured whereas salts of cuprous (Cu^{+}) ion are colourless.

27. Name the oxometal anions of the first series of the transition metals in which the metal exhibits the oxidation state equal to its group number. **NCERT**

28. Calculate the 'spin only' magnetic moment of $M^{2+}(aq)$ ion. $(Z = 27)$. **NCERT**

Short Answer Type II Questions

3 Marks

29. The halides of transition elements become more covalent with increasing oxidation state of the metal. Why? **NCERT Exemplar**

30. How would you account for the following? **NCERT**

(i) Of the d^4 species, Cr^{2+} is strongly reducing agent while manganese (III) is strongly oxidising agent.

(ii) Cobalt (II) is stable in aqueous solution but in the presence of complexing reagents, it is easily oxidised.

(iii) The d^1 configuration is very unstable in ions.

31. Explain why transition metals form complex compounds? **ISC 2012**

32. Explain the following:

(i) Why do transition metal ions possess a great tendency to form complexes?

(ii) The paramagnetic character in 3*d*-transition series elements increases upto Mn and then decreases. **ISC 2015**

33. Explain why,

(i) transition elements form alloys?

(ii) Zn^{2+} salts are white whereas Cu^{2+} salts are coloured?

(iii) transition metals and their compounds act as catalyst? **ISC 2019**

34. Explain the following: **ISC 2020**

(i) Transition metals and their compounds generally exhibit a paramagnetic behaviour.

(ii) There is an increase in density of elements from titanium $(Z = 22)$ to copper $(Z = 29)$ in the 3*d*-series of transition elements.

(iii) $K_2Cr_2O_7$ acts as a powerful oxidising agent in acidic medium.

35. Calculate the number of unpaired electrons in the following gaseous ions Mn^{3+}, Cr^{3+}, V^{3+} and Ti^{3+}. Which one of these is the most stable in aqueous solution? **NCERT**

36. Iron is ferromagnetic in nature. Explain why? **ISC 2011**

37. What is meant by disproportionation? Give two examples of disproportionation reaction in aqueous solution. **NCERT**

Long Answer Type Questions

5 Marks

38. What are the characteristics of the transition elements and why are they called transition elements? Which of the *d*-block elements may not be regarded as the transition elements? **NCERT**

39. Compare the general characteristics of the first series of the transition metals with those of the second and third series metals in the respective vertical columns. Give special emphasis on the following points. **NCERT**

(i) Electronic configuration

(ii) Oxidation states

(iii) Ionisation enthalpies

(iv) Atomic size

40. Comment on the statement that elements of the first transition series possess many properties different from those of heavier transition elements. **NCERT**

41. What can be inferred from the magnetic moment values of the following complex species? **NCERT**

Examples	Magnetic moment (BM)
$K_4[Mn(CN)_6]$	2.2
$[Fe(H_2O)_6]^{2+}$	5.3

42. Write down the number of $3d$-electron in each of the following ions; Ti^{2+}, V^{2+}, Cr^{3+}, Mn^{2+}, Fe^{2+}, Fe^{3+}, Co^{2+}, Ni^{2+} and Cu^{2+}. Indicate how would you expect the five $3d$-orbitals to be occupied for these hydrated ions (octahedral)? **NCERT**

Hints & Solutions

1. (i) $3d^{10}4s^1$. (ii) (+)2
(iii) (a) paramagnetic, diamagnetic
(iv) $\sqrt{35}$, i.e. 5.92 B.M. (v) coke, carbon monoxide.

2. (i) (d) Transition metal, which have low oxidation number show the oxidising nature because of great tendency to lose the electron.

(ii) (c) The electronic configuration of Mn is

$$_{25}Mn = [Ar]3d^5 4s^2$$

$$\therefore \quad Mn^{4+} = [Ar]\, 3d^3$$

Thus, three unpaired electrons are present.

$\therefore$ Spin only magnetic moment, $\mu = \sqrt{n(n+2)}$

$$\because \quad n = 3$$

$$\therefore \quad \mu = \sqrt{3(3+2)}$$

$$= \sqrt{15} = 3.87 = 4 \text{ BM}$$

(iii) (a) MnO is ionic due to lower oxidation state.

(iv) (b) $ZnSO_4$ is diamagnetic and colourless. Zn is in +2 oxidation state.

$$_{30}Zn^{2+} = 3d^{10}$$

All electrons are paired, hence diamagnetic and colourless.

3. (c) $\because \mu = \sqrt{n(n+2)}$, n = No. of unpaired electron

$Cr^{3+}(Z = 24), 3d^3 4s^0, \mu = \sqrt{3(3+2)} = \sqrt{15}$

$Fe^{2+}(Z = 26), 3d^6 4s^0, \mu = \sqrt{4(4+2)} = \sqrt{24}$

$Ni^{2+}(Z = 28), 3d^8 4s^0, \mu = \sqrt{2(2+2)} = \sqrt{8}$

$Mn^{2+}(Z = 25), 3d^5 4s^0, \mu = \sqrt{5(5+2)} = \sqrt{35}$

4. Silver in its +1 oxidation state, exhibits $4d^{10}\, 5s^0$ configuration. But in some compounds, it also shows +2 oxidation state, so the configuration becomes $4d^9\, 5s^0$. Here, d-orbital is not completely filled. Therefore, silver is a transition element. (1)

5. The electronic configuration of chromium atom ($Z = 24$) is

$1s^2, 2s^2, 2p^6, 3s^2, 3p^6, 4s^1, 3d^5$ (1)

6. Due to lanthanoid contraction, the atomic radii of the second and third rows of transition elements is almost same. So, they resemble each other much more as compared to first row elements and show similar characteristics. (1)

7. Zinc has stable ground state due to its completely filled d-orbitals. It therefore, has least tendency to form metallic bonds, in the series, thus requires least enthalpy of atomisation to get atomised. (1)

8. Manganese shows maximum number of oxidation states (EC : $3d^5, 4s^2$), i.e. + 2, + 3, + 4, + 5, + 6, + 7 in its compounds due to maximum number of unpaired electrons. (1)

9. Mn^{2+} compounds are more stable due to half-filled d-orbitals. Fe^{2+} compounds are comparatively less stable as they have six electrons in its outermost orbitals. So, they tend to lose one electron from Fe^{2+} and get stable $3d^5$ configuration. (1)

10. Oxygen and fluorine both have small size and high value of electronegativity. So, they can oxidise the metal to their highest oxidation states. (1)

11. The electronic configuration of

$Cu^+ = 1s^2, 2s^2, 2p^6, 3s^2, 3p^6, 4s^0, 3d^{10}$

and $Cu^{2+} = 1s^2, 2s^2, 2p^6, 3s^2, 3p^6, 4s^0, 3d^9$

In Cu^+ ion, all electrons are paired. Here Cu^+ is diamagnetic in nature. Whereas, Cu^+ has one unpaired electron thus, shows paramagnetic character. (1)

12. The transition metal ions having completely filled d-orbitals or completely empty d-orbitals are colourless or white. Since, Zn^{2+} possesses completely filled d-orbitals as electronic configuration of Zn^{2+} is $1s^2, 2s^2, 2p^6, 3s^2, 3p^6, 3d^{10}$. Thus, its salts are white or colourless. On the other hand, Cu^{2+} possesses an unpaired electron as electronic configuration is $1s^2 2s^2 2p^6 3s^2 3p^6 3d^9$.

Thus, it undergoes d-d transition. Hence, Cu^{2+} salts are coloured. (1)

13. The compounds which are formed when small atoms like H, C, N etc, are trapped inside the interstitial spaces of crystal lattices of transition metals are called interstitial compounds.

14. Electronic configuration of the given ions are :

(i) $Cr^{3+}(Z = 24) = 1s^2\, 2s^2\, 2p^6\, 3s^2 3p^6 3d^3$

Here, $1s^2\, 2s^2\, 2p^6\, 3s^2 3p^6$ refers to the electronic configuration of $[Ar]^{18}$, thus electronic configuration of Cr^{3+} can be written as $Cr^{3+} = [Ar]\, 3d^3$.

For (ii), (iii) and (iv): Refer to table on page 136. (Electronic configuration of d-block elements).

$(4 \times ½ = 2)$

15. Generally, atomic radii of transition elements belonging to a particular series decreases with increase in atomic number. As atomic number increases, the added electron enters in $(n-1)d$ subshell and thus, the shielding effect increases along with increase in nuclear charge. However, the decrease in size with increase in nuclear charge due to increase in atomic number is counter balanced by the increased shielding effect of $(n-1)d$ electrons. Hence, in a given transition series, there is no significant changes in the atomic radii of elements with increase in atomic number. (2)

16. The most common +2 oxidation state of first half of first row transition elements becomes more and more stable with increasing atomic number because 3*d*-orbitals acquire only one electron in each of five 3*d*-orbitals (i.e. remain half-filled) and the electronic repulsion is the least and nuclear charge increases. In 2nd half of first row transition element, electrons starts pairing up in 3*d*-orbital, thus the stability of + 2 oxidation decreases after Mn^{2+}. (2)

17. The use of 3*d* electron for formation of bond increases from Sc to Mn, causing the increase in oxidation state up to +7. This is because the number of unpaired electrons increases from Sc to Mn. As the number of unpaired electrons decreases from Fe to Cu so does the oxidation state. (2)

18. In aqueous solution, copper (I) undergoes disproportionation reaction.

$$2Cu^{+}(aq) \longrightarrow Cu^{2+} + Cu(s)$$

The highest stability of Cu^{2+} ion in aqueous solution is due to negative enthalpy of hydration.
Hence, Cu^{+} is not known (or unstable) in aqueous solution. (2)

19. Electronic configuration of Cu is $[Ar]\,3d^{10}4s^1$. When copper atom loses 1 electron, it exhibits + 1 oxidation state and forms Cu^{+} ion with stable $3d^{10}$ configuration. So, copper metal in the first transition series tends to have + 1 oxidation state to achieve a stable configuration. **(2)**

20. **Hint** Ions having d^0 or d^{10} configuration are colourless. Refer to text on page 268 (Formaion of coloured ions).

21. (i) $La(OH)_3$ is more basic than $Lu(OH)_3$ due to lanthanide contraction. The size of lanthanoid ions decreases from $La^{3+}$to Lu^{3+}, the covalent character of the hydroxides increases and hence the basic strength decreases as we move from $La^{3+}$to Lu^{3+}.

(ii) Most of the transition metals and their compounds act as a catalyst because of the variable oxidation states and the presence of vacant *d*-orbitals due to which they can form a variety of unstable intermediates.
Further, large surface area of transition metals also attributes to their catalytic property. Thus, the reactants are adsorbed on their surface and come closer to each other facilitating the reaction process.

22. (i) The paramagnetic nature of any compound is due to unpaired electron. The salts of $Cu^{2+}$are paramagnetic because it has one unpaired electrons.
Electronic configuration of $Cu^{2+}$is [Ar] $3d^9 4s^0$.
Electronic configuration of Cu^{+} is [Ar] $3d^{10}4s^0$.
Here, Cu^{+} has $3d^{10}\,4s^0$ electronic configuration, it has no unpaired electrons hence diamagnetic.

(ii) Manganese in +2 oxidation state form stable compounds than iron in +2 oxidation state.
$Mn^{2+} = 1s^2\,2s^2\,2p^6\,3s^2\,3p^6\,3d^5$ (half-filled *d*-orbital)
$Fe^{2+} = 1s^2\,2s^2\,2p^6\,3s^2\,3p^6\,3d^6$
Mn^{2+}compounds are more stable due to half-filled *d*-orbitals. Fe^{2+}compounds are comparatively less stable as they have six electrons in their 3*d*-orbitals.

23. (i) Mn^{2+} ion has half-filled configuration, i.e. $3d^5$, while Fe^{2+} ion does not (i.e. $3d^6$). Therefore, Mn^{2+} ion is more stable than Fe^{2+} ion.

(ii) Ion which does not have unpaired electrons does not impart colour to the solution. La^{3+} has $5d^0 6s^0$ and Lu^{3+} has $4f^{14}5d^0 6s^0$ configuration. Thus, both do not have unpaired electron. Thus, they do not shown any colour in their solution.

24. (i) Because it has incompletely filled *d*-orbitals in one of its oxidation states, i.e. Cu^{2+} ($[Ar]3d^9$). **(1)**

(ii) Cr^{2+} is a stronger reducing agent than Fe^{2+} as when Cr^{2+} losses one electron, it forms Cr^{3+} with electronic configuration d^3 while Fe^{2+} changes to Fe^{3+} with electronic configuration d^5 which is highly stable. Thus, Cr^{2+} can loose more than one electron, but Fe^{2+} can loose only one electron. (1)

25. (i) As zinc, cadmium and mercury of group 12 have completely filled *d*-orbitals in their common oxidation states, thus they are not regarded as transition metals, but they are studied along with the chemistry of the transition metals.

(ii) The transition metals form a large number of complex compound due to the comparatively smaller size of the metal ions, their high charge density and vacant *d*-orbitals for bond formation.

26. (i) Due to lanthanoid contraction, there is a small difference in the size of Zr and Hf. So, there is difference in some properties of lanthanoids like solubility, degree of hydration and complex formation. These differences enable the separation of lanthanoids by ion exchange method.

(ii) Cu^{2+} ion has an electronic configuration $3d^9$ whereas Cu^{+} ion has an $3d^{10}$. Hence, an unpaired electron is present in Cu^{2+} due to which $d-d$ electronic transition takes place. The energy of excitation corresponds to the frequency of light absorbed. The colour observed corresponds to the complementary colour of the light absorbed. In contrast, due to lack of unpaired electrons Cu^{+} is colourless.

27. $[ScO_2]^-$: Group number = Oxidation state of Sc = 3
$[TiO_3]^{2-}$: Group number = Oxidation state of Ti = 4
$[VO_3]^-$: Group number = Oxidation state of V = 5
$[Cr_2O_7]^{2-}$: Group number = Oxidation state of Cr = 6
$[CrO_4]^{2-}$: Group number = Oxidation state of Cr = 6
$[MnO_4]^-$: Group number = Oxidation state of Mn = 7 (2)

28. $\mu = 3.87$ BM
[Same method as example 2 on page 267 to 268.] (Magnetic properties). (2)

29. This problem is based on the concept of Fajans' rule. As the oxidation state increases, size of the ion of transition element decreases. As per Fajans' rule, when the size of metal ion decreases, covalent character of the bond formed increases. Therefore, the halide of transition elements become more covalent with increasing oxidation state of the metal. (3)

30. (i) The electronic configuration of Cr^{2+} is $3d^4 4s^0$. After loosing one electron, it changes to Cr^{3+} whose configuration is $3d^3$ t_{2g}^3 which is a more stable configuration and, hence it can act as a reducing agent. While Mn^{3+} after gaining one electron becomes Mn^{2+} whose electronic configuration is $3d^5 4s^0$ which highly stable configuration. Thus, it act as an oxidising agent. (1)

(ii) Cobalt (III) ion has greater tendency to form complexes than cobalt (II) ion. Hence, in presence of ligands Co(II) changes to Co (III), i.e. is easily oxidised. (1)

(iii) Ions of transition metals with d^1 configuration tend to lose one electron to acquire d^0 configuration that is they are unstable. Therefore, such ions (with d^1) undergo either oxidation or disproportionation, hence unstable. (1)

31. Transition metal form a large number of complex compounds due to the following reasons :
(i) Small size (ii) High nuclear charge
(iii) Availability of vacant d-orbitals of suitable energy for accommodating the lone pair of electrons donated by the ligands. (3)

32. (i) Due to small size of transition metal atoms or their cations and high effective nuclear charge, they have a high positive charge density on them. This high positive charged density makes the atoms or cation to attract the lone pair of electrons from the ligand and transition metal cation or atoms have vacant d-orbital in which they can accommodate the lone pair of electrons donated by ligands and thus can form $L \rightarrow M$ coordinate bonds. (1½)

(ii) Paramagnetic character increases with the increase in the number of unpaired electrons. The larger is the number of unpaired electron in central atom or ion greater is the paramagnetic character. Since, from Sc to Mn number of unpaired electron increases and then from Fe to Zn decreases hence, paramagnetic character also increases from Sc to Mn and then decreases from Fe to Zn. (1½)

33. (i) The atomic radii of the transition elements in any series are not much different from each other. As a result, they can very easily replace each other in the lattice and form solid solutions over an appreciable composition range. Such solid solution are called alloys.

(ii) Zn^{2+} salts have a completely filled set of d-orbitals ($3d^{10}$), while Cu^{2+} has an incompletely filled set of d - orbitals ($3d^9$), and therefore, $d-d$-transition is possible in Cu^{2+}, leading to blue colour.

(iii) Many transition metals and their compounds are used as catalyst because the catalytic activity is due to their ability to adopt multiple oxidation states and to form complexes. Transition metals, because of their variable valencies sometimes form unstable intermediate compounds and provide a new path with lower activation energy for the reaction and thus acts as a catalyst.

34. (i) Transition metals have one or more unpaired electron. So, they readily occur paramagnetic in nature.

(ii) While going from left to right in a period, the radii of transition elements remain similar but their atomic masses increases gradually. As a result, their density increases correspondingly.

(iii) $K_2Cr_2O_7$ act as an oxidising agent in acidic medium because it itself get reduced and helps in oxidation. Equation involved is as follows :

$$Cr_2O_7^{2-} + 14H^+ + 6e^- \longrightarrow 2Cr^{3+} + 7H_2O \quad (E° = 1.33\,V)$$

35. Mn^{3+} ($Z = 25$) = [Ar] $3d^4$ [1|1|1|1|]

Cr^{3+} ($Z = 24$) = [Ar] $3d^3$ [1|1|1| |]

V^{3+} ($Z = 23$) = [Ar] $3d^2$ [1|1| | |]

Ti^{3+} ($Z = 22$) = [Ar] $3d^1$ [1| | | |]

Cr^{3+} is the most stable among these in aqueous solution because it has half-filled t_{2g} level ($= t_{2g}^3$). (3)

36. Ferromagnetism is a special case of paramagnetism in which a substance acquires a permanent magnetic moment.

Paramagnetism is due to the presence of unpaired electrons in $(n-1)d$ orbital. As number of unpaired electrons increases, paramagnetism increases. Iron is much more paramagnetic than rest of the elements due to more number of unpaired electrons [$3d^6 4s^2$] and hence, it is termed as ferromagnetic. It is used to prepare permanent magnets. (3)

37. In a disproportionation reaction, same substance undergoes oxidation (increase in oxidation number) as well as reduction (decrease in oxidation number) resulting in the formation of two different products. (1)

e.g.
(i) Mn (VI) becomes unstable relative to Mn (VII) and Mn (IV) in acidic solution. (1)

$$3\overset{+6}{Mn}O_4^{2-} + 4H^+ \longrightarrow 2\,\overset{+7}{Mn}O_4^- + \overset{+4}{Mn}O_2 + 2H_2O$$

(ii) Many Cu (I) compounds are unstable in aqueous solution and undergo disproportionation as follows:

$$2Cu^+(aq) \longrightarrow Cu^{2+} + Cu(s)$$ (1)

38. Refer to text on page 136 to 138 (General properties of the transition elements) (*d*-block). They are called transition elements because of their position between s and *p*-block elements. Zinc due to presence of fully-filled *d*-orbitals (d^{10} electronic configuration) may not be regarded as transition elements. (5)

39. (i) **Electronic configuration** The elements in the same vertical column generally have similar electronic configuration $[ns^2(n-1)d^{1-10}]$. Although, the first series has only two exceptions,

$$Cr = 3d^5\, 4s^1 \text{ and } Cu = 3d^{10}4s^1$$

Second transition series have five exceptions,

$Mo = 4d^5 5s^1$, $Nb = 4d^4 5s^1$,

$Rh = 4d^8 5s^1$, $Pd = 4d^{10} 5s^0$

$Ag = 4d^{10} 5s^1$

Third transition series has three exceptions,

$W = 4f^{14}5d^4 6s^2$, $Pt = 4f^{14}5d^9 6s^1$

$Au = 4f^{14}5d^{10}6s^1$ (2)

(ii) **Oxidation states** Refer to text on pages 137 and 138. (Variable valency and oxidation states.) (1)

(iii) **Ionisation enthalpies** The first ionisation enthalpy in each series generally increase gradually as we move from left to right. (1)

Though some exceptions are observed in each series. The first ionisation enthalpies of some elements in the second (4*d*) series are higher, while some of them have lower value than the elements of 3*d*-series in the same vertical column. (1)

(iv) **Atomic size** Generally, ions of the same charge or atoms in a given series show progressive decrease in radius with increasing atomic number though the decrease is quite small. But the size of the atoms of the 4*d*-series is larger than the corresponding elements of the 3*d*-series whereas those of corresponding elements of the 5*d*-series are nearly the same as those of 4*d*-series due to lanthanoid contraction. (1)

40. The heavier transition elements belong to fourth (4*d*), fifth (5*d*) and sixth (6*d*) transition series. Their properties are expected to be different from the elements belonging to the first (3*d*) series due to the following reasons:

(i) Atomic radii of heavier transition elements (4*d* and 5*d* series) are larger than those of the corresponding elements of the first transition series though those of 4*d* and 5*d*-series are very close to each other. (1)

(ii) Ionisation enthalpies of 5*d*-series are higher than the corresponding elements of 3*d* and 4*d*-series. (1)

(iii) Enthalpies of atomisation of 4*d*-and 5*d*-series are higher than the corresponding elements of the first series. (1)

(iv) Melting and boiling points of heavier transition elements are greater than those of the first transition series due to stronger intermetallic bonding. (1)

(v) The elements of the first transition series generally form low spin or high spin complexes, depending upon the strength of ligand field.

However, the heavier transition elements form low spin complexes irrespective of the strength of the ligand field. (1)

41. Magnetic moment $(\mu) = \sqrt{n(n+2)}$ BM

For $n = 1$, $\mu = \sqrt{1(1+2)} = \sqrt{3} = 1.73 \text{BM} \approx 2$

For $n = 2$, $\mu = \sqrt{2(2+2)} = \sqrt{8} = 2.83 \text{ BM} \approx 3$

For $n = 3$, $\mu = \sqrt{3(3+2)} = \sqrt{15} = 3.87 \text{ BM} \approx 4$

For $n = 4$, $\mu = \sqrt{4(4+2)} = \sqrt{24} = 4.90 \text{BM} \approx 5$

For $n = 5$, $\mu = \sqrt{5(5+2)} = \sqrt{35} = 5.92 \text{ BM} \approx 6$ (1)

In $K_4[Mn(CN)_6]$, Mn is in +2 oxidation state, i.e. given value of μ (2.2 BM $\approx$ 2) indicates the presence of one unpaired electron.

Since, CN^- is a strong field ligand. Hence, when CN^- ligands approach Mn^{2+} ion, the electrons in 3*d* pair up. Hybridisation involved is d^2sp^3 forming inner orbital octahedral complex.

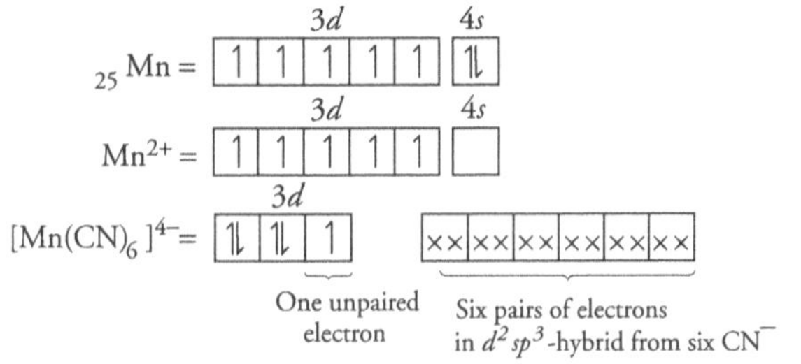

(2)

In $[Fe(H_2O)_6]^{2+}$, Fe is in +2 oxidation state. Given, μ = 5.3 BM ($\approx$ 5), shows that there are four unpaired electrons. Since, H_2O is a weak ligand.

Hence, the electrons in 3*d* do not pair up when the ligands, i.e. H_2O molecules, approach. To accommodate the electrons donated by H_2O molecules, the hybridisation is sp^3d^2. Hence, it will be an outer orbital octahedral complex.

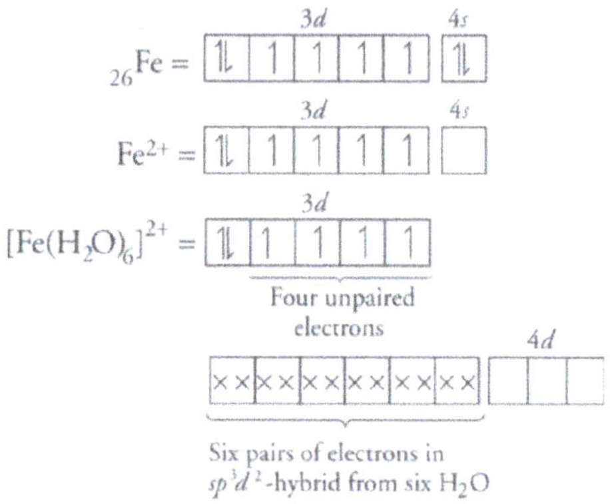

(2)

42. All the ions form complex of the type $[M(H_2O)_6]^{n+}$. As water is a weak field ligand, therefore, in case of octahedral complex, pairing will not takes place, hence each t_{2g} and e_g orbital will be first singly occupied [In octahedral t_{2g} (d_{xy}, d_{yz}, d_{zx}) set is of lower energy and e_g $(d_{z^2}, d_{x^2-y^2})$ is of higher energy]. (2)

Ions	Configuration	Number of 3d electrons	Number of unpaired electrons	Occupancy of 3d-orbitals
Ti^{2+}	$3d^2$	2	2	t_{2g}^2
V^{2+}	$3d^3$	3	3	t_{2g}^3
Cr^{3+}	$3d^3$	3	3	t_{2g}^3
Mn^{2+}	$3d^5$	5	5	$t_{2g}^3e_g^2$
Fe^{2+}	$3d^6$	6	4	$t_{2g}^4e_g^2$
Fe^{3+}	$3d^5$	5	5	$t_{2g}^3e_g^2$
Co^{2+}	$3d^7$	7	3	$t_{2g}^5e_g^2$
Ni^{2+}	$3d^8$	8	2	$t_{2g}^6e_g^2$
Cu^{2+}	$3d^9$	9	1	$t_{2g}^6e_g^3$

(3)

TOPIC 02 Important Compounds and Applications of Transition Elements

Potassium Permanganate, $KMnO_4$

It is a powerful oxidising agent in solution state and acts as a strong bleaching agent.

Preparation

(i) Potassium permanganate is prepared by pyrolusite (MnO_2) ore. When pyrolusite ore is fused with alkali metal hydroxide in the presence of air or an oxidising agent like KNO_3, potassium manganate is formed.

$$2MnO_2 + 4KOH + O_2 \longrightarrow \underset{\text{Potassium manganate}}{2K_2MnO_4} + 2H_2O$$

Potassium manganate (K_2MnO_4) is of green colour which disproportionate in a neutral or acidic solution to produce potassium permanganate.

$$3MnO_4^{2-} + 4H^+ \longrightarrow 2MnO_4^- + MnO_2 + 2H_2O$$

$$\text{or } 3K_2MnO_4 + 4H^+ \longrightarrow \underset{\text{Potassium permanganate}}{2KMnO_4} + MnO_2 + 2H_2O + 4K^+$$

(ii) Commercially, it is prepared by alkaline oxidative fusion of MnO_2 followed by electrolytic oxidation of manganate (VI).

$$MnO_2 \xrightarrow[\text{Oxidised with air or } KNO_3]{\text{Fused with KOH}} \underset{\text{Manganate ion}}{MnO_4^{2-}}$$

$$MnO_4^{2-} \xrightarrow[\text{in alkaline solution}]{\text{Electrolytic oxidation}} \underset{\text{Permanganate ion}}{MnO_4^-}$$

(iii) In the laboratory, a manganese (II) ion salt is oxidised by peroxodisulphate to permanganate.

$$MnO_4^{2-} \longrightarrow MnO_4^- + e^-$$

$$2Mn^{2+} + 5S_2O_8^{2-} + 8H_2O \longrightarrow 2MnO_4^- + 10SO_4^{2-} + 16H^+$$

(vi) Dark purple crystals are formed which are isostructural with $KClO_4$.

Structure

(i) The manganate, MnO_4^{2-} and permanganate, MnO_4^- are tetrahedral, the green MnO_4^{2-} is paramagnetic with one unpaired electron but the purple MnO_4^- is diamagnetic.

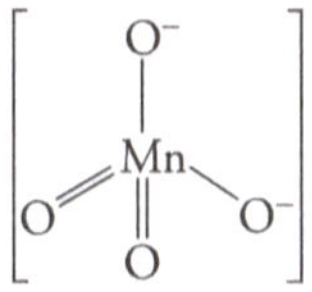

Tetrahedral manganate ion (green) (Paramagnetic)

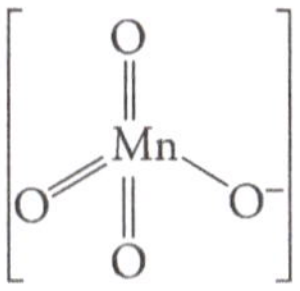

Tetrahedral permanganate ion (purple)

(ii) The π-bonding takes place by overlapping of *p*-orbitals of oxygen with *d*-orbitals of manganese.

Physical Properties

(i) It is dark purple coloured (the deep purple colour of $KMnO_4$ is due to charge transfer from O to Mn) crystalline solid. It is moderately soluble in water (6.4 g/100 g of H_2O at 293 K).

(ii) It is stored in dark coloured bottles because it gets decomposed in the presence of sunlight.

(iii) It has weak paramagnetism which depends upon temperature.

Chemical Properties

(i) **Effect of Heat** On heating, it decomposes at 513 K and O_2 is evolved.

$$2KMnO_4 \xrightarrow{513\text{ K}} K_2MnO_4 + MnO_2 + O_2$$

(ii) Potassium permanganate ($KMnO_4$) produces nascent oxygen in solution state, which is the cause of its bleaching and oxidising properties. Its important reactions are as follows :

Bleaching Action of $KMnO_4$ in Different Solution

(a) **Neutral solution**

$$2KMnO_4 + H_2O \longrightarrow 2KOH + 2MnO_2 + 3[O]$$
$$MnO_4^- + 2H_2O + 3e^- \longrightarrow MnO_2 + 4OH^-$$

(b) **Alkaline solution**

$$2KMnO_4 + 2KOH \longrightarrow 2K_2MnO_4 + H_2O + [O]$$
$$MnO_4^- + e^- \longrightarrow MnO_4^{2-}$$

(c) **Acidic solution**

$$2KMnO_4 + 3H_2SO_4 \longrightarrow K_2SO_4 + 2MnSO_4 + 3H_2O + 5[O]$$
$$MnO_4^- + 8H^+ + 5e^- \longrightarrow Mn^{2+} + 4H_2O$$

(iii) **Oxidation Reactions of Acidified** $KMnO_4$

(a) **Iodide to iodine**

$$[MnO_4^- + 8H^+ + 5e^- \longrightarrow Mn^{2+} + 4H_2O] \times 2$$
$$[2I^- \longrightarrow I_2 + 2e^-] \times 5$$
$$2MnO_4^- + 10I^- + 16H^+ \longrightarrow 2Mn^{2+} + 5I_2 + 8H_2O$$

(b) **Ferrous to ferric**

$$MnO_4^- + 8H^+ + 5e^- \longrightarrow Mn^{2+} + 4H_2O$$
$$[\underset{\text{(Green)}}{Fe^{2+}} \longrightarrow \underset{\text{(Yellow)}}{Fe^{3+}} + e^-] \times 5$$
$$MnO_4^- + 5Fe^{2+} + 8H^+ \longrightarrow Mn^{2+} + 5Fe^{3+} + 4H_2O$$

(c) **Oxalate to carbon dioxide** (at 333 K)

$$[MnO_4^- + 8H^+ + 5e^- \longrightarrow Mn^{2+} + 4H_2O] \times 2$$
$$[C_2O_4^{2-} \longrightarrow 2CO_2 + 2e^-] \times 5$$
$$2MnO_4^- + 5C_2O_4^{2-} + 16H^+ \longrightarrow 2Mn^{2+} + 10CO_2 + 8H_2O$$

(d) **Hydrogen sulphide to sulphur**

$$H_2S \longrightarrow 2H^+ + S^{2-}$$
$$[MnO_4^- + 8H^+ + 5e^- \longrightarrow Mn^{2+} + 4H_2O] \times 2$$
$$[S^{2-} \longrightarrow S + 2e^-] \times 5$$
$$2MnO_4^- + 5S^{2-} + 16H^+ \longrightarrow 2Mn^{2+} + 5S + 8H_2O$$

(iv) **Oxidation Reaction in Basic Medium** It oxidise potassium iodide to potassium iodate.

$$2KMnO_4 + H_2O \longrightarrow 2MnO_2 + KOH + 3O$$
$$KI + 3O \longrightarrow 2KIO_3$$
$$2KMnO_4 + KI + H_2O \longrightarrow 2MnO_2 + 2KOH + KIO_3$$

(v) **Oxidation Properties in Neutral Medium** It oxidiser hydrogen sulphide to sulphur.

$$2KMnO_4 + H_2O \longrightarrow 2KOH + 2MnO_2 + 30$$
$$[H_2S + O \longrightarrow H_2O + S] \times 3$$
$$2KMnO_4 + 3H_2S \longrightarrow 2KOH + 2MnO_2 + 2H_2O + 3S$$

Uses

In analytical chemistry, it is used as an oxidant in the preparation of organic compounds, bleaching of wool, cotton, silk, decolourisation of oils.

In case HCl is used, it is oxidised to Cl_2 and in cleaning surgical instruments in hospitals.It is used in volumetric analysis of for the estimation of ferrous salts, oxalates, iodides etc.

Note $KMnO_4$ is not used as primary standard solution. This is due to the fact that it is difficult to obtain it in the pure state and free from traces of MnO_4^-. That's why it is always first standardised with a standard solution of oxalic acid

$Cr_2O_7^{2-}$ oxidises nitrites, NO_2^- to nitrates, NO_3^-.

$$Cr_2O_7^{2-} + 8H^+ + 3NO_2^- \longrightarrow 2Cr^{3+} + 3NO_3^- + 4H_2O$$

Potassium dichromate does not act as an oxidising agent in basic and neutral medium.

(iv) **Use in Redox Titration : Estimation**

$K_2Cr_2O_7$ is determined volumetrically using Fe^{2+} or I^- (Iodometrically)

$$Cr_2O_7^{2-} + 6Fe^{2+} + 14H^+ \longrightarrow 2Cr^{3+} + 7H_2O$$

$$Cr_2O_7^{2-} \equiv 6Fe^{2+}$$

$$Cr_2O_7^{2-} + 6I^- + 14H^+ \longrightarrow 2Cr^{3+} + 3I_2 + 7H_2O$$

$$I_2 + 2S_2O_3^{2-} \longrightarrow S_4O_6^{2-} + 2I^-$$

Note Sodium dichromate, like potassium dichromate, is also an excellent oxidising agent and it being highly water soluble is extensively used as an oxidising agent in organic chemistry.

Uses

It is used as an oxidising agent, disinfectant, in volumetric analysis, for tanning of leather and in chromyl chloride test.

Applications of Transition Metals

(i) Iron and steel are the most important construction materials.

(ii) TiO is used in pigment industry.

(iii) MnO_2, Zn, Ni and Cd are used in battery industries.

(iv) Cu, Ag and Au are used for making coins and ornaments.

(v) V_2O_5 is used as a catalyst in the manufacture of sulphuric acid.

(vi) $TiCl_4$ with $Al(CH_3)_3$ is used in the manufacture of polythene.

(vii) Iron catalyst is used in Haber's process for the manufacture of ammonia.

(viii) Ni catalyst is used for hydrogenation of fats.

(ix) Light sensitive properties of AgBr are used in photographic industries.

(x) Steel, titanium nitride, titanium carbide, etc., are used for making artificial joint replacement of bones.

Topic Practice 2

Very Short Answer Type Questions

1 Mark

1. Fill in the Blanks

(i) Oxidation state of Mn in $KMnO_4$ is ....

(ii) Oxidation state of Cr in $K_2Cr_2O_7$ is ....

(iii) In alkaline medium $Cr_2O_7^{2-}$ ions, exist as .... ion.

(iv) The given compound .... (a), is an oxidising agent. It changes its colour to orange-red, so that its pH becomes .... (b)

In the above sentence (a) and (b) are

(a) $K_2Cr_2O_7, <>$ (b) $K_2Cr_2O_7, >>$

(c) $KMnO_4, <>$ (d) $KMnO_4, >>$

2. Objective Type Questions

(i) Acidified potassium permanganate solution is decolor by

(a) bleaching power (b) white vitriol

(c) Mohr's salt (d) microcosmic salt

(ii) $KMnO_4$ acts as an oxidising agent in alkaline medium. When alkaline $KMnO_4$ is treated with KI, iodide ion is oxidised to

(a) I_2 (b) IO^-

(c) IO_3^- (d) IO_4^-

(iii) At pH >>, the colour of $K_2Cr_2O_7$ is

(a) Orange (b) yellow

(c) green (d) black

(iv) When $KMnO_4$ is heated with acidified oxalic acid, gas bubbles are evolved. These gas bubbles are evolved due to the formation of

(a) SO_2 (b) CO_2

(c) SO_3 (d) O_2 **ISC 2024**

3. Match Column I with II and choose the correct code.

	Column I	Column II
A.	Use of $K_2Cr_2O_7$	(i) (+) 6
B.	Use of $KMnO_4$	(ii) (+) 7
C.	Oxidation number of CrO_4^{2-}	(iii) in making Baeyer's reagent.
D.	Oxidation number of MnO_4^-	(iv) used in chromyl chloride test.

Codes

	A	B	C	D
(a)	(i)	(ii)	(iii)	(iv)
(b)	(iv)	(iii)	(i)	(ii)
(c)	(iv)	(iii)	(ii)	(i)
(d)	(iii)	(iv)	(i)	(ii)

Short Answer Type II Questions

(2 Marks)

4. Give balanced equation for the following reaction:
Potassium permanganate is heated with concentrated hydrochloric acid. **ISC 2017**

5. Potassium iodide treated with acidified potassium permanganate solution. **ISC 2013**

6. Give the balanced equation for acidified potassium permanganate and oxalic acid **ISC 2012**

7. Explain why does colour of $KMnO_4$ disappear when oxalic acid is added to its solution in acidic medium? **NCERT Exemplar**

8. Complete and balance the following chemical equations:
   (i) $Fe^{2+} + MnO_4^- + H^+ \rightarrow$
   (ii) $MnO_4^- + H_2O + I^- \rightarrow$

9. Give balanced equation for the following reaction:
Potassium dichromate is treated with acidified ferrous sulphate solution. **ISC 2016**

10. Describe the oxidising action of potassium dichromate and write the ionic equations for its reactions with (i) iodide and (ii) H_2S.

11. Describe the oxidising action of potassium dichromate and write the ionic equations for its reaction with (i) iodide (ii) iron (II) solution and (iii) H_2S. **NCERT**

12. Which trivalent ion has maximum size in the lanthanoid series, i.e.
lanthanum ion (La^{3+}) to lutetium ion (Lu^{3+})?
(At. no. of lanthanum = 57 and lutetium = 71) **ISC 2019**

13. Explain why, Cu^{2+} is paramagnetic but Cu^+ is diamagnetic? (at. no. of Cu = 29) **ISC 2019**

14. Complete the following chemical reaction equations:
   (i) $MnO_4^-(aq) + C_2O_4^{2-}(aq) + H^+(aq) \longrightarrow$
   (ii) $Cr_2O_7^{2-}(aq) + Fe^{2+}(aq) + H^+(aq) \longrightarrow$

15. Complete and balance the following chemical equations **ISC 2023**
   (i) $KMnO_4 + H_2SO_4 + KI \longrightarrow$ .... + ... + ...
   (ii) $K_2Cr_2O_7 + H_2SO_4 + H_2S \longrightarrow$ .... + ... + 6.........

Short Answer Type II Questions

(3 Marks)

16. Explain why? [3]
   (i) Mn^{2+} is more stable than Fe^{2+} towards oxidation to+3 state. (Atomic number of Mn=25, Fe=26)
   (ii) Transition elements usually form coloured ions.
   (iii) Zr and Hf exhibit similar properties. (Atomic number of Zr = 40, Hf = 72)

Or

Complete and balance the following chemical equations. **ISC 2018**
   (i) $KMnO_4 + KI + H_2SO_4 \longrightarrow$ .... + ... + ... + ...
   (ii) $K_2Cr_2O_7 + H_2SO_4 + H_2S \longrightarrow$ .... + ... + ... + ...
   (iii) $KMnO_4 + H_2SO_4 + FeSO_4 \longrightarrow$ .... + ... + ... + ...

17. How does potassium dichromate prepared from a sample of chromite ore? Give the balanced equations for the chemical reactions involved.

18. Complete and balance the following chemical equations.
   (i) $KMnO_4 + H_2SO_4 + H_2C_2O_4 \longrightarrow - + - + - + -$
   (ii) $K_2Cr_2O_7 + H_2SO_4 + KI \longrightarrow - + - + - + -$
   (iii) $K_2Cr_2O_7 + H_2SO_4 + FeSO_4 \longrightarrow - + - + - + -$
ISC 2019

19. When orange solution containing $Cr_2O_7^{2-}$ ion is treated with an alkali, a yellow solution is formed and when H^+ ions are added to yellow solution, an orange solution is obtained. Explain, why does this happen? **NCERT Exemplar**

Long Answer Type Questions

(5 Marks)

20. Describe the preparation of potassium permanganate. How does the acidified permanganate solution react with (i) iron (II) ion, (ii) SO_2 and (iii) oxalic acid?
Write the ionic equations for the reactions. **NCERT**

21. When chromite ore is fused with sodium carbonate in free access of air and the product is dissolved in water, a yellow solution of compound (*A*) is obtained. On acidifying the yellow solution with sulphuric acid, compound (*B*) is crystallised out. When compound (*B*) is treated with KCl, orange crystals of compound (*C*) crystallise out. Identify (*A*), (*B*) and (*C*) and write the reactions involved.

Hints & Solutions

1. (i) (+)7 (ii) (+)6 (iii) CrO_4^{2-} ion

(iv) (a) $K_2Cr_2O_7$, <>.

$\therefore K_2Cr_2O_7$ changes to orange red an adding H^+ ions, so that its pH becomes ><

2. (i) (c) $FeSO_4(NH_4)_2SO_4\ 6H_2O$ (Mohr's salt).

$$2KMnO_4 + 8H_2SO_4 + 10FeSO_4 \longrightarrow K_2SO_4 + 2MnSO_4 + 5Fe_2(SO_4)_3 + 8H_2O$$

(ii) (c) $2MnO_4^- + H_2O + I^- \xrightarrow{\text{Alkali}} 2MnO_2 + 2OH^- + IO_3^-$.

(iii) At pH >>, i.e. in basic medium, the colour of $K_2Cr_2O_7$ is formed to be yellow. The reaction occurs is as follows:

$$\underset{\text{(Orange red)}}{Cr_2O_7^{2-}} + H_2O \rightleftharpoons \underset{\substack{\text{(Yellow)}\\ \text{(pH, >>)}}}{2CrO_4^{2-}} + 2H^+$$

(iv) (b) These gas bubbles are evolved due to the formation of CO_2 gas.

$$2MnO_4^- + 5C_2O_4^{2-} + 16H^+ \longrightarrow 2Mn^{2+} + 10CO_2 + 8H_2O$$

3. (b) A → (iv), B → (iii), C → (i), D → (ii)

(A) $K_2Cr_2O_7$ is used in chromyl chloride test for the detection of Cl^- ions.

(B) $KMnO_4$ is used in making Bayer's reagent, which is an alkaline dilute solution of $KMnO_4$.

(C) Oxidation state of Cr in CrO_4^{2-} is (+)6.

(D) Oxidation state of Mn in MnO_4^- is (+)7.

4. $\underset{\text{(Conc.)}}{HCl} + KMnO_4 \longrightarrow KCl + MnCl_2 + Cl_2 + H_2O$ (1)

5. An acidified $KMnO_4$ solution oxidised potassium iodide to iodine.

$$2KMnO_4 + 3H_2SO_4 \longrightarrow K_2SO_4 + 2MnSO_4 + 3H_2O + 5O$$

$$[2KI + 2H_2SO_4 \longrightarrow 2K_2SO_4 + 2HI] \times 5$$

$$[2HI + O \longrightarrow H_2O + I_2] \times 5$$ (2)

$$2KMnO_4 + 8H_2SO_4 + 10KI \longrightarrow 6K_2SO_4 + 2MnSO_4 + 8H_2O + 5I_2$$

6. $KMnO_4$ oxidises oxalic acid (or oxalates) to carbon dioxide.

$$2KMnO_4 + 3H_2SO_4 \longrightarrow K_2SO_4 + 2MnSO_4 + 3H_2O + 5O$$

$$\left[\begin{array}{l}COOH\\ |\\ COOH\end{array} + O \longrightarrow 2CO_2 + H_2O\right] \times 5$$

$$2KMnO_4 + 3H_2SO_4 + 5\underset{\text{Oxalic acid}}{\begin{array}{l}COOH\\ |\\ COOH\end{array}} \longrightarrow K_2SO_4 + 2MnSO_4 + 8H_2O + 10CO_2$$ (2)

7. $2MnO_4^- + 16H^+ + 5C_2O_4^{2-} \rightarrow 2Mn^{2+} + 8H_2O + 10CO_2$

MnO_4^- ion gets reduced to Mn^{2+} ion and oxalic acid oxidises to CO_2 due to which the colour of $KMnO_4$ disappear. (2)

8. (i) $5Fe^{2+} + MnO_4^- + 8H^+ \rightarrow Mn^{2+} + 5Fe^{3+} + 4H_2O$ (1)

(ii) $2MnO_4^- + H_2O + I^- \rightarrow IO_3^- + 2MnO_2 + 2OH^-$ (1)

9.
$$\underset{\text{Ferrous sulphate}}{6FeSO_4} + \underset{\text{Potassium dichromate}}{K_2Cr_2O_7} + \underset{\text{Sulphuric acid}}{7H_2SO_4} \longrightarrow \underset{\text{Ferric sulphate}}{3Fe_2(SO_4)_3} + \underset{\text{Potassium sulphate}}{K_2SO_4} + \underset{\text{Chromium sulphate}}{Cr_2(SO_4)_3} + \underset{\text{Water}}{7H_2O}$$ (2)

10. Potassium dichromate is a strong oxidising agent. In acidic solution, its oxidising action is represented as:
$Cr_2O_7^{2-} + 14H^+ + 6e^- \longrightarrow 2Cr^{3+} + 7H_2O$

Ionic equations

(i) **Reaction of** $K_2Cr_2O_7$ **with** I^-

$Cr_2O_7^{2-} + 14H^+ + 6I^- \longrightarrow 2Cr^{3+} + 3I_2 + 7H_2O$ (1)

(ii) **Reaction of** $K_2Cr_2O_7$ **with** H_2S

$Cr_2O_7^{2-} + 8H^+ + 3H_2S \longrightarrow 2Cr^{3+} + 3S + 7H_2O$ (1)

11. Refer to text on page 148-149 (Chemical properties) (2)

12. Among trivalent ions in the lanthanoid seriesh, there is a gradual decrease in ionic size due to lanthanoid contraction.

Therefore, size of La^{3+} is more than that of Lu^{3+}, i.e. La^{3+} has ionic size 106 pm (approx.) and of Lu^{3+} has ionic size less than 86 pm.

13. The electronic configuration of copper (Cu), $(Z = 29)$ is, $[Ar]\,4s^1 3d^{10}$.

For Cu^+ ion we have fully-filled $3d^{10}$ configuration, whereas Cu^{2+} ion has $3d^9$ configuration and has one unpaired electron in its $3d$ - subshell.

Therefore, Cu^+ is diamagnetic, whereas Cu^{2+} is paramagnetic in nature.

14. (i) $2MnO_4^- + 5C_2O_4^{2-} + 16H^+ \longrightarrow 2Mn^{2+} + 8H_2O + 10CO_2$ (1)

(ii) $Cr_2O_7^{2-}(aq) + 6Fe^{2+}(aq) + 14H^+(aq) \longrightarrow 2Cr^{3+} + 6Fe^{3+} + 7H_2O$ (1)

15. (i) $2KMnO_4 + 10KI + 8H_2SO_4 \longrightarrow 6K_2SO_4 + 2MnSO_4 + 5I_2 + 8H_2O$

(ii) $K_2Cr_2O_7 + 4H_2SO_4 + 3H_2S \longrightarrow K_2SO_4 + Cr_2(SO_4)_3 + 3S + 7H_2O$

16. (i) Electronic configuration of Mn^{2+} is $3d^5$ which is half-filled and hence stable. Therefore, third ionisation enthalpy is very high, i.e. third electron cannot be lost easily. In case of Fe^{2+}, electronic configuration is $3d^6$. Hence, it can lose electron easily to give stable half-filled configuration, i.e. $3d^5$. (1)

(ii) Most of the complexes of transition elements are coloured. This is because of the absorption of radiation from visible light region to promote an unpaired electron from one of the *d*-orbitals to another. The ions of transition elements absorb the radiation of a particular wavelength and the rest is reflected, imparting colour to the solution. (1)

(iii) Due to lanthanoid contraction, Hf ($Z = 72$) has similar size to that of Zr ($Z = 40$). Hence, their properties are similar and therefore, occur together. (1)

Or (i) $2KMnO_4 + 10KI + 3H_2SO_4 \longrightarrow K_2SO_4 + 2MnSO_4 + 8H_2O + 5I_2$ (1)

(ii) $K_2Cr_2O_7 + 4H_2SO_4 + 3H_2S \longrightarrow K_2SO_4 + Cr_2(SO_4)_3 + 7H_2O + 3S$ (1)

(iii) $2KMnO_4 + 8H_2SO_4 + 10FeSO_4 \longrightarrow K_2SO_4 + 2MnSO_4 + 5Fe_2(SO_4)_3 + 8H_2O$ (1)

17. Potassium dichromate is generally manufactured from chromite ore $FeO \cdot Cr_2O_3$ or $FeCr_2O_4$.

The steps involved are:

(i) Finely powdered chromite ore is mixed with Na_2CO_3 and quicklime. The mixture is roasted in a reverberatory furnace in the presence of excess of air. On account of roasting, a yellow mass containing sodium chromate is obtained.

$$4\,FeCr_2O_4 + O_2 \longrightarrow 2\ FeO_3 + 4Cr_2O_3$$
$$4Cr_2O_3 + 8Na_2CO_3 + 6O_2 \longrightarrow 8\,Na_2CrO_4 + 8CO_2$$
$$4FeCr_2O_4 + 8Na_2CO_3 + 7O_2 \longrightarrow 2\,Fe_2O_3 + 8\,Na_2CrO_4 + 8CO_2$$

(ii) Sodium chromate obtained is treated with concentrated sulphuric acid where it is converted into sodium dichromate.

$$2Na_2CrO_4 + H_2SO_4 \longrightarrow Na_2Cr_2O_7 + Na_2SO_4 + H_2O$$

The solution is concentrated when less soluble sodium sulphate $Na_2SO_4 \cdot 10H_2O$ crystallises out. This solution is filtered hot. The solution is now cooled till sodium dichromate crystals ($Na_2Cr_2O_7 \cdot 2H_2O$) separates out. (1)

(iii) Hot concentrated solution of sodium dichromate is treated with calculated amount of potassium chloride and the mixture is cooled till orange crystals of potassium dichromate are obtained.

$$Na_2Cr_2O_7 + 2KCl \longrightarrow K_2Cr_2O_7 + 2NaCl \quad (1)$$

18. (i) $2KMnO_4 + 5H_2C_2O_4 + 3H_2SO_4 \xrightarrow{60°C} 2MnSO_4 + 10\,CO_2 + K_2SO_4 + 8H_2O$

(ii) $K_2Cr_2O_7 + 6KI + 7H_2SO_4 \longrightarrow 3I_2 + Cr_2(SO_4)_3 + 4K_2SO_4 + 7H_2O$

(iii) $K_2Cr_2O_7 + 7H_2SO_4 + 6FeSO_4 \longrightarrow 3Fe_2(SO_4)_3 + K_2SO_4 + Cr_2(SO_4)_3 + 7H_2O$

19. When orange solution containing $Cr_2O_7^{2-}$ ion is treated with an alkali, a yellow solution of CrO_4^{2-} is obtained. In the same way, when H^+ ions are added to yellow solution, an orange solution is obtained due to interconversion.

$$\underset{\text{Dichromate (Orange)}}{Cr_2O_7^{2-}} \underset{H^+}{\overset{OH^-}{\rightleftharpoons}} \underset{\text{Chromate (Yellow)}}{CrO_4^{2-}}$$ (3)

20. Refer to text on pages 146 and 147 (Potassium permanganate $KMnO_4$, preparation, oxidation reaction of acidified $KMnO_4$).

21. Compounds *A*, *B* and *C* are:

A : Na_2CrO_4 ; *B* : $Na_2Cr_2O_7$; *C* : $K_2Cr_2O_7$ (2)

The reactions involved are as follows :

$4\,FeCr_2O_4 + 8Na_2CO_3 + 7\,O_2 \longrightarrow 8\,Na_2CrO_4 + 2Fe_2O_3 + 8\,CO_2$ (1)

$2\,Na_2CrO_4 + 2H^+ \longrightarrow Na_2Cr_2O_7 + 2Na^+ + H_2O$ (1)

$Na_2Cr_2O_7 + 2KCl \longrightarrow K_2Cr_2O_7 + 2\,NaCl$ (1)

TOPIC 03 Inner-Transition Elements

The elements in which differentiating electron enters in $(n-2)f$ subshell are called **f-block elements.** They are also called **inner-transition elements** because in periodic table they are placed inside the transition elements. These elements are divided into two series

(a) $4f$-series or lanthanides (b) $5f$-series or actinides

Lanthanoids

The series involving the filling of $4f$- orbitals following lanthanum is called lanthanoid series. This series contain 14 elements from Ce ($Z=58$) to Lu ($Z=71$).

General Characteristics of Lanthanoids

Some general properties of lanthanoids are discussed below:

1. Appearance

Lanthanoids are silvery white soft metals which tarnish rapidly in air. The hardness increases with increasing atomic number (samarium is steel hard).

2. Electronic Configuration

General electronic configuration of lanthanoids are $6s^2$ $5d^{0\text{-}1}4f^{1\text{-}14}$. In these elements, last electron enters into the $4f$-orbital till Yb($4f^{14}$). Only cerium, gadolinium and lutetium have electron in $5d$-orbital as well.

Electronic Configurations of Lanthanum and Lanthanoids

Atomic number	Name	Symbol	Outer electronic configurations
57	Lanthanum	La	$5d^1\ 6s^2$
58	Cerium	Ce	$4f^1\ 5d^1\ 6s^2$
59	Praseodymium	Pr	$4f^3\ 6s^2$
60	Neodymium	Nd	$4f^4\ 6s^2$
61	Promethium	Pm	$4f^5\ 6s^2$
62	Samarium	Sm	$4f^6\ 6s^2$
63	Europium	Eu	$4f^7\ 6s^2$
64	Gadolinium	Gd	$4f^7\ 5d^1\ 6s^2$
65	Terbium	Tb	$4f^9\ 6s^2$
66	Dysprosium	Dy	$4f^{10}\ 6s^2$
67	Holmium	Ho	$4f^{11}\ 6s^2$
68	Erbium	Er	$4f^{12}\ 6s^2$
69	Thulium	Tm	$4f^{13}\ 6s^2$
70	Ytterbium	Yb	$4f^{14}\ 6s^2$
71	Lutetium	Lu	$4f^{14}\ 5d^1\ 6s^2$

3. Density and Melting Point

Lanthanoids are highly dense metals and have high melting point (1000 to 1200 K). Sm has exceptionally high melting point of 1623 K.

4. Atomic and Ionic Radii

The atomic and ionic radii decrease from lanthanum to lutetium. This is due to the unique property of lanthanoids which is known as lanthanoid contraction.

(i) Lanthanoid Contraction

(a) The filling of $4f$-orbital before $5d$-orbital results in a regular decrease in atomic radii called lanthanoid contraction. The factor responsible for the lanthanoid contraction is similar to that of ordinary transition series, i.e. the imperfect shielding of one electron by another in the same set of orbitals.

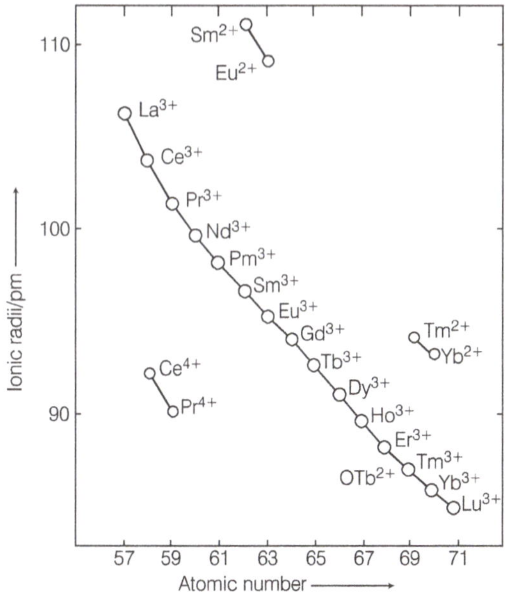

Trends in ionic radii of lanthanoids

However, the shielding of one $4f$-electron by another is less than that of one d-electron by another due to peculiar shapes of $4f$-orbitals and as the nuclear charge increases along the series, there is fairly regular decrease in the size of the entire $4f^n$-orbitals.

(b) The decrease in atomic radii is not regular but the decrease in ionic radii of their M^{3+} ions are quite regular as represented by the following graph.

(ii) Consequences of Lanthanoid Contraction

(a) **Basic character of oxides and hydroxides** Due to the lanthanoid contraction, the covalent nature of Ln—OH bond increases as the basic character of oxides and hydroxides decreases from $La(OH)_3$ to $Lu(OH)_3$.

(b) **Similarity in the size or radii of elements of second and third transition series** Because of lanthanoid contraction, elements which follow the third transition series are considerably smaller than that would otherwise be expected.

The normal size increases from Sc →Y → La and disappears after lanthanoids. Thus, pairs of elements such as Zr/Hf, Nb/Ta and Mo/W are almost identical in size. Due to almost similar size, such pairs have very similar properties which make their separation difficult and hence, also called chemical twin.

(c) **Separation of lanthanoids** Due to lanthanoid contraction, there is a small difference in the size of lanthanoids.

So, there is slight difference in some properties of lanthanoids like solubility, degree of hydration and complex formation. These similarities enable the separation of lanthanoids difficult.

5. Oxidation States

The most stable oxidation state of lanthanoids is +3. Oxidation states +2 and +4 also exist but they relapse to +3, e.g. La and Ce show +3 and +4 oxidation state to attain $4f^0$ configuration, whereas Eu, Gd, and Tb attain $4f^7$ configuration in +2, +3 and +4 oxidation state respectively Sm^{2+}, Eu^{2+} lose one electron to attain +3 state and hence are good reducing agents.

Similarly, Yb^{2+} and Lu^{3+} with f^{14} configuration act as a reductant and Tb^{4+} with half-filled *f*-orbitals acts as an oxidant.

While Ce^{4+}, Pr^{4+} in aqueous solution gain one electron to attain +3 state and hence are oxidising agents. There is a large gap in energy of $4f$- and $5d$-subshells and thus, the number of oxidation states of lanthanoids is limited.

6. Metallic Property

They have typical metallic structure and are good conductors of heat and electricity.

7. Ionisation Enthalpy

The first ionisation enthalpies of lanthanoids are around 600 kJ mol^{-1}, the second about1200 kJmol^{-1} comparable with those of calcium. The variation of the third ionisation enthalpies indicates that the exchange enthalpy consideration (as in $3d$-orbital of 1st transition series) appears to impart a certain degree of stability to empty, half-filled and completely filled *f*-orbitals as indicated by the abnormally low third ionisation enthalpies of La, Gd, Lu.

8. Alloy Formation

With other metals especially Fe they easily form alloys, e.g. alloy **mischmetal** of rare earth element (94%-95%), iron (upto 5%) and traces of S, C, Ca and Al. Pyrophoric alloys contain Ce (40.5%), La + neodymium (44%), Al, Ca and S.

9. Complex Formation

Lanthanoids have low density due to large size and high charge. As a result, they have poor tendency to form complex.

10. Colour

Several trivalent (M^{3+}) lanthanide ions are coloured in solid state as well as in aqueous solution. Colour of member of this series arise due to f-f electronic transition, as f-subshells are partially filled.

Note Lanthanide ions with xf electrons have a similar colour to those with $(14-x)$ of electrons, e.g. La^{3+} and Lu^{3+} are colourless, Eu^{3+} and Tb^{3+} are pale pink etc. (See table given below).

11. Magnetic Properties

Many lanthanide ions are paramagnetic due to the presence of unpaired electrons in the $4f$-orbital (except Ce^{4+}, Lu^{3+} and Yb^{3+}). There is difference in calculating the magnetic moment of these elements with respect to transition elements.

Hence, both spin as well as orbital moments give contribution and μ_{eff} is calculated.

$$\mu_{eff} = \sqrt{4s(s+1) + l(l+1)} \text{ B.M}$$

where, l is orbital quantum number and s is the spin quantum number.

$\mu_{eff} = \sqrt{N(N+2)}$ B.M. for N unpaired electrons.

The Colour and Magnetic Moment of Lanthanide (III) Ions

Ion	Colour (aqua complex)	Electronic configuration	N (unpaired electrons)	Magnetic moment of N unpaired electrons/ μ BM	
				Calculated (only total spin) $\sqrt{N(N+2)}$	Observed
La^{3+}	Colourless	$4f^0$	0	00	0
Ce^{3+}	Colourless	$4f^1$	1	1.73	2.3 – 2.5
Pr^{3+}	Green	$4f^2$	2	2.83	3.4 – 3.6
Nd^{3+}	Lilac	$4f^3$	3	3.87	2.5 – 3.6
Pm^{3+}	Yellow	$4f^4$	4	4.90	2.70
Sm^{3+}	Yellow	$4f^5$	5	5.92	1.5 – 1.6
Eu^{3+}	Pale pink	$4f^6$	6	6.93	3.4 – 3.6
Gd^{3+}	Colourless	$4f^7$	7	7.94	7.8 – 8.0
Tb^{3+}	Pale pink	$4f^8$	6	6.93	9.4 – 9.6
Dy^{3+}	Yellow	$4f^9$	5	5.92	10.4 – 10.5
Ho^{3+}	Pale yellow	$4f^{10}$	4	4.90	10.3 – 10.5
Er^{3+}	Rose-red (pink)	$4f^{11}$	3	3.87	9.4 – 9.6
Tm^{3+}	Pale-green	$4f^{12}$	2	2.83	7.1 – 4.4
Yb^{3+}	Colourless	$4f^{13}$	1	1.73	4.4-4.9
Lu^{3+}	Colourless	$4f^{14}$	0	0.00	0

12. Chemical Reactivity

(i) They are highly electropositive and reactive. All of them burn in air to form oxides Ln_2O_3 (cerium gives CeO_2). Powdered cerium is even pyrophoric. Ytlerbium usually forms a protective oxide coating on it and remains unattacked by air even at 1273 K.

$$4Ln + 3O_2 \longrightarrow 2Ln_2O_3$$

(ii) They combine with H_2 on gentle heating and form hydrides, have defected lattice and are non-stoichiometric.

$$2Ln + 3H_2 \longrightarrow 2LnH_3$$

(iii) They from trihalides on burning with halogens but Ce and Tb give CeF_4 and TbF_4 respectively.

$$2Ln + 3X_2 \longrightarrow 2LnX_3$$

(iv) Complex fluorides of Pr(IV), Nd(IV) and Dy(IV) are also formed.

(v) They react with H_2O form hydroxide and liberate H_2 gas.

$$Ln + H_2O \longrightarrow Ln(OH)_3 + H_2\uparrow$$

The hydroxides are ionic and basic. They are less basic than $Ca(OH)_2$ but more basic than amphoteric $Al(OH)_3$. The base strength decreases from $Ce(OH)_3$ to $Lu(OH)_3$.

(vi) Lanthanides on reaction with carbon at high temperature (approx. 2500°C) form carbides of the type Ln_2C, Ln_2C_3 and LnC_2.

$$Ln + C \xrightarrow{2773\text{ K}} LnC_2$$

(vii) With sulphur they form sulphide as follows:

$$2Ln + 3S \longrightarrow Ln_2S_3$$

(viii) When heated with nitrogen gas, they form nitride as

$$2Ln + N_2 \longrightarrow 2LnN$$

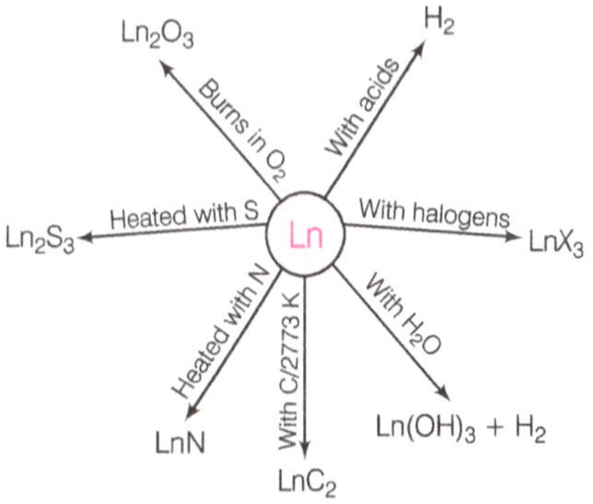

Chemical reactions of the lanthanoids

Uses

(i) Lanthanoids are used for the production of alloy steels for plates and pipes.

(ii) Mischmetal alloy of lanthanoid is used in Mg-based alloy to produce bullets, shell and lighter flint.

(iii) Mixed oxides of lanthanoids are used as catalyst in cracking of petroleum.

(iv) Some lanthanum oxides are used as phosphorus in television screens.

Actinoids

These are the elements in which last electron filled in $5f$-orbitals. The actinoids are radioactive elements and the earlier members possess relatively long half-lives while the latter ones have half-life values ranging from a day to 3 min. The latter members could be prepared only in nanogram quantities.

General Characteristics of Actinoids

Some properties of actinoids are discussed below:

1. Electronic Configuration

The general electronic configuration is $5f^{1-14}6d^{0-2}7s^2$. The irregularities in the electronic configuration of actinoids is due to the stabilities of f^0, f^7 and f^{14} occupancies of 5 f-orbitals.

Electronic Configuration of Actinoids

Atomic number	Name	Symbol	Outer electronic structure
89	Actinium	Ac	$6d^1 7s^2$
90	Thorium	Th	$6d^1 7s^2$
91	Protactinium	Pa	$5f^2 6f^1 7s^2$
92	Uranium	U	$5f^3 6d^1 7s^2$
93	Neptunium	Np	$5f^4 6d^1 7s^2$
94	Plutonium	Pu	$5f^6 7s^2$
95	Americium	Am	$5f^7 7s^2$
96	Curium	Cm	$5f^7 6d^1 7s^2$
97	Berkelium	Bk	$5f^9 7s^2$
98	Californium	Cf	$5f^{10} 7s^2$
99	Einsteinium	Es	$5f^{11} 7s^2$
100	Fermium	Fm	$5f^{12} 7s^2$
101	Mendelevium	Md	$5f^{13} 7s^2$
102	Nobelium	No	$5f^{14} 7s^2$
103	Lawrencium	Lr	$5f^{14} 6d^1 7s^2$

2. Ionic Size

The radii of trivalent and quadrivalent ions of actinoids contract slightly with increasing atomic number due to **actinoid contraction**. This contraction results from poor shielding experienced by $5f$-electrons.

3. Oxidation States

Actinoids show a variety of oxidation states such as +2 +3, +4, +5, +6 and +7 due to comparable energies of $5f$, $6d$ and $7s$ energy levels. The dominant oxidation state of actinoids is +3 which show increasing stability for the heavier elements.

4. Magnetic Properties

Actinoids are strongly paramagnetic. Their magnetic moments are smaller than the theoretically predicted values as the $5f$-electrons of actinoids are less effectively shielded which results in quenching of orbital combination.

5. Colour of the Ions

Actinoid ions are generally coloured due to f-f transition. Ions having $5f^0$, $5f^1$ and $5f^7$ configuration are colourless. It depends upon the number of unpaired electrons in $5f$-orbitals.

Colours of M^{3+} and M^{4+} Actinoid Cations

M^{3+}/M^{4+}	Valence of shell configuration of the cation	Number of unpaired electrons (n)	Colour
Ac^{3+}	$5f^0 6d^0 7s^0$	0	Colourless
U^{3+}	$5f^3 6d^0 7s^0$	3	Red
Np^{3+}	$5f^4 6d^0 7s^0$	4	Purple
Pu^{3+}	$5f^5 6d^0 7s^0$	5	Violet
Am^{3+}	$5f^6 6d^0 7s^0$	6	Pink
Cm^{3+}	$5f^7 6d^0 7s^0$	7	Colourless
Th^{4+}	$5f^0 6d^0 7s^0$	0	Colourless
Pa^{4+}	$5f^1 6d^0 7s^0$	1	Colourless
U^{4+}	$5f^2 6d^0 7s^0$	2	Green
Np^{4+}	$5f^3 6d^0 7s^0$	3	Yellowish green
Pu^{4+}	$5f^4 6d^0 7s^0$	4	Orange
Am^{4+}	$5f^5 6d^0 7s^0$	5	Red

6. Complex Formation

Actinoids have greater tendency to form complexes due to higher nuclear charge and smaller size of their atoms.

7. Reactivity

Actinoids are more electropositive and are reactive. Their reactivity increases with increase in atomic number. They tarnish rapidly in air, forming an oxide coating which is protective in case of Th but less for the other elements. The dominant feature of the actinides is their nuclear instability as they have tendency to undergo spontaneous fission and decay becomes more pronounced with the heavier elements. The radioactivity of Th and U is probably responsible for much of the earth's internal heat. The metals react with most non-metals especially on heating, but resist alkali attack and are less reactive towards acids than might be expected. Concentrated HCl react rapidly but concentrated HNO_3 makes Th, U and Pu passive, which can be prevented in presence of F^-. With boiling water or steam, H_2 is obtained and metal is converted into oxide.Metals react rapidly with H_2 forming hydrides which are decomposed by H_2O.

Uses

The most useful actinides are thorium, uranium and plutonium. Thorium is used in the atomic reactors and in the treatment of cancer, uranium is used as nuclear fuel. Plutonium, also can be used as fuel.

Comparison of Actinoids and Lanthanoids

Actinoids and lanthanoids shows resemblance in some of their properties as well as difference in their properties which are as follows:

Similarities between Lanthanoids and Actinoids

There are some similarities between lanthanoids and actinoids, which are:

(i) Both exhibit +3 oxidation state predominantly.
(ii) Both are electropositive and have high reactivity.
(iii) Like lanthanoid contraction, there is actinoid contraction also.
(iv) They show ion exchange behaviour.
(v) In both series, *f*-orbitals are being progressively filled.

Difference between Lanthanoids and Actinoids

The important points of distinction between them are tabulated as follow:

Difference between Lanthanoids and Actinoids

Property	Lanthanoids	Actinoids
Oxidation states	They show mainly +3 oxidation state. +2 and +4 oxidation states also exist.	In addition to +3 oxidation state, actinoids also show higher oxidation states like +4, +5, +6 and +7.
Binding energies	Binding energies of 4*f* are higher.	Binding energies of 5*f* are lower.
Shielding effect	They have poor shielding effect.	They have even poor shielding effect than lanthanoids.
Magnetic properties	They are paramagnetic and their magnetic properties can be easily explained.	They are also paramagnetic, but their magnetic properties cannot be easily explained.
Chemical reactivity		
(i) Tendency to form complexes	Less	More
(ii) Radioactivity	Except promethium, these are non-radioactive substances.	These are radioactive substances.
(iii) Basic character	These are less basic.	These are more basic.

Topic Practice 3

Very Short Answer Type Questions

1 Mark

1. Fill in the Blanks

(i) Elements from atomic number 57 to 71 are called .... (*A*) and from 89 to 103 are called ....(*A*).

In the above sentence (*A*) and (*B*) are

(a) transition elements, lanthanoids
(b) *p*-block elements, actinoids
(c) lanthanoids, actinoids
(d) actinoids, lanthanoids

(ii) Element europium has atomic number......... .

(iii) Atomic number of element lutetium is ....

(iv) The last member of actinoid series with atomic number 103 is ....

2. Objective Type Questions

(i) Arrange Ce^{3+}, La^{3+}, Pm^{3+} and Yb^{3+} in increasing order of their ionic radii.

(a) $Yb^{3+} < Pm^{3+} < Ce^{3+} < La^{3+}$
(b) $Ce^{3+} < Yb^{3+} < Pm^{3+} < La^{3+}$
(c) $Yb^{3+} < Pm^{3+} < La^{3+} < Ce^{3+}$
(d) $Pm^{3+} < La^{3+} < Ce^{3+} < Yb^{3+}$

(ii) Lanthanoid contraction is caused due to

(a) the appreciable shielding on outer electrons by 4*f* electrons from the nuclear charge
(b) the appreciable shielding on outer electrons by 5*d* electrons from the nuclear charge
(c) the same effective nuclear charge from Ce to Lu
(d) the imperfect shielding on outer electrons by 4*f* electrons from the nuclear charge

(iii) Identify the incorrect statement among the following.

(a) *d*-block elements show irregular and erratic chemical properties among themselves
(b) La and Lu have partially filled *d*-orbitals and no other partially filled orbitals
(c) The chemistry of various lanthanoids is similar
(d) 4*f* and 5*f*-orbitals are equally shielded

3. Match Coloumn I with Column II and choose the correct option using the codes given below:

	Column I (Symbol)		Column II (Atomic Number)
A.	Pr	(i)	95
B.	Yb	(ii)	93
C.	Np	(iii)	70
D.	Am	(iv)	59

Codes

	A	B	C	D		A	B	C	D
(a)	(i)	(ii)	(iii)	(iv)	(b)	(iv)	(iii)	(ii)	(i)
(c)	(iv)	(iii)	(i)	(ii)	(d)	(ii)	(i)	(iii)	(iv)

4. What are the different oxidation states exhibited by lanthanoids? **NCERT**

5. State the common oxidation state of **ISC 2011**

(i) lanthanoids (ii) actinoids

6. Name a member of the lanthanoid series which is well known to exhibit +4 oxidation state.

Short Answer Type I Questions

2 Marks

7. Name the members of the lanthanoid series which exhibit + 4 oxidation states and those which exhibit +2 oxidation states. Try to correlate this type of behaviour with the electronic configuration of these elements. **NCERT**

8. Use Hund's rule to derive the electronic configuration of Ce^{3+} ion and calculate its magnetic moment on the basis of 'spin only' formula. **NCERT**

9. Although, Zr belongs to 4*d* and Hf belongs to 5*d* transition series but it is quite difficult to separate them, why? **NCERT Exemplar**

10. Actinoid contraction is greater from element to element than lanthanoid contraction. Why? **NCERT**

11. The chemistry of the actinoid elements is not so smooth as that of the lanthanoids. Justify this statement by giving some examples from the oxidation state of these elements. **NCERT**

Chapter Practice

Very Short Answer Type Questions

1 Mark

1 **Fill in the Blank**

(i) The general outermost electronic configuration for d-block elements is ………… .

(ii) The d-block element, which is liquid at room temperature is ………… .

(iii) The maximum oxidation state, exibit by the element of $3d$-series member is ………… .

(iv) Between lanthanoids and actinoids, more number of oxidation-states is shown by.

2 **Objective Type Questions**

(i) Zinc does not show variable valency like d-block elements because

(a) it is low melting
(b) its d-orbital is complete
(c) it is a soft metal
(d) two electrons are present in the outermost orbit

(ii) Among of the following outermost configurations of transition metals, which shows the highest oxidation state?

(a) $3d^5 4s^1$ (b) $3d^3 4s^2$
(c) $3d^5 4s^2$ (d) $3d^6 4s^2$

(iii) The highest magnetic moment is shown by the transition metal ion with the outer electronic configuration.

(a) $3d^2$ (b) $3d^7$ (c) $3d^5$ (d) $3d^9$

(iv) Amongst TiF_6^{2-}, CoF_6^{3-}, Cu_2Cl_2 and $NiCl_4^{2-}$, the colourless species are (atomic number Ti = 22, Co = 27, Cu = 29, Ni = 28)

(a) CoF_6^{3-} and $NiCl_4^{2-}$ (b) TiF_6^{2-} and CoF_6^{2-}
(c) Cu_2Cl_2 and $NiCl_4^{2-}$ (d) TiF_6^{2-} and Cu_2Cl_2

3 Match Column I with Column II and choose the correct option using the codes given below

	Column I (Element)		Column II (Atomic number)
A.	V (Vanadium)	i.	93
B.	Zr (Zirconium)	ii.	40
C.	Ce (Cerium)	iii.	23
D.	Np (Neptunium)	iv.	58

Codes

	A	B	C	D
(a)	(i)	(ii)	(iii)	(iv)
(b)	(iv)	(iii)	(ii)	(i)
(c)	(ii)	(iii)	(i)	(iv)
(d)	(iii)	(ii)	(iv)	(i)

4 Why does the transition element scandium ($Z = 21$) not exhibit variable oxidation states?

5 Explain the large difference in melting point of Cr (1920°C) and Zn (420°C).

6 Calculate the 'spin only' magnetic moment of $M^{2+}(aq)$ ion. ($Z = 27$).

7 Why does copper metal not replace hydrogen from acid?

8 Why are the $E^{\ominus}$ values of Mn, Zn more negative than expected?

9 The atomic size of Fe, Co and Ni are nearly same. Explain with reason.

10 Why Zn^{2+} salts are white while Ni^{2+} salts are blue?

11 Out of $[Sc(H_2O)_6]^{3+}$ and $[Ti(H_2O)_6]^{3+}$ ions, which is coloured and why? Give reason.

12 What factors led to the appearance of colour in the transition elements?

13 Draw the structures of manganate ion and permanganate ion.

14 Write the formula of compound in which transition metal is in +6 oxidation state.

15 In chromic acid, (CrO_3), Cr has d^0 configuration but it is bright orange coloured solid, why?

Assertion and Reason

Directions (Q. Nos. 16-20) In the following questions an Assertion (A) is followed by a corresponding Reason (R). Use the following keys to choose the appropriate answer.

(a) Both (A) and (R) are correct, (R) is the correct explanation of (A).
(b) Both (A) and (R) are correct, (R) is not the correct explanation of (A).
(c) (A) is correct; (R) is incorrect.
(d) (A) is incorrect; (R) is correct.

Potassium Dichromate, $K_2Cr_2O_7$

It is used in leather industry and acts as an oxidant for the preparation of many azo compounds.

Preparation

Potassium dichromate is prepared by chromite ore ($FeCr_2O_4$).

(i) When chromite ore is fused with sodium or potassium carbonate in free access of air.

$$4FeCr_2O_4 + 8Na_2CO_3 + 7O_2 \longrightarrow 2Fe_2O_3 + \underset{\text{Sodium chromate}}{8Na_2CrO_4} + 8CO_2$$

(ii) Yellow solution of sodium chromate is filtered and acidified with sulphuric acid to give orange sodium dichromate solution.

$$2Na_2CrO_4 + 2H^+ \longrightarrow \underset{\substack{\text{Sodium dichromate}\\\text{(Orange)}}}{Na_2Cr_2O_7} + 2Na^+ + H_2O$$

$K_2Cr_2O_7$ is prepared by treating the solution of $Na_2Cr_2O_7$ with KCl because sodium dichromate is more soluble than potassium dichromate.

$$Na_2Cr_2O_7 + 2KCl \longrightarrow \underset{\substack{\text{Potassium}\\\text{dichromate}}}{K_2Cr_2O_7} + 2NaCl$$

Orange coloured crystals of $K_2Cr_2O_7$ separates out. In the solution, chromate ions exist in equilibrium with dichromate ions. Depending on the pH of solution, equilibrium shifts in the forward and backward direction. The oxidation state of chromium in chromate and dichromate ion is same.

In alkaline medium,

$$Cr_2O_7^{2-} + 2OH^- \longrightarrow 2CrO_4^{2-} + H_2O$$

In acidic medium,

$$2CrO_4^{2-} + 2H^+ \longrightarrow Cr_2O_7^{2-} + H_2O$$

Structure

The structure of chromate ion ($Cr_2O_4^{2-}$) is tetrahedral and dichromate ion ($Cr_2O_7^{2-}$) consists of two tetrahedral sharing one corner with Cr—O—Cr bond angle of 126°.

(i) **Dichromate ion** ($Cr_2O_7^{2-}$)

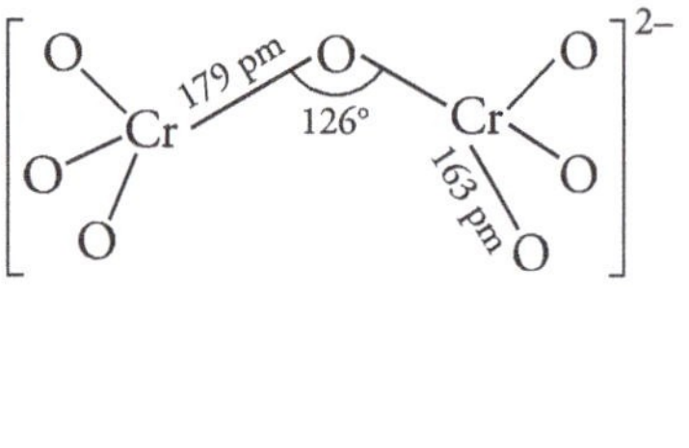

(ii) **Chromate ion** (CrO_4^{2-})

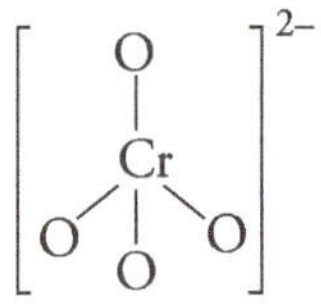

Physical Properties

(i) It is a crystalline ionic solid having bright, reddish-orange colour.

(ii) It is odourless, with density around 2.67 g cm^{-3}.

(iii) It is soluble in water and insoluble in alcohol, acetone etc.

Chemical Properties

(i) **Effect of heat** When potassium dichromate is strongly heated, it decomposes to give oxygen.

$$\underset{\text{Orange red}}{4K_2Cr_2O_7(s)} \xrightarrow{\Delta} \underset{\text{Yellow}}{4K_2CrO_4(s)} + 2Cr_2O_3(s) + 3O_2$$

(ii) **Inter Conversion of Chromate and Dichromate (K_2CrO_4 and $K_2Cr_2O_7$)** On acidifying the K_2CrO_4 solution, the colour changes to orange-red due to the reformation of dichromate.

$$2K_2CrO_4 + H_2SO_4 \longrightarrow K_2Cr_2O_7 + K_2SO_4 + H_2O$$

or $$2CrO_4^{2-} + 2H^+ \longrightarrow Cr_2O_7^{2-} + H_2O$$

Reason for inter conversion In dichromate solution, the orange-red $Cr_2O_7^{2-}$ ions are invariably in equilibrium with yellow CrO_4^{2-} ions.

$$\underset{\text{Orange-red}}{Cr_2O_7^{2-}} + H_2O \rightleftharpoons \underset{\text{Yellow}}{2CrO_4^{2-}} + 2H^+$$

(iii) **Oxidising Nature in Acidic Medium** Potassium dichromate is a strong oxidising agent in acidic medium and used as a primary standard solution in volumetric analysis in acidic medium,

$$Cr_2O_7^{2-} + 14H^+ + 6e^- \longrightarrow 2Cr^{3+} + 7H_2O, (E° = 1.33\ V)$$

Thus, acidified potassium dichromate oxidises iodides to iodine, sulphides to sulphur, iron (II) salts to iron (III) and tin (II) to tin (IV).

$$6I^- \longrightarrow 3I_2 + 6e^- \qquad 3H_2S \longrightarrow 6H^+ + 3S + 6e^-$$

$$6Fe^{2+} \longrightarrow 6Fe^{3+} + 6e^- \qquad 3Sn^{2+} \longrightarrow 3Sn^{4+} + 6e^-$$

The full ionic equation may be obtained by adding half reaction for potassium dichromate ($K_2Cr_2O_7$) to half reaction for reducing agent.

16 **Assertion** (A) Zinc is not regarded as a transition element.

Reason (R) In zinc, 3*d* orbitals are completely filled in its ground state as well as in its oxidised state.

17. **Assertion** (A) Zn do not show any characteristic properties of transition elements except complex formation.

Reason (R) Zinc has completely filled 3*d*-subshell.

18 **Assertion** (A) Highest oxidation state of manganese in fluoride is +4 (MnF_4) but highest oxidation state in oxides is +7(Mn_2O_7).

Reason (R) Fluorine stabilises lower oxidation state.

19 **Assertion** (A) HCl is not used to make the medium acidic in oxidation reactions of $KMnO_4$ in acidic medium.

Reason (R) $KMnO_4$ acts as a reducing agent in the presence of HI.

20 **Assertion** (A) CrO_3 is bright orange colour solid.

Reason (R) In chromic acid (CrO_3) Cr has d^0 configuration.

Case-Study

21 In the periodic table, the elements are classified into mainly four blocks, i.e. *s*, *p*, *d* and *f*. The *d*-block elements are called **transition elements**. The *s*-block contains the elements of the group 3-12. They possess properties that are ransitional between the *s* and *p*-block elements. Cd, Hg do not exhibit characteristic erties of transition elements. All the s belongs to this section are metals. T four rows of the transition elements inv ng of 3*d*, 4*d*, 5*d* and 6*d* orbitals.

(i) e transition element scandium no able oxidation state?

(ii) Why ch a typical hard metal while mercury is

(iii) What is the com oxidation state of Cu, Ag and Au?

22 The *d*-block, which lies be en *s* and *p*-blocks contains, elements of group 2, in which *d*-orbitals are progressively fi n each of four long periods of periodic table. T e elements are also called **transition elemen** metals.

The elements constituting the *f*-block are those in which 4*f* and 5*f*-orbitals are progressively filled. They are place in a separate panel at the bottom of the periodic table. The elements of *f*-block are also called inner-transition elements.

(i) Transition metal are very good catalyst. Why?

(ii) Out of $La(OH)_3$ and $Lu(OH)_3$, which is more basic and why?

(iii) Why NbF_4 is paramagnetic while NbX_4 (X = Cl, or, I) are diamagnetic?

Short Answer Type I Questions (2 Marks)

23 Reactivity of transition elements decreases almost regularly from Sc to Cu. Why?

24 Why there is striking similarities (horizontal and vertical) among successive members of the transition series?

25 (i) Why Cu^+ salts are colourless, while Cu^{2+} salts are coloured?

(ii) The elements of *d*-series exhibit a larger number of oxidation states than the elements of *f*-series. Explain.

26 Chromium is a typical hard metal while mercury is a liquid. Why?

27 What happens, when

(i) $KMnO_4$ is heated? (ii) $K_2Cr_2O_7$ is heated?

28 Why fluorine is stabilises in low oxidation states of transition metals?

29 Complete the following equations :

(i) $2MnO_4^- + 5S^{2-} + 16H^+ \longrightarrow$

(ii) $Cr_2O_7^{2-} + 2OH^- \longrightarrow$

30 Write the oxidation reaction of iodide to iodate ion by potassium permanganate.

31 Explain why $Cr_2O_7^{2-}$ ion is a powerful oxidant in acidic medium but weak oxidant in basic medium?

32 (i) In the titration of Fe^{2+} ions with $KMnO_4$ in acidic medium, dil. H_2SO_4 is used but not the dil. HCl. Why?

(ii) Arrange the following oxides of Mn in the order of their decreasing acidic nature.

$MnO, Mn_2O_3, Mn_3O_4, MnO_2, Mn_2O_7$.

33 What happens when

(i) H_2S reacts with acidified $K_2Cr_2O_7$ solution?

(ii) ethanol is oxidised with acidified $K_2Cr_2O_7$ solution?

Short Answer Type II Questions

3 Marks

34 How would you account for the following?

(i) Copper (I) is diamagnetic, whereas copper (II) is paramagnetic.

(ii) What is the common oxidation state of Cu, Ag, Au?

(iii) The d^1-configuration is very unstable in ions.

35 Give examples and suggest reasons for the following features of the transition metal chemistry.

(i) The lowest oxide of transition metal is basic; the highest is amphoteric/acidic.

(ii) A transition metal exhibits highest oxidation state in oxides and fluorides.

(iii) The highest oxidation state is exhibited in oxoanions of a metal.

36 Although Cu^+ does not exist in solution state, but CuCl (s) is formed in the presence of Cl^- ions in aqueous solution of Cu(*s*) and Cu^{2+}. Explain.

37 Explain the following:

(i) The paramagnetic character in 3*d* transition series increases upto Cr and then decreases.

(ii) Transition metals are very good catalyst.

(iii) Transition metals form a large number of interstitial compounds.

38 The $E°$ value with respect of electrodes of chromium ($Z = 24$), manganese ($Z = 25$) and iron ($Z = 26$) are

$Cr^{3+} / Cr^{2+} = -0.4$ V; $Mn^{3+} / Mn^{2+} = 1.5$ V

$Fe^{3+} / Fe^{2+} = +0.8$ V

On the basis of the above information, compare the feasibilities of further oxidation of their +2 oxidation state.

39 Which oxoanion (among VO_4^{3-}, CrO_4^{2-}, MnO_4^{2-} or FeO_4^{2-}) is strongest oxidant and which is weak oxidant?

40 Write the chemical equations for the following reactions:

(i) Oxidation of nitrite ion by MnO_4^- in acidic medium.

(ii) Acidification of potassium chromate solution.

(iii) Disproportionation of Mn(VI) in acidic solution.

41 Write the chemical equations for the following reactions :

(i) Disproportionation of Mn^{2+} in acidic medium.

(ii) Disproportionation of MnO_4^{2-} in alkaline medium.

(iii) Disproportionation of MnO_4^{2-} in acidic medium.

42 (i) How $KMnO_4$ can be obtained from MnO_2, KOH and KNO_3?

(ii) K_2PtCl_6 is a well known compound whereas corresponding Ni compound is not known. State the reason for it.

43 Chromium is used extensively in steel alloys. It is extracted from its ore chromite ($FeCr_2O_4$), which contains chromium in +3 oxidation state.

(i) Give the electronic configuration of the elements iron and chromium.

(ii) What is the oxidation state of iron in chromite?

44 Complete the following reactions:

(i) $MnO_4^-(aq) + S_2O_3^{2-}(aq) + H_2O\,(l) \longrightarrow$

(ii) $Cr_2O_7^{2-}(aq) + H_2S\,(g) + H^+(aq) \longrightarrow$

(iii) $MnO_4^-(aq) + Fe^{2+}(aq) + H^+(aq) \longrightarrow$

45 Describe the factors on which the stability of an oxidation state of lanthanoid elements depends.

46 The first few members of the series are quite reactive. They usually form oxides and hydroxides. Complete the following reactions of lanthanoids.

(i) $Ln \xrightarrow{\text{Heated with N}}$ (ii) $Ln \xrightarrow{\text{With halogens}}$ (iii) $Ln \xrightarrow{\text{Burns in } O_2}$

47 (i) NbF_4 is paramagnetic while NbX_4 (X = Cl, Br, I) are diamagnetic, why?

(ii) Out of $La(OH)_3$ and $Lu(OH)_3$, which is more basic and why?

Long Answer Type Questions

5 Marks

48 (i) Write the steps involved in the preparation of

(a) $K_2Cr_2O_7$ from Na_2CrO_4.

(b) $KMnO_4$ from K_2MnO_4.

(ii) What is the effect of lanthanoid contraction on the chemistry of the lanthanoids?

49 (i) A blackish brown coloured solid *A* which is an oxide of manganese, when fused with alkali metal hydroxide and an oxidising agent like KNO_3, produces a dark green coloured compound *B* which on disproportionation in neutral and acidic solution gives a purple coloured compound *C*. Identify *A*, *B* and *C* and write the reaction involved when compound *C* is heated to 513 K.

(ii) (a) $E^\circ_{M^{3+}/M^{2+}}$ values for the first series of transition elements are given below:

$E°$(V)	Ti	V	Cr	Mn	Fe	Co
M^{3+}/M^{2+}	−0.37	−0.26	−0.41	+1.57	+0.77	+1.97

Identify the two strongest oxidising agents in the aqueous solution from the above data.

(b) Copper (I) ion is not known in aqueous solution. Explain.

(c) In this series the highest oxidation state of a metal is exhibited in its oxide. Identify the metal.

Answers

1 (i) $(n-1)d^{1-10}$, ns^{1-2} (ii) mercury (Hg)
(iii) manganese (Mn) (iv) actinoids

2 (i) (b) Zn have complete d-orbital, i.e. $3d^{10}4s^2$.

(ii) (c) In the first transition series Mn$[3d^5,4s^2]$ shows the maximum oxidation state of 7.

(iii) (c) Magnetic moment depend upon the number of unpaired electron and $3d^5$configuration corresponds to maximum number of unpaired electrons.

(iv) (d) Transition metal ions having unpaired electrons are coloured while those which have no unpaired electron are colourless.

- In TiF_6^{2-}; Ti^{4+}; $[Ar]3d^0$;0 unpaired electron; colourless
- In Cu_2Cl_2; Cu^+; $[Ar]3d^{10}$;0 unpaired electrons; colourless
- In CoF_6^{3-}; Co^{3+}; $[Ar]3d^6$;4 unpaired electrons; coloured
- $NiCl_4^{2-}$; N; $[Ar]3d^8$;2 unpaired electrons; coloured

3 (d) (A) ⟶ (iii), (B)⟶(ii), (C)⟶(iv), (D)⟶(i)

4 Electronic configuration of Sc $=3d^1 4s^2$ it loses 1 electron from d-orbital and 2 electrons from s-orbital to form Sc^{3+} ion to form Sc^{3+} ion whose configuration is equivalent with argon. So, it doesn't have many electrons in
d-orbital to show variable state. Hence, it shows +3 as the only oxidation state. (1)

5 **Hint** Cr : $3d^5 4s^2$, Zn : $3d^{10}4s^2$ (1)

6 Magnetic moment, $\mu = \sqrt{n(n+2)}$ BM (½)

Electronic configuration of $M = [Ar]3d^7 4s^2$

$$M^{2+} = [Ar]\,3d^7 4s^0$$

So, $\mu = \sqrt{n(n+2)} = \sqrt{3(3+2)} = \sqrt{15} = 3.89$ BM (½)

7 As copper is less reactive than hydrogen. (1)

8 Negative E^- values of Mn^{2+} and Zn^{2+} are related to stabilities of half-filed and completely filled configuration respectively. (1)

9 **Hint** Addition of electrons in the d-subshell increases the screening effect.

10 Electronic configuration of $Zn^{2+} = 3d^{10}4s^0$

= | ⇅ | ⇅ | ⇅ | ⇅ | ⇅ |

Electronic configuration of $Ni^{2+} = 3d^8 4s^0$

= | ⇅ | ⇅ | ⇅ | ↑ | ↑ |

Compounds that contains unpaired electrons are coloured. (1)

11 **Hint** Compounds that contains unpaired electrons are coloured. (1)

12 **Hint** (i) d-d transitions, (ii) Charge transfer. (1)

13

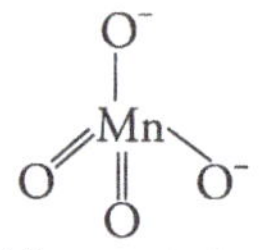

Manganate ion

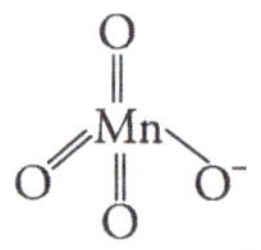

Permanganate ion (1)

14 K_2MnO_4 (1)

15 Due to charge transfer. (1)

16 (a) Both (A and (R) are true and (R) is the correct explaination of (A).

17 (a) The $3d$-subshell of zinc is completely filled in ground state as well as in their oxidation state. Thus, does not show any characteristic properties of transition elements except complex formation. Thus, both (A) and (R) are correct and (R) is correct explanation of (A).

18 (c) Highest oxidation state of manganese in fluoride is +4 (MnF_4) but highest oxidation state in oxides is $+7(Mn_2O_7)$.

The reason is that in covalent compounds fluorine can form single bond while oxygen forms double bond.

Thus, (A) is correct, (R) is incorrect.

19 (c) HCl is not used to make the medium acidic in oxidation reactions of $KMnO_4$ in acidic medium. The reason is that if HCl is used, the oxygen produced from $KMnO_4$ + HCl is partly utilised in oxidising HCl to Cl_2 which itself acts as an oxidising agent and partly oxidises the reducing agent.

20 (b) Both (A) and (R) are correct, (R) is not the correct explanation of (A).

21 (i) Outer electronic configuration of Sc $= 3d^1 4s^2$. Hence, it shows +3 as the only oxidation state.

(ii) Cr have $3d^5 4s^1$. Hence, metallic bonds are very strong.
In Hg, all the d-orbitals are fully filled. Hence, the metallic bonds are very weak.

(iii) The common oxidation state of Cu, Ag, Au is H.

22 (i) Refer to text on page 139.

(ii) **Hint:** Size of lanthanoid ions decrease from La^{3+} and Lu^{3+}.

(iii) **Hint** : Using Fajans' rule.

23 **Hint** This is due to increase in electronegativity and ionisation energy on moving from Sc to Cu.

24 This is because of the fact that along a horizontal row, electrons enters an incomplete inner shell while outer shell remains unchanged. In vertical columns, similarities are due to similar electronic configurations. (2)

25 (i) **Hint** $Cu^+ = 3d^{10}$ and $Cu^{2+} = 3d^9$.

As Cu^{2+} has one unpaired electron thus it will be colored. (1)

(ii) Refer to text on pages 137-138 (Topic-1, Variable valency and oxidation state). (1)

26 **Hint** Cr have $3d^5 4s^1$. Hence, metallic bonds are very strong.

27 (i) Refer to text on pages 147 (Topic-2, Chemical properties). (1)

(ii) Refer to text on pages 147. (Topic-2, Chemical properties). (1)

28 **Hint** Fluorine can form only single bonds.

29 (i) Refer to text on page 147. (Topic-2, Chemical properties, hydrogen sulphide to sulphur). (1)

(ii) Refer to text on page 147 (Topic-2, Preparation). (1)

30 Refer to text on page 147 (Topic-2, Chemical properties). (2)

31 Refer to text on page 148 (Topic-2, Chemical properties). (2)

32 (i) $KMnO_4$ in presence of dil. H_2SO_4 acts as oxidising agent and oxygen, thus produced oxidises ferrous salt to ferric salt.

$$2KMnO_4 + 8H_2SO_4 + 10FeSO_4 \longrightarrow K_2SO_4 + 2MnSO_4 + 5Fe(SO_4)_3 + 8H_2O \quad (½)$$

$KMnO_4$ is presence of dil.HCl also acts as oxidising agent but oxygen produced is used up partly for oxidation of HCl.

$$2KMnO_4 + 4HCl \longrightarrow 2KCl + 2MnCl_2 + 2H_2O + 6[O] \quad (½)$$

$$2HCl + [O] \longrightarrow H_2O + Cl_2$$

(ii) $Mn_2O_7 > MnO_2 > Mn_2O_3 > Mn_3O_4 > MnO$ (1)

33 (i) Refer to text on page 148. (Topic-2, Chemical properties). (1)

(ii) $CH_3CH_2OH + K_2Cr_2O_7 \xrightarrow{\Delta} CH_3COOH$ (Acidified) (1)

34 (i) **Hint** $Cu^+ = 3d^{10}$ and $Cu^{2+} = 3d^9$ (1)

(ii) Common oxidation state of Cu, Ag and Au is +1. (1)

(iii) As after loosing 1 more electron it will become stable. All elements with d^1 configuration are either reducing agent or undergo disproportionation. (1)

35 (i) With increase in the oxidation state of a given transition metal, the covalent character of its compound increases and thus, acidic character also increases. Therefore, lowest oxide of transition metal is basic and the highest is amphoteric/acidic. (1)

(ii) Refer to text on pages 137-138 (Topic-1, Variable valency and oxidation state). (1)

(iii) Due to high electronegativity and multiple bond formation of oxygen atom, metal atom exhibits highest oxidation state in oxoanions. (1)

36 **Hint** Cu^{2+} ion is stable in aqueous solution. (3)

37 (i) Refer to text on page 138 (Topic-1, Magnetic properties). (1)

(ii) Refer to text on page 139 (Topic-1, Catalytic properties). (1)

(iii) Refer to text on page 139 (Topic-1, Formation of interstitial compounds). (1)

38 **Hint** Order of stability of +2 oxidation state (3)

$$= Cr^{2+} < Fe^{2+} < Mn^{2+}$$

39 Strongest oxidant = MnO_4^{2-}, weakest oxidant = VO_4^{3-}

40 (i) $2MnO_4^- + 5NO_2^- + 6H^+ \rightarrow 2Mn^{2+} + 5NO_3^- + 3H_2O$ (1)

(ii) Refer to text on page 148 (Topic-2, Chemical properties). (1)

(iii) **Hint** $3MnO_4^{2-} + 4H^+ \rightarrow MnO_2 + 2MnO_4^- + 2H_2O$ (1)

41 (i) Refer to text on pages 147. (Topic-2, Chemical properties). (1)

(ii) $3MnO_4^{2-} + 2H_2O \rightarrow MnO_2 + 2MnO_4^- + 4OH^-$ (1)

(iii) Refer to text on pages 147. (Topic-2, Chemical properties). (1)

42 (i) Refer to text on page 146. [Topic-2, Potassium dichromate ($K_2Cr_2O_7$) preparation]. (1½)

(ii) This is because Pt^{4+} is more stable than Ni^{4+} as the sum of four ionisation enthalpies of Pt is more than that of Ni. (1½)

43 (i) Fe : $[Ar]_{18} 3d^6 4s^2$ (1)

Cr : $[Ar]_{18} 3d^5 4s^1$

(ii) **Hint** Oxidation state of Fe = + 2 (2)

44 (i) $8MnO_4^- + 3S_2O_3^{2-} + H_2O \rightarrow 8MnO_2 + 6SO_4^{2-} + 2OH^-$ (1)

(ii) Refer to text on page 148. (Topic-2, Chemical properties : Oxidising nature in acidic medium). (1)

(iii) Refer to text on page 148 (Topic-2, Chemical properties). (1)

45 Refer to text on page 154 (Topic-3, Oxidation state). (3)

46 Refer to text on pages 155 (Topic-3, Chemical reactivity).

47 (i) **Hint** The compound which have unpaired electrons is paramagnetic in nature and if it has paired electrons, then it is diamagnetic.

(ii) Refer to text on page 154 (Topic-3, Consequences of lanthonoid contraction).

48 (i) (a) Refer to text on page 148 (Topic-2, Potassium dichromate ($K_2Cr_2O_7$) Preparation).

(b) Refer to text on page 146 (Topic-2, Potassium permanganate $KMnO_4$ Preparation). (1)

(ii) Refer to text on page 154 (Topic-3, Lanthanoid contraction). (1)

49 **Hint** $A = MnO_2$ (pyrolusite), $B = K_2MnO_4$, $C = KMnO_4$ (2)

(ii) (a) Mn and CO (1)

(b) Refer to text on pages 137-138 (Topic-1, Variable valency and oxidation states). (1)

(c) Manganese (1)

RELATED ONLINE VIDEOS

Visit : https://youtu.be/baTbKrL1QPg
OR Scan the Code

Visit : https://youtu.be/pucta3AiBOM
OR Scan the Code

Visit : https://youtu.be/lb4NlWjYDl8
OR Scan the Code

CHAPTER

05

Coordination Compounds

'Certain elements, that include mostly transition metals, have exceptional ability to bond with other charged or neutral atoms or molecules to form addition compounds through coordination bonds. The complex structure, thus formed, is known as **coordination complex** or **coordination compound**.

These are combinedly known as **addition compounds** and play important roles in natural process as well as in our daily life.

- Coordination Compounds: Nomenclature and Isomerism
- Bonding and Magnetic Behaviour
- Metal Carbonyls, Stability and Significance of Coordination Compounds

TOPIC 01 Coordination Compounds : Nomenclature and Isomerism

Addition Compounds

When two or more stable compounds combine together in stoichiometric ratio, then the compound formed is called addition compound. On the basis of how the addition compounds dissociate, these are classified into two main types, namely, coordination compounds and double salts.

Coordination Compounds

Addition compounds which exhibit properties completely different from their constituents and retain their identity even in solution state are called coordination compounds.

Coordination compounds can be described as, those addition compounds in which a central metal atom or ion is permanently attached to certain atoms or groups of atoms called ligands. These ligands are capable of donating atleast a pair of electrons to the central metal atom a ion and get attached to it is by coordinate bond.

e.g. Potassium hexacyanoferrate (II), $K_4[Fe(CN)_6]$, when dissolved in water gives four $K^+$and one $[Fe(CN)_6]^{4-}$ ions in the solution. This solution does not show any properties of Fe^{2+} or CN^-ions.

Double Salts

These are the addition compounds which are stable in the solid state but break up into constituents in dissolved state. These compounds show some properties of their constituent ions too.

It contains two salts in equimolar ratio which are crystallised together and form their saturated solution. e.g. Mohr's Salt, $FeSO_4 \cdot (NH_4)_2SO_4 \cdot 6H_2O$, when dissolved in water gives Fe^{2+}, NH_4^+ and SO_4^{2-} ions and shows the properties of these ions during their respective tests.

Difference between double salts and coordination compounds

Double salts	Coordination compounds
They lose their identity in solution.	They don't completely lose their identity in solution.
They exist only in solid state and dissociate into ions in aqueous solution or in other solvent.	They exist in solid state as well as ions when dissolved in water or any other solvent. They don't dissociate into simple ions completely.
Their properties are essentially the same as those of its constituent compounds.	Their properties are different from their constituents.
In a double salt, metal ions exhibit their normal valency.	In a complex compound or coordination compound, metal ion satisfies two types of valencies called primary and secondary valencies.
e.g. Mohr's salt $[FeSO_4 \cdot (NH_4)_2 SO_4 \cdot 6H_2O]$, potash alum$[K_2SO_4 \cdot Al_2(SO_4)_3 \cdot 24H_2O]$, etc.	e.g. $[Ni(NH_3)_6]Cl_2$, $K_4[Fe(CN)_6]$, etc.

Definitions of Some Important Terms Used in Coordination Compounds

Coordination Entity

Coordination entity constitutes a central metal atom or ion attached to a fixed number of ions or molecules. It may be positive, negative or neutral. e.g. $[CoCl_3(NH_3)_3]$ is a coordination entity in which cobalt ion is surrounded by three NH_3 molecules and three Cl^- ions. Other examples are $[Fe(CN)_6]^{4-}$, $[Co(NH_3)_6]^{3+}$, $[Ni(CO)_4]$ and $[PtCl_2(NH_3)_2]$.

Central Metal Atom or Ion

In a coordination entity, the metal atom or ion to which a fixed number of ions/groups are bounded in a definite geometrical arrangements around it, is called central metal atom or ions. e.g. In $[NiCl_2(H_2O)_4]$, $[CoCl(NH_3)_5]^{2+}$ and $[Fe(CN)_6]^{3-}$, Ni^{2+}, Co^{3+} and Fe^{3+} respectively are central metal or ions which are also called Lewis acids.

Ligands

Molecules or ions which donate a lone pair of electron to the central atom or ion are called ligands. These are the ions or molecules bound to the central atom/ion through coordinate bond in the coordination entity. These ligands are a Lewis bases. These may be simple ions such as Cl^-, small molecules such as H_2O or NH_3, larger molecules such as $H_2NCH_2CH_2NH_2$ or even molecules, such as proteins.

Ligands are classified into three categories on the basis of charge:

(i) Neutral ligands $H_2\ddot{O}$, CO, $\ddot{N}H_3$, NO, etc.

(ii) Negative ligands F^-, Cl^-, Br^-, I^-, OH^-, CN^-, SO_4^{2-}, etc.

(iii) Positive ligands NO^+, NO_2^+, $NH_2—NH_3^+$, etc.

On the basis of denticity (donor sites/number of ligating groups), ligands are classified as follows:

(i) **Unidentate** When a ligand is bonded through one donor site to central metal atom/ion, it is said to be unidentate ligand, e.g. Cl^-, CO, NH_3, H_2O, etc.

(ii) **Didentate or Bidentate** When a ligand is bonded through two donor sites to central metal atom/ion, it is said to be didentate ligand, e.g., 2-ethanediamine($NH_2—CH_2—CH_2—NH_2$) or $C_2O_4^{2-}$ (oxalate), etc.

(iii) **Polydentate** The ligands which contains three or more donor atoms, are called polydentate ligands, e.g. ethylenediaminetetraacetate ion ($EDTA^{4-}$). It is an important hexadentate ligand. It can bind through two nitrogen and four oxygen atom to a central metal ion.

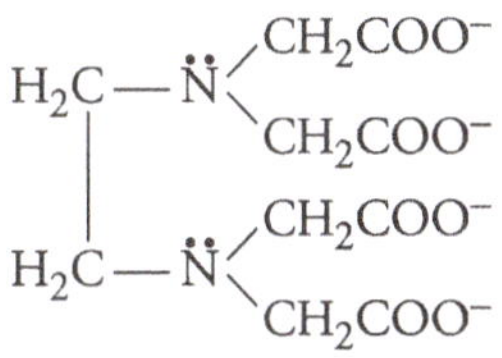

Structure of ($EDTA^{4-}$)

(iv) **Ambidentate Ligands** When a ligand is bonded through two different atoms, it is said to be ambidentate ligand, e.g. NO_2^-, SCN^-, CN^-

NO_2^- ion can coordinate either through nitrogen or oxygen to central metal ion.

Similarly, SCN^- ion can coordinate through sulphur or nitrogen atom.

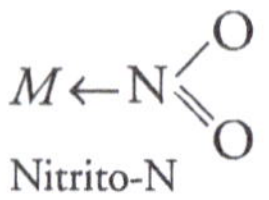

Nitrito-N

$M \leftarrow O—N{=}O$

Nitrito-O

$M \leftarrow SCN$ Thiocyanato

$M \leftarrow NCS$ Isothiocyanato

(v) **Chelating Ligands** When a di- or polydentate ligand uses its two or more donor sites to bind a single metal ion, in such a way that it forms a five or six membered ring is called a chelating ligand and the ring is called chelates.

The chelating ligands form more stable complexes than the unidentate analogs because when chelation occurs, entropy decreases and the process becomes more favourable.

e.g.

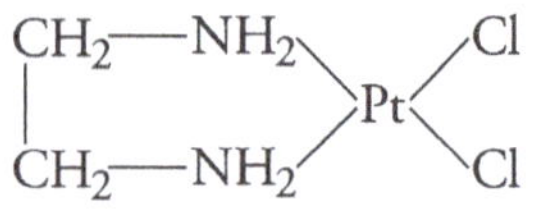

Structure of $[Pt(en)Cl_2]$

Coordination Number (CN)

(i) The total number of ligand donor atoms, attached directly to the metal ion in a complex is called coordination number.

e.g. $[Co(NH_3)_6]^{3+}$, CN of Co = 6

$[Ni(CO)_4]$, CN of Ni = 4

$[Co(en)_3]^{3+}$, CN of Co = 3 × 2 = 6

(∵ en ethane-1,2-diammine is didentate)

$[Fe(C_2O_4)_3]^{3+}$, CN of Fe = 3 × 2 = 6

(∵ $C_2O_4^{2-}$ is didentate)

(ii) π(pi) bonds, if formed between the ligand and the central atom/ion, are not counted for the coordination number.

(iii) The coordination number is determined only by the number of sigma (σ) bonds formed by the ligand with atom/ion.

Coordination Sphere and Counter Ions

The central atom/ion and the ligands attached to it are enclosed in the square bracket and are collectively known as coordination sphere. The ionisable groups are written outside the bracket and are known as counter ions or ionisation sphere, e.g. in $K_4[Fe(CN)_6]$, the coordination sphere is $[Fe(CN)_6]^{4-}$ and the counter ion is $4K^+$.

For example in the coordination complex $[Cr(NH_3)_6]Cl_3$, the coordination entity is $[Cr(NH_3)_6]^{3+}$ and the counter ions are Cl^-.

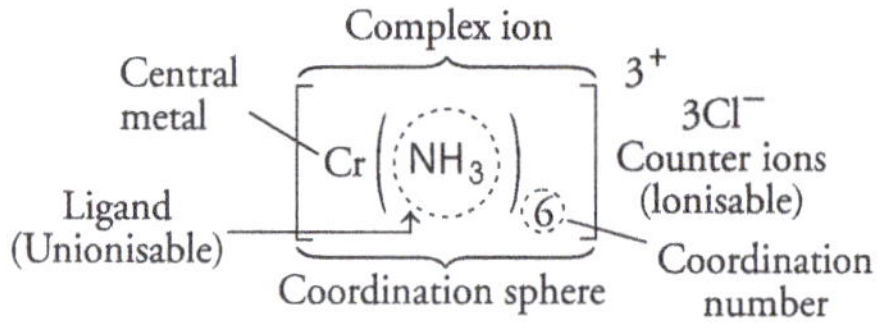

Coordination Polyhedron

It is the spatial arrangement of the ligand atoms which are directly attached to the central atom/ion. The most common coordination polyhedra are octahedral, square planar and tetrahedral.

e.g. $[Co(NH_3)_6]^{3+}$ is octahedral, $[Ni(CO)_4]$ is tetrahedral and $[PtCl_4]^{2-}$ is square planar.

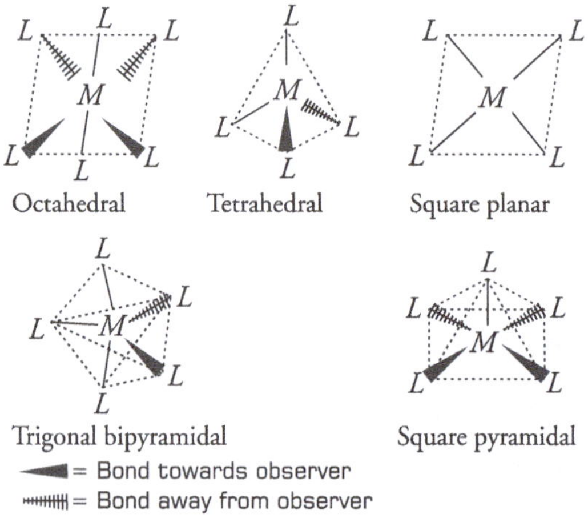

Shapes of different coordination polyhedra, where, M is central atom/ ion and L is a unidentate ligand

Homoleptic and Heteroleptic Complexes

Complexes in which a metal is bound to only one kind of donor groups, e.g. $[Co(NH_3)_6]^{3+}$ are known as homoleptic complexes.

Complexes in which a metal is bound to more than one kind of donor groups, e.g. $[Co(NH_3)_4Cl_2]^+$ are known as heteroleptic complexes.

Charge on the Complex Ion

The charge carried by a complex ion is the algebraic sum of the charges carried by the central metal ion and the total ligands attached to the central metal ion. e.g.

In the complex ion, $[Ag(CN)_2]^-$, Ag^+ ion carries a charge of +1 and each CN^- ion carries a charge of −1. Therefore, the net charge on complex ion $[Ag(CN)_2]^-$ is one negative $(+1-2=-1)$.

Oxidation Number of Central Atom

Oxidation number of central atom in a complex is defined as the charge it would carry when all the ligands are removed along with electron pairs which are shared with central atom.

The oxidation number is represented by a Roman numeral in parenthesis following the name of the coordination entity.

e.g. In $[Cu(CN)_4]^{3-}$, oxidation number of Cu is +1 and it is written as Cu(I). Oxidation number of central atom is a charge on central atom.

Effective Atomic Number (EAN)

EAN of the metal in complex is given by

$$EAN = Z - (ON) + 2(CN)$$

(where, ON is oxidation number, CN is the coordination number and Z is the atomic number).

EAN can also be given by

$$EAN = Z(ON) + 2(\text{ligands})$$

(assuming that each ligand is unidentate.)

Nomenclature of Coordination Compounds

The formulae and names adopted for the coordination entities are based on the recommendations of the International Union of Pure and Applied Chemistry (IUPAC).

The rules for the nomenclature of coordination compounds are as follows:

1. Formulae of Mononuclear Coordination Entities

The formula of a compound is a shorthand tool used to provide basic information about the constitution of the compound in a concise and convenient manner.

Mononuclear coordination entities contain a single central metal atom.

Following rules are applied while writing the formulae:

(i) The central atom is listed first.

(ii) The ligands are then listed in alphabetical order. The placement of a ligand, in the list does not depend on its charge.

(iii) Polydentate ligands are also listed alphabetically. In case of abbreviated ligand, the first letter of the abbreviation is used to determine the position of the ligand in the alphabetical order.

(iv) The formula for the entire coordination entity, whether charged or not, is enclosed in square brackets. When ligands are polyatomic, their formulae are enclosed in parentheses. Ligand abbreviations are also enclosed in parenthesis.

(v) There should be no space between the ligands and the metal within a coordination sphere.

(vi) When the formula of a charged coordination entity is to be written without that of the counter ion, the charge is indicated outside the square brackets as a right superscript with the number before the sign. e.g. $[Co(CN)_6]^{3-}$, $[Cr(H_2O)_6]^{3+}$, etc.

(vii) The charge of the cation(s) is balanced by the charge of the anion(s).

Note IUPAC, in 2004, recommends that ligands will be sorted alphabetically. Charge has no role in it.

2. Naming of Mononuclear Coordination Compounds

The names of coordination compounds are derived by following the principles of additive nomenclature, i.e. the groups that surround the central atom must be identified in the name. They are listed as prefixes to the name of the central atom along with any appropriate multipliers.

The following rules are used while naming coordination compounds:

(i) The cation is named first in both positively and negatively charged coordination entities.

(ii) The ligands are named in an alphabetical order before the name of the central atom/ion. (This procedure is reversed from writing formula).

(iii) Names of the anionic ligands end in -'o', those of neutral and cationic ligands are the same except aqua for H_2O, ammine for NH_3, carbonyl for CO and nitrosyl for NO. These are placed within enclosing marks ( ).

(iv) Prefixes mono, di, tri, etc., are used to indicate the number of the individual ligands in the coordination entity. When the names of the ligands include a numerical prefix, then the terms, *bis, tris, tetrakis* are used, the ligand to which they refer is placed in parenthesis. e.g. $[NiCl_2(PPh_3)_2]$ is named as dichloro*bis*- (triphenylphosphine)nickel(II).

(v) Oxidation state of the metal in cation, anion or neutral coordination entity is indicated by Roman numeral in parenthesis.

(vi) If the complex ion is a cation, the metal is named same as the element, e.g. Co in a complex cation is called cobalt and Pt is called platinum. If the complex ion is an anion, the name of the metal ends with the suffix—'ate', e.g. Co in a complex anion, $[Co(SCN)_4]^{2-}$ is called cobaltate. For some metals, the Latin names are used in the complex anions, e.g. ferrate for Fe.

(vii) The neutral complex molecule is named similar to that of the complex cation. e.g.

- $[Pt(NH_3)_2Cl(NO_2)]$ is named as Diamminechloridonitrito-N-platinum(II)

Name of some common ligands

Neutral ligands		Negative ligands	
Formula	**Name as ligand**	**Formula**	**Name as ligand**
OH_2	Aqua		
NH_3	Ammine	F^- (fluoride)	Fluorido
CO	Carbonyl	Cl^-	Chlorido
NO	Nitrosyl	Br^-	Bromido
NH_2CH_3	Methylamine	I^-	Iodido
NC_5H_5 or Py	Pyridine	O^{2-} (oxide)	Oxido
$N(C_2H_5)_3$	Triethylamine	OH^- (hydroxide)	Hydroxido
$N(CH_3)_3$	Trimethylamine	CN^- (cyanide)	Cyanido*
$P(C_6H_5)_3$	Triphenyl Phosphine	NC^-	Isocyanido*
PH_3	Phosphine	S^{2-}	Sulphidido
Positive ligands NO_2^+	Nitronium	H^-	Hydridido
$NH_2—NH_3^+$	Hydrozinium	SO_4^{2-}	Sulphato
NO^+	Nitrosonium	$C_2O_4^{2-}$	Oxalato
		NO_2^-	Nitro
		ONO^-	Nitrito
		CO_3^{2-}	Carbonato

Note Ambident, underlined atoms are electron donating.

Example 1 Write down the IUPAC names of the following coordination compounds.

(i) $[Co(NH_3)_5Cl]Cl_2$ (ii) $K_2[PdCl_4]$ **NCERT Intext**

Sol. (i) $[CO(NH_3)_5Cl]Cl_2$

↑ Metal atom; ↑ ↑ Ligands; ↑ Counter ion

Let the oxidation state of Co be x.

$$x + (0) \times 5 + (-1) \times 1 + (-1) \times 2 = 0$$

$$x + 0 - 3 = 0 \qquad x = +3$$

So, the name of the complex is pentaamminechloridocobalt (III) chloride. **(1½)**

(ii) $K_2[PdCl_4]$

↑ Counter ion; ↑ Metal atom; ↑ Ligand; ↑ Coordination number

Let the oxidation state of Pd be x.

$$(+1)\,2 + x + (-1)\,4 = 0$$

$$2 + x - 4 = 0$$

$$\Rightarrow \qquad x = +2$$

So, the name of the complex is potassiumtetrchloridopalladate (II). **(1½)**

Example 2 Write the formulae for the following coordination compounds.

(i) Tetraamminediaquacobalt(III) chloride

(ii) Potassium tetracyanonickelate(II)

(iii) *Tris* (ethan-1, 2-diamine) chromium(III) chloride

(iv) Amminebromidochloridonitrito-N-platinate(II)

(v) Dichlorido *bis*-(ethane-1, 2-diamine) platinum(IV) nitrate

(vi) Iron(III) hexacyanoferrate(II) **NCERT Intext**

Sol. (i) Tetraamminediaqua (Ligand) cobalt (III) (Metal) chloride (Counter ion)

$[\overset{III}{Co}(NH_3)_4(H_2O)_2]Cl_x$

To find the value of x, we have to find the charge on the complex.

$$[\overset{III}{Co}(NH_3)_4(H_2O)_2]^+$$

$$\Rightarrow \qquad +3 + 4 \times 0 + 2 \times 0 = x$$

$$x = +3$$

So, the formula of the complex is $[Co(NH_3)_4(H_2O)_2]Cl_3$.

(ii) Potassium (Counter ion) tetracyano (Ligand) nickelate (II) (Metal)

$K_x[\overset{II}{Ni}(CN)_4]$

To find the value of x, find the charge on the complex.

$[Ni(CN)_4]^{x-}$ (as K^+ is positive)

$$+2 + (-1) \times 4 = -x$$

$$-x = -2 \quad \text{or} \quad x = +2$$

So, the formula of the complex is $K_2[Ni(CN)_4]$.
Similarly,

(iii) $[Cr(en)_3]Cl_3$

(iv) $[Pt(NH_3)BrCl(NO_2)]^-$

(v) $[PtCl_2(en)_2](NO_3)_2$

(vi) $Fe_4[Fe(CN)_6]_3$ $\left(6 \times \frac{1}{2} = 3\right)$

Isomerism in Coordination Compounds

Compounds having same molecular formula but different structures are called **isomers** and this phenomenon is called **isomerism**. Coordination compounds show two major types of isomerism; structural isomerism and stereoisomerism.

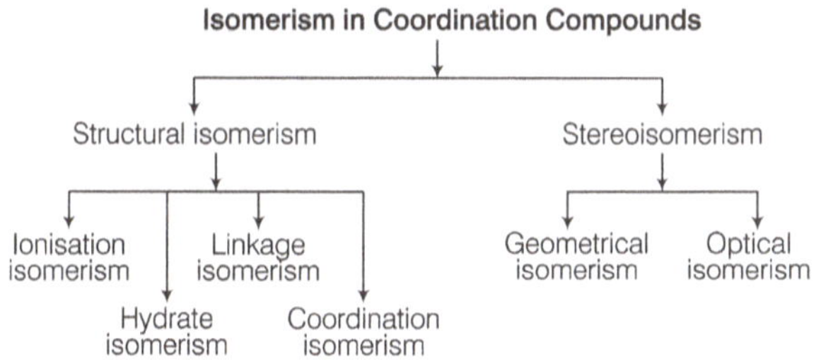

Structural Isomerism

The coordination compounds having same chemical formula but different structural arrangement are known as structural isomers. These isomers have different bonding pattern. It is further subdivided into following two types :

1. Linkage Isomerism

It is shown by the coordination compounds containing ambidentate ligand such as NO_2, SCN, etc. SCN which can bind to metal through N and S as *M*—NCS and *M*—SCN, respectively. Similarly, NO_2 can bind either by N or by O of NO_2, e.g.

$$\underset{\text{(Yellow)}}{[Co(NH_3)_3(NO_2)]Cl_2} \text{ and } \underset{\text{(Blue)}}{[Co(NH_3)_3ONO]Cl_2}.$$

2. Coordination Isomerism

It arises from the interchange of ligands between cationic and anionic entities of different metal ions present in a complex, e.g. $[Co(NH_3)_6][Cr(CN)_6]$ in which the NH_3 ligands are bound to Co^{3+} and the CN^- ligand to Cr^{3+} and in its coordination isomer, in $[Cr(NH_3)_6][Co(CN)_6]$, the NH_3 ligands are bound to Cr^{3+} and CN^- ligands to Co^{3+}.

3. Ionisation Isomerism

It arises when compounds give different ions in the solution although they have same composition. It arises when the counter ion in a complex salt is itself a potential ligand and can displace a ligand which can then become the counter ion, e.g.

$$\underset{\text{(Red)}}{[Co(NH_3)_5SO_4]Br} \text{ and } \underset{\text{(Violet)}}{[Co(NH_3)_5Br]SO_4}.$$

4. Hydrate Isomerism or Solvate Isomerism

This type of isomerism arises in case where water is involved as a solvent. Solvate isomers differ by whether or not a solvent molecule is directly bonded to the metal ion or merely present as free solvent molecules in the crystal lattice, e.g. *aqua* complex $[Cr(H_2O)_6]Cl_3$ (violet) and its solvate isomer $[Cr(H_2O)_5Cl]Cl_2 \cdot H_2O$ (grey, green).

Stereoisomerism

Coordination compounds having same molecular as well as structural formulae but different arrangement in space in the polyhedral are called stereoisomers. This phenomenon is called stereoisomerism. It is further subdivided into two types:

1. Geometrical Isomerism

Heteroleptic complexes with coordination numbers 4 and 6 show this type of isomerism. It arises due to the difference in the geometrical arrangement of the ligands around the central metal ion. When same ligands occupy the adjacent position in the polyhedra, it is known as *cis*-isomer whereas when same ligands occupy the opposite position in the polyhedra, it is known as *trans*-isomer.

A square planar complex of the type $[MX_2L_2]$ (*X* and *L* are unidentate) shows these two geometrical isomers, e.g.

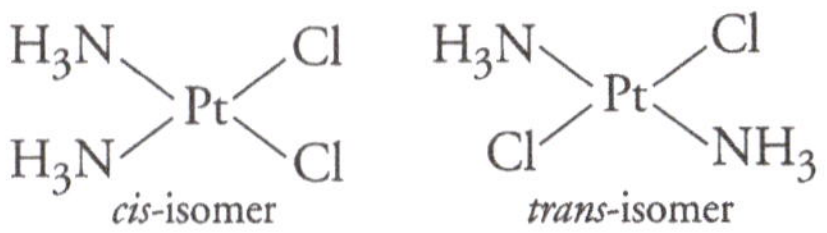

Geometrical isomers of $[Pt(NH_3)_2Cl_2]$

Note

cis-isomer of $[Pt(NH_3)_2Cl_2]$ is also known as *cis*-platin which is used as an anticancer drug in the chemotherapy process of cancer treatment.

Geometrical Isomerism in Complexes having Coordination Number 4

Square planar complex of the type [*MABXL*] (*ABXL* are unidentate ligands) shows three isomers-two *cis* and one *trans*.

Such isomerism is not possible in a tetrahedral complexes but similar behaviour or isomerism is possible in octahedral complexes of the type $[MX_2L_4]$ in which two ligands X may be oriented *cis* or *trans* to each other, e.g.

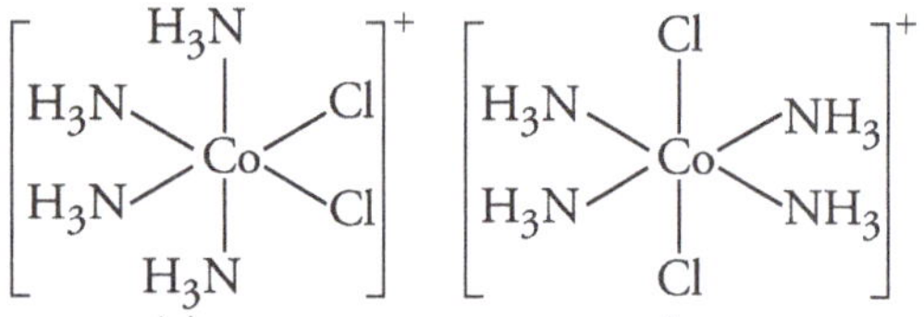

cis-isomer *trans*-isomer

Geometrical isomers of $[Co(NH_3)_4Cl_2]^+$

Geometrical Isomerism in Complexes Coordination Number 6

Octahedral coordination entities of the type $[Ma_3b_3]$ shows geometrical isomerism. When three donor atoms of same ligands are occupying adjacent position in the polyhedra, it is known as **facial** (*fac*) **isomer.**

Whereas when three same ligands are occupying position around the meridian of the octahedral, it is known as **meridional** (*mer*) **isomer,** e.g.

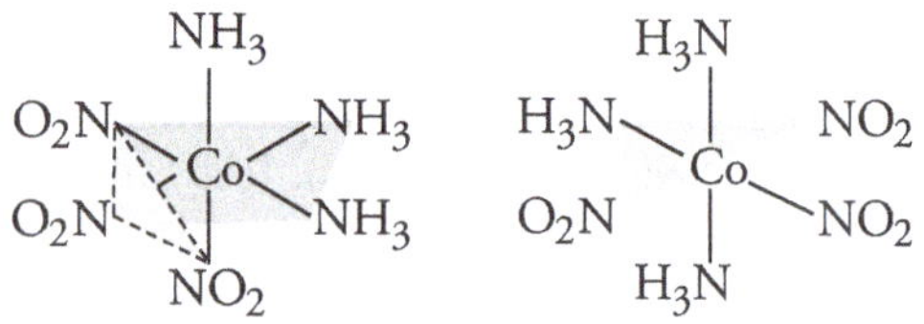

fac *mer*

Facial (fac) and meridional (mer) isomers of $[Co(NH_3)_3(NO_2)_3]$

Hence, these isomers differ in one or more physical or chemical properties.

Note

Tetrahedral complex does not show geometrical isomerism because the relative positions of unidentate ligands attached to the central metal atom are the same with respect to each other.

2. Optical Isomerism

The compounds which do not have a plane of symmetry show optical isomerism. The optically active isomers have non-superimposable mirror images or which cannot be superimposed on one another and the molecules which cannot be superimposed are called **chiral** molecules.

The two forms called *dextro* (*d*) or *laevo* (*l*), depending upon the direction they rotate the plane of polarised light in a polarimeter, are called **enantiomers.**

The isomer which rotate the plane of polarised light to the right is called ***dextro*** (*d*) rotatory whereas the isomer which rotate the plane of polarised light to the left is called ***laevo*** (*l*) rotatory. An equimolar mixture of *dextro* (*d*) and *laevo* (*l*) rotatory isomers is called **racemic mixture.**

Optical isomerism is commonly shown by the octahedral complexes involving didentate ligands.

e.g. For $[Co(en)_3]^{3+}$ two isomers can be represented as :

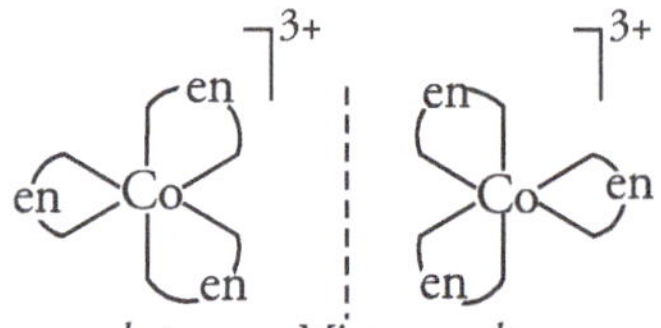

dextro Mirror *laevo*

Optically active isomers of cis-$[Co(en)_3]^{3+}$

In a coordination entity of the type $[PtCl_2(en)_2]^{2+}$, only the *cis*-isomer shows optical activity.

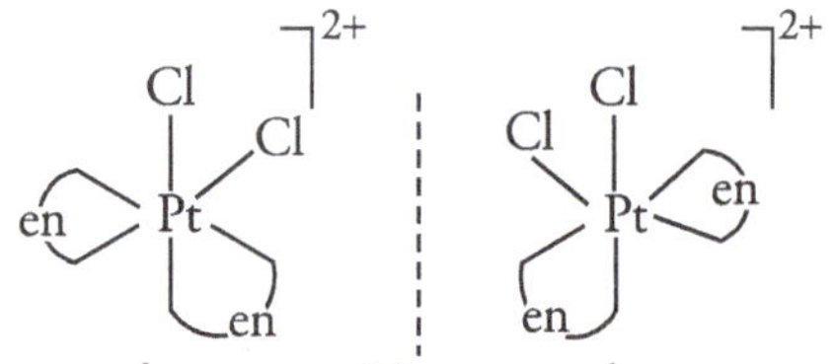

dextro Mirror *laevo*

Optically active isomers of cis-$[PtCl_2(en)_2]^{2+}$

Some examples of octahedral complexes showing optical isomerism are given below:

(i) **Type** $[M(AA)_3]$

e.g. $[Co(en)_3]^{3+}$, $[Cr(ox)_3]^{3-}$.

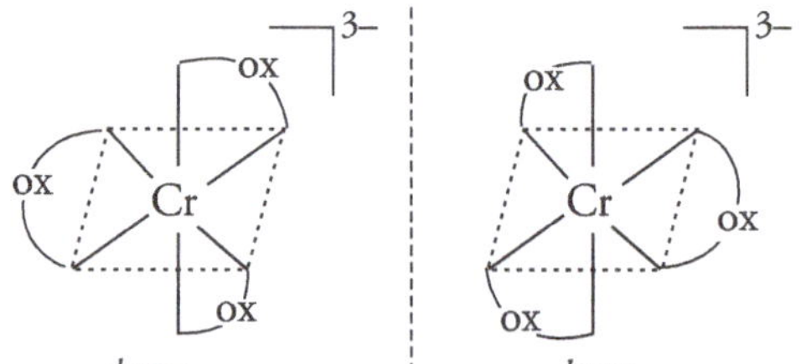

dextro *laevo*

Mirror

Optically active isomers of cis-$[Cr(ox)_3]^{3-}$

(ii) **Type** $[M(AA)_2X_2]^{n+}$ or $[M(AA)_2XY]^{n+}$

e.g. *cis*-$[Co(en)_2Cl_2]^+$, *cis*-$[Pt(en)_2Cl_2]^+$, *cis*-$[Cr(ox)_2Cl_2]^{3-}$

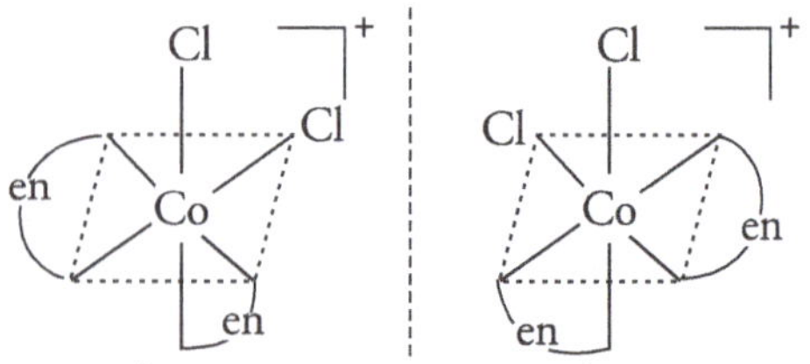

dextro Mirror *laevo*

Optically active isomers of cis-$[Co(en)_2Cl_2]$

(iii) **Type** $[M(AA)X_2Y_2]$

e.g. $[Co(en)(NH_3)_2Cl_2]^+$

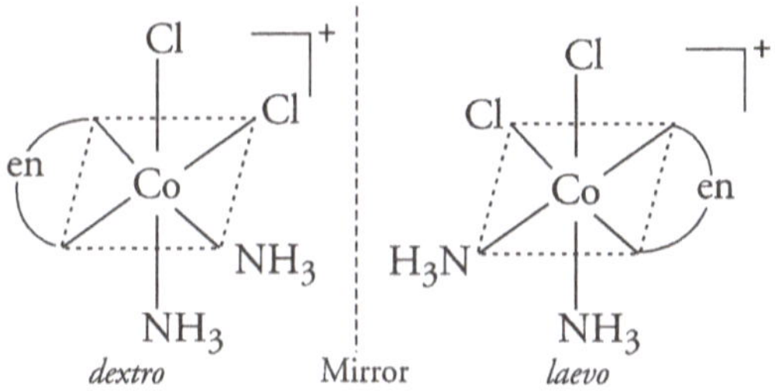

Optically active isomers of cis-$[Co(NH_3)_2(en)Cl_2]$

Werner's Theory of Coordination Compounds

Alfred Werner (1866-1919), a Swiss chemist was the first to formulate his ideas about the structures of coordination compounds in 1898.

He proposed the concept of a **primary valency** and a **secondary valency** for a metal ion. Binary compounds such as $CrCl_3$, $CoCl_2$ and $PdCl_2$ have primary valency of 3, 2 and 2 respectively.

In a series of compounds of cobalt (III) chloride with ammonia, it was found that some of the chloride ions could be precipitated as AgCl on adding excess $AgNO_3$ solution in cold but some remained in the solution.

(i) 1 mole of $CoCl_3 \cdot 6NH_3$ (yellow) gave 3 moles of AgCl.

(ii) 1 mole of $CoCl_3 \cdot 5NH_3$ (purple) gave 2 moles of AgCl.

(iii) 1 mole of $CoCl_3 \cdot 4NH_3$ (green) gave 1 mole of AgCl.

(iv) 1 mole of $CoCl_3 \cdot 4NH_3$ (violet) gave 1 mole of AgCl.

On the basis of results of conductivity measurement in solution, above observations can be explained, if

(i) all six groups either Cl^- ions or NH_3 molecules or both, remain bonded to cobalt ion during reaction.

(ii) the compounds are formulated to form a single entity which does not dissociate in the reaction condition as:

Formulation of cobalt (III) chloride-ammonia complexes

Colour	Formula	Solution conductivity corresponds to
Yellow	$[Co(NH_3)_6]^{3+}\ 3Cl^-$	1 : 3 electrolyte
Purple	$[CoCl(NH_3)_5]^{2+}\ 2Cl^-$	1 : 2 electrolyte
Green	$[CoCl_2(NH_3)_4]^+\ Cl^-$	1 : 1 electrolyte
Violet	$[CoCl_2(NH_3)_4]^+\ Cl^-$	1 : 1 electrolyte

Werner called secondary valency for the number of groups bounded directly to the metal ion. In each of the above complexes secondary valencies are six.

Postulates of Werner's Theory

(i) In coordination compounds, metal has two types of linkages (valencies)-primary and secondary in a complex.

(ii) Primary valency is equal to the oxidation number of central metal ion. It is non-directional and ionisable. It is satisfied by **negative** ions, e.g. in $CrCl_3$, the primary valency is three.

(iii) Secondary valency is equal to the coordination number of central atom/ion. It is directional and non-ionisable. It is commonly satisfied by neutral molecules or negative ions and is always fixed for a metal. Each metal ion has a fixed number of secondary valency.

e.g. $[Co(NH_3)_6]^{3+}$ has octahedral shape.

(iv) The ions or groups bounded by the secondary linkages to the metal have characteristic spatial arrangements called coordination polyhedra.

e.g. Structure of $[CoCl_2(NH_3)_4]^+Cl^-$ is as follows:

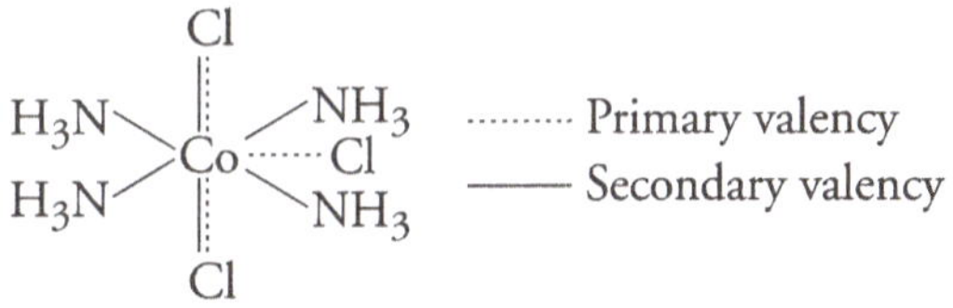

The solid and dotted lines together indicate Cl-atom satisfying both primary and secondary valencies.

(v) Werner further postulated that octahedral, tetrahedral and square planar geometrical shapes are more common in coordination compounds of transition metals thus, $[Co(NH_3)_6]^{3+}$,$[CoCl\ (NH_3)_5]^{2+}$ and $[CoCl_2\ (NH_3)_4]^+$are octahedral entities, while $[Ni\ (CO)_4]$ and $[PtCl_4]^{2-}$ are tetrahedral and square planar, respectively.

Topic Practice 1

Very Short Answer Type Questions

(1 Mark)

1. **Fill in the Blanks**

   (i) The coordination number and oxidation state of the complex $K_4[Fe(CN)_6]$ are .... and .... respectively. **ISC 2023**

   (ii) EDTA is used in the treatment of .... while *cis*-platin is used in the treatment of .... **ISC 2024**

   (iii) Coordination compounds strucutre was first proposed by .... **ISC 2009**

   (iv) Mohr's salt, $[FeSO_4.(NH_4)_2SO_4.6H_2O]$ is .... (*A*) while $[Ni(NH_3)_6]Cl_2$ is a .... (*B*).

   Consider the above sentence and identify (*A*) and (*B*).

   (a) Complex, double salt

   (b) double salt, complex

   (c) double salt, double salt

   (d) complex, complex

2. **Objective Type Questions**

   (i) In the complexes $[Fe(CN)_6]^{3-}$ and $[Pt(en)(H_2O)_2(NO_2)(Cl)]^{2+}$, the respective oxidation numbers of central metal atoms are

   (a) + 3 and + 4 (b) + 6 and + 4

   (c) + 6 and + 3 (d) + 3 and + 3 **ISC 2015**

   (ii) Among the following coordination compounds, the one giving a white precipitate with $BaCl_2$ solution is **ISC 2012**

   (a) $[Cr(H_2O)_5Br]SO_4$ (b) $[Cr(H_2O)_5SCN]$

   (c) $[Co(NH_3)_5SO_4]Br$ (d) $[Pt(NH_3)_6Cl_4]$

3. Math Column (I) with Column (II) and choose the correct option using the codes given below :

Column I (Species)		Column II (Number of ions produced in aqueous solution)
A. $Co(NH_3)_6 \cdot Cl_3$	(i)	4
B. $Co(NH_3)_5 \cdot Cl_2$	(ii)	3
C. $CoCl_2(NH_3)_4 \cdot Cl$	(iii)	2
D. $CoCl_2(NH_3)_4$	(iv)	0

Codes

	A	B	C	D		A	B	C	D
(a)	(i)	(ii)	(iii)	(iv)	(b)	(iv)	(iii)	(ii)	(i)
(c)	(i)	(ii)	(iv)	(iii)	(d)	(i)	(iii)	(iv)	(ii)

4. Correct the following statement by changing the underlined part of sentence.

   In a coordination complex, donation of electron pair takes place from the central metal atom to the ligands. **ISC 2009**

5. Write the coordination number and oxidation state of platinum in the complex $[Pt(en)_2Cl_2]$.

6. Write the IUPAC names of the following coordination compounds:

   (i) $[Cr(NH_3)_4(H_2O)_2]Cl_3$

   (ii) $[PtCl_2(NH_3)_4][PtCl_4]$ **ISC 2015**

7. Give the IUPAC name of the following coordination compounds :

   (i) $K_2[Zn(OH)_4]$

   (ii) $[Co(NH_3)_5(CO_3)]Cl$ **ISC 2013**

8. Give the IUPAC name for the following :

   (i) $Na_3[AlF_6]$

   (ii) $[Co(NH_3)_6]Cl_3$ **ISC 2011**

9. Write the formula of the following compounds :

   (i) Triamminetriaquachromium (III) chloride

   (ii) Potassiumhexacyanoferrate (III) **ISC 2014**

10. Write the formula of the following compounds:

    (i) Potassium trioxalatoaluminate (III)

    (ii) Hexaaquairon (II) sulphate. **ISC 2017**

11. Write the formula of the following coordination compounds :

    (i) Tetracarbonylnickel (0)

    (ii) Potassiumdicyanoargentate (I) **ISC 2010**

12. Write the formula of the following coordination compounds :

    (i) Potassiumtetracyanonickelate (0)

    (ii) Triamminetrinitrocobalt (III) **ISC 2012**

13. Draw the structural isomer of $[Co(NH_3)_5NO_2]Cl_2$ and name the type of isomerism. **ISC 2012**

14. Name the types of isomerism shown by the following pairs of compounds:

    (i) $Cu(NH_3)_4)[PtCl_4]$ and $[Pt(NH_3)_4][CuCl_4]$

    (ii) $[Co(en)_2Cl_2]^+$ and $[Co(en)_2Cl_2]^+$ **ISC 2017**

15. Draw the geometrical isomers exhibited by the compound $[PtCl_2(NH_3)_2]$. **ISC 2010**

16. Write the oxidation number of cobalt in $K[Co(CO)_4]$. **NCERT**

17. How many geometrical isomers are possible in the following coordination entities?
   (i) $[Cr(C_2O_4)_3]^{3-}$
   (ii) $[Co(NH_3)_3Cl_3]$ **NCERT**

18. How many ions are produced from the complex, $Co(NH_3)_6Cl_2$ in solution? **NCERT**

Short Answer Type I Questions (2 Marks)

19. Name the type of isomerism when ambidentate ligands are attached to central metal ion. Give two examples of ambidentate ligands. **NCERT Exemplar**

20. Give the evidence that $[Co(NH_3)_5Cl]SO_4$ and $[Co(NH_3)_5SO_4]Cl$ are ionisation isomers. **NCERT Intext**

21. Name the type of isomerism shown by the following pair of compounds :
   (i) $[CoCl(H_2O)(NH_3)_4]Cl_2$ and $[CoCl_2(NH_3)_4]Cl\cdot H_2O$
   (ii) $[Pt(NH_3)_4][PtCl_6]$ and $[Pt(NH_3)_4Cl_2][PtCl_4]$ **ISC 2014**

22. What type of structural isomers are $[Co(NH_3)_5Br]SO_4$ and $[Co(NH_3)_5SO_4]Br$? Give a chemical test to distinguish the isomer. **ISC 2013**

23. Name the type of isomerism shown by the following pair of compounds, $[PtCl_2(NH_3)_4]Br_2$ and $[PtBr_2(NH_3)_4]Cl_2$. Give a chemical test to distinguish between the given pair of isomers. **ISC 2010**

24. Name the type of isomerism shown by the following pairs of coordination compounds.
   (*i*) $[Co(NH_3)_5NO_2]Cl_2$ and $[Co(NH_3)_5ONO]Cl_2$
   (*ii*) $[Cr(H_2O)_5Cl]Cl_2\cdot H_2O$ and $[Cr(H_2O)_4Cl_2]Cl\cdot 2H_2O$ **ISC 2009**

25. Write all the geometrical isomers of $[Pt(NH_3)(Br)(Cl)(py)]$ and how many of these will exhibit optical isomers? **NCERT**

26. A complex of the type $[M(AA)_2X_2]^{n+}$ is known to be optically active. What does this indicate about the structure of the complex? Give one example of such complex. **NCERT Exemplar**

27. $FeSO_4$ solution mixed with $(NH_4)_2SO_4$ solution in 1:1 molar ratio gives the test of Fe^{2+} ion but $CuSO_4$ solution mixed with aqueous ammonia in 1 : 4 molar ratio does not give the test of Cu^{2+} ion. Why? **NCERT**

28. Aqueous copper sulphate solution (blue in colour) gives
   (i) a green precipitate with aqueous potassium fluoride.
   (ii) a bright green solution with aqueous potassium chloride.

   Explain these experimental results. **NCERT**

29. When a coordination compound $CoCl_3\cdot 6NH_3$ is mixed with $AgNO_3$, three moles of AgCl are precipitated per mole of the compound. Write the structural formula and IUPAC name of the coordination compound. **ISC 2019**

30. A coordination compound $CoCl_3\cdot 4H_2O$ precipitates silver chloride when treated with silver nitrate. The molar conductance of its solution corresponds to a total of two ions. Write the structural formula of the compound and name it. **NCERT Exemplar**

31. What is the coordination entity formed when excess of aqueous KCN is added to an aqueous solution of copper sulphate? Why is it that no precipitate of copper sulphide is obtained when $H_2S(g)$ is passed through this solution? **NCERT**

32. $CoSO_4Cl\cdot 5NH_3$ exists in two isomeric forms '*A*' and '*B*'. Isomer '*A*' reacts with $AgNO_3$ to give white precipitate, but does not react with $BaCl_2$. Isomer '*B*' gives white precipitate with $BaCl_2$ but does not react with $AgNO_3$.

   Answer the following questions.
   (i) Identify '*A*' and '*B*' and write their structural formulae.
   (ii) Name the type of isomerism involved.
   (iii) Give the IUPAC name of '*A*' and '*B*'. **NCERT Exemplar**

Short Answer Type II Questions (3 Marks)

33. (i) Write the IUPAC names of the following:
   (a) $K_3[Fe(C_2O_4)_3]$ (b) $[Co(NH_3)_5Cl]SO_4$
   (ii) $[Fe(CN)_6]^{4-}$ is a coordination complex ion.
   (a) Calculate the oxidation number of iron in the complex.
   (b) Is the complex ion diamagnetic or paramagnetic?
   (c) What is the hybridisation state of the central metal atom?
   (d) Write the IUPAC name of the complex ion. **ISC 2019**

34. Explain with two examples for each of the following.
Coordination entity, ligand, coordination number, coordination polyhedron, homoleptic and heteroleptic. **NCERT**

35. What is meant by unidentate, didentate and ambidentate ligands? Give two examples for each. **NCERT**

36. Using IUPAC forms, write the systematic names of the following:
(i) $[Ni(NH_3)_6]Cl_2$ (ii) $[Co(en)_3]^{3+}$
(iii) $[Ni(CO)_4]$ **NCERT**

37. Write the IUPAC name of the following coordination compounds.
(i) $[Cr(NH_3)_3Cl_3]$ (ii) $K_3[Fe(CN)_6]$
(iii) $[CoBr_2(en)_2]^+$ (en = ethylene diamine)

38. Using IUPAC norms, write the systematic names of the following.
(i) $[Co(NH_3)_6]Cl_3$
(ii) $[Pt(NH_3)_2Cl(NH_2CH_3)]Cl$
(iii) $[Ti(H_2O)_6]^{3+}$ **NCERT**

39. Using IUPAC norms, write the formulae for the following:
(i) Tetrahydroxozincate(II)
(ii) Potassium tetrachloridopalladate(II)
(iii) Diamminedichloridoplatinum(II)
(iv) Potassium tetracyanonickelate(II)
(v) Pentaamminenitrito-O-cobalt(III)
(vi) Hexaamminecobalt(III) sulphate **NCERT**

40. Specify the oxidation number of metal in the following coordination entities. **NCERT**
(i) $[Co(H_2O)(CN)(en)_2]^{2+}$ (ii) $[CoBr_2(en)_2]^+$
(iii) $[PtCl_4]^{2-}$

41. Draw the structures of optical isomers of
(i) $[Cr(C_2O_4)_3]^{3-}$ (ii) $[PtCl_2(en)_2]^{2+}$
(iii) $[Cr(NH_3)_2Cl_2(en)]^+$ **NCERT**

42. Draw all the isomers (geometrical and optical) of
(i) $[CoCl_2(en)_2]^+$ (ii) $[Co(NH_3)Cl(en)_2]^{2+}$
(iii) $[Co(NH_3)_2Cl_2(en)]^+$ **NCERT**

43. Explain the bonding in coordination compounds in terms of Werner's postulates. **NCERT**

44. Name of the type of isomerism exhibited by the following pairs of compounds :
(a) $[Co(ONO)(NH_3)_5]^{2+}$ and $[Co(NO_2)(NH_3)_5]^{2+}$
(b) $[Cr(H_2O)_4Cl_2]Cl \cdot 2H_2O$ and $[Cr(H_2O)_5Cl]Cl_2 \cdot H_2O$
(c) $[Co(NH_3)_6][Cr(CN)_6]$ and $[Cr(NH_3)_6][Co(CN)_6]$ **ISC 2020**

Long Answer Type Questions

5 Marks

45. List various types of isomerism possible for coordination compounds, giving an example of each. **NCERT**

46. Indicate the types of isomerism exhibited by the following complexes and draw the structures for these isomers.
(i) $K[Cr(H_2O)_2(C_2O_4)_2]$ (ii) $[Co(en)_3]Cl_3$
(iii) $[Co(NH_3)_5(NO_2)](NO_3)_2$
(iv) $[Pt(NH_3)(H_2O)Cl_2]$ **NCERT Intext**

47. (i) Write the IUPAC names of the following complexes :
(a) $[Cu(NH_3)_4]SO_4$ (b) $[Co(en)_2Cl_2]$
(c) $K_3[Al(C_2O_4)_3]$
(ii) With reference to the coordination complex ion $[Fe(H_2O)_6]^{2+}$ answer the following : (Atomic number of Fe = 26)
(a) Give the IUPAC name of the complex ion.
(b) What is the oxidation number of the central metal atom?
(c) How many unpaired electrons are there in the complex ion?
(d) State the type of hybridisation of the complex ion. **ISC 2020**

48. (i) Name the type of isomerism exhibited by the following pairs of compounds.
(a) $[Co(NH_3)_5(ONO)]Cl_2$ and $[Co(NH_3)_5(NO_2)]Cl_2$
(b) $[Cr(H_2O)_5Cl]Cl_2.H_2O$ and $[Cr(H_2O)_4Cl_2]Cl.2H_2O$
(c) $[Pt(NH_3)_4Cl_2]Br_2$ and $[Pt(NH_3)_4Br_2]Cl_2$
(ii) Write the IUPAC names of the following complexes
(a) $[Co(NH_3)_4(H_2O)_2]Cl_3$
(b) $K_2[Ni(CN)_4]$ **ISC 2023**

49. (i) A coordination compound has a formula $CoCl_3 \cdot 4NH_3$. It precipitates silver ions as AgCl and its molar conductance corresponds to a total of two ions.

Based on this information, answer the following questions.

(a) Deduce structural formula of the complex compound.

(b) Write the IUPAC name of the complex compound.

(c) Draw the geometrical isomers of the complex compound.

(ii) Give a chemical test to show that $[Co(NH_3)_5Cl]SO_4$ and $[Co(NH_3)_5SO_4]Cl$ are ionisation isomers. **ISC 2024**

50. (i) Write the IUPAC names of the following :

(a) $[Co(NH_3)_4SO_4]NO_3$

(b) $K[Pt(NH_3)Cl_3]$

(ii) What type of isomerism is exhibited by the following pairs of compounds?

(a) $[PtCl_2(NH_3)_4]Br_2$ and $[PtBr_2(NH_3)_4]Cl_2$

(b) $[Cr(SCN)(H_2O)_5]^{2+}$ and $[Cr(NCS)(H_2O)_5]^{2+}$

(iii) How does $K_2[PtCl_4]$ get ionised when dissolved in water? Will it form precipitate, when $AgNO_3$ solution is added to it? Give a reason for your answer. **ISC 2017**

Hints & Solutions

1. (i) 6, 2 (ii) lead poisoning; cancer (iii) Werner.

(iv) (A) Double salt

(B) Complex

2. (i) (a) $[Fe(CN)_6]^{3-}$

Let, oxidation number of Fe = x

$$x + 6 \times (-1) = -3$$

$$\Rightarrow \quad x = +3$$

$[Pt(en)(H_2O)_2(NO_2)(Cl)]^{2+}$

Let, oxidation number of Pt = x,

$$x + (0) + 2(0) + (-1) + (-1) = +2$$

$$\Rightarrow \quad x = +4$$

(ii) (a) $[Cr(H_2O)_5Br]SO_4$ gives a white precipitate of $BaSO_4$ when reacted with $BaCl_2$ solution, as it gives SO_4^{2-} ions in solution. Hence, option (a) is correct.

3. (a) (A) → (i), (B) → (ii), (C) → (iii), (D) → (iv)

4. In a coordination complex, donation of electron pair takes place from the ligands to the central metal atom. (1)

5. Coordination number of platinum in the complex. $[Pt(en)_2Cl_2]$ is 6 as en is a bidentate ligand. Let the oxidation state of Pt is x.

$$\therefore \quad x + 0 + 2(-1) = 0$$

$$x = +2$$

Thus, oxidation state of Pt is +2 (1)

6. IUPAC name

(i) $[Cr(NH_3)_4(H_2O)_2]Cl_3$
Tetraamminediaquachromium (III) chloride (1/2)

(ii) $[PtCl_2(NH_3)_4][PtCl_4]$
Tetraamminedichloroplatinum (IV) tetrachloroplatinate (II) (1/2)

7. (i) Potassiumtetrahydroxyzincate (II) (1/2)

(ii) Pentaamminecarbonatocobalt (III) chloride (1/2)

8. (i) Sodiumhexafluoroaluminate (III) (1/2)

(ii) Hexaamminecobalt (III) chloride (1/2)

9. (i) $[Cr(NH_3)_3(H_2O)_3]Cl_3$ (1/2)

(ii) $K_3[Fe(CN)_6]$ (1/2)

10. (i) $K_3[Al(ox)_3]$ or $K_3[Al(C_2O_4)_3]$ (1/2)

(ii) $[Fe(H_2O)_6]SO_4$ (1/2)

11. (i) $[Ni(CO)_4]$

(ii) $K[Ag(CN)_2]$ (1)

12. (i) $K_4[Ni(CN)_4]$

(ii) $[Co(NH_3)_3(NO_2)_3]$ (1)

13. The isomerism is linkage isomerism, as NO_2 is ambidentate ligand. Here, in NO_2^- ion, either nitrogen or an oxygen atom may act as donor. (1/2)

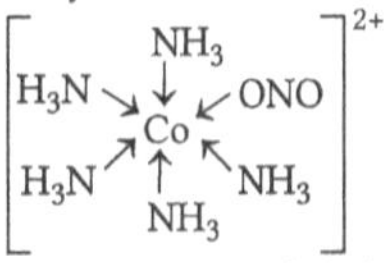

Pentaamminenitrito-O-cobalt (III) ion

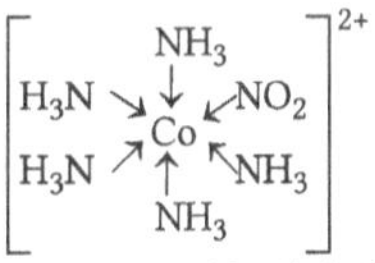

Pentaamminenitrito-N-cobalt (III) ion (1/2)

14. (i) Coordination isomerism (1/2)

(ii) Geometrical or *cis-trans* isomerism. (1/2)

15. Coordination number is 4. $[PtCl_2(NH_3)_2]$ exists in two forms. These are cis and trans forms.

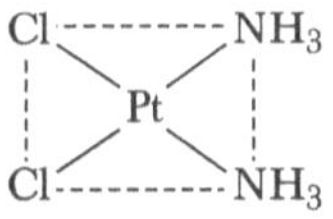

cis-isomer

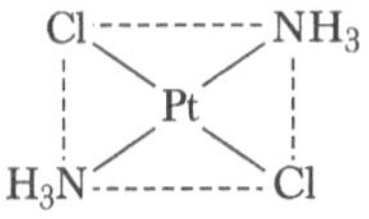

trans-isomer (1)

16. $K[Co(CO)_4]$

Let the oxidation number of Co be x.

$1 + x + 4 \times (0) = 0, \; x = -1$

17. (i) No geometrical isomer is possible. (1/2)

(ii) Two geometrical isomers are possible for $[Co(NH_3)_3Cl_3]$.

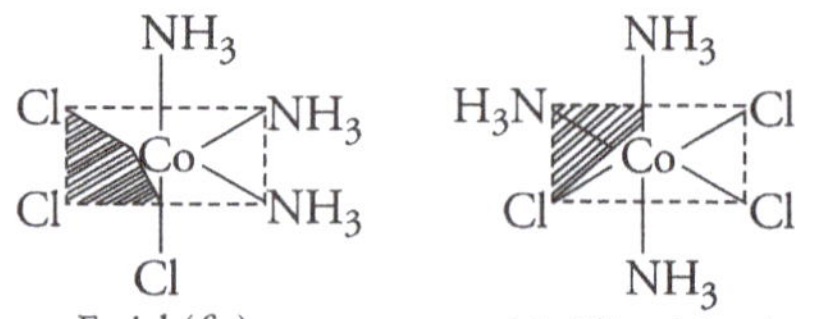

Facial (*fac*) Meridional (*mer*) (1/2)

18. The complex will dissociate in aqueous solution to produce three ions.

$Co(NH_3)_6Cl_2(aq) \longrightarrow [Co(NH_3)_6]^{2+} + 2Cl^-$ (1)

19. Ligands having more than one different binding position are known as ambidentate ligands. e.g. SCN has two different binding positions S and N, NO_2 has two different binding positions N and O.

Coordination compounds containing ambidentate ligands are considered to show linkage isomerism due to the presence of two different binding positions. (2)

20. We dissolve both the compounds in water in different test tubes. To both the test tubes

Case I Add $BaCl_2$ solution, one compound gives white ppt. indicating the presence of SO_4^{2-} ions. The other compound does not give white precipitate, indicating the absence of SO_4^{2-} ions.

$[Co(NH_3)_5Cl]SO_4 + BaCl_2(aq) \longrightarrow [Co(NH_3)_5Cl]Cl_2 + \underset{\text{White ppt.}}{BaSO_4(s)}$

$[Co(NH_3)_5SO_4]Cl + BaCl_2(aq) \rightarrow$ No reaction (1)

Case II Add $AgNO_3$ solution to both the compounds in separate test tubes.

Only II compound gives white precipitate and not I, due to the absence of Cl^- as counter ion.

$[Co(NH_3)_5SO_4]Cl + AgNO_3(aq) \longrightarrow [Co(NH_3)_5SO_4]NO_3 + \underset{\text{White ppt.}}{AgCl(s)}$

$[Co(NH_3)_5Cl]SO_4 + AgNO_3(aq) \longrightarrow$ No reaction

These two test prove that the given two compounds are a pair of ionisation isomers. (1)

21. (i) In both compounds the difference is in the number of water molecule which is present as ligand (i.e. in coordination sphere) and as molecule of water of crystallisation (i.e. outside the coordination sphere). Hence, they are called hydrate isomers. (1)

(ii) In these compounds, both positive and negative ions of salt are complex ions and the two isomers differ in the distribution of ligands in cation and anion. Hence, they are coordination isomers. (1)

22. The compounds will give different ions in solution, although they have same composition. Hence, they represent ionisation isomers.

These compounds ionise in solution as given below :

$[CoBr(NH_3)_5]\ SO_4 \longrightarrow [CoBr(NH_3)_5]^{2+} + SO_4^{2-}$

$[Co(SO_4)(NH_3)_5]Br \longrightarrow [Co(SO_4)(NH_3)_5]^+ + Br^-$ (1)

The complex $[CoBr(NH_3)_5]\ SO_4$ is red violet and its aqueous solution gives a white precipitate of $BaSO_4$ with $BaCl_2$, thus confirming the presence of $SO_4^{\ 2-}$ ions in the solution, whereas the complex $[Co(SO_4)(NH_3)_5]Br$ is red in colour and its aqueous solution gives a light yellow precipitate of AgBr with $AgNO_3$, thus confirming the presence of Br^- ions in the solution.

$\underset{\text{Red violet}}{[CoBr(NH_3)_5]SO_4} + BaCl_2 \longrightarrow$ White ppt. due to SO_4^{2-} ion

$\underset{\text{Red}}{[Co(NH_3)_5SO_4]Br} + BaCl_2 \longrightarrow$ No ppt. (1)

23. They show ionisation isomerism. It is because both compounds give different ions in solution although they have same composition,

$[PtCl_2(NH_3)_4]\ Br_2 \overset{H_2O}{\rightleftharpoons} [PtCl_2(NH_3)_4]^{2+} + 2Br^-$

$[PtBr_2(NH_3)_4]Cl_2 \overset{H_2O}{\rightleftharpoons} [Pt\ Br_2(NH_3)_4]^{2+} + 2Cl^-$ (1)

Test When reacted with $AgNO_3$, they give different colour.

$[PtCl_2(NH_3)_4]Br_2 + AgNO_3 \longrightarrow \underset{\text{Pale yellow ppt.}}{AgBr}$

$[PtBr_2(NH_3)_4]Cl_2 + AgNO_3 \longrightarrow \underset{\text{White ppt.}}{AgCl}$ (1)

24. (i) In both compounds, ambident ligand NO_2 is present. In $[Co(NH_3)NO_2]Cl_2$, NO_2 is coordinated through N and in $[Co(NH_3)_5ONO]Cl_2$, NO_2 is coordinated through O. Hence, they show linkage isomerism. (1)

(ii) These isomers differ from each other in number of water molecules coordinated to central metal atom, i.e. (Cr). So, they show hydrate isomerism. (1)

25. There are three geometrical isomers of $[Pt(NH_3)Br(Cl)(py)]$ (These structures are obtained by fixing the position of one ligand, i.e. NH_3 and placing at the *trans*-position w.r.t any one of the remaining three ligands one by one. Two of these are *cis* and one is *trans*).

(i)
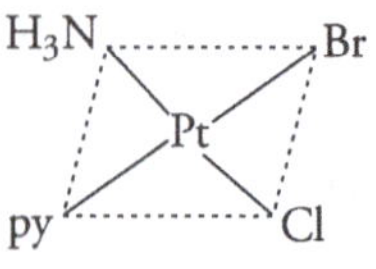

(ii)
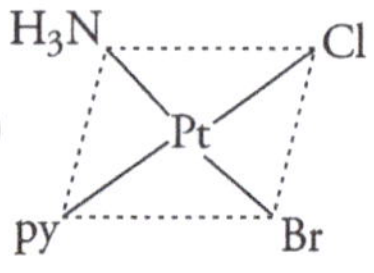

(½)

(iii)
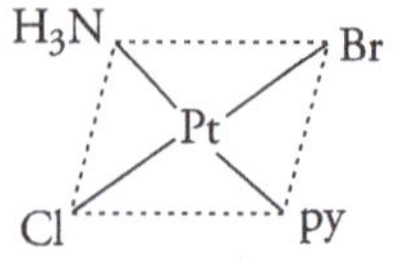

(½)

Optical isomerism is not exhibited by the compound with CN=4 and square planar geometry because of the presence of horizontal plane of symmetry. (1)

26. An optically active complex of the type $[M(AA)_2X_2]^{n+}$ indicates that the two mirror images are non-superimposable.
e.g. *cis*- $[Pt(en)_2Cl_2]^{2+}$ or *cis*- $[Co(en)_2Cl_2]^+$

For the structure refer to text on page 297 [Optical isomerism (ii)]. (2)

27. When $FeSO_4$ and $(NH_4)_2SO_4$ solutions are mixed in 1:1 molar ratio, Mohr's salt (a double salt) is formed.

$$FeSO_4(aq) + (NH_4)_2SO_4(aq) \longrightarrow FeSO_4 \cdot (NH_4)_2SO_4 \cdot 6H_2O$$

$$FeSO_4 \cdot (NH_4)_2SO_4 \cdot 6H_2O \rightleftharpoons Fe^{2+}(aq) + 2NH_4^+(aq) + 2SO_4^{2-}(aq) + 6H_2O$$

As a double salt is formed, so it will retain the properties of, its constituents and hence gives the test of Fe^{2+}ion. (1)

$$CuSO_4(aq) + 4NH_3(aq) \longrightarrow [Cu(NH_3)_4]SO_4$$

As a coordination complex is formed so, its properties would be different from that of their constituents and hence will not give the test of Cu^{2+} ion. (1)

28. Aqueous copper sulphate (blue) is $[Cu(H_2O)_4]SO_4$.

$$[Cu(H_2O)_4]SO_4 \longrightarrow \underset{\text{Blue}}{[Cu(H_2O)_4]^{2+}} + SO_4^{2-}$$

$[Cu(H_2O)_4]^{2+}$is a labile complex in which H_2O ligand get easily replaced by F^- ions of KF and by Cl^- ions of KCl.

(i) $[Cu(H_2O)_4]^{2+}(aq) + 4F^-(aq) \longrightarrow \underset{\text{Green ppt.}}{[CuF_4]^{2-}} + 4H_2O$ (1)

(ii) $[Cu(H_2O)_4]^{2+}(aq) + 4Cl^-(aq) \longrightarrow \underset{\text{(Bright green ppt.)}}{[CuCl_4]^{2-}} + 4H_2O$

29. On mixing the coordination compound, $CoCl_3.6NH_3$ with $AgNO_3$, three moles of AgCl are precipitated. It indicates the presence of three chlorine atom outside the coordination sphere, i.e 3 moles of chlorine are ionisable. Therefore, structural formula of the given complex is: $[Co(NH_3)_6]Cl_3$

IUPAC name of the complex is :

Hexaammine cobalt (III) Chloride

30. Formation of white precipitate with $AgNO_3$ shows that atleast one Cl^- ion is present outside the coordination sphere. Moreover, only two ions are obtained in solution, so only one Cl^- is present outside the sphere. Thus, the structural formula of the complex is $[Co(H_2O)_4Cl_2]Cl$ and its IUPAC name is tetraaquadichloridocobalt (III) chloride. (2)

31. When excess of KCN(*aq*) is mixed with $CuSO_4(aq)$, a complex named potassiumtetracyanocuprate (II) is formed. (1)

$$\underset{\text{(Excess)}}{5KCN(aq)} + CuSO_4(aq) \longrightarrow \underset{\text{(Soluble)}}{K_3[Cu(CN)_4]\,(aq)} + K_2SO_4\,(aq)$$

There is no precipitate of copper sulphide when $H_2S(g)$ is passed through this solution. This is because coordination complex is formed so it will loose all the properties of its constituents. (1)

32. '*A*' gives precipitate with $AgNO_3$, so in it Cl is present outside the coordination sphere.

'*B*' gives precipitate with $BaCl_2$, so in it SO_4^{2-} is present outside the coordination sphere.

(i) So, *A* - $[Co(NH_3)_5\ SO_4]Cl$
B- $[Co(NH_3)_5Cl]\ SO_4$

(ii) Ionisation isomerism (as give different ions when subjected to ionisation.)

(iii) *A*, Pentaamminesulphatocobalt (III) chloride.
B, Pentaamminechloridocobalt (III) sulphate. (2)

33. (i) (a) $K_3[Fe(C_2O_4)_3]$
Potassiumtrioxalato ferrate (III)

(b) $[Co(NH_3)_5Cl]SO_4$
Pentammine chlorocobalt (III) sulphate

(ii) $[Fe(CN)_6]^{4-}$ ion

(a) Oxidation number of iron in the complex, $[Fe(CN)_6]^{4-}$

$$x + 6(-1) = -4,\ x - 6 = -4 \Rightarrow x = 6 - 4 = 2$$

(b) In the complex $[Fe(CN)_6]^{4-}$, iron exists in the + 2 oxidation state. Electronic configuration of Fe^{2+} is $4s^0 3d^6$. As CN^- is a strong field ligand, it causes the pairing of the unpaired 3*d* electrons. Hence, it is diamagnetic.

(c) In the given complex, hybridisation state of the central metal atom is d^2sp^3.

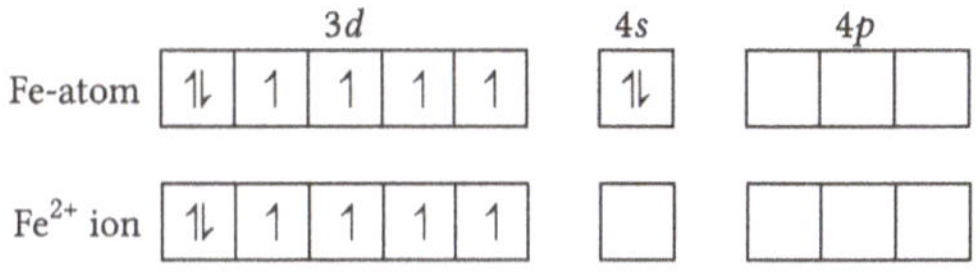

CN^- is a strong field ligand, thus it can pair the unpaired electrons of Fe^{2+}.

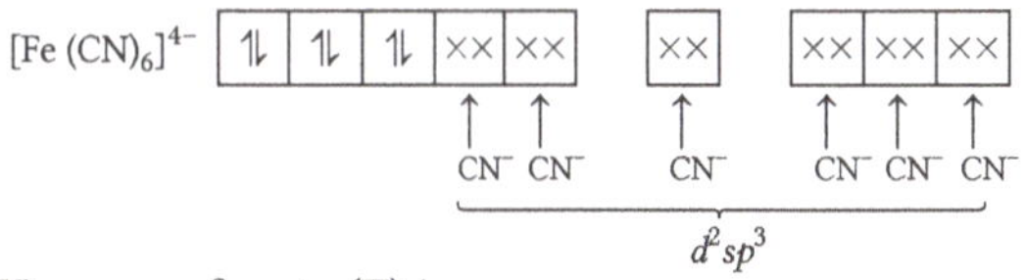

(d) Hexacyanoferrate (II) ion.

34. Refer to text on pages 167 and 168. (Definitions of some important terms used in coordination compounds). (3)

35. Refer to text on pages 167 and 168 (Ligands).

36. (i) Hexaamminenickel(II) chloride (1)
(ii) *Tris*-(ethane-1, 2-diamine)cobalt(III) ion (1)
(iii) Tetracarbonylnickel (0) (1)

37. (i) Triamminetrichloridochromium(III) (1)
(ii) Potassium hexacyanoferrate(III) (1)
(iii) Dibromido*bis*-(ethane-1, 2-diamine) cobalt (III) ion (1)

38. (i) Hexaamminecobalt(III) chloride (1)
(ii) Diamminechlorido (methylamine) platinum(II) chloride (1)
(iii) Hexaaquatitanium(III) ion (1)

39. (i) $K_2[Zn(OH)_4]$ (ii) $K_2[PdCl_4]$
(iii) $[Pt(NH_3)_2Cl_2]$ (iv) $K_2[Ni(CN)_4]$ (3)
(v) $[Co(NH_3)_5(ONO)]^{2+}$ (vi) $[Co(NH_3)_6]_2(SO_4)_3$

40.

Coordination entities	Oxidation state	
(i) $[Co(H_2O)(CN)(en)_2]^{2+}$	+3	(1)
(ii) $[CoBr_2(en)_2]^+$	+3	(1)
(iii) $[PtCl_4]^{2-}$	+2	(1)

41. (i) $[Cr(C_2O_4)_3]^{3-}$ Refer to text on page 172. (Optical isomerism (i)). (1)
(ii) Refer to text on pages 172 and 173. (Optical isomerism). (1)
(iii) $[Cr(NH_3)_2Cl_2(en)]^+$ (only *cis*-isomer shows optical activity) (1)

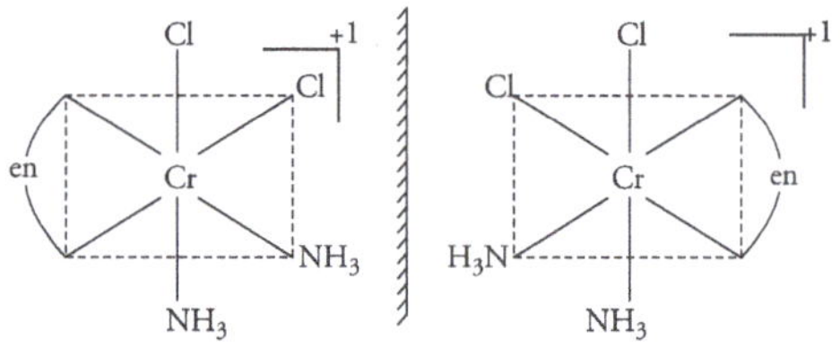

d-form l-form

42. (i) $[CoCl_2(en)_2]^+$ has two geometrical isomers. Further, *cis*-form shows optical isomerism.
Refer to text on page 172 (Optical isomerism (ii)). (1)
(ii) $[Co(NH_3)Cl(en)_2]^{2+}$

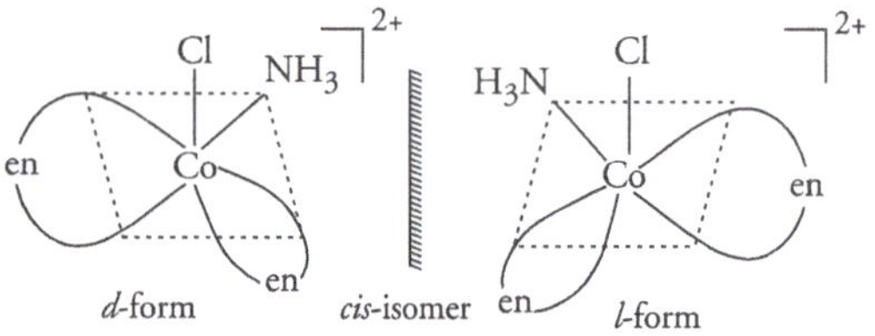

d-form *cis*-isomer *l*-form

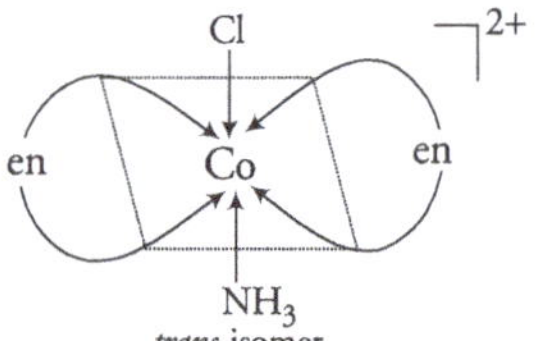

trans-isomer (1)

(iii) $[Co(NH_3)_2Cl_2(en)]^+$. It has 4 geometrical isomers

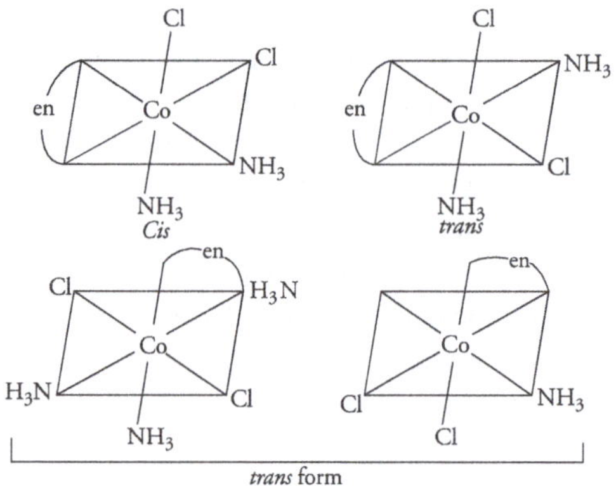

trans form

Fot its optical isomers
Refer to text on page 173. [Optical isomerism (iii)]. (1)

43. Refer to text on page 173 [Werner's theory of coordination compounds (iii)]. (3)

44. (a) Linkage isomerism.
(b) Hydrate isomerism.
(c) Coordination isomerism.

45. Refer to text on pages 171 and 172 (Isomerism in coordination compounds). (3)

46. It exists as both geometrical (*cis* and *trans*) and optical isomers.
(a) Geometrical isomers

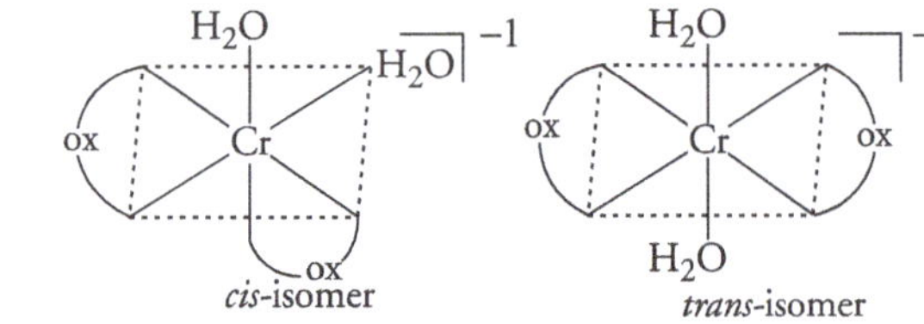

cis-isomer *trans*-isomer (1)

(b) Optical isomers of *cis-form*

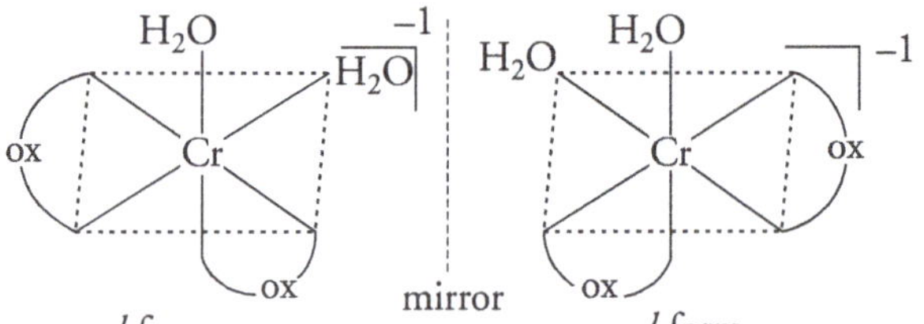

d-form *l*-form (1)

(ii) It shows two optical isomers.

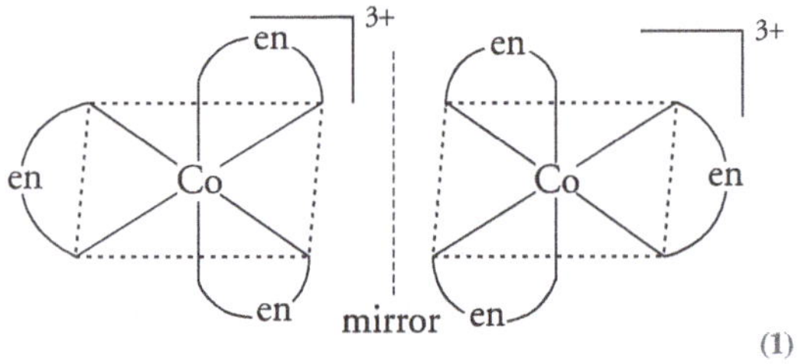

(1)

(iii) **Ionisation isomers**
$[Co(NH_3)_5(NO_2)](NO_3)_2$,
$[Co(NH_3)_5(NO_3)](NO_2)(NO_3)$
Linkage isomers
$[Co(NH_3)_5(NO_2)](NO_3)_2$,
$[Co(NH_3)_5(ONO)](NO_3)_2$ (1)

(iv) **Geometrical isomers** (*cis* and *trans*)

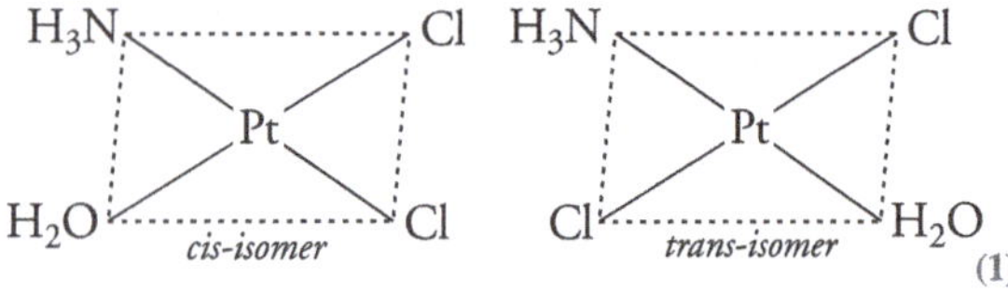

(1)

47. (i) (a) Tetraamminecopper (II) sulphate

(b) Dichlorido *bis*-(ethane-1, 2-diammine) cobalt (II)

(c) Potassium trioxalatoaluminate (III)

(ii) (a) Hexaaqua iron (II) ion.

(b) Oxidation number is + 2.

(c) In $[Fe(H_2O)_6]^{2+}$, four unpaired electrons are present.

$[Fe(H_2O)_6]^{2+}$, Fe is in + 2 oxidation state

3*d*

$Fe^{2+}(3d^6, 4s^0)$ = 

(d) sp^3d^2-hybridisation

Refer to page no. 184 (Table).

48. (i) (a) In both compounds, ambidentate ligand NO_2 is present. In $[Co(NH_3)_5(ONO)]Cl_2$ complex ONO is attached through O with Co while in $[Co(NH_3)_5(NO_2)]Cl_2$ complex NO_2 is attached through N with Co. Hence, they show linkage isomerism.

(b) Given compounds will have different no. of water molecules in coordination sphere which are directly attacked to metal ion. Hence, they show hydration isomerism.

(c) Given compounds will give different number of ions in solution, although they have same composition. Hence, they show ionisation isomerism.

(ii) (a) Tetraamine diaquacobalt (III) chloride.

(b) Potassium tetracyanonickelate (II).

49. (i) It is given that $CoCl_3 \cdot 4NH_3$ precipitates silver ions as AgCl and its molar conductance corresponds to a total of two ions. Thus, the formula of the compound will be $[CoCl_2(NH_3)_4]Cl$ as it satisfies both the conditions.

(a) The structural formula of the complex compound is $[CoCl_2(NH_3)_4]Cl$.

(b) IUPAC name = Tetraamminedichloridocobalt(III) chloride

(c) Geometrical isomers of $[CoCl_2(NH_3)_4]Cl$ are as follows

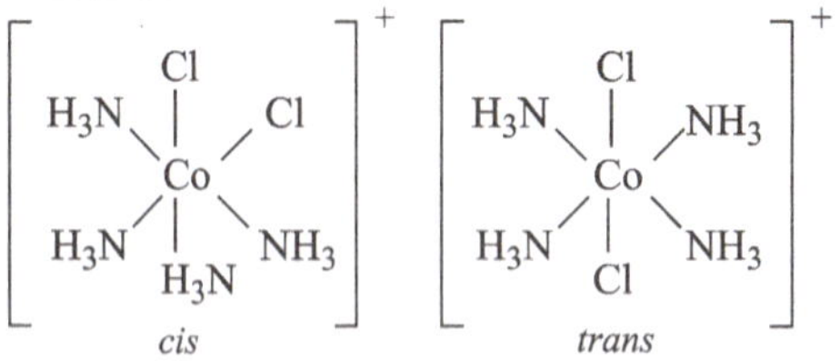

cis *trans*

(ii) The $[Co(NH_3)_5SO_4]Cl$ complex gives white precipitate with silver nitrate solution while $[Co(NH_3)_5Cl]SO_4$ does not gives such precipitate. This shows that $[Co(NH_3)_5SO_4]Cl$ and $[Co(NH_3)_5Cl]SO_4$ are ionisation isomers.

50. (i) (a) Tetraaminesulphatecobalt (III) nitrate. (1)

(b) Potassium amminetrichloridoplatinate (II). (1)

(ii) (a) Given compounds will give different ions in solution, although they have same composition. Hence, they exhibit ionisation isomerism. (1)

(b) In both compounds, ambidentate ligand SCN is present. In $[Cr(SCN)(H_2O)_5]^{2+}$ complex SCN is attached through S with Cr while in $[Cr(NCS)(H_2O)_5]^{2+}$ complex NCS is attached through N with Cr. Hence, they show linkage isomerism. (1)

(iii) $K_2[PtCl_4]$ ionise in solution as follows :

$$K_2[PtCl_4] \longrightarrow 2K^+ + [PtCl_4]^{2-}$$

The compound does not ionise to give free chloride ion, therefore it will not form precipitate when $AgNO_3$ solution is added to it. (1)

TOPIC 02 Bonding and Magnetic Behaviour

Bonding in Coordination Compounds

Werner was the first to explain the nature of bonding in coordination compounds but his theory was not able to answer the basic questions like :

(a) Why only some elements can form coordination compounds?

(b) Why the directional properties are exhibited by the bonds in coordination compounds?

(c) Why magnetic and optical properties are unique characteristic for coordination compounds?

Many approaches have been put forth to explain the nature of bonding in coordination compounds. These are Valence Bond Theory (VBT), Crystal Field Theory (CFT), Ligand Field Theory (LFT) and Molecular Orbital Theory (MOT).

Valence Bond Theory

This theory was put forward by L. **Pauling** in 1930 to explain the shapes of the complexes.

The main points of this theory are as follows:

(i) Central atom/ion makes available required number of empty orbitals.

(ii) These orbitals undergo hybridisation by using $(n-1)d$, ns, np or ns, np, nd orbitals of central atom/ion under the influence of ligands to give same number of hybrid orbitals of equal energy and definite geometry, such as linear, trigonal planar tetrahedral, square planar and octahedral etc. The hybridisation and geometry are given in the following table :

Hybridisation and geometry of complexes

C.N.	Hybridisation	Bond Angle	Geometry	Examples
2	sp	180°	Linear	$[Ag(NH_3)_2]^+$, $[Ag(CN)_2]^-$
3	sp^2	120°	Trigonal bipyramidal	$[HgI_3]^-$
4	sp^3	109°28′	Tetrahedral	$[Ni(CO)_4]$, $[ZnCl_4]^{2-}$, $[Zn(NH_3)_4]^{2+}$
4	dsp^2	90°	Square planar	$[Pt(NH_3)_4]^{2+}$, $[Cu(CN)_4]^{2-}$
5	dsp^3 or sp^3d	120°, 90°	Trigonal bipyramidal	$[Fe(CO)_5]$, $[MoCl_5]$, $[CuCl_5]^{3-}$
5	d^2sp^3 or sp^3d^2	90°	Octahedral	$[Fe(CN)_6]^{4-}$, $[Fe(CN)_6]^{3-}$, $[Co(NH_3)_6]^{3+}$, $[PtCl_6]^{2-}$, $[Cr(NH_3)_6]^{3+}$

(iii) Ligands must have one sigma orbital containing lone pair of electrons, so that it can donate to form bond with metal ion.

Structures and Shapes of Complexes on the Basis of Valence Bond Theory

1. Octahedral Complexes

Octahedral complexes involve one s, three p and two d-orbitals. They can form inner orbital and outer orbital complexes. When the complex formed involves the inner $(n-1)$ d-orbitals for hybridisation, the complex is called **inner orbital complex.**

These complexes usually contain lesser number of unpaired electrons. Therefore, they are also called low spin or spin paired complex, e.g. $[Ni(CN)_4]^{2-}$ and $[Co(NH_3)_6]^{3+}$.

When the complex formed involves the outer nd-orbital for hybridisation, the complex is called **outer orbital complex.** Such complexes possess higher number of unpaired electrons. Thus, they are reffered to as **high spin** or **spin free complex.**

Let us take some examples to explain octahedral complexes. These are as follows :

(i) **$[Co(NH_3)_6]^{3+}$** In this complex, oxidation state of cobalt is +3 and electronic configuration of Co^{3+} ion is $[Ar]^{18}3d^6$.

Its hybridisation scheme can be shown as:

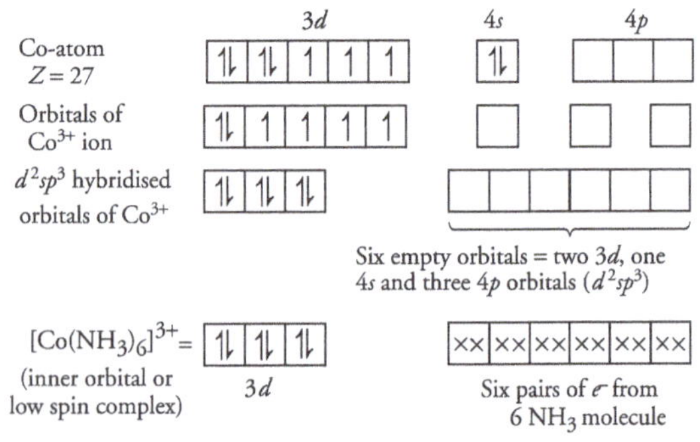

Six pairs of electrons one from each NH_3 molecule, occupy the six hybrid orbitals. Thus, complex has octahedral (d^2sp^3) geometry.

(ii) $[CoF_6]^{3-}$ In $[CoF_6]^{3-}$, outer orbital $4d$ is used in hybridisation. Thus, it is called outer orbital or high spin or spin free complex.

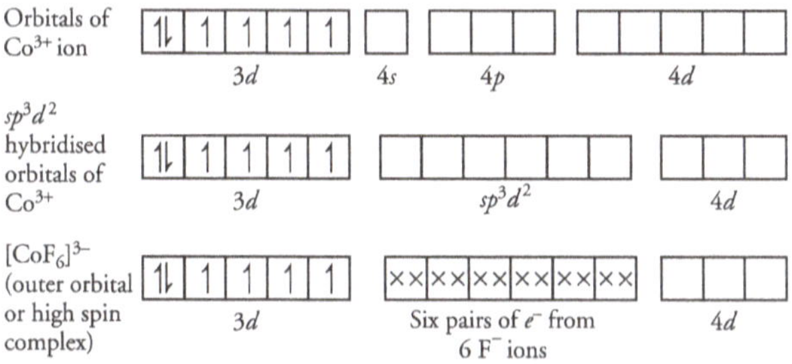

Six pairs of electrons one from each F^- ion occupy the six hybrid orbitals. Thus, the complex has octahedral geometry (sp^3d^2) and is paramagnetic because of the presence of four unpaired electrons.

2. Tetrahedral Complexes

In tetrahedral complexes, one s and three p-orbitals are hybridised to form four equivalent orbitals oriented tetrahedrally. Let us take an example to explain tetrahedral complexes.

$[NiCl_4]^{2-}$ In this complex ion, oxidation state of Ni is +2 and its valence shell configuration is $[Ar]^{18} 3d^8$.

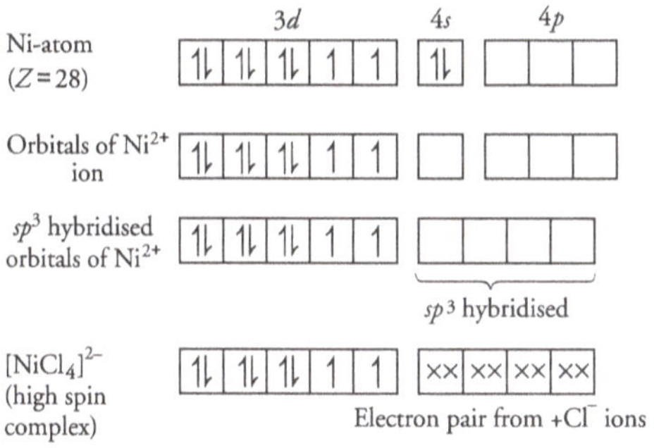

Each Cl^- ion donates a pair of electrons. The compound is paramagnetic, because it contains two unpaired electrons. Similarly, $[Ni(CO)_4]$ has tetrahedral geometry but it is diamagnetic because nickel is in zero oxidation state and contains no unpaired electrons.

3. Square Planar Complexes

Square planar complexes involve one d, one s and two p-orbitals for bonding. The hybridisation involved is dsp^2. Let us take an example to understand it clearly.

e.g. $[Ni(CN)_4]^{2-}$ has square planar shape.

Ni atom (ground state) $=[Ar] 3d^8, 4s^2, 4p^0$

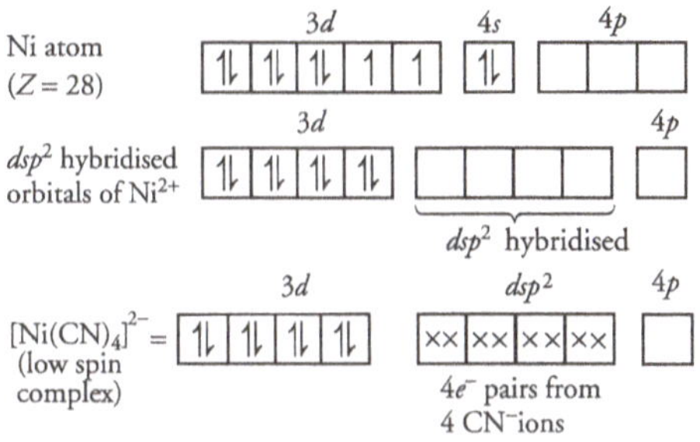

Each of the hybridised orbitals receive a pair of e^-s from CN^- ion. The compound is diamagnetic.

Magnetic Properties of Coordination Compounds

Magnetic nature of coordination compounds is due to the presence of unpaired electrons in molecules. The magnetic moment of coordination compounds can be measured by the magnetic susceptibility experiments. The results can be used to obtain information about the structures of metal complexes. Spin only magnetic moment (μ) can be calculated as $=\sqrt{n(n+2)}$ B.M.

where, n is the number of unpaired electrons.

Some complications revealed on the basis of critical study of magnetic data of coordination compounds are as follows:

(i) For metal ions upto three electrons in d-orbital (Ti^{3+}, V^{3+}, Cr^{3+}), two vacant d-orbitals are available for octahedral hybridisation using $4s$ and $4p$-orbitals. The magnetic behaviour of these free ions and their coordination entities is similar.

(ii) When more than three $3d$ electrons are present, the required pair of $3d$ orbitals for octahedral hybridisation are not directly available because of Hund's rule, e.g. for d^4 (Cr^{2+}, Mn^{3+}), d^5 (Mn^{2+}, Fe^{3+}), d^6(Fe^{2+}, Co^{3+}) cases, a vacant pair of d-orbitals result only by pairing of $3d$ electrons which leaves two, one and zero unpaired electrons, respectively.

(iii) The magnetic data agree with maximum spin pairing in many cases with coordination compound containing d^6 ions. However, with species containing d^4 and d^5 ions have complications.

Some examples are given below :

- $[Mn(CN)_6]^{3-}$ has magnetic moment of two unpaired electrons while $[MnCl_6]^{3-}$ has a paramagnetic moment of four unpaired electrons.

- $[Fe(CN)_6]^{3-}$ has paramagnetic moment of one unpaired electron while $[FeF_6]^{3-}$ has a paramagnetic moment of five unpaired electrons.

This is explained by VBT in terms of formation of inner orbital (d^2sp^3 hybridisation) and outer orbital (sp^3d^2hybridisation) coordination entities. $[Mn(CN)_6]^{3-}$, $[Fe(CN)_6]^{3-}$ and $[Co(C_2O_4)_3]^{3-}$ are inner orbital complexes. While $[MnCl_6]^{3-}$, $[FeF_6]^{3-}$ and $[CoF_6]^{3-}$ are outer orbital complex.

Limitations of VBT

Although valence bond theory is advantageous to explain formation, structures and magnetic properties of coordination compounds but it comes with few limitations, listed as follows:

(i) It is based on the number of assumptions.

(ii) It does not distinguish between weak and strong ligands.

(iii) It does not give quantitative interpretations of magnetic data.

(iv) It does not give a quantitative interpretation of the thermodynamic or kinetic stabilities of coordination compounds.

(v) It fails to explain relative energies of different shapes.

(vi) It does not explain the colour and spectral properties of the 4-coordination compounds.

(vii) It fails to predict the exact tetrahedral and square planar structures of 4-coordinate complexes.

Description of Some Important Metal Complexes Using VBT

Ion/Complex	Central metal ion	Configuration of metal ion	Hybridisation of metal ion involved	Geometry of the complex	Number of unpaired electrons	Magnetic behaviour
$[Ti(H_2O)_6)]^{3+}$	Ti^{3+}	d^1	d^2sp^3	Octahedral	1	Paramagnetic
$[V(H_2O)_6]^{3+}$	V^{3+}	d^2	d^2sp^3	Octahedral	2	Paramagnetic
$[Cr(H_2O)_6]^{3+}$	Cr^{3+}	d^3	d^2sp^3	Octahedral	3	Paramagnetic
$[Cr(NH_3)_6]^{3+}$	Cr^{3+}	d^3	d^2sp^3	Octahedral	3	Paramagnetic
$[MnF_6]^{3-}$	Mn^{3+}	d^4	sp^3d^2	Octahedral	4	Paramagnetic
$[Mn(CN)_6]^{3-}$	Mn^{3+}	d^4	d^2sp^3	Octahedral	2	Paramagnetic
$[MnCl_4]^{2-}$	Mn^{2+}	d^5	sp^3	Tetrahedral	5	Paramagnetic
$[FeF_6]^{3-}$	Fe^{3+}	d^5	sp^3d^2	Octahedral	5	Paramagnetic
$[Fe(H_2O)_6]^{3+}$	Fe^{3+}	d^5	sp^3d^2	Octahedral	5	Paramagnetic
$[Fe(CN)_6]^{3-}$	Fe^{3+}	d^5	d^2sp^3	Octahedral	1	Paramagnetic
$[Fe(CN)_6]^{4-}$	Fe^{2+}	d^6	d^2sp^3	Octahedral	0	Diamagnetic
$[FeCl_4]^{2-}$	Fe^{2+}	d^6	sp^3	Tetrahedral	4	Paramagnetic
$[Co(NH_3)_6]^{3+}$	Co^{3+}	d^6	d^2sp^3	Octahedral	0	Diamagnetic
$[CoF_6]^{3-}$	Co^{3+}	d^6	sp^3d^2	Octahedral	4	Paramagnetic
$[Ni(CO)_4]$	Ni	$3d^8,4s^2$	sp^3	Tetrahedral	0	Diamagnetic
$[Ni(CN)_4]^{2+}$	Ni^{2+}	d^8	dsp^2	Square planar	0	Diamagnetic
$[NiCl_4]^{2-}$	Ni^{2+}	d^8	sp^3	Tetrahedral	2	Paramagnetic
$[Ni(H_2O)_6]^{2+}$	Ni^{2+}	d^8	sp^3d^2	Octahedral	2	Paramagnetic
$[CuCl_4]^{2+}$	Cu^{2+}	d^9	sp^3	Tetrahedral	1	Paramagnetic
$[Zn(NH_3)_4]^{2+}$	Zn^{2+}	d^{10}	sp^3	Tetrahedral	0	Diamagnetic
$[Pt(NH_3)Cl_2]$	Pt^{2+}	d^2	dsp^2	Square planar	0	Diamagnetic

Crystal Field Theory(CFT)

This theory was proposed by H. Bethe and van Vleck in 1930. L. Orgel in 1952, gave a much more satisfactory explanation for the bonding and the properties of complexes. The crystal field theory (CFT) is an electrostatic model which considers the metal-ligand bond to be ionic arising purely from electrostatic interactions between the metal ion and the ligand.

The main points of this theory are as follows:

(i) The transition metal ion is surrounded by the ligands with lone pairs of electrons and the complex is a combination of central ion surrounded by other ions or molecules or dipoles, e.g. ligands.

(ii) All types of ligands are regarded as point charges in case of anions and as dipoles in case of neutral molecules.

(iii) The interactions between the metal ion and the negative ends of anion (or ion dipoles) is purely electrostatic, i.e. the bond between the metal and ligand is considered to be 100% ionic.

(iv) The ligands surrounding the metal ion produce electrical field and this electrical field influences the energies of the orbitals of central metal ion, particularly *d*-orbitals.

(v) In the case of free metal ion, all five *d*-orbitals have the same energy. Orbitals having the same energies are called degenerate orbitals.

(vi) The five degenerate *d*-orbitals of the metal ion split into different sets of orbital having different energies in the presence of electrical field of ligands. This is called **crystal field splitting**.

(vii) The crystals field splitting will be different in different
structures having different coordination numbers.

(viii) To understand the crystal field theory, it is essential to understand the disposition of the five *d*-orbitals in space and the geometrical arrangement of the ligands around the central metal ion. This concept can be illustrated with the complexes having coordination number 6 and 4 (which are very common).

Crystal Field Splitting in Octahedral Coordination Entities

(i) In an octahedral coordination entity with six ligands surrounding the metal atom/ion, there will be repulsion between the electrons in metal *d*-orbitals and the electrons (or negative charges) of the ligands.

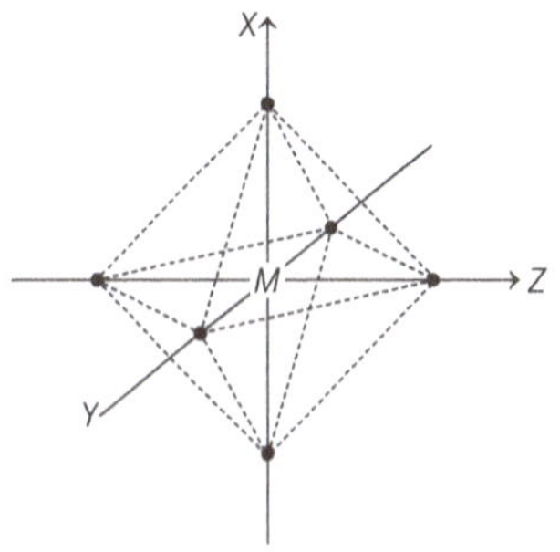

Six ligands at the corners of an octaheadron surrounding the metal ion M^{n+}

(ii) Thus, the $d_{x^2-y^2}$ and d_{z^2} orbitals which point towards the axis along the direction of the ligand will experience more repulsion and will be raised in energy and the d_{xy}, d_{zx} and d_{yz} orbitals which are directed between the axis will be lowered in energy relative to the average energy in the spherical crystal field.

(iii) Thus, the degeneracy of the *d*-orbitals has been removed due to ligand-metal electron repulsions in the octahedral complex to yield three orbitals of lower energy, t_{2g} set and two orbitals of higher energy, e_g set. This splitting of the degenerate levels due to the presence of ligands in a definite geometry is termed as crystal field splitting and it is denoted by Δ_o (the subscript *o* is for octahedral).

(iv) The difference of energy between the two sets of degenerate orbitals as a result of crystal field splitting is known as **Crystal Field Stabilisation Energy** (CFSE) and it is denoted by Δ_o (the subscript *o* is for octahedral).

(v) Thus, the energy of the two e_g orbitals will increase by (3/5) Δ_o and that of the three t_{2g} will decrease by (2/5)Δ_o.

The splitting of *d*-orbitals in an octahedral crystal field can be seen in following diagram.

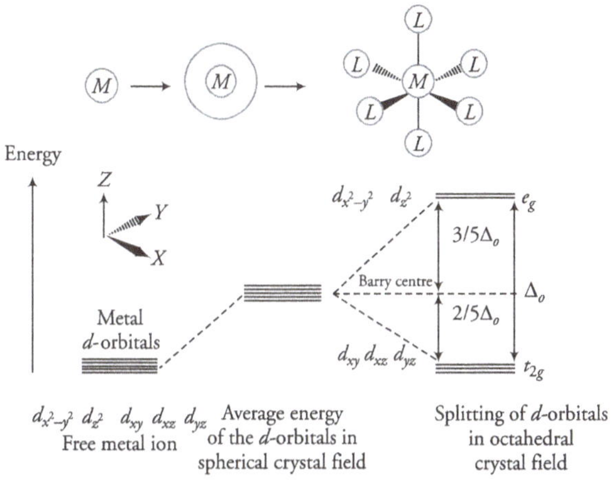

d-orbital splitting in an octahedral crystal field

Here, CFSE can be calculated as:

$$CFSE = [-0.4x + 0.6y]\Delta_o$$

Where, Δ_o = CFS in octahedral complex

x = Number of electrons in t_{2g} orbitals

y = Number of unpaired electrons in e_g orbitals

Spectrochemical Series

The crystal field splitting, Δ_o, depends upon the field produced by the ligand and charge on the metal ion. Some ligands are able to produce strong fields in which, the splitting will be large whereas others produce weak fields and consequently result in small splitting of *d*-orbitals.

So, ligands can be arranged in a series in the order of increasing field strength. This series is known as spectrochemical series.

e.g. $I^- < Br^- < SCN^- < Cl^- < S^{2-} < F^- < OH^- < C_2O_4^{2-}$
$< H_2O < NCS^- < EDTA^{4-} < NH_3 < en < CN^- < CO$

It is an experimentally determined series, based on the absorption of light by complexes with different ligands.

Upto d^3, electrons are filled according to Aufbau principle and Hund's rule. For d^4 ions, two possible patterns of electron distribution arise:

(i) The fourth electron could either enter the t_{2g} level and pair with an existing electron, or

(ii) It could avoid paying the price of the pairing energy by occupying the e_g level.

These possibilities depend on the relative magnitude of the crystal field splitting, Δ_o and the pairing energy, P (P represents the energy required for electron pairing in a single orbital). The two options are given below:

If $\Delta_o < P$, it will be a high spin complex. If $\Delta_o > P$, it will be a low spin complex. Strong field ligands form low spin complexes. Weak field ligands form high spin complex. Calculations show that d^4 to d^7 coordination entities are more stable for strong field as compared to weak field cases.

Crystal Field Splitting in Tetrahedral Coordination Entities

For tetrahedral complex, coordination number is four (4) i.e. four ligands are present around the central atom at alternate corners of the imaginary cube (as shown in the fig).

Four ligands around the metal-ion in tetrahedral cube.

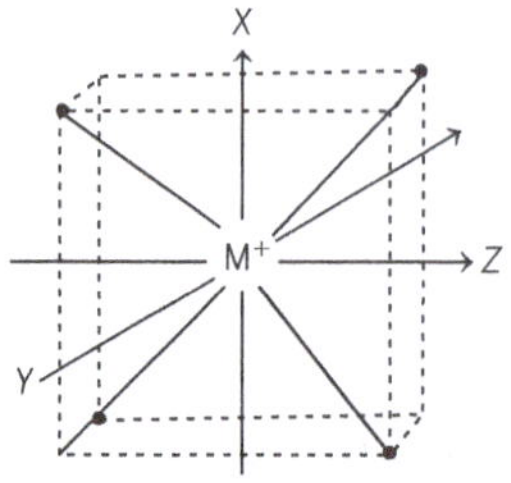

Four ligands around the metal-ion in tetrahedral cube

In tetrahedral coordination entity formation, the *d*-orbital splitting is inverted and is smaller as compared to the octahedral field splitting.

It can be easily illustrated from the given figure.

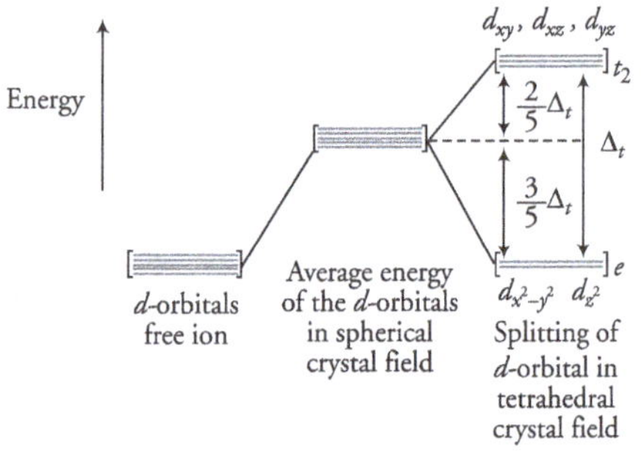

d-orbital splitting in a tetrahedral crystal field

Here, CFSE can be calculated as:

$$CFSE = [-0.6x + 0.4y]\Delta_t$$

Where, Δ_t = CFS in tetrahedral complex

x = Number of electons in *e*-orbitals.

y = Number of electrons in t_2-orbitals.

For the same metal, the same ligands and metal-ligand bond distances, it can be shown that $\Delta_t = (4/9)\Delta_o$. Consequently, the orbital splitting energies are not sufficiently large for forcing pairing and, therefore, low spin configurations for tetrahedral complexes are rarely observed.

Colour in Coordination Compounds

When light of certain frequency falls on the complex, it absorbs light from visible range for transition of electron from lower to higher level. Colour of the compound is complementary to the colour of absorbed light. This is known as *d-d* transition.

e.g. The complex $[Ti(H_2O)_6]^{3+}$ appears violet in colour due to the transition of electron from t_{2g} level to the e_g level ($t_{2g}^1 e_g^0 \rightarrow t_{2g}^0 e_g^1$).

It can be easily understood by following energy diagram

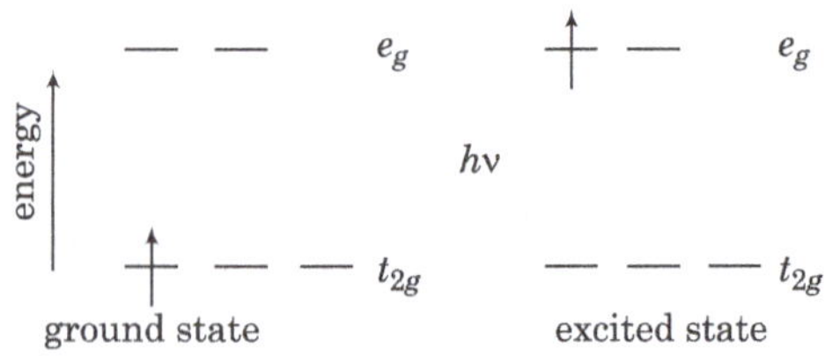

Transition of an electron in $Ti(H_2O)_6]^{3+}$

It is important to note that in the absence of ligand, crystal field splitting does not occur and hence the substance is colourless, e.g. anhydrous $CuSO_4$ is white, while $CuSO_4 \cdot 5H_2O$ is blue.

Effect of Ligand on the Colour of a Complex

Ligand plays an important role in exhibiting the colour to the complex. This can be easily illustrated by considering the example of $[Ni(H_2O_6]^{2+}$ complex which forms when nickel (II) chloride is dissolved in water. If the didendate ligand, ethane –1, 2– diamine (en) is progressively added in the molar ratio en : Ni, 1 : 1, 2 : 1, 3 : 1; complexes with different colours were formed.

Limitations of CFT

CFT is successful in explaining the colour, magnetic properties, the effects of weak and strong field ligands in coordination compounds.

However, it has the following limitations:

(i) As the ligands are point charges, the anionic ligands should exert the greatest splitting effect. Actually, the anionic ligands are found at the low end of the spectrochemical series.

(ii) CFT treats the metal-ligand bond as purely ionic and it does not take into account the covalent character of bonding between the ligand and the central atom.

Note Valence bond theory consider the *M*—*L* bond as covalent while crystal field theory consider the *M*—*L* bond to be ionic.

Topic Practice 2

Very Short Answer Type Questions

(1 Mark)

1. Fill in the Blanks

(i) According to valence bond theory, the outer octahedral complex has .... hybridisation.

(ii) Outer orbital complexes involve .... hybridisation and are ...... spin complexes. **ISC 2020**

(iii) Square planar complex's show .... hybridisation.

(iv) According to crystal field splitting strong field ligands form .... spin complex.

(v) Field strength of Cl^- is .... than that of NH_3 as ligand.

2. Objective Type Questions

(i) The metal complex ion that is paramagnetic is (Atomic number of Fe = 26, Cu = 29, Co = 27 and Ni = 28)

(a) $[Fe(CN)_4]^{2-}$ (b) $[Co(NH_3)_6]^{3+}$
(c) $[Ni(CN)_4]^{2-}$ (d) $[Cu(NH_3)_4]^{2+}$ **ISC 2024**

(ii) The complex ion $[Ni(CN)_4]^{2-}$ is

(a) square planar and diamagnetic
(b) tetrahedral and paramagnetic
(c) square planar and paramagnetic
(d) tetrahedral and diamagnetic **ISC 2017**

(iii) Which one of the following complex is an outer orbital complex? (Atomic number : Mn = 25, Fe= 24, Co = 27, Ni = 28)

(a) $[Fe(CN)_6]^{4-}$ (b) $[Mn(CN)_6]^{6-}$
(c) $[Co(NH_3)_6]^{3+}$ (d) $[Ni(NH_3)_6]^{3+}$

(iv) In which of following octahedral complexes of Co (atomic number = 27), will have highest magnitude of Δ_o?

(a) $[Co(CN)_6]^{3-}$ (b) $[Co(C_2O_4)_3]^{3-}$
(c) $[Co(H_2O)_6]^{3+}$ (d) $[Co(NH_3)_6]^{3+}$

(v) For an octahedral complex, which of the following *d*-electron configuration will give maximum CFSE?

(a) High spin d^6 (b) Low spin d^4
(c) Low spin d^5 (d) High spin d^7

(vi) Among $Ni(CO)_4$, $[Ni(CN)_4]^{2-}$, $[NiCl_4]^{2-}$ species, the hybridisation states of the Ni atom are respectively (Atomic number of Ni = 28)

(a) sp^3, dsp^2, dsp^2 (b) sp^3, dsp^2, sp^3
(c) sp^3, sp^3, dsp^2 (d) dsp^2, sp^3, sp

(vii) The hybridisation of the iron atom in $[Fe(CN)_6]^{3-}$ complex is **ISC 2010**

(a) sp^3 (b) d^2sp^3
(c) sp^3d^2 (d) dsp^2

3. Match Column I with Column II and choose the correct option using the codes given below :

Column I (Species)		Column II (Hybridisation)	
(A)	$[V(H_2O)_6]^{3+}$	(i)	dsp^2
(B)	$[FeF_6]^{3-}$	(ii)	sp^3
(C)	$[FeCl_4]^{2-}$	(iii)	sp^3d^2
(D)	$[Ni(CN)_4]^{2+}$	(iv)	d^2sp^3

Codes

	A	B	C	D
(a)	(i)	(ii)	(iii)	(iv)
(b)	(iv)	(iii)	(ii)	(i)
(c)	(iii)	(iv)	(ii)	(i)
(d)	(iv)	(iii)	(i)	(ii)

4. State the hybridisation and magnetic property of $[Fe(CN)_6]^{3-}$ ion according to the valence bond theory. **ISC 2015**

5. For the complex ion of $[Co(NH_3)_6]^{3+}$
   (i) state the hybridisation of the complex.
   (ii) state the magnetic nature of the complex.

6. For the complex ion $[Fe(CN)_6]^{3-}$, state
   (i) the geometry of the ion.
   (ii) the magnetic property of the ion. **ISC 2013**

Short Answer Type I Questions

2 Marks

7. Why do compounds having similar geometry have different magnetic moment? **NCERT Exemplar**

8. On the basis of crystal field theory, explain why Co(III) forms paramagnetic octahedral complex with weak field ligands whereas it forms diamagnetic octahedral complex with strong field ligands. **NCERT Exemplar**

9. Why are different colours observed in octahedral and tetrahedral complex for the same metal and same ligands? **NCERT Exemplar**

10. $[CoF_6]^{3-}$ is a coordination complex ion
    (i) What is the oxidation number of cobalt in the complex?
    (ii) How many unpaired electrons are there in the complex?
    (iii) State the magnetic behaviour of the complex.
    (iv) Give the IUPAC name of the complex. **ISC 2012**

11. For the coordination complex ion $[Co(NH_3)_6]^{3+}$.
    (i) Give the IUPAC name of the complex ion.
    (ii) What is the oxidation number of cobalt in the complex ion?
    (iii) State the type of hybridisation of the complex ion.
    (iv) State the magnetic behaviour of the complex ion. **ISC 2017**

12. What is the relationship between observed colour of the complex and the wavelength of light absorbed by the complex? **NCERT Exemplar**

Short Answer Type II Questions

3 Marks

13. Using the valence bond approach, predict the shape, hybridisation and magnetic behaviour of $[Ni(CO)_4]$. (Atomic number of Ni = 28) **ISC 2020**

14. Explain on the basis of valence bond theory that $[Ni(CN)_4]^{2-}$ ion with square planar structure is diamagnetic and the $[NiCl_4]^{2-}$ ion with tetrahedral geometry is paramagnetic. **NCERT Intext**

15. Explain $[Co(NH_3)_6]^{3+}$ is an inner orbital complex whereas $[Ni(NH_3)_6]^{2+}$ is an outer orbital complex. **NCERT Intext**

16. Predict the number of unpaired electrons in the square planar $[Pt(CN)_4]^{2-}$ ion. **NCERT Intext**

17. Amongst the following ions which one has the highest magnetic moment value?
    (i) $[Cr(H_2O)_6]^{3+}$ (ii) $[Fe(H_2O)_6]^{2+}$
    (iii) $[Zn(H_2O)_6]^{2+}$ **NCERT**

18. $[NiCl_4]^{2-}$ is paramagnetic while $[Ni(CO)_4]$ is diamagnetic though both are tetrahedral. Why? **NCERT Intext**

19. $[Cr(NH_3)_6]^{3+}$ is paramagnetic while $[Ni(CN)_4]^{2-}$ is diamagnetic. Why? **NCERT**

20. (i) Write the formula of the following coordination compound:
    Iron (III) hexacyanoferrate(II)
    (ii) What type of isomerism is exhibited by the complex $[Co(NH_3)_5Cl]SO_4$?
    (iii) Write the hybridisation and number of unpaired electrons in the complex $[CoF_6]^{3-}$. (Atomic number of Co = 27)

21. (i) For the complex ion $[Fe(CN)_6]^{3-}$, state
    (a) the type of hybridisation.
    (b) the magnetic behaviour
    (c) the oxidation number of the central metal atom.
    (ii) Write the IUPAC name of $[Co(en)_2Cl_2]^+$ ion and draw the structures of its geometrical isomers.

22. For the complex ion of $[Fe(CN)_6]^{3-}$
    (i) Show hybridisation diagramatically.
    (ii) Is it an inner orbital complex or an outer orbital complex?
    (iii) State its magnetic property. **ISC 2011**

23. Draw the figure to show the splitting of *d*-orbitals in an octahedral crystal field. **NCERT**

24. What is the crystal field stabilisation energy? How does the magnitude of Δ_o decide the actual configuration of *d*-orbital in a coordination entity? **NCERT**

Or What is meant by crystal field splitting energy? On the basis of crystal field theory, write the electronic configuration of d^4 in terms of t_{2g} and e_g in an octahedral field when

(i) $\Delta_o > P$ (ii) $\Delta_o < P$

25. The hexaaquamanganese (II) ion contains five unpaired electrons, while the hexacyano manganese (II) ion contains only one paired electron. Explain using crystal field theory. **NCERT Intext**

26. $[Fe(CN)_6]^{4-}$ and $[Fe(H_2O)_6]^{2+}$ are of different colours in dilute solutions. Why? **NCERT**

Long Answer Type Questions

5 Marks

27. Discuss the nature of bonding in the following coordination entities on the basis of valence bond theory. **NCERT**

(i) $[Fe(CN)_6]^{4-}$ (ii) $[FeF_6]^{3-}$

(iii) $[Co(C_2O_4)_3]^{3-}$ (iv) $[CoF_6]^{3-}$

28. Write down the IUPAC name for each of the following complexes and indicate the oxidation state, electronic configuration and coordination number. Also give stereochemistry and magnetic moment of the complex.

(i) $K[Cr(H_2O)_2(C_2O_4)_2]\cdot 3H_2O$

(ii) $[Co(NH_3)_5Cl]Cl_2$

(iii) $[CrCl_3(py)_3]$

(iv) $Cs[FeCl_4]$

(v) $K_4[Mn(CN)_6]$ **NCERT**

Hints & Explanations

1. (i) sp^3d^2 (ii) sp^3d^2, high (iii) dsp^2 (iv) low spin (v) less

2. (i) (d) The $[Cu(NH_3)_4]^{2+}$ complex is paramagnetic as Cu^{2+} has d^4 configuration.

(ii) (a) Square planar and diamagnetic.

(iii) (d) The complex in which *nd*-orbitals are used in hybridisation are called outer orbital complex.

$[Ni(NH_3)_6]^{2+}$ =

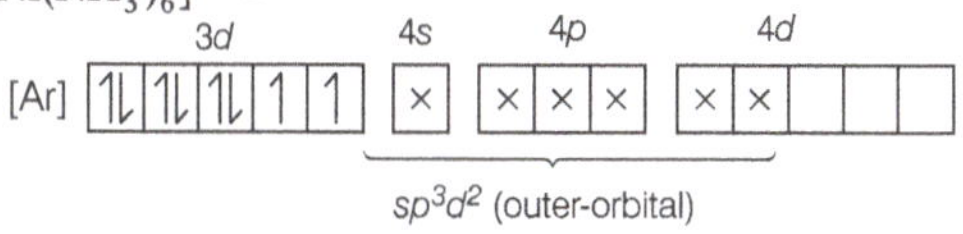

(iv) (a) CFSE (crystal field splitting energy) for octahedral complex, Δ_o depends on the strength of negative ligand. As CN^- is strongest ligand among all.

Therefore, magnitude of Δ_o will be highest in case of $[Co(CN)_6]^{3-}$.

(v) (c) $\Delta_o = -0.4 \times n_{t_{2g}} + 0.6 \times n_{e_g}$

[where, n=number of electrons]

(i) For high spin d^6, Δ_o (CFSE) $= -0.4\times4 + 0.6\times2 = -0.4$

(ii) For low spin d^4, Δ_o(CFSE) $= -0.4\times4 + 0.6\times0 = 1.6$

For low spin d^5, Δ_o(CFSE) $= -0.4\times5 + 0.6\times0 = -2.0$

For high spin d^7, Δ_o(CFSE) $= -0.4\times5 + 0.6\times2 = -0.8$

The calculations reveal that maximum CFSE is for low spin d^5 configuration.

(vi) (b) In $Ni(CO)_4$, Ni is sp^3-hybridised. Its oxidation state is zero. CO is strong field ligand so it causes pairing. It is diamagnetic. In $[Ni(CN)_4]^{2-}$, nickel is in +2 oxidation state and CN^- also causes pairing of electrons hence, it is dsp^2-hybridised and diamagnetic. In $[NiCl_4]^{2-}$, Ni is in 2+ oxidation state. Cl^- is weak field ligand. It does not cause pairing hence it is sp^3-hybridised and paramagnetic.

(vii) (b) Coordination number of complex is 6. So, hybridisation could be d^2sp^3 or sp^3d^2 but as CN^- is a strong field ligand, hence will form inner orbital complex. Hence, option (b) is correct.

3. (b) (A) → (iv), (B) → (iii), (C) → (ii), (D) → (i)

4. In $[Fe(CN)_6]^{3-}$, Fe^{3+} has electronic configuration of $3d^5 4s^0$.

Fe^{3+}

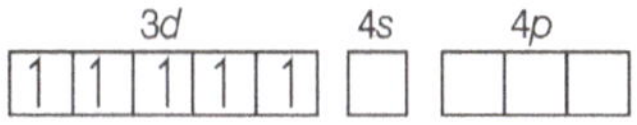

As CN^- is a strong ligand, it causes pairing of electrons.

$[Fe(CN)_6]^{3-}$

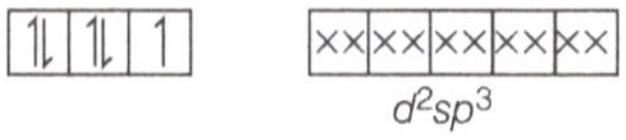

has d^2sp^3-hybridisation and octahedral structure and shows paramagnetic character due to the presence of unpaired electron. **(1)**

5. **Oxidation number of Co in the complex** $[Co(NH_3)_6]^{3+}$ is $x + 6\times(0) = +3$, $x = +3$

Electronic configuration of Co is $[Ar]3d^7 4s^2$.

Co atom

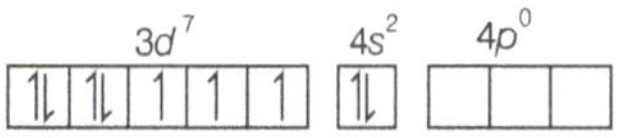

Co^{3+} ion

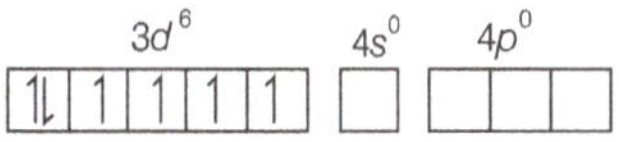

NH_3 is a strong field ligand, it causes pairing of $3d^6$ electrons.

Thus, Co^{3+} ion

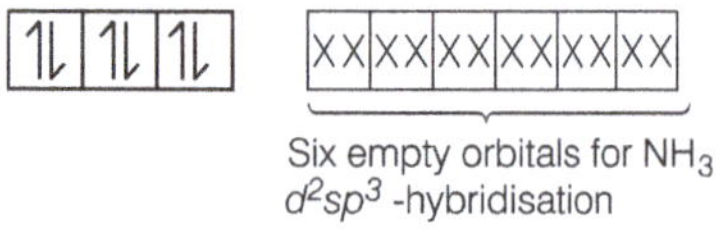

(i) Coordination number of the complex is 6. Hence, hybridisation is d^2sp^3. (½)

(ii) All electrons are paired. So, it is diamagnetic. (½)

6. **Oxidation number of Fe in the complex,** $[Fe(CN)_6]^{3-}$ is $\quad x + 6(-1) = -3 \Rightarrow \quad x = +3$

Electronic configuration of Fe is $[Ar]3d^6\, 4s^2$.

Fe atom

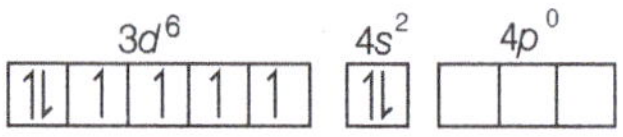

Fe^{3+} ion

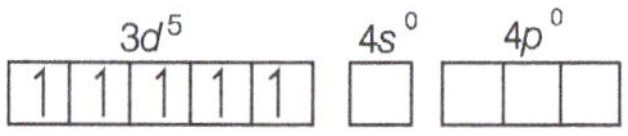

CN^- being strong field ligand, paired up the d-electrons of the metal. Thus,

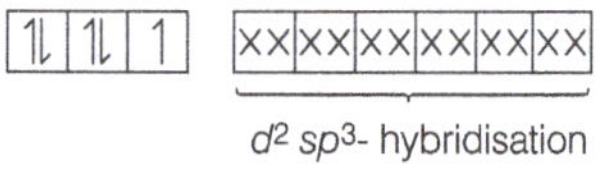

(i) Coordination number of the complex is 6. Hence, hybridisation is d^2sp^3, so geometry is octahedral. (1\2)

(ii) Since, there is one unpaired electron, so it is paramagnetic. (1\2)

7. It is due to the presence of weak or strong field ligands in complexes. If CFS is high, the complex will show low value of magnetic moment and *vice-versa*, e.g. $[CoF_6]^{3-}$ and $[Co(NH_3)_6]^{3+}$, the former is paramagnetic, and the latter is diamagnetic because F^- is a weak field ligand and NH_3 is a strong field ligand while both have similar geometry.

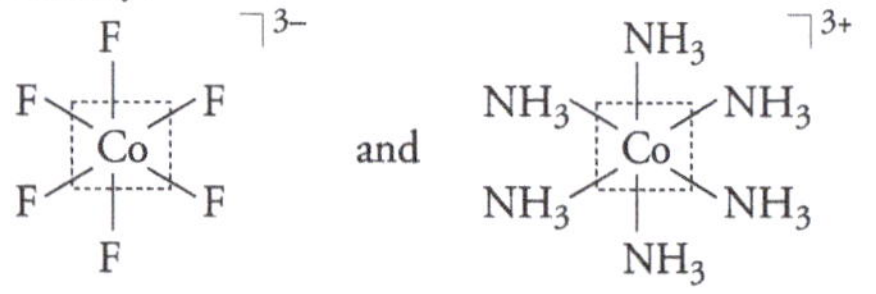

(2)

8. With weak field ligands, $\Delta_o < P$, (pairing energy) so, the electronic configuration of Co (III) will be $t_{2g}^4\, e_g^2$, i.e. it has 4 unpaired electrons and is paramagnetic.

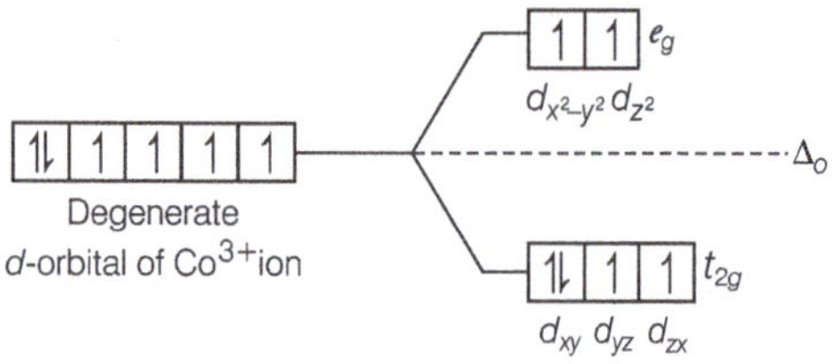

(1)

With strong field ligands $\Delta_o > P$ (pairing energy), so pairing occurs thus, the electronic configuration will be $t_{2g}^6 e_g^0$. It has no unpaired electrons and is diamagnetic.

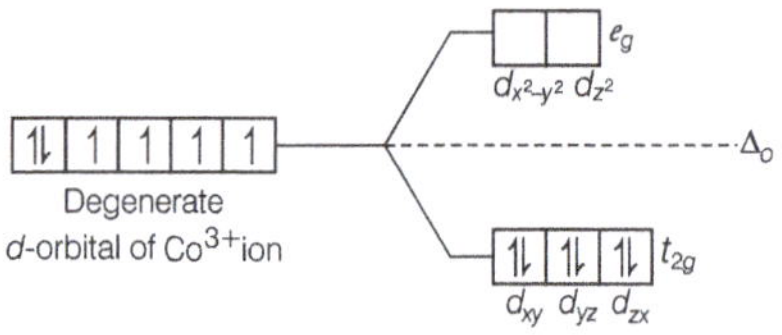

(1)

9. Extent of splitting of d-orbitals is different in octahedral and tetrahedral field. CFS in octahedral and tetrahedral are closely related as: $\Delta_t = \left(\frac{4}{9}\right)\Delta_o$

where, Δ_t = crystal field splitting in tetrahedral field
Δ_o = crystal field splitting in octahedral field Wavelength of light and CFS are related to each other by formula

$$\Delta_o = E = \frac{hc}{\lambda} \quad \Rightarrow \quad E \propto \frac{1}{\lambda}$$

So, higher wavelength of light is absorbed in octahedral complexes than tetrahedral complexes for same metal and ligands. Thus, different colours are observed. (2)

10. (i) Let the oxidation number of Co in the complex ion $[CoF_6]^{3-}$ is x, then

$$x + 6(-1) = -3 \Rightarrow x = +3$$ (½)

(ii) Electronic configuration of Co = $[Ar]\, 3d^7, 4s^2$

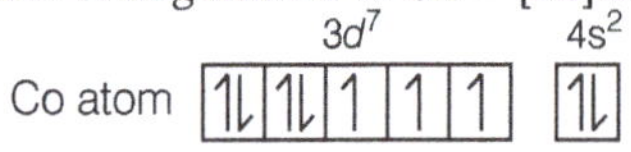

For Co^{3+} = [Ar] $3d^6$, 4s°

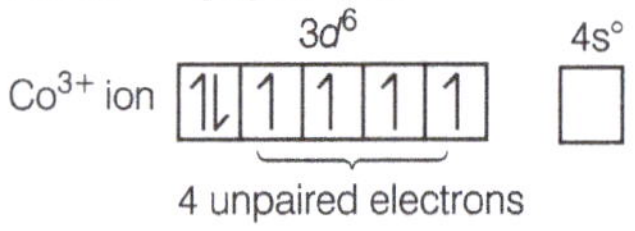

Therefore, there are 4 unpaired electrons. (½)

(iii) It contains four unpaired electrons. So, it is paramagnetic. (½)

(iv) Hexaflouridocobalt (III) ion. (½)

11. (i) Hexaammine cobalt (III) ion (½)

(ii) Oxidation number of Co in the complex $[Co(NH_3)_6]^{3+}$ is $\quad x \times 6 \times (0) = +3$ (½)

$$x = +3$$

(iii) Electronic configuration of Co is $[Ar]3d^7 4s^2$.

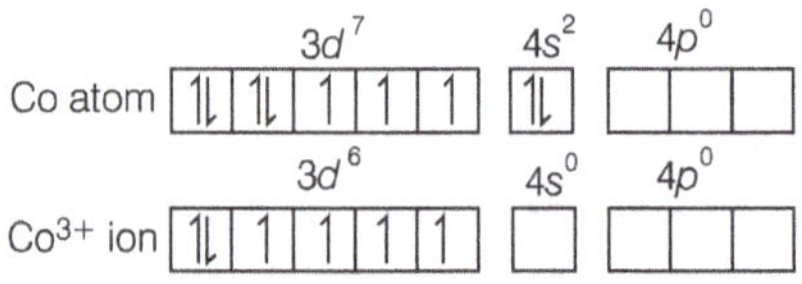

NH_3 is a strong field ligand, it causes pairing of $3d^6$ electrons. Thus,

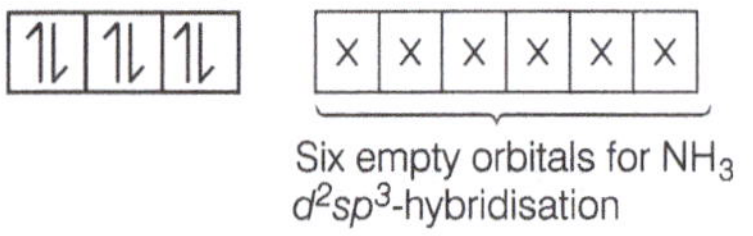

Coordination number of the complex is 6. Hence, hybridisation is d^2sp^3. (½)

(iv) All electrons are paired. So, it is diamagnetic. (½)

12. When white light falls on the complex, some part of it is absorbed. Higher the crystal field splitting, lower will be the wavelength absorbed by the complex. The observed colour of complex is the colour generated from the wavelength left over.

e.g. If green light is absorbed, the complex appears red.

In terms of crystal field theory, suppose there is an octahedral complex with empty e_g level and unpaired electrons in the t_{2g} level in ground state.

If the unpaired electron absorbs light corresponding to blue-green region, it will excite to e_g level and the complex will appear violet in colour. (2)

13. Refer to page no. 184 (Description of some important metal complexes).

14. For $[Ni(CN)_4]$: Refer to text on page 183 (Square planar complex). (½)

For $[NiCl_4]$: Refer to text on page 183 (Tetrahedral complex) (1½)

15. $[Co(NH_3)_6]^{3+}$: Refer to text on pages 182 and 183 Structure and shapes of complexes on the basis of valence bond theory octahedral complexes). (1½)

$[Ni(NH_3)_6]^{2+}$ =

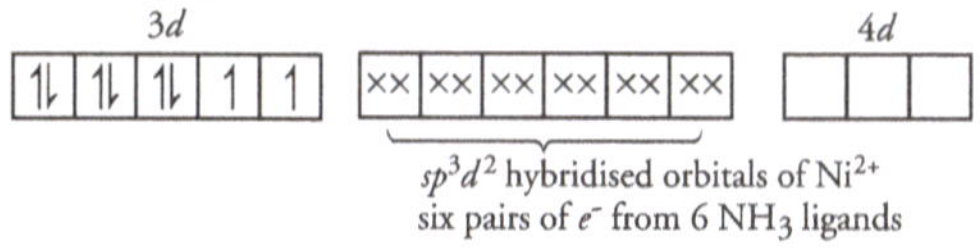

Since, $(n-1)d$-orbitals are not available. So, the nd-orbitals are used in bond formation, i.e. in hybridisation, the complex is called outer orbital complex. (1½)

16. $_{78}Pt$ is present in group 10 of the periodic table. Its outer configuration is $5d^9 6s^1$. (1)

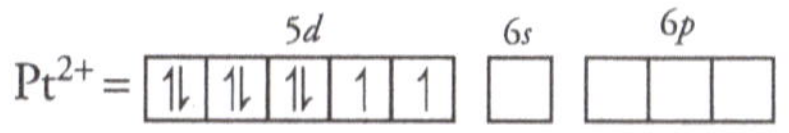

CN^- is a strong field ligand. Therefore, it causes pairing of $5d$-electrons.

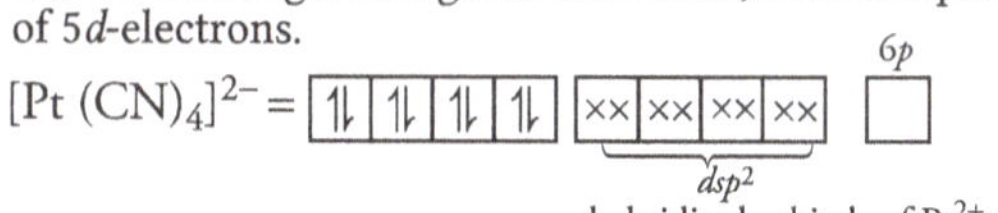

(1)

For square planar shape, the hybridisation is dsp^2. Hence, the unpaired electrons in $5d$-orbital pair up to make one d-orbital empty for dsp^2 hybridisation. Thus, there is **no unpaired electron**. (1)

17. Electronic configuration of

(i) $Cr^{3+} = 3d^3$, unpaired $e^-(n) = 3$ (1/2)

(ii) $Fe^{2+} = 3d^6$, $n = 4$ (1/2)

(iii) $Zn^{2+} = 3d^{10}$, $n = 0$ (1/2)

From, $\mu = \sqrt{n(n+2)}$ BM (1/2)

As $\mu \propto n$, therefore Fe^{2+} contains maximum number of unpaired electrons, thus has the highest magnetic moment value. (1)

18. In $[NiCl_4]^{2-}$, Ni is +2 oxidation state with the configuration in $3d^8 4s^0$. Cl^- is a weak ligand. It cannot pair up the electrons in 3d orbitals. Hence, it is paramagnetic. In $[Ni(CO)_4]$, Ni is in zero oxidation state with the configuration $3d^8\ 4s^2$. In the presence of strong field ligand CO the 4s electrons shift to 3d to pair up 3d electrons. Thus, there is no unpaired electron present. Hence, it is diamagnetic. (3)

19. $[Cr(NH_3)_6]^{3+}$, Cr is present in + 3 oxidation state with electronic configuration $3d^3 4s^0$ are available for hybridisation, therefore no pairing will occur in this case.

Cr^{3+}

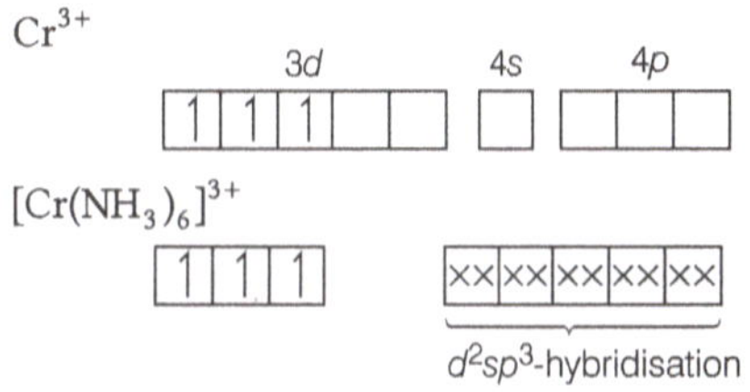

As it contains three unpaired electrons so it is paramagnetic in nature. **(1½)**

For $[Ni(CN)_4]^{2-}$ refer to text on page 183 (square planar complexes). (1½)

20. (i) Iron (III) hexacyanoferrate (II) has formula– $Fe_4[Fe(CN)_6]_3$. (1)

(ii) $[Co(NH_3)_5Cl]SO_4$ exhibit ionisation isomers. Its ionisation isomer is $[Co(NH_3)_5SO_4]Cl$. (1)

(iii) $[CoF_6]^{3-}$: Oxidation state of cobalt is +3.

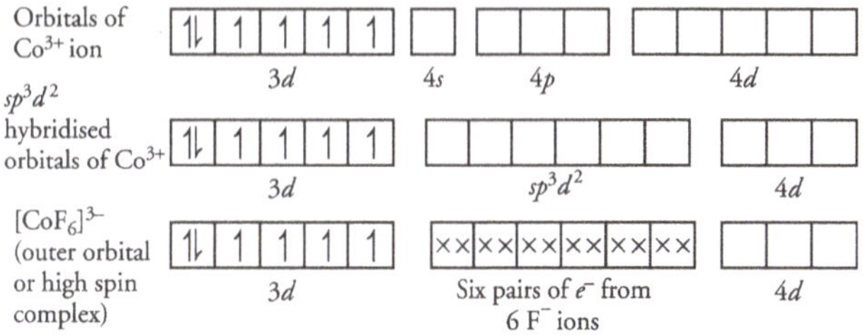

Six pairs of electrons one from each F^- ion occupy the six hybrid orbitals. Thus, the complex has octahedral geometry (sp^3d^2). (1)

21. (i) (a) In $[Fe(CN)_6]^{3-}$ complex,

Let the oxidation number of Fe is x

$\therefore x + 6(-1) = -3,\ x = +3$

Thus, Fe is present as Fe^{3+}.

Electronic configuration of $Fe^{3+} = 3d^5 4s^0$

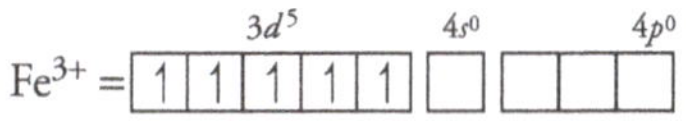

CN^- being strong field ligand, pair up the unpaired d-electrons. Thus, two $3d$-orbitals are now available for CN^- ions.

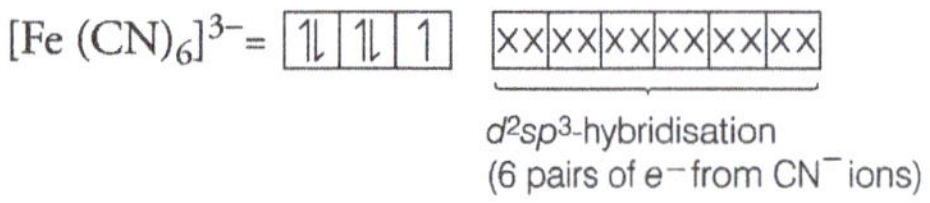

∴ The hybridisation is d^2sp^3. (½)

(b) Since, one electron remains unpaired, the complex is paramagnetic. (½)

(c) Oxidation number as calculated in (i) is +3. (½)

(ii) $[Co(en)_2Cl_2]^+$ **IUPAC name** Dichlorido *bis*-(ethane-1, 2 diamine) cobalt (III) ion. Structure of its geometrical isomers (cis and *trans*) are given below :

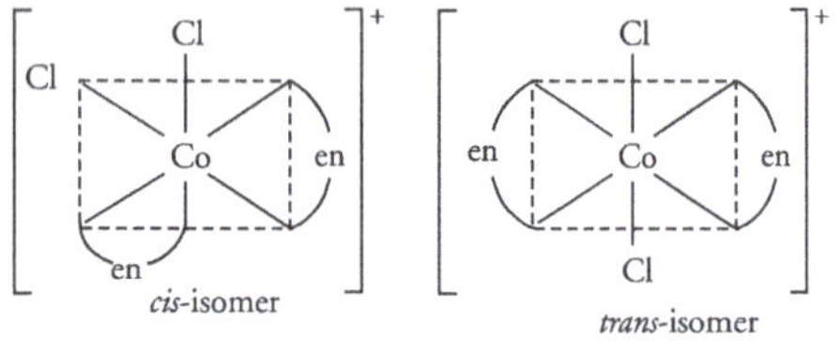

(1½)

22. (i) Let the oxidation number of Fe in the complex ion $[Fe(CN)_6]^{3-}$ be x.

Then, $x + 6(-1) = -3 \Rightarrow x = +3$

Electronic configuration

$\Rightarrow$ $Fe = [Ar]\,3d^6 4s^2$

For Fe^{3+}
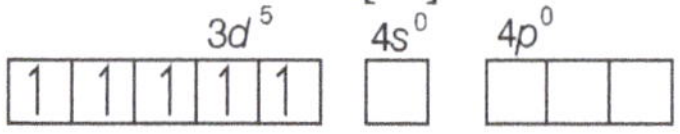

CN⁻ being strong field ligand, paired up the d-electrons of the metal

For d^2sp^3 hybridisation,

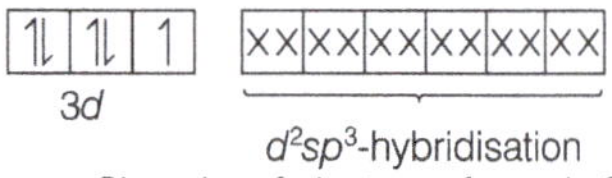

d^2sp^3-hybridisation
Six pairs of electrons from six CN^- ions (1)

(ii) It is an inner orbital complex as inner $(n-1)$ d-orbitals take part in hybridisation. (1)

(iii) It is paramagnetic due to the presence of unpaired electron. (1)

23. Refer to text on pages 185 and 186 (Crystal field splitting in octahedral coordination etities).

24. Refer to text on pages 185 and 186 (Crystal field splitting in octahedral coordination entities).

25. CN^- is a strong field ligand (thus, causes pairing) and H_2O is a weak field ligand. Mn (II) ion has $3d^5$ configuration. In the presence of H_2O molecules (acting as weak field ligand), the distribution of these five electrons in d orbitals is t_{2g}^3, e_g^2, i.e. all the electrons remain unpaired to form a high spin complex. (1)

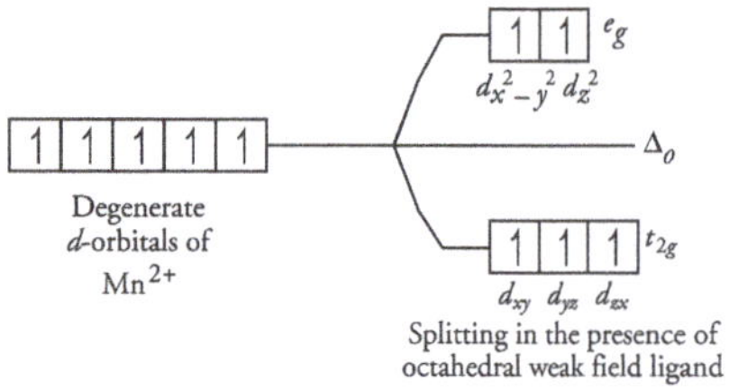

(1)

However, in the presence of CN^- (acting as strong field ligands), pairing of electronses occur and the distribution of these electrons in d-orbitals is t_{2g}^5, e_g^0, i.e. two t_{2g} orbitals contain paired electrons, while the third t_{2g} orbital contains one unpaired electron. The complex formed is a low spin complex.

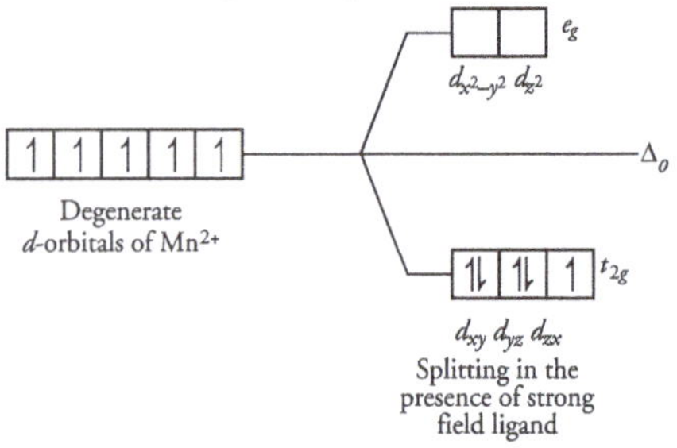

(1)

26. In both the complex compounds, Fe is in +2 oxidation state with configuration $3d^6$, i.e. it has four unpaired electrons. In the presence of weak H_2O ligands, the unpaired electrons do not pair up but in the presence of strong ligand CN^-, they get paired up. Then no unpaired electron is left. Due to this difference in the number of unpaired electrons, both complex ions have different colours.

$[Fe(H_2O)_6]$
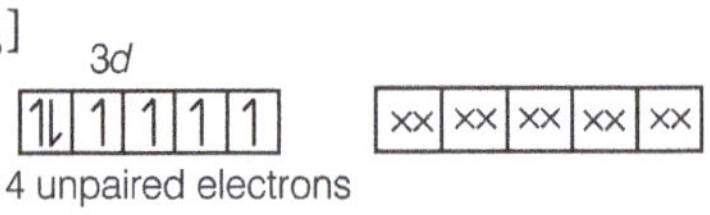

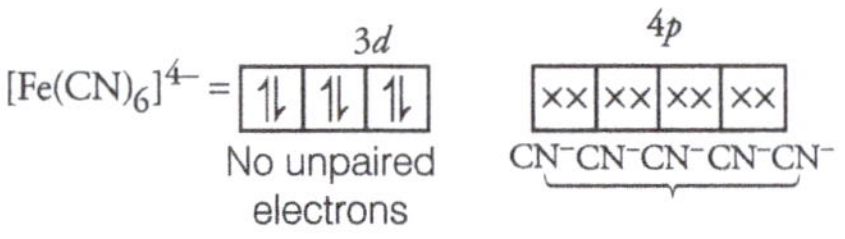

(3)

27. (i) $[Fe(CN)_6]^{4-}$: In this complex, Fe is present as Fe^{2+}.

$Fe = [Ar]\,3d^6 4s^2$

Outer configuration of $Fe^{2+} = 3d^6 4s^0$

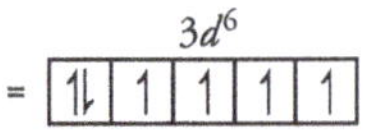

CN^- being strong field ligand, pair up the unpaired d-electrons. Thus, two $3d$-orbitals are now available for CN^- ions.

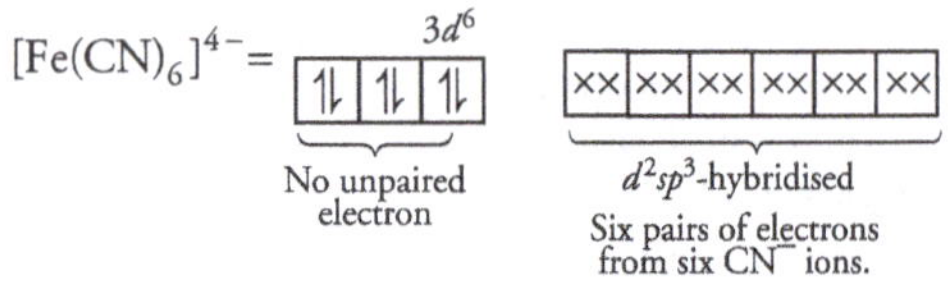

Since, all the electrons are paired, the complex is diamagnetic. Moreover, $(n-1)$ d-orbitals are involved in bonding. So, it is an inner orbital or low spin complex. (1½)

(ii) $[FeF_6]^{3-}$ In this complex, the oxidation state of Fe is + 3. $Fe^{3+} = 3d^5 4s^0$

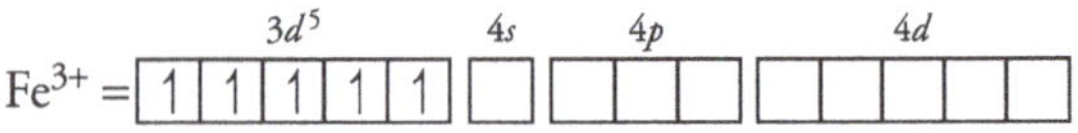

F^- is a weak field ligand, so no pairing occurs. Thus, 3*d*-orbitals are not available to take part in bonding.

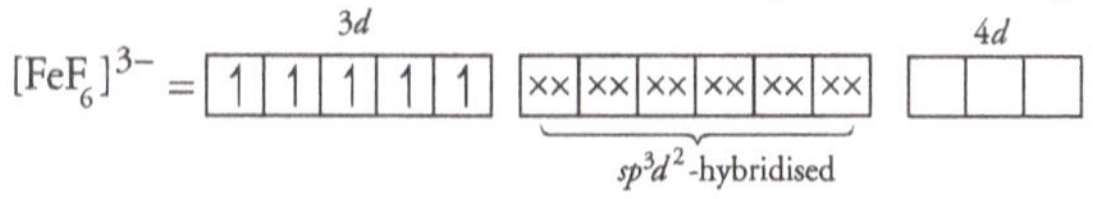

Six pairs of e^- from six F^- ions. Because of the presence of five unpaired electrons, the complex is paramagnetic. Moreover, *nd*-orbitals are involved in bonding, so it is an outer orbital or high spin complex. (1½)

(iii) $[Co(C_2O_4)_3]^{3-}$ In this complex, the oxidation state of Co is +3. Outer configuration of $Co = 3d^7 4s^2$

$$Co^{3+} = 3d^6\ 4s^0$$

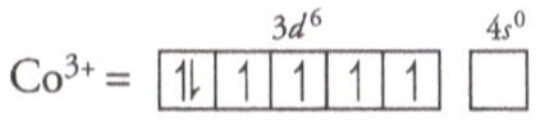

Oxalate ion being a strong field ligand pair up the 3*d*-electrons, thus two out of the five 3*d*-orbitals are available for oxalate ions.

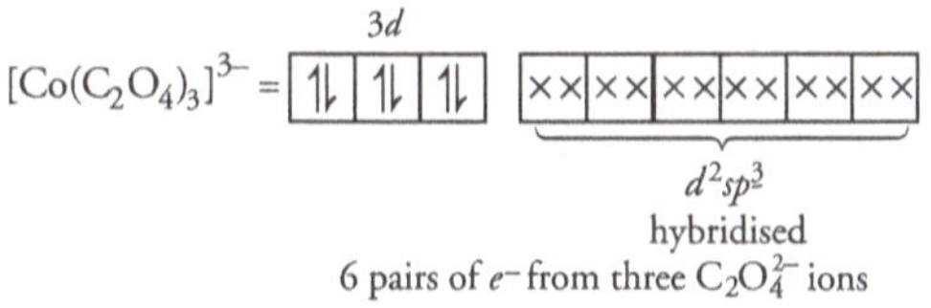

Since, all the electrons are paired, hence this complex is diamagnetic. It is an inner orbital complex because of the involvement of $(n-1)$ *d*-orbital for bonding. (1)

(iv) Refer to text on pages 182 and 183. (1)
(Structures and shapes of complexes on the basis of VBT, octahedral complexes).

28. (i) $K[Cr(H_2O)_2(C_2O_4)_2]. 3H_2O$

IUPAC name Potassium diaquadiooxalatochromate (III) hydrate; **Coordination number** (CN) = 6,

Shape = octahedral

oxidation state or Cr

$$+1 + x + (0)\times 2 + (-2)2 + 3(0) = `0 + 1 + x - 4 = 0$$
$$x = +3$$

EC of $Cr^{3+} = 3d^3 = t_{2g}^3 . e_g^0$

Unpaired electrons $(n) = 3$

Magnetic moment $(\mu) = \sqrt{n(n+2)} = \sqrt{3(3+2)} = 3.87$ BM

This complex exhibits geometrical isomerism and exists in following *cis-trans* forms.

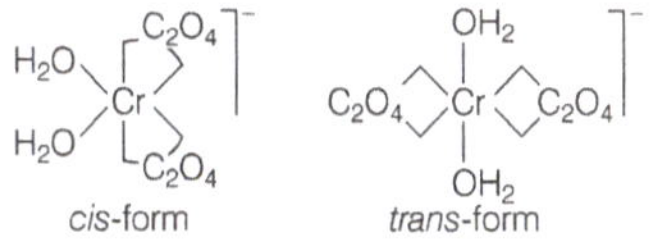

cis-form *trans*-form

cis-form can be resolved into *d* and *l*-form (i.e. optical isomers).

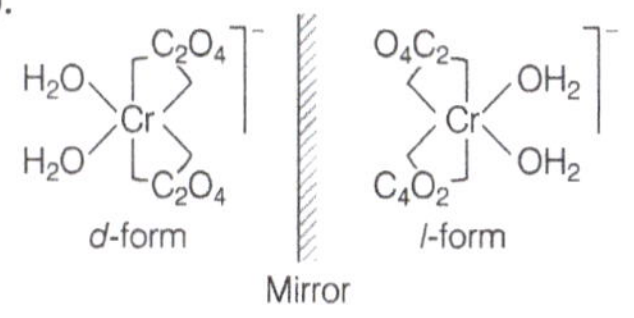

(1)

(ii) $[Co(NH_3)_5Cl]Cl_2$

IUPAC name Pentaamminechloridocobalt (III) chloride

Oxidation state of Co can be calculated as:

$$x + (0)5 + (-1) + (-1)2 = 0$$
$$x - 3 = 0$$
$$x = +3$$

Coordination number (CN) = 5 + 1 = 6 (number of monodentate ligands)

Outer electronic configuration (EN) of Co^{3+}

$$= 3d^6 = t_{2g}^6 e_g^0$$

Number of unpaired electrons, $n = 0$
(all electrons are paired).

So, **magnetic moment,** $\mu = \sqrt{n(n+2)}$ BM

$$= \sqrt{0(0+2)} \text{ BM}$$
$$= 0 \text{ BM}$$

This complex does not exhibit geometrical as well as optical isomerism. (1)

(iii) $CrCl_3(py)_3$

IUPAC name Trichloridotripyridinechromium (III)

Oxidation state of Cr $x + (-1)\times 3 + (0)3 = 0$

$$x = +3$$

Coordination number (CN) = 6

Outer electronic configuration of Cr $= 3d^3 (t_{2g}^3 e_g^0)$

Number of unpaired electrons = 3

So, **magnetic moment,** $\mu = \sqrt{n(n+2)}$ BM

$$= \sqrt{3(3+2)} = \sqrt{15} = 3.87 \text{ BM}$$

This complex exists in *fac* and *mer*-forms, i.e. exhibit geometrical isomerism. (In *fac* form, similar groups occupy adjacent positions while in *mer*- isomer the same ligands occupy position around the meridian of the octahedral).

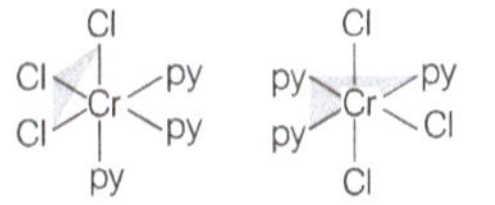

fac-form (facial form) *mer*-form (meridional form)

(iv) $Cs[FeCl_4]$

IUPAC name Caesium tetrachloridoferrate (III)

Oxidation state of Fe

$$+1 + x + (-1)4 = 0$$
$$x - 3 = 0$$
$$x = +3$$

Coordination number, (CN) = 4

Outer electronic configuration of Fe $= 3d^5 (t_{2g}^3 e_g^2)$

Number of unpaired electrons = 5

∴**Magnetic moment,** $\mu = \sqrt{n(n+2)}$ BM

$$= \sqrt{5(5+2)} = \sqrt{35} = 5.92 \text{ BM}$$

It is a tetrahedral complex, so it does not exhibit geometrical or optical isomerism. (stereoisomerism). (1)

(v) $K_4[Mn(CN)_6]$

IUPAC name Potassium hexacyanomanganate (II)

Oxidation state of Mn in $K_4[Mn(CN)_6]$

$$(+1)4 + x + (-1)6 = 0$$
$$x - 2 = 0$$
$$x = +2$$

Coordination number (CN) = 6

Outer electronic configuration of Mn $= 3d^5 [t_{2g}^5 e_g^0]$

(as CN^- is a strong field ligand)

Number of unpaired electrons = 1

Magnetic moment, $\mu = \sqrt{n(n+2)}$ BM $= \sqrt{1(1+2)}$BM

$= \sqrt{3} = 1.73$ BM

This complex does not exhibit stereoisomerism.

TOPIC 03 Stability and Significance of Coordination Compounds

Stability of Coordination Compounds

The stability of a complex or coordination compound refers to the extent upto which it exists in a solution as coordination sphere. Factors affecting the stability of complex are :

(i) **Charge on the Central Metal Ion** Greater the charge on the central metal ion, greater the stability of complex.

(ii) **Nature of the Metal Ion** Groups 3, 6 and inner transition elements form stable complexes when donor atoms of the ligands are N, O and F. The elements after group 6 of the transition metals form stable complexes when the donor atoms of the ligands are the heavier members of N, O and F family.

(iii) **Basic Nature of the Ligands** Greater the basic strength, greater is the stability of the complex.

(iv) **Presence of Chelate Rings** Its presence increases the stability of the complex. It is called chelate effect. It is maximum for the 5 and 6 membered rings. Chelating ligands form more stable complex than monodentate ligands.

(v) **Effect of Multidentate Cyclic Ligands** If the ligands are π multidentate and cyclic without any steric effect, the stability of the complex get increased.

Stability Constant

Stability of a complex is measured in terms of stability constant. It is actually the magnitude of equilibrium constant of the complex formation reaction.

It is of two types :

1. Stepwise Stability Constant

A complex is formed in a stepwise additive attachment of ligand to the metal. Equilibrium constant for every step is known as stepwise stability constant of a complex and is denoted by k_n (where, n can take any integer value from 1 to infinity).

2. Overall Stability Constant

The equilibrium constant of overall formation of complex in a reaction is called overall stability constant which denoted by K. It is given as:

$$[M(H_2O)_n] + nL \rightleftharpoons ML_n + nH_2O$$
$$K = \frac{[ML_n]}{[M(H_2O)_n][L]^n}$$

Consider the following chemical reaction

$$M + 4L \rightleftharpoons ML_4; K = [ML_4]/[M][L]^4$$

where, K is the overall stability constant. Overall stability constant is the equilibrium constant for net reaction. The stepwise stability constant can be given as:

$$M + L \rightleftharpoons ML, k_1 = [ML]/[M][L]$$
$$ML + L \rightleftharpoons ML_2, k_2 = [ML_2]/[ML][L]$$
$$ML_2 + L \rightleftharpoons ML_3, k_3 = [ML_3]/[ML_2][L]$$
$$ML_3 + L \rightleftharpoons ML_4, k_4 = [ML_4]/[ML_3][L]$$

where, k_1, k_2 etc., are referred to as stepwise stability constants.

The stepwise stability constants and overall constants are related as:

$$K = k_1 \times k_2 \times k_3 \times k_4 \text{ or more generally}$$

and $K = k_1 \times k_2 \times k_3 \times k_4 \cdots k_n$

e.g. $Cu^{2+} + NH_3 \rightleftharpoons Cu(NH_3)^{2+}$,

$$k_1 = [Cu(NH_3)^{2+}]/[Cu^{2+}][NH_3]$$

$$Cu(NH_3)^{2+} + NH_3 \rightleftharpoons Cu(NH_3)_2^{2+},$$

$$k_2 = [Cu(NH_3)_2^{2+}]/[Cu(NH_3)]^{2+}[NH_3], \text{etc.}$$

Also, $K = [Cu(NH_3)_4^{2+}]/[Cu^{2+}][NH_3]^4$

Significance of Coordination Compounds

Due to their complex structures, coordination compounds hold very important significance in the natural as well as man-made realms.

Important applications of these compounds are discussed below:

1. In Biological Systems

(i) Haemoglobin, the oxygen carrier in blood, is a coordination compound of Fe^{2+} with porphyrin ring.

(ii) The pigment chlorophyll in plants, responsible for photosynthesis, is a coordination compound of Mg^{2+} with porphyrin.

(iii) Vitamin-B_{12} also called cobalamin, is a coordination compound of cobalt.

2. In Medicinal Chemistry

(i) The platinum complex *cis*-$[Pt(NH_3)_2Cl_2]$, commonly known as *cis*-platin, is used in the treatment of cancer.

(ii) EDTA complex of calcium is used in the treatment of lead poisoning.

(iii) The excess of copper and iron present in animal system are removed by the chelating ligands D-penicillamine and desferrioxime B *via* the formation of complexes.

3. In Analytical Chemistry

(i) Detection of Cu^{2+}.

(ii) Estimation of hardness of water.

(iii) Ni^{2+} is detected by the formation of a red complex with dimethyl glyoxime (DMG).

(iv) The separation of Ag^+ and Hg^{2+} in group I is based on the fact that AgCl dissolves in NH_3, while Hg_2Cl_2 makes an insoluble black substance with it.

4. In the Extraction/Metallurgy of Metals

(i) Extraction of various metals from their ore involves complex formation, e.g. silver and gold are extracted from their ore by dissolving it in NaCN.

(ii) Also used for the purification of metals, e.g. Mond's process for the purification of nickel, in which impure Ni is converted to $[Ni(CO)_4]$ which is decomposed to yield pure nickel.

5. In other Areas

(i) Electroplating of metals involves the complex salts as electrolyte.

(ii) The complexes are used in homogeneous and heterogeneous catalysis, e.g. Wilkinson catalyst $[(Ph_3P)_3RhCl]$ is used for the hydrogenation of alkenes.

(iii) These are used as an antiknock, e.g. $[(C_2H_5)_4Pb]$.

(iv) In photography, the developed film is fixed by washing with hypo solution which dissolves the undecomposed AgBr to form a complex ion, $[Ag(S_2O_3)_2]^{3-}$.

Topic Practice 3

Very Short Answer Type Questions

1 Mark

1. Fill in the Blanks

(i) Greater the charge on the central metal ion, ... the stability of complex.

(ii) Greater the .... strength of the ligand, greater is the stability of the complex.

(iii) Presence of ...., increases the stability of complex.

(iv) The intermediate activated complex in a chemical reaction is highly .... due to .... energy. **ISC 2023**

(v) The pigment, chlorophyll in plants is responsible for ....

(vi) Vitamin B_{12} is a .... compound or complex.

2. Objective Type Questions

(i) The stabilisation of coordination compounds due to chelation is called the chelate effect. Which of the following is the most stable complex species? **[NCERT Exemplar]**

(a) $[Fe(CO)_5]^{3-}$
(b) $[Fe(CN)_6]^{3-}$
(c) $[Fe(C_2O_4)_3]^{3-}$
(d) $[Fe(H_2O)_6]^{3+}$

(ii) What is the ratio of uncomplexed to complexed Zn^{2+} ion in a solution that is 10 M in NH_3, if the stability constant of $[Zn(NH_3)_4]^{2+}$ is 3×10^9?

(a) 3.3×10^{-9} (b) 3.3×10^{-11}

(b) 3.3×10^{-14} (d) 3×10^{-13}

(iii) Among the following, the most stable species is

(a) $[MnF_6]^{3-}$ (b) $[Fe(CN)_6]^{3-}$

(b) $[Co(NH_3)_6]^{3+}$ (d) $[Fe(C_2O_4)_3]^{3-}$

3. If (*M*) is a metal ion and (*L*) is the ligand. Match Column (I) with Column (II) and choose the correct option using the codes given below :

Column (I)		Column (II)	
A.	$M + L \rightleftharpoons ML,$	(i)	$K = [ML]/[M][L]$
B.	$ML + L \rightleftharpoons ML_2$	(ii)	$K = [ML_4]/[ML_3][L]$
C.	$ML_2 + L \rightleftharpoons ML_3$	(iii)	$K = [ML_3]/[ML_2][L]$
D.	$ML_3 + L \rightleftharpoons ML_4$	(iv)	$K = [ML_2]/[ML][L]$

Codes

	A	B	C	D
(a)	(i)	(ii)	(iii)	(iv)
(b)	(iv)	(iii)	(ii)	(i)
(c)	(i)	(iii)	(iv)	(ii)
(d)	(i)	(iv)	(iii)	(ii)

Short Answer Type I Questions

2 Marks

4. Calculate the overall complex dissociation equilibrium constant for the $[Cu(NH_3)_4]^{2+}$ ions, given that β_4 for this complex is 2.1×10^{13}.

NCERT Intext

5. Discuss briefly giving an example in each case, the role of coordination compounds in

(i) biological systems

(ii) medicinal chemistry

(iii) analytical chemistry

(iv) extraction/metallurgy of metals **NCERT**

Short Answer Type II Questions

3 Marks

6. What is meant by stability of a coordination compound in solution? State the factors which govern stability of complexes. **NCERT**

Hints & Explanations

1. (i) greater/more (ii) basic (iii) chelate rings (iv) unstable, high (v) photosynthesis (vi) coordinate

2. (i) (c) $C_2O_4^{2-}$ is didentate ligand that forms chelates.

Thus, $[Fe(C_2O_4)_3]^{3-}$ is the most stable complex species.

(ii) (b) $Zn^{2+} + 4NH_3 \rightleftharpoons [Zn(NH_3)_4]^{2+}$

$$K_f = \frac{[Zn(NH_3)_4]^{2+}}{[Zn^{2+}][NH_3]^4} = 3 \times 10^9$$

$$\therefore \quad \frac{[Zn(NH_3)_4]^{2+}}{[Zn^{2+}]} = [NH_3]^4 \times 3 \times 10^9$$

$$\therefore \quad \frac{[Zn^{2+}]}{[Zn(NH_3)_4]^{2+}} = 3.3 \times 10^{-14}$$

(iii) (d) $[Fe(C_2O_4)_3]^{3-}$ is the most stable species due to formation of chelate ring by bidentate $(C_2O_4)^{2-}$ ligand.

3. (d) (A) → (i) (B) → (iv) (C) → (iii) (D) → (ii)

4. Dissociation constant is the reciprocal of the stability constant, β_4. Overall complex dissociation equilibrium

constant $= \frac{1}{\beta_4}$ (1)

$$= \frac{1}{2.1 \times 10^{13}} = 4.7 \times 10^{-14}$$ (1)

5. Refer to text on pages 195 (Significance of coordination compounds) (2)

6. Refer to text on page 194 (Stability of coordination compounds) (3)

SUMMARY

- Addition compounds are formed when two or more stable compounds combine together in stoichiometric ratio.
- Coordination compounds do not dissociate and retain their identity in solution, e.g. $K_4[Fe(CN)_6]$
- **Double salts** dissociate and lose their identity in solution, e.g. Mohr's salt.
- **Coordination entity** contains central metal atom/ion surrounded by fixed number of ions or molecules.
- Ions/molecules which donate their lone pair of electrons to central metal ion are called **ligands**.They may be positive, negative or neutral.
- On the basis of number of donor atoms present, ligands are classified as monodentate,bidentate or polydentate.
- The number of ligands bonded to the metal is called **coordination number.**

  CN = number of ligands × denticity
- **Oxidation number** is the charge carried by central metal atom/ion if all the ligands are removed.
- **IUPAC Nomenclature**
  - **For Anionic Complexes** : Counter ion name + ligand name with quantity in alphabetical order + metal name + ate + (OS of metal)
  - **For Cationic/Neutral Complexes** : Ligand no. + ligand name (alphabetically) + metal name + (OS of metal) + counter ion name (if present)

    H_2O-aqua, NO-nitrosyl, Cl^- - chlorido, CN^- - cyano, etc.
- **Structural isomerism** is due to difference in structural arrangement.
- **Ionisation isomerism** This is shown by isomers which give different ions in solution or in molten state, e.g.

  $[Co(NH_3)_5SO_4]Br$ and $[Co(NH_3)_5Br]SO_4$.
- **Linkage isomerism** is due to presence of ambident ligands like NO_2, SCN etc.
- **Coordination isomerism** arises when interchange of ligands between cationic and anionic entities of different metal ions present in a complex, takes place, e.g. $[Co(NH_3)_6][Co(CN)_6]$.
- **Hydrate isomerism** is due to difference in H_2O molecules inside the sphere.
- **Stereoisomers** have same molecular formula but different spatial arrangements.
- **Geometrical isomerism** is shown by complexes of the type MA_2B_2, $MABCD$, MA_2B_4 etc. but not by tetrahedral complexes.
- **Optical isomerism** is shown by complexes which don't have a plane of symmetry.
- According to **Werner's theory,** primary valency is ionisable but secondary valency (coordination number) is not.
- **Valence bond theory** (VBT) explains the formation, magnetic behaviour and geometrical shapes of coordination compounds. It fails to provide quantitative interpretation of magnetic properties.

  By this theory, property of a complex can be calculated as:
  - Predict the OS of central metal atom/ion.
  - Write EC of central metal atom/ion.
  - Pair up the *d*-electron, if ligand is strong like CN^-, CO, NH_3 etc.
  - Fill ligands in empty *d*-orbitals and predict hybridisations and structure as.

Orbital Used	Hybridisation	Structure
$1s + 3p$	sp^3	Tetrahedral
$1d + 1s + 2p$	dsp^3	Square planar
$2d + 1s + 3p$	sp^3d^2	Octahedral

  - If unpaired electron, (s) are present, then paramagnetic otherwise diamagnetic
  - $(n-1)d$ – orbital used by ligand = inner orbital while *nd*-orbital used by ligand = outer orbital complx.
- **Crystal field theory** (CFT) is based on the effect of different crystal on degeneracy of *d*-orbital energies of central metal ion.
- Here, *d*-orbital of metal splits into $d_{x^2-y^2}$, and d_{z^2} (i.e. e_g set) and d_{xy}, d_{yz}, d_{zx} (i.e. t_{2g} set).

  For tetrahedral, $e_g < t_{2g}$; For Octahedral, $e_g > t_{2g}$
  - If $\Delta_o < P$, then complex is high spin or weak field.
  - If $\Delta_o > P$, then complex is low spin or strong field.
- CFT provides quantitative estimation of orbital separation energies, magnetic moments and stability parameters.
- **Stability** is measured in terms of stepwise stability constant. A complex is more stable if a metal has more charge, if chelate is formed and ligand is more basic.

For Mind Map

Visit : https://goo.gl/g5c2mD OR **Scan the Code**

Chapter Practice

Very Short Answer Type Questions

1 Mark

1 Fill in the Blanks

(i) When $FeSO_4.(NH_4)_2SO_4.6H_2O$ dissolved in water, it gives ......*A*......, ...*B*...... and ......*C*...... ions.
Identify *A*, *B* and *C*?

(ii) Oxidation number of Cu in $[Cu(CN)_4]^{3-}$ is ....

(iii) Valence bond theory for coordinate compounds was put forward by ....

(iv) Oxidation state of Ni in $[Ni(CO)_4]$ is ....

2 Objective Type Questions

(i) In the compound lithium tetrahydridoaluminate, the ligand is

(a) H^+ (b) H^-
(c) H (d) None of these

(ii) Which of the following compounds is not coloured?

(a) $Na_2[CuCl_4]$ (b) $K_4[Fe(CN)_6]$
(c) $K_3[Fe(CN)_6]$ (d) $Na_2[CdCl_4]$

(iii) Which of the following complexes formed by Cu^{2+} ions is most stable? **[NCERT Exemplar]**

(a) $Cu^{2+} + 4NH_3 \rightleftharpoons [Cu(CN)_4]^{2-}, \log K = 11.6$
(b) $Cu^{2+} + 4CN^- \rightleftharpoons [Cu(CN)_4]^{2-}, \log K = 27.3$
(c) $Cu^{2+} + 2en \rightleftharpoons [Cu(en)_2]^{2+}, \log K = 15.4$
(d) $Cu^{2+} + 4H_2O \rightleftharpoons [Cu(H_2O)_4]^{2+}, \log K = 8.9$

3 Match Column I and Column II and choose the correct option using the codes given below :

Column I		Column II	
A.	$[Ni(CN)_4]^{2-}$	(i)	Ti^{4+}
B.	Chlorophyll	(ii)	sp^3, paramagnetic
C.	*Ziegler-Natta* catalyst	(iii)	non-planar
D.	$[NiCl_4]^{2-}$	(iv)	Mg^{2+}
E.	Deoxyhaemoglobin	(v)	Planar
		(vi)	dsp^2; diamagnetic

Codes

	A	B	C	D	E
(a)	(vi)	(iv)	(i)	(ii)	(iii)
(b)	(ii)	(iv)	(i)	(ii)	(iii)
(c)	(ii)	(iv)	(i)	(vi)	(v)
(d)	(vi)	(iv)	(i)	(ii)	(v)

4 What is the coordination number of Fe in $[Fe(CN)_6]^{4-}$?

5 Write the IUPAC name of $[Co(NH_3)_5ONO]^{2+}$.

6 Write the oxidation number of Pt in
$$[PtCl_2(NH_3)_2]$$

7 Write the IUPAC name of $[PtCl_6]^{2-}$.

8 How many ions are produced from the complex $[Cr(H_2O)_6]Cl_3$ in solution?

9 Give the examples of two coordination complexes where central metal atom has coordination number

(i) 4 (ii) 6

10 Which type of isomerism is exhibited by $[Co(NH_3)_3(NO_2)_3]$?

11 Give one example for each.

(i) Neutral ligand of carbon
(ii) Positive ligand of nitrogen

12 An element '*X*' has one unpaired electron. Calculate its magnetic moment.

13 Write an important factor on which the crystal field splitting depends.

14 What is the basis of formation of the spectrochemical series?

15 Arrange the following complex ions in the increasing order of crystal field splitting energy
$[Fe(CN)_6]^{4-}$, $[Fe(CO)_5]$, $[Fe(en)_3]^{3+}$

16 If an element have high positive charge then what will be its affect on the stability of complex?

Assertion-Reason

■ **Directions** (Q. Nos. 17-21) In the following questions an Assertion (A) is followed by a corresponding Reason (R). Use the following keys to choose the appropriate answer.

(a) Both (A) and (R) are correct but (R) is the correct explanation of (A).

(b) Both (A) and (R) are correct but (R) is not the correct explanation of (A).
(c) (A) is correct but (R) is incorrect.
(d) (A) is incorrect but (R) is correct.

17. **Assertion** (A) In the coordination compound $[Co(H_2NCH_2CH_2NH_2)_3]_2$, ethane-1,2-diamine is a neutral ligand.
Reason (R) Oxidation number of Co in the complex ion is +3.

18. **Assertion** (A) The stability of $[Ni(en)_3]Cl_2$ is more than that of $[Ni(NH_3)_6]Cl_2$.
Reason (R) The geometry of Ni is trigonal bipyramidal in $[Ni(en)_3]Cl_2$.

19. **Assertion** (A) Tetrahedral complexes do not show geometrical isomerism.
Reason (R) The relative positions of the unidentate ligands attached to the central metal atom are the same with respect to each other.

20. **Assertion** (A) Complexes of MX_6 and MX_5L type (X and L are unidentate) do not show geometrical isomerism. **NCERT Exemplar**
Reason (R) Geometrical isomerism is not shown by complexes of coordination number 6.

21. **Assertion** (A) $[Ni(CN)_4]^{2-}$ is square planar and diamagnetic. **NCERT Exemplar**
Reason (R) It has no unpaired electrons due to presence of strong field ligand.

Case-Study

22. Werner, a swiss chemist in 1892 prepared and characterised a large number of coordination compounds and studied their physical and chemical behaviour. He proposed that in coordination compounds, metals possess two types of valencies, i.e. primary valencies which are normally ionisable and secondary valencies which are non-ionisable.

In a series of compounds of cobalt (III) chloride with ammonia, it was found that some of the chloride ions could be precipitated as AgCl on adding excess of $AgNO_3$ solution, but some remained in solution. The number of ions furnished by a complex in a solution can be determined by precipitation reactions.

The measurement of molar conductance of solutions of coordination compounds helps to estimate the number of ions formed by the compound in solution.

(i) Assign the secondary valency for the compound $NiCl_2 \cdot 6H_2O$ which precipitate 2 moles of AgCl with excess of $AgNO_3$.
(ii) The compound $CoCl_3 \cdot 4NH_3$ contains only one Cl^- ion that is precipitated immediately on the addition of Ag^+ ions. Write the structural formula of the compound.
(iii) When 1 mole of $CrCl_3 \cdot 6H_2O$ is treated with excess of $AgNO_3$, 3 moles of AgCl are obtained. What is the formula of the complex ?

23. Coordination compounds are widely present in the minerals, plant and animal worlds and are known to play many important functions in the area of analytical chemistry, metallurgy, biological systems and medicine.

Alfred Werner's theory postulated the use of two types of linkage (primary and secondary), by a metal atom/ion in a coordination compound. He predicted the geometrical shapes of a large number of coordination entities using the property of isomerism.

The Valence Bond Theory (VBT) explains the formation, magnetic behaviour and geometrical shapes of coordination compounds. If, however, fails to describe the optical properties of these compounds.

The Crystal Field Theory (CFT) explains the effect of different crystals fields (provided by the ligands taken as point charges) on the degeneracy or *d*-orbital energies of the central metal atom/ion.

Answer the following questions. **CBSE 2023**

(i) When a coordination compound $NiCl_2 \cdot 6H_2O$ is mixed with Ag NO_3 solution, 2 moles of AgCl are precipitated per mole of the compound. Write the structural formula of the complex and secondary valency for nickel ion.
(ii) Write the IUPAC name of the ionisation isomer of $[Co(NH_3)_5(SO_4)]Cl$.
(iii) Give reasons Low spin tetrahedral complexes are not formed.

Short Answer Type I Questions

(2 Marks)

24 A complex of the type $[M(AA)_2X_2]^{n+}$ is known to be optically active. What does this indicate about the structure of complex? Give one example of such complex.

25 Write the structures and names of all stereoisomers of the following compounds:
(i) $[Co(en)_3]Cl_3$ (ii) $[Pt(NH_3)_2Cl_2]$

26 The complexes $[Co(NH_3)_6]$ $[Cr(CN)_6]$ and $[Cr(NH_3)_6]$ $[Co(CN)_6]$ are the examples of which type of isomerism? State its definition.

27 How many isomers can be formed for the complex $[Co(C_2O_4)_2(NH_3)_2]$?

28 A solution containing 0.319 g of complex $CrCl_3 \cdot 6H_2O$ was passed through cation exchanger and the solution given out was neutralised by 28.5 mL of 0.125 M of NaOH. What is the correct formula of complex?

29 What is crystal field splitting among octahedral and tetrahedral crystal fields? In which case, the magnitude of crystal field splitting is larger?

30 Give the name, the stereochemistry and the magnetic behaviour of the following complexes.
(i) $[Co(NH_3)_5Cl]Cl_2$ (ii) $K_2[Ni(CN)_4]$

31 Give the formula of each of the following coordination compound entities.
(i) Co^{3+} ion is bound to one Cl^-, one NH_3 molecule and two bidentate ethylenediamine (en) molecules.
(ii) Ni^{2+} ion is bound to two water molecules and two oxalate ions.

32 List down the major factors which affect the stability of coordination complexes.

33 Explain the following.
(i) Complex that is used as an anti-knock.
(ii) Complex of calcium used in the treatment of lead poisoning.

Short Answer Type II Questions (3 Marks)

34 Giving a suitable example for each, explain the following.
(i) Linkage isomerism (ii) Chelating ligand

35 Draw all the possible isomers (structural and stereoisomeric) having the composition $[CrBrCl(NH_3)_4]$.

36 Square planar complexes of MX_2L_2 type with coordination number of 4 exhibit geometrical isomerism whereas tetrahedral complexes with similar composition do not. Why?

37 Draw the diagram showing splitting of d-orbital in tetrahedral complex.

38 Name the compound $[Fe(H_2O)_5NO]^{2+}$ and explain the magnetic properties of $[Fe(H_2O)_5NO]^{2+}$ and oxidation state of iron in this complex.

39 Using valence bond theory, explain the following in relation to the complexes, given below : $[Mn(CN)_6]^{3-}$, $[Cr(H_2O)_6]^{3+}$.
(i) Type of hybridisation
(ii) Magnetic behaviour
(iii) Inner or outer orbital complex

40 Compare the following complexes with respect to structural shapes of units, magnetic behaviour and hybrid orbitals involved in units.
(i) $[Ni(CN)_4]^{2-}$
(ii) $[NiCl_4]^{2-}$
(iii) $[CoF_6]^{3-}$
(Atomic number of Ni = 28, Co = 27)

41 $[Co(NH_3)_6]^{3+}$ and $[CoF_6]^{3-}$, both the complexes contain cobalt in +3 oxidation state, but $[Co(NH_3)_6]^{3+}$ is diamagnetic while $[CoF_6]^{3-}$ is paramagnetic with magnetic moment 4.90 BM. Explain.

42 Give detailed description of CFT for different types of ligand and explain how CFT explain colour of coordination compound? Use suitable examples to explain.

43 Explain the hybridisation, geometry, magnetic properties, IUPAC nomenclature and comparative stability of $[Fe(CN)_6]^{4-}$ and $[Fe(CN)_6]^{3-}$.

44 Explain the following :
(i) Low spin octahedral complexes of nickel are not known.
(ii) CO is a stronger ligand than NH_3 for many metals.

45 $PtCl_4$ and NH_3 may form five complexes, $A(PtCl_4 \cdot 6NH_3)$, $B(PtCl_4 \cdot 5NH_3)$, $C(PtCl_4 \cdot 4NH_3)$, $D(PtCl_4 \cdot 3NH_3)$ and $E(PtCl_4 \cdot 2NH_3)$. One mole of each A, B, C, D and E reacts with excess of $AgNO_3$ to yield 4, 3, 2 and 1 mole(s) of AgCl respectively, while E gives, no AgCl. The conductance of their solutions are in the order $A > B > C > D > E$. On the basis of Werner's theory, write their structure and give the total number of ions given by one complex.

46 Indicate the types of isomerism exhibited by the following complexes and draw the structures for these isomers.

(i) $[Co(NH_3)_5NO_3]SO_4$ (ii) $[CoCl(NH_3)_4(H_2O)]Br_2$
(iii) $[Cr(H_2O)_5(SCN)]^{2+}$ (iv) $[Co(en)_3]$ $[Cr(CN)_6]$
(v) $[Pt\ NH_3Cl\ (Py)_2]$

Long Answer Type Questions

(5 Marks)

47 A metal ion M^{n+} having d^4 valence electronic configuration combines with three bidentate ligands to form a octahedral complex compound. Assuming $\Delta_o > P$.

(i) Draw the diagram showing d-orbital splitting during this complex formation.

(ii) Write the electronic configuration of the valence electrons of the metal M^{n+} ion in terms of t_{2g} and e_g.

(iii) What type of hybridisation will M^{n+} ion have?

48 $[Ti(H_2O)_6]^{3+}$ absorbs light of wavelength 500 nm. Name one ligand which would form Ti(III) complex absorbing light of lower wavelength than 500 nm and one ligand which would form a complex absorbing light of wavelength higher than 500 nm.

49 Predict the number of unpaired electrons, the magnetic moments for each of the following complex.

(i) $[Fe(CN)_6]^{4-}$

(ii) $[Cr(NH_3)_6]^{2+}$

(iii) $[Sc(H_2O)_6]^{3+}$

Answers

1 (i) (A) Fe^{2+}, (B) NH_4^+, and (C) SO_4^{2-}
(ii) (+) 1
(iii) L. Pauling
(iv) zero

2 (i) (b) In $LiAlH_4$, the ligand is H^-.
(ii) (d) $Na_2[CdCl_4]$ is not coloured due to completely filled $4d^{10}$ orbitals
(iii) (b) Stability $\propto \log K$.
The complex of Cu^{2+} which has highest value of $\log K$ is most stable.

3 (a) A→(vi), B→(iv). C→(i), D→(ii), E→(iii)

(a) $[Ni(CN)_4]^{2-}$

$$Ni(28) = [Ar]3d^8 4s^2$$
$$Ni^{2+} = [Ar]3d^8, 4s^0$$

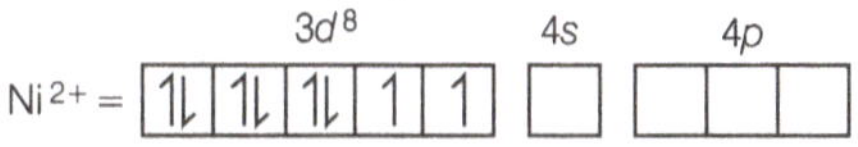

Since, CN^- is a strong field ligand, it causes pairing of electrons.

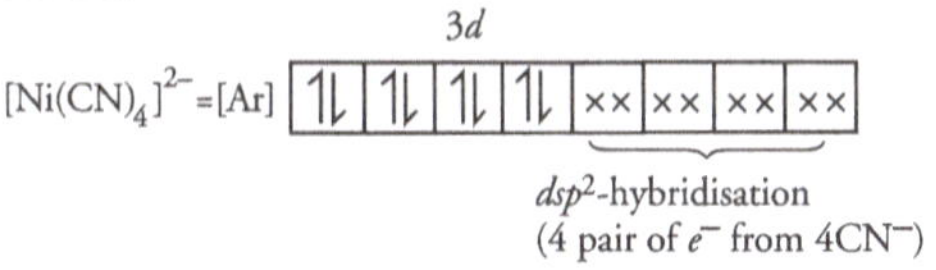

No unpaired e^- is present, therefore complex is diamagnetic.

(b) Chlorophyll contains Mg^{2+} ion.

(c) *Ziegler-Natta* catalyst is $Ti^{4+} + (C_2H_5)_3Al$

(d) $[NiCl_4]^{2-}$

In this case, Cl^- is a weak field ligand, so doesn't cause pairing. Hence,

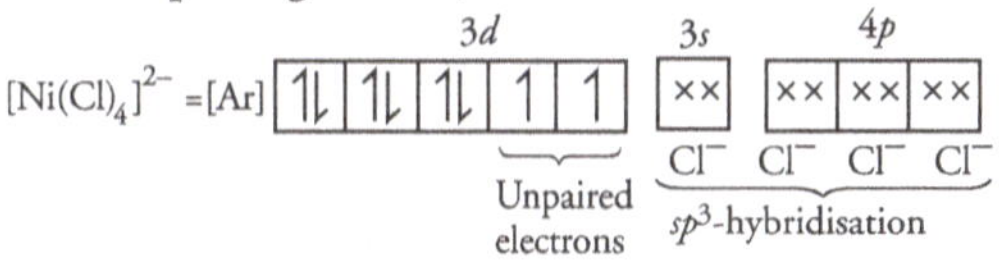

Due to the presence of unpaired electrons, it is paramagnetic.

(e) Deoxyhaemoglobin is non-planar while oxyhaemoglobin is planar.

4 Coordination number of Fe is 6. (1)

5 Pentaamminenitrito–O–cobalt (III) ion. (1)

6 Let the oxidation number of Pt in a complex be x.
$$x + (-1) \times 2 + (0) \times 2 = 0$$
$$x = +2$$ (1)

7 Hexochloroplatinate (IV) ion.

8 $[Cr(H_2O)_6]Cl_3 \rightleftharpoons [Cr(H_2O)_6] + 3Cl^-$

Thus, 4 ions are formed. (1)

9 Coordination number 4 = $[Pt(NH_3)_2Cl_2]$ (½)

Coordination number 6 = $[Co(NH_3)_4Cl_2]^+$ (½)

10 Linkage isomerism. $[Co(NH_3)_2(NO_2)_3]$ and $[Co(NH_3)_3(ONO)_3]$ (1)

11 (i) CO (ii) NO^+ (1)

12 Using formula, $\mu = \sqrt{n(n+2)}$ BM = 1.73 BM (2)

13 Crystal field spliting depends upon the field produced by the ligand and charge on the metal ion. (2)

14 Refer to text on page 186 (Topic-2, Spectrochemical series). (1)

15 Increasing order of field strength. (2)

$$en < CN^- < CO$$

Hint Stronger is the ligand more will be the CFSE.

16 **Hint** Greater is the charge on metal ion, greater is the stability of the complex. (2)

17 (*b*) Ethane-1, 2-diamine is a neutral ligand as it carries no charge. Oxidation number of Co in the complex ion is +3. Both (A) and (R) are correct but (R) is not the correct explanation of (A).

18 (*c*) $[Ni(en)_3]Cl_2$ is more stable than $[Ni(NH_3)_6]Cl_2$, because $[Ni(en)_3]Cl_2$ is a chelating compound which are more stable than complexes with unidentate ligands as the dissociation of complex involves breaking of two bonds instead of one.

$[Ni(en)_3Cl_2]$ show octahedral geometry with d^8 configuration. (A) is correct but (R) is incorrect.

19 (*a*) Tetrahedral complexes do not show geometrical isomerism because the relative positions of the unidentate ligands attached to the central metal atom are same with respect to each other. Both (A) and (R) are correct and R is correct explanation of (A).

20 (*c*) (A) is correct but (R) is incorrect.

Complexes of MX_6 and MX_5L type (X and L are unidentate) do not show geometrical isomerism due to presence of plane of symmetry.

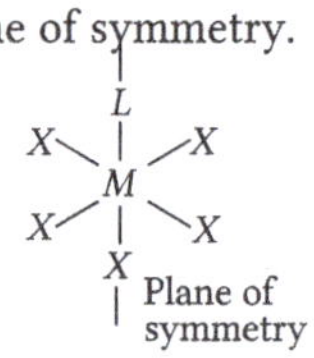

21 (*a*) $[Ni(CN)_4]^{2-}$ is square planar and is diamagnetic.

$$Ni \rightarrow 3d^8\ 4s^2; \quad Ni^{2+} \rightarrow 3d^8\ 4s^0$$

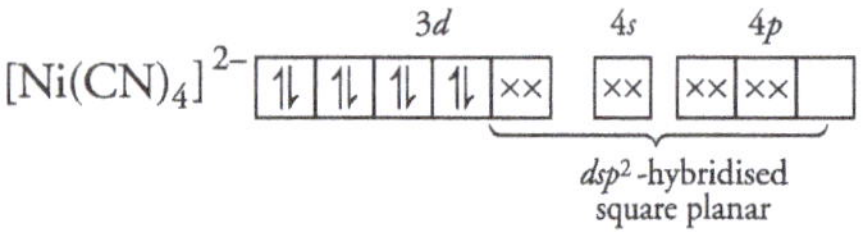

∴ This complex has no unpaired electron.

Both (A) and (R) are correct and (R) is the correct explanation of (A).

22 (i) 6

(ii) The coordination number of Co-atom is 6 and only one Cl^- ion is precipitated on the addition of Ag^+ ions, hence it contains only one Cl^- ion outside the coordination sphere and thus structure of compound is $[Co(NH_3)_4Cl_2]Cl$.

(iii) 1 mole of $AgNO_3$ precipitates one free chloride ion (Cl^-).

Here, 3 moles of AgCl are precipitated by excess of $AgNO_3$. Hence, there must be three free Cl^- ions. So, the formula of the complex can be $[Cr(H_2O)_6]Cl_3$.

23 (i) The structural formula of the complex is $[Ni(H_2O)_6]Cl_2$.

(ii) Pentaamminesulphatecobalt (II)chloride

(iii) For tetrahedral complexes, the crystal field stabilisation energy is lower that pairing energy. Thus, low spin tetrahedral complexes are not formed.

24 Refer to text on page 172 (Topic-1, Optical isomerism). (2)

25 Refer to text on pages 171 and 172. (Topic-1, Stereoisomerism). (2)

26 It is a coordination isomerism. For definition. Refer to text on page 171 (Topic - 1, Structural isomerism, coordination isomerism). (2)

27

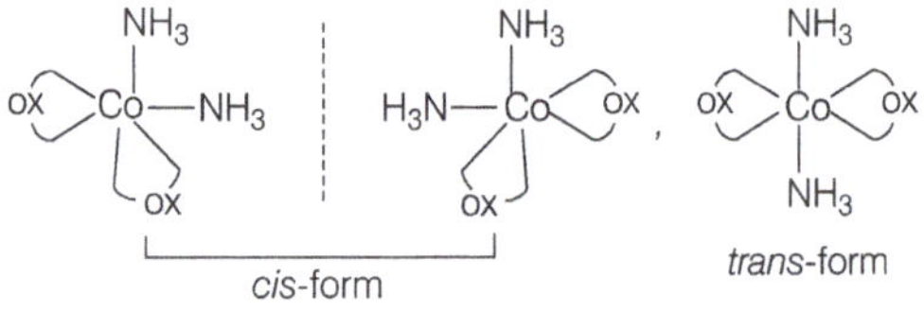

Thus, it has 3 isomers.

28 **Hint:** The correct formula of the complex will be $[Cr(H_2O)_6]Cl_3$. (2)

29 Refer to text on pages 185 and 186 (Topic - 2, Crystal field splitting in octahedral and tetrahedral entities) (2)

30 (i) Refer to solution 28 (ii) on page 193 (Topic - 2) (2)

(ii) $K_2[Ni(CN)_4]$

IUPAC name Potassium tetracyononickelete (II)

Oxidation state of Ni

$$(+1)2 + x + (-1)4 = 0$$
$$+4 + x - 4 = 0$$
$$x - 2 = 0$$
$$x = +2$$

- Coordination number, (CN) = 4
- Outer electronic configuration of $Ni^{2+} = 3d^8\ (e_g^4 t_{2g}^4)$
- Number of unpaired electrons (n) = 0 (All electrons are paired)
- Magnetic moment, $\mu = \sqrt{n(n+2)}$ BM

$$\mu = \sqrt{0(0+2)} \text{ BM}$$
$$\mu = 0 \text{ BM}$$

- Paramagnetic.
- It is a tetrahedral complex, so it does not exhibit geometrical or optical isomerism.

31 (i) $[Co(NH_3)(Cl)(en)_2]^{2+}$ (1)

(ii) $[Ni\ (H_2O)_2\ (ox)_2]^{2-}$ (1)

32 Refer to text on page 194 (Topic - 3, Stability of coordination compounds).

33 Refer to text on pages 195 (Topic - 3, Significance of coordination compounds).

34 (i) Refer to text on page 171-172 (Topic - 1, Structural isomerism, linkage isomerism). (1½)

(ii) Refer to text on page 168 (Chelating ligands). (1½)

35 Refer to text on pages 171-172 (Topic - 1, Structural and stereoisomerism). (3)

36 Refer to text on pages 171-172 (Topic - 1, Structural and stereoisomerism). (3)

37 Refer to text on page 186 (Topic - 2, Crystal field splitting in tetrahedral coordination entities). (3)

38 **Hint** Pentaaquanitrosyl iron (II) ion.
Oxidation state of Fe =+ 2 and is paramagnetic in nature. (3)

39 Refer to text on pages 182 and 183 (Topic - 2, Structure and shapes of complexes on the basis of valence bond theory).

40 Refer to text on pages 182 and 183 (Topic - 2, Structure and shapes of complexes on the basis of valence bond theory).

41 Refer to text on pages 183 and 184 (Topic - 2, Magnetic properties of coordination compounds).

42 Refer to text on pages 186 and 187 (Topic - 2, Spectrochemical series, colour in coordination compound).

43 Refer to text on pages 182-183 (Topic- 2, Structure and shapes of complexes on the basis of valence bond theory)

44 (i) Ni usually exist in +2 oxidation state in its octahedral complexes. The electronic configuration of Ni^{+2} ion is $[Ar]3d^8 4s^0$ ($t_{2g}^6 e_g^2$ strong ligands causes pairing of e^-s and form low spin complexes, but in this case after pairing also, two unpaired electrons are left in the e_g set and will, there form high spin complexes and not low spin complexes irrespective of ligand. (1½)

(ii) According to ligand field theory, π - acceptor ligands are the stronger ligand and the π- donating ligand is weak field ligand.
NH_3 is a π- donor in comparison to CO which is a π-acceptor ligand. Thus, CO acts as stronger ligand than NH_3 for many metals. (1½)

45 Refer to text on page 173 (Topic - 1, Werner's theory of coordination compounds). (3)

46 Refer to text on pages 171-172 (Topic - 1, Structural and stereoisomerism.) (3)

47 Refer to text on pages 185-186 (Topic - 2, Crystal field splitting in octahedral coordination entities). (5)

48 **Hint** CFSE $\propto \frac{1}{\lambda}$,
[Strong ligand will have more CFSE, hence will absorbs less wavelength and *vice-versa*]. (5)

49 Refer to text on pages 183-184 (Topic - 2, Magnetic properties of coordination compounds). (5)

RELATED ONLINE VIDEOS

Visit : https://youtu.be/ft5yMiS-PyY
OR **Scan the Code**

Visit : https://youtu.be/BNzEaqQkszo
OR **Scan the Code**

Visit : https://youtu.be/f7reOyv_wP0
OR **Scan the Code**

CHAPTER

06

Haloalkanes and Haloarenes

The replacement of hydrogen atom in a hydrocarbon, aliphatic or aromatic, by halogen atom (s) results in the formation of alkyl halide (haloalkane) and aryl halide (haloarene), respectively. Halogenated compounds persist in the environment due to their resistance to breakdown by soil bacteria.

In this chapter, we will study the important methods of preparation, physical and chemical properties of **organo-halogen compounds.**

- Classification, Nomenclature and Nature of Haloalkanes and Haloarenes
- Methods of Preparation of Haloalkanes and Haloarenes
- Properties of Haloalkanes and Haloarenes
- Polyhalogen Compounds

TOPIC 01 Haloalkanes (Alkyl Halides)

Haloalkanes contain halogen atom(s) attached to the sp^3-hybridised carbon atom of an alkyl group. Since, halogen atoms are more electronegative than the carbon atom, the carbon-halogen bond of alkyl halide is polarised.

Due to this reason, they undergo a number of chemical reaction $-\overset{|}{\underset{|}{C}}^{\delta+}-\overset{\delta-}{X}$.

They have general formula $R-X$ (where, $X = F, Cl, Br, I$). They are represented by the formula $C_nH_{2n+1}X$ $(n = 1, 2, 3...)$

Classification

Haloalkanes may be classified as follows :

On the Basis of Number of Halogen Atoms

Depending on the number of halogen atoms in their structures, haloalkanes may be mono, di, tri or polyhalogen (tetra, penta, etc.) compounds.

Monohaloalkane	Dihaloalkane	Trihaloalkane
CH_3X or C_2H_5X	CH_2X-CH_2X	$CH_2X-CHX-CH_2X$

(where, X = F, Cl, Br, I)

On the Basis of Nature of Carbon of C—*X* Bond

Monohalo compounds may further be classified according to the hybridisation of the carbon atom to which halogen is bonded, as discussed below :

1. Compounds Containing sp^3 C—*X* Bond

These are classified into following types :

(i) **Alkyl Halides** or **Haloalkanes** *(R—X)* Here, the halogen atom (*X*) is bonded to an alkyl group (*R*). They form a homologous series of compounds represented by the formula $C_nH_{2n+1}X$.

They are further classified as primary (1°), secondary (2°) or tertiary (3°) depending upon the nature of carbon atom to which the halogen is attached.

e.g. 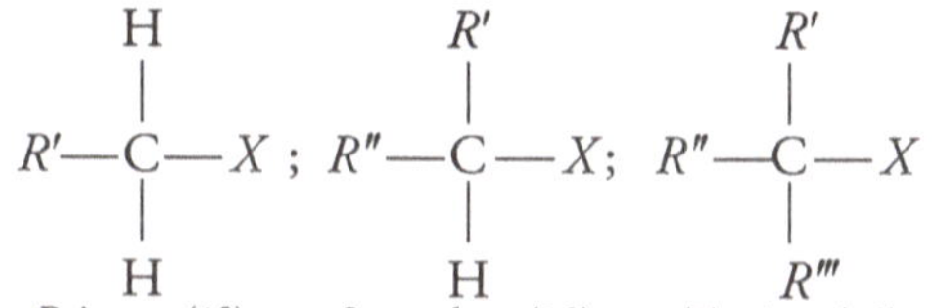

Primary (1°) Secondary (2°) Tertiary (3°)

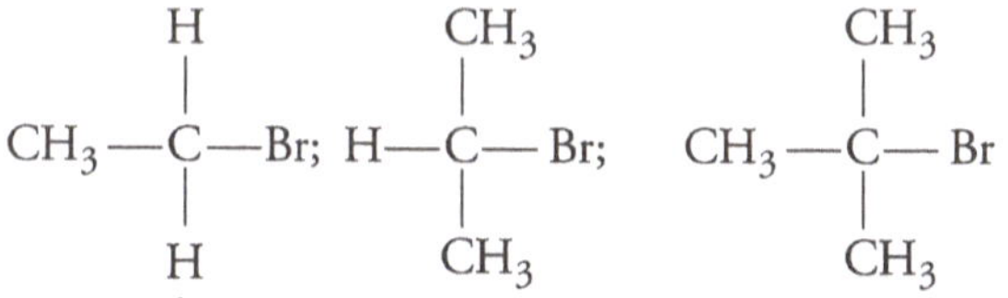

Bromoethane (Primary or 1°) 2-bromopropane (Secondary or 2°) 2-bromo-2-methylpropane (Tertiary or 3°)

(ii) **Allylic Halides** Here, the halogen is bonded to the sp^3-hybridised carbon atom next to carbon-carbon double bond which is also called allylic carbon. Hence, these halides are called allylic halides.

e.g. 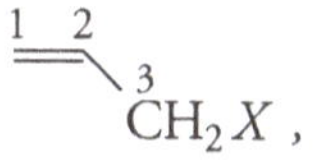

3-haloprop-1-ene (Allyl halide)

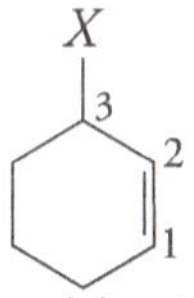

3-halocyclohex-1-ene

$CH_2{=}CH{-}CH_2{-}Cl$,

3-chloroprop-1-ene

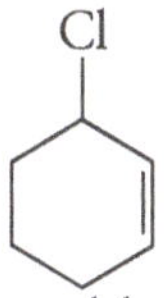

3-chlorocyclohex-1-ene

2. Compounds Containing sp^2 C—*X* Bond

In these compounds, halogen is directly attached to one of the doubly bonded carbon atom $(-\overset{|}{C}{=}\overset{|}{C}-X)$.

e.g. **Vinylic halide** in which halogen atom is bonded to the sp^2-hybridised carbon of one of the carbon atoms of a double bond, i.e. vinylic carbon.

e.g. 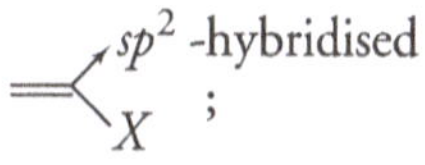

Haloethene (Vinyl halide) ;

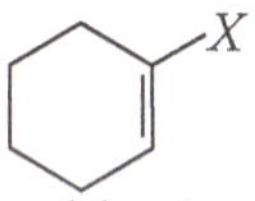

1-halocyclohex-1-ene

Nomenclature

1. For Monosubstituted Haloalkane

The **common names** of alkyl halides are derived by naming the alkyl group followed by the name of halide (chloride, bromide, etc). Here, the prefixes *n*-, *iso*-, *sec*-, *tert*-, etc., are used. In **IUPAC system,** alkyl halides are named as halosubstituted hydrocarbons, i.e. haloalkanes. The names are written by prefixing the word 'halo' to the name of alkane corresponding to the longest continuous carbon chain having the halogen atom.

e.g. $CH_3CH_2CH_2I$;

Common name *n*-propyl iodide
IUPAC name (1-iodopropane)

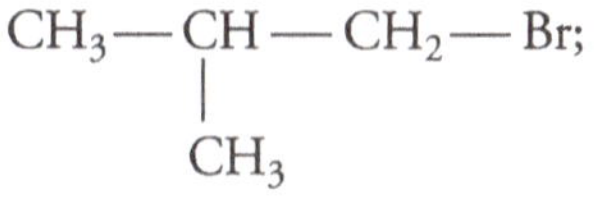

Common name *iso*-butyl bromide
IUPAC name (1-bromo-2-methylpropane)

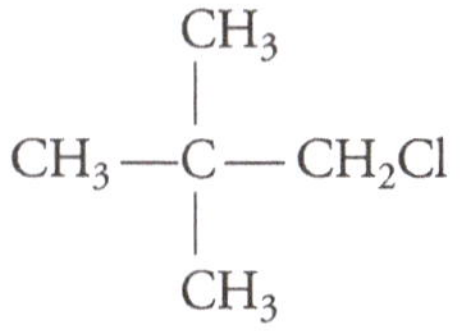

Common name *neo*-pentyl chloride
IUPAC name (1-chloro-2, 2-dimethylpropane)

2. For Disubstituted Haloalkane

The dihaloalkanes having the same type of halogen atoms are named as alkylidene or alkylene dihalides. The dihalo compounds having same type of halogen atoms are further classified as:

(i) ***Geminal* Halides** Here halogen atoms are present on the same carbon atom.

(ii) ***Vicinal* Halides** Here halogen atoms are present on the adjacent carbon atoms.

In common name system, *gem*-dihalides are named as alkylidene halides, whereas *vic*-dihalides are named as alkylene dihalides. In IUPAC system, they are named as dihaloalkanes.

e.g.

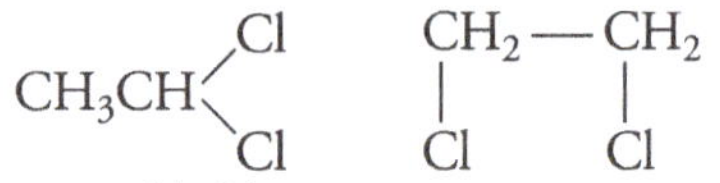

	gem-dihalide	*vic*-dihalide
Common name	Ethylidene chloride	Ethylene dichloride
IUPAC name	1,1-dichloroethane	1,2-dichloroethane

Common and IUPAC Names of Some Halides

Structure	Common Name	IUPAC Name
$CH_3\ CH_2\ CH_2F$	*n*-propyl fluoride	1-fluoropropane
$(CH_3)_3CCH_2$—Br	*neo*-pentyl bromide	1-bromo-2,2-dimethyl propane
$CH_3CH_2CH\ (Cl)\ CH_3$	*sec*-butyl chloride	2-chlorobutane
$(CH_3)_3C$— Br	*tert*-butyl bromide	2-bromo-2-methyl propane
$CH_2=CH$— CH_2Br	Allyl bromide	3-bromopropene
$CH_2=CHCl$	Vinyl chloride	Chloroethene

Example 1 Write the IUPAC names of the following compound: $(CCl_3)_3CCl$ **NCERT**

Sol.

(i) We follow the following steps:

I. To write the IUPAC name, we first expand the structure of the compound as follows:

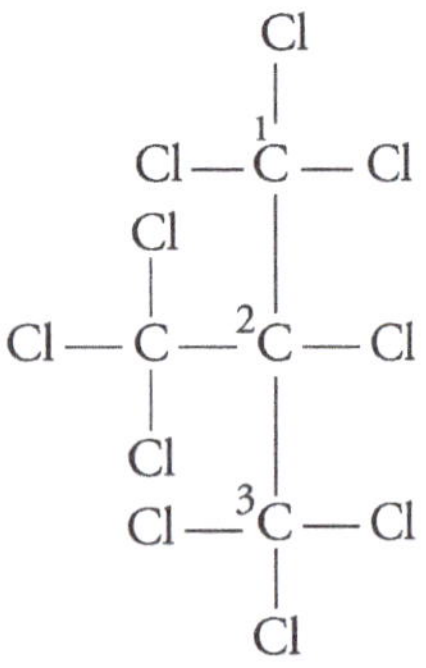

II. Now we do the numbering of the carbon chain, specifically from the end where functional group is nearer and/or more in number. In this case, numbering from both the ends is equivalent.

III. Then we write the IUPAC name, counting the functional groups and their positions.

Thus, the name of the given structure is 2-(trichloromethyl)-1,1,1,2,3,3,3,-heptachloropropane.

Nature of C—X Bond

Electronegativity of halogen atom is greater than that of carbon atom due to which the shared pair of electron in C—X bond lies closer to the halogen atom.

As a result, the halogen atom bears a partial negative charge whereas, the carbon atom bears a partial positive charge.

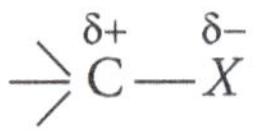

As we go down in 17th group of the periodic table, the size of halogen atom increases, fluorine atom is the smallest and iodine atom is the largest. Consequently, the carbon-halogen bond length also increases from C—F to C—I.

Further, as we move from F to I, the electronegativity of the halogen decreases, therefore the polarity of the C—X bond decreases accordingly.

Carbon-Halogen (C—X) Bond Lengths, Bond Enthalpies and Dipole Moments

Bond between carbon and halogen	Bond length/pm	C—X Bond enthalpies / kJ mol^{-1}	Dipole moment/Debye
CH_3 — F	139	452	1.847
CH_3 — Cl	178	351	1.860
CH_3 — Br	193	293	1.830
CH_3 — I	214	234	1.636

Methods of Preparation of Haloalkanes

Haloalkanes can be prepared from wide range of organic compounds through various methods.

Some important methods of preparation are discussed below:

1. Preparation from Alkanes and Halogen

(By Free Radical Halogenation)

Alkanes react with halogens (Cl_2 and Br_2) in the presence of UV light to form haloalkanes. The reaction proceeds through free radical mechanism and gives a complex mixture of isomeric mono and polyhaloalkanes which are difficult to separate as pure compounds.

e.g. $$CH_3CH_2CH_2CH_3 \xrightarrow[\text{or Heat}]{Cl_2\,/\,\text{UV light}} CH_3CH_2CH_2CH_2Cl + CH_3\underset{\displaystyle Cl}{\underset{|}{C}}HCH_2CH_3$$

The relative amounts of these isomeric haloalkanes depend upon the nature of the halogen and the number and type of hydrogen atoms (1°, 2° and 3°) which are being substituted. For the ease of substitution, various hydrogens follow the sequence as: 3° > 2° > 1°

2. Preparation from Alkenes

(i) **Addition of Hydrogen Halides** On reaction with hydrogen halide, an alkene is converted to the corresponding alkyl halide.

e.g. 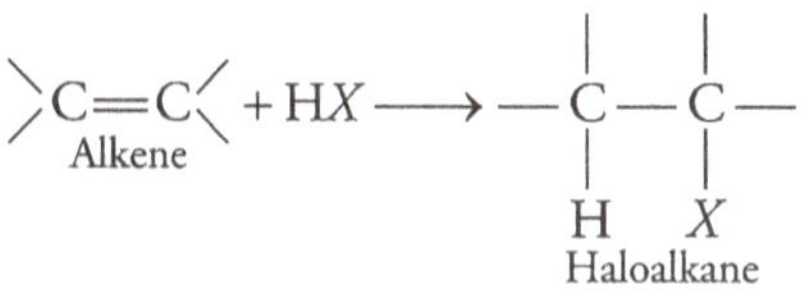

The decreasing order of reactivity of the halogen acids is HI > HBr > HCl > HF

In case of addition to symmetrical alkenes, only one addition product is formed. But in case of addition to unsymmetrical alkenes, Markovnikov's rule is followed, e.g. propene yields two products but only one predominates according to Markovnikov's rule.

$$\underset{\text{Propene}}{CH_3CH{=}CH_2} + HI \longrightarrow \underset{\substack{\text{1-iodopropane}\\\text{(Minor)}}}{CH_3CH_2CH_2I}$$

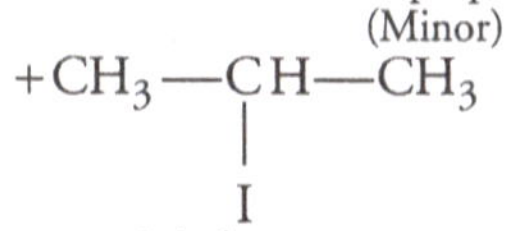

2-iodopropane
(Major)

However, in the presence of a peroxide, the addition of HBr to an unsymmetrical alkene, proceeds in contrary to the Markovnikov's rule. This effect is known as **Kharash effect or peroxide effect**.

$$\underset{\text{Propene}}{CH_3CH{=}CH_2} + HBr \xrightarrow{\text{Peroxide}} \underset{\text{1-bromopropane}}{CH_3CH_2CH_2Br}$$

It is informally called as ***anti*-Markovnikov's addition.**

(ii) **Addition of Halogens** In the laboratory, addition of bromine (Br_2) to an alkene in CCl_4 results in discharge of reddish-brown colour of bromine.

It is an important method for the detection of double bond in a molecule. The addition results in the synthesis of *vic*-dibromides which are colourless.

On adding Br_2 or Cl_2 to alkenes, the addition occurs at the double bond forming *vic*-dihalides.

e.g. 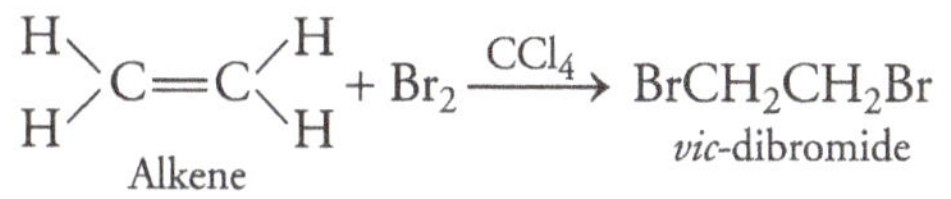

3. Preparation from Alcohols

This is the most convenient method for the preparation of haloalkanes in the laboratory. In this method, the hydroxyl group of an alcohol is replaced by halogen on reaction with concentrated halogen acids, phosphorus halides or thionyl chloride.

Different reagents can be used to get haloalkanes from alcohols as described below:

(i) **By the Action of Halogen Acids** Haloalkanes are prepared by the treatment of alcohols with halogen acids as follows:

$$\underset{\text{Alcohol}}{ROH} + \underset{\text{Halogen acid}}{HX} \longrightarrow \underset{\text{Haloalkane}}{RX} + \underset{\text{Water}}{H_2O}$$

The rate of reaction depends on the nature of alcohol as well as the halogen acid.

- The reaction of primary (1°) and secondary (2°) alcohols with halogen acids require the presence of a catalyst, $ZnCl_2$ which acts as a Lewis acid and helps in the cleavage of C—O bond. Chloroalkanes are prepared by the action of hydrochloric acid to the primary and secondary alcohols in the presence of anhydrous zinc chloride (**Groove's process**).

$$\underset{\text{Ethyl alcohol (1°)}}{CH_3CH_2OH} + HCl(g) \xrightarrow{\text{Anhydrous } ZnCl_2} \underset{\text{Ethyl chloride}}{CH_3CH_2Cl} + H_2O$$

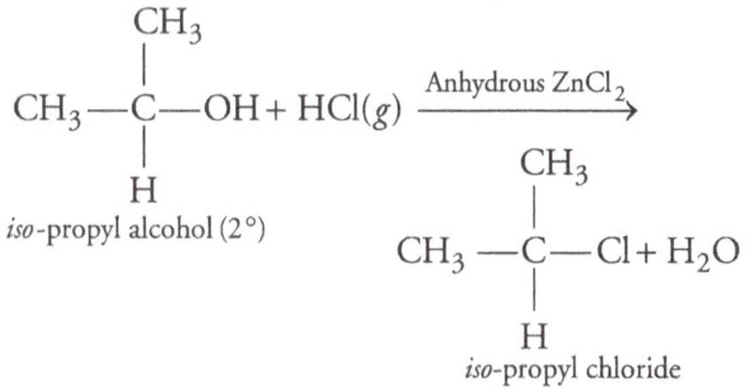

Tertiary alcohols are very reactive and therefore, their reactions are conducted by simply shaking with concentrated HCl at room temperature even in the absence of zinc chloride.

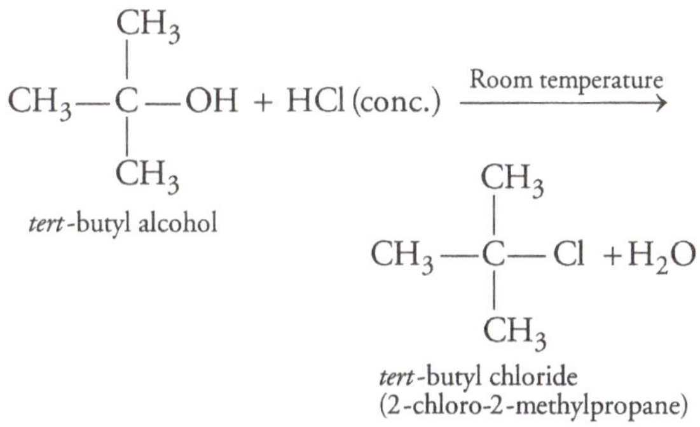

- Bromoalkanes are prepared by heating an alcohol with constant boiling of HBr (48%) in the presence of conc. H_2SO_4, which acts as a catalyst.

$$\underset{\text{Ethyl alcohol}}{CH_3CH_2OH} + HBr \xrightarrow[\Delta]{\text{Conc. } H_2SO_4} \underset{\text{Ethyl bromide}}{CH_3CH_2Br} + H_2O$$

HBr can also be generated in *situ* by the action of conc. H_2SO_4 on KBr or NaBr.

$$\underset{\text{Ethyl alcohol}}{CH_3CH_2OH} + KBr + H_2SO_4 \xrightarrow{\Delta} \underset{\text{Ethyl bromide}}{CH_3CH_2Br} + KHSO_4 + H_2O$$

- Iodoalkanes are prepared by heating an alcohol with constant boiling HI (57%).

$$\underset{\text{Ethyl alcohol}}{CH_3CH_2OH} + HI \xrightarrow{\text{Reflux}} \underset{\text{Iodoethane}}{CH_3CH_2I} + H_2O$$

HI can also be generated in *situ* by the action of 95% phosphoric acid on KI.

$$\underset{\text{Ethyl alcohol}}{CH_3CH_2OH} + KI + \underset{\text{Phosphoric acid}}{H_3PO_4} \xrightarrow{\Delta} \underset{\text{Iodoethane}}{CH_3CH_2I} + KH_2PO_4 + H_2O$$

This reaction gives good yield of alkyl iodides.

(ii) **By the Action of Phosphorus Halides**

- Chloroalkanes are obtained by the action of PCl_5 or PCl_3 on alcohols.

$$R\text{—}OH + PCl_5 \longrightarrow R\text{—}Cl + POCl_3 + HCl$$

$$\underset{\text{Ethyl alcohol}}{CH_3CH_2OH} + PCl_5 \longrightarrow \underset{\text{Chloroethane}}{CH_3CH_2Cl} + \underset{\text{Phosphoryl chloride}}{POCl_3} + HCl$$

$$\underset{\text{Ethyl alcohol}}{3CH_3CH_2OH} + PCl_3 \longrightarrow \underset{\text{Chloroethane}}{3CH_3CH_2Cl} + \underset{\text{Phosphorous acid}}{H_3PO_3}$$

- Bromoalkanes and iodoalkanes are prepared by the reaction of PBr_3 and PI_3, respectively with the alcohols. PBr_3 and PI_3 are usually generated in *situ* by the reaction of red phosphorus with bromine and iodine, respectively.

$$R\text{—}OH \xrightarrow{\text{Red P}/X_2} R\text{—}X \text{ (where, } X = \text{Br, I)}$$

$$CH_3\text{—}OH \xrightarrow{\text{Red P}/Br_2} CH_3\text{—}Br$$

(iii) **By the Action of Thionyl Chloride** Chloroalkanes are prepared by refluxing the alcohols with $SOCl_2$ in the presence of pyridine.

$$\underset{\text{Ethyl alcohol}}{CH_3CH_2OH} + \underset{\text{Thionyl chloride}}{SOCl_2} \xrightarrow{\text{Pyridine}} \underset{\text{Chloroethane}}{CH_3CH_2Cl} + SO_2\uparrow + HCl\uparrow$$

This method is usually preferred since both the products of this reaction (SO_2 and HCl) are escapable gases. Hence, the reaction gives pure alkyl halide.

Note The above three methods are not applicable for the preparation of aryl halides because the C—O bond in phenol has a partial double bond character and is difficult to break being stronger than a single bond.

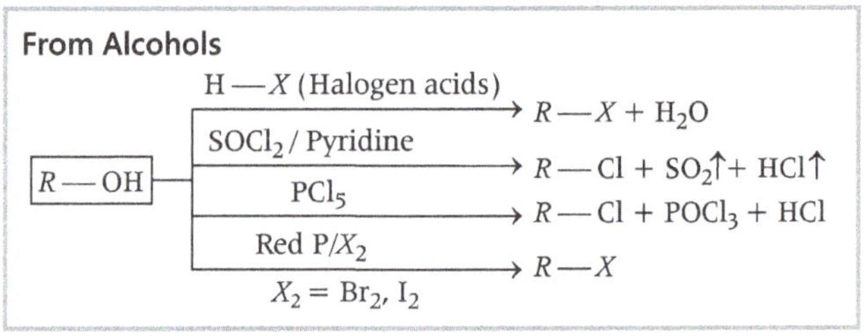

4. Preparation by Halogen Exchange Method

Alkyl iodides are often prepared by the reaction of alkyl chlorides/bromides with NaI in dry acetone. This reaction is known as **Finkelstein reaction.**

$$R\text{—}X + NaI \longrightarrow R\text{—}I + NaX \quad [X = \text{Cl, Br}]$$

e.g. $$CH_3CH_2Br + NaI \xrightarrow[\Delta]{\text{Acetone}} CH_3CH_2I + NaBr$$

NaBr or NaCl, thus formed gets precipitated in dry acetone which facilitates the forward reaction according to **Le-Chatelier's principle.**

Fluoroalkanes are best prepared by treating alkyl chloride/bromide in the presence of a metallic fluoride such as AgF, Hg_2F_2, CoF_2 or SbF_3. This reaction is known as **Swarts reaction.**

$$\underset{\text{Methyl bromide}}{CH_3Br} + \underset{\text{Silver fluoride}}{AgF} \longrightarrow \underset{\text{Fluoromethane}}{CH_3F} + AgBr$$

5. Preparation from Silver Salts of Acids

Generally, bromoalkanes are prepared by refluxing the silver salts of acids with bromine in CCl_4. This reaction is known as **Borodine-Hunsdiecker reaction.** The reaction can be depicted as:

$$CH_3CO\overset{-}{O}\overset{+}{Ag} + Br_2 \xrightarrow{CCl_4} \underset{\text{Methyl bromide}}{CH_3Br} + CO_2\uparrow + AgBr$$

Physical Properties of Haloalkanes

Some of the important physical properties of haloalkanes are as follows :

(i) **Physical State** Chloride, bromide, fluoride of methane and chloride of ethane are gases at room temperature, rest alkyl halides upto C_{18} are colourless liquids and beyond it, are colourless solids.

(ii) **Solubility** Haloalkanes have polar nature but are insoluble in polar solvents like water because they have no ability to form H-bonds with water.

However, these are soluble in organic solvents like ether, benzene etc.

(iii) **Melting and Boiling Points** Due to greater polarity as well as higher molecular mass as compared to the parent hydrocarbon, the intermolecular forces of attraction (dipole-dipole and van der Waals') are stronger in the halogen derivative. As a result, the boiling point of chlorides, bromides and iodides are considerably higher than those of the hydrocarbons of comparable molecular mass. For the same alkyl group, boiling point increases as the atomic mass of the halogen increases and hence, the magnitude of the van der Waals' forces of attraction increases.

$$RI > RBr > RCl > RF$$

For the same halogen atom, the boiling point increases with increase in the size of the alkyl group.

$$CH_3X < CH_3CH_2X < CH_3CH_2CH_2X < CH_3CH_2CH_2CH_2X \text{ (where, } X = F, Cl, Br, I)$$

For isomeric alkyl halides, boiling point decreases with branching due to decrease in surface area of the alkyl halide and hence, the magnitude of van der Waals' forces of attraction decreases.

$$CH_3CH_2CH_2CH_2Cl > CH_3CH_2\underset{\substack{|\\Cl}}{CH}CH_3 > (CH_3)_2CHCH_2Cl > (CH_3)_3CCl$$

Boiling point increases with decrease in the number of halogen atom.

$$CH_3Cl < CH_2Cl_2 < CHCl_3 < CCl_4$$

Chemical Reactions of Haloalkanes

Due to the presence of a polar C—X bond, haloalkanes are highly reactive compounds. The reactions may be divided into following categories:

Nucleophilic Substitution Reactions

When a nucleophile (i.e. electron rich species) stronger than the halide ion, reacts with haloalkane having a partial positive charge on the carbon atom bonded to halogen, a substitution reaction takes place. Since, the substitution reaction is initiated by a nucleophile, hence it is called nucleophilic substitution reaction.

$$\ddot{Nu}^- + \;>\overset{\delta+}{C}-\overset{\delta-}{X} \longrightarrow \;>C-Nu + X^-$$

Various nucleophilic substitution reactions are as follows:

(i) **Reaction with Aqueous NaOH** Haloalkanes react with boiling aqueous alkali like NaOH or KOH to give alcohols.

For Example,

$$\underset{\text{Ethyl bromide}}{C_2H_5Br} + NaOH(aq) \rightarrow \underset{\text{Ethyl alcohol}}{C_2H_5OH} + NaBr$$

(ii) **Reaction with Water** Haloalkanes are hydrolysed to alcohols by boiling water.

$$R\boxed{X + H}OH \longrightarrow \underset{\text{Alcohol}}{ROH} + HX$$

$$\underset{\text{Ethyl bromide}}{C_2H_5\boxed{Br + H}OH} \longrightarrow \underset{\text{Ethyl alcohol}}{C_2H_5OH} + HBr$$

(iii) **Reaction with Sodium Iodide** Alkyl chlorides or bromides on treatment with NaI in acetone undergo halogen exchange to give alkyl iodides.

$$C_2H_5Cl \xrightarrow[\text{Acetone}]{\text{NaI}} C_2H_5I + NaCl$$

$$C_2H_5Br \xrightarrow[\text{Acetone}]{\text{NaI}} C_2H_5I + NaBr$$

This reaction is called **Finkelstein reaction.**

(iv) **Reaction with Ammonia (Formation of Amines)** Haloalkanes on heating with ethanolic ammonia under pressure gives primary amine.

The primary amine thus formed react futher with alkyl halides and gives 2°, 3° amines and quaternary ammonium salts.

e.g.

$$\underset{\text{Ethyl bromide}}{C_2H_5Br} + NH_3 \longrightarrow \underset{\substack{\text{Ethylamine}\\(1^\circ \text{ amine})}}{C_2H_5NH_2} + HBr$$

$$C_2H_5NH_2 + C_2H_5Br \longrightarrow \underset{\substack{\text{Diethylamine}\\(2^\circ \text{ amine})}}{(C_2H_5)_2NH} + HBr$$

$$(C_2H_5)_2NH + C_2H_5Br \longrightarrow \underset{\substack{\text{Triethylamine}\\(3^\circ \text{ amine})}}{(C_2H_5)_3N} + HBr$$

$$(C_2H_5)_3N + C_2H_5Br \longrightarrow \underset{\text{Tetraethyl ammonium bromide (Quaternary salt)}}{[(C_2H_5)_4N]^+Br^-}$$

This reaction is called **ammonolysis.**

(v) **Reaction with Potassium Cyanide (Formation of Cyanides)** Haloalkanes on reaction with alcoholic solution of KCN give alkyl cyanides.

$$\underset{\text{Ethyl bromide}}{C_2H_5Br} + KCN(alc.) \longrightarrow \underset{\text{Ethyl cyanide}}{C_2H_5CN} + KBr$$

(vi) **Reaction with Silver Cyanide (Formation of Isocyanides)** Aqueous alcoholic silver cyanide when heated with haloalkanes, it gives alkyl isocyanides.

$$\underset{\text{Ethyl bromide}}{C_2H_5Br} + AgCN(aq, alc.) \longrightarrow \underset{\text{Ethyl isocyanide}}{C_2H_5NC} + AgBr$$

(vii) **Reaction with Potassium Nitrite** When haloalkanes are heated with aqueous alcoholic solution of KNO_2, alkyl nitrite are produced as major product.

$$\underset{\text{Ethyl bromide}}{C_2H_5Br} + \underset{\text{Pot. nitrite}}{K{-}O{-}N{=}O} \longrightarrow \underset{\text{Ethyl nitrite}}{C_2H_5{-}O{-}N{=}O} + KBr$$

(viii) **Reaction with Silver Nitrite** When haloalkanes are heated with an ethanolic solution of $AgNO_2$, nitro alkanes are produced as major product.

$$\underset{\text{Ethyl bromide}}{C_2H_5Br} + \underset{\text{Silver nitrite}}{Ag{-}O{-}N{=}O} \longrightarrow \underset{\text{Ethylnitrite}}{C_2H_5{-}N\!\overset{\nearrow O}{\underset{\searrow O}{}}} + AgBr$$

(ix) **Reaction with Silver Salt of Acids** (Formation of Ester) Haloalkanes on reaction with an ethanolic solution of silver salts of a carboxylic acid give esters.

$$\underset{\text{Silver acetate}}{CH_3{-}\overset{\overset{\displaystyle O}{\|}}{C}{-}O}\boxed{Ag + Br}C_2H_5 \xrightarrow{\Delta} \underset{\text{Ethyl acetate}}{CH_3{-}\overset{\overset{\displaystyle O}{\|}}{C}{-}OC_2H_5} + AgBr\downarrow$$

(x) **Reduction** Haloalkanes on reduction with $LiAlH_4$ give alkanes.

$$4C_2H_5Br + LiAlH_4 \longrightarrow \underset{\text{Ethane}}{4C_2H_6} + AlBr_3 + LiBr$$

Nucleophilic Substitution Reaction of Alkyl halide with Different Reagents

Reagent	Nucleophile (Nu^-)	Substitution product (R—Nu)	Class of main product
NaOH(KOH)	HO^-	ROH	Alcohol
H_2O	H_2O	ROH	Alcohol
NaOR'	$R'O^-$	ROR'	Ether
NaI	I^-	R—I	Alkyl iodide
NH_3	NH_3	$R\,NH_2$	Primary amine
$R'NH_2$	$R'NH_2$	$RNHR'$	*sec*-amine
$R'R''NH$	$R'R''NH$	$RNR'R''$	*tert*-amine
KCN	$\bar{C} \equiv N:$	RCN	Nitrile (cyanide)
AgCN	Ag— CN:	RNC (isocyanide)	Isonitrile
KNO_2	O=N—O^-	R—O—N=O	Alkyl nitrite
$AgNO_2$	Ag—$\ddot{O}$—N=O	R— NO_2	Nitroalkane
R'COOAg	$R'COO^-$	R'COOR	Ester
$LiAlH_4$	H^-	RH	Hydrocarbon
R'—M^+	R'^-	RR'	Alkane

Groups like cyanides and nitrites possess two nucleophilic centres and are called **ambident nucleophiles.** Cyanide group is a hybrid of two contributing structures and therefore, can act as nucleophile in two different ways

$$[\,^-{:}C \equiv N{:} \leftrightarrow {:}C{=}\bar{\ddot{N}}\,].$$

When it links through carbon atom, it results in formation of **alkyl cyanides,** while that through nitrogen atom, it results in formation of **isocyanides.**

Similarly, in nitrite ion. There are two different points of linkage ($^-O{-}\ddot{N}{=}O$). The linkage through oxygen results in **alkyl nitrites** while that through nitrogen atom, results in **nitroalkanes.**

Note Among alkyl halides, iodide ion is the best leaving group and hence, iodoalkanes undergo nucleophilic substitution reactions at the fastest rate in comparison to fluoroalkane, as fluoride ion is the poorest leaving group. Better the leaving group, more facile is the nucleophilic substitution reaction.

Example 1 Haloalkanes react with KCN to form alkyl cyanides while AgCN forms isocyanides as the chief product. Why?

Sol. K^+CN^- is predominantly ionic and provide cyanide ions in solution. Although, both carbon and nitrogen atoms are in position to donate electron pairs, the attack takes place mainly through carbon atom and not through nitrogen atom. Since, C— C bond is more stable than C— N bond. However, Ag— CN is mainly covalent in nature and only electron pair of nitrogen is available for bond formation . As a result, alkyl isocyanides are the chief products.

Example 2 Haloalkanes react with KNO_2 to form alkyl nitrites while $AgNO_2$ forms nitroalkanes as the chief product. why?

Sol. KNO_2 (or $O{=}N{-}O^-K^+$) is predominantly ionic and one of the oxygen atom have a negative charge. Nucleophilic attack through this negatively charged oxygen atom on the alkyl halides mainly gives alkyl nitrites. In contrast, $AgNO_2$ is a covalent compound and both oxygen and nitrogen atoms carry lone pair of electrons. Since, nitrogen is less electronegative than oxygen, therefore, lone pair of electrons of nitrogen is more easily available for bond formation. As a result, nitroalkanes are the chief products.

Mechanism

The nucleophilic substitution reactions proceed by the following two different mechanisms :

1. Bimolecular Nucleophilic Substitution (S_N2)

When two molecules take part in determining the rate of the reaction, it is called bimolecular nucleophilic substitution (S_N2). Here, the rate depends upon the concentration of both the reactants. e.g. The reaction between CH_3Cl and hydroxide ion to yield methanol and chloride ion follow a second order kinetics.

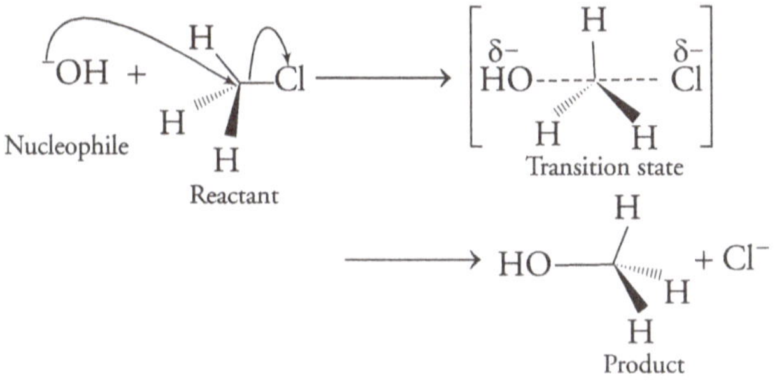

This can be represented diagrammatically as shown below :

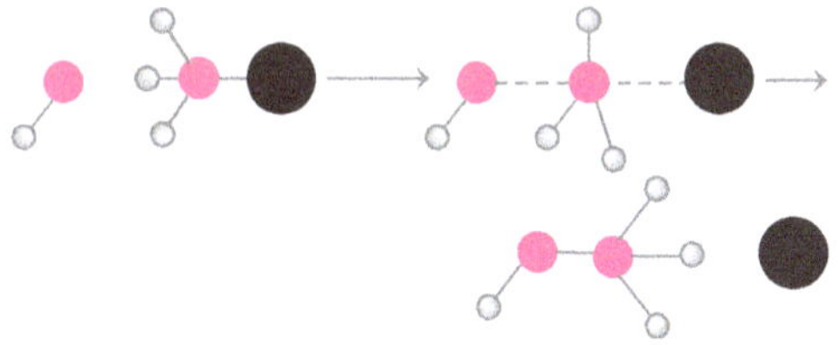

For Colour Fig. Scan

Grey dot represents the incoming hydroxide ion and black dot represents the outgoing halide ion

Mechanism In S_N2 mechanism, the incoming nucleophile approaches the alkyl halide (CH_3X) molecule and starts interacting with it due to which the carbon-halide ($C{-}X$) bond starts breaking and a new carbon-nucleophile ($C{-}OH$) bond starts forming. These two processes take place simultaneously in a single step and no intermediate is formed.

Such reaction occurs through the formation of a transition state. In transition state, the C-atom is simultaneously bonded to incoming nucleophile and also to the outgoing leaving group, i.e. carbon is bonded to five atoms. Thus, this state is unstable and results in the formation of the product.

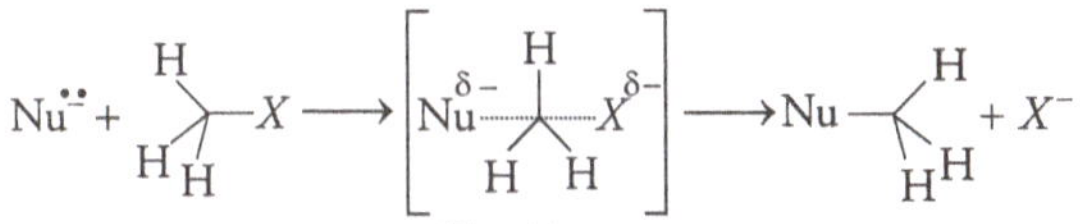

Transition state

In S_N2 reactions, the attack of nucleophile (i.e. Nu^-) occurs from the backside and the leaving group leaves from the front side. As this happens, the configuration of C-atom under attack invert in the same way as an umbrella is turned inside out when caught in a strong wind, while the leaving group is pushed away, this process is called **inversion of configuration** or **Walden inversion** and is a characteristic feature of S_N2 reaction.

Tertiary halides are least reactive because of the presence of bulky groups which hinders the approaching nucleophiles. Non-polar solvents favour S_N2 mechanism.

Thus, the order of reactivity of alkyl halides toward S_N2 reactions is as follows :

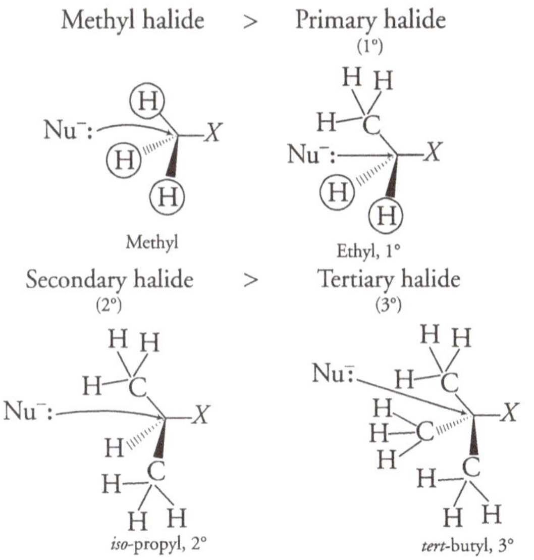

Steric effects in S_N2 reaction

2. Unimolecular Nucleophilic Substitution (S_N1)

When only one molecule is involved in determining the rate of the reaction, it is called unimolecular nucleophilic substitution. Such type of reactions are generally carried out in polar protic solvents such as water, alcohol, acetic acid, etc., because they stabilise the carbocation by solvation.

Mechanism

S_N1 *reaction occurs via two steps :*

In ***step*** **I**, formation of carbocation takes place due to the heterolytic cleavage of —C—X bond. This step is slow and reversible (rate determining step). This step involves only one reactant, i.e. alkyl halide, therefore, rate of reaction depends only on the concentration of alkyl halide and not on the concentration of nucleophile.

In ***step*** **II**, nucleophile attack the carbocation formed in step I and the substitution reaction completes.

e.g. The reaction between *tert*-butyl bromide and hydroxide ion yield *tert*-butyl alcohol.

$$(CH_3)_3C—Br + OH^- \longrightarrow (CH_3)_3COH + Br^-$$

Step I Formation of carbocation intermediate

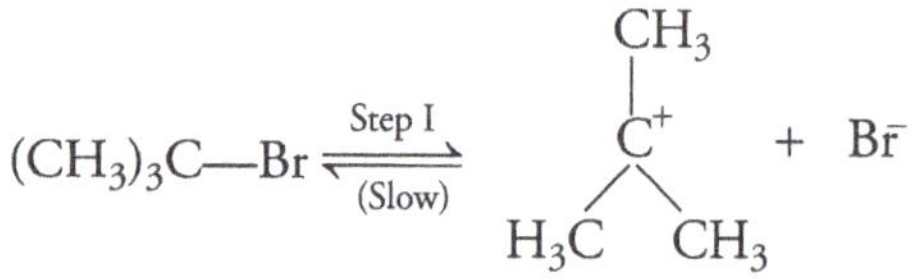

Step II Attack of nucleophile on carbocation formed

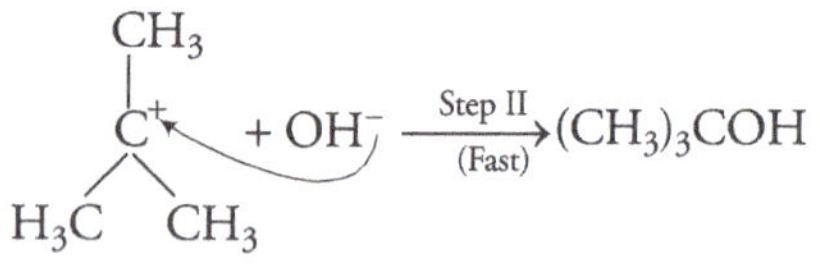

Greater the stability of carbocation, greater will be its ease of formation of product from alkyl halide and faster will be the rate of reaction. That's why, 3° alkyl halides undergo S_N1 reaction very fast because of high stability of 3° carbocations.

Therefore, the order of reactivity of alkyl halides toward S_N1 reactions is as follows:

Methyl halide < Primary halide < Secondary halide < Tertiary halide.

We can sum up the order of reactivity of alkyl halide towards S_N1 and S_N2 reactions as follows:

S_N1 reactivity increases ←

Tertiary halide, Secondary halide, Primary halide, CH_3X

→ S_N2 reactivity increases

- For a given alkyl group, the reactivity of the halide, $R—X$ follows the same order in both the mechanisms, S_N1 and S_N2.

$$R—I > R—Br > R—Cl > R—F$$

Difference between S_N1 and S_N2 Reaction

Characteristics	S_N1	S_N2
Number of steps	It is a two step mechanism.	It is a one step mechanism.
Nature	Ionic in nature.	Non-ionic in nature.
Molecularity	Unimolecular reaction.	Bimolecular reactions.
Strength of nulceophile	Low concentration of OH^- favours this mechanism.	High concentration of OH^- favours this mechanism.
Effect of solvent	Polar solvent favours it.	Non-polar solvent favours it.
Stereochemistry	Racemisation takes place.	Inversion of configuration takes place.

Stereochemical Aspects of Nucleophilic Substitution Reactions

S_N2 reaction proceeds with the complete stereochemical inversion while S_N1 reaction proceeds with racemisation.

Before discussing this concept, we need to learn some stereochemical principles and notations. These are as follows:

(i) Plane Polarised Light and Optical Activity

A beam of ordinary light consists of electromagnetic waves vibrating in all planes in space. When this light is passed through a nicol prism, it becomes plane polarised light, which vibrates only in one plane.

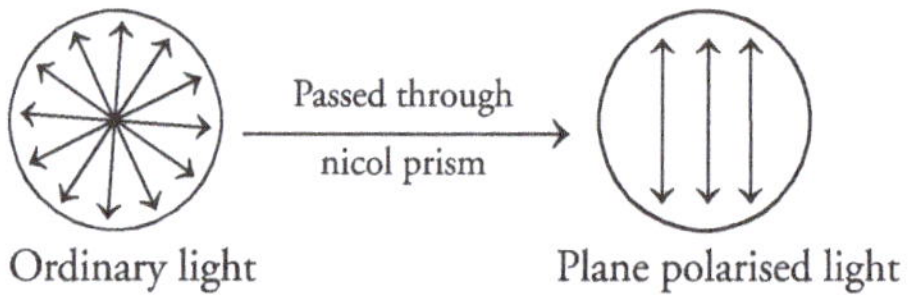

Polarisation of ordinary light

When the solutions of certain organic compounds are placed in the path of plane polarised light, they rotate the path of the light either to left or right, such substances are called **optically active substances.**

A substance which rotates the plane polarised light to the right is called **dextrorotatory** or ***d*-form** and is indicated by placing a positive (+) sign before the degree of rotation.

The substance which rotates the plane polarised light towards the left is called **laevorotatory** or ***l*-form** and is indicated by placing a negative (–) sign before the **degree of rotation**.

Such *d*-and *l*-forms of compound are called **optical isomers** and the phenomenon is called **optical isomerism.**

(ii) Specific Rotation

It is defined as the rotation of plane of polarised light by a solution of 10 cm (1 dm) and unit concentration (1 g/mL) for the given wavelength of the light at the given temperature.

Specific rotation, $\boxed{[\alpha]_{\lambda}^{t} = \dfrac{\alpha_{obs}}{e \times C}}$

Where, α_{obs} = Measured rotation expressed in degree
l = Length of the tube containing the solution in decimeter
C = Concentration in g/mL of solution
t = Temperature in degree celsius
λ = Wavelength of the light.

(iii) Molecular Asymmetry, Chirality and Enantiomers

The four valencies of carbon atom are directed towards the corners of regular tetrahedron and if all the atoms or groups attached to a carbon atom are different, such carbon atom is called **asymmetric carbon atom** or **stereocentre.** The resulting molecule would lack symmetry and the molecule is called **asymmetric molecule**. The asymmetry of the molecule is responsible for the optical activity in such organic compounds.

All molecules or objects have mirror images. An object or molecule which is not superimposable on its mirror image is called **chiral** and this property is called **chirality,** e.g. human hand.

The objects which are superimposable on their mirror images are called **achiral**. Let us take two simple molecules, propan-2-ol and butan-2-ol and their mirror images. Propan-2-ol does not contain asymmetric carbon atom. Therefore, it is achiral.

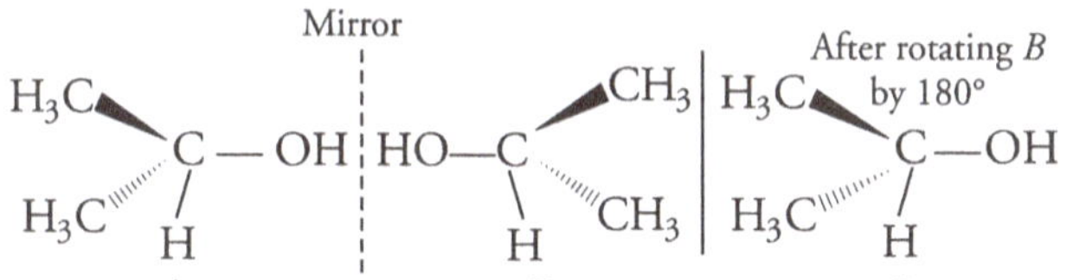

A *B* *C*

The structure *C* is superimposable on *A*.

Butan-2-ol molecule contains asymmetric carbon atom and as expected is chiral.

It has non-superimposable mirror images as shown in the figure:

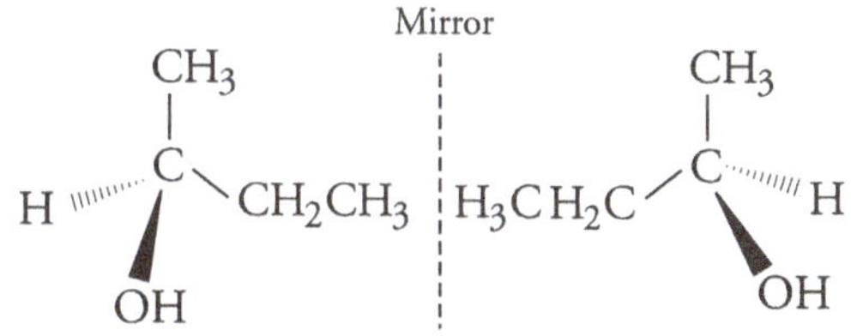

Some common examples of chiral molecules are :

2-chlorobutane : $(CH_3CH(Cl)CH_2CH_3)$,
2,3-dihydroxy propanal : (OHC—CHOH—CH_2OH),
bromochloroiodomethane : (BrClCHI),
2-bromopropanoic acid : (H_3C—CHBr—COOH).

The optical isomers which are non-superimposable mirror images of each other are called **enantiomers** and the phenomenon is called **enantiomerism.**

The enantiomers have identical physical and chemical properties but differs with respect to the rotation of plane polarised light. If one of the enantiomer is dextrorotatory then other will be laevorotatory.

Racemic Mixtures and Racemisation

A mixture containing two enantiomers in equal proportions will have zero optical rotation, as the rotation due to one isomer will be cancelled by the rotation due to the other isomer. Such a mixture is called **racemic mixture.** It is represented as *dl* or ± forms and will be optically inactive. The process of converting *d* - or *l*-form of an optically active compound into racemic form (*dl*) is called racemisation.

Retention

When the relative spatial arrangement of bonds to an asymmetric centre in a chiral molecule remains the same before and after the reaction, the reaction is said to occur with **retention of configuration**, e.g.

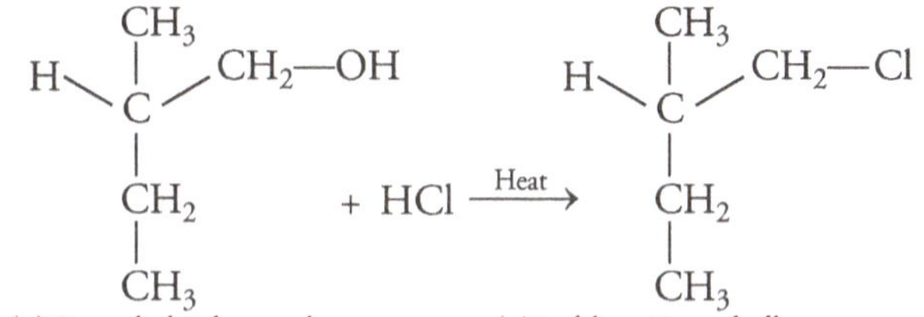

(–) 2-methyl-1-butanol (+)1-chloro-2-methylbutane

In the above example, no bond at the asymmetric carbon is broken, and the product will have the same general configuration of groups around the stereocentre as that of reactants. Therefore, the reaction proceeds with retention of configuration inspite of change of optical rotation from (–) to (+).

Inversion

If the relative spatial arrangement of bonds at an asymmetric carbon atom becomes opposite as compared to reactant after the reaction, then the reaction is called **inversion**.

Stereochemical Aspects of S_N2 Reaction

In S_N2 mechanism, the nucleophile attacks on the side opposite to one where halogen atom is present. Therefore, S_N2 reaction is always accompanied by inversion of configuration, that is called as **Walden inversion.**

e.g. When (–) 2-halobutane is allowed to react with potassium hydroxide, (+) butane-2-ol is formed with the —OH group occupying the position opposite to what bromide had occupied.

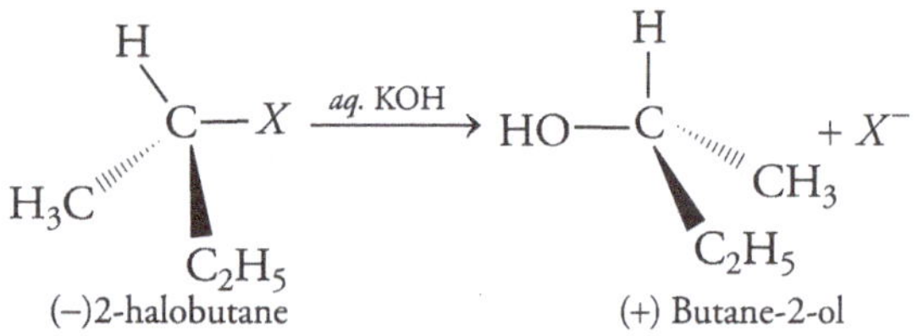

Thus, S_N2 reaction of optically active alkyl halides is always accompanied by the inversion of configuration.

Stereochemical Aspects of S_N1 Reaction

In S_N1 reactions, if the alkyl halide is optically active, the product obtained is a racemic mixture. The intermediate carbocation formed in slowest step being sp^2-hybridised is planar (achiral) species .

Therefore, the attack of the nucleophile OH^- can occur from both the faces with equal ease of forming a mixture of two enantiomers. Thus, S_N1 reaction of optically active alkyl halides are accompanied by racemisation.

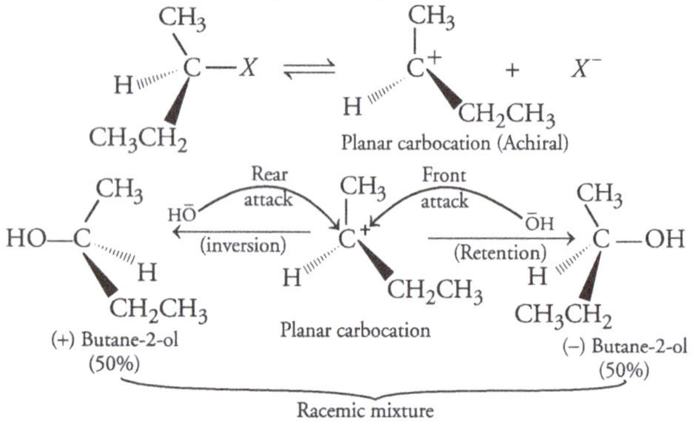

Elimination Reactions : Dehydrohalogenation (Formation of Alkenes)

When a haloalkane with β-hydrogen atom is heated with alc. KOH solution, then alkene is formed. In this reaction, hydrogen is eliminated from β-carbon and the halogen is lost from α-carbon atom. As a result, an alkene is formed as a product. Due to the involvement of elimination of β-hydrogen atom, the process is often called as β-elimination.

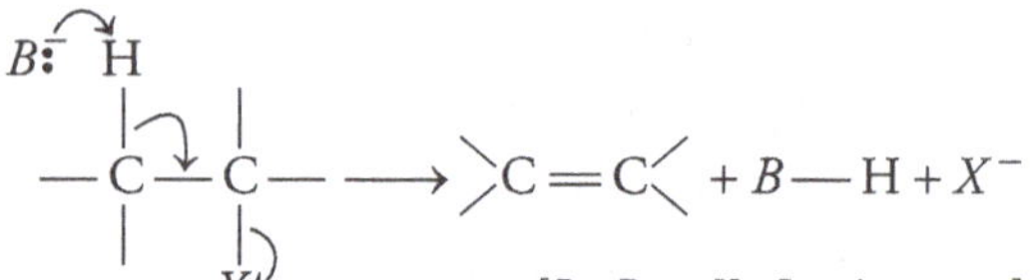

[*B* = Base; *X* = Leaving group]

e.g. $H—CH_2—CH_2Br + KOH\ (alc.) \xrightarrow{Heat} CH_2{=}CH_2 + KBr + H_2O$

If there is possibility for the formation of more than one alkene due to the availability of more than one β-hydrogen atoms, usually one alkene is formed as the major product. This occurs according to the **Saytzeff rule**, which can be summarised as "in dehydrohalogenation reactions, the preferred product is that alkene which has the greater number of alkyl groups attached to the doubly bonded carbon atoms".

e.g. 2-bromopentane gives pent-2-ene as the major product.

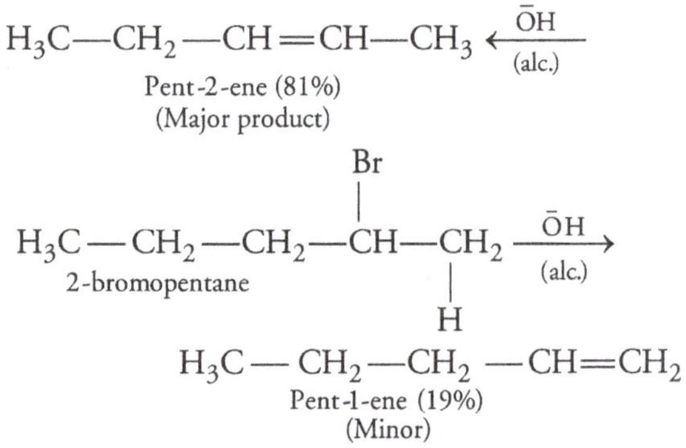

Elimination *versus* Substitution

When alkyl halide reacts with nucleophile, it may undergo either substitution *via* S_N1 and S_N2 or elimination reaction.

It depends upon the following factors :

(i) **Nature of Alkyl Halide** Primary alkyl halide will prefer S_N2 reaction, i.e. nucleophilic substitution reaction *via* S_N2 mechanism. Secondary alkyl halide can undergo substitution or elimination depending upon the strength of the nucleophile. Tertiary alkyl halide will undergo substitution or elimination depending upon the stability of carbocation or the more substituted alkene.

(ii) **Strength and Size of the Nucleophile or Base** A bulkier nucleophile will carry out the elimination more easily than substitution as it prefers to act as a base and abstracts a proton rather than approaching a tetravalent carbon atom (due to steric reasons) and *vice-versa*. Stronger nucleophiles like $C_2H_5O^-$ will bring out the elimination whereas, nucleophiles like OH^- will bring out the substitution.

(iii) **The conditions of the reaction such as temperature, pressure, etc.**

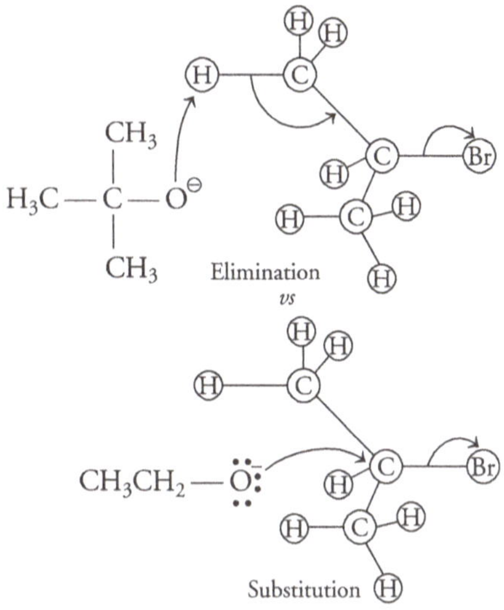

Reaction with Metals

Most organic chlorides, bromides and iodides react with certain metals to give compounds containing carbon-metal bonds. Such compounds are known as **organometallic compounds.**

1. Action with Magnesium

(Formation of Grignard Reagents)

Victor Grignard in 1900 discovered an important class of organometallic compounds, i.e. alkyl magnesium halide, $R—MgX$ which is commonly called Grignard reagents.

The Grignard reagents are obtained by the reaction of haloalkanes with magnesium metal in presence of dry ether.

$$CH_3CH_2Br + Mg \xrightarrow{\text{Dry ether}} \underset{\text{Grignard reagent}}{CH_3CH_2\,MgBr}$$

In the Grignard reagent, the carbon-magnesium bond is covalent but highly polar, with carbon pulling electrons from electropositive magnesium, the magnesium halogen bond is essentially ionic.

$$\overset{\delta^-}{R}—\overset{\delta^+}{Mg}\,\overset{\delta^-}{X}$$

These are highly reactive and react with any source of proton to give hydrocarbons. Even alcohols, amines, water are sufficiently acidic to convert them to corresponding hydrocarbons.

$$RMgX + H_2O \longrightarrow RH + Mg(OH)X$$

Due to its high reactivity, it is necessary to avoid even traces of moisture from a Grignard reagent.

On the other hand, this could be considered as one of the methods for converting halides to hydrocarbons.

2. Action with Sodium (Wurtz Reaction)

The reactions in which alkyl halides react with sodium in the presence of dry ether to form hydrocarbons containing double the number of carbon atoms present in the halide, are known as **Wurtz reaction.**

$$2RX + 2Na \xrightarrow{\text{Dry ether}} R—R + 2NaX$$

Topic Practice 1

Very Short Answer Type Questions

1 Mark

1. **Fill in the Blanks**
   (i) Presence of two halogen atoms of same type in the structure of haloalkanes are called ....
   (ii) When halogen atom is bonded with the sp^3-hybrid carbon atom, next to carbon-carbon double bond, molecule is called ....
   (iii) IUPAC name of a molecule having three carbon atoms and two bromine atoms on the second carbon is called ....
   (iv) The reaction of chlorine with methane in presence of sunlight is a .... reaction which involve .... fission of the C—H bond.
   (v) Use of $SOCl_2$ in presence of pyridine for the reaction with alcohols is preferred to get chloroalkanes because the by products are .... and .... gases.
   (vi) Alkanes give haloalkanes with halogens in the presence of UV - light. This reaction proceeds through .... mechanism.

2. **Objective Type Questions**
   (i) Which of the following is an example of *geminal* halide?
   (a) $CH_3—CH_2—CH_2—Cl$
   (b) $CH_3—\underset{Cl}{CH}—\underset{Cl}{CH}—CH_3$
   (c) $CH_3—\underset{Cl\;\;Cl}{C}—CH_2—CH_3$
   (d) $CH_3—\underset{Cl}{CH}—\underset{Cl}{CH}—CH_2—Cl$

(ii) If R = alkyl group in which of the following species, halogen (X) atom is attached with the secondary carbon atom.

(a) $R—CH_2—X$ (b) $R—CH(R)—X$

(c) $R—C(R)(R)—X$ (d) $R—C(R)(R)—C—X$

(iii) IUPAC name of $CH_2 = CH—CH_2—Br$ is

(a) 1-bromo 2- propene (b) 3-bromopropene
(c) 3-bromopropane (d) 1-bromo-2-propane

(iv) Preparation of alkyl halides in laboratory is least preferred by

(a) halide exchange
(b) treatment of alcohols
(c) addition of hydrogen halides to alkenes
(d) direct halogenation of alkanes

(v) Tertiary alkyl halides are practically inert to substitution by S_N2 mechanism because of

(a) insolubility (b) instability
(c) inductive effect (d) steric hindrance

(vi) In the addition of HBr to propene in the absence of peroxide, the first step involves the addition of

(a) H^+ (b) Br^- (c) H^- (d) Br

(vii) Chloromethane on treatment with excess of ammonia yields mainly

(a) N, N - dimethylmethanamine $CH_3—N(CH_3)_2$
(b) N - methylmethanamine ($CH_3—NH—CH_3$)
(c) methanamine (CH_3NH_2)
(d) mixture containing all these in equal proportion

3. Match the reactants (in Column I) with their products (in Column II) and choose the correct option using the codes given below :

Column I	Column II
A. C_2H_5Cl + moist Ag_2O	(i) CH_3CH_2ONO
B. C_2H_5Cl + aqueous ethanolic AgCN	(ii) C_2H_4
C. C_2H_5Cl + aqueous ethanolic $AgNO_2$	(iii) CH_3CH_2OH
D. C_2H_5Cl + ethanolic KOH	(iv) CH_3CH_2NC

Codes

	A	B	C	D
(a)	(ii)	(iii)	(iv)	(i)
(b)	(i)	(iv)	(ii)	(iii)
(c)	(iii)	(iv)	(i)	(ii)
(d)	(iv)	(i)	(iii)	(ii)

4. How can the following conversion be brought about methyl chloride to acetone? **ISC 2016**

5. Suggest a possible mechanism for the following reaction:

$$n\text{-BuBr} + KCN \xrightarrow{EtOH, H_2O} n\text{-BuCN}$$ **ISC 2009, 2008**

6. (i) Identify the chiral molecule in the following pair:

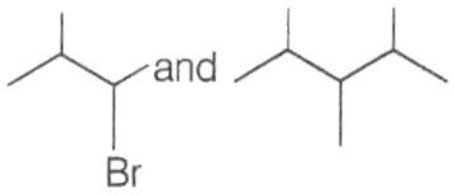

(ii) Write the structure of the alkene formed by dehydrohalogenation of 1 - bromine - 1 methylcyclohexane with alcoholic KOH.

7. Write the IUPAC name of

$CH_3CH = CH—C(CH_3)(Br)—CH_3$

8. Write the IUPAC name of the following compound.

$CH_3—CH(Cl)—CH_2—CH = CH_2$

9. Out of 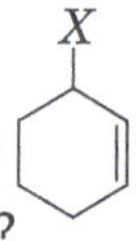 and 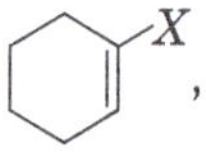, which is an allylic halide?

10. Write the structure of 3-bromo-2-methylprop-1-ene.

11. Give the IUPAC name of the following compound.

$CH_2 = C(CH_3)—CH_2Br$ *Or* 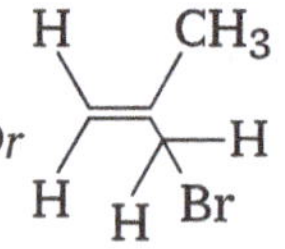

12. Write the IUPAC name of $(CH_3)_2CH \cdot CH(Cl)CH_3$.

13. Write the structure of the compound 4-*tert*-butyl-3-iodoheptane. **NCERT Intext; NCERT**

14. Identify the products A and B formed in the following reaction.

$CH_3—CH_2—CH = CH—CH_3 + HCl \longrightarrow A + B$ **NCERT Exemplar**

15. What happens when ethyl chloride is treated with aqueous KOH? **NCERT**

16. Out of $CH_3-\underset{\underset{CH_3}{|}}{CH}-CH_2-Cl$ and

$CH_3-CH_2-\underset{\underset{CH_3}{|}}{CH}-Cl$,

which one is more reactive towards S_N1 reaction and why?

17. Which would undergo S_N2 reaction faster in the following pair and why?

CH_3-CH_2-Br and $CH_3-\overset{\overset{CH_3}{|}}{\underset{\underset{Br}{|}}{C}}-CH_3$

Short Answer Type I Questions

2 Marks

18. Write the IUPAC name of the following compounds.

(i) $CH_3-\overset{\overset{F}{|}}{\underset{\underset{C_2H_5}{|}}{C}}-CH_2-\overset{\overset{Cl}{|}}{\underset{\underset{C_2H_5}{|}}{C}}-CH_3$

(ii) $CH_3-\overset{\overset{CH_3}{|}}{\underset{\underset{CH_3}{|}}{C}}-\underset{\underset{Cl}{|}}{CH}-CH_3$

19. Give the IUPAC names of the following compounds:

(i) $CH_3CH(Cl)CH(Br)CH_3$

(ii) $CHF_2CBrClF$

(iii) $ClCH_2C\equiv CCH_2Br$ **NCERT**

20. Write the structures of different dihalogen derivatives of propane. **NCERT Intext**

21. A hydrocarbon, C_5H_{10} does not react with chlorine in dark but gives a single monochlorocompound, C_5H_9Cl in bright sunlight. Identify the hydrocarbon. **NCERT**

22. How will you carry out the following conversions?

2-bromopropane to 1-bromopropane

23. Write the structure of the major organic products in each of the following reactions.

(i) $CH_3CH_2CH_2Cl + NaI \xrightarrow[\text{Heat}]{\text{Acetone}}$

(ii) $CH_3CH_2CH_2OH + SOCl_2 \xrightarrow{\text{Pyridine}}$

(iii) $CH_3CH_2CH=CH_2 + HBr \xrightarrow{\text{Peroxide}}$

(iv) $CH_3CH=\underset{\underset{CH_3}{|}}{C}(CH_3) + HBr \longrightarrow$ **NCERT**

24. Arrange each set of compounds in the order of increasing boiling points.

(i) Bromomethane, bromoform, chloromethane, dibromomethane

(ii) 1-chloropropane, *iso*-propyl chloride, 1-chlorobutane **NCERT Intext**

25. The treatment of alkyl chlorides with aqueous KOH, leads to the formation of alcohols but in the presence of alcoholic KOH, alkenes are major products. Explain. **NCERT**

26. Among the following alcohols, which will yield the corresponding alkyl chloride on reaction with concentrated HCl at room temperature?

$CH_3-CH_2-\underset{\underset{CH_3}{|}}{CH}-CH_2OH$,

$CH_3CH_2-\overset{\overset{CH_3}{|}}{\underset{\underset{CH_3}{|}}{C}}-OH$,

$CH_3-CH_2-CH_2-\underset{\underset{CH_3}{|}}{CH}-OH$

27. (i) Which alkyl halide from the following pair is chiral and undergoes faster towards S_N2 reaction?

(a) 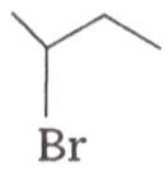

(b) 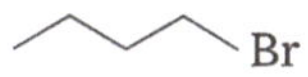

(ii) Out of S_N1 and S_N2, which reaction occurs with

(a) inversion of configuration?

(b) racemisation?

28. Which compound in each of the following pairs will react faster in S_N2 reaction with OH^- and why?

(i) CH_3Br or CH_3I

(ii) $(CH_3)_3CCl$ or CH_3Cl **NCERT**

29. *Tert*-butylbromide reacts with *aq.* NaOH by S_N1 mechanism while *n*-butylbromide reacts by S_N2 mechanism. Why? **NCERT Exemplar**

30. Write the balanced chemical equations for the following name reactions **ISC 2023**
(i) Wurtz reaction
(ii) Finkelstein reaction

Short Answer Type II Questions

3 Marks

31. Name the following halides according to the IUPAC system and classify them as alkyl, allyl, benzyl (primary, secondary, tertiary), vinyl or aryl halides.
(i) $CH_3C(Cl)(C_2H_5)CH_2CH_3$
(ii) $CH_3CH{=}C(Cl)CH_2CH(CH_3)_2$
(iii) $CH_3CH{=}CHC(Br)(CH_3)_2$ **NCERT**

32. Draw the structures of major monohalo products in each of the following reactions.

(i) 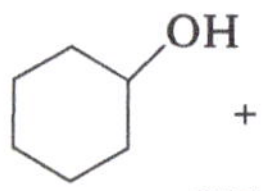 $+ SOCl_2 \longrightarrow$

(ii) 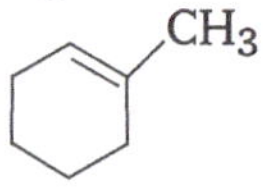 $+ HI \longrightarrow$

(iii) $CH_3CH_2Br + NaI \longrightarrow$

(iv)  $+ Br_2 \xrightarrow[\text{UV-light}]{\text{Heat}}$

33. Explain,
(i) why alkyl halides, though polar, are immiscible with water?
Or why is the solubility of haloalkanes in water very low? **NCERT Exemplar**
(ii) why Grignard reagents should be prepared under anhydrous conditions? **NCERT**

34. What happens, when
(i) ethyl chloride is treated with $AgNO_2$?
(ii) 2-bromopentane is treated with alcoholic KOH?
Write the chemical equations in support of your answer.

35. Primary alkyl halide C_4H_9Br (*A*) reacts with alcoholic KOH to give compound *B*. Compound *B* is reacted with HBr to give *C*, which is an isomer of *A*. When *A* is reacted with sodium metal, it gives compound *D*, C_8H_{18} which is different from the compound formed when *n*-butyl bromide is reacted with sodium. Give the structural formula of *A* and write the equations for all the reactions. **NCERT**

36. Identify *A*, *B*, *C*, *P*, *Q*, *R* and *R'* in the following:

(i) 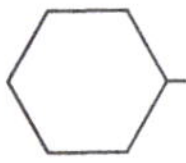 $—Br + Mg \xrightarrow{\text{Dry ether}} A \xrightarrow{H_2O} B$

(ii) $R—Br + Mg \xrightarrow{\text{Dry ether}} C \xrightarrow{D_2O} CH_3\underset{\displaystyle D}{\underset{|}{C}}HCH_3$

(iii) 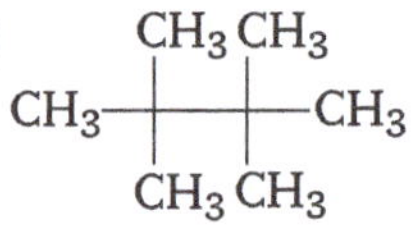 $\xleftarrow{\text{Na/Ether}} R'–X \xrightarrow{Mg} P \xrightarrow{H_2O} Q$

NCERT Intext

37. Give reasons:
(i) *n*-butyl bromide has higher boiling point than *t*-butyl bromide.
(ii) Racemic mixture is optically inactive.

38. Following compounds are given to you:
2-bromopentane, 2-bromo-2-methylbutane, 1-bromopentane
(i) Write the compound which is most reactive towards S_N2 reaction.
(ii) Write the compound which is optically active.
(iii) Write the compound which is most reactive towards β-elimination reaction.

39. Give reasons for the following:
(i) Ethyl iodide undergoes S_N2 reaction faster than ethyl bromide.
(ii) (±) 2-butanol is optically inactive.
(iii) C—*X* bond length in halobenzene is smaller than C—*X* bond length in CH_3—*X*.
Or The C— Cl bond length in chlorobenzene is shorter than that in CH_3Cl.

Long Answer Type Questions

5 Marks

40. Name the following halides according to IUPAC system and classify them as alkyl, allyl, benzyl (primary, secondary, tertiary), vinyl or aryl halides.
(i) $(CH_3)_2CHCH(Cl)CH_3$
(ii) $CH_3CH_2CH(CH_3)CH(C_2H_5)Cl$
(iii) $CH_3CH_2C(CH_3)_2CH_2I$
(iv) $CH_3CH(CH_3)CH(Br)CH_3$
(v) $CH_3C(C_2H_5)_2CH_2Br$ **NCERT**

41. Write a chemical reaction to depict the preparation of haloalkane from each of the following.
(i) Ethyl alcohol (ii) Propane

42. How can the following conversions be carried out?
(i) Ethyl chloride to propanoic acid
(ii) Ethanol to propane nitrile
(iii) 1-bromopropane to 2-bromopropane
(iv) 2-chlorobutane to 3,4-dimethylhexane
(v) 2-methyl-1-propene to 2-chloro-2-methylpropane **NCERT**

Hints & Solutions

1 (i) dihalides
(ii) allylic halide
(iii) *gem*-dihalides, i.e. 2, 2-dibromopropane
(iv) The reaction of chlorine with methane is a substitution reaction, which involves homolytic fission of the C—H bond.

$$CH_4 + Cl_2 \xrightarrow{\text{Sunlight}} CH_3Cl + HCl$$

(v) $SO_2(g)$ and $HCl(g)$
(vi) free radical mechanism

2 (i) (c) $CH_3—C(Cl)(Cl)—CH_2—CH_3$ is an example of *geminal* dihalide, because it has two halogen atoms on the same carbon atom.
(ii) (b) $R—CH(R)—X$ is the correct answer because in this structure, halogen atom is bonded with the carbon atom which is directly bonded with two carbon atoms.
(iii) (b) IUPAC name is 3-bromopropene.
(iv) (d) Preparation of alkyl halide is least preferred by direct halogenation of alkanes because a mixture of monohalogen, dihalogen, trihalogen and tetrahalogen substituted product is obtained by this method. These are difficult to separate.

$$CH_4 \xrightarrow[h\nu]{Cl_2} CH_3Cl \xrightarrow[h\nu]{Cl_2} CH_2Cl_2 \xrightarrow{Cl_2}$$

$$CHCl_3 \xrightarrow[h\nu]{Cl_2} CCl_4$$

(v) (d) Steric hindrance due to bulky alkyl groups prevent the backside attack of S_N2.
(vi) (a) Addition of HBr to an alkene is an electrophilic addition reaction. Here, the first step involves the addition of H^+.
(vii) (c) Chloromethane (CH_3Cl) on reaction with excess of ammonia (NH_3) gives product methanamine ($CH_3—NH_2$).

3 (c) A→(iii), B →(iv), C →(i), D →(ii)

S.No.	Reactants	Products
A.	C_2H_5Cl, moist Ag_2O	CH_3CH_2OH
B.	C_2H_5Cl, aqueous ethanolic AgCN	CH_3CH_2NC
C.	C_2H_5Cl, aqueous ethanolic $AgNO_2$	CH_3CH_2ONO
D.	C_2H_5Cl, ethanolic KOH	C_2H_4

4 $\underset{\text{Methyl chloride}}{CH_3Cl} \xrightarrow[\text{Ether}]{Mg} \underset{\text{Methyl magnesium chloride}}{CH_3MgCl}$

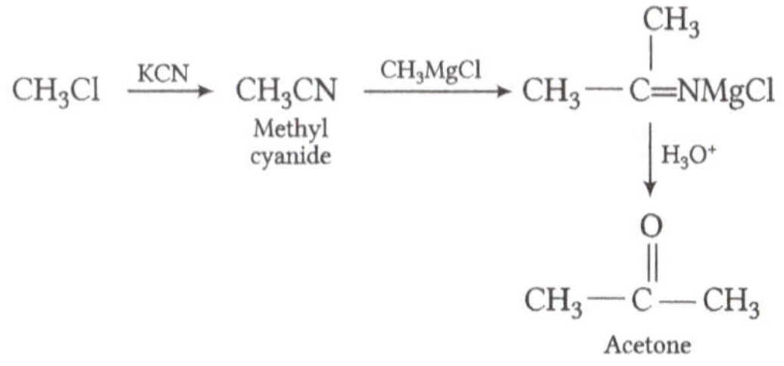

5 **Key idea**
(i) Write the resonating structures of KCN.
(ii) Due to the presence of polar solvent, find the possibility, which product will be formed preferentially.

KCN is a reagent that gives CN^- ion as nucleophile in aqueous medium.

Resonating forms of KCN

$$K^+[:\bar{C}{\equiv}N:] \longleftrightarrow K^+[:C{=}\ddot{\bar{N}}:]$$

$$K^+CN^- + CH_3CH_2CH_2\overset{\delta+}{CH_2}\overset{\delta-}{Br} \longrightarrow CH_3CH_2CH_2CH_2CN + KBr$$

or n-BuBr + KCN ⟶ n-BuCN + KBr

CN^- is an ambident nucleophile therefore, it can attack either through C-atom or through N-atom. Since, C— C is a stronger bond than C—N bond, therefore it's attack occurs through C to form n-butyl cyanide.

6 (i) A molecule which completely lacks symmetry is called chiral. The mirror images of such molecules are non-superimposable.
Molecule (i) is chiral in given structures as the mirror images are

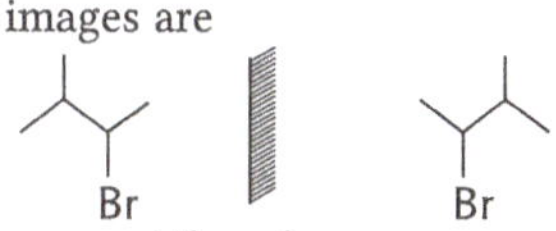

Mirror image
(Non-superimposble)

(ii)

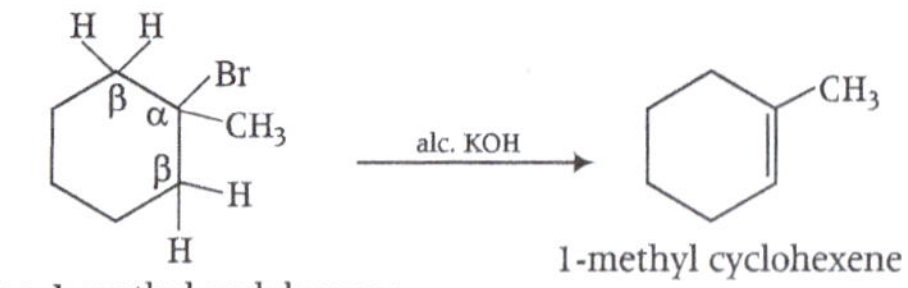

1-bromo-1-methyl cyclohexane   1-methyl cyclohexene

β-hydrogen on each side of Br atom are equivalent, because of which only one alkene will be formed.

7 4-bromo-4-methylpent-2-ene

8 $\overset{5}{C}H_3-\overset{4}{C}H(Cl)-\overset{3}{C}H_2-\overset{2}{C}H=\overset{1}{C}H_2$

4-chloropent-1-ene

9 In allylic halides, the halogen is bonded to the sp^3-hybridised carbon atom next to a carbon-carbon double bond. Thus, 3-halocyclohex-1-ene is an allylic halide.

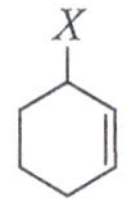

3-halocyclohex-1-ene

10 The structure of 3-bromo-2-methylprop-1-ene is

$BrCH_2-C(CH_3)=CH_2$

11 $\overset{1}{C}H_2=\overset{2}{C}(CH_3)-\overset{3}{C}H_2Br$

IUPAC name : 3-bromo-2-methylprop-1-ene

12 $(\underset{4}{H_3C})(H_3C)\underset{3}{C}H-\underset{2}{C}H(Cl)-\underset{1}{C}H_3$

IUPAC name : 2-chloro-3-methylbutane

13 $\overset{1}{C}H_3-\overset{2}{C}H_2-\overset{3}{C}H(I)-\overset{4}{C}H(C(CH_3)_3)-\overset{5}{C}H_2\overset{6}{C}H_2\overset{7}{C}H_3$

(4-substituent: $H_3C-C(CH_3)-CH_3$)

4-*tert*-butyl-3-iodoheptane

14 In the given reaction, addition occurs and following two products (*A* and *B*) are possible.

$H_3C-CH_2-CH=CH-CH_3+HCl\longrightarrow$

$CH_3-CH_2-CH_2-CH(Cl)-CH_3$

2-chloropentane (*A*)

$+\ CH_3-CH_2-CH(Cl)-CH_2-CH_3$

3-chloropentane (*B*)

15 Ethyl chloride being a primary alkyl halide undergoes bimolecular nucleophilic substitution (S_N2) reaction leading to the formation of ethanol.

$$C_2H_5Cl+KOH(aq)\longrightarrow C_2H_5OH+KCl$$

16 $CH_3-CH_2-CH(CH_3)-Cl$ will undergo S_N1 reaction faster because it is a secondary alkyl halide and forms a secondary carbocation that can stabilise itself more than primary carbocation.

17 On steric hindrance grounds, 1° alkyl halides are more reactive than *tert*-alkyl halides in S_N2 reactions. Thus, CH_3-CH_2-Br reacts at a faster rate than $(CH_3)_3CBr$ in S_N2 reaction, because it is a primary halide, i.e. less hindered.

18 (i) 3-chloro-5-fluoro-3,5-dimethylheptane

(ii) 2-chloro-3,3-dimethylbutane (halogen is preferred over alkyl group while naming).

19 To write the IUPAC name, draw the structures, find the longest carbon chain, give the numbers and name them.

(i) $\overset{4}{C}H_3-\overset{3}{C}H(Cl)-\overset{2}{C}H(Br)-\overset{1}{C}H_3$

IUPAC name: 2-bromo-3-chlorobutane

(ii) $CHF_2CBrClF$

IUPAC name: 1-bromo-1-chloro-1,2,2-trifluoroethane

(iii) $Cl-\overset{4}{C}H_2-\overset{3}{C}\equiv\overset{2}{C}-\overset{1}{C}H_2-Br$

IUPAC name: 1-bromo-4-chlorobut-2-yne

20 The structures of different dihalogen derivatives of propane are :

(i) $Br-\overset{1}{C}H_2-\overset{2}{C}H_2-\overset{3}{C}H_2-Br$

1, 3 - dibromopropane (I)

(ii) $Br-\overset{1}{C}H_2-\overset{2}{C}H(Br)-\overset{3}{C}H_3$,

1, 2-dibromopropane (II)

(iii) $\overset{3}{C}H_3-\overset{2}{C}H_2-\overset{1}{C}H(Br)-Br$

1, 1 - dibromopropane (III)

(iv) $\overset{3}{C}H_3-\overset{2}{C}(Br)_2-\overset{1}{C}H_3$

2, 2-dibromopropane (IV)

21 Enlist the possibilities of structures for molecular formula, C_5H_{10} which react in dark and in sunlight. In the given reaction,

(i) Molecular formula C_5H_{10} can be either alkene or cycloalkane.

(ii) Since, the hydrocarbon does not react with chlorine in dark, hence, it is not an alkene but is a cycloalkane.

(iii) Since, it forms only single monochloro derivative in bright sunlight, all the H-atoms should be identical. So, it is a cyclopentane.

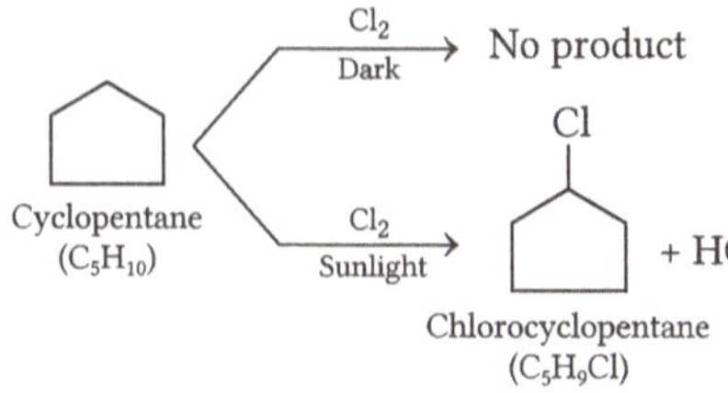

22 2-bromopropane to 1-bromopropane

$$CH_3-\underset{\underset{Br}{|}}{CH}-CH_3 \xrightarrow{\text{Alc.KOH}} CH_3-CH=CH_2 \xrightarrow{\text{HBr, peroxide}} CH_3CH_2CH_2Br$$

23 (i) $\underset{\text{1-chloropropane}}{CH_3CH_2-CH_2-Cl} + NaI \xrightarrow[\text{Heat}]{\text{Acetone}} CH_3CH_2CH_2I + NaCl$ (1/2)

(ii) $\underset{\text{Propan-1-ol}}{CH_3CH_2CH_2OH} + SOCl_2 \xrightarrow{\text{Pyridine}} \underset{\text{1-chloropropane}}{CH_3CH_2CH_2Cl} + SO_2\uparrow + HCl\uparrow$ (1/2)

(iii) $\underset{\text{But-1-ene}}{CH_3CH_2-CH=CH_2} + HBr \xrightarrow{\text{Peroxide}} \underset{\text{1-bromobutane}}{CH_3CH_2CH_2CH_2Br}$ (1/2)

(iv) $CH_3CH=\overset{\overset{CH_3}{|}}{C}-CH_3 + HBr \xrightarrow[\text{rule}]{\text{Markovnikov's}} CH_3-CH_2-\underset{\underset{Br}{|}}{\overset{\overset{CH_3}{|}}{C}}-CH_3$

2-bromo -2-methyl butane

(1/2)

24 (i) For the same alkyl group, boiling point increases with the size of the halogen atom. Thus, boiling point of bromomethane is higher than that of chloromethane. Further, the boiling point increases as the number of halogen atoms increases.

Thus, the boiling point of bromoform with three Br atoms is highest followed by dibromomethane with two Br atoms while that of bromomethane containing only one Br atom is lowest. Therefore, the arrangement of the given compounds in the order of increasing boiling points is as follows:

CH_3Cl (chloromethane) $< CH_3Br$ (bromomethane) $< CH_2Br_2$ (dibromomethane) $< CHBr_3$(bromoform). (1)

(ii) For the same halogen, boiling point increases with an increase in the size of the alkyl group. Thus, the boiling point of 1-chlorobutane is higher than those of 1-chloropropane and isopropyl chloride. Further, the boiling point decreases as the branching increases. Thus, the boiling point of chloropropane is higher than isopropyl chloride.

Therefore, the arrangement of the given compounds in the order of increasing boiling points is as follows:

$(CH_3)_2CHCl$ (*iso*-propyl chloride or 2-chloropropane)
$< ClCH_2CH_2CH_3$ (1-chloropropane)
$< ClCH_2CH_2CH_2CH_3$ (1-chlorobutane)

25 In the presence of water, KOH dissociates completely into OH^- ions which, being a strong nucleophile, brings about substitution on alkyl halides and produce alcohols from alkyl halides. Further, in the aqueous solution, OH^- ions are highly solvated (hydrated). This solvation reduces the basic character of OH^- ions which therefore, fails to abstract a H-atom from the β-carbon of the alkyl chloride to form an alkene. In alcoholic medium, solution also contains $C_2H_5O^-$, ethoxide ions in addition to OH^- ions. Being a stronger base than OH^-, they abstract H^+ ion from β-C-atom, giving rise to an alkene as a major product (dehydrohalogenation).

26 3° alcohols are very reactive and hence, their reactions with conc. HCl takes place even at room temperature. (2)

27 (i) (a) 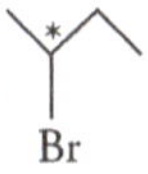 is chiral. (1/2)

(b)  undergoes faster towards S_N2 reaction as it is a primary halide. (1/2)

(ii) (a) S_N2 reaction occurs with inversion of configuration.

(b) S_N1 reaction proceeds with racemisation.

28 (i) CH_3Br and CH_3I both are primary halogen compounds. The reactivity will depend upon the size of the halogen atom. Iodine is a better leaving group because of larger size, therefore, CH_3I will react faster than CH_3Br. (1)

(ii) Out of $(CH_3)_3CCl$ and CH_3Cl, the molecule being a primary halide, i.e. CH_3Cl, will react faster with OH^- because in S_N2 reaction, 1° halide reacts faster than 3° halide.

29 *Tert*-butylbromide reacts with *aq.* NaOH as follows:

$$\underset{\substack{\textit{tert}\text{-butylbromide}\\(3^\circ\text{ alkyl halide})}}{H_3C-\underset{\underset{CH_3}{|}}{\overset{\overset{CH_3}{|}}{C}}-Br} \xrightarrow{S_N1} \underset{\substack{3^\circ\text{ carbocation}\\(\text{More stable})}}{H_3C-\underset{\underset{CH_3}{|}}{\overset{\overset{CH_3}{|}}{C^+}}} + Br^-$$

$$H_3C-\underset{\underset{CH_3}{|}}{\overset{\overset{CH_3}{|}}{C^+}} + OH^- \longrightarrow H_3C-\underset{\underset{CH_3}{|}}{\overset{\overset{CH_3}{|}}{C}}-OH$$

tert-butylbromide when treated with aqueous NaOH, it forms *tert*-carbocation which is more stable intermediate. This intermediate is further attacked by OH^- ion. (1)

As *tert*-carbocation is highly stable, so *tert*-butylbromide follows S_N1 mechanism.

In case of *n*-butylbromide, primary carbocation is formed which is least stable, so it does not follow S_N1 mechanism. Here, steric hindrance is very less, so it follows S_N2 mechanism. In S_N2 mechanism, OH^- will attack from backside and a transition state is formed.

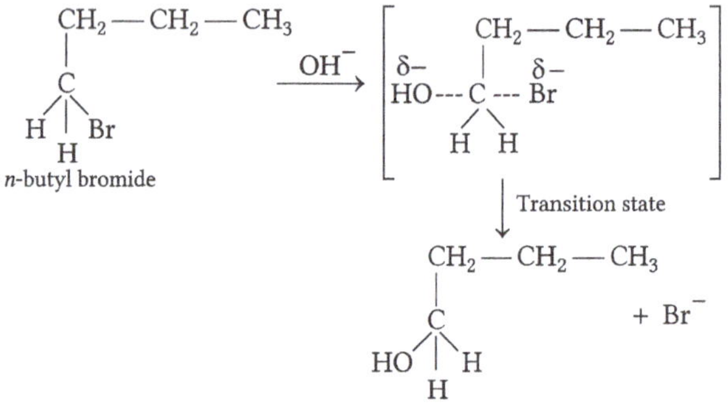

n-butyl alcohol

30 (i) **Wurtz reaction** Alkyl halide reacts with alkyl halide and undergoes coupling when treated with sodium metal in the presence of dry ether of form alkane.

$$\underset{\text{Alkyl halide}}{R{-}X} + \underset{\text{Alkyl halide}}{R{-}X} \xrightarrow{\text{Na, Dry ether}} \underset{\text{Alkane}}{R{-}R}$$

(iii) **Finkelstein reaction** Alkyl iodide are often prepared by the reaction of chlorides/bromides with NaI in dry acetone.

$$R{-}X + \text{NaI} \xrightarrow[\text{Reflux}]{\text{Acetone}} R{-}I + \text{Na}X$$

31 (i)

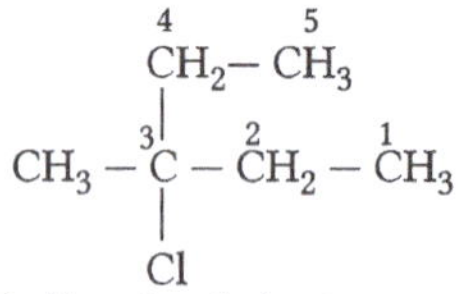

3-chloro-3-methylpentane
(Tertiary alkyl halide)

(3 × 1 = 3)

(ii)

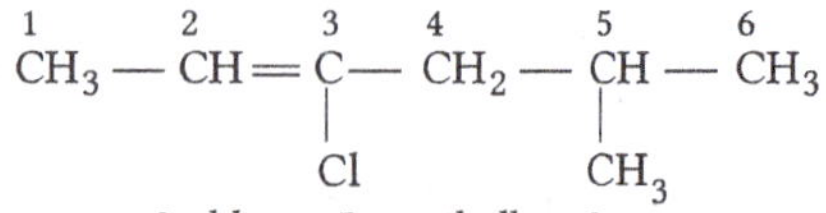

3-chloro - 5 - methylhex-2-ene
(Vinyl halide)

(iii)

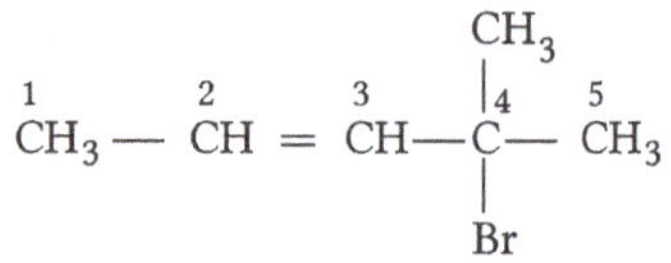

4- bromo -4-methylpent-2-ene
(Allyl halide)

32 (i)

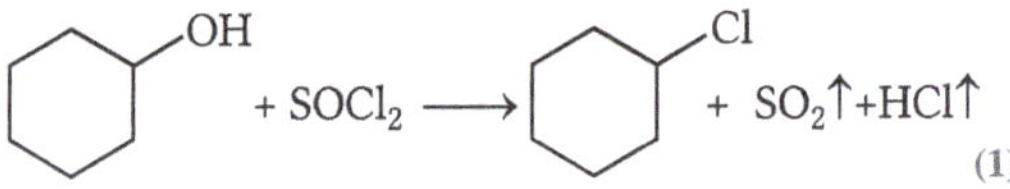

(1)

(ii)

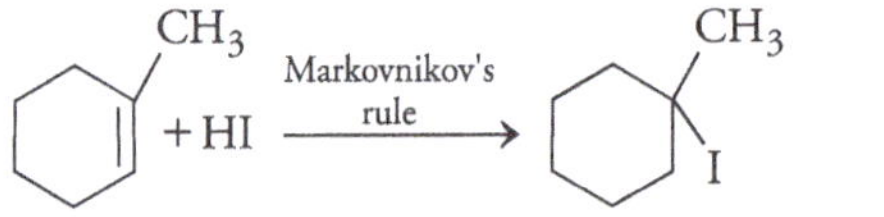

1-methyl cyclohexene　　1-iodo-1-methyl cyclohexane

According to Markovnikov's rule, iodine will add to the carbon atom having less number of hydrogen atoms.

(iii) $$\underset{\text{Bromoethane}}{CH_3CH_2Br} + NaI \longrightarrow \underset{\text{Iodoethane}}{CH_3CH_2I} + NaBr$$

Iodide ion is a strong nucleophile, so it displaces bromide ion. (½)

(iv)

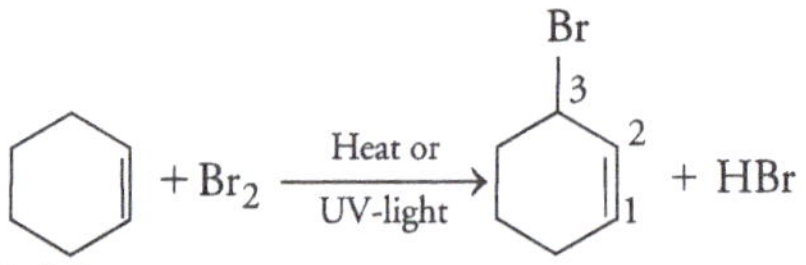

Cyclohexene　　3-bromocyclohexene

(½)

Under the conditions specified above, allylic halogenation takes place. Addition reaction can take place only at room temperature.

33

> **Key idea**
> (i) Strong intermolecular H-bonding exist among water molecules.
> (ii) Consider the reactive nature of Grignard reagents with water.

(i) Water molecules have enough strong intermolecular H-bonding which is difficult to be broken by alkyl halides, though they are polar in nature as well. Therefore, alkyl halides do not dissolve in water and form separate layers. (1½)

(ii) Grignard reagents ($R{-}Mg{-}X$) are readily decomposed by water to produce alkanes. That is why, they should be prepared under anhydrous conditions. Instead, ether is used as a solvent during the preparation of Grignard reagent. (1½)

$$R{-}Mg{-}X + H_2O \longrightarrow \underset{\text{Alkane}}{R{-}H} + Mg\begin{matrix} X \\ OH \end{matrix}$$

34 (i) $CH_3CH_2Cl + AgNO_2 \longrightarrow CH_3CH_2NO_2 + AgCl$ (1)

(ii) When 2-bromopentane is treated with alcoholic KOH, it undergoes dehydrohalogenation leading to the formation of two or more different products depending upon the number of different types of β-hydrogen available. The more highly substituted alkene (i.e. having lesser number of hydrogen atoms on the doubly bonded carbon atoms) is the major product of dehydrohalogenation. This is in accordance to Saytzeff rule. (1)

$$\underset{\text{2-bromopentane (has 2 }\beta\text{-H-atoms)}}{CH_2(H)-CH(Br)-CH(H)-CH_2-CH_3} \xrightarrow{\text{Alc.KOH}} \underset{\text{pent-2-ene (Major)}}{CH_3-CH{=}CH-CH_2-CH_3} + \underset{\text{Pent-1-ene (Minor)}}{CH_2{=}CH-CH_2-CH_2CH_3}$$ (1)

35 Two possible isomers of given primary alkyl halide, C_4H_9Br are:

$$\underset{\substack{[I] \\ (1^\circ)}}{CH_3-CH_2-CH_2-CH_2-Br}\ ;\ \underset{\substack{[II] \\ (1^\circ)}}{CH_3-CH(CH_3)-CH_2-Br}$$ (1)

According to the question, compound *A* on reaction with sodium does not give the same product produced by *n*-butyl bromide. So, *A* cannot be [I].

$$\underset{n\text{-butyl bromide}}{2CH_3-CH_2-CH_2-CH_2-Br} + 2Na \xrightarrow{\text{Ether}} \underset{n\text{-octane (not formed in the reaction)}C_8H_{18}}{CH_3-CH_2-CH_2-CH_2-CH_2-CH_2-CH_2-CH_3}$$ (1)

Now, [II] must be the correct isomer. Hence, the overall equations for all the reactions are:

$$\underset{\substack{iso\text{-butyl bromide} \\ \text{(1-bromo-2-methyl propane)} \\ (A)}}{CH_3-CH(CH_3)-CH_2-Br} \xrightarrow{\text{KOH(alc.)}} \underset{\substack{\text{2-methyl propene} \\ (B)}}{CH_3-C(CH_3){=}CH_2} + KBr + H_2O \xrightarrow{\text{HBr}} \underset{\substack{\text{2-bromo-2-methyl} \\ \text{propane} \\ (C)}}{CH_3-C(Br)(CH_3)-CH_3}$$

$$\underset{(A)}{2CH_3-CH(CH_3)-CH_2-Br} + 2Na \xrightarrow[\text{Wurtz reaction}]{\text{Dry ether}} \underset{\substack{\text{2,5-dimethyl hexane} \\ C_8H_{18}\,(D)}}{CH_3-CH(CH_3)-CH_2-CH_2-CH(CH_3)-CH_3}$$ (1)

36 (i) Haloalkanes react with Mg in dry ether to form Grignard reagents ($RMgX$), which react with water to form hydrocarbons.

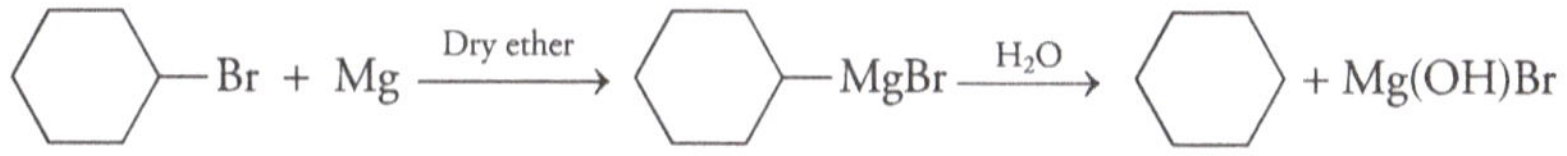

Bromocyclohexane — Cyclohexyl magnesium bromide [*A*] (Grignard reagent) — Cyclohexane [*B*] (1½)

(ii) In this reaction,

R is $CH_3-CH(CH_3)-$ group. $$\underset{iso\text{-propyl bromide}}{CH_3-CH(CH_3)-Br} + Mg \xrightarrow{\text{Dry ether}} \underset{\substack{iso\text{-propyl magnesium} \\ \text{bromide }[C] \\ \text{(Grignard reagent)}}}{CH_3-CH(CH_3)-MgBr} \xrightarrow{D_2O} \underset{\text{2-deuteropropane}}{CH_3-CH(CH_3)-D} + Mg(OD)Br$$ (1½)

(iii) Haloalkanes react with Na in dry ether to give hydrocarbons containing double number of C-atoms. (2)

$$\underset{\text{2,2,3,3- tetramethylbutane}}{CH_3-C(CH_3)_2-C(CH_3)_2-CH_3} \xleftarrow[\text{Wurtz reaction}]{\text{Na/dry ether}} CH_3-C(CH_3)_2-X \xrightarrow{\text{Mg}} \underset{\substack{\text{Grignard reagent} \\ [P]}}{CH_3-C(CH_3)_2-MgX} \xrightarrow{H_2O} \underset{\substack{\text{2-methylpropane} \\ [Q]}}{CH_3-C(CH_3)_2-H} + Mg(OH)X$$

37 (i) For isomeric alkyl halides, the boiling points decrease with branching because with branching, the surface area of the alkyl halide decrease and hence, the magnitude of van der Waals' forces of attraction decreases. Therefore, *n*-butyl bromide ($CH_3CH_2CH_2CH_2Br$) has higher boiling than *tert*-butyl bromide, (1½)

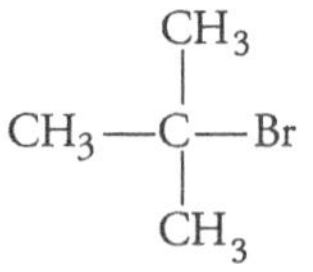

(ii) Racemic mixture contains two enantiomers, i.e. *d* and *l*- forms in equal proportions and possesses zero optical rotation as the rotation of plane polarised light due to one isomer will be cancelled by the rotation due to the other isomer. Thus, the mixture will be optically inactive. (1½)

38 (i) S_N2 reactions involve the formation of transition state. Higher the steric hindrance, lesser the stability of transition state and lower is their reactivity towards S_N2.

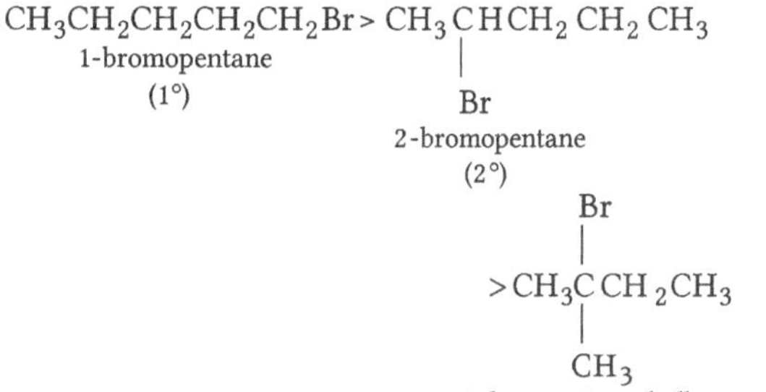

1-bromopentane (1°) > 2-bromopentane (2°) > 2-bromo-2-methylbutane (3°) (1)

(ii) Among the given compounds, 2-bromopentane is optically active due to the presence of chiral carbon (*)

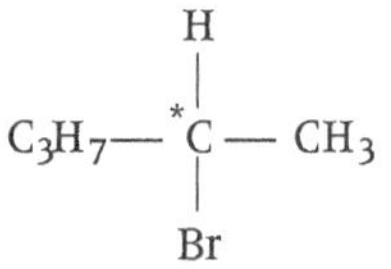

Note A chiral carbon have four different groups or atoms attached separately to its four valencies. (1)

(iii) 2-bromo-2-methylbutane is most reactive towards β-elimination reaction because in this case, more substituted alkene is the major product. (1)

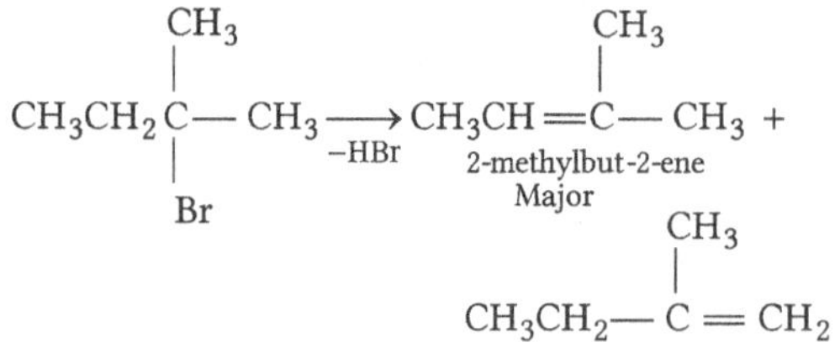

2-methylbut-2-ene (Major)

2-methylbut-1-ene (Minor)

39 (i) Iodide is a better leaving group because of its larger size than bromide, therefore, ethyl iodide undergoes S_N2 reaction faster than ethyl bromide. (1)

(ii) (±) 2-butanol is a racemic mixture. It is a mixture which contains two enantiomers in equal proportion and thus, have zero optical rotation due to internal compensation. Therefore, it is optically inactive. (2)

(iii) In halobenzene (like chlorobenzene), the lone pair of electrons on halogen atom is delocalised on the benzene ring. As a result, C — *X* bond (C — Cl bond in case of chlorobenzene) acquires some double bond character while in $CH_3—X$, C—*X* bond is a pure single bond. Therefore, C—*X* bond in halobenzene is shorter than in $CH_3—X$. (2)

40 (i)

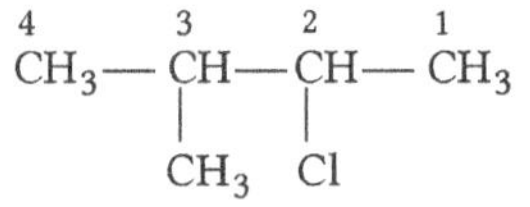

2-chloro -3-methylbutane
(Secondary alkyl halide) (5 × 1 = 5)

(ii)

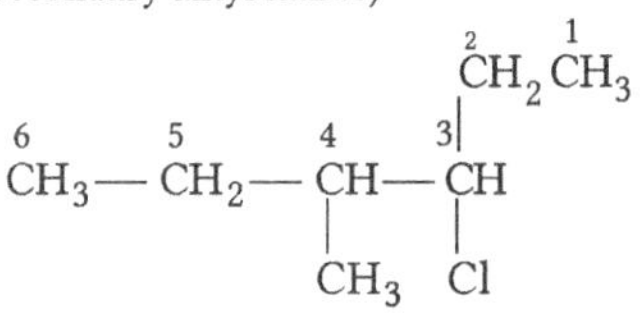

3-chloro-4-methylhexane
(Secondary alkyl halide)

(iii)

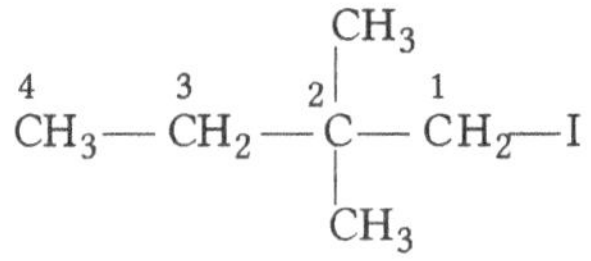

1-iodo -2,2-dimethylbutane
(Primary alkyl halide)

(iv)

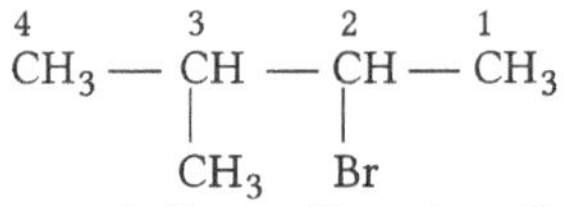

2-bromo-3-methylbutane (Secondary alkyl halide)

(v)

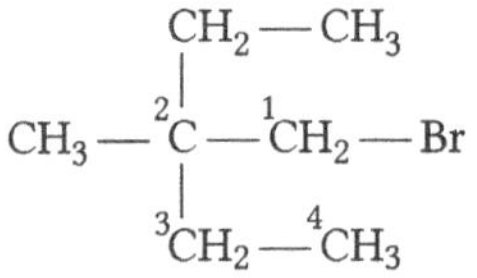

1-bromo-2-ethyl-2-methylbutane
(Primary alkyl halide)

41 (i) Refer to text on page 207 (Preparation from alcohols). (2)

(ii) Refer to text on page 206 (Preparation from alkanes). (3)

42 (i) $CH_3—CH_2—Cl \xrightarrow{KCN} CH_3—CH_2—C \equiv N$

Ethyl chloride (Chloroethane) → Ethylnitrile (Cyanopropane)

$\xrightarrow{2H_2O/H^+} CH_3—CH_2—COOH$

Propanoic acid

(ii) $CH_3—CH_2—OH \xrightarrow{\text{Red P/I}_2} CH_3—CH_2—I \xrightarrow{KCN} CH_3—CH_2—CN$

Ethanol → Iodoethane → Propane nitrile

(iii) $CH_3CH_2CH_2Br \xrightarrow[\Delta]{\text{KOH (alc.)}} CH_3CH{=}CH_2 \xrightarrow{HBr} CH_3CH(Br)—CH_3$

1-bromopropane → Prop-1-ene → 2-bromopropane

(iv) $2CH_3—CH_2—CH(CH_3)—Cl + 2Na \xrightarrow[\text{Wurtz reaction}]{\text{Dry ether}} CH_3—CH_2—CH(CH_3)—CH(CH_3)—CH_2—CH_3 + 2NaCl$

2-chlorobutane → 3, 4-dimethylhexane

(v) $CH_3—C(CH_3){=}CH_2 \xrightarrow{HCl} CH_3—C(Cl)(CH_3)—CH_3$

2-methyl-1-propene → 2-chloro-2-methylpropane

(5 ×1= 5)

TOPIC 02 Haloarenes (Aryl Halides)

Haloarenes are the aromatic compounds in which halogen replaces hydrogen atom(s) of benzene ring. These are also known as **aryl halide** . The carbon atom to which halogen is attached is sp^2-hybridised.

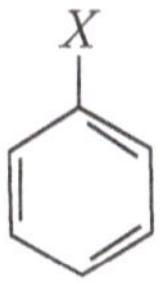

(where, X =Br, Cl, I, F))

Classification

Haloarenes may be classified as follows:

On the Basis of Number of Halogen Atoms

Depending on the number of halogen atoms directly attached to benzene ring. Haloarenes may be mono, di, tri or polyhalogen (tetra, penta, etc.) compounds.

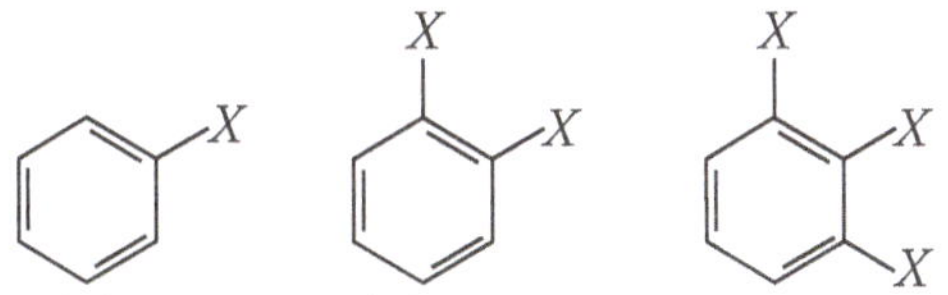

Monohaloarene Dihaloarene Trihaloarene

(where, X = F, Cl, Br, I)

On the Basis of Nature of Carbon of C—X Bond

In these benzylic halides, the halogen atom is bonded to the sp^3-hybridised carbon atom next to an aromatic ring, i.e. to a benzylic carbon. Here, the halogen is attached to the side chain of benzene ring.

e.g.

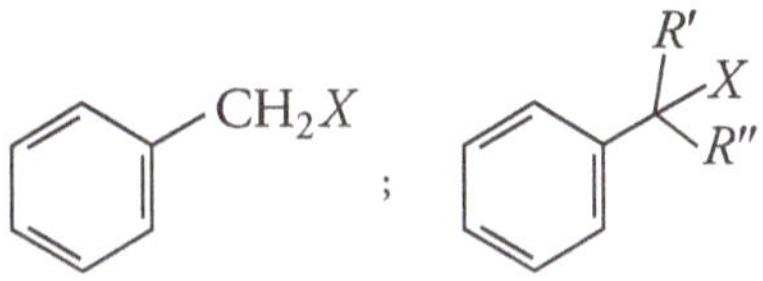

(1°) [If R' = CH R'' = H(2°) If R' = R'' = CH_3(3°)]

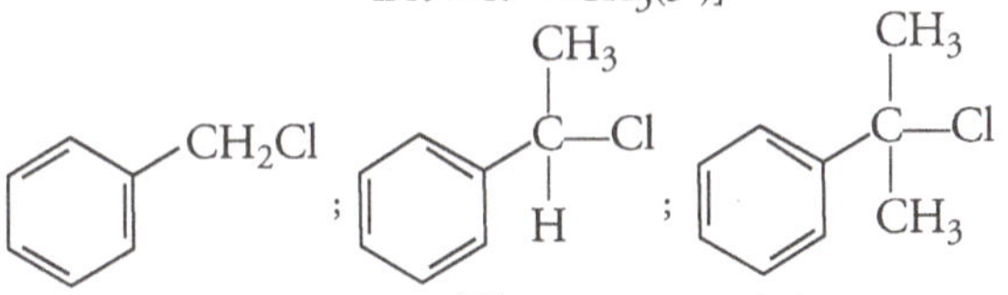

(1°) (2°) (3°)

Nomenclature

They are named by prefixing 'halo' before the name of the aromatic hydrocarbon.

Haloarenes are the common as well as IUPAC names of aryl halides. For dihalogen derivatives, the prefixes *o*-, *m*-, *p*- are used in common system but in IUPAC system, the numerals 1,2; 1,3 and 1,4 are used respectively.

Common and IUPAC names some haloarenes are as follows:

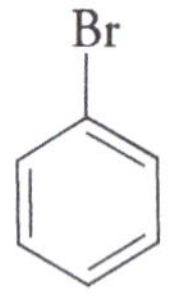
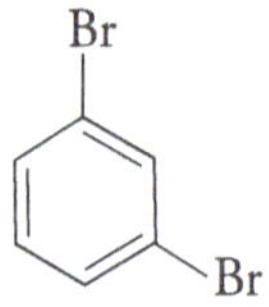

Common name	Bromobenzene	*m*-dibromobenzene
IUPAC name	Bromobenzene	1,3-dibromobenzene

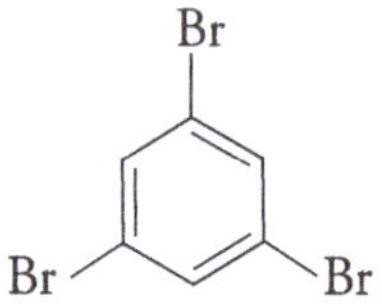
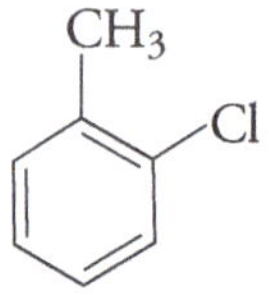

Common name	*sym*-tribromobenzene	*o*-chlorobenzene
IUPAC name	1,3,5-tribromobenzene	1-chloro-2-methylbenzene or 2-chlorotoluene

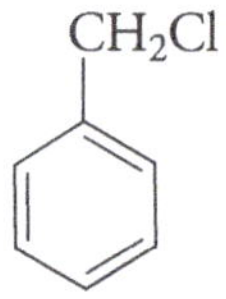

Common name	Benzyl chloride
IUPAC name	Chlorophenylmethane

Nature of C—X Bond

In haloarenes, sp^2 hybridised carbon of benzene is bonded to halogen and C—X bond is also polar as in haloalkanes due to higher electronegativity of halogen. Apart from this, lone pairs of electrons of halogen atom are involved in resonance with benzene ring. So, this C—X bond acquires partial double bond character.

The C—X bond of haloarenes is less polar than C—X bond of haloalkanes. This is supported by the fact that dipole moment of chlorobenzene ($\mu = 1.69$ D) is little lower than that of CH_3Cl ($\mu = 1.83$ D). The C—X bond of haloarene is usually shorter than haloalkane.

The reason for this occurrence is that haloarenes are more electron rich, due to the presence of double bonds, than haloalkanes and the benzene ring as a whole due to resonance is strongly attracted towards electronegative halogen atoms.

Preparation of Haloarenes

Haloarenes can be prepared by the following methods :

By Electrophilic Substitution of Aromatic Hydrocarbons

Aryl chlorides and bromides can be easily prepared by electrophilic substitution of arenes with chlorine and bromine, respectively in dark, at ordinary temperature in the presence of a Lewis acid catalysts such as iron or ferric halides or aluminium halides ($FeCl_3$, $FeBr_3$, $AlCl_3$). Lewis acid is used to generate the electrophile, i.e. Cl^+ and Br^+ which reacts with aryl halide.

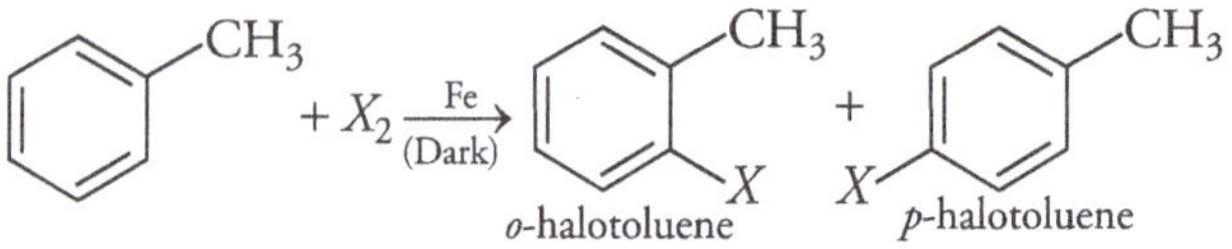

o-halotoluene *p*-halotoluene

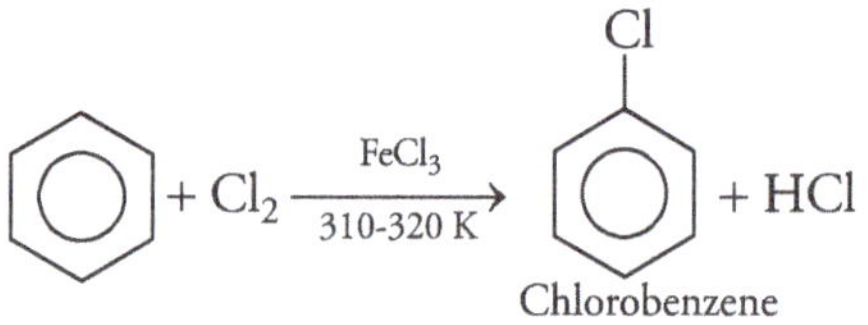

Chlorobenzene

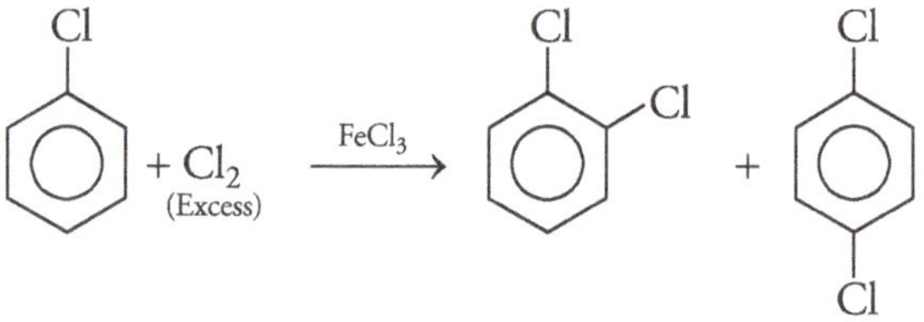

o-dichlorobenzene (Minor) *p*-dichlorobenzene (Major)

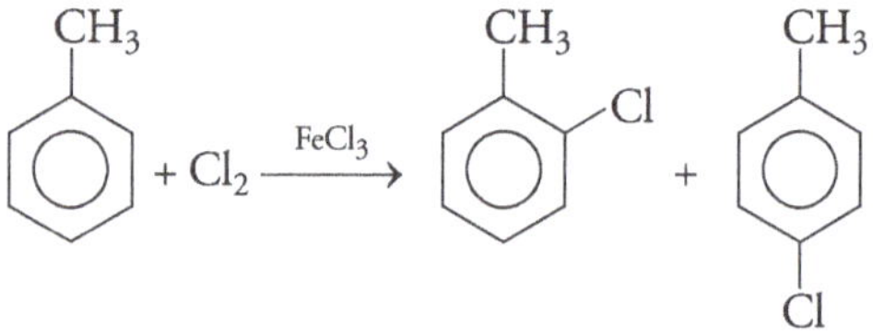

o-chlorotoluene *p*-chlorotoluene

o and *p* -isomers can be easily separated due to large difference in their melting points.

Reaction with iodine is reversible and require the presence of an oxidising agent (HNO_3, HIO_4) to oxidise the HI formed during iodination.

The reaction with fluorine is violent and uncontrollable, hence fluoroarene cannot be prepared by direct fluorination of aromatic hydrocarbon.

From Diazonium Salts (Sandmeyer's and Gattermann Reaction)

The diazonium salt is prepared by treating aniline dissolved in cold aqueous mineral acid with an aqueous solution of sodium nitrite at low temperature (0-5°C). Bromo and chloroarenes can be prepared by treating a freshly prepared diazonium salt solution with cuprous bromide or cuprous chloride.

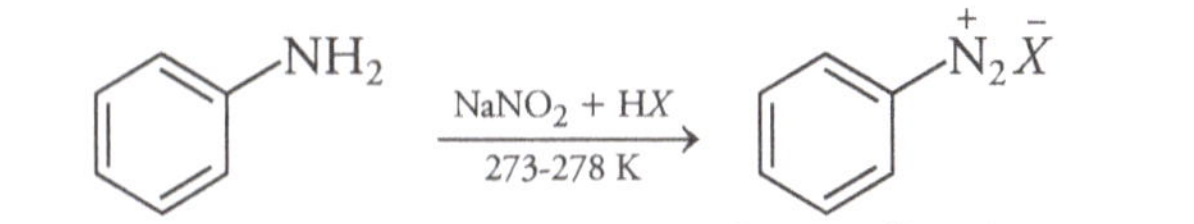

Benzene diazonium halide

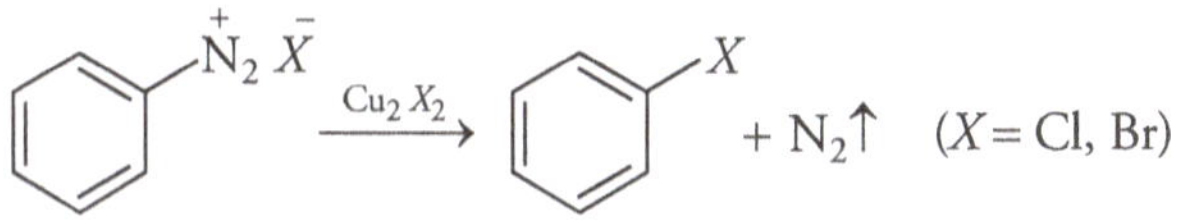

Aryl halide

Replacement of the diazonium group by iodine is done simply by shaking the diazonium salt with potassium iodide.

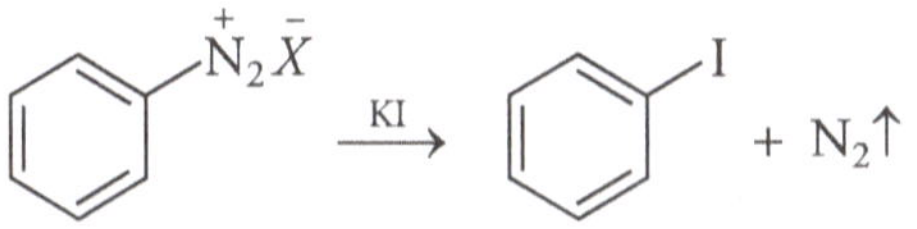

The Sandmeyer's reaction has been modified by using copper powder in place of cuprous halide. This reaction is called **Gattermann reaction.**

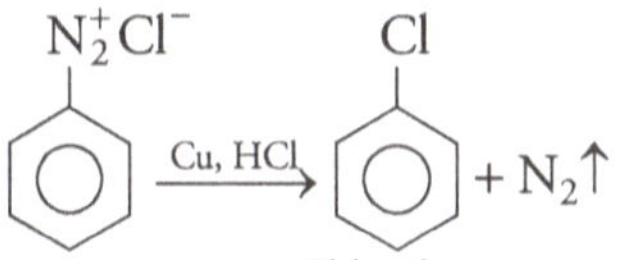

Chlorobenzene

If the diazonium group is replaced using fluoroboric acid, the reaction is called **Balz-Schiemann reaction.**

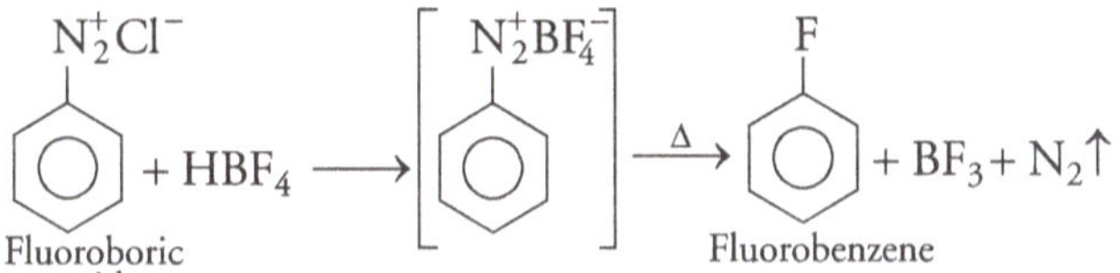

Fluoroboric acid   Fluorobenzene

Physical Properties

Some of the important physical properties of haloarenes are as follows:

(i) **Physical State** Haloarenes are colourless liquids or crystalline solids.

(ii) **Melting and Boiling Points** Molecules of organic halogen compounds are generally polar. Due to greater polarity and higher molecular mass as compared to the parent hydrocarbon, the intermolecular forces of attraction (dipole-dipole and van der Waals') between molecules are stronger in the halogen derivatives.

Boiling point of haloarenes generally follow the following trends :

Iodoarene > Bromoarene > Chloroarene

- Generally, the boiling points of chloro, bromo and iodo compounds increases as the number of halogen atom increases.
- Boiling points of isomeric dihalobenzenes are nearly the same.

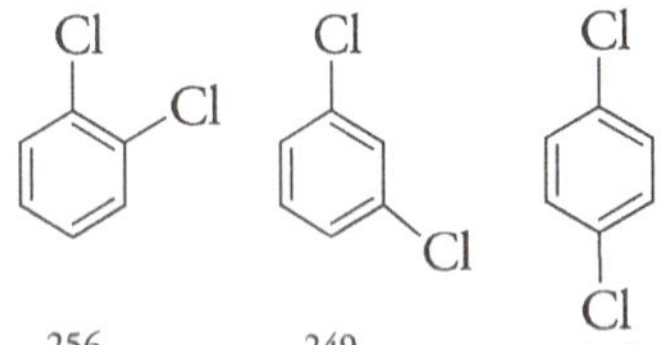

mp/K	256	249	323
bp/K	453	446	448

However, the *p*-isomers have high melting point as compared to their *o* and *m*-isomers. This is due to the symmetry of *p*-isomers that fits in the crystal lattice better as compared to *o* and *m*-isomers.

(iii) **Density** Density is directly proportional to the mass of any compound, therefore density increases as we move from chloro to iodo compounds.

(iv) **Solubility** Haloarenes are polar but immiscible with water because these cannot form hydrogen bonds with water (due to weaker force of attraction). As a result, solubility of haloarenes are low.

(v) **Stability** The stability also decreases as the strength of C—X bond decreases (RF > RBr > RCl > RI).

(vi) **Dipole Moment** As the electronegativity of the halogen decreases from Cl to I, dipole moment also decreases whereas fluorides have lower dipole moment than chlorides because of very small size of F which outweighs the effect of greater electronegativity.

Chemical Properties

Some important chemical properties of haloarenes are as follows:

Nucleophilic Substitution Reactions

Nucleophilic substitution reactions in aryl halides occur only under drastic conditions. This is because haloarenes are chemically less reactive towards nucleophilic substitution reactions (than haloalkanes) due to the following reasons:

(i) **Resonance Effect** In haloarenes, like chlorobenzene, the lone pair of electrons on halogen atom are in conjugation with π-electrons of the ring and hence, these are delocalised on the benzene ring as shown below:

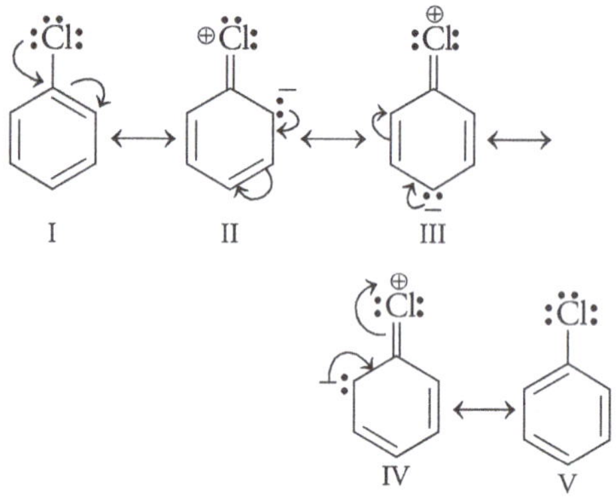

As a result of resonance, C—Cl bond acquires a partial double bond character. Thus, the bond cleavage in haloarene is difficult than haloalkane (where carbon is attached to halogen by a pure single bond) and thus, they are less reactive towards nucleophilic substitution reaction.

(ii) **Difference in Hybridisation of Carbon Atom in C—*X* Bond** In haloalkanes, the carbon atoms attached to halogen is sp^3-hybridised while in haloarenes, it is sp^2-hybridised .

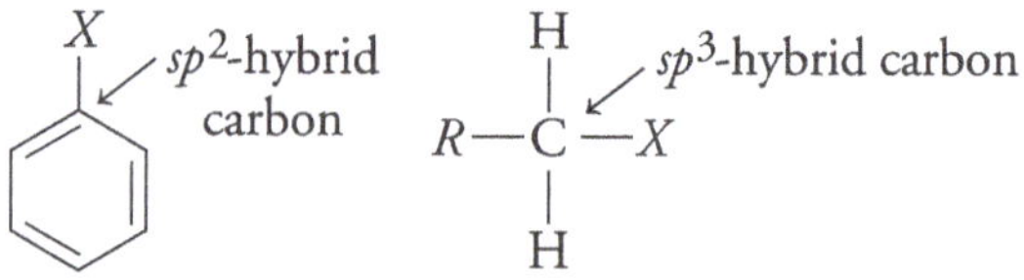

The sp^2-hybridised C-atom with greater *s*-character is more electronegative. It can hold the electron pair of the bond more tightly than the sp^3-hybridised C-atom with less *s*-character. As a result, the C—*X* bond in haloarenes (169 pm) is shorter than in haloalkanes (177 pm). Since, it is difficult to break a shorter (C—*X*) bond than a longer and therefore, haloarenes are less reactive than haloalkanes towards nucleophilic substitution reaction.

(iii) **Instability of Phenyl Cation** In haloarenes, the phenyl cation formed as a result of self-ionisation will not be stabilised by resonance, hence S_N1 mechanism cannot occur.

(iv) **Repulsion between the Electron Rich Attacking Nucleophiles and Electron Rich Arenes** Because of electron rich arenes, electron rich nucleophile will not approach closely for the attack due to repulsion.

Mechanism

On the basis of kinetic studies, we observed that nucleophilic substitution reactions of aryl halides, having electron withdrawing group at *o*-and *p*-positions with respect to halogen atom, take place in two steps :

(i) In the first step, the nucleophile *Z* attacks on the carbon atom, attached to halogen atom to form a carbanion which is resonance stabilised as shown below:

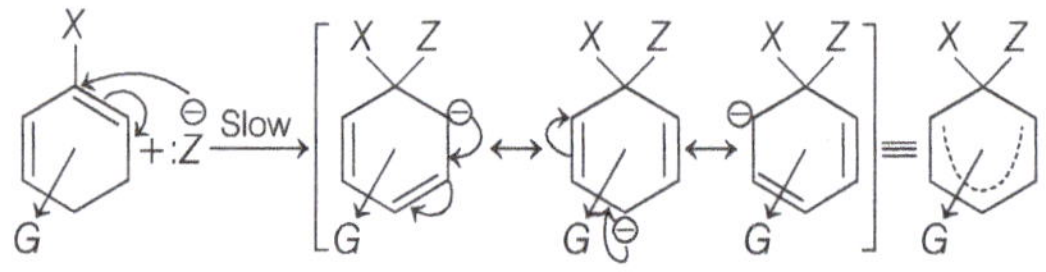

G=electron withdrawing group

When intermediate carbanion is being formed, the state of hydridization of carbon changes from sp^2 to sp^3 and because of this, the aromatic character of benzene ring gets destroyed. Therefore, activation energy of this step is high and thus, it has slow rate and act as rate determining step.

(ii) The carbanion formed in the first step changes to the product by another transition state. In this step, halide ion is lost and the product develops an aromatic character. E_{act} for this step is low. Thus, this step is fast and will not affect the overall rate of reaction.

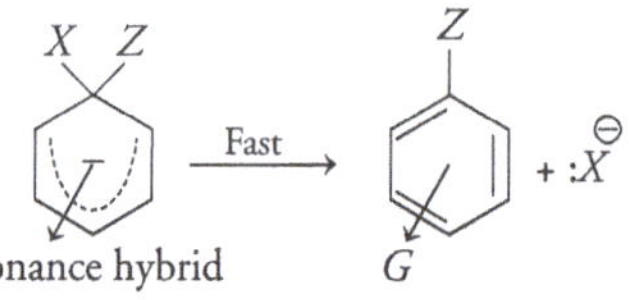

As slow, i.e rate determining step does not involve in the breaking of carbon halogen bond, unlike alkyl halides there is hardly substitution reaction and this has been actually found to the true. In order to explain the effect of substitutents on orientation, a comparison of the carbanions formed during the attack at *ortho*, *para* and *meta* nitrochlorobenzenes by a nucleophile OH^- given below.

Substitution by Hydroxyl Group

Chlorobenzene when heated in *aq*. NaOH solution at a temperature of 623 K and a pressure of 300 atm, phenol is formed.

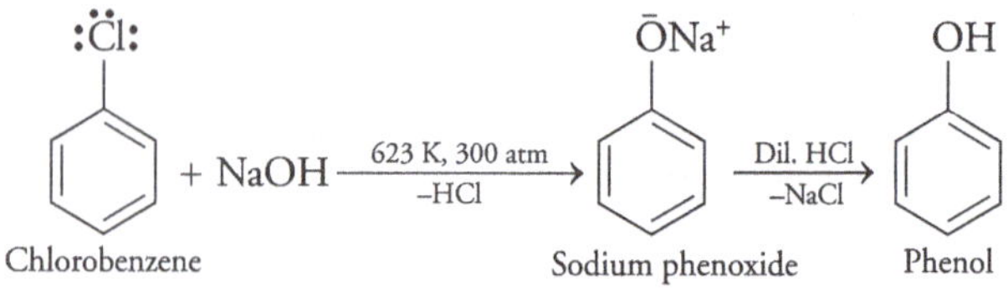

The presence of electron withdrawing groups such as $—NO_2$, $—CN$ at *o* and *p*-positions of haloarenes with respect to halogen greatly activates the benzene ring towards nucleophilic substitution.

Further, greater the number of such groups at *o*-and *p*-positions with respect to halogen, more reactive is the haloarene.

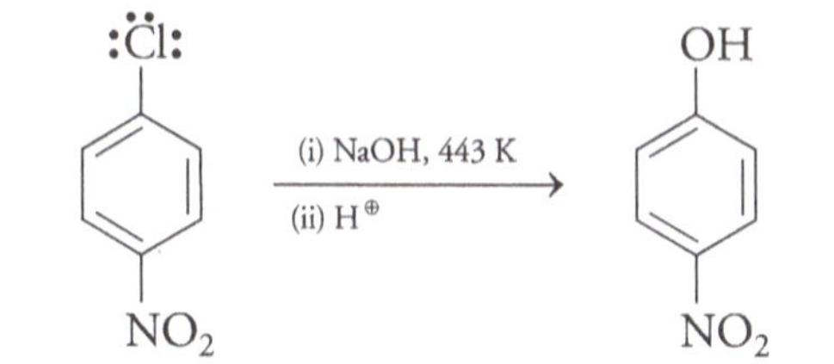

1-chloro-4-nitrobenzene p-nitrophenol

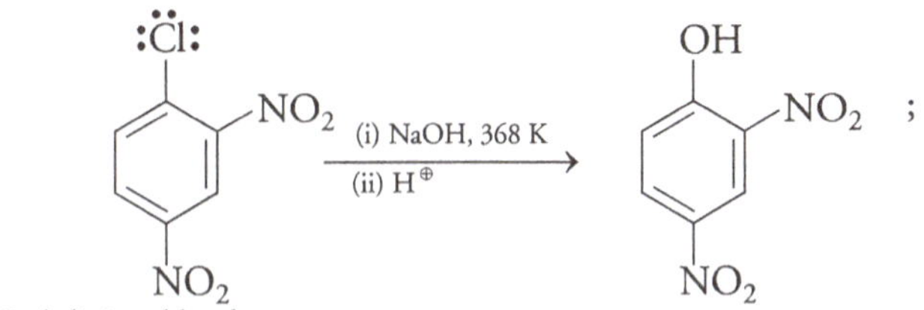

2, 4-dinitrochlorobenzene 2, 4-dinitrophenol

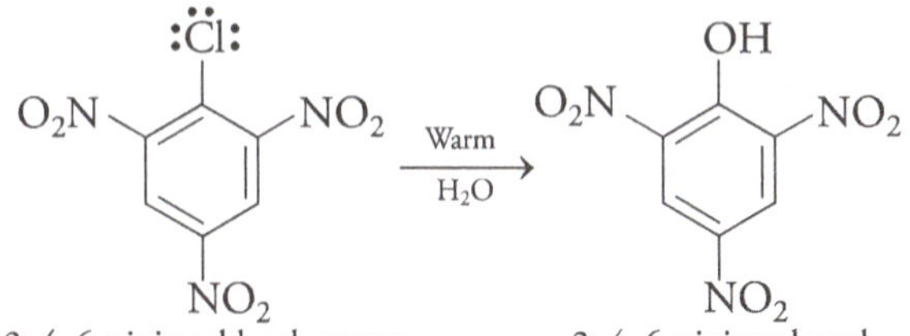

2, 4, 6-trinitrochlorobenzene 2, 4, 6-trinitrophenol (Picric acid)

The $—NO_2$ group at *m*-position to the chlorine has no effect on reactivity.

Mechanism

The presence of NO_2 groups at *o*- and *p*-positions withdraw electrons from benzene ring and facilitates the attack of nucleophile on haloarenes. The carbanion formed is stabilised through resonance as depicted below:

(i) NO_2 at *para*-position

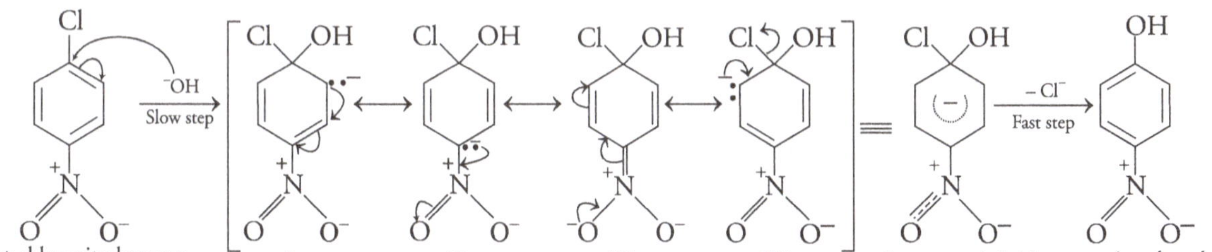

p-chloronitrobenzene I II III IV Resonance hybrid p-nitrophenol

(ii) NO_2 at *ortho*-position

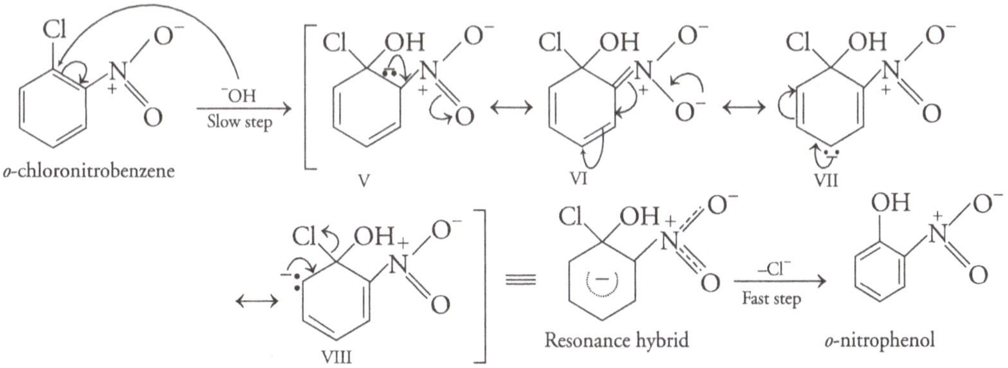

(iii) NO_2 at *meta*-position

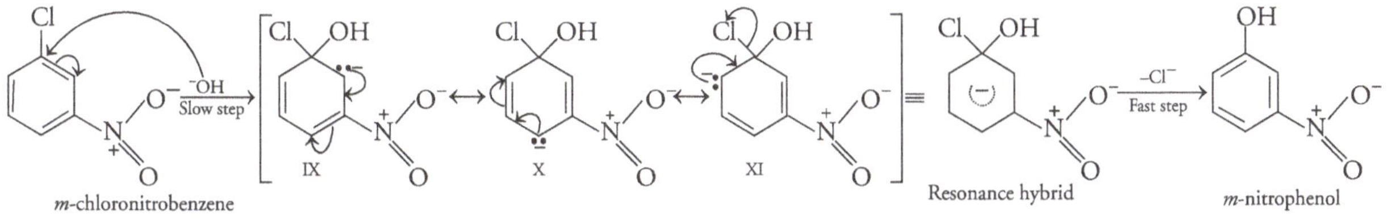

Note In the above structures showing NO_2 at *meta*-position, there is no such structure in which the negative charge is present on carbon atom bearing the —NO_2 group. Therefore, the presence of nitro group at *meta*-position does not stabilise the negative charge. Hence, no effect on reactivity is observed by the presence of —NO_2 group at *meta*-position.

Substitution by —NH_2 Group

Chlorobenzene in presence of strong base such as $NaNH_2$ undergoes nucleophilic substitution reaction.

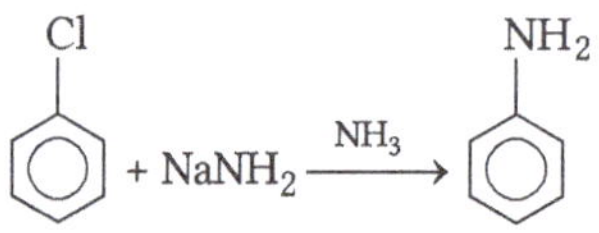

Mechanisin

Various steps involved in the mechanism are as follows:

Step 1 Abstraction of *ortho*-proton of chlorobenzene. In chlorobenzene, the presence of highly electronegative chlorine makes the *ortho*-hydrogen acidic and this hydrogen is easily taken away as a proton by strong base like amide ion (NH_2^-).

Step 2 Elimination of chloride ion formation of benzyne intermediat. Here, the electronegative chlorine stabilises the carbanion through its *I*-effect. The carbanion undergoes loss of a chloride ion that results in the formation of highly reactive intermediate called benzyne

Step 3 The benzyne intermediate is highly unstable and highly reactive. It easily attack by .

Step 4 Proton abstraction by carbanion formation of substituted product.

Electrophilic Substitution Reactions

Haloarenes undergo the usual electrophilic reactions of the benzene ring such as halogenation, nitration, sulphonation and Friedel-Crafts reactions. In these reactions, stronger electrophile replaces weaker electrophile.

The electrophilic substitution reactions in haloarenes occur slowly and require more drastic conditions. This is due to the *ortho* and *para*-directing influence of halogen atom attached to a benzene ring which can be understood by the following resonating structures of halobenzene.

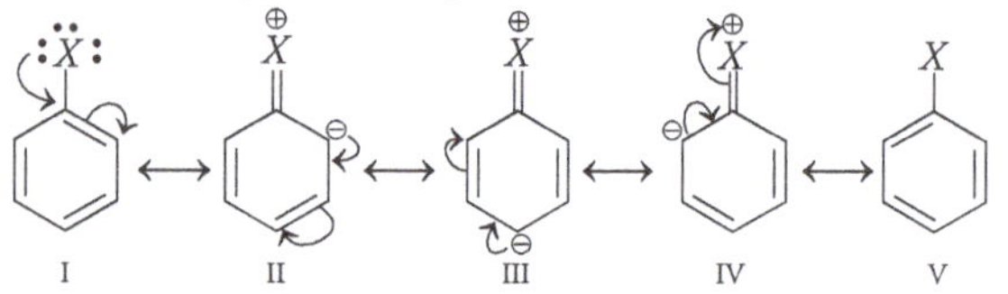

Thus, due to resonance, the electron density increases more at *o* and *p*-positions than at *m*-positions. Hence, electrophilic reactions occur at *o* and *p*-position. The halogen atom has the tendency to withdraw electrons due to which electron density on benzene ring decreases (–*I*-effect) and the ring gets deactivated. Hence, electrophilic substitution in haloarene occurs at a slower rate.

Mechanism

In electrophilic substitution reactions the formation of an intermediate carbocation occurs in slow step, which can act as rate determining step and the factors which stabilise the intermediate carbocation, favour the electrophilic substitution.

Halogens attached directly to a benzene ring show dual nature. The lone pair of electrons present on halogens show delocalisation with π-electrons of the benzene ring. When this electron release towards the benzene ring, due to + *R*-effect stabilises the carbocation formed by ortho and *para*-attack.

(i) Attack at *ortho*-position

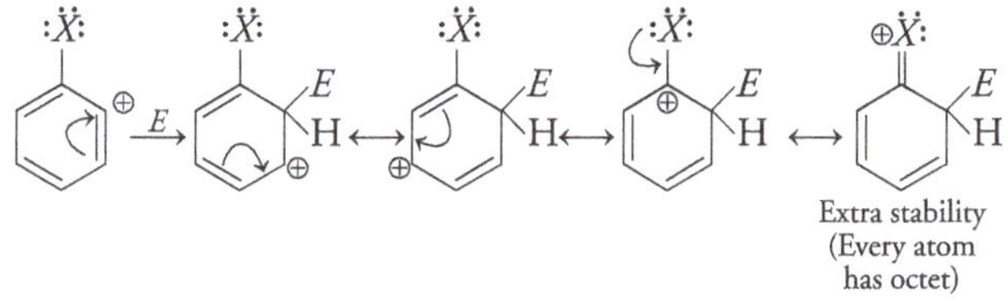

(ii) Attack at *para*-position

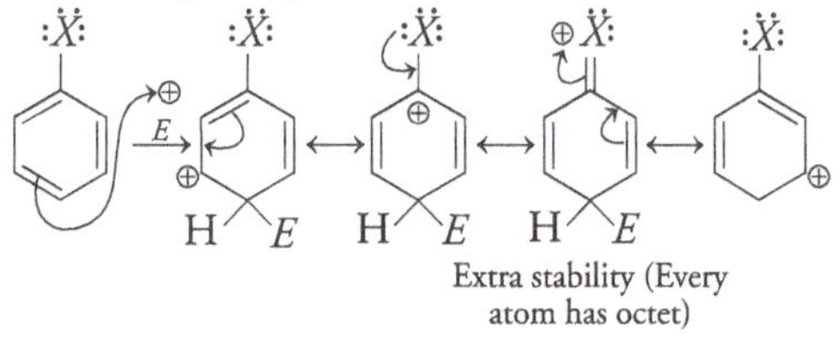

(iii) Attack at *meta*-position

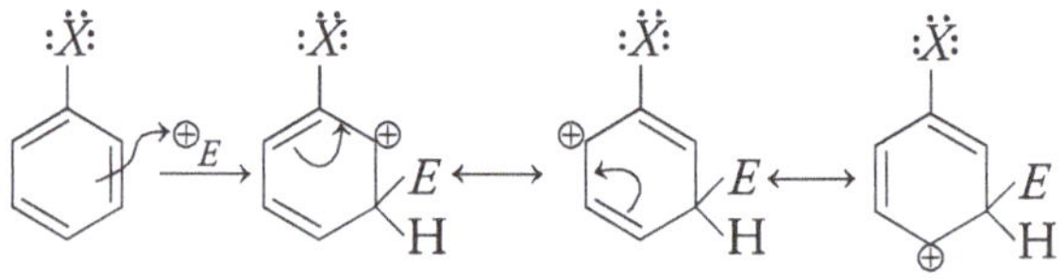

Halogens also withdraw the electrons from benzene ring because–*I*-effect of halogen atom, that destabilises the carbocation formed during the electrophilic substitution.

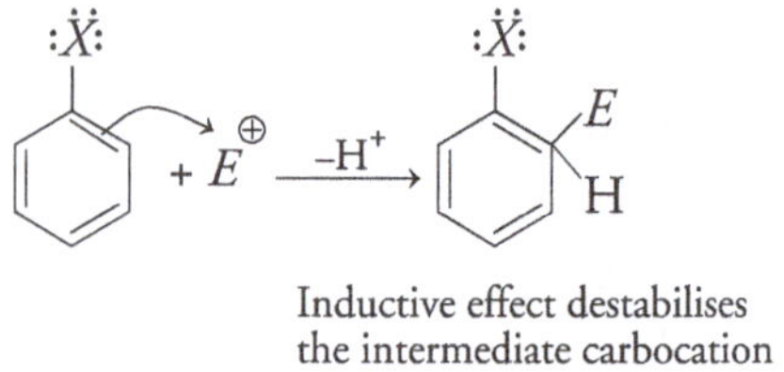

E = Electrophile (NO_2^+, X^+, R^+ etc.)

The inductive effect is quite stronger. Hence, halogens are **deactivating**. The resonance effect will oppose the inductive effect for the attack at *ortho* and *para*-positions and, hence makes the deactivation less for *ortho* and *para* -attack.

Hence, electrophilic substitution is preferred at *ortho* and *para*-positions. Thus, halogens are deactivating at *ortho* and *para*-directing. The intermediate carbocation obtained in the first step (which is a resonance hybrid of various structures), then loses a proton to form the product.

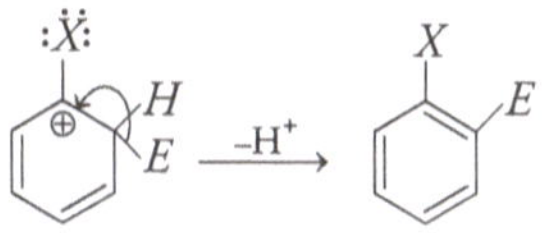

Important electrophiles needed in the reaction can be generated as follows :

(i) $FeCl_3 + Cl:Cl \longrightarrow FeCl_4^- + Cl^+$

(ii) $HONO_2 + 2H.HSO_4 \longrightarrow H_3O^+ + 2HSO_4^- + \overset{+}{N}O_2$

(iii) $2H_2SO_4 \longrightarrow H_3\overset{+}{O} + SO_3^+ + HSO_4^-$

(iv) $R—\overset{O}{\overset{\|}{C}}—Cl + AlCl_3 \longrightarrow AlCl_4^- + R—\overset{O}{\overset{\|}{C}}^+$

Other Common Electrophilic Substitution Reactions

The common electrophilic substitution reactions of haloarenes are depicted as below:

1. Halogenation

This reaction takes place by reacting haloarenes with halogens in the presence of ferric salt.

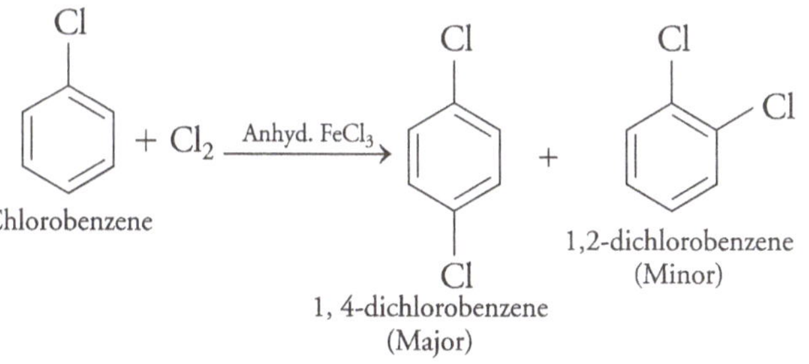

2. Nitration

This reaction takes place by heating haloarenes with conc.HNO_3 in the presence of conc.H_2SO_4.

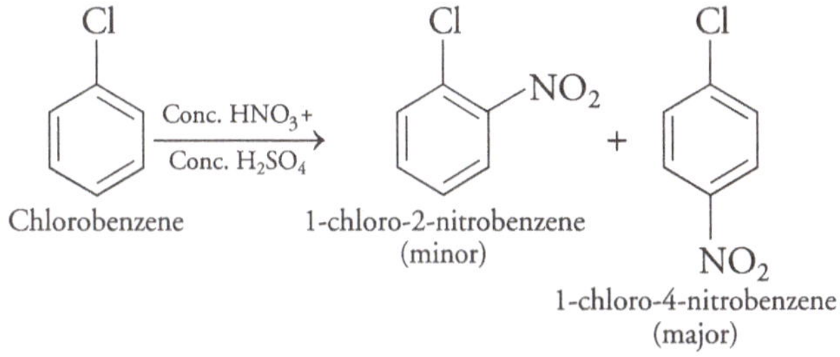

3. Sulphonation

This reaction takes place by heating haloarenes with conc.H_2SO_4.

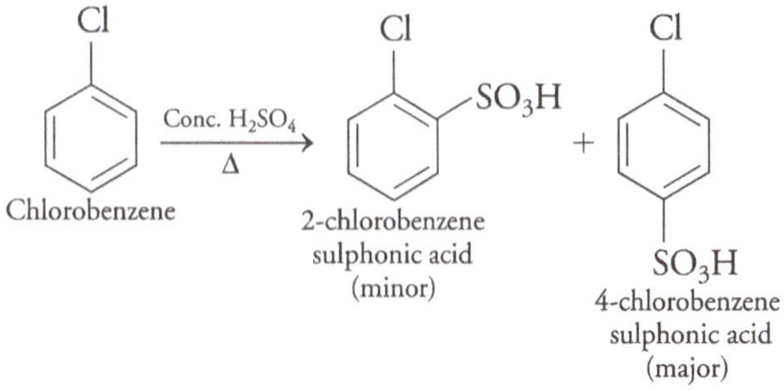

4. Friedel-Craft's Reactions

This reaction is carried out by treating haloarenes with alkyl chloride or acyl chloride in the presence of anhydrous $AlCl_3$ acting as a catalyst.

There are two main types of Friedel-Crafts reactions:

(i) Alkylation

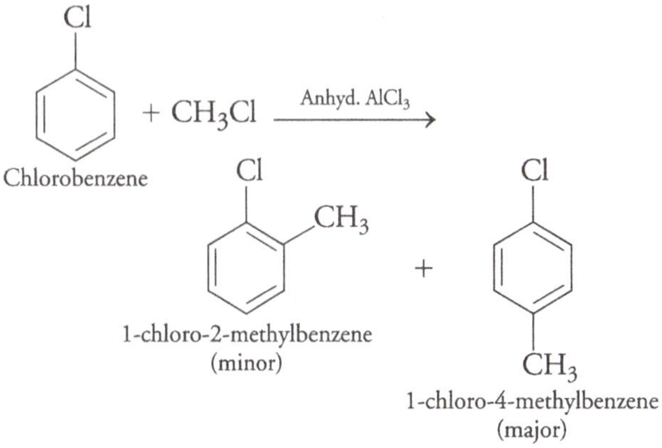

(ii) **Acylation**

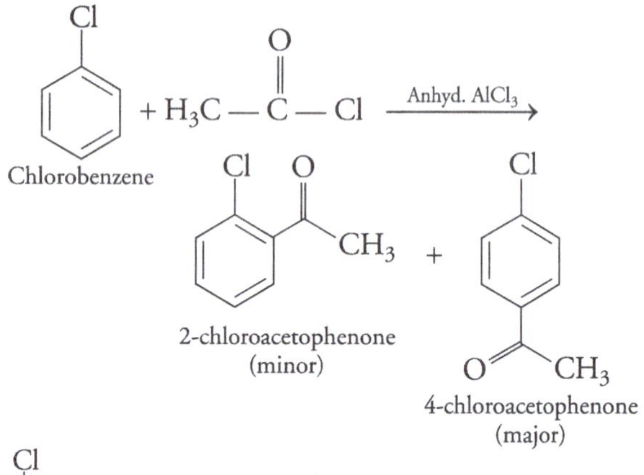

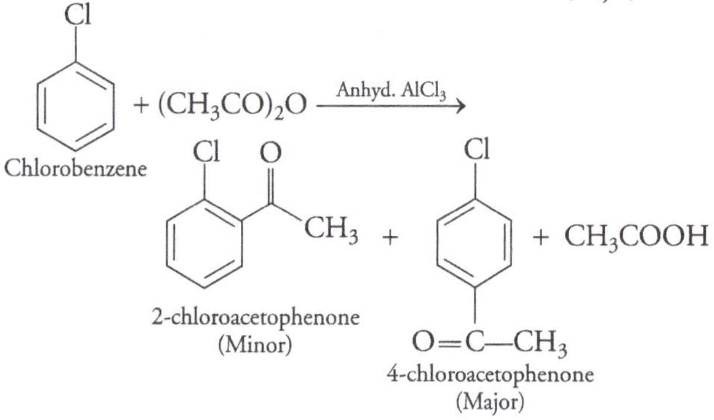

Reaction with Metals

1. Wurtz-Fittig Reaction

When aryl halide is heated with alkyl halide in the presence of sodium in dry ether, halogen atom is replaced by alkyl group and alkylarene is formed. This reaction is called Wurtz-Fittig reaction.

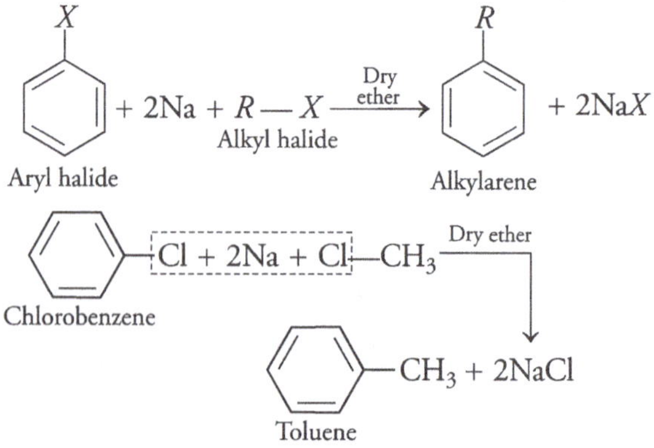

2. Fittig Reaction

When haloarenes react with sodium in the presence of dry ether, two aryl groups are joined together and diphenyl is formed. This reaction is called Fittig reaction.

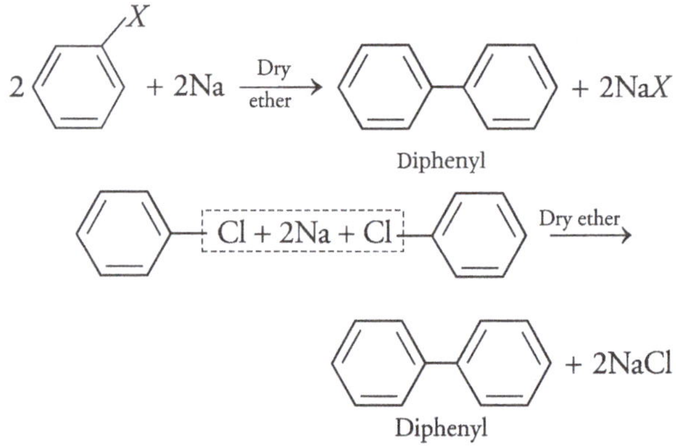

3. Addition Reaction with Magnesium

When haloaren reacts with magnesium then Grignard reagent is formed. Like alkyl halides, aryl bromides and iodides also react with magnesium in dry ether to form Grignard reagent.

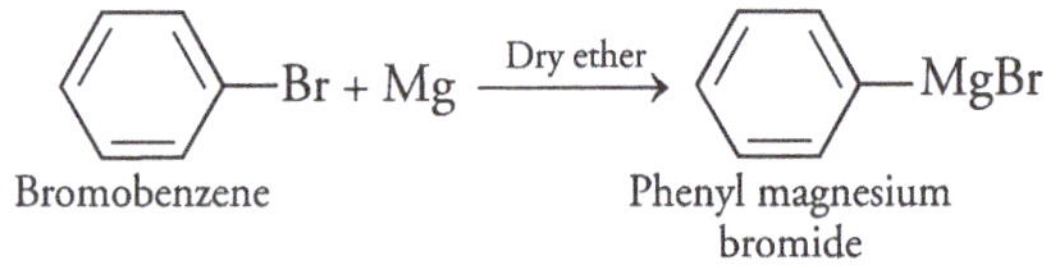

4. Reaction with Lithium

Bromo and iodo arenes react with lithium metal in the presence of dry ether to form their corresponding organometallic compounds.

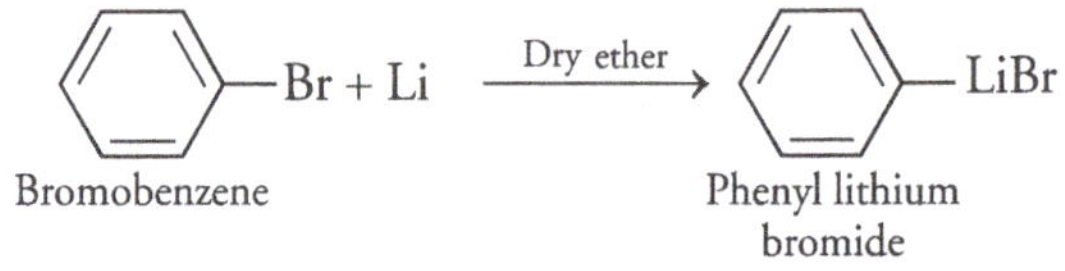

5. Reaction with Copper Powder

When iodobenzene is heated with copper powder in a sealed tube, diphenyl is formed. This reaction is called **Ullmann reaction**.

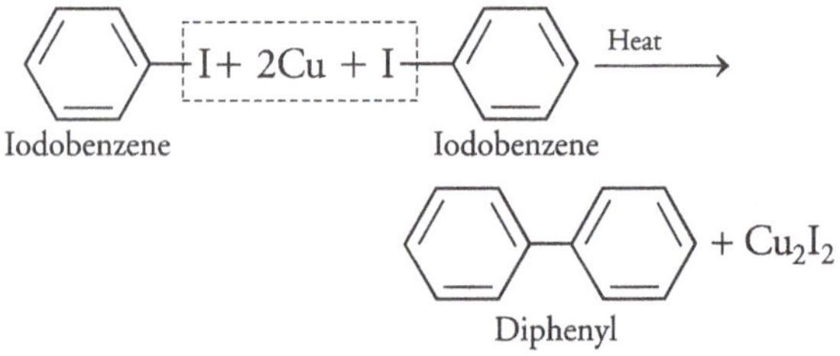

Reduction

On reduction of haloarenes, hydrocarbons are formed.

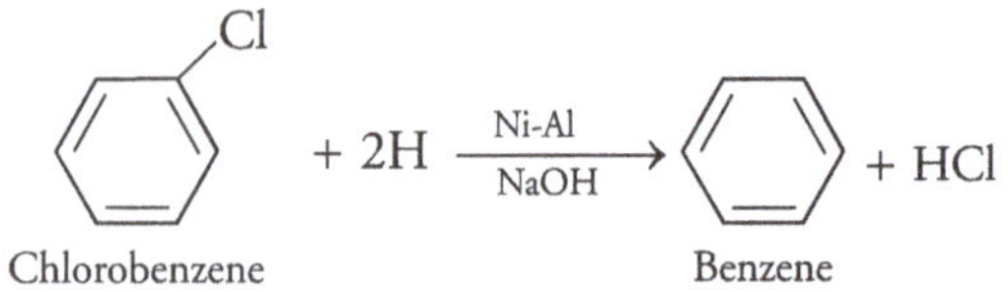

Topic Practice 2

Very Short Answer Type Questions

1 Mark

1. **Fill in the Blanks**

(i) 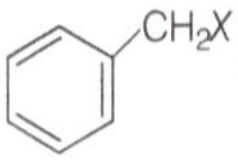 is known as ....

(ii) 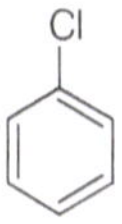 is ....

(iii) 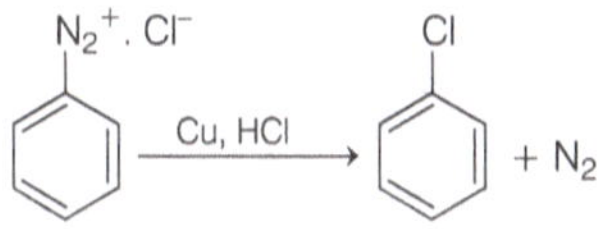

The reaction is known as ....

(iv) 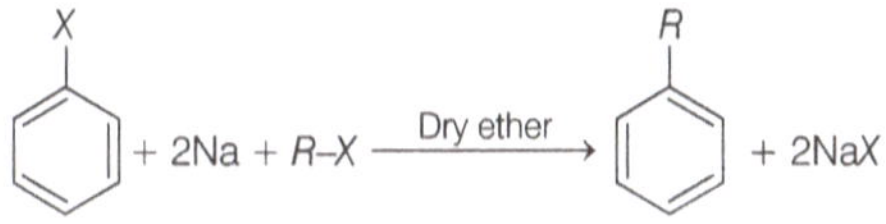

The reaction is called ....

2. **Objective Type Questions**

(i) p - nitrobromobenzene can be converted to p-amino nitrobenzene using $NaNH_2$. The reaction proceeds *via* intermediate named

(a) carbocation (b) carbanion
(c) benzyne (d) dianion

(ii) 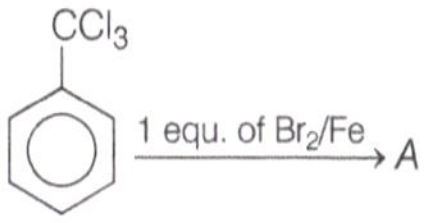

Compound A is

(a) 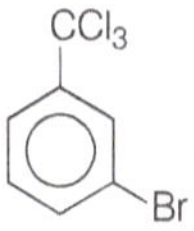 (b) 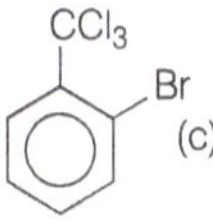 (c) 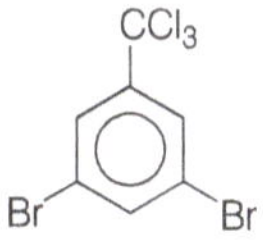 (d) 

(iii) o-methoxy bromobenzene is treated with sodamide and then with NH_3. The product formed is

(a) o-methoxy bromobenzene
(b) aniline
(c) methoxy benzene
(d) m-methoxy aniline

(iv) Reaction of $C_6H_5CH_2Br$ with aqueous sodium hydroxide follows **NCERT Exempler**

(a) S_N1 mechanism
(b) S_N2 mechanism
(c) Any of the above two depending upon the temperature of reaction
(d) Saytzeff rule

3. Match Column I with Column II and choose the correct option using the codes given below :

	Column I (Reaction)		Column II (Name)
A.	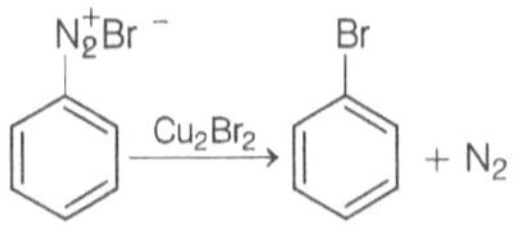	(i)	Fitting reaction
B.	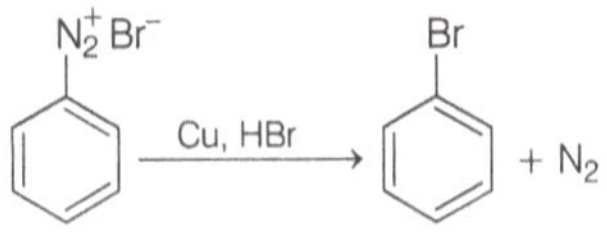	(ii)	Balz - Schiemann reaction
C.	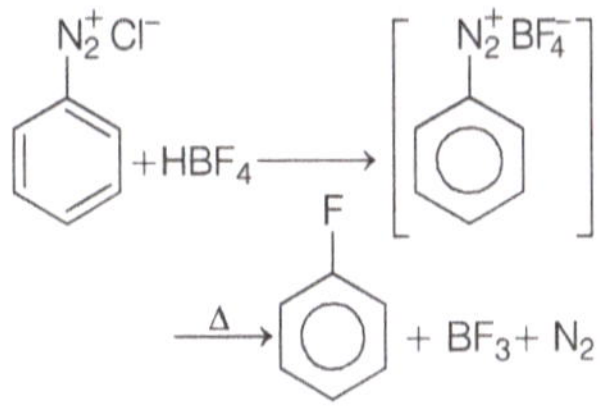	(iii)	Gattermann reaction
D.	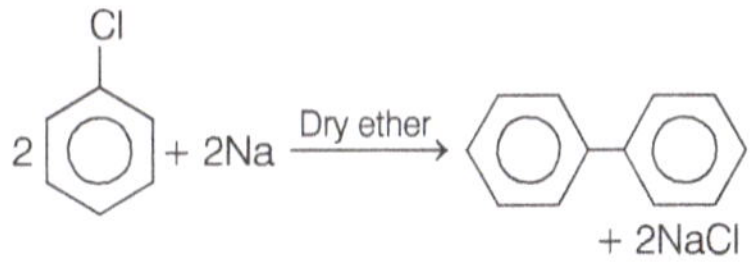	(iv)	Sandmeyer's reaction

Codes

	A	B	C	D		A	B	C	D
(a)	(i)	(ii)	(iii)	(iv)	(b)	(iv)	(iii)	(ii)	(i)
(c)	(i)	(ii)	(iv)	(iii)	(d)	(ii)	(i)	(iii)	(iv)

4. Write the IUPAC name of the following compound.

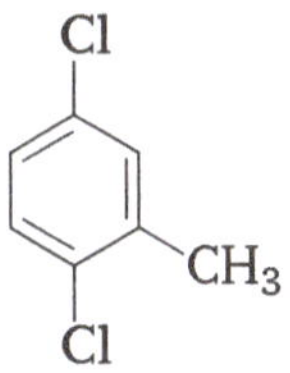

5. Give the IUPAC names of the following compounds.

$CH_3C(p\text{-}ClC_6H_4)_2CH(Br)CH_6$ **NCERT**

6. Write the structure of 2, 4-dinitrochlorobenzene. **Delhi 2017**

7. Write the structures of the following organic halogen compounds.

1-bromo-4-*sec*-butyl-2-methylbenzene

NCERT Intext

8. Out of *o* and *p*-dibromobenzene, which one has higher melting point and why? **NCERT Exemplar**

9. Give the balanced equation for the following name reaction: Wurtz-Fittig reaction **ISC 2016**

10. How can the following conversions be brought about ? Chlorobenzene to phenol **ISC 2015**

11. What will be the product formed when chlorobenzene is heated with sodium metal in the presence of dry ether? **ISC 2015**

12. Give the balanced equation, aniline treated with mixture of HNO_2 and excess of HCl at low temperature. **ISC 2002**

13. Identify the products *A* and *B* formed in the following reaction. molecular formula C_7H_8, is treated with Cl_2 in the presence of $FeCl_3$. **NCERT Exemplar**

Short Answer Type I Questions

(2 Marks)

14. Name the following halides according to the IUPAC system and classify them as benzyl (primary, secondary, tertiary), aryl halides.
(i) *p* - $ClC_6H_4CH_2CH(CH_3)_2$
(ii) *m* - $ClCH_2C_6H_4CH_2C(CH_3)_3$
(iii) *o* -Br — $C_6H_4CH(CH_3)CH_2CH_3$ **NCERT**

15. Write the structures of the following organic halogen compounds.
(i) *p*-bromochlorobenzene
(ii) 2-(2-chlorophenyl)-1-iodooctane **NCERT**

16. Draw the structures of major monohalo products in the following reactions :

(i) 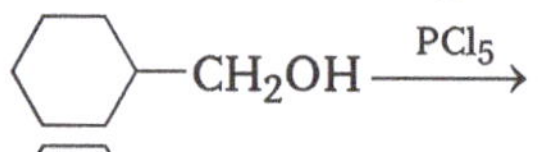

(ii) 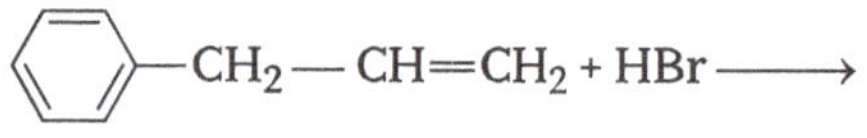

17. How will you bring the following conversions?
(i) Benzene to biphenyl **ISC 2024**
(ii) Iodoform to acetylene

18. How will you carry out the following conversions
Benzene to *p*-chloronitrobenzene

19. Why aryl halides cannot be prepared by the reaction of phenol with HCl in the presence of $ZnCl_2$?

20. Write the structure of the major organic product in each of the following reactions:

$$C_6H_5ONa + C_2H_5Cl \longrightarrow$$

21. Bring out the following conversions.
Chlorobenzene to 2-chloroacetophenone

22. Explain,
why the dipole moment of chlorobenzene is lower than that of cyclohexyl chloride?

23. Which of the following compound/s will have the highest melting point and why?

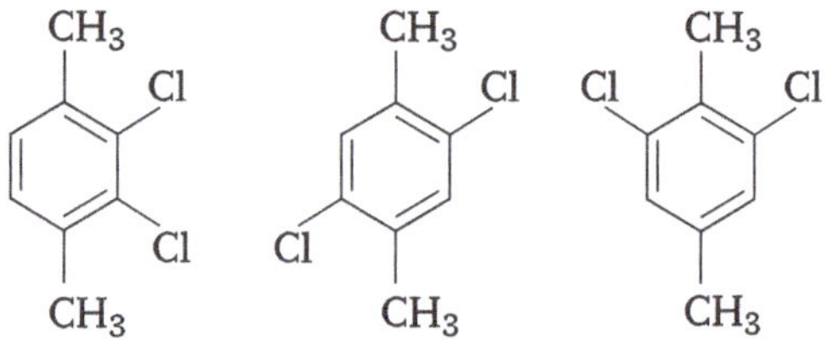

(I) (II) (III)

24. Give chemical equations for each of the following. **ISC 2023**
(i) Ethyl chloride is treated with aqueous KOH solution.
(ii) Chlorobenzene is treated with ammonia at 573 K and high pressure.

25. Write the balanced chemical equation for each of the following: **ISC 2019**
(i) Chlorobenzene treated with ammonia in the presence of Cu_2O at 475 K and 60 atm.
(ii) Ethyl chloride treated with alcoholic potassium hydroxide.

26. Account for the following :
Electrophilic substitution reactions in haloarenes occur slowly.

27. Draw the structures of major monohalo products in each of the following reactions.

(i) 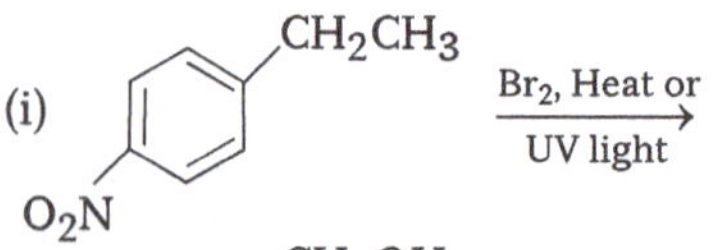

(ii) 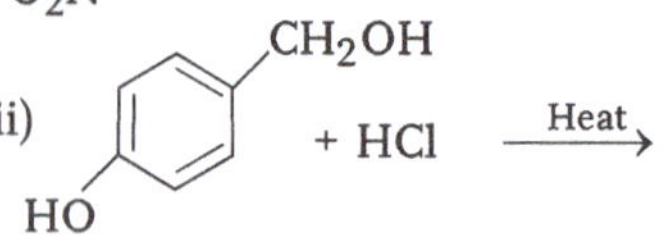

28. What happens, when chlorobenzene is treated with $Cl_2 / FeCl_3$?
Write the chemical equations in support of your answer.

Short Answer Type II Questions
(3 Marks)

29. Give reasons for the following :
C—*X* bond length in halobenzene is smaller than C—*X* bond length in CH_3—*X*.

Or

The C— Cl bond length in chlorobenzene is shorter than that in CH_3Cl.

30. Illustrate Sandmeyer's reaction with the help of a suitable example.

31. How will you convert the following? **ISC 2020**
(i) Chlorobenzene to biphenyl
(ii) Propene to 1-bromopropane
(iii) Chlorobenzene to aniline

32. Give reasons:
The presence of nitro group (—NO_2) at *o*/*p*-positions, increases the reactivity of haloarenes towards nucleophilic substitution reactions.

Long Answer Type Questions
(5 Marks)

33. Write a chemical reaction to depict the preparation of haloarene from each of the following.
(i) Toluene
(ii) Aniline

34. What happens, when
(i) bromobenzene is treated with Mg in the presence of dry ether?
(ii) chlorobenzene is subjected to hydrolysis?

Hints & Solutions

1. (i) benzyl halide (ii) chlorobenzene
(iii) Gattermann reaction (iv) Wurtz - Fittig reaction

2. (i) (c) Aryl halides, in presence of strong base like $NaNH_2$, gives nucleophilic substitution reaction through benzyne intermediate.

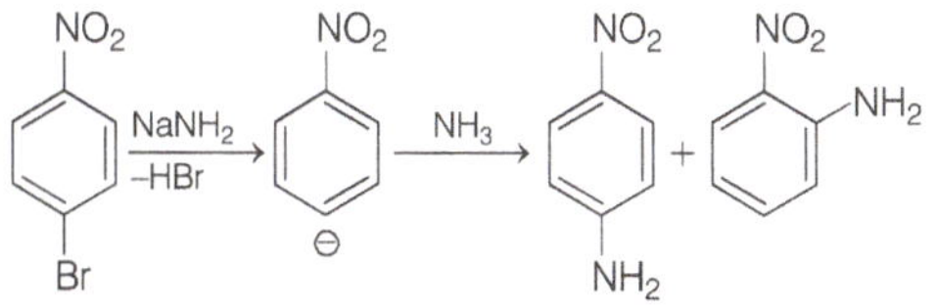

(ii) (a) Due to presence of 3Cl-atoms, the ring is highly deactivating, the product is

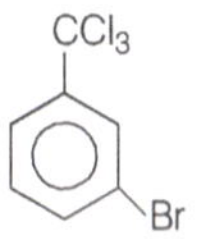

(iii) (d)

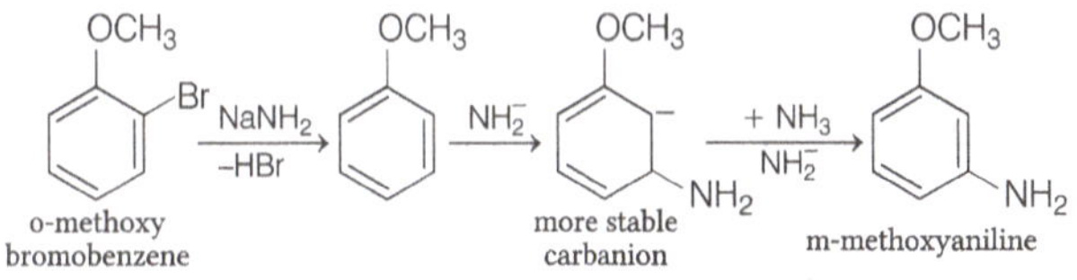

(iv) (a) $C_6H_5\overset{+}{C}H_2$ is stable cation, so favours the progress of reaction by S_N1 mechanism.

3. (b) (A) → (iv), (B) → (iii), (C) → (ii), (D) → (i)

4. IUPAC name of the given compound

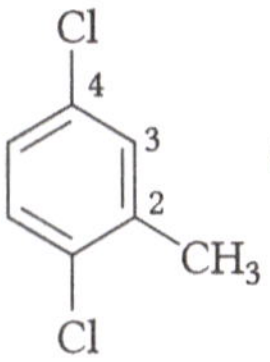

is 1,4-dichloro-2-methylbenzene

5.

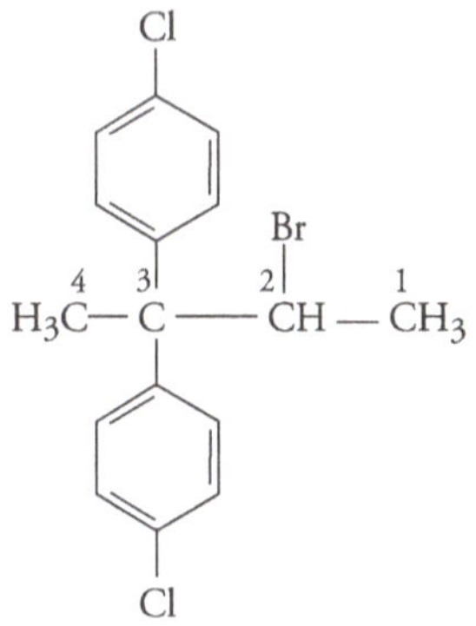

6. The structure of 2,4-dinitrochlorobenzene is

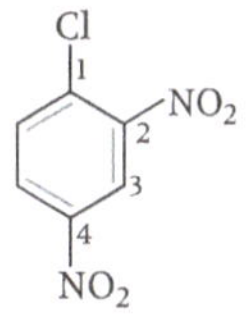

7.

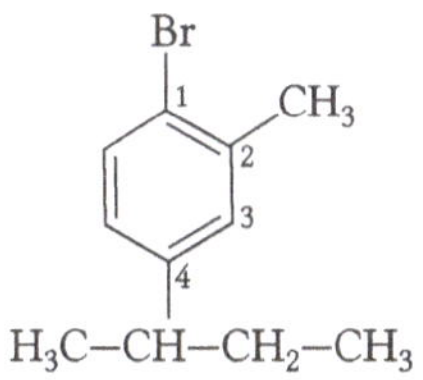

1-bromo-4-sec-butyl-2-methylbenzene

8. *p*-dibromobenzene has higher melting point than its *o*-isomer due to symmetry of *p*-isomer that fits in the crystal lattice better than the *o*-isomer. Hence, *p*-isomer has higher melting point than *o*-isomer (or *m*-isomer).

9. Wurtz-Fittig reaction

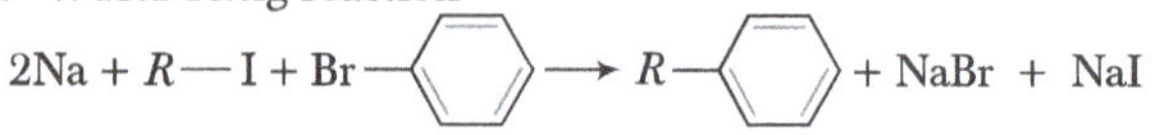

10.

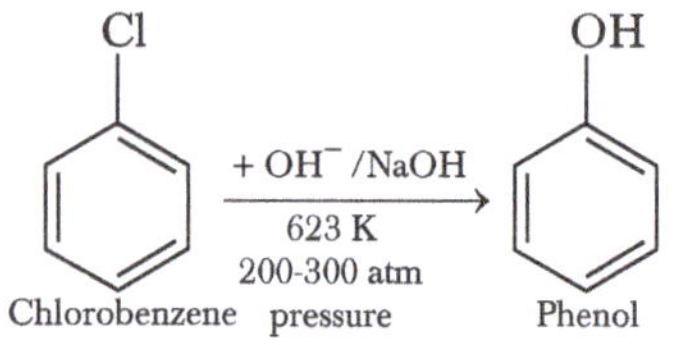

11. Chlorobenzene is heated with sodium metal in the presence of dry ether gives diphenyl compound.

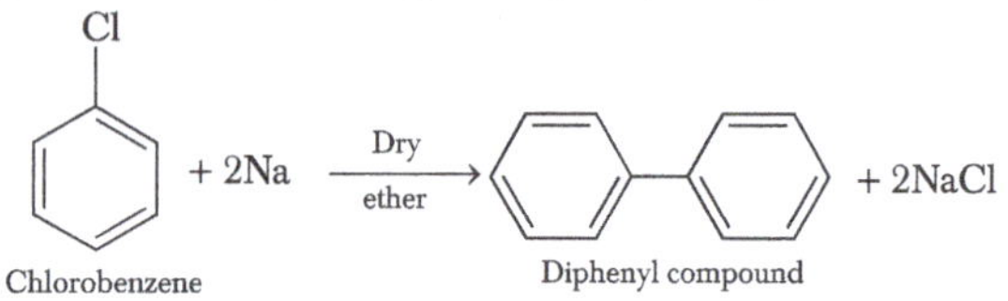

12. Benzene diazonium chloride is obtained by treating aniline with HNO_2 ($NaNO_2$ + HCl) at 273-278 K.

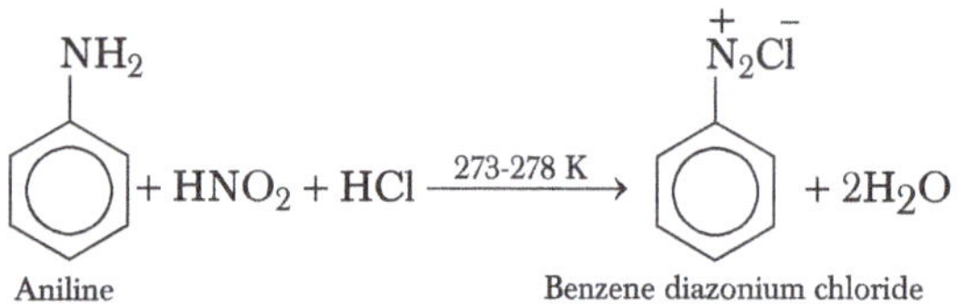

13.

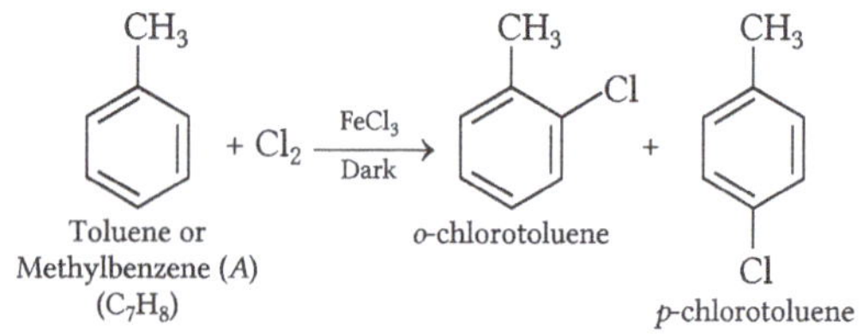

14. (i)

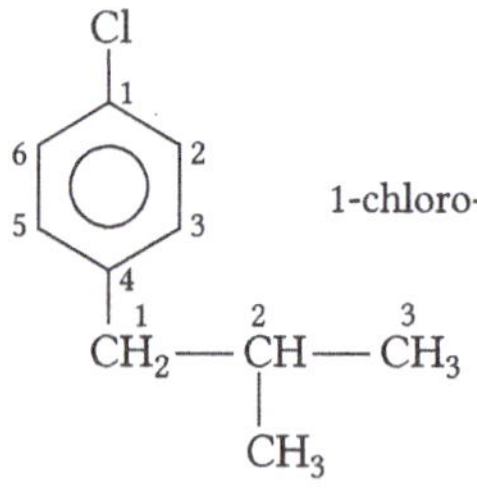

1-chloro-4-(2-methylpropyl) benzene (Aryl halide)

(ii)

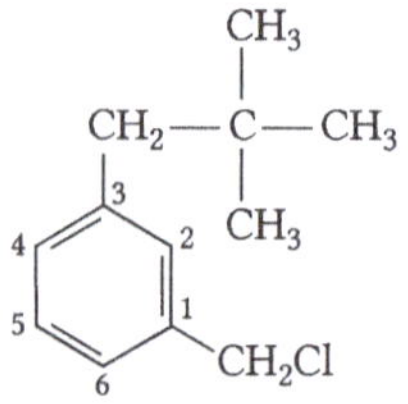

1-chloromethyl-3 (2, 2-dimethylpropyl) benzene (Benzyl halide)

(iii)

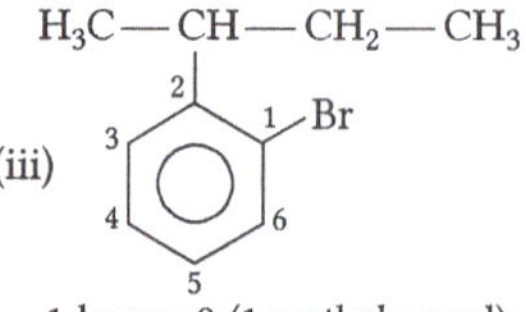

1-bromo-2-(1-methylpropyl) benzene (Aryl halide)

15. (i)

p-bromochlorobenzene

(ii)

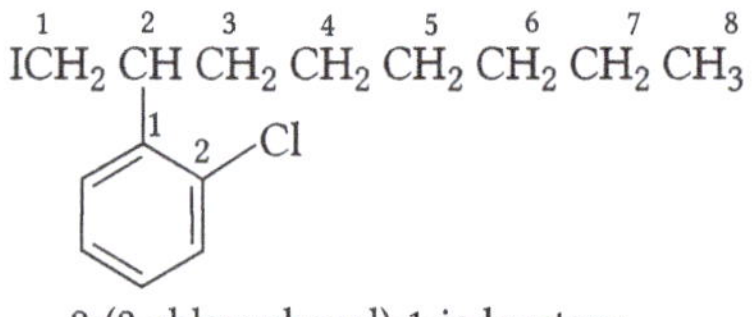

2-(2-chlorophenyl)-1-iodooctane

16. (i)

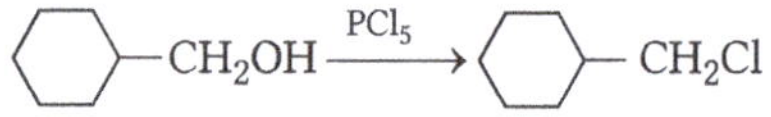

(1)

(ii)

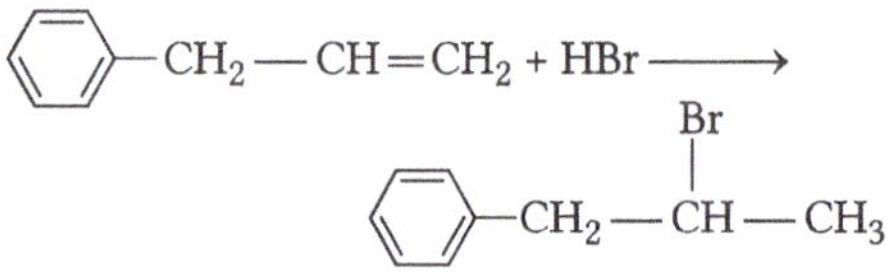

(1)

17. (i) Benzene to biphenyl

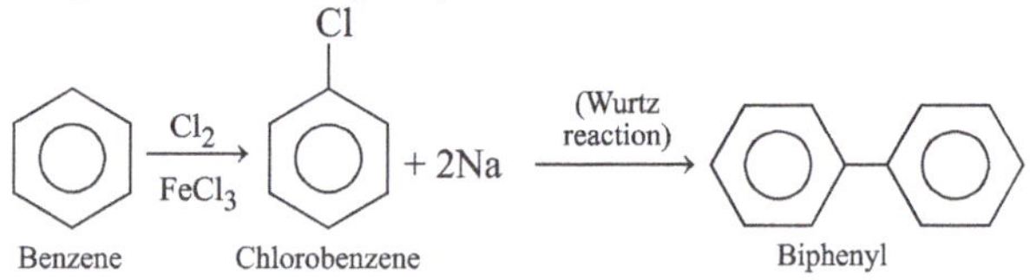

(ii) Iodoform to acetylene

$$2CHI_3 + 6Ag \longrightarrow CH \equiv CH + 6AgI\downarrow$$

18. Benzene to *p*-chloronitrobenzene

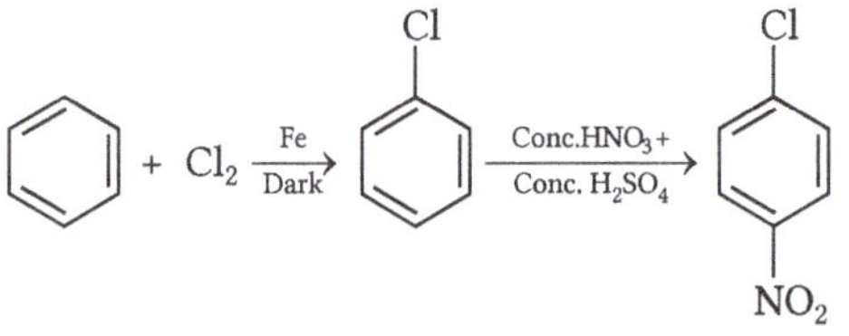

19. Due to resonance in phenol, C—O bond of phenol has some partial double bond character, which strengthens the bond. So, it is difficult to break this C—O bond of phenol while the C—O bond of alcohol is purely single bond and comparatively weaker bond. So, alkyl halides can be prepared by the reaction of alcohols with HCl in the presence of $ZnCl_2$ while aryl halides cannot be prepared by the reaction of phenol with HCl in the presence of $ZnCl_2$.

$$\underset{\text{Phenol}}{C_6H_5OH} \xrightarrow[ZnCl_2]{HCl} \text{No reaction}$$

$$\underset{\text{Alcohol}}{RCH_2OH} \xrightarrow[ZnCl_2]{HCl} \underset{\text{Alkyl chloride}}{RCH_2Cl} + H_2O \qquad (2)$$

20. $$\underset{\text{Sodium phenoxide}}{C_6H_5\overset{-}{O}\overset{+}{Na}} + \underset{\text{Chloroethane}}{C_2H_5Cl} \xrightarrow[\text{synthesis}]{\text{Williamson's}} \underset{\text{Phenyl ethyl ether}}{C_6H_5—O—C_2H_5} + NaCl$$

21. 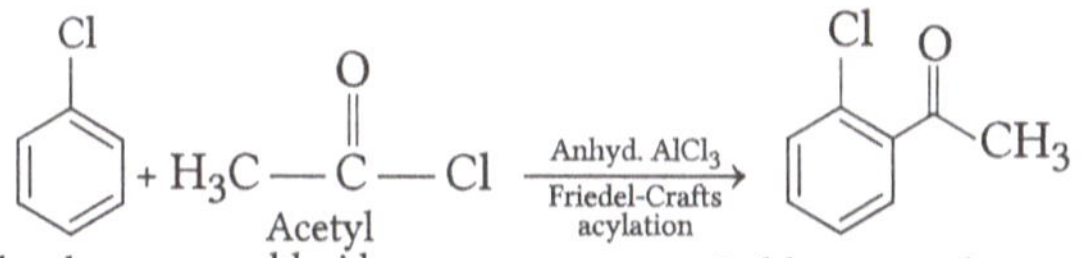

Chlorobenzene, Acetyl chloride → 2-chloroacetophenone

22.

Key idea

(i) Find the hybridisation of C-atoms in chlorobenzene and cyclohexyl chloride and electronegativity to find the bond polarity and thus, dipole moment.

(ii) Strong intermolecular H-bonding exist among water molecules.

(iii) Consider the reactive nature of Grignard reagents with water.

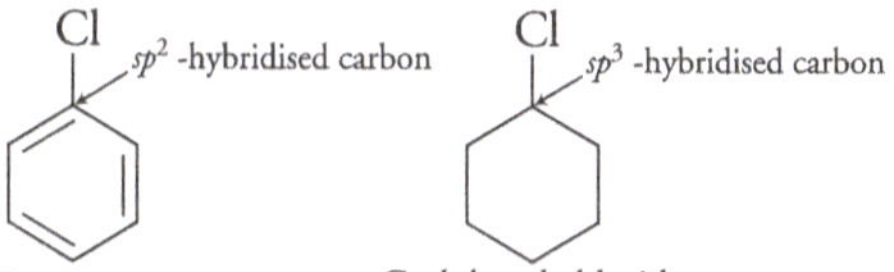

Chlorobenzene   Cyclohexyl chloride

Due to sp^2-hybridisation of C-atom in chlorobenzene, C-atom is more electronegative (greater *s*-character) whereas in cyclohexyl chloride, C-atom is sp^3 hybridised, i.e. less electronegative (lesser *s*-character). So, polarity of C—Cl bond in chlorobenzene is less than the C—Cl bond in cyclohexyl chloride.

Further, due to delocalisation of lone pair of electrons of Cl-atom over the benzene ring, C—Cl bond in chlorobenzene acquires some double bond character while C—Cl bond in cyclohexyl chloride is a pure single bond.

Thus, C—Cl bond in chlorobenzene is shorter than in cyclohexyl chloride. As dipole moment is a product of charge and distance, therefore, the dipole moment of chlorobenzene is lower than that of cyclohexyl chloride. **(1)**

23. Compound (II) is most symmetrical because it has both CH_3 groups and Cl atoms *para*- to each other. Therefore, it fits in the crystal lattice better than the other two isomers and hence it has the higher melting point.

24. (i) $CH_3CH_2Cl \xrightarrow{Aq.\ KOH} CH_3CH_2OH$

(ii) 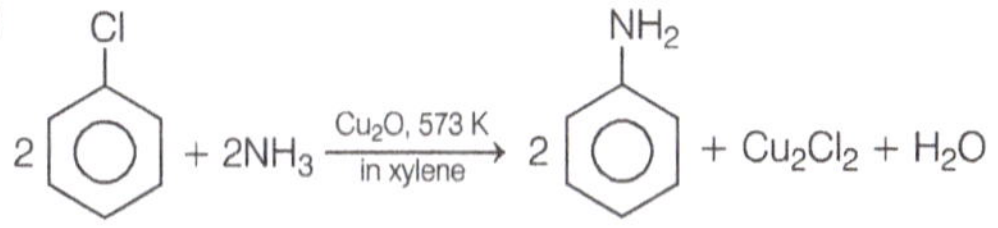

25. (i) Chlorobenzene when treated with ammonia in the presence of Cu_2O at 475 K and 60 atm pressure form aniline.

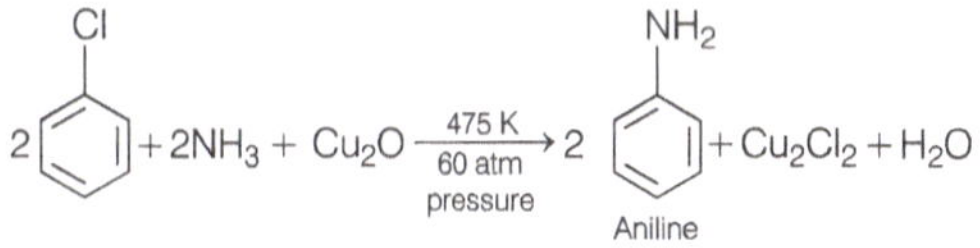

Aniline

(ii) When ethyl chloride is treated with alcoholic KOH, it undergoes elimination reaction to form ethene.

$$C_2H_5Cl + KOH \longrightarrow C_2H_4 + KCl + H_2O$$

26. Refer to text on page 230 (Electrophilic substitution reactions).

27. (i) 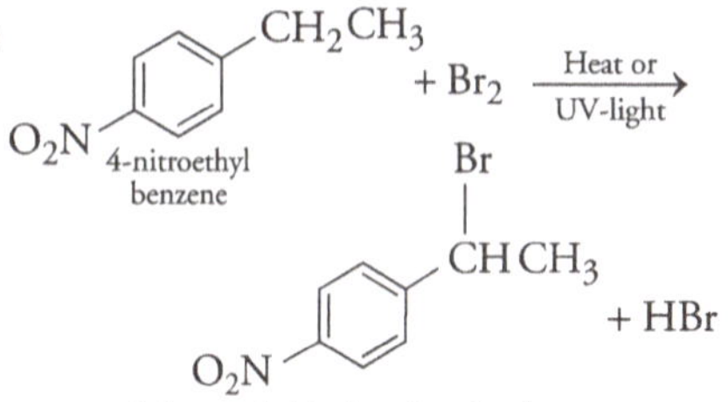

4-nitroethyl benzene → 1-bromo-1-(4-nitrophenyl) ethane

Bromination does not take place on benzene ring.

(ii) 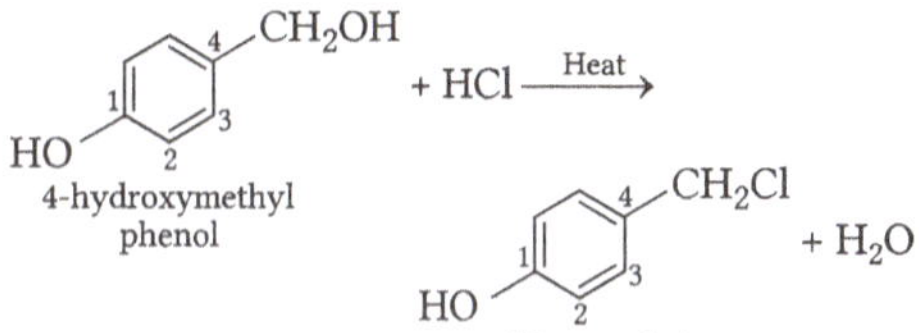

4-hydroxymethyl phenol → 4-chloromethyl phenol

Note Phenolic —OH group is not replaced by —Cl group.

28. 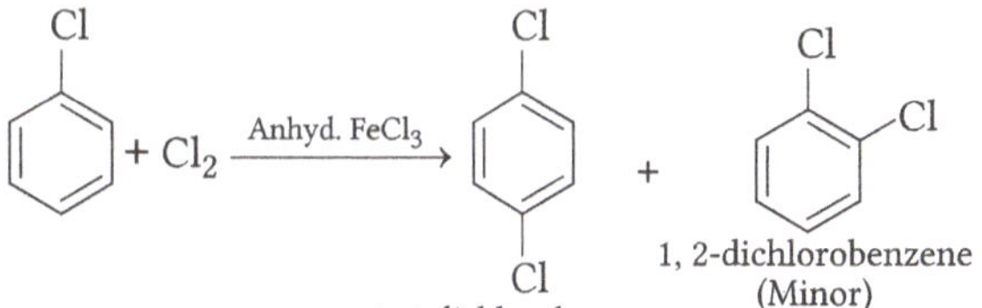

1, 4-dichlorobenzene (Major)   1, 2-dichlorobenzene (Minor)

29. In halobenzene (like chlorobenzene), the lone pair of electrons on halogen atom is delocalised on the benzene ring. As a result, C — *X* bond (C — Cl bond in case of chlorobenzene) acquires some double bond character while in $CH_3—X$, C—*X* bond is a pure single bond. Therefore, C—*X* bond in halobenzene is shorter than in $CH_3—X$.

30. Mixing the solution of freshly prepared diazonium salt with cuprous chloride or cuprous bromide, results in the replacement of the diazonium group by —Cl or —Br.

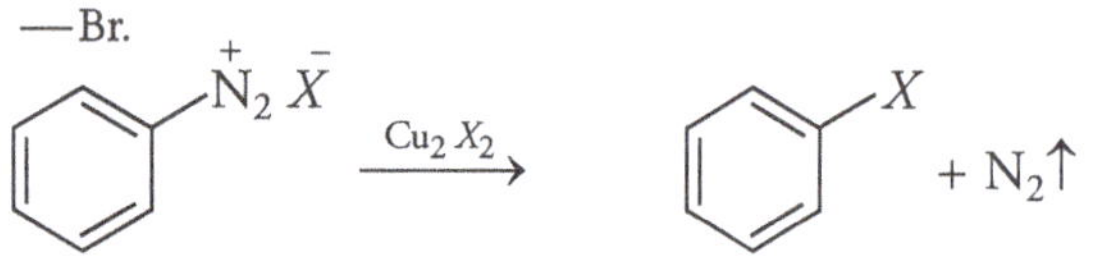

Aryl halide

(X = Cl, Br)

31. (i) Refer to page no. 232 (Fittig reaction).

(ii) $CH_3CH{=}CH_2 + HBr \longrightarrow CH_3CH_2CH_2Br + CH_3\underset{\underset{Br}{|}}{C}H{-}CH_3$

Propene; 1-bromo propane (minor); 2-bromo propane (major)

(iii)

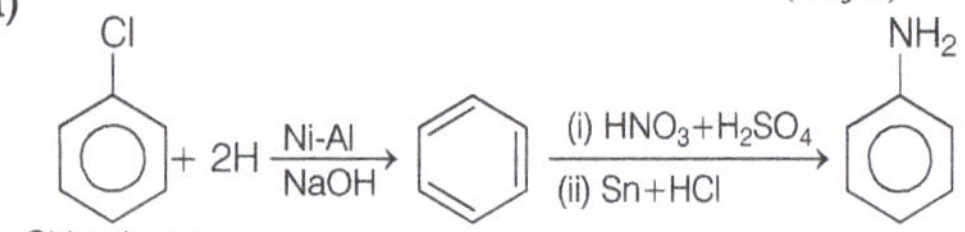

Chlorobenzene → Benzene → Aniline

32. Refer to text on page 228 and 229 (Substitution by hydroxyl group).

33. (i) Refer to text on page 226 (By electrophilic substitution of aromatic hydrocarbons).

(ii) Refer to text on page 226 and 227 (From diazonium salt).

34. (i) Phenyl magnesium bromide is formed.

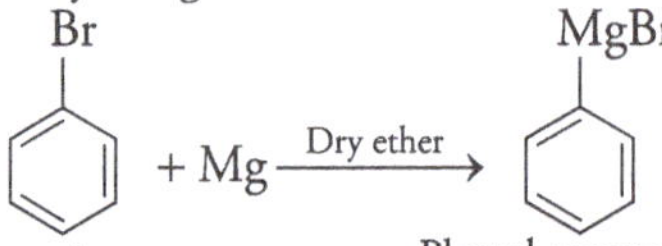

Bromobenzene → Phenyl magnesium bromide (Grignard reagent)

(ii) At room temperature and pressure, no reaction occurs but when chlorobenzene is heated with 6-8 % NaOH solution at 623K under 320 K atmospheric pressure, phenol is obtained.

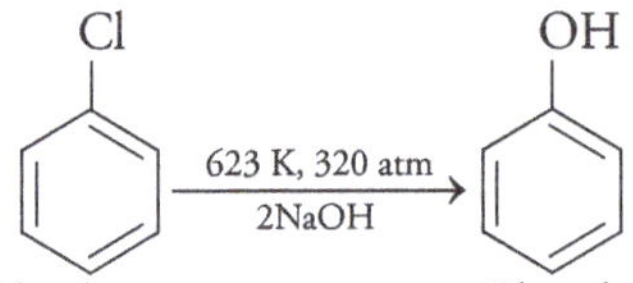

Chlorobenzene → Phenol

TOPIC 03 Polyhalogen Compounds

Carbon compounds having more than one halogen atom are usually referred to as polyhalogen compounds. Many of these compounds are useful in industry and agriculture. Some important polyhalogen compounds are described as follows :

Dichloromethane

(Methylene Chloride, CH_2Cl_2)

It is colourless, sweet smelling volatile liquid, having low boiling point of 313 K and specific gravity of 1.37. It is prepared industrially by the direct chlorination of methane in the presence of diffused sunlight.

$$CH_4 + 2Cl_2 \xrightarrow{h\nu} CH_2Cl_2 + 2HCl$$

Uses

It is used

(i) as a solvent and also as a paint remover.
(ii) as a propellant in aerosols.
(iii) as a metal cleaning and finishing solvent.
(iv) as refrigerant and dewaxing agent.
(v) as a process solvent in the manufacture of drugs.

Harmful Effects (Physiological Effects)

Some of the important harmful effects of methylene chloride are as follows:

(i) It harms the human central nervous system.
(ii) Exposure to low levels of methylene chloride in air can lead to slightly impaired hearing and vision.
(iii) Exposure to high levels of methylene chloride can cause dizziness, nausea, tingling and numbness in the fingers and toes.
(iv) Direct contact with skin causes intense burning and mild redness of the skin.
(v) Direct contact with eyes can burn the cornea.

Trichloromethane

(Chloroform, $CHCl_3$)

Trichloromethane is commonly known as chloroform. It is a colourless liquid with sweet odour. It is non-flammable but its vapour burns with green flame. $CHCl_3$ causes unconsciousness when vapours are inhaled for sufficient time.

Preparation

In industry, $CHCl_3$ is produced by heating a mixture of chlorine and either chloromethane or methane.

CH_3CH_2OH on reaction with moist bleaching powder is converted into $CHCl_3$.

$$CaOCl_2 + H_2O \longrightarrow Ca(OH)_2 + Cl_2$$

$$Cl_2 + H_2O \longrightarrow 2HCl + O \text{ (Oxidising agent)}$$

$$CH_3CH_2OH + O \longrightarrow CH_3CHO + H_2O$$

$$CH_3CHO + 3Cl_2 \longrightarrow \underset{\text{Chloral}}{CCl_3CHO} + 3HCl$$

$$2CCl_3CHO + Ca(OH)_2 \longrightarrow 2CHCl_3 + (HCOO)_2Ca$$

Chemical Properties

Some of the important reactions of chloroform are as follows :

(i) **Oxidation** Chloroform is slowly oxidised by air in the presence of light to an extremely poisonous gas, carbonyl chloride also called phosgene. It is therefore stored in dark coloured bottles. These bottles are completely filled with chloroform upto the brim and are properly stoppered to keep air out.

$$2CHCl_3 + O_2 \xrightarrow{\text{Sunlight}} \underset{\text{Phosgene}}{2COCl_2} + 2HCl$$

1% ethanol is added so, as to convert phosgene gas to diethyl carbonate which is non-volatile and non-toxic.

$$\underset{\text{Phosgene}}{COCl_2} + 2C_2H_5OH \longrightarrow \underset{\text{Diethyl carbonate}}{(C_2H_5)_2CO_3} + 2HCl$$

(ii) **Reduction** Partial reduction of chloroform is carried out with zinc and hydrochloric acid that converts chloroform to methylene chloride. But when zinc dust and water is used then is completely reduced to methane.

$$CH_4 \xleftarrow[\text{6[H]}]{\text{Zn/H}_2\text{O}, \; -\text{HCl}} CHCl_3 \xrightarrow[\text{2[H]}^+]{\text{Zn/HCl-C}_2\text{H}_5\text{OH}} CH_2Cl_2$$

$$CCl_4 \xrightarrow{\text{Fe/H}_2\text{O}} CHCl_3$$

(iii) **Halogenation** When chlorine is passed through chloroform in the presence by sunlight, it forms carbon tetrachloride.

$$CHCl_3 + Cl_2 \xrightarrow{h\nu} \underset{\text{Tetrachloromethane}}{CCl_4}$$

(iv) **Hydrolysis** Chloroform reacts with *aq.* KOH or NaOH and undergoes hydrolysis to form sodium or potassium salts of formic acid.

$$CHCl_3 + 4NaOH \longrightarrow HCOO^-Na^+ + 3NaCl + 2H_2O$$

(v) **Nitration** It reacts with HNO_3 to form chloropicrin. Which is used as an insecticide.

$$Cl_3C{-}H + HO{-}NO_2 \longrightarrow \underset{\substack{\text{(Nitro chloroform)}\\ \text{Chloropicrin}}}{Cl_3C{-}NO_2} + H_2O$$

(vi) **Reaction with acetone** It condenses with acetone in presence of KOH to form chloretone, a sleep-inducing medicine (hypnotic).

$$CHCl_3 + \underset{\text{Acetone}}{CH_3{-}\overset{\overset{\large O}{\|}}{C}{-}CH_3} \xrightarrow{\text{KOH}} \underset{\text{Chloretone}}{CH_3\overset{\overset{\large CH_3}{|}}{\underset{\underset{\large CCl_3}{|}}{C}}{-}OH}$$

(vii) **Reaction with Ag powder**

$$CHCl_3 + 6Ag + CHCl_3 \longrightarrow CH{\equiv}CH + 6AgCl$$

(viii) **Reimer-Tiemann reaction** On refluxing alkaline solution of phenol with $CHCl_3$ at 330 K, and on subsequent acidification, *o*-hydroxy- benzaldehyde (salicylaldehyde) is obtained. It is called **Reimer-Tiemann** reaction, *o*-isomer predominates but is separated from *p*-isomer by steam-distillation.

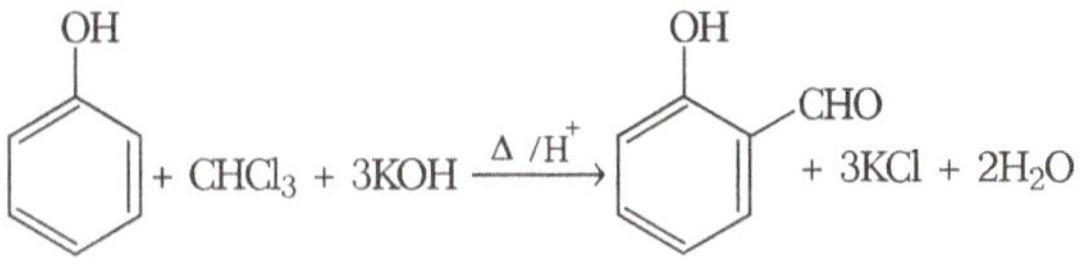

Salicylaldehyde

If *o*-position is already occupied, aldehyde group goes to *p*-position.

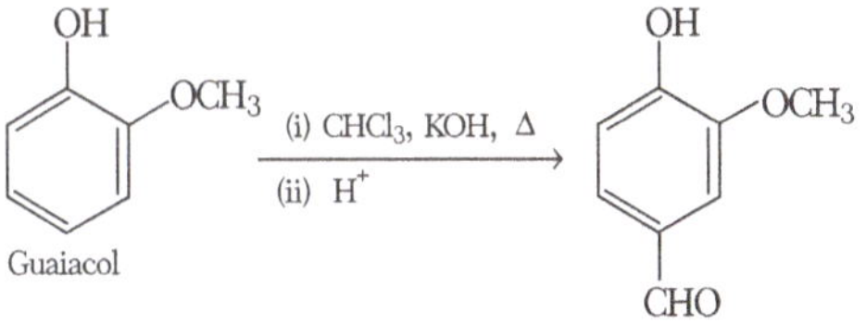

Guaiacol Vanillin

(ix) **Carbylamine reaction** On heating $CHCl_3$ with ethanolic KOH and anilin (or 1° amine RNH_2), phenyl isocyanide is formed a is readily detected by its nauseating odour. It is called **isocyanide** or **carbylamine** test of 1° amine RNH_2.

$$CHCl_3 + 3KOH + RNH_2 \xrightarrow{\Delta} RNC + 3KCl + 3H_2O$$

Uses

It is used

(i) as a solvent for fats, alkaloids, iodine and other substances.
(ii) as a laboratory reagent.
(iii) in the preparation of chloropicrin, chloretone, etc.
(iv) in medicines.
(v) in the production of freon refrigerant, *R*-22.
(vi) as an anaesthetic but now it has been replaced by other anaesthetics such as ether.

Harmful Effects (Physiological Effects)

(i) Chloroform affect the central nervous system. Inhaling it, 900 ppm (in air) for a short time, causes dizziness, fatigue and headache.
(ii) Chronic exposure to chloroform damages liver and kidney due to the formation of phosgene gas inside the body.
(iii) Skin develop sore if immersed directly into the chloroform.

Preservation of Chloroform

To prevent the oxidation of chloroform, it is preserved in the following ways :

(i) Chloroform is stored in dark coloured bottles to protect it from sunlight to avoid their oxidation.
(ii) These bottles are completely filled with chloroform upto the brim and are properly stoppered to keep air out.
(iii) 1% ethanol is added so, as to convert phosgene gas to diethyl carbonate which is non-volatile and non-toxic.

$$\underset{\text{Phosgene}}{COCl_2} + 2C_2H_5OH \longrightarrow \underset{\text{Diethyl carbonate}}{(C_2H_5)_2CO_3} + 2HCl$$

Triiodomethane (Iodoform, CHI_3)

It is a yellow coloured crystalline solid with characteristic unpleasant odour.

Laboratory Preparation

It can be obtained by heating ethyl alcohol or acetone with NaOH and iodine or Na_2CO_3 and iodine.

$$2NaOH + I_2 \longrightarrow NaI + \underset{\text{Sodium hypoiodide}}{NaOI} + H_2O$$

$$\underset{\text{Ethanol}}{C_2H_5OH} + NaOI \xrightarrow{\text{Oxidation}} CH_3CHO + NaI + H_2O$$

$$\underset{\text{Ethanal}}{CH_3CHO} + 3NaOI \xrightarrow{\text{Iodination}} CI_3CHO + 3NaOH$$

$$\underset{\text{Triiodo ethanal}}{CI_3CHO} + NaOH \xrightarrow{\text{Hydrolysis}} CHI_3\downarrow + HCO\overset{-}{O}\overset{+}{N}a$$

The complete reaction may be written as :

$$CH_3CH_2OH + 4I_2 + 6NaOH \longrightarrow CHI_3 + 5NaI + HCO\overset{-}{O}\overset{+}{N}a + 2H_2O$$

When sodium carbonate is used in place by NaOH

$$CH_3CH_2OH + 4I_2 + 3Na_2CO_3 \longrightarrow CHI_3\downarrow + 3NaI + HCO\overset{-}{O}\overset{+}{N}a + 3CO_2 + 2H_2O$$

Physical Properties

(i) It is pale yellow solid having melting point 392 K.
(ii) The compound has a characteristic odour.
(iii) It is insoluble in water but readily soluble in alcohol and ether.

Chemical Properties

Various chemical properties are as follows :

(a) **Reaction with alc. KOH** On boiling with KOH solution, potassium formate is formed as shown below:

$$CHI_3 + 3KOH \xrightarrow[-3KI]{} \left[CH\begin{matrix}OH\\OH\\OH\end{matrix}\right] \xrightarrow[-H_2O]{} \underset{\text{Formic acid}}{HCOOH} \xrightarrow[KOH]{} \underset{\text{Potassium formate}}{HCOO\overset{+}{K}} + H_2$$

(b) Reaction with amines (carbylamine reaction)
An offensive smell of isocyanide is obtained when iodoform is heated with primary amine and potassium hydroxide.

$$CHI_3 + CH_3NH_2 + 3KOH \xrightarrow{\text{heat}} CH_3NC + 3KI + 3H_2O$$

(c) **Reduction** With red phosphorus and conc. HI, it is reduced to methylene iodide.

$$CHI_3 + 2H \xrightarrow{P+HI} \underset{\text{Methylene iodide}}{CH_2I_2} + HI$$

(d) **Heating with silver powder** On heating with silver powder, it forms acetylene.

$$2CHI_3 + 6Ag \xrightarrow{\Delta} \underset{\text{Acetylene}}{H{-}C{\equiv}C{-}H} + 6AgI$$

(e) **With silver nitrate** When heated with alcoholic silver nitrate solution, it forms yellow precipitate. This reaction shows that iodoform is relatively unstable.

(f) **Oxidation** It undergoes oxidation in presence of air, light and moisture to give iodine.

$$4CHI_3 + 5O_2 \xrightarrow[\text{moisture}]{\text{Air, light}} 4CO_2 + 6I_2 + 2H_2O$$

Uses

It is used

(i) as an antiseptic due to the liberation of free iodine.

$$4CHI_3 + 5O_2 \xrightarrow[\text{Heat}]{} 6I_2 + 4CO_2 + 2H_2O$$

But due to its unpleasant smell, it has been replaced by other formulations containing iodine.

(ii) in the manufacture of pharmaceuticals.

Tetrachloromethane

(Carbon Tetrachloride, CCl_4)

It is colourless oily liquid with sickly smell. Its boiling point is 350 K. It is formed from chloroform as follows:

$$CHCl_3 + Cl_2 \xrightarrow{h\nu} CCl_4 + HCl$$

Uses

It is used

(i) in large quantities, in the manufacture of refrigerants and propellants for aerosol cans.

(ii) as a feed stock in the synthesis of chlorofluoro carbons (freons) and other chemicals.

(iii) as a cleaning fluid, degreasing agent and spot remover.

(iv) as fire extinguisher.

Harmful Effects (Physiological Effects)

(i) Exposure to CCl_4 causes liver cancer in humans.

(ii) The most common effects are dizziness, light headedness, nausea and vomiting which can cause permanent damage to nerve cells. In severe cases, these effects can lead to coma, unconsciousness or even death.

(iii) Exposure of CCl_4 vapours can make heartbeat irregular or even can stop it. When brought in contact with eyes, it may cause irritation in eyes.

(iv) It is also harmful to environment. When it is released in air, it rises in the atmosphere and depletes the ozone layer. Depletion of ozone layer increases the human exposure to UV rays which lead skin cancer, eye diseases and disorders and possible disruption of the immune system.

Freons

Chlorofluorocarbon compounds (CFC) of methane and ethane are collectively known as freons. They are extremely stable, unreactive, non-toxic, non-corrosive and easily liquefiable gases. Freon-12 (dichlorodifluoromethane, CCl_2F_2) is one of the most common freons in industrial use. It is manufactured from tetrachloromethane by **Swarts reaction.**

$$3CCl_4 + 2SbF_3 \xrightarrow{SbCl_5} 2SbCl_3 + \underset{\text{Freon-12}}{3CCl_2F_2}$$

Uses

(i) These are used as refrigerants in refrigerators and in air conditioning.

(ii) These are used as propellants for aerosols and foams to spray out deodorants, cleansers, shaving creams, hair sprays and insecticides.

(iii) In stratosphere, freon is able to initiate chain reactions that can result in depletion of ozone layer. Since, freon has been found to be one of the factors responsible for the depletion of ozone layer, they are being replaced by other harmless compounds in many countries.

Harmful Effects (Environmental Effects)

Most freons make its way into the atmosphere, where it undergoes photochemical decomposition and initiates radical chain reactions for depletion of the ozone layer. Therefore, the use of freons as propellants and refrigerants has been drastically discouraged.

p,p′-dichlorodiphenyltrichloroethane

(DDT)

DDT, the first chlorinated organic insecticide, was originally prepared in 1873. **Paul Muller** was awarded the Nobel prize in medicine and physiology in 1948 for this discovery. It is a white powder, insoluble in water but soluble in oil.

The structure of DDT is :

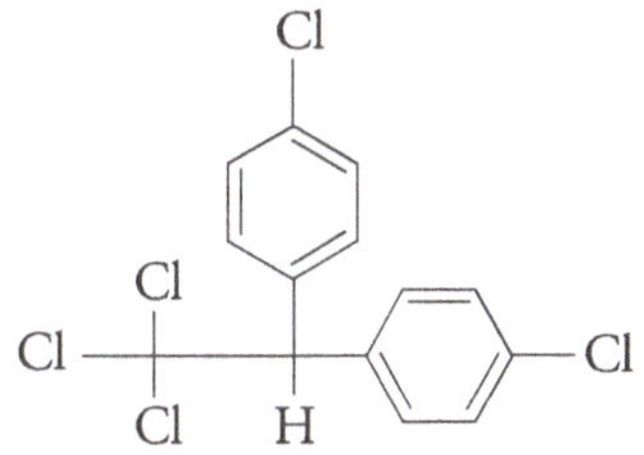

Uses

(i) DDT is a cheap but powerful insecticide.

(ii) It is popularly very effective against anopheles, mosquitoes (causes malaria) and lices which carry typhus.

Harmful Effects

(Environmental and Physiological Effects)

DDT is non-biodegradable and extremely stable compound which acts as water pollutant and kills aquatic animals thus imbalancing the water ecosystem. When higher animals (including humans) feed on dead fishes killed by DDT, it enters in their food chains. DDT gets stored in fat tissues of animal and increases in amount over the time. Researches have shown that such deposition in long run may cause cancer and other harmful diseases. Hence, DDT has been banned in many countries but it is still in use, due to its magical effects of controlling disease, in most of the developing countries.

Topic Practice 3

Very Short Answer Type Questions

1 Mark

1. Fill in the Blanks

(i) The addition of small quantity of ethanol to chloroform prevents the formation of .... and converts it into the harmless compound .... **ISC 2024**

(ii) It is an iodo-compound and used as an antiseptic. The compound liberate free iodine with oxygen the compound can be ....

(iii) A .... precipitate is obtained on adding iodine and sodium hydroxide to.........

(iv) .... are used as refrigerants in refrigerators and air-conditioning.

(v) *p, p′*-dichlorodiphenyl trichloroethane is commonly abbreviated as ....

(vi) DDT is a powerful .... but is non-biodegradable, therefore it is an extremely .... compound.

2. Objective Type Questions

(i) Acetone is mixed with bleaching powder to give

(a) chloroform (b) acetaldehyde
(c) ethanol (d) phosgene

(ii) Hydrolysis of trichloromethane with aqueous KOH gives

(a) methanol (b) acetic acid
(c) ethanol (d) formic acid

(iii) On being warmed with silver powder, chloroform gives

(a) C_6H_6 (b) C_4H_4
(c) C_2H_2 (d) CH_3Cl

(iv) The product formed when aniline is warmed with chloroform and caustic potash. **ISC 2010, 2002**

(a) Phenyl chloride (b) Methyl isocyanide
(c) Phenyl isocyanide (d) Nitrophenol

3. Match Column I with Column II and choose the correct option using the codes given below :

	Column I		Column II
A.	$CHCl_3 + O_2 \xrightarrow{\text{Sunlight}}$	(i)	DDT
B.	$CHCl_3 + Cl_2 \xrightarrow{h\nu}$	(ii)	Freon-12
C.	$CCl_4 + SbF_3 \xrightarrow{SbCl_5}$	(iii)	Carbon tetrachloride
D.	Chloral + chlorobenzene $\xrightarrow{H_2SO_4\text{(conc.)}}$	(iv)	Phosgene

Codes

	A	B	C	D
(a)	(i)	(ii)	(iii)	(iv)
(b)	(iv)	(iii)	(ii)	(i)
(c)	(iv)	(iii)	(i)	(ii)
(d)	(iii)	(iv)	(ii)	(i)

Short Answer Type I Questions

2 Marks

4. Write the balanced equation for the preparation of DDT. **ISC 2008**

5. Correct the following statement :
When acetone is treated with bleaching powder, acetaldehyde is obtained. **ISC 2007**

6. Write the chemical equation for the following reaction :
Acetone with sodium hypoiodite.

7. Complete the following reaction and name the reaction.

$$C_3H_7NH_2 + CHCl_3 + 3KOH\text{ (alc.)} \xrightarrow{\Delta} \ldots + 3KCl + 3H_2O$$

ISC 2010, 2002

Long Answer Type Questions

(5 Marks)

8. Name the following polyhalogen compounds.
   (i) Compound that act as a propellant in aerosols.
   (ii) Compound that is used in the preparation of chloropicrin.
   (iii) Compound that act as fire extinguisher.
   (iv) Compound that is a cheap insecticide.
   (v) Compound that is used in hair sprays.

Hints & Solutions

1. (i) phosgene; diethyl carbonate
   (ii) The iodo - compound is CHI_3. It is used as an antiseptic and give free I_2 on reaction with oxygen.
   (iii) yellow, methyl ketone
   (iv) Freons (i.e chlorofluorocarbons)
   (v) DDT
   (vi) insecticide, stable

2. (i) (a) $CaOCl_2 + H_2O \longrightarrow Ca(OH)_2 + Cl_2$

$$CH_3COCH_3 + 3Cl_2 \longrightarrow CCl_3COCH_3 + 3HCl$$

$$2CCl_3COCH_3 + Ca(OH)_2 \longrightarrow 2CHCl_3 + (CH_3COO)_2Ca$$

(ii) (d)

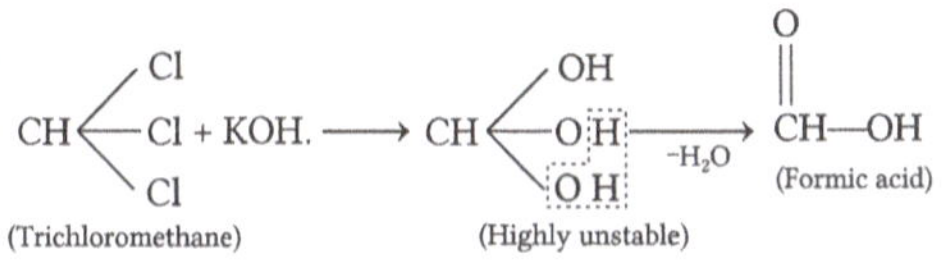

(iii) (c) $2CHCl_3 + 6Ag \xrightarrow{\Delta} CH \equiv CH + 6AgCl$

(iv) (c) **Phenyl isocyanide** In carbylamine reaction, when chloroform is warmed with aniline and alcoholic caustic potash, phenyl isocyanide is obtained which has an extremely offensive smell.

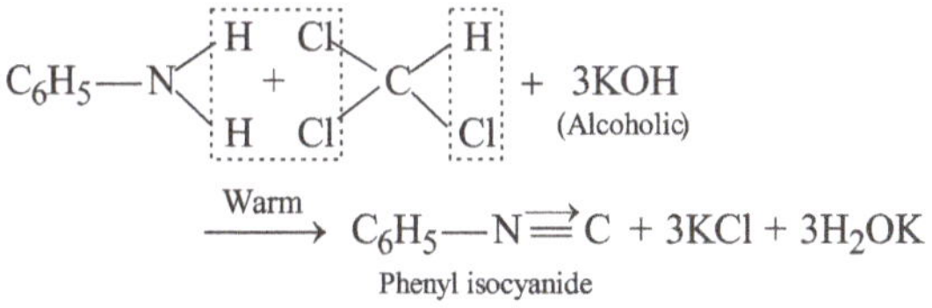

Hence, option (c) is correct.

3. (b) (A) → (iv), (B) → (iii), (C) → (ii), (D) → (i)

4. DDT is prepared by heating chlorobenzene with chloral in the presence of concentrated sulphuric acid.

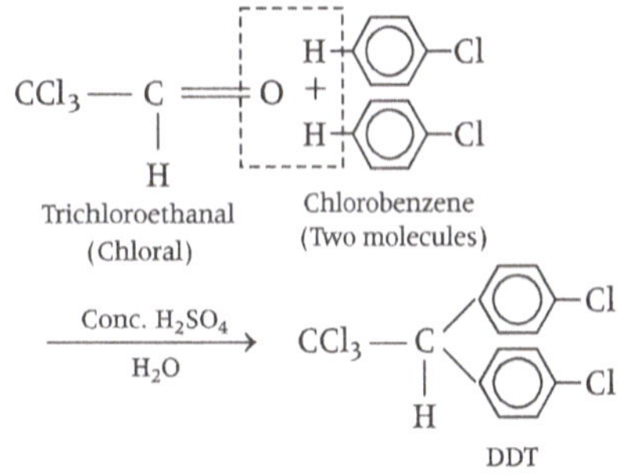

(2)

5. When acetone is treated with bleaching powder, **chloroform** is obtained. (2)

$$\underset{\text{Bleaching powder}}{CaOCl_2} + H_2O \longrightarrow \underset{\text{Chlorine}}{Cl_2} + Ca(OH)_2$$

$$\underset{\text{Acetone}}{CH_3-\overset{O}{\overset{\|}{C}}-CH_3} + 3Cl_2 \longrightarrow CCl_3-\overset{O}{\overset{\|}{C}}-CH_3 + 3HCl$$

$$2Ca(OH)_2 + 2CCl_3-\overset{O}{\overset{\|}{C}}-CH_3 \longrightarrow \underset{\text{Chloroform}}{2CHCl_3} + \underset{\text{Calcium acetate}}{(CH_3COO)_2Ca}$$

6. In the preparation of iodoform, sodium hypoiodite can also be used in place of sodium hydroxide with acetone. (2)

$$CH_3COCH_3 + 3NaOI \longrightarrow CH_3COCI_3 + 3NaOH$$

$$CH_3COCI_3 + NaOH \longrightarrow CH_3CO\overset{-}{O}\overset{+}{Na} + CHI_3$$

7. $C_3H_7NH_2 + CHCl_3 + 3KOH\,(alc.) \xrightarrow{\Delta}$ (2)

$$\underset{\text{Propyl isocyanide}}{C_3H_7N \rightleftarrows C} + 3KCl + 3H_2O \text{ (Carbylamine reaction)}$$

When chloroform is warmed with a suitable aromatic or aliphatic primary amine and alcoholic caustic potash, corresponding isocyanide is formed which has extremely offensive smell.

8. (i) Carbon tetrachloride (CCl_4) (ii) Chloroform ($CHCl_3$)
   (iii) Carbon tetrachloride (CCl_4) (iv) DDT
   (v) Freons ($5 \times 1 = 5$)

SUMMARY

- Organic compounds formed by the replacement of one or more hydrogen atoms of aliphatic hydrocarbon, by an equal number of halogen atoms are called **haloalkanes**. **Haloarenes** are compounds having halogen atom directly attached to the aromatic ring.
- In IUPAC system, these are written by prefixing the word 'halo' to the name of the longest straight chain alkane.
- Haloarenes are the common as well as IUPAC names of aryl halides. For dihalogen derivatives, the prefixes, *o* -, *m* - and *p* - are used in common system but in IUPAC system the numerals 1, 2; 1, 3 and 1, 4 are used.
- **Preparation** (Haloalkanes)

Method	Reaction involved
(i) From alcohols (substitution)	$RCH_2OH + HX \longrightarrow RCH_2X + H_2O$, $R—OH \xrightarrow[(P_4/X_2)]{PX_3} R—X + H_3PO_3$, $R—OH + SOCl_2 \xrightarrow{\Delta} R—Cl + SO_2\uparrow + HCl\uparrow$
(ii) From alkanes (halogenation)	$CH_4 \xrightarrow{Cl_2/h\nu} CH_3Cl + CH_2Cl_2 + CHCl_3 + CCl_4$
(iii) From alkenes (addition) • Addition of hydrogen halides	$R—\overset{H}{C}=\overset{H}{C}—R + HX \longrightarrow R—\underset{H}{\overset{H}{C}}—\underset{H}{\overset{H}{C}}—R'$
• Addition of halogen	$H_2C=CH_2 + Br_2 \xrightarrow{CCl_4} BrCH_2—CH_2Br$
• Allylic substitution of alkenes	$CH_3CH_2CH=CH_2 + X_2 \xrightarrow[\text{or NBS}]{773\ K} CH_3\underset{X}{CH}—CH=CH_2 + HX$
(iv) By halide exchange reaction	$H_3C—Br + AgF \xrightarrow[\text{acetone}]{\text{Dry}} H_3C—F + AgBr$ (Swarts reaction)

- **Physical Properties of Haloalkanes**
  - **Haloalkanes** Polar in nature, insoluble in polar solvents like water as they do not have the ability to form hydrogen bond with water, density increases with increase in the number of alkyl groups.

- **Preparation of Haloarenes**

(i) Halogenation

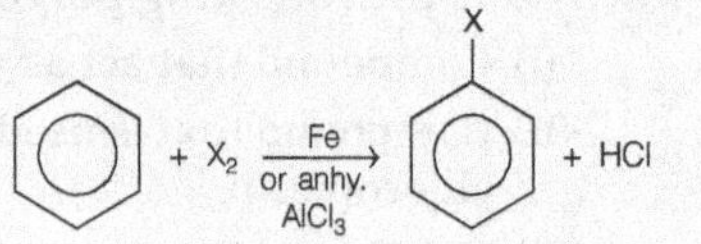

(ii) From benzene diazonium salts

Sandmeyer's reaction

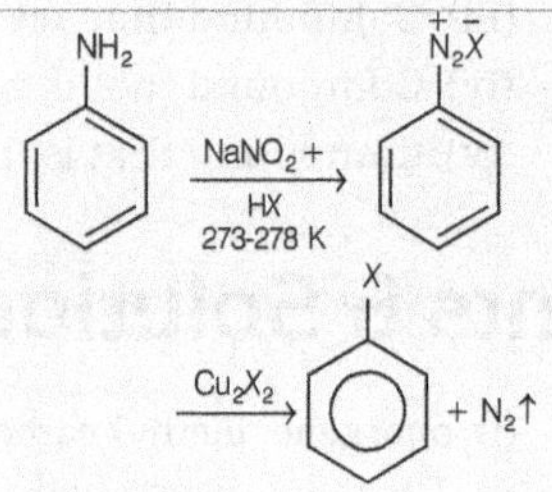

Gattermann reaction

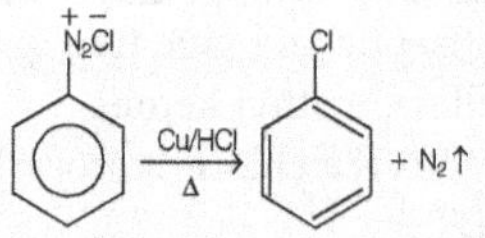

Balz-Schiemann reaction

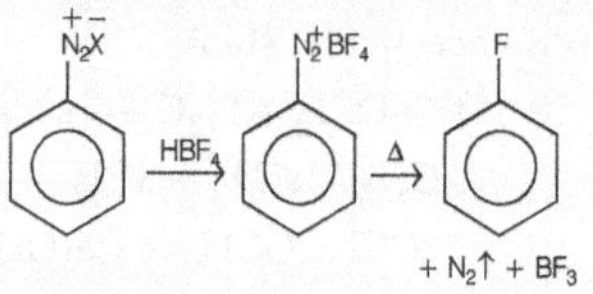

- **Physical Properties of Haloarenes**
  - **Haloarenes** They are solids, less polar compounds, insoluble in water but soluble in organic solvents like ethanol and ether.
  - Boiling point increases as the size of halogen atom increases and also as the size of aryl group increases.
  - When alkyl group is same, melting point increases as size of halogen increases. For dihalobenzenes, *p*-isomer has high melting point as its molecules pack closely in the crystal lattice.
  - The dipole moments of haloarenes increases in the order; fluorobenzene < chlorobenzene < bromobenzene < iodobenzene.
  - Aryl halides, give nucleophilic substitution, elimination reaction, reduction reaction with metals and Friedel-Craft's alkylation.
- **Polyhalogen compounds**
  - **Dichloromethane** It is colourless, sweet smelling, volatile liquid, having low boiling point of 313 K and specific gravity of 1.37. It is used as solvent, paint remover, propellant, refrigerant and dewaxing agent.
  - **Chloroform** $CHCl_3$ is slowly oxidised by air in the presence of light to an extremely poisonous gas carbonyl chloride, also known as phosgene.
  - **Iodoform** CHI_3 is yellow coloured crystalline solid with characteristic unpleasant odour.
  - **Tetrachloromethane** CCl_4 is a colourless, oily liquid with sickly smell.
  - **Freons** CFC of methane and ethane are collectively known as freons.

For Mind Map
Visit : https://goo.gl/ztM6wh OR **Scan the Code**

Chapter Practice

Very Short Answer Type Questions

1 Mark

1 Fill in the Blanks

(i) IUPAC name of *m* -dibromobenzene is ......

(ii) In IUPAC system, benzyl chloride is known as ....

(iii) $2C_2H_5Br + 2Na \xrightarrow{\text{Dry ether}} (P)$

in the above reaction main, main product (P) is ....

(iv) When C_2H_5Cl react with $AgNO_2$, the name of the main product formed is ....

2 Objective Type Questions

(i) $C_6H_6Cl_6$ can be obtained from

(a) HCl and benzene

(b) Cl_2, benzene and $AlCl_3$

(c) NaOCl and benzene

(d) Cl_2 and benzene in diffused light

(ii) 1 - chlorobutane on reaction with alcoholic potash gives

(a) but-1-ene (b) but-2-ene

(c) butan-1-ol (d) butan-2-ol

(iii) S_N1 reaction of alkyl halide leads to

(a) retention of configuration

(b) racemisation

(c) inversion of configuration

(d) None of the above

(iv) 1-2 dibromoethane reacts with alcoholic KOH to yield a product *X*. The hybridisation state of the carbons present in *X* respectively, are

(a) sp,sp (b) sp^3,sp^3

(c) sp^3,sp^2 (d) sp^2,sp^2

3 Match Column I with Column II and choose the correct option using the codes given below :

	Column I (Reaction)		Column II (Main product)
A.	$C_6H_6 + Cl_2 \xrightarrow[310-320\ K]{FeCl_3}$	(i)	$C_6H_4(CH_3)Cl$
B.	$C_6H_5Cl + Cl_2 \xrightarrow{FeCl_3}$	(ii)	$C_6H_{13}Cl$
C.	$C_6H_5 - CH_3 + Cl_2 \xrightarrow{FeCl_3}$	(iii)	C_6H_5Cl
D.	$C_6H_{13}Cl + PCl_3 \longrightarrow$	(iv)	$C_6H_4Cl_2$

Codes

	A	B	C	D		A	B	C	D
(a)	(i)	(ii)	(iii)	(iv)	(b)	(iv)	(iii)	(ii)	(i)
(c)	(iii)	(iv)	(i)	(ii)	(d)	(iv)	(iii)	(i)	(ii)

4 Among the following, which is not an allylic halide?

3-bromo-2-methylpropene, 4-bromobut-1-ene and 3-bromo-2-methylbut-1-ene.

5 Among the following, which nomenclature is not according to the IUPAC system?

1-bromoprop-2-ene, 2-methyl-3 phenylpentane and 5-oxohexanoic acid.

6 Write the IUPAC name of the following compound

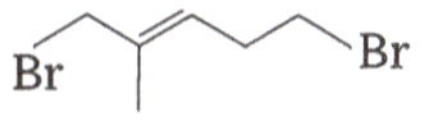

7 Write the IUPAC name of the compound $(CH_3)_3CCH_2Br$.

8 Write the structure of the compound 1-chloro-4-ethylcyclohexane.

9 Write the structure of the following compound, 2-chloro-3-methylpentane **NCERT Intext; NCERT**

10 Write the structure of 1-bromo-4-chlorobut-2-ene.

11 What is *A* in the following reaction?

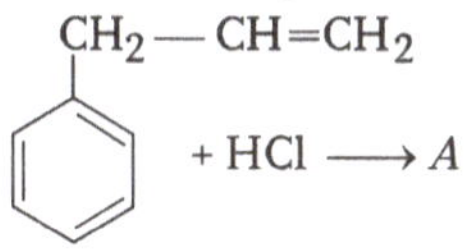

12 How can the following conversion be carried out?

Aniline to bromobenzene.

13 Arrange the following compounds in the order of increasing boiling points. Chloromethane, chloroform, iodomethane, bromomethane.

14 Write a chemical reaction in which iodide ion displaces diazonium group from diazonium salt.

15 Why iodoform has appreciable antiseptic property?

16 In the following pairs of halogen compounds, which compound undergoes S_N2 reaction faster?

and

17 An alcohol having molecular formula, $C_4H_{10}O$ is optically active. What is its structure?

18 What happens when CH_3—Br is treated with KCN?

19 A solution of KOH hydrolyses $CH_3CHClCH_2CH_3$ and $CH_3CH_2CH_2CH_2Cl$. Which one of these is more easily hydrolysed?

20 What is the IUPAC name of DDT? Why is its use banned in many countries?

Assertion and Reason

Directions (Q. Nos. 21-25) In the following questions, an Assertion (A) is followed by a corresponding. Reason (R). Use the following keys to choose the appropriate answer.

(a) Both (A) and (R) are correct, (R) is the correct explanation of (A).

(b) Both (A) and (R) are correct, (R) is not the correct explanation of (A).

(c) (A) is correct but (R) is incorrect.

(d) (A) is incorrect but (R) is correct.

21. **Assertion** (A) Phosphorus chlorides (tri and penta) are preferred over thionyl chloride for the preparation of alkyl chlorides from alcohols.

Reason (R) Thionyl chloride give pure alkyl halides.

22 **Assertion** (A) Alkyl halides are insoluble in water.

Reason (R) Alkyl halides have halogen attached to sp^3 hybridised carbon.

23 **Assertion** (A) Hydrolysis of (–)-2-bromooctane proceeds with inversion of configuration.

Reason (R) This reaction proceeds through the formation of a carbocation.

24 **Assertion** (A) Aryl iodides can be prepared by reaction of arenes with iodine in the presence of an oxidising agent.

Reason (R) Oxidising agent oxidises I_2 into HI.

25 **Assertion** (A) Presence of a nitro group at *ortho* or *para* position increases the reactivity of haloarenes towards nucleophilic substitution.

Reason (R) Nitro group, being an electron withdrawing group decreases the electron density over the benzene ring.

Case Study

26. The polarity of C—*X* bond of alkyl halides is responsible for their nucleophilic substitution, elimination and their reaction with metal atoms to form organometallic compounds.

Alkyl halides are prepared by the free radical halgenation of alkanes, addition of halogen acids to alkenes, replacement of —OH group of alcohols with halogen using phosphorus halides, thionyl chloride or halogen acids. Aryl halides are prepared by electrophilic substitution of arenes.

Nucleophilic substitution reactions are categorised into S_N1 and S_N2 on the basis of their kinetic properties. Chirality has a profound role in understanding the S_N1 and S_N2 mechanism.

Answer the following questions

(i) What happens when bromobenzene is treated with Mg in the presence of dry ether ?

(ii) Which compound in each of the following pairs will react faster in S_N1 reaction with $\overline{OH}$?

(a) $CH_2{=}CH—CH_2—Cl$ or $CH_3—CH_2—CH_2—Cl$

(b) $(CH_3)_3C—Cl$ or CH_3Cl

(iii) Write the equations for the preparation of 1-iodobutane from

(a) 1-chlorobutane (b) but-1-ene

27. In S_N2 mechanism, the nucleophile attacks on the side opposite to one where halogen atom is present. Therefore, S_N2 reaction is always accompanied the inversion of configuration, that is referred to as **Walden inversion**.

S_N2 reaction of optically active alkyl halides is always accompanied by the inversion of configuration.

In S_N1 mechanism, if the alkyl halide is optically active, the product obtained is a racemic mixture. The intermediate carbocation formed in slowest step being sp^2-hybridised is planar (achiral) species.

Therefore, the attack of the nucleophile can occur from both the faces with equal case of forming a mixture of two enantiomers. Thus, S_N1 reaction of optically active alkyl halides are accompanied by racemisation.

The following questions are multiple choice questions. Choose the most appropriate answer.

(i) The following haloalkanes are hydrolysed in presence of *aq.* KOH.
  (I) 1-chlorobutane
  (II) 2-chloro-2-methylpropane
  Which of the above is most likely to give
  (a) an inverted product?
  (b) a racemic mixture?
  Justify your answer.

(ii) Optically active 2-bromobutane, on treatment with NaI in acetone gives a product, which does not show optical activity. Give reason.

(iii) An optically active compound with molecular formula of $C_7H_{15}Br$ reacts with aqueous KOH to give a racemic mixture of products. Write the mechanism involved for this reaction.

Short Answer Type I Questions

(2 Marks)

28 Account for the following :
  (i) *p*-dibromobenzene has higher melting point than *o*-dibromobenzene.
  (ii) *n*-butyl bromide reacts faster than *t*-butyl bromide through S_N2 mechanism.

29 Why is iodination of benzene difficult?

30 Write the mechanism of the following reaction.

$$CH_3CH_2OH \xrightarrow{HBr} CH_3CH_2Br + H_2O$$

31 Complete the following reactions.

(i) 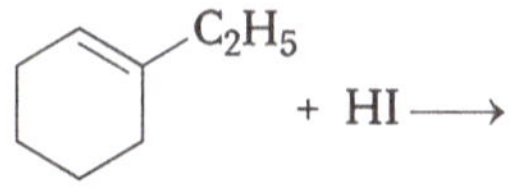

(ii) $CH_3CH_2CH=CH_2 + HBr \longrightarrow$

32 Suggest a possible reason for the following observations:
  (i) The order of reactivity of haloalkanes is $RI > RBr > RCl$.
  (ii) *Neo*-pentyl chloride, $(CH_3)_3C-CH_2Cl$ does not follow S_N2 mechanism.

33 P, Q, R and S undergoes S_N2 reaction with KI in acetone. What is the order of the rate of reaction?

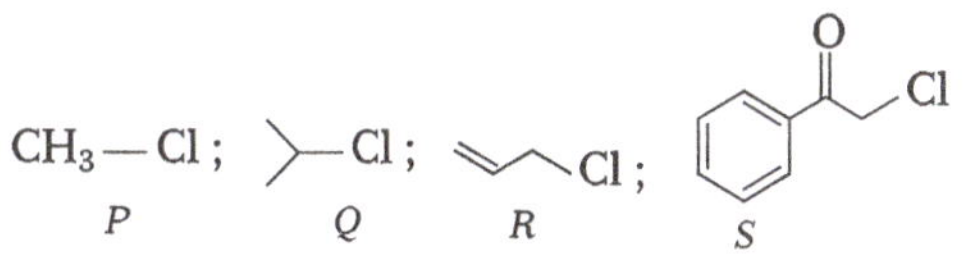

P *Q* *R* *S*

34 Why are haloarenes more stable than haloalkanes and undergo electrophilic substitution reaction at *o*- and *p*-position?

35 Write the reaction for the formation of each of the following.
  (i) Dichloromethane (ii) Phosgene

36 Write one physiological and environmental effect for each of the following.
  (i) Tetrachloromethane
  (ii) DDT

37 How are polyhalogens different from other organic halogens? Explain with example.

38 Give the IUPAC names of the following compounds.

(i) $H_3C-\overset{CH_3}{\underset{CH_3}{C}}-CH_2Cl$

(ii) $CH_3CH=\underset{CH_3}{C}-\underset{Br}{CH}-CH_3$

(iii) $(CH_3)_3CCH_2-CH_2Cl$

(iv) $CH_3-\overset{C_2H_5}{\underset{Cl}{C}}-CH_2-\overset{C_2H_5}{\underset{Cl}{C}}-CH_3$

39 (i) Allyl chloride is hydrolysed more readily than *n*-propylchloride. Why?
  (ii) Cyanide ion acts as an ambident nucleophile. From which end, it acts as a stronger nucleophile in aqueous medium and why?

40 Out of $C_6H_5CHClC_6H_5$ and $C_6H_5CH_2Cl$, which is more easily hydrolysed by aqueous KOH? **NCERT**

41 Diphenyls are potential threat to the environment. How are these produced from aryl halides? **NCERT Exemplar**

Short Answer Type II Questions

(3 Marks)

42 Classify the haloalkanes on the basis of hybridisation of their $C-X$ bonds alongwith examples.

43 Write the IUPAC name, structure and one isomer for each of the following compounds.
  (i) *tert*-butyl bromide
  (ii) Allyl chloride

44 Which one of the following pair undergo S_N1 reaction faster and why?

$H_2C = CHCHClCH_3$ or $CH_3 - CH_2CHClCH_3$

45 How will you obtain monobromobenzene from aniline? Give reaction.

46 Give reasons for the following observations.

(i) Out of chlorobenzene and chloromethane, which is more reactive towards nucleophilic substitution reaction?

(ii) Racemisation occurs in S_N1 reaction.

47 How would you differentiate between S_N1 and S_N2 mechanisms of the substitution reactions? Give one example of each.

48 How will you bring about the following conversions?

(i) 1-bromobutane to 2-bromobutane

(ii) Aniline to chlorobenzene

(iii) Ethanol to ethyl fluoride

49 Explain the formation of the two products in the following reaction:

$CH_3\,CH{=}CHCH_2\,Cl + H_2\,O \longrightarrow$
$CH_3\,CH{=}CHCH_2\,OH + CH_3\,CH(OH)CH{=}CH_2$

50 (i) Why is ether preferred over chloroform as anaesthetic agent?

(ii) Name the polyhalogen which is used to prepare chloropicrin?

51 Classify the following compounds as primary, secondary and tertiary halides.

(i) 1-bromobut-2-ene

(ii) 4-bromopent-2-ene

(iii) 2-bromo-2-methylpropane **NCERT Exemplar**

52 Write the equations for the preparation of 1-iodobutane from **NCERT**

(i) 1-butanol (ii) 1-chlorobutane (iii) but-1-ene

53 (i) Why are haloalkanes more reactive towards nucleophilic substitution reaction than haloarenes?

Or Chlorobenzene is extremely less reactive towards a nucleophilic substitution reaction. Give two reasons for the same.

Or Why aryl halides are less reactive towards nucleophilic substitution reactions than alkyl halides?

(ii) Which of the following two substances undergo S_N1 reaction faster and why? **NCERT Exemplar**

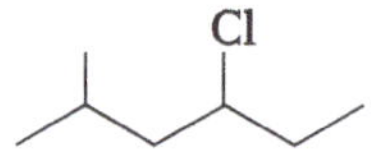

Or

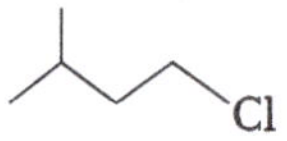

54 Arrange the compounds of each set in the order of reactivity towards S_N2 displacement. **NCERT**

(i) 2-bromo-2-methylbutane, 1-bromopentane, 2-bromopentane

(ii) 1-bromo-3-methylbutane, 2-bromo-2-methyl butane, 2-bromo-3-methylbutane

(iii) 1-bromobutane, 1-bromo-2, 2-dimethylpropane, 1-bromo-2-methylbutane, 1-bromo-3-methyl butane

55 What will be the major organic product of the following reactions?

(i) 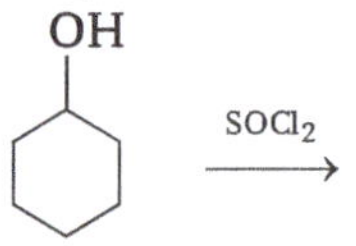

(ii) $CH_3-C(CH_3)_2-Br \xrightarrow[\text{Ethanol, heat}]{KOH}$

(iii) $CH_3CH{=}C(CH_3)_2 \xrightarrow{HBr}$

Long Answer Type Questions

5 Marks

56 (i) What are enantiomers? Draw the structures of the possible enantiomers of 3-methylpent-1-ene.

(ii) Optically active 2-bromobutane, on treatment with NaI in acetone gives a product, which does not show optical activity. Give reason.

(iii) An optically active compound with molecular formula of C_7H_{15} Br, reacts, with aqueous KOH to give a racemic mixture of products. Write the mechanism involved for this reaction.

57 The following reaction gives two products:

$C_6H_5CH_2CHClC_6H_5 \xrightarrow[\text{heat}]{\text{Alc.KOH}}$

Explain the formation of the products and write their structures.

58 (i) Account for the following :

(a) Use of DDT was banned in United States in 1973.

(b) Alkyl halides prefer to undergo dehydrohalogenation in the presence of a strong base such as Na metal, instead of undergoing Wurtz reaction.

(ii) What happens, when

(a) ethyl chloride is treated with aqueous KCN?

(b) chlorobenzene is subjected to hydrolysis?

Answers

1 (i) 1, 3-dibromobenzene
(ii) Chlorophenylmethane
(iii) C_4H_{10} (butane)
(iv) $C_2H_5NO_2$(nitroethane)

2 (i) (d) $C_6H_6 + 3Cl_2 \xrightarrow{\text{Diffused sunlight}} C_6H_6Cl_6$

(ii) (a) $CH_3CH_2CH_2CH_2Cl \xrightarrow{\text{Alc.KOH}}$
$CH_3CH_2—CH = CH_2 + KCl + H_2O$

(iii) (b) S_N1 reaction proceeds through the formation of planar intermediate carbocation, which can undergo the attack of incoming nucleophile from both the sides giving racemised product.

(iv) (a) Alkyl halides give elimination reaction with alcoholic KOH and yield an alkene and then an alkyne (from dihalides).

$$\underset{\text{1, 2-dibromoethane}}{Br—CH_2—CH_2—Br} \xrightarrow[\Delta]{\text{Alc. KOH}} \underset{\text{Acetylene}}{\overset{sp}{C}H \equiv \overset{sp}{C}H}$$

Hence, product has both *sp*-hybridised carbon.

3 (c) (A) → iii (B) → iv (C) → i (D) → ii

4 4-bromobut-1-ene

5 1-bromoprop-2-ene

6 1, 5- dibromo-2-methylpent-2-ene

7 1- bromo-2,2-dimethylpropane

8 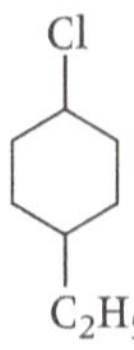

9 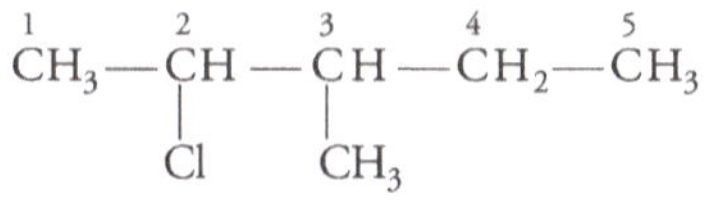

10 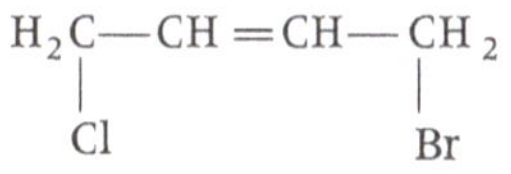

11 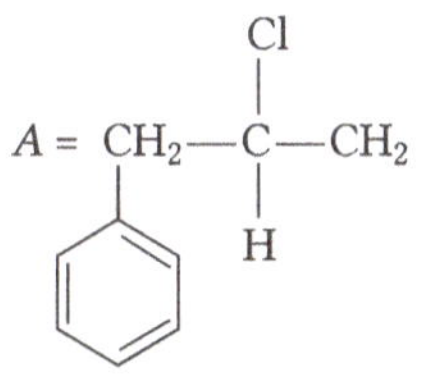

12 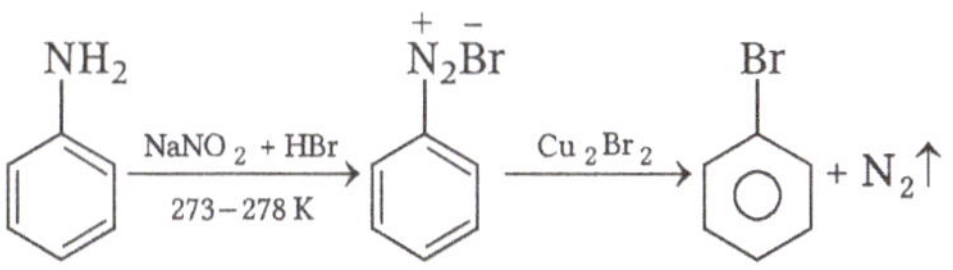

13 Chloroform>Iodomethane>Bromomethane >Chloromethane

14 Replacement of the diazonium group by iodine is done simply by shaking the diazonium salt with potassium iodide.

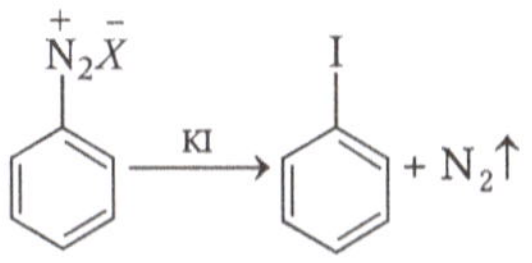

15 Iodoform has appreciable antiseptic properties due to the liberation of free iodine.

$$CHI_3 + 5O_2 \xrightarrow[\text{heat}]{SO_2} 6I_2\uparrow + 4CO_2 + 2H_2O$$

16  compound undergoes faster S_N2 reaction.

17 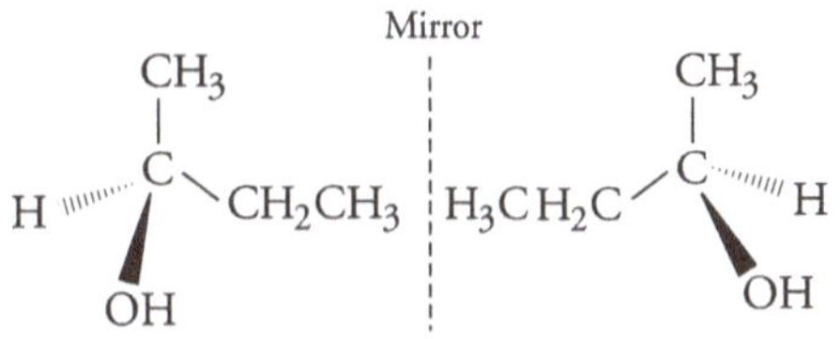

18 When CH_3Br is treated with KCN then methyl cyanide (CH_3CN) is formed.

$$CH_3Br + KCN \longrightarrow CH_3CN + KBr$$

19 $CH_3CHClCH_2CH_3$ upon ionisation gives more stable 2° carbocation while $CH_3CH_2CH_2CH_2Cl$ gives less stable 1° carbocation.

20 The IUPAC name of DDT is 2, 2-*bis*-(4-chlorophenyl)-1, 1, 1-trichloroethane. It is non-biodegradable and extremely stable compound which act as a water pollutant and kills aquatic animals, thus imbalancing the water ecosystem.

21 (d) (A) is not correct but (R) is correct. In fact, the use of thionyl chloride is preferred over phosphorus chlorides for preparing haloalkanes from alcohols because the other products of the reaction, HCl(*g*) and $SO_2(g)$ being gases escape out leaving behind pure haloalkane.

22 (b) Here, both (A) and (R) are true but (R) is not the correct explanation of (A).

Alkyl halides are insoluble in water because they are unable to form hydrogen bonds with water or break pre-existing hydrogen bonds.

23 (c) Assertion is correct but reason is incorrect.

Correct Reason This reaction proceeds through S_N2 mechanism, in which $\overset{-}{O}H$ ion, attacks at 180° to the halogen atom of 2-bromooctane which leads to the inversion of configuration.

24 (d) Aryl halides are less reactive towards nucleophilic substitution reactions because of the carbon halogen bond in aryl halides has partial double bond character.

25 (a) Nitro group being an electron withdrawing group, decreases the electron density of benzene ring thus increasing the reactivity of haloarenes towards nucleophilic substitution.

26 (i) When bromobenzene is treated with Mg in the presence of dry ether, phenyl magnesium bromide is formed.

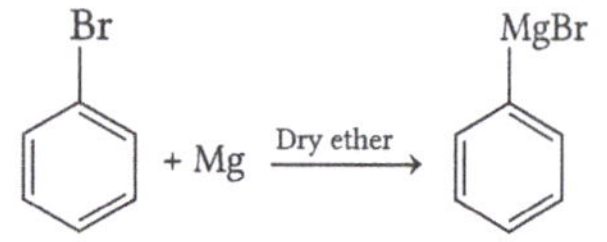

(ii) (a) $CH_2{=}CH{-}CH_2Cl$, Allylic halides show high reactivity towards S_N1 reaction because carbocation formed gets stabilised through resonance.

(b) Out of $(CH_3)_3C{-}Cl$ and CH_3Cl, the molecule being a tertiary halide i.e, $(CH_3)C{-}Cl$ will react faster with $\overline{OH}$ because in because in S_N1 reaction, 3° halide reacts faster than 1° halide.

(iii) (a) $\underset{\text{1-chlorobutane}}{CH_3CH_2CH_2CH_2Cl} + KI \xrightarrow{\text{Acetone}} \underset{\text{1-iodobutane}}{CH_3CH_2CH_2CH_2I} + KCl\downarrow$

(b) $\underset{\text{But-1-ene}}{CH_3CH_2CH{=}CH_2} + HBr \xrightarrow{\text{Peroxide}}$

$CH_3CH_2CH_2CH_2Br \xrightarrow[\text{KI}]{\text{Acetone}} \underset{\text{1-iodobutane}}{CH_3CH_2CH_2CH_2I}$

27 (i) (I) Inverted product will be given by 1 chlorobutane as it udnergoes S_N2 reaction.

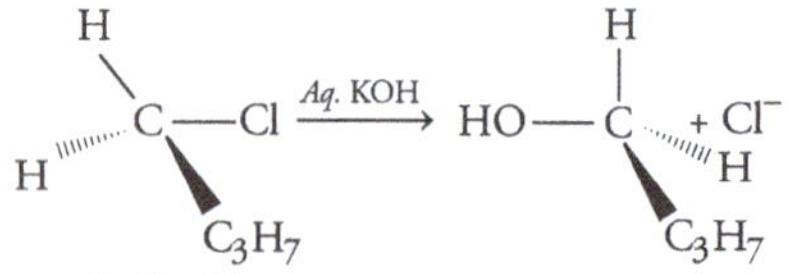

1-chlorobutane

(II) Racemic mixture will be given by 2-chloro-2-methylpropane as it undergoes S_N1 reaction.

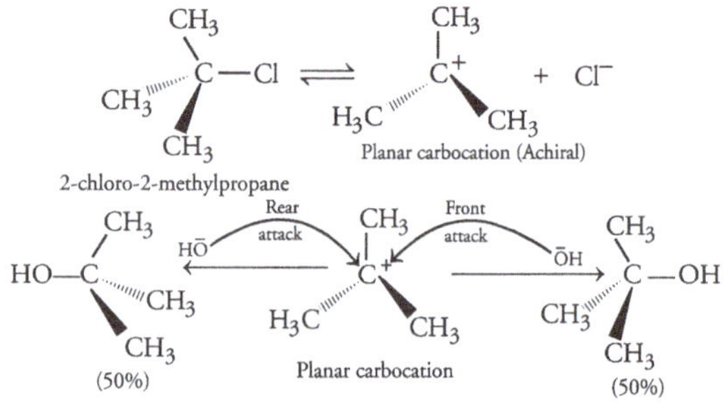

(ii)

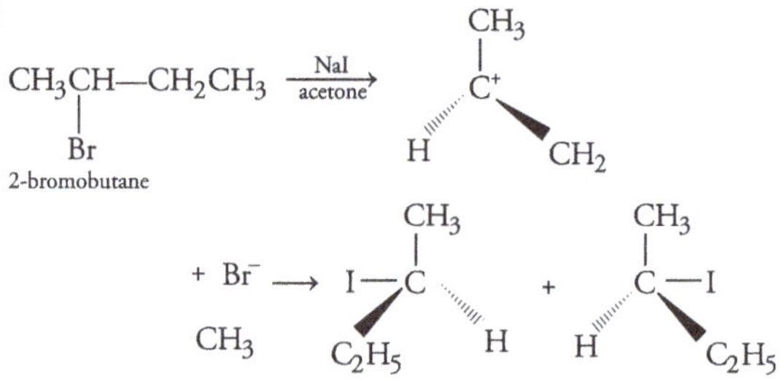

This follows a S_N1 reaction mechanism. The product obtained is a racemic mixture which is optically inactive.

(iii) An optically active compound has to be chiral (asymmetric molecule). Possible optically active structure of $C_7H_{15}Br$ should also be a 3° alkyl halide as it has to undergo S_N1 mechanism to get product a racemic mixture.

So, the suitable structure is

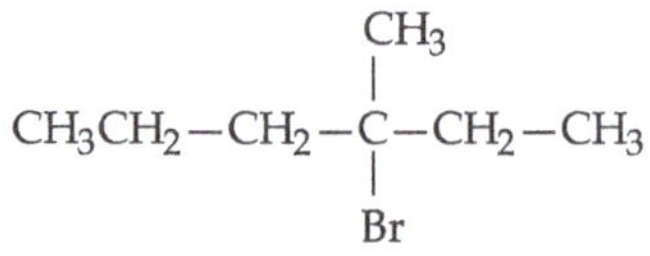

Mechanism

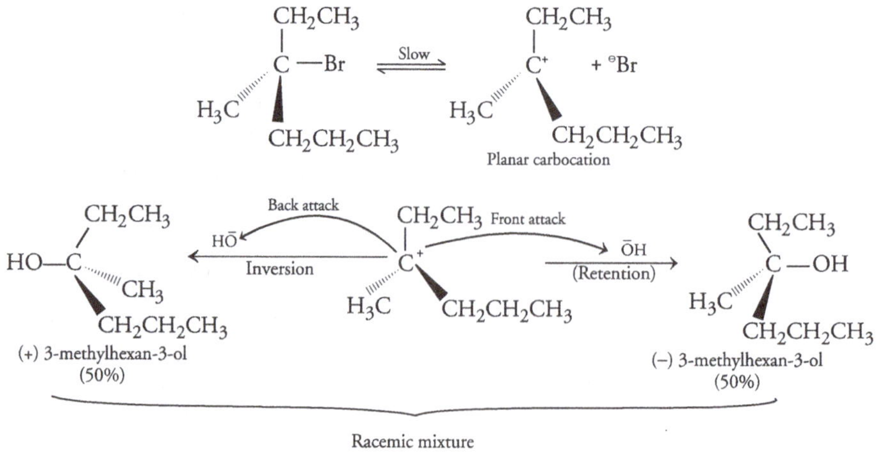

28 (i) Refer to text on page 227 (Topic-2, Physical properties of haloarenes).
(ii) Refer to text on page 221 (Topic-1, S_N2 mechanism).

29 Refer to text on page 226. (Topic-2. By electrophilic substitution of aromatic hydrocarbon).

30

$$C_2H_5—\ddot{O}H + H^+ \longrightarrow C_2H_5—\overset{+}{\ddot{O}}H_2$$

$$X^- + R-\overset{+}{O}H_2 \longrightarrow C_2H_5-X + H_2O$$

31 (i) 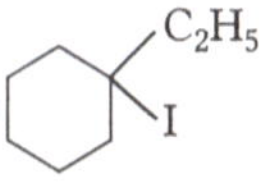 (ii) $CH_3CH_2\underset{\underset{Br}{|}}{C}HCH_3$

32 (i) The order of reactivity of haloalkanes is $RI > RBr > RCl$. As we down the group, i.e. from $Cl \rightarrow I$, atomic size increases and RI bond length weakens. Hence, RI is most reactive.
(ii) **Hint** Neo-pentyl chloride does not follow S_N2 mechanism due to presence of bulky group. It readily gives elimination reaction.

33 Refer to text on page 211 (Topic-1, S_N2 Mechanism).

34 Refer to text on pages 227 and 228. (Topic-2, Nucleophilic substitution reactions).

35 (i) $CH_4 + 2Cl_2 \xrightarrow{hv} CH_2Cl_2 + 2HCl$
(ii) $2CHCl_3 + O_2 \xrightarrow{hv} 2COCl_2 + 2HCl$

36 (i) Refer to text on page 238 and 239 (Topic-3, Trichloromethane)
(ii) Refer to text on page 241 and 242 (Topic 3, DDT)

37 Refer to text on page 238 (Topic-3, Polyhalogen compounds).

38 (i) 1-chloro-2, 2-dimethylpropane
(ii) 4-bromo-3-methylpent-2-ene
(iii) 1-chloro-3, 3-dimethylbutane
(iv) 3, 5-dichloro-3, 5-dimethylheptane

39 (i) Ease of hydrolysis depends upon the stability of carbocation formed. In case of allyl chloride, the carbocation is resonance stabilised, that's why hydrolysed more easily.
(ii) Refer to text on pages 209 and 210 (Topic-1, Nucleophilic substitution reactions).

40 In S_N1 reaction, $C_6H_5CHClC_6H_5$ gets hydrolysed more easily than $C_6H_5CH_2Cl$.
However, under S_N2 reaction, $C_6H_5CH_2Cl$ (with lesser steric hindrance) gets hydrolysed more easily than $C_6H_5CHClC_6H_5$. Refer to text on pages 209 and 210 (Topic-1, Nucleophilic substitution reactions).

41 In environment, diphenyl is formed during the incomplete combustion of mineral oil and coal. It is present in the exhaust gases of vehicles and in exhaust air from residential and industrial heating devices.
Acute exposure to high levels of diphenyl has been observed to cause eye and skin irritation and toxic effect on the liver, kidneys and central/peripheral nervous system. Kidneys of animals are also affected due to the ingestion of biphenyls. **Fittig reaction** (Preparation of diphenyls from aryl halides). Refer to text on page 232 (Topic-2, Reaction with metals).

42 Refer to text on pages 204 and 205 (Topic-1, Classification).

43 (i) Refer to text on pages 205 and 206 (Topic-1, Nomenclature).
(ii) Allyl chloride ($CH_2 = CH - CH_2Cl$)
Isomer of $CH_2 = CH–CH_2Cl$ (allyl chloride) is
$CH_3 - CH = CH–Cl$ (1-chloroprop-1-ene)

44 **Hint** $CH_2 = CHCHClCH_3$, due to the delocalisation of electrons.

45 Refer to text on page 226 and 227 (Topic-2, Sandmeyer's reaction).

46 (i) **Hint** : Chloromethane as it is an aliphatic halide.
(ii) Refer to text on pages 209 and 210 (Topic-1, Nucleophilic substitution reaction).

47 Refer to text on page 212 S_N2 (Topic-1, Table : Difference between S_N1 and S_N2 reaction).

48 (i) **Hint** : Dehydrohalogenation followed by Markovnikov's addition.
(ii) Refer to text on page 226 and 227 (Topic-3, Sandmeyer's reaction).
(iii) $CH_3CH_2OH + SOCl_2 \xrightarrow{\text{Pyridine}} CH_3CH_2Cl + SO_2\uparrow + HCl\uparrow$

$$CH_3CH_2Cl + AgF \longrightarrow CH_3CH_2F + AgBr$$

49 1-chlorobut-2-ene undergoes hydrolysis in warm water to give a mixture of these allylic alcohols.

$$CH_3CH = CHCH_2Cl \xrightarrow{H_2O} \underset{\text{But-2-en-1-ol}}{CH_3CH = CHCH_2OH} + \underset{\text{But-3-en-1-ol}}{CH_3\overset{\overset{OH}{|}}{C}HCH = CH_2}$$

The two products can be explained by an S_N1 mechanism that produces an allylic cation that can react with water at either 1 or 3 position.

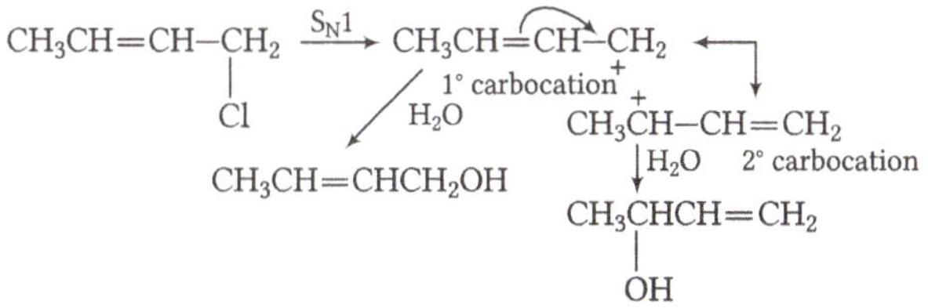

50 (i) Refer to text on page 238 and 239. (Topic-3, Trichloromethane).
(ii) Chloroform

51 (i) Primary halide (ii) Secondary halide
(iii) Tertiary halide

52 (i) $\underset{\text{1-butanol}}{CH_3CH_2CH_2CH_2OH} + HI \xrightarrow{ZnCl_2} \underset{\text{1-iodobutane}}{CH_3CH_2CH_2CH_2I}$

(ii) $CH_3CH_2CH_2CH_2Cl + NaI \xrightarrow{\text{Dry acetone}} CH_3CH_2CH_2CH_2I + NaCl$
1-chlorobutane → 1-iodobutane

(iii) $CH_3CH_2CH{=}CH_2 + HBr \xrightarrow{\text{Peroxide}}$
But-1-ene

$CH_3CH_2CH_2CH_2Br \xrightarrow[\text{Dry acetone}]{NaI} CH_3CH_2CH_2CH_2I$
1-bromobutane → 1-iodobutane

53 (i) Refer to text on pages 227 and 228. (Topic-2, Nucleophilic substitution reactions).

(ii) In S_N1 reaction, reactivity depends upon the stability of intermediate carbocation. A secondary carbocation is more stable than primary carbocation.

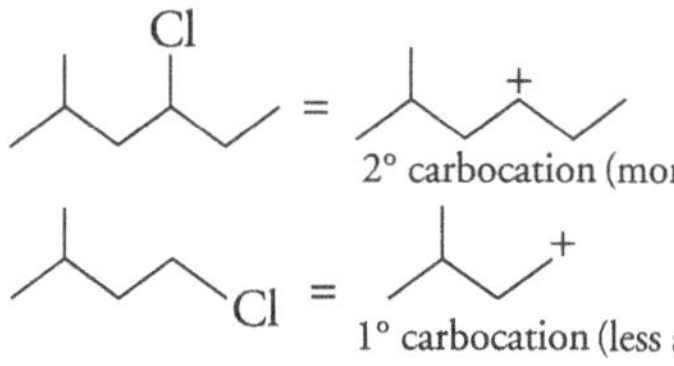

2° carbocation (more stable)

1° carbocation (less stable)

Former carbocation being secondary, is more stable than the latter being primary. Hence, it undergoes S_N1 reaction faster.

54 (i) $CH_3CH_2CH_2CH_2CH_2Br > CH_3CH(Br)CH_2CH_2CH_3 > CH_3C(Br)(CH_3)CH_2CH_3$
1-bromopentane (1°) > 2-bromopentane (2°) > 2-bromo -2-methylbutane (3°)

(ii) $CH_3CH(CH_3)CH_2CH_2Br > CH_3{-}CH(Br){-}CH(CH_3){-}CH_3 > CH_3{-}C(Br)(CH_3){-}CH_2{-}CH_3$
1-bromo-3-methyl butane (1°) > 2-bromo-3-methyl butane (2°) > 2-bromo-2-methylbutane (3°)

(iii) $CH_3CH_2CH_2CH_2Br > CH_3CH(CH_3)CH_2CH_2Br >$
1-bromobutane (1°) > 1-bromo-3-methyl butane (1°) >

$CH_3CH_2CH(CH_3)CH_2Br > CH_3{-}C(CH_3)_2{-}CH_2Br$
1-bromo-2-methylbutane (1°) > 1-bromo-2,2-dimethylpropane (1°) (1)

55 (i)

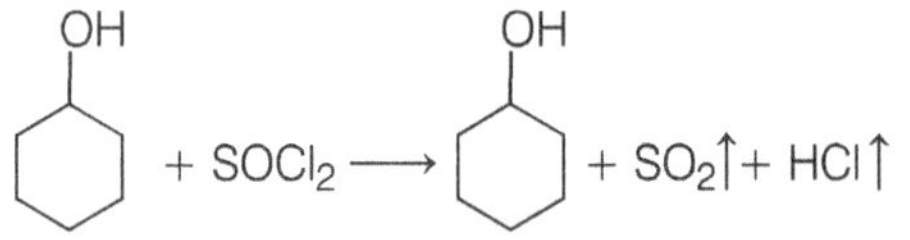

(ii) $CH_3{-}C(CH_3)_2{-}Br \xrightarrow{\text{Eth. KOH}} H_3C{-}C(=CH_2){-}CH_3 + KBr$
(Major)

(iii) $CH_3{-}CH{=}C(CH_3){-}CH_3 \xrightarrow{HBr} CH_3{-}CH_2{-}C(CH_3)(Br){-}CH_3$ (1)

56 (i) Refer to text on page 213 (Topic-1, Molecular asymmetry chirality and enantioiners).

(ii) **Hint** $CH_3CH_2{-}C(H)(CH_3){-}C(H){=}CH_2$ ¦ $H_2C{=}C(H){-}C(H)(CH_3){-}CH_2CH_3$

(iii) Refer to text on page 209 (Topic-1, Nucleophilic substitution reaction).

57 $(H_5C_6)(H)C{=}C(C_6H_5)(H)$ + $(H_5C_6)(H)C{=}C(H)(C_6H_5)$
cis *trans*

58 (i) (a) Refer to text on page 241 and 242 (Topic-3, DDT).

(b) Refer to text on page 215 (Topic-1, Reaction with metals).

(ii) (a) $C_2H_5Cl + KCN \longrightarrow C_2H_5CN + KCl$

(b) $C_6H_5Cl \xrightarrow{H_2O/H^+} C_6H_5OH$

RELATED ONLINE VIDEOS

Visit : https://youtu.be/QdCFwENjlOU
OR **Scan the Code**

Visit : https://youtu.be/fGXNN8DCsCg
OR **Scan the Code**

Visit : https://youtu.be/eYlsgW6EFtw
OR **Scan the Code**

CHAPTER

07

Alcohols, Phenols and Ethers

Alcohols and phenols are formed by replacing one hydrogen atom from a hydrocarbon (aliphatic or aromatic) by —OH group. They have a variety of applications in industry as well as in day-to-day life. Similarly, ether plays an important role in pharmacology and medicines, especially for the use of anaesthetics. They are quite volatile. They are also used as solvents and plasticisers.

- Alcohols
- Phenols
- Ethers

TOPIC 01 Alcohols

An alcohol contains one or more hydroxyl group(s) (—OH), directly attached to carbon atom(s) of an aliphatic system the compound obtained are called **alcohols** having general formula, $C_nH_{2n+1}OH$.

Classification

On the basis of number of —OH groups present in the molecule

(i) **Monohydric** Alcohols having one hydroxyl group (—OH) attached to the carbon atom of a compound are monohydric.

e.g.

$\underset{\text{Methanol}}{CH_3OH}$, $\underset{\text{Ethanol}}{CH_3CH_2OH}$

(ii) **Dihydric** Alcohols having two hydroxyl groups (—OH) attached to the two carbon atoms of a compound are dihydric. They are called as diols.

e.g.

CH_2—OH
|
CH_2
|
CH_2—OH

Propane-1,3-diol

(iii) **Trihydric** Alcohols having three hydroxyl groups (—OH) attached to the three carbon atoms of a compound, are trihydric. They are called **triols**.

e.g.

$$\begin{array}{c} CH_2OH \\ | \\ CHOH, \\ | \\ CH_2OH \end{array}$$

Glycerol

(iv) **Polyhydric** Alcohols that have more than three —OH groups are said to be polyhydric alcohols.

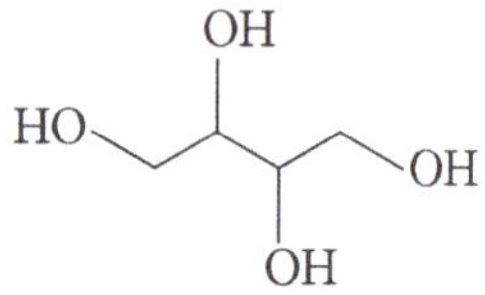

Erythritol

Note The two or more —OH groups must be present at different carbon atoms. If they are present at same carbon atom, it leads to the removal of water molecule.

$$H_2C\begin{array}{l} OH \\ OH \end{array} \xrightarrow[\text{Water}]{\text{Loses}} HCHO(\text{stable})$$

- *On the basis of position of —OH group in the carbon chain*

(i) **Primary Alcohols** In primary (1°) alcohols, the carbon which carries the —OH group, is attached with only one alkyl group, i.e. they contain $—CH_2OH$ group. e.g.

$$\underset{\text{Ethanol}}{CH_3—CH_2—OH}, \quad \underset{\text{2-methylpropan-1-ol}}{CH_3—\underset{\underset{CH_3}{|}}{CH}—CH_2—OH}$$

(ii) **Secondary Alcohols** In secondary (2°) alcohols, the carbon carrying —OH group is joined directly to two alkyl groups, which may or may not be same. In other words, they have $>$CHOH group. e.g.

$$\underset{\text{Propan-2-ol}}{CH_3—\overset{\overset{OH}{|}}{CH}—CH_3}, \quad \underset{\text{Butan-2-ol}}{CH_3—\overset{\overset{OH}{|}}{CH}—CH_2—CH_3}$$

(iii) **Tertiary Alcohols** In tertiary (3°) alcohols, the carbon atom holding the —OH group is attached directly to **three** alkyl groups, which may or may not be same. In other words, they have $>$C—OH group.

$$\underset{\text{2-methylpropan-2-ol}}{CH_3—\overset{\overset{OH}{|}}{\underset{\underset{CH_3}{|}}{C}}—CH_3}, \quad \underset{\text{2-methylbutan-2-ol}}{CH_3—CH_2—\overset{\overset{OH}{|}}{\underset{\underset{CH_3}{|}}{C}}—CH_3}$$

Alcohol is of $(3-n)°$ where n is the number of H at carbon that carries OH group. CH_3OH is always 1°.

Nomenclature

The **common name** of an alcohol is derived from common name of alkyl group and adding the word alcohol to it.

e.g. $CH_3OH \rightarrow \underbrace{CH_3 \text{ (methyl group)} + \text{alcohol}}_{\downarrow}$

Methyl alcohol

In **IUPAC system**, the name of an alcohol is derived from the name of the alkane from which the alcohol is derived, by replacing 'e' of alkane with the suffix 'ol'. The position of substituents are indicated by numerals.

Steps for writing the IUPAC name of the alcohols are as follows:

(i) Select the longest carbon chain (parent chain) containing —OH group.
(ii) The selected longest chain is numbered from the end nearest to the hydroxyl group.
(iii) Replace the 'e' of alkane by adding suffix 'ol'.
(iv) The positions of the —OH group and other substituents are indicated by using the numbers of carbon atoms to which these are attached.
(v) For naming polyhydric alcohols, the 'e' of alkane is retained and the ending or suffix 'ol' is added.
(vi) Indicate the number of —OH groups by adding prefix like di, tri, etc., before 'ol'.

Common and IUPAC Name of Some Alcohols

Compound	Common name	IUPAC name
CH_3OH	Methyl alcohol	Methanol
CH_3CH_2OH	Ethyl alcohol	Ethanol
$CH_3CH_2CH_2OH$	*n*-propyl alcohol	Propan-1-ol
$CH_3—\overset{\overset{OH}{\vert}}{CH}—CH_3$	*iso*-propyl alcohol	Propan-2-ol
$CH_3CH_2CH_2CH_2—OH$	*n*-butyl alcohol	Butan-1-ol

Compound	Common name	IUPAC name
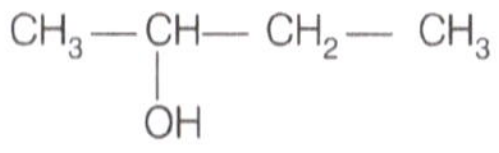	*sec*-butyl alcohol	Butan-2-ol
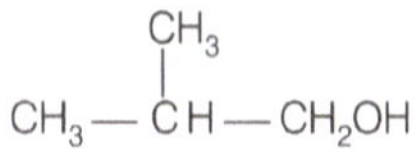	*iso*-butyl alcohol	2-methyl propan-1-ol
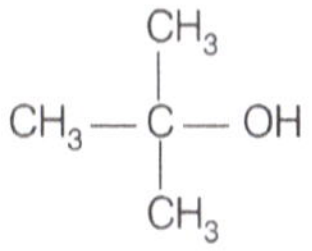	*tert*-butyl alcohol	2-methyl propan-2-ol
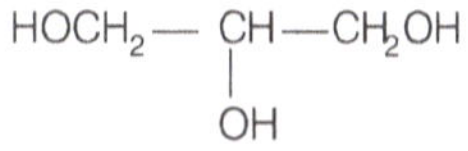	Glycerol	Propane-1, 2, 3-triol

Example 1 Name the following compounds according to IUPAC system.

(i) 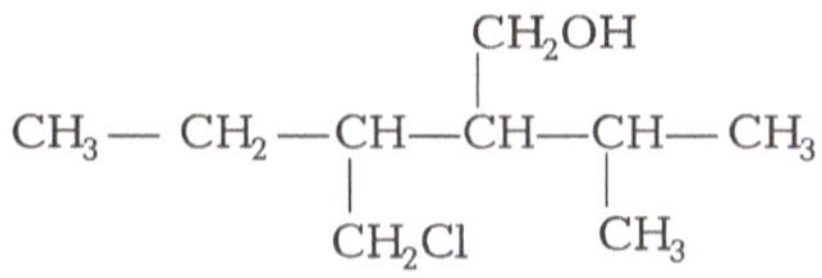

(ii) 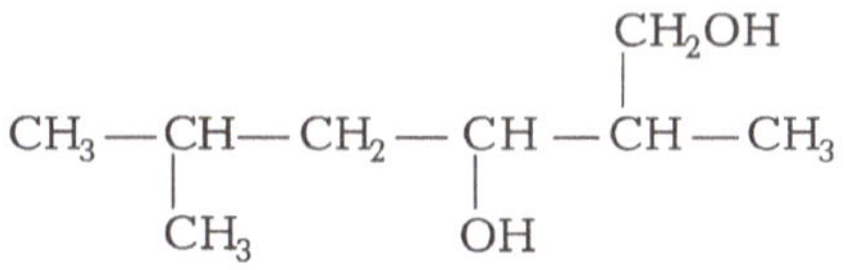

(iii) 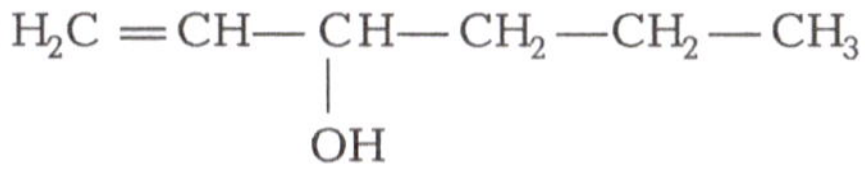

(iv) 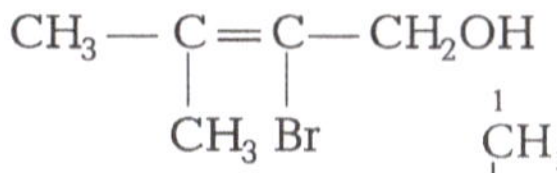

NCERT Intext

Sol. (i) 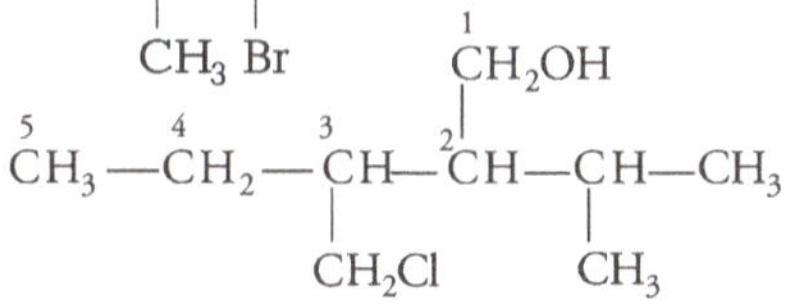

3-chloromethyl-2-isopropylpentan-1-ol

(ii) 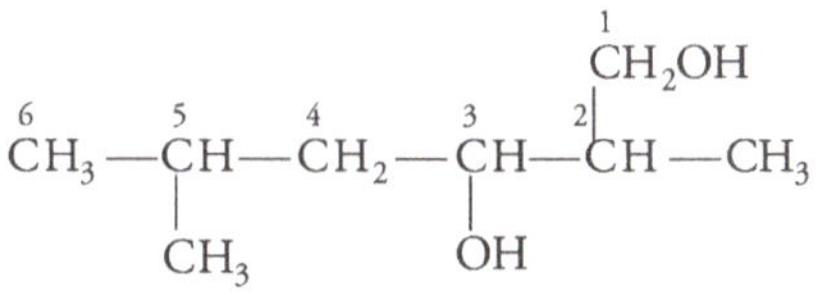

2, 5-dimethylhexane-1, 3-diol

(iii) 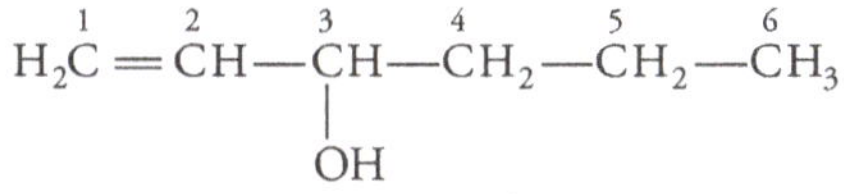

Hex-1-en-3-ol

(iv) 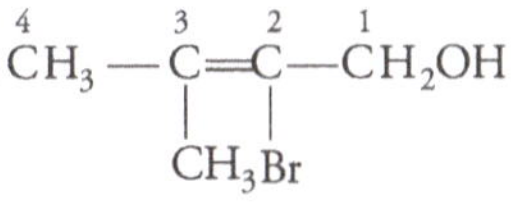

2-bromo-3-methylbut-2-en-1-ol

Structure

The structure of an alcohol resembles the structure of water with an alkyl group replacing one of the hydrogen atoms of water. Both have sp^3-hybridised oxygen atoms, but the C—O—H bond angle in methanol (108.9°) is considerably larger than the H—O—H bond angle in water (104.5°) because the methyl group is much larger than a hydrogen atom. The bulky methyl group counter acts the bond angle compression caused by non-bonding (lone) electron pairs of oxygen. The O—H bond lengths are about the same in water and methanol (0.96 Å) but the C—O bond is considerably longer (1.4 Å), reflecting the larger covalent radius of carbon compared to hydrogen.

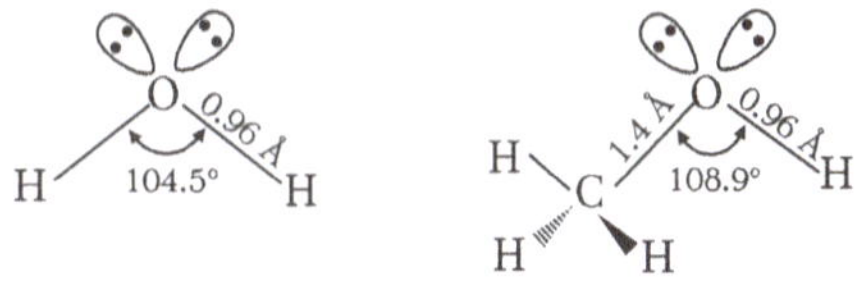

Structure of water and methyl alcohol

Methods of Preparation

These are prepared by the following methods:

1. From Alkenes

Direct Hydration of Alkenes

The term hydration refers to the addition of a molecule of water. Alkenes react with water in the presence of acid as catalyst to form alcohols. In case of unsymmetrical alkenes, the addition of water takes place in accordance with Markovnikov's rule. This rule states that negative part of the water molecule, i.e. OH^- part gets attached to that carbon atom which possesses lesser number of hydrogen atoms.

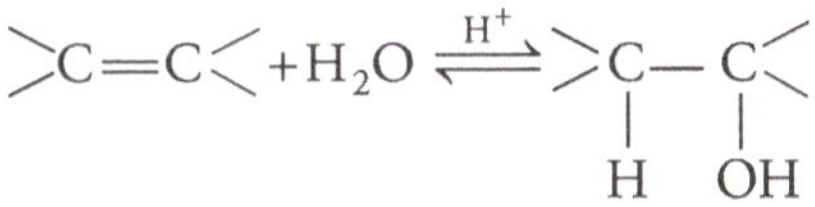

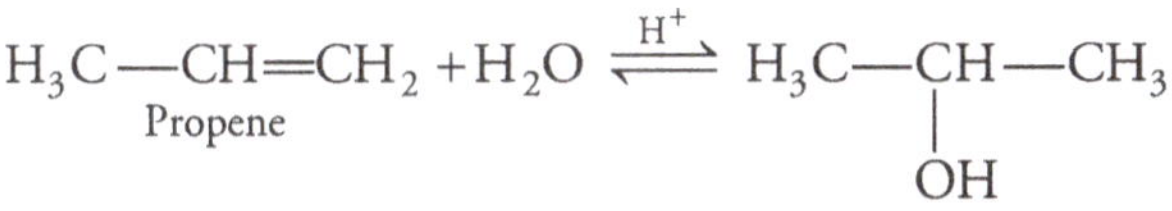

Propene   Propan-2-ol

Indirect Hydration of Alkenes

In this method, sulphuric acid and alkene react at elevated temperature and under pressure to form sulfate esters. The rate of absorption of alkenes is increased by agitation of liquid. Further the sulfate esters are hydrolyzed to alcohol.

$$RCH{=}CH_2 + H_2SO_4 \longrightarrow R\underset{\substack{|\\ OSO_2OH}}{C}HCH_3 + (R\overset{\substack{CH_3\\ |}}{C}HO)_2SO_2$$

$$\xrightarrow[H_2SO_4]{H_2O} R\underset{\substack{|\\ OH}}{CH}{-}CH_3$$

Note In case of unsymmetrical alkenes, the addition of H_2SO_4 takes place in accordance with Markovnikov's rule.

By Hydroboration-Oxidation

Diborane $(BH_3)_2$ reacts with alkenes to give trialkyl boranes as addition product which upon subsequent oxidation by H_2O_2 in the presence of aqueous sodium hydroxide give alcohols.

$$\underset{\text{Propene}}{CH_3{-}CH{=}CH_2} + \underset{\text{Diborane}}{(H{-}BH_2)_2} \longrightarrow$$

$$CH_3{-}\underset{\substack{\vdots\\ H}}{CH}{-}\underset{\substack{\vdots\\ BH_2}}{CH_2} \xrightarrow{CH_3-CH=CH_2}$$

$$(CH_3{-}CH_2{-}CH_2)_2BH \xrightarrow{CH_3-CH=CH_2}$$

$$\underset{\text{Trialkylborane}}{(CH_3{-}CH_2{-}CH_2)_3B} \xrightarrow[3H_2O_2,\ OH^-]{H_2O}$$

$$B(OH)_3 + 3\underset{\text{Propan-1-ol}}{CH_3{-}CH_2{-}CH_2{-}OH}$$

Here, the addition of borane to the double bond takes place in such a manner that the boron atom gets attached to the sp^2 carbon carrying greater number of hydrogen atoms. The alcohols seem to have been formed by the addition of water to the alkene in a way **opposite to the Markovnikov's rule**. In this reaction, alcohol is obtained in excellent yield.

2. From Reduction of Carbonyl Compounds

By the Reduction of Aldehydes and Ketones

Aldehydes and ketones are reduced to the corresponding alcohols by:

(i) Addition of H_2 in the presence of a finely divided catalyst like Pt, Pd, Ni or Ru metals (catalytic hydrogenation).

$$R{-}CHO + H_2 \xrightarrow{Ni/Pd} R{-}CH_2OH$$

$$\underset{\text{Acetaldehyde}}{CH_3CHO} + H_2 \xrightarrow{Ni/Pd} \underset{\text{Ethanol (1°)}}{CH_3CH_2OH}$$

(ii) In presence of complex metal hydrides such as $LiAlH_4$, $NaBH_4$, etc. aldehydes yield primary alcohols whereas ketones give secondary alcohols.

$$\underset{\text{Ketone}}{\overset{R}{\underset{R'}{>}}C{=}O} \xrightarrow{NaBH_4} \underset{\text{2° alcohol}}{\overset{R}{\underset{R'}{>}}CH{-}OH}$$

$$\underset{\text{Aldehyde}}{R{-}CHO} \xrightarrow{LiAlH_4} \underset{\text{1°alcohol}}{R{-}CH_2OH}$$

$$\underset{\text{Ethanal}}{CH_3CHO} \xrightarrow{LiAlH_4} \underset{\text{Ethanol}}{CH_3CH_2OH}$$

$$\underset{\text{Acetone}}{\overset{H_3C}{\underset{H_3C}{>}}C{=}O} \xrightarrow{LiAlH_4} \underset{\text{Propan-2-ol (2°)}}{\overset{H_3C}{\underset{H_3C}{>}}CH{-}OH}$$

By the Reduction of Carboxylic Acids and Esters

Carboxylic acids are reduced to primary alcohols by lithium aluminium hydride, a strong reducing agent.

$$R{-}COOH \xrightarrow[\text{(ii) } H_3O^+]{\text{(i) } LiAlH_4} RCH_2OH$$

$$C_6H_5{-}COOH \xrightarrow[\text{(ii) } H_3O^+]{\text{(i) } LiAlH_4} \underset{\text{Benzyl alcohol}}{C_6H_5{-}CH_2OH}$$

In this reaction, excellent yield of alcohols are obtained. However, $LiAlH_4$ is an expensive reagent and therefore, used for preparing special chemicals only.

Commercially, acids are reduced to alcohols by converting them to esters, which on catalytic hydrogenation usually at high temperature and pressure give a mixture of two alcohols.

$$\underset{\text{Carboxylic acid}}{RCOOH} \xrightarrow[H^+]{R'OH} \underset{\text{Ester}}{RCOOR'} \xrightarrow[\text{Catalyst}]{H_2/\text{Copper chromite}} \underset{\text{Alcohol}}{RCH_2OH + R'OH}$$

3. From Grignard Reagents

Aldehydes and ketones react with Grignard reagent to form alcohol in two steps :

These are as follows:

Step I This step involves the nucleophilic addition of Grignard reagent to the carbonyl group to form an adduct.

Step II This step involves the hydrolysis of an adduct to yield an alcohol.

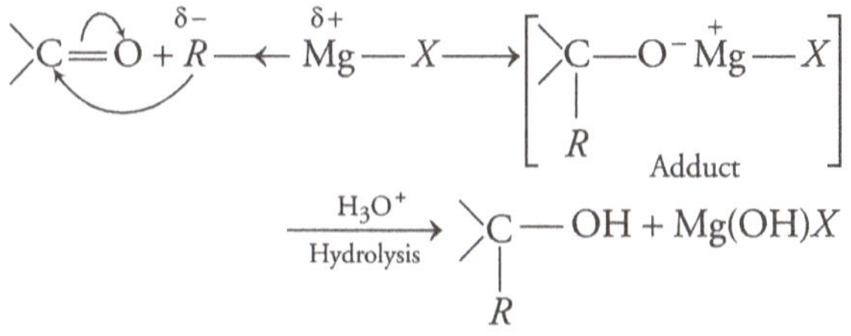

The overall reactions using different aldehydes and ketones are as follows:

$$\underset{\text{Formaldehyde}}{HCHO} + RMgX \longrightarrow RCH_2OMgX \xrightarrow{H_2O/H^+} \underset{1^\circ \text{ alcohol}}{RCH_2OH} + Mg(OH)X$$

$$\underset{\text{Aldehyde}}{RCHO} + R'MgX \longrightarrow R{-}CH(R'){-}\overset{-}{O}\overset{+}{M}gX \xrightarrow{H_2O/H^+} \underset{2^\circ \text{ alcohol}}{R{-}CH(R'){-}OH} + Mg(OH)X$$

$$\underset{\text{Ketone}}{RCOR'} + R''MgX \longrightarrow R{-}C(R')(R''){-}\overset{-}{O}\overset{+}{M}gX \xrightarrow{H_2O/H^+} \underset{3^\circ \text{ alcohol}}{R{-}C(R')(R''){-}OH} + Mg(OH)X$$

Only formaldehyde yields primary alcohol on reaction with Grignard reagents whereas all other aldehydes and ketones give secondary and tertiary alcohols, respectively.

4. Hydrolysis of Alkyl Halide

Haloalkanes when treated with aqueous solution of an alkali (NaOH/KOH) give corresponding alcohols.

$$\underset{\text{Haloalkane}}{R{-}X} + KOH(aq) \longrightarrow \underset{\text{Alcohol}}{R{-}OH} + KX$$

5. From Aliphatic Primary Amines

Aliphatic primary amines react with nitrous acid to give primary alcohol.

$$NaNO_2 + HCl \xrightarrow{0-3^\circ C} \underset{\text{Nitrous acid}}{HNO_2} + NaCl$$

$$R{-}NH_2 + HNO_2 \xrightarrow{0-3^\circ C} R{-}OH + N_2\uparrow + H_2O$$

But this is not a good method for the preparation of 1° alcohols because a mixture of alkenes, alkyl halides, aldehydes are also produced along with alcohols, e.g. methyl amine gives ether and methyl nitrite.

Physical Properties

The alcohols consist of two parts :

(i) Alkyl or aryl group and (ii) Hydroxyl group

Their properties are chiefly due to hydroxyl (—OH) group. The nature of alkyl or aryl groups simply modify these properties.

Some important physical properties are as follows :

1. Physical State

At room temperature, lower alcohols are colourless liquids with distinct smell and burning taste. The higher members are colourless, odourless waxy solids.

2. Boiling Points

The boiling points of alcohols increase with increase in number of C-atoms (due to increase in van der Waals' forces). In alcohols, the boiling point decreases with increase of branching in carbon chain because of decrease in van der Waals' forces with decrease in surface area. The —OH group in alcohols is involved in intermolecular hydrogen bonding or H-bonding due to which they exist as associated molecules and hence, have higher boiling points.

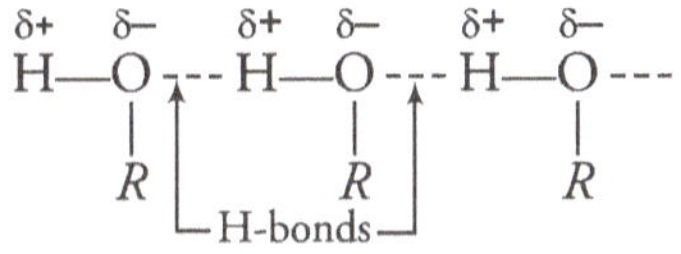

Boiling points of alcohols are usually higher in comparison to hydrocarbons, ethers, haloalkanes and haloarenes of comparable molecular masses. This is mainly due to the presence of intermolecular H-bonding in them which is absent in ethers and hydrocarbons.

C_2H_5OH	CH_3OCH_3	$CH_3CH_2CH_3$
Ethanol	Methoxy methane	Propane
Molecular mass = 46	Molecular mass = 46	Molecular mass = 44
Boiling point = 351 K	Boiling point = 248 K	Boiling point = 231 K

3. Solubility

The solubility of alcohols in water is due to their ability to form H-bonds with water molecules. Solubility decreases with increase in size of alkyl/aryl (i.e. hydrophobic) groups.

However, solubility of isomeric alcohols increases with branching due to decrease in surface area of hydrophobic part. Many lower molecular mass alcohols are miscible with water in all proportions.

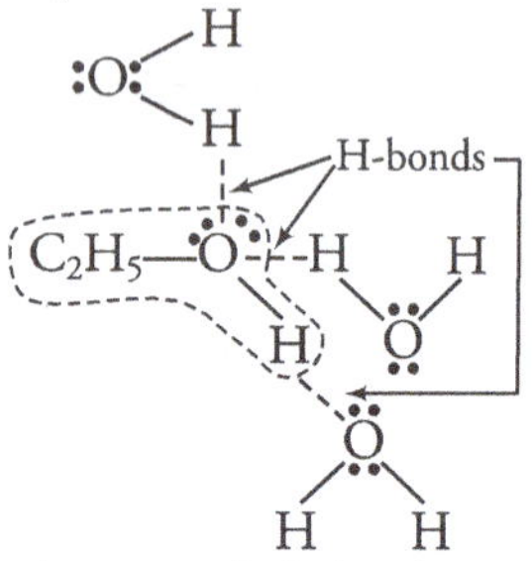

H-bonding between alcohol and water molecules

Chemical Properties

1. Acidic Nature

Alcohols behave as weak acids and ionise to a very small extent as shown below :

$$R\text{—OH} \rightleftharpoons \underset{\text{Alkoxide ion}}{R\text{—O}^-} + H^+$$

Acidic strength of alcohols is even less than that of water.

$$\underset{\text{Base}}{R\text{—}\ddot{\text{O}}:^{\ominus}} + \underset{\text{Acid}}{\text{H—}\ddot{\text{O}}\text{—H}} \longrightarrow \underset{\text{Conjugate acid}}{R\text{—O—H}} + \underset{\text{Conjugate base}}{{}^{\ominus}:\ddot{\text{O}}\text{H}}$$

The acidic character of alcohols is due to the polar nature of O—H bond. An electron-releasing group ($—CH_3, —C_2H_5$) increases electron density on oxygen, tending to decrease the polarity of O—H bond. This effect decreases the acid strength. For this reason, the acid strength of alcohols decreases in the following order:

$$\underset{1°}{R \rightarrow CH_2OH} > \underset{2°}{R_2 \rightarrow CHOH} > \underset{3°}{R_3 \rightarrow C\text{—OH}}$$

2. Reaction with Active Metals (Sodium)

When an alcohol is treated with sodium or potassium, the O—H bond gets cleaved and a metal alkoxide is formed with the evolution of hydrogen gas.

$$2R\text{—OH} + 2Na \longrightarrow \underset{\text{Sodium alkoxide}}{2R\overset{-}{O}\overset{+}{Na}} + H_2\uparrow$$

3. Reaction with Metal Hydrides

Alcohols react with metal hydrides to form metal alkoxides with the evolution of hydrogen gas.

$$CH_3OH + NaH \longrightarrow CH_3\overset{-}{O}\overset{+}{Na} + H_2\uparrow$$

4. Reaction with Acid Chlorides and Acid Anhydrides (Acylation)

Alcohols react with acid chlorides or acid anhydrides in the presence of bases like pyridine to form esters. This reaction is called **acylation reaction.**

$$\underset{\text{Acid chloride}}{R\text{—}\overset{O}{\overset{\|}{C}}\text{—Cl}} + \underset{\text{Alcohol}}{H\text{—O—}R'} \xrightarrow[\text{base}]{\text{Pyridine}} \underset{\text{Ester}}{R\text{—}\overset{O}{\overset{\|}{C}}\text{—O—}R'} + HCl$$

$$\underset{\text{Acid anhydride}}{R\text{—}\overset{O}{\overset{\|}{C}}\text{—O—}\overset{O}{\overset{\|}{C}}\text{—}R} + \underset{\text{Alcohol}}{H\text{—O—}R'} \xrightarrow{\text{Pyridine}} \underset{\text{Ester}}{R\text{—}\overset{O}{\overset{\|}{C}}\text{—O—}R'} + \underset{\text{Acid}}{R\text{—}\overset{O}{\overset{\|}{C}}\text{—OH}}$$

5. Reaction with Carboxylic Acid (Esterification)

Alcohols react with carboxylic acid in the presence of concentrated sulphuric acid to form esters. This reaction is called **esterification.**

$$\underset{\text{Acid}}{R\text{—}\overset{O}{\overset{\|}{C}}\text{—OH}} + \underset{\text{Alcohol}}{HOR'} \underset{H_2SO_4}{\overset{\text{Conc.}}{\rightleftharpoons}} \underset{\text{Ester}}{R\text{—}\overset{O}{\overset{\|}{C}}\text{—}OR'} + H_2O$$

Mechanism

The reaction is said to proceed through "**nucleophilic addition-elimination**" and gives best result in the presence of mineral acids. The **nucleophilic addition-elimination pathway with acid catalysed condition** for esterification can be said to proceed as follows :

Step I Initially the H^+ of mineral acid attacks on O-atom of carbonyl part of —COOH group. Such an attack is said to create unit positive charge on C-atom of this group so that nucleophile can attack on it easily as :

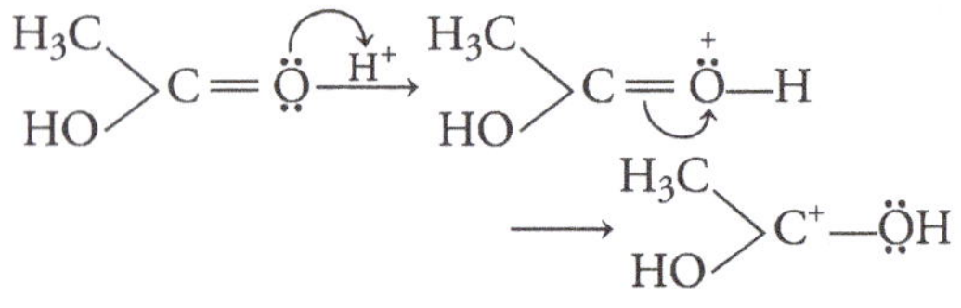

Step II Now the oxygen of alcohol donates its lone pair to positively charged C-atom of carbonium ion as :

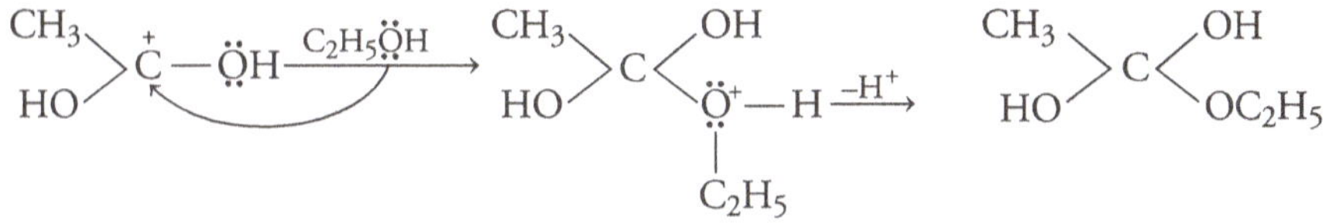

Step III The H^+ liberated in step II attacks on the oxygen of —OH group, taking the lone pair from it, thus

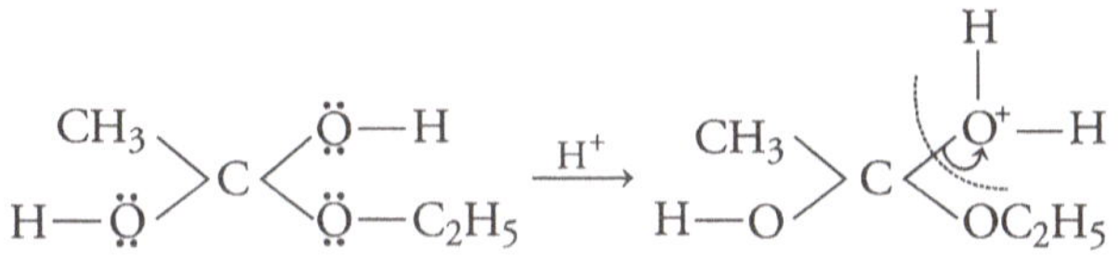

This results in liberation of water molecule and formation of another carbonium ion as :

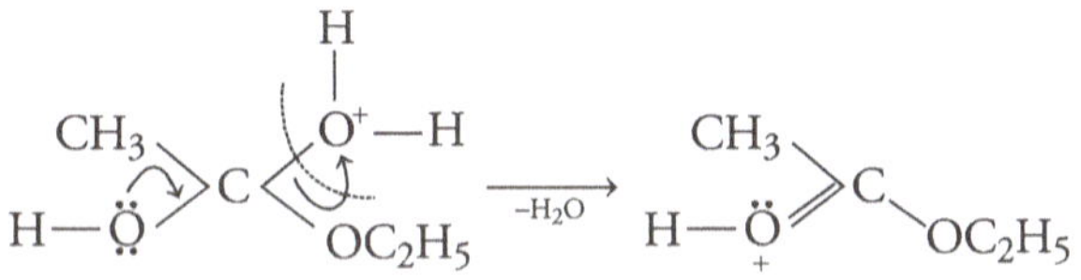

This carbonium ion stabilises itself as:

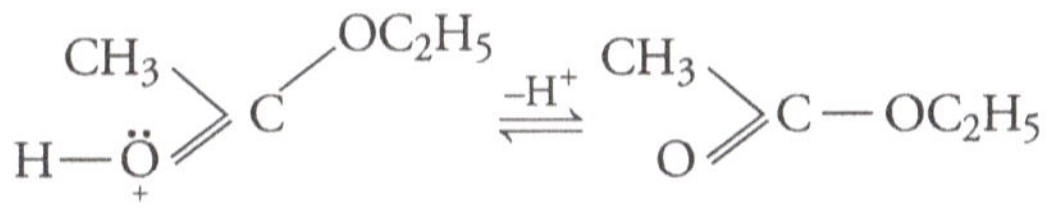

6. Reaction with Thionyl Chloride

Alcohols react with thionyl chloride in the presence of pyridine to form chloroalkanes.

$$\underset{}{R\text{—}OH} + \underset{\text{Thionyl chloride}}{SOCl_2} \xrightarrow{\text{Pyridine}} \underset{\text{Chloroalkane}}{R\text{—}Cl} + SO_2\uparrow + HCl\uparrow$$

7. Reaction with Hydrogen Halides

Alcohols react with hydrogen halides to form the corresponding haloalkanes.

$$R\text{—}OH + HX \longrightarrow \underset{\text{Haloalkane}}{R\text{—}X} + H_2O$$

8. Reaction with Phosphorus Halides

Alcohols react with phosphorus halides, PCl_3, PCl_5, etc., to form corresponding haloalkanes.

$$CH_3CH_2OH + PCl_5 \longrightarrow \underset{\text{Chloroethane}}{CH_3CH_2Cl} + \underset{\text{Phosphorus oxychloride}}{POCl_3} + HCl\uparrow;$$

$$3CH_3CH_2OH + PCl_3 \longrightarrow \underset{\text{Chloroethane}}{3CH_3CH_2Cl} + \underset{\text{Phosphorus acid}}{H_3PO_3}$$

9. Oxidation

Primary and secondary alcohols are easily oxidised by $Na_2Cr_2O_7$ / $K_2Cr_2O_7$ /acidified $KMnO_4$ to form aldehydes and ketones containing same number of carbon atoms respectively. This process involves the formation of carbon-oxygen double bond with cleavage of O — H and C — H bonds.

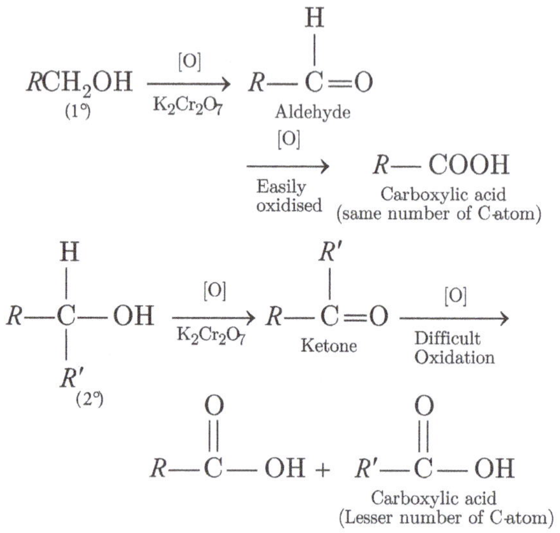

Tertiary alcohols, when subjected to vigorous oxidation with nitric acid give ketone containing lesser number of carbon atoms.

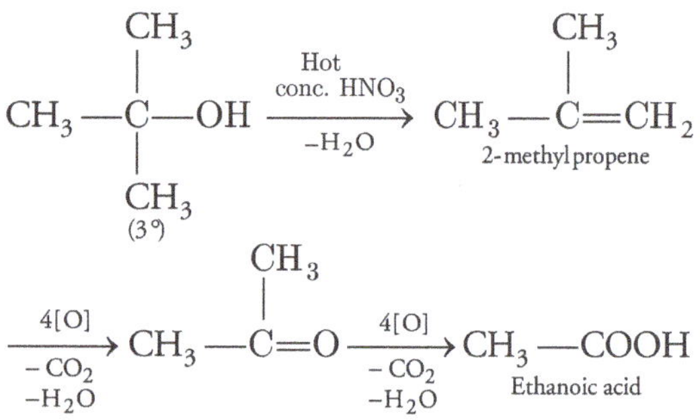

10. Dehydration

Alcohols undergo dehydration (i.e. removal of a molecule of water) to form alkenes on treatment with a protic acid such as H_2SO_4 or H_3PO_4 or catalysts such as anhydrous $ZnCl_2$ or Al_2O_3.

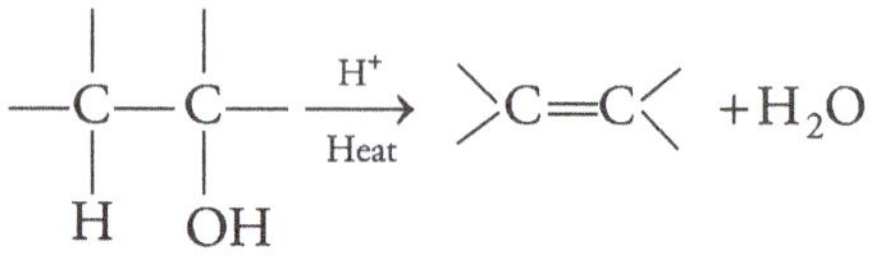

Ethanol undergoes dehydration by heating with conc. H_2SO_4 at 443 K.

$$\underset{\substack{\text{Ethyl alcohol}\\(1^\circ\text{ alcohol})}}{CH_3-CH_2OH} \xrightarrow[443\text{ K}]{\text{Conc. }H_2SO_4} \underset{\text{Ethylene}}{CH_2=CH_2} + H_2O$$

Secondary and tertiary alcohols are dehydrated under mild conditions.

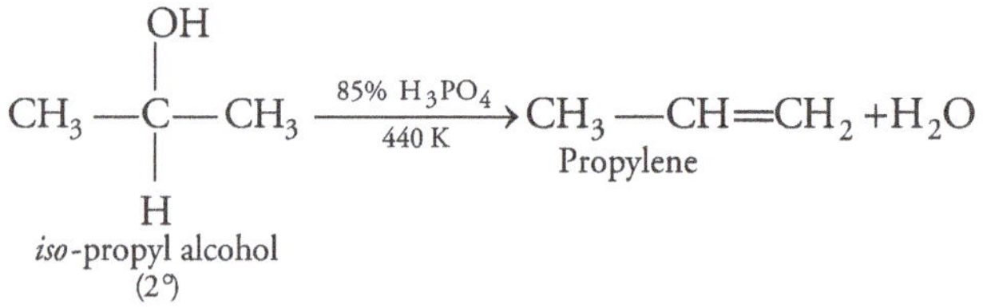

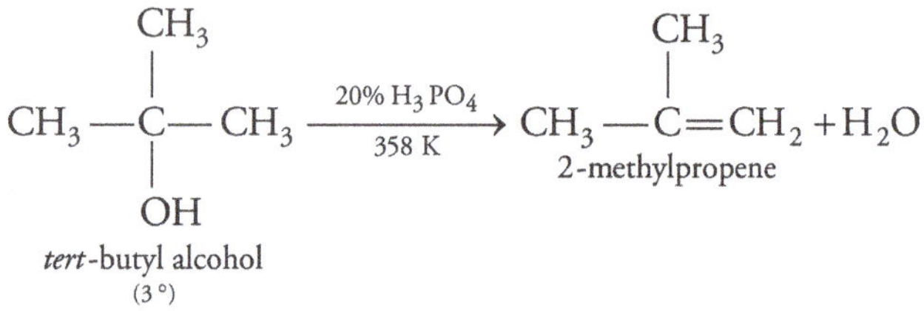

Order for ease of dehydration is:

3° alcohol > 2° alcohol > 1° alcohol.

Mechanism

The mechanism of dehydration of ethanol involves the following steps:

Step I **Formation of Protonated Alcohol**

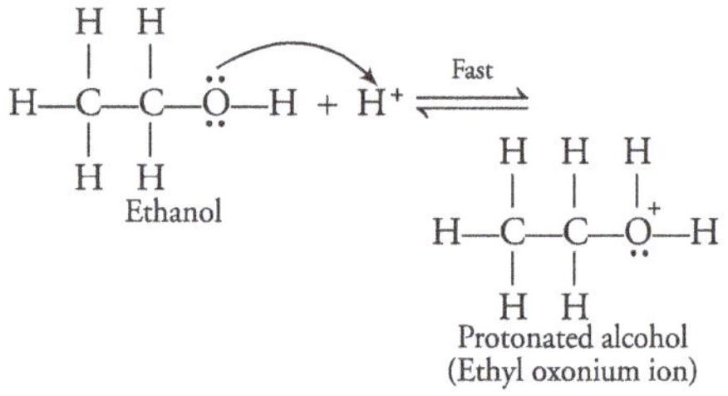

Step II **Formation of Carbocation**

It is the slowest step and hence, it is the rate determining step of the reaction.

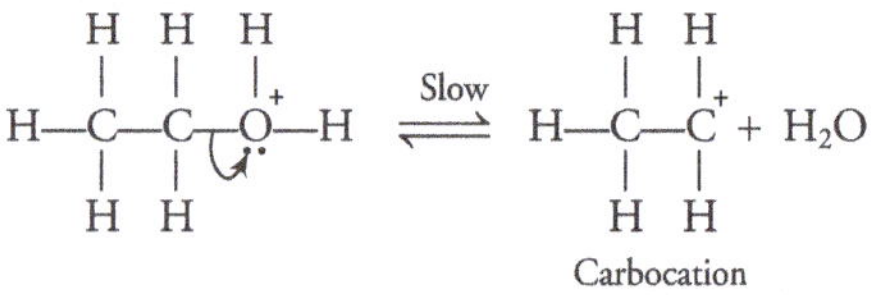

Note Tertiary carbocations are more stable and therefore, are easier to form than secondary and primary carbocations. Tertiary alcohols are the easiest to dehydrate.

Step III Formation of ethene by the elimination of a proton.

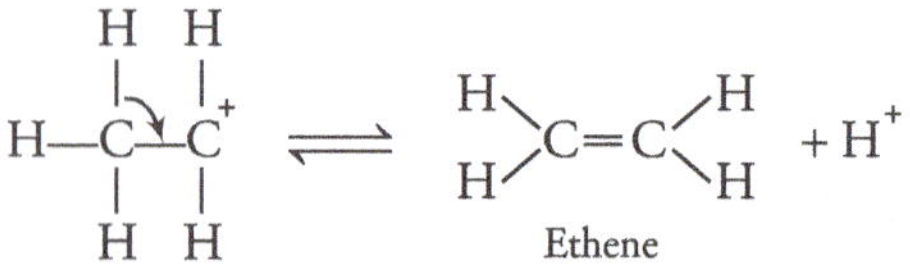

The acid used in step I is released in step III. To drive the equilibrium to the right, ethene is removed as it is formed.

Some Commercially Important Alcohols

Methanol and ethanol are some of the commercially important alcohols. *These are discussed below:*

Methanol (CH_3OH)

It is also known as 'wood spirit', as it was produced by the destructive distillation of wood.

Preparation (Bosch Process)

Now-a-days, methanol is produced by the catalytic hydrogenation of carbon monoxide at high pressure and temperature in the presence of $ZnO - Cr_2O_3$ catalyst.

$$CO + 2H_2 \xrightarrow[\substack{200-300\text{ atm}\\575-673\text{ K}}]{ZnO-Cr_2O_3} \underset{\text{Methyl alcohol or methanol}}{CH_3—OH}$$

Properties

Methanol is a colourless liquid with a boiling point of 337 K. It is highly poisonous in nature and ingestion of even small quantities of methanol can cause blindness and large quantities cause even death.

Uses

It is used as a solvent in paints, varnishes and in formaldehyde formation, as an antioxidant.

Ethanol (C_2H_5OH)

Ethanol is a volatile, flammable, colourless liquid having chemical formula C_2H_5OH.

Preparation

It is obtained commercially by the fermentation of sugar present in molasses, sugarcane or fruits like grapes.

$$\underset{\text{Sucrose}}{C_{12}H_{22}O_{11}} + H_2O \xrightarrow{\text{Invertase}} \underset{\text{Glucose}}{C_6H_{12}O_6} + \underset{\text{Fructose}}{C_6H_{12}O_6}$$

$$\underset{\text{Glucose or Fructose}}{C_6H_{12}O_6} \xrightarrow{\text{Zymase}} \underset{\text{Ethanol}}{2C_2H_5OH} + 2CO_2\uparrow$$

Fermentation takes place in anaerobic conditions, i.e. in the absence of air. Carbon dioxide is released during fermentation. If air gets into fermentation mixture, the oxygen of air oxidises ethanol to ethanoic acid which destroys the taste of alcoholic drinks.

Properties

It is a colourless liquid with boiling point of 351 K. It is harmful for central nervous system. It can affect judgement, can cause nausea, loss of consciousness and can be fatal.

Uses

It is used as a solvent in paint industry and in wine making. 100% ethanol is called absolute alcohol. Commercial alcohol is made unfit for drinking by mixing in it some copper sulphate (to give it colour) and pyridine (a foul smelling liquid). It is known as **denaturation** of alcohol. Now a days, large quantities of ethanol are obtained by the hydration of ethene.

Note Absolute alcohol is 100% ethanol that is prepared from rectified spirit (ethanol) by azeotropic distillation.

Distinction Tests between Primary, Secondary and Tertiary Alcohols

Lucas Test

A small quantity of unknown alcohol is added to Lucas reagent (anhyd. $ZnCl_2$ + conc. HCl) at room temperature and the mixture is shaken.

A tertiary alcohol forms turbidity immediately, secondary alcohol forms turbidity within five minutes and primary alcohol shows no turbidity at room temperature.

$$\underset{3^\circ\text{ alcohol}}{R_3COH} \xrightarrow[\text{anhyd . }ZnCl_2]{\text{Conc.HCl +}} \underset{\text{Turbidity appears immediately}}{R_3CCl} + H_2O$$

$$\underset{2^\circ\text{ alcohol}}{R_2CHOH} \xrightarrow[\text{anhyd . }ZnCl_2]{\text{Conc.HCl +}} \underset{\text{Turbidity appears in 5 min}}{R_2CHCl}$$

$$\underset{1^\circ\text{ alcohol}}{RCH_2OH} \xrightarrow[\text{anhyd . }ZnCl_2]{\text{Conc.HCl +}} \text{No reaction}$$

Conversion of Alcohols

(i) **Conversion of a Lower Alcohol into a Higher Alcohol**

$$\underset{\text{Lower alcohol}}{R—OH} \xrightarrow[-H_2O]{HI} RI \xrightarrow[-KI]{KCN} RCN \xrightarrow[\text{Reduction}]{4[H]} RCH_2NH_2 \xrightarrow{HNO_2} \underset{\text{Higher alcohol}}{RCH_2OH}$$

(ii) **Conversion of Higher Alcohol into a Lower Alcohol**

$$\underset{\text{Higher alcohol}}{RCH_2OH} \xrightarrow[K_2Cr_2O_7]{[O]} RCHO \xrightarrow{[O]} RCOOH \xrightarrow{NaOH} RCO\overset{-}{O}\overset{+}{Na}$$

$$\xrightarrow[\text{Heat}]{NaOH + CaO} Na_2CO_3 + RH \xrightarrow{Cl_2} R—Cl \xrightarrow{aq.\ KOH} \underset{\text{Lower alcohol}}{R—OH} + Na_2CO_3$$

(iii) **Conversion of Primary Alcohol to a Secondary Alcohol**

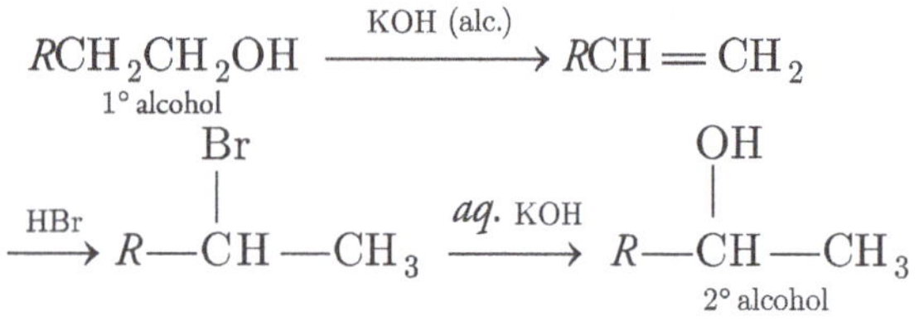

(iv) **Conversion of Secondary Alcohol to a Tertiary Alcohol**

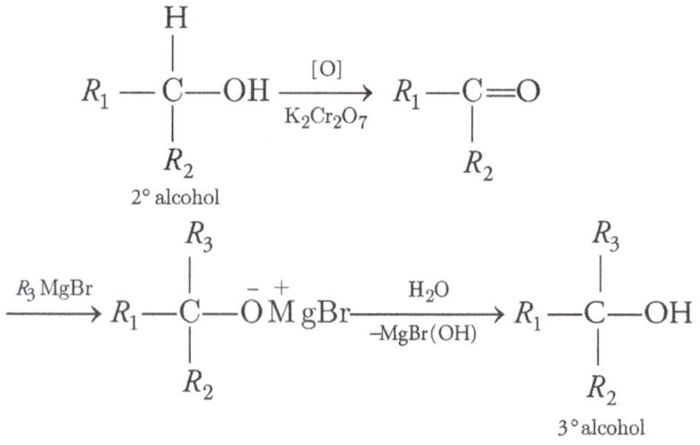

(v) **Conversion of Primary Alcohol to a Tertiary Alcohol**

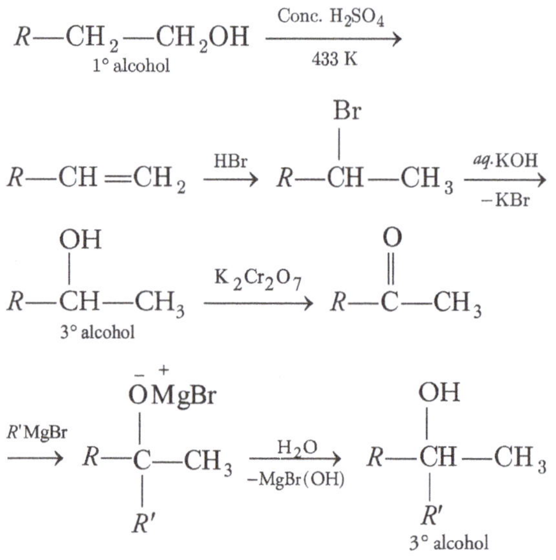

Topic Practice 1

Very Short Answer Type Questions

1 Mark

1. Fill in the Blanks

(i) ......is an example of trihydric alcohol and ...... is an example of dihydric alcohol. **ISC 2011**

(ii) ......and ......are functional isomers. **ISC 2009**

(iii) Aldehyde gives .... alcohol whereas ketone gives .... alcohol on reduction.

(iv) The dehydration of ethyl alcohol with conc. H_2SO_4 at 140°C mainly yields .... while at 170°C the main product formed is .... **ISC 2024**

(v) The primary alcohols are easily oxidised first into .... and then into .... **ISC 2023**

(vi) A mixture of conc. HCl and anhydrous $ZnCl_2$ is called .... which shows maximum reactivity with .... alcohol. **ISC 2019**

2. Objective Type Questions

(i) When acetaldehyde is treated with Grignard reagent, followed by hydrolysis the product formed is **ISC 2015**

(a) primary alcohol
(b) secondary alcohol
(c) carboxylic acid
(d) tertiary alcohol

(ii) The compound which is optically active is **ISC 2015**

(a) 1-butanol
(b) 2-butanol
(c) 1-propanol
(d) 2-methyl-1-propanol

(iii) When oxalic acid is heated with glycerol, we get **ISC 2009**

(a) formic acid (b) acetic acid
(c) lactic acid (d) tartaric acid

(iv) When acetone is treated with Grignard's reagent, followed by hydrolysis, the product formed is

(a) secondary alcohol (b) tertiary alcohol
(c) primary alcohol (d) aldehyde

3. Match the following Columns and choose the correct option using the codes given below :

Column I	Column II
A. Antifreeze used in car engine	(i) Glycerol
B. Solvent used in perfumes	(ii) Methanol
C. Wood spirit	(iii) Ethylene glycol
D. By product of soap industry used in cosmetics	(iv) Ethanol

Codes

	A	B	C	D		A	B	C	D
(a)	(iii)	(iv)	(ii)	(i)	(b)	(i)	(iii)	(iv)	(ii)
(c)	(i)	(ii)	(iii)	(iv)	(d)	(iv)	(ii)	(iii)	(i)

4. Write the IUPAC name of the given compound:

$$HO—CH_2—CH=\underset{\displaystyle |\atop CH_3}{C}—CH_3$$

5. Write IUPAC name of the following compound.

$$HO—CH_2—\underset{\displaystyle |\atop OH}{CH}—CH_2—OH$$

6. Write the IUPAC name of the following compound.

$$CH_3—CH—CH—\underset{\displaystyle |\atop OH}{CH}—CH_2—CH_3$$

7. Give IUPAC name of the following compound :

$$H_2C=CH—\underset{\displaystyle |\atop OH}{CH}—CH_2—CH_2—CH_3$$

8. Write the IUPAC name of

$$H_3C—\underset{\displaystyle |\atop CH_3}{CH}—CH_2—\underset{\displaystyle |\atop OH}{CH}—\underset{\displaystyle |\atop CH_3}{CH}—CH_2OH$$

9. Give IUPAC name of the following compound.

$$H_3C—\underset{\displaystyle |\atop CH_3}{C}=\underset{\displaystyle |\atop Br}{C}—CH_2—OH$$

10. Write the IUPAC name of the compound given below:

$$CH_3—CH_2—\underset{\displaystyle |\atop CH_3}{C}=\underset{\displaystyle |\atop CH_2OH}{C}—OH$$

NCERT Exemplar

11. Alcohols are comparatively more soluble in water than hydrocarbons of comparable molecular masses. Explain this fact. **NCERT**

12. Lower alcohols are water soluble whereas, higher alcohols are water insoluble. Give reason.

13. Name the alcohol that is used to make the following ester:

$$CH_3—\overset{\displaystyle O\atop \|}{C}—O—\underset{\displaystyle |\atop CH_3}{CH}—CH_3$$

14. Of the two hydroxy organic compounds, ROH and $R'OH$, the first one is basic and other one is acidic in behaviour. How is R different from R'?

15. Suggest a reagent for the following conversion:

NCERT Exemplar

(a) 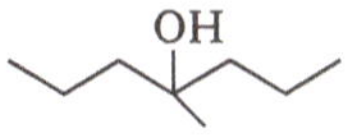

(b) 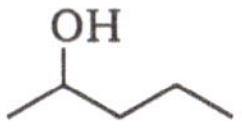

Short Answer Type I Questions

2 Marks

16. Draw the structure of hex-1-en-3-ol compound.

17. Draw the structural formula of 2-methylpropan-2-ol molecule.

18. Give reason for the following:

The C — O — H bond angle in alcohols is slightly less than the tetrahedral angle (109° 28′).

19. How will you convert
   (i) propene to propan-1-ol?
   (ii) ethanal to propan-2-ol?

20. How do you convert the following?
Propan-2-ol to 2-methylpropan-2-ol

21. How would you obtain ethane-1, 2-diol from ethanol?

22. How could you convert ethanol to ethene?

23. Write the mechanism of acid dehydration of ethanol to yield ethene. **NCERT**

Or Explain the mechanism of the following reaction:

$$CH_3—CH_2—OH \xrightarrow[443\,K]{H^+} CH_2=CH_2 + H_2O$$

24. Write the mechanism of the following reaction:

$$CH_3CH_2OH \xrightarrow{HBr} CH_3CH_2Br + H_2O$$

25. How will you convert the following?
Propan-2-ol to propanone

26. An organic compound *A* with molecular formula $C_3H_8O_3$ reacts with oxalic acid to give *B*. *B* gives a silver mirror with Tollen's reagent and reduces acidified potassium permangantate solution.

Identify *A* and *B* and give the reaction of *B* with acidified $KMnO_4$ solution.

27. Why is the reactivity of all the three classes of alcohols with conc. HCl and $ZnCl_2$ (Lucas reagent) different? **NCERT Exemplar**

28. Give a reason for each of the following.
  (i) Ethoxy ethane does not react with sodium, but ethanol does.
  (ii) Methoxy ethane with conc. HI at 373 K gives C_2H_5OH and CH_3I but not CH_3OH and C_2H_5I.
ISC 2024

29. Identify the compounds [*A*], [*B*] and [*C*] in each of the following reactions.
  (i) $C_2H_5OH \xrightarrow{PCl_5} [A] \xrightarrow{KCN} [B] \xrightarrow{H_3O^+} C_2H_5COOH \xrightarrow[\Delta]{NH_3} [C]$
  (ii) $C_6H_5OH \xrightarrow{Zn/Dust} [A] \xrightarrow[Anhy.\ AlCl_3]{CH_3Cl} [B] \xrightarrow[K_2Cr_2O_7 + H_2SO_4]{[O]} [C]$
ISC 2024

30. (i) Write a chemical test to distinguish between ethanol and phenol.
  (ii) Give a chemical reaction to convert acetaldehyde into secondary propyl alcohol.
ISC 2024

31. (i) How will you obtain the following (give balanced chemical equations)?
  (a) Benzene from phenol.
  (b) Iodoform from ethanol.

Or

  (ii) How will you obtain the following (give balanced chemical equations)?
  (a) Salicylaldehyde from phenol.
  (b) Propan -2- ol from Grignard's reagent.
ISC 2019

Short Answer Type II Questions
3 Marks

32. Classify the following as primary, secondary and tertiary alcohols.
  (i) 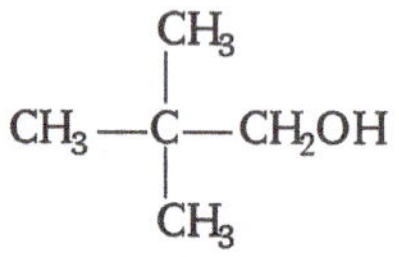
  (ii) $H_2C{=}CH{-}CH_2OH$
  (iii) $CH_3{-}CH_2{-}CH_2{-}OH$
NCERT Intext

33. Predict the products of the following reactions.
  (i) $CH_3 - CH{=}CH_2 \xrightarrow[(ii)\ 3H_2O/OH^-]{(i)\ B_2H_6} ?$
  (ii) $CH_3CH_2OH \xrightarrow{Cu/573\ K}$

34. Show how will you synthesise pentan-1-ol using an alkyl halide? **NCERT**

35. Predict the major product of acid catalysed dehydration of butan-1-ol **NCERT Intext**

36. Name the reagent in the following reactions :
  (i) Oxidation of primary alcohol to a carboxylic acid.
  (ii) Oxidation of primary alcohol to an aldehyde.
  (iii) Benzyl alcohol to benzoic acid.
  (iv) Dehydration of propan-2-ol to propene.
  (v) Butan-2-one to butan-2-ol.
  (vi) Reduction of acetaldehyde to ethanol. **NCERT**

37. Give the structures of the products you would expect when each of the following alcohol reacts with
  (a) Butan-1-ol
  (b) 2-methylbutan-2-ol
  (i) HCl-$ZnCl_2$
  (ii) HBr
  (iii) $SOCl_2$

38. How may be the following transformation carried out (in not more than six steps)? Ethyl alcohol to vinyl acetate.

39. Draw the structure and name the product formed if the following alcohols are oxidised. Assume that an excess of oxidising agent is used.
  (i) Butan-1-ol
  (ii) Butan-2-ol
  (iii) 2-methylpropan-1-ol

40. Account for the following **ISC 2023**
  (i) Phenol is a stronger acid than aliphatic alcohols.
  (ii) Ethanol gives iodoform reaction, whereas methanol does not give iodoform reaction.
  (iii) Ethers should not be distilled to dryness.

41. Give a chemical test to distinguish between the following pairs of compounds. **ISC 2024**
  (i) Ethanol and methanol
  (ii) Ethanol and ethanal
  (iii) Propan-2-ol and 2-methyl propan-2-ol

Long Answer Type Questions
5 Marks

42. Show how would you synthesise the following alcohols from alkenes?
  (i) 4-methyl heptan-4-ol
  (ii) Pentan-2-ol

43. (i) When 3-methylbutan-2-ol is treated with HBr, the following reaction takes place:

$$CH_3-CH(CH_3)-CH(\ddot{O}H)-CH_3 \xrightarrow{HBr} CH_3-C(Br)(CH_3)-CH_2-CH_3$$

Give a mechanism for this reaction.

(ii) What is meant by hydroboration-oxidation reaction? Illustrate it with an example. **NCERT**

44. (i) How are the following conversions carried out?

(a) Propene $\rightarrow$ Propan-2-ol

(b) Ethyl magnesium chloride $\rightarrow$ Propan-1-ol

(c) Methyl magnesium bromide $\rightarrow$ 2-methyl propan-2-ol. **NCERT**

(ii) Explain why propanol has higher boiling point than that of butane? **NCERT**

45. (i) Explain with reason:

Solubility of alcohols in water decreases with increase in molecular mass.

(ii) How would you obtain :

2-methylpropan-2-ol from 2-methylpropene?

46. How would you obtain the following :

(i) Benzoquinone from phenol?

(ii) 2-methyl propan-2-ol from methyl magnesium bromide ?

(iii) Propan-2-ol from propene?

(a) $C_2H_5OH \xrightarrow[\Delta]{Cu} A \xrightarrow{Dil.\ NaOH} B$

(b) 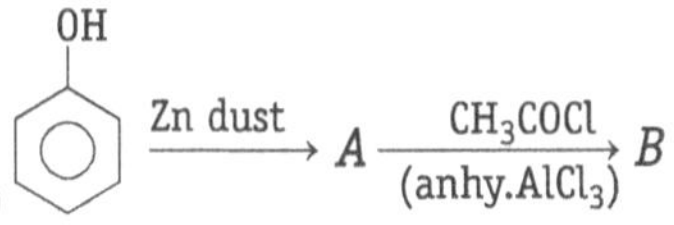

Hints & Solutions

1. (i) Glycerol, glycol (ii) Ethanol, dimethyl ether (iii) primary, secondary (iv) diethyl ether, ethene (v) aldehyde, carboxylic acid (vi) Lucas reagent, tertiary

2. (i) $\rightarrow$ (b), (ii) $\rightarrow$ (b), (iii) $\rightarrow$ (a), (iv) $\rightarrow$ (b)

3. (a) A $\rightarrow$ (iii), B $\rightarrow$ (iv), C $\rightarrow$ (ii), (D) $\rightarrow$ (i)

4. $\overset{1}{HO-CH_2}-\overset{2}{CH}=\overset{3}{C}(CH_3)-\overset{4}{CH_3}$

IUPAC name 3-methylbut-2-en-1-ol

5. Propane-1, 2, 3 -triol.

6. $\overset{4}{CH_3}-\overset{3}{CH}-\overset{2}{CH}-\overset{1}{CH}(OH)-CH_2-CH_3$

2-ethylbutanol

7. $\overset{1}{H_2C}=\overset{2}{CH}-\overset{3}{CH}(OH)-\overset{4}{CH_2}-\overset{5}{CH_2}-\overset{6}{CH_3}$

Hex-1-en-3-ol

8. $\overset{6}{H_3C}-\overset{5}{CH}(CH_3)-\overset{4}{CH_2}-\overset{3}{CH}(OH)-\overset{2}{CH}(CH_3)-\overset{1}{CH_2OH}$

2,5-dimethylhexane-1,3-diol

9. $\overset{4}{H_3C}-\overset{3}{C}(CH_3)=\overset{2}{C}(Br)-\overset{1}{CH_2}-OH$

2-bromo-3-methyl but-2-en-1-ol

10. The **IUPAC name** of the given compound is

$$\overset{5}{H_3C}-\overset{4}{CH_2}-\overset{3}{C}(CH_3)=\overset{2}{C}(OH)-\overset{1}{CH_2}-OH$$

3-methylpent-2-ene-1,2-diol

11. Alcohols can form H-bonds with water and break the H-bonds already existing between water molecules. Therefore, they are water soluble.

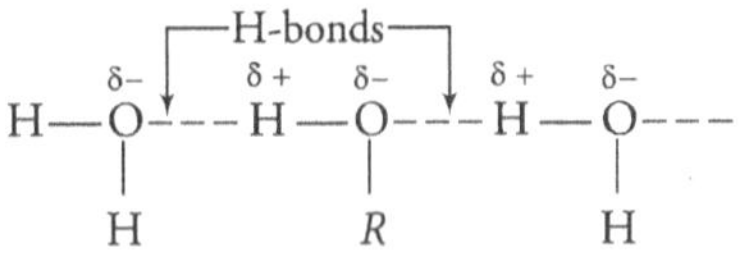

On contrary, hydrocarbons cannot form H-bonds with water and thus, are insoluble in water.

12. Lower alcohols can form H-bonds with water whereas in higher alcohols, due to the presence of larger hydrocarbon part, H-bonding is inefficient.

13. $CH_3-CH(OH)-CH_3$

Propan-2-ol

14. *R* must be a group having more electron density than H, i.e. having +*I*-effect whereas *R'* must be having –*I*- effect.

15. The complex of CrO_3, pyridine and HCl, i.e. PCC (pyridinium chlorochromate), oxidises $>CHOH$ to $>C=O$ without carrying out oxidation of double bond.

16. $\overset{6}{CH_3}-\overset{5}{CH_2}-\overset{4}{CH_2}-\overset{3}{CH}(OH)-\overset{2}{CH}=\overset{1}{CH_2}$

Hex-1-en-3-ol

17. $\overset{1}{C}H_3-\overset{2}{C}(OH)(CH_3)-\overset{3}{C}H_3$

2-methylpropan-2-ol

18. Refer to text on page 255 (Structure). **(1)**

19. (i) Propene to propan-1-ol

$$\underset{\text{Propene}}{CH_3CH{=}CH_2} + HBr \xrightarrow{\text{Peroxide}} \underset{\text{Propyl bromide}}{CH_3CH_2CH_2Br}$$

$$\xrightarrow{aq.\ KOH} \underset{\text{Propan-1-ol}}{CH_3-\overset{3}{C}H_2-\overset{2}{C}H_2-\overset{1}{O}H}$$ (1)

(ii) Refer to text on pages 256 and 257 (From Grignard reagent).

20. (i) Propan-2-ol to 2-methylpropan-2-ol

$$\underset{\text{Propan-2-ol}}{CH_3-CH(OH)-CH_3} \xrightarrow[-H_2O]{K_2Cr_2O_7/H_2SO_4,\ [O]} \underset{\text{Acetone}}{CH_3-\overset{O}{\overset{\|}{C}}-CH_3} \xrightarrow{CH_3MgBr}$$

$$\underset{\text{Adduct}}{\left[CH_3-C(\overset{-}{O}\overset{+}{M}gBr)(CH_3)-CH_3\right]} \xrightarrow[-Mg(OH)Br]{H^+/H_2O} \underset{\text{2-methylpropan-2-ol}}{CH_3-C(OH)(CH_3)-CH_3}$$ (1)

21. $CH_3CH_2OH \xrightarrow[443\ K]{Conc.\ H_2SO_4}$

$$CH_2{=}CH_2 \xrightarrow{Cl_2} \underset{\ \ Cl\qquad\ Cl}{CH_2-CH_2} \xrightarrow[KOH]{aq.} \underset{\ \ OH\qquad OH}{CH_2-CH_2}$$

22. $$\underset{\text{Ethanol}}{CH_3CH_2OH} \xrightarrow[\substack{443\ K\\ \text{(Dehydration)}}]{Conc.\ H_2SO_4} \underset{\text{Ethene}}{CH_2{=}CH_2} + H_2O$$

23. Refer to text on page 260 (Dehydration). (2)

24. The mechanism of the given reaction can be predicted as:

Step 1 $HBr \longrightarrow H^+ + Br^-$

Step 2 $CH_3-CH_2-\ddot{O}H + H^+ \longrightarrow$

$$CH_3-CH_2-\overset{+}{O}H_2 \xrightarrow[S_N2\ \text{reaction}]{Br^-} \underset{\text{Bromoethane}}{CH_3-CH_2Br} + H_2\ddot{O}$$ (2)

25. Refer to text on page 259 and 260 (Oxidation).

26. *A* is glycerol $CH_2OH-CHOH-CH_2OH$.

B is formic acid (HCOOH).

When *B* reacts with acidified $KMnO_4$ solution, the later gets decolourised.

$$2KMnO_4 + 3H_2SO_4 + 5HCOOH \longrightarrow 2MnSO_4 + 8H_2O + 5CO_2$$ **(1)**

27. The reaction of alcohols with Lucas reagent (conc. HCl and $ZnCl_2$) follows S_N1 mechanism which depends upon the stability of carbocations (intermediate). More stable is the intermediate carbocation, more reactive is the alcohol.

Tertiary carbocations are most stable among the three classes of carbocations and the order of the stability of carbocation is $3° > 2° > 1°$. This order, in turn, reflects the order of reactivity of three classes of alcohols, i.e. $3° > 2° > 1°$.

Thus, as the stability of carbocations are different so the reactivity of all the three classes of alcohols with Lucas reagent is different. (2)

28. (a) Alcohols react with active metals like Na to produce corresponding alkoxides with the evolution hydrogen gas. This show that alcohols are acidic in nature (and can donate a proton to a stronger base).

Whereas diethyl ether does not contain any ionic functional groups nor can deprotonate readily. Thus, in the absence of available hydrogen atoms or other ionic species, the sodium ions will not react.

(b) In case of unsymmetrical ethers having two different alkyl groups, the alcohol and the alkyl halide formed depends on the nature of the alkyl group. In methoxy ethane, alkyl groups are present, thus, lower alkyl group forms alkyl iodide (CH_3I) and higher alkyl group forms alcohol, i.e. C_2H_5OH. This is an example of S_N2 reaction.

29. (i) $$C_2H_5OH \xrightarrow{PCl_5} \underset{(A)}{C_2H_5Cl} \xrightarrow{KCN} \underset{(B)}{C_2H_5-CN}$$

$$\xrightarrow{H_3O^+} C_2H_5COOH \xrightarrow[\Delta]{NH_3} \underset{(C)}{CH_3-CH_2-\overset{O}{\overset{\|}{C}}-NH_2}$$

(ii)

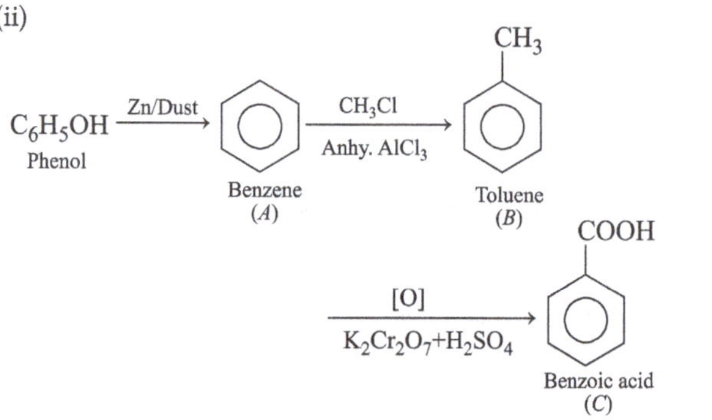

30. (i) Iodoform test can be used distinguish between ethanol and phenol.

$$\underset{\text{Ethanol}}{CH_3CH_2OH} + 4NaOI \longrightarrow \underset{\substack{\text{Iodoform}\\ \text{(Yellow ppt.)}}}{CHI_3} + HCOONa + NaI + H_2O + 2NaOH$$

$$\underset{\text{Phenol}}{C_6H_5OH} + NaOH \longrightarrow \text{No yellow ppt.}$$

(ii) Conversion of acetaldehyde to secondary propyl alcohol.

$$\underset{\text{(Acetaldehyde)}}{CH_3-\overset{H}{\overset{|}{C}}=O} + CH_3MgBr \longrightarrow CH_3-\underset{CH_3}{\underset{|}{\overset{H}{\overset{|}{C}}}}-OMgBr$$

$$\xrightarrow[\text{Hydrolysis}]{H_2O/H^+} \underset{\text{(Secondary propyl alcohol)}}{CH_3-\underset{CH_3}{\underset{|}{\overset{H}{\overset{|}{C}}}}-OH} + Mg\begin{matrix} OH \\ Br \end{matrix}$$

31. (i) (a) Benzene from phenol

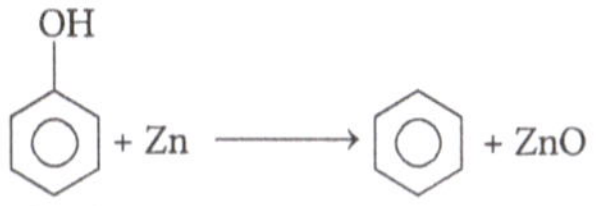

Phenol   Benzene

(b) Iodoform from ethanol

$$\underset{\text{Ethanol}}{C_2H_5OH} + 4I_2 + 6NaOH \xrightarrow{\Delta} \underset{\text{Iodoform}}{CHI_3} + HCOONa + 5NaI + 5H_2O$$

Or

(i) (a) Salicyladehyde from phenol

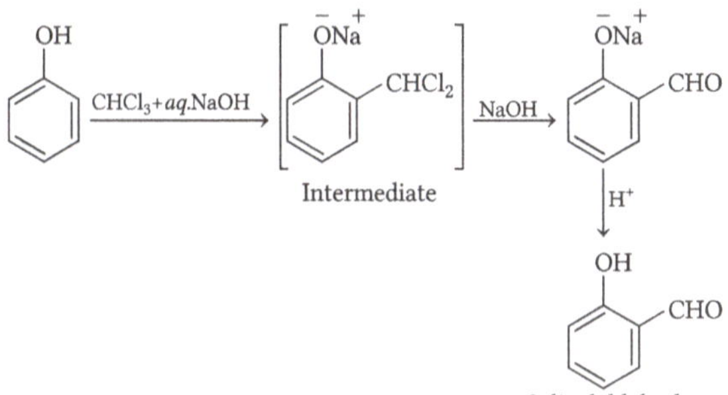

Salicylaldehyde

This reaction is known as Reimer-Tiemann reaction.

(b) Propan-2-ol from Grignard's reagent.

$$CH_3CHO \xrightarrow[\text{(ii) } H_2O/H^+]{\text{(i) } CH_3MgX} \underset{\text{Propan-2-ol}}{CH_3-\underset{CH_3}{\underset{|}{CH}}-OH} + Mg\begin{matrix} OH \\ X \end{matrix}$$

32. Primary alcohols-(i), (ii), (iii) $\left(6 \times \frac{1}{2} = 3\right)$

33. (i) $CH_3-CH=CH_2 \xrightarrow[\text{(ii) } 3H_2O/OH^-]{\text{(i) } B_2H_6} \underset{\text{Propanol}}{CH_3-CH_2-CH_2OH}$

(ii) $CH_3CH_2OH \xrightarrow{Cu/573\ K} \underset{\text{Ethanal}}{CH_3CHO}$

34. Refer to text on page 257 (Hydrolysis of alkyl halide). (2)

35. $\underset{\text{Butan-1-ol}}{CH_3CH_2CH_2CH_2-\ddot{\underset{\cdot\cdot}{O}}H} \xrightarrow{+H^+} \underset{\text{Protonated alcohol}}{CH_3CH_2CH_2CH_2-\overset{+}{\underset{\cdot\cdot}{O}}H_2}$

$$\xrightarrow{-H_2O} \underset{1^\circ \text{ carbocation}}{CH_3CH_2-\underset{H}{\underset{|}{C}}H-\overset{+}{C}H_2} \xrightarrow{1,2\text{-hydride shift}}$$

$$\underset{\substack{2^\circ \text{ carbocation (II)} \\ \text{(More stable)}}}{CH_3-CH_2-\overset{\oplus}{C}H-CH_3} \xrightarrow[-H^+]{}$$

$$\underset{\substack{\text{But-1-ene} \\ \text{(Minor)}}}{CH_3CH_2CH=CH_2} + \underset{\substack{\text{But-2-ene} \\ \text{(Major)}}}{CH_3-CH=CH-CH_3} \qquad (1½)$$

36. (i) Acidified $K_2Cr_2O_7$ (followed by hydrolysis with dil. H_2SO_4)

(ii) Pyridinium chlorochromate (PCC)

(iii) Acidified or alkaline $KMnO_4$ (followed by hydrolysis with dil. H_2SO_4) (iv) 85% H_3PO_4 at 440 K

(v) Ni/H_2 or $NaBH_4$ or $LiAlH_4$

(vi) Ni/Pd $\left(6 \times \frac{1}{2} = 3\right)$

37. (i) **With HCl-ZnCl$_2$** (Lucas reagent)

(a) $\underset{\text{Butan-1-ol}}{CH_3CH_2CH_2CH_2-OH} + \underset{\text{(Conc.)}}{HCl} \xrightarrow{\text{Anhy. } ZnCl_2}$

No reaction at room temperature (1/2)

(b) $\underset{\text{2-methylbutan-2-ol}}{CH_3-\underset{OH}{\underset{|}{\overset{CH_3}{\overset{|}{C}}}}-CH_2CH_3} + HCl \xrightarrow{\text{Anhy. } ZnCl_2}$

$$\underset{\substack{\text{2-chloro-2-methylbutane} \\ \text{(White turbidity)}}}{CH_3-\underset{Cl}{\underset{|}{\overset{CH_3}{\overset{|}{C}}}}-CH_2CH_3} + H_2O \qquad (1/2)$$

(ii) **With HBr**

(a) $\underset{\text{Butan-1-ol}}{CH_3CH_2CH_2CH_2OH} + HBr \xrightarrow{\text{Heat}}$

$$\underset{\text{1-bromobutane}}{CH_3CH_2CH_2CH_2Br} + H_2O \qquad (1/2)$$

(b) $\underset{\text{2-methylbutan-2-ol}}{CH_3-\underset{OH}{\underset{|}{\overset{CH_3}{\overset{|}{C}}}}-CH_2CH_3} + HBr \xrightarrow{\text{Heat}}$

$$\underset{\text{2-bromo-2-methylbutane}}{CH_3-\underset{Br}{\underset{|}{\overset{CH_3}{\overset{|}{C}}}}-CH_2CH_3} + H_2O \qquad (1/2)$$

(iii) **With $SOCl_2$**

(a) $CH_3CH_2CH_2CH_2OH + SOCl_2 \xrightarrow{Heat} CH_3CH_2CH_2CH_2Cl + SO_2\uparrow + HCl$
Butan-1-ol → 1-chlorobutane (1/2)

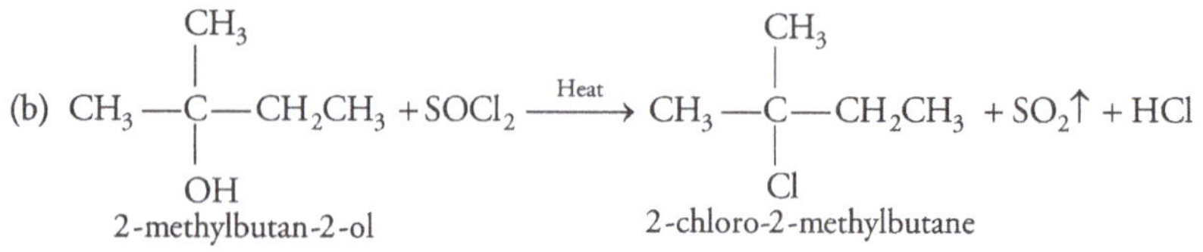

(1/2)

38. $CH_3CH_2OH \xrightarrow[\Delta]{Conc.\,H_2SO_4} CH_2=CH_2 \xrightarrow{NaNH_2} Na^+-\overset{-}{C}\equiv C-H \xrightarrow[CH_3COOH]{Hg(CH_3COO)_2} CH_2=CH-OCOCH_3$
Ethyl alcohol, Ethene, Vinyl acetate (3)

39. (i) $CH_3CH_2CH_2CH_2OH \xrightarrow[\substack{Oxidation\\KMnO_4\,(alk.)}]{[O]} CH_3CH_2CH_2COOH$
Butan-1-ol → Butanoic acid (1)

(ii)

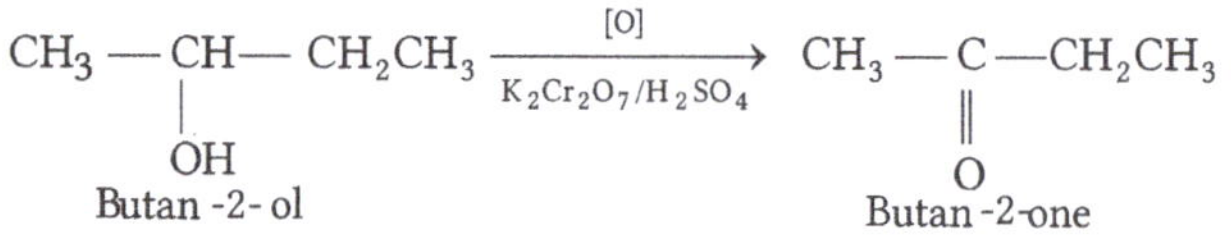

(1)

(iii)

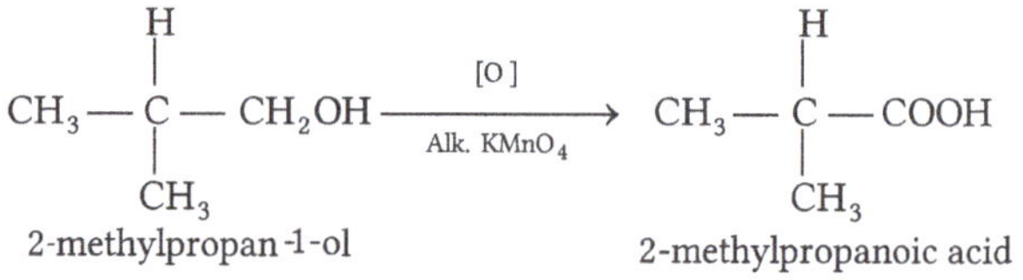

(1)

40. (i) Phenol is a stronger acid due to the presence of polar $-OH$ group and resonance stabilisation of phenoxide ion. This resonance stabilisation of phenoxide ion makes phenol more acidic than aliphatic alcohols.

(ii) Compounds that can be oxidised to methyl ketone or having methyl group attached to carbonyl carbon can give haloform reaction. Thus, ethyl alcohol (ethanol) can be oxidised to ethanal which contains methyl keto group but methyl alcohols do not as it cannot be oxidised to methyl keto group.

(iii) Ethers are not distilled to dryness for the fear of explosion due to formation of peroxides. Peroxides are highly explosive and are less volatile than ethers.

41. (i) **Ethanol and methanol** Ethanol gives positive iodoform test when warmed with iodine in presence of NaOH while methanol does not.

$$CH_3CH_2OH \xrightarrow{3I_2+4\,NaOH} CHI_3 + HCOO^-Na^+ + 5NaI + 5H_2O$$

$$CH_3-OH \xrightarrow{NaOH,\,I_2} \text{No reaction}$$

(ii) **Ethanol and ethanal** Ethanal gives positive Tollen's test while ethanol does not.

$$CH_3-\overset{\overset{O}{||}}{C}-H + 2[Ag(NH_3)_2]^+ + 3\overset{-}{O}H \longrightarrow CH_3-\overset{\overset{O}{||}}{C}-OH + 2Ag\downarrow + 4NH_3 + 2H_2O$$

Acetic acid

$$CH_3CH_2-OH + 2[Ag(NH_3)_2]^+ + 3\overset{-}{O}H \longrightarrow \text{No reaction}$$

(iii) **Propan-2-ol and 2-methylpropan-2-ol** Propan-2-ol when passed over heated copper at 573 K, a ketone is formed.

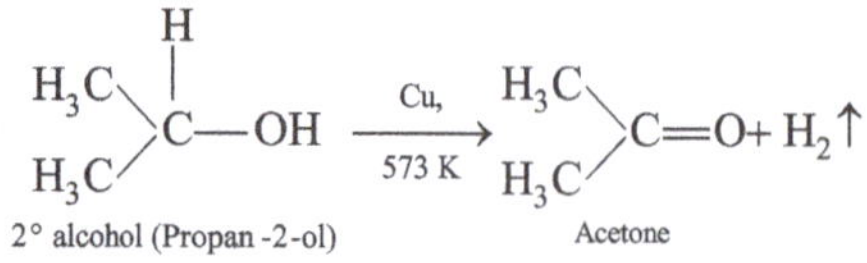

whereas, when 2-methylpropan-2-ol passed over heated copper at 573 K, it gives an alkene.

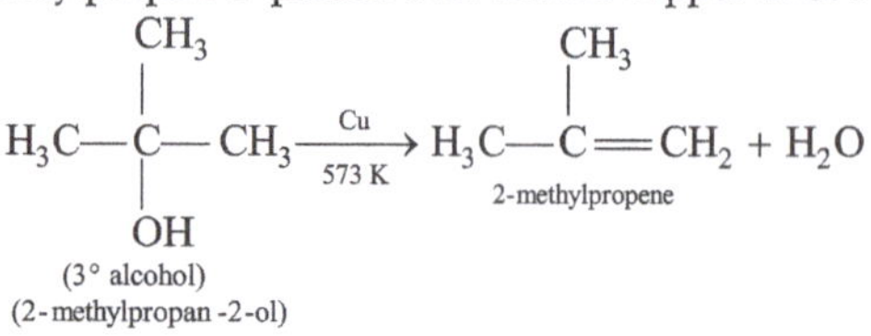

42. (i) When we add H_2O to 4-methylhept-3-ene in the presence of an acid, we get 4-methylheptan-4-ol. (1)

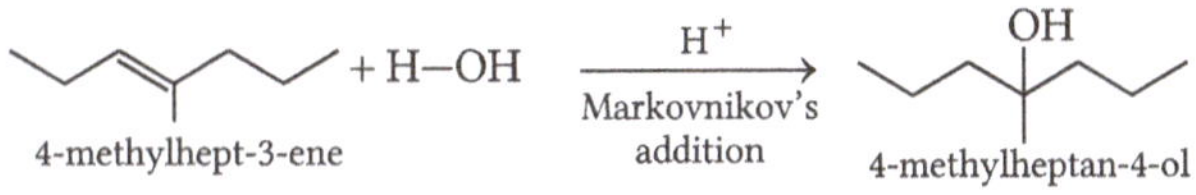

(1)

(ii) On adding H_2O to pent-1-ene in presence of acid, we get pentan-2-ol.

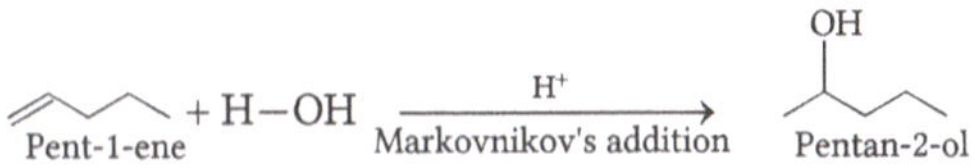

(1)

43. (i) We get a 2° carbocation on protonation of 3-methylbutan-2-ol followed by the loss of H_2O. It is rearranged by 1, 2-hydride shift to more stable 3° carbocation (II). Nucleophilic attack by Br^- ion on this carbocation (II) gives the final product. (1)

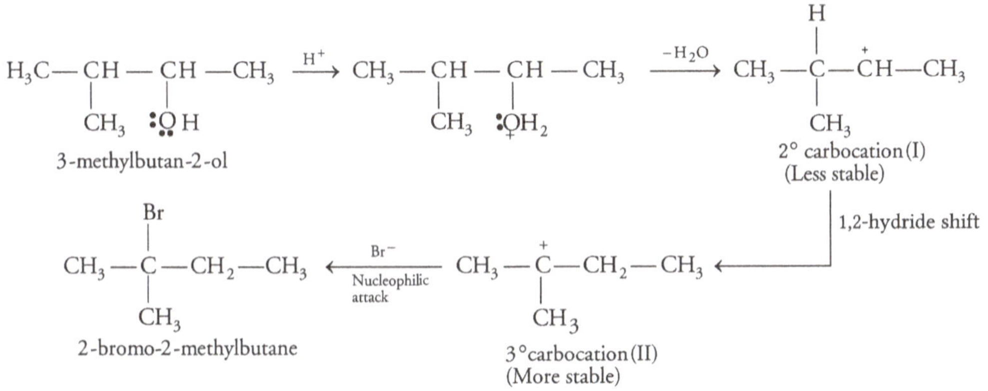

(2)

(ii) Refer to text on page 256. (By hydroboration oxidation) (2)

44.

(i) (a) Propene ⟶ Propan-2-ol

$$\underset{\text{Propene}}{CH_3-CH=CH_2} \xrightarrow{H^+/H_2O} \underset{\text{Propan-2-ol}}{CH_3-\underset{OH}{\underset{|}{CH}}-CH_3}$$

(1)

(b) Ethyl magnesium chloride ⟶ Propan-1-ol

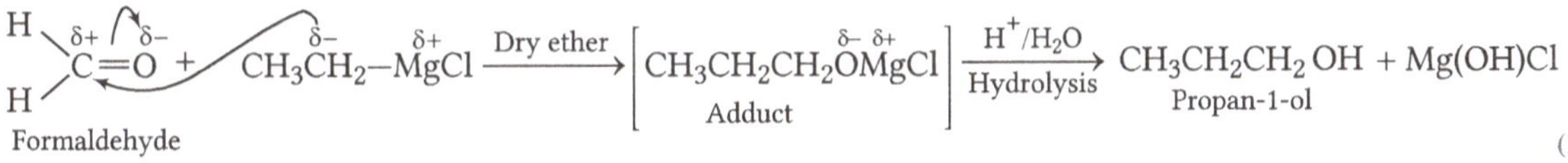

(1)

(c) Methyl magnesium bromide ⟶ 2-methylpropan-2-ol

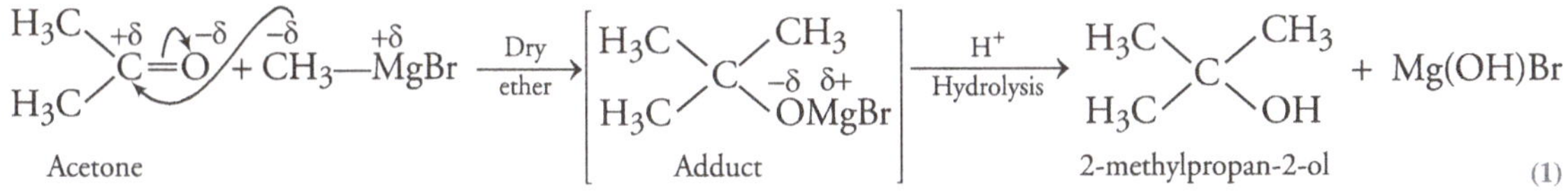

(1)

(ii) Refer to text on page 257 (Physical properties : Boiling points).

45. (i) Refer to text on pages 257 and 258 (Physical properties solubility).

(ii) Refer to text on page 260 (Dehydration)

46. (i)

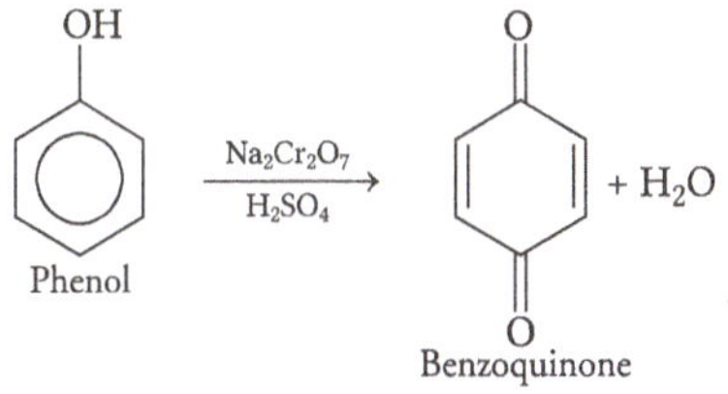

(ii) 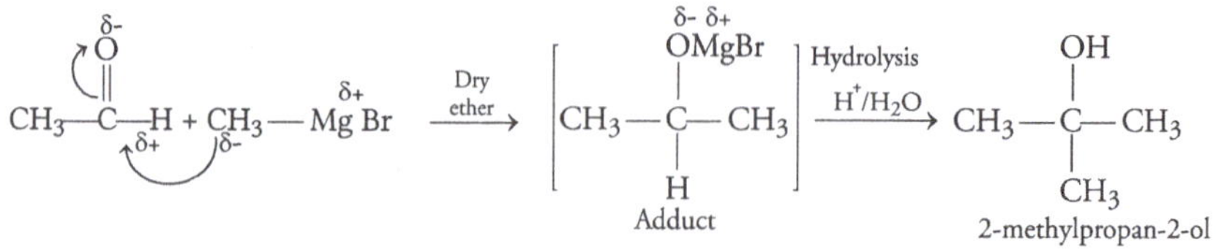

(iii) 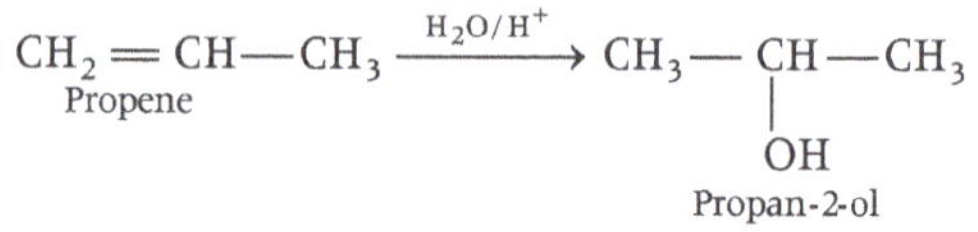

TOPIC 02 Phenols

A phenol contains —OH group(s), directly attached to carbon atom(s) of an aromatic system having general formula is (Ar—OH), where Ar is phenyl group (or aromatic ring).

Classification

Phenols may be classified on the basis of number of —OH *groups present. These are as follows:*

1. Monohydric Phenols

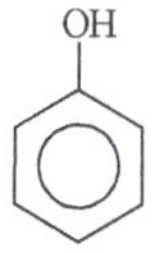

Phenol

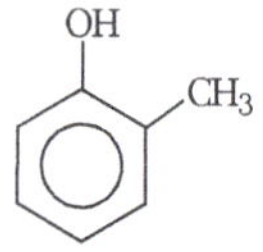

o-cresol

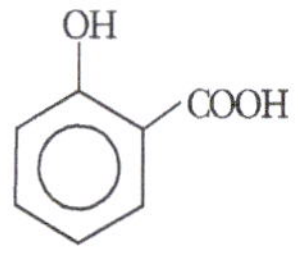

Salicylic acid

2. Dihydric Phenols

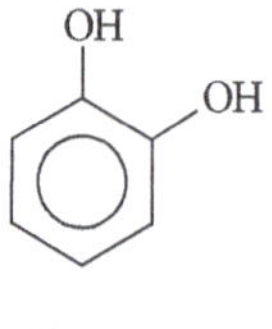

1,2-dihydroxy benzene (catechol)

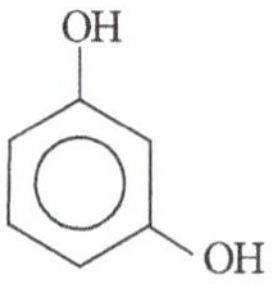

1, 3-dihydroxy benzene (resorcinol)

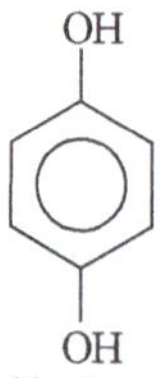

1, 4-dihydroxybenzene (quinol)

3. Trihydric Phenols

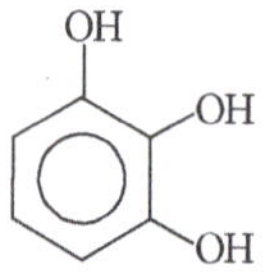

1, 2, 3-trihydroxy benzene (pyrogallol)

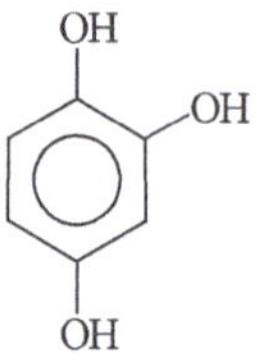

1, 2, 4-trihydroxy benzene (hydroxyquinol)

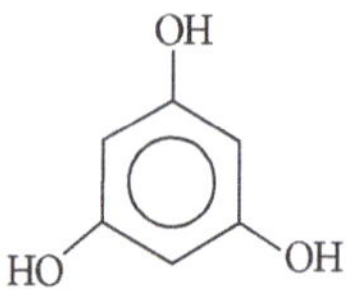

1, 3, 5-trihydroxybenzene (phloroglucinol)

Nomenclature

The name phenol is given to simplest hydroxy derivative of benzene and it is also an accepted IUPAC name.

As the structure of phenol involves a benzene ring in its substituted compounds, the terms *ortho* (1, 2-disubstituted), *meta* (1,3-disubstituted) and *para* (1,4-disubstituted) are often used in the common names.

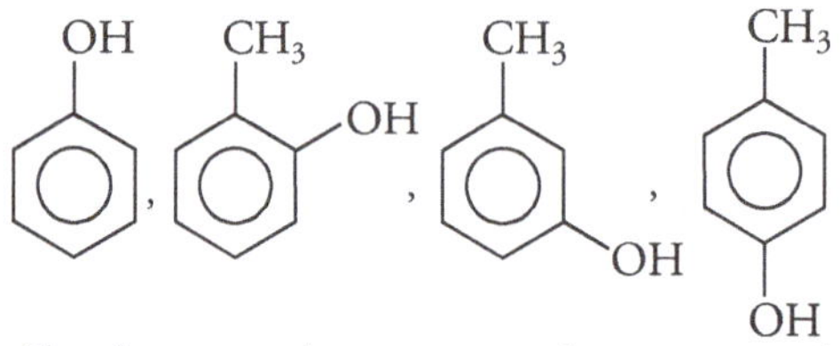

Common name	Phenol	*o*-cresol	*m*-cresol	*p*-cresol
IUPAC name	Phenol	2-methyl phenol	3-methyl phenol	4-methylphenol

Example 1 Name the following compounds according to IUPAC system.

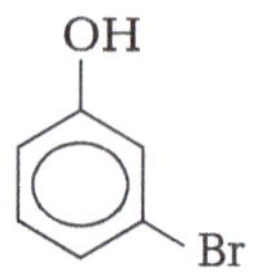

Sol.

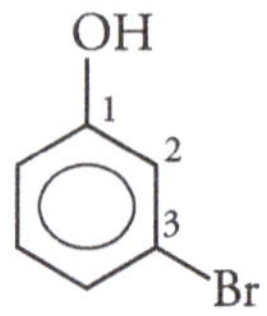

IUPAC name : 3-bromophenol

Structure

In phenols, the —OH group is attached to sp^2 hybridised carbon atom of aromatic ring. This C—O bond is formed by the overlapping of sp^3 orbital of oxygen with sp^2 hybridised orbital of carbon of benzene ring. The carbon-oxygen bond length (136 pm) in phenol is slightly less than that in methanol.

This is due to

(i) partial double bond character on account of the conjugation of unshared electron pairs of oxygen with the aromatic ring.

(ii) sp^2 hybridised state of carbon to which oxygen is attached.

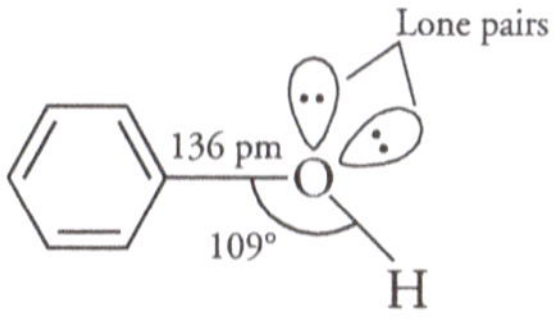

Structure of phenol

Methods of Preparation

Phenols are also called **carbolic acid**. It was first isolated in the early 19th century from coaltar. Now a days, it is commercially produced synthetically. In the laboratory, phenols are prepared from benzene derivatives using any of by the following methods:

1. From Benzene Sulphonic Acid

When benzene is sulphonated with oleum ($H_2S_2O_7$ = conc. $H_2SO_4 + SO_3$), then benzene sulphonic acid is formed which gets further converted to sodium phenoxide, on heating with molten sodium hydroxide. Acidification of sodium phenoxide gives phenol.

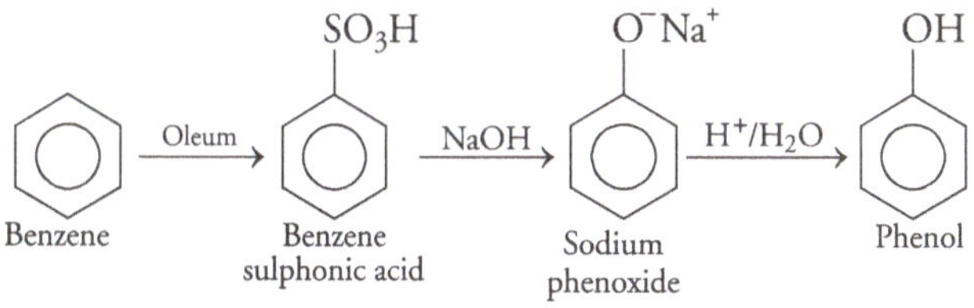

2. From Chlorobenzene (Dow's Process)

Chlorobenzene on fusion with NaOH at 623 K and 320 atm pressure gives sodium phenoxide which on acidification yields phenol.

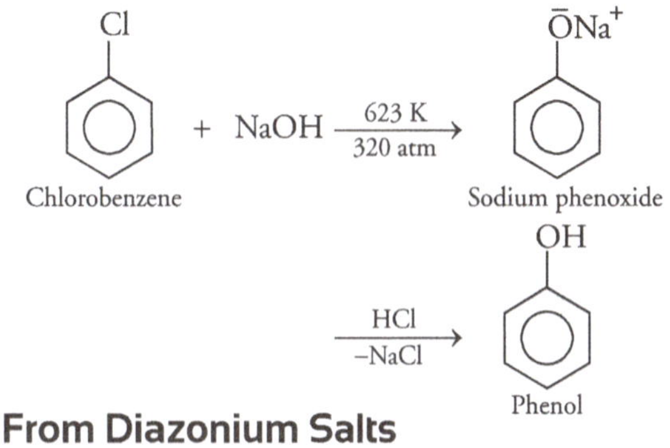

3. From Diazonium Salts

A diazonium salt of aromatic amine (i.e. aniline) is formed by treating amine with nitrous acid ($NaNO_2 + HCl$) at 273-278 K. Diazonium salts on hydrolysis with warm water or dilute acids give phenols.

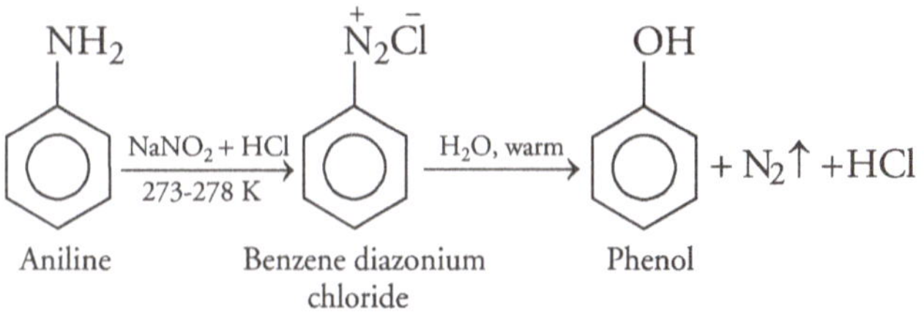

4. From Cumene

Cumene (*iso*-propyl benzene) on aerial oxidation form cumene hydroperoxide which upon subsequent hydrolysis with dilute acid gives phenol and propanone (acetone). Acetone (a by-product) is obtained in large quantities.

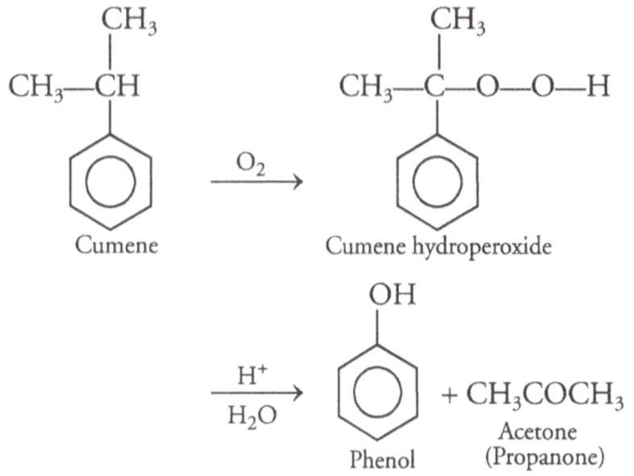

Physical Properties

Some important physical properties are as follows :

1. Physical state

At room temperature, pure phenols are either colourless liquids or solids and usually turn reddish-brown due to atmospheric oxidation.

2. Boiling points

The boiling points of phenols increases with increase in number of C-atoms (due to increase in van der Waals' forces). In phenols, the boiling point decreases with increase of branching in carbon chain because of decrease in van der Waals' forces with decrease in surface area. The —OH group in phenols is involved in intermolecular hydrogen bonding or H-bonding due to which they exist as associated molecules and hence, have higher boiling points.

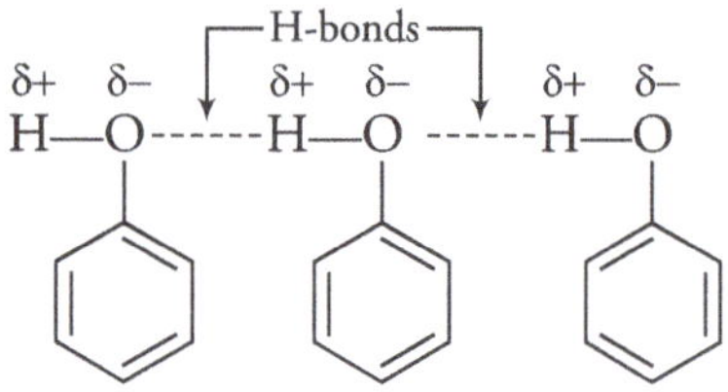

Boiling points of phenols are usually higher in comparison to hydrocarbons, ethers, haloalkanes and haloarenes of comparable molecular masses.

This is mainly due to the presence of intermolecular H-bonding in them which is absent in ethers and hydrocarbons.

CH_3OCH_3	$CH_3CH_2CH_3$
Methoxy methane	Propane
Molecular mass = 46	Molecular mass = 44
Boiling point = 248 K	Boiling point = 231 K

3. Solubility

The solubility of alcohols and phenols in water is due to their ability to form H-bonds with water molecules. Solubility decreases with increase in size of alkyl/aryl (i.e. hydrophobic) groups. However, solubility of isomeric alcohols increases with branching due to decrease in surface area of hydrophobic part.

Chemical Properties

Chemical reactions shown by phenols are as follows:

1. Acidic Character of Phenol

Phenols behave as weak acids. Phenols react with alkali metals and their hydroxides to form salts.

The acidic character of phenols is mainly due to the presence of polar—OH group and resonance stabilisation of phenoxide ion.

$$2C_6H_5OH + 2Na \longrightarrow 2C_6H_5\overset{-}{O}\overset{+}{Na} + H_2$$

$$C_6H_5OH + NaOH \longrightarrow C_6H_5\overset{-}{O}\overset{+}{Na} + H_2O$$

Phenoxide ion is resonance stabilised which makes the phenol more acidic than alcohols. An electron withdrawing group increases the acidic strength of phenol. The effect is more pronounced at *o*- and *p*-positions while the presence of an electron releasing group decreases the acidic strength of phenol.

2. Electrophilic Aromatic Substitution

Phenols undergo electrophilic aromatic substitution reaction readily because —OH group attached to the benzene ring activates the benzene ring towards electrophilic substitution. Further, it directs the incoming group to *ortho* and *para* positions in the ring as these positions become electron rich due to the resonance effect. Common electrophilic aromatic substitution reactions taking place in phenol are:

(i) Bromination (Halogenation)

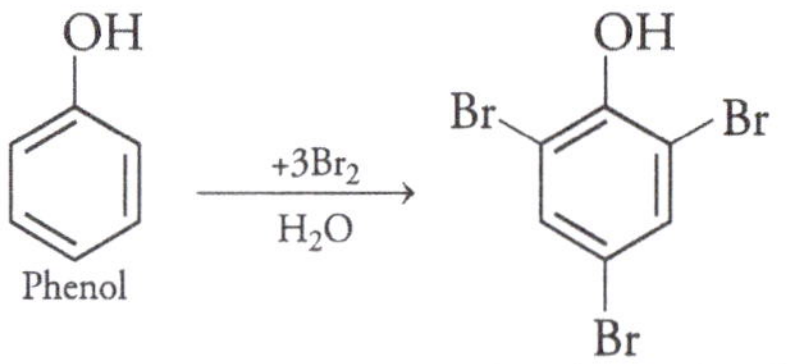

2,4,6-tribromophenol
(Picric acid)

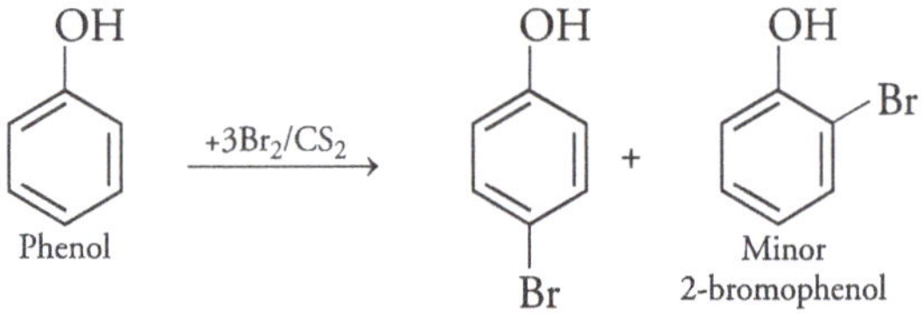

Major
4-bromophenol

Minor
2-bromophenol

(ii) Nitration

In the presence of HNO_3 (dil.), it gives *ortho* and *para* product but with HNO_3 (conc.), it forms picric acid.

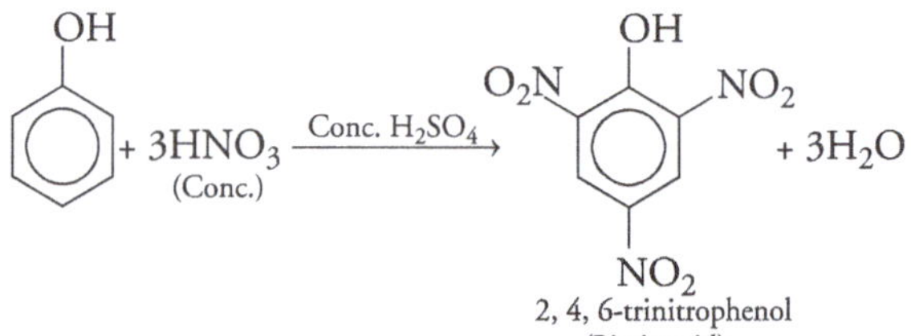

2, 4, 6-trinitrophenol
(Picric acid)

(iii) Sulphonation

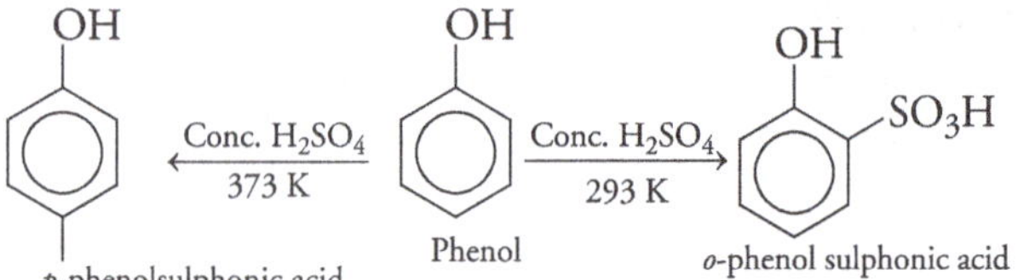

p-phenolsulphonic acid
(Major product)

o-phenol sulphonic acid
(Major product)

3. **Kolbe's Reaction** (Formation of Salicylic Acid)

Phenoxide ion produced by treating phenol with NaOH is more reactive than phenol towards electrophilic aromatic substitution. Hence, it undergoes electrophilic substitution with weak electrophile, CO_2.

o-hydroxybenzoic acid is formed as the main product.

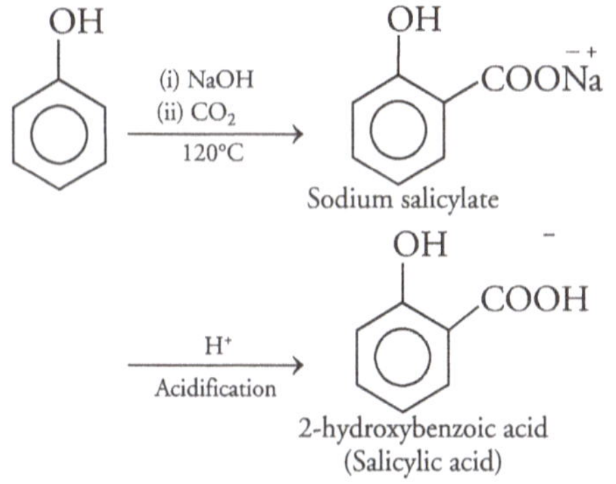

4. **Reimer-Tiemann Reaction**

On treating phenol with $CHCl_3$ (chloroform) in the presence of sodium hydroxide, a —CHO group is introduced at *ortho* position of benzene ring. This reaction is called **Reimer-Tiemann reaction**. In this reaction, electrophile is dichlorocarbene ($:CCl_2$).

The intermediate substituted benzal chloride is hydrolysed in the presence of alkali to produce salicylaldehyde.

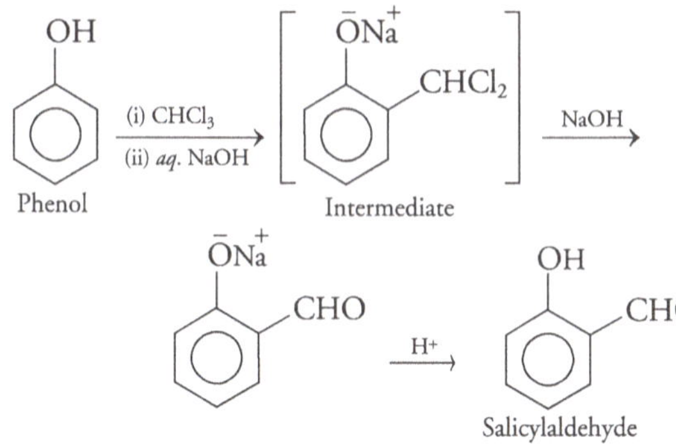

5. Reaction of Phenol with Zinc Dust

Phenol is converted to benzene on heating with zinc dust.

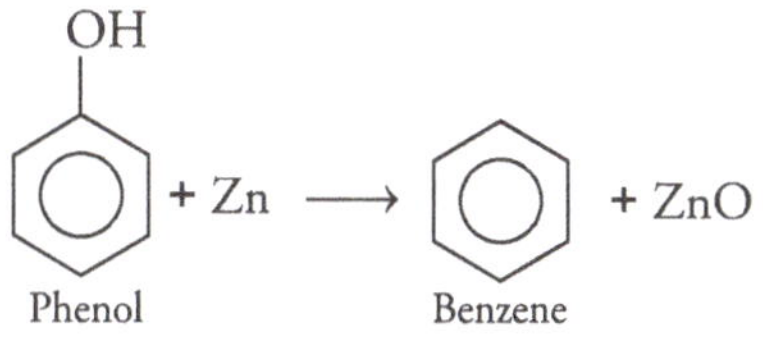

6. **Oxidation**

Oxidation of phenol with chromic acid produces a conjugated diketone known as benzoquinone.

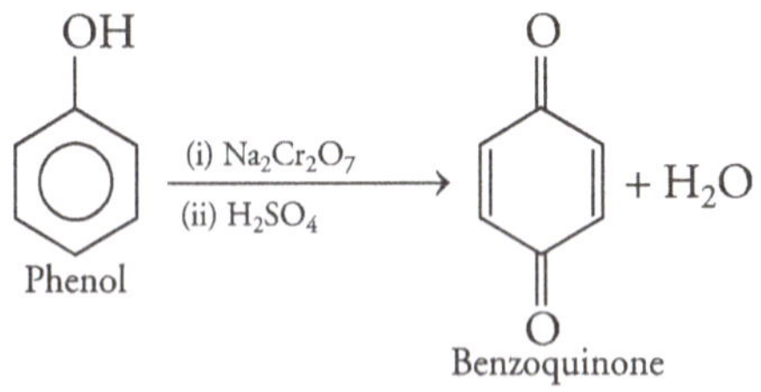

In the presence of air, phenol undergoes oxidation and gives dark-coloured mixtures containing quinones.

7. **Friedel-Crafts Acylation** (Fries Rearrangement)

When esters of phenols are heated with aluminium chloride, the acyl group migrates from the phenolic oxygen to an *o*-or *p*-position of the ring, thus yield a ketone. This reaction is called Fries rearrangement.

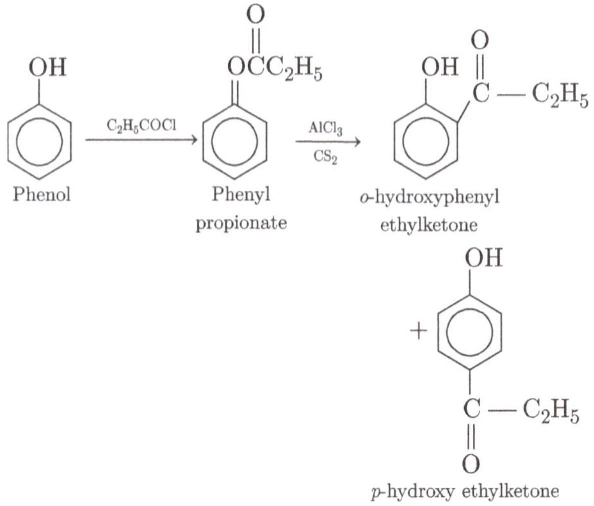

Note In some cases, rearrangement appears to involve generation of an acylium ion $R\ CO^+$ which then attacks the ring as in ordinary Friedel-Crafts acylation.

8. **Reaction with PCl_5**

The replacement of —OH group of phenol by a halogen atom is quite difficult and the yield of chlorobenzene is very poor.

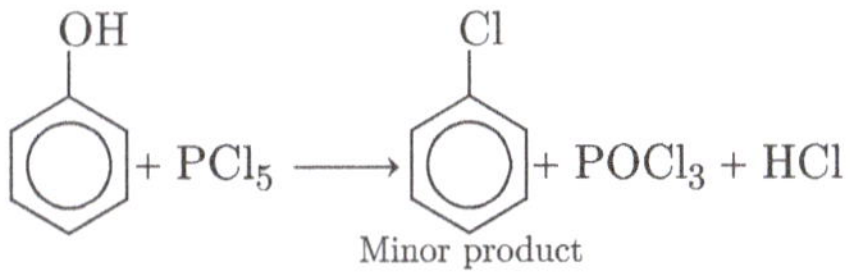

9. **Reaction with Acetyl Chloride and Acetic Anhydride**

Phenol reacts with acid chlorides and anhydrides in alkaline solution to form phenylesters. This reaction is known as **acylation**.

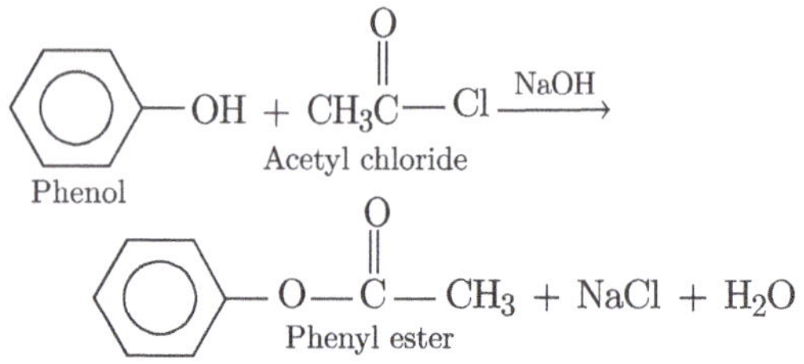

Uses

Phenols are used as an antiseptic and disinfectant in soaps, in making of drugs, azo dyes, as a preservative for inks, in the manufacturing of picric acid. It is also used as an explosive.

Test for Phenols

(i) **$FeCl_3$ Test** Phenols react with neutral $FeCl_3$ and give violet coloured water soluble complex $[Fe(OC_6H_5)_6]^{3-}$.

$$6C_6H_5OH + FeCl_3 \rightarrow 3H^+ + [Fe(OC_6H_5)_6]^{3-} + 3HCl$$

(ii) **Azo Dye Test** This reaction gives bright coloured azo dyes.

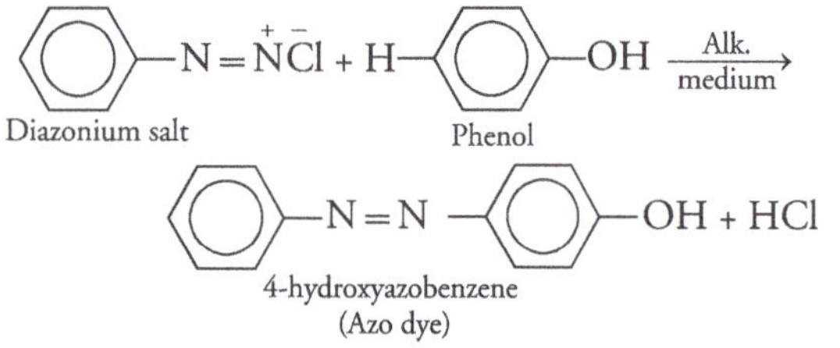

Topic Practice 2

Very Short Answer Type Questions

(1 Mark)

1. Fill in the Blanks

(i) Phenol on .... with chromic acid gives ....

(ii) Phenol is .... because of resource stabilisation of its conjugate base namely ....

(iii) Phenol when distilled with zinc dust gives ....

2. Objective Type Questions

(i) IUPAC name of *m*- cresol is ....

(a) 3-methylphenol (b) 3-chlorophenol
(c) 3-methoxyphenol (d) benzene-1, 3-diol

(ii) Which of the following compounds will react with sodium hydroxide solution in water?

(a) C_6H_5OH (b) $C_6H_5CH_2OH$
(c) $(CH_3)_3COH$ (d) C_2H_5OH

(iii) Which of the following species can act as the strongest base?

(a) $^{\ominus}OH$ (b) $^{\ominus}OR$
(c) $^{\ominus}OC_6H_5$ (d) 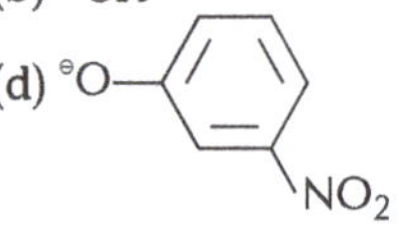

3. Match the structures of the compounds given in Column I with the name of the compounds given in Column II and choose the correct answer using the codes given below :

	Column I		Column II
A.	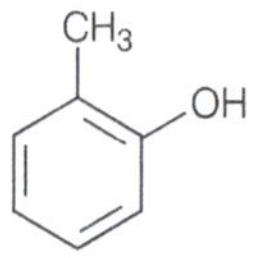	(i)	Hydroquinone
B.	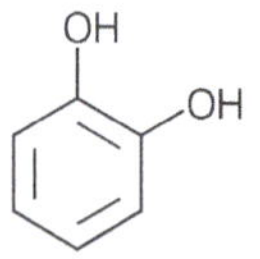	(ii)	Phenetole
C.	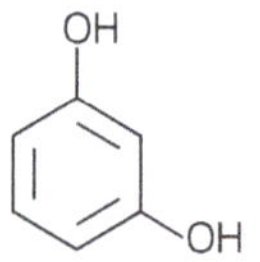	(iii)	Catechol
D.		(iv)	*o*-cresol
E.	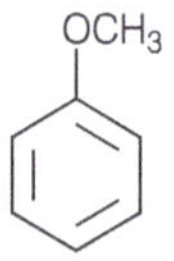	(v)	Quinone
F.	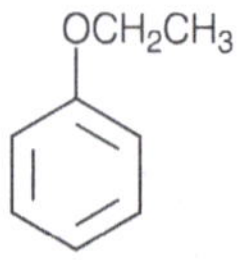	(vi)	Resorcinol
		(vii)	Anisole

Structure labels — A: CH_3, OH; B: OH, OH; C: OH, OH; D: OH, OH; E: OCH_3; F: OCH_2CH_3

Codes

	A	B	C	D	E	F
(a)	(i)	(iii)	(iv)	(v)	(vi)	(ii)
(b)	(iv)	(iii)	(vi)	(i)	(vii)	(ii)
(c)	(i)	(iv)	(v)	(ii)	(ii)	(vii)
(d)	(i)	(ii)	(vi)	(iv)	(iii)	(v)

4. Write the IUPAC name of the given compound:

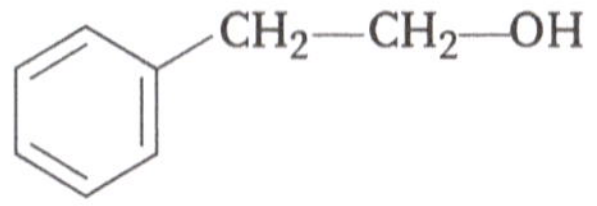

5. Write the IUPAC name of the following compounds

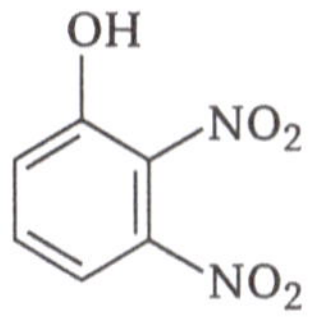

6. Give the structure of the molecule of a compound whose IUPAC name is 1-phenylpropan-2-ol. **NCERT**

7. Write the IUPAC name of the given compound.

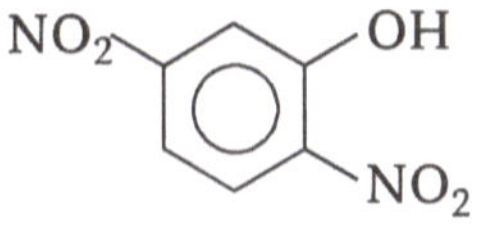

8. *o*-nitrophenol has lower boiling point than *p*-nitrophenol. Explain.

Or Which of the following isomers is more volatile? *o*-nitrophenol or *p*-nitrophenol **NCERT Exemplar**

9. Why do phenols not give the protonation reaction readily?

10. Write the equation involved in the acetylation of salicylic acid.

11. How will you convert phenol to salicylic acid? **ISC 2004**

12. In Kolbe's reaction, instead of phenol, phenoxide ion is treated with CO_2. Why?

13. Give the balanced equation for the following name reaction : Reimer–Tiemann reaction **ISC 2015**

Or Give balanced equation for the preparation of salicylaldehyde from phenol. **ISC 2013**

Or

Give an example (equation) for the following name reaction:
Reimer-Tiemann reaction **ISC 2011**

Or

Give balanced chemical equation when phenol is heated with chloroform and sodium hydroxide. **ISC 2009**

14. How is toluene obtained from phenol?

Short Answer Type I Questions

(2 Marks)

15. Write the equation and name the following reaction Phenol with acetyl chloride in the presence of .

16. How will you convert phenol to picric acid? Write the relevant equation.

17. Give reason:
Phenol boils at higher temperature than haloarenes of comparable molecular mass.

18. Both methanol and phenol have —OH group but the dipole moment of methanol (1.71 D) is higher than that of phenol (1.54 D). Why?

19. How can you convert benzene to phenol? **ISC 2012**

20. How will you bring about the following conversion?
Phenol to benzoic acid **ISC 2009**

21. Explain why is *ortho*-nitrophenol more acidic than *ortho*-methoxyphenol? **NCERT**

22. *Ortho* and *para*-nitrophenols are more acidic than phenol. Draw the resonance structures of the corresponding phenoxide ions. **NCERT Intext**

Or

Explain why *p*-nitrophenol is more acidic than phenol?

23. Give reason, why phenol is more easily nitrated than benzene?

24. Arrange the following compounds in the increasing order of their acidic strength :
p-cresol, *p*-nitrophenol, phenol

25. Give equations of the following reactions.
(i) Bromine in CS_2 with phenol.
(ii) Dilute HNO_3 with phenol.
(iii) Treating phenol with chloroform in the presence of aqueous NaOH. **NCERT**

26. How will you convert the following
(i) Phenol to 2, 4, 6-tribromophenol
(ii) Phenol to picric acid

27. How will the following be obtained ? (Give chemical equations)
(a) Ethanol from Grignard's reagent.
(b) Diethyl ether from sodium ethoxide. **ISC 2023**

28. Convert the following by giving chemical equations for each.
(i) Ethyl bromide to diethyl ether
(ii) Phenol to salicylaldehyde **ISC 2024**

29. Explain the following reaction with an example.
Kolbe's reaction

30. Describe the chemical test to distinguish between ethanol and phenol.

Short Answer Type II Questions

(3 Marks)

31. Classify the following as primary, secondary and tertiary alcohols.

(i) 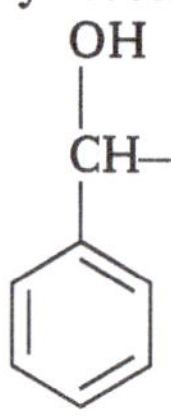
(ii) 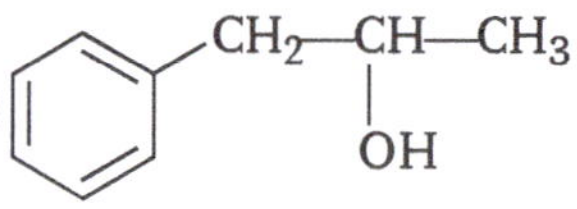

(iii) 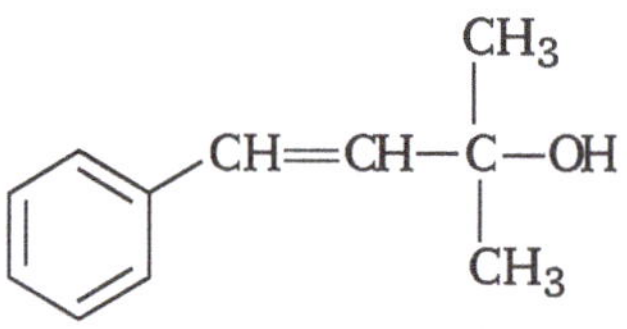

NCERT Intext

32. Give the structures and IUPAC names of monohydric phenols of molecular formula C_7H_8O. **NCERT**

33. Give one chemical test to distinguish between the following pairs of compounds:
Acetone and phenol **ISC 2013**

34. Give one test to distinguish between phenol and benzoic acid. **ISC 2004**

35. Show how will you synthesise
(i) 1-phenyl ethanol from a suitable alkene?
(ii) cyclohexyl methanol using an alkyl halide by an S_N2 mechanism? **NCERT**

36. Predict the major product of acid catalysed dehydration of 1-methyl cyclohexanol **NCERT Intext**

Long Answer Type Questions

(5 Marks)

37. (i) Show how would you synthesise the following alcohols from alkenes?

(a) 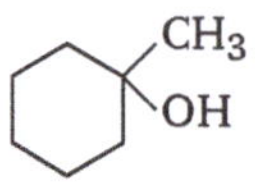 (b) 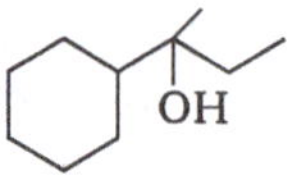

(ii) While separating a mixture of *ortho* and *para* nitrophenols by steam distillation, name the isomer which will be steam volatile. Give reason. **NCERT**

38. (i) Explain with reason:
(a) Presence of electron withdrawing group increases the acidic character of phenol.
(b) Phenol is more acidic than ethanol.
(ii) How would you obtain picric acid from phenol?

Hints & Solutions

1. (i) oxidation, *p*-benzoquinone
(ii) acidic, phenoxide ion (iii) benzene
2. (i) → (b), (ii) → (a), (iii) → (b)
3. (b) A → (iv), B → (iii), C→ (vi), D.→(i) E→(vii), F.→ (ii)
4. **IUPAC name** 2-phenylethanol (1)
5. 2,3-dinitrophenol
6. $\overset{3}{CH_3}-\overset{2}{CH}(OH)-\overset{1}{CH_2}-C_6H_5$
7. 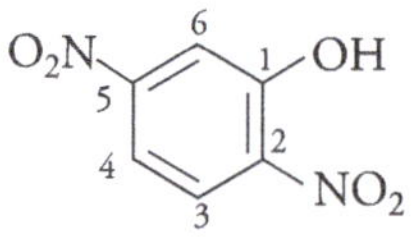

IUPAC name 2,5-dinitrophenol

8. In *o*-nitrophenol, intramolecular H-bonding exists which makes it more volatile whereas in *p*-nitrophenol, intermolecular hydrogen bonding exists, which makes it less volatile. That's why, *o*-nitrophenol has lower boiling point than *p*-nitrophenol.
9. In phenols, the lone pairs of electrons on the oxygen atom are delocalised over the benzene ring due to resonance and hence, are not easily available for protonation to destabilise O—H bond thus, making protonation difficult.
10. 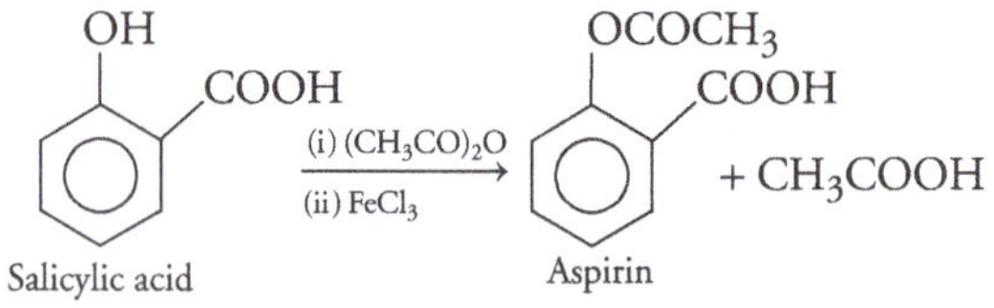

11. Phenol to salicylic acid
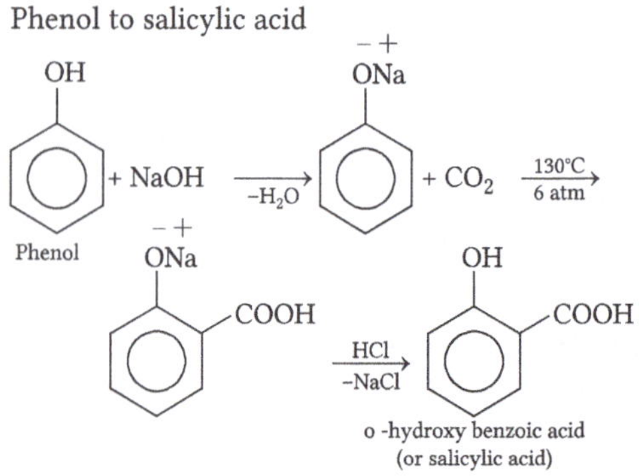

This reaction is named as Kolbe's reaction.

12. Phenoxide ion is more reactive than phenol towards electrophilic aromatic substitution and can undergo electrophilic substitution easily with CO_2, which is a weak electrophile.

13. Reimer-Tiemann reaction

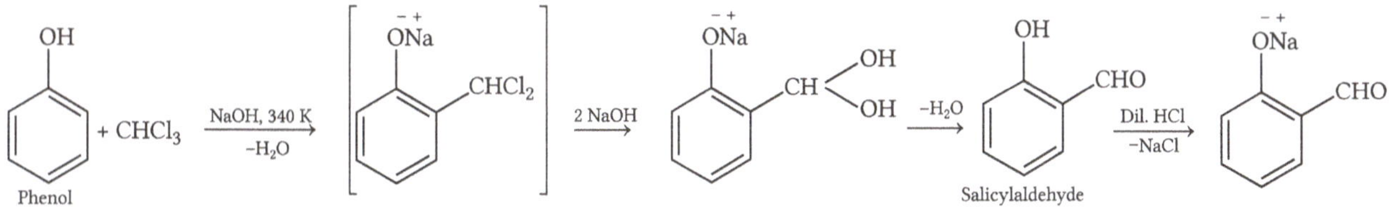

14.

15. Phenols undergo Friedel-Crafts acylation reaction when treated with acetyl chloride in the presence of   to give the mixture of *o* - and *p* -derivatives.

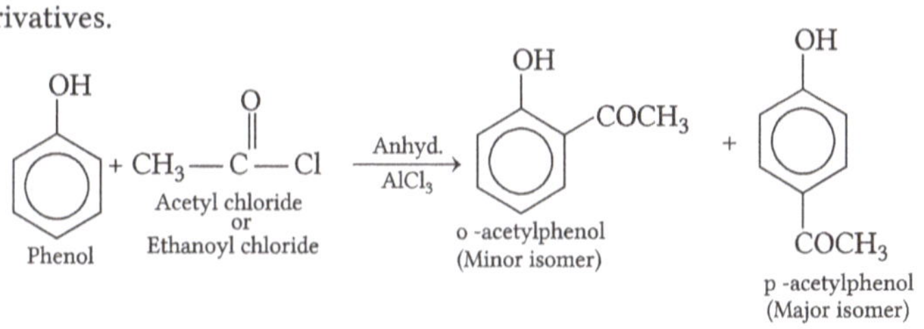

16. When nitration of phenol is carried out with conc. nitric acid in the presence of conc. sulphuric acid then picric acid (2, 4, 6-trinitrophenol) is obtained.

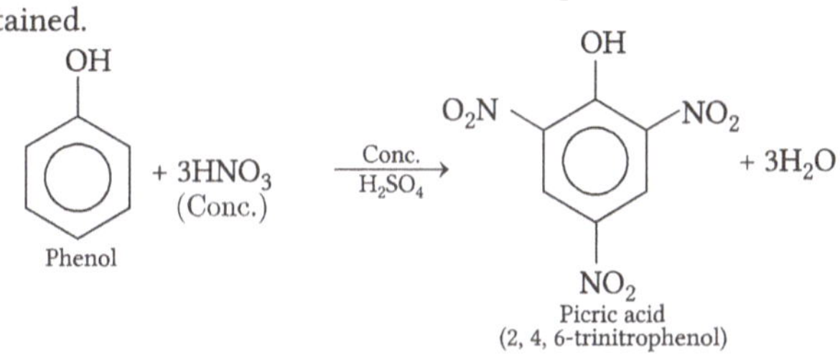

17. Refer to text on page 271 and 272 (Physical properties-Boiling points).

18. **Hint** In phenol, C – O bond is less polar due to electron withdrawing effect of the benzene ring whereas in methanol, C—O bond is more polar due to electron releasing effect of —CH_3 group. (2)

19. **Benzene to phenol**

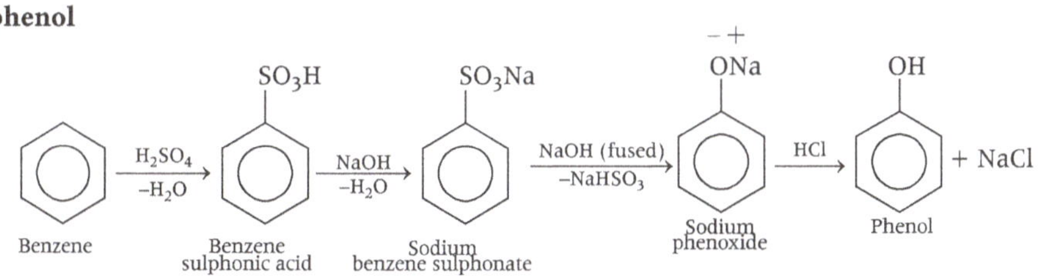

20. **Phenol to benzoic acid**

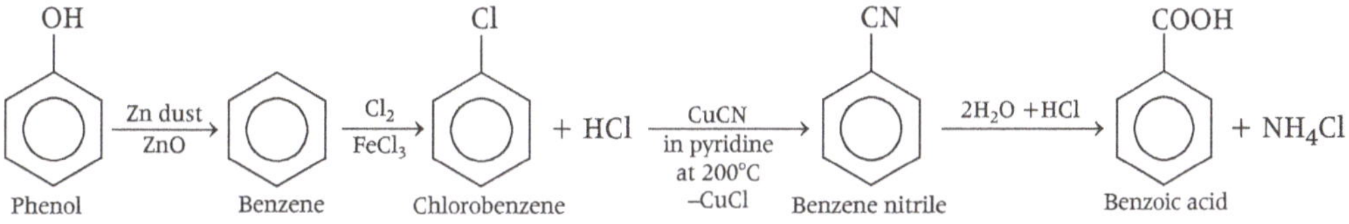

21. Nitro (NO_2) group is electron withdrawing whereas methoxy (OCH_3) group is electron releasing in nature. *o*-nitrophenol produces H^+ ions easily but methoxyphenol does not. This is because *o*-nitrophenoxide ion is stabilised due to resonance. This is not true with *o*-methoxyphenoxide ion. The two negative charges repel each other thereby destabilising it.

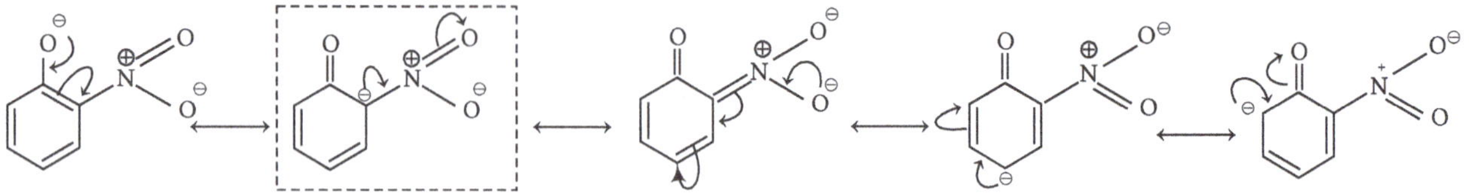

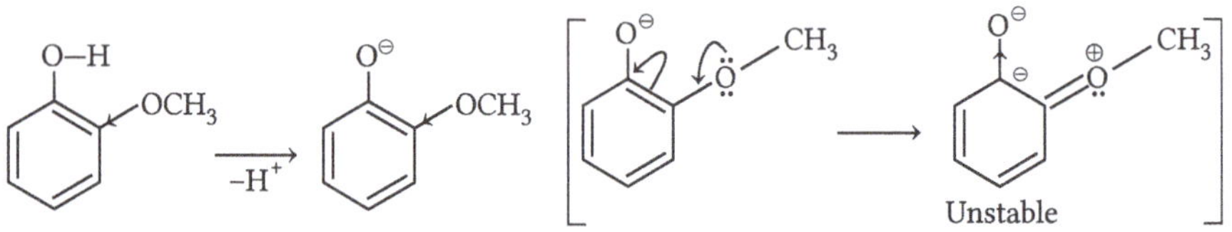

(2)

22. Resonating structures of *o*-nitrophenoxide ions that are formed by the loss of proton from *o*-nitrophenol are as follows:

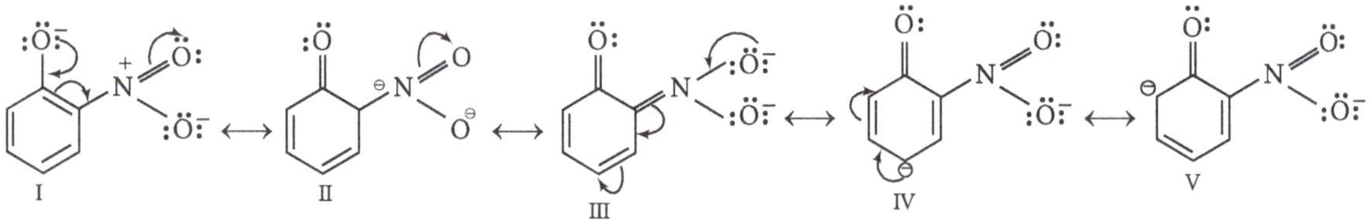

(½)

Resonating structures of *p*-nitrophenoxide ions that are formed by the loss of proton from *p*-nitrophenol are as follows:

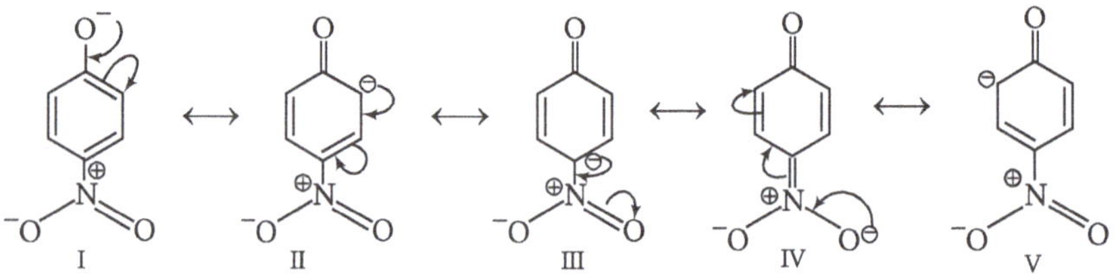

(½)

Resonating structures of phenoxide ions that are formed by the loss of proton from phenol are as follows:

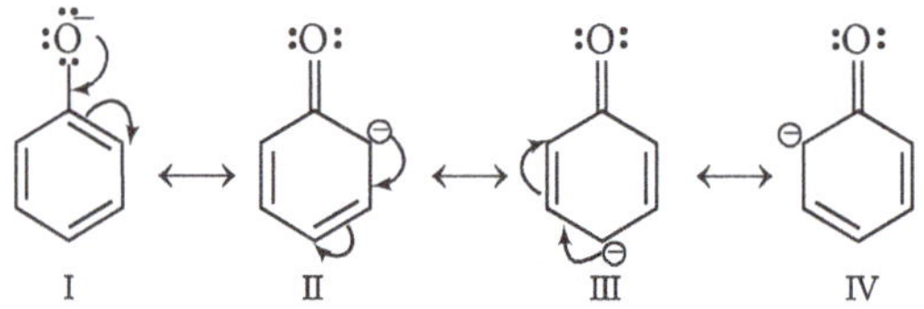

(1/2)

It is clearly evident from the above structures that due to $-R$-effect of — NO_2 group, *o*-and *p*-nitrophenoxide ions are more stable than phenoxide ions. Consequently, *o*- and *p*-nitrophenols are more acidic than phenols. (1/2)

23. In phenol, — OH group activates the benzene ring and increases the electron density at *ortho* and *para* positions. Hence, nitration (an electrophilic substitution) can be carried out easily.

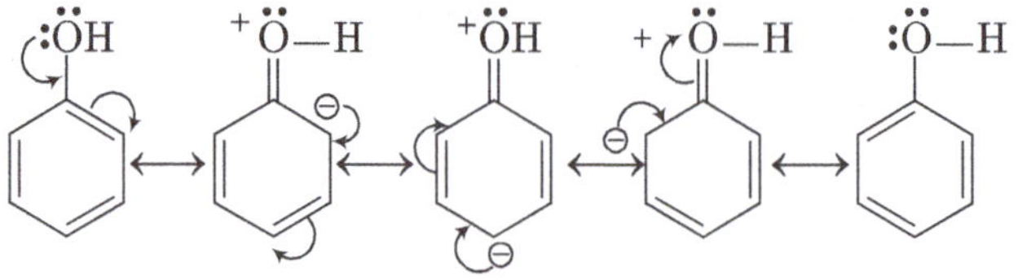

While in benzene, no such activating group is present, thus nitration is carried out under only special conditions.

24. (i) Electron withdrawing groups such as $—NO_2$, increases the acidic character while electron releasing group such as $— CH_3$ decreases the acidic character. Thus, the increasing order of acidic strength is

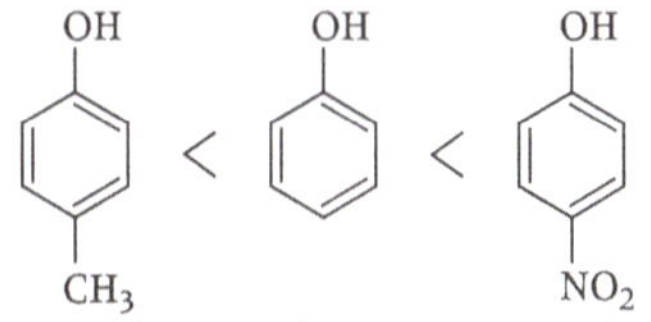

(p-cresol) (Phenol) (p-nitrophenol)

25. (i) Refer to text on page 272 (Bromination).
(ii) Refer to text on page 272 (Nitration).
(iii) Refer to text on page 273 (Reimer-Tiemann reaction).

$\left(4 \times \frac{1}{2} = 2\right)$

26. (i)

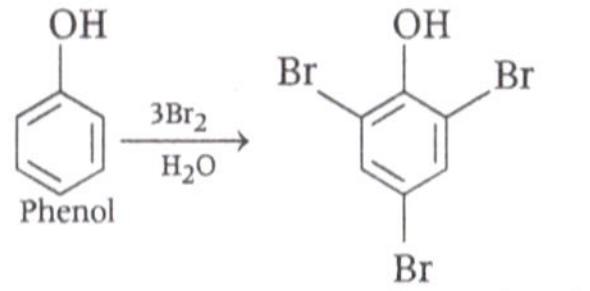

2, 4,6-tribromophenol

(ii) Refer to text on page 272 (Bromination).

27. (i) When methanal reacts with methyl magnesium bromide in presence of dry ether to give a complex which on hydrolysis gives ethanol.

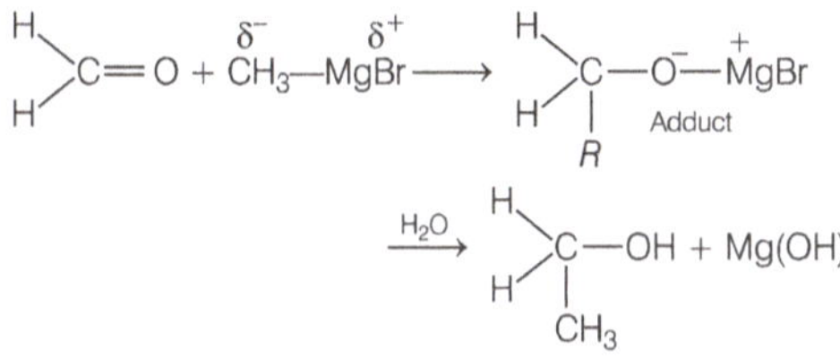

(ii) Williamson's synthesis

$$CH_3—CH_2—O—CH_2—CH_3 + NaBr$$
Diethyl ether

28. (i) **Ethyl bromide to diethyl ether**

$$\underset{\text{Ethyl bromide}}{CH_3CH_2Br} + \underset{\text{Sodium ethoxide}}{NaO—C_2H_5} \longrightarrow \underset{\text{Diethyl ether}}{CH_3CH_2—O—CH_2CH_3} + NaBr$$

(ii) **Phenol to salicylaldehyde**

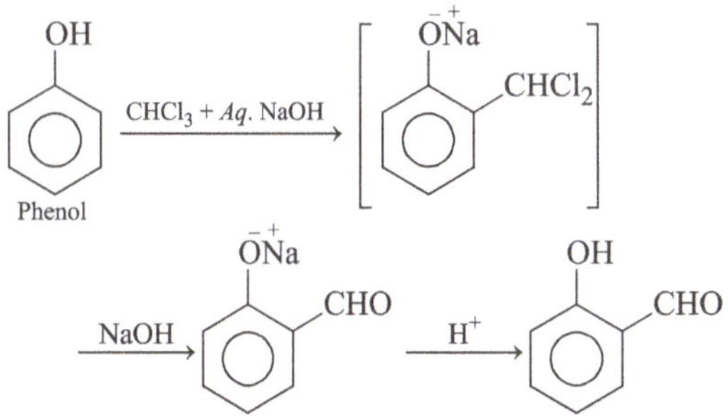

Salicylaldehyde

29. Refer to text on page 273 (Kolbe reaction).

30. Ethanol when warmed with $NaOH + I_2$, gives yellow ppt. of iodoform while phenol does not give this test.

$$\underset{\text{Ethanol}}{CH_3CH_2OH} + 4NaOI \longrightarrow \underset{\substack{\text{Iodoform}\\\text{(Yellow ppt.)}}}{CHI_3\downarrow}$$
$$+ HCOO^-Na^+ + NaI + H_2O + 2NaOH$$

$$\underset{\text{Phenol}}{C_6H_5OH} + NaOH \longrightarrow \text{No yellow ppt.}$$

(2)

31. Secondary alcohols-(i), (ii) Tertiary alcohols-(iii)

32. The phenolic compound with molecular formula C_7H_8O, has three isomers that are as follows:

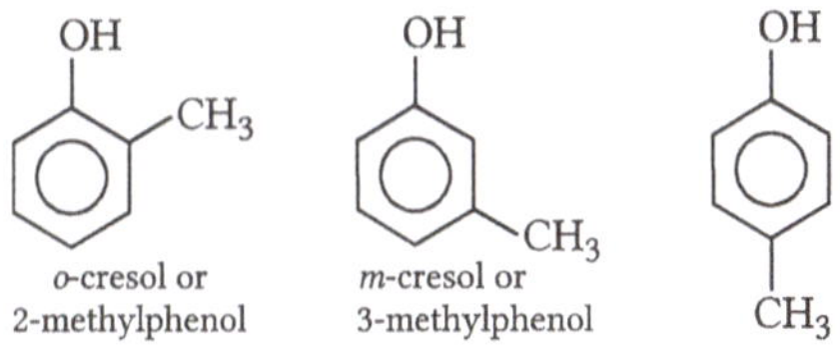

o-cresol or 2-methylphenol | m-cresol or 3-methylphenol | p-cresol or 4-methylphenol

$(3 \times 1 = 3)$

33. Following methods can be used to distinguish acetone and phenol:

(i) Phenol gives violet colour with neutral $FeCl_3$ solution while acetone does not give this test.

$$C_6H_5OH + FeCl_3 \longrightarrow \text{Violet colour}$$
$$CH_3COCH_3 + FeCl_3 \longrightarrow \text{No reaction}$$

(ii) Acetone has methyl group linked to the carbonyl carbon atom which is oxidised by sodium hypohalite to sodium salt of ethanoic acid and iodoform while phenol does not give this test.

$$CH_3—\overset{\overset{\displaystyle O}{\|}}{C}—CH_3 \xrightarrow{3NaOI} CH_3CO\overset{-}{O}\overset{+}{Na} + CHI_3\downarrow + 3NaOH$$

$$C_6H_5OH \xrightarrow{NaOI} \text{No reaction}$$

34. Following methods are used distinguish phenol and benzoic acid.

(i) **Sodium hydrogen carbonate test** Benzoic acid reacts with sodium hydrogen carbonate to evolve brisk effervescence of CO_2 while phenol does not react.

$$C_6H_5COOH + NaHCO_3 \longrightarrow C_6H_5CO\overset{-}{O}\overset{+}{Na} + H_2O + CO_2\uparrow$$

(ii) **$FeCl_3$ test** Phenol gives violet colour with neutral solution while benzoic acid gives buff coloured ppt.

$$3C_6H_5OH + FeCl_3 \longrightarrow \underset{\text{(Violet colour)}}{[(C_6H_5O)_3\,Fe]^{3-}} + 3\,HCl$$

$$3\,C_6H_5COOH + FeCl_3 \longrightarrow \underset{\text{(Buff coloured ppt.)}}{[Fe(C_6H_5COO)_3]} + 3HCl$$

35. (i) On adding H_2O to ethenyl benzene in the presence of dil. H_2SO_4, we get 1-phenyl ethanol.

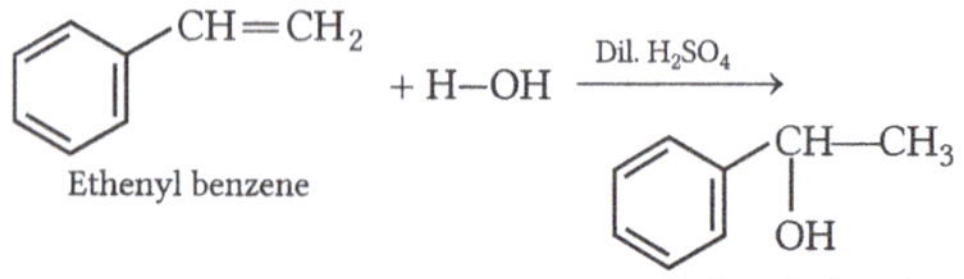

(1)

(ii) Hydrolysis of cyclohexyl methyl bromide by aqueous NaOH gives cyclohexyl methanol.

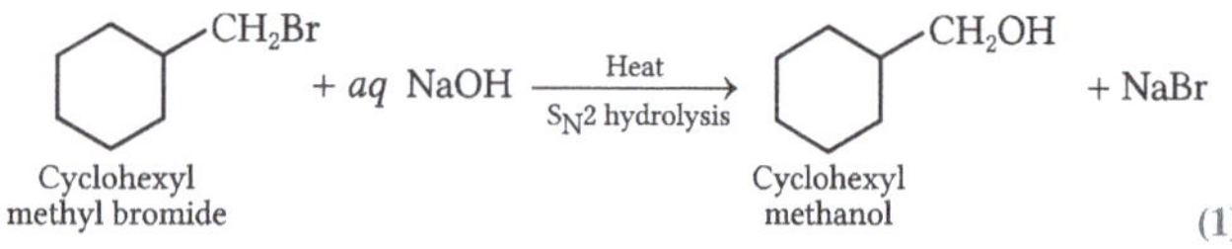

(1)

36.

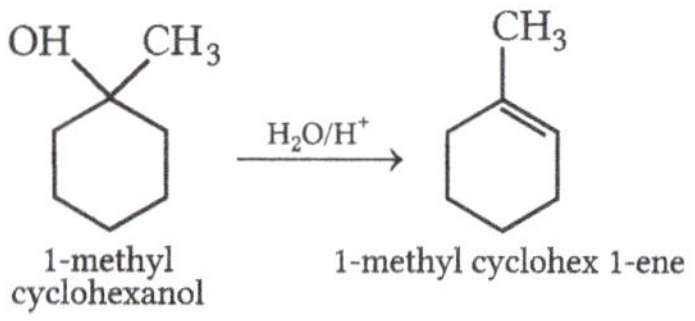

(1½)

37. (i) (a) On adding H_2O to 1-methylcyclohexene in the presence of acid, we get 1-methylcyclohexan-1-ol.

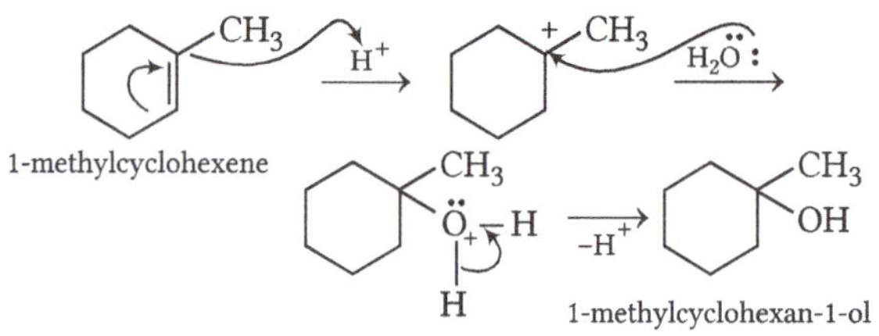

(b) When we add H_2O to 2-cyclohexylbut-2-ene or 2-cyclohexylidenebutane, in the presence of an acid, the product obtained is same, i.e. 2-cyclohexylbutan-2-ol.

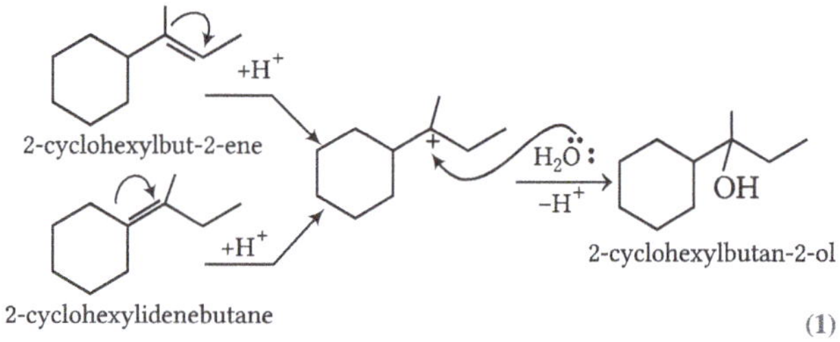

(1)

(ii) *o*-nitrophenol is steam volatile due to intramolecular H-bonding and hence, can be separated by steam distillation from *p*-nitrophenol, which is not steam volatile. (1)

38. (i) (a) Refer to text on page 272 (Acidic character of phenol).

(b) Refer to text on page 272 (Acidic character of phenol).

(ii) Refer to text on page 272 (Nitration).

TOPIC 03 Ethers

The substitution of a hydrogen atom in a hydrocarbon (aliphatic/aromatic) by an alkoxy (O*R*)/aryloxy (OAr) group yield ethers.

General formula; $C_nH_{2n+2}O$.

e.g. $$\underset{\text{Alkane}}{R—H} \xrightarrow[+\,OR]{-\,H} \underset{\text{Ether}}{R—OR}$$

$$Ar—H \xrightarrow[+\,OR]{-\,H} \underset{\text{Ether}}{Ar—O—R}$$

Classification

Ethers can be classified as :

(i) **Simple or Symmetrical Ethers** Same alkyl or aryl groups are attached to the oxygen atom.

e.g. $$\underset{\text{Dimethyl ether}}{CH_3OCH_3}$$

$$\underset{\text{Diethyl ether}}{C_2H_5OC_2H_5}$$

(ii) **Unsymmetrical Ethers** Different alkyl or aryl groups are attached to the oxygen atom.

e.g. $$\underset{\text{Methyl phenyl ether}}{C_6H_5—O—CH_3}$$

$$\underset{\text{Methyl ethyl ether}}{C_2H_5—O—CH_3}$$

Nomenclature

In IUPAC system, ethers are named as alkoxy alkane. Ethereal oxygen along with smaller alkyl group is called alkoxy.

Larger alkyl group is considered as a part of alkane. Common names of ethers are derived from the names of alkyl or aryl groups written as a separate word in an alphabetical order and adding the word 'ether'.

Common and IUPAC Names of Some Ethers

Compound	Common name	IUPAC name
CH_3OCH_3	Dimethyl ether	Methoxymethane
$C_2H_5OC_2H_5$	Diethyl ether	Ethoxyethane
$CH_3OCH_2CH_2CH_3$	Methyl *n*-propyl ether	1-methoxypropane
$C_6H_5OCH_3$	Methyl *n*-phenyl ether (anisole)	Methoxybenzene
$C_6H_5OCH_2CH_3$	Ethyl phenyl ether (phenetole)	Ethoxybenzene
$C_6H_5O(CH_2)_6—CH_3$	Heptyl phenyl ether	1-phenoxyheptane
$CH_3O—\underset{\underset{CH_3}{\vert}}{CH}—CH_3$	Methyl *iso*-propyl ether	2-methoxypropane
$C_6H_5—O—CH_2—CH_2—\underset{\underset{CH_3}{\vert}}{CH}—CH_3$	Phenyl *iso*-pentyl ether	3-methylbutoxybenzene
$CH_3—O—CH_2—CH_2—OCH_3$	—	1, 2-dimethoxyethane
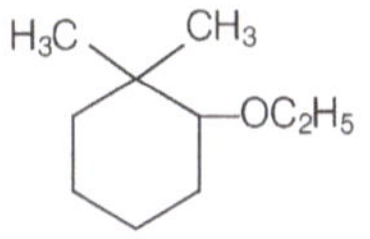	—	2-ethoxy-1,1-dimethyl cyclohexane

Example 1 Write the IUPAC names of the following compounds.

(i) $CH_3—O—CH_2—\underset{\underset{CH_3}{\vert}}{CH}—CH_3$

(ii) $C_6H_5—O—C_2H_5$

(iii) $C_6H_5—O—C_7H_{15}(n\text{-})$

(iv) $CH_3—CH_2—O—\underset{\underset{CH_3}{\vert}}{CH}—CH_2CH_3$ **NCERT**

Sol.

(i) 1-methoxy-2-methylpropane (ii) Ethoxybenzene

(iii) 1-phenoxyheptane (iv) 2-ethoxybutane

Structure

In ethers, the four electron pairs, i.e. the two bond pairs and two lone pairs of electrons on oxygen are arranged in approximate tetrahedral arrangement.

Bond angle is slightly greater than tetrahedral angle because of the repulsive interaction between two bulky (—*R*) groups.

The C—O bond length (141 pm) is almost the same as in alcohols, e.g. methoxy methane.

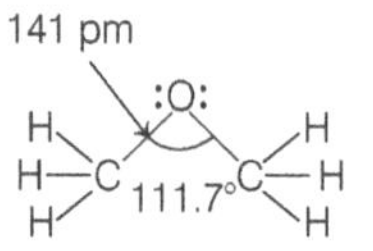

Methods of Preparation of Aliphatic and Aryl Ethers

Ethers can be prepared by the following methods :

1. Dehydration of Alcohols

Alcohols undergo dehydration in the presence of protic acids such as H_2SO_4, H_3PO_4.

Formation of the reaction product, alkene or ether depends upon the reaction conditions, e.g. ethanol is dehydrated to ethoxyethane at 413 K in the presence of sulphuric acid.

$$\underset{\text{Ethanol (Excess)}}{2C_2H_5OH} \xrightarrow[413\text{ K}]{\text{Conc. } H_2SO_4} \underset{\text{Ethoxyethane}}{C_2H_5—O—C_2H_5} + H_2O$$

2. Williamson's Ether Synthesis

This is one of the best and important laboratory methods for the preparation of symmetrical and unsymmetrical ethers. In this method, an alkyl halide is allowed to react with sodium alkoxide.

$$\underset{\text{Alkyl halide}}{R—X} + \underset{\text{Sodium alkoxide}}{R'—\ddot{\underset{\cdot\cdot}{O}}^{-}\overset{+}{Na}} \longrightarrow \underset{\text{Ether}}{R—\ddot{\underset{\cdot\cdot}{O}}—R'} + \underset{\text{Sodium halide}}{NaX}$$

Ethers containing substituted alkyl groups (secondary or tertiary) may be prepared by this method. This reaction involves S_N2 attack of an alkoxide ion on primary alkyl halide. Better results are obtained, if the alkyl halide is primary.

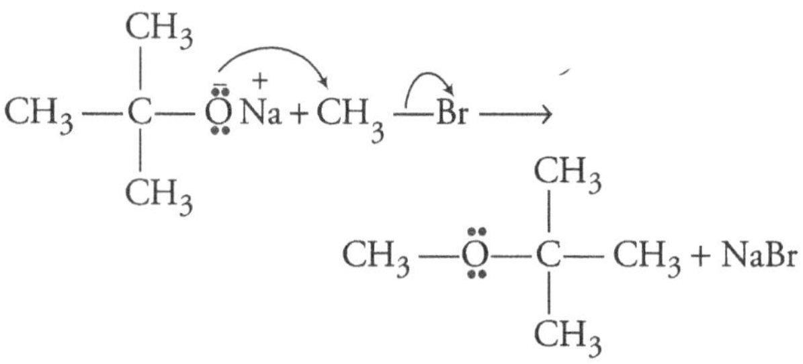

In case of 2° and 3° alkyl halides, due to steric hindrance, elimination competes over substitution and alkenes are formed. It is because alkoxides are not only nucleophiles but strong bases as well. These react with alkyl halides leading to the elimination reaction.

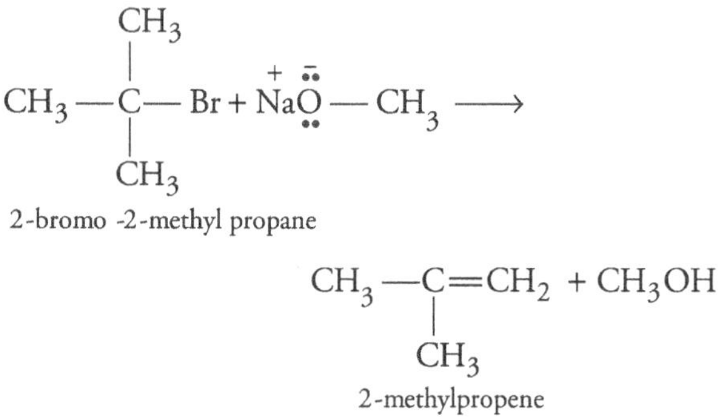

Phenols are also converted to ethers by this method. In this method, phenol is used as the phenoxide moiety.

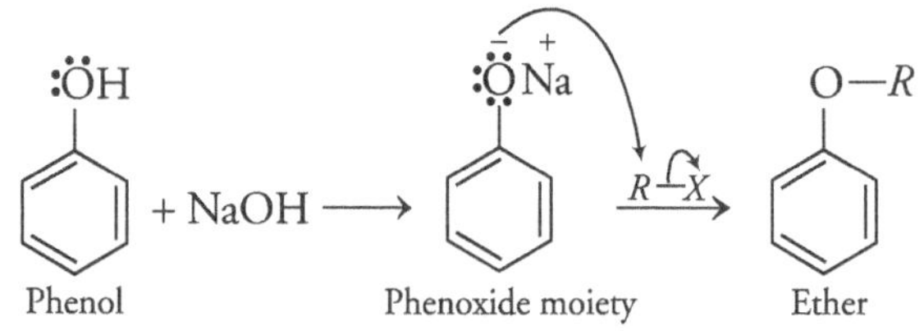

Note For the synthesis of unsymmetrical ethers, a proper choice of reactants is necessary. This method cannot be used for preparing diaryl ethers. It is also not applicable for tertiary alkyl halide as they yield alkene instead of ethers.

3. Reaction of Alkyl Halides with Dry Silver Oxide

When alkyl halide is heated with silver oxide, symmetrical ether is formed.

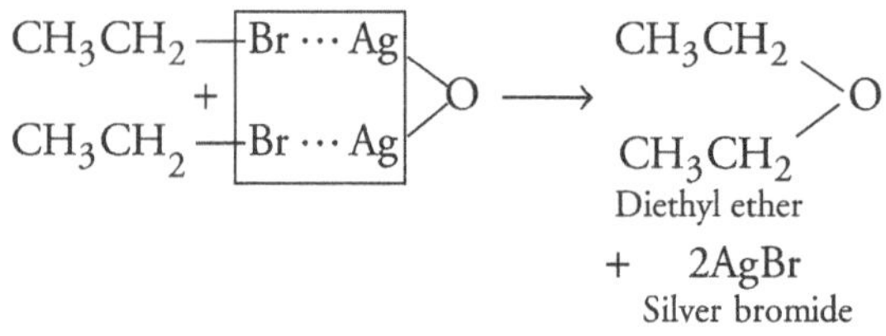

4. From Grignard Reagent

Higher ethers can be prepared by treating α-haloethers with suitable Grignard reagent.

$$\underset{\text{Chloromethoxy methane}}{CH_3—O—CH_2Cl} + CH_3MgI \xrightarrow{\text{Dry ether}} \underset{\text{Ethyl methyl ether}}{CH_3—OCH_2CH_3} + \underset{\text{Chloromagnesium iodide}}{Mg(Cl)I}$$

Physical Properties of Aliphatic and Aryl Ethers

Some of the important physical properties of aliphatic ethers and aryl ethers are as follows :

(i) Dimethyl ether and ethylmethyl ethers are gases at ordinary temperature whereas higher ones are liquids with characteristic smell.

(ii) The C—O bonds in ethers are polar, therefore ethers have a net dipole moment.

(iii) Boiling points of ethers are much lower than the boiling points of alcohols. The large difference in boiling points of alcohols and ethers is due to the presence of H-bonding in alcohols. The boiling points of ethers are comparable to alkanes of comparable molecular masses due to their low polarity.

Formula	Nomenclature	Bp/K
$CH_3(CH_2)_3CH_3$	*n*-pentane	309.1
$C_2H_5—O—C_2H_5$	Ethoxy ethane	307.6
$CH_3(CH_2)_3—OH$	Butan -1-ol	390

(iv) Lower ethers (upto three carbon atoms) are soluble in water and their miscibility with water resembles those of alcohols of the same molecular mass.

Both Ethoxy ethane and Butan-1-ol are miscible to almost the same extent, i.e. 7.5 and 9 g per 100 mL H_2O, respectively while pentane is essentially immiscible with H_2O. This is due to the fact that just like alcohols, oxygen of ether can also form H-bonds with water molecule.

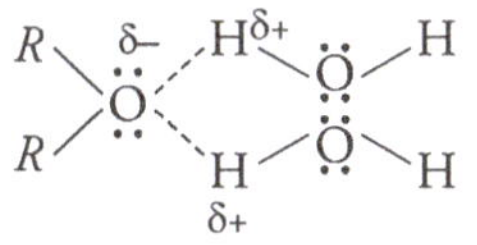

Chemical Properties of Aliphatic Ethers

Some of the important chemical reactions of ethers are as follows :

1. Reactions with Chlorine

When ethers react with Cl_2 or Br_2 in dark, substitution takes place mainly at α - C atom.

$$\underset{\text{Ether}}{R'CH_2—O—R} + Cl_2 \xrightarrow{\text{Dark}} \underset{\text{Chloroether}}{R'CHCl—O—R} + HCl$$

In the presence of light and excess of Cl_2, all H-atoms of ether are substituted by halogen atom to form perchlorodialkyl ether.

$$CH_3—CH_2—O—CH_2—CH_3 + \underset{\text{Excess}}{10Cl_2} \xrightarrow[-10HCl]{\text{Light}} \underset{\text{Perchlorodiethyl ether}}{CCl_3—CCl_2—O—CCl_2—CCl_3}$$

2. Formation of Peroxides (Oxidation)

In contact with air or O_2, ethers form peroxides which are unstable compounds.

$$CH_3CH_2OCH_2CH_3 \xrightarrow[\text{Light}]{O_2(\text{air})} \underset{\text{1-ethoxyethylhydroperoxide}}{CH_3—\underset{\underset{H—O—O}{|}}{CH}—O—CH_2CH_3}$$

3. Reaction with Halogen Acids (HX)

In cold, alkyl halide and alcohol are formed.

$$\underset{\text{Ether}}{R—O—R} + \underset{(X = \text{I or Br})}{HX} \xrightarrow{\text{Cold}} \underset{\text{Alcohol}}{ROH} + \underset{\text{Alkyl halide}}{RX}$$

$$\underset{\text{Diethyl ether}}{C_2H_5—O—C_2H_5} + HI \xrightarrow{\text{Cold}} \underset{\text{Iodoethane}}{C_2H_5I} + \underset{\text{Ethanol}}{C_2H_5OH}$$

With excess of halogen acids, 2 molecules of alkyl halides are formed.

$$R—O—R + \underset{\text{Excess}}{2\,HX} \xrightarrow{\Delta} 2RX + H_2O\,;$$

$$\underset{\text{Diethyl ether}}{C_2H_5—O—C_2H_5} + \underset{\text{Excess}}{2HI} \xrightarrow{\Delta} 2C_2H_5I + H_2O$$

4. Reaction with PCl_5

Alkyl chlorides are formed by the cleavage of C—O bond.

$$R—O—R + PCl_5 \xrightarrow{\Delta} \underset{\text{Alkyl chloride}}{2R—Cl} + POCl_3$$

Chemical Properties of Aryl Ethers

Aryl ethers readily undergoes electrophilic substitution reaction. *These are as follows.*

Electrophilic Substitution Reaction

Alkoxy group (—O*R*) is *ortho, para* directing and activates the aromatic ring towards electrophilic substitution and directs the incoming electrophile at *o*-and *p*-positions (because of the negative charges at *o*-and *p*-positions indicate the more electron density at these positions).

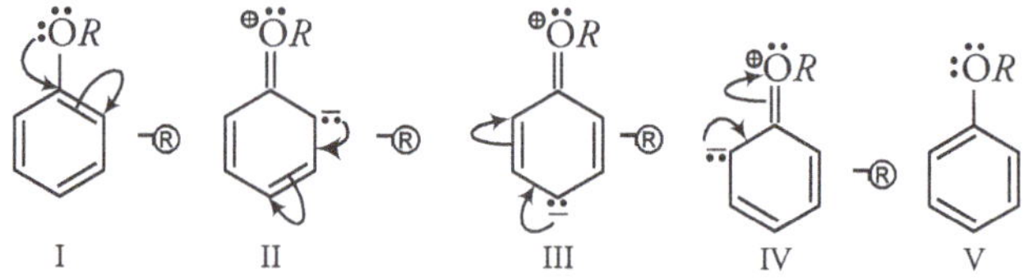

Important electrophilic substitution reactions are as follows:

1. Halogenation

Phenylalkyl ethers undergo usual halogenation in the benzene ring, e.g. anisole undergoes bromination with bromine in ethanoic acid even in the absence of iron (III) bromide catalyst. It is due to the activation of benzene ring by the methoxy group. Halide group is introduced at *o*-and *p*-positions of the ring. *p*-isomer is obtained in 90% yield.

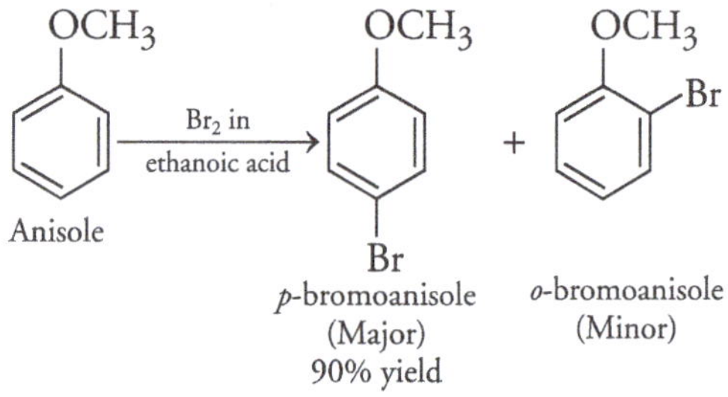

2. Friedel-Crafts Reaction

Anisole undergoes Friedel-Crafts reaction, i.e. the alkyl and acyl groups are introduced at *o*- and *p*-positions by reaction with alkyl and acyl halides in the presence of anhydrous aluminium chloride (a Lewis acid) as catalyst.

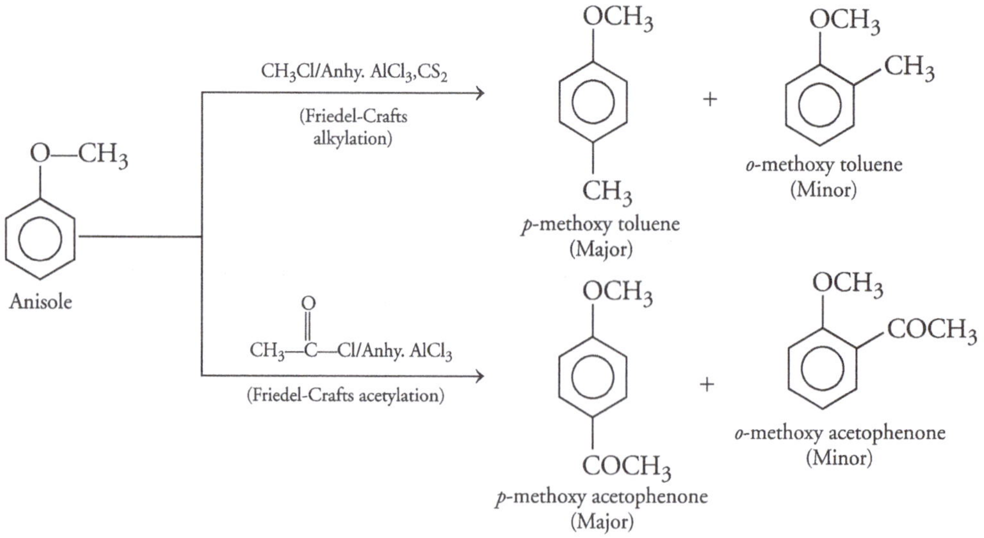

3. Nitration

Anisole reacts with a mixture of concentrated sulphuric acid and nitric acids to yield a mixture of *ortho* and *para* nitroanisole.

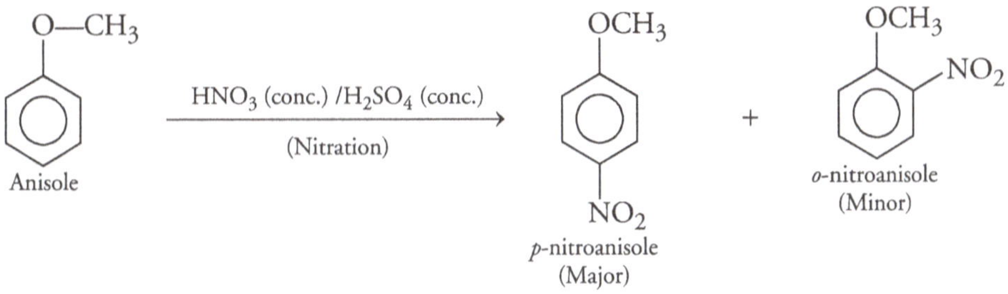

Uses

Some of the important uses of ethers are as follows :

(i) Dimethyl ether is used as refrigerant and as solvent at low temperatures.
(ii) Used as an industrial solutions for oils, resins, gums, etc.
(iii) As an extracting solvent in laboratory and industry because of their almost inert nature and good dissolving power.
(iv) Diphenyl ether is used as heat transfer medium because of its high boiling point.

Topic Practice 3

Very Short Answer Type Questions

1 Mark

1. Fill in the Blanks

(i) .... and .... are functional isomers. **ISC 2009**

(ii) Aromatic ether is prepared by heating .... with alkyl halide.

(iii) In ether, the bond angle is slightly .... than the tetrahedral angle.

2. Objective Type Questions

(i) IUPAC name of the compound $CH_3-\underset{CH_3}{\underset{|}{CH}}-OCH_3$......

(a) 1-methoxy-1-methylethane **NCERT Exemplar**
(b) 2-methoxy-2-methylethane
(c) 2-methoxypropane
(d) *iso*-propylmethyl ether

(ii) Formation of diethyl ether from ethanol is based on
(a) dehydration reaction
(b) dehydrogenation reaction
(c) hydrogenation reaction
(d) heterolytic fission reaction

(iii) Which of the following ethers on reaction with HI in cold leads to the formation of methyl alcohol?
(a) Ethyl methyl ether (b) Methyl propyl ether
(c) *Iso*-propyl methyl ether
(d) *Tert*-butyl methyl ether

3. The reactants given in Column I react with HI and gives products given in Column II. Match the following Columns and choose the option using the codes given below :

	Column I		Column II
A.	$CH_3—O—CH_3$	(i)	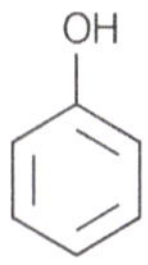 $+ CH_3I$
B.	$\begin{matrix}CH_3\\CH_3\end{matrix}\!>CH-O-CH_3$	(ii)	$CH_3-\underset{CH_3}{\overset{CH_3}{C}}-I + CH_3OH$
C.	$H_3C-\underset{CH_3}{\overset{CH_3}{C}}-O-CH_3$	(iii)	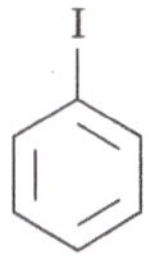 $+ CH_3OH$
D.	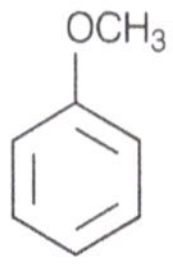	(iv)	$CH_3—OH + CH_3I$
		(v)	$\begin{matrix}CH_3\\CH_3\end{matrix}\!>CH—OH + CH_3I$

Codes

	A	B	C	D		A	B	C	D
(a)	(i)	(iii)	(iv)	(v)	(b)	(iv)	(v)	(ii)	(i)
(c)	(i)	(ii)	(iii)	(iv)	(d)	(v)	(iii)	(iv)	(i)

4. Write the IUPAC name of the given compound.

$$CH_3—\underset{\displaystyle CH_3}{\underset{|}{CH}}—CH_2—O—CH_2—CH_3$$

5. Write the IUPAC name of the following compound.

$$CH_3—O—\overset{\displaystyle CH_3}{\overset{|}{\underset{\displaystyle CH_3}{\underset{|}{C}}}}—CH_3$$

6. Write the IUPAC name of the following compound.

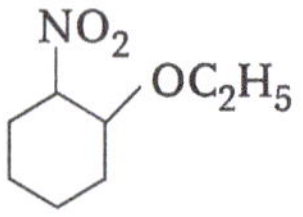

7. Write the equation involved in the Williamson's ether synthesis.

8. Give reason: $(CH_3)_3C—O—CH_3$ on reaction with HI gives $(CH_3)_3C—I$ and $CH_3—OH$ as the main products and not $(CH_3)_3C—OH$ and $CH_3—I$.

9. How do you convert phenol to anisole?

10. Dimethyl ether is completely soluble in water but diethyl ether is soluble in water to small extent. Why?

11. Give the balanced equation for the following reaction : Diethyl ether with phosphorus pentachloride. **ISC 2016**

12. Give the balanced equation for the following reaction : Sodium ethoxide is treated with ethyl bromide. **ISC 2014**

13. Give the balanced equation for the following reaction :
Chlorine is passed through diethyl ether. **ISC 2010**

14. Give the name of the following reaction. **ISC 2009**

$$\longrightarrow$$

15. Give the chemical test to distinguish: dimethyl ether and ethyl alcohol. **ISC 2016**

Short Answer Type I Questions (2 Marks)

16. Draw the structures of the compounds whose IUPAC names are as follows:
 (i) 1-ethoxypropane
 (ii) 2-ethoxy-3-methylpentane **NCERT**

17. Write the structure of three ethers with molecular formula $C_4H_{10}O$. **ISC 2016**

18. Explain the following with an example.
 (i) Williamson's ether synthesis
 (ii) Unsymmetrical ether **NCERT**

19. Select the ether which cannot be prepared by Williamson's synthesis and state why?
Divinyl ether, dicyclohexyl ether,
1-propoxy-2-methyl propane, propyl -*sec*-butyl ether.

20. Write the names of reagents and equations for the preparation of the following ethers by Williamson's synthesis.
 (i) 1-propoxypropane (ii) Ethoxybenzene
 (iii) 2-methoxy-2-methylpropane
 (iv) 1-methoxyethane **NCERT**

21. Write the reaction of Williamson's synthesis of 2-ethoxy-3-methylpentane, starting from ethanol and 3-methylpentan-2-ol. **NCERT Intext**

22. Which of the following is an appropriate set of reactants for the preparation of 1-methoxy-4-nitrobenzene and why?

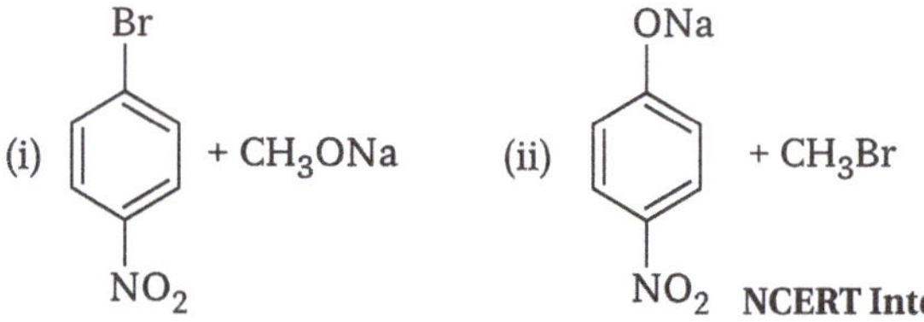

NCERT Intext

23. Give reason for the higher boiling point of ethanol in comparison to methoxy methane. **NCERT**

Or

Explain why alcohols and ethers of comparable molecular mass, have different boiling points? **NCERT Exemplar**

24. Explain, why $O=C=O$ is non-polar while $R—O—R$ is polar? **NCERT Exemplar**

25. How will you bring about the following conversion?
Diethyl ether to ethanol. **ISC 2008**

26. Explain the fact that in aryl alkyl ether,
 (i) the alkoxy group activates the benzene ring towards electrophilic substitution and
 (ii) it directs the incoming substituents to *ortho* and *para*-positions in benzene ring. **NCERT**

27. Complete the following reactions :
 (i) Chlorobenzene to phenol

(ii) Diethyl ether to ethanol **ISC 2015**

28. Predict the products of the following reactions:

(i) $CH_3—CH_2—CH_2—O—CH_3 + HBr \longrightarrow$

(ii) 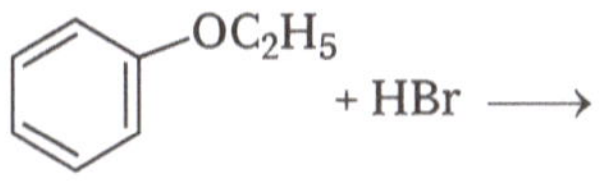

(iii) 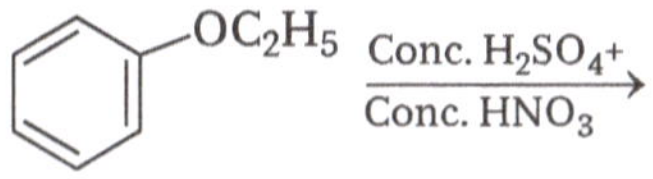

(iv) $(CH_3)_3C—OC_2H_5 \xrightarrow{HI}$

29. (i) Convert propanol to 1-propoxy propane.

(ii) Give the structure and IUPAC name of the major product, obtained in the following reaction:

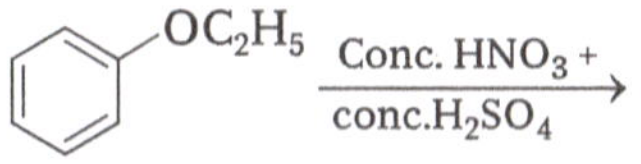

30. State the products of the following reactions:

(i) $CH_3CH_2CH_2CH_2OCH_3 + HBr \longrightarrow$

(ii) $C_2H_5—O—C(CH_3)_3 \xrightarrow{HI}$

Short Answer Type II Questions (3 Marks)

31. (i) Give the IUPAC name of

$$C_6H_5—O—CH_2—\underset{\displaystyle CH_3}{\underset{|}{CH}}—CH_3$$

(ii) Write the mechanism of acid dehydration of ethanol to yield ether :

$$2CH_3CH_2OH \xrightarrow[413\ K]{H^+} CH_3CH_2OCH_2CH_3$$

32. (i) What happens, when $CH_3—O—CH_3$ is heated with HI?

(ii) Give the products for the following reactions:

(a) 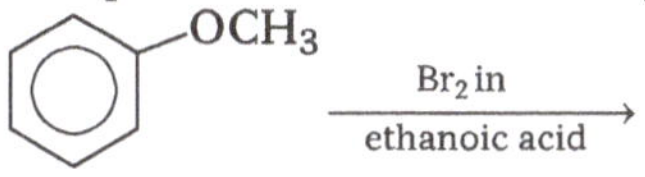

(b) 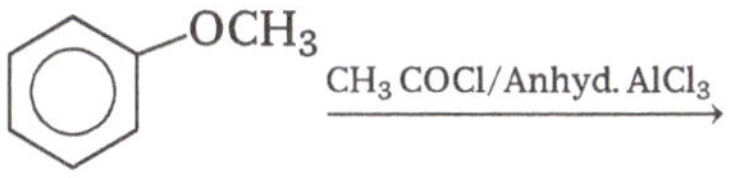

33. Complete the following reactions:

(i) $\begin{matrix} CH_3CH_2—Br \\ CH_3CH_2—Br \end{matrix} + \begin{matrix} Ag \\ Ag \end{matrix}\!\!>\! O \longrightarrow A$

(ii) $CH_3—O—CH_2Cl + CH_3MgI \xrightarrow{\text{Dry ether}} B$

34. Compound A having molecular formula $C_4H_{10}O$, is found to be soluble in concentrated sulphuric acid. It does not react with sodium metal or potassium permanganate. On heating with excess of HI, it gives a single alkyl halide. Deduce the structure of compound A and explain all the reactions.

35. Write the equation for the reaction of hydrogen iodide with

(i) 1-propoxy propane

(ii) methoxy benzene and

(iii) benzyl ethyl ether **NCERT**

36. Illustrate with examples, the limitations of the Williamson's synthesis for the preparation of certain types of ethers. **NCERT**

37. The following is not an appropriate reaction for the preparation of *tert*-butyl methyl ether:

$$CH_3ONa + (CH_3)_3\ C—Cl \longrightarrow (CH_3)_3\ C—OCH_3\ \text{(Minor)}$$

(i) What would be the major product of the given reaction?

(ii) Write a suitable reaction for the preparation of *tert*-butyl methyl ether, specifying the names of reagents used. Justify your answer in both cases.

38. How is 1-propoxy propane synthesised from propan-1-ol ? Write the mechanism of this reaction. **NCERT**

Long Answer Type Questions (5 Marks)

39. (i) Predict the product(s) of the following reaction

$$C_6H_5COCH_3 \xrightarrow{C_6H_5MgBr} A \xrightarrow{H^+/H_2O} B$$

(ii) Explain why anisole does not undergo nucleophilic substitution reactions?

40. Preparation of ethers by acid-catalysed dehydration of secondary and tertiary alcohols is not a suitable method. Give reason. **NCERT**

41. Write equation of the following reactions. **NCERT**

(i) Friedel-Crafts reaction (alkylation in anisole)

(ii) Nitration of anisole

(iii) Bromination of anisole in ethanoic acid

(iv) Friedel-Crafts reaction (acetylation of anisole)

42. (i) Give balanced chemical equations for the following reactions :

(a) Phenol is treated with ice cold alkaline solution of benzene diazonium chloride.

(b) Diethyl ether is treated with phosphorus pentachloride.

(c) Ethyl alcohol is treated with thionyl chloride.

(ii) Give one chemical test each to distinguish between the following pairs of compounds :

(a) Ethanol and dimethyl ether

(b) Propan-1-ol and propan-2-ol **ISC 2020**

43. (i) Write chemical equations to illustrate the following name reactions :

(a) Williamson's synthesis

(b) Esterification reaction

(c) Reimer-Tiemann reaction

(ii) Identify the compounds *A* and *B* in the given reactions: **ISC 2020**

(a) $C_2H_5OH \xrightarrow[\Delta]{Cu} A \xrightarrow{\text{Dil. NaOH}} B$

(b)

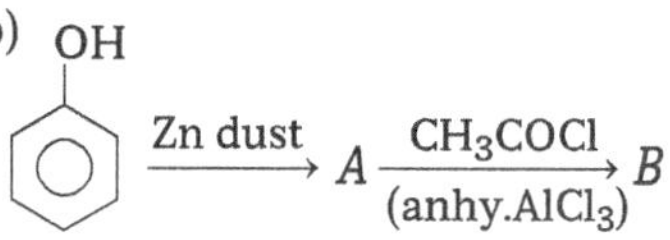

Hints & Solutions

1. (i) Alcohol and ether
(ii) phenoxide ion
(iii) greater

2. (i) → (c), (ii) → (a), (iii) → (d)

3. (b) A → (iv), B → (v), C → (ii), D → (i)

4. $\overset{3}{C}H_3—\overset{2}{C}H(CH_3)—\overset{1}{C}H_2—O—CH_2—CH_3$

IUPAC name 1-ethoxy-2-methylpropane

5. Given, compound is $CH_3—O—C(CH_3)_2—CH_3$

The IUPAC name is 2-methoxy-2-methylpropane.

6. 1-ethoxy-2-nitrocyclohexane.

7. $2CH_3X + CH_3\ddot{O}Na \longrightarrow CH_3OCH_3 + NaX$

8. In case of unsymmetrical ethers having two different alkyl groups, the alcohol and the alkyl halide formed depends on the nature of the alkyl group.

If one of the alkyl group is tertiary, the alkyl halide is formed from the tertiary alkyl group due to stability of tertiary carbocation. Since, reaction now follows S_N1 mechanism.

$$CH_3—C(CH_3)_2—OCH_3 + HI \xrightarrow{S_N1} \underset{\text{Methyl alcohol}}{CH_3—OH} + \underset{\textit{Tert}\text{-butyl iodide}}{CH_3—C(CH_3)_2—I}$$

This is due to the reason that the reaction occurs *via* S_N1 mechanism and the formation of products is controlled by the stability of the carbocation.

9.

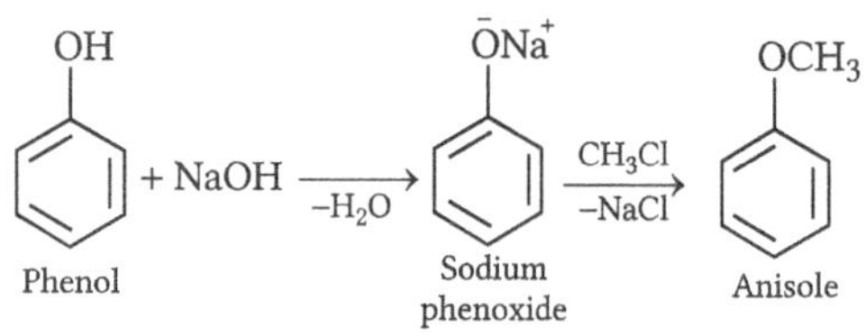

10. Both dimethyl ether and diethyl ether form weak hydrogen bonds with water which accounts for their solubility in water. However, in diethyl ether, the hydrophobic hydrocarbon part is larger than dimethyl ether and therefore, limits the hydrogen bond formation.

11. $$\underset{\text{Diethyl ether}}{C_2H_5—O—C_2H_5} + PCl_5 \xrightarrow{\Delta} \underset{\text{Ethyl chloride}}{2C_2H_5Cl} + \underset{\text{Phosphoryl chloride}}{POCl_3}$$

12. $$\underset{\text{Sodium ethoxide}}{C_2H_5\overset{-}{O}\overset{+}{Na}} + \underset{\text{Ethyl bromide}}{C_2H_5Br} \longrightarrow \underset{\text{Diethyl ether}}{C_2H_5OC_2H_5} + NaBr$$

13. With , substitution takes place at α-C atom.

$$\underset{\text{Diethyl ether}}{CH_3CH_2—O—CH_2CH_3} \xrightarrow[-HCl]{+Cl_2}$$

$$\underset{\alpha\text{-chlorodiethyl ether}}{CH_3CHClOCH_2CH_3} \xrightarrow[-HCl]{+Cl_2} \underset{\alpha,\alpha'\text{-dichlorodiethyl ether}}{CH_3CHCl\cdot OCHClCH_3}$$

14. The given reaction is Williamson's synthesis used for the preparation of ether.

15. Ethyl alcohol gives yellow precipitate during iodoform test, while dimethyl ether does not give such test.

$$CH_3CH_2OH + 6NaOH + 4I_2 \longrightarrow CHI_3(\downarrow) + HCO\overset{-}{O}\overset{+}{Na} + 5NaI + 5H_2O$$

$$CH_3—O—CH_3 + 6NaOH + 4I_2 \longrightarrow \text{No reaction}$$

16. (i) $CH_3CH_2—O—CH_2CH_2—CH_3$

(ii) $CH_3—CH(OCH_2—CH_3)—CH(CH_3)—CH_2—CH_3$ (2 × 1 = 2)

17. Structures of ethers having molecular formula $C_4H_{10}O$,

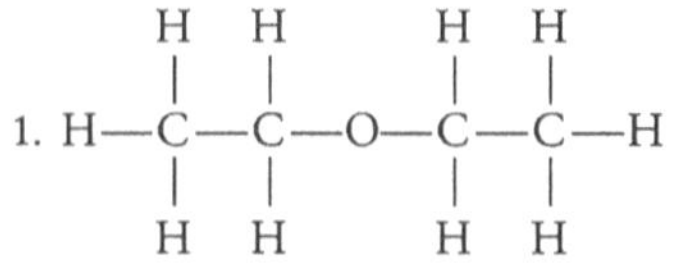

Diethyl ether

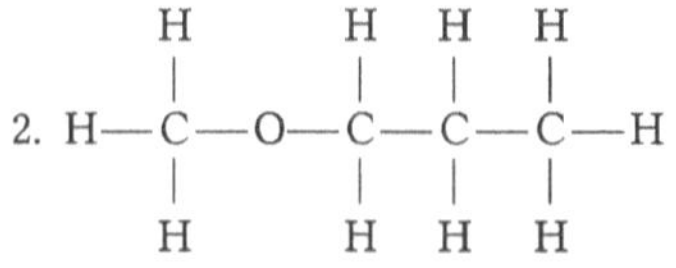

Methyl propyl ether

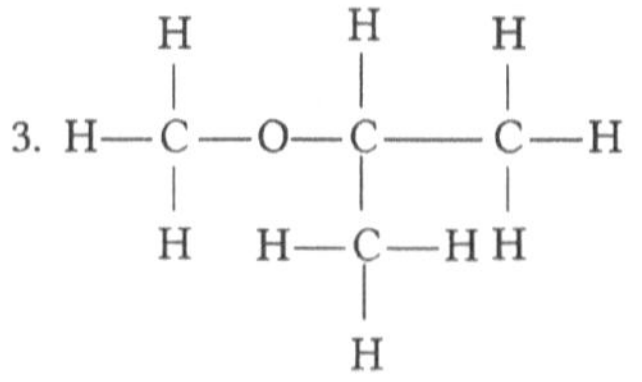

Methyl isopropyl ether

18. (i) Refer to text on page 282 (Williamson's ether synthesis).

(ii) Refer to text on page 281 (Unsymmetrical ether).

19. Refer to text on page 282 (Williamson's ether synthesis).

20. (i) $CH_3CH_2CH_2O^- — Na^+ + CH_3CH_2CH_2—Br$
Sodium propoxide 1-bromopropane

$\xrightarrow{\text{Heat}} CH_3CH_2CH_2—O—CH_2CH_2CH_3 + NaBr$
1-propoxypropane

(ii)

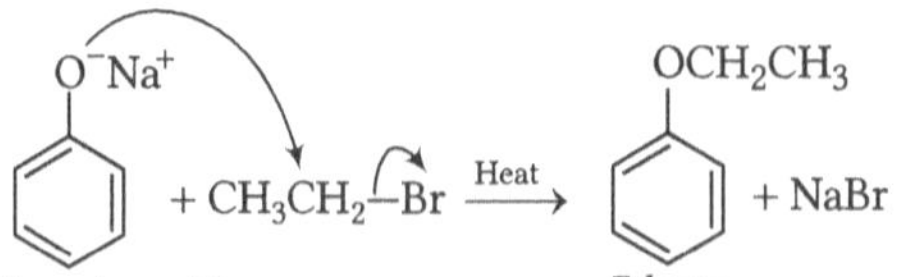

Sodium phenoxide Ethoxy benzene

(iii)

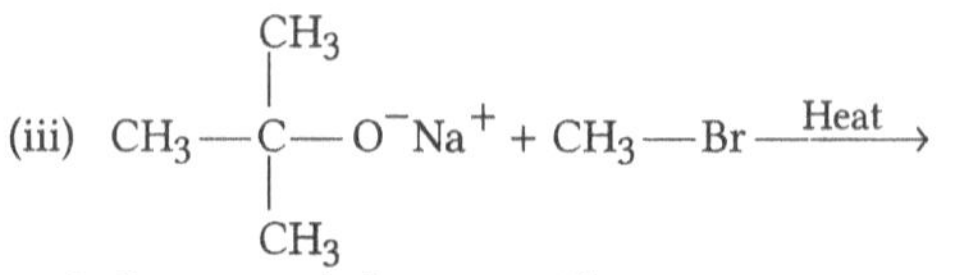

Sodium-2-methyl-2-propoxide

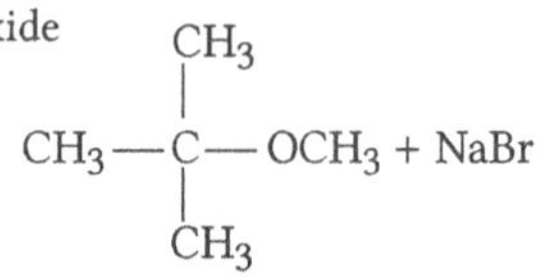

2-methoxy-2-methylpropane

(iv) $CH_3CH_2—\overset{-}{O}\overset{+}{Na} + CH_3—Br \xrightarrow{\text{Heat}}$
Sodium ethoxide Bromomethane

$CH_3CH_2—O—CH_3 + NaBr$
1-methoxyethane $\left(4 \times \frac{1}{2} = 2\right)$

21. Alkyl halide should be primary for Williamson's synthesis. Hence, alkyl halide is derived from ethanol and the alkoxide ion from 3-methylpentan-2-ol.

$CH_3CH_2OH + HBr \xrightarrow{\Delta} CH_3CH_2Br + H_2O$
Ethanol Ethyl bromide

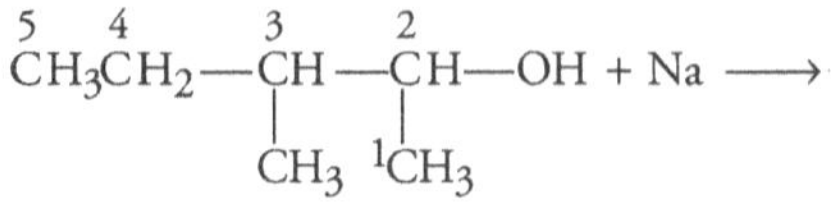

3-methylpentan-2-ol (1)

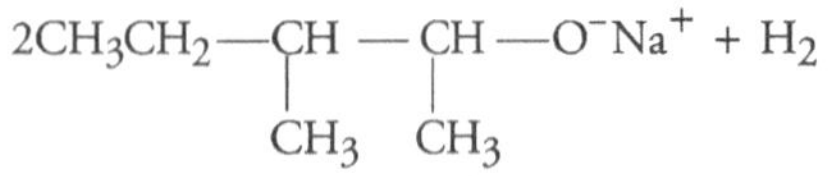

Sodium-3-methyl-2-pentoxide

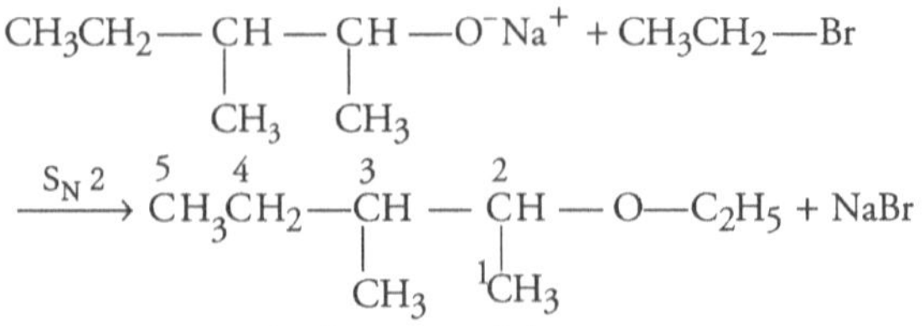

2-ethoxy-3-methylpentane (1)

22.

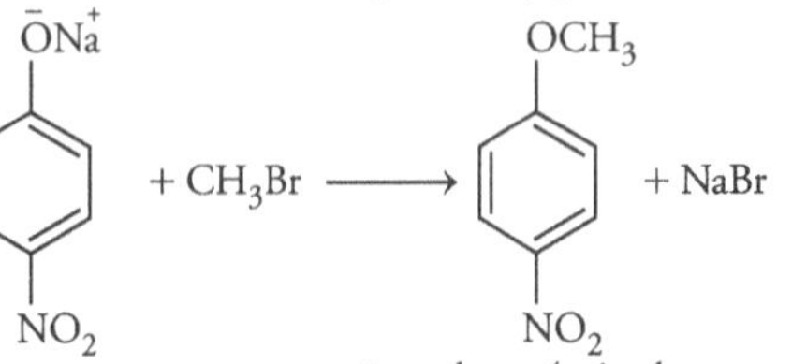

1-methoxy-4-nitrobenzene (1)

This reaction involves the preparation of ether by Williamson's synthesis. It takes place *via* S_N2 attack of an alkoxide ion on primary alkyl halide because here the alkyl halide used is primary.

Moreover in method (i) the C—Br bond has some double bond character. (1)

23. Refer to text on page 283 (Physical properties of aliphatic and aryl ethers).

24. CO_2 is a linear molecule. The dipole moment of two C = O bonds are equal and opposite. Hence, they cancel each other. So, the dipole moment of CO_2 is zero and it is a non-polar molecule.

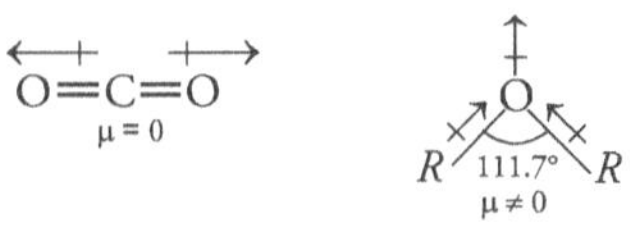

While for ethers, two dipoles are pointing in the same direction. These two dipoles do not cancel the effect of each other.

Therefore, there is a finite resultant dipoles and hence, *R*—O—*R* is a polar molecule. (2)

25. Diethyl ether to ethanol

(i) **By Hydrolysis** When diethyl ether is boiled with steam, ethanol is formed.

$$C_2H_5—O—C_2H_5 + HOH \longrightarrow 2C_2H_5OH$$

(ii) **With H_2SO_4** When boiled with dil. H_2SO_4 under pressure, ether forms alcohol.

$$C_2H_5—O—C_2H_5 + H_2O \xrightarrow[\Delta,]{\text{Dil. } H_2SO_4} 2\,C_2H_5OH$$

26. (i) In aryl alkyl ethers, $+R$-effect of the alkoxy group ($—OR$) increases the electron density on the benzene ring thereby, activating the benzene ring towards electrophilic substitution reactions.

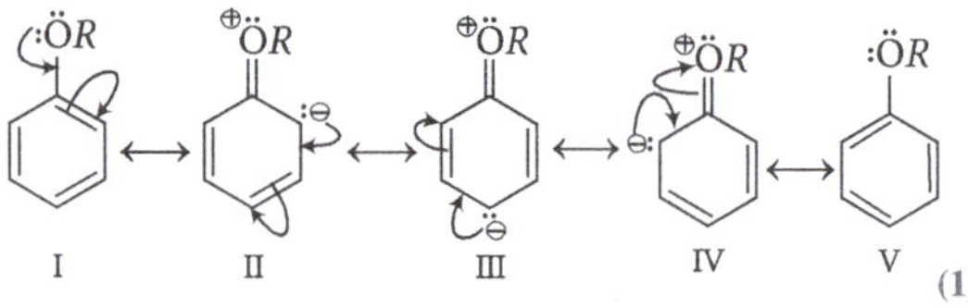

(1)

(ii) Refer to text on page 284 (Electrophilic substituion reaction). (1)

27. (i)

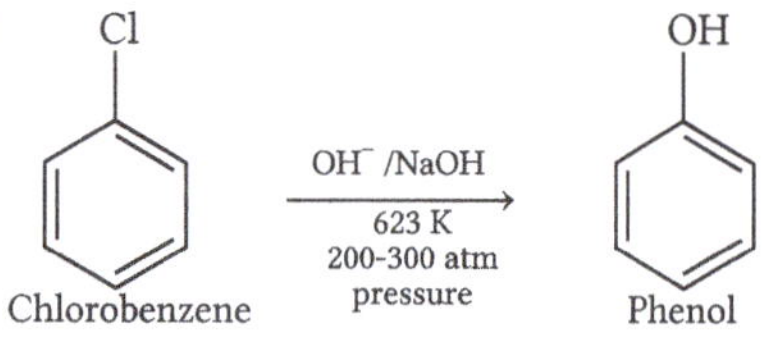

(ii) Diethyl ether to ethanol

$$\underset{\text{Diethyl ether}}{C_2H_5—O—C_2H_5} + HI \xrightarrow{\Delta} \underset{\text{Ethanol}}{C_2H_5OH} + C_2H_5I$$

28. (i) $\underset{\text{Methoxy propane}}{CH_3—CH_2—CH_2—O—CH_3} + HBr \longrightarrow$

$$\underset{\text{Propanol}}{CH_3—CH_2—CH_2—OH} + CH_3Br$$

(ii)

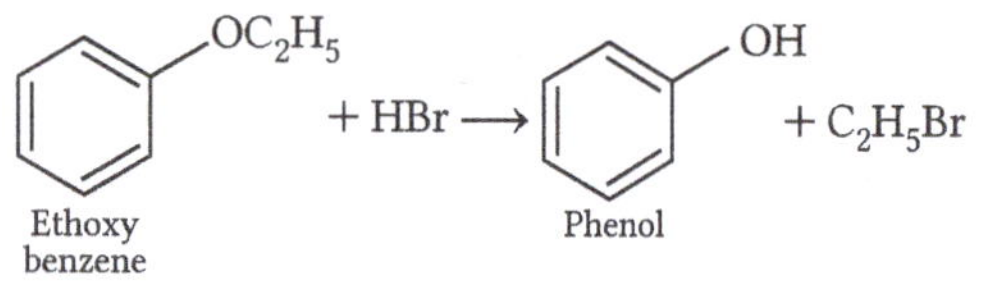

(iii)

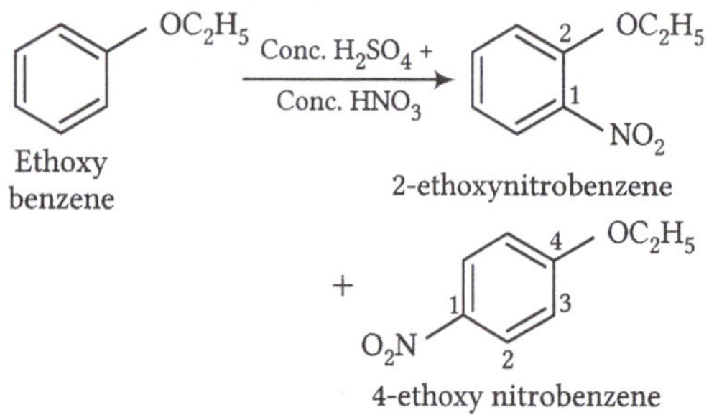

(iv) $\underset{t\text{-butyl ethyl ether}}{(CH_3)_3C—OC_2H_5} \xrightarrow{HI}$

$$\underset{t\text{-butyl iodide}}{(CH_3)_3C—I} + \underset{\text{Ethanol}}{C_2H_5OH} \qquad \left(4 \times \frac{1}{2} = 2\right)$$

29. (i) Refer to text on page 282 (Dehydration of alcohols) (1)

(ii)

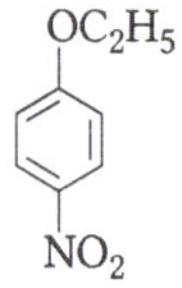

p-ethoxynitrobenzene (Major) (1)

30. (i) Refer to text on pages 283 and 284 (Reaction with halogen acid). (1)

(ii) Refer to text on pages 283 and 284 (Reaction with halogen acids)

31. (i) Refer to text on page 281 (Nomenclature). (1)

(ii) $CH_3—CH_2—\ddot{O}—H + H^+ \longrightarrow CH_3—CH_2—\overset{+}{O}(H)—H$

$CH_3CH_2—\ddot{O}(H) + CH_3—CH_2—\overset{+}{O}H_2 \longrightarrow CH_3CH_2—\overset{+}{O}(H)—CH_2CH_3 + H_2O$

$CH_3CH_2—\overset{+}{O}(H)—CH_2CH_3 \longrightarrow CH_3CH_2—O—CH_2CH_3 + H^+$ (2)

32. (i) $CH_3—O—CH_3 + HI \longrightarrow CH_3—OH + CH_3—I$ (1)

(ii) Refer to text on page 284 (Halogenation and Friedel-Crafts reaction).

33. (i) Refer to text on 283 (Reaction of alkyl halide with dry silver oxides). (1)

(ii) Refer to text on 283 (From Grignard reagent). (2)

34. (i) As compound A does not react with sodium metal or potassium permanganate, it cannot be an alcohol. (1/2)

(ii) As compound A dissolves in conc. H_2SO_4, it may be an ether. (1/2)

(iii) As compound A on heating with excess of HI, gives a single alkyl halide, therefore compound A must be a symmetrical ether. (1)

(iv) The only symmetrical ether having molecular formula $C_4H_{10}O$ is diethyl ether. Thus, compound A is diethyl ether, $CH_3—CH_2—O—CH_2—CH_3$.

$$CH_3CH_2—O—CH_2CH_3 \xrightarrow{\text{Conc. } H_2SO_4} \underset{\text{Soluble oxonium salt}}{\left[CH_3—CH_2—\overset{+}{O}(H)—CH_2—CH_3\right]} HSO_4^-$$

$$\underset{\text{Diethyl ether}}{\underset{(A)}{CH_3CH_2OCH_2CH_3}} \xrightarrow[\Delta]{HI} \underset{\text{Ethyl iodide}}{2\,CH_3CH_2—I}$$ (1)

35. (i) $CH_3CH_2CH_2—O—CH_2CH_2CH_3 \xrightarrow[373\ K]{HI}$
1-propoxy propane

$CH_3CH_2CH_2—OH + CH_3CH_2CH_2—I$ (1)
Propan-1-ol 1-iodopropane

(ii)

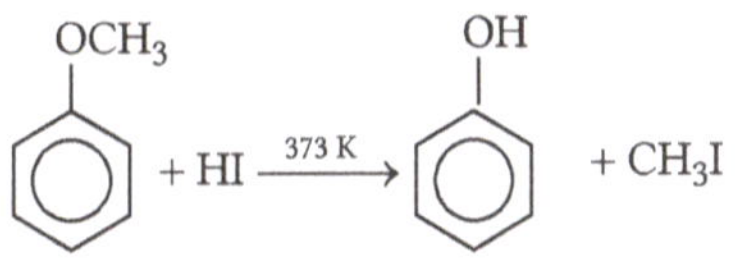

(1)

(iii)

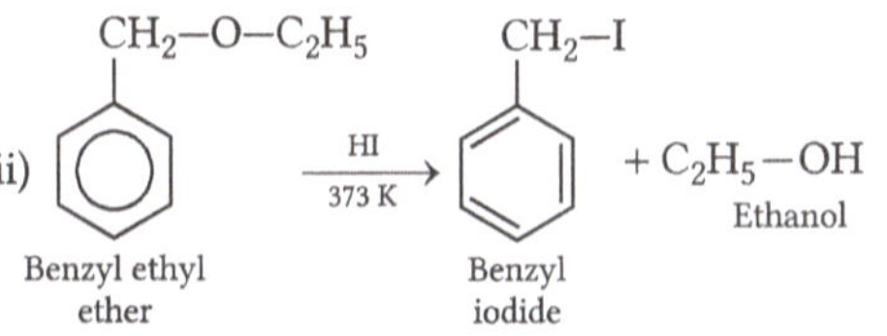

(1)

36. (i) Williamson's synthesis is not applicable for tertiary alkyl halides as they yield alkenes instead of ethers. The reaction of CH_3ONa with $(CH_3)_3C—Br$ gives exclusively 2-methylpropene. (1)

$$(CH_3)_3C—Br + Na—\ddot{O}—CH_3 \longrightarrow CH_3—\underset{CH_3}{\underset{|}{C}}=CH_2 + NaBr$$

tert-butylbromide 2-methylpropene (1)

(ii) Aryl and vinyl halides cannot be used as substrates because of their low reactivity in nucleophilic substitution. (1)

37. (i) The major product obtained is $CH_3—\overset{CH_3}{\overset{|}{C}}=CH_2$

(ii) Refer to text on page 282 (Williamson's ether synthesis).

38. Two methods can be employed for this preparation:

(i) *Via* Williamson's synthesis

(a) $3CH_3CH_2CH_2OH + PBr_3 \longrightarrow 3CH_3CH_2CH_2Br + H_3PO_3$
Propan-1-ol 1-bromopropane

(b) $2CH_3CH_2CH_2OH + 2Na \longrightarrow 2CH_3CH_2CH_2O^-Na^+ + H_2$
Propan-1-ol Sodium propoxide

$CH_3CH_2CH_2O^-Na^+ + CH_3CH_2CH_2—Br \xrightarrow[Heat]{Dry\ ether}$
Sodium propoxide 1-bromopropane

$CH_3CH_2CH_2—O—CH_2CH_2CH_3 + NaBr$
1-propoxypropane (1)

(ii) By the dehydration of propan-1-ol with conc. H_2SO_4 at 413 K.

$CH_3CH_2CH_2OH + H^+ \longrightarrow CH_3CH_2CH_2—\overset{+}{\ddot{O}}H_2$
Propan-1-ol Protonated propan-1-ol

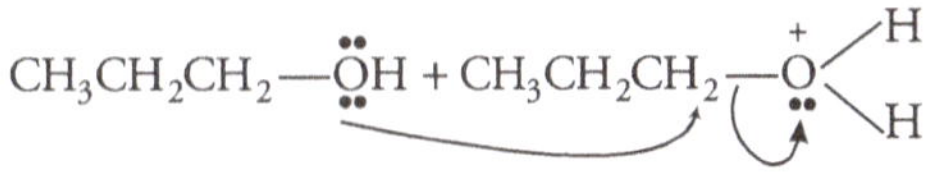

$\xrightarrow[-H_2O,\ -H^+]{413\ K} CH_3CH_2CH_2—O—CH_2CH_2CH_3$
1-propoxypropane (1)

39.

(i)

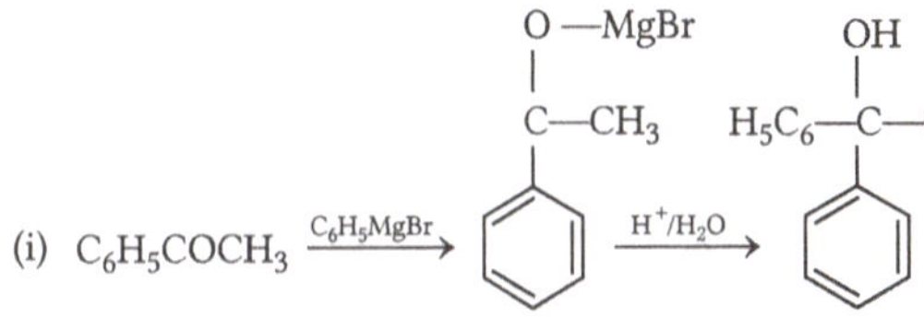

(ii) Since, in anisole $—OCH_3$ is electron releasing group which increases electron density on benzene.

Due to which is not possible for incoming nucleophile to approach the ring. Refer to text on page 284 (Electrophilic substitution reaction)

40. Under acid catalysed dehydration, 2° and 3° alcohols give alkenes rather than ethers.

The reason is that due to steric hindrance, nucleophilic attack by the alcohol molecule on the protonated alcohol molecule does not occur.

Instead protonated 2° and 3° alcohols lose a water molecule to form stable 2° and 3° carbocations. These carbocations prefer to lose a proton to form alkenes rather than undergoing nucleophilic attack by alcohol molecule to form ethers. (1)

$$CH_3—\overset{CH_3}{\overset{|}{CH}}—OH \xrightarrow{H^+} CH_3—\overset{CH_3}{\overset{|}{CH}}—\overset{+}{O}H_2$$

Propan-2-ol (2° alcohol) Protonated propan-2-ol

$$\xrightarrow{-H_2O} CH_3—\overset{CH_3}{\overset{|+}{CH}}$$

iso-propyl carbocation (1)

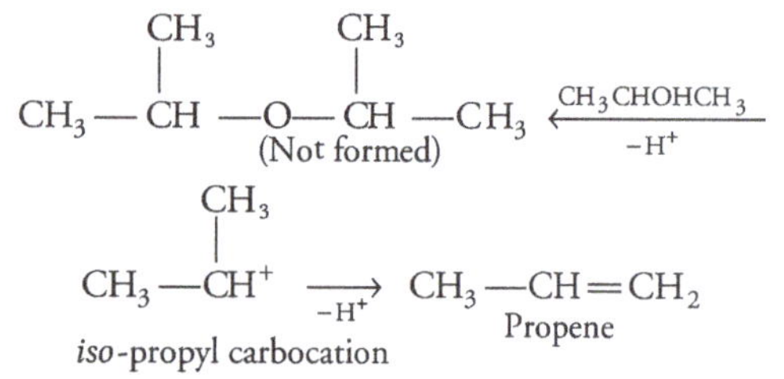

(1)

41. (i) Refer to text on page 284.
[Friedel-Crafts reaction (alkylation)].
(ii) Refer to text on page 285 (Nitration).
(iii) Refer to text on page 284 (Friedel-Crafts acetylation).

42. (i) (a) Refer to page no. 287 (Azo dye test).

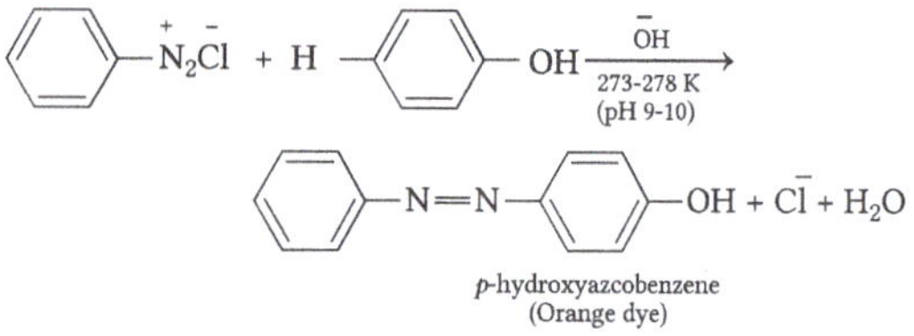

(b) Refer to page no. 284 (Reaction with PCl_5).
(c) Refer to page no. 259 (Reaction with thionyl chloride).

(ii) (a) Refer to page no. 286 (Q.15).
(b) Propan-1-ol (1° alcohol) and propan-2-ol (2° alcohol) can be distinguished by the oxidation using Cu. 1° alcohols yeild aldehyde while 2° alcohol yeild ketone

$$\underset{\text{Propan-1-ol}}{CH_2CH_2CH_2OH} \xrightarrow[570\text{ K}]{Cu} \underset{\text{Aldehyde}}{CH_3CH_2CHO} + H_2$$

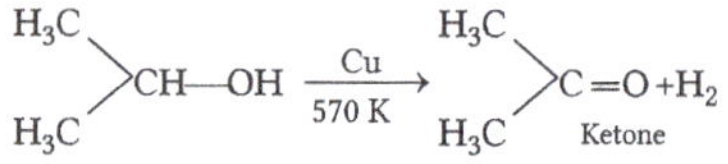

43. (i) (a) Refer to page no. 282
(Williamson's ether synthesis).
(b) Refer to page no. 258 (Esterification).
(c) Refer to page no. 273
(Reimer-Tiemann reaction).

(ii) (a)

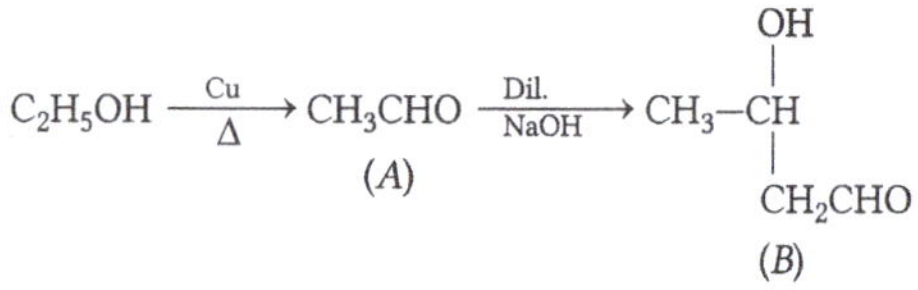

(b)

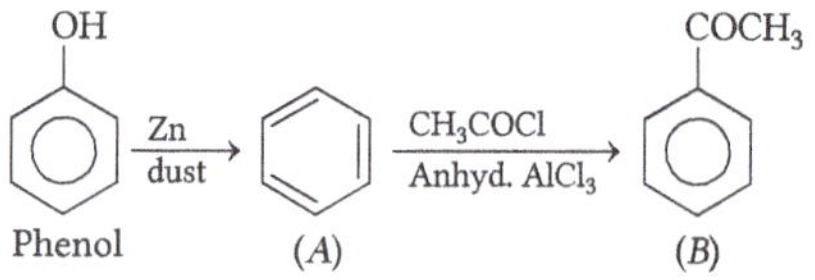

SUMMARY

- Alcohols are hydroxy organic compounds of the alkanes with general formula $C_nH_{2n+2}O$ or $C_nH_{2n+1}OH$.
- Alcohols are named by replacing the terminal '–e' of the corresponding alkane name by –'ol'
- Alcohols exhibit chain, position, functional and optical isomerism.

Methods of Preparation of Alcohols

	Method	Reaction involved
1.	Hydration of alkenes	$(CH_3)_2C{=}CH_2 + H_2O \longrightarrow (CH_3)_3C{-}OH$
2.	Hydroboration oxidation	$3R{-}CH{=}CH_2 + BH_3 \xrightarrow[\text{DIGLYME}]{\text{THF or}} (RCH_2CH_2)_3B \xrightarrow{H_2O_2} RCH_2CH_2OH$
3.	Reduction of aldehydes, ketones, acids and acid derivatives	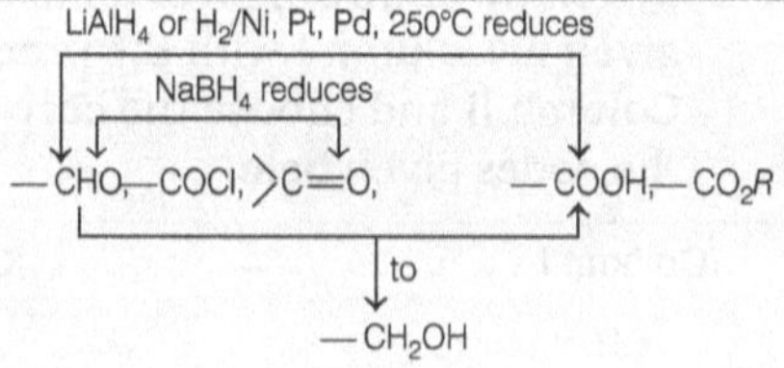
4.	From Grignard's reagent	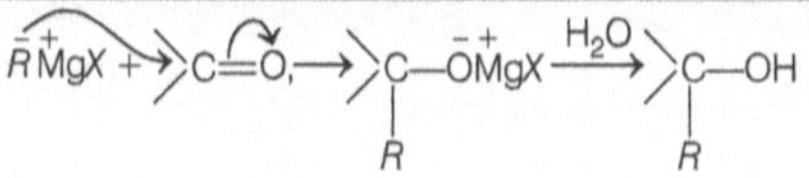
5.	From hydrolysis of alkyl halide	$R{-}X + KOH(aq) \longrightarrow ROH + KX$
6.	From aliphatic primary amines	$R{-}NH_2 + HNO_2 \xrightarrow{0-3°C} R{-}OH + N_2\uparrow H_2O$

Physical Properties of Alcohols

- Lower alcohols are colourless, toxic liquids whereas the higher members are waxy solids.
- The boiling point of alcohol is always higher than the corresponding ether, hydrocarbon and haloalkane due to the presence of hydrogen bonding.

Distinction between 1°, 2° and 3° Alcohols

Name of the test and procedure	1° alcohol	2° alcohol	3° alcohol
Lucas test Alcohol is treated with Lucas reagent (equimolar mixture of anhy. $ZnCl_2$ and conc.HCl)	does not react	Produces turbidity after 5 min	Produces turbidity immediately
Dehydrogenation Cu or Ag are used for dehydrogenation	Produces aldehyde	Produces ketone	Dehydrated to give alkene

- **Methanol** is a colourless liquid and boils at 373 K. It is highly poisonous in nature. Ingestion of even small quantities of methanol is hazardous and large quantities causes even death.
- **Ethanol** is a good industrial solvent. It is a colourless liquid with boiling point 351 K. It is used as a solvent in paint industry.

- The class of organic compounds which contain a hydroxyl group, attached directly to an aromatic ring, are known as phenols.

Methods of Preparation of Phenols

	Methods	Reactions involved
1.	Dow process (by hydrolysis)	$PhX \xrightarrow[340°C,\,150\text{ atm}]{\text{aq.NaOH}} PhO^-Na^+ \xrightarrow{H_2O/H^+} PhOH$
2.	Cumene process	$PhCH(CH_3)_2 \xrightarrow[H_2O/H^+]{O_2\text{ catalyst}} PhOH + CH_3COCH_3$
3.	From diazonium salts	$PhN^+ \equiv NX^- \xrightarrow{H_2O/H^+} PhOH + N_2\uparrow + HX$
4.	Fusion of alkali metal salt of sulphonic acid	$PhSO_3^-Na^+ + NaOH \xrightarrow{\text{Fuse}} PhO^-Na^+ \xrightarrow{H_2O/H^+} PhOH$
5.	From Grignard's reagent	$PhMgBr \xrightarrow{[O]} PhOMgBr \xrightarrow{H_2O/H^+} PhOH$

Physical Properties of Phenols

- Colourless, crystalline, deliquescent liquid or solid.
- Characteristic carbolic odour, sparingly soluble in water
- Capable of forming intermolecular H-bonding with water and among themselves.

Ethers

- Ethers are the organic compounds having two alkyl groups bounded to an oxygen atom with general molecular structure of $R{-}O{-}R'$.
- IUPAC nomenclature $\underbrace{R}_{\substack{\text{Alkane}\\ \text{(larger group)}}} — \underbrace{O{-}R'}_{\substack{\text{Alkoxy}\\ \text{(smaller group)}}}$, $CH_3O{-}CH_2CH_3$ Methoxy ethane (right) ethoxy methane (wrong)

Preparation of Ethers

1.	By dehydration of alcohols	$2ROH \xrightarrow[\Delta\ 413K]{H_2SO_4} R{-}O{-}R + H_2O$
2.	Williamson's synthesis	$R{-}Br + R'ONa \longrightarrow ROR' + NaBr$ (R is generally 1°, or benzyl with 3° R, alkene is the major product)
3.	Reaction of alkyl halides with dry silver oxide	$2RX + Ag_2O \xrightarrow{\Delta} R{-}O{-}R + 2AgX$
4.	From Grignard reagent	$CH_3OCH_2Cl + CH_3MgI \xrightarrow{\text{Dry ether}} CH_3OCH_2CH_3 + Mg(Cl)I$

Physical Properties of Ethers

- Colourless liquids with ethereal smell, lower boiling point than isomeric alcohols.
- Ethers upto three carbon atoms are soluble in water due to the formation of intermolecular H-bonding.

For Mind Map

Visit : https://goo.gl/P2xKQn OR **Scan the Code**

Chapter Practice

Very Short Answer Type Questions

1 Mark

1 Fill in the Blanks

(i) .... and .... are functional isomers.

(ii) Phenol on .... with chromic acid gives ....

(iii) .... is an example of trihydric alcohol and .... is an example of dihydric alocohol.

(iv) Aldehyde gives .... alcohol whereas ketone gives .... alcohol.

(v) Glycerol is a .... alcohol and is used in making ....

2 Objective Type Questions

(i) Which of the following compounds is aromatic alcohol?

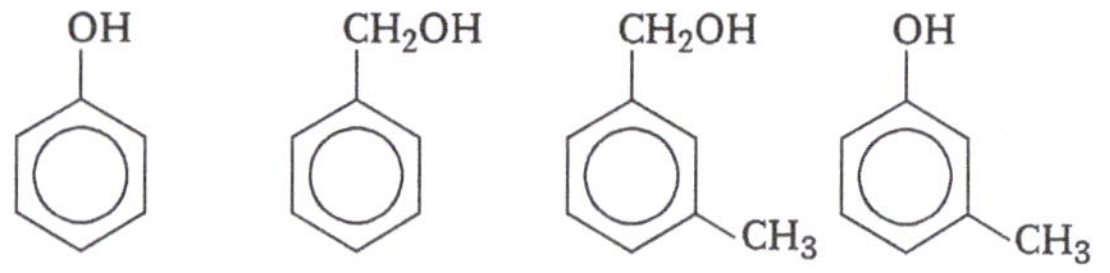

(A) (B) (C) (D)

(a) A, B, C, D (b) A, D (c) B, C (d) A

(ii) Give IUPAC name of the compound given below :

$$CH_3—\underset{|}{\underset{Cl}{CH}}—CH_2—CH_2—\underset{|}{\underset{OH}{CH}}—CH_3$$

(a) 2-chloro-5-hydroxyhexane
(b) 2-hydroxy-5-chlorohexane
(c) 5-chlorohexan-2-ol
(d) 2-chlorohexan-5-ol

(iii) Mark the correct order of decreasing acid strength of the following compounds.

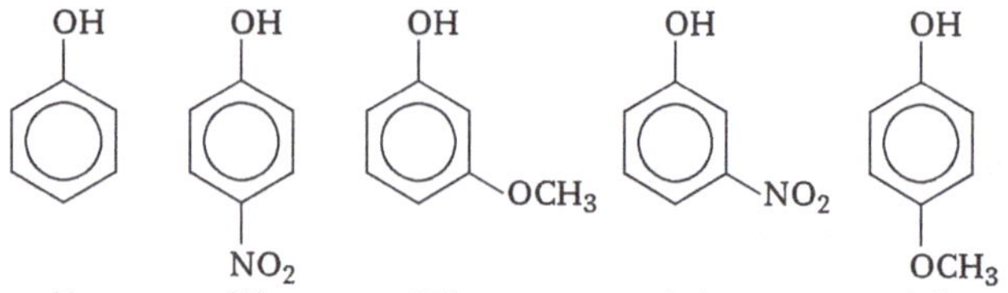

(I) (II) (III) (IV) (V)

(a) V > IV > II > I > III
(b) II > IV > I > III > V
(c) IV > V > III > II > I
(d) V > IV > III > II > I

(iv) IUPAC name of the compound $CH_3-\underset{|}{\underset{CH_3}{CH}}-OCH_3$ is ....

(a) 1-methoxy-1-methylethane
(b) 2-methoxy-2-methylethane **[NCERT Exemplar]**
(c) 2-methoxypropane
(d) isopropylmethyl ether

3 Match the following reactants and reagents given in Column I with the products given in Column II and choose the correct option from the codes given below.

	Column I		Column II
A.	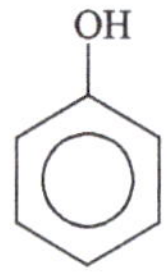 + Zn	(i)	Benzene
B.	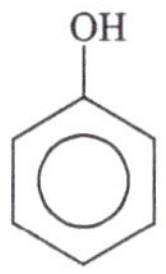 $\xrightarrow[H_2SO_4]{Na_2Cr_2O_7}$	(ii)	Salicylaldehyde
C.	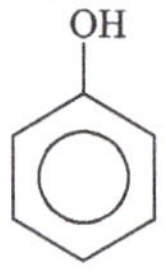 $\xrightarrow[\text{(ii) NaOH, (iii) } H^{\oplus}]{\text{(i) } CHCl_3 + aq.\ NaOH}$	(iii)	Benzoquinone

Codes

	A	B	C		A	B	C
(a)	(iii)	(i)	(ii)	(b)	(i)	(iii)	(ii)
(c)	(i)	(ii)	(iii)	(d)	(iii)	(ii)	(i)

4 What is the IUPAC name of the following compounds?

(i) $\underset{|}{\underset{OH}{CH_2}}—\underset{|}{\underset{OH}{CH}}—\underset{|}{\underset{OH}{CH_2}}$ (ii) $CH_3CH_2CH_2—OCH_2CH_3$

5 Name the starting material used in the industrial preparation of phenol.

6 Give reason.

The boiling points of alcohols decreases with increase in branching of the alkyl chain.

7 Arrange the following compounds in the increasing order of acidity:

$CH_3OH, H_2O, HC \equiv CH$

8 Name a reagent which converts 1° alcohols exclusively to corresponding aldehydes.

9. How will you convert phenol to picric acid? Write the relevant equation.

10 What is the order of reactivity of HCl, HBr and HI with alcohols?

11 How will you confirm that whether a given –OH group is alcoholic or phenolic?

12 Why aryl halides cannot be used for the formation of ethers?

13 Why are higher ethers insoluble in water?

14 Write the equation and name the following reaction: Phenol with acetyl chloride in the presence of $AlCl_3$.

15 A reaction is given below:

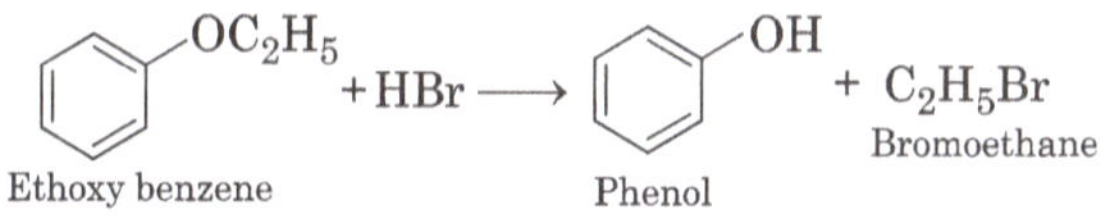

What is the name of this reaction?

Assertion-Reason

Directions (Q. Nos. 16-20) In the following questions an Assertion (A) is followed by a corresponding Reason (R). Use the following keys to choose the appropriate answer.

(a) Both (A) and (R) are correct, (R) is the correct explanation of (A).
(b) Both (A) and (R) are correct, (R) is not the correct explanation of (A).
(c) (A) is correct; (R) is incorrect.
(d) (A) is incorrect; (R) is correct.

16. **Assertion** (A) In alcohols, the boiling point decreases with decrease in branching of the carbon chain.

Reason (R) There is the decrease in van der Waals' forces between the number of carbon atoms with decrease in the surface area.

17. **Assertion** (A) *o*-nitrophenol is less volatile than *p*-nitrophenol.

Reason (R) There is intramolecular hydrogen bonding in *o*-nitrophenol and intermolecular hydrogen bonding in *p*-nitrophenol.

18. **Assertion** (A) Addition reaction of water to but-1-ene in acidic medium yields butan-2-ol.

Reason (R) Addition of water in acidic medium proceeds through the formation of primary carbanion.

19. **Assertion** (A) Like bromination of benzene, bromination of phenol is also carried out in the presence of Lewis acid.

Reason (R) Lewis acid polarises the bromine molecule.

20. **Assertion** (A) IUPAC name of the compound

$CH_3—\underset{\displaystyle CH_3}{\underset{|}{CH}}—O—CH_2—CH_2—CH_3$ is 2-ethoxy-2-methylethane.

Reason (R) In IUPAC nomenclature, ether is regarded as hydrocarbon derivative in which a hydrogen atom is replaced by —*OR* or —OAr group [where, *R* = alkyl group and Ar = aryl group].

Case-Study

21. Phenols are the compounds that possess a hydroxyl group directly attached to an aromatic carbocylic nucleus. Phenol is the trivial name for monohydroxybenzene.

The *o*-, *m*- and *p*-cresols are monohydroxytoluenes and are distinct in their properties and reactions from the isomeric side chain hydroxy compound, benzyl alcohol, which is a typical aromatic alcohol.

Simple monohydric phenols are either corrosive liquids or low melting solids. The dihydric and trihydric phenols are solids.

The mono-hydroxy compounds are only slightly soluble in water but are miscible with organic solvents.

Water solubility increases and solubility in organic solvent decreases with the introduction of additional hydroxyl groups. They are all characterised by and distinguished from the aliphatic or aromatic alcohols by their different solubility in aqueous alkali.

(i) Name the reagent used in the bromination of phenol to give 2, 4, 6-tribromophenol.
(ii) What are the products obtained on reaction of phenol with dil. HNO_3?

(iii) Complete the reaction,

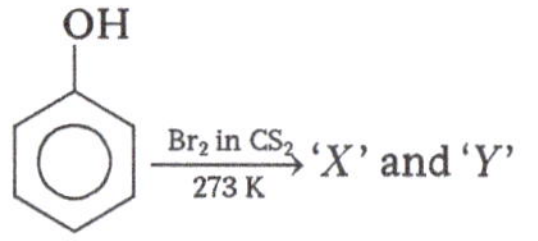

22. Alcohols and phenols consist of two parts, an alkyl/aryl group and a hydroxyl group. The properties of alcohols and phenols are chiefly due to the hydroxyl group.

Alcohol consumption, particularly heavier drinking is an important risk factor for many health problems and thus, is a major contributor to the global burden of disease. Infact, alcohol is a necessary underlying cause for more than 30 conditions and a contributing factor to many more.

The most common disease categories that are entirely or partly caused by alcohol consumption include infectious diseases cancer, diabetes, neuropsychiatric diseases, cardiovascular disease, liver and pancrease disease.

Phenol is historical disinfectant with continued use in industry laboratories, and some health care settings.

Phenol is a protoplasmic poison that can result in multisystem organ failure in severe toxicity. This activity will describe the mechanism of toxicity of phenols, the expected clinical manifestations of phenol toxicity and the management of phenol poisoned patients.

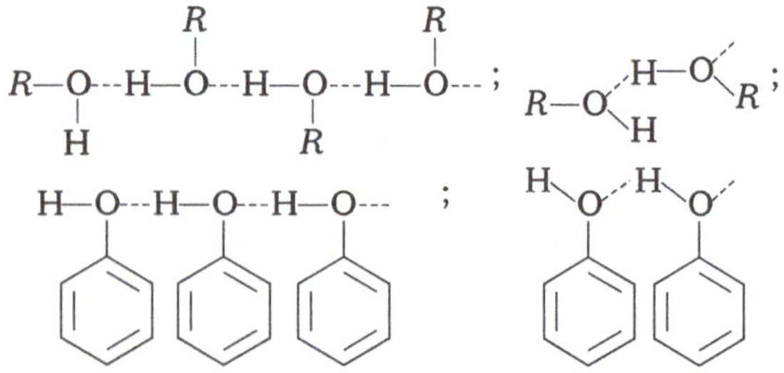

(i) Write the decreasing boiling point of the following alcohols.
(a) 1-pentanol,
(b) 2-methyl-2-butanol,
(c) 3-methyl-2-butanol

(ii) Write the increasing order of the basicity of the following compounds.

$H_2O, OH^-, CH_3OH, CH_3O^-$

(iii) Which among the following alcohols will have the highest boiling point?
Methanol, 2-butanol, Butan-1-ol, 2-methyl-2-propanol

Short Answer Type I Questions
2 Marks

23 What is the order of acidic character of 1°, 2° and 3° alcohols? Give reason.

24 Why are alcohols and phenols soluble in water? What happens to their solubility when bulky alkyl groups are present in them?

25 What is the main product obtained when vapours of *t*-butyl alcohol are react with hot conc. HNO_3? Give reaction also.

26 Give balanced equation and explain what happens, when phenol is treated with bromine water?

27 Name the compound with molecular formula C_7H_8O which on treatment with Br_2 water, readily gives a precipitate of $C_7H_5OBr_3$.

28 In the reaction,

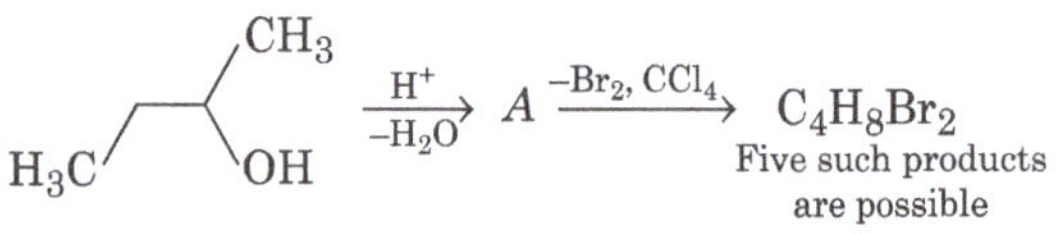

How many isomer(s) of *A* is/are possible?

29 Give one chemical test to distinguish between the following pairs of compounds:
Acetone and phenol

30 How will you distinguish between the following compounds?

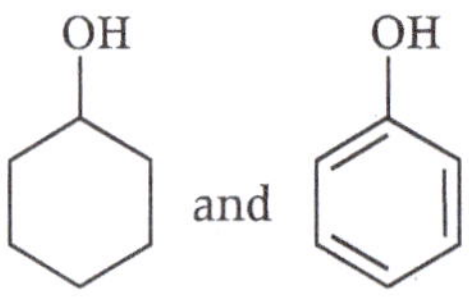

31 Give one test to distinguish between phenol and benzoic acid.

32 Methyl tertiary butyl ether is an important additive of gasoline. How it can be prepared using Williamson's synthesis?

33 Name the alkyl halide and alkoxide ion used to prepare 2-(benzyloxy)propane. Write the equations involved.

34 Considering sodium acetate (NaOAc) and 2-naphthol (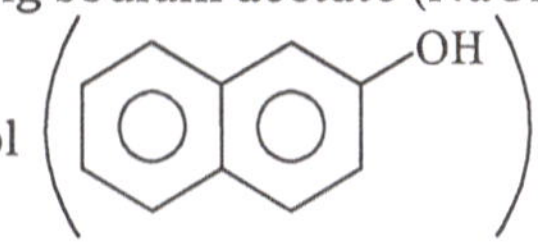) as solutes, explain which of the following solvent can dissolve these solutes?

(i) Diethyl ether (ii) Water

35 What happens when anisole is heated with HI?

36 How will you bring about the following conversion?
Phenol to benzoic acid

37 How will you convert phenol to salicylic acid?

38 *Iso*-propyl benzene is oxidised in the presence of air to compound *A*. When compound *A* is treated with dilute mineral acid, which aromatic compound is formed?

39 Explain why alcohols do not react with NaBr but when H_2SO_4 is added, they form alkyl bromides?

40 Arrange the following compounds in the decreasing order of their boiling points.

$C_2H_5—O—C_2H_5$, $CH_3—O—C_2H_5$, 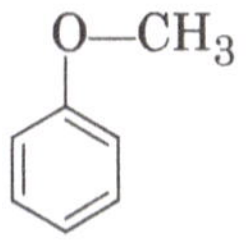

(I) (II) (III)

Short Answer Type II Questions

3 Marks

41 Give the reaction of alcohols with phosphorus trihalides and hydrogen halides.

42 Complete the following equations and name the products formed.

(i) $C_6H_5OH + Br_2 \xrightarrow{H_2O}$

(ii) $(CH_3)_2C{=}O \xrightarrow{LiAlH_4}$

(iii) $C_6H_5OH + CHCl_3 \xrightarrow[340\ K]{aq.\ NaOH}$

43 How will you convert

(i) phenol to 4-bromophenol?

(ii) phenol to 2-hydroxy benzoic acid?

44 How will you distinguish between the following pair by suitable chemical tests? butan-1-ol and butan-2-ol.

45 Why 2,4,6-trinitrophenol is a strong acid? How is it prepared from phenol?

46 How does Lucas reagent help in the distinction of primary, secondary and tertiary alcohols? Discuss the reactions involved.

47 Give the industrial uses of methanol and ethanol.

48 (i) How can diethyl ether be prepared from the following?

(a) Ethyl iodide

(b) Ethyl alcohol

Write the chemical equation in each case.

(ii) How is ethyl alcohol obtained from molasses?

49 Discuss the following:

(i) Cleavage of ethers by acids

(ii) Acidity of phenols

50 Write the main product(s) in each of the following reactions:

(i) $CH_3—C(CH_3)_2—O—CH_3 + HI \longrightarrow$

(ii) $CH_3—CH{=}CH_2 \xrightarrow[(ii)\ 3H_2O_2/OH^-]{(i)\ B_2H_6}$

(iii) $C_6H_5OH \xrightarrow[(ii)\ CO_2,\ H^+]{(i)\ aq.\ NaOH}$

Long Answer Type Questions

5 Marks

51 (i) How is phenol obtained from

(a) aniline

(b) benzene sulphonic acid?

(ii) How it can be converted into

(a) salicylaldehyde

(b) benzoquinone

52 (i) Identify the product when $CH_3CH{=}CH—CH_2—CH_2—C({=}O)—CH_3$ reacts with following reagents:

(a) $LiAlH_4/D_2O$ (b) $NaBH_4$ (c) C_2H_5MgBr

(ii) Write the structure and mechanism of the product formation in the following reaction:

$PhCH_2—O—CH(Ph)_2 \xrightarrow{aq\ HI}$

Answers

1. (i) ethanol, dimethyl ether
   (ii) oxidation, *p*-benzoquinone
   (iii) glycerol, glycol
   (iv) primary, secondary
   (v) trihydric, explosive
2. (i) (c), (ii) (c), (iii) (b), (iv) (c)
3. (b) A →(i), B →(iii), C →(ii)
4. (i) Propane-1,2,3-triol
   (ii) Ethoxypropane
5. Cumene is the starting material used in the industrial preparation of phenol.
6. In alcohols, the boiling point decreases with increase of branching in carbon chain because of decrease in van der Waals' forces with decrease in surface area.
7. The correct order is : $HC \equiv CH > H_2O > CH_3OH$
8. **Hint** PCC
9. When nitration of phenol is carried out with conc. nitric acid in the presence of conc. sulphuric acid then picric acid (2, 4, 6-trinitrophenol) is obtained.

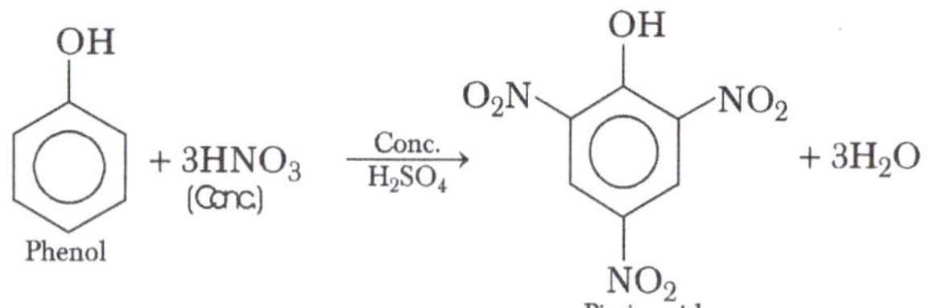

Picric acid (2, 4, 6-trinitrophenol)

10. HI > HBr > HCl
11. **Hint Reaction with $FeCl_3$:** Phenol gives positive test while alcohol does not.
12. Aryl halides can not be used for the formation of ethers because they are less reactive toward nucleophilic substitution reactions.
13. Higher ethers are immiscible with H_2O due to the presence of large hydrocarbon part.
14. Phenols undergo Friedel Crafts acylation reaction when treated with acetyl chloride in the presence of $AlCl_3$ to give the mixture of *o* - and *p* -derivatives.

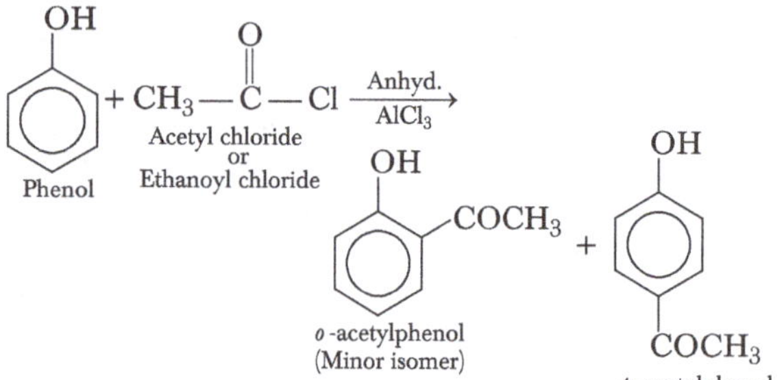

o-acetylphenol (Minor isomer) *p*-acetylphenol (Major isomer)

15. Hydrohalogenation of ethers.
16. (*d*) The boiling point of alcohols and phenols increases with increase in the number of carbon atoms (increase in van der Waals' forces).
    In alcohols, the boiling point decreases with increase of branching in carbon chain (because of decrease in van der Waals' forces with decrease in surface area). Hence, (A) is incorrect but (R) is correct.
17. (*d*) *o*-nitrophenol is more volatile due to intramolecular hydrogen bonding, while *p*-nitrophenol is less volatile due to intermolecular hydrogen bonding which causes the association of molecules. Hence, (A) is incorrect but (R) is correct.

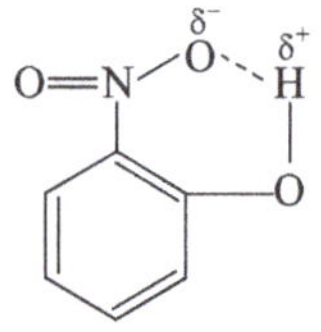

o-nitrophenol (intramolecular H-bonding)

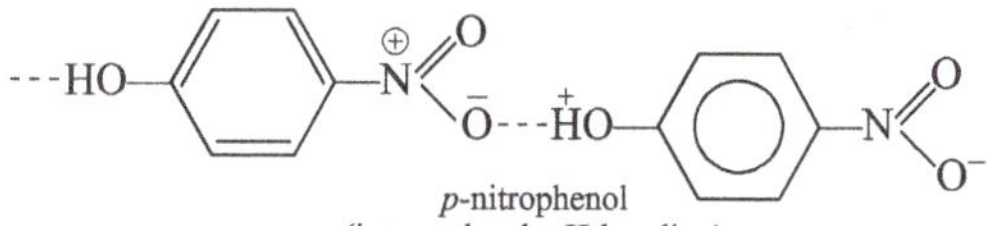

p-nitrophenol (intermolecular H-bonding)

18. (*c*) Addition of water to but-1-ene in acidic medium yields butan-2-ol. It is as follows

$$\underset{\text{But-1-ene}}{CH_3—CH_2—CH=CH_2} + H_2O \xrightarrow{H_2SO_4}$$

$$CH_3—CH_2—\underset{\underset{OSO_3H}{|}}{CH}—CH_3 \xrightarrow{H_2SO_4}$$

$$\underset{\text{Butan-2-ol}}{CH_3—CH_2—\underset{\underset{OH}{|}}{CH}—CH_3} + H_2SO_4 \longrightarrow$$

Addition of H_2O to unsymmetrical alkenes takes place in accordance with the Markownikoff's rule *via* the formation of carbocation. Hence, (A) is correct but (R) is incorrect.

19. (*d*) (A) is incorrect statement but (R) is correct statement.
    Correct (A) Bromination of benzene but not of phenol is carried out in presence of a Lewis acid.
    In case of phenol, the polarisation of bromine molecule takes place even in the absence of Lewis acid. It is due to the highly activating effect of OH group attached to the benzene ring.
20. (*d*) (A) is incorrect statement but (R) is correct statement.
    Correct (A) The IUPAC name of the given compound is 1-(2-propoxy) propane.
21. (i) Aqueous bromine.
    (ii)

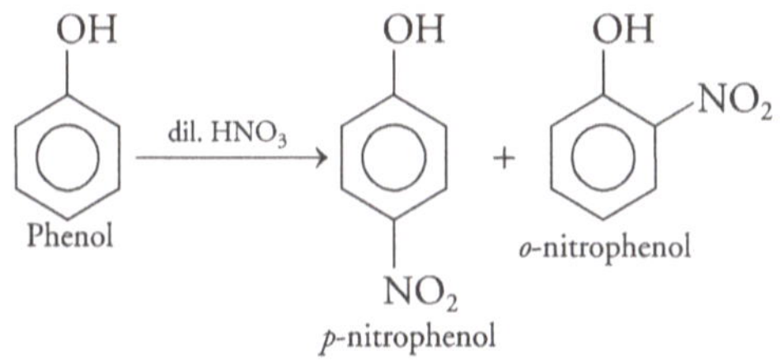

(iii)

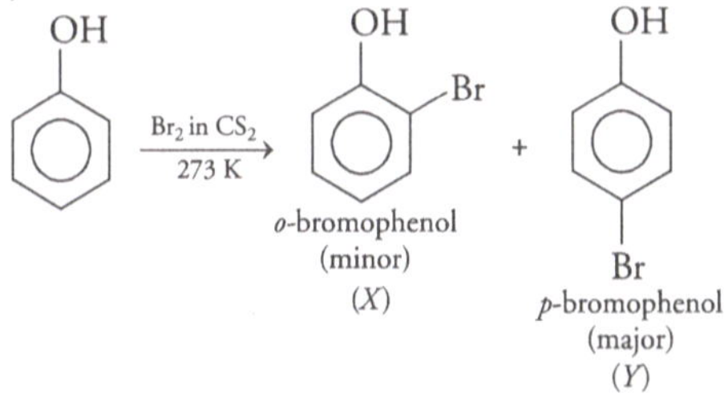

22. (i) (a) $CH_3—CH_2—CH_2—CH_2—CH_2—OH$
1-pentanol

(b) $CH_3—CH_2—C(CH_3)(OH)—CH_3$
2-methyl-2-butanol

(c) $CH_3—CH(CH_3)—CH(OH)—CH_3$
3-methyl-2-butanol

The boiling point decreases with increase of branching in carbon chain because of decrease in van der Waals' forces with decrease in surface area. Therefore, order of decreasing boiling point is : I > III > II.

(ii) Basicity can be described as the tendency to donate electrons by a chemical species. $OH^{\ominus}$ and CH_3O^- having a negative charge possess more tendency to donate electrons than H_2O and CH_3OH. $—CH_3$ shows $+I$ effect, hence $CH_3O^{\ominus}$ is the most basic among the four group and also CH_3OH is more basic than H_2O due to the same (R).
Hence, the correct order of increasing basicity is :

$$H_2O < CH_3OH < OH^- < CH_3O^-.$$

(iii) The boiling point of alcohols increases with increase in no. of carbon atoms and decreases with increase in branching in carbon chain. Therefore, butanol has the highest boiling point among the given options.

23. Refer to text on page 258 (Topic 1, Acidic nature).

24. Refer to text on pages 257-258 (Topic 1, Solubility).

25. Refer to text on pages 259 and 260 (Topic-1, Oxidation).

26. Reaction of phenol with bromine water produces white ppt. of 2, 4, 6-tribromophenol.

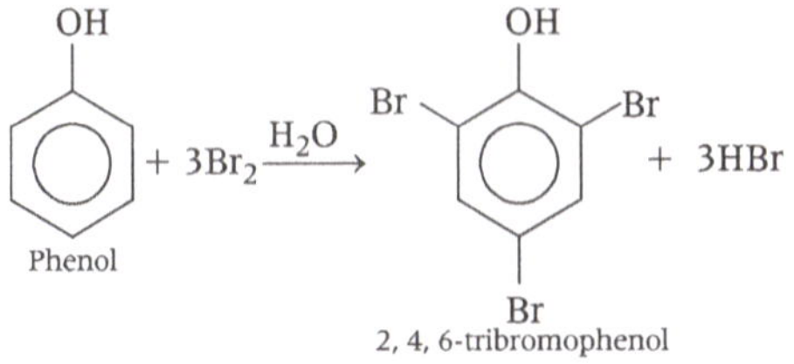

27. **Hint** $C_6H_5CH_2OH$ (Benzyl alcohol)

28. **Hint** 2 isomers are possible.

29. (i) Phenol gives violet colour with neutral $FeCl_3$ solution while acetone does not give this test.

$$C_6H_5OH + FeCl_3 \longrightarrow \text{Violet colour}$$
$$CH_3COCH_3 + FeCl_3 \longrightarrow \text{No reaction}$$

(ii) Acetone has methyl group linked to the carbonyl carbon atom which is oxidised by sodium hypohalite to sodium salt of ethanoic acid and iodoform while phenol does not give this test.

$$CH_3—\overset{O}{\overset{\|}{C}}—CH_3 \xrightarrow{3NaOI} CH_3CO\overset{-}{O}\overset{+}{Na} + CHI_3\downarrow + 3NaOH$$

$$C_6H_5OH \xrightarrow{NaOI} \text{No reaction}$$

30. Phenol gives violet colouration with $FeCl_3$ solution while cyclohexanol does not react.

31. (i) **Sodium hydrogen carbonate test** Benzoic acid reacts with sodium hydrogen carbonate to evolve brisk effervescence of CO_2 while phenol does not react.

$$C_6H_5COOH + NaHCO_3 \longrightarrow C_6H_5CO\overset{-}{O}\overset{+}{Na} + H_2O + CO_2\uparrow$$

(ii) **test** Phenol gives violet colour with neutral $FeCl_3$ solution while benzoic acid gives buff coloured ppt.

$$3C_6H_5OH + FeCl_3 \longrightarrow \underset{\text{(Violet colour)}}{[(C_6H_5O)_3\ Fe]^{3-}} + 3\ HCl$$

$$3\ C_6H_5COOH + FeCl_3 \longrightarrow \underset{\text{(Buff coloured ppt.)}}{Fe\ (C_6H_5COO)_3} + 3\ HCl$$

32. Refer to text on pages 282 (Topic-3, Williamson synthesis).

33. $(CH_3)_2CHBr$ and $C_6H_5\overset{-}{O}\overset{+}{Na}$

34. (i) 2-naphthol is dissolved in diethyl ether
(ii) Sodium acetate is dissolved in H_2O

35. **Hint** Phenol is formed.

36. Phenol to benzoic acid.

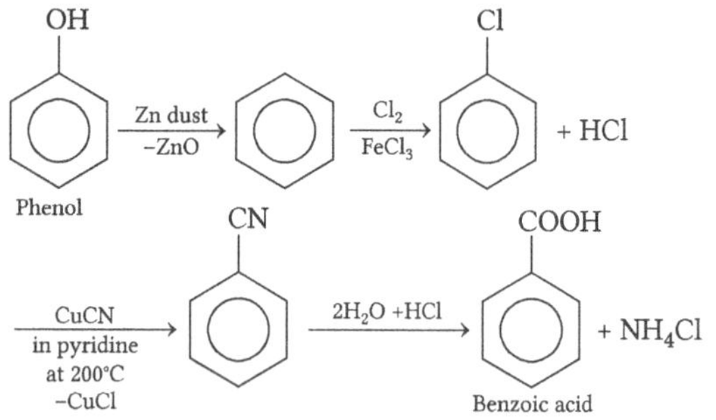

37. Phenol to salicylic acid

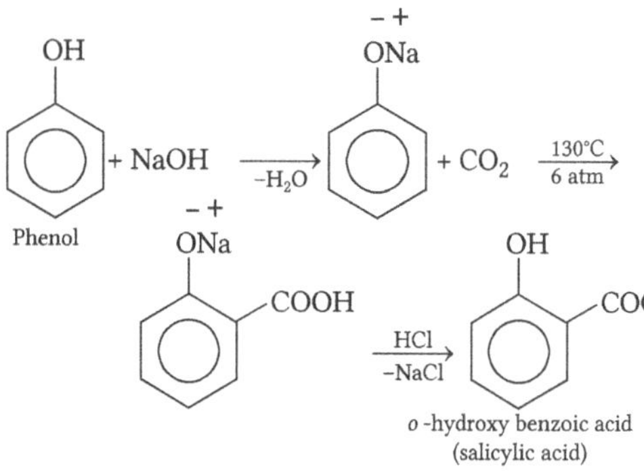

This reaction is named as Kolbe's reaction.

38. Compound is phenol.

39. OH^- being a strong base is a bad leaving group. When H_2SO_4 is added, protonation of alcohol occurs, i.e —OH is converted into—$\overset{+}{O}H_2$.

40. Refer to text on page 283 (Topic-3, Physical properties)
Hint (iii) > (i) > (ii)

41. (i) Refer to text on page 259 (Topic-1, Reaction with phosphorous halide).
(ii) $ROH + HX \longrightarrow RX + H_2O$

42.
(i) 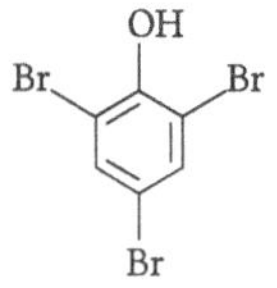
(ii) $H_3C—\underset{\displaystyle OH}{\underset{|}{HC}}—CH_3$

(iii) Refer to text on page 273 (Topic-2, Reimer-Tiemann reaction).

43. (i) 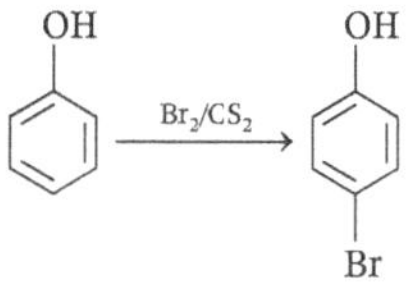

(ii) Refer to text on page 273 (Topic-2, Kolbe's reaction).

44. Refer to text on pages 261 and 262 (Topic-1, Distinction between primary, secondary and tertiary alcohols).

45. Refer to text on pages 272 (Topic-2, Nitration).

46. Refer to text on pages 261-262 (Topic-1, Distinction between primary, secondary and tertiary alcohols).

47. Refer to text on page 261 (Topic-1, Some commercially important alcohols).

48. (i) Refer to text on page 282 (Topic-3, Dehydration of alcohols and Williamson's synthesis).
(ii) Refer to text on page 261 (Topic-1, Ethanol).

49. (i) Refer to text on pages 283 and 284 (Topic-3, Reaction with halogen acids).
(ii) Refer to text on page 272 (Topic-1, Acidic character of phenol).

50. (i) Refer to text on pages 283 and 284 (Topic-3, Reaction with halogen acid).
(ii) Refer to text on page 255 (Topic-1, Direct hydration of alkanes).
(iii) Refer to text on page 273 (Topic-2, Kolbe reaction).

51. (i) (a) Refer to text on page 271 (Topic-2, From diazonium salt).
(b) Refer to text on page 271 (Topic-2, From benzene sulphonic acid).
(ii) (a) Refer to text on page 273 (Topic-2, Reimer-Tiemann reaction).
(b)Refer to text on page 273 (Topic-2, Oxidation).

52. (i) (a) Refer to text on page 256 (Topic-1, From reduction carbonyl compound).
(b) $CH_3CH = CH—CH_2—CH_2—\overset{\displaystyle OH}{\overset{|}{HC}}—CH_3$
(c) Refer to text on pages 256 and 257 (Topic-1, From Grignard reagent).
(ii) Refer to text on pages 283 and 284 (Topic-3, Reaction with halogen acid).

RELATED ONLINE VIDEOS

Visit : https://youtu.be/ZKbUKlhO0Yg
OR **Scan the Code**

Visit : https://youtu.be/nQ7QSV4JRSs
OR **Scan the Code**

Visit : https://youtu.be/SPI7DILFMHg
OR **Scan the Code**

CHAPTER 08

Aldehydes, Ketones and Carboxylic Acids

- Aldehydes and Ketones
- Carboxylic Acids

The compounds containing carbonyl group i.e. carbon-oxygen double bond (represented as $>C=O$) are known as **carbonyl compounds**.

Depending upon the atoms or group of atoms attached on either sides of the carbonyl group, these compounds are divided into three major classes, i.e. aldehydes, ketones and carboxylic acids.

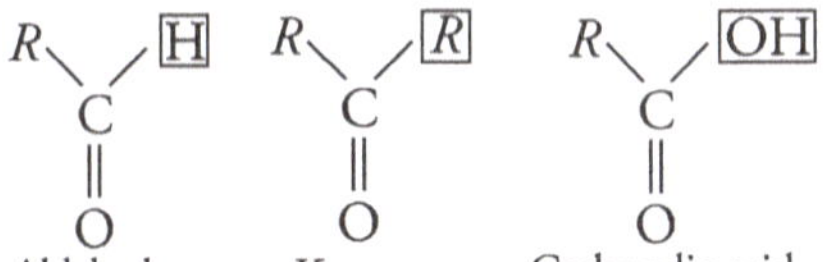

Aldehyde Ketone Carboxylic acid

TOPIC 01 Aldehydes and Ketones

In aldehydes, the carbonyl group is bonded to a carbon and hydrogen, while in ketones, it is bonded to the two carbon atoms. General formula; $C_nH_{2n}O$. e.g.

Aldehyde Ketone

Aldehydes and ketones are the simplest and most important carbonyl compounds.

Classification

Depending on the nature of groups attached to the carbonyl group, aldehydes and ketones are classified as below:

Aldehydes

Aldehydes are classified as :

(i) **Aliphatic Aldehyde** In which an alkyl group or a H-atom is attached to an aldehydic (—CHO) group, e.g. formaldehyde (HCHO), acetaldehyde (*R*CHO).

(ii) **Aromatic Aldehyde** In which an aryl group is attached to an aldehydic (—CHO) group, e.g. benzaldehyde (C_6H_5CHO).

e.g.

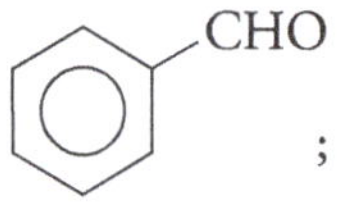

; CH_3CHO

Benzaldehyde   Acetaldehyde

$$\underset{\gamma}{H_3C}-\underset{\beta}{\overset{\overset{\displaystyle Br}{|}}{CH}}-\underset{\alpha}{CH_2}-\overset{\overset{\displaystyle O}{\|}}{C}-H$$

β-bromobutyraldehyde

Ketones

Ketones are classified as follows:

On the basis of carbon atoms attached to $>C{=}O$ group, ketones are classified as:

(i) **Symmetrical** Same alkyl or aryl groups attached to $C{=}O$ ketones, e.g. CH_3COCH_3.

(ii) **Unsymmetrical** Different alkyl or aryl groups are attached to $C{=}O$ ketones, e.g. $CH_3COC_2H_5$.

On the basis of alkyl or aryl nature of group attached to carbonyl group, ketones are classified as:

(i) **Aliphatic ketones** When both the groups attached to the carbonyl group are alkyl group, then they are called aliphatic ketones.

$$CH_3-\overset{\overset{\displaystyle O}{\|}}{C}-CH_3 \qquad C_2H_5-\overset{\overset{\displaystyle O}{\|}}{C}-CH_3$$

Propanone   Butan-2-one

(ii) **Aromatic ketones** These are further classified as aryl-alkyl ketones and diaryl ketones. When carbonyl groups attached to an aryl and an alkyl group, then ketone is called **aryl-alkyl ketone,** while when both groups are aryl groups then ketone is termed as **diaryl ketone.**

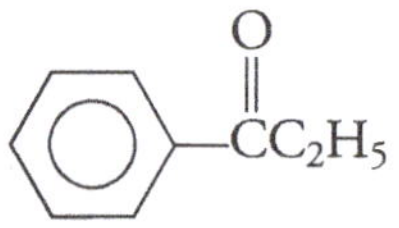

Ethylphenyl ketone (Aryl-alkyl ketone)

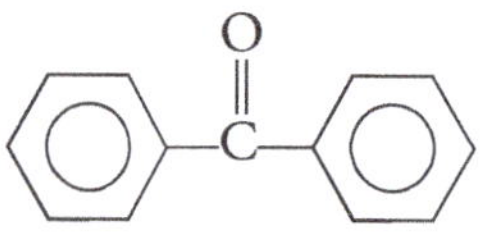

Diphenyl ketone (Diaryl ketone)

Nomenclature

There are two systems of nomenclature of aldehydes and ketones. These are as follows :

Common Names

(i) Common names of aldehydes are derived from common names of carboxylic acids (—COOH) just by replacing the ending '-ic' of carboxylic acid with aldehyde. The location of the substituent in the carbon chain is indicated by Greek letters α, β, γ, δ, etc. The α-carbon being the one directly linked to the $>C{=}O$ group, β - carbon the next and so on.

(ii) The common names of ketones are derived by naming the two alkyl or aryl groups bonded to the carbonyl group in alphabetical order. Alkyl phenyl ketones are usually named by adding the acyl group as prefix to phenone. The locations of substituents are indicated by Greek letters αα′, ββ′, etc., beginning with the carbon atoms next to the carbonyl group, indicated as αα′. e.g.

$$Cl-\overset{\alpha'}{CH_2}-\overset{\overset{\displaystyle O}{\|}}{C}-\overset{\alpha}{CH_2}-Cl,$$

α, α′-dichloroacetone

$$Cl-\overset{\alpha}{CH_2}-\overset{\overset{\displaystyle O}{\|}}{C}-\overset{\alpha'}{CH_2}\overset{\beta'}{CH_2}Br,$$

β′-bromoethyl-α-chloromethylketone

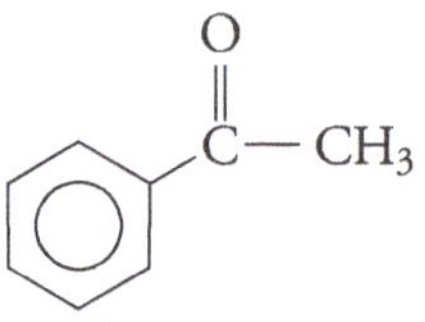

Acetophenone

IUPAC Names

The IUPAC names of open chain aliphatic aldehydes and ketones are derived from the names of the corresponding alkanes by replacing the ending 'e' with '-al' and '-one' respectively.

In aldehydes, the longest carbon chain is numbered from the carbon of the aldehyde group whereas numbering of carbon chain starts from the end nearer to the carbonyl group in ketones.

The substituents are prefixed in alphabetical order along with numerals indicating their positions in the carbon chain. The same applies to cyclic ketones, where the carbonyl carbon is numbered one. When the aldehydic group is attached to a ring, the suffix **'carbaldehyde'** is added after the full name of cycloalkane.

The numbering of the ring carbon atoms start from the carbon atom attached to the aldehyde group. The name of the simplest aromatic aldehyde carrying the aldehyde group on a benzene ring is **benzenecarbaldehyde** or **benzaldehyde**. However, the common name benzaldehyde is also accepted by IUPAC.

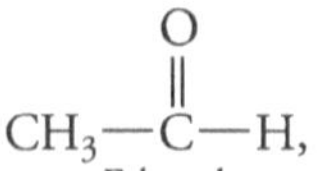
Ethanal

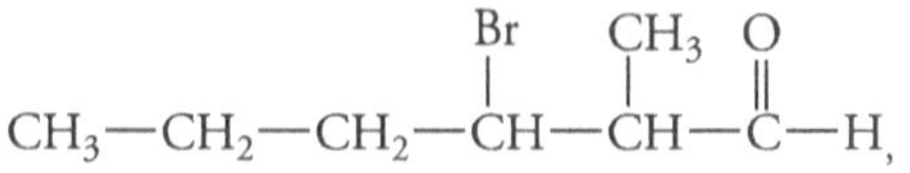
3-bromo-2-methylhexan-1-al

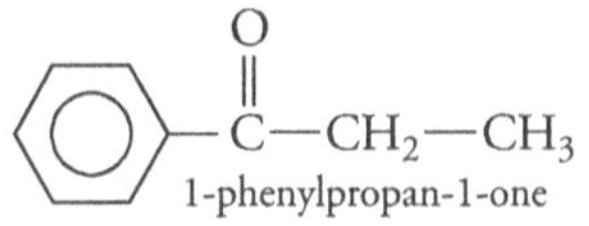
1-phenylpropan-1-one

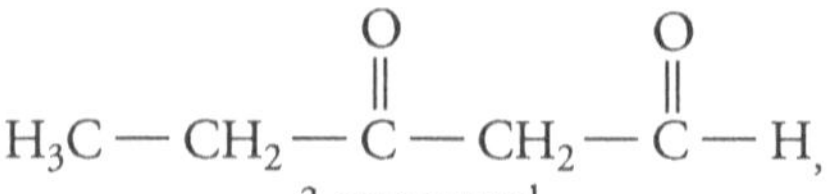
3-oxopentanal

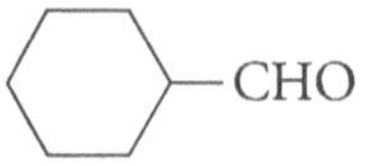
Cyclohexane carbaldehyde

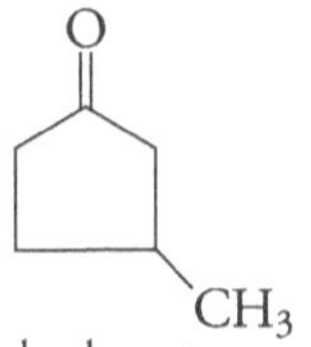
3-methylcyclopentanone

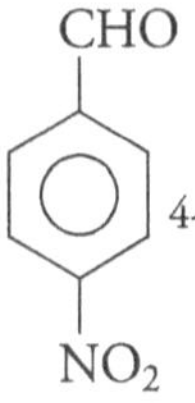
4-nitrobenzaldehyde, or 4-nitrobenzene carbaldehyde

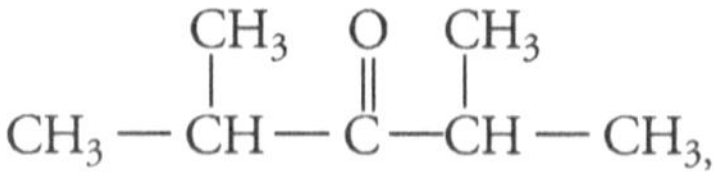
2, 4-dimethylpentan-3-one

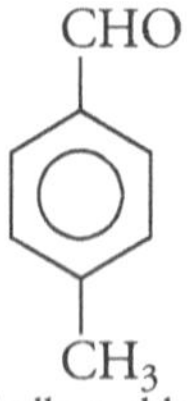
4-methylbenzaldehyde (or *p*-methylbenzaldehyde)

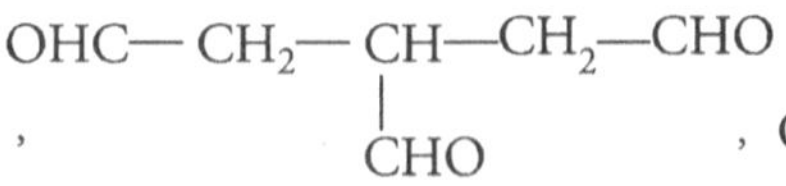
Propane-1,2,3-tricarbaldehyde

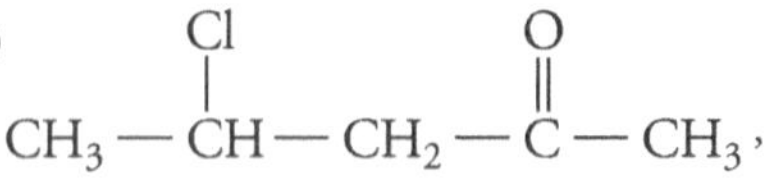
4-chloropentan-2-one

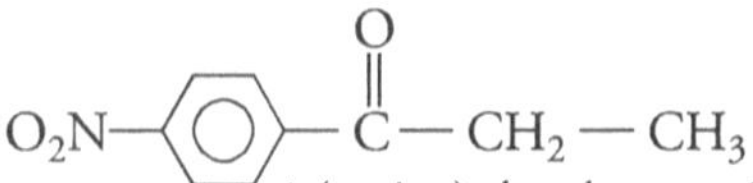
1-(*p*-nitro) phenyl propan-1-one or *p*-nitropropiophenone

Common and IUPAC Names of Some Aldehydes and Ketones

Structural formula	Common name	IUPAC name
Aldehydes		
HCHO	Formaldehyde	Methanal
$CH_3—CHO$	Acetaldehyde	Ethanal
$CH_3—CH_2—\overset{\alpha}{C}H(CH_3)—CHO$	α-methylbutyraldehyde	2-methylbutanal
$(CH_3)_2CHCHO$ or $CH_3—CH(CH_3)—CHO$	*iso* butyraldehyde	2-methylpropanal
$CH_3—CH_2—CH_2—CH_2—CHO$	Valeraldehyde	Pentanal
$CH_2=CH—CHO$	Acrolein	Prop-2-en-1-al
$CH_3—\overset{\alpha}{C}H(OCH_3)—CHO$	α-methoxypropionaldehyde	2-methoxypropanal
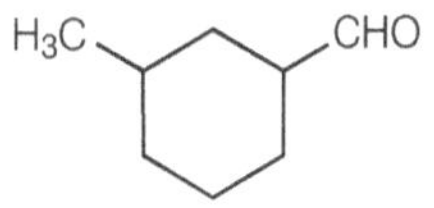	γ-methylcyclohexanecarbaldehyde	3-methylcyclohexanecarbaldehyde

Structural formula	Common name	IUPAC name
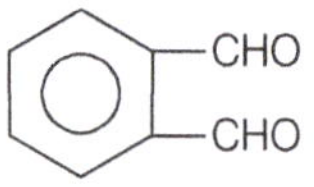	Phthaldehyde	Benzene-1,2-dicarbaldehyde
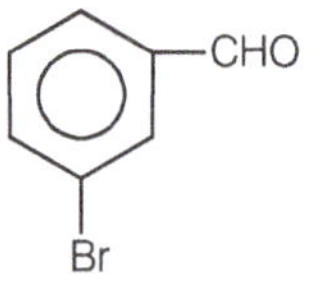	*m*-bromobenzaldehyde	3-bromobenzenecarbaldehyde or 3-bromobenzaldehyde
$CH_3—CH=CH—CHO$	Crotonaldehyde	But-2-enal
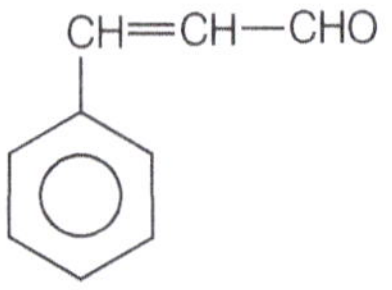	Cinnamaldehyde	3-phenylprop-2-enal
Ketones		
CH_3COCH_3	Acetone	Propanone
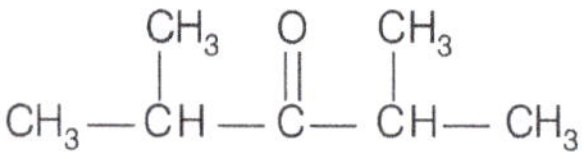	Diisopropyl ketone	2, 4-dimethylpentan-3-one
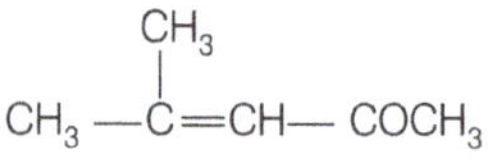	Mesityl oxide	4-methylpent-3-en-2-one
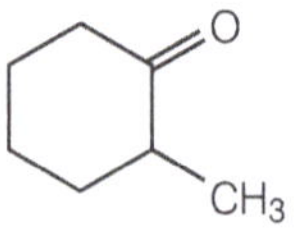	α-methylcyclohexanone	2-methylcyclohexanone

Example 1 Draw the structures of the following compounds.

(i) α-methoxypropionaldehyde (ii) 3-hydroxybutanal
(iii) 2-hydroxycyclopentane carbaldehyde (iv) 4-oxopentanal
(v) Di-sec-butylketone (vi) 4- fluoroacetophenone

NCERT Intext

Sol. (i) 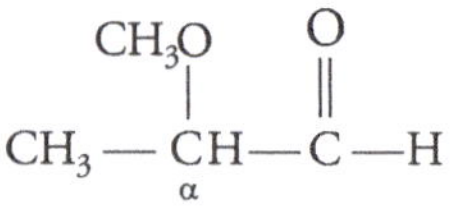 (α-methoxypropionaldehyde)

(ii) 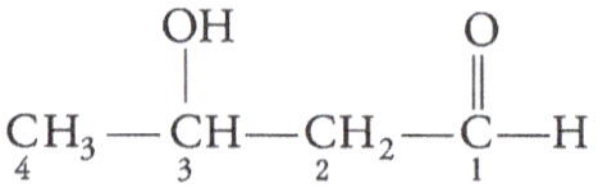 (3-hydroxybutanal)

(iii) 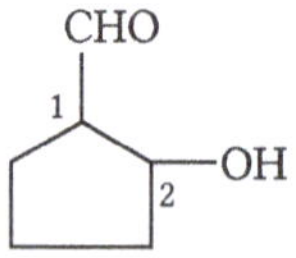 (2-hydroxycyclopentane carbaldehyde)

(iv) 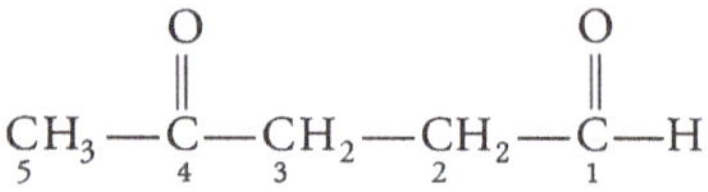 (4-oxopentanal)

(v) 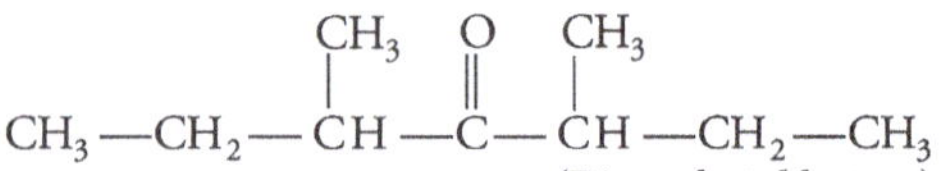 (Di-sec-butyl ketone)

(vi) 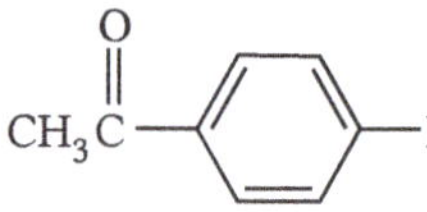 (4- fluoroacetophenone)

Structure

The carbonyl carbon atom is sp^2- hybridised and forms 3 sigma (σ) bonds. The fourth valence electron of carbon remains in its p-orbital where it forms a π-bond by overlapping with p-orbital of an oxygen. The oxygen atom also have two non-bonding electron pairs. Thus, carbonyl carbon and three atoms attached to it lie in the same plane and π-electron cloud is above and below this plane. It possesses a trigonal coplanar structure with bond angles of $120°$.

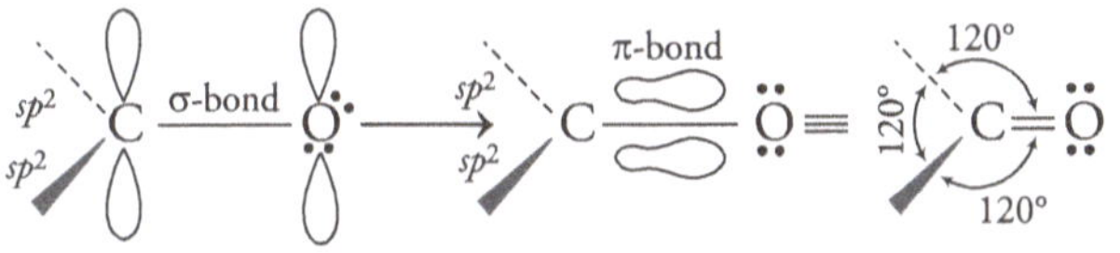

Orbital diagram for the formation of carbonyl group

Methods of Preparation

Some important methods of preparation of aldehydes and ketones are discussed below:

Preparation of both Aldehydes and Ketones

These are prepared by the following methods:

1. From Alcohol

(i) By oxidation of alcohols with $K_2Cr_2O_7/H_2SO_4$ or $KMnO_4/KOH$.

$$\underset{1^\circ\text{alcohol}}{RCH_2OH} + [O] \xrightarrow{K_2Cr_2O_7/H_2SO_4} \underset{\text{Aldehyde}}{R\text{—}CHO} + H_2O$$

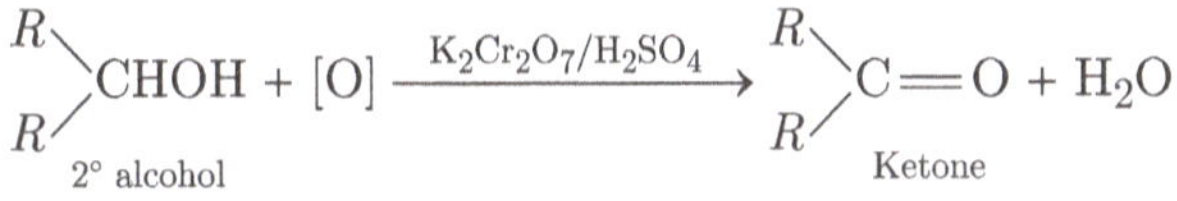

(ii) By catalytic dehydrogenation of alcohols with Cu at 573 K.

$$\underset{1^\circ\text{alcohol}}{R\text{—}CH_2OH} \xrightarrow{Cu/573\ K} \underset{\text{Aldehyde}}{R\text{—}CHO} + H_2$$

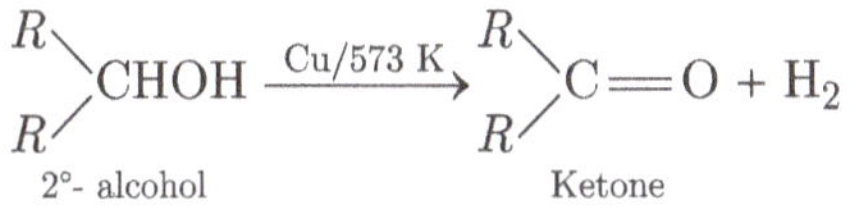

2. From Alkenes (Ozonolysis)

Ozonolysis of alkenes followed by the reaction with zinc dust and water gives aldehydes, ketones or both depending on the substitution pattern of the alkene.

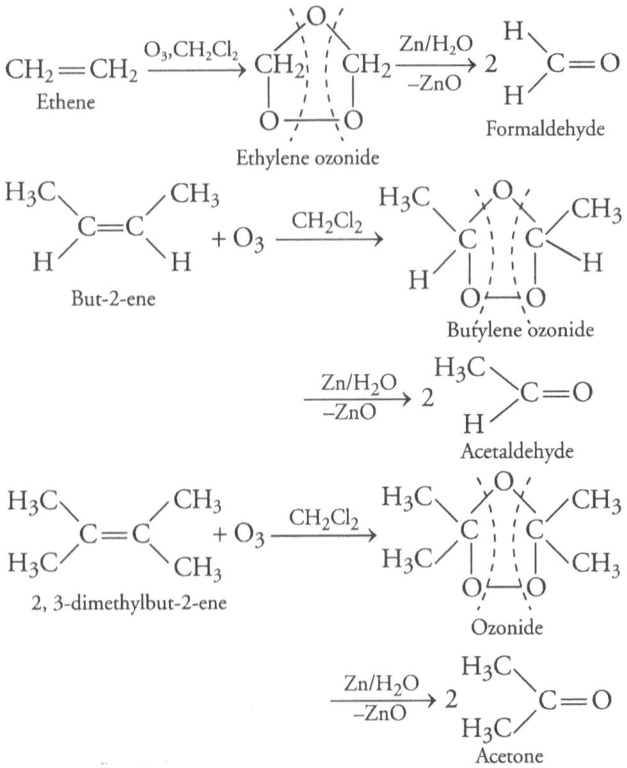

3. From Hydration of Alkynes

Addition of water to ethyne in the presence of dil. H_2SO_4 and $HgSO_4$ gives acetaldehyde. All other alkynes give ketones in the reaction.

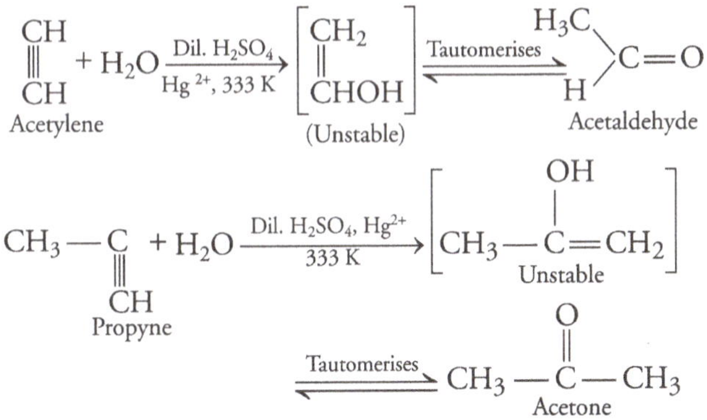

4. From Calcium Salts of Carboxylic Acids

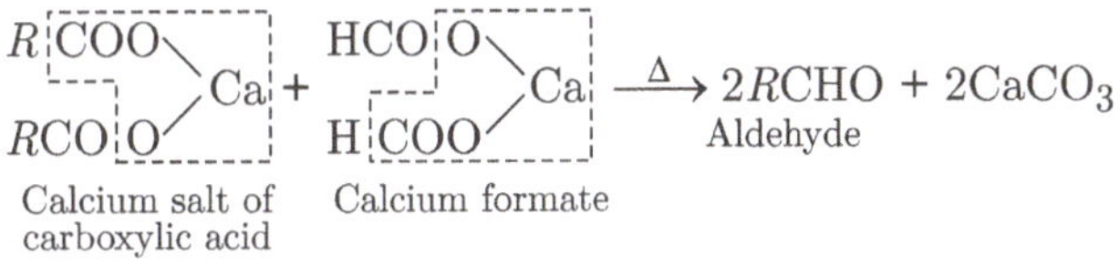

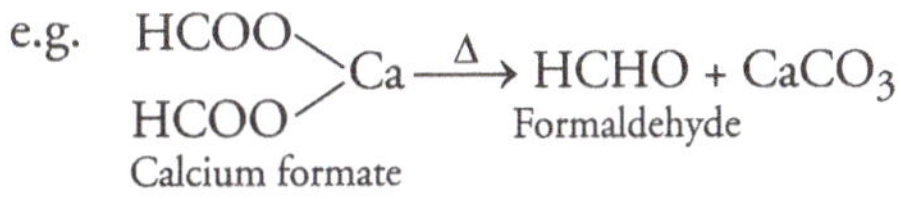

$$\underset{\text{Calcium acetate}}{\begin{matrix}CH_3COO\\CH_3COO\end{matrix}\!\!>Ca} + \underset{\text{Calcium formate}}{Ca<\!\!\begin{matrix}OOCH\\OOCH\end{matrix}} \xrightarrow{\Delta} 2\underset{\text{Acetaldehyde}}{\begin{matrix}CH_3\\H\end{matrix}\!\!>C{=}O} + 2CaCO_3$$

$$\underset{\text{Calcium acetate}}{\begin{matrix}CH_3COO\\CH_3COO\end{matrix}\!\!>Ca} \xrightarrow{\Delta} \underset{\text{Acetone}}{\begin{matrix}CH_3\\CH_3\end{matrix}\!\!>C{=}O} + CaCO_3$$

Note Instead of Ca salts, Mg, Ba and Th salts may also be used in the above method.

Preparation of Aldehydes

Some important methods for the preparation of only aldehydes are given below :

1. From Acyl Chloride (Rosenmund's Reduction)

Acyl chloride or acid chloride is hydrogenated in the presence of palladium catalyst supported over and partially poisoned by the addition of sulphur or barium sulphate. This reaction is called **Rosenmund reduction.**

$$\underset{\text{Acetyl chloride}}{CH_3-\overset{\overset{\displaystyle O}{\|}}{C}-Cl} \xrightarrow[\text{Pd/BaSO}_4\text{, S}]{H_2} \underset{\text{Acetaldehyde}}{CH_3-\overset{\overset{\displaystyle O}{\|}}{C}-H}$$

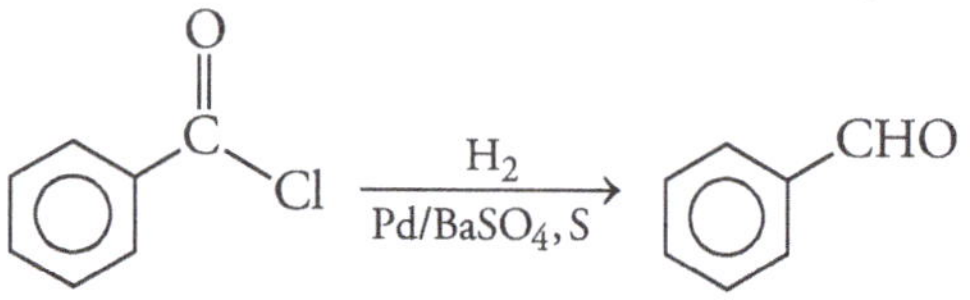

Benzoyl chloride Benzaldehyde

Formaldehyde cannot be prepared by this method because formyl chloride, HCOCl is unstable at room temperature. $BaSO_4$ and sulphur acts as a poison to the Pd catalyst and thus, prevents the aldehyde from being further reduced to alcohols.

2. From Nitriles (Stephen Reaction)

Nitriles are reduced to corresponding imine with stannous chloride in the presence of hydrochloric acid, which on hydrolysis give corresponding aldehyde.

$$\underset{\text{Nitrile}}{RCN} + SnCl_2 + HCl \longrightarrow \underset{\text{Imine}}{RCH{=}NH} \xrightarrow{H_3O^+} \underset{\text{Aldehyde}}{RCHO}$$

This reaction is called **Stephen reaction.**

Alternatively, diisobutylaluminium hydride, $[(CH_3)_2CHCH_2]_2AlH$ is abbreviated as $AlH(i\text{-Bu})_2$ or DIBAL-H is used to reduce nitriles (selectively) to imines which upon hydrolysis give aldehydes.

$$RCN \xrightarrow{\text{(i) AlH}(i\text{-Bu})_2} \underset{\text{Imine}}{RCH{=}NH} \xrightarrow[\text{Hydrolysis}]{\text{(ii) H}_2\text{O}} \underset{\text{Aldehyde}}{RCHO} + NH_3$$

$$\underset{\text{Hex-4-en-1-nitrile}}{CH_3-CH{=}CH-CH_2CH_2CN} \xrightarrow[\text{(ii) H}_2\text{O}]{\text{(i) AlH}(i\text{-Bu})_2} \underset{\text{Hex-4-en-1-al}}{CH_3-CH{=}CH-CH_2CH_2-CHO}$$

3. From Esters

Esters are also reduced to aldehydes with DIBAL-H.

$$\underset{\text{Ethyl undecanoate}}{\underset{\text{(Ester)}}{CH_3(CH_2)_9-\overset{\overset{\displaystyle O}{\|}}{C}-OC_2H_5}} \xrightarrow[\text{(ii) H}_2\text{O}]{\text{(i) DIBAL-H}} \underset{\text{Undecanal}}{CH_3(CH_2)_9-\overset{\overset{\displaystyle O}{\|}}{C}-H}$$

4. From Hydrocarbons

Aromatic aldehydes (benzaldehyde and its derivatives) can be prepared from aromatic hydrocarbons (discussed on pg-313).

Preparation of Ketones

Some important methods for the preparation of ketones are given below :

1. From Acyl Chlorides (Reaction with Dialkyl Cadmium)

Acyl chlorides, on treatment with dialkyl cadmium gives ketones.

$$\underset{\text{Grignard reagent}}{2R-Mg-X} + CdCl_2 \xrightarrow{\text{Dry ether}} \underset{\text{Dialkyl cadmium}}{R_2Cd} + 2Mg(X)Cl$$

$$\underset{\text{Acyl chloride}}{2R'-\underset{\underset{\displaystyle O}{\|}}{C}-Cl} + \underset{\text{Dialkyl cadmium}}{R_2Cd} \xrightarrow{\text{Dry ether}} 2R'-\underset{\underset{\displaystyle O}{\|}}{C}-R + CdCl_2$$

e.g. $$\underset{\text{Acetyl chloride}}{2CH_3-\overset{\overset{\displaystyle O}{\|}}{C}-Cl} + \underset{\text{Diethyl cadmium}}{(CH_3CH_2)_2Cd} \xrightarrow{\text{Dry ether}} \underset{\text{Butanone}}{2CH_3-\overset{\overset{\displaystyle O}{\|}}{C}-CH_2CH_3} + CdCl_2$$

2. From Nitriles

When a nitrile is treated with Grignard reagent followed by hydrolysis yields a ketone.

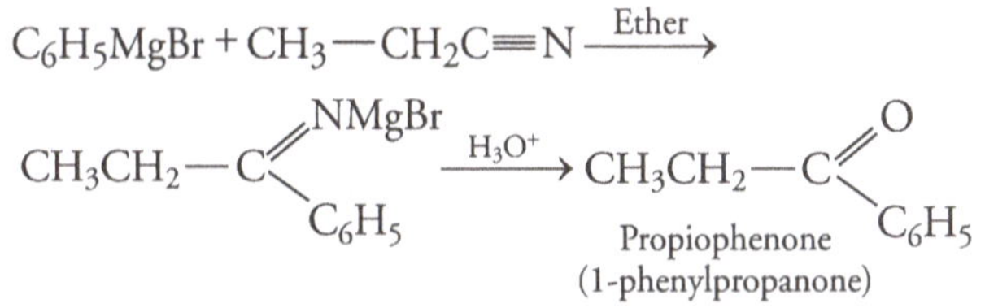

3. From Benzene or Substituted Benzene

When benzene or substituted benzene is treated with acid chloride in the presence of anhydrous aluminium chloride, a corresponding ketone is obtained.

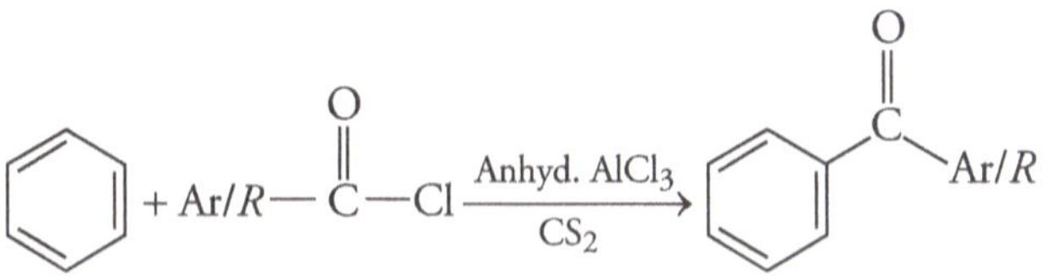

This reaction is known as **Friedel-Crafts acylation reaction.**

Physical Properties

The physical properties of aldehydes and ketones are as follows:

1. Physical State

Methanal is a gas at room temperature. Ethanal is a volatile liquid. Other aldehydes and ketones are liquid or solid at room temperature.

2. Boiling Point

Boiling points of aldehydes and ketones are higher than hydrocarbons and ethers of comparable molecular masses because weak intermolecular association arises due to dipole-dipole interactions. Also, their boiling points are lower than those of alcohols of similar molecular masses due to the absence of intermolecular hydrogen bonding.

3. Solubility

Lower members of aldehydes and ketones like methanal, ethanal and propanone are miscible with water in all proportions because they form hydrogen bond with water.

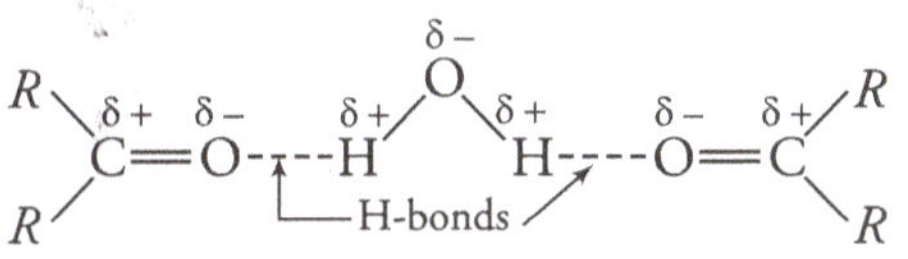

However, the solubility of aldehydes and ketones decreases when the length of alkyl chain increases. All aldehydes and ketones are fairly soluble in organic solvents like benzene, ether, methanol, chloroform, etc.

4. Odour

Lower aldehydes have sharp pungent (unpleasant) odours. The odour becomes less pungent with increase in molecular size. Many naturally occurring aldehydes and ketones are used in blending of perfumes and flavouring agents

Chemical Properties

Aldehydes and ketones are highly reactive compounds. Since, both of these possess the same functional group, i.e. polarised carbonyl group, they undergo a number of common reactions.

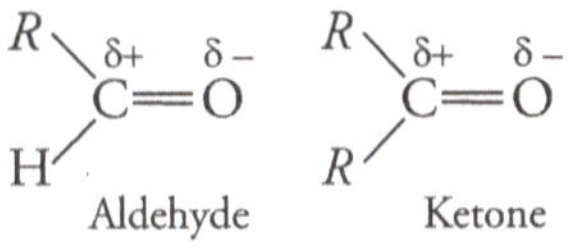

Some important reactions of aldehydes and ketones are as follows:

Nucleophilic Addition Reactions

Both alkenes and carbonyl compounds, i.e. aldehydes and ketones are unsaturated compounds. However, unlike alkenes which undergo electrophilic addition reactions, aldehydes and ketones undergo nucleophilic addition reactions.

Mechanism

Carbonyl group being polar (due to greater electronegativity of oxygen as compared to carbon), behaves as an electrophile in the presence of nucleophile.

Thus, the nucleophile readily attacks the electrophilic carbon atom of carbonyl group in the direction perpendicular to the plane of sp^2-hybridised orbitals of carbonyl carbon.

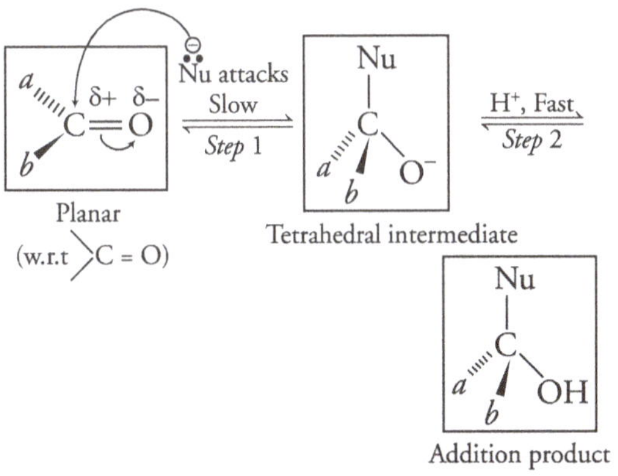

Nucleophilic attack on carbonyl carbon

The hybridisation of carbon changes from sp^2 to sp^3 in this process and tetrahedral alkoxide intermediate is formed. The intermediate then picks up a proton either from the solvent (usually H_2O) or from the reagent to give electrically neutral addition product. The net result is addition of Nu^- and H^+ across the carbon oxygen double bond.

Relative Reactivities

Aldehydes are more reactive towards nucleophilic addition reactions than ketones due to the following reasons:

(i) **Inductive Effect** Since, an alkyl group has electron donating (+*I*) inductive effect. Hence, greater the number of alkyl groups attached to carbonyl group, greater the electron density on carbonyl carbon. Thus, it lowers the attack of nucleophile that results in a decrease in reactivity.

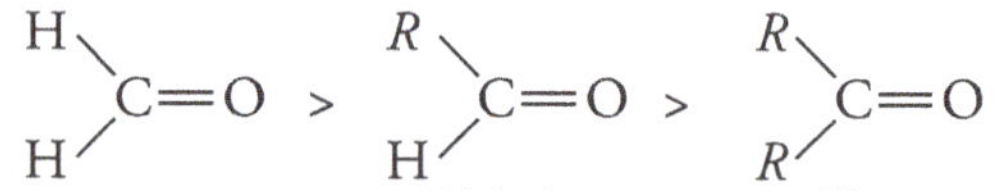

Formaldehyde Aldehyde Ketone

(ii) **Steric Effect** As the number of alkyl group attached to carbonyl carbon increases, the attack of nucleophile on carbonyl group becomes more and more difficult due to steric hindrance. Therefore, due to the presence of two bulky alkyl (or *R*) groups, the attack of nucleophile is hindered and hence, ketones are less reactive than aldehydes.

Thus, the reactivity of the following carbonyl compounds decreases as:

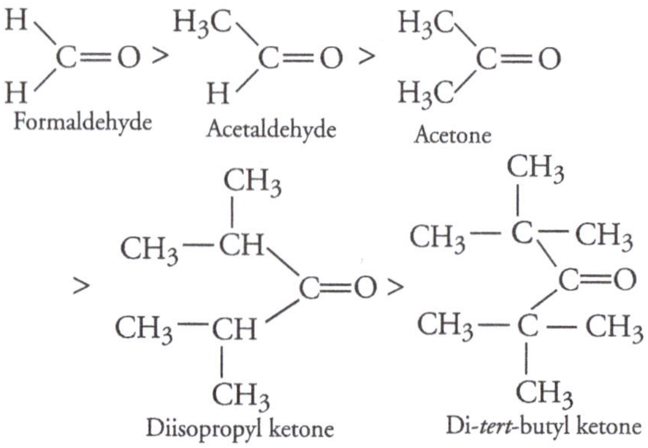

Reactivity of Aromatic Aldehydes and Ketones

In general, aromatic aldehydes and ketones are less reactive than the corresponding aliphatic analogues because electron donating resonance effect (+*R*-effect) of the benzene ring increases the electron density on the carbonyl carbon. This makes the carbonyl carbon less electrophilic.

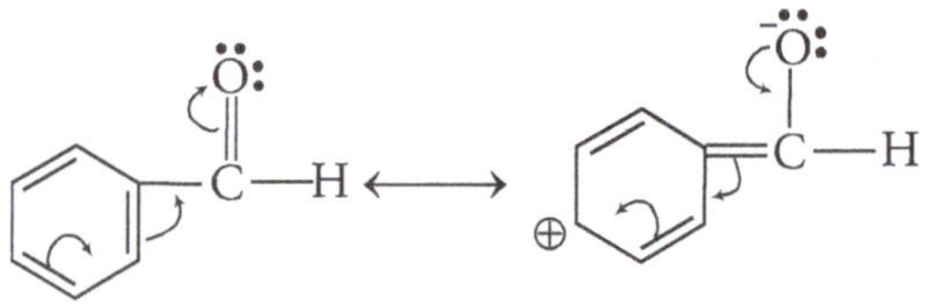

However, amongst aromatic aldehydes and ketones, aromatic aldehydes are more reactive than alkyl aryl ketones which in turn are more reactive than diaryl ketones.

$$C_6H_5CHO > C_6H_5COCH_3 > C_6H_5COC_6H_5$$

Some Important Examples of Nucleophilic Addition Reactions

1. Addition of Hydrogen Cyanide (HCN)

Aldehydes and ketones on reaction with HCN give cyanohydrins. This reaction is very slow with pure HCN. So, it is catalysed by a base and the generated CN^- being a stronger nucleophile readily attacks on carbonyl-carbon to yield corresponding cyanohydrin.

$$H\overset{\ominus}{O} + H-CN \rightleftharpoons :\bar{C}N + H_2O$$

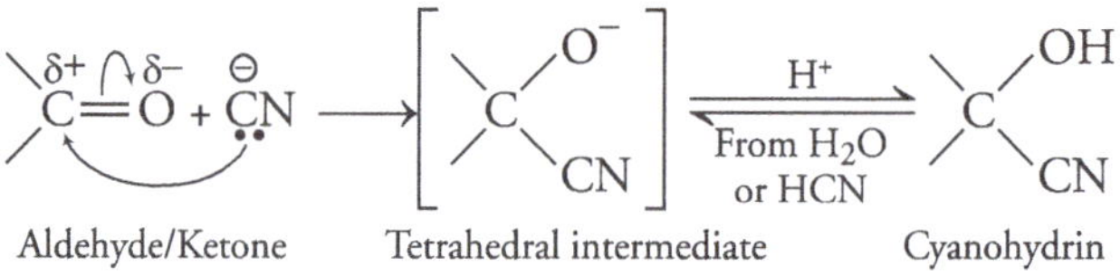

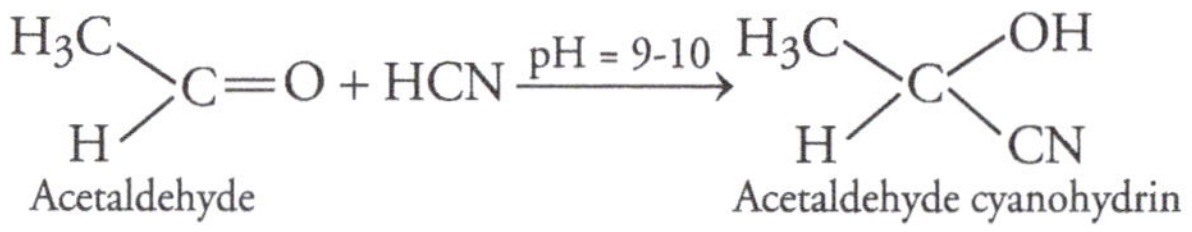

Cyanohydrins are useful synthetic intermediate. e.g.

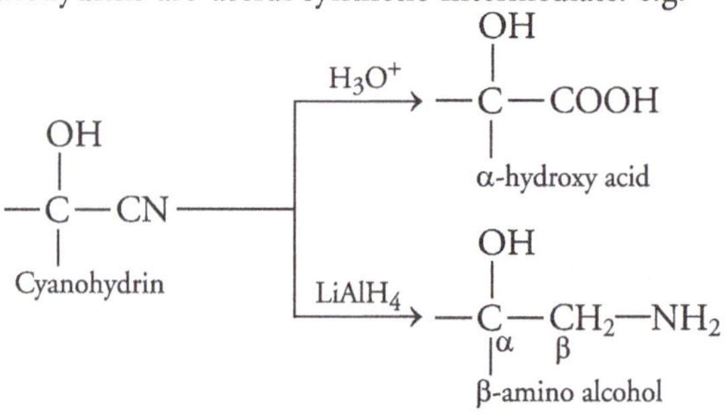

2. Addition of Sodium Hydrogen Sulphite ($NaHSO_3$)

Most of the aldehydes and aliphatic methyl ketones which are not sterically hindered, on reaction with $NaHSO_3$ give bisulphite addition product.

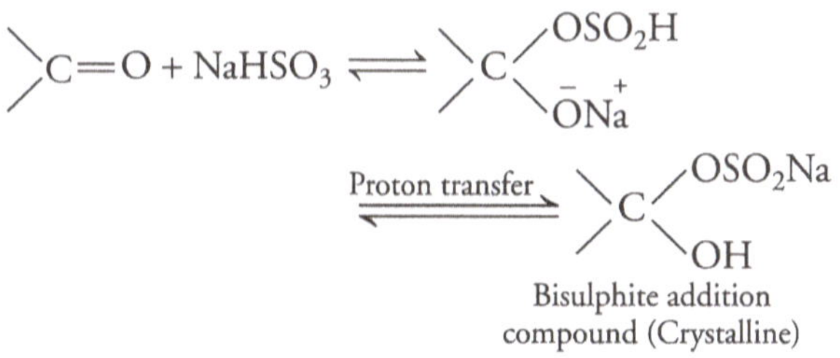

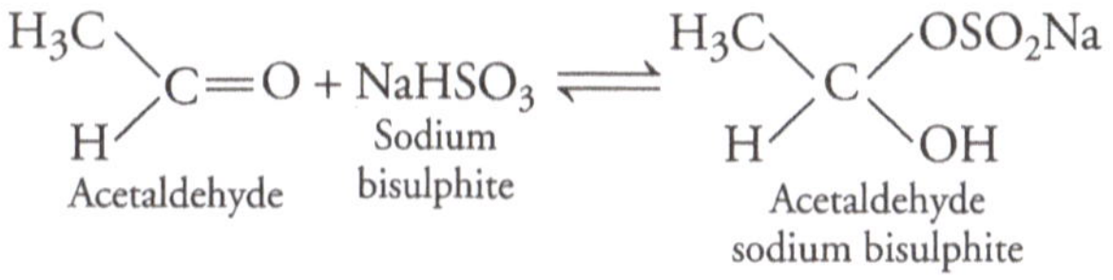

The position of the equilibrium lies largely to the right hand side for most aldehydes and to the left for most ketones due to steric reasons.

The bisulphite addition compound is water soluble and can be converted back to the original carbonyl compound by treating it with dilute mineral acid or alkali.

Therefore, these are useful for separation and purification of aldehydes.

3. Addition of Grignard Reagents

Aldehydes and ketones on reaction with Grignard reagent give addition products which upon hydrolysis with water or dilute mineral acids give alcohols. The type of alcohol formed depends upon the aldehyde or ketone used (formaldehyde $\rightarrow 1^\circ$ alcohols, other aldehydes $\rightarrow 2^\circ$ alcohols and ketones $\rightarrow 3^\circ$ alcohols) (discussed in chapter 11).

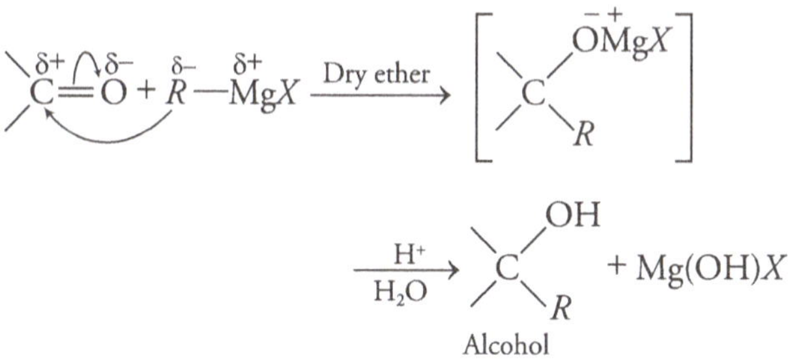

4. Addition of Alcohols

Aldehydes react with one equivalent of a monohydric alcohol in the presence of dry HCl gas to yield alkoxy alcohol intermediate known as **hemiacetals**. Hemiacetals on further reaction with one more molecule of alcohol give **acetals**. (Hemiacetals are alkoxy alcohols while acetals are *gem*-dialkoxy compounds).

e.g.

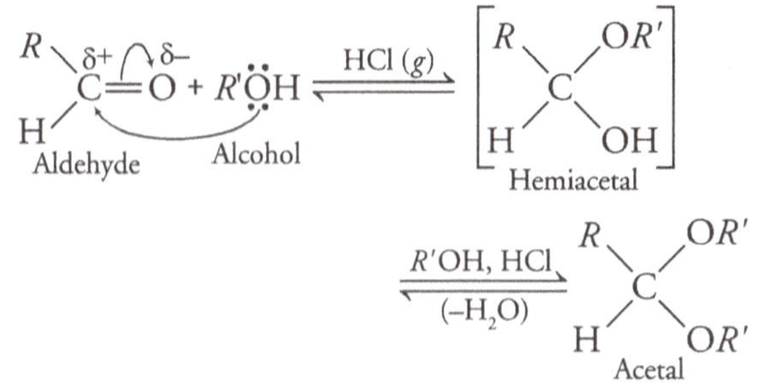

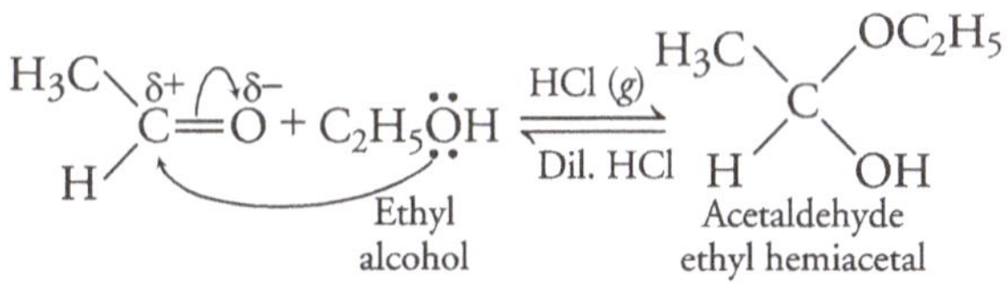

In this reaction, dry HCl gas protonates the oxygen atom of the carbonyl compound, thereby increasing the electrophilicity of the carbonyl carbon and hence facilitating the nucleophilic attack by the alcohol molecule. Ketones, however, do not react with monohydric alcohols but they react with dihydric alcohol such as ethylene glycol to give cyclic **ketals**.

e.g.

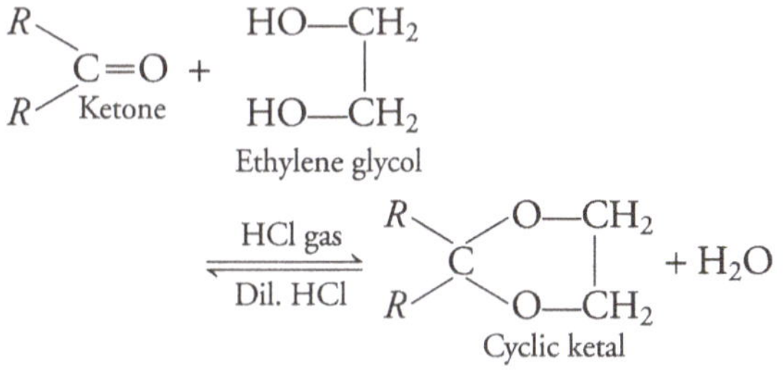

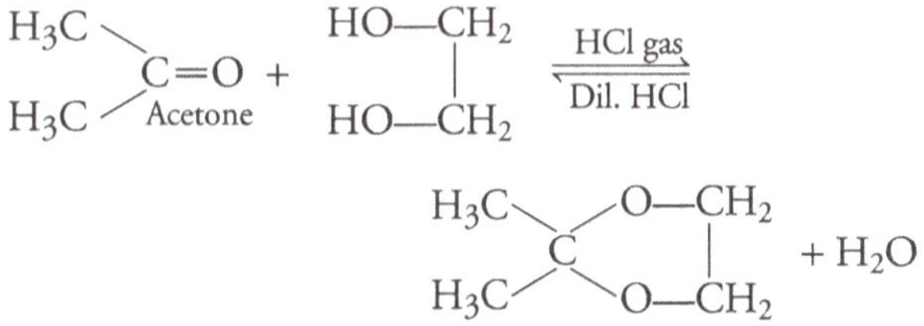

Note Acetals and ketals are hydrolysed by dilute acids and generate original aldehydes and ketones respectively.

Nucleophilic Addition Elimination Reactions

These are two step reactions involving addition followed by elimination of some small molecules. Their first step is similar to nucleophilic addition reactions. Examples of nucleophilic addition elimination reaction are as follows:

Addition of Ammonia and its Derivatives

Aldehydes and ketones react with ammonia and a number of its derivatives, $H_2N—Z$ in weakly acidic medium to form compounds containing $>C=N$ group. These reactions are reversible and catalysed by acid. The equilibrium favours the product formation due to rapid dehydration of the intermediate to form $>C=N—Z$ type compounds.

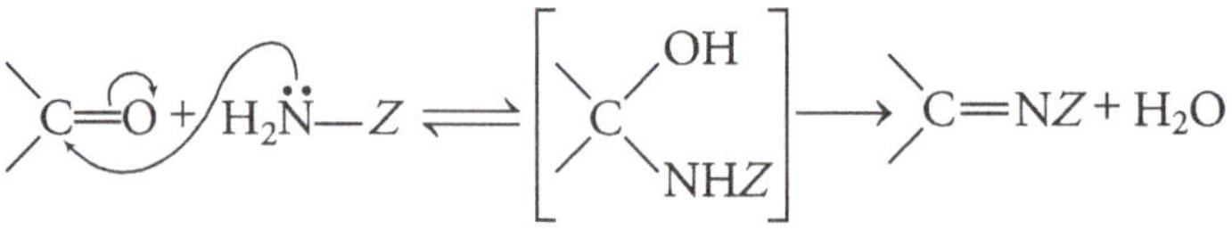

(where, Z = H, alkyl, aryl, — OH, — NH_2, — $NHCONH_2$ and —NH— 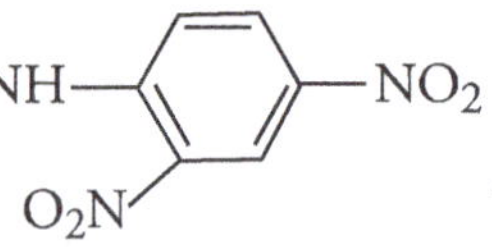)

The reactions of carbonyl group with substituted N-derivatives can be summarised as:

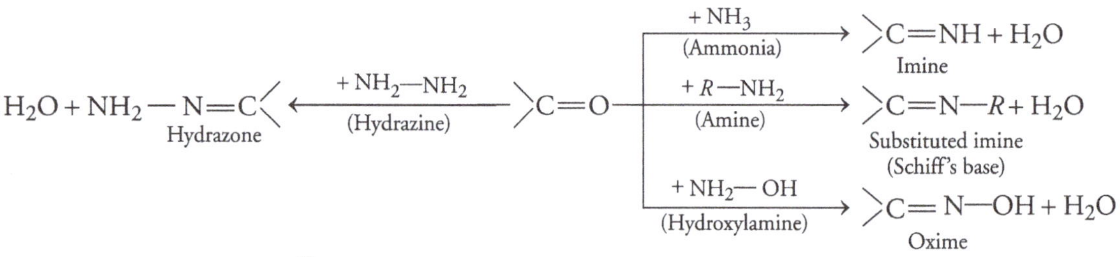

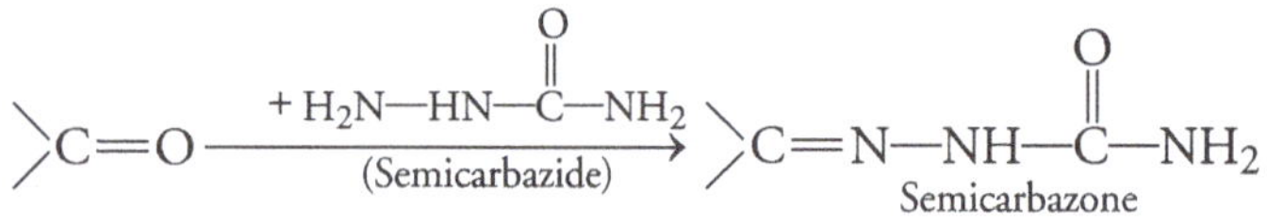

Note 2,4-dinitrophenyl hydrazine is **Brady's reagent**. Aldehydes and ketones react with it to form yellow, orange or red ppt. of 2,4-dinitrophenyl hydrazone. These are useful for the characterisation of aldehydes and ketones.

Example 2 Predict the products of the following reactions:

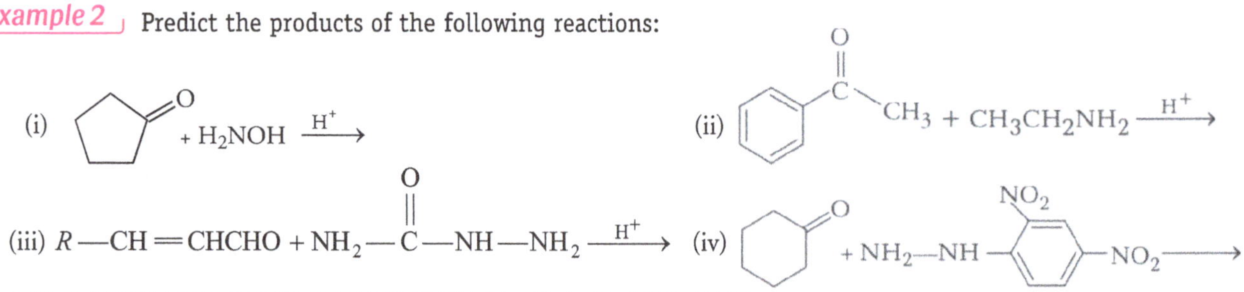

Hint Elimination of H_2O from carbonyl and amine group and formation of C=N bond.

Sol.

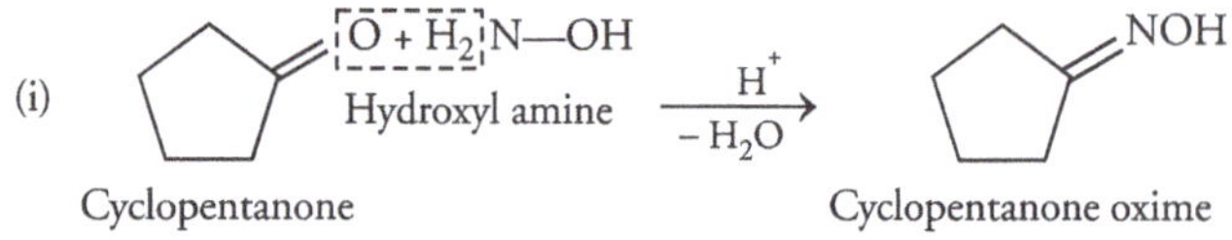

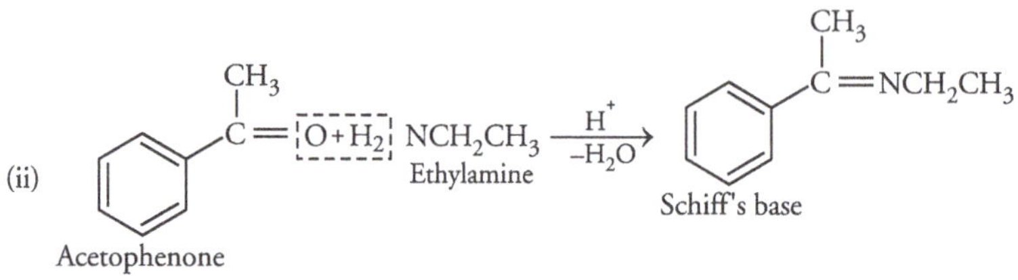

(iii) $R{-}CH{=}CH{-}CHO + H_2N{-}NH{-}\overset{\overset{\displaystyle O}{\|}}{C}{-}NH_2$

Unsaturated aldehyde, Semicarbazide

$$\xrightarrow[-H_2O]{H^+} RCH{=}CH{-}CH{=}N{-}NH{-}\overset{\overset{\displaystyle O}{\|}}{C}{-}NH_2$$

Semicarbazone

(iv) 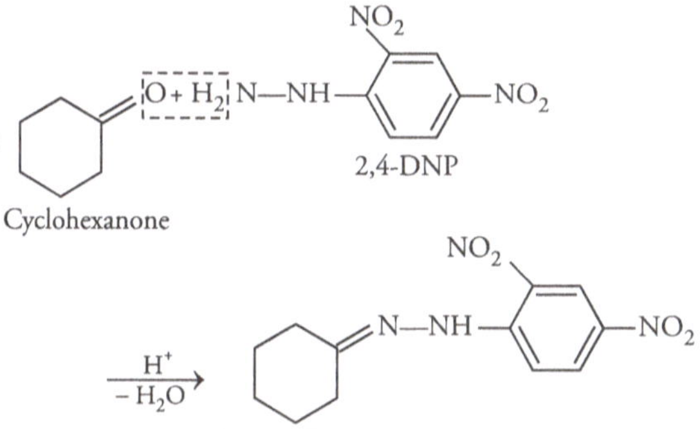

2,4-DNP derivative of cyclohexanone

Note Reaction (iv) is used to test the presence of carbonyl group.

Oxidation Reactions

Aldehydes differ from ketones in their oxidation reactions. Aldehydes are easily oxidised to carboxylic acids containing the same number of carbon atom because aldehydes contain H-atom attached to carbonyl group, which can be converted into —OH group without involving the cleavage of any other bond.

Thus, they are oxidised not only by strong oxidising agents like HNO_3, $KMnO_4$ and $K_2Cr_2O_7$ but also by weak oxidising agents like Tollen's reagent, Fehling's solution and Benedict's reagent.

$$R{-}CHO \xrightarrow{[O]} R{-}COOH$$

Unlike aldehydes, ketones do not contain H-atom attached to $\rangle C{=}O$ group and hence, they cannot be oxidised by weak oxidising agent.

1. Reactions with Strong Oxidising Agents

Ketones are generally oxidised by strong oxidising agents like HNO_3, acidified $KMnO_4$, acidified $K_2Cr_2O_7$ at high temperature. Their oxidation involves carbon-carbon bond cleavage with the formation of a mixture of carboxylic acids each containing lesser number of carbon atoms than the original ketone.

$$R{-}\overset{1}{C}H_2{-}\underset{\underset{\displaystyle O}{\|}}{\overset{2}{C}}{-}\overset{3}{C}H_2{-}R' \xrightarrow{[O]} R{-}COOH + R'{-}CH_2COOH$$

(By cleavage of $C_1{-}C_2$ bond)

Or $R{-}CH_2COOH + R'{-}COOH$

(By cleavage of $C_2{-}C_3$ bond)

$$\underset{(3\,C)}{CH_3{-}\overset{\overset{\displaystyle O}{\|}}{C}{-}CH_3} + 3[O] \xrightarrow{\text{Conc. } HNO_3} \underset{(1C)}{HCOOH} + \underset{(2C)}{CH_3{-}COOH}$$

$$\underset{1}{CH_3}{-}\underset{2}{\overset{\overset{\displaystyle O}{\|}}{C}}{-}\underset{3}{CH_2}{-}\underset{4}{CH_2}{-}\underset{5}{CH_3} \xrightarrow[H_2SO_4]{K_2Cr_2O_7}$$

Pentan-2-one

$\xrightarrow[\text{cleavage}]{C_2{-}C_3 \text{ bond}}$ CH_3COOH + $CH_3{-}CH_2{-}COOH$
Acetic acid (Major product), Propionic acid (Minor product)

$\xrightarrow[\text{cleavage}]{C_1{-}C_2 \text{ bond}}$ $HCOOH$ + $CH_3CH_2CH_2COOH$
Formic acid, Butyric acid

Note In case of unsymmetrical ketones, e.g. pentan-2-one, the keto group stays preferentially with smaller alkyl group (Popoff's rule).

2. Reactions with Mild Oxidising Agents

The mild oxidising agents given below are used to distinguish aldehydes from ketones.

(i) **Tollen's Test** Tollen's reagent is an ammoniacal solution of silver nitrate. When an aldehyde is heated with freshly prepared Tollen's reagent, a bright silver mirror is produced due to the formation of silver metal. Aldehydes are oxidised to the corresponding carboxylate anion. The reaction occurs in alkaline medium.

$$\underset{\text{Aldehyde}}{RCHO} + \underset{\text{Tollen's reagent}}{2[Ag(NH_3)_2]^+} + 3OH^- \xrightarrow{\Delta} RCOO^- + \underset{\text{Silver mirror}}{2Ag\downarrow} + 2H_2O + 4NH_3\uparrow$$

The silver thus formed shines like mirror. Hence, this test is called **silver mirror test.**

Note Both aliphatic and aromatic aldehydes reduce Tollen's reagent.

(ii) **Fehling's Test** Fehling's reagent is a mixture of two solutions, i.e. Fehling's solution *A* and *B*. Fehling's solution *A* is an aqueous copper sulphate and Fehling's solution *B* is an alkaline sodium potassium tartarate (Rochelle salt). These two solutions are mixed in equal amounts before test. When an aldehyde is heated with Fehling's reagent, a reddish-brown precipitate is obtained. Aldehydes are oxidised to corresponding carboxylate anion.

$$\underset{\text{Aldehyde}}{RCHO} + \underset{\text{Fehling's solution}}{2Cu^{2+} + 5OH^-} \xrightarrow{\Delta} RCOO^- + \underset{\text{Red-brown ppt.}}{Cu_2O\downarrow} + 3H_2O$$

Note Aromatic aldehydes do not reduce Fehling's solution.

(iii) **Benedict's Test** Benedict's solution is an alkaline solution of Cu^{2+} ions complexed with citrate ions. (whereas, Fehling's solution is an alkaline solution of Cu^{2+} ions complexed with tartarate ions.) Benedict's solution reacts in the same way as Fehling's solution.

3. Haloform Reaction

Aldehydes and ketones having atleast one methyl group linked to the carbonyl carbon atom (methyl ketones) are oxidised by sodium hypohalite to sodium salts of corresponding carboxylic acids having one carbon atom less than that of carbonyl compound. The methyl group is converted into haloform. This oxidation does not affect a carbon-carbon double bond, if present in the molecule.

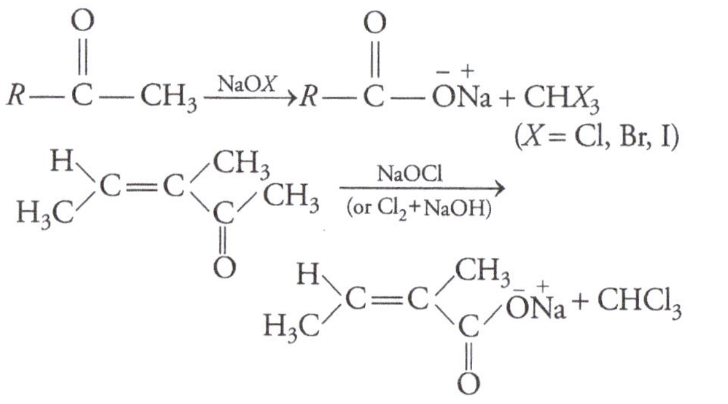

Iodoform reaction with sodium hypoiodite is also used for the detection of CH_3CO — group or $CH_3CH(OH)$ — group which produces CH_3CO — group on oxidation.

Example 3 Complete the following reaction:

$$CH_3CH_2CH_2COCH_3 \xrightarrow[H^+/H_2O]{I_2/NaOH} ?$$

Sol. $\underset{\text{Pentan-2-one}}{CH_3CH_2CH_2COCH_3} \xrightarrow[H^+/H_2O]{I_2/NaOH} \underset{\text{Butanoic acid}}{CH_3CH_2CH_2COOH} + \underset{\text{Iodoform}}{CHI_3} \downarrow$

Reduction Reactions

Aldehydes and ketones can be reduced to a variety of compounds under different conditions. Reduction various reactions are as follows:

1. Reduction to Alkanes

The carbonyl group of an aldehyde or ketone is reduced to methylene group to form a hydrocarbon.

This can be achieved by either one of the following two reactions:

(i) **Clemmensen Reduction** It involves the reduction of carbonyl group ($>C=O$) to $>CH_2$ group and it is carried out in the presence of Zn amalgam and conc. HCl.

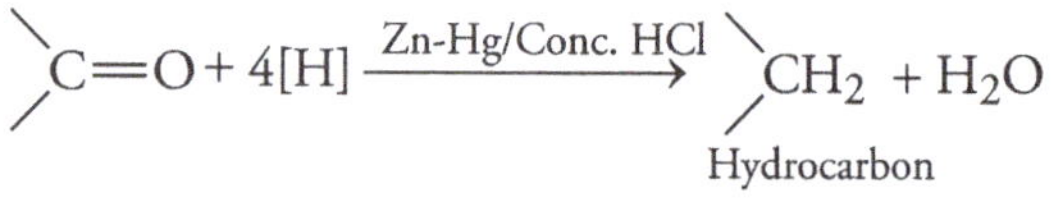

It is widely used for the reduction of aldehydes and ketones which are sensitive to alkalies.

(ii) **Wolff-Kishner Reduction** In this method, the aldehyde or ketone is heated with hydrazine and KOH or NaOH in high boiling solvent such as ethylene glycol. It is used when carbonyl compounds are sensitive to acids.

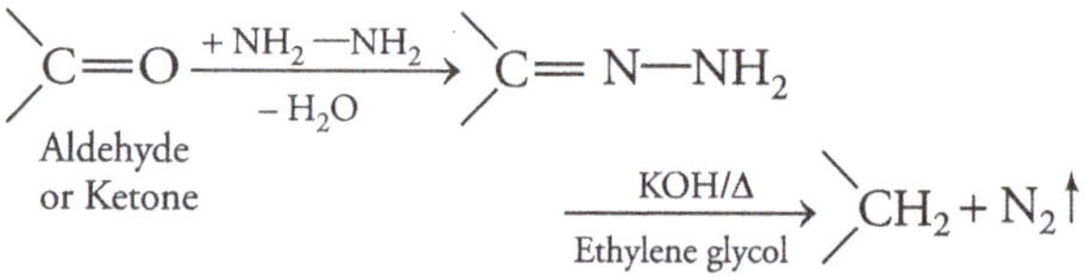

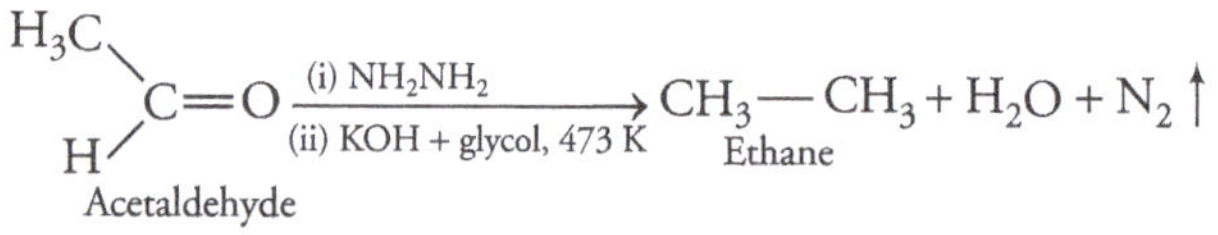

(iii) **Reduction with HI and Red P** Aldehydes and ketones on heating with HI (hydroiodic acid) and red P at 423 K are reduced to their corresponding alkanes.

$$CH_3CHO + 4HI \xrightarrow{\text{Red P, 423 K}} CH_3—CH_3 + H_2O + 2I_2$$

$$CH_3COCH_3 + 4HI \xrightarrow[\text{423 K}]{\text{Red P}} CH_3CH_2CH_3 + H_2O + 2I_2$$

2. Reduction to Alcohols

Aldehydes and ketones are reduced to 1° and 2° alcohols, respectively. It is carried out either catalytically (H_2 + Ni /Pt /Pd) or chemically ($LiAlH_4$ or $NaBH_4$).

$$\underset{\text{Aldehyde}}{R—CHO} + 2[H] \xrightarrow[\text{or } NaBH_4]{LiAlH_4} \underset{1^\circ\text{alcohol}}{R—CH_2—OH}$$

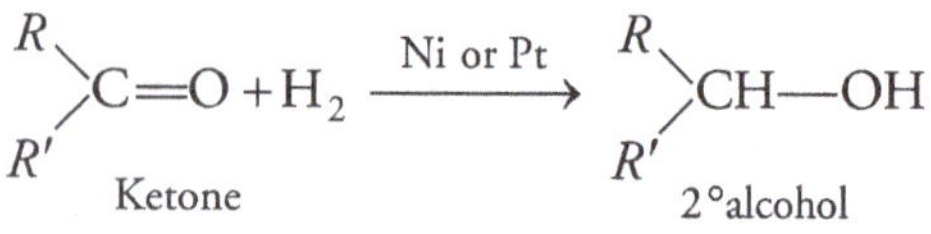

Base Catalysed Reactions (Reactions due to α-Hydrogen)

The aldehydes and ketones undergo a number of reactions due to the acidic nature of α-H which in turn is due to the strong electron withdrawing effect of $\gt C{=}O$ group.

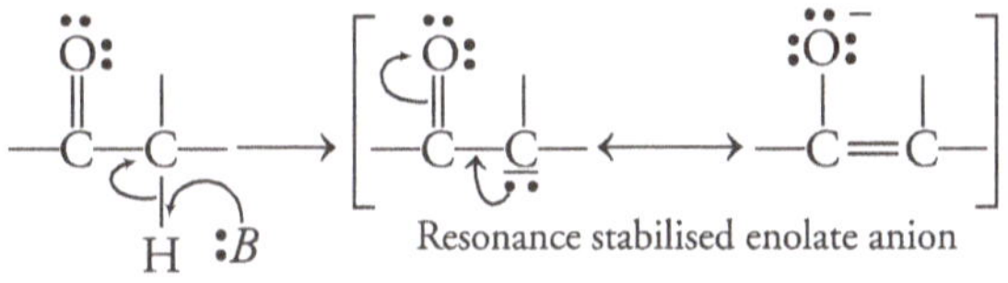

Resonance stabilised enolate anion

1. Aldol Condensation

Aldehydes and ketones containing at least one α-H atoms undergo aldol condensation in the presence of dilute alkali as catalyst to form β -hydroxy aldehyde or β- hydroxy ketone, e.g.

$$\underset{\text{Ethanal}}{2CH_3{-}CHO} \underset{}{\overset{\text{Dil. NaOH}}{\rightleftharpoons}} \underset{\substack{\text{3-hydroxybutanal}\\\text{(Aldol)}}}{CH_3{-}\underset{OH}{\underset{|}{C}H}{-}CH_2{-}CHO} \xrightarrow[-H_2O]{\Delta} \underset{\substack{\text{But-2-enal}\\\text{(Aldol condensation product)}}}{CH_3{-}CH{=}CH{-}CHO}$$

$$\underset{\text{Propanone}}{2CH_3{-}CO{-}CH_3} \overset{Ba(OH)_2}{\rightleftharpoons} \underset{\substack{\text{Diacetone alcohol or ketol}\\\text{4-hydroxy-4-methylpentan-2-one}}}{CH_3{-}\overset{CH_3}{\overset{|}{\underset{OH}{\underset{|}{C}}}}{-}CH_2CO{-}CH_3} \xrightarrow[-H_2O]{\Delta} \underset{\substack{\text{4-methylpent-3-en-2-one}\\\text{(Aldol condensation product)}\\\text{(Mesityl oxide)}}}{CH_3{-}\overset{CH_3}{\overset{|}{C}}{=}CHCO{-}CH_3}$$

β-hydroxy aldehydes or ketones are collectively called aldols or ketols and the reaction is called **aldol condensation.** Aldols readily lose water to give α, β-unsaturated carbonyl compounds which are aldol condensation product. Though ketones give ketol compounds containing a keto group and alcoholic group, yet the name aldol is used for the condensation product of two molecules of ketones due to their similarity with aldehydes.

Note Formaldehyde (HCHO), benzaldehyde (C_6H_5CHO) and benzophenone ($C_6H_5COC_6H_5$) do not undergo aldol condensation as they do not contain α-H atoms.

Mechanism

Step I Formation of resonance stabilised enolate anion (carbanion).

$$\underset{\underset{H}{|}}{\overset{\alpha}{C}H_2}{-}\overset{O}{\overset{\|}{C}}{-}H + OH^- \longrightarrow \underset{\text{Carbanion (Enolate ion)}}{\overset{\ominus}{C}H_2{-}\overset{O}{\overset{\|}{C}}{-}H}$$

Step II Attack of carbanion on carbonyl carbon of the second molecule of aldehydes to form alkoxide ion.

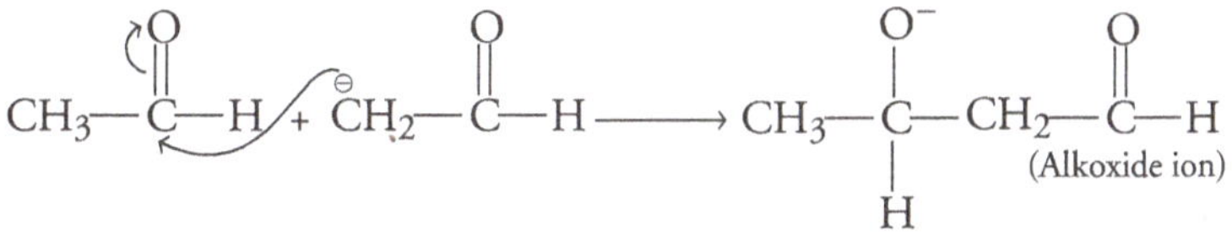

Step III Proton uptake from the solvent to yield aldol.

$$CH_3{-}\overset{O^-}{\overset{|}{\underset{H}{\underset{|}{C}}}}{-}CH_2{-}\overset{O}{\overset{\|}{C}}{-}H \xrightarrow[H_2O]{H^+} \underset{\text{Aldol}}{CH_3{-}\overset{OH}{\overset{|}{C}H}{-}CH_2{-}\overset{O}{\overset{\|}{C}}{-}H}$$

Step IV Heating of aldol gives α, β-unsaturated compound.

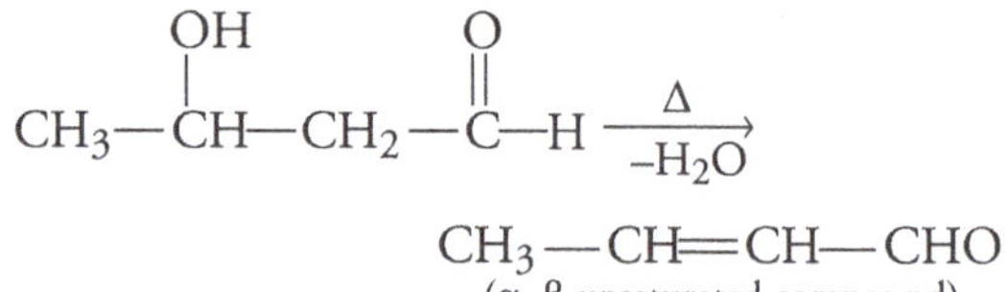

2. Crossed-Aldol Condensation

Aldol condensation may also occur between the molecules of different aldehydes or different ketones or one aldehyde and one ketone provided they contain α-H atoms. Such aldol condensation is called **crossed-aldol condensation or mixed aldol condensation**. When two different aldehydes each containing α-H atoms undergo crossed-aldol condensation, several products are obtained.

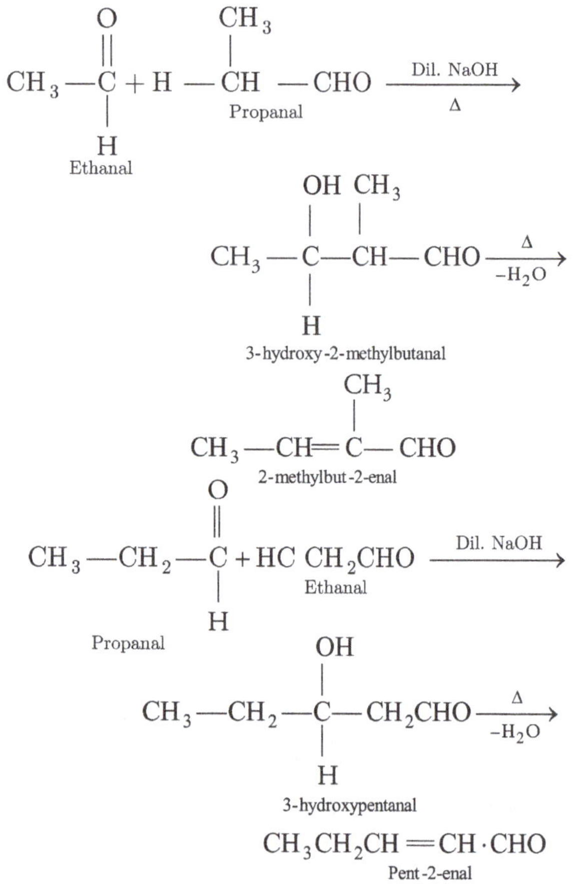

- Thus two main product are formed during the crossed-aldol condensation of ethanal and propanal which are pent-2-enal and 2-methylbut-2-enal.
- Cross-aldol condensation reactions are of great synthetic use if one of the carbonyl compound do not possess α-H atom.

Other Reactions

1. Cannizzaro Reaction

Aldehydes which do not have α-H atom undergo self oxidation and reduction (disproportionation) reactions on heating with conc. alkali. In this reaction, one molecule of aldehyde is reduced to alcohol while another molecule is oxidised to salt of carboxylic acid.

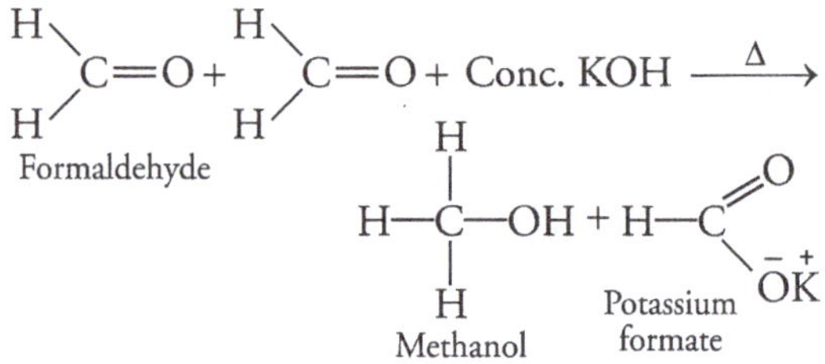

Mechanism

Step I Rapid addition of $\bar{O}H$ to one molecule of aldehyde results in the formation of a hydroxy alkoxide ion

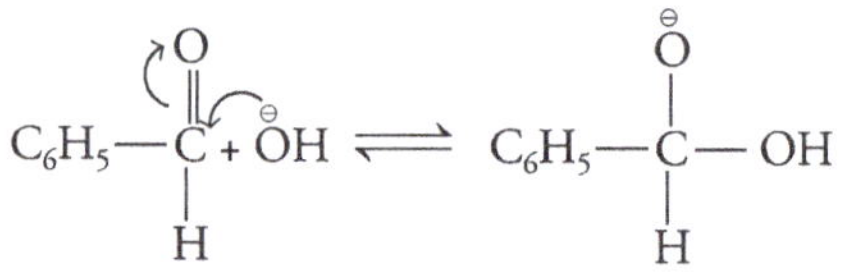

Step II Hydroxy alkoxide ion acts as a hydride-ion donor to the second molecule of aldehyde. In the final step of the reaction, the acid and the alkoxide ion exchange proton for reasons of stability.

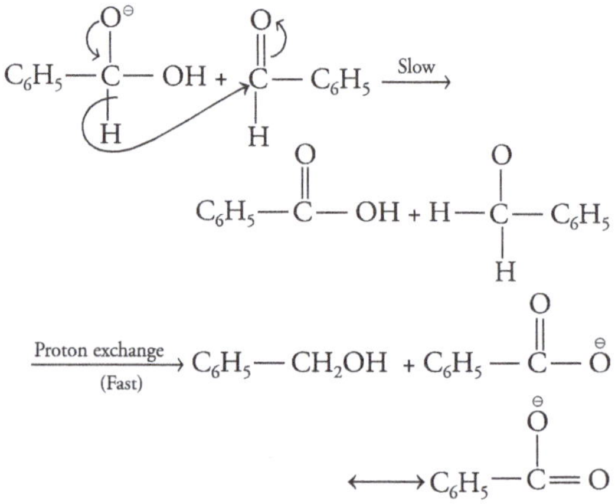

Uses

Some of the important uses of aldehydes and ketones are as follows:

(i) They are used as solvents, starting materials and reagents for the synthesis of other products in chemical industry.

(ii) Formalin (40% solution of formaldehyde) solution is used to preserve biological specimens and in making bakelite, urea-formaldehyde glues and other polymeric products.

(iii) Acetaldehyde is used primarily as a starting material in the manufacture of acetic acid, ethyl acetate, vinyl acetate, polymers and drugs.

(iv) Some of the aldehydes and ketones are used for preparing materials like adhesives, paints, resins, perfumes, plastics, fabrics, etc.

Distinction Tests

Test to Differentiate between Formaldehyde and Acetaldehyde

Test	Formaldehyde	Acetaldehyde
Heat the compound with (Iodine) I_2 and NaOH.	No ppt. is obtained	A pale yellow ppt. of iodoform with a characteristic odour is obtained.

Tests to Differentiate between Acetaldehyde and Acetone

Reaction	Acetaldehyde	Acetone
With Schiff's reagent	Gives pink colour	Does not give pink colour.
With Fehling's solution	Gives red ppt. of Cu_2O	No reaction
With Tollen's reagent	Gives silver mirror	No reaction
With alkaline sodium nitroprusside solution	Gives deep red colour	Red colour changes to yellow
With conc. NaOH solution.	Forms brown resinous mass	No reaction

Aromatic Aldehyde

[Benzaldehyde (C_6H_5CHO)]

It is commercially known as **oil of bitter almonds.**

Methods of Preparation

Various preparation methods are as follows :

(1) In **laboratory** benzaldehyde is prepared from toluene by oxidation with chromyl chloride

Chromyl chloride oxidises methyl group to a chromium complex which on hydrolysis gives corresponding benzaldehyde.

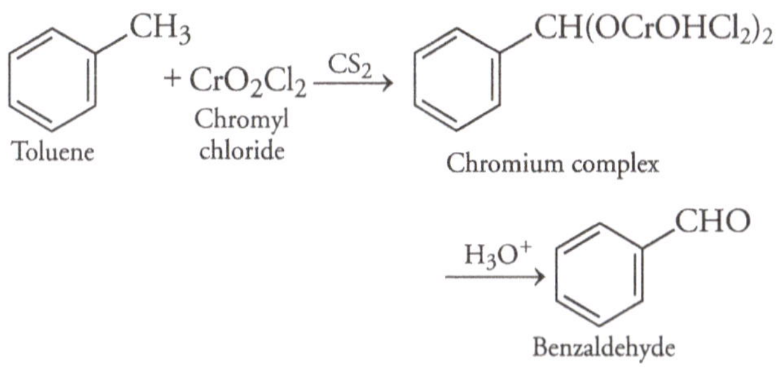

This reaction is called **Etard reaction.**

(2) Benzaldehyde can also be prepared by the reaction of toluene with CrO_3 and side chain chlorination of toluene. The chemical reaction is as follows:

(i) By use of CrO_3

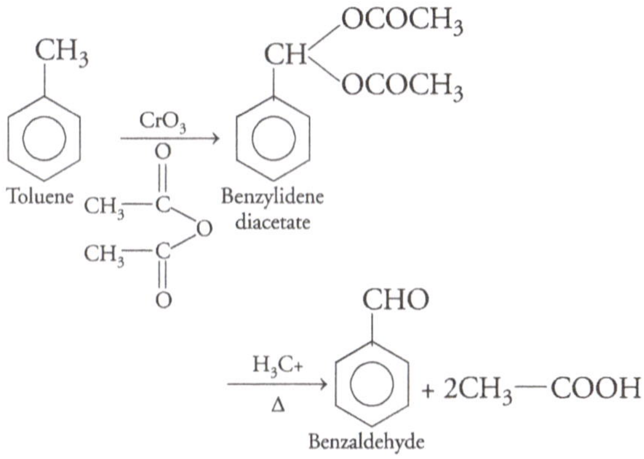

(ii) **By side chain chlorination** followed by hydrolysis:

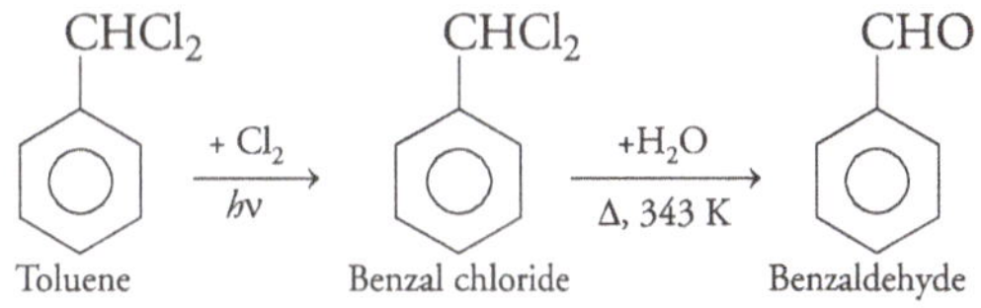

(iii) **By Gattermann-Koch reaction** When benzene or its derivative is treated with carbon monoxide and hydrogen chloride in the presence of anhydrous aluminium chloride or cuprous chloride, it gives benzaldehyde or substituted benzaldehyde. This reaction is known as **Gattermann-Koch reaction.**

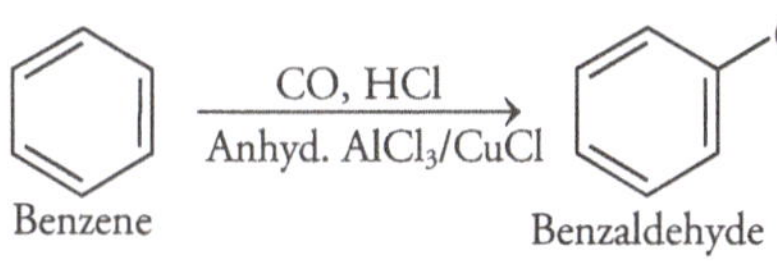

Physical Properties

Benzaldehyde is a colourless liquid with bitter almond-like odour. It is soluble in organic solvents like ethanol, diethyl ether etc. It is steam volatile. It's boiling point is 179°C. Aromatic aldehydes and ketones are less reactive than aliphatic carbonyl compounds. Due to $-R$ effect of carbonyl group, there is delocalisation of π-electrons and thus, conjugation of carbonyl carbon with aryl ring reduces the electrophilic reactivity of carbonyl carbon.

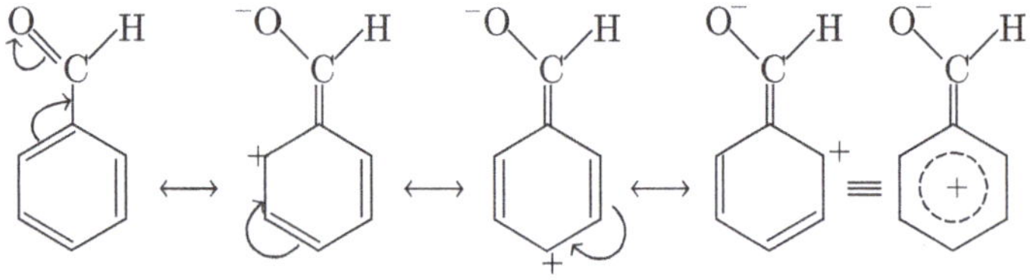

Chemical Properties

1. Oxidation

It gets oxidised to benzoic acid in the presence of dil. HNO_3 or alkaline $KMnO_4$.

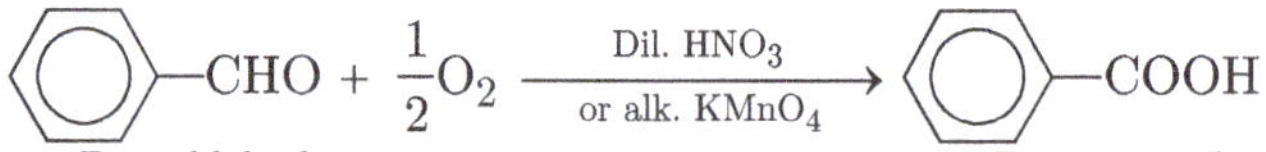

Benzaldehyde　　Benzoic acid

2. Reduction

It is reduced to benzyl alcohol.

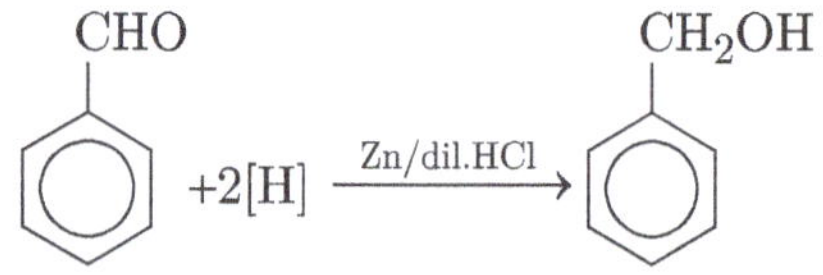

Benzaldehyde　　Benzyl alcohol

3. Nucleophilic Addition Reactions

(i) **With HCN**

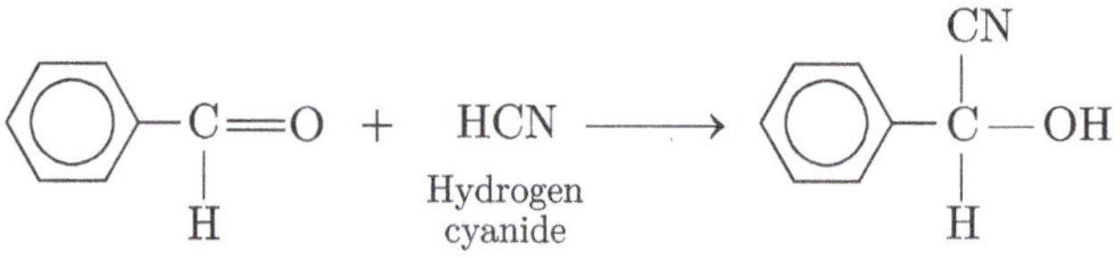

Benzaldehyde　　Benzaldehyde cyanohydrin

(ii) **With $NaHSO_3$**

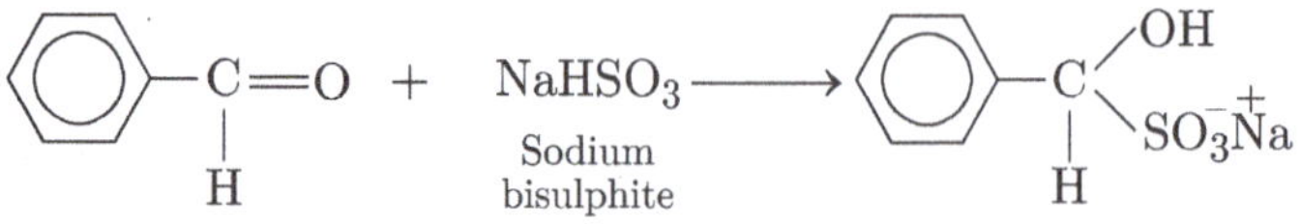

Benzaldehyde　　Benzaldehyde bisulphite compound

4. Nucleophilic Addition Elimination Reaction

These are two step reactions involving addition followed by elimination of some small molecules. Their first step is similar to nucleophilic addition reaction. Some examples are given below:

(i) **With Ammonia** It reacts with NH_3 to form complex product called **hydrobenzamide.**

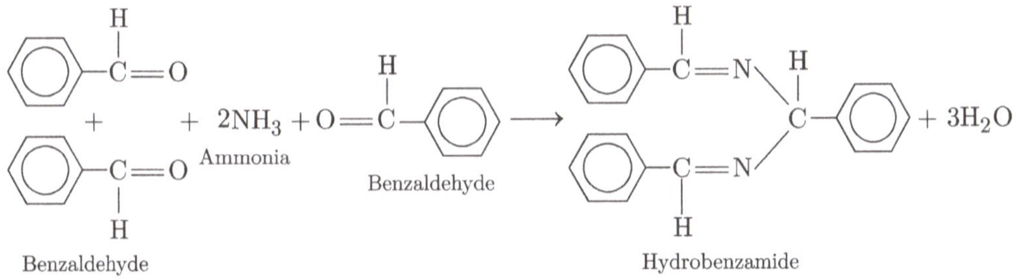

(ii) **With Hydroxyl Amine**

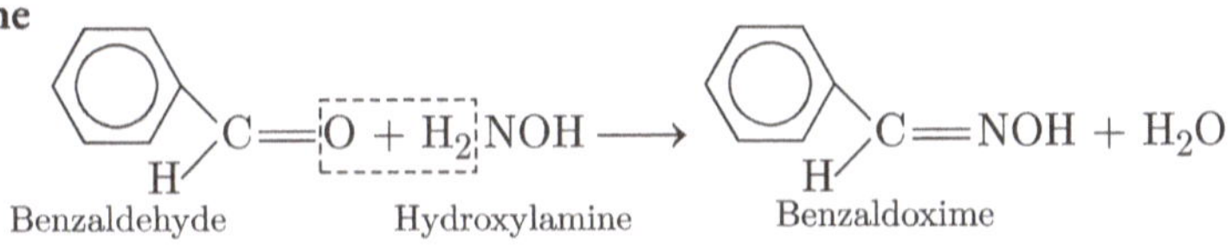

(iii) **With Hydrazine**

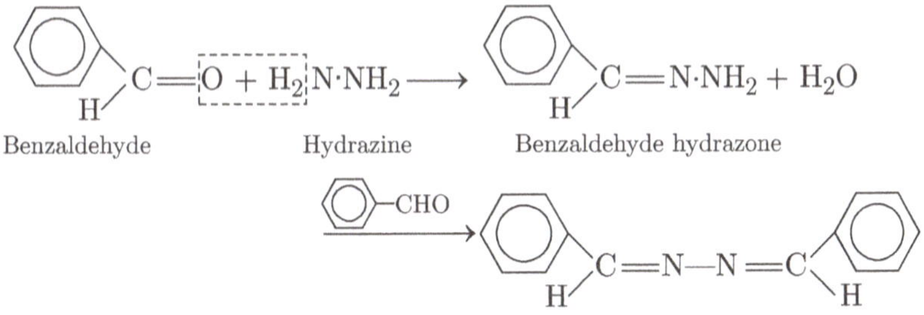

(iv) **With Phenyl Hydrazine**

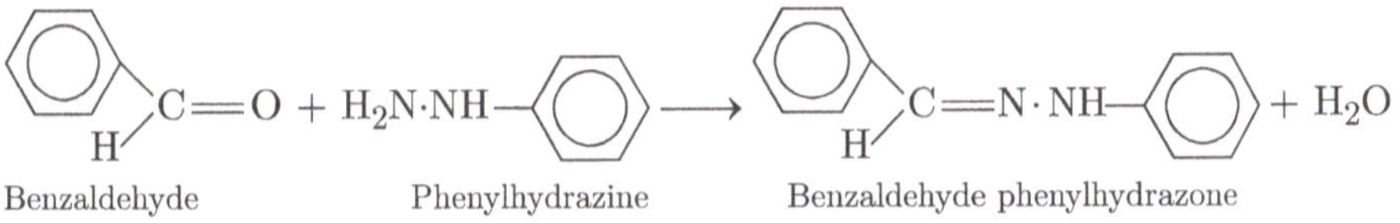

(v) **With 2,4-dinitrophenyl Hydrazine**

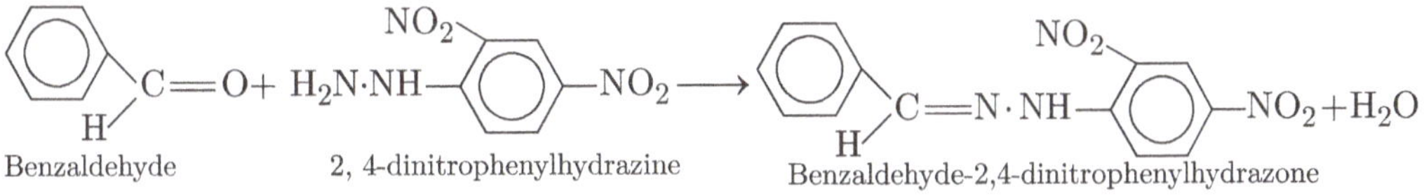

5. Reaction with PCl_5

Benzaldehyde on reaction with PCl_5 readily forms benzyl chloride and $POCl_3$.

$$\underset{\text{Benzaldehyde}}{C_6H_5CHO} + PCl_5 \longrightarrow \underset{\text{Benzal chloride}}{C_6H_5CHCl_2} + POCl_3$$

6. Cannizzaro's Reaction

When benzaldehyde is heated with strong alkali solution, it undergoes simultaneous oxidation and reduction forming salt of benzoic acid and benzyl alcohol.

$$\underset{\text{Benzaldehyde}}{2C_6H_5CHO} + \underset{\text{Conc.}}{NaOH} \longrightarrow \underset{\text{Benzyl alcohol}}{C_6H_5CH_2OH} + \underset{\text{Sodium benzoate}}{C_6H_5COONa}$$

7. Benzoin Condensation

When two molecules of benzaldehyde are heated with an alcoholic solution of KCN, they undergoes self-condensation to form benzoin.

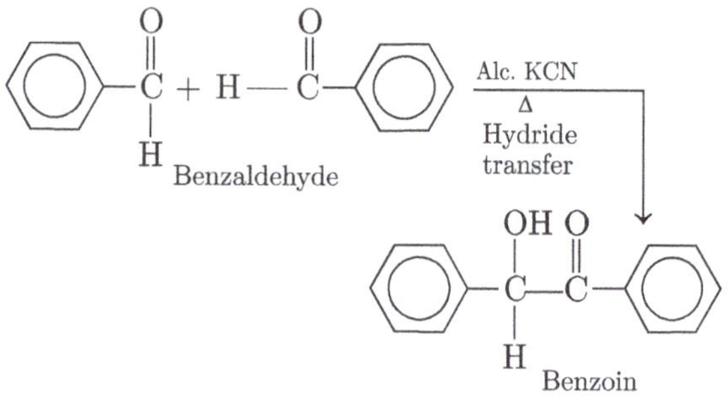

This reaction is called benzoin condensation.

8. Perkin's Reaction

When benzaldehyde is heated with aliphatic acid anhydride in the presence of sodium salt of the acid corresponding to the anhydride, they form α, β-unsaturated acid on hydrolysis.

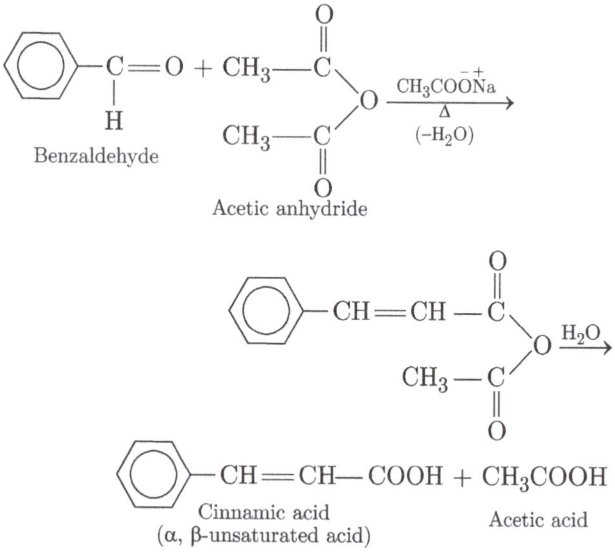

9. Electrophilic Substitution Reactions

— CHO group is deactivating *m*-directing group.

(i) **Halogenation**

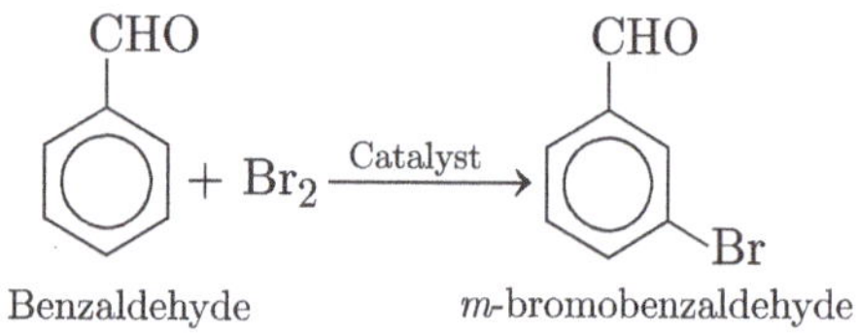

(ii) **Nitration**

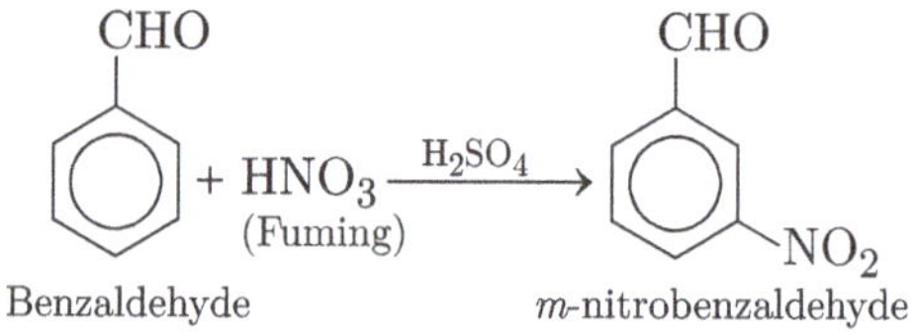

(iii) **Sulphonation**

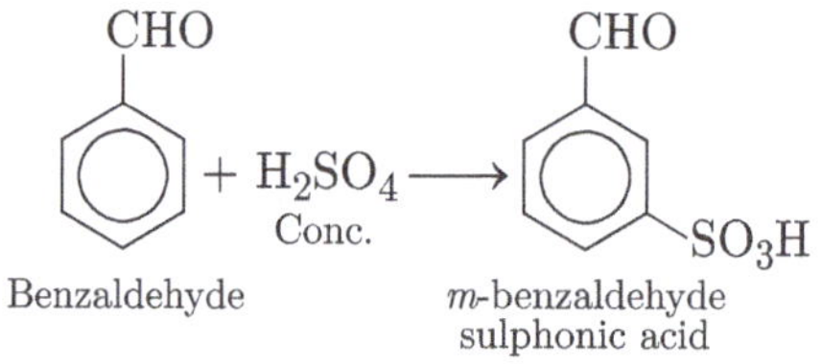

Distinction Tests

Distinction between Aromatic Aldehyde and Aliphatic Aldehyde

Reaction	Aliphatic aldehyde	Aromatic aldehyde
1 Fehling's solution test	Red ppt. of Cu_2O is formed.	No red ppt.
2. Benedict's solution test	Red ppt. of Cu_2O is formed.	No red ppt.

Uses

(i) as a flavouring essence in perfumery.
(ii) in the manufacture of dyes.
(iii) in the synthesis of cinnamic acid, cinnamaldehyde etc

Topic Practice 1

Very Short Answer Type Questions

1 Mark

1. **Fill in the Blanks**
   (i) Benzaldehyde undergoes ...... reaction on treatment with concentrated sodium hydroxide because it has .... **ISC 2001**
   (ii) Acetaldehyde in the presence of dilute alkali gives ...... and the reaction is called .... **ISC 2005**
   (iii) Acetaldehyde reacts with HCN to give ......which on hydrolysis gives .... **ISC 2008**
   (iv) Benzaldehyde when treated with an alcoholic solution ... forms .... . **ISC 2013**
   (v) Propanone on reaction with zinc-amalgam is presence of conc. HCl gives .... and the reaction is known as .... reduction. **ISC 2023**

2. **Objective Type Questions**

(i) When acetic acid reacts with calcium hydroxide and the product is dry distilled the compound formed is **ISC 2012**

(a) calcium acetate (b) acetone
(c) acetaldehyde (d) acetic anhydride

(ii) Calcium acetate on heating gives ....'*A*'.... which gives ....'*B*'.... on heating with iodine and sodium hydroxide solution.
In the above sentence, '*A*' and '*B*' are
(a) aldehyde, chloroform (b) acetone, iodoform
(c) aldehyde, iodoform (d) acetone, iodine tincture **ISC 2017**

(iii) An aqueous solution of $CH_3CO\overset{-}{O}\overset{+}{N}a$ is ......'*A*'...... due to .....'*B*'...... .
In the above sentence, '*A*' and '*B*' are
(a) acidic, anionic hydrolysis
(b) basic, cationic hydrolysis
(c) acidic, cationic hydrolysis
(d) basic, anionic hydrolysis **ISC 2017**

(iv) Benzaldehyde undergoes ....'*A*'... reaction due to .... '*B*'... of α-hydrogen atom.
In the above sentence, '*A*' and '*B*' respectively are:
(a) Cannizzaro, absence (b) Rosenmund's, presence
(c) Cannizzaro, presence (d) Rosenmund's, absence

3. Match the common names given in column I with the IUPAC names given in column II and choose the correct option using the codes given below:

	Column I (Common names)		Column II (IUPAC names)
A.	Cinnamaldehyde	(i)	Pentanal
B.	Acetophenone	(ii)	Prop-2-en-al
C.	Valeraldehyde	(iii)	4-methylpent-3-en-2-one
D.	Acrolein	(iv)	3-phenylprop-2-en-al
E.	Mesityl oxide	(v)	1-phenylethanone

Codes

	A	B	C	D	E
(a)	(iv)	(iii)	(ii)	(v)	(i)
(b)	(i)	(ii)	(iv)	(iii)	(v)
(c)	(iv)	(v)	(i)	(ii)	(iii)
(d)	(i)	(ii)	(iii)	(iv)	(v)

4. Draw the molecular structure of the compound 4-methylpent-3-en-2-one.

5. Write the reaction to prepare acetaldehyde from hydrogen gas and acid chloride.

6. How will you carry out the following conversion? Ethanol to acetone.

7. Arrange the following compounds in the increasing order of their boiling points.
CH_3CHO, CH_3CH_2OH, CH_3OCH_3, $CH_3CH_2CH_3$

8. How can the following conversion be brought about acetaldehyde to propan-2-ol. **ISC 2017**

9. Give balanced equation for the reaction of acetaldehyde with hydroxylamine. **ISC 2017**

10. Give the balanced equation for the following reaction :
Acetone reacts with hydrogen in the presence of heated copper. **ISC 2011**

11. Write the formula of the product formed when formaldehyde reacts with ammonia and name the product. **ISC 2012**

Or Write the balanced equation for the formation of urotropine.

12 Write the balanced equation of the following reaction : **ISC 2008**
Acetone and phosphorus pentachloride

13. Explain the following with at least one example :
Haloform reaction **ISC 2007**

14. Give balanced equations for aldol condensation. **ISC 2015**

15. Name the following reaction and write balanced equation :
Acetaldehyde with dilute sodium hydroxide **ISC 2002**

16. Write balanced chemical equations for the following reaction and name the reaction.
Benzaldehyde is treated with 50% sodium hydroxide solution. **ISC 2013, 2002**

17. Give one chemical test to distinguish between the following pair of compounds:
Acetaldehyde and benzaldehyde

18. Give a chemical test to distinguish between acetaldehyde and acetone. **ISC 2007, 2000**

19. Give one test to distinguish between acetaldehyde and formaldehyde. **ISC 2006**

20. Give one chemical test to distinguish between the following pair of compounds:
Acetone and phenol **ISC 2013**

Short Answer Type I Questions

2 Marks

21. Alkenes, $\rangle C{=}C\langle$ and carbonyl compounds, $\rangle C{=}O$ both contains π-bond but alkenes show electrophilic addition reactions whereas carbonyl compounds show nucleophilic addition reactions. Explain. **NCERT Exemplar**

22. Arrange the following compounds in the increasing order of their reactivity towards nucleophilic addition reactions.
(i) Ethanal, propanal, propanone, butanone
(ii) Benzaldehyde, *p*-tolualdehyde, *p*-nitrobenzaldehyde, acetophenone **NCERT Intext**

23. (i) Benzaldehyde is less reactive than propionaldehyde. Why? **ISC 2024**
(ii) In the preparation of ethanal by the oxidation of ethanol, ethanal should be removed immediately as it is formed. Why?

24. How will the following be converted ? (Give chemical equations) **ISC 2023**
(i) Acetaldehyde to acetone
(ii) Formaldehyde to urotropine

25. Give an example (equation) for each of the following name reactions :
(i) Aldol condensation **ISC 2023**
(ii) Rosenmund's reduction **ISC 2011, 2007**

26. Write the reactions involved in the following reactions: **ISC 2023**
(i) Clemmensen reduction
(ii) Cannizzaro reaction

27. Write the structural formulae and names of the four possible aldol condensation products from propanal and butanal. In each case, indicate which aldehyde served as electrophile and which as nucleophile? **NCERT**

28. Complete the following reaction sequence.

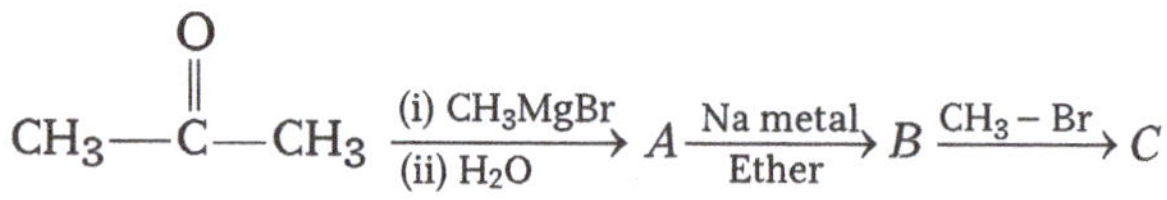

NCERT Exemplar

29. Can Gattermann-Koch reaction be considered similar to Friedel-Crafts acylation? Discuss. **NCERT Exemplar**

30. Write the equations involved in the following reactions :
(i) Wolff-Kishner reduction. (ii) Etard reaction.

31. Benzaldehyde can be obtained from benzal chloride. Write the reactions for obtaining benzal chloride and then benzaldehyde from it. **NCERT Exemplar**

32. Name the electrophile produced in the reaction of benzene with benzoyl chloride in the presence of anhydrous $AlCl_3$. Name the reaction also. **NCERT Exemplar**

33. Ethyl benzene is generally prepared by acetylation of benzene followed by the reduction and not by direct alkylation. Think of a possible reason. **NCERT Exemplar**

34. When liquid '*A*' is treated with a freshly prepared ammoniacal silver nitrate solution, it gives bright silver mirror. The liquid forms a white crystalline solid on treatment with sodium hydrogen sulphite. Liquid '*B*' also forms a white crystalline solid with sodium hydrogen sulphite but it does not give test with ammoniacal silver nitrate. Which of the two liquids is aldehyde? Write the chemical equations of these reactions also. **NCERT Exemplar**

Short Answer Type II Questions

3 Marks

35. Write the IUPAC names of the following ketones and aldehydes. Wherever possible, give their common names.
(i) $CH_3CO(CH_2)_4CH_3$
(ii) $CH_3CH_2CHBrCH_2CH(CH_3)CHO$
(iii) $CH_3(CH_2)_5CHO$
(iv) $Ph—CH=CH—CHO$
(v) 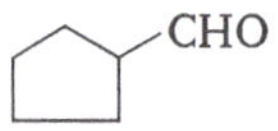

(vi) PhCOPh **NCERT**

36. Draw the structures of the following derivatives.
(i) 2,4-dinitrophenylhydrazone of benzaldehyde
(ii) Cyclopropanone oxime
(iii) Acetaldehyde dimethylacetal
(iv) Semicarbazone of cyclobutanone
(v) Ethylene ketal of hexan-3-one
(vi) Methyl hemiacetal of formaldehyde **NCERT**

37. Give the balanced equations for the following reactions :
(i) Phenol heated with chloroform and sodium hydroxide. **ISC 2009**
(ii) Acetaldehyde reacted with phenyl hydrazine.

38. Give balanced chemical equations for the following reactions. **ISC 2019**
(i) Acetaldehyde reacts with hydrogen cyanide.
(ii) Acetone reacts with phenyl hydrazine.

39. Give one reason each for the following :
Acetone reacts with hydroxylamine to form only one product which has no geometrical isomer,

but acetaldehyde reacts with hydroxylamine to form a product which has two geometrical isomers. **ISC 2007**

40. Which of the following compounds would undergo aldol condensation and/or Cannizzaro reaction or neither of these two reactions. Write the structures of the expected products of aldol condensation or Cannizzaro reaction.

(i) Methanal (ii) 2-methyl pentanal
(iii) Benzaldehyde (iv) Benzophenone
(v) Cyclohexanone (vi) 1-phenyl propanone
(vii) Phenyl acetaldehyde (viii) Butan-1-ol
(ix) 2,2-dimethyl butanal **NCERT**

41. An organic compound C_2H_4O gives red precipitate when heated with Fehling solution. It also undergoes aldol condensation in the presence of dilute NaOH. **ISC 2024**

(i) Identify the organic compound and write its IUPAC name.
(ii) Which compound will be formed when this organic compound reacts with hydroxylamine?
(iii) What is observed when the compound, referred to in subpart (i), is heated with ammoniacal silver nitrate?

42. How will you convert ethanal into the following compounds?

(i) Butane-1,3-diol (ii) But-2-enal
(iii) But-2-enoic acid **NCERT**

43. An organic compound with molecular formula $C_9H_{10}O$, forms 2,4-DNP derivative, reduces Tollen's reagent and undergoes Cannizzaro reaction. On vigorous oxidation, it gives 1,2-benzene dicarboxylic acid. Identify the compound. **NCERT**

44. An organic compound contains 69.77% carbon, 11.63% hydrogen and rest oxygen. The molecular mass of the compound is 86. It does not reduce Tollen's reagent but forms an addition compound with sodium hydrogen sulphite and gives positive iodoform test. On vigorous oxidation, it gives ethanoic acid and propanoic acid. Write the possible structure of the compound. **NCERT**

45. An organic compound [*A*], having a specific smell forms two compounds [*B*] and [*C*] by reacting with conc. sodium hydroxide. The molecular formula of compound [*B*] is C_7H_8O, which forms compound [*A*] again on oxidation. Compound [*C*] forms benzene on heating with soda lime.

Write the structures of compounds [*A*], [*B*] and [*C*]. Also, write the reactions involved. **ISC 2024**

Long Answer Type Questions

5 Marks

46. Write the structures of three compounds which have the same molecular formula of but have different functional groups. **ISC 2006**

47. Give one test to distinguish between the following pair. Write the relevant equation.
Acetophenone and benzophenone **ISC 2014**

48. (i) Write the products formed when CH_3CHO reacts with the following reagents:
(a) HCN
(b) $H_2N—OH$
(c) CH_3CHO in the presence of dilute NaOH.

(ii) Write the chemical equations to illustrate the following name reactions.
(a) Rosenmund's reduction
(b) Cannizzaro reaction

(iii) Out of $CH_3CH_2—CO—CH_2—CH_3$ and $CH_3CH_2—CH_2—CO—CH_3$, which gives iodoform test?

49. How will you carry out the following conversion? Acetaldehyde to *iso* -propyl alcohol **ISC 2002, 2000**

50. Give balanced equations for the following reactions :

(i) Acetaldehyde is heated with hydroiodic acid in the presence of red phosphorus.
(ii) Calcium acetate is subjected to dry distillation.
(iii) Benzaldehyde is treated with sodium bisulphite. **ISC 2014**

51. (i) Write chemical equations to illustrate the following name reactions.
(a) Aldol condensation
(b) Cannizzaro's reaction
(c) Benzoin condensation

(ii) Identify the compounds *A* and *B* in the given reactions.

(a) 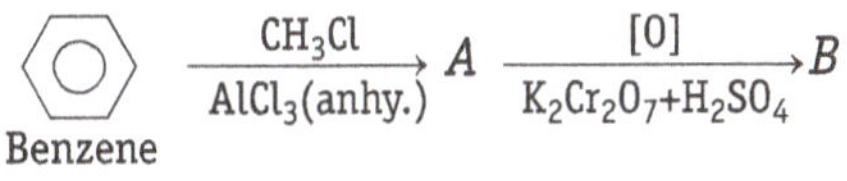

(b) $CH_3COCH_3 \xrightarrow[HNO_3(conc.)]{[O]} A \xrightarrow{PCl_5} B$

ISC 2019

52. Predict the products formed when cyclohexane carbaldehyde reacts with following reagents:
(i) PhMgBr and then H_3O^+
(ii) Tollen's reagent
(iii) Semicarbazide and weak acid
(iv) Excess ethanol and acid
(v) Zinc amalgam and dilute hydrochloric acid **NCERT**

53. (i) How will you bring about the following conversion in not more than two steps?
(a) Propanone to propene
(b) Ethanol to 3-hydroxybutanal
(c) Benzene to *m*-nitroacetophenone
(d) Bromobenzene to 1-phenylethanol
(e) Benzaldehyde to benzophenone
(f) Benzaldehyde to α-hydroxy phenylacetic acid
(ii) Arrange the following compounds in the increasing order of their property as indicated:
Acetaldehyde, acetone, di-*tert*-butyl ketone, *tert*-butyl methyl ketone (reactivity towards HCN) **NCERT**

54. Complete each synthesis by giving missing starting material, reagent or products.

(i) $\underset{\text{Benzaldehyde}}{C_6H_5CHO} \xrightarrow{H_2NCONHNH_2}$

(ii) 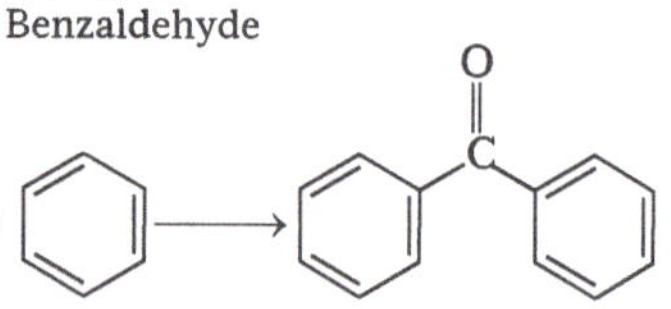

(iii) 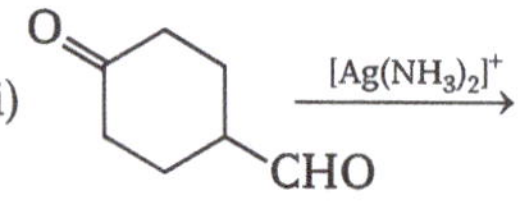

(iv) 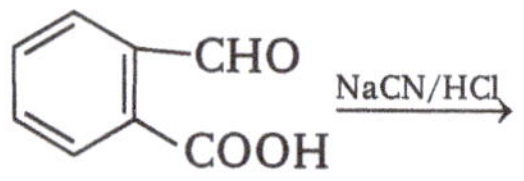

(v) $C_6H_5CHO + CH_3CH_2CHO \xrightarrow{\text{Dil. NaOH}}$

(vi) 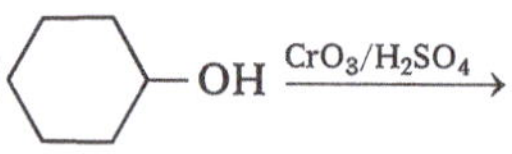

(vii) 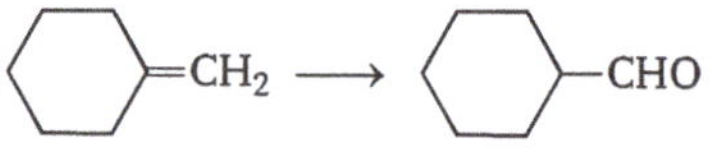

(viii) 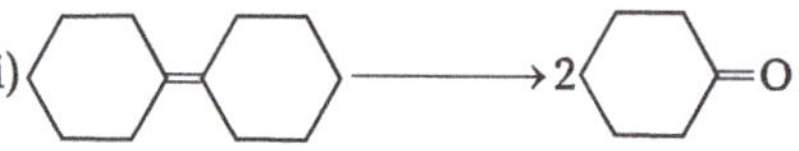

(ix) 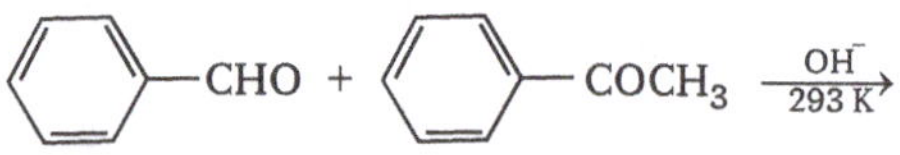

(x) 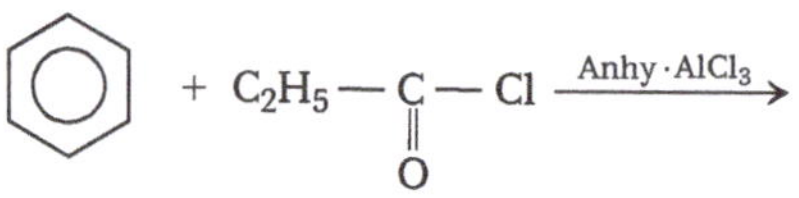

Hints & Solutions

1. (i) Cannizzaro, no α-hydrogen atoms
(ii) aldol, aldol condensation
(iii) acetaldehyde cyanohydrin, lactic acid
(iv) potassium cyanide, benzoin
(v) propane, Clemmensen

2. (i) (b), (ii) (b), (iii) (d), (iv) (b)

3. (c) A→(iv), B→(v), C→(i), D→(ii), E→(iii)

4. $\overset{1}{H_3C}-\overset{2}{\underset{\|}{C}}(=O)-\overset{3}{CH}=\overset{4}{C}(CH_3)-\overset{5}{CH_3}$

4-methylpent-3-en-2-one

5. Acid chloride (e.g. acetyl chloride) can be reduced to aldehyde (e.g. acetaldehyde) with hydrogen gas in boiling xylene using palladium as catalyst supported by $BaSO_4$ and partially poisoned by the addition of sulphur.

$$\underset{\text{Acetyl chloride}}{CH_3-\overset{O}{\overset{\|}{C}}-Cl} + H_2 \xrightarrow[\text{Boiling xylene}]{Pd/BaSO_4, S} \underset{\text{Acetaldehyde}}{CH_3-\overset{O}{\overset{\|}{C}}-H} + HCl$$

6. Ethanol to acetone

$$CH_3CH_2OH \xrightarrow{PCl_5} CH_3CH_2Cl \xrightarrow{KCN} CH_3CH_2CN$$
$$\xrightarrow{\text{Reduction}} CH_3CH_2CH_2NH_2 \xrightarrow[H_2O]{HNO_2}$$
$$CH_3CH_2CH_2OH \xrightarrow{PCl_5} CH_3CH_2CH_2Cl \xrightarrow[KOH]{Alc.}$$
$$CH_3CH=CH_2 \xrightarrow[Hg^{2+}]{Dil. H_2SO_4} CH_3-\underset{\underset{O}{\|}}{C}-CH_3$$

7. $CH_3CH_2CH_3 < CH_3OCH_3 < CH_3CHO < CH_3CH_2OH$

Stronger the attractive forces, higher is the boiling point. Hydrocarbons are non-polar having weakest attractive forces, ethers are polar and aldehydes have strong dipolar interaction. Alcohols have maximum intermolecular forces due to the presence of H-bonding.

8. $$\underset{\text{Acetaldehyde}}{CH_3CHO} \xrightarrow{CH_3MgBr} \left[\underset{\text{Addition product}}{CH_3-\overset{OMgBr}{\overset{|}{CH}}-CH_3}\right]$$
$$\xrightarrow[-Mg(OH)Br]{H^+/H_2O} \underset{\text{Propan-2-ol}}{CH_3-\overset{OH}{\overset{|}{CH}}-CH_3}$$

9. $\underset{\text{Acetaldehyde}}{CH_3CHO} + \underset{\text{Hydroxylamine}}{NH_2OH} \longrightarrow CH_3-CH=NOH + H_2O$

10.

$$\underset{\text{Acetone}}{(CH_3)_2CO} + H_2 \xrightarrow[573\text{ K}]{\text{Heated Cu}} \underset{\textit{Iso}\text{-propyl alcohol}}{(CH_3)_2CHOH}$$

11. Formaldehyde reacts with ammonia to form hexamethylene tetraamine. Also, known as urotropine.

$$\underset{\text{Formaldehyde}}{6HCHO} + 4NH_3 \longrightarrow \underset{\substack{\text{(Urotropine)}\\ \text{hexamethylenetetraamine}}}{(CH_2)_6N_4} + 6H_2O$$

12.

$$\underset{\text{Acetone}}{(H_3C)_2C{=}O} + \underset{\substack{\text{Phosphorus}\\ \text{penta Chloride}}}{PCl_5} \longrightarrow \underset{\text{2, 2-dichloro propane}}{(H_3C)_2CCl_2} + POCl_3$$

13. Aldehydes and ketones having $CH_3—\overset{O}{\overset{\|}{C}}—$ group can be oxidised with sodium hypohalite [NaOX] to give a haloform (CHX) and the salt of carboxylic acid. This reaction is called haloform reaction. e.g.

$$CH_3—\overset{O}{\overset{\|}{C}}—CH_3 + 3I_2 + 4NaOH \longrightarrow \underset{\text{Yellow ppt.}}{CHI_3\downarrow} + CH_3—\overset{O}{\overset{\|}{C}}—\overset{-}{O}\overset{+}{Na} + 3NaI + 3H_2O$$

14. Aldehydes and ketones containing α H-atoms undergo aldol condensation in presence of dilute alkali as catalyst, e.g.

$$2\,CH_3—CHO \xrightarrow{\text{Dil.NaOH}} \underset{\substack{\text{3-hydroxybutanal}\\ \text{(Aldol)}\\ \text{(Aldol condensation product)}}}{CH_3—\underset{OH}{\underset{|}{CH}}—CH_3—CHO}$$

15.

$$2\,\underset{\text{Acetaldehyde}}{CH_3—\overset{O}{\overset{\|}{C}}—H} + \text{Dil. NaOH} \longrightarrow \underset{\substack{\text{3-hydroxybutanal}\\ \text{(Aldol)}}}{CH_3—\underset{H}{\underset{|}{\overset{OH}{\overset{|}{C}}}}—CH_2CHO}$$

(2)

This reaction is called aldol condensation.

16.

$$\underset{\text{Benzaldehyde}}{C_6H_5CHO} + C_6H_5CHO \xrightarrow{\text{50\% NaOH}} \underset{\text{Benzyl alcohol}}{C_6H_5CH_2OH} + \underset{\text{Sodium benzoate}}{C_6H_5COO^-Na^+}$$

(2)

This reaction is known as Cannizzaro reaction.

17. **Acetaldehyde and benzaldehyde** Acetaldehyde reacts as reducing agent which reduces Fehling solution. The aldehyde gets oxidised to carboxylate ion and Cu^{2+} is reduced to cuprous oxide.

$$\underset{\text{Acetaldehyde}}{CH_3—\underset{O}{\underset{\|}{C}}—H} + 2\,Cu^{2+} + 5OH^- \longrightarrow \left[\underset{\text{Carboxylate ion}}{CH_3—\overset{O}{\overset{\|}{C}}—O^-}\right]$$

Benzaldehyde is not oxidised by Fehling solution.

18. **Acetaldehyde and acetone** Acetaldehyde gives a silver mirror test when heated with Tollen's reagent.

$$\underset{\text{Acetaldehyde}}{CH_3CHO} + \underset{\text{Tollen's reagent}}{2[Ag(NH_3)_2]^+OH^-} \longrightarrow CH_3COONH_4 + \underset{\text{Silver miror}}{2Ag\downarrow} + 3NH_3 + H_2O$$

Acetone does not give this test as it is a ketone.

19. They are distinguished by iodoform test. When heated gently with iodine and caustic alkali, acetaldehyde (due to the presence of $CH_3—\overset{O}{\overset{\|}{C}}—$ group) gives a yellow ppt. of iodoform with a characteristic smell.

$$\underset{\text{Acetaldehyde}}{CH_3CHO} + 3I_2 + 4NaOH \longrightarrow \underset{\substack{\text{Iodoform}\\ \text{Yellow ppt.}}}{CHI_3\downarrow} + HCO\overset{-}{O}\overset{+}{Na} + 3NaI + 3H_2O$$

Formaldehyde does not give this test. (2)

20. Acetone gives iodoform test while phenol does not. Acetone gives a yellow ppt of iodoform when heated with in the presence of an alkali, while phenol does not contain $CH_3—\underset{O}{\underset{\|}{C}}—$ group, so do not give this test.

21. Refer to text on pages 306 and 307 (Nucleophilic addition reactions).

22. (i) Butanone < propanone < propanal < ethanal

(ii) Acetophenone < *p*-tolualdehyde < benzaldehyde < *p*-nitrobenzaldehyde (1)

23. (i) The carbon atom of carbonyl group of benzaldehyde is less electrophilic than carbon atom of the carbonyl group present in propionaldehyde. As the polarity of $>C{=}O$ group is reduced in benzaldehyde due to resonance hence it is less reactive.

(ii) In oxidation of ethanol to ethanal, is the formed ethanal is readily oxidised to carboxylic acid if allowed to remain in the reaction mixture. Therefore, ethanal should be removed immediately as it is formed.

24. (i)

$$CH_3CHO \xrightarrow[\text{[O]}]{K_2Cr_2O_7/H^+} CH_3COOH \xrightarrow{Ca(OH)_2} (CH_3COO)_2Ca \xrightarrow{\text{Heat}} CH_3COCH_3$$

(ii) Formaldehyde reacts with ammonia to form hexamethylene tetraamine (urotropine).

$$6HCHO + 4NH_3 \longrightarrow (CH_2)_6N_4 + 6H_2O$$

25. (i) **Aldol condensation** (2 × 1 = 2)

$$CH_3-\overset{O}{\overset{\|}{C}}H + \overset{H}{\overset{|}{C}}H_2-CHO \xrightarrow[\text{Heat}]{\text{Dil. NaOH}} CH_3-\overset{OH}{\overset{|}{C}}H-CH_2-CHO$$

Acetaldehyde → Aldol

(ii) **Rosenmund's reduction**

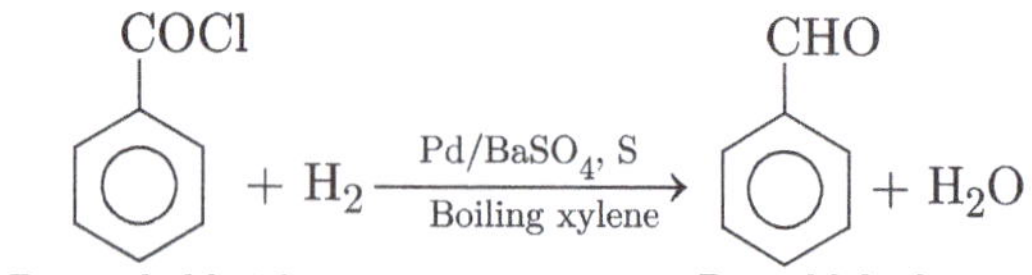

Benzoyl chloride → Benzaldehyde

26. (i) **Clemmensen reduction** It involves reduction of carbonyl group of an aldehyde or ketone to methylene group to form a hydrocarbon. Clemmensen reduction is carried out in presence of Zn amalgam and conc. HCl. e.g.

$$>C=O + 4[H] \xrightarrow{\text{Zn-Hg/ conc. HCl}} >CH_2 + H_2O$$

Hydrocarbon (1)

It is widely used for the reduction of aldehydes and ketones which are sensitive to alkalies.

(ii) **Cannizzaro reaction** Aldehydes which do not have α-H atoms undergo Cannizzaro reaction on treatment with conc. alkali. In this reaction, one molecule of aldehyde is reduced to alcohol while another molecule is oxidised to salt of carboxylic acid.

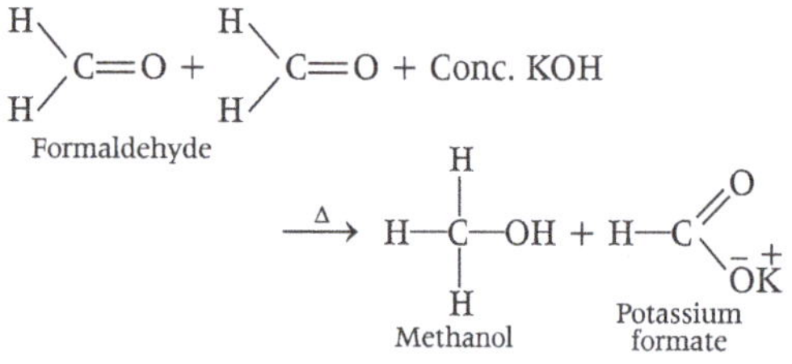

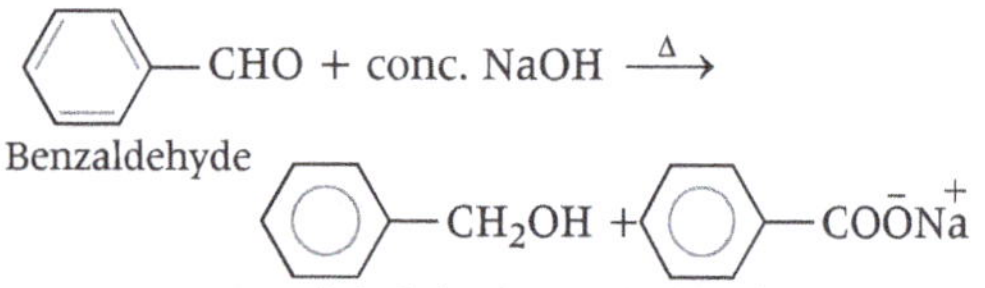

Benzyl alcohol Sodium benzoate (1)

27. (i) Propanal acts as both nucleophile and electrophile.

$$CH_3CH_2CHO + CH_3CH_2CHO \longrightarrow \overset{5}{C}H_3\overset{4}{C}H_2\overset{OH}{\overset{|}{\overset{3}{C}H}}-\overset{CH_3}{\overset{|}{\overset{2}{C}H}}-\overset{1}{C}HO$$

Propanal → 3-hydroxy-2-methylpentanal

(ii) Butanal serves as both nucleophile and electrophile.

$$CH_3CH_2CH_2CHO + CH_3CH_2CH_2CHO \longrightarrow \overset{6}{C}H_3\overset{5}{C}H_2\overset{4}{C}H_2-\overset{OH}{\overset{|}{\overset{3}{C}H}}-\overset{CH_2CH_3}{\overset{|}{\overset{2}{C}H}}\overset{1}{C}HO$$

Butanal → 2-ethyl-3-hydroxyhexanal

(iii) Propanal serves as electrophile and butanal as nucleophile.

$$CH_3CH_2CHO + CH_3CH_2CH_2CHO \longrightarrow \overset{5}{C}H_3\overset{4}{C}H_2-\overset{OH}{\overset{|}{\overset{3}{C}H}}-\overset{CH_2CH_3}{\overset{|}{\overset{2}{C}H}}\overset{1}{C}HO$$

Propanal, Butanal → 2-ethyl-3-hydroxypentanal

(iv) Butanal serves as electrophile and propanal as nucleophile.

$$CH_3CH_2CH_2CHO + CH_3CH_2CHO \longrightarrow \overset{6}{C}H_3\overset{5}{C}H_2\overset{4}{C}H_2-\overset{OH}{\overset{|}{\overset{3}{C}H}}-\overset{CH_3}{\overset{|}{\overset{2}{C}H}}-\overset{1}{C}HO$$

Butanal, Propanal → 3-hydroxy-2-methyl hexanal

(4 × 1/2 = 2)

28.

$$CH_3-\overset{O}{\overset{\|}{C}}-CH_3 \xrightarrow[\text{(ii) } H_2O]{\text{(i) } CH_3MgBr} \underset{(A)}{CH_3-\overset{OH}{\overset{|}{\underset{CH_3}{\underset{|}{C}}}}-CH_3} \xrightarrow[\text{Ether}]{\text{Na-metal}}$$

$$\underset{(B)}{CH_3-\overset{\bar{O}\overset{+}{Na}}{\overset{|}{\underset{CH_3}{\underset{|}{C}}}}-CH_3} \xrightarrow[-NaBr]{CH_3-Br} \underset{(C)}{CH_3-\overset{O-CH_3}{\overset{|}{\underset{CH_3}{\underset{|}{C}}}}-CH_3}$$

(C) 2-methyl-2-methoxy propane (2)

29. In Gattermann-Koch reaction, benzene or its derivative is treated with CO and HCl in the presence of anhydrous aluminium chloride to produce benzaldehyde. In this reaction, CO and HCl combine to form HCOCl, i.e. formyl chloride which gets substituted on benzene by the replacement of H-atom.

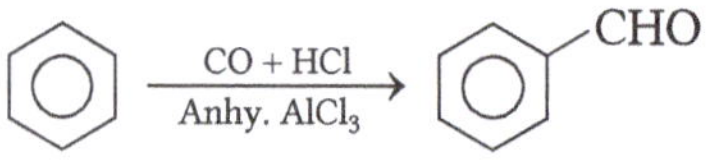

While in Friedel-Crafts acylation, acyl group is also transferred to carbon of benzene and acyl benzene is obtained as a result. This can be done by reaction of benzene with acyl chloride in the presence of anhydrous $AlCl_3$.

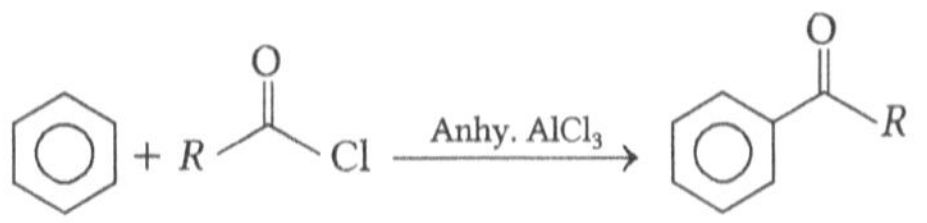

As, formyl chloride is unstable in nature. So, it can be prepared *in situ* by treating CO and HCl in the presence of anhy. $AlCl_3$ by only Gattermann-Koch reaction, not by Friedel-Crafts reaction. Since, in both the reactions, acylation takes place, hence, Gattermann-Koch reaction can be considered similar to Friedel-Crafts acylation. (2)

30. (i) **Wolff-Kishner Reduction**

Carbonyl group are easily reduce by hydrazine followed by heating with strong base like alkali to $>CH_2$.

$$>C{=}O \xrightarrow[-H_2O]{NH_2NH_2} >C{=}N{-}NH_2$$

Ketone or aldehyde

$$\xrightarrow[\text{Ethylene glycol}]{KOH} >CH_2 + N_2\uparrow$$

(1)

(ii) **Etard Reaction**

Toluene reacts with chromyl chloride in presence of CS_2 followed by hydrolysis produces benzaldehyde.

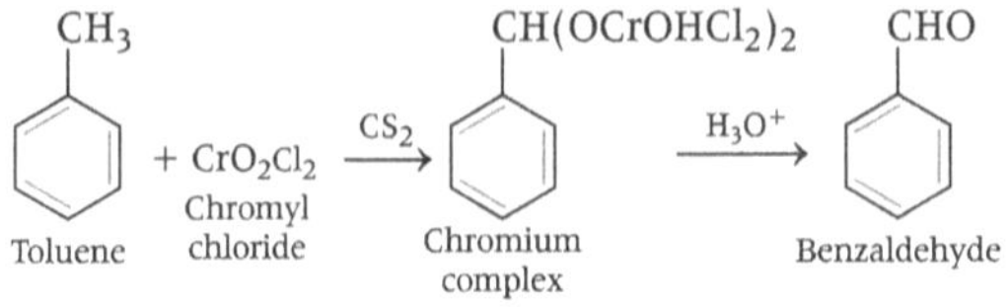

(1)

31. It is the commercial method for preparing benzaldehyde. Benzal chloride can be obtained by photochlorination of toluene, i.e. chlorination of toluene in the presence of sunlight. Then, benzal chloride on heating with boiling water produces benzaldehyde as shown below: (2)

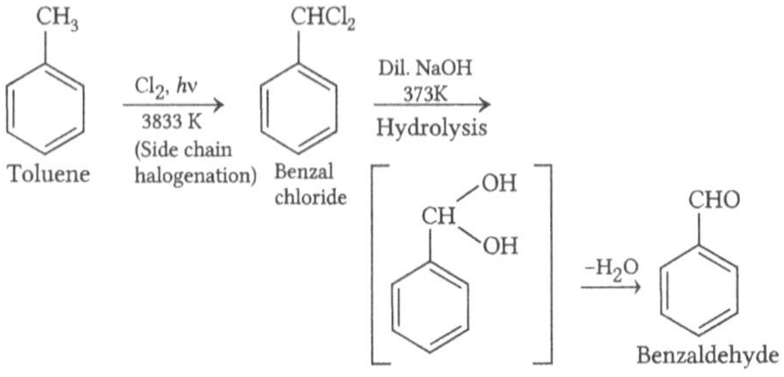

32. Benzene, on reaction with benzoyl chloride gives benzophenone through an intermediate benzoylinium cation. (1)

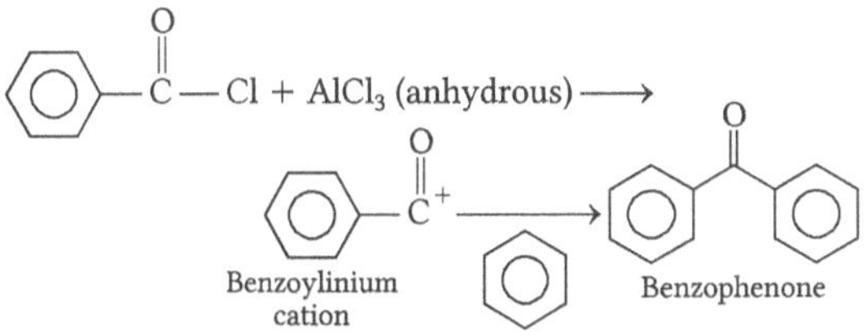

This is an example of **Friedel-Craft's acylation reaction.** (1)

33. Preparation of ethyl benzene from acylation of benzene yields acetophenone which on reduction gives ethyl benzene. The complete reactions can be shown as:

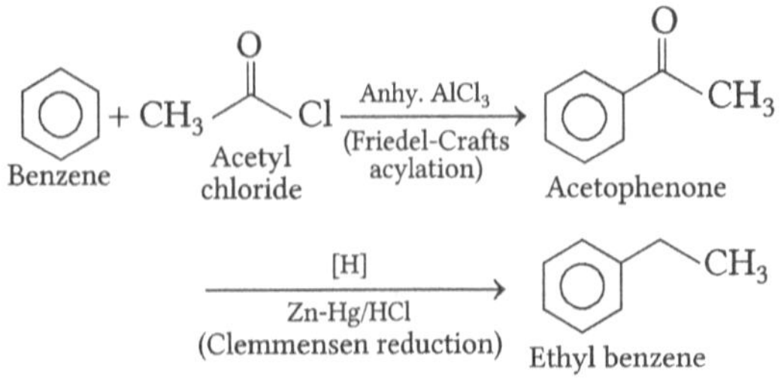

The direct alkylation cannot be performed because polysubstitution product is formed.

Due to disadvantage of polysubstitution, the Friedel-Crafts alkylation reaction is not used for the preparation of alkyl benzene. Instead of that, Friedel-Crafts acylation is used. (2)

34. Since, the liquid *A* reduces ammoniacal silver nitrate (Tollen's reagent), hence *A* is aldehyde and *B* does not give test with ammoniacal silver nitrate, thus, *B* is a ketone. Further, *B* forms a white crystalline solid on treatment with sodium hydrogen sulphite. This suggests that *B* is a methyl ketone. (1)

(i)

$$>C{=}O + NaHSO_3 \rightleftharpoons >C{<}^{OSO_2H}_{\overset{-}{O}\overset{+}{Na}} \underset{\text{transfer}}{\overset{\text{Proton}}{\rightleftharpoons}} >C{<}^{OSO_2Na}_{OH}$$

Aldehyde or ketone; Sodium hydrogen sulphite; Bisulphite addition compound (White crystalline solid)

(ii) $RCHO + 2\,[Ag(NH_3)_2]NO_3 + 2NH_4OH$

$$\longrightarrow RCOOH + \underset{\text{Silver mirror}}{2Ag\downarrow} + H_2O + 4NH_3 + 2\,NH_4NO_3$$

Note Aldehyde and ketone both gives white crystalline solid with sodium hydrogen sulphite but only aldehyde gives Tollen's test and Fehling's test. (1)

35.

S.No.	Structure	IUPAC name	Common name
(i)	$CH_3CO(CH_2)_4CH_3$	Heptan- 2-one	Methyl *n*-pentyl ketone
(ii)	$CH_3CH_2CHBrCH_2$ $CH(CH_3)CHO$	4-bromo-2-methyl hexanal	γ-bromo-α-methyl caproaldehyde
(iii)	$CH_3(CH_2)_5CHO$	Heptanal	Heptanaldehyde
(iv)	$PhCH{=}CH{-}CHO$	3-phenylprop -2-enal	β-phenylacrolein
(v)	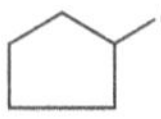 CHO	Cyclopentane carbaldehyde	Cyclopentane carbaldehyde
(vi)	PhCOPh	Diphenylmethanone	Benzophenone

$\left(6 \times \frac{1}{2} = 3\right)$

36.

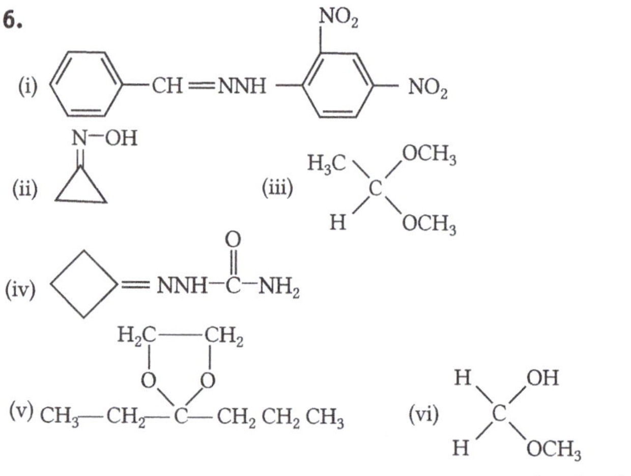

$\left(6 \times \frac{1}{2} = 3\right)$

37. (i)

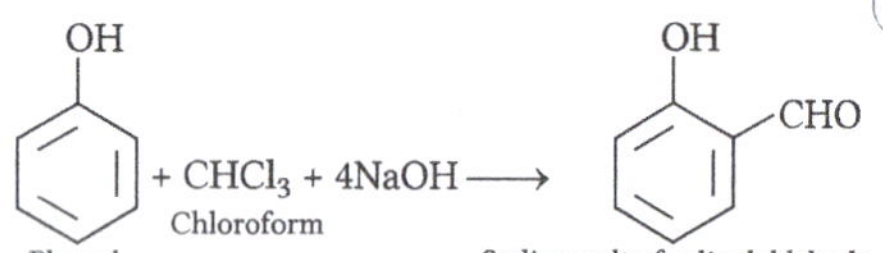

Phenol   Chloroform   Sodium salt of salicylaldehyde (Major isomer)

+ $3NaCl + 3H_2O$ (1½)

(ii) $CH_3CHO + H_2N \cdot NHC_6H_5 \longrightarrow$
Acetaldehyde   Phenylhydrazine

$CH_3CH = N \cdot NHC_6H_5 + H_2O$
Phenylhydrazone (1½)

38. (i) Acetaldehyde reacts with hydrogen cyanide.

Acetaldehyde   Hydrogen cyanide   Ethane cyanohydrin

Above reaction is a nucleophilic addition reaction when acetaldehyde reacts with hydrogen cyanide, it gives ethane cyanohydrin.

(ii) Acetone reacts with phenyl hydrazine.

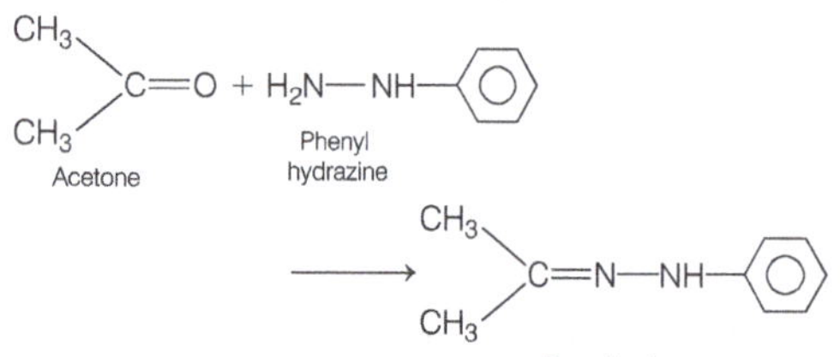

Acetone   Phenyl hydrazine   Phenyl hydrazone

When acetone reacts with phenyl hydrazine. It gives phenl hydrazone as a product.

39. This is because when acetone reacts with $—NH_2OH$, acetoxime formed has two identical groups, $—CH_3$ attached to carbon with which N forms a double bond. This does not fulfill conditions for geometrical isomerism. But when acetaldehyde reacts with NH_2OH, acetaldoxime is formed which has two different groups attached to C forming double bond with nitrogen. Therefore, it exhibits geometrical isomerism.

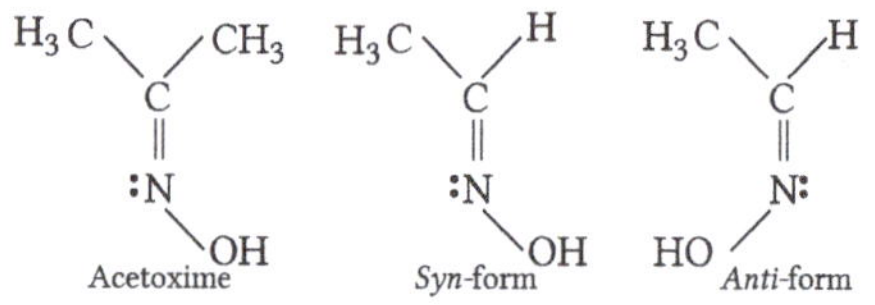

Acetoxime   *Syn*-form   *Anti*-form (3)

40. Compounds which undergo aldol condensation (having α-hydrogen atom) are follows :

(ii) **2-methylpentanal**

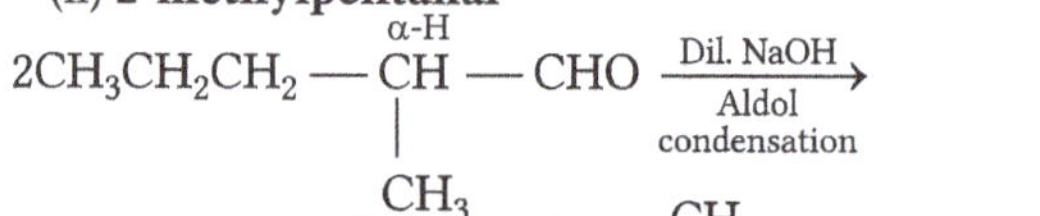

2-methylpentanal

3-hydroxy-2, 4-dimethyl 2-propylheptanal

(v) **Cyclohexanone**

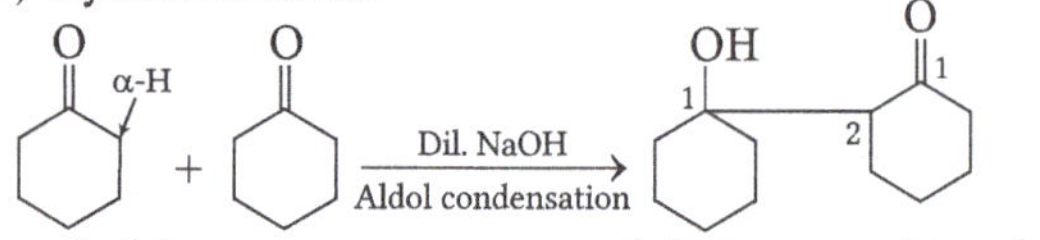

Cyclohexanone   2-(1-hydroxy-1-cyclohexyl) cyclohexan-1-one

(vi) **1-phenyl propanone**

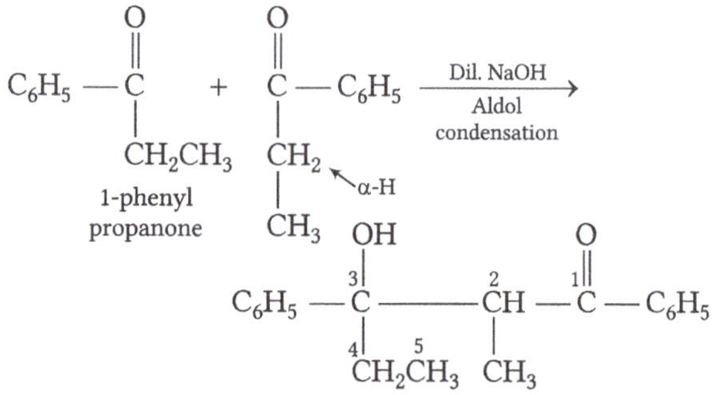

1-phenyl propanone

3-hydroxy-2-methyl-1, 3-diphenylpentan-1-one

(vii) **Phenyl acetaldehyde**

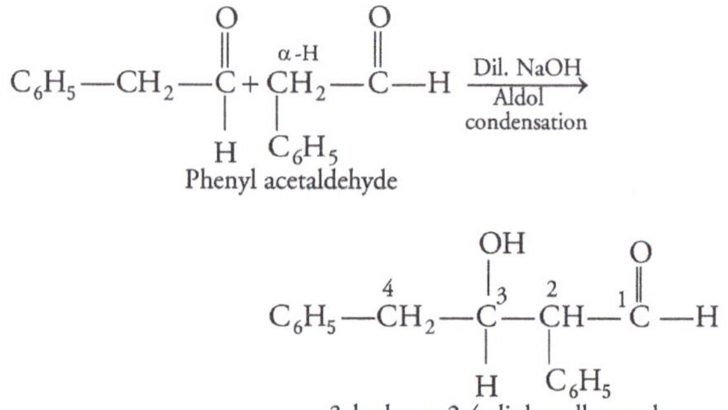

Phenyl acetaldehyde

3-hydroxy-2,4-diphenylbutanal

Compounds which undergo Cannizzaro reaction (only aldehydes without α-hydrogen atoms)

(i) **Methanal** Refer to text on page 314 (Cannizzaro reaction).

(iii) **Benzaldehyde** Refer to text on page 314. (Cannizzaro reaction).

(ix) **2, 2-dimethylbutanal**

$$2\,CH_3CH_2-\underset{CH_3}{\overset{CH_3}{\underset{|}{\overset{|}{C}}}}-CHO \xrightarrow[\text{Cannizzaro reaction}]{\text{Conc. NaOH}}$$

2, 2-dimethylbutanal

$$\overset{4}{C}H_3\,\overset{3}{C}H_2-\underset{CH_3}{\overset{CH_3}{\underset{|}{\overset{|}{\overset{2}{C}}}}}-\overset{1}{C}H_2OH + \overset{4}{C}H_3\,\overset{3}{C}H_2-\underset{CH_3}{\overset{CH_3}{\underset{|}{\overset{|}{\overset{2}{C}}}}}-\overset{1}{C}O\overset{-}{O}\overset{+}{N}a$$

2, 2-dimethylbutan-1-ol   Sodium-2, 2-dimethylbutanoate

Compounds which neither undergo Cannizzaro nor aldol reaction are

(iv) **Benzophenone** It is a ketone, so it does not undergo Cannizzaro reaction without α-hydrogen. It cannot participate in aldol condensation.

(viii) **Butan-1-ol** It is an alcohol. So, it cannot participate in any of the above two reactions. $(3 \times 1 = 3)$

41. (i) According to the given information that C_2H_4O gives red ppt. with Fehling solution and undergoes aldol condensation in presence of dil. NaOH. This means C_2H_4O is an aldehyde having an α-H atom. Thus, it can be CH_3-CHO. Its IUPAC name is ethanal.

$$\underset{\text{Ethanal}}{CH_3CHO} + \underset{\text{Fehling solution}}{2Cu^{2+}} + 4\overset{+}{O}H \xrightarrow{\Delta} \underset{\text{Acetic acid}}{CH_3-\overset{O}{\overset{||}{C}}-OH} + \underset{\text{Red ppt.}}{Cu_2O\downarrow} + 2H_2O$$

$$\underset{\text{Ethanol}}{2CH_3-\overset{O}{\overset{||}{C}}-H} \xrightarrow[(H_2O)]{\text{Dil. NaOH}} \underset{\text{3-hydroxybutanal}}{CH_3-\overset{OH}{\overset{|}{C}H}-CH_2-\overset{O}{\overset{||}{C}}-H}$$

(ii) Reaction of ethanal with hydroxylamine.

$$CH_3-\overset{O}{\overset{||}{C}}-H + \underset{\text{Hydroxylamine}}{H_2N-OH} \xrightarrow{\overset{+}{H}} \underset{\text{Acetaldoxime}}{CH_3-\underset{H}{\underset{|}{C}}=N-OH} + H_2O$$

(iii) Reaction of ethanal with ammoniacal silver nitrate.

$$CH_3-\overset{O}{\overset{||}{C}}-H + \underset{\text{(Tollen's reagent)}}{2[Ag(NH_3)_2]^+} + 2\overset{-}{O}H \xrightarrow{\Delta} \underset{\text{Acetic acid}}{CH_3-\overset{O}{\overset{||}{C}}-OH} + 2Ag\downarrow + 4NH_3 + H_2O$$

42. (i) $\underset{\text{Ethanal}}{2CH_3CHO} \xrightarrow[\text{(Aldol condensation)}]{\text{Dil. NaOH}} \underset{\text{3-hydroxybutanal}}{\overset{4}{C}H_3\,\overset{3}{C}HOH-\overset{2}{C}H_2-CHO}$

$\xrightarrow[\text{(Reduction)}]{NaBH_4} \underset{\text{Butane-1, 3-diol}}{\overset{4}{C}H_3-\overset{3}{C}HOH-\overset{2}{C}H_2-\overset{1}{C}H_2OH}$ (1)

(ii) Refer to text on page 313 (Crossed-aldol condensation). (1)

(iii) $\underset{\text{Ethanal}}{2CH_3CHO} \xrightarrow[\text{(ii)}-H_2O,\ \Delta]{\text{(i) Dil. NaOH}}$

$CH_3CH=CHCHO \xrightarrow{\text{Alk. }KMnO_4} \underset{\text{But-2-enoic acid}}{CH_3CH=CHCO_2H}$ (1)

43. (i) As the given compound with molecular formula $C_9H_{10}O$, forms a 2,4-DNP derivative and reduces Tollen's reagent, thus it must be an aldehyde.

(ii) As it undergoes Cannizzaro reaction, hence —CHO group is directly attached to the benzene ring.

(iii) On vigorous oxidation, it gives 1,2-benzenedicarboxylic acid. Therefore, it must be an *ortho*-substituted benzaldehyde and the only *o*-substituted aromatic aldehyde which have $C_9H_{10}O$ molecular formula is *o*-ethyl benzaldehyde. (1½)

Reactions involved:

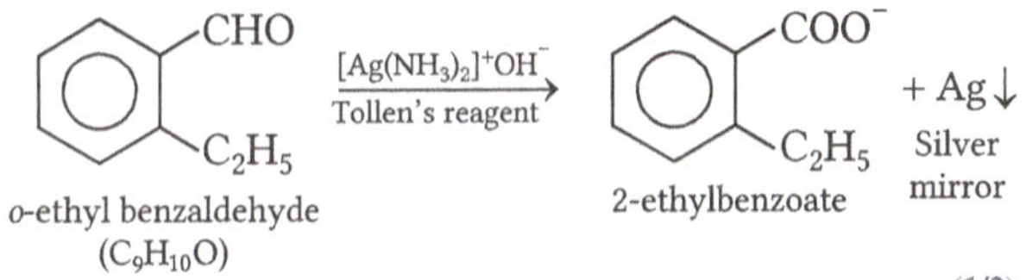

(1/2)

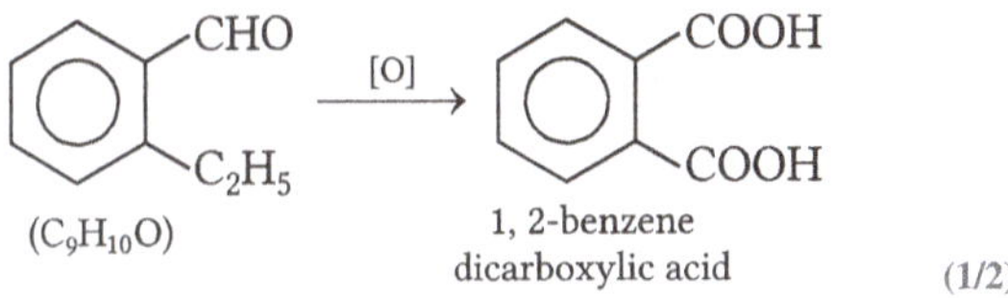

(1/2)

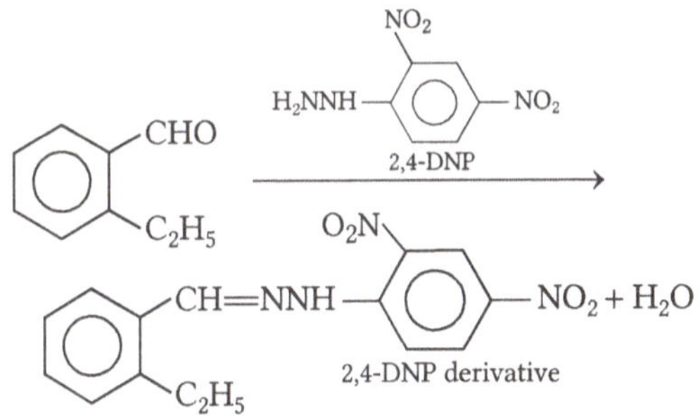

(1/2)

44. C = 69.77%, H = 11.63%, O = 100 − (69.77 + 11.63) = 18.6%

Element	Percentage (*x*)	Molar mass (*y*)	Moles (*x*/*y*)	Simple ratio
C	69.77	12	5.81	5
H	11.63	1	11.63	10
O	18.60	16	1.16	1

Empirical formula of given compound = $C_5H_{10}O$ (1)

Empirical formula mass = $5\times 12+10\times 1+1\times 16=86$

$$n=\frac{86}{86}=1$$

$\therefore$ Molecular formula = $(C_5H_{10}O)_1 = C_5H_{10}O$ (1)

Since, it does not give Tollen's test but gives positive iodoform test, hence it is a methyl ketone, i.e. have $-COCH_3$ group. Since, on oxidation, it gives ethanoic acid and propanoic acid, it is pentan-2-one.

$$\underset{\text{Pentan-2-one}}{CH_3-\overset{\overset{\displaystyle O}{\|}}{C}-CH_2CH_2CH_3} \xrightarrow{[O]} \underset{\text{Ethanoic acid}}{CH_3COOH} + \underset{\text{Propanoic acid}}{CH_3CH_2COOH}$$

Hence, the compound is pentan-2-one. (1)

45. It is given that the molecular formula of B is C_7H_8O. The possible compound having this molecular formula may be benzyl alcohol ($C_6H_5CH_2OH$), anisole ($C_6H_5OCH_3$), *ortho*, *meta* or *para*-cresol ($CH_3-C_6H_4OH$).

- *o*, *m*, *p*-cresol on oxidation give complex products and anisol cannot be easily oxidised. Thus, the compound (B) must be benzyl alcohol.
- It is given that compound (B) forms compound (A) on oxidation, which has characteristic smell, that means compound (D) may be benzaldehyde.
- Benzaldehyde (A) on treatment with NaOH undergoes Cannizzaro reaction to give compounds (B) and (C). We know that compound (B) is benzyl alcohol, therefore compound (C) may be sodium benzoate ($C_6H_5CO\overset{-}{O}\overset{+}{Na}$).

Also, it is given that compound (C) forms benzene on heating with soda lime. Thus, it confirm that compound (C) must be sodium benzoate ($C_6H_5CO\overset{-}{O}\overset{+}{Na}$). The chemical equation of all the reactions involved are as follows.

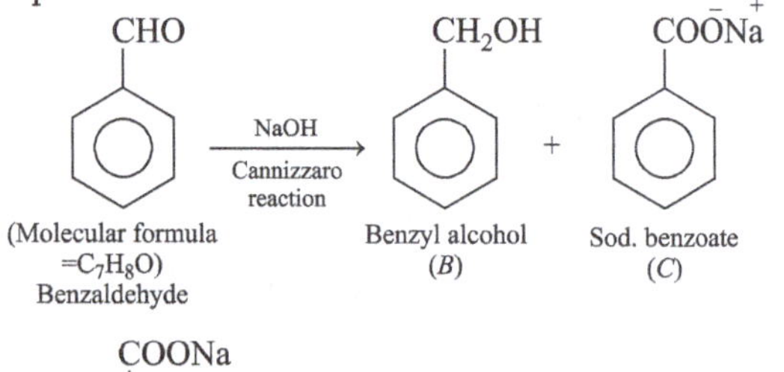

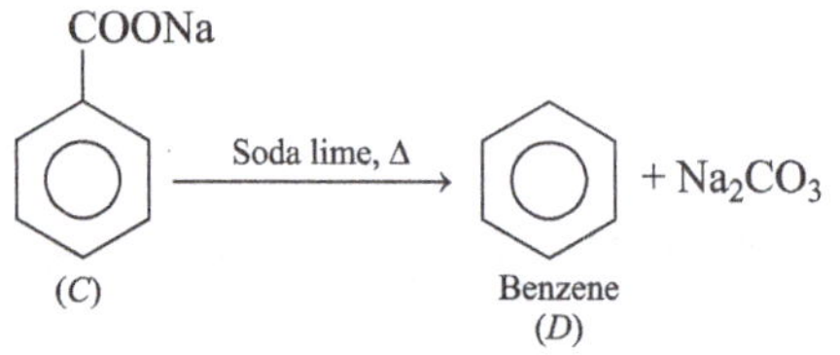

Thus, $A = C_6H_5CHO$, Benzaldehyde

$B = C_6H_5CH_2OH$, Benzyl alcohol

$C = C_6H_5COONa$, Sodium benzoate

$D = C_6H_5$, Benzene

46. (i) Butanal : $CH_3CH_2CH_2CHO$ (An aldehyde)

(ii) Butanone : $CH_3COCH_2CH_3$ (A ketone)

(iii) Butenol : $CH_2=CH-CH_2-CH_2OH$ (An unsaturated alcohol).

47. Acetophenone and benzophenone These can be distinguished by the iodoform test. Acetophenone ($C_6H_5COCH_3$) due to the presence of $CH_3\overset{\overset{\displaystyle O}{\|}}{C}-$ group gives yellow ppt. of iodoform on treatment with NaOI. While benzophenone ($C_6H_5COC_6H_5$) does not respond to this test.

$$C_6H_5COCH_3 + 3NaOI \longrightarrow \underset{\text{Sodium benzoate}}{C_6H_5CO\overset{-}{O}\overset{+}{Na}} + \underset{\substack{\text{Iodoform}\\\text{(Yellow ppt.)}}}{CHI_3\downarrow} + 2NaOH$$

$\longrightarrow$ No yellow ppt. of

48. (i) (a) Refer to text on page 308 (Addition of HCN).

(b) Refer to text on pages 310 (Addition of NH_3 and its derivative).

(c) Refer to text on pages 313 (Aldol condensation reaction). (3)

(ii) (a) Refer to text on page 306 (Rosenmund's reduction).

(b) Refer to text on page 314 (Cannizzaro reaction) (2)

(iii) $CH_3CH_2-CH_2-CO-CH_3$ gives iodoform test as it contains CH_3CO- group. (1)

49.

$$\underset{\text{Acetaldehyde}}{CH_3-\overset{\overset{\displaystyle O}{\|}}{C}-H} \xrightarrow{CH_3MgI} CH_3-\underset{\underset{\displaystyle CH_3}{|}}{\overset{\overset{\displaystyle \overset{-}{O}\overset{+}{Mg}I}{|}}{C}}-H$$

$$\xrightarrow{H_2O} \underset{\textit{Iso}\text{-propyl alcohol}}{CH_3-\underset{\underset{\displaystyle CH_3}{|}}{\overset{\overset{\displaystyle OH}{|}}{C}}-H} + Mg\begin{smallmatrix}OH\\I\end{smallmatrix}$$

50. (i) $\underset{\text{Acetaldehyde}}{CH_3CHO} + 4HI \xrightarrow[423\ K]{\text{Red P}} \underset{\text{Ethane}}{CH_3CH_3}$ (1)

(ii) $\underset{\text{Calcium acetate}}{\begin{matrix}CH_3COO\\CH_3COO\end{matrix}\!>\!Ca} \xrightarrow{\text{Dry distillation}} \underset{\text{Acetone}}{\begin{matrix}CH_3\\CH_3\end{matrix}\!>\!C=O} + CaCO_3$ (2)

(iii)

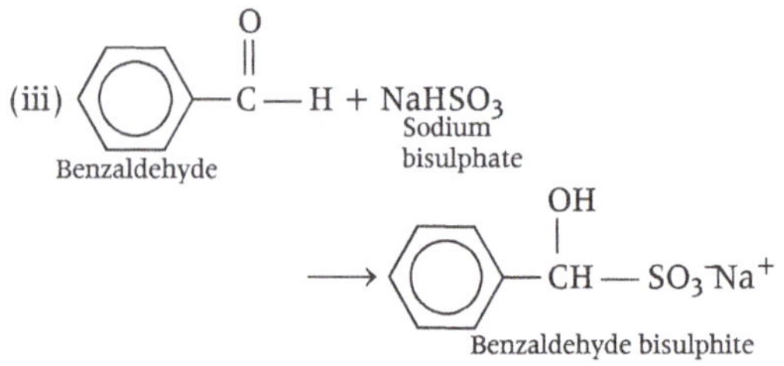

(2)

51. (i) (a) **Aldol condensation**

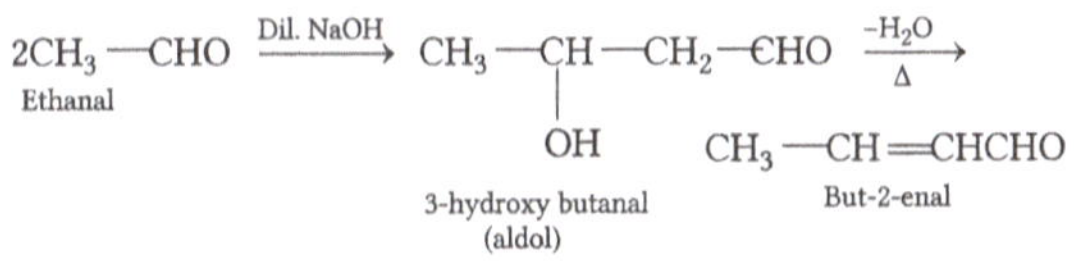

This reaction is exhibited by those aldehydes and ketones which have atleast one α- hydrogen.

(b) **Cannizzaro's reaction**

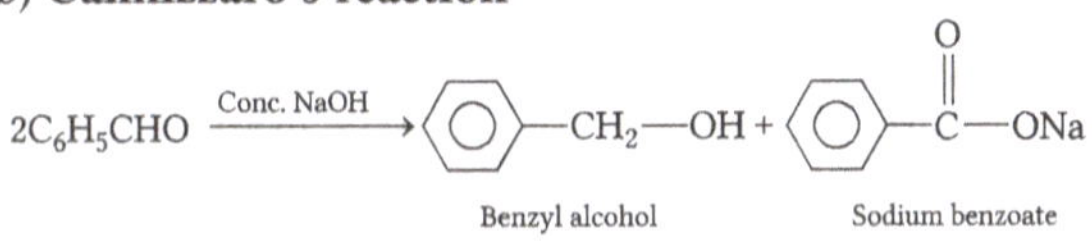

Aldehydes which do not have any α-hydrogen atom, undergo self oxidation and reduction reaction on treatment with concentrated alkali.

(c) **Benzoin condensation** It is a reaction between two benzaldehyde.

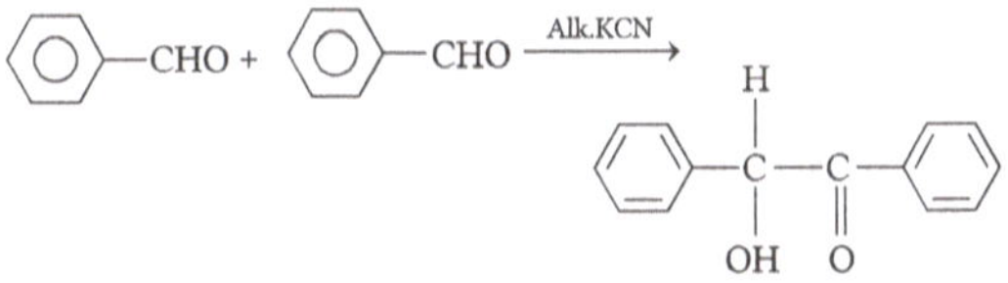

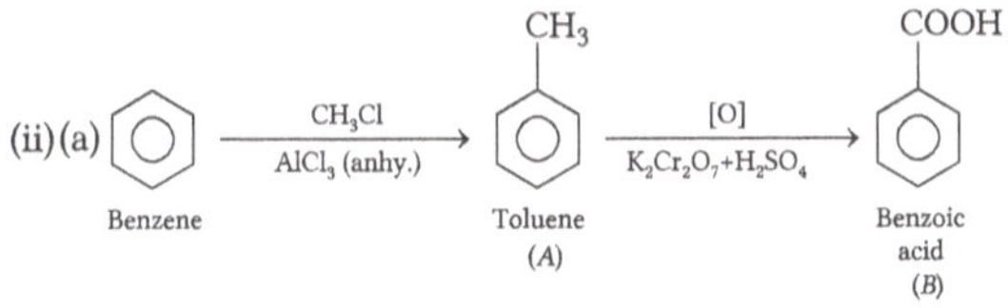

(b)

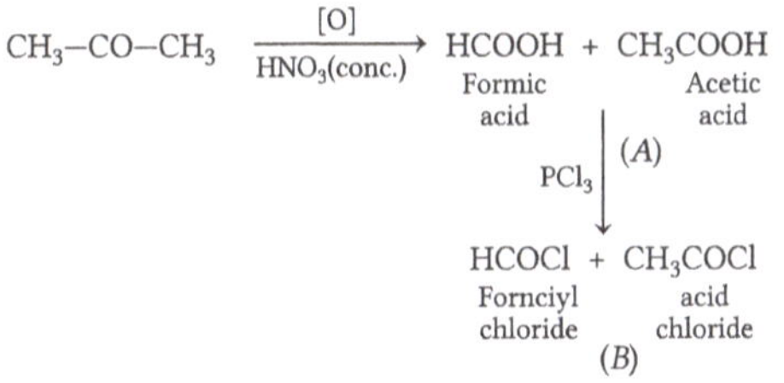

52.

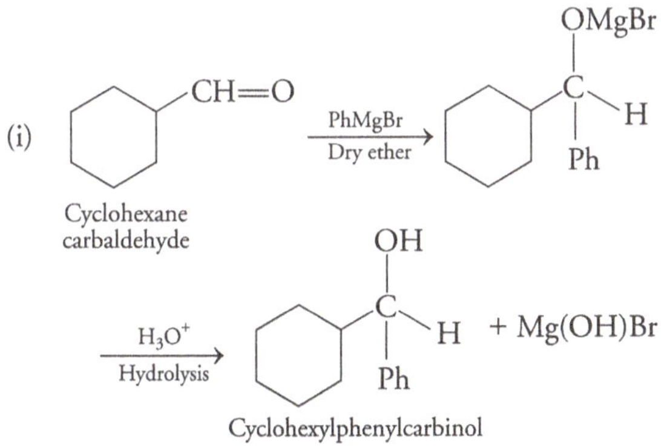

(ii) Refer to text on page 310 (Tollen's test).

(iii) Refer to text on pages 310 and 311 (Addition of ammonia and its derivatives).

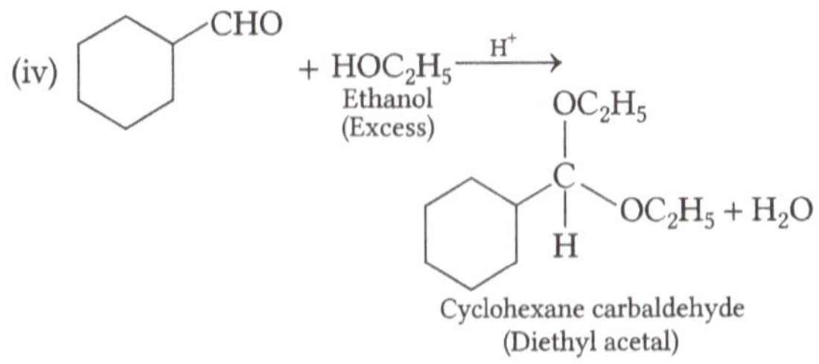

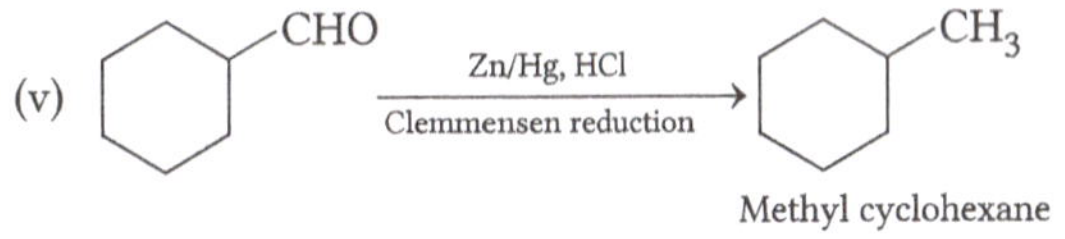

(5 × 1 = 5)

53.(i)(a) **Propanone to propene**

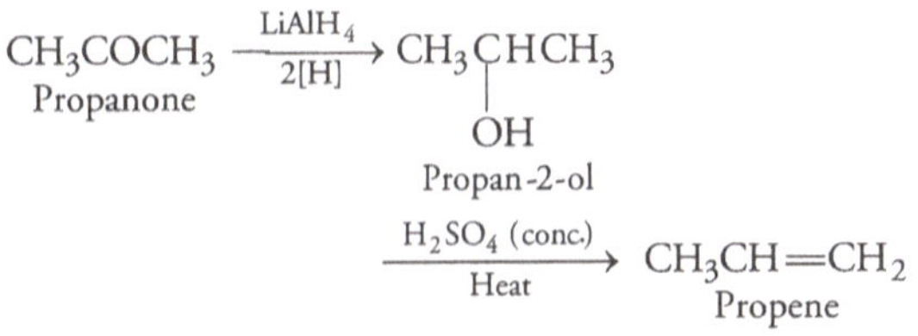

(b) **Ethanol to 3-hydroxybutanal**

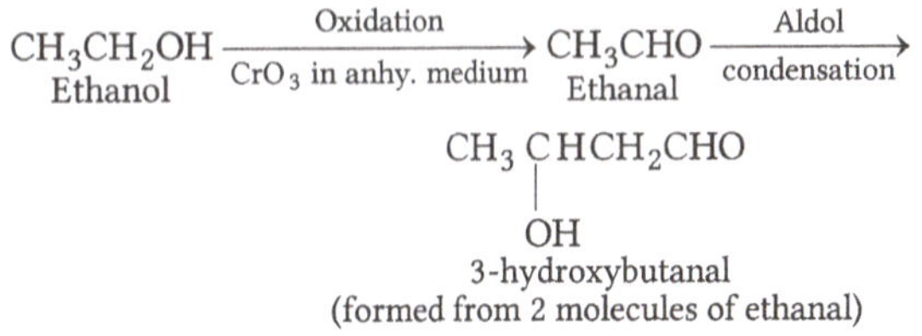

(c) **Benzene to *m*-nitroacetophenone**

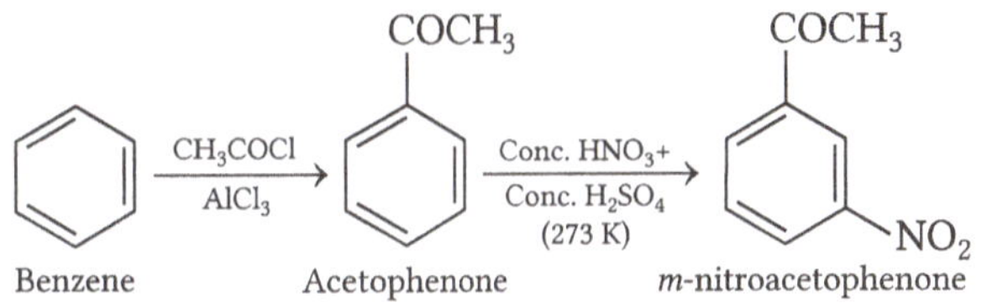

(d) **Bromobenzene to 1-phenylethanol**

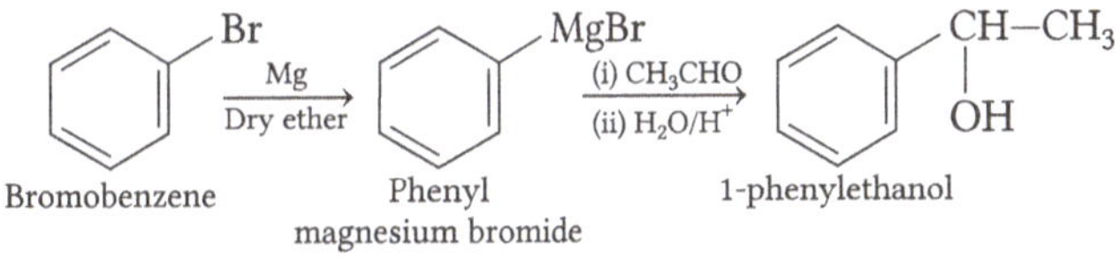

(e) **Benzaldehyde to benzophenone**

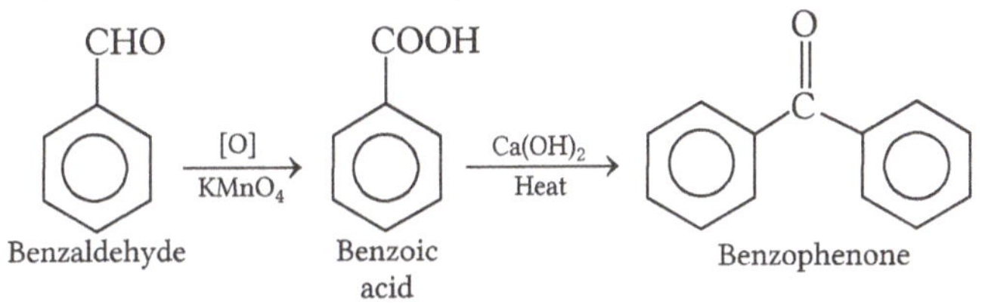

(f) **Benzaldehyde to α-hydroxyphenylacetic acid**

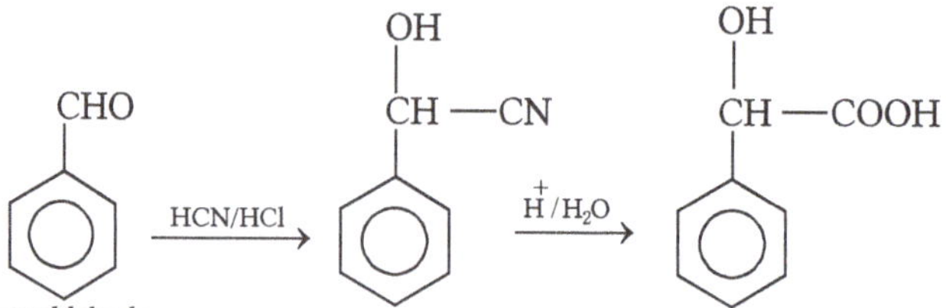

Benzaldehyde α-hydroxy phenylacetic acid

$\left(6 \times \frac{1}{2} = 3\right)$

(ii) The reactivity of carbonyl compounds towards HCN addition decreases as the $+I$-effect of the alkyl group(s) increases or the presence of bulkier alkyl group increases, which causes steric hindrance to the nucleophilic attack by CN^- at the carbonyl carbon. Thus, the reactivity decreases in the order:

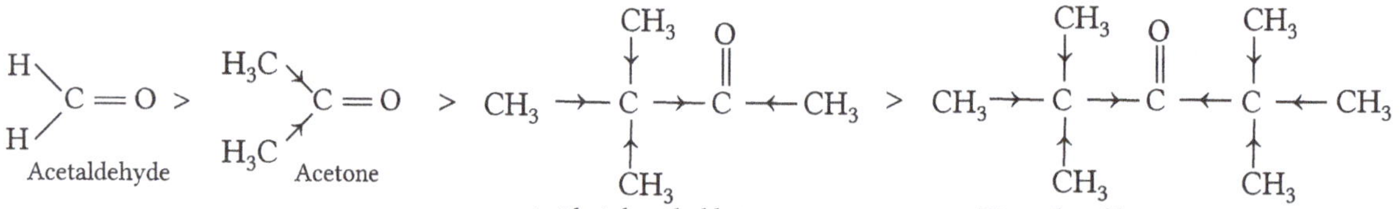

Acetaldehyde Acetone *tert*-butyl methyl ketone Di-*tert*-butyl ketone

$+I$-effect increases →

Steric hindrance due to bulkier group increases →

Reactivity towards HCN addition reaction decreases (2)

54. (i) Refer to text on page 310 (Addition of ammonia and its derivatives).

(ii) 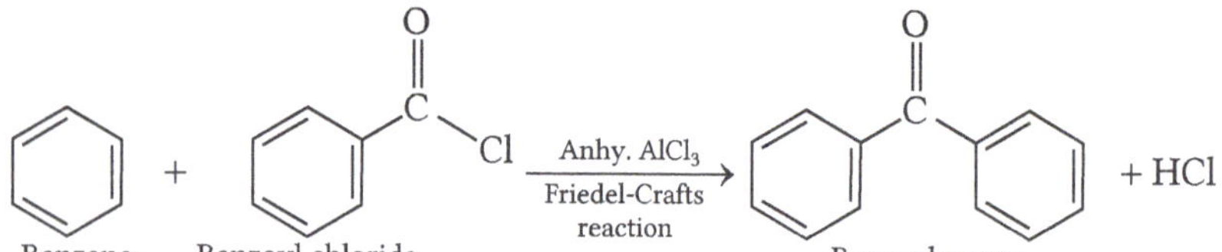

Benzene Benzoyl chloride Benzophenone

(iii) 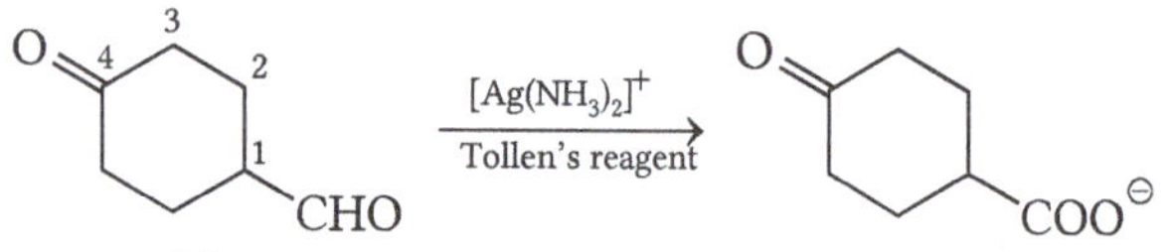

4-oxocyclohexane carbaldehyde 4-oxocyclohexane carboxylate anion

(iv) 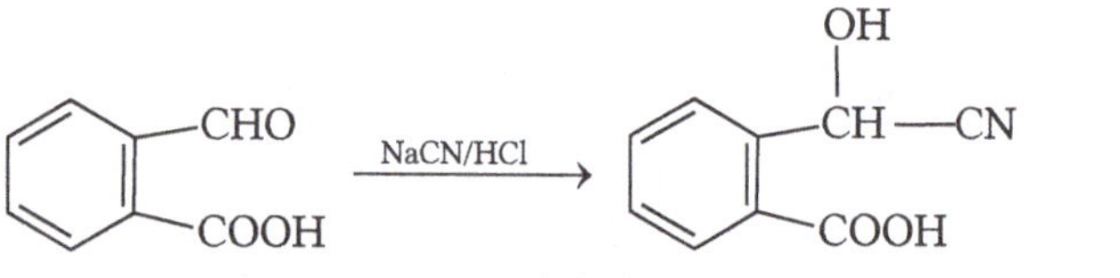

2-(1-hydroxycyanomethyl) benzoic acid

(v) $C_6H_5CHO + H_2C(CH_3)-CHO \xrightarrow{\text{Dil. NaOH}/\Delta} C_6H_5-\overset{3}{C}H=\overset{2}{C}(CH_3)-\overset{1}{C}HO$

Propanal 2-methyl-3-phenylprop-2-en-1-al

(vi) 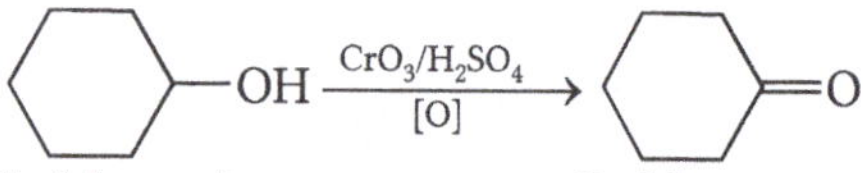

Cyclohexanol Cyclohexanone

(vii) 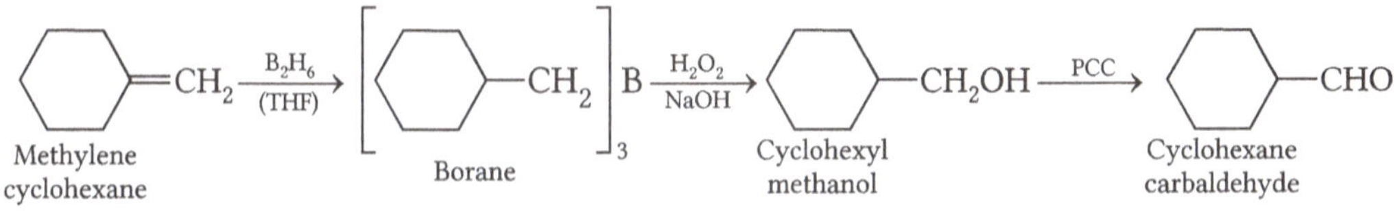

(viii) 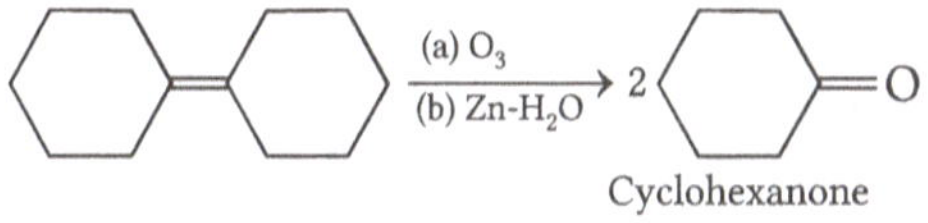

(ix) 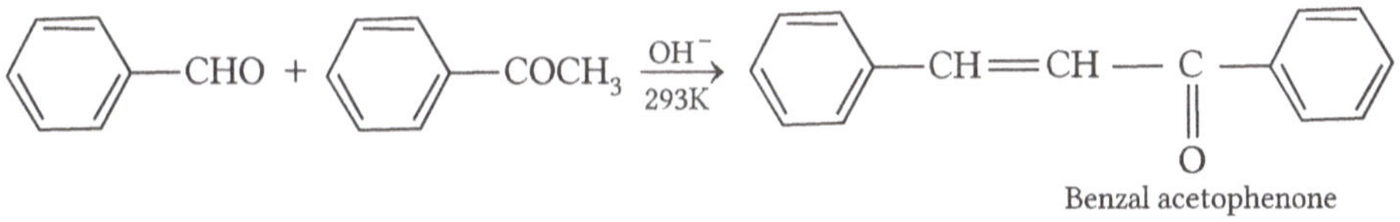

(x) 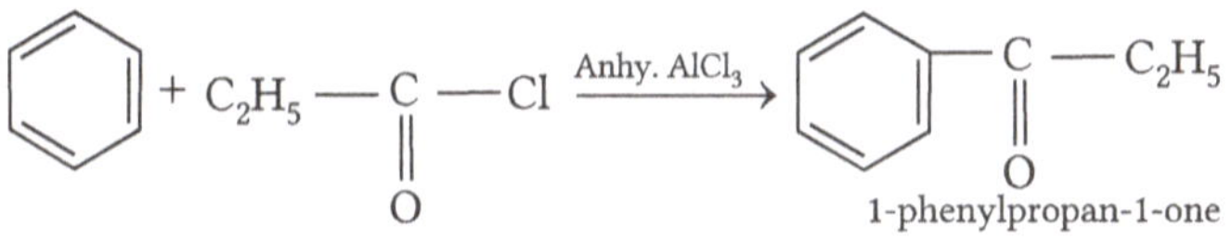

$\left[10 \times \frac{1}{2} = 5\right]$

TOPIC 02 Carboxylic Acids

The carbon compounds containing a carboxyl functional group, —COOH are known as carboxylic acids. **General formula** is $C_nH_{2n+1}COOH$ carboxyl group consists of a carbonyl group attached to a hydroxyl group, hence it is named as carboxyl.

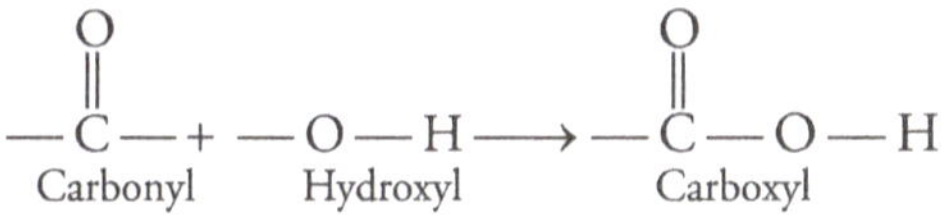

Some higher members of aliphatic carboxylic acids (C_{12} - C_{18}) known as **fatty acids**, occur in natural fats as esters of glycerol.

When carbonyl group gets attached with groups like —O*R*, —NH_2, —*X* and —OCO*R*, the compounds are called **derivatives of carboxylic acids** and known by the name, **ester, amide, acyl halide** and **acid anhydride** respectively.

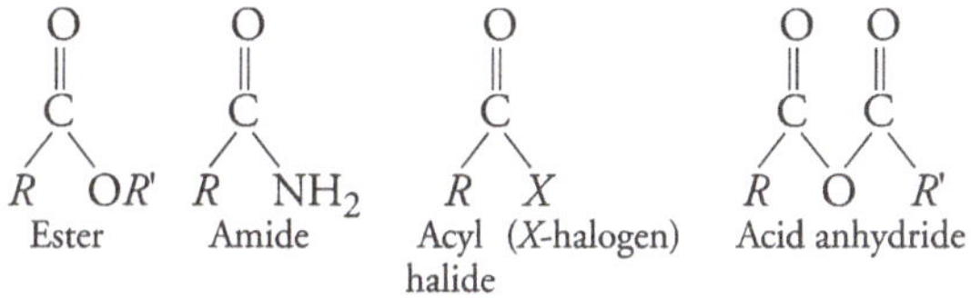

Classification

Carboxylic acids (R—COOH) are classified as follows :

1. Classification Based on Nature of Group Attached to the Carboxyl group

It is of two types:

(i) **Aliphatic carboxylic acids** When alkyl group or hydrogen atom is attached to carboxylic group, then it is termed as aliphatic carboxylic acid, e.g. acetic acid (CH_3COOH) and formic acid (HCOOH).

(ii) **Aromatic carboxylic acids** When aryl group is attached to carboxylic group, then it is termed as aromatic carboxylic acid, e.g. benzoic acid (C_6H_5COOH).

2. Classification Based on Number of Carboxyl Groups

It includes both aliphatic and aromatic acids and may be classified as follows:

(i) **Monocarboxylic acids** When carboxylic acids contain one —COOH group, then it is termed as monocarboxylic acids, e.g. acetic acid (CH_3COOH), *n*-butyric acid ($CH_3CH_2CH_2COOH$).

(ii) **Dicarboxylic acids** When carboxylic acids contain two — COOH groups, then it is termed as dicarboxylic acids,

e.g. oxalic acid [COOH | COOH], malonic acid [CH_2(COOH)(COOH)].

(iii) **Tricarboxylic acids** These contain three — COOH groups, e.g. citric acid.

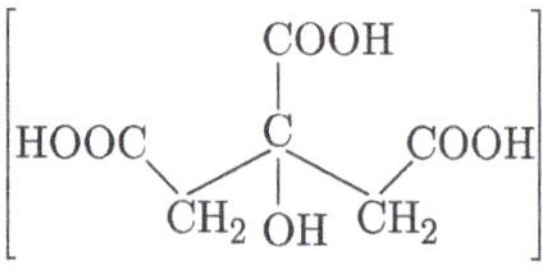

Nomenclature

Carboxylic acids are named by two systems:

1. Common System

In common system, the common names end with the suffix -'ic acid' and have been derived from Latin or Greek names of their natural sources. e.g. Formic acid (HCOOH) was first obtained from red ants (Latin : *formica* means ant), acetic acid (CH_3COOH) from vinegar (Latin : *acetum* means vinegar), butyric acid ($CH_3CH_2CH_2COOH$) from rancid butter (Latin : *butyrum* means butter).

2. IUPAC System

(i) **For naming the compounds containing only one carbonyl group** IUPAC name of carboxylic acid is alkanoic acid. Thus, in IUPAC system, their names are derived by replacing the terminal 'e' from the name of corresponding straight chain alkane by suffix 'oic acid'. In numbering, the carbon chain, the carboxylic carbon is numbered one. e.g.

$CH_3—CH(CH_3)—CH_2—COOH$
3-methylbutanoic acid

$CH_3—CH(Br)—COOH$
2-bromopropanoic acid

$C_6H_5—CH{=}CH—COOH$
3-phenylprop-2-enoic acid

(ii) **For naming the compounds containing more than one carboxyl group**, the alkyl chain is numbered and the number of carboxyl groups are indicated by adding the multiplicative prefix sueh as dicarboxylic acid, tricarboxylic acid, etc., to the name of parent alkyl chain. The position of — COOH groups are indicated by the arabic numeral before the multiplicative prefix.

Nomenclature

Carboxylic acids are named by two systems:

1. Common System

In common system, the common names end with the suffix -'ic acid' and have been derived from Latin or Greek names of their natural sources. e.g. Formic acid (HCOOH) was first obtained from red ants (Latin : *formica* means ant), acetic acid (CH_3COOH) from vinegar (Latin : *acetum* means vinegar), butyric acid ($CH_3CH_2CH_2COOH$) from rancid butter (Latin : *butyrum* means butter).

2. IUPAC System

(i) **For naming the compounds containing only one carbonyl group** IUPAC name of carboxylic acid is alkanoic acid. Thus, in IUPAC system, their names are derived by replacing the terminal 'e' from the name of corresponding straight chain alkane by suffix 'oic acid'. In numbering, the carbon chain, the carboxylic carbon is numbered one. e.g.

(ii) **For naming the compounds containing more than one carboxyl group**, the alkyl chain is numbered and the number of carboxyl groups are indicated by adding the multiplicative prefix sueh as dicarboxylic acid, tricarboxylic acid, etc., to the name of parent alkyl chain. The position of — COOH groups are indicated by the arabic numeral before the multiplicative prefix.

IUPAC Names and Structures of some Carboxylic Acids

Structure	Common name	IUPAC name
HCOOH	Formic acid	Methanoic acid
CH_3COOH	Acetic acid	Ethanoic acid
CH_3CH_2COOH	Propionic acid	Propanoic acid
$CH_3CH_2CH_2COOH$	Butyric acid	Butanoic acid
$(CH_3)_2CHCOOH$	*iso*-butyric acid	2-methylpropanoic acid
HOOC— COOH	Oxalic acid	Ethanedioic acid
HOOC— CH_2— COOH	Malonic acid	Propanedioic acid
HOOC— $(CH_2)_2$— COOH	Succinic acid	Butanedioic acid
HOOC— $(CH_2)_3$— COOH	Glutaric acid	Pentanedioic acid
HOOC— $(CH_2)_4$— COOH	Adipic acid	Hexanedioic acid
HOOC—CH_2—CH(COOH)—CH_2—COOH	—	Propane-1,2,3-tricarboxylic acid

Structure	Common name	IUPAC name
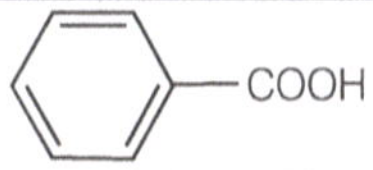	Benzoic acid	Benzene carboxylic acid (Benzoic acid)
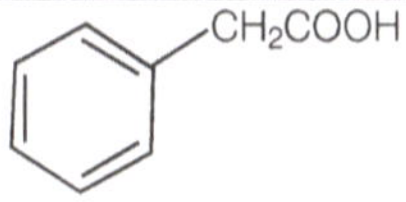	Phenylacetic acid	2-phenylethanoic acid
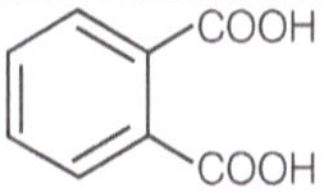	Phthalic acid	Benzene-1, 2-dicarboxylic acid

Example 1 Give the IUPAC names of the following compounds.

(i) $PhCH_2CH_2COOH$ (ii) $(CH_3)_2C{=}CHCOOH$

(iii) 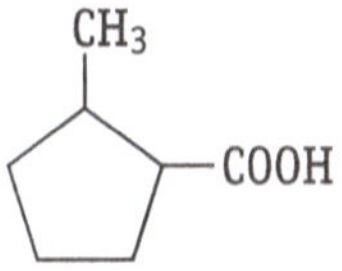 (iv) 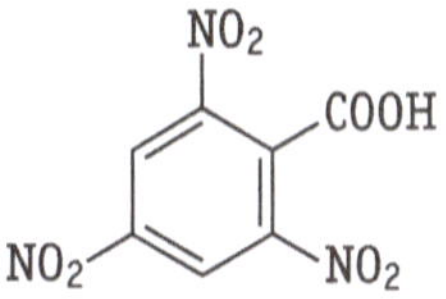

NCERT Intext

Sol. (i) $\overset{3}{Ph—CH_2}—\overset{2}{CH_2}—\overset{1}{COOH}$
3-phenylpropanoic acid

(ii) $\overset{4}{CH_3}\overset{3}{C}(CH_3)=\overset{2}{CH}—\overset{1}{COOH}$
3-methylbut-2-en-1-oic acid

(iii) 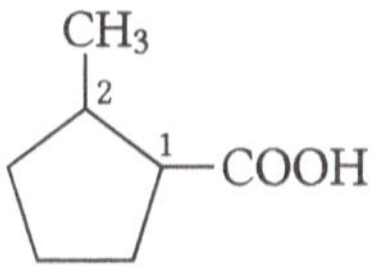
2-methylcyclopentane carboxylic acid

(iv) 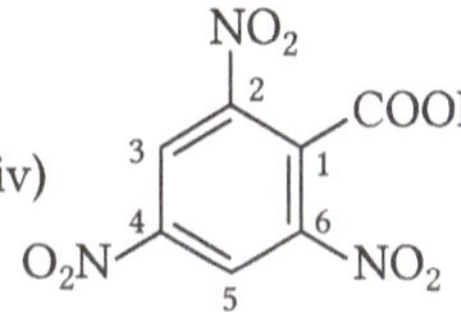
2,4,6-trinitrobenzoic acid

Structure

In carboxylic acids, the bonds attached to the carboxyl carbon are in one plane and are separated by about 120°. The carboxylic carbon is less electrophilic than carbonyl carbon because of the following possible resonance structures:

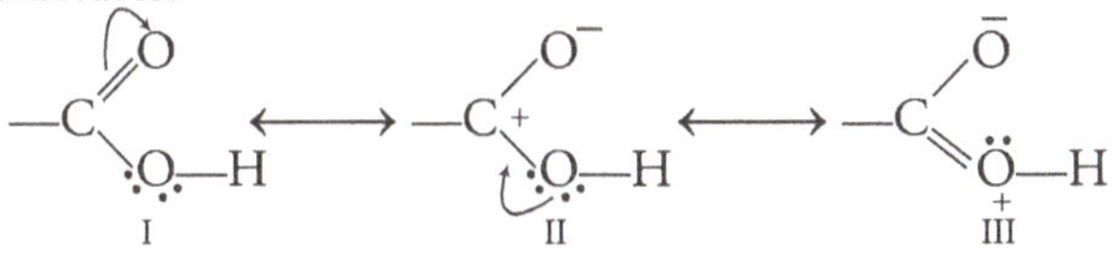

In structures (I) and (III), carboxyl carbon is electrically neutral. As a result, the carboxyl carbon of resonance hybrid is less positive. However, like carbonyl group, carboxyl group is also polar due to the resonance structures (II) and (III).

Methods of Preparation

Carboxylic acids are prepared by the following methods:

From Primary Alcohols and Aldehydes

Primary alcohols and aldehydes are readily oxidised to corresponding carboxylic acids with common oxidising agents such as potassium permanganate ($KMnO_4$) in neutral, acidic or alkaline medium or by potassium dichromate ($K_2Cr_2O_7$) and chromium trioxide (CrO_3) in acidic medium (Jones reagent).

$$RCH_2OH \xrightarrow[\text{(ii)}H_3O^+]{\text{(i) Alkaline } KMnO_4} RCOOH$$

$$\underset{\text{Decan-1-ol}}{CH_3(CH_2)_8CH_2OH} \xrightarrow{CrO_3,\,H_2SO_4} \underset{\text{Decanoic acid}}{CH_3(CH_2)_8COOH}$$

Carboxylic acids are also prepared from aldehydes by the use of mild oxidising agents like Tollen's reagent.

$$\underset{\text{Acetaldehyde}}{CH_3CHO} \xrightarrow[\text{Tollen's reagent}]{[O]} \underset{\text{Acetic acid}}{CH_3COOH}$$

From Nitriles and Amides

Nitriles are first hydrolysed to amides and then to acids in the presence of H^+ or $\bar{O}H$ as catalyst. Mild reaction conditions are used to stop the reaction at the amide stage.

$$R—CN \xrightarrow[H_2O]{\overset{+}{H} \text{ or } \bar{O}H} R—\overset{O}{\overset{\|}{C}}—NH_2 \xrightarrow[\Delta]{\overset{+}{H} \text{ or } \bar{O}H} RCOOH + NH_3\uparrow$$

$$\underset{\text{Ethanamide}}{CH_3CONH_2} \xrightarrow[H_3O^+]{\Delta} \underset{\text{Ethanoic acid}}{CH_3COOH} + NH_3\uparrow$$

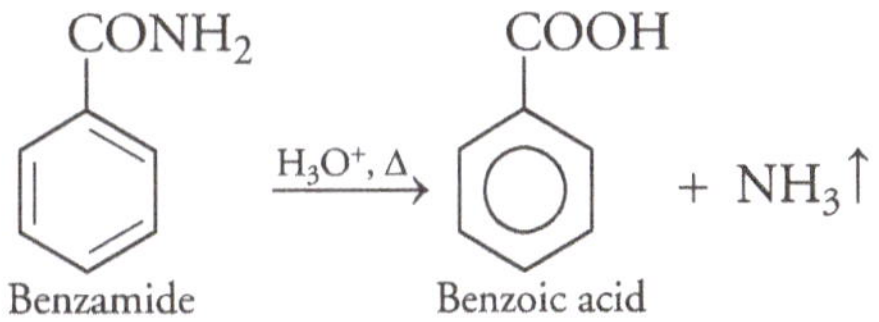
Benzamide Benzoic acid

From Alkyl Benzene

Aromatic acids are obtained by vigorous oxidation of alkyl benzene with chromic acids or acidic or alkaline $KMnO_4$. During oxidation, the aromatic nucleus remains intact but the entire chain is oxidised to —COOH group irrespective of the length of carbon chain.

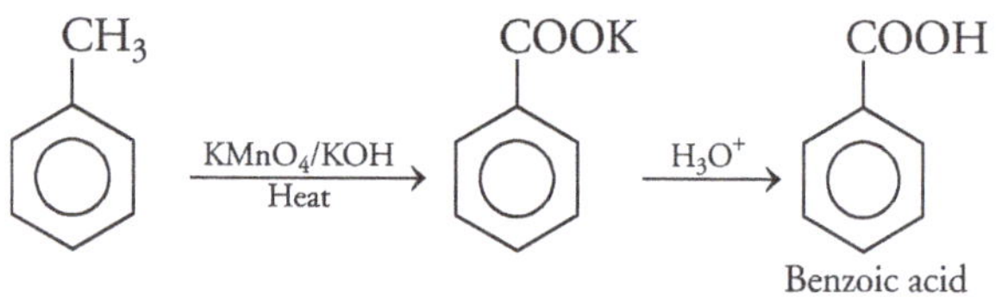

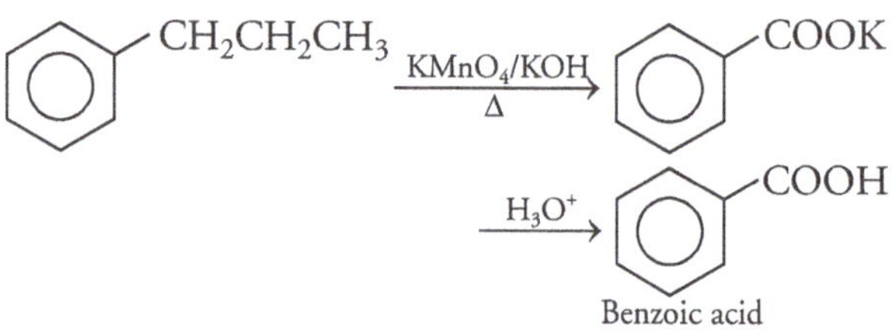

From Grignard Reagents

Grignard reagents react with dry ice (CO_2) in ethereal solution to produce salts of carboxylic acids, which on acidification with mineral acids give corresponding carboxylic acids.

$$R\text{—}MgX + O{=}C{=}O \xrightarrow{\text{Dry ether}} \underset{\text{Adduct}}{R\text{—}\overset{\displaystyle O}{\overset{\|}{C}}\text{—}\overset{-}{O}\overset{+}{M}gX} \xrightarrow[-Mg(OH)X]{H^+/H_2O} R\text{—}COOH$$

$$\underset{\text{Methyl magnesium bromide}}{CH_3MgBr} + O{=}C{=}O \xrightarrow{\text{Dry ether}} \underset{\text{Addition product}}{\left[CH_3\text{—}\overset{\displaystyle O}{\overset{\|}{C}}\text{—}\overset{-}{O}\overset{+}{M}gBr\right]} \xrightarrow{H^+/H_2O} \underset{\text{Ethanoic acid}}{CH_3\text{—}\overset{\displaystyle O}{\overset{\|}{C}}\text{—}OH} + Mg\begin{matrix}OH\\Br\end{matrix}$$

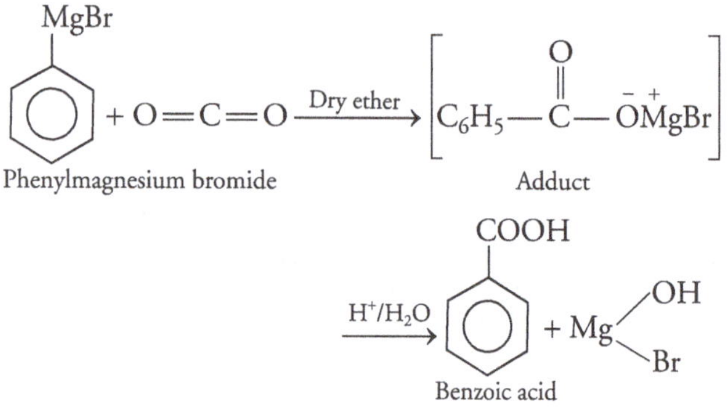

Note As nitriles and Grignard reagents can be prepared from alkyl halides, thus, the last two methods (from alkyl benzenes and Grignard reagents) listed above are very useful for converting alkyl halides into corresponding carboxylic acids having one carbon atom more than that present in alkyl halides (i.e. ascending the series).

Example 2 Show how each of the following compounds can be converted to benzoic acid?
(i) Ethyl benzene (ii) Acetophenone
(iii) Bromobenzene (iv) Phenylethene (styrene)

NCERT Intext

Sol.

(i)

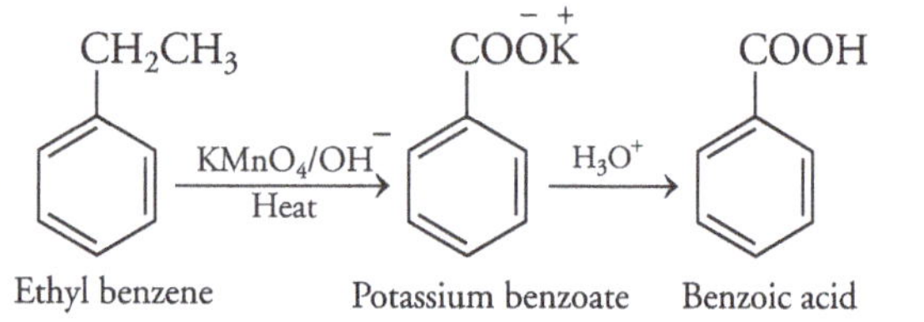

(ii)

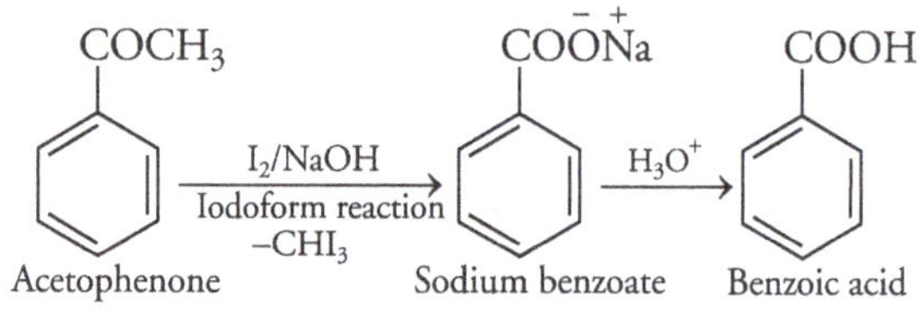

(iii)

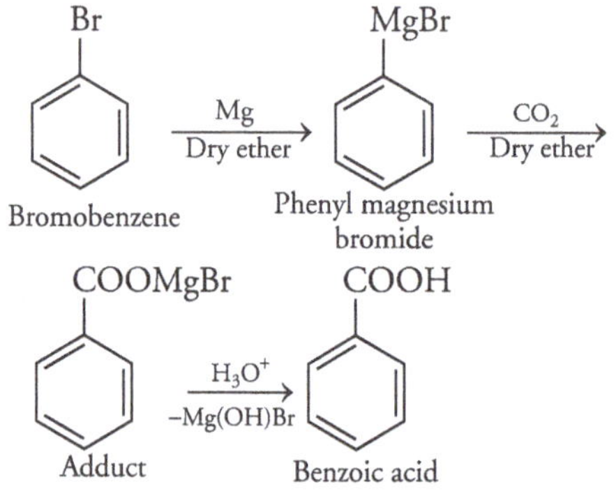

(iv)

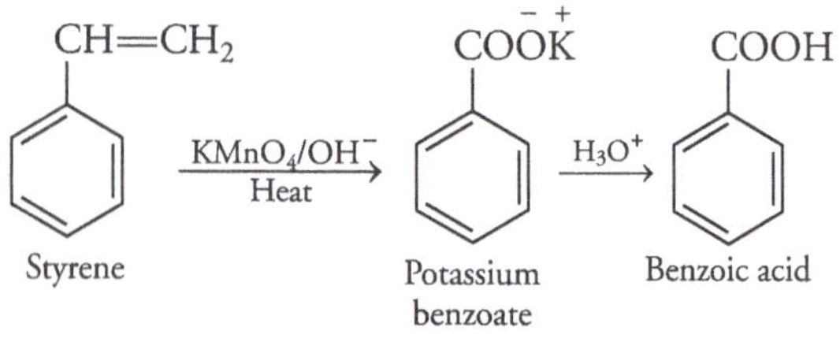

Physical Properties

The physical properties of carboxylic acids are described below:

(i) **Physical State** Aliphatic carboxylic acids upto nine carbon atoms are colourless liquids at room temperature with unpleasant odours while higher carboxylic acids are wax like solids and odourless due to their low volatility.

(ii) **Solubility** Simple aliphatic carboxylic acids having upto four carbon atoms are miscible with water because of hydrogen bond formation with water. Solubility decreases with increase in the number of carbon atoms which is due to increased hydrophobic interaction of hydrocarbon part. Carboxylic acids are also soluble in less polar organic solvents like benzene, ether, alcohol, chloroform, etc.

(iii) **Boiling Point** As compare to hydrocarbons, aldehydes, ketones and carboxylic acids have higher boiling points because they have high extent of hydrogen bonding with water, due to which they exists as associated molecules.

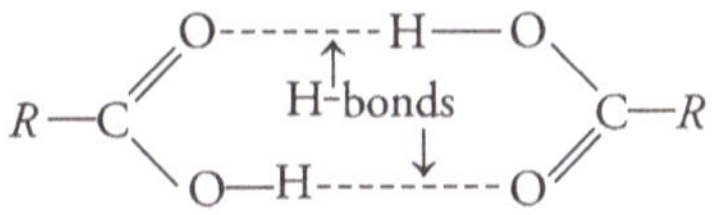

Dimer

In vapour state or in aprotic solvent

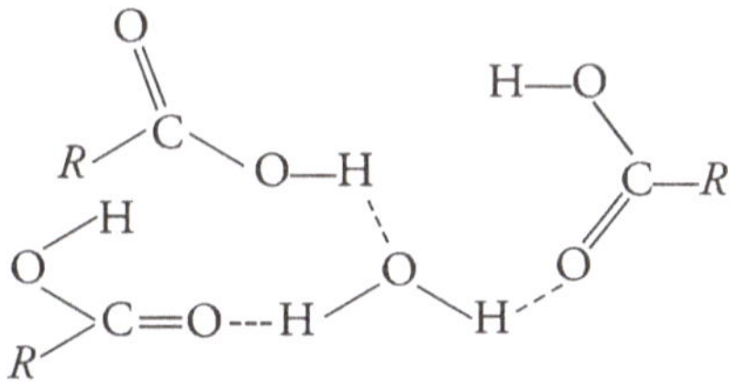

Hydrogen bonding (dotted) of R COOH with H_2O

The hydrogen bonds are not broken completely even in the vapour phase. Infact, most carboxylic acids exist as dimer in the vapour phase or in aprotic solvent.

(iv) **Melting Point** The melting point of aliphatic carboxylic acids do not show a regular pattern rather they show oscillation or alteration effect, i.e. melting point of an acid containing even number of carbon atoms is higher than the next member containing odd number of carbon atoms.

Chemical Properties

Chemical properties of carboxylic acids are characteristic of carboxyl group and the alkyl or the aryl group. The reactions of carboxylic acids are classified as follows:

Reactions Involving H-atom of the Carboxyl Group

1. Acidic Nature of Carboxylic Acids

Like alcohols, carboxylic acids also evolve hydrogen with metals and form salts with alkalies similar to phenols. However, unlike phenols, they react with weaker bases like sodium carbonate and hydrogen carbonate to evolve carbon dioxide.

Reactions Showing Acidic Character of —COOH Group

(a) **With active metal** (Na)

$$2R\text{—COOH} + 2\text{Na} \longrightarrow \underset{\text{Sodium carboxylate}}{2R\text{—CO}\overset{-}{\text{O}}\overset{+}{\text{Na}}} + \text{H}_2$$

(b) **With alkali**

$$R\text{—COOH} + \text{NaOH} \longrightarrow R\text{—CO}\overset{-}{\text{O}}\overset{+}{\text{Na}} + \text{H}_2\text{O}$$

(c) **With carbonates**

$$R\text{COOH} + \text{Na}_2\text{CO}_3 \longrightarrow 2R\text{CO}\overset{-}{\text{O}}\,\text{Na}^+ + \text{CO}_2 + \text{H}_2\text{O}$$

(d) **With bicarbonates**

$$R\text{COOH} + \text{NaHCO}_3 \longrightarrow R\text{—CO}\overset{-}{\text{O}}\overset{+}{\text{Na}} + \text{H}_2\text{O} + \text{CO}_2\uparrow$$

In aqueous solution, carboxylic acids ionise and exist in dynamic equilibrium between the resonance stabilised carboxylate ions and the hydronium ions.

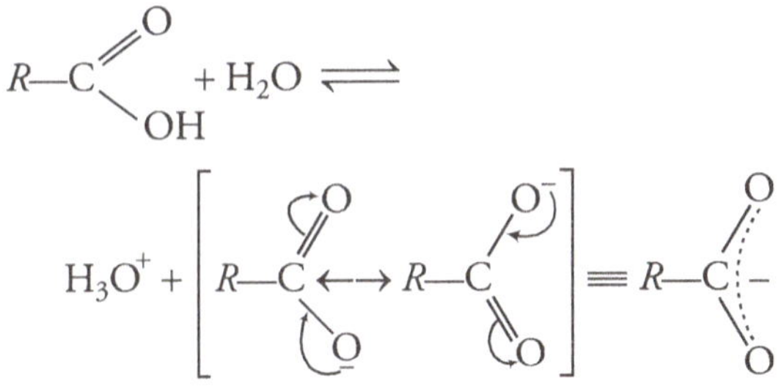

For the above reaction:

$$K_{\text{eq}} = \frac{[\text{H}_3\text{O}^+][R\text{COO}^-]}{[\text{H}_2\text{O}][R\text{COOH}]};$$

$$K_a = K_{\text{eq}}[\text{H}_2\text{O}] = \frac{[\text{H}_3\text{O}^+][R\text{COO}^-]}{[R\text{COOH}]}$$

where, K_{eq} is equilibrium constant and K_a is the acid dissociation constant.

The strength of an acid is usually indicated by its pK_a value rather than its K_a value.

$$\text{p}K_a = -\log K_a$$

Smaller the pK_a, stronger is the acid. Strong acids have pK_a values < 1. Trifluoroacetic acid is the strongest organic acid (pK_a of $CF_3COOH = 0.23$). pK_a of hydrochloric acid, benzoic and acetic acid are –7.0, 4.19 and 4.76, respectively.

The acids with pK_a values between 1 and 5 are considered to be moderately strong acids, weak acids have pK_a values between 5 and 15 and extremely weak acids have pK_a values >15.

Carboxylic acids are weaker than mineral acids but they are stronger acids than alcohols and many simple phenols.

Cause of Acidic Nature of Carboxylic Acids

Carboxylic acids may be regarded as a resonance hybrid of the structures I and II.

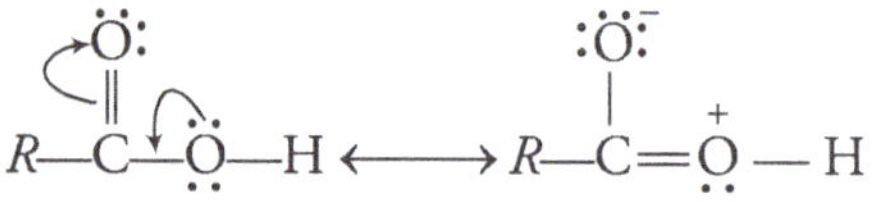

(I) (II)

Acidic nature of carboxyl group is due to the breaking of O—H bond as positively charged oxygen weakens the bond. Carboxylate anion formed by the removal of a proton is also stabilised by resonance.

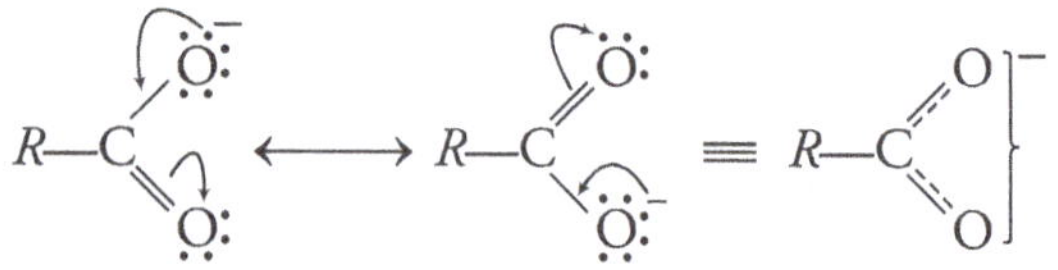

(III) (IV) (V)

Resonance stabilisation of carboxylate anion is more than that of undissociated carboxylic acid. Therefore, greater stability of carboxylate ion is responsible for the acidic character of carboxylic acids.

Carboxylic acids are more acidic than alcohols because carboxylate anions are more stable than alkoxide ions, so carboxylic acids have strong tendency to release a proton.

Similarly, carboxylic acids are stronger acids than phenols because carboxylate ion is much more resonance stabilised than phenoxide ion as negative charge is delocalised over two electronegative O-atoms in carboxylate anion while in phenol, negative charge is delocalised over only one O-atom.

Effect of Substituents on the Acidity of Carboxylic Acids

Substituents may affect the stability of the conjugate base and thus, also affect the acidity of the carboxylic acids.

Electron Withdrawing Groups (EWGs) increase the stability of the carboxylate ion by dispersing the negative charge through resonance effects on the conjugate while electron donating groups (EDGs) decrease the stability of the carboxylate ion by intensifying the negative charge.

Acidity of carboxylic acids increases due to the presence of Electron Withdrawing Groups (EWGs)

Acidity of carboxylic acids decreases due to the presence of Electron Donating Groups (EDGs)

The effect of the following substituent groups in the increasing acidity order is:

$$Ph < I < Br < Cl < F < CN < NO_2 < CF_3$$

$$\therefore\ FCH_2COOH > ClCH_2COOH >$$
$$BrCH_2COOH > HCOOH > PhCOOH >$$
$$PhCH_2COOH > CH_3COOH > CH_3CH_2COOH$$

As the $+I$-effect of electron donating group increases the relative acidic strength decreases as:

$$—CH_3 < —C_2H_5 < —CH(CH_3)_2 < — C(CH_3)_3 \ (+I\text{-effect increases})$$

$$\underset{\text{Acetic acid}}{CH_3COOH} > \underset{\text{Propionic acid}}{CH_3CH_2COOH} >$$

$$\underset{\text{Isobutyric acid}}{(CH_3)_2CHCOOH} > \underset{\text{2,2-dimethyl propanoic acid}}{(CH_3)_3COOH}$$

(Relative acidic strength decreases)

> **Order of Decreasing Acidity of Different Carboxylic Acids Based On pK_a Value**
>
> $CF_3COOH > CCl_3COOH > Cl_2CHCOOH > O_2NCH_2COOH >$
> $NC—CH_2COOH > FCH_2COOH > ClCH_2COOH >$
> $BrCH_2COOH > ICH_2COOH > HCOOH > ClCH_2CH_2COOH >$
> $C_6H_5COOH > C_6H_5CH_2COOH > CH_3COOH > CH_3CH_2COOH$

Direct attachment of groups such as phenyl or vinyl to the carboxylic acid, increases the acidity of corresponding carboxylic acid, contrary to the decrease expected due to resonance effect shown below:

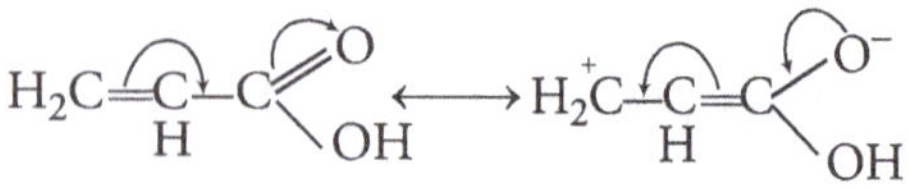

sp^2-hybridised carbon is more electronegative than that of sp^3-hybridised carbon. Therefore, as the hybridisation of carbon atom directly attached to —COOH, change from $sp^3 \longrightarrow sp^2 \longrightarrow sp$, the acidic strength increases in the order

$\underset{sp^3}{CH_3COOH} < CH_2{=}\underset{sp^2}{CH}COOH < \underset{sp^2}{C_6H_5COOH} < HC{\equiv}\underset{sp}{C}{-}COOH$

Benzoic acid is stronger acid than acrylic acid ($CH_2{=}CHCOOH$) because delocalisation destroys the aromatic character of the benzene ring.

Acidic strength of few substituted aromatic acids in the decreasing order are:

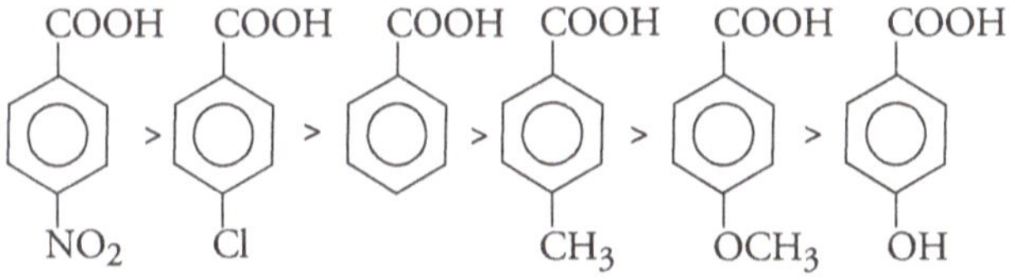

Reactions Involving —OH Part of the Carboxyl Group

1. Formation of Acid Chlorides

Carboxylic acids can be converted into the corresponding acid chlorides by treating with PCl_5, PCl_3 or $SOCl_2$.

(i) Reaction with Phosphorus Pentachloride

$$\underset{\text{Carboxylic acid}}{R{-}\overset{\overset{\displaystyle O}{\|}}{C}{-}OH} + \underset{\text{Phosphorus pentachloride}}{PCl_5} \longrightarrow \underset{\text{Acid chloride}}{R{-}\overset{\overset{\displaystyle O}{\|}}{C}{-}Cl} + \underset{\text{Phosphorus oxychloride}}{POCl_3} + HCl$$

(ii) Reaction with Phosphorus Trichloride

$$3\underset{\text{Carboxylic acid}}{R{-}\overset{\overset{\displaystyle O}{\|}}{C}{-}OH} + \underset{\text{Phosphorus trichloride}}{PCl_3} \longrightarrow 3\underset{\text{Acid chloride}}{R{-}\overset{\overset{\displaystyle O}{\|}}{C}{-}Cl} + \underset{\text{Phosphorus acid}}{H_3PO_3}$$

(iii) Reaction with Thionyl Chloride

$$\underset{\text{Carboxylic acid}}{R{-}\overset{\overset{\displaystyle O}{\|}}{C}{-}OH} + \underset{\text{Thionyl chloride}}{SOCl_2} \longrightarrow \underset{\text{Acid chloride}}{R{-}\overset{\overset{\displaystyle O}{\|}}{C}{-}Cl} + SO_2\uparrow + HCl\uparrow$$

2. Formation of Esters

When carboxylic acids heated with alcohols in the presence of conc. H_2SO_4 or dry HCl gas, esters are formed.

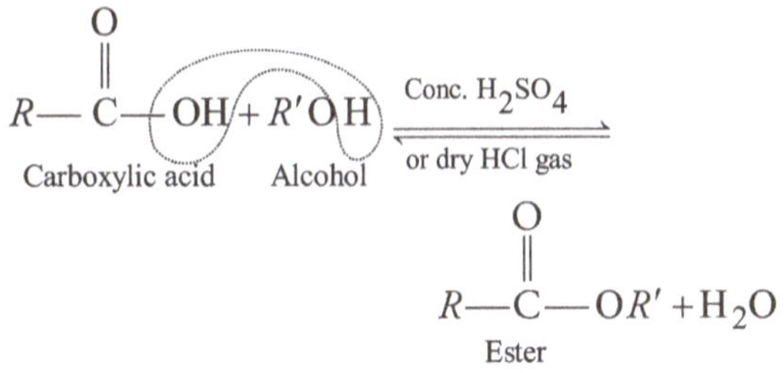

This reaction is reversible in nature and is called **esterification.**

3. Formation of Amides

Carboxylic acids react with ammonia to form ammonium salts which upon heating form acid amides.

e.g.

$$\underset{\text{Carboxylic acid}}{R{-}\overset{\overset{\displaystyle O}{\|}}{C}{-}OH} + \underset{\text{Ammonia}}{NH_3} \longrightarrow \underset{\text{Ammonium carboxylate}}{R{-}\overset{\overset{\displaystyle O}{\|}}{C}{-}O^-\overset{+}{N}H_4} \xrightarrow{\text{Heat}} \underset{\text{Acid amide}}{R{-}\overset{\overset{\displaystyle O}{\|}}{C}{-}NH_2} + H_2O$$

4. Formation of Acid Anhydrides

Carboxylic acids on heating in the presence of a strong dehydrating agent such as phosphorus pentaoxide, P_2O_5 or H_2SO_4 form corresponding acid anhydrides.

e.g.

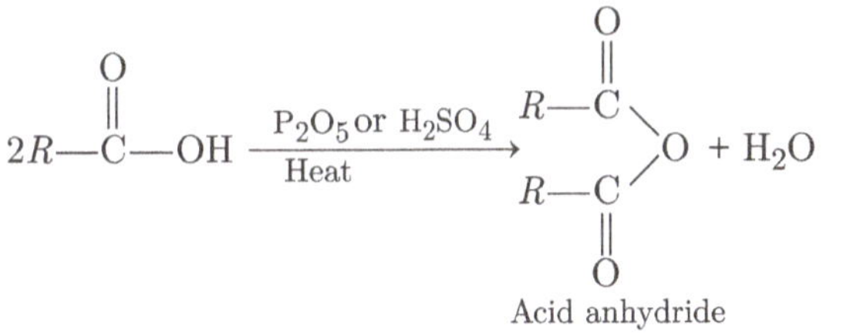

Reactions Involving Carboxyl Group

1. Decarboxylation (Removal of — CO_2 Group)

(i) By Heating Sodium Salt of the Acid With Sodalime

$$\underset{\text{Sodium salt of carboxylic acid}}{R{-}\overset{\overset{\displaystyle O}{\|}}{C}{-}\overset{-}{O}\overset{+}{N}a} + NaOH \xrightarrow[\text{Heat}]{\text{CaO}} \underset{\text{Alkane}}{R{-}H} + Na_2CO_3$$

(ii) **By electrolysis of Aqueous Solution of Sodium or Potassium Salt**

Complete Reaction :

$$2R\overset{-\ +}{COONa} \longrightarrow \underset{\text{Carboxylate ion}}{2RCOO^-} + 2Na^+$$

At anode $\underset{\text{Carboxylate ion}}{2RCOO^-} \longrightarrow \underset{\text{Alkane}}{R—R} + 2CO_2 + 2e^-$

At cathode

$$2H_2O \rightleftharpoons 2H^+ + 2OH^-, (2H^+ + 2e^- \longrightarrow H_2)$$

This process is known as **Kolbe's electrolysis.**

2. Reduction

(i) **Partial Reduction to Alcohols**

$$\underset{\text{Carboxylic acid}}{RCOOH} + 2H_2 \xrightarrow[\text{(or } LiAlH_4)]{\text{Copper chromite}} \underset{\text{Alcohols}}{RCH_2OH} + H_2O$$

(ii) **Complete Reduction to Alkanes**

$$\underset{\text{Carboxylic acid}}{RCOOH} + 6HI \xrightarrow[\text{Heat}]{\text{Red P}} \underset{\text{Alkane}}{RCH_3} + 3I_2 + 2H_2O$$

Reactions Involving Alkyl Group of Carboxylic Acid

Hell-Volhard Zelinsky Reaction (Halogenation)

Carbodylic acids (except formic acid) react with chlorine or bromine in presence of small amount of red phosphorus gives α-halogenated carboxylic acids.

$$\underset{\text{Acetic acid}}{CH_3COOH} \xrightarrow[(-HCl)]{Cl_2,\ \text{Red P}} \underset{\text{Monochloro acetic acid}}{CH_2ClCOOH}$$

$$\xrightarrow[(-HCl)]{Cl_2,\ \text{Red P}} \underset{\text{Dichloro acetic acid}}{CHCl_2COOH} \xrightarrow[-HCl]{Cl_2,\ \text{Red P}} \underset{\text{Trichloro acetic acid}}{CCl_3COOH}$$

This reaction is called **Hell-Volhard Zelinsky** (HVZ) reaction.

Ring Substitution Reactions

Aromatic carboxylic acids undergo electrophilic substitution reactions in which the carboxyl group acts as a deactivating and *meta*-directing group.

However, they do not undergo Friedel-Crafts reaction because the carboxyl group is deactivating and the catalyst aluminium chloride (Lewis acid) gets bonded to the carboxyl group.

(i) **Halogenation**

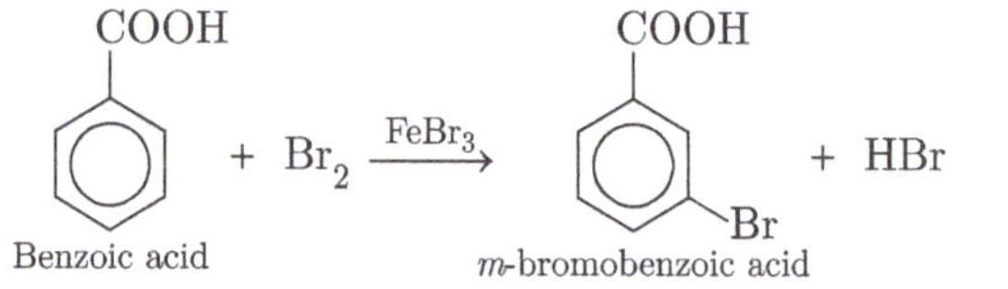

(ii) **Nitration**

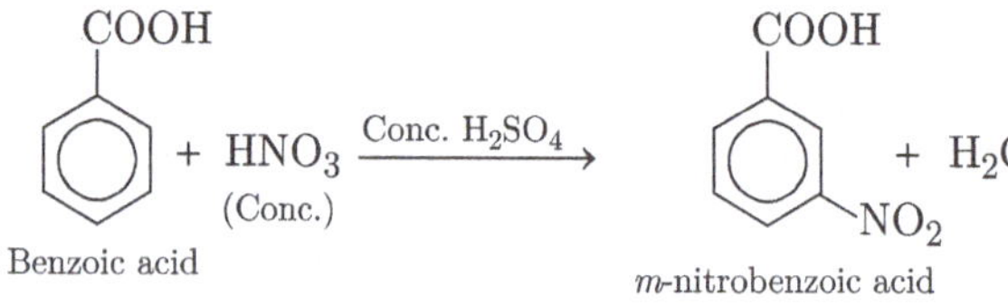

(iii) **Sulphonation**

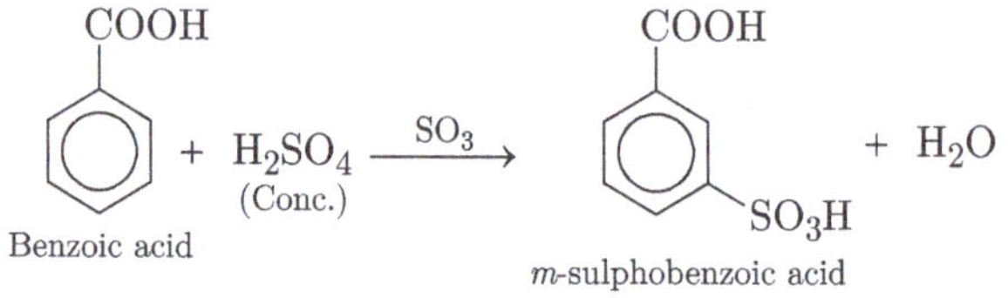

Tests for Acids

Some important tests used to distinguish acids are as follows :

Formic Acid

(i) It gives silver mirror or black precipitate with Tollen's reagent.

(ii) It gives red precipitate with Fehling's solution.

(iii) It decolourises pink colour of acidified $KMnO_4$.

Acetic Acid

(i) It liberates carbon dioxide gas with bicarbonates and carbonates.

(ii) With ferric chloride, it produces wine red colour.

(iii) When warmed with ethyl alcohol and conc. H_2SO_4, a pleasant fruity odour of ethyl acetate is formed.

3. Benzoic Acid

(i) It dissolves in water on boiling but separates out in the form of white shining leaflets on cooling.

(ii) Benzoic acid (neutral solution) gives buff coloured precipitate with $FeCl_3$.

(iii) On warming it with a little alcohol and conc. H_2SO_4, a fragrant odour of ethyl benzoate is obtained.

Uses

Some important uses of acids are as follows :

1. Formic Acid

(i) As an antiseptic.

(ii) For dye baths in textiles.

(iii) As a coagulating agent in rubber industry.
(iv) For the preservation of fruits

2. Acetic Acid

(i) As a solvent for resins, cellulose, etc.
(ii) In the production of dyes, perfumes, esters, acetone, etc.
(iii) For the manufacture of cellulose acetate which is used for making packaging materials, varnishes, rayon, etc.

3. Benzoic Acid

(i) As a food preservative either in the pure form or mostly in the form of sodium benzoate.
(ii) As urinary antiseptic in medicine.
(iii) In the manufacture of antiseptics and dyes.

Topic Practice 2

Very Short Answer Type Questions

1 Mark

1. Fill in the Blanks

(i) ...... is more acidic than acetic acid because of ...... effect. **ISC 2003**

(ii) Hydrolysis of methyl propanoate gives ... and .... **ISC 2012**

(iii) Benzoic acid is soluble in ..... water

2. Objective Type Questions

(i) When acetic acid is reacted with calcium hydroxide and the product is distilled dry, the compound formed is **ISC 2012**

(a) calcium acetate (b) acetone
(c) acetaldehyde (d) acetic anhydride

(ii) Effervescence takes place when sodium carbonate solution is added to **ISC 2003**

(a) formaldehye (b) acetaldehyde
(c) acetic acid (d) phenol

(iii) In the equation, $CH_3COOH + Cl_2 \xrightarrow[-HCl]{\text{Red P}} A$,

The compound A is **ISC 2016**

(a) CH_3CH_2Cl (b) $ClCH_2COOH$
(c) CH_3Cl (d) CH_3COCl

(iv) When oxalic acid is heated with glycerol, we get. **ISC 2009**

(a) formic acid (b) acetic acid
(c) lactic acid (d) tartaric acid

3. Match the acids given in Column I with their correct IUPAC names given in Column II and choose the correct option using the codes given below :

Column I (Acids)		Column II (IUPAC names)	
A.	Phthalic acid	(i)	Hexane-1, 6-dioic acid
B.	Oxalic acid	(ii)	Benzene-1, 2-dicarboxylic acid
C.	Succinic acid	(iii)	Pentane-1, 5-dioic acid
D.	Adipic acid	(iv)	Butane-1, 4-dioic acid
E.	Glutaric acid	(v)	Ethane-1, 2-dioic acid

Codes

	A	B	C	D	E
(a)	(ii)	(v)	(iv)	(i)	(iii)
(b)	(ii)	(iv)	(iii)	(i)	(v)
(c)	(i)	(v)	(iv)	(iii)	(ii)
(d)	(i)	(iii)	(iv)	(iii)	(v)

4. Starting with Grignard's reagent, how will you prepare propanoic acid? **ISC 2016**

5. The aqueous solution of sodium acetate is basic. Explain. **ISC 2015**

6. Name the reagents used in the following reaction.

$$C_6H_5—CH_2—CH_3 \xrightarrow{?} C_6H_5—COO^-K^+$$

7. Correct the following statement:
Chloroacetic acid is more acidic than acetic acid because of the $-M$ effect. **ISC 2007**

8. Arrange the following compounds in the increasing order of their property as indicated.
$Cl—CH_2—COOH$, $F—CH_2—COOH$, $CH_3—COOH$ (acidic character) **NCERT Exemplar**

9. What happens when methylbenzene is oxidised with alkaline $KMnO_4$?

10. Write the reagents required in the following reaction: $CH_3—COOH \xrightarrow{?} CH_3—CONH_2$

11. Predict the product of the following reaction:

$$CH_3COONa \xrightarrow[\Delta]{NaOH/CaO} ?$$

12. Complete the following reaction:

$$CH_3COOH \xrightarrow{Br_2/P}$$

13. Give the balanced equation for the following name reaction. Benzoin condensation **ISC 2016**

14. Give the balanced equations for the following reaction:
Kolbe's electrolytic reaction **ISC 2014**

15. Give the balanced equation for the following reaction: Benzoic acid and phosphorus pentachloride. **ISC 2012**

16. Give one example for the following name reaction:
Hell-Volhard-Zelinsky (HVZ) reaction. **ISC 2023, 2010**

17. Give the balanced equation for the following reaction: Formic acid is heated with Tollen's reagent. **ISC 2009**

18. Give the balanced equation for the following reaction:
Sucrose is warmed with concentrated nitric acid. **ISC 2007, 2000**

19. Write the chemical equation for the following reaction and name the main product:
Oxalic acid with glycerol at 260°C. **ISC 2005**

20. Give simple chemical tests to distinguish between the following pair of compounds.
Benzoic acid and phenol.

21. Give chemical test to distinguish acetaldehyde and acetic acid. **ISC 2017**

22. Give the chemical test to distinguish between formaldehyde and acetaldehyde. **ISC 2016**

23. Give one test to distinguish between acetone and acetic acid. **ISC 2006**

24. Give the chemical equation.
Acetic acid is treated with ethanol and a drop of conc. H_2SO_4. **ISC 2019**

Short Answer Type I Questions

(2 Marks)

25. How will you convert the following?
(i) Ethanal to 2-hydroxy propanoic acid
(ii) Toluene to benzoic acid

26. Identify the products *A*, *B* and *C*.

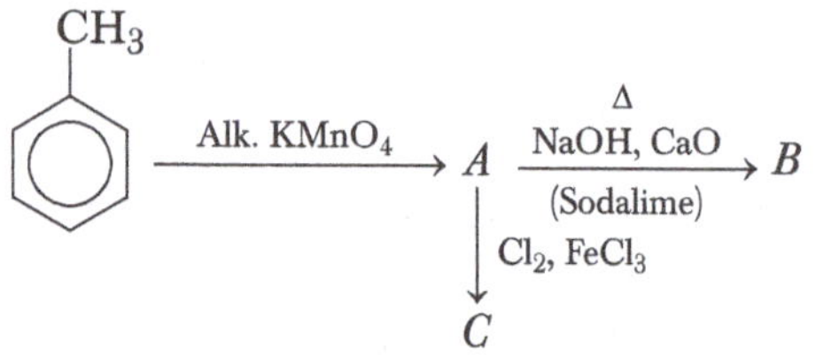

27. How will you bring about the following conversion?
Formic acid to oxalic acid. **ISC 2008, 2003**

28. Predict the products of the following reactions:
(i) $C_6H_5—CH_3 \xrightarrow[\text{(ii) } H^+]{\text{(i) } KMnO_4/\ KOH} ?$
(ii)

29. Identify the compounds [*A*] and [*B*] in the reactions given below. **ISC 2024**
(i) $C_6H_6 \xrightarrow[AlCl_3 \text{ (anhy.)}]{CH_3Cl} [A] \xrightarrow[KrCr_2O_7 + H_2SO_4]{[O]} [B]$
(ii) $CH_3—CHOH—CH_3 \xrightarrow[K_2Cr_2O_7 + H_2SO]{[O]} [A] \xrightarrow{NH_2OH} [B]$

30. Arrange the following compounds in the increasing order of their property as indicated.
(i) $CH_3\ CH_2CH(Br)COOH$, $CH_3CH(Br)CH_2COOH$, $(CH_3)_2CHCOOH$, $CH_3CH_2CH_2COOH$ (acidic strength).
(ii) Benzoic acid, 4-nitrobenzoic acid, 3,4-dinitro benzoic acid, 4-methoxy benzoic acid (acidic strength). **NCERT**

31. How will you carry out the following conversion?
Acetic acid to methane **ISC 2002**

32. How can the following conversion be brought about? Propanoic acid to ethylamine. **ISC 2013**

33. How will you distinguish between the following pair of compounds? Give one good chemical test. Oxalic acid and acetic acid. **ISC 2009**

34. Compound *A* was prepared by the oxidation of compound *B* with alkaline $KMnO_4$. Compound *A* on reduction with lithium aluminium hydride gets converted back to compound *B*. When compound *A* is heated with compound *B* in the presence of H_2SO_4, it produces fruity smell of compound *C*. To which family, the compounds *A*, *B* and *C* belongs to? **NCERT Exemplar**

35. An aromatic carboxylic acid [*A*] which readily sublimes on heating, produces compound [*B*] on treatment with PCl_5. Compound [*B*], when reduced in the presence of Pd catalyst over $BaSO_4$ poisoned by sulphur in xylene solution gives compound [*C*].When compound [*C*] is condensed in the presence of alcoholic KCN, it gives compound [*D*]. (Molecular formula of compound [*D*] is $C_{14}H_{12}O_2$). Identify the compounds [*A*], [*B*], [*C*] and [*D*]. **ISC 2023**

36. Write the reactions involved in the following:
(i) Hell-Volhard-Zelinsky reaction
(ii) Decarboxylation reaction **Delhi 2017**

37. Give one chemical test to distinguish between the following pair of compounds:
Formic acid and acetic acid. **ISC 2013**

38. Give one chemical test each to distinguish between the following pairs of compounds.

(i) Acetone and benzaldehyde. **ISC 2019**

(ii) Phenol and benzoic acid.

Short Answer Type II Questions

(3 Marks)

39. Identify the compounds A, B, C and D in the given reaction. **ISC 2019**

$$HC \equiv CH \xrightarrow[Hg^{2+}/H_2SO_4]{H_2O} A \xrightarrow[K_2Cr_2O_7 + H_2SO_4]{[O]} B \xrightarrow{Ca(OH)_2} C \xrightarrow[\text{Dry distillation}]{\text{Heat}} D$$

40. Identify the compounds A, B and C in the following reaction.

$$CH_3—Br \xrightarrow{Mg / Ether} [A] \xrightarrow[\text{(ii) Water}]{\text{(i) } CO_2} [B] \xrightarrow{CH_3OH / H^+} [C]$$

NCERT Exemplar

41. Account for the following :

(i) $Cl—CH_2COOH$ is a stronger acid than CH_3COOH.

(ii) Carboxylic acids do not give reactions of carbonyl group.

42. Identify the compounds A, B and C :

(i) $C_6H_5COOH \xrightarrow{PCl_5} A \xrightarrow{H_2-Pd/BaSO_4} B \xrightarrow[\text{distilled}]{KCN(alc.)} C$

(ii) $H—C \equiv C—H \xrightarrow[Dil.H_2SO_4 + HgSO_4]{H_2O} A \xrightarrow[[Ni]]{H_2} B \xrightarrow[Conc.\ H_2SO_4]{140°C} C$

43. Identify the compounds A, B and C.

(i) $C_2H_5OH \xrightarrow{PCl_5} A \xrightarrow{KCN} B \xrightarrow{H_3O^+} C_2H_5COOH \xrightarrow[\Delta]{NH_3} C$

(ii) $C_6H_5COOH \xrightarrow{SOCl_2} A \xrightarrow{NH_3} B \xrightarrow{Br_2/KOH} C$ **ISC 2016**

44. Identify A to F.

$$A \xrightarrow{LiAlH_4} C_2H_5OH \xrightarrow{PBr_3} B \xrightarrow{KCN} C \longrightarrow C_3H_7NH_2 \xrightarrow[H_2O]{HNO_2} E \xrightarrow[K_2Cr_2O_7/H^+]{[O]} F$$

ISC 2011

Long Answer Type Questions

(5 Marks)

45. Give simple chemical tests to distinguish between the following pairs of compounds.

(i) Benzaldehyde and benzoic acid.

(ii) Propanal and propanone **All India 2014**

46. An organic compound A has the molecular formula C_7H_6O. When A is treated with NaOH followed by acid hydrolysis, it gives two products B and C. When B is oxidised, it gives A, when A and C are each treated separately with PCl_5, they give two different products D and E.

(i) Identify A, B, C, D and E.

(ii) Give the chemical reaction when A is treated with NaOH and name the reaction. **ISC 2016**

47. An organic compound $[A]$ having molecular formula $C_4H_{10}O$ forms a compound $[B]$ with molecular formula C_4H_8O on oxidation. Compound $[B]$ gives a positive iodoform test. The reaction of compound $[B]$ with CH_3MgBr followed by hydrolysis gives compound $[C]$ with molecular formula $C_5H_{12}O$.
Identify the compounds $[A]$, $[B]$ and $[C]$. Write the reaction for the conversion of compound $[A]$ and compound $[B]$. **ISC 2024**

48. An aliphatic unsaturated hydrocarbon (A) when treated with $HgSO_4 / H_2SO_4$ yields a compound (B) having molecular formula C_3H_6O. (B) on oxidation with concentrated HNO_3 gives two compounds (C) and (D). Compound (C) when treated with PCl_5 gives compound (E). (E) when reacts with ethanol gives a sweet smelling liquid (F). Compound (F) is also formed when (C) reacts with ethanol in the presence of concentrated H_2SO_4.

(i) Identify the compound A, B, C, D, E and F.

(ii) Give the chemical equation for the reaction of (C) with chlorine in the presence of red phosphorus and name the reaction. **ISC 2017**

49. How will you prepare the following compounds from benzene? You may use any inorganic reagent and any organic reagent, having not more than one carbon atom.

(i) Methyl benzoate (ii) *m*-nitrobenzoic acid

(iii) *p*-nitrobenzoic acid (iv) Phenylacetic acid

(v) *p*-nitrobenzaldehyde **NCERT**

50. (i) Account for the following:

(a) Electrophilic substitution in benzoic acid takes place at *meta* position.

(b) Carboxylic acids do not give characteristic reactions of carbonyl group.

(ii) Give simple chemical test to distinguish between the following pairs of compounds:

(a) Acetophenone and benzaldehyde

(b) Benzoic acid and ethylbenzoate

Or

(i) Write structures of *A*, *B*, *C* and D in the following reaction sequence:

$$CH_3COCl \xrightarrow{H_2/Pd\text{-}BaSO_4} A \xrightarrow{\text{Dil. NaOH}} B \xrightarrow{\Delta} C$$

$$A \xrightarrow{CH_3MgBr/H_3O^+} D$$

(ii) Arrange the following compounds in the increasing order of their boiling points:

CH_3CHO, CH_3CH_2OH, CH_3OCH_3, CH_3COOH

51. How will you carry out the following conversion? Acetic acid to propionic acid. **ISC 2002**

52. (i) How will you convert

(a) acetonitrile to acetic acid?

(b) propanone to 2-methylpropan-2-ol?

(ii) Give reasons:

(a) Electrophilic substitution in benzoic acid takes place at *meta* position.

(b) Carboxylic acids are higher boiling liquids than aldehydes, ketones and alcohols of comparable molecular masses.

Or (i) Write the products of the following reactions:

(a) 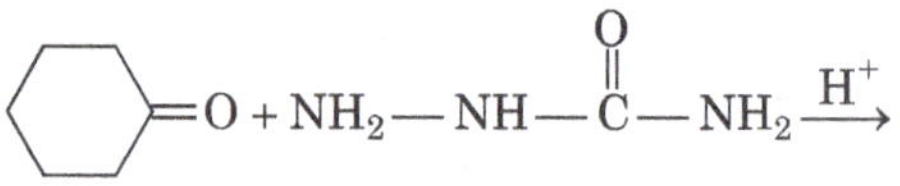

(b) $CH_3MgBr + CO_2 \xrightarrow[H_3O^+]{\text{Dry ether}}$

(c) $CH_3CH_2COOH + Br_2 \xrightarrow{\text{Red Phosphorus}}$

(ii) Write a simple chemical test to distinguish between the following pairs of compounds.

(a) Propanal and propanone

(b) Benzaldehyde and Benzoic acid **Delhi 2017C**

53. Give the simple chemical tests to distinguish between the following pairs of compounds.

(i) Acetophenone and benzophenone

(ii) Phenol and benzoic acid

(iii) Benzoic acid and ethyl benzoate

(iv) Pentan-2-one and pentan-3-one

(v) Ethanal and propanal **NCERT**

Hints & Solutions

1. (i) Benzoic acid, negative inductive
(ii) methanol, propanoic acid (iii) hot.

2. (i) → b, (ii) → c, (iii) → b, (iv) → a

3. (a) A → (ii) B → (v) C → (iv) D → (i) E → (iii)

4. $\underset{\text{Grignard's reagent}}{C_2H_5—MgCl} \xrightarrow[\text{(ii) } H_3O^+]{\text{(i) } CO_2} \underset{\text{Propanoic acid}}{C_2H_5—\overset{O}{\overset{||}{C}}—OH}$

5. Because, when it reacts with water, it produces strong base, i.e. NaOH which makes the solution basic.

6. $C_6H_5—CH_2—CH_3 \xrightarrow{KMnO_4\text{-}KOH} C_6H_5—CO\overset{-}{O}K^+$

7. The correct statement is :
Chloroacetic acid is more acidic than acetic acid because of the –*I*-effect of Cl group.

8. The correct increasing order of acidic character of carboxylic acids is :

$$CH_3—\overset{O}{\overset{||}{C}}—OH < \overset{Cl}{\overset{|}{C}H_2}—\overset{O}{\overset{||}{C}}—OH < \overset{F}{\overset{|}{C}H_2}—\overset{O}{\overset{||}{C}}—OH$$

F being more electronegative, produces greater–*I*- effect than Cl atom due to which F-atom withdraws electron from O—H bond and thereby making O—H bond weaker and hence, facilitates the release of H^+ ion from O—H bond. Hence, FCH_2COOH is stronger acid than $ClCH_2COOH$ and CH_3COOH. In CH_3COOH, due to +*I*-effect of methyl group, electron density in O—H bond increases. As a result, release of H^+ ions from acetic acid becomes more difficult.

9. Benzoic acid is obtained.

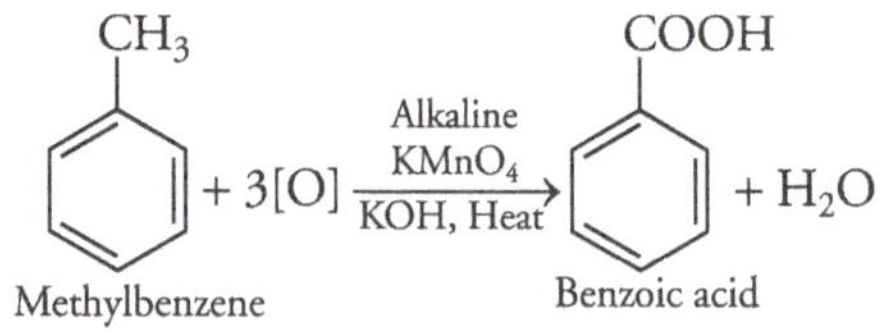

10. $CH_3—COOH \xrightarrow[-H_2O]{NH_3/\text{Heat}} CH_3—CONH_2$

11. $CH_3CO\overset{-}{O}\overset{+}{Na} \xrightarrow[\Delta]{NaOH/CaO} CH_3—H + Na_2CO_3$

12. $\underset{\text{Acetic acid}}{CH_3COOH} \xrightarrow{Br_2/P} \underset{\alpha\text{-bromoacetic acid}}{\underset{Br}{\underset{|}{C}H_2}—COOH}$

13. Benzoin condensation

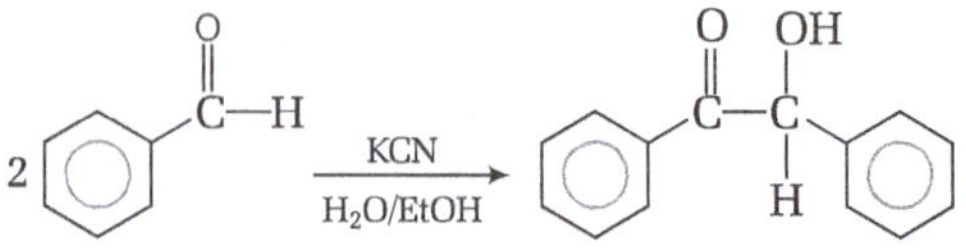

14. Kolbe's electrolytic reaction can be proceed as follows:

Let us take an example

$$\underset{\text{Sodium acetate}}{2CH_3\overset{-\ +}{COONa}} \longrightarrow \underset{\text{Acetate ion}}{2CH_3COO^-} + 2Na^+$$

At anode,

$$\underset{\text{Acetate ion}}{2CH_3COO^-} \longrightarrow \underset{\text{Ethane}}{CH_3{-}CH_3} + 2CO_2 + 2e^-$$

At cathode,

$$2H_2O \rightleftharpoons 2H^+ + 2\,OH^-$$

$$2H^+ + 2e^- \longrightarrow H_2$$

$$2Na^+ + 2\,OH^- \longrightarrow 2NaOH$$

15. The balanced chemical equation is

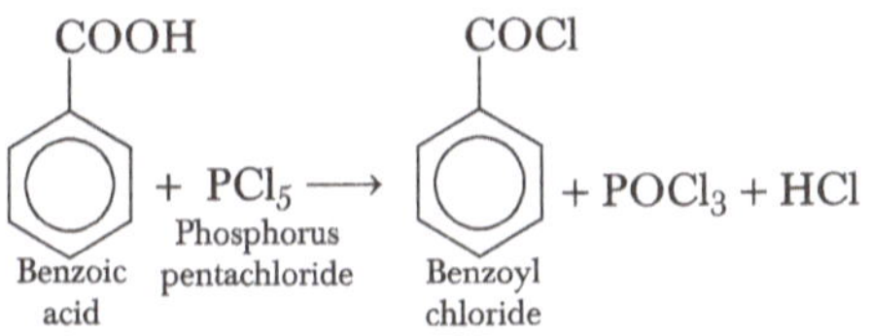

16. Hell-Volhard-Zelinsky (HVZ) **reaction** Reaction of acetic acid with chlorine in the presence of little phosphorus in which α-H to the carboxylic group get substituted by chlorine.

$$\underset{\text{Acetic acid}}{CH_3COOH} \xrightarrow[-HCl]{+Cl_2(P)} \underset{\text{Monochloro acetic acid}}{CH_2ClCOOH} \xrightarrow[-HCl]{+Cl_2(P)}$$

$$\underset{\text{Dichloroacetic acid}}{CHCl_2COOH} \xrightarrow[-HCl]{+Cl_2(P)} \underset{\text{Trichloroacetic acid}}{CCl_3COOH}$$

17. $$\underset{\text{Formic acid}}{HCOOH} + \underset{\text{Tollen's reagent}}{2[Ag(NH_3)_2]^+NO_3^-} + H_2O \longrightarrow 2NH_4NO_3 + (NH_4)_2CO_3 + \underset{\text{Silver mirror}}{2Ag\downarrow}$$

18. The balanced chemical equation is

$$\underset{\text{Sucrose}}{C_{12}H_{22}O_{11}} \xrightarrow[\text{Conc. } HNO_3,\ V_2O_5]{18\,[O]} 6\ \underset{\text{Oxalic acid}}{\begin{matrix} COOH \\ | \\ COOH \end{matrix}} + 5\,H_2O$$

19. Allyl alcohol is formed as:

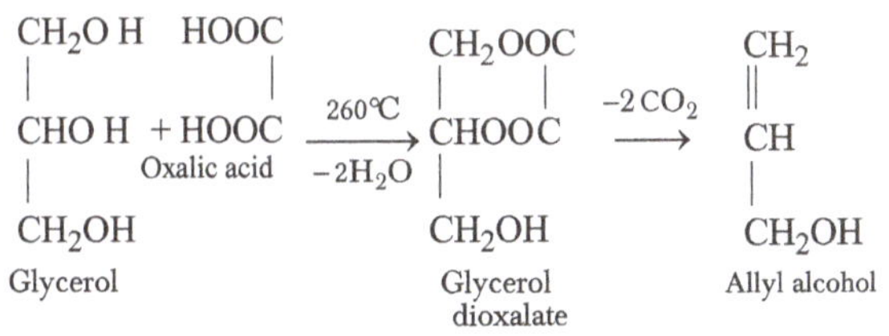

20. Benzoic acid and phenol Benzoic acid reacts with sodium bicarbonate to produce effervescence of carbon dioxide whereas phenol does not.

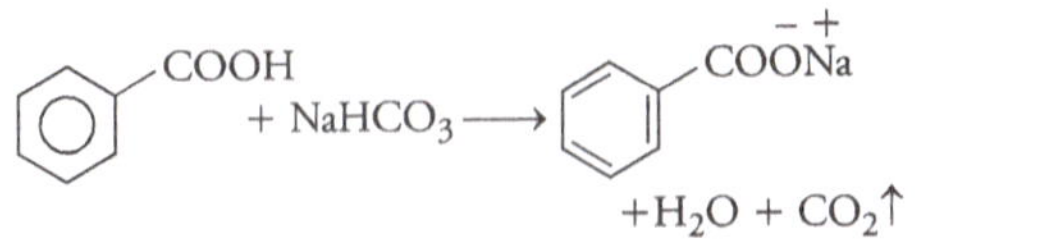

21. Tollen's test—Acetaldehyde reduces Tollen's reagent to give shining silver mirror but acetic acid does not.

$$\underset{\text{Acetaldehyde}}{CH_3CHO} + \underset{\text{Tollen's reagent}}{2[Ag(NH_3)_2]^+} + 3OH^- \longrightarrow \underset{\text{Acetate ion}}{CH_3COO^-} + \underset{\text{Silver mirror}}{2Ag\downarrow} + 2H_2O + 4NH_3$$

$$CH_3COOH \xrightarrow{\text{Tollen's reagent}} \text{No reaction}$$

22. Iodoform test When formaldehyde and acetaldehyde are treated with iodine in the presence of alkali, acetaldehyde gives yellow precipitate of iodoform, but formaldehyde does not give such precipitate.

$$CH_3CHO + 4NaOH + 3I_2 \longrightarrow CHI_3\downarrow + HCO\overset{-\ +}{ONa} + 3NaI + 3H_2O$$

$$HCHO + 4NaOH + 3I_2 \longrightarrow \text{No Iodoform test}$$

23. Acetic acid when heated with ethyl alcohol in the presence of conc. H_2SO_4, it gives a fruity smell of an ester, ethyl ethanoate.

$$\underset{\text{Acetic acid}}{CH_3COOH} + C_2H_5OH \xrightarrow[\text{Conc. } H_2SO_4]{\Delta \text{ with}} \underset{\text{Ethyl ethanoate}}{CH_3COOC_2H_5} + H_2O$$

while acetone does not give this test.

24. Acetic acid is treated with ethanol and a drop of conc. H_2SO_4.

$$\underset{\text{Acetic acid}}{CH_3COOH(l)} + \underset{\text{Ethanol}}{C_2H_5OH(l)} \xrightarrow{\Delta,\ \text{Conc. } H_2SO_4} \underset{\text{Ethyl acetate}}{CH_3COOC_2H_5(l)} + \underset{\text{Water}}{H_2O(l)}$$

When acetic acid reacts with ethanol in the presence of conc. H_2SO_4 the product will be ester (ethyl acetate).

25. (i) **Ethanal to 2-hydroxy propanoic acid**

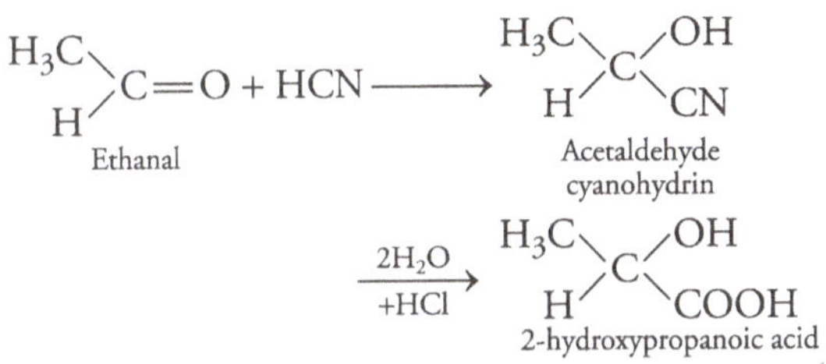

(1)

(ii) **Toluene to benzoic acid**

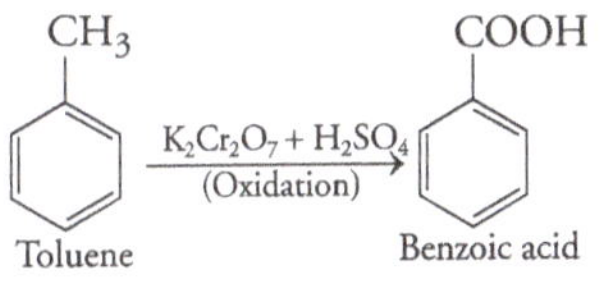

(1)

26. The products are:

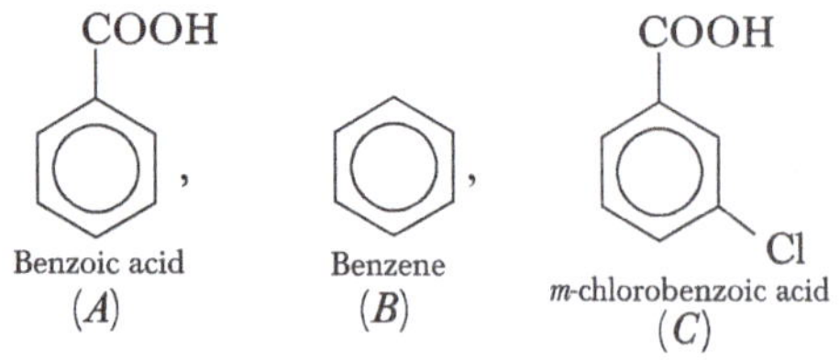

27. Formic acid is first treated with NaOH solution to get sodium formate which is then heated to 390°C to form sodium oxalate. It is then form calcium oxalate which on hydrolysis with dil. H_2SO_4 gives oxalic acid.

$$\underset{\text{Formic acid}}{HCOOH} + NaOH \longrightarrow HCO\overset{-}{O}\overset{+}{Na} + H_2O$$

$$\underset{\text{Sodium formate}}{2HCO\overset{-}{O}\overset{+}{Na}} \xrightarrow{390°C} (COONa)_2 + H_2\uparrow$$

$$\underset{\text{Sodium oxalate}}{(COONa)_2} + CaCl_2 \longrightarrow \underset{\text{Calcium oxalate}}{(COO)_2Ca} + 2NaCl$$

$$(COO)_2Ca + \underset{\text{(Dil.)}}{H_2SO_4} \longrightarrow \underset{\text{Oxalic acid}}{(COOH)_2} + CaSO_4\downarrow$$

28. (i)

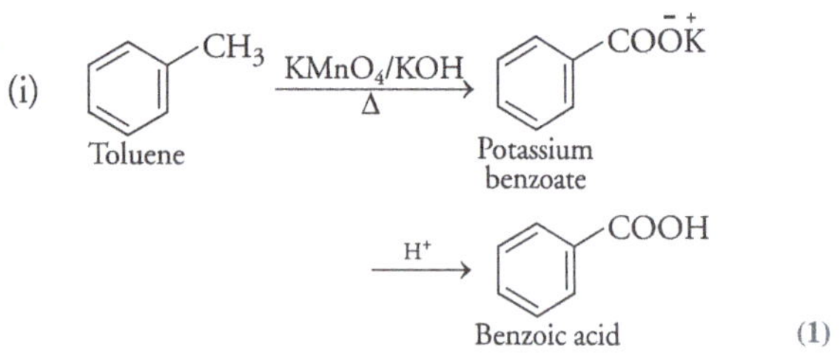

(1)

(ii)

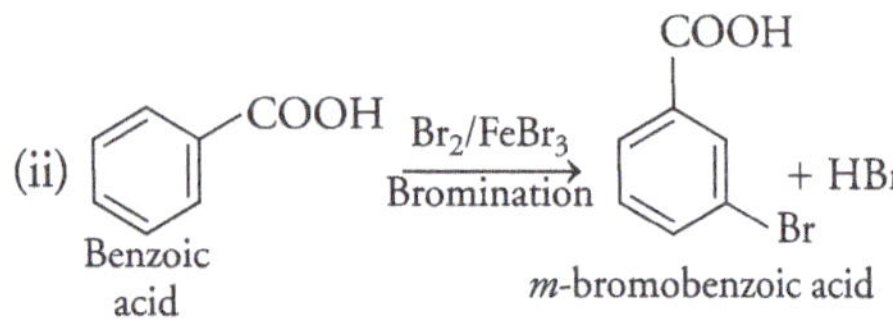

(1)

29. (i)

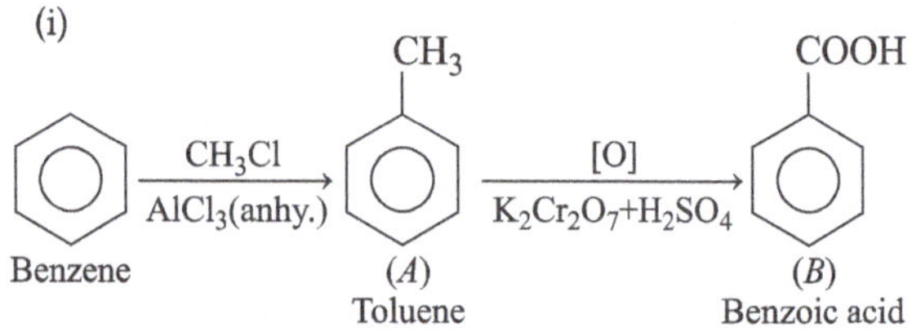

(ii) $$\underset{\text{Propan-2-ol}}{CH_3-\overset{\overset{OH}{|}}{CH}-CH_3} \xrightarrow[K_2Cr_2O_7 + H_2SO_4]{[O]} \underset{\substack{\text{Acetone}\\(A)}}{CH_3-\overset{\overset{O}{||}}{C}-CH_3}$$

$$\xrightarrow{NH_2OH} \underset{\substack{\text{Acetoxime}\\(B)}}{(H_3C)_2C{=}N-OH} + H_2O$$

30. (i) As $+I$- effect of isopropyl group is more than that of n-propyl group, therefore, $(CH_3)_2CHCOOH$ is a weaker acid than $CH_3CH_2CH_2COOH$.

Since, $-I$- effect decreases with distance, therefore, $CH_3CH_2CH(Br)COOH$ is a stronger acid than $CH_3CH_2CH(Br)CH_2COOH$.

Hence, increasing order of acidic strength is:
$(CH_3)_2CHCOOH < CH_3CH_2CH_2COOH$
$< CH_3CH(Br)CH_2COOH$
$< CH_3CH_2CH(Br)COOH$ (1)

(ii) Electron donating group ($-OCH_3$) decreases the acidic strength therefore, 4-methoxy benzoic acid is a weaker acid than benzoic acid whereas electron withdrawing group ($-NO_2$) increases the same therefore, both 4-nitrobenzoic acid and 3,4-dinitrobenzoic acid are stronger acids than benzoic acid.

Further, due to the presence of an additional $-NO_2$ group at m-position with respect to COOH group, 3,4-dinitrobenzoic acid is a little stronger acid than 4-nitrobenzoic acid.

Hence, increasing order of acidic strength is

4-methoxy benzoic acid < benzoic acid < 4-nitrobenzoic acid < 3,4-dinitrobenzoic acid. (1)

31. When acetic acid is treated with caustic soda, it produces sodium salt of acetic acid. When it is refluxed in the presence of slaked lime, hydrocarbon is produced.

$$\underset{\text{Acetic acid}}{CH_3COOH} \xrightarrow{NaOH} CH_3-\overset{\overset{O}{||}}{C}-\overset{-}{O}\overset{+}{Na}$$

$$+ H_2O \xrightarrow{CaO} \underset{\text{Methane}}{CH_4} + \underset{\text{Sodium carbonate}}{Na_2CO_3}$$

32. To convert propanoic acid to ethylamine, the following steps are applied:

(i) Propanoic acid is converted into amide through a suitable catalyst such as NH_4OH and heat.

(ii) Amide is converted into primary amine through Br_2 / KOH (Hoffmann bromamide reaction).

$$\underset{\text{Propanoic acid}}{CH_3CH_2COOH} \xrightarrow{NH_4OH} CH_3CH_2COONH_4$$

$$\xrightarrow{\Delta} CH_3CH_2CONH_2 \xrightarrow[\substack{\text{Hofmann}\\\text{bromamide reaction}}]{Br_2/KOH} \underset{\text{Ethylamine}}{CH_3CH_2NH_2}$$

33. Oxalic acid decolourises acidified potassium permanganate solution while acetic acid does not.

34. $$\underset{\substack{(B)\\\text{Alcohol}}}{RCH_2OH} \xrightarrow[{[O]}]{\text{Alkaline } KMnO_4} \underset{\substack{(A)\\\text{Carboxylic acid}}}{RCOOH}$$

$$\underset{\substack{\text{Carboxylic acid}\\(A)}}{RCOOH} \xrightarrow{LiAlH_4} \underset{\substack{\text{Alcohol}\\(B)}}{RCH_2OH}$$

$$\underset{\text{Acid}}{RCOOH} + \underset{\text{Alcohol}}{RCH_2OH} \underset{\Delta}{\overset{H_2SO_4}{\rightleftharpoons}} \underset{\substack{\text{Ester}\\(C)\\\text{(Fruity smell)}}}{RCOOCH_2R} + H_2O$$ (2)

35.

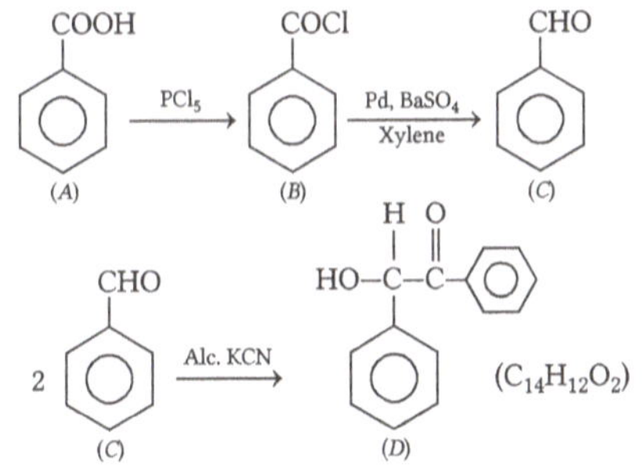

36. (i) **Hell-Volhard-Zelinsky reaction**

Carboxylic acids having α-hydrogen are halogenated at the α-position. On treatment with chlorine or bromine in the presence of small amount of red phosphorus, it gives α-halocarboxylic acids. The reaction is known as Hell-Volhard-Zelinsky reaction.

$$R\text{—}CH_2\text{—}COOH \xrightarrow[\text{(ii) } H_2O]{\text{(i) } X_2/\text{Red phosphorus}} \underset{\text{α-halocarboxylic acid}}{R\text{—}\underset{X}{\underset{|}{CH}}\text{—}COOH}$$

(where, X = Cl, Br) (1)

(ii) **Decarboxylation reaction**

Decarboxylation is a chemical reaction that takes place in carboxylic acid by the release of carbon dioxide (CO_2). It is an example of the cleavage of a carbon-carbon single bond.

(a) **Using sodalime**

$$R\text{—}CO\overset{-}{O}\overset{+}{Na} \xrightarrow[\text{Heat}]{\text{NaOH and CaO}} \underset{\text{Alkane}}{R\text{—}H} + Na_2CO_3$$

(In sodalime, the ratio of NaOH and CaO is 3 : 1.)

(b) **Electrolytic decarboxylation**

(Kolbe electrolysis)

$$2RCOO^-Na^+ + 2H_2O \xrightarrow{\text{Electrolysis}} R\text{—}R + 2CO_2 + H_2 + 2NaOH$$

At anode

$$2RCOO^- \longrightarrow 2RCOO^\bullet \longrightarrow 2R^\bullet + 2CO_2\uparrow$$

$$R^\bullet + R^\bullet \xrightarrow{-2e^-} \underset{\text{Alkane}}{R\text{—}R}\uparrow$$

At cathode

$$H_2O + e^- \longrightarrow OH^- + H^\bullet$$

$$2H^\bullet \longrightarrow H_2\uparrow$$

Decarboxylation of silver salts of carboxylic acids in presence of bromine **(Hunsdiecker reaction)**.

$$CH_3COOH \xrightarrow[\text{(ii) } AgNO_3]{\text{(i) } NH_4OH} CH_3CO\overset{-}{O}Ag^+$$

$$\xrightarrow{Br_2/CCl_4} CH_3Br + AgBr + CO_2 \quad (1)$$

37. Formic acid gives silver mirror test with Tollen's reagent while acetic acid does not give this test.

$$\underset{\text{Formic acid}}{HCOOH} + \underset{\text{Tollen's reagent}}{2\,[Ag(NH_3)_2]^+ NO_3^-} + H_2O \longrightarrow 2NH_4NO_3 + (NH_4)_2CO_3 + \underset{\text{Silver mirror}}{2Ag\downarrow}$$

$$\underset{\text{Acetic acid}}{CH_3COOH} + \underset{\text{Tollen's reagent}}{2\,[Ag(NH_3)_2]^+ NO_3^-} + H_2O \longrightarrow \text{No reaction}$$

38. (i) Acetone and benzaldehyde by Tollen's test

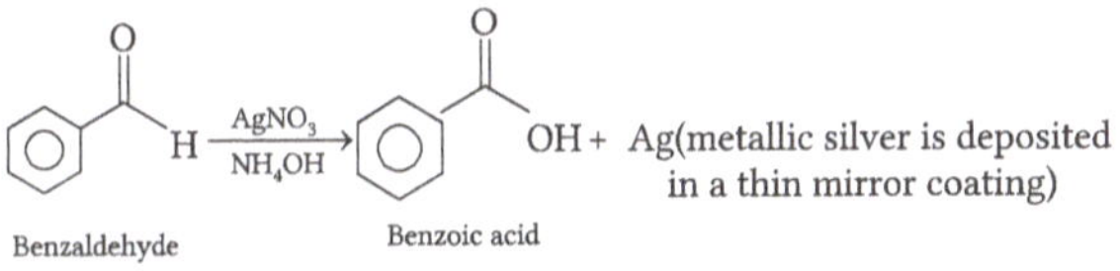

A silver mirror is formed when benzaldehyde reacts with Tollen's reagent.

No such compound is formed on reaction of the tollen's reagent with acetone.

(ii) Phenol and benzoic acid by sodium bicarbonate test,

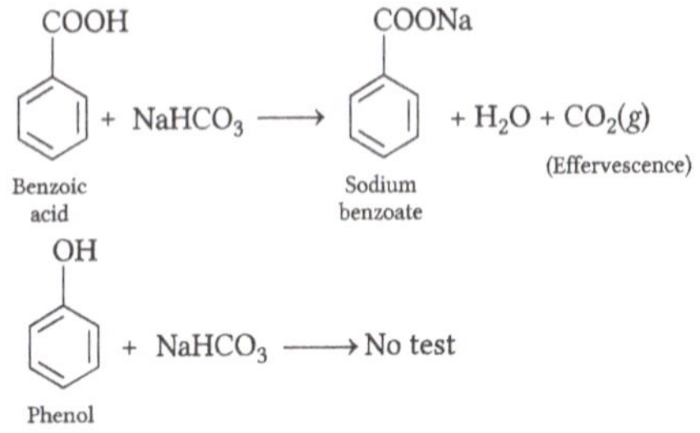

Benzoic acid reacts with sodium bicarbonate to produce effervescence of carbon dioxide, whereas phenol does not.

39. $$HC\equiv CH \xrightarrow[Hg^{2+}/H_2SO_4]{H_2O} \left[\begin{array}{c} CH_2 \\ \| \\ CHOH \end{array}\right] \xrightarrow{\text{Tautomerises}} \underset{\text{(Acetaldehyde) (A)}}{\begin{array}{l} CH_3 \\ H \end{array}\!\!>C=O}$$

$$\underset{(A)}{CH_3\text{—}CHO} \xrightarrow[K_2Cr_2O_7 + H_2SO_4]{[O]} \underset{(B)}{\underset{\text{(Acetic acid)}}{CH_3COOH}}$$

$$\underset{(B)}{CH_3COOH} \xrightarrow{Ca(OH)_2} \underset{(C)}{(CH_3COO)_2Ca}$$

$$\underset{(C)}{(CH_3COO)_2Ca} \xrightarrow[\text{Dry distillation}]{\Delta} \underset{(D)}{\underset{\text{(Acetone)}}{\begin{array}{l} CH_3 \\ CH_3 \end{array}\!\!>C=O}} + CaCO_3$$

∴ (A) = CH_3—CHO (acetaldehyde)

(B) = CH_3COOH (acetic acid)

(C) = Calcium acetate, i.e. $(CH_3COO)_2Ca$

(D) = Acetone, i.e. $\begin{array}{l} CH_3 \\ CH_3 \end{array}\!\!>C=O$

40. Complete chemical conversion can be done as:

$$\underset{\text{Bromomethane}}{CH_3-Br} \xrightarrow{Mg/Ether} \underset{\substack{[A] \\ \text{Methyl magnesium} \\ \text{bromide}}}{CH_3MgBr} \xrightarrow[\text{(ii) Water}]{\text{(i) } CO_2}$$

$$\underset{\substack{(B) \\ \text{Ethanoic acid}}}{CH_3COOH} \xrightarrow{CH_3OH/H^+} \underset{\substack{(C) \\ \text{Methyl ethanoate}}}{CH_3COOCH_3}$$

Hence, $A = CH_3MgBr$, $B = CH_3COOH$,

$$C = CH_3-\overset{\overset{\displaystyle O}{||}}{C}-O-CH_3$$ (3)

41. (i) $Cl-CH_2COOH$ is a stronger acid than CH_3COOH. It is because $-Cl$ group exhibits $-I$-effect which makes the carboxylate ion more stable. Higher the stability of carboxylate ion, easier is the removal of proton from the carboxylic acid and stronger is the acid. In CH_3COOH, $-CH_3$ group has $+I$-effect which destabilised it. Hence, CH_3COOH is a weaker acid. (1½)

(ii) Carboxylic acids contain carbonyl group but do not show the reactions of carbonyl group such as nucleophilic addition reaction like aldehydes and ketones.

Because of the presence of lone pair of electrons on the O-atom of OH group, the electrophilic character of carbonyl carbon by resonance decreases, hence the partial positive charge on carbonyl carbon atom is reduced and therefore, they do not show nucleophilic addition reactions. (1½)

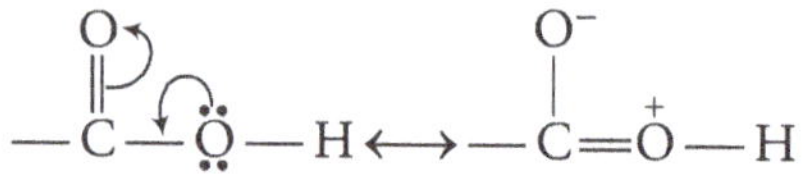

42. (i) $C_6H_5COOH \xrightarrow{PCl_5} \underset{(A)}{C_6H_5COCl} \xrightarrow[Pd/BaSO_4]{H_2} \underset{(B)}{C_6H_5CHO}$

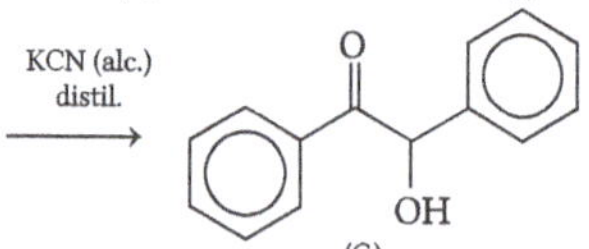

(C)

(ii) $H-C\equiv C-H \xrightarrow[\text{Dil.}H_2SO_4+HgSO_4]{H_2O} \underset{(A)}{CH_3-\overset{\overset{\displaystyle O}{||}}{C}-H}$

$\xrightarrow[Ni]{H_2} \underset{(B)}{CH_3\,CH_2\,OH} \xrightarrow[\text{Conc.}H_2SO_4]{140°C} \underset{(C)}{CH_2=CH_2}$

43. (i) $C_2H_5OH \xrightarrow{PCl_5} \underset{(A)}{C_2H_5Cl} + POCl_3 + HCl$;

$\underset{(A)}{C_2H_5Cl} \xrightarrow{KCN} \underset{(B)}{C_2H_5CN} \xrightarrow{H_3O^+} C_2H_5COOH$

$C_2H_5COOH \xrightarrow[\Delta]{NH_3} \underset{(C)}{C_2H_5COONH_4}$

(ii) $\underset{\substack{\text{Benzoic acid} \\ (A)}}{C_6H_5COOH} \xrightarrow{SOCl_2} \underset{\substack{\text{Benzoyl chloride} \\ (A)}}{C_6H_5COCl} + HCl + SO_2$;

$\underset{\substack{\text{Benzamide} \\ (B)}}{C_6H_5CONH_2} \xrightarrow{KOH/Br_2} \underset{\substack{\text{Aniline} \\ (C)}}{C_6H_5NH_2}$

44. Substances from *A* to *F* are:

- *A* is acetic acid (CH_3COOH)
- *B* is ethyl bromide (C_2H_5Br).
- *C* is ethyl cyanide (C_2H_5CN).
- *D* is H_2 / Pt or $LiAlH_4$.
- *E* is propyl alcohol (C_3H_7OH).
- *F* is propionic acid (C_2H_5COOH).

45. (a) **Benzaldehyde and benzoic acid**

$NaHCO_3$ test Benzoic acid being an acid reacts with $NaHCO_3$ solution, to produce brisk effervescence due to evolution of CO_2 while benzaldehyde does not give this test.

$$C_6H_5COOH + NaHCO_3 \longrightarrow C_6H_5CO\overset{-}{O}\overset{+}{Na} + CO_2\uparrow + H_2O;$$

$$C_6H_5CHO \xrightarrow{NaHCO_3 \text{ solution}} \text{No effervescence}$$

(b) **Propanal and propanone** Propanone responds to iodoform test whereas propanal (CH_3CH_2CHO), does not due to the absence of CH_3CO- group.

$$\underset{\text{Propanone}}{CH_3COCH_3} + \underset{\substack{\text{Sodium} \\ \text{hypoiodite}}}{3NaOI} \xrightarrow[\text{Heat}]{NaOH,\ I_2}$$

$$\underset{\substack{\text{(Yellow ppt.)} \\ \text{Iodoform}}}{CHI_3}\downarrow + \underset{\substack{\text{Sodium} \\ \text{acetate}}}{CH_3CO\overset{-}{O}\overset{+}{Na}} + 2NaOH$$ (3)

46. (*i*) For predicting structural formula of C_7H_6O, (A) we use DBI (Double Bond Index)

DBI

$$= \frac{\text{Number of hydrogen atoms in alkane} - \text{Given H - atoms}}{2}$$

$$= \frac{(7 \times 2) + 2 - 6}{2}$$

$$= \frac{10}{2} = 5$$

DBI = 5, means there should be either one ring and four double bonds. Hence, the compound would be

The organic compound *A* is benzaldehyde (C_6H_5CHO).

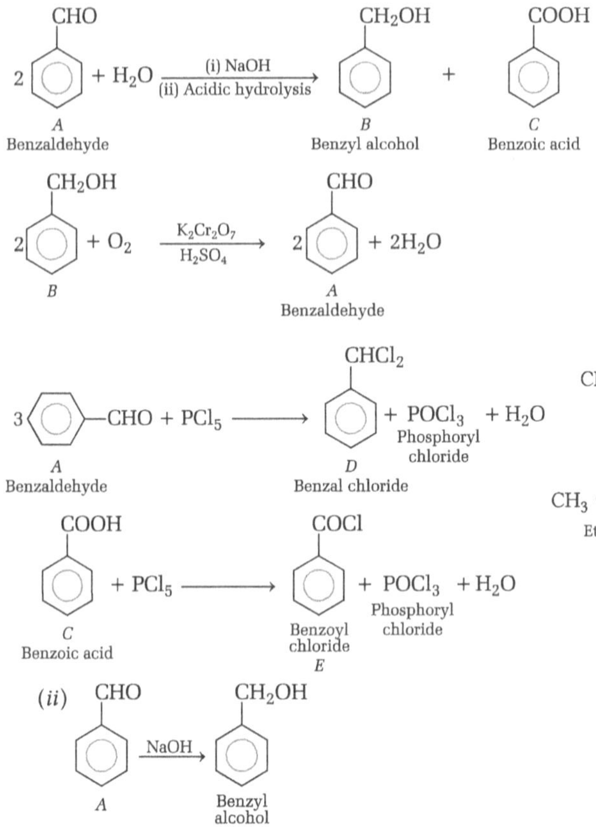

Thus, this is Cannizzaro reaction.

47. According to the given question compound *B*, i.e. C_4H_8O gives positive iodoform test. Thus, it is a ketone containing $CH_3-\overset{O}{\overset{\|}{C}}-$ group. As only one aldehyde, i.e. acetaldehyde gives positive iodoform test, hence, the formula of *B* may be $CH_3-\underset{O}{\underset{\|}{C}}-CH_2CH_3$

As *B* is formed by the oxidation of *A*, thus *A* must be an alcohol. Thus, the formula of alcohol forming *B* is

$$CH_3-\underset{H}{\underset{|}{\overset{OH}{\overset{|}{C}}}}-CH_2CH_3$$, i.e. butanol.

The reaction involve is

$$\underset{(A)}{CH_3-\overset{OH}{\overset{|}{CH}}-CH_2CH_3} \xrightarrow[\text{agent}]{\text{Mild oxidising}} \underset{(B)}{CH_3-\overset{O}{\overset{\|}{C}}-CH_2CH_3}$$

The reaction of (*B*) with CH_3MgBr followed by hydrolysis gives (*C*). The reaction is given as

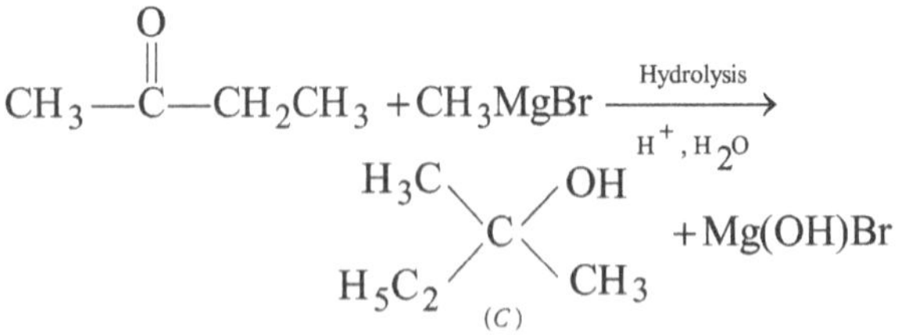

Thus, compounds *A*, *B* and *C* are butanol, butan-2-one and 2-methylbutan-2-ol respectively.

48. (i) The reaction takes place as follows :

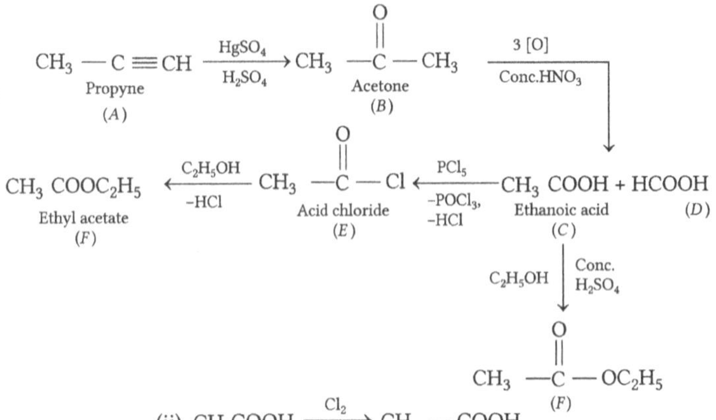

(ii) $$CH_3COOH \xrightarrow[\text{Red P}]{Cl_2} \underset{Cl}{\underset{|}{CH_2}}-COOH$$

2-chloro ethanoic

49. (i) **Benzene to methyl benzoate**

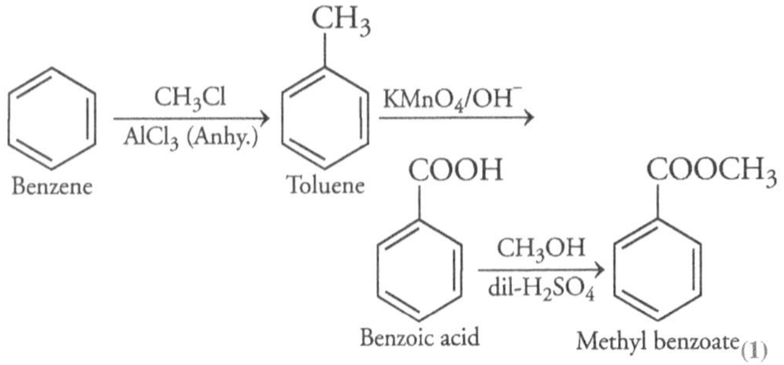

(1)

(ii) **Benzene to *m*-nitrobenzoic acid**

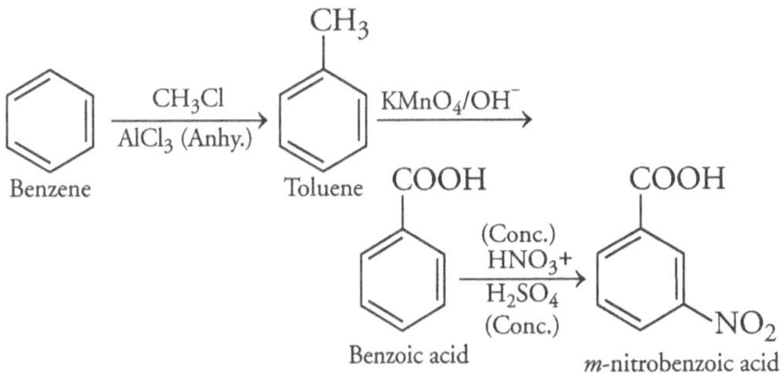

(1)

(iii) **Benzene to p-nitrobenzoic acid**

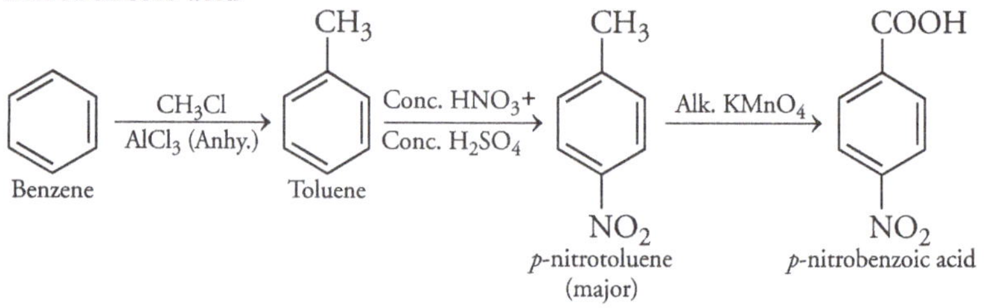

(1)

(iv) **Benzene to phenylacetic acid**

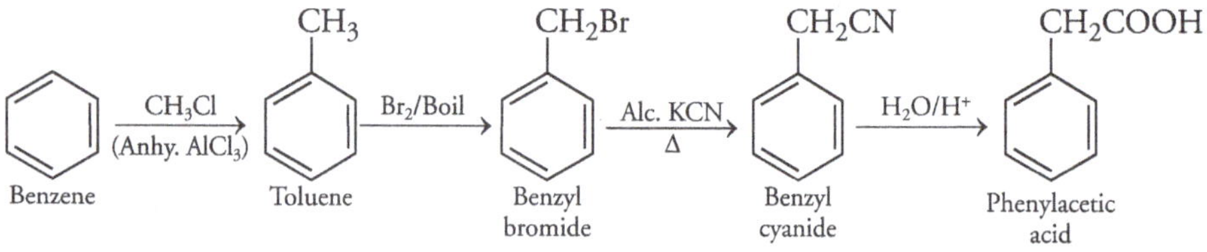

(1)

(v) **Benzene to p-nitrobenzaldehyde**

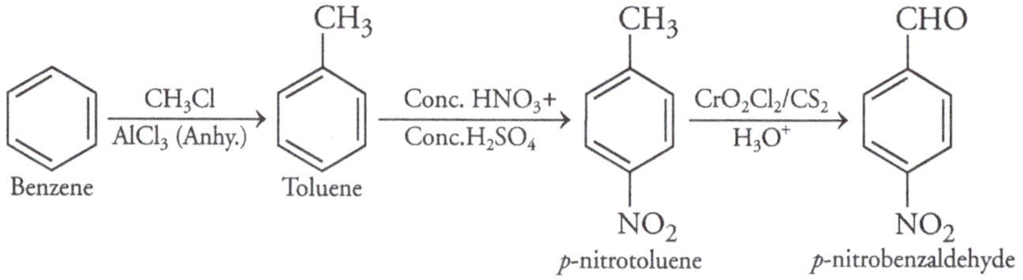

(1)

50. (i) (a) Electrophilic substitution in benzoic acid takes places at *meta* position because carboxylic group is a deactivating group. The presence of electron withdrawing carboxylic group results in a decreased electron density at *o* – and *p* – position.

(b) Due to resonance, electrophilicity of carbonyl carbon is reduced. (2½)

(ii) (a) Add NaOH and I_2 to both the compounds and heat them. Acetophenone forms yellow precipitate of iodoform while benzaldehyde does not.

(b) Add $NaHCO_3$ solution to both the compounds. Benzoic acid will give effervescence and liberate CO_2 while ethylbenzoate does not. (2½)

Or

(i)

$$CH_3COCl \xrightarrow{H_2/Pd\text{-}BaSO_4} \underset{(A)}{CH_3CHO} \xrightarrow{\text{Dil. NaOH}} \underset{(B)}{CH_3-\underset{\substack{|\\OH}}{CH}-CH_2CHO}$$

$$\underset{(A)}{CH_3CHO} \xrightarrow{CH_3MgBr/H_3O^+} \underset{(D)}{CH_3-\underset{\substack{|\\CH_3}}{CH}-OH}$$

$$(B) \xrightarrow{\Delta} \underset{(C)}{CH_3-CH=CHCHO}$$

(4)

(ii) The correct increasing order of the boiling points is : $CH_3-O-CH_3 < CH_3CHO < CH_3CH_2OH < CH_3COOH$ (1)

51.

$$\underset{\text{Acetic acid}}{2CH_3COOH} \xrightarrow{Ca(OH)_2} \underset{\text{Calcium acetate}}{\begin{matrix}CH_3COO\\CH_3COO\end{matrix}\!\!>\!Ca} \xrightarrow[\text{with }(HCOO)_2Ca]{\text{Distillation}} \underset{\text{Acetaldehyde}}{CH_3CHO} \xrightarrow[\text{Reduction}]{LiAlH_4} \underset{\text{Ethyl alcohol}}{CH_3CH_2OH} \xrightarrow{P+I_2}$$

$$\underset{\text{Ethyl iodide}}{CH_3CH_2I} \xrightarrow{KCN} \underset{\text{Ethyl nitrile}}{CH_3CH_2CN} \xrightarrow[\text{Hydrolysis}]{H^+/H_2O} \underset{\text{Propionic acid}}{CH_3CH_2COOH}$$

(2)

Chapter Practice

Very Short Answer Type Questions

1 Mark

1 Fill in the Blanks

(i) Complete the following reaction :

$$\ldots\ldots + 3I_2 + 4KOH \longrightarrow CHI_3 + CH_3CO\overset{-}{O}\overset{+}{K} + 3KI + 3H_2O$$

(ii) Acetic acid on reduction with $LiAlH_4$ yields ......

(iii) Acetic acid is a ...... acid than formic acid due to ...... effect of methyl group.

(iv) Acetic acid in treatment with sodium carbonate liberates ......

(v) Urotropine is formed by the action of ...... on ......

(vi) Tollen's reagent gives ...... with acetaldehyde.

2 Objective Type Questions

(i) Iodoform test is given by

(a) formaldehyde (b) benzaldehyde
(c) methyl ketones (d) All of these

(ii) When acetaldehyde is treated with Grignard reagent, followed by hydrolysis the product formed is

(a) primary alcohol (b) secondary alcohol
(c) carboxylic acid (d) tertiary alcohol

(iii) The compound which gives a positive haloform test and a positive Fehling solution test is

(a) acetone (b) acetaldehyde
(c) formaldehyde (d) diethyl ether

(iv) Benzaldehyde when heated with an alcoholic solution of potassium cyanide, forms

(a) benzyl alcohol (b) benzoin
(c) hydrobenzamide (d) benzoic acid

(v) Addition of water to alkynes occurs in acidic medium and in the presence of Hg^{2+} ions as a catalyst. Which of the following products will be formed on addition of water to but-1-yne under these conditions?

(a) $CH_3-CH_2-CH_2-\overset{O}{\overset{\|}{C}}-H$

(b) $CH_3-CH_2-\overset{O}{\overset{\|}{C}}-CH_3$

(c) $CH_3-CH_2-\overset{O}{\overset{\|}{C}}-OH + CO_2$

(d) $CH_3-\overset{O}{\overset{\|}{C}}-OH + H-\overset{O}{\overset{\|}{C}}-H$

(vi) Which of the following compounds is most reactive towards nucleophilic addition reactions?

(a) $CH_3-\overset{O}{\overset{\|}{C}}-H$ (b) $CH_3-\overset{O}{\overset{\|}{C}}-CH_3$

(c) 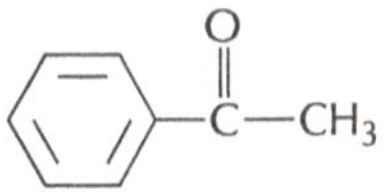 (d) 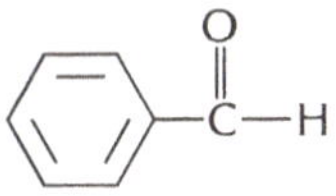

3 Matching Type Questions

(i) Match the reactions given in Column I with the suitable reagents given in Column II and choose the correct option using the codes given below:

Column I (Reactions)		Column II (Reagents)	
A.	Benzophenone → Diphenylmethane	(i)	$LiAlH_4$
B.	Benzaldehyde → 1-phenylethanol	(ii)	DIBAL-H
C.	Cyclohexanone → Cyclohexanol	(iii)	Zn(Hg)/Conc.HCl
D.	Phenyl benzoate → Benzaldehyde	(iv)	C_2H_5MgBr

Codes

	A	B	C	D
(a)	(i)	(iii)	(iv)	(ii)
(b)	(iii)	(iv)	(i)	(ii)
(c)	(i)	(iii)	(ii)	(iv)
(d)	(i)	(ii)	(iii)	(iv)

(ii) Match the example given in Column I with the name of the reaction in Column II and choose the correct option using the codes given below:

	Column I (Example)	Column II (Reaction)
A.	$CH_3-\overset{O}{\overset{\|\|}{C}}-Cl + H_2 \xrightarrow{Pd-C/BaSO_4} CH_3-\overset{O}{\overset{\|\|}{C}}-H$	(i) Friedel-Crafts acylation
B.	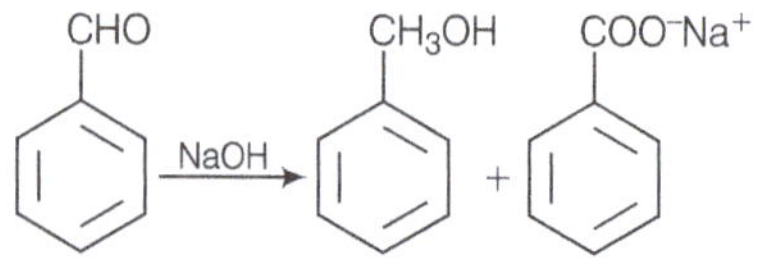	(ii) HVZ-reaction
C.	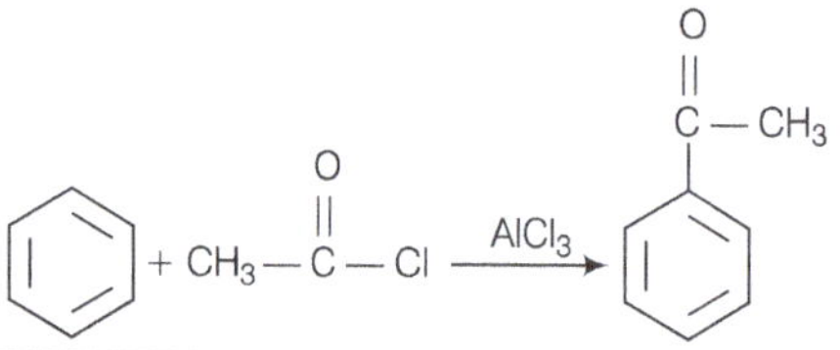	(iii) Aldol condensation
D.	$R-CH_2-COOH \xrightarrow{Br_2/Red\,P} R-\underset{Br}{\underset{\|}{CH}}-COOH$	(iv) Cannizzaro's reaction
E.	$CH_3-CN \xrightarrow[(ii)\,H_2O/H^+]{(i)\,SnCl_2/HCl} CH_3CHO$	(v) Rosenmund's reduction
F.	$2CH_3CHO \xrightarrow{NaOH} CH_3-CH=CHCHO$	(vi) Stephen's reaction

Codes

	A	B	C	D	E	F
(a)	(v)	(iv)	(i)	(ii)	(vi)	(iii)
(b)	(iii)	(i)	(ii)	(iv)	(vi)	(v)
(c)	(i)	(ii)	(iii)	(iv)	(v)	(vi)
(d)	(iv)	(ii)	(iii)	(i)	(v)	(vi)

4 Why there is a large difference in the boiling points of butanal and butan-1-ol?

5 Dipole moment of CH_3CH_2CHO (propanal) (2.5 D) is greater than that of but-1-ene (0.30 D). Why?

6 Oxidation of ketones involve carbon-carbon bond cleavage. Name the products formed on the oxidation of 2,5-dimethyl hexan-3-one.

7 Name any two reagents which are used to distinguish between aldehydes and ketones.

8 How can the following conversions be carried out?

Acetaldehyde to formaldehyde

9 How can the following conversion be brought about?

2-propanol to acetoxime

10 Carry out the following conversion:

Methyl chloride to acetic acid.

11 Carry out the following conversion:

Benzene to benzoic acid.

12 pK_a of chloroacetic acid is lower than pK_a of acetic acid. Why?

13 Why is C—O bond shorter in *R*COOH than in *R*CHO?

14 Complete the following reaction:

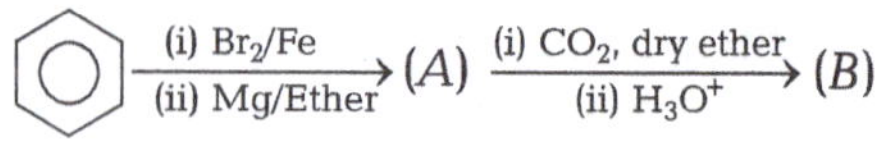

15 Consider the following reaction:

$$2R-\overset{O}{\overset{\|\|}{C}}-OH \xrightarrow[P_2O_5,\,\Delta]{H^+,\,\Delta} \text{Product } (A)$$

Identify the product *A*.

16 Give one example of the following name reaction.

Benzoin condensation.

17 Correct the following statements by changing the underlined part of the sentence (Do not change the whole sentence).

(i) Acetone gives a white precipitate on treatment with sodium chloride.

(ii) Acetaldehyde undergoes Cannizzaro's reaction on treatment with dilute alkali.

18 Draw the structures of vanillin, cinnamaldehyde and salicylaldehyde.

19 What is Clemmensen reduction?

Or Illustrate the following name reaction giving suitable example: Clemmensen reduction

20 Complete the reaction,

Assertion-Reason

Directions (Q. Nos. 23-34) In the following questions. an Assertion (A) is followed by a corresponding Reason (R). Use the following keys to choose the appropriate answer.

(a) Both (A) and (R) are correct and (R) is the correct explanation of (A).

(b) Both (A) and (R) are correct but (R) is not the correct explanation of (A).

(c) (A) is correct but (R) is incorrect.

(d) (A) is incorrect but (R) is correct.

21. **Assertion** (A) α-hydrogen atoms of carbonyl compounds are acidic.

Reason (R) The strong electron releasing effect of the carbonyl group make the stabilisation of the conjugate base by the resonance.

22. **Assertion** (A) The solubility of aldehydes and ketones in water decreases with increase in the size of alkyl group.

Reason (R) Alkyl groups are electron-repelling groups.

23. **Assertion** (A) Aromatic aldehydes and formaldehyde undergo Cannizzaro reaction.

Reason (R) Aromatic aldehydes are almost as reactive as formaldehyde.

24. **Assertion** (A) IUPAC name of $HOOC \leftarrow CH_2 \rightarrow_2 COOH$ is butane-dioic acid.

Reason (R) In compounds containing more than one carboxyl group, '-e' of the alkane is retained, and prefix 'di' is added to the term-'oic'.

25. **Assertion** (A) A carboxylate ion ($RCOO^-$) is stabilised by resonance to a greater extent as compared to the acid ($RCOOH$).

Reason (R) The contributing structures of $RCOO^-$ are equivalent, while those of $RCOOH$ are not.

Case-Study

26. An unknown aldehyde '*A*' on reacting with alkali gives a β-hydroxy aldehyde, which loses water to form an unsaturated aldehyde, 2-butenal. Another aldehyde '*B*' undergoes disproportionation reaction in the presence of conc. alkali to form products *C* and *D*. *C* is an aryl alcohol with the formula, C_7H_8O.

(i) Identify *A* and *B*?

(ii) Write the sequence of reactions involved and also the name of the reaction.

(iii) Name the product, when '*B*' reacts with zinc amalgam and hydrochloric acid.

27. An organic monobasic acid $(A)(C = 60.87\%, H = 4.35\%)$ is found to produce violet colour with neutral $FeCl_3$ solution. When the organic acid is heated with a mixture of NaOH and CaO it produces another product (*B*) which again also gives violet colour with $FeCl_3$. *B* when heated with zinc dust produces product (*C*) which on treatment with CO, HCl in presence of anhyd. $AlCl_3$ gives *D*. *D* reacts with hydroxylamine to give *E*.

(i) The monobasic acid *A* is ....

(ii) What are the products *B* and *C* in the reaction?

(iii) What do we call the conversion of product *C* to *D*?

Short Answer Type I Questions

2 Marks

28 Give one good chemical test to distinguish between the following pair of compounds:
Oxalic acid and benzoic acid. **ISC 2018**

29 Sodium bisulphite is used for the purification of aldehydes and ketones. Explain.

30 Di-*tert*-butyl ketone does not give a $NaHSO_3$ adduct but acetone does. Give reason.

31 Why is it necessary to control the pH during the reaction of aldehydes and ketones with ammonia derivatives?

32 Write the products of oxidation of
(i) pentan-2-one and (ii) pentan-3-one.
Are the major products same or different? Explain.

33 Complete the following reaction and explain the formation of products.
(i) $HCOOH \xrightarrow{\text{Conc. } H_2SO_4}$
(ii) $CH_3COOH + CH_3OH \xrightarrow{\text{Conc. } H_2SO_4}$

34 Why benzoic acid does not undergo Friedel-Crafts reaction?

35 An aldehyde $A(C_{11}H_8O)$, which does not undergo self aldol condensation, gives benzaldehyde and 2 moles of B on ozonolysis. Compound B on oxidation with silver ion gives oxalic acid. Identify the compounds A and B.

36 Identify the missing compounds in the following reaction sequence :

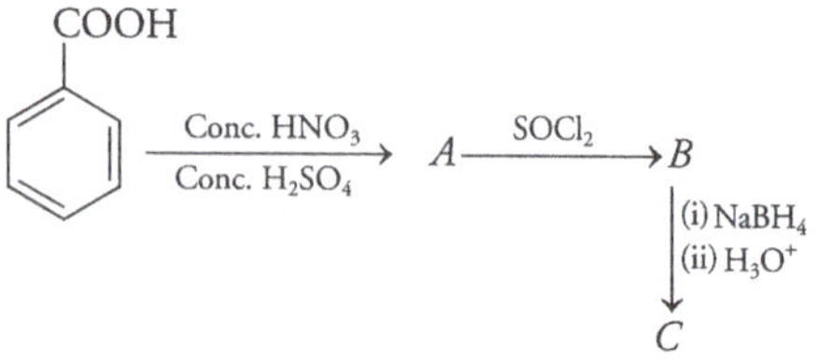

37 Write balanced chemical equations for the following and name the reactions occurring in each case :
(i) Benzaldehyde reacts with an alcoholic solution of potassium cyanide.
(ii) Propanone is treated with iodine and excess of alkali and warmed. **ISC 2018**

38 Write the balanced equations for the reaction of ammonia with formaldehyde, acetaldehyde and acetone. **ISC 2001**

39 How will you bring about the following conversions?

(i) 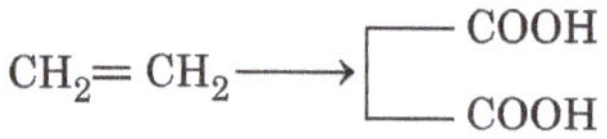

(Succinic acid)

(ii) 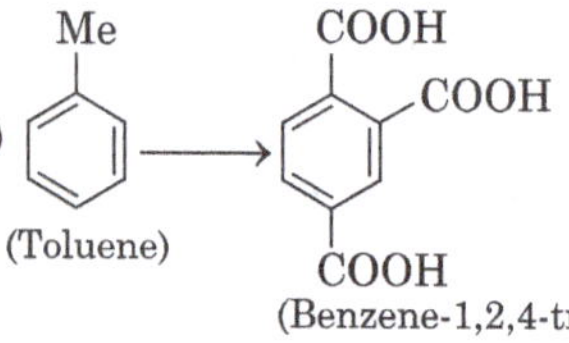

(Toluene)
(Benzene-1,2,4-tricarboxylic acid)

40 Complete the following reactions :

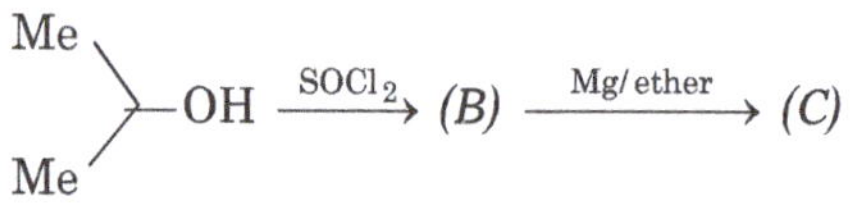

41 Describe the following:
(i) Cannizzaro reaction
(ii) Cross-aldol condensation **NCERT**

42 Which acid of each pair shown here would you expect to be stronger?
(i) CH_3COOH or CH_2FCOOH
(ii) CH_2FCOOH or $CH_2ClCOOH$
(iii) $CH_2FCH_2CH_2COOH$ or CH_3CHFCH_2COOH
(iv) 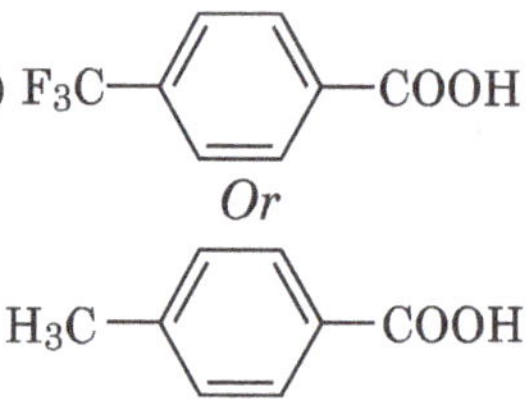

Short Answer Type II Questions

3 Marks

43 (i) Give the structures of the following:
(a) Phthalldehyde
(b) 3-methyl cyclohexane carbaldehyde
(c) 3-methylbut-2-enoic acid

(ii) Write the IUPAC names of the following structures:

(a) 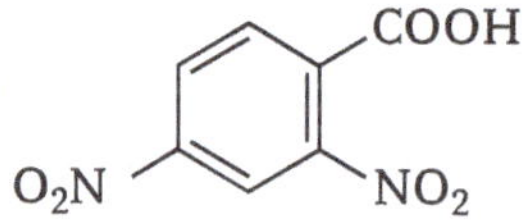

(b) 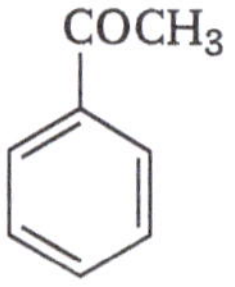

(c) 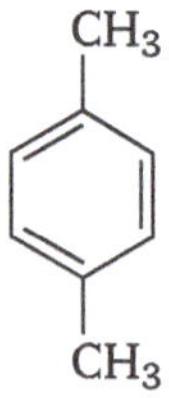

44 Give names of the reagents to bring about the following transformations:
(i) Benzoyl chloride to benzaldehyde
(ii) Benzene to benzaldehyde
(iii) Benzene to acetophenone

45 Complete the following equations, giving the names of the reactants and the products.

(i) $C_6H_6 + \ldots \xrightarrow{\text{Anhy. } AlCl_3} C_6H_5COCH_3$

(ii) $(CH_3)_2CO \xrightarrow{LiAlH_4}$

46 What is α-hydrogen in a carbonyl compounds? Write the similarities and differences on the reactivity of the compounds CH_3CHO and C_6H_5CHO with the reagents:
(i) NaOH (ii) Tollen's reagent

47 Acetone on reaction with HCN gives one compound, whereas acetaldehyde gives two compounds that are difficult to separate. Explain why?

48 Show how each of the following compounds can be converted to benzoic acid?
(i) Benzamide (ii) Propyl benzene

49 Account for the following differences in the acidic character of the following.
(i) $Me_3C—CH_2—COOH > Me_3SiCH_2COOH$
(ii) $H_2C{=}CHCH_2COOH > CH_3CH_2COOH$
(iii) $N{\equiv}C—CH_2COOH > CH_3COCH_2—COOH$

50 Give the balanced equations for the following name reactions :
(*i*) Rosenmund's reaction
(*ii*) Formaldehyde is treated with ammonia

51 Write down the IUPAC and common name for the following.

(i) 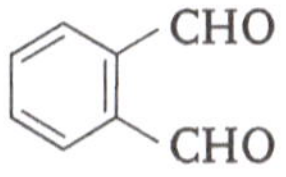

(ii) 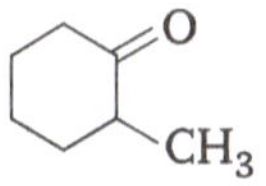

(iii) $CH_2{=}CHCHO$

52 Write the chemical equations to illustrate the following name reactions.
(i) Wolff-Kishner reduction
(ii) Aldol condensation
(iii) Cannizzaro reaction

Long Answer Type Questions

5 Marks

53 Write the balanced chemical equation for the following reaction:
(i) Oxalic acid is treated with acidified potassium permanganate solution.
(ii) Benzoic acid is treated with a mixture of concentrated nitric acid and concentrated sulphuric acid.
(iii) Methyl magnesium iodide is treated with carbon dioxide and the product hydrolysed in acidic medium.

54 What is meant by the following terms? Give an example of the reaction in each case.
(i) Hemiacetal (ii) Oxime
(iii) Ketal (iv) Imine
(v) Schiff's base

55 Differentiate between the following:
(i) Propanoic acid and acrylic acid ($CH_2{=}CH—COOH$)
(ii) 2-bromopropanoic acid ($CH_3CHBrCOOH$) and pyruvic acid ($CH_3COCOOH$).
(iii) Malonic acid $\left(\begin{array}{c} COOH \\ | \\ CH_2 \\ | \\ COOH \end{array}\right)$ and succinic acid $\left(\begin{array}{c} CH_2COOH \\ | \\ CH_2COOH \end{array}\right)$.

56 An organic compound (*P*) having molecular formula $C_9H_{10}O$, form an orange precipitate (*Q*) with 2,4-DNP reagent. Compound (*P*) gives a yellow precipitate (*R*) when heated in the presence of iodine and NaOH along with a colourless compound (*S*). (*P*) neither reduce Tollen's reagent or Fehling's solution nor it decolourises bromine water. On drastic oxidation of (*P*) with chromic acid, a carboxylic acid (*T*) having molecular formula $C_7H_6O_2$ is obtained. Deduce the structures of the compounds (*P*) to (*T*).

57 An organic compound *A* has the molecular formula C_7H_6O. When *A* is treated with NaOH followed by acid hydrolysis, it gives two products *B* and *C*. When *B* is oxidised, it gives *A*. When *A* and *C* are each treated separately with PCl_5, they give two different products *D* and *E*.
(i) Identify *A*, *B*, *C*, *D* and *E*.
(ii) Give the chemical reaction when *A* is treated with NaOH and name the reaction.

58 An organic compound *A* with molecular formula C_7H_8 on oxidation by chromyl chloride in the presence of CCl_4 gives a compound *B* which gives positive Tollen's test.
The compound B on treatment with NaOH followed by acid hydrolysis gives two products

C and *D*. *C* on oxidation gives *B* which on further oxidation gives *D*. The compound *D* on distillation with sodalime gives a hydrocarbon *E*.

Below 60°C, concentrated nitric acid reacts with *E* in the presence of concentrated sulphuric acid forming a compound *F*. Identify the compounds *A*, *B*, *C*, *D*, *E* and *F*.

59 Write any three mild oxidising agents that are used to distinguish aldehydes from ketones and explain the reactions involved.

60 $(A)\ C_6H_{12} \xrightarrow{HCl} (B)C_6H_{13}Cl + (C), C_6H_{13}Cl$

$(B) \xrightarrow{\text{Alcoholic KOH}} (D)$,

$(D) \xrightarrow{\text{Ozonolysis}} (E)$, (Negative Fehling's solution test)

$(A) \xrightarrow{\text{Ozonolysis}} (F) + (G)$,

(Positive Tollen's test for both)

$(F) + (G) \xrightarrow{\text{Conc. NaOH}}$ HCOONa + A primary alcohol

Identify the compounds (*A*) to (*G*).

Answers

1 (i) CH_3COCH_3 (ii) ethyl alcohol
(iii) weaker, $+I$ (iv) Carbon dioxide
(v) formaldehyde, ammonia (vi) silver mirror

2 (i) → c (ii) → b (iii) → b (iv) → b (v) → b (vi) → a

3 (i) (b) **A** → (iii) **B** → (iv) **C** → (i) **D** → (ii)
(ii) (a) **A** → (v) **B** → (iv) **C** → (i) **D** → (ii) **E** → (vi) **F** → (iii)

4 Boiling point of butanal is lower that butan-1-ol due to the absence of intermolecular hydrogen bonding.

5 **Hint** Due to the presence of $>C=O$ (polar group) in propanal.

6 **Hint** $CH_3-\underset{\underset{CH_3}{|}}{CH}-COOH$, $CH_3-\overset{\overset{CH_3}{|}}{\underset{\underset{H}{|}}{C}}-CH_2COOH$

7 **Hint** Tollen's reagent and Fehling's reagent.

8 $\underset{\text{Acetaldehyde}}{CH_3CHO} \xrightarrow[K_2Cr_2O_7 + H_2SO_4]{[O]} CH_3COOH$

$\longrightarrow CH_3COONH_4 \xrightarrow{\Delta} CH_3CONH_2 \xrightarrow{+}$

$CH_3NH_2 \longrightarrow CH_3OH \xrightarrow[\Delta,]{Cu} \underset{\text{Formaldehyde}}{HCHO}$

9 Following steps will be taken:
(i) First convert propan-2-ol to acetone by catalytic dehydrogenation with Cu at 573 K.
(ii) Then, convert acetone to acetoxime by addition of hydroxylamine.
Propan-2-ol to acetoxime

$\underset{\text{Propan-2-ol}}{CH_3CHOHCH_3} \xrightarrow[,\ 573\ K]{} \underset{\text{Acetone}}{CH_3COCH_3}$

$\longrightarrow \underset{\text{Acetoxime}}{(CH_3)_2C=NOH} + H_2O$

10 The conversion of methyl chloride to acetic acid have the following steps:

$\underset{\text{Methyl chloride}}{CH_3Cl} + 2Na + Cl\cdot CH_3 \longrightarrow CH_3\cdot CH_3 + 2NaCl$

$CH_3\cdot CH_3 + Cl_2 \xrightarrow{h\nu} C_2H_5Cl + HCl$

$C_2H_5Cl + \underset{(aq.)}{KOH} \longrightarrow C_2H_5OH + KCl$

$C_2H_5OH + O_2 \xrightarrow[H_2SO_4]{K_2Cr_2O_7} \underset{\text{Acetic acid}}{CH_3COOH} + H_2O$

11 The conversion of benzene to benzoic acid have the following steps:

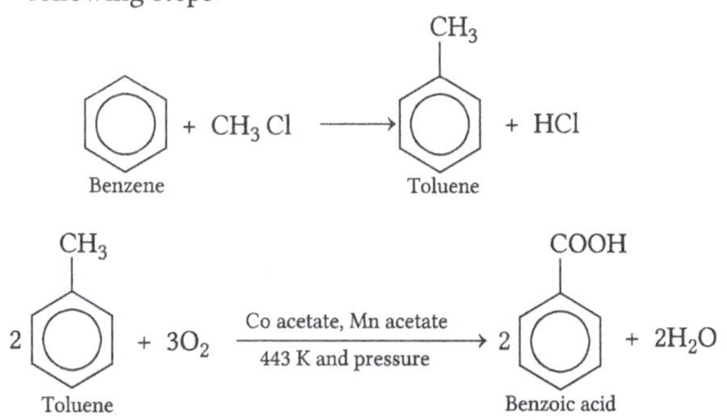

12 pK_a of chloroacetic acid is lower that pK_a of acetic acid because acidity of carboxylic acids increases due to the presence of electron withdrawing groups.

13 The C— O bond is shorter in *R*COOH than in *R*CHO due to the following possible resonance structures :

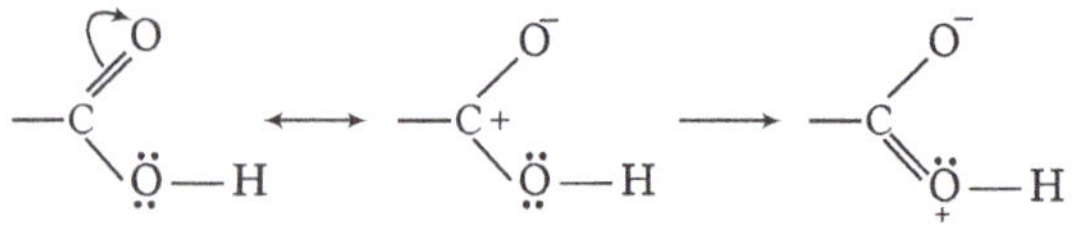

14 **Hint**

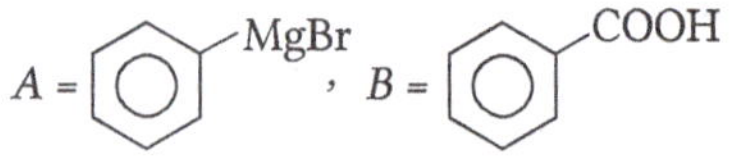

15.

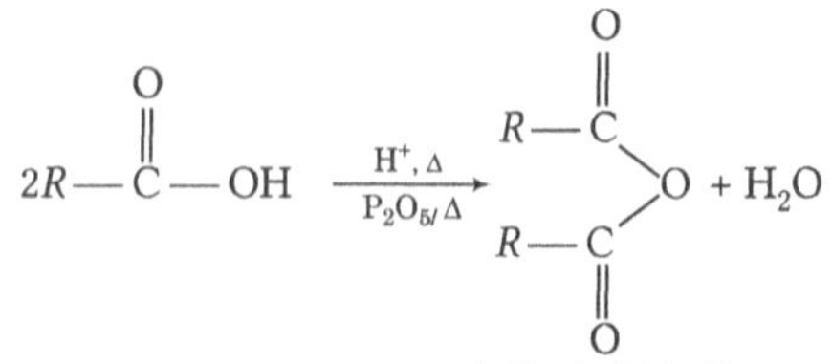

Acid anhydride (A)

16. **Benzoin condensation** Two benzaldehyde molecules on heating with potassium cyanide solution undergoes self condensation to form benzoin. This reaction is called benzoin condensation.

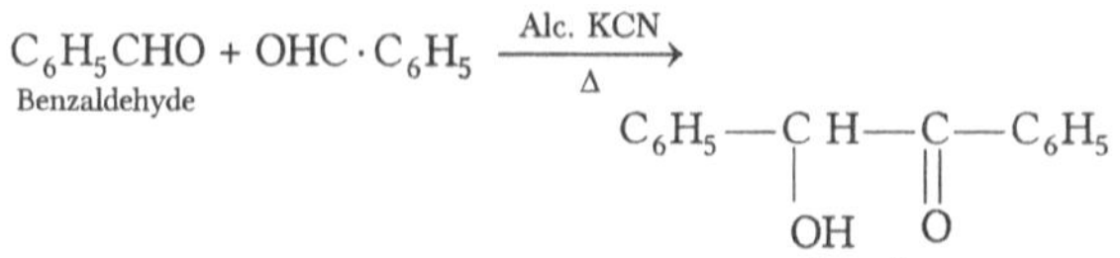

17. (i) Acetone gives a white precipitate on treatment with **sodium bisulphate**.

(ii) Acetaldehyde undergoes **aldol condensation** on treatment with dilute alkali.

18.

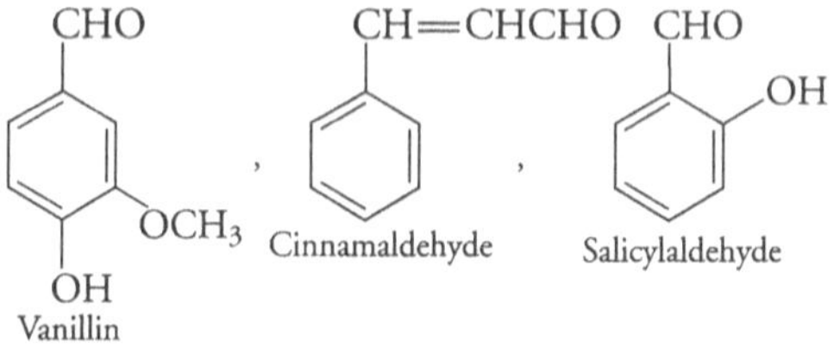

19 **Clemmenson reduction** involves the reduction of carbonyl group form $\rangle C=O$ to $\rangle CH_2$ group and it is carried out in the presence of Zn-Hg amalgam and conc. HCl.

$$\rangle C=O + 4\,[H] \xrightarrow{\text{Zn-Hg/Conc. HCl}} \rangle CH_2 + H_2O$$

Hydrocarbon

20

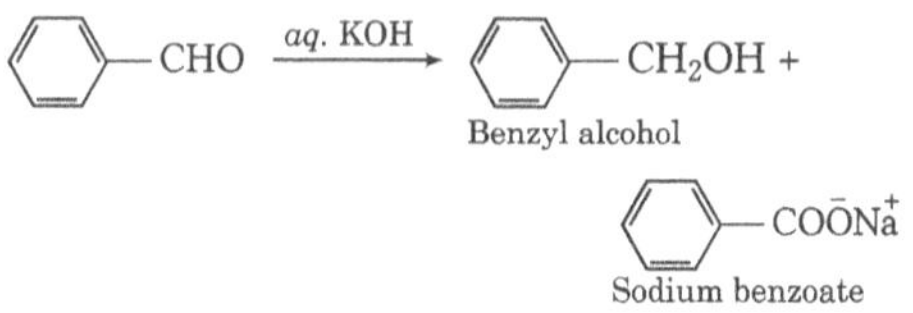

21 (c) The acidity of α-hydrogen atoms of carbonyl compounds is due to the strong electron withdrawing effect of the carbonyl group and resonance stabilisation of the conjugate base.

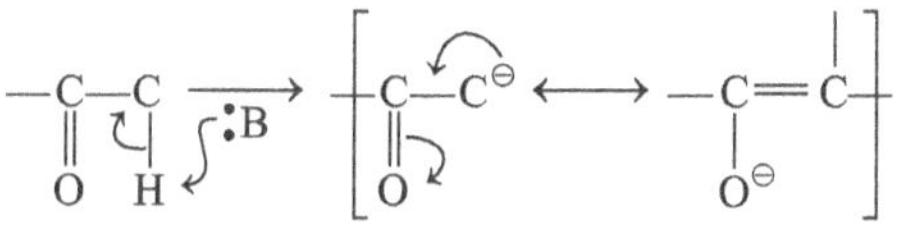

Hence, (A) is correct but (R) is incorrect.

22 (c) The solubility of aldehydes and ketones decreases when the length of alkyl chain increases because of the increase in the magnitude of non-polar (hydrophobic) part in the molecule.

23 (c) Aromatic aldehydes are less reactive than aliphatic aldehyde like formaldehyde. Cannizzaro's reaction is shown by aldehydes which do not contain any α-H atom. Such aldehydes in the presence of concentrated solution of an alkali undergo self oxidation-reduction to give a mixture of alcohol and a salt of the carboxylic acid. For example, formaldehyde (HCHO) gives methanol and sodium methanoate.

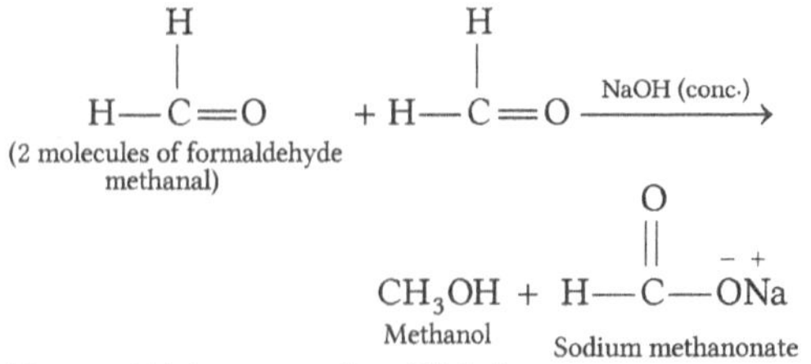

Hence, (A) is correct but (R) is incorrect.

24 (a) IUPAC name of $HOOC \leftarrow CH_2 \rightarrow_2 COOH$ is butane-dioic acid. For compounds containing more than one carboxyl group, the ending '-e' of the alkane is retained. The number of carboxyl groups are indicated by adding the multiplicative prefix, di, tri etc., to the term 'oic'. Thus, both (A) and (R) is correct and (R) is the correct explanation of (A).

25 (a) Both (A) and (R) are correct and (R) is the correct explanation of (A).

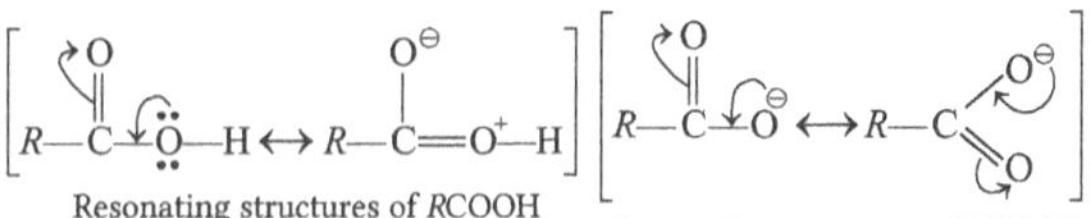

Resonating structures of RCOOH (non-equivalent)

Resonating structures of $RCOO^-$ (equivalent)

26 (i) *A* is CH_3CHO (ethanal) and *B* is C_6H_5CHO (benzaldehyde).

(ii) $$\underset{[A]}{2CH_3CHO} \xrightleftharpoons{NaOH} CH_3—\overset{OH}{CH}—CH_2CHO \xrightarrow{-H_2O} \underset{\text{But-2-enal}}{CH_3—CH=CH—CHO}$$

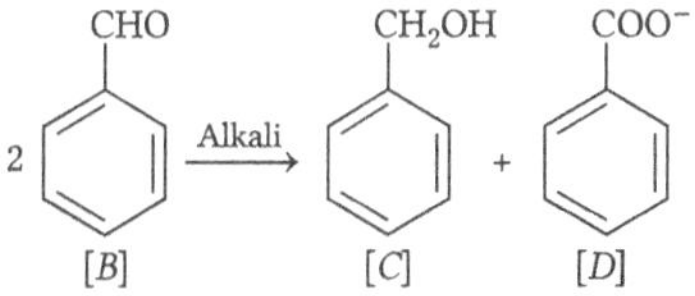

(*A*) undergoes aldol condensation.

(*B*) undergoes Cannizzaro reaction.

(iii) Toluene

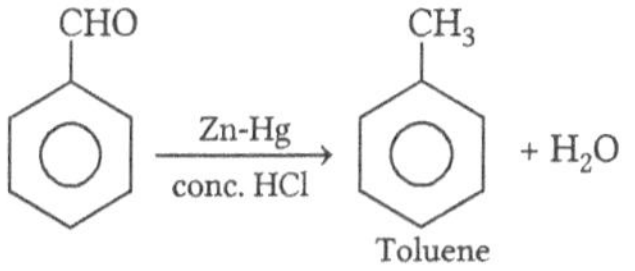

Toluene

This reaction is called as Clemmensen reduction.

27 $C = 60.87\%$ $H = 4.35\%$ $O = 100 - (60.87 + 4.35) = 34.78\%$

Element	%	Molar mass	Moles (n)	$y = \frac{n}{2.17}$
C	60.87	12	5.07	$2.34 \times 3 = 7$
H	4.35	1	4.35	$2 \times 3 = 6$
O	34.78	16	2.17	$1 \times 3 = 3$

Empirical formula of $A = C_7H_6O_3$.
Since, acid (A) gives violet colour with neutral $FeCl_3$ solution, it must be a phenol.

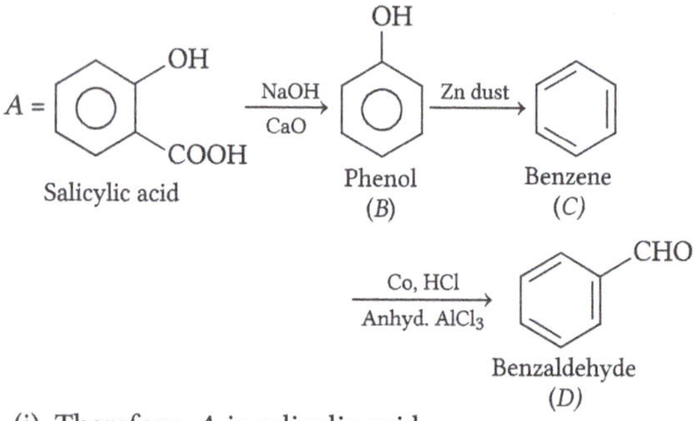

(i) Therefore, A is salicylic acid.
(ii) B is phenol and C is benzene.
(iii) Conversion of benzene to benzaldehyde on treatement with CO, HCl in the presence of anhyd. $AlCl_3$ is called Gattermann-Koch reaction.

28 Oxalic acid decolourised hot solution of acidified $KMnO_4$ whereas benzoic acid does not give this test.

29 Refer to text on pages 308 and 309 (Topic 1, Addition of $NaHSO_3$).

30 **Hint** Due to steric hinderance caused by the bulky *tert*-butyl groups, the bisulphite ion cannot easily approach the carbonyl group for addition.

31 **Hint** NH_3 is a base. In acidic medium, it can form anilinium ion.

32 Refer to text on page 311 (Topic 1, Oxidation reactions).

33 (i) $CO + H_2O$

(ii) $CH_3\,O{-}\overset{\overset{O}{\|}}{C}CH_3$

34 Refer to text on page 338 (Ring substitution reaction).

35 **Hint** Aldehyde A is

A = CH=CH—C≡C—CHO,

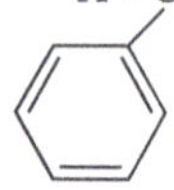

B is OHC—COOH

36

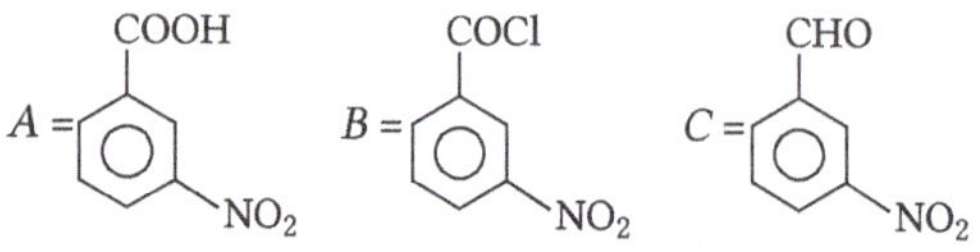

37. (i)

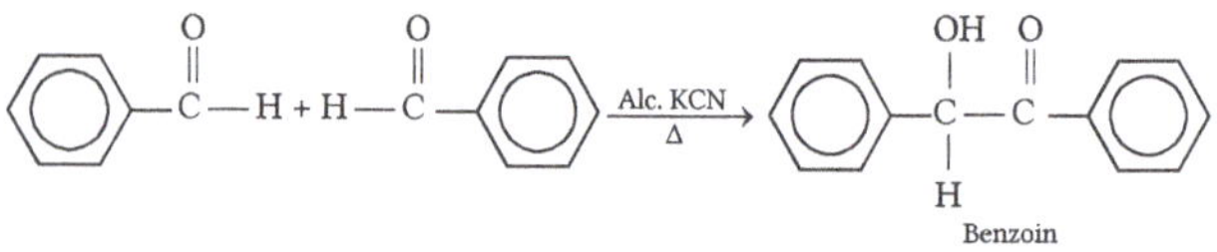

This reaction is **benzoin condensation.**

(ii) $\underset{\text{Propanone}}{CH_3COCH_3} + 3I_2 + 4NaOH \xrightarrow{\Delta} \underset{\text{Iodoform}}{CHI_3}\downarrow + CH_3CO\overset{-}{O}\overset{+}{Na} + 3NaI + 4H_2O$

This reaction is **iodoform reaction.**

38. **Ammonia with formaldehyde**

$$6HCHO + 4NH_3 \longrightarrow 6H_2O + \underset{\text{Hexamethylene tetraamine (Urotropine)}}{(CH_2)_6N_4},$$

Ammonia with acetaldehyde

$$\underset{\text{Acetaldehyde}}{CH_3\cdot CH{=}O} + H{-}NH_2 \longrightarrow \underset{\text{Acetaldehyde ammonia}}{CH_3{-}\overset{\overset{H}{|}}{\underset{\underset{NH_2}{|}}{C}}{-}OH}$$

Ammonia with acetone

$$\underset{\text{Acetone}}{(H_3C)_2CO} + \underset{\text{Ammonia}}{NH_3} \xrightarrow{\text{Low temp.}} CH_3{-}\overset{\overset{NH_2}{|}}{\underset{\underset{CH_3}{|}}{C}}{-}OH$$

$$(H_3C)_2CO + NH_3 \xrightarrow{\text{High temp.}} (H_3C)_2C(NH_2)CH_2COCH_3 + H_2O$$

39 (i) $CH_2{=}CH_2 \xrightarrow{Br_2} Br\,CH_2\,CH_2\,Br \xrightarrow{CN^-}$

$$NC\,CH_2\,CH_2\,CN \xrightarrow{H_3O^+} \begin{matrix} CH_2{-}COOH \\ | \\ CH_2{-}COOH \end{matrix}$$

(ii) **Hint** Alkylation followed by oxidation.

40 $B = (CH_3)_2CH_2{-}Cl$ $C = (Me)_2{-}MgCl$

41 (i) **Cannizzaro reaction** Refer to text on pages 314 and 315 (Topic 1, Cannizzaro reaction).
(ii) **Cross aldol condensation** Refer to text on page 314 (Topic 1, Cross -aldol condensation)

42 (i) CH_2FCOOH is a stronger acid.
(ii) CH_2FCOOH is a stronger acid.
(iii) CH_3CHFCH_2COOH is a stronger acid.
(iv) F_3C—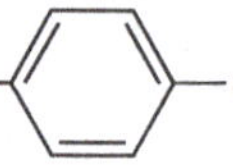—COOH is a stronger acid.

43 Hint

(a) 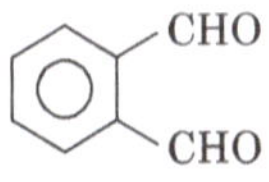 (b) 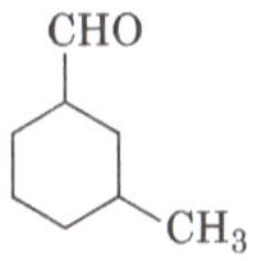

(c) $CH_3-\overset{\overset{CH_3}{|}}{C}=CH-COOH$

(ii) (a) 2, 4-dinitrobenzoic acid
(b) Acetophenone (c) 4-methyltoluene.

44 (i) Refer to text on page 306 (Topic 1, Preparation of aldehydes).
(ii) Refer to text on page 306 (Topic 1, Preparation of aldehydes).
(iii) Refer to text on pages 306 and 307 (Topic 1, Preparation of ketones).

45 (i) CH_3COCl (ii) $(CH_3)_2CHOH$

46 Refer to text on page 313.
(i) CH_3CHO will give aldol condensation with NaOH while C_6H_5CHO does not.
(ii) CH_3 CHO gives positive test with Tollen's reagent whereas C_6H_5CHO does not.

47 Refer to text on page 308 (Topic 1, Addition of hydrogen cyanide HCN).

48 (i) Refer to text on pages 333 and 334 (Topic 2, Methods of preparation from nitriles).
(ii) Refer to text on pages 333 and 335 (Topic 2, Methods of preparation).

49 Hint
(i) Carbon is more electronegative than silicon.
(ii) sp^2-hybridised carbon is more electronegative than sp^3-hybridised carbon.
(iii) sp-hybridised carbon of $C\equiv N$ is more electronegative than sp^2- hybridised carbon of $C=O$.

50 (i) Rosenmund's reaction

$$CH_3-\overset{\overset{O}{||}}{C}-Cl+H_2 \xrightarrow[\text{Boiling xylene}]{\text{Pd, BaSO}_4} CH_3-\overset{\overset{O}{||}}{C}-H+HCl$$

(ii) When formaldehyde is treated with ammonia, then urotropine is formed.

$$6H-\overset{\overset{O}{||}}{C}-H+4NH_3 \longrightarrow \underset{\text{Urotropine}}{(CH_2)_6N_4}+6H_2O$$

51 Refer to text on pages 303 and 304 (Topic 1).

52 (i) Refer to text on page 312 (Topic 1, Reduction to hydrocarbons).
(ii) Refer to text on pages 313 and 314 (Topic 1, Reactions due to α-hydrogen).
(iii) Refer to text on pages 314 (Topic 1, Cannizzaro reaction).

53 The balanced chemical equations for the given reactions are as follows:

(i) $$5\underset{\text{Oxalic acid}}{\begin{array}{c}COOH\\|\\COOH\end{array}} + \underset{\text{Potassium permanganate}}{2KMnO_4} + 3H_2SO_4 \longrightarrow K_2SO_4 + \underset{\text{(Colourless)}}{2MnSO_4} + 10CO_2 + 8H_2O$$

(ii) 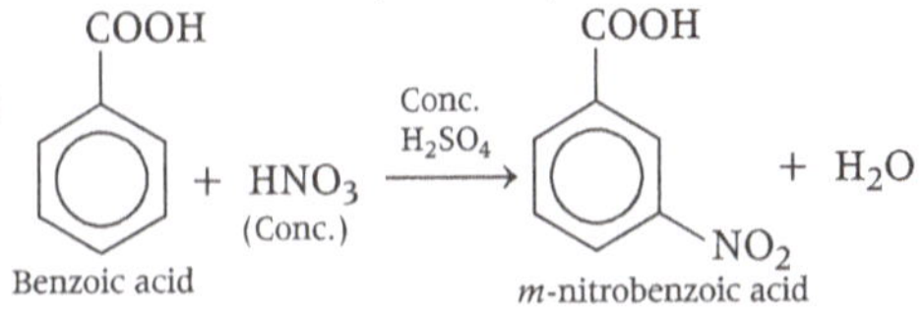

(iii) $$\underset{\text{Carbon dioxide}}{O=C=O} + \underset{\text{Methyl magnesium iodide}}{CH_3-Mg-I} \longrightarrow CH_3-\overset{\overset{OH}{|}}{CH}-CH_3$$

$$O=\overset{\overset{CH_3}{|}}{C}-OMgI \xrightarrow{H_2O/H^+} \underset{\text{Acetic acid}}{CH_3-\overset{\overset{O}{||}}{C}-OH} + \underset{\text{Hydroxy magnesium iodide}}{Mg\begin{array}{l}OH\\I\end{array}}$$

54 (i) Refer to text on page 309 (Topic 1, Addition of alcohols).
(ii) Refer to text on pages 310 and 311 (Topic 1, Addition of ammonia and its derivative).
(iii) Refer to text on page 309 (Topic 1, Addition of alcohols).
(iv) Refer to text on pages 310 and 311 (Topic 1, Addition of ammonia and its derivative).
(v) **Schiff 's base** When an aldehyde or ketone reacts with primary aliphatic or aromatic amines, the compound formed is called Schiff 's base or azomethine.

$$\underset{\text{Aldehyde}}{R-CH=O} + \underset{\text{Primary amine}}{H_2N-R'} \xrightarrow{H^+} \underset{\text{Schiff 's base}}{R-CH=N-R'} + H_2O$$

55 (i) **Hint** Acrylic acid is stronger than propanoic acid (acidity depends upon stability of its conjugate base).
(ii) **Hint** EWG increases the acidity of carboxylic acids.
(iii) **Hint** pK_a value of succinic acid is higher than pK_a value of malonic acid.

RELATED ONLINE VIDEOS

Visit : https://youtu.be/0gSxDgzw7eE OR Scan the Code	**Visit :** https://youtu.be/50vJAPMwVsw OR Scan the Code
Visit : https://youtu.be/PiSFMeicf8 OR Scan the Code	**Visit :** https://youtu.be/sd3YfPbPTgY OR Scan the Code

56

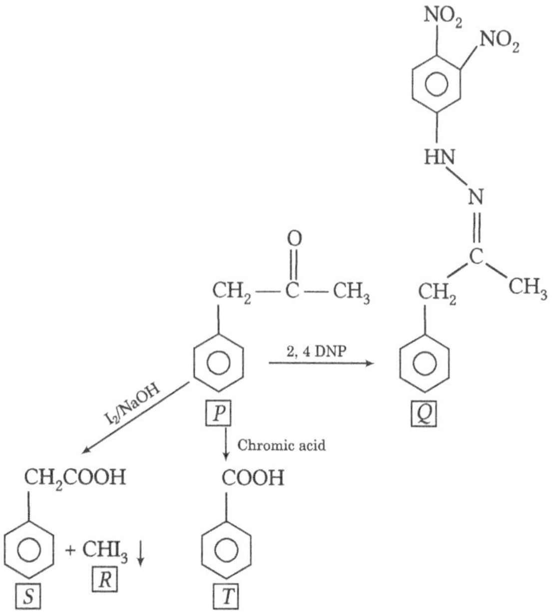

57 (i) The organic compound A, C_7H_6O is benzaldehyde,

C_6H_5CHO or 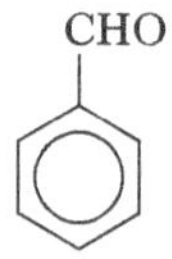

i.e.

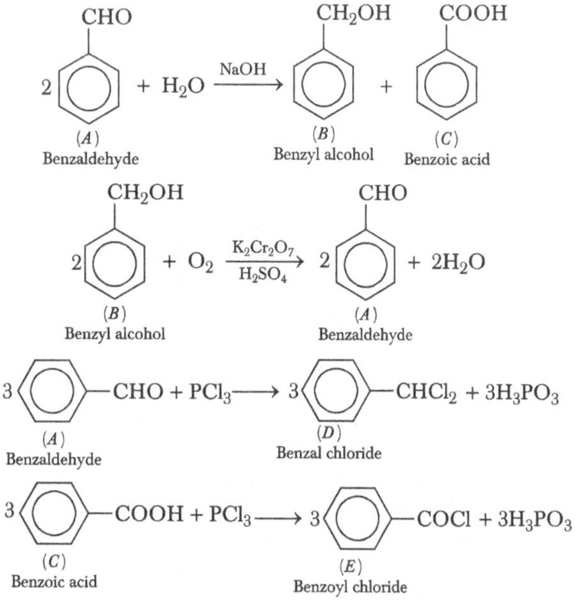

Thus, *A* is benzaldehyde.
B is benzyl alcohol. *C* is benzoic acid.
D is benzal chloride. *E* is benzoyl chloride.

(ii) When benzaldehyde reacts with sodium hydroxide then the benzyl alcohol and sodium benzoate are formed. This reaction is known as **Cannizzaro reaction.**

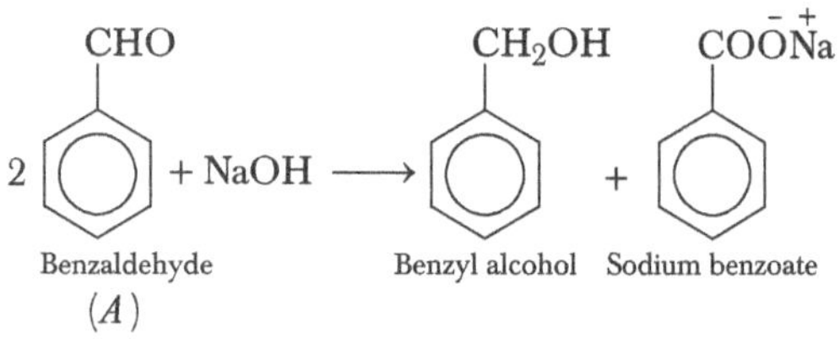

58 Compound A must be toluene and B should be benzaldehyde (as it gives positive Tollen's test).

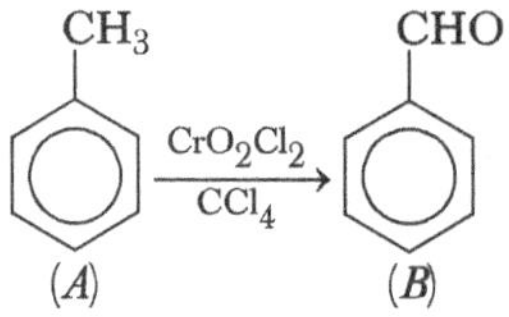

(*A*) $C_6H_5CHO \longrightarrow$ Benzaldehyde (*B*)
Compound *B* (C_6H_5CHO) on treatment with NaOH followed by acid hydrolysis gives two products, benzyl alcohol (*C*) and sodium benzoate (*D*).
This is **Cannizzaro reaction.**

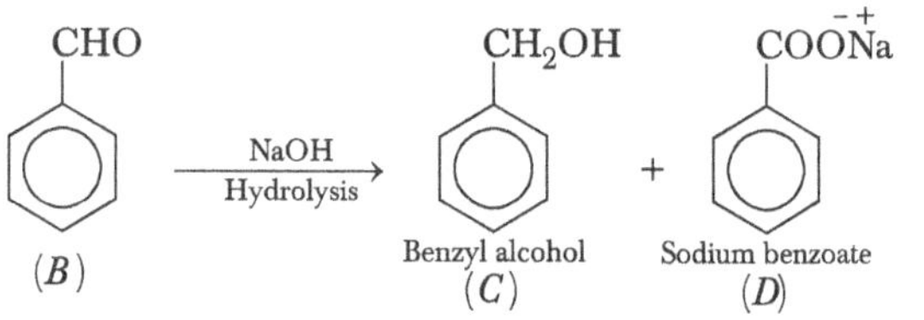

Compound *C* on oxidation gives *B*, which on further oxidation gives *D*. *i.e.*

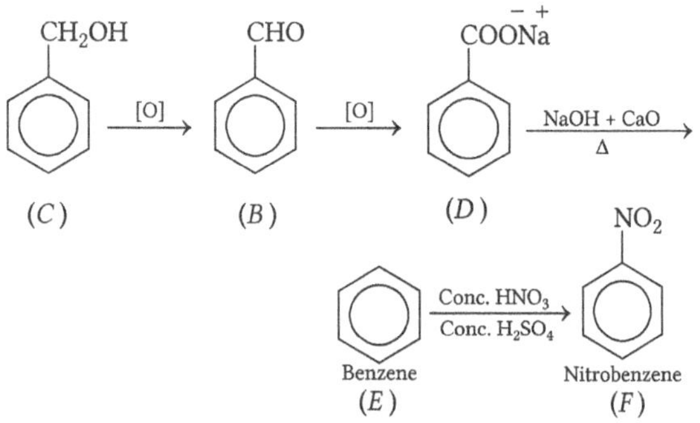

59 Refer to text on pages 311 and 312 (Topic 1, Reactions with mild oxidising agents).

60

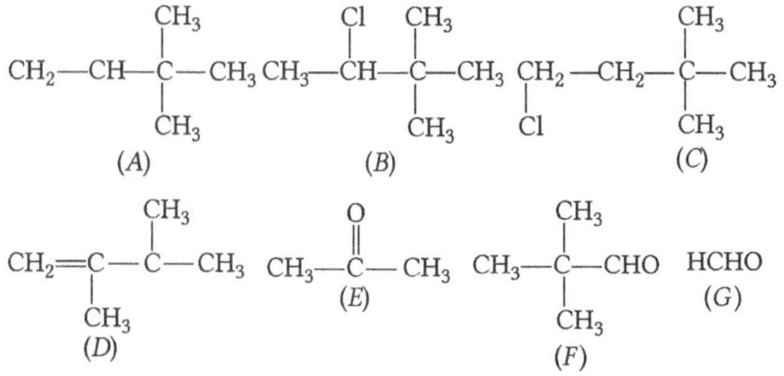

CHAPTER

09

Organic Compounds Containing Nitrogen

Amines constitute one of the most important class of organic compounds. These are derived by replacing one or more hydrogen atom(s) of ammonia molecule by **alkyl** or **aryl groups**. That's why, these are also known as derivatives of ammonia. They occur among proteins, vitamins, alkaloids and hormones.

- Structure, Classification Nomenclature and Preparation of of Amines
- Properties of Amines
- Diazonium salts

TOPIC 01 Structure, Classification, Nomenclature and Preparation of Amines

Structure

Structure of amines is described below:

(i) Like ammonia, nitrogen atom of amines is trivalent and carries an unshared pair of electrons. Therefore, the N orbitals in amines are sp^3-hybridised and the geometry of amines is pyramidal.

(ii) The ground state electronic configuration of N is $1s^2, 2s^2, 2p_x^1 2p_y^1 2p_z^1$. Here, one 2*s*-orbital and three 2*p*-orbitals are hybridised to form four sp^3-hybridised orbitals, three of them have one electron each and the fourth orbital has one lone pair of electrons.

(iii) Each of the three sp^3-hybridised orbitals of nitrogen overlap with orbitals of carbon or hydrogen depending upon the composition of the amines. The fourth orbital of N contains an unshared pair of electrons, in all amines.

(iv) Due to the presence of unshared pair of electrons, the angle C—N—*E* (where *E* is C or H) is less than 109.5°. e.g. In trimethylamine, angle is 108°.

(v) Due to the presence of lone pair of electrons on nitrogen which can be donated, amines act as a nucleophile.

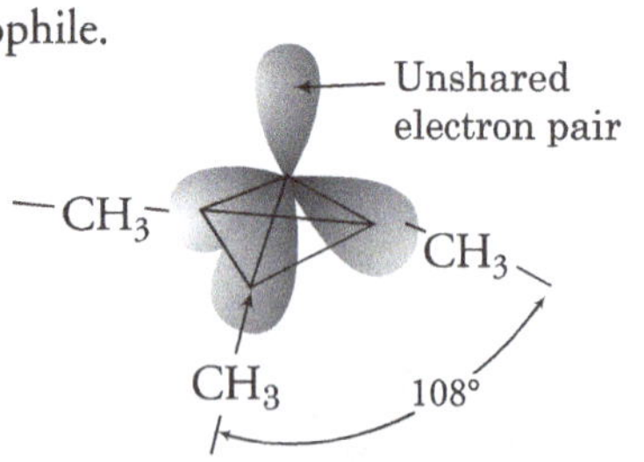

Pyramidal shape of trimethylamine

Classification

Amines are the derivatives of ammonia, obtained by the replacement of hydrogen atoms by alkyl/aryl groups. Thus, they are classified as:

(i) When one of the hydrogen atoms in ammonia is replaced by an alkyl group its called **aliphatic amines**. (General formula for aliphatic amine is $C_nH_{2n+1} \cdot NH_2$.)

(ii) When one of the hydrogen atoms in ammonia is replaced by an aromatic ring it is known as **aromatic amine** or aniline. General formula for aniline is $Ar—NH_2$. (where, Ar is aromatic ring.)

These aliphatic and aromatic amines are classified as primary (1°), secondary (2°) and tertiary (3°) depending upon the number of hydrogen atoms in ammonia molecule replaced by alkyl (*R*) or aryl (Ar) groups. Thus, we can show the sequence of classification of amine from ammonia.

$$\underset{\text{Ammonia}}{NH_3} \xrightarrow[+R]{-H} \underset{\text{Primary (1°)}}{R—NH_2} \xrightarrow[+R']{-H} \underset{\text{Secondary (2°)}}{R—NH—R'} \xrightarrow[+R'']{-H} \underset{\text{Tertiary (3°)}}{R—N(R')(R'')}$$

Degree and Functional Group of Various Amines

S. No.	Amine	*n* (no. of H-atoms attached to N)	Type of amine	Functional group	General formula
1.	$R—N(H)—H$	2	1° (primary)	$—NH_2$	$C_nH_{2n+1}NH_2$
2.	R_2NH	1	2° (secondary)	$—NH—$	$C_nH_{2n+2}NH$
3.	R_3N	0	3° (tertiary)	$>N—$	$C_nH_{2n+3}N$

Note There is another class of a amine compounds known as quaternary ammonium compounds $\left[H—\overset{H}{\underset{H}{N}}—H\right]^+ X^-$

- Amines can also be classified into simple and mixed amines
- **Simple amines** When all the alkyl/aryl groups are same, the amines are said to be simple amines. e.g. $\underset{2°\ \text{amine}}{(CH_3)_2NH}$, $\underset{3°\ \text{amine}}{(CH_3CH_2)_3N}$
- **Mixed amines** When all the alkyl/aryl groups are different, the amines are said to be mixed amines.

e.g. $\underset{\text{Ethylmethyl amine (2°)}}{CH_3—NH—CH_2CH_3}$,

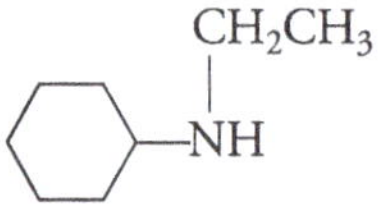

Cyclohexyl ethyl amine (2°)

Nomenclature

Rules and steps to be followed while naming of the amines are given below:

(i) In common system, an aliphatic amine is named by adding suffix 'amine' to the name of the alkyl group attached to the nitrogen atom, e.g. methylamine.

(ii) In 2° and 3° amines, when two or more groups are the same, the prefix di or tri is used before the name of the alkyl group.

e.g. $\underset{\text{Trimethylamine}}{CH_3—N(CH_3)—CH_3}$

(iii) In IUPAC system, amines are named as alkanamines, derived by the replacement of 'e' of alkane by word 'amine'.

e.g. $\underset{\text{Methanamine}}{CH_3NH_2}$, $\underset{\text{N, N-dimethylmethanamine}}{CH_3—N(CH_3)—CH_3}$

(iv) If more than one amino group is present at different positions in the parent chain, then by assigning number, their positions are specified to the carbon atoms bearing $—NH_2$ groups and the terminal '*e*' of the name of the parent hydrocarbon is retained.

e.g. $\underset{\text{Ethane-1,2-diamine}}{H_2N—CH_2—CH_2—NH_2}$

(v) The simplest **arylamine/aromatic amine** in which the $—NH_2$ group is directly attached to the benzene ring, i.e. $C_6H_5NH_2$ is called **aniline** and the substituted aromatic amines are named as derivatives of aniline. e.g.

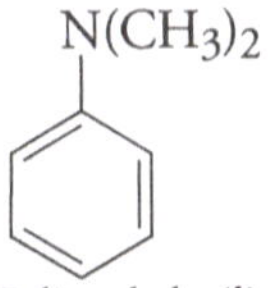

N, N-dimethylaniline

(vi) In IUPAC system, the terminal 'e' of arene is replaced by 'amine'. e.g. $C_6H_5—NH_2$(Benzenamine)

Nomenclature of Some Important Alkanamines and Arylamines

Amine	Common name	IUPAC name
$CH_3—CH_2—NH_2$	Ethylamine	Ethanamine
$CH_3—CH_2—CH_2—NH_2$	*n*-propylamine	Propan-1-amine
$CH_3—\underset{NH_2}{\underset{\mid}{CH}}—CH_3$	Isopropylamine	Propan-2-amine
$CH_3—\underset{H}{\underset{\mid}{N}}—CH_2—CH_3$	Ethylmethylamine	N-methylethanamine
$CH_3—\underset{CH_3}{\underset{\mid}{N}}—CH_3$	Trimethylamine	N,N-dimethylmethanamine
$C_2H_5—\underset{C_2H_5}{\underset{\mid}{N}}—\overset{1}{C}H_2—\overset{2}{C}H_2—\overset{3}{C}H_2—\overset{4}{C}H_3$	N,N-diethylbutylamine	N,N-diethylbutan-1-amine
$NH_2—\overset{1}{C}H_2—\overset{2}{C}H{=}\overset{3}{C}H_2$	Allylamine	Prop-2-en-1-amine
$NH_2—(CH_2)_6—NH_2$	Hexamethylenediamine	Hexane-1,6-diamine
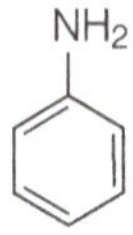	Aniline	Aniline or Benzenamine
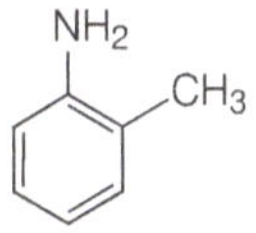	*o*-toluidine	2-aminotoluene
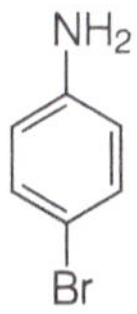	*p*-bromoaniline	4-bromobenzenamine or 4-bromoaniline
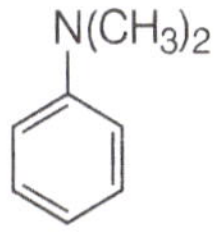	N,N-dimethylaniline	N,N-dimethylbenzenamine

Preparation of Amines

Amines are prepared by the following methods:

1. By the Ammonolysis of Alcohols

When vapours of a mixture of alcohol and ammonia are passed over heated alumina or thoria (ThO_2) at 620 K, a mixture of amines is obtained. This process of cleavage of C — OH bond by ammonia molecule is called ammonolysis of alcohols.

All the three types of amines are obtained, by this method

$$\underset{\text{Methanol}}{CH_3OH} + NH_3 \xrightarrow[(350°C)]{Al_2O_3} \underset{1°\text{amine}}{CH_3NH_2} + H_2O$$

$$CH_3NH_2 + CH_3OH \longrightarrow \underset{2°\text{ amine}}{(CH_3)_2NH} + H_2O$$

$$(CH_3)_2NH + CH_3OH \longrightarrow \underset{3°\text{amine}}{(CH_3)_3N} + H_2O$$

In excess of NH_3, primary amines may be obtained in good yield.

2. Ammonolysis of Alkyl Halides

This reaction is a nucleophilic substitution reaction in which ammonia acting as a nucleophile, displaces the halogen atom. This process of cleavage of C—*X* bond by ammonia is called ammonolysis. Alkyl or benzyl or aryl halides on reaction with ethanolic solution of ammonia undergoes nucleophilic substitution reaction because in these halides, carbon-halogen bond is easily cleaved by a nucleophile. This reaction is also knwon as Hofmann's ammonolysis reaction.

$$\underset{\text{Ammonia}}{:NH_3} + \underset{\text{Alkyl halide}}{R—X} \xrightarrow[\text{Sealed tube}]{373\text{ K}} \underset{\substack{\text{Substituted}\\ \text{ammonium salt}}}{R—\overset{+}{N}H_3X^-} \xrightleftharpoons{NH_3} \underset{1°\text{amine}}{RNH_2}$$

$$\underset{(1°)}{RNH_2} \xrightarrow{RX} \underset{(2°)}{R_2NH} \xrightarrow{RX} \underset{(3°)}{R_3N} \xrightarrow{RX} \underset{\substack{\text{Quaternary}\\ \text{ammonium salt}}}{R_4\overset{+}{N}\overset{-}{X}}$$

This primary amine behaves as a nucleophile and on subsequent reaction with alkyl halide forms
2°, 3° amines and finally forms quaternary ammonium salt.
This method cannot be used for the preparation of arylamine (unless benzene ring is activated by EWG at *o*- and *p*-positions). The free amine can be obtained from the ammonium salt by the treatment with a strong base.

$$R—\overset{+}{N}H_3\overset{-}{X} + NaOH \longrightarrow R—NH_2 + H_2O + Na^+X^-$$

the order of reactivity of halides with NH_3 is

$$R—I > R—Br > R—Cl > R—F$$

Example 1 Write reactions of the final alkylation product of aniline with excess of methyl iodide in the presence of sodium carbonate solution.

Sol. **Hofmann's ammonolysis reaction** In the presence of excess of methyl iodide, aniline (primary amine) forms quaternary ammonium salt.

$$\underset{\text{Aniline}}{C_6H_5\ddot{N}H_2} + CH_3—I \longrightarrow \underset{\substack{\text{N-methylanilinium iodide}\\ \text{(Intermediate)}}}{[C_6H_5\overset{+}{N}H_2CH_3]\,I^-}$$

$$2[C_6H_5\overset{+}{N}H_2CH_3]\,\overset{-}{I} + Na_2CO_3 \longrightarrow \underset{\text{N-methylaniline}}{2C_6H_5NHCH_3} + 2NaI + CO_2 + H_2O$$

$$C_6H_5\ddot{N}HCH_3 \xrightarrow[Na_2CO_3]{CH_3I} \underset{\text{N, N-dimethylaniline}}{C_6H_5N(CH_3)_2}$$

$$C_6H_5\ddot{N}(CH_3)_2 + CH_3—I \longrightarrow \underset{\text{N, N, N-trimethylanilinium iodide}}{[C_6H_5\overset{+}{N}(CH_3)_3]I^-}$$

$$2[C_6H_5\overset{+}{N}(CH_3)_3]\,\overset{-}{I} + Na_2CO_3 \rightarrow \underset{\substack{\text{N, N, N-trimethyl}\\ \text{anilinium carbonate}}}{[C_6H_5\overset{+}{N}(CH_3)_3]_2\,CO_3^{2-}} + 2NaI$$

3. From Cyanide (By the Reduction of Nitriles)

Reduction of nitriles with lithium aluminium hydride ($LiAlH_4$) or catalytic hydrogenation produces primary amines. This method is used to prepare amines containing one carbon atom more than the starting amine.

$$R—C{\equiv}N \xrightarrow[LiAlH_4\text{ or }Na(Hg)\,/\,C_2H_5OH]{\text{Raney Ni}/H_2} R—CH_2—NH_2$$

4. From Amide (By Hofmann's Bromamide Degradation Reaction)

This reaction is used for preparing amine containing one carbon less than the starting amide. This method was developed for the preparation of primary amines by reacting an amide with Br_2 / Cl_2 in an aqueous or ethanolic solution of NaOH/KOH.

In this reaction, migration of an alkyl or aryl group takes place from carbonyl carbon of the amide to the N-atom.

$$R—\overset{\overset{\large O}{\|}}{C}—NH_2 + Br_2 + 4NaOH \longrightarrow R—NH_2 + Na_2CO_3 + 2NaBr + 2H_2O$$

e.g. $$\underset{\text{Amide}}{CH_3CH_2CONH_2} + Br_2 + 4NaOH \longrightarrow \underset{\text{Amine}}{CH_3CH_2NH_2} + Na_2CO_3 + 2NaBr + 2H_2O$$

5. By the Reduction of Nitro Compounds

Both aliphatic and aromatic primary amines can be prepared by the reduction of nitro compounds either catalytically with H_2 in the presence of Raney Ni, Pt or Pd or chemically with active metal in acidic medium like Sn or Fe in HCl.

e.g. $$\underset{\text{Nitromethane}}{CH_3NO_2} + 3H_2 \xrightarrow[\text{Ethanol}]{\text{Raney Ni/Pt}} \underset{\text{Methylamine}}{CH_3NH_2} + 2H_2O$$

Reduction with Fe scrap and HCl is preferred because $FeCl_2$ formed, gets hydrolysed to release HCl during the reaction. Therefore, only a small amount of HCl is needed to initiate the reaction.

6. Gabriel Phthalimide Synthesis

When a phthalimide is treated with ethanolic KOH, it forms potassium salt of phthalimide which on heating with alkyl halide followed by alkaline hydrolysis forms corresponding primary amines.

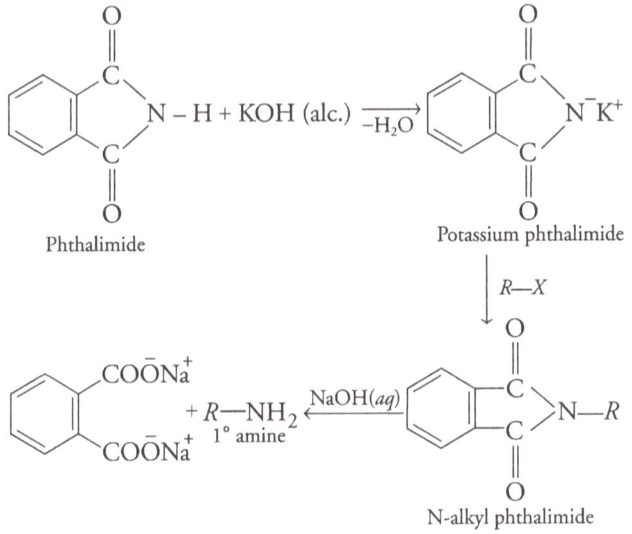

This method produces only primary amines without the traces of secondary or tertiary amines. So, this method is preferred for the synthesis of primary amines.

Note This method is not useful for the preparation of aromatic primary amines because aryl halides do not undergo nucleophilic substitution with the anion formed by phthalimide.

7. By the Reduction of Amides

On reduction with $LiAlH_4$, amides yield amines.

e.g. $$R-\overset{\overset{\displaystyle O}{\|}}{C}-NH_2 \xrightarrow[\text{(ii) } H_2O]{\text{(i) } LiAlH_4\text{, ether}} R-CH_2-NH_2$$

$$\underset{\text{Acetamide}}{CH_3CONH_2} \xrightarrow[\text{(ii) } H_2O]{\text{(i) } LiAlH_4\text{, ether}} \underset{\text{Ethylamine}}{CH_3CH_2NH_2}$$

Topic Practice 1

Very Short Answer Type Questions

(1 Mark)

1. Fill in the Blanks

(i) When acetamide is treated with bromine and caustic soda it gives .... as the main product and the reaction is called ....

ISC 2011

(ii) Gabriel phthalimide synthesis is used for the synthesis of .... amine.

(iii) Acetamide on treatment with .... and .... forms methylamine.

2. Objective Type Questions

(i) Which of the following is a 3° amine?
(a) 1 - methylcyclohexylamine
(b) Triethylamine
(c) *Tert*-butylamine
(d) N - methylaniline

(ii) The correct IUPAC name for $CH_2 = CHCH_2NHCH_3$ is
(a) allyl methylamine
(b) 2 - amino - 4 - pentene
(c) 4 - aminopent - 1 - ene
(d) N - methylprop - 2 -en- 1 amine

(iii) Which of the following reagents would not be a good choice for reducing an aryl nitro compound to an amine?
(a) H_2 (excess) / Pt
(b) $LiAlH_4$ in ether
(c) Fe and HCl
(d) Sn and HCl

(iv) The reaction of ethanamide with alcoholic sodium hydroxide and bromine gives

ISC 2024

(a) ethylamine
(b) methylamine
(c) propylamine
(d) aniline

3. Match the reactions given in Column I with the statements given in Column II and choose the correct option using the codes given below.

	Column I		Column II
A.	Ammonolysis	(i)	Amine with lesser number of carbon atoms
B.	Gabriel phthalimide synthesis	(ii)	Detection test for primary amines.
C.	Hofmann bromamide reaction	(iii)	Reaction of phthalimide with KOH and R—X
D.	Carbylamine reaction	(iv)	Reaction of alkylhalides with NH_3

Codes

	A	B	C	D
(a)	(iv)	(i)	(ii)	(iii)
(b)	(i)	(ii)	(iii)	(iv)
(c)	(iv)	(iii)	(i)	(ii)
(d)	(i)	(iv)	(ii)	(iii)

4. Give the name of any two naturally occurring amines.

5. Draw the structure of N-methylethanamine.

6. Write the IUPAC name of the following compound.

$$CH_3-\underset{\displaystyle NH_2}{\underset{|}{CH}}-CH_2-CHO$$

7. Write the IUPAC name of the following compound:

$$(CH_3)_2N-CH_2\,CH_3$$

8. Write the IUPAC name of the following compound:

$$(CH_3CH_2)_2\,NCH_3$$

9. Write the IUPAC name of the following compound:

$$NH_2CH_2-CH=CH_2$$

10. Write the IUPAC name of the following compound.

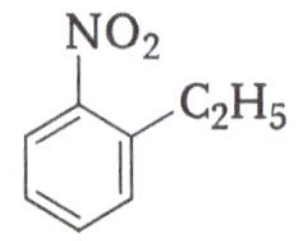

11. Write down the IUPAC name of

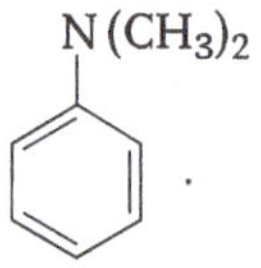

NCERT Exemplar

12. Draw the structure of prop-2-en-1-amine.

Or

Write the IUPAC name and structure of allyl amine.

13. Write the IUPAC name of the following compound:

$$CH_3-CH_2-CH_2-CH_2-N\begin{matrix}\diagup CH_3\\ \diagdown CH_3\end{matrix}$$

14. Write the main product of the following reaction:

$$CH_3-\underset{\displaystyle O}{\underset{||}{C}}-NH_2 \xrightarrow{Br_2\,+\,NaOH}$$

15. Convert benzoic acid to aniline.

16. How would you convert the following Methylamine to ethylamine

17. How will you convert the acetic anhydride to methylamine

18. What is the best reagent to convert nitrile to primary amine? **NCERT Exemplar**

19. Write the balanced chemical equation for the following reaction and also name the reaction:
Acetamide is heated with bromine and sodium hydroxide solution.

Or

Give one example of the following reaction.
Hofmann's degradation

Or

Name the following reaction and write balanced equation:
Acetamide with bromine in the presence of potassium hydroxide

Short Answer Type I Questions

(2 Marks)

20. Classify the following amines as primary, secondary or tertiary.

(i) 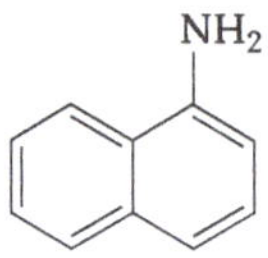 (ii) 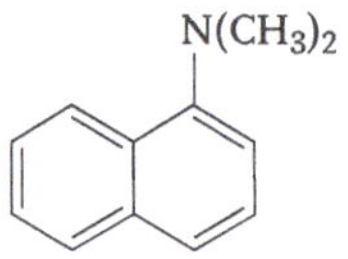

(iii) $(C_2H_5)_2CHNH_2$
(iv) $(C_2H_5)_2NH$ **NCERT Intext**

21. Write the IUPAC names of the following compounds and classify them into primary, secondary and tertiary amines. **NCERT**
(i) $(CH_3)_2CHNH_2$ (ii) $CH_3(CH_2)_2NH_2$

22. Write the IUPAC names of the following compounds and classify them into primary, secondary and tertiary amines.
(i) $C_6H_5NHCH_3$
(ii) $(CH_3CH_2)_2-N-CH_3$ **NCERT**

23. Write the IUPAC names of the following compounds and classify them into primary, secondary and tertiary amines.
(i) $CH_3NHCH(CH_3)_2$
(ii) $(CH_3)_3\,CNH_2$ **NCERT**

24. Give the structures of *A*, *B* and *C* in the following reaction.

$$CH_3CH_2I \xrightarrow{NaCN} A \xrightarrow[\text{Partial hydrolysis}]{OH^-} B \xrightarrow{NaOH + Br_2} C$$ **NCERT**

25. Give the structures A, B and C in the following reaction.

$$CH_3CN \xrightarrow{H_2O/H^+} A \xrightarrow[\Delta]{NH_3} B \xrightarrow{Br_2 + KOH} C$$

26. How will you convert the following?
(i) Nitrobenzene into aniline
(ii) Ethanoic acid into methanamine

27. How can the following conversion be brought about?
Nitrobenzene to 2, 4, 6-tribromoaniline. **ISC 2014**

28. How will you carry out the following conversion?
Acetamide to ethylamine **ISC 2003**

29. How will you carry out the following conversion? Write the balanced equation and name the reaction.
Acetamide to methylamine **ISC 2001, 2000**

30. Identify A and B in the following reaction.

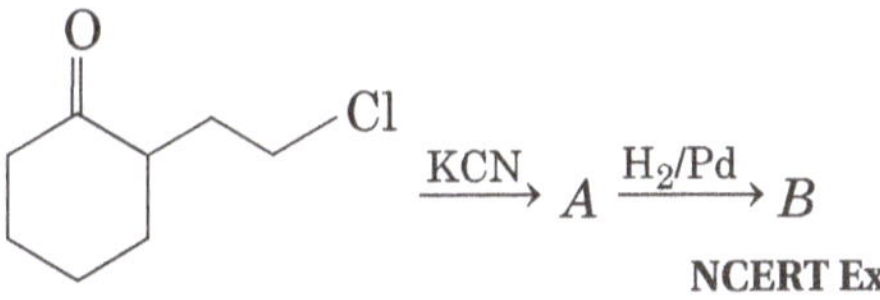

NCERT Exemplar

Short Answer Type II Questions

3 Marks

31. Identify the reagents, X, Y and Z

$$C_2H_5Cl \xrightarrow{X} C_2H_5CN \xrightarrow{Y}$$

$$C_2H_5CH_2NH_2 \xrightarrow{Z} C_2H_5CH_2NHCOCH_3$$

32. (i) Give the structures of different isomeric amines corresponding to the molecular formula, $C_4H_{11}N$.
(ii) Write the IUPAC names of all the isomers.
(iii) What type of isomerism is exhibited by different pairs of amines? **NCERT Intext**

33. In the reduction of nitro compounds, why Fe scrap and HCl is preferred over other metals?

34. Name the reagent used in the following reactions.

(i) $R—C \equiv N \xrightarrow{A} RCH_2NH_2$

(ii) 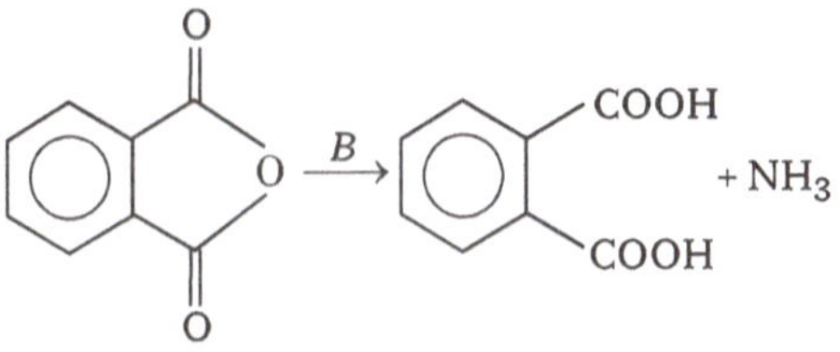

(iii) $C_6H_5NO_2 + 3H_2 \xrightarrow{C} C_6H_5NH_2 + 2H_2O$

35. Write short notes on the following.
(i) Hofmann bromamide reaction **ISC 2015**
(ii) Ammonolysis
(iii) Gabriel phthalimide synthesis
NCERT

36. How can the following conversion be brought about?
Ethylamine to methylamine **ISC 2010, 2000**

37. How can the following conversion be brought about? Benzene to acetanilide **ISC 2010**

38. Which type of reagents are good choice for reducing an aryl nitro compound to an amine?

Hints & Explanations

1. (i) methylamine, Hofmann's degradation
(ii) primary
(ii) Br_2, KOH

2. (i) b , (ii) d, (iii) c
(iv) (b)

3. (c) (A) → (iv), B → (iii), C → (i), D → (ii)

4. Alkaloids and proteins. (1)

5. $\overset{2}{C}H_3—\overset{1}{C}H_2—NH—CH_3$
N-methylethanamine (1)

6. $CH_3—CH(NH_2)—CH_2—CHO$

IUPAC name 3-amino-1-butanal or 3-aminobutanal (1)

7. Given compound, $H_3C—N(CH_3)—CH_2CH_3$

IUPAC name N, N-dimethyl ethanamine. (1)

8. Given compound is $H_3CH_2C—N(CH_3)—CH_2CH_3$

IUPAC name N-ethyl, N-methylethanamine. (1)

9. The IUPAC name for $NH_2CH_2—CH=CH_2$ is prop-2-en-1-amine. (1)

10.

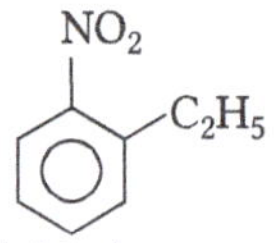

2-ethylnitrobenzene (1)

11. During naming of N-substituted amine, substituted group present at N is added as suffix N-alkyl in IUPAC nomenclature. (1)

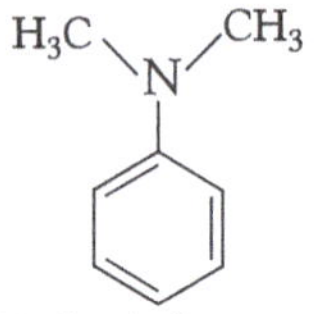

N, N-dimethylbenzenamine

12. $\overset{3}{C}H_2=\overset{2}{C}H—\overset{1}{C}H_2NH_2$
Prop-2-en-1-amine (1)

13. N, N-dimethylbutan-1-amine (1)

14. $CH_3—\underset{\underset{O}{\|}}{C}—NH_2 \xrightarrow[\text{Hofmann bromamide reaction}]{Br_2 + NaOH} CH_3NH_2$ (1)

$+ Na_2CO_3 + 2NaBr + 2H_2O$

15.

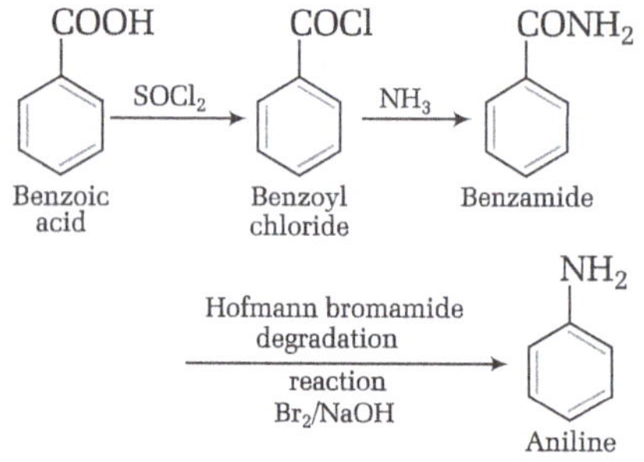

(1)

16. Methylamine to ethylamine

$\underset{\text{Methylamine}}{CH_3NH_2} \xrightarrow{HNO_2} CH_3OH \xrightarrow{PCl_5} CH_3Cl$

$\xrightarrow{NaCN} CH_3CN \xrightarrow{LiAlH_4} \underset{\text{Ethylamine}}{CH_3CH_2NH_2}$ (1)

17. Acetic anhydride to methylamine

$\underset{\text{Acetic anhydride}}{(CH_3CO)_2O} \xrightarrow[-CH_3COOH]{NH_3} \underset{\text{Ethanamide}}{CH_3—\overset{\overset{O}{\|}}{C}—NH_2}$

$\xrightarrow[\text{Hofmann bromamide reaction}]{Br_2 + KOH} \underset{\text{Methylamine}}{CH_3NH_2}$ (1)

18. The best reagent to reduce nitriles is sodium/alcohol or $LiAlH_4$ and the product of this reduction is primary amine. (1)

19. **Hofmann's degradation** Conversion of acetamide to methylamine by the action of bromine and potassium hydroxide.

$\underset{\text{Acetamide}}{CH_3CONH_2} + Br_2 + 4KOH \longrightarrow$

$\underset{\text{Methylamine}}{CH_3NH_2} + 2KBr + K_2CO_3 + 2H_2O$ (1)

20. (i) Primary (ii) Tertiary
(iii) Primary (iv) Secondary $\left(4 \times \frac{1}{2} = 2\right)$

21. (i) Propan-2-amine (1°) (ii) Propanamine (1°) (2)

22. (i) N-methylbenzenamine (2°)
(ii) N-ethyl-N-methylethanamine (3°) (2)

23. (i) N-methylpropan-2-amine (2°)
(ii) 2-methylpropan-2-amine (1°) (2)

24. $\underset{\text{Ethyl iodide}}{CH_3CH_2I} \xrightarrow{NaCN} \underset{\underset{A}{\text{Ethyl cyanide}}}{CH_3CH_2CN} \xrightarrow[\text{Partial hydrolysis}]{OH^-}$

$\underset{\underset{B}{\text{Propionamide}}}{CH_3CH_2CONH_2} \xrightarrow[\text{Hofmann bromamide degradation}]{NaOH + Br_2} \underset{\underset{C}{\text{Ethylamine}}}{CH_3CH_2NH_2}$ (2)

25. $CH_3CN \xrightarrow{H_2O/H^+} \underset{A}{CH_3COOH} \xrightarrow[\Delta]{NH_3}$

$\underset{B}{CH_3CONH_2} \xrightarrow[\text{Hofmann bromamide degradation}]{Br_2 + 4KOH} \underset{C}{CH_3NH_2}$ (2)

26. (i) **Nitrobenzene into aniline**

$\underset{\text{Nitrobenzene}}{C_6H_5NO_2} + 3H_2 \xrightarrow[\text{or Fe + HCl}]{Sn + HCl} \underset{\text{Aniline}}{C_6H_5NH_2} + 2H_2O$ (1)

(ii) **Ethanoic acid into methanamine**

$\underset{\text{Ethanoic acid}}{CH_3COOH} \xrightarrow{SOCl_2} \underset{\text{Ethanoyl chloride}}{CH_3COCl} \xrightarrow{NH_3(\text{excess})}$

$\underset{\text{Ethanamide}}{CH_3CONH_2} \xrightarrow[\text{(Hofmann bromamide reaction)}]{Br_2/KOH} \underset{\text{Methanamine}}{CH_3NH_2}$ (1)

27. Nitrobenzene to 2, 4, 6-tribromoaniline

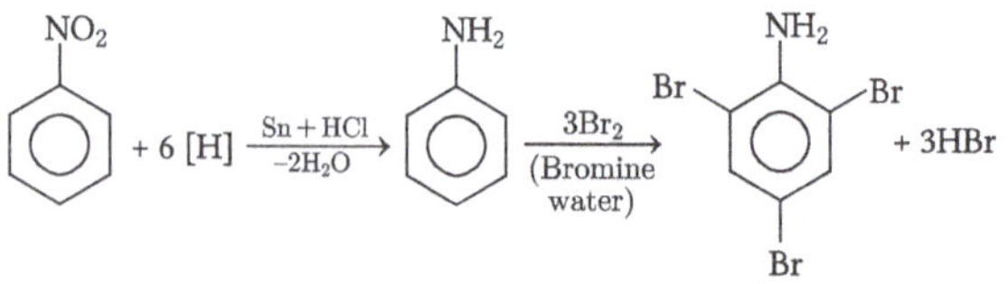

2, 4, 6-tribromoaniline (2)

28. Acetamide to ethylamine

$\underset{\text{Acetamide}}{CH_3—\overset{\overset{O}{\|}}{C}—NH_2} \xrightarrow[P_2O_5]{\Delta} \underset{\text{Mehyl cyanide}}{CH_3C\equiv N} + H_2O$

$\xrightarrow[LiAlH_4]{+4[H]} \underset{\text{Ethylamine}}{CH_3CH_2NH_2}$ (2)

29. Acetamide can be converted to methylamine by the reaction of acetamide with bromine in the presence of alkali solution. (½)

Reaction

$$CH_3CONH_2 + Br_2 + 4KOH \longrightarrow CH_3NH_2 + 2KBr + K_2CO_3 + 2H_2O \quad (1)$$

Name of the reaction is **Hofmann bromamide reaction.** (½)

30.

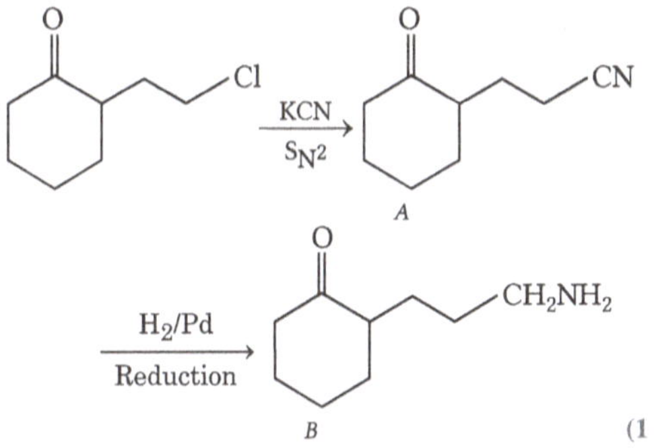

(1 × 2 = 2)

31. $C_2H_5Cl \xrightarrow[{[X]}]{KCN} C_2H_5CN \xrightarrow[{[Y]}]{Na/C_2H_5OH} C_2H_5CH_2NH_2 \xrightarrow[{[Z]}]{(CH_3CO)_2O} C_2H_5CH_2NHCOCH_3$

$X = KCN$, $Y = Na / C_2H_5OH$, $Z = (CH_3CO)_2O$ (3)

32. (i) and (ii) Eight isomers of $C_4H_{11}N$ are:

(a) $\overset{4}{C}H_3—\overset{3}{C}H_2—\overset{2}{C}H_2—\overset{1}{C}H_2—NH_2$
Butan-1-amine (Primary)

(b) $\overset{3}{C}H_3—\overset{2}{C}H(CH_3)—\overset{1}{C}H_2—NH_2$
2-methyl propan-1-amine (Primary)

(c) $\overset{4}{C}H_3—\overset{3}{C}H_2—\overset{2}{C}H(\overset{1}{C}H_3)—NH_2$
Butan-2-amine (Primary)

(d) $CH_3—\overset{2}{C}(\overset{1}{C}H_3)(\overset{3}{C}H_3)—NH_2$
2-methyl propan-2-amine (Primary)

(e) $C_2H_5—N(C_2H_5)—H$
N-ethyl ethanamine (Secondary)

(f) $C_3H_7—N(CH_3)—H$
N-methyl propan-1-amine (Secondary)

(g) $CH_3—CH(CH_3)—NH—CH_3$
N-methyl propan-2-amine (Secondary)

(h) $CH_3—N(C_2H_5)—CH_3$
N, N-dimethyl ethanamine (Tertiary) (2)

(iii) Isomerism exhibited by different amines are:

(a) **Chain isomers**, i.e. have different carbon chains, (a) and (b), (c) and (d) [as discussed in part (i) and (ii)]

(b) **Position isomers**, i.e. functional group occupy different positions, (b) and (c), (b) and (d), (a) and (d).

(c) **Metamers**, i.e. different alkyl groups are attached to the same functional group, (e) and (f), (g) and (e).

(d) **Functional isomers**, i.e. they have different functional groups. All the three categories (1°, 2° and 3°) of amines are the functional isomers of each other. (1)

33. Refer to text on pages 365 (By the reduction of nitro compounds).

34. (i) $LiAlH_4$ (1)

(ii) KOH (1)

(iii) Fe/HCl (1)

35. Refer to text on pages 364 and 365 (Preparation of amines).

36. (i) For conversion of Ethylamine to methylamine Following steps will be taken

$$\underset{\text{Ethylamine}}{CH_3CH_2 \cdot NH_2} \xrightarrow[-NH_2, -H_2O]{+HNO_2} \underset{\text{Ethanol}}{CH_3CH_2OH} \xrightarrow[\Delta]{Cu/573K} \underset{\text{Acetaldehyde}}{CH_3CHO} \xrightarrow[KMnO_4]{\text{Alkaline}} \underset{\text{Acetic acid}}{CH_3COOH} \xrightarrow{SOCl_2}$$

$$\underset{\text{Acetyl chloride}}{CH_3COCl} \xrightarrow[-H_2O]{NH_3/\Delta} \underset{\text{Acetamide}}{CH_3CONH_2}$$

$$\xrightarrow[\Delta \text{ (Hofmann bromamide reaction)}]{Br_2 + NaOH} \underset{\text{Methylamine}}{CH_3NH_2} + 2NaBr + Na_2CO_3 + 2H_2O$$
(3)

37. For conversion of benzene to acetanilide following steps will be taken

$$\underset{\text{Benzene}}{C_6H_6} \xrightarrow[-H_2O]{HNO_3/H_2SO_4} \underset{\text{Nitrobenzene}}{C_6N_5NO_2} \xrightarrow[(Sn + HCl), -2H_2O]{4[H]}$$

$$\underset{\text{Aniline}}{C_6H_5NH_2} \xrightarrow[-HCl]{CH_3COCl} \underset{\text{Acetanilide}}{C_6H_5NHCOCH_3}$$
(3)

38. Following reagent are good choice for reducing an aryl nitro compound to an amine.

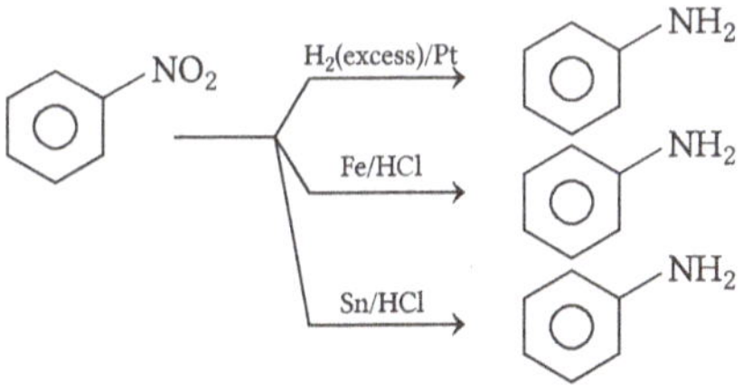

(3)

TOPIC 02 Properties of Aliphatic Amines and Aniline

Physical Properties

Physical properties of amines are as follows:

1. Colour and Odour

(i) Pure amines are colourless liquids but develop colour on keeping in air or on storage due to atmospheric oxidation.

(ii) The lower aliphatic amines are gases and smell like ammonia.

(iii) Primary amines with three or more carbon atoms are liquids with fishy odours and higher ones are solid. Aromatic amines are toxic in nature.

2. Solubility

(i) Lower aliphatic amines can form hydrogen bonds with water molecules and hence are soluble in water.

(ii) Solubility of amines decreases with increase in molar mass due to increase in the hydrophobic part which retard the formation of H-bonds and hence, higher amines containing six or more carbon atoms are insoluble in water.

(iii) Since, the electronegativity of nitrogen (3.0) is lower than oxygen (3.5), amines form weaker H-bond than alcohols and carboxylic acids.

3. Boiling Point

(i) Amines are polar and hence form intermolecular H-bonds and therefore, they have higher boiling points.

(ii) This intermolecular association depends upon the extent of H-bonding. 1° amines have two, 2° amines have one, while 3° amines have no hydrogen bonded to nitrogen.

(iii) Therefore, the order of boiling point of amines is 1° amines > 2° amines > 3° amines.

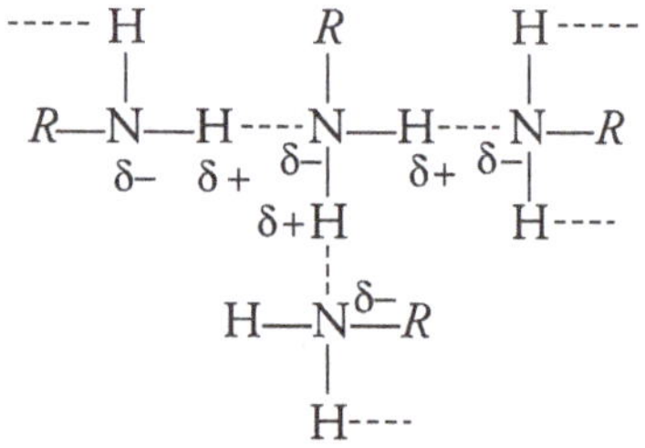

Intermolecular hydrogen bonding in primary amines

Since, the electronegativity of nitrogen is lower than oxygen, amines form weaker H-bond than alcohol. Thus, they have less boiling point than alcohols.

Boiling point of amines, alcohols and alkanes of almost the same molar mass are as shown below:

Comparison of boiling points of amines, alcohols and alkanes of almost similar molecular mass

S.No.	Compound	Molar mass	Boiling point/K
1.	n-$C_4H_9NH_2$	73	350.8
2.	$(C_2H_5)_2NH$	73	329.3
3.	$C_2H_5N(CH_3)_2$	73	310.5
4.	$C_2H_5CH(CH_3)_2$	72	300.8
5.	n-C_4H_9OH	74	390.3

Basic Character of Amines

Lone pair of electrons on N atom is responsible for the basic character of amines. Hence, they act as Lewis base.

Basic character of amines are described below:

Basic character of amine can be better understood in terms of their K_b and pK_b values as explained below:

$$R—\ddot{N}H_2 + H_2O \rightleftharpoons R—\overset{+}{N}H_3 + \overset{-}{O}H$$

$$K = \frac{[R—\overset{+}{N}H_3][\overset{-}{O}H]}{[R—NH_2][H_2O]}$$

$$\text{or} \quad K[H_2O] = \frac{[R—\overset{+}{N}H_3][\overset{-}{O}H]}{[R—NH_2]}$$

$$K_b = \frac{[R—\overset{+}{N}H_3][\overset{-}{O}H]}{[R—NH_2]}$$

$$pK_b = -\log K_b$$

Larger the value of K_b or smaller the value of pK_b, stronger is the base.

e.g. K_b p-toluidine (12.0×10^{-10}) > m-toluidine (5×10^{-10}) > aniline (4.2×10^{-10}) > o-toluidine (2.6×10^{-10})

pK_b $(CH_3)_2NH$ (3.27) > CH_3NH_2 (3.38) > $(CH_3)_3N$ (4.22)

pK_b values of amines in aqueous phase

Name of amine	pK_b
Methanamine	3.38
N-methylmethanamine	3.27
N,N-dimethylmethanamine	4.22
Ethanamine	3.29
N-ethylethanamine	3.00
N,N-diethylethanamine	3.25
Benzenamine	9.38
Phenylmethanamine	4.70
N-methylaniline	9.30
N,N-dimethylaniline	8.92

Comparison of Basic Strength of Alkyl Amines, Ammonia and Aniline (Basic Strength)

Aliphatic amines are stronger bases than ammonia due to $+I$-effect (electron-donating power) of alkyl groups ouring to which electron density on nitrogen atom increases and hence, they can easily donate their electrons. pK_b values of ammonia is 4.75 and pK_b values of aliphatic amine lies between the range 3 to 4.22.

Aliphatic amine **Ammonia**

$CH_3 \rightarrow NH_2$ (+ I-effect)

$H-\ddot{N}-H$ with H below N (no + I- effect)

On the other hand, aromatic amines (aniline) are weaker bases than ammonia due to electron withdrawing nature of aryl group.

Structure-Basicity Relationship of Amines

Basic character of amines depends upon the ease for the formation of cation by accepting a proton from acid. The more stable the cation is relative to the amine, more basic is the amine.

Alkanamine *versus* Ammonia

The reaction of an alkanamine and ammonia with a proton is used to compare their basicity.

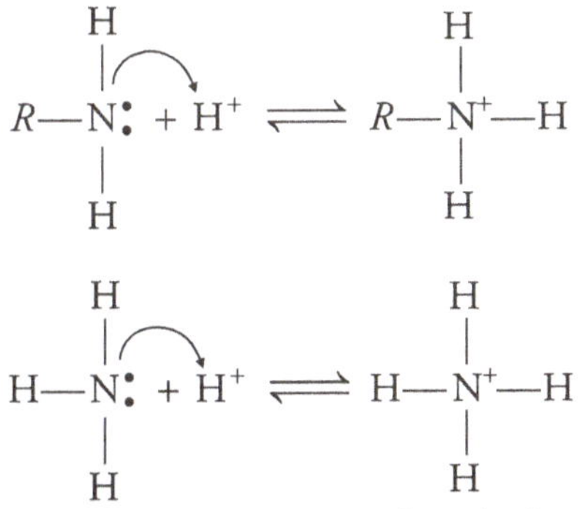

Ammonium ion

Due to electron releasing nature of alkyl group, it pushes electrons towards nitrogen and makes the unshared electron pair more available for sharing with the proton of the acid.

The substituted ammonium ion formed from the amine gets stabilised due to dispersal of the positive charge by the $+I$-effect of alkyl group.

Thus, basic nature of amine increases with increase in the number of alkyl group.

Order of basicity of amines in gaseous phase and aqueous phase are as follows:

Tertiary amine > Secondary amine > Primary amine > Ammonia

Ammonia < Tertiary amine < Primary amine < Secondary amine (due to steric effect)

Arylamines *versus* Ammonia

pK_b value of aniline is quite high due to the following reasons:

(i) As, NH_2 group is directly attached to benzene ring, the lone pair of electrons gets delocalised inside the benzene ring and thus, it is less available for protonation. Therefore, aromatic amines (aniline) are weaker bases than ammonia.

(ii) If we consider the resonating structures, then we know that greater the number of resonating structures, greater is the stability. Thus, more will be the basic character.

The resonating structures of aniline are as follows:

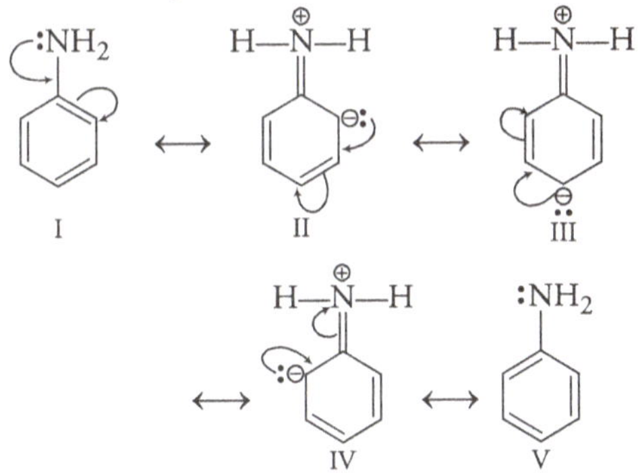

Resonating structures of aniline

In anilinium ion, there are two resonating structures, therefore, it is less stable than aniline (five resonating structures).

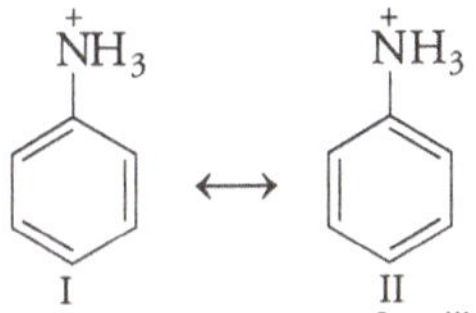

Resonating structures of anilinium ion

(iii) **Effect of substitueuts on the basic strength of aniline** In case of substituted aniline, electron releasing groups like $—CH_3$, $—OCH_3$, $—NH_2$ increase the basic strength whereas electron withdrawing groups like $—NO_2$, $—X$, $—COOH$ decrease the basic strength.

Chemical Reactions

Amines are very reactive due to the difference in electronegativity between nitrogen and hydrogen atoms and due to the presence of unshared pair of electrons over N-atom. The number of hydrogen atoms attached to the N-atom decides the course of reactions of amine, that is why, amines different differ in many reactions.

Some of the reactions of amines are described below:

1. Basic Nature

(i) **Action with water**

$$RNH_2 + H_2O \rightleftharpoons RNH_3 \cdot OH \rightleftharpoons [RNH_3]^+ + OH^-$$

$$R_2NH + H_2O \rightleftharpoons R_2NH_2 \cdot OH \rightleftharpoons [R_2NH_2]^+ + OH^-$$

$$R_3N + H_2O \rightleftharpoons R_3NH \cdot OH \rightleftharpoons [R_3NH]^+ + OH^-$$

(ii) **Action with acids** They form salts with acids.

$$C_2H_5NH_2 + HCl \longrightarrow \underset{\text{Ethylamine hydrochloride}}{[C_2H_5NH_3]^+Cl^-}$$

2. Alkylation

Amines undergo alkylation on reaction with alkyl halides.

$$\underset{\text{Ethylamine}}{CH_3CH_2NH_2} + \underset{\text{Ethyl bromide}}{CH_3CH_2Br} \longrightarrow \underset{\text{Diethylamine}}{(CH_3CH_2)_2NH} + HBr$$

$$\underset{\text{Diethylamine}}{(CH_3CH_2)_2NH} + \underset{\text{Ethyl bromide}}{CH_3CH_2Br} \longrightarrow \underset{\text{Triethyl amine}}{(CH_3CH_2)_3N} + HBr$$

$$\xrightarrow{CH_3CH_2Br} \underset{\text{Tetraethylammonium bromide}}{(CH_3CH_2)_4\overset{+}{N}Br^-}$$

Mechanism

$$CH_3CH_2\ddot{N}H_2 + CH_3—CH_2—Br \longrightarrow$$

$$(CH_3CH_2)_2\overset{+}{N}H_2\,Br^- \xrightarrow{\text{Base}} (CH_3CH_2)_2NH + HBr$$

The process of conversion of a 1° amines into quaternary ammonium salt is called Hofmann exhaustive alkylation.

3. Acylation

Aliphatic and aromatic primary and secondary amines react with acid chlorides, anhydrides and esters by nucleophilic substitution reaction.

This reaction is considered as replacement of hydrogen atom of $—NH_2$ or $>NH$ group by acyl group. This reaction is known as acylation.

The reaction is carried out in the presence of a base stronger than amine like pyridine, which removes HCl so formed and shifts the equilibrium towards right hand side. The product obtained by acylation reactions is known as amides.

Mechanism

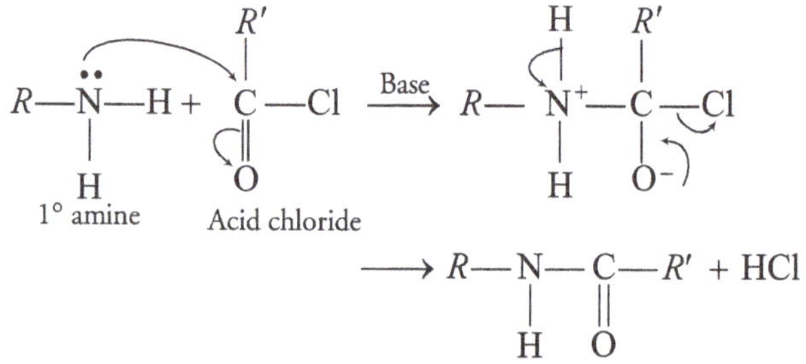

N-substituted amide

4. Benzoylation

The introduction of benzoyl group ($C_6H_5—\overset{O}{\overset{\|}{C}}—$) by the replacement of H-atom of amino group, in a molecule is called benzoylation.

$$\underset{\text{Methanamine}}{CH_3NH_2} + \underset{\text{Benzoyl chloride}}{C_6H_5COCl} \longrightarrow \underset{\text{N-methylbenzamide}}{CH_3NHCOC_6H_5} + HCl$$

Benzoylation of amines in the presence of NaOH is known as Schotten-Baumann reaction.

Note At room temperature, amines react with carboxylic acid to form corresponding salts.

5. Carbylamine Reaction (Isocyanide test)

Primary amines on heating with chloroform and ethanolic potassium hydroxide form isocyanides or carbylamines which have foul smell. This reaction is called carbylamine reaction or isocyanide test. These reactions are used to test primary amines. In general,

$$\underset{\text{Amine}}{R—NH_2} + \underset{\text{Chloroform}}{CHCl_3} + 3KOH \xrightarrow{\Delta} \underset{\text{Alkyl or aryl isocyanide}}{R—NC} + 3KCl + 3H_2O$$

$$\underset{\text{Methylamine}}{CH_3—NH_2} + CHCl_3 + 3KOH \xrightarrow{\Delta} \underset{\text{Methyl isocyanide}}{CH_3—NC} + 3KCl + 3H_2O$$

Secondary and tertiary amines (both aliphatic and aromatic) do not give this test. Hence, this test is used to distinguish 1° amine from 2° and 3° amines.

Distinction between Primary, Secondary and Tertiary Amines

	Tests	Primary amine	Secondary Amine	Tertiary amine
(i)	Action with nitrous acid ($NaNO_2$ + HCl)	N_2 is given out with the formation of alcohols. $R—NH_2 + HONO \longrightarrow R—OH + N_2 + H_2O$	Nitrosoamines are obtained which give Libermann's nitroso test $R_2NH + HONO \longrightarrow R_2N—N{=}O + H_2O$ Nitrosoamine	They remain dissolved forming amine nitrite salt which decomposes on warming to nitrosoamine and alcohol. $R_3N + HONO \longrightarrow R_3NHNO_2 \longrightarrow R_2N{\cdot}NO + R—OH$
(ii)	Carbylamine reaction (with $CHCl_3$ and alc. KOH)	Give foul smelling carbylamine $R—NH_2 + CHCl_3 + \underset{\text{alc.}}{3KOH} \longrightarrow \underset{\text{Carbylamine}}{RNC} + 3KCl + 3H_2O$	No reaction	No reaction
(iii)	Hinsberg's test (with benzene sulphonyl chloride)	N - alkyl benzene sulphoamide is obtained. It is soluble in alkali. 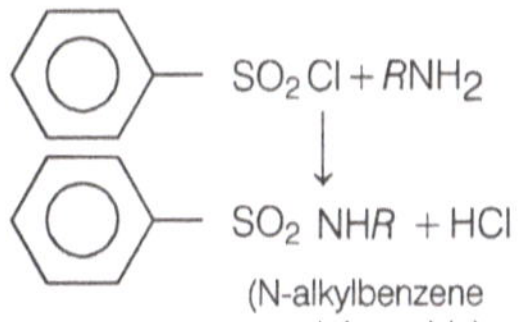 (N-alkylbenzene sulphoamide) (N- alkyl benzene sulphoamide) (soluble in alkali)	N, N-dialkylbenzene sulphoamide is obtained. It is insoluble in alkali 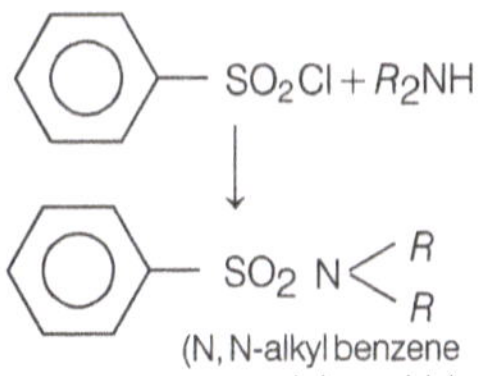 (N, N-alkyl benzene sulphoamide) (soluble in alkali)	No reaction

6. Reaction with Nitrous Acid

Primary, secondary and tertiary amines react differently with nitrous acid which is prepared in situ from a mineral acid and sodium nitrite.

(i) Primary Amines

When primary aliphatic amines react with nitrous acid, diazonium salts are formed which being unstable, liberate nitrogen gas quantitatively and alcohols.

Quantitative evolution of nitrogen is used in the estimation of amino acid and proteins.

$$R—NH_2 + HNO_2 \xrightarrow{NaNO_2 + HCl} \left[R—\overset{+}{N}_2\overset{-}{Cl}\right] \xrightarrow{H_2O} \underset{\text{Alcohols}}{R—OH} + N_2\uparrow + HCl$$

(ii) Secondary Amines

Secondary amines react with nitrous acid to form a yellow green oily layer of N-nitrosoamines.

Nitrosoamines warmed with phenol and conc. H_2SO_4 produced green colour solution which turms deep blue on adding alkali.

$$R_2NH + HONO \longrightarrow \underset{\text{Nitrosoamine}}{R_2N—N{=}O} + H_2O$$

It is a test for secondary amine. This reaction is also called Liebermann's nitrosoamine test.

(iii) Tertiary Amines

Tertiary amines readily dissolve in nitrous acid forming crystalline trialkyl ammonium nitrite.

$$R_3N + HNO_2 \longrightarrow \underset{\text{Trialkyl ammonium nitrite}}{R_3\overset{+}{N}HNO_2^-}$$

Reaction with Aryl Sulphonyl Chloride (Hinsberg's test)

(i) Primary amine when reacts with benzene sulphonyl chloride (Hinsberg's reagent), it yields N-ethylbenzene sulphonamide. Hydrogen atom attached to nitrogen is strongly acidic due to the presence of strong electron withdrawing sulphonyl group, hence, it is soluble in alkali.

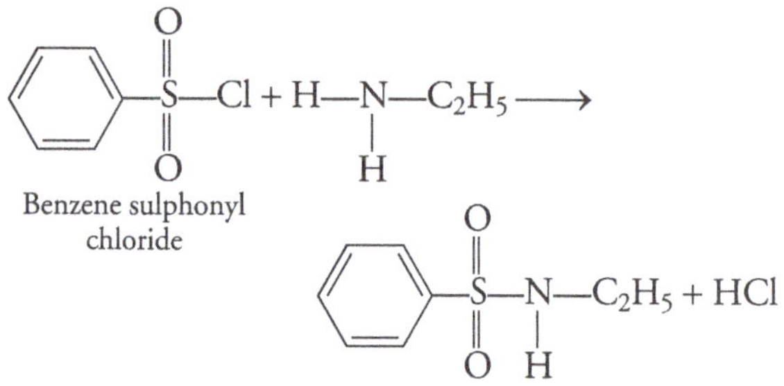

Benzene sulphonyl chloride

N-ethylbenzene sulphonamide (Soluble in alkali)

(ii) Secondary amine when reacts with benzene sulphonyl chloride, it yields N,N-diethylbenzene sulphonamide. Since, it does not have any H-atom attached to N-atom, it is not acidic and hence, insoluble in alkali.

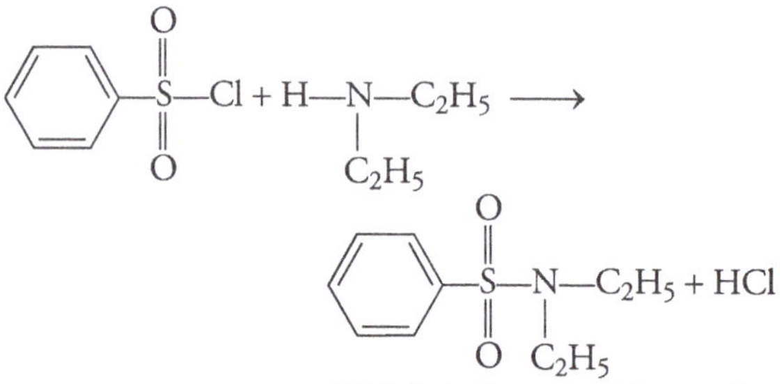

N,N-diethylbenzene sulphonamide (Insoluble in alkali)

(iii) Tertiary amines do not react with benzene sulphonyl chloride. This property of amine reacting with benzene sulphonyl chloride in a different way is used for the distinction of 1°, 2° and 3° amines and also for the separation of a mixture of amines. Now-a-days, benzene sulphonyl chloride is replaced by *p*-toluene sulphonyl chloride.

Uses of Amines

(i) Aliphatic amines are used as solvents and intermediates in the manufacture of drugs.

(ii) They are used as reagents in organic synthesis.

(iii) Aromatic amines are used in the formation of polymers, dyes and drugs.

Aniline [$C_6H_5NH_2$]

Preparation of Aniline

Aromatic nitro compounds can be reduced to corresponding aromatic amine, i.e. aniline by metal/acid reducing agent combination.

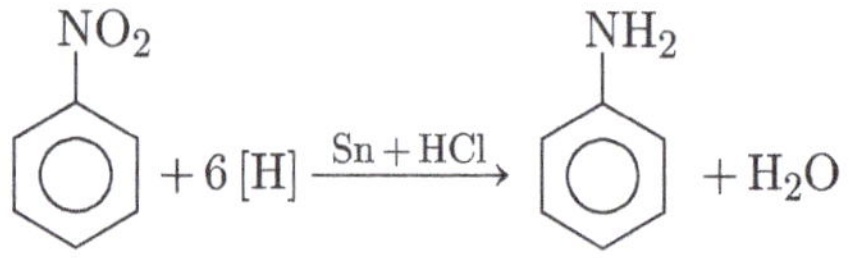

Nitrobenzene Aniline

Physical Properties of Aniline

(i) Pure aniline is a steam volatile colourless oily liquid but gets darken rapidly on exposure to air.

(ii) It is sparingly soluble in water but dissolves in organic solvent like alcohol, chloroform and ether.

(iii) It is highly toxic in nature.

(iv) It has a boiling point of 475 K.

Chemical Properties of Aniline

1. Basicity of Aromatic Amines (Aniline)

Aniline is weaker base than aliphatic amines and NH_3 because of the delocalisation of the lone pair of 'N' atom of amino group in the benzene ring which makes the electrons unavailable for proton atom.

Among aromatic amines, the order of basic strength is:

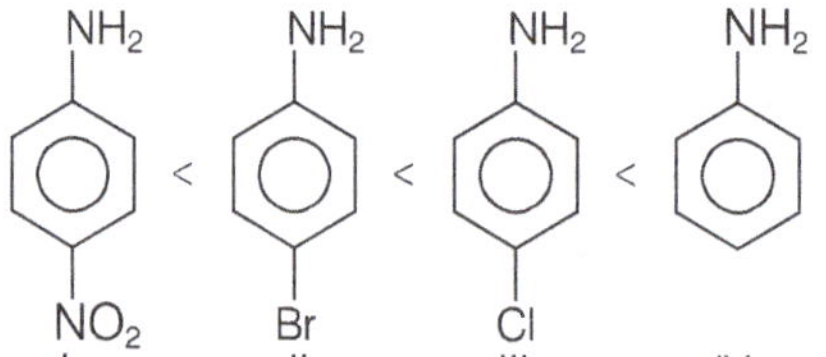

I II III IV

(Due to the presence of electron withdrawing group (—NO_2) on the aromatic ring, I shows minimum basic strength)

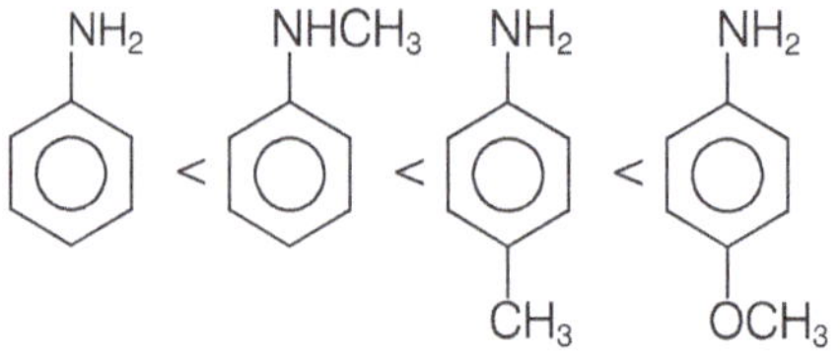

I II III IV

(Due to the presence of electron releasing group (—OCH_3) on aromatic ring, IV shows maximum basic strength)

o-substituted amines are usually weaker base than aniline due to *ortho* effect which is due to steric hinderance and electronic factors.

The base strengthening effect of $+I$-group and the base weakening effect of $-I$-group is more pronounced at *p*-position than at *m*-position. Thus, the basicity order is

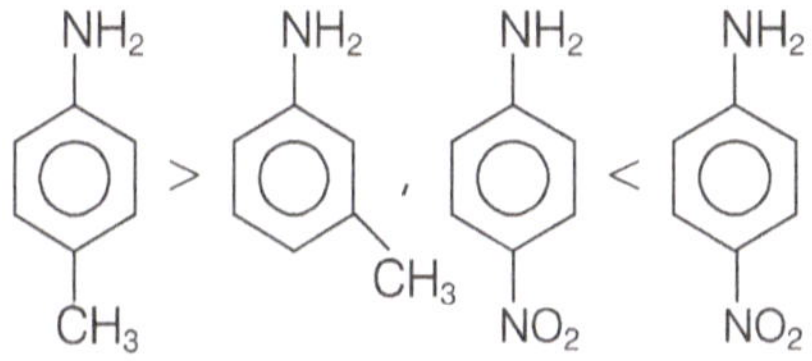

Note Aliphatic amines are more basic than aromatic amines because in aromatic amines, lone pair of electrons present on nitrogen takes part in resonance, hence not available for donation whereas in aliphatic amines, it is available.

The N-alkyl substituted arylamines are more basic than the corresponding parent alkylamines.

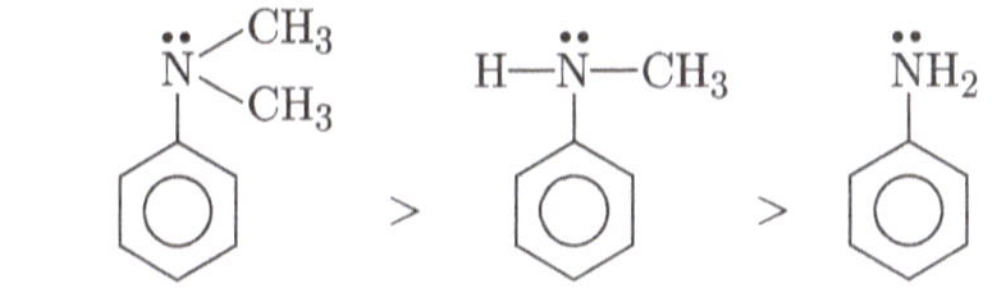

N, N-dimethylaniline   N-methylaniline   Aniline

N-aryl substituted arylamines are less basic than the corresponding arylamines, as more resonance occur in N-aryl substituted arylamines than arylamines.

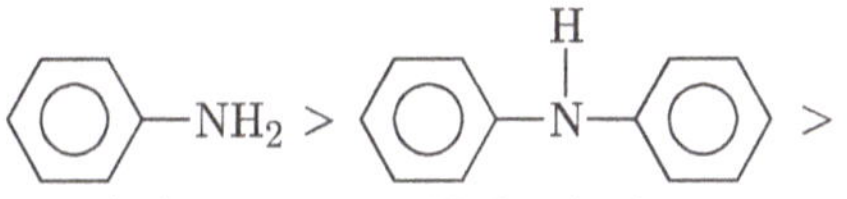

Aniline   N-phenylaniline

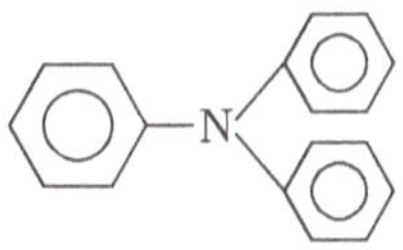

N, N-diphenylaniline

2. Reaction with HCl and H_2SO_4

(Basic Nature)

Aromatic amines form salt with acids. This shows their basic nature. However, these are less basic as compared to aliphatic amines due to delocalisation of electrons.

$$\underset{\text{Benzamine}}{C_6H_5NH_2} + HCl \longrightarrow \underset{\text{Anilinium chloride}}{C_6H_5NH_2 \cdot HCl}$$

$$\underset{\text{Benzamine}}{2C_6H_5NH_2} + H_2SO_4 \longrightarrow \underset{\text{Anilinium sulphate}}{(C_6H_5NH_2)_2 \cdot H_2SO_4}$$

3. Alkylation

Aromatic amines react with alkyl halides to give respective secondary and tertiary amines.

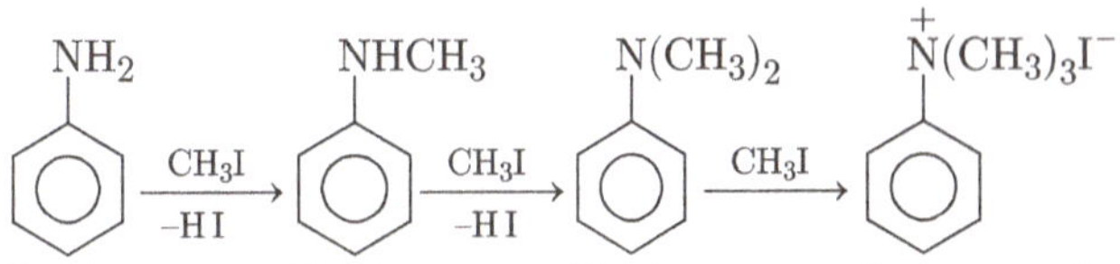

1° amine   2° amine   3° amine   Quaternary salt

4. Acetylation

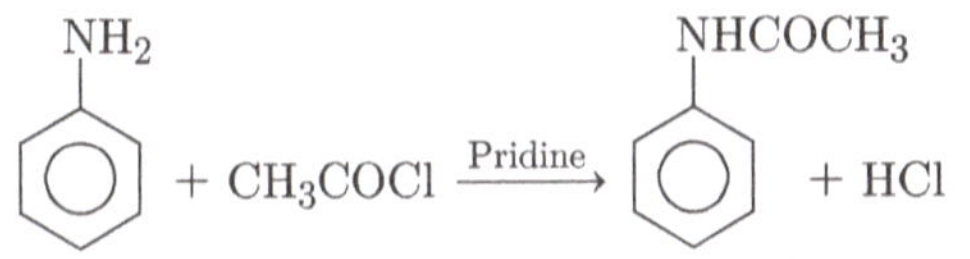

N-phenylacetamide

5. Benzoylation

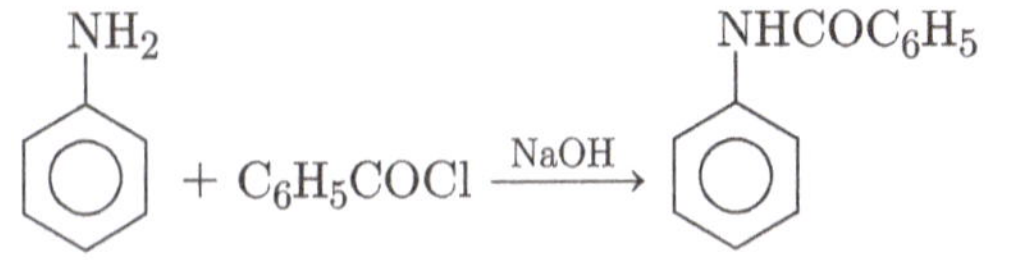

Benzamine   N-phenylbenzamide

6. Carbylamine Reaction

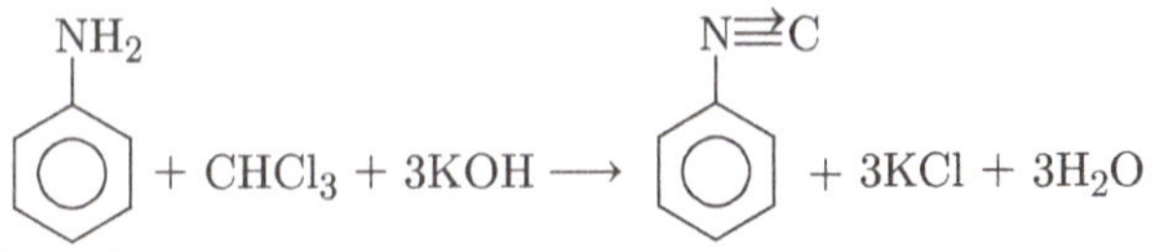

Benzamine   Phenyl isocyanide

7. Coupling Reaction (Diazotisation)

Aromatic amines with diazonium salt at low temperature form azo dyes (brilliant coloured azo compounds).

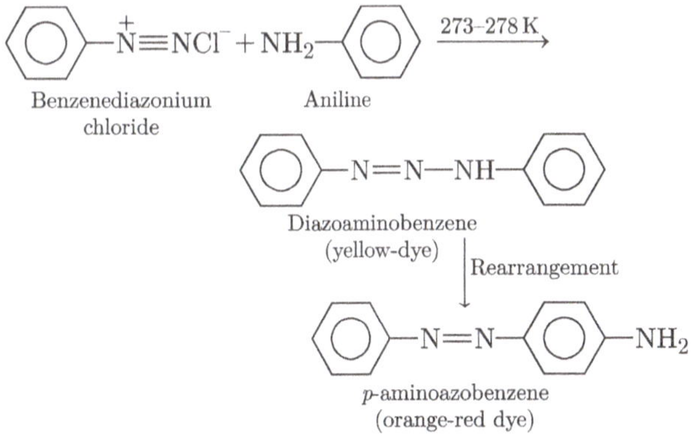

Note Diazonium salt can be prepared by reacting aniline with nitrous acid ($NaNO_2$ + HCl) at low temperatures (273-278K).

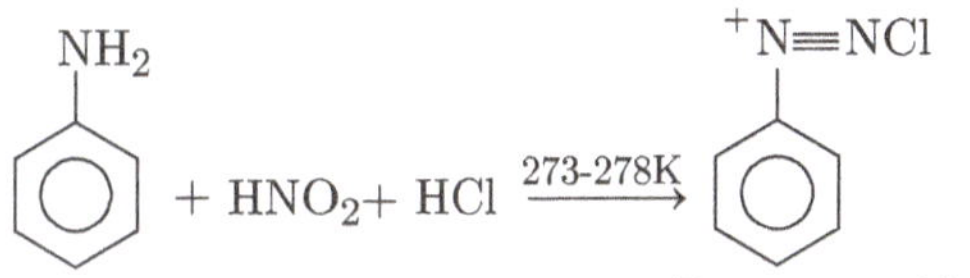

(Diazonium salt)

Electrophilic Substitution Reactions

In aniline, electron density at *ortho* and *para*-positions with respect to —NH_2 group is high. Therefore, this group is *ortho* or *para*-directing and a powerful activating group.

1. Halogenation (Bromination)

In the absence of catalyst, aniline on treatment with bromine water forms 2, 4, 6-tribromoaniline.

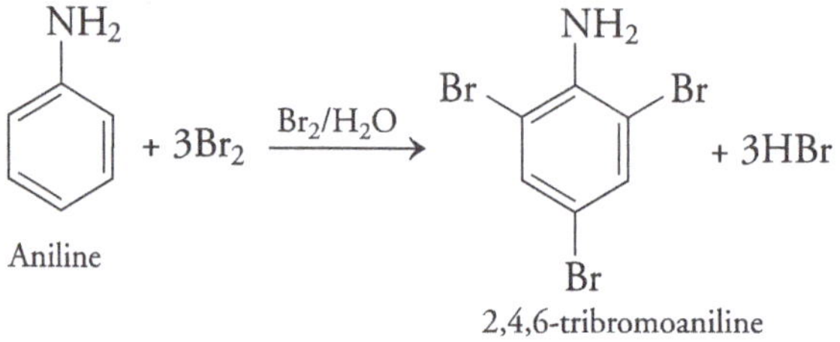

The main problem encountered during electrophilic substitution reaction of aromatic amine is that they have very high reactivity towards substitution at *ortho* and *para*-positions. In order to get monohalogenated derivative, the activating effect of —NH_2 group was controlled by acetylation with acetic anhydride and then halogenation is carried out. After halogenation, the acetyl group is removed by hydrolysis.

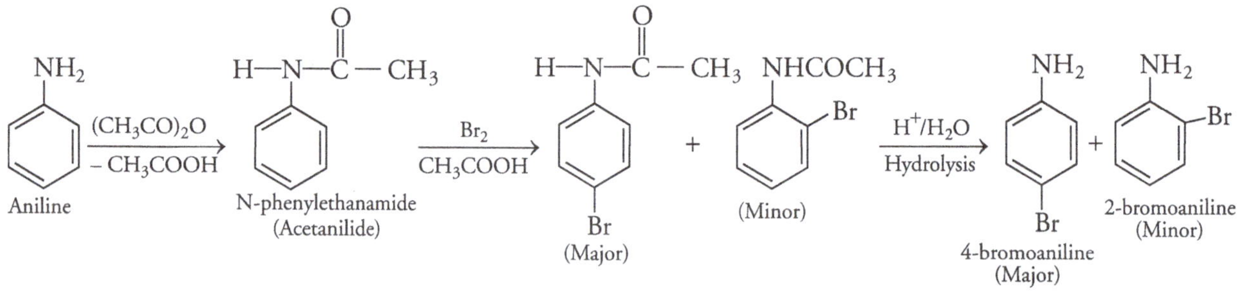

The lone pair of electrons on nitrogen of acetanilide interacts with oxygen atom due to resonance as shown below:

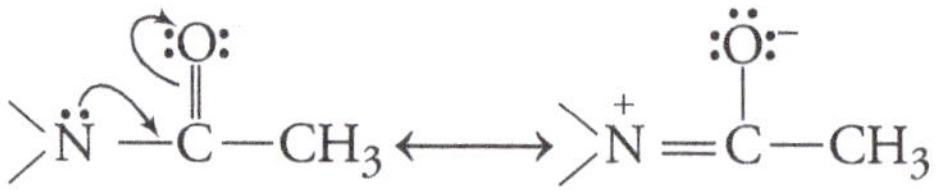

Hence, the lone pair of electrons on nitrogen is less available for donation to benzene ring by resonance, therefore activating effect of $>NHCOCH_3$ group is less than that of amine group.

2. Nitration

In strongly acidic medium, aniline on nitration gives a mixture of *ortho*, *para* and significant amount of *meta*-nitroaniline. Aniline is protonated to form anilinium ion which is a *m*-directing group under strongly acidic medium.

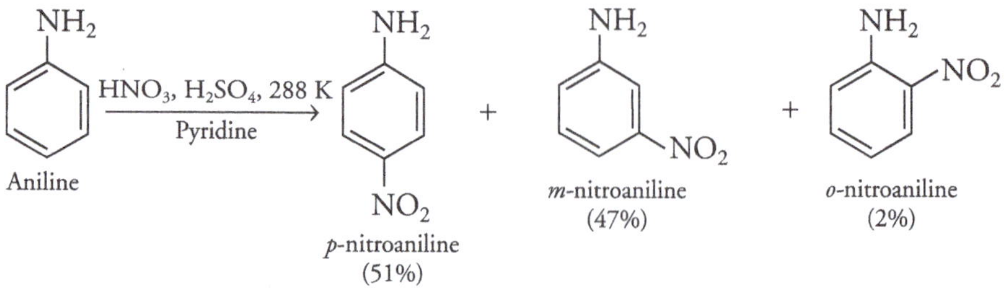

By protecting the $—NH_2$ group by acetylation with acetic anhydride, the reaction can be controlled and only *p*-nitro derivative as the major product is obtained.

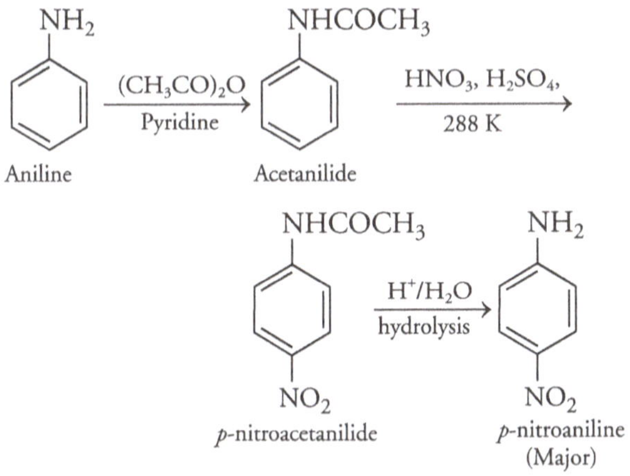

3. Sulphonation

Aniline when react with concentrated H_2SO_4, it forms anilinium hydrogen sulphate which on heating with H_2SO_4 at 455-475 K forms *p*-aminobenzene sulphonic acid (sulphanilic acid).

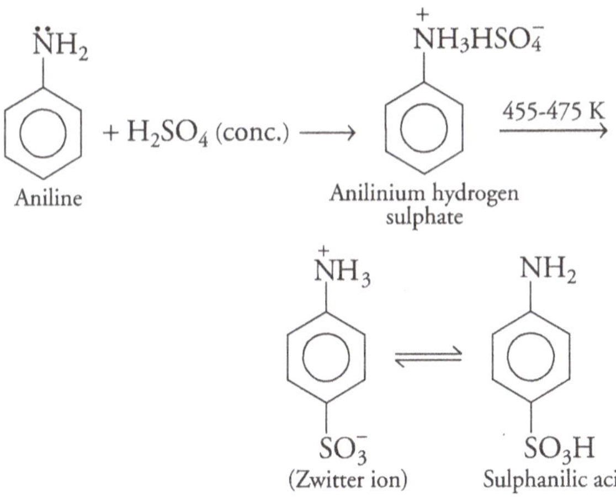

Note Aniline does not undergo Friedel-Crafts reaction (alkylation and acetylation) due to salt formation with anhydrous $AlCl_3$, the Lewis acid, which is used as a catalyst. As a result, nitrogen of aniline acquires positive charge and hence acts as a strong deactivating group for further reaction.

Zwitter ion The ion which contains both positive and negative charges and also contains acidic and basic groups in the same molecule is known as Zwitter ion. e.g.

Structure of Zwitter ion

Tests for Aniline

1. Nitrous Acid Test

Aromatic primary amines also react with nitrous acid $HNO_2(NaNO_2 + HCl)$ but at low temperatures.

$$C_6H_5—NH_2 \xrightarrow[273\text{-}278\ K]{NaNO_2 + 2HCl} C_6H_5—N_2^+\bar{C}l + NaCl + 2H_2O$$

Secondary and tertiary aromatic amines also react with nitrous acid in different manner.

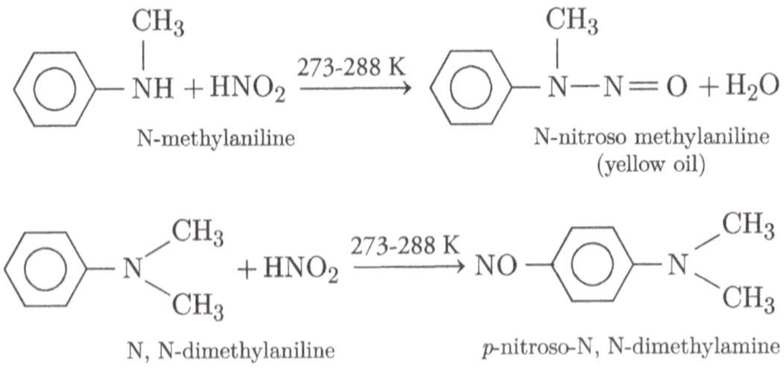

2. Azo Dye Test

This test is used to distinguish aromatic primary (1°) amines from aliphatic 1° amines. Aniline on treatment with HNO_2 $(NaNO_2 + dil. HCl)$ followed by the treatment with alkaline solution of β-naphthol forms an orange or red dye.

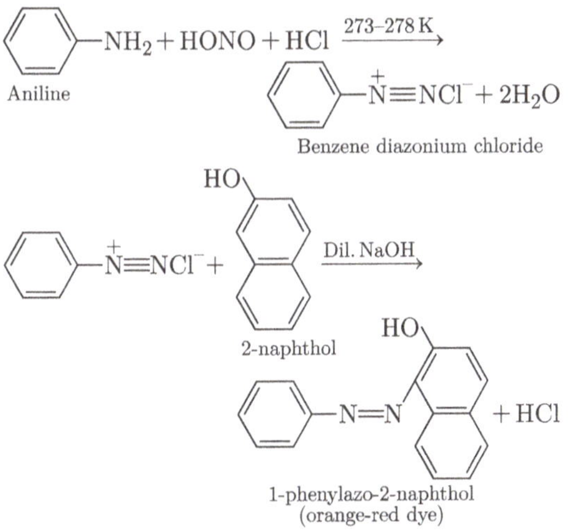

Aliphatic amines, i.e. ethylamine does not form dye. It gives brisk effervescence due to evolution of N_2.

Uses of Aniline

(i) It is used in the preparation of benzenediazonium chloride.

(ii) It is used in the preparation of Schiff's bases, sulpha drugs.

(iii) It is used as solvent in rubber industry.

Topic Practice 2

Very Short Answer Type Questions

1 Mark

1. Fill in the Blanks.

(i) methylamine is more .... than ammonia because of .... effect. **ISC 2002**

(ii) basicity of aniline is .... than that of ammonia because of ...... **ISC 2002**

(iii) Primary amines on reaction with nitrous acid form ....

2. Objective Type Questions

(i) The product formed when aniline is warmed with chloroform and caustic potash is **ISC 2010**

(a) Phenyl chloride (b) methyl isocyanide
(c) Phenyl isocyanide (d) Nitro phenol

(ii) An example of an electrophile is **ISC 2009, 2003**

(a) NO_2^+ (b) NO_2^- (c) NO_2 (d) NO_3^-

(iii) On heating an aliphatic primary amine with chloroform and alcoholic potassium hydroxide, the organic compound formed is an **ISC 2020**

(a) alkyl isocyanide
(b) alkanol
(c) alkanal
(d) alkyl cyanide

(iv) Which of the following compound will not undergo azo coupling reaction with benzene diazonium chloride?

(a) Aniline
(b) Phenol
(c) Anisole
(d) Nitrobenzene

(v) Which of the following is the weakest Bronsted base?

(a) 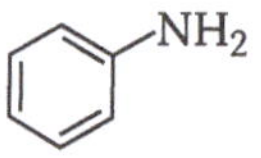

(b) 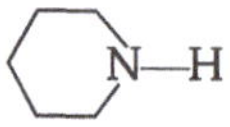

(c) 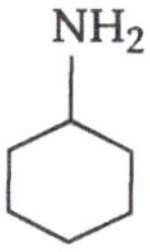

(d) CH_3NH_2

(vi) The reaction of a primary amine with chloroform and ethanolic KOH is called **ISC 2023**

(a) Carbylamine reaction
(b) Kolbe's reaction
(c) Reimer- Tiemann reaction
(d) Wurtz- Fittig reaction

3. Match the following Columns and choose the correct option using the codes given below.

(A)	Carbylamine	(i)	Benzene sulphonyl chloride
(B)	Hinsberg's reagent	(ii)	Obnoxious smell
(C)	Conversion of amide to amine	(iii)	Secondary amines
(D)	Libermann's nitroso test	(iv)	Hofmann-bromamide reaction

Coder

	A	B	C	D
(a)	(i)	(ii)	(iv)	(iii)
(b)	(i)	(ii)	(iii)	(iv)
(c)	(ii)	(i)	(iv)	(iii)
(d)	(ii)	(i)	(iv)	(iii)

4. Arrange the following compounds in the increasing order of basic strength.

$C_6H_5NH_2, C_6H_5NHCH_3, C_6H_5CH_2NH_2$

5. In the following reaction, which species behave as a Lewis base?

$$R—\ddot{N}H_2 + H—X \rightleftharpoons R—\overset{+}{N}H_3X^-$$

6. What is the role of pyridine in the acylation reaction of amines? **NCERT Exemplar**

7. Complete the following reaction

$CH_3CH_2NH_2 + CHCl_3 + \text{alc. } 3KOH \longrightarrow$ **All India 2013**

Or

Give the balanced equation for carbylamine reaction. **ISC 2016**

Or

Explain the following with at least one example Carbylamine reaction **ISC 2000**

8. How will you convert the following? Aniline into N-phenylethanamide (write the chemical equations involved)

9. Complete the following reaction.

$C_6H_5NH_2 + H_2SO_4$ (conc.) $\longrightarrow$ **NCERT**

10. Give the balanced equation for the following reaction Aniline is treated with benzoyl chloride. **ISC 2000**

11. How will you distinguish between primary, secondary and tertiary amines by Hinsberg's test? **ISC 2017**

12. Give the chemical test to distinguish between the following pair of compounds, ethylamine and dimethylamine.

Short Answer Type I Questions

2 Marks

13. State one reason for each of the following.
    (i) Alkylamine is soluble in water, whereas arylamine is insoluble in water.
    (ii) Methylamine is a stronger base than methyl alcohol. **ISC 2023**

14. Give reasons for the following.
    (i) pK_b of aniline is more than that of methylamine.
    (ii) Ethylamine is soluble in water whereas aniline is not. **ISc 2020 NCERT**

15. Give reason. Direct nitration of aniline is not possible **ISC 2007**

16. Complete the following acid-base reactions and name the products.
    (i) $CH_3—CH_2—CH_2—NH_2 + HCl \longrightarrow$
    (ii) $(C_2H_5)_3N + HCl \longrightarrow$ **NCERT Intext**

17. Why is NH_2 group of aniline acetylated before carrying out nitration? **NCERT Exemplar**

18. Write the chemical reaction of aniline with benzoyl-chloride and also write the name of the product obtained. **NCERT Intext**

19. Write shortnotes on the following
    (i) Acylation (ii) Carbylamine reaction **NCERT**

20. Give the balanced equations for following reactions.
    (i) Ethylamine with nitrous acid
    (ii) Aniline with acetyl chloride **ISC 2016**

21. Complete the following reactions.
    (i) $C_6H_5NH_2 + CHCl_3 + \text{alc. } 3KOH \longrightarrow$
    (ii) $C_6H_5NO_2 \xrightarrow{Fe/HCl} A \xrightarrow[273\text{ K}]{HNO_2} B$ **NCERT**

22. Give the balanced equations for following reactions
    (i) How will you convert ethylamine to methylamine?
    (ii) Aniline is treated with nitrous acid and HCl at low temperature **ISC 2016**

23. How will you convert
    (i) Nitromethane into dimethylamine?
    (ii) Propanoic acid into ethanoic acid? **NCERT**

24. Suggest a route by which the following conversion can be accomplished.

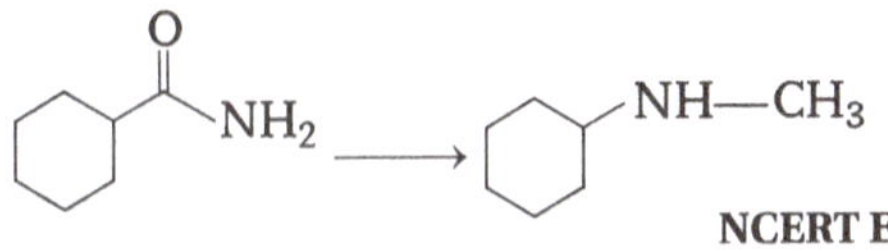

NCERT Exemplar

25. Account for the following.
    (i) Methylamine in water reacts with ferric chloride to precipitate hydrated ferric oxide.
    (ii) Aniline does not undergo Friedel-Crafts reaction. **NCERT**

26. Illustrate the following reactions by giving one suitable example in each case.
    (i) Coupling reaction
    (ii) Acetylation of ethylamine **ISC 2024**

27. Complete the following reactions.
    (i) $C_6H_5NH_2 + 3Br_2(aq) \longrightarrow$
    (ii) $C_6H_5NH_2 + (CH_3CO)_2O \longrightarrow$ **NCERT**

28. Complete and balance the following equations :
    (i) $C_6H_5NH_2 + CH_3COCl \longrightarrow ... + ...$
    (ii) $C_2H_5NH_2 + HNO_2 \longrightarrow ... + ... + ...$ **ISC 2020**

29. Give one chemical test to distinguish between the following pairs of compounds.
    (i) Aniline and benzylamine
    (ii) Aniline and N-methyl aniline **NCERT**

30. Give the chemical test to distinguish between the following pair of compounds
    Aniline and ethylamine **ISC 2014**

31. Give one good chemical test to distinguish between the following pair of organic compounds
    Methyl amine and dimethyl amine **ISC 2011**

32. Draw the structures of different isomers corresponding to the molecular formula, C_3H_9N. Write the IUPAC names of the isomers which will liberate nitrogen gas on treatment with nitrous acid. **NCERT Intext**

Short Answer Type II Questions

3 Marks

33. Account for the following:
    (i) Primary amines ($R—NH_2$) have higher boiling point than tertiary amines (R_3N).
    (ii) $(CH_3)_2NH$ is more basic than $(CH_3)_3N$ in an aqueous solution.

34. Arrange the following.

(i) in the decreasing order of basic strength in gas phase
$C_2H_5NH_2, (C_2H_5)_2NH, (C_2H_5)_3N$ and NH_3.

(ii) in the increasing order of boiling point
$C_2H_5OH, (CH_3)_2NH, C_2H_5NH_2$. **NCERT**

(iii) in the increasing order of solubility in water
$C_6H_5NH_2, (C_2H_5)_2NH, C_2H_5NH_2$.

35. Arrange the following compounds in the ascending order of their basic strength and give reasons for your answer
Methylamine, Aniline, Ethylamine, Diethyl ether **ISC 2015**

36. Arrange the following:

(i) in the decreasing order of pK_b values
$C_2H_5NH_2, C_6H_5NHCH_3, (C_2H_5)_2NH$ and $C_6H_5NH_2$.

(ii) in the increasing order of basic strength
$C_6H_5NH_2, C_6H_5N(CH_3)_2, (C_2H_5)_2NH$ and CH_3NH_2.

(iii) In the increasing order of basic strength.

(a) Aniline, *p*-nitroaniline and *p*-toluidine

(b) $C_6H_5NH_2, C_6H_5NHCH_3, C_6H_5CH_2NH_2$ **NCERT**

37. Arrange the following in the increasing order of their basic strength.

(i) $C_2H_5NH_2, C_6H_5NH_2, NH_3, C_6H_5CH_2NH_2$ and $(C_2H_5)_2NH$

(ii) $C_2H_5NH_2, (C_2H_5)_2NH, (C_2H_5)_3N, C_6H_5NH_2$

(iii) $CH_3NH_2, (CH_3)_2NH, (CH_3)_3N, C_6H_5NH_2, C_6H_5CH_2NH_2$ **NCERT Intext**

38. Give reasons for the following:

(i) Aniline does not undergo Friedel-Crafts reaction. **ISC 2024**

(ii) $(CH_3)_2NH$ is more basic than $(CH_3)_3N$ in an aqueous solution.

(iii) Primary amines have higher boiling point than tertiary amines.

39. Account for the following:

(i) Although, amino group is *o*-and *p*-directing in aromatic electrophilic substitution reactions, aniline on nitration gives a substantial amount of *m*-nitroaniline.

(ii) Gabriel phthalimide synthesis is preferred for synthesising primary amines. **NCERT**

40. Give reasons for the following:

(i) Acetylation of aniline reduces its activation effect.

(ii) CH_3NH_2 is more basic than $C_6H_5NH_2$.

(iii) Although $—NH_2$ is *o*/*p*-directing group, yet aniline on nitration gives a significant amount of *m*-nitroaniline.

41. How will you convert:

(i) ethanamine into methanamine?

(ii) ethanoic acid into propanoic acid?

(iii) methanamine into ethanamine? **NCERT**

42. How will you convert

(i) ethanoic acid into methanamine?

(ii) hexane nitrile into 1-aminopentane?

(iii) methanol into ethanoic acid? **NCERT**

43. Give the structures of *A*, *B* and *C* in the following reactions.

(i) $CH_3CH_2Br \xrightarrow{KCN} A \xrightarrow{LiAlH_4} B \xrightarrow[0°C]{HNO_2} C$

(ii) $CH_3COOH \xrightarrow[\Delta]{NH_3} A \xrightarrow{NaOBr} B \xrightarrow{NaNO_2 / HCl} C$

NCERT

44. Write the reactions of

(i) aromatic and

(ii) aliphatic primary amines with nitrous acid. **NCERT**

45. Write the main products of the following reactions.

(i) $CH_3CH_2NH_2 \xrightarrow[(0°C)]{HNO_2}$

(ii) 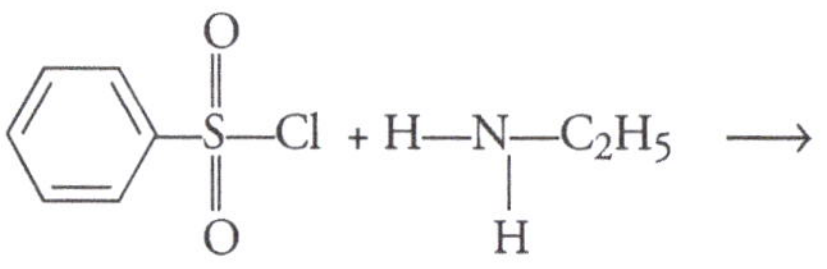

(iii) 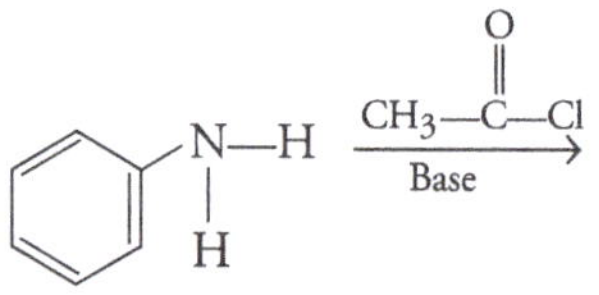

NCERT

46. Accomplish the following conversions.

(i) Benzyl chloride to 2-phenylethanamine

(ii) Chlorobenzene to *p*-chloroaniline **NCERT**

47. How can the following conversions be brought about:

(i) Acetic acid to methylamine.

(ii) Aniline to benzene. **ISC 2017**

48. Give two test to distinguish between aniline and dimethyl aniline. **ISC 2003**

49. How will you distinguish between the following pair of compounds?
Give one chemical test.
Ethylamine and acetamide. **ISC 2009**

Long Answer Type Questions

(5 Marks)

50. (i) Write the structure of main products when aniline reacts with the following reagents :
(a) Br_2 water **ISC 2019**
(b) HCl
(c) $(CH_3CO)_2O$/pyridine

(ii) Arrange the following in the increasing order of their boiling point :
$C_2H_5NH_2$, C_2H_5OH, $(CH_3)_3N$

(iii) Give a simple chemical test to distinguish between the following pair of compounds $(CH_3)_2NH$ and $(CH_3)_3N$

51. Write the balanced equations of the following reactions
(i) Aniline and bromine water
(ii) Ethylamine and nitrous acid
(iii) Acetic anhydride and ammonia **ISC 2008**

52. How can primary, secondary and tertiary aliphatic amines be distinguished by reaction with HNO_2 ($NaNO_2$ +)? **ISC 2000**

Hints & Explanations

1. (i) Basic, inductive $(+I)$
(ii) Less, resonance
(iii) Primary alcohols

2. (i) (c) (ii) (a)
(iii) (a)
(iv) (d) (v) (a) (vi) (a)

3. (d) A-(ii), B-(i), C-(iv), D-(iii)

4. Increasing order of basic strength

$$C_6H_5NH_2 < C_6H_5NHCH_3 < C_6H_5CH_2NH_2$$ (1)

5. Primary amine (1)

6. Pyridine being a base, is used to remove the side product, i.e. HCl from reaction mixture.

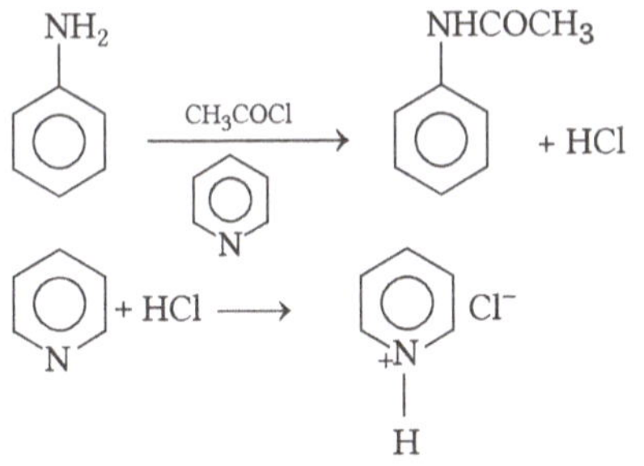

(1)

7. **Carbylamine reaction** When primary amines are treated with alcoholic KOH and chloroform, corresponding carbylamine is formed, e.g. methylamine gives methyl carbylamine.

e.g. $\underset{\text{Methylamine}}{CH_3NH_2} + 3\,KOH + CHCl_3 \longrightarrow \underset{\text{Methyl carbylamine}}{CH_3NC} + 3KCl + 3H_2O$ (1)

8.

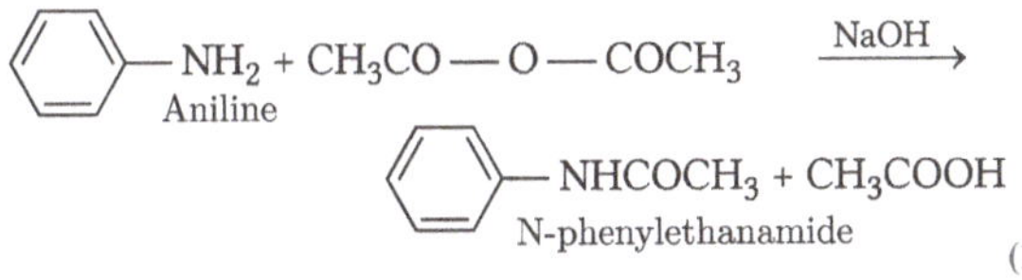

(1)

9. $C_6H_5NH_2 + H_2SO_4(\text{Conc.}) \longrightarrow C_6H_5\overset{+}{N}H_3HSO_4^- \xrightarrow{455-475K} \underset{p\text{-isomer (major product)}}{C_6H_5NH_2SO_3H}$ (1)

10.

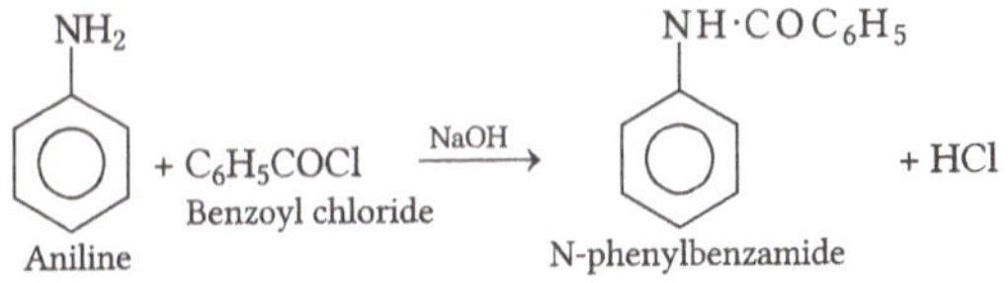

(1)

11. Refer to test on page 374 (Reaction with Aryl sulphonyl chloride, Hinsberg reagent) (1)

12. Ethylamine gives carbylamine test, i.e. on treatment with alcoholic KOH and chloroform, followed by heating, it gives offensive odour of ethyl isocyanide. Dimethylamine does not give this test.

$$C_2H_5NH_2 + CHCl + 3KOH \xrightarrow{\Delta} C_2H_5NC + 3KCl + 3H_2O$$ (1)

13. (i) Alkylamine is soluble in water because it forms hydrogen bonds (intermolecular) with water.
On the other hand, arylamine is insoluble because of presence of benzene, i.e. hydrophobic. Thus, not soluble in water.

(ii) In methylamine ($MeNH_2$), nitrogen is less electronegative than oxygen in methyl alcohol. So, methylamines can easily donate a lone pair of electrons to a proton of an acid.

14. (i) In aniline, the electron pair on nitrogen atom is involved in conjugation with ring and is less available for protonation than that in methylamine. Therefore, pK_b value of aniline is more than that of methylamine and thus aniline is less basic (as higher the pK_b value, weaker is the base). (1)

(ii) Ethylamine is soluble in water due to hydrogen bonding.

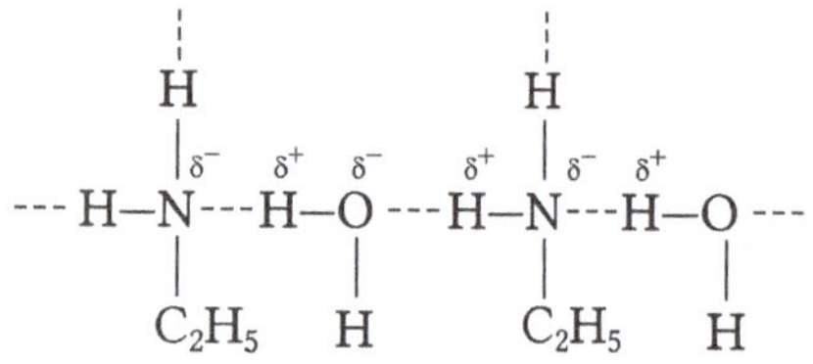

In aniline, due to bulky hydrocarbon part, the extent of hydrogen bonding is less and it is not soluble in water. (1)

15. Direct nitration of aniline gives oxidation products alongwith some nitro derivatives because HNO_3 is a strong oxidising agent therefore, direct nitration is not possible. (2)

16. (i) $CH_3—CH_2—CH_2—\ddot{N}H_2 + H—Cl \longrightarrow$ (*n*-propylamine)

$CH_3—CH_2—CH_2—\overset{+}{N}H_3\overset{-}{Cl}$ (*n*-propyl ammonium chloride) (1)

(ii) $(C_2H_5)_3\ddot{N} + H—Cl \longrightarrow (C_2H_5)_3\overset{+}{N}HCl^-$

Triethylamine → Triethylammonium chloride (1)

17. As HNO_3 is a strong oxidising agent, direct nitration of aniline gives oxidation products alongwith some nitro derivatives. Thus, NH_2 group of aniline is acetylated before carrying out nitration.
For reaction, refer to text on pages 376 and 377 (Nitration). (2)

18. The entire reaction sequence can be written as :

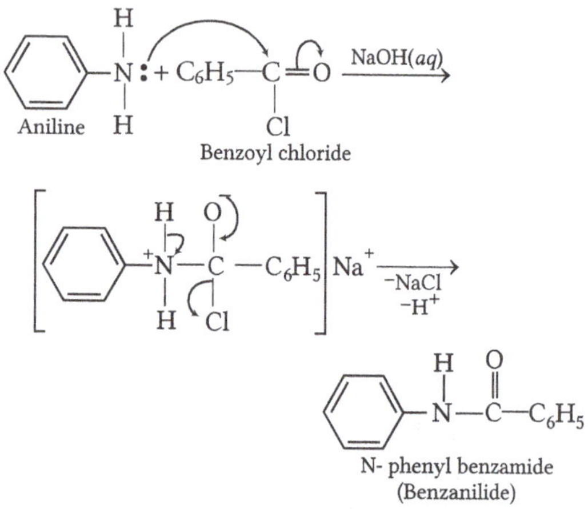

(2)

19. Refer to text on pages 372 and 373 (Chemical reactions). (2)

20. (i) $CH_3CH_2NH_2 + HNO_2 \longrightarrow$ (Ethylamine)

$CH_3CH_2OH + H_2O + N_2\uparrow$ (Ethylalcohol) (1)

(ii) $C_6H_5NH_2 + CH_3COCl \longrightarrow$ (Aniline, Acetyl chloride)

$CH_3CONHC_6H_5 + HCl$ (Phenyl acetamide) (1)

21. (i) $C_6H_5NH_2 + CHCl_3 + \text{Alc. } 3KOH \xrightarrow{\Delta} C_6H_5NC + 3KCl + H_2O$ (1)

(ii) $C_6H_5NO_2 \xrightarrow{Fe/HCl} \underset{(A)}{C_6H_5NH_2} \xrightarrow[273\,K]{HNO_2} \underset{(B)}{C_6H_5\overset{+}{N_2}\overset{-}{Cl}}$ (1)

22. (i) $CH_3—CH_2—NH_2 + HNO_2 \xrightarrow{278\text{-}278K}$ (Ethylamine)

$CH_3—CH_2—OH + N_2\uparrow + H_2O$

$CH_3—CH_2—OH + [O] \xrightarrow[\text{Dil. } H_2SO_4, \Delta]{K_2Cr_2O_7} CH_3COOH + H_2O$

$CH_3COOH \xrightarrow{SOCl_2} CH_3COCl \xrightarrow{NH_3}$

$CH_3CONH_2 \xrightarrow[\text{Hofmann-bromamide degradation}]{Br_2 + NaOH} CH_3NH_2$ (1)

(ii) When aniline is treated with nitrous acid and HCl at 0-5°C temperature, then benzene diazonium salt is formed.

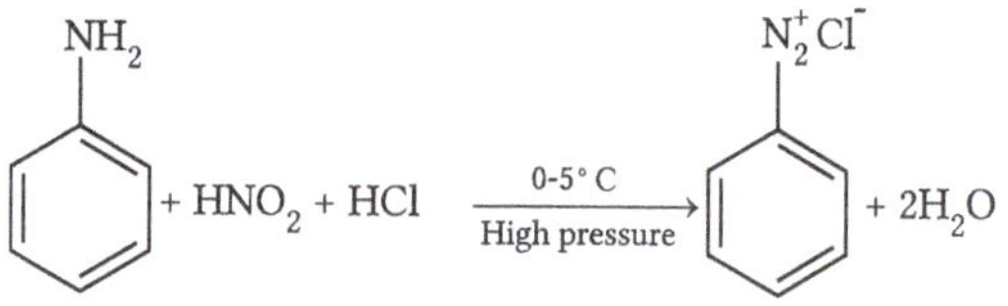

(1)

23. Nitromethane into dimethylamine

(i) $CH_3NO_2 \xrightarrow[{[H]}]{Sn/HCl} CH_3NH_2 \xrightarrow{CHCl_3/KOH}$

Nitromethane → Aminomethane

$CH_3NC \xrightarrow[{[H]}]{Na/C_2H_5OH} CH_3NHCH_3$

Methyl isocyanide → Dimethylamine (1)

(ii) Propanoic acid into ethanoic acid

$CH_3CH_2COOH \xrightarrow{NH_3/\text{Heat}} CH_3CH_2CONH_2$

Propanoic acid → Propanamide

$\xrightarrow{Br_2/KOH} CH_3CH_2NH_2 \xrightarrow[-N_2, -H_2O]{HONO}$ (Ethylamine)

$CH_3CH_2OH \xrightarrow[{[O]}]{K_2Cr_2O_7/H_2SO_4} CH_3CHO$

Ethanol → Ethanal

$\xrightarrow[{[O]}]{K_2Cr_2O_7/H_2SO_4} CH_3COOH$ (Ethanoic acid) (1)

24. Complete conversion can be performed as :

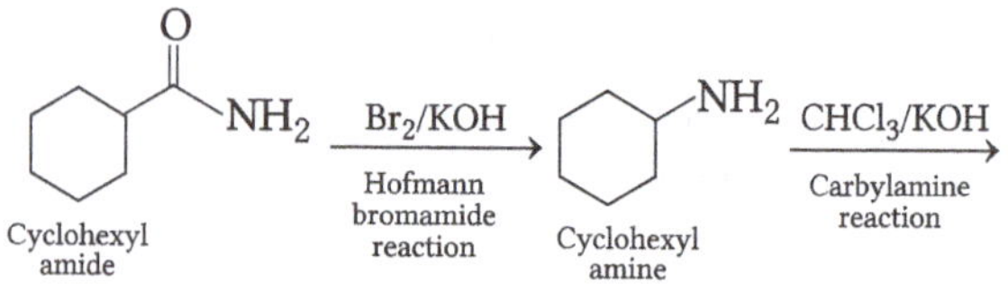

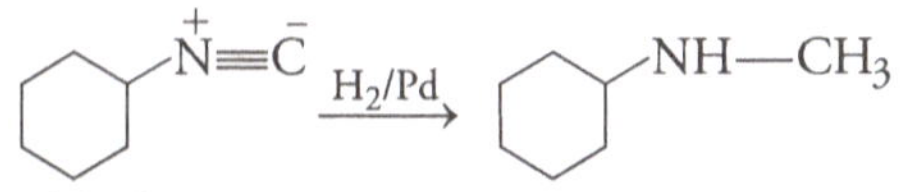

Cyclohexyl isocyanide → Cyclohexyl methylamine (2)

25. (i) Methylamine being more basic than water, accepts a proton from water and OH^- ions are produced which further reacts with ferric ion to give brown ppt. of hydrated ferric oxide.

$$\underset{\text{Methylamine}}{CH_3\ddot{N}H_2} + H—OH \longrightarrow CH_3\overset{+}{N}H_3 + OH^-$$

$$FeCl_3 \longrightarrow Fe^{3+} + 3Cl^-$$

$$2Fe^{3+} + 6OH^- \longrightarrow 2Fe(OH)_3 \text{ or } \underset{\substack{\text{Hydrated ferric}\\ \text{oxide}\\ \text{(Brown ppt.)}}}{Fe_2O_3 \cdot 3H_2O}$$ (1)

(ii) Refer to text on page 377 (Sulphonation, Note)

$$\underset{\substack{\text{Aniline}\\ \text{(Lewis base)}}}{C_6H_5\ddot{N}H_2} + \underset{\text{(Lewis acid)}}{AlCl_3} \longrightarrow \underset{\text{(Complex)}}{[C_6H_5NH_2]^+ [AlCl_3]^-}$$ (1)

26. (i) **Coupling reaction**

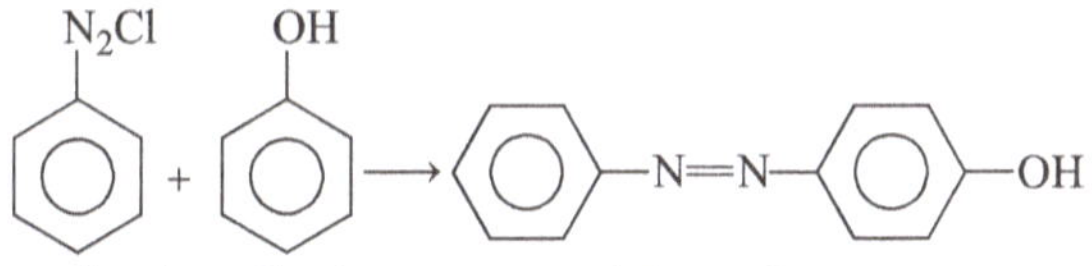

Benzene diazonium chloride + Phenol → *p*-hydroxyazobenzene

(ii) **Acetylation of ethylamine**

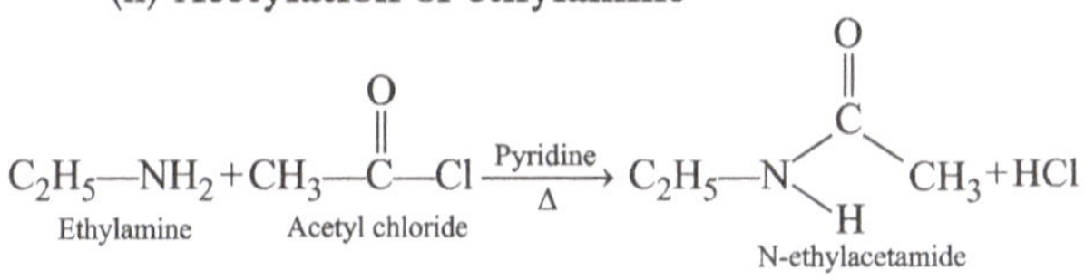

Ethylamine, Acetyl chloride, N-ethylacetamide

27. (i) $C_6H_5NH_2$ $3Br_2 \xrightarrow{aq}$

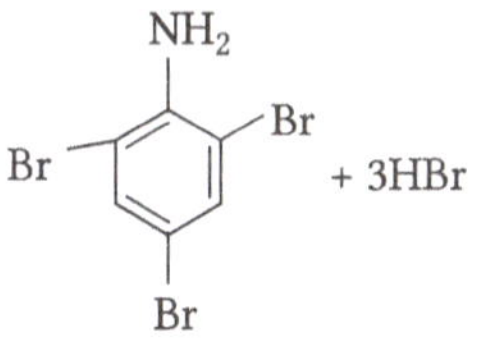

(1)

(ii) $\underset{\text{Aniline}}{C_6H_5NH_2} + \underset{\substack{\text{Ethanoic}\\ \text{anhydride}}}{(CH_3CO)_2O} \longrightarrow$

$$\underset{\substack{\text{N-phenylethanamide}\\ \text{or acetanilide}}}{H_5C_6NHCOCH_3} + \underset{\substack{\text{Ethanoic}\\ \text{acid}}}{CH_3COOH}$$ (1)

28. (i) Refer to page no. 380 [Q. 45 (iii)]

(ii) Refer to page no. 380 [Q. 45 (i)].

29. (i) **Nitrous acid test** Aniline with HNO_2 (from $NaNO_2$ + HCl) gives benzene diazonium chloride which is stable at 273-278 K and hence, does not decompose to give N_2 gas.

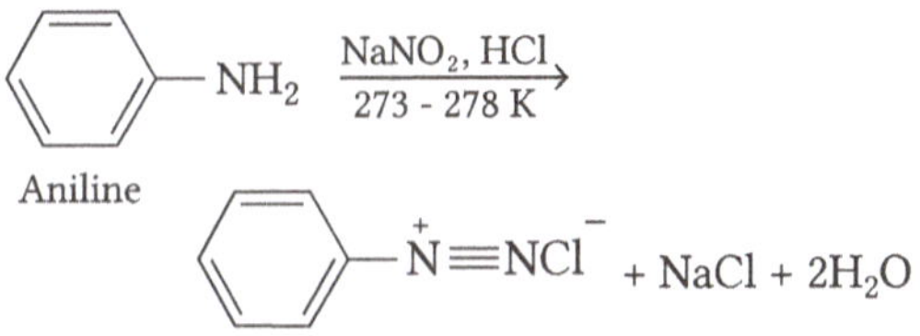

Aniline → Benzene diazonium chloride (1/2)

While benzylamine reacts with HNO_2, it give diazonium salt which being unstable at low temperature decomposes and gives N_2 gas.

$$C_6H_5CH_2NH_2 \xrightarrow{NaNO_2/HCl} \underset{\text{(Unstable)}}{[C_6H_5CH_2—\overset{+}{N}\equiv NCl^-]}$$

$$\xrightarrow{H_2O} \underset{\text{Benzyl alcohol}}{C_6H_5CH_2OH} + N_2\uparrow + HCl$$ (1/2)

(ii) Aniline is a primary aromatic amine while N-methyl aniline is a secondary aromatic amine. So, they can be distinguished by carbylamine test.(1)

For test, refer to text on pages 372 and 373 (Carbylamine reaction).

30. Aniline and ethylamine are distinguished by **azo-dye** test which are as follows :

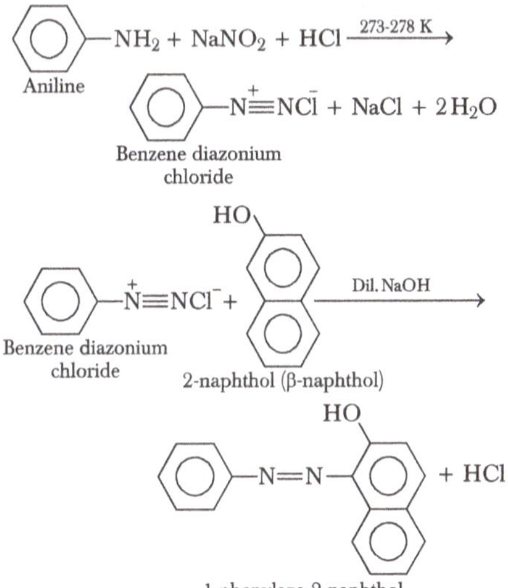

1-phenylazo-2-naphthol (Orange-red dye)

Ethylamine does not form any dye and therefore does not show any colour when treated with β-naphthol. (2)

31. **Key Idea** *Primary amines give carbylamine test.*

Methylamine(1°) and dimethyl amine(2°) can be distinguished by carbylamine test.

Methylamine when heated with chloroform and alcoholic potassium hydroxide, it forms methyl isocyanide commonly known as carbylamine which can be recognised by its offensive odour but this test is not responded by dimethyl amine because it is secondary amine.

$$CH_3NH_2 + CHCl_3 + 3KOH \longrightarrow CH_3CN + 3KCl + 3H_2O$$

(2)

32. Four structural isomers of C_3H_9N are possible.

$CH_3—CH_2—CH_2—NH_2$,
Propan-1-amine
(1° amine)

$CH_3—NH—C_2H_5$, N-methyl ethanamine (2° amine)

$CH_3—\underset{|}{C}H—CH_3$ with NH_2 on the central carbon
Propan-2-amine
(1° amine) (1)

Only 1° amines react with HNO_2 to give N_2 gas, i.e.

$$\underset{\text{Propan-1-amine}}{CH_3—CH_2—CH_2—NH_2} + HONO \longrightarrow \underset{\text{Propan-1-ol (Major product)}}{CH_3—CH_2—CH_2OH} + N_2\uparrow + H_2O$$

$$\underset{\text{Propan-2-amine}}{(H_3C)_2CH—NH_2} + HONO \longrightarrow \underset{\text{Propan-2-ol (Major product)}}{(H_3C)_2CH—OH} + N_2\uparrow + H_2O$$ (1)

33. (i) Intermolecular hydrogen bonding is present in primary amines ($R—NH_2$) but not in tertiary amines (R_3N), so primary amines have higher boiling point than tertiary amines. (1½)

(ii) Basic strength of $(CH_3)_2NH$ and $(CH_3)_3N$ depends upon the stabilisation of their conjugate acids by a number of factors such as H-bonding, steric hindrance of alkyl groups and +*I*-effect of alkyl groups.

The first two factors are favourable for 2° amines, hence $(CH_3)_2NH$ is a stronger base than $(CH_3)_3N$. (1½)

34. (i) $(C_2H_5)_3N > (C_2H_5)_2NH > C_2H_5NH_2 > NH_3$ (1)

(ii) $(CH_3)_2NH < C_2H_5NH_2 < C_2H_5OH$ (1)

(iii) $C_6H_5NH_2 < (C_2H_5)_2NH < C_2H_5NH_2$ (1)

35. Basic strength

diethyl ether < aniline < methylamine < ethylamine.

In aliphatic amines, due to the presence of electron donating alkyl group, electron density on nitrogen increases. Hence, lone pair is easily available for protonation.

In aniline, the lone pair of nitrogen is in conjugation with benzene and less available for protonation hence, aniline is less basic than aliphatic amine and ethers are inert in nature due to stable C—O—C bond. (3)

36. (i) $C_6H_5NH_2 > C_6H_5NHCH_3 > C_2H_5NH_2 > (C_2H_5)_2NH$ (1)

(ii) $C_6H_5NH_2 < C_6H_5N(CH_3)_2 < CH_3NH_2 < (C_2H_5)_2NH$ (1)

(iii) (a) *p*-nitroaniline < aniline < *p*-toluidine

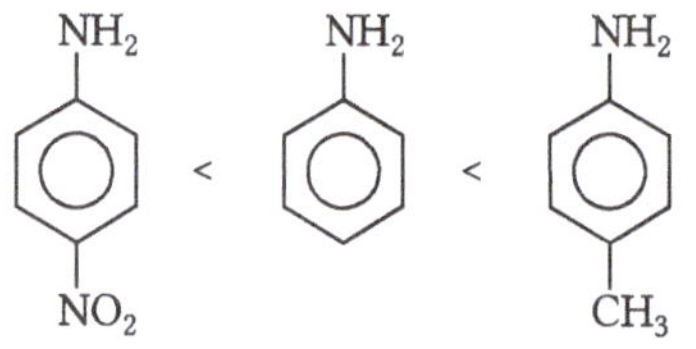

(1/2)

(b) $C_6H_5NH_2 < C_6H_5NHCH_3 < C_6H_5CH_2NH_2$ (1/2)

37. (i) $C_2H_5NH_2 < NH_3 < C_6H_5CH_2NH_2 < C_2H_5NH_2 < (C_2H_5)_2NH$ (1)

(ii) $C_6H_5NH_2 < (C_2H_5)_3N < C_2H_5NH_2 < (C_2H_5)_2NH$ (1)

(iii) $C_6H_5NH_2 < C_6H_5CH_2NH_2 < (CH_3)_3N < CH_3NH_2 < (CH_3)_2NH$ (1)

38. (i) Aniline being a Lewis base, react with the Lewis acid $AlCl_3$ used in Friedel-Crafts reaction and produce a complex salt.

$$C_6H_5 \cdot NH_2 + AlCl_3 \longrightarrow C_6H_5 \cdot \overset{+}{N}H_2 \cdot AlCl_3^-$$ (1)

As a result nitrogen of aniline requires positive charge and hence acts as a storng deactivating group. Hence, it does not show Friedel-Crafts reaction.

(ii) In aqueous solution, basic nature depends on + *I*-effect, H-bonding and steric-effect.

The combined effect shows that $(CH_3)_2 \cdot NH$ is more basic than $(CH_3)_3 \cdot N$ as H-bonding is more in case of $(CH_3)_2 \cdot NH$ than in $(CH_3)_3N$, which predominates over the stability due to +*I*- effect of three — CH_3 groups. (1)

(iii) Primary amines (1°) show two-hydrogen bonds whereas tertiary amines (3°) show no hydrogen bonding.

Thus, the net attractive force in case of primary amines is more than that of tertiary amines. Hence, primary amines have higher boiling point than that of tertiary amines. (1)

39. (i) Nitration is usually carried out with a mixture of conc. HNO_3 and conc. H_2SO_4. So, in the presence of these acids, aniline gets protonated to form anilinium ion.

Therefore, in the presence of these acids, the reaction mixture consists of aniline and anilinium ion. $—NH_2$ group in aniline is o, *p*-directing and activating, whereas the $\overset{+}{N}H_3$ group in anilinium ion is *m*-directing and deactivating. Now, nitration of aniline mainly gives *p*-nitroaniline due to steric hindrance at *o*-position, the nitration of anilinium ion gives *m*-nitroaniline. In actual practice approx. 1 : 1 mixture of *p*-nitroaniline and *m*-nitroaniline is obtained. (2)

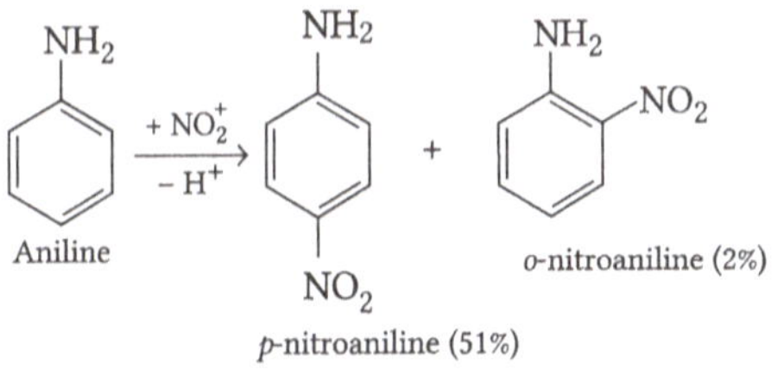

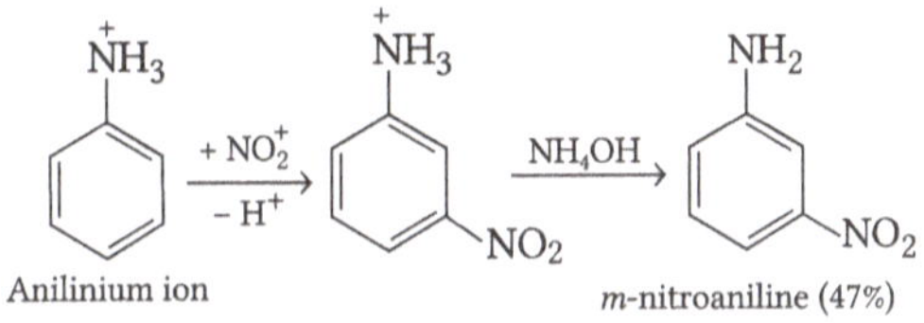

(ii) Gabriel phthalimide synthesis produces primary amines only without the traces of secondary or tertiary amines. So, this method is preferred for the synthesis of primary amines.

Refer to text on page 365 (Gabriel phthalimide synthesis). (1)

40. (i) Due to electron withdrawing effect of the acetyl group, the lone pair of electrons on N-atom is attracted by $COCH_3$ group.

As a result, lone pair of electrons on N-atom is not exclusively available for donation to the benzene ring and hence, activating effect of the — NH_2 group is reduced. (1)

(ii) In aniline ($C_6H_5NH_2$), the electron pair on nitrogen atom is involved in conjugation with ring and is less available for protonation than that in methylamine (CH_3NH_2). Therefore, aniline is less basic than methylamine.

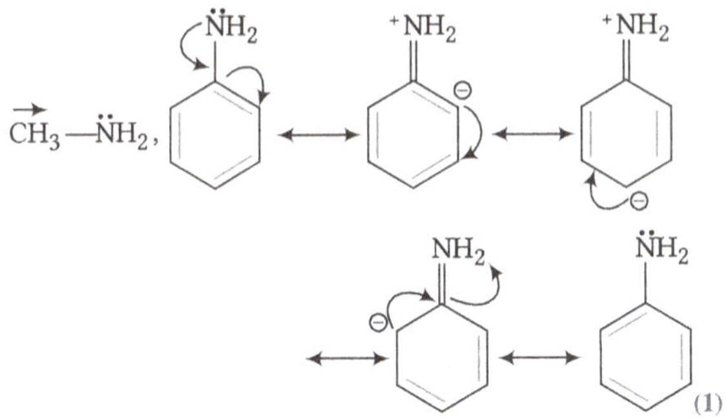

(1)

(iii) Nitration is usually carried out with a mixture of conc. HNO_3 and conc. H_2SO_4. So in the presence of these acids, aniline gets protonated to form anilinium ion. Therefore, the reaction mixture consists of aniline and anilinium ion.

— NH_2 group in aniline is *o*, *p*-directing and activating, whereas the $\overset{+}{N}H_3$ group in anilinium is *m*-directing and deactivating. Now, nitration of aniline mainly gives *p*-nitroaniline due to steric hindrance at *o*-position and the nitration of anilinium ion gives *m*-nitroaniline.

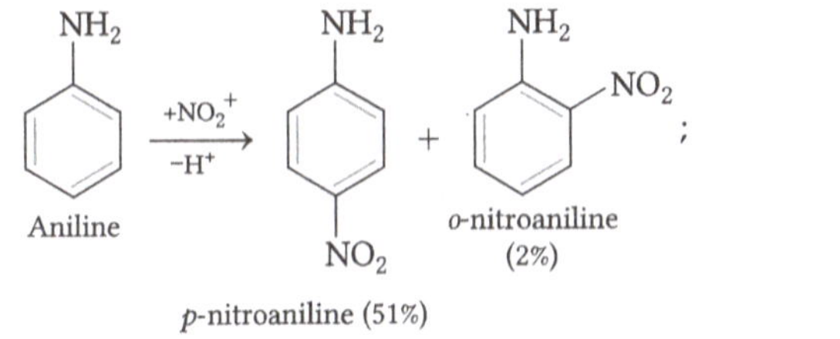

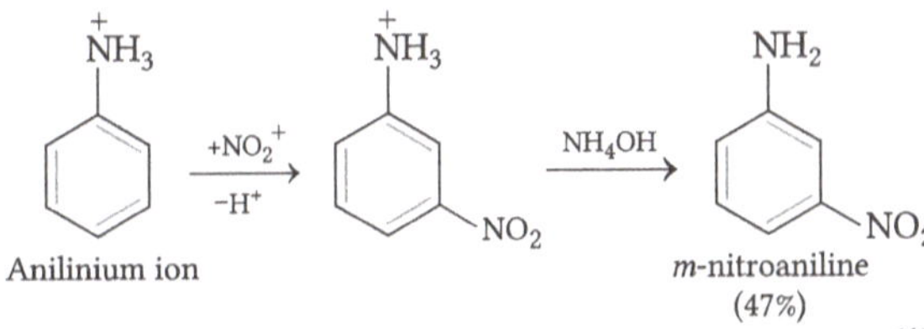

(1)

41. (i) Ethanamine into methanamine

$$\underset{\text{Ethanamine}}{CH_3CH_2NH_2} \xrightarrow[-N_2,\,-H_2O]{HONO} \underset{\text{Ethanol}}{CH_3CH_2OH} \xrightarrow[K_2Cr_2O_7/H_2SO_4]{[O]} CH_3CHO \xrightarrow[K_2Cr_2O_7/H_2SO_4]{[O]} CH_3COOH$$

$$\xrightarrow[\text{Heat}]{NH_3} \underset{\text{Ethanamide}}{CH_3CONH_2} \xrightarrow{Br_2/KOH} \underset{\text{Methanamine}}{CH_3NH_2}$$ (1)

(ii) Ethanoic acid into propanoic acid

$$\underset{\text{Ethanoic acid}}{CH_3COOH} \xrightarrow{LiAlH_4} \underset{\text{Ethanol}}{CH_3CH_2OH} \xrightarrow{\text{Red P}/I_2}$$

$$\underset{\text{Iodoethane}}{CH_3CH_2I} \xrightarrow{KCN(alc.)} \underset{\text{Propane nitrile}}{CH_3CH_2CN} \xrightarrow{H_2O/H^+} \underset{\text{Propanoic acid}}{CH_3CH_2COOH}$$ (1)

(iii) Methanamine into ethanamine

$$\underset{\text{Methanamine}}{CH_3NH_2} \xrightarrow[-N_2,\,-H_2O]{HONO} \underset{\text{Methanol}}{CH_3OH} \xrightarrow{\text{Red P}/I_2}$$

$$\underset{\text{Methyl iodide}}{CH_3I} \xrightarrow{KCN(alc.)} \underset{\text{Ethane nitrile}}{CH_3CN} \xrightarrow[4[H]]{Na/C_2H_5OH/\text{Reduction}} \underset{\text{Ethanamine}}{CH_3CH_2NH_2}$$ (1)

42. (i) Ethanoic acid into methanamine (1)

$$\underset{\text{Ethanoic acid}}{CH_3COOH} \xrightarrow{SOCl_2} \underset{\text{Ethanoyl chloride}}{CH_3COCl} \xrightarrow{NH_3\text{ (excess)}}$$

$$\underset{\text{Ethanamide}}{CH_3CONH_2} \xrightarrow[\text{Hofmann bromamide reaction}]{Br_2/KOH} \underset{\text{Methanamine}}{CH_3NH_2}$$ (1)

(ii) Hexane nitrile into 1-aminopentane

$$\underset{\text{Hexane nitrile}}{CH_3(CH_2)_4CN} \xrightarrow[\text{Partial hydrolysis}]{H_3O^+} \underset{\text{Hexanamide}}{CH_3(CH_2)_4CONH_2}$$

$$\xrightarrow[\text{Hofmann bromamide reaction}]{Br_2/KOH} \underset{\text{1-aminopentane}}{CH_3(CH_2)_4NH_2}$$ (1)

(iii) Methanol into ethanoic acid

$$\underset{\text{Methanol}}{CH_3OH} \xrightarrow{PCl_5} \underset{\text{Chloromethane}}{CH_3Cl} \xrightarrow{KCN(alc.)}$$

$$\underset{\text{Ethane nitrile}}{CH_3CN} \xrightarrow{H_3O^+} \underset{\text{Ethanoic acid}}{CH_3COOH}$$ (1)

43. (i) $$\underset{\text{Ethyl bromide}}{CH_3CH_2Br} \xrightarrow{KCN} \underset{\text{Ethyl cyanide (A)}}{CH_3CH_2CN} \xrightarrow{LiAlH_4}$$

$$\underset{\substack{n\text{-propylamine} \\ (B)}}{CH_3CH_2CH_2NH_2} \xrightarrow[0°C]{HNO_2} \underset{\substack{n\text{-propyl alcohol} \\ (C)}}{CH_3CH_2CH_2OH}$$ (1 ½)

(ii) $$\underset{\text{Acetic acid}}{CH_3COOH} \xrightarrow[\text{Heat}]{NH_3} \underset{\substack{\text{Acetamide} \\ (A)}}{CH_3CONH_2} \xrightarrow{NaOBr}$$

$$\underset{\substack{\text{Methyl amine} \\ (B)}}{CH_3NH_2} \xrightarrow{NaNO_2/HCl} \underset{\substack{\text{Methanol} \\ (C)}}{CH_3OH}$$ (1 ½)

44. Refer to text on pages 373 and 375 (Peaction with nitrous acid and note). (3)

45. (i) $$\underset{\text{Ethylamine}}{CH_3CH_2NH_2} + HNO_2 \xrightarrow{0°C} \underset{\text{Ethyl alcohol}}{CH_3CH_2OH} + N_2\uparrow + H_2O$$ (1)

(ii) Refer to text on page 374 (Reaction with aryl sulphonyl chloride). (1)

(iii)

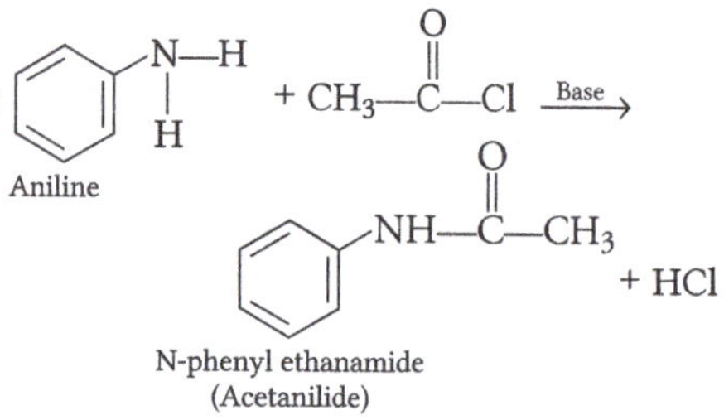

(1)

46. (i)

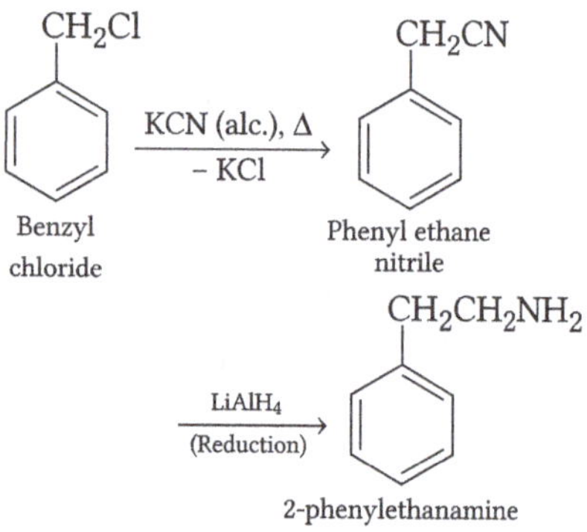

(ii)

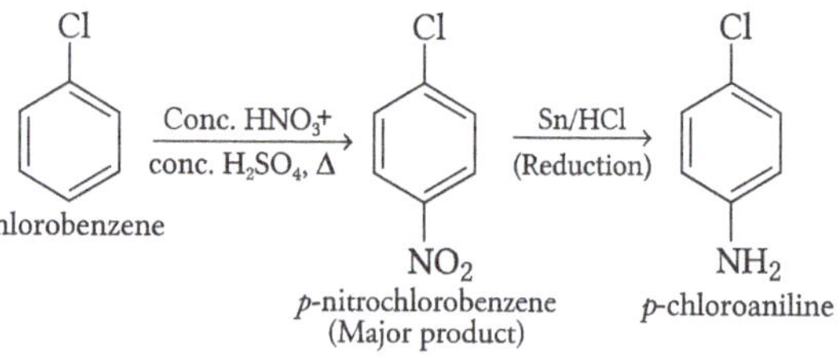

47. (i) $$\underset{\text{Acetic acid}}{CH_3COOH} \xrightarrow{NH_3} \underset{\text{Ammonium acetate}}{CH_3CO\overset{-}{O}\overset{+}{N}H_4}$$

$$\xrightarrow[-H_2O]{\Delta} \underset{\text{Acetamide}}{CH_3CONH_2} \xrightarrow{Br_2/KOH} \underset{\text{Methylamine}}{CH_3NH_2}$$ (1½)

(ii)

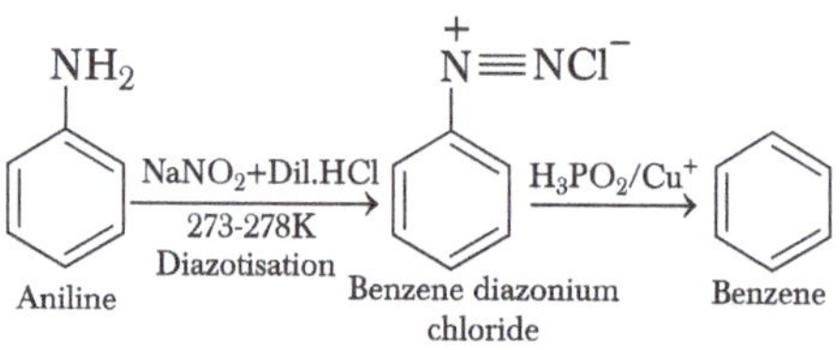

(1½)

48. Carbylamine Reaction

Aniline [1°amine]	Dimethyl aniline [2°amine]
Aniline gives foul smell of phenyl isocyanide, when heated with chloroform and KOH. $C_6H_5NH_2 + CHCl_3 + 3KOH \longrightarrow C_6H_5NC + 3KCl + 3H_2O$	No characteristic observation.
Dye test	
On diazotisation and coupling with alkaline β-naphthol, aniline forms an orange red dye.	No characteristic observation.

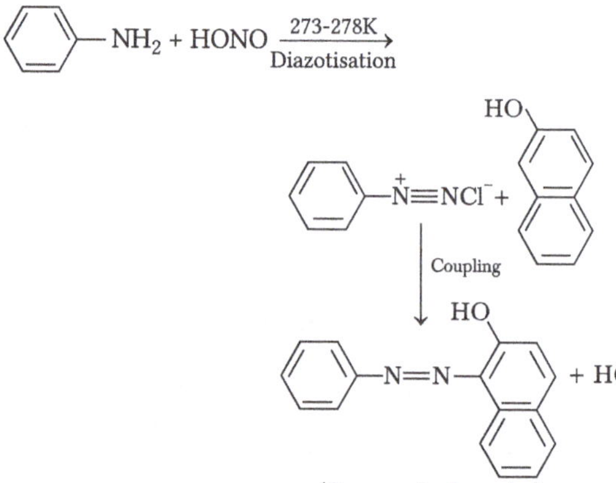

(Orange-red coloure dye)

49. Ethylamine (1° amine) when heated with chloroform and alcoholic KOH it forms ethyl carbylamine which has peculiar offensive smell. Acetamide (acid amide) does not give this test. (3)

$$C_2H_5NH_2 + CHCl_3 + 3KOH \longrightarrow \underset{\text{offensive smell}}{C_2H_5NC} + 3KCl + 3H_2O$$

50. (i) (a)

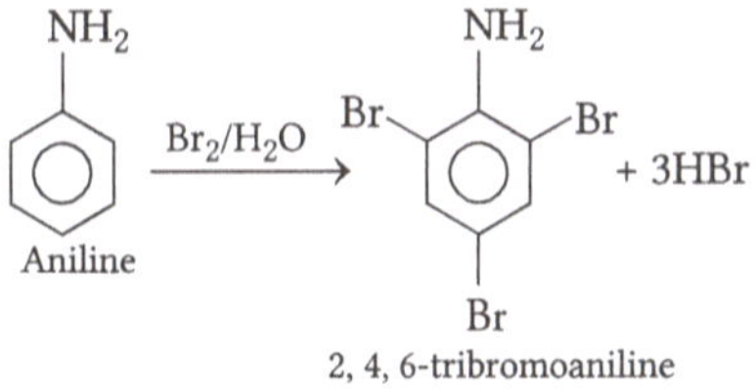

(1/2)
(1/2)
(1/2)

(b)

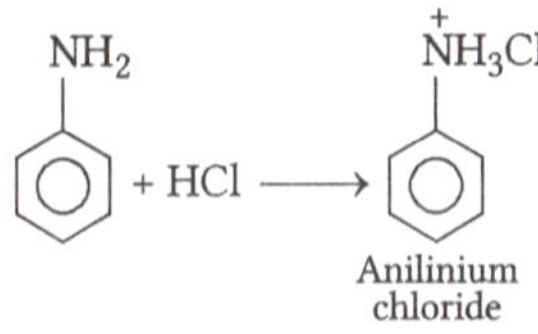

(c)

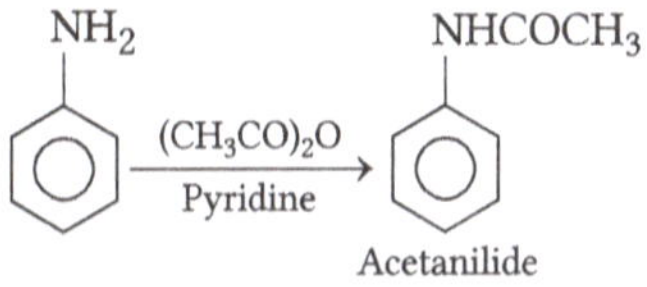

(ii) Alcohols have higher boiling point as compared to that of amines, because oxygen being more electronegative atom, forms strong hydrogen bond as compared to that of nitrogen.

In tertiary amine, there is no hydrogen bond formation due to the absence of H-atoms and hence, has the lowest boiling point.

Therefore, increasing order of boiling point

$(CH_3)_3N < C_2H_5NH_2 < C_2H_5OH$ (1 ½)

(iii) $(CH_3)_2NH$ and $(CH_3)_3N$ are secondary and tertiary amines respectively. These are distinguished by Hinsberg's reagent which gives sulphonamide with secondary amines and no reaction takes place out with tertiary amines. $(CH_3)_2NH$ reacts with benzene sulphonyl chloride is as follows:

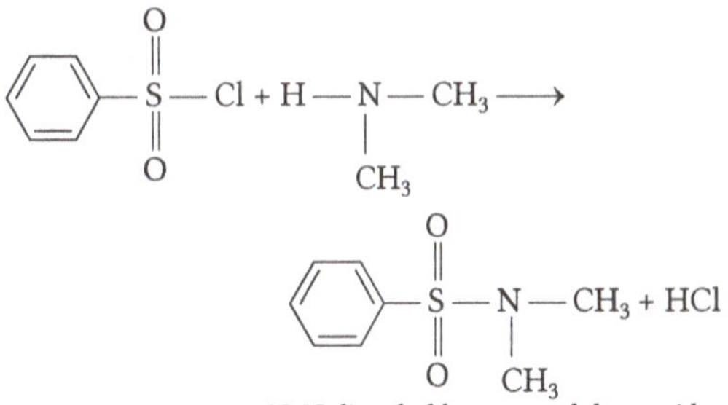

N, N-dimethyl benzene sulphonamide (2)

51. (i)

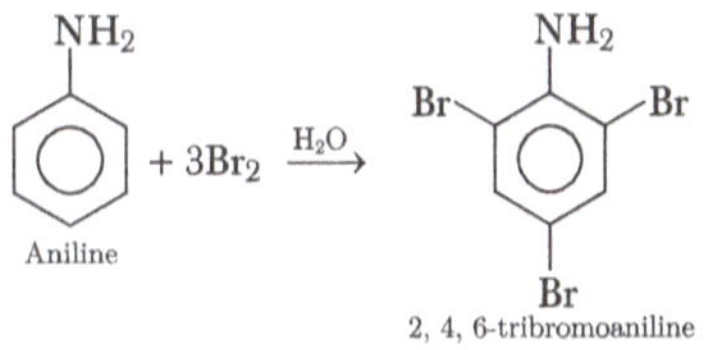

(1½)

(ii) $\underset{\text{Ethylamine}}{C_2H_5NH_2} + HNO_2 \longrightarrow \underset{\text{Ethanol}}{C_2H_5OH} + N_2\uparrow + H_2O$ (1½)

(iii) $\underset{\text{Acetic anhydride}}{(CH_3CO)_2O} + NH_3 \longrightarrow \underset{\text{Acetic acid}}{CH_3COOH} + \underset{\text{Acetamide}}{CH_3CONH_2}$ (2)

52. Refer to text on page 373 (Reaction with nitrous acid).

TOPIC 03

Cyanides, Isocyanides and Diazonium Salts

Cyanides and Isocyanides

The cyanide group is an ambident group and can attach itself to H through both C as well as N-atom.

HCN exists in the following two tautomeric forms

$$\underset{\text{Hydrogen cyanide}}{H—C\equiv N} \rightleftharpoons \underset{\text{Hydrogen isocyanide}}{H—N\overset{\rightarrow}{\equiv}C}$$

The functional group in cyanides is $—C\equiv N$ and is called **cyano** or **nitrile group**, while that in isocyanides is $—N\overset{\rightarrow}{\equiv}C$ and is called **isocyano** or **isonitrile** or **carbylamine** group.

Nomenclature

In the common system, the cyanides are named as alkyl cyanides. In the IUPAC system, cyanides are named as alkane nitriles. e.g.

$$CH_3—C\equiv N$$

Common name Methyl cyanide
IUPAC name Ethanenitrile

$$CH_3—CH_2—C\equiv N$$

Common name Ethyl cyanide
IUPAC name Propanenitrile

In the common system, the isocyanides are named as alkyl isocyanides or aryl isocyanides. In the IUPAC system, the isocyanides are named as alkyl carbylamines.

e.g. $CH_3—N\overset{\rightarrow}{\equiv}C$ $\quad$ $CH_3—CH_2—N\overset{\rightarrow}{\equiv}C$

Common name Methyl isocyanide $\quad$ Ethyl isocyanide
IUPAC name Ethylcarbylamine $\quad$ Methylcarbylamine

Methods of Preparation

1. Cyanides

(i) **From alkyl halides** When an alkyl halide is heated with an alcoholic solution of sodium or potassium cyanide, alkyl cyanides are obtained.

$$RX + K^+CN^-(\text{alc.}) \xrightarrow{\Delta} R—C\equiv N + K^+X^-$$

(ii) **From acid amides** When an acid amide is heated with P_2O_5 or $SOCl_2$, the amide undergoes dehydration to give corresponding cyanide.

$$R—\overset{\overset{\displaystyle O}{\|}}{C}—NH_2 \xrightarrow[\Delta]{P_2O_5 \text{ or } SOCl_2} R—C\equiv N + H_2O$$

2. Isocyanides

(i) **From alkyl halides** When an alkyl halide is treated with an alcoholic solution of silver cyanide, alkyl isocyanide is formed.

$$RX + AgCN(\text{alc.}) \longrightarrow R—N\overset{\rightarrow}{\equiv}C + AgX$$

(ii) **From primary amines** When a suitable primary amine is heated with chloroform and alcoholic potassium hydroxide solution, alkyl isocyanide is formed. This reaction is known as **carbylamine reaction.**

$$\underset{\text{Primary amine}}{R—NH_2} + CHCl_3 + 3KOH(\text{alc.}) \xrightarrow{\Delta} \underset{\text{Alkyl isocyanide}}{R—N\overset{\rightarrow}{\equiv}C} + 3KCl + 3H_2O$$

Note Distinction between Cyanides and Isocyanides

- Cyanides are soluble in water whereas isocyanides are sparingly soluble in water.
- Cyanides have pleasant smell whereas isocyanides have offensive smell.
- Cyanides on complete reduction give 1° amine whereas isocyanides give 2° amine.

Diazonium Salts

Diazonium salts are a group of organic compounds, having the general formula, $Ar\overset{+}{N}_2\bar{X}$, where Ar is abbreviated for the aryl group and $\bar{X}$ may be $Cl^-, Br^-, HSO_4^-, NO_3^-$, etc.

Nomenclature

The $\overset{+}{N}_2$, (i.e. $—\overset{+}{N}\equiv N$) is called diazo group. These are named by adding the suffix diazonium to the name of the parent hydrocarbon from which they are derived followed by the name of anion. e.g. $C_6H_5\overset{+}{N}_2\bar{C}l$ is benzene diazonium chloride, $C_6H_5N_2^+HSO_4^-$ is benzene diazonium hydrogen sulphate.

Stability

Primary aliphatic amines form highly unstable alkyl diazonium salts. Primary aromatic amines form arene diazonium salts, which are stable for a short time in solution at low temperature (0-5°C).

The stability of arene diazonium salt is due to the dispersal of the positive charge over the benzene ring.

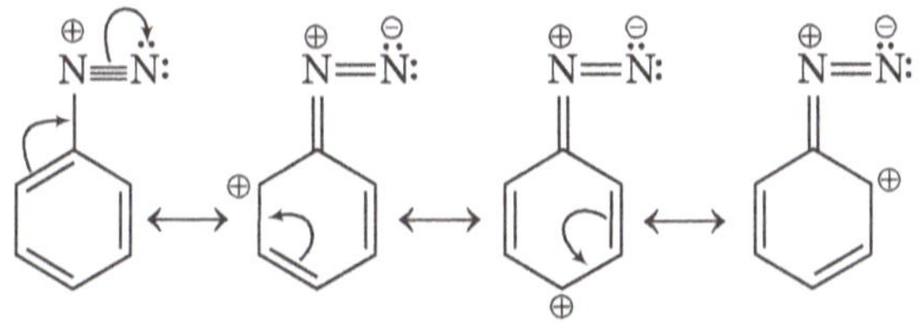

Note Resonance stabilisation is not possible in diazonium salts of aliphatic amines.

Methods of Preparation

Benzene diazonium chloride is prepared by the reaction of aniline with nitrous acid (which is produced by the reaction of $NaNO_2$ and HCl) at 273-278 K or 0-5°C.

$$C_6H_5NH_2 + NaNO_2 + 2HCl \xrightarrow{273\text{-}278\text{ K}} C_6H_5\overset{+}{N}_2\bar{Cl} + NaCl + 2H_2O$$

The conversion of primary aromatic amines into their diazonium salts is called **diazotisation**. Due to its unstability, the diazonium salt is not generally stored and is used immediately after its preparation.

Physical Properties

Benzene diazonium chloride is colourless and readily soluble in water. Hence, physical properties of diazonium salts can be described as follows:

(i) Diazonium salts are generally colourless, crystalline solids.

(ii) These are readily soluble in water and stable in cold water. They react with water when warmed.

(iii) These are unstable and exploit in dry state, hence used in solution state.

(iv) Their aqueous solutions are neutral to litmus and conduct electricity due to the presence of ions.

(v) Benzene diazonium fluoroborate is water insoluble and stable at room temperature.

Chemical Reactions

The chemical reactions of diazonium salts can be divided into two categories:

1. Reactions Involving Displacement of Nitrogen

Diazonium group being a very good leaving group, is substituted by other groups such as Cl^-, Br^-, I^-, CN^- and OH^- from the aromatic ring. The nitrogen thus formed escapes from the reaction mixture as a gas. Some important reactions are as follows:

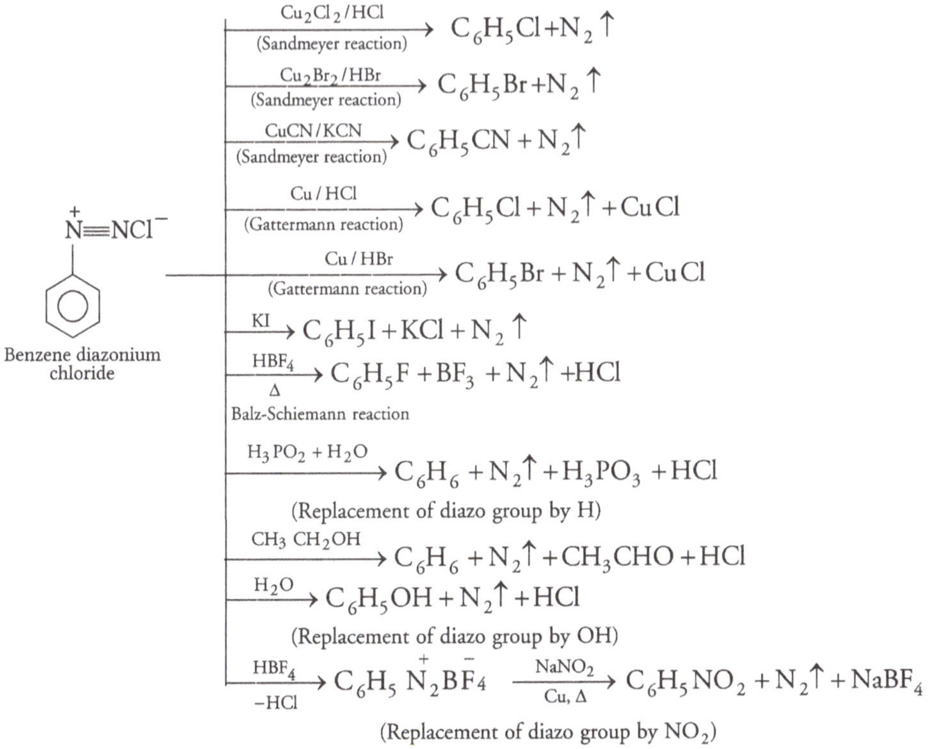

2. Reactions Involving Retention of Diazo Group (Coupling Reactions)

Benzene diazonium chloride reacts with phenol in which phenol molecule at its *para*-position is coupled with diazonium salt to give the product *p*-hydroxy azobenzene, hence the reaction is known as coupling reaction.

The azo products obtained having both the aromatic rings joined through the —N=N— bonds, are coloured and used as dyes.

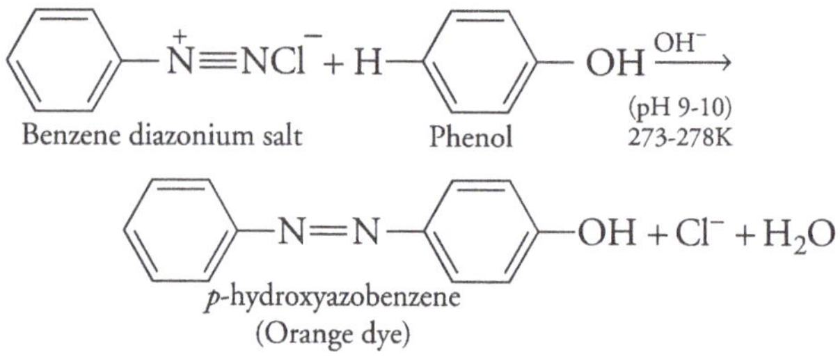

Similarly, the reaction of diazonium salt with aniline gives *p*-aminoazobenzene (yellow dye).

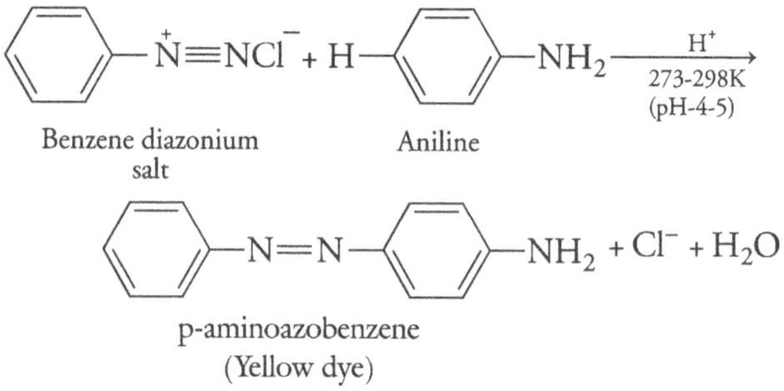

Importance of Diazonium Salts in the Synthesis of Aromatic Compounds

These are important in the synthesis of aromatic compounds due to the following facts:

(i) These are very good intermediates for the introduction of —F, —Cl, —OH, —CN, —NO_2, etc., into the aromatic ring.

(ii) Similarly, aryl fluorides and iodides cannot be prepared by the direct halogenation. Cyano group cannot be introduced by nucleophilic substitution reaction but cyanobenzene can be prepared from diazonium salts.

(iii) Thus, replacement of diazo group by the other group is helpful in preparing those aromatic compounds which cannot be prepared by the direct substitution in benzene.

Topic Practice 3

Very Short Answer Type Questions

(1 Mark)

1. Fill in the Blanks

(i) Diazonium salts are a group of organic compounds having the general formula is ....

(ii) Aliphatic diazonium salts are highly .... whereas arene diazonium salts are ...... for a short time in solution at low temperature.

(iii) Resonance stabilisation is not possible in diazonium salts of ...... amines.

2. Objective Type Questions

(i) Which of the following undergoes diazotisation?
(a) Aniline (b) Methylamine
(c) Ethylamine (d) All of these **ISC 2017**

(ii) In order to prepare a 1° amine from an alkyl halide with simultaneous addition of one CH_2 group in the carbon chain, the reagent used as source of nitrogen is ....
(a) sodium amide, $NaNH_2$
(b) sodium azide, NaN_3
(c) potassium cyanide, KCN
(d) potassium phthalimide $C_6H_4(CO)_2N^-K^+$

(iii) The reaction $Ar\overset{+}{N}_2Cl^- \xrightarrow{Cu/HCl} ArCl + N_2 + CuCl$ is named as ....
(a) Sandmeyer reaction (b) Gattermann reaction
(c) Claisen reaction (d) Carbylamine reaction

3. Match the compounds given in Column I with the items given in Column II and choose the correct option using the codes given below.

Column I		Column II	
A.	Benzene sulphonyl chloride	(i)	Zwitter ion
B.	Sulphanilic acid	(ii)	Hinsberg reagent
C.	Alkyl diazonium salts	(iii)	Dyes
D.	Aryl diazonium salts	(iv)	Conversion to alcohols

Codes

	A	B	C	D
(a)	(i)	(ii)	(iv)	(iii)
(b)	(ii)	(i)	(iv)	(iii)
(c)	(i)	(ii)	(iii)	(iv)
(d)	(ii)	(iii)	(iv)	(i)

4. How can the following conversion be brought about? Acetic acid to methyl cyanide. **ISC 2014**

5. What is a diazo group?

6. Diazonium salts of aromatic amines are more stable than those of aliphatic amines. Explain. **NCERT**

7. Benzene diazonium salts are more stable than alkyl diazonium salts. Give reason.

8. Write a short note on diazotisation. **NCERT**

9. Convert benzene to benzene diazonium chloride. **ISC 2016**

10. The conversion of primary aromatic amines into diazonium salts is known as

11. Why diazonium group gets easily substituted by other groups?

12. Give balanced equation for the following reaction given below :
Aniline is treated with a mixture of $NaNO_2$ and excess of HCl at low temperature. **ISC 2007**

13. Complete the following reaction.
$C_6H_5N_2Cl + C_2H_5OH \longrightarrow$ **NCERT**

14. Define Gattermann reaction.

15. Give balanced equation for the following name reaction Balz-Schiemann's reaction **ISC 2014**

16. Complete the following reaction and name the intermediate products *A*, *B* and *C* **ISC 2006**

NO_2
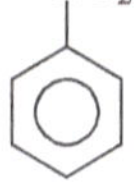
$+ Cl_2 \xrightarrow{FeCl_3} [A] \xrightarrow{Sn/HCl} [B] \xrightarrow{NaNO_2+HCl} [C]$

17. Write a short note on coupling reaction.

Or

Explain the coupling reaction. **NCERT**

18. Benzene diazonium chloride is not stored and used immediately after its preparation. Give reason.

Short Answer Type I Questions

2 Marks

19. Complete the following reactions.
(i) $C_6H_5N_2^+Cl^- \xrightarrow[\text{(Room temperature)}]{H_2O}$

(ii) NH_2

$\xrightarrow{NaNO_2/HCl} \xrightarrow[H_2O/H^+]{\text{Boiling}}$

20. Complete the following reactions.
(i) $C_6H_5N_2Cl + H_3PO_2 + H_2O \longrightarrow$
(ii) $C_6H_5N_2Cl \xrightarrow[\text{(ii) } NaNO_2/Cu]{\text{(i) } HBF_4}$ **NCERT**

21. State the reagents for the following conversion
Benzene $\xrightarrow{[A]}$ Nitrobenzene $\xrightarrow{[B]}$
Aniline $\xrightarrow{[C]}$ Aniline hydrochloride
$\xrightarrow{[D]}$ Benzene diazonium chloride **ISC 2008**

22. Give balanced equations for the following:
(i) Ethylamine is heated with chloroform and alcoholic solution of potassium hydroxide.
(ii) Benzene diazonium chloride is treated with ice cold solution of aniline in acidic medium. **ISC 2019**

Short Answer Type II Questions

3 Marks

23. Write the major product(s) in the following reactions.
(i) $C_6H_5—NO_2 \xrightarrow{Sn/HCl} ?$
(ii) $N_2^+ Cl^-$
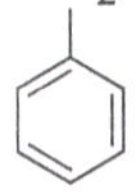
$\xrightarrow{Cu_2Cl_2/HCl} ?$
(iii) $CH_3CONH_2 \xrightarrow{Br_2/KOH(aq)} ?$

24. Write the structures of compounds *A*, *B* and *C* in the following reactions.
(i) $CH_3—COOH \xrightarrow{NH_3/\Delta} A \xrightarrow{Br_2/KOH(aq)} B \xrightarrow{CHCl_3 + \text{alc. } KOH} C$
(ii) $C_6H_5N_2^+BF_4^- \xrightarrow[\Delta]{NaNO_2/Cu} A \xrightarrow{Fe/HCl} B \xrightarrow{CH_3COCl/\text{pyridine}} C$

25. Identify *A*, *B* and *C* in the following reactions
(i) $CH_3CH_2Cl \xrightarrow{KCN} A \xrightarrow{H_2/Ni} B \xrightarrow{CH_3COCl/\text{Base}} C$
(ii) $C_6H_5N_2^+ Cl^- \xrightarrow{HBF_4} A \xrightarrow[\Delta]{NaNO_2/Cu} B \xrightarrow{Sn/HCl} C$

26. Identify the compounds *A*, *B*, *C*, *D*, *E* and *F* required for the following conversion **ISC 2014**
$C_6H_5NO_2 \xrightarrow{[A]} C_6H_5NH_2 \xrightarrow{[B]}$
$C_6H_5N_2^+Cl^- \xrightarrow{[C]} C_6H_5Cl \xrightarrow{[D]}$
$C_6H_5OH \xrightarrow{H_2SO_4} [E] + [F]$

27. How will you carry out the following conversion?
Aniline to chlorobenzene **ISC 2002**

28. Accomplish the following conversions.
(i) Aniline to 2, 4, 6-tribromofluorobenzene
(ii) Nitrobenzene to benzoic acid
(iii) Benzene to *m*-bromophenol **NCERT**

29. Accomplish the following conversions.
(i) Aniline to *p*-bromoaniline
(ii) Benzamide to toluene
(iii) Aniline to benzyl alcohol **NCERT**

30. Give the structures of *A*, *B* and *C* in the following reactions.

(i) $C_6H_5\overset{+}{N}_2Cl^- \xrightarrow{CuCN} A \xrightarrow{H_2O/\ H^+} B \xrightarrow[\Delta]{NH_3} C$

(ii) $C_6H_5NO_2 \xrightarrow{Sn + HCl} A \xrightarrow[273\ K]{NaNO_2 + HCl} B \xrightarrow[\Delta]{H_2O/H^+} C$

NCERT

31. Convert
(i) 3-methyl aniline into 3-nitrotoluene.
(ii) aniline into 1, 3, 5-tribromobenzene.
NCERT Intext

32. Write the products *A* and *B* in the following.

(i) 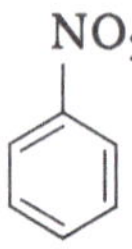 $\xrightarrow{Sn/HCl} A \xrightarrow{CHCl_3 + aq.\ NaOH} B$

(ii) 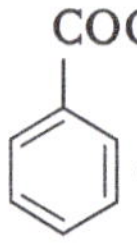 $\xrightarrow{NH_3} A \xrightarrow{Heat} B$

(iii) $C_6H_5\overset{+}{N}_2Cl^- \xrightarrow{Cu/HCl} A \xrightarrow{Cl_2/FeCl_3} B$

33. Give the structures of *A*, *B* and *C* in the following reactions.

(i) $C_6H_5NO_2 \xrightarrow{Fe\ /\ HCl} A \xrightarrow[273\ K]{NaNO_2 + HCl} B \xrightarrow[\Delta]{H_2O\ /\ H^+} C$

(ii) $C_6H_5NO_2 \xrightarrow{Fe\ /\ HCl} A \xrightarrow[273\ K]{HNO_2} B \xrightarrow{C_6H_5OH} C$ **NCERT**

34. Give one chemical test to distinguish between the following pairs of compounds.
(i) Methylamine and dimethylamine
(ii) Secondary and tertiary amines
(iii) Ethylamine and aniline **NCERT**

Long Answer Type Questions

5 Marks

35. Identify *A*, *B*, *C*, *D* and *E* **ISC 2003**

$C_6H_5CONH_2 \xrightarrow{Br_2/KOH} [A] \xrightarrow[\text{(ii) Steam}]{\text{(i) } NaNO_2/HCl} [B] \xrightarrow[\text{Ice cold}]{C_6H_5N_2Cl} [C]$

$[B] \xrightarrow{CuCl_3 + KOH} [D]$

$[B] \xrightarrow{CH_3COOH} [E]$

36. Identify *A*, *B*, *C*, *D* and *E*, **ISC 2001**

$\text{Benzoic acid} \xrightarrow[\text{Heat}]{NH_3} [A] \xrightarrow{Br_2/KOH} [B] \xrightarrow[\text{Ice cold}]{NaNO_2 + HCl} [C] \xrightarrow[HCl]{CuCl} [D]$

$[E] \xrightarrow{Sn/HCl} [B]$

37. Identify the compounds [*A*], [*B*] and [*C*] in the following reactions **ISC 2023**

(i) $CH_3COOH \xrightarrow[\Delta]{NH_3} [A] \xrightarrow{Br_2 + KOH} [B]$

$[A] \xrightarrow{CHCl_3 + NaOH(alc.)} [C]$

(ii) $CH_3Br \xrightarrow{KCN} [A] \xrightarrow{LiAlH_4} [B] \xrightarrow[273K]{HNO_2} [C]$

38. How will the following be converted ? (Give chemical equations)
(i) Ethyl bromide to ethyl isocyanide.
(ii) Aniline to benzene diazonium chloride.
(iii) Benzene diazonium chloride to phenol.
ISC 2023

39. (i) Write the structures of main products when benzene diazonium chloride reacts with the following reagents :
(a) $H_3PO_2 + H_2O$ (b) $CuCN/KCN$ (c) H_2O

(ii) Arrange the following in the increasing order of their basic character in an aqueous solution :
$C_2H_5NH_2$, $(C_2H_5)_2NH$, $(C_2H_5)_3N$

(iii) Give a simple chemical test to distinguish between the following pair of compounds:
$C_6H_5—NH_2$ and $C_6H_5—NH—CH_3$

40. An aromatic compound '*A*' of molecular formula C_7H_7ON undergoes a series of reactions as shown below.

Write the structures of *A*, *B*, *C*, *D* and *E* in the following reactions.

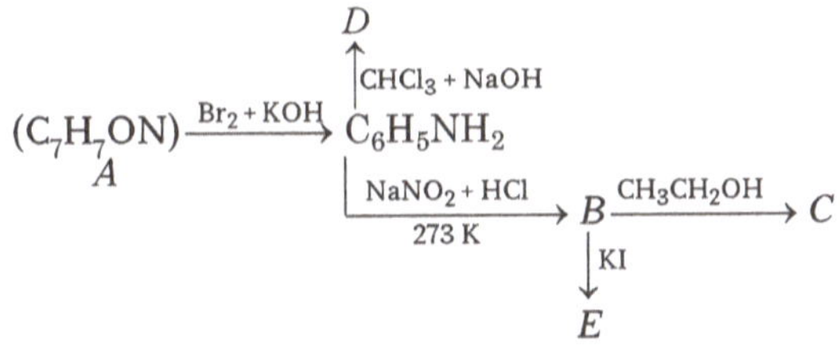

41. A hydrocarbon '*A*' (C_4H_8) on reaction with HCl gives a compound '*B*' (C_4H_9Cl), which on reaction with 1 mole of NH_3 gives compound '*C*' ($C_4H_{11}N$). On reacting with $NaNO_2$ and HCl followed by the treatment with water, compound '*C*' yields an optically active alcohol, '*D*'. Ozonolysis of '*A*' gives 2 moles of acetaldehyde. Identify compounds '*A*' to '*D*'. Explain the reactions involved.

Hints & Solutions

1. (i) $Ar\overset{+}{N}_2X^-$ (ii) unstable, stable (iii) aliphatic

2. (i)→(a), (ii)→(c), (iii)→(b)

3. (b) A → (ii), B → (i), C → (iv), D → (iii)

4. $\underset{\text{Acetic acid}}{CH_3COOH} \xrightarrow[\text{(ii) Heat}]{\text{(i) } NH_3} CH_3CONH_2 \xrightarrow{P_2O_5,\Delta} \underset{\text{Methyl cyanide}}{CH_3CN}$

5. $\overset{+}{N}_2\,(-\overset{+}{N}\equiv N)$

6. Diazonium salts of aromatic amines are more stable than those of aliphatic amines due to the delocalisation of the positive charge on the benzene ring as shown below by the resonating structures.

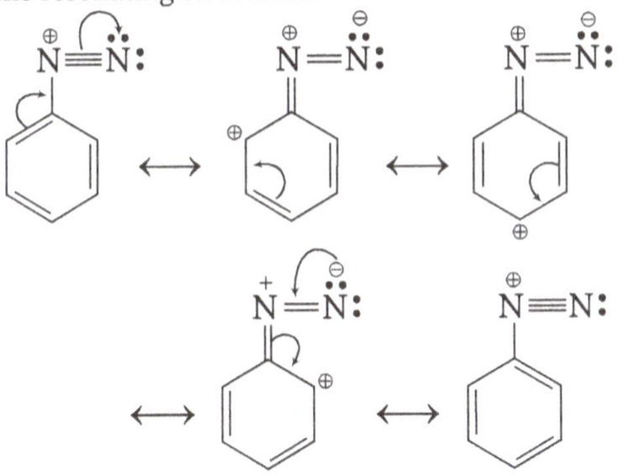

7. Due to the dispersal of positive charge over benzene ring.

8. The conversion of primary aromatic amines into their diazonium salts is called diazotisation.

9.

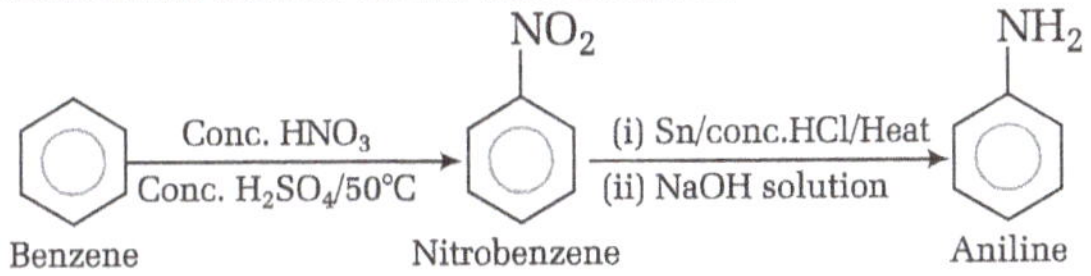

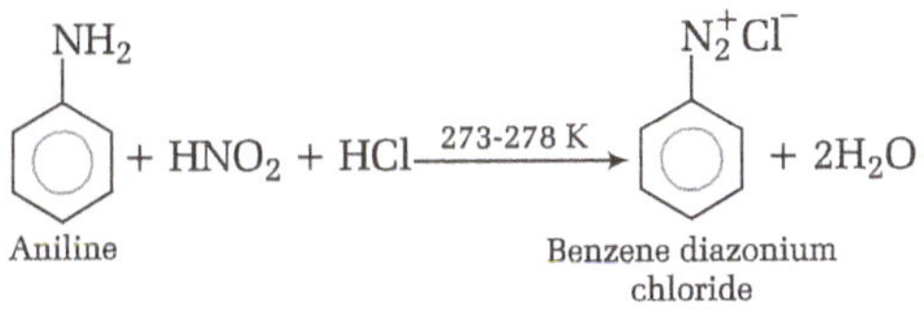

10. The conversion of primary aromatic amines into diazonium salts is known as diazotisation.

11. Because it is a good leaving group.

12. $C_6H_5NH_2 + HNO_2 + HCl$

$$\xrightarrow[\text{HCl at low temperature}]{NaNO_2} C_6H_5\overset{+}{N}\equiv N\overset{-}{Cl} + 2H_2O$$

13. $C_6H_5N_2Cl + C_2H_5OH \longrightarrow C_6H_6 + CH_3CHO + N_2\uparrow + HCl$

14. The introduction of chlorine or bromine can also be introduced in the benzene ring by treating the diazonium salt solution with corresponding halogen acid in the presence of copper powder.This is referred a **Gattermann reaction.**

$$C_6H_5N_2^+Cl^- \xrightarrow{Cu/HCl} C_6H_5Cl + N_2\uparrow + CuCl$$

15. Balz-Schiemann's reaction

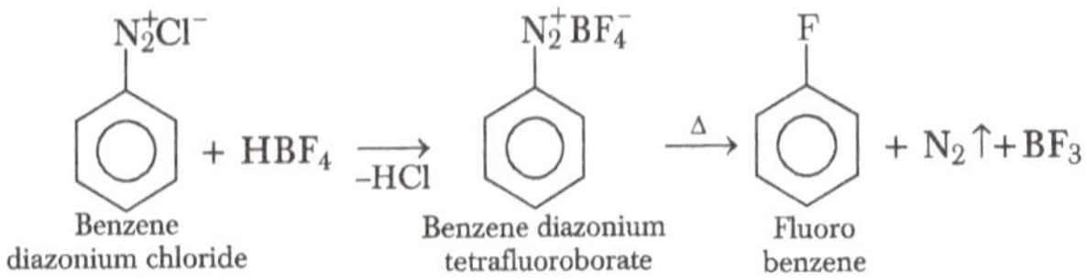

16.

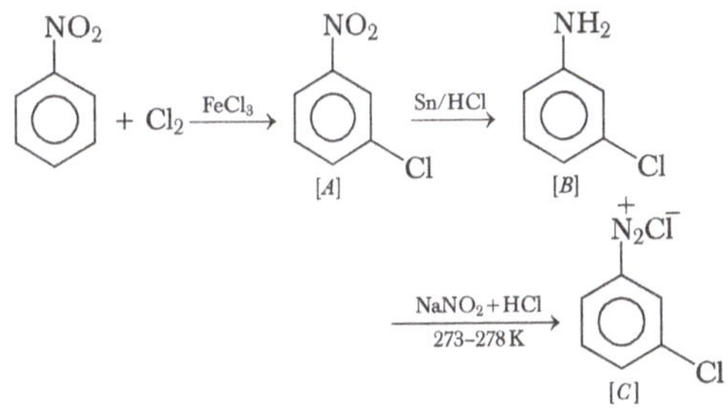

A is *m*-chloronitrobenzene.
B is *m*-chloroaniline.
C is *m*-chlorobenzene diazonium chloride.

17. Coupling reaction is the reaction of benzene diazonium chloride with phenol in which phenol molecule at its *para*-position is coupled with diazonium salt.

18. Benzene diazonium chloride is unstable or stable for a very short time in a solution at low temperature. Due to its unstability, it is used immediately after its preparation.

19. (i) $C_6H_5N_2^+Cl \xrightarrow[\text{Room temperature}]{H_2O} \underset{\text{Phenol}}{C_6H_5OH} + N_2\uparrow + HCl$ (1)

(ii)

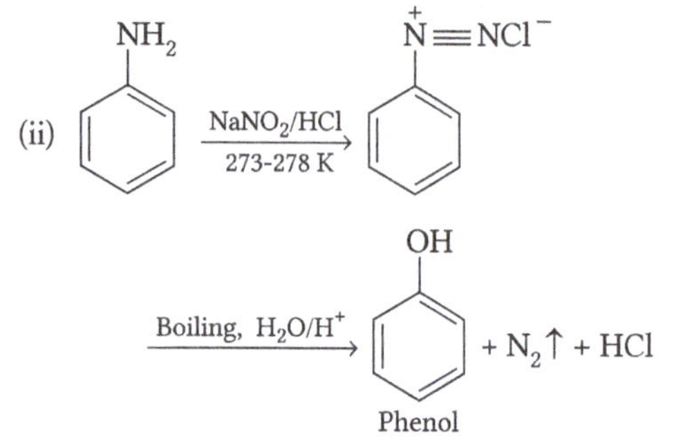

(1)

20. Refer to text on pages 389 (Reactions involving displacement of nitrogen). (2)

21. Benzene $\xrightarrow[(A)]{}$ Nitrobenzene $\xrightarrow[[B]]{}$ Aniline $\xrightarrow[[C]]{}$ Aniline hydrochloride $\xrightarrow[[D]5°]{O_2+}$ Benzene diazonium chloride (2)

22. (ii) $\underset{\text{Ethylamine}}{CH_3CH_2NH_2} + \underset{\text{Chloroform}}{CHCl_3} + 3KOH(Alc.) \xrightarrow{\Delta}$

$$\underset{\text{(Ethyl isocyanide)}}{CH_3CH_2-N \rightleftarrows C} + 3KCl + 3H_2O$$

(iii)

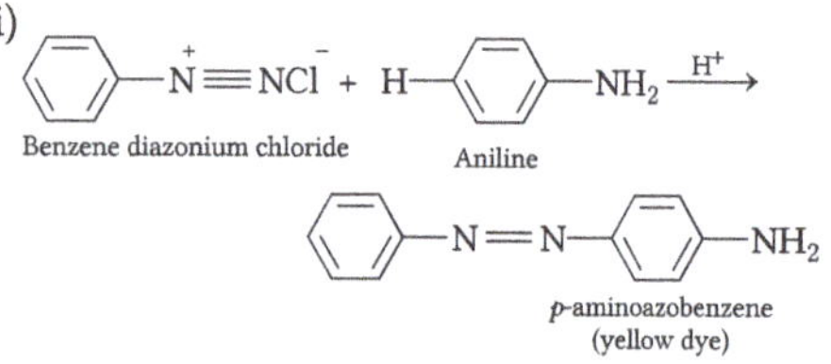

23. (i) $C_6H_5-NO_2 \xrightarrow{Sn/HCl} \underset{\text{Aniline}}{C_6H_5\cdot NH_2}$ (1)

(ii)

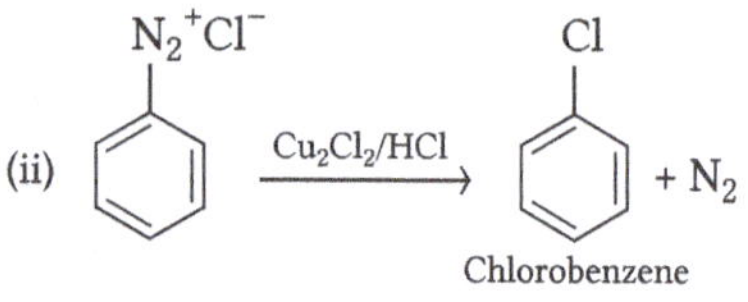

(1)

(iii) $CH_3CONH_2 \xrightarrow{Br_2/KOH(aq)} CH_3NH_2 + K_2CO_3 + 2KBr + 2H_2O$ (1)

24. (i) $\underset{\text{Acetic acid}}{CH_3COOH} \xrightarrow[-H_2O]{NH_3/\Delta} \underset{\text{Acetamide (A)}}{CH_3CONH_2} \xrightarrow{Br_2/KOH(aq)}$

$\underset{\substack{\text{Methylamine}\\(B)}}{CH_3NH_2} \xrightarrow{CHCl_3 + \text{alc. KOH}} \underset{\substack{\text{Methyl isocyanide}\\(C)}}{CH_3NC}$ (1½)

(ii) $C_6H_5N_2^+BF_4^- \xrightarrow[-N_2,-NaBF_4]{NaNO_2/Cu,\Delta} \underset{\substack{\text{Nitrobenzene}\\(A)}}{C_6H_5NO_2} \xrightarrow[\text{Reduction}]{Fe/HCl}$

$\underset{\substack{\text{Aniline}\\(B)}}{C_6H_5NH_2} \xrightarrow[-HCl]{CH_3COCl/pyridine} \underset{\substack{\text{Acetanilide}\\(C)}}{C_6H_5NHCOCH_3}$ (1½)

25. (i) $CH_3CH_2Cl \xrightarrow{KCN} \underset{(A)}{CH_3CH_2CN} \xrightarrow{H_2/Ni} \underset{(B)}{CH_3CH_2NH_2}$

$\xrightarrow{CH_3COCl/Base} \underset{(C)}{CH_3CH_2CH_2NHCOCH_3}$

(ii) $C_6H_5N_2^+Cl^- \xrightarrow{HBF_4} \underset{(A)}{C_6H_5N_2^+BF_4^-} \xrightarrow[\Delta]{NaNO_2/Cu}$

$\underset{(B)}{C_6H_5NO_2} \xrightarrow{Sn/HCl} \underset{(C)}{C_6H_5NH_2}$ $\left(6\times\frac{1}{2}=3\right)$

26.

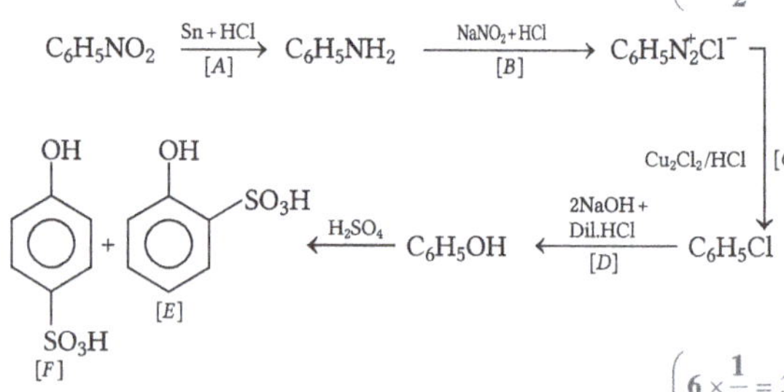

$\left(6\times\frac{1}{2}=3\right)$

27. Key Idea *Aniline to chlorobenzene*

(i) Diazotisation (ii) Gattermann reaction

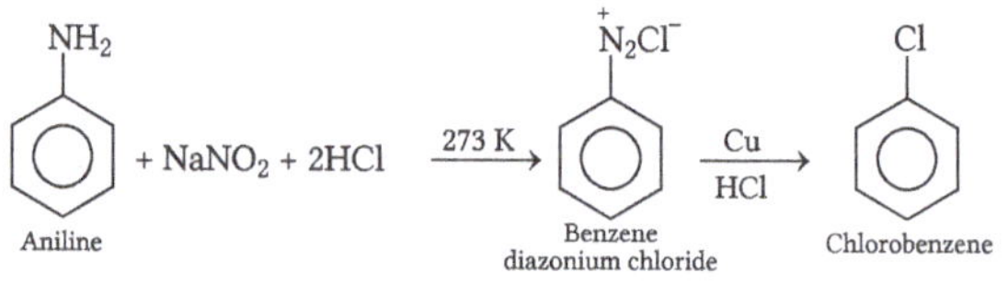

(3)

28. (i)

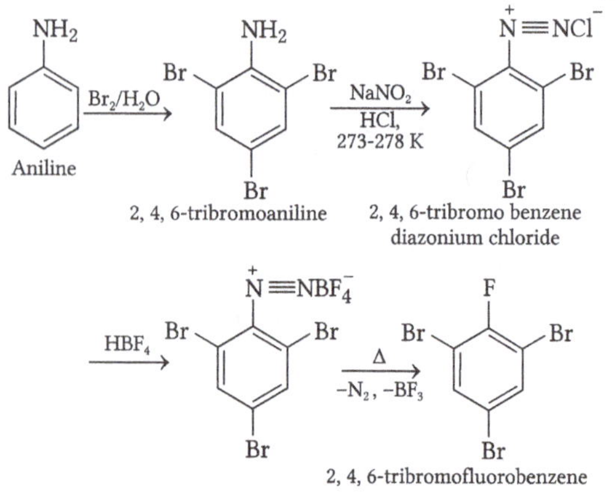

(1)

(ii)

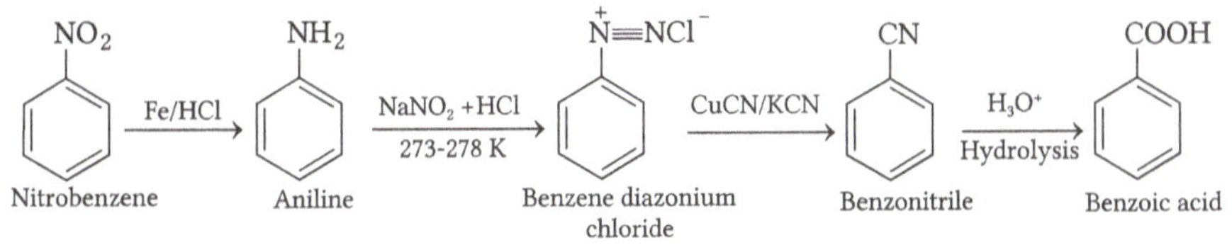

(1)

(iii)

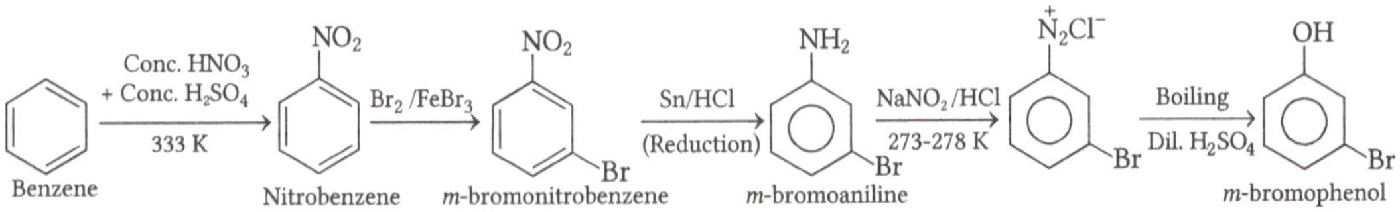

(1)

29. (i)

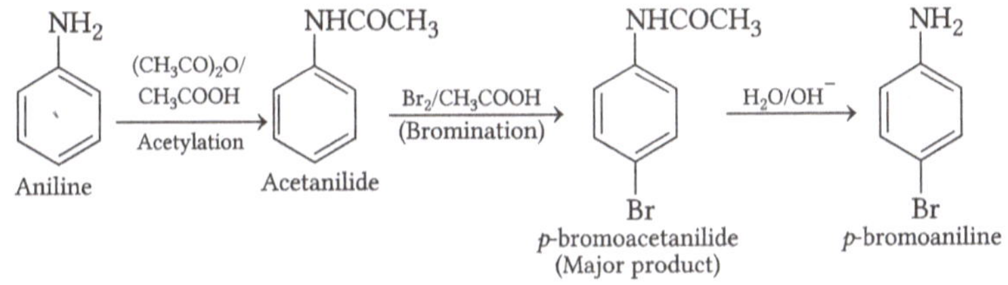

(1)

(ii)

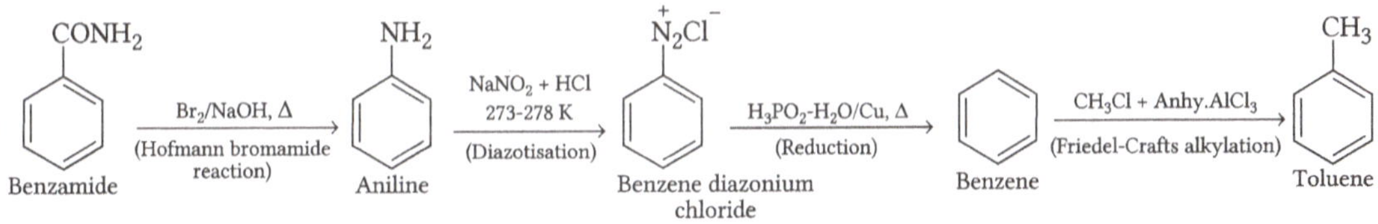

(1)

(iii)

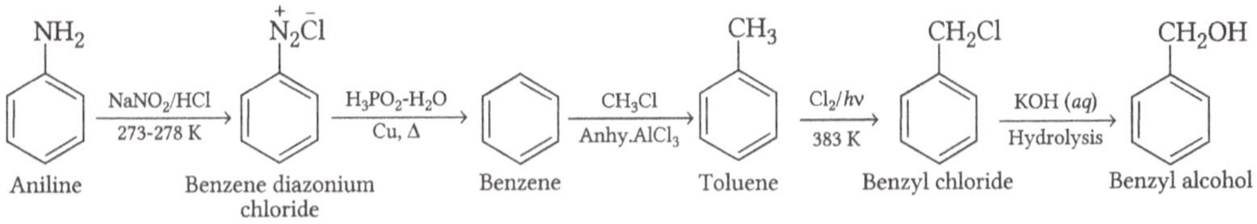

(1)

30. (i) $C_6H_5N_2^+Cl^- \xrightarrow{CuCN} \underset{\text{Benzonitrile } (A)}{C_6H_5CN} \xrightarrow{H_2O/H^+} \underset{\text{Benzoic acid } (B)}{C_6H_5COOH} \xrightarrow[\Delta]{NH_3} \underset{\text{Benzamide } (C)}{C_6H_5CONH_2}$ (1 ½)

(ii)

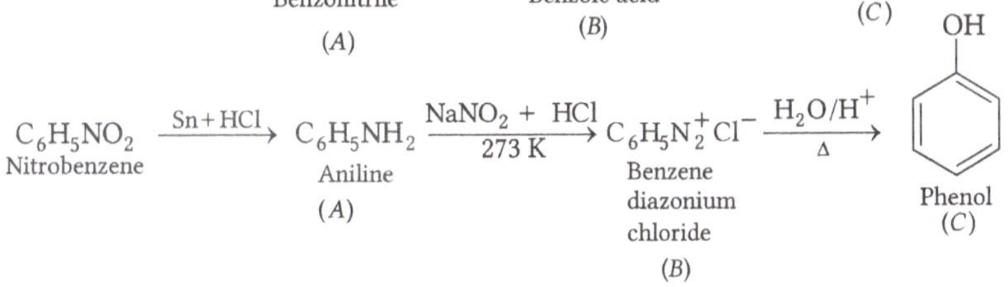

(1 ½)

31. (i)

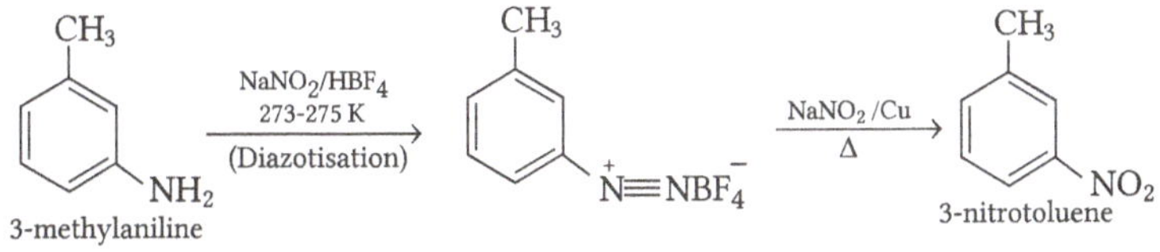

(1 ½)

(ii)

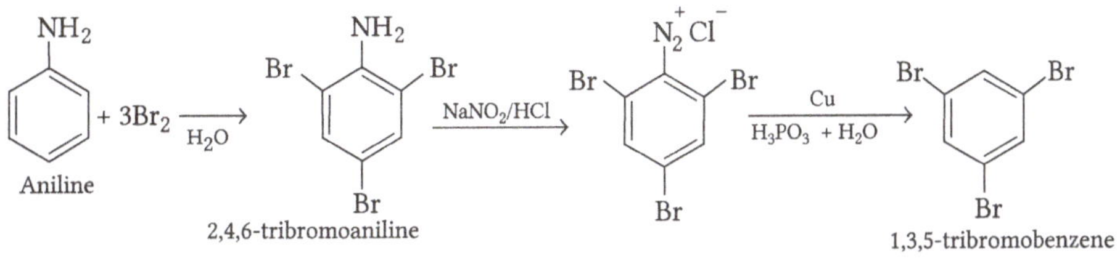

(1 ½)

32.

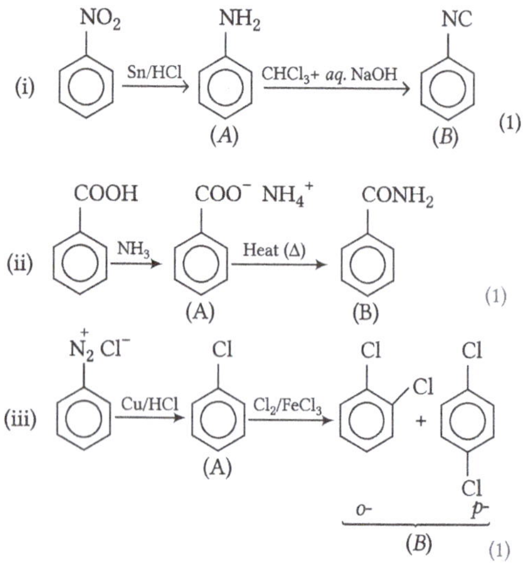

33. (i) $C_6H_5NO_2$ (Nitrobenzene) $\xrightarrow{Fe/HCl}$ $C_6H_5NH_2$ (Aniline, (A)) $\xrightarrow[273\text{ K}]{NaNO_2 + HCl}$

$C_6H_5\overset{+}{N}\equiv NCl^-$ (Benzene diazonium chloride (B)) $\xrightarrow[\Delta]{H_2O/H^+}$ C_6H_5OH (Phenol (C))

(1 ½)

(ii) $C_6H_5NO_2 \xrightarrow{Fe/HCl}$ $C_6H_5NH_2$ (Aniline (A)) $\xrightarrow[273\text{ K}]{HNO_2}$

$C_6H_5—\overset{+}{N}\equiv NCl^-$ (Benzene diazonium chloride (B)) $\xrightarrow[\text{Coupling reaction}]{C_6H_5OH}$

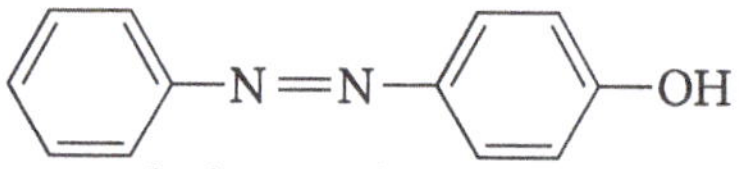

p-hydroxy azobenzene
(C)

(1 ½)

34. (i) **Carbylamine test** Methylamine is a primary amine, therefore it gives carbylamine test. When heated with an alcoholic solution of KOH and $CHCl_3$, it gives offensive smell of methyl isocyanide.

For reaction, refer to text on pages 372 and 373.

Since, dimethylamine is a secondary amine hence, it does not give this test.

$(CH_3)_2NH$ (Dimethylamine (2° amine)) $\xrightarrow[\Delta]{CHCl_3/KOH(alc.)}$ No reaction

(1)

(ii) They can be distinguished by **Liebermann nitrosoamine** test.

Secondary (2°) amines on treatment with HNO_2, give yellow coloured oily N-nitrosoamines.

$(CH_3CH_2)_2NH$ (Diethylamine (2° amine)) + HO—N=O (Nitrous acid) ⟶ $(CH_3CH_2)_2N—N=O + H_2O$ (N-nitrosodiethylamine (Yellow colour))

N-nitrosodiethylamine, on warming with a crystal of phenol and conc. H_2SO_4, gives a green solution which when made alkaline with aqueous NaOH turns deep blue and then red on dilution.

Tertiary amines do not give this test. (1)

(iii) Ethylamine ($CH_3CH_2NH_2$) is a primary aliphatic amine while aniline ($C_6H_5NH_2$) is a primary aromatic amine.

With the reaction of nitrous acid (HNO_2).

Ethylamine gives a brisk effervescence of N_2 gas with the formation of alcohol.

$CH_3CH_2NH_2 + HONO$ (Ethylamine) $\xrightarrow[\text{Dil. HCl(273-278 K)}]{NaNO_2}$ $CH_3CH_2OH + N_2\uparrow + H_2O$ (Ethanol)

Whereas, aniline gives benzene diazonium chloride which on treatment with alkaline solution of β-naphthol (2-naphthol) gives an orange dye (azo dye test). (1)

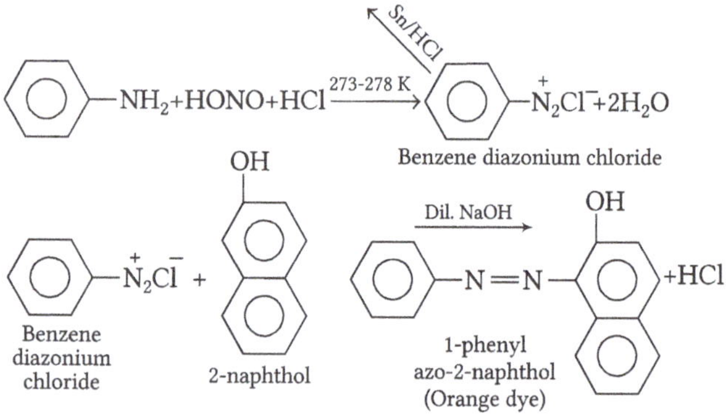

35. $C_6H_5CONH_2 \xrightarrow{Br_2/KOH} C_6H_5NH_2$ [A]

$C_6H_5NH_2$ [A] $\xrightarrow{CHCl_3+KOH}$ C_6H_5NC [D]

$C_6H_5NH_2$ [A] $\xrightarrow{\text{(i) } NaNO_2/HCl \text{ (ii) Steam}}$ C_6H_5OH [B]

C_6H_5OH [B] $\xrightarrow[\text{Ice cold}]{C_6H_5\overset{+}{N_2}\bar{Cl}}$ $C_6H_5—N=N—C_6H_5OH$ (p-hydroxyazobenzene (an azo dye) [C])

C_6H_5OH [B] $\xrightarrow{CH_3COOH}$ $CH_3COOC_6H_5$ [E]

(5 × 1 = 5)

36.

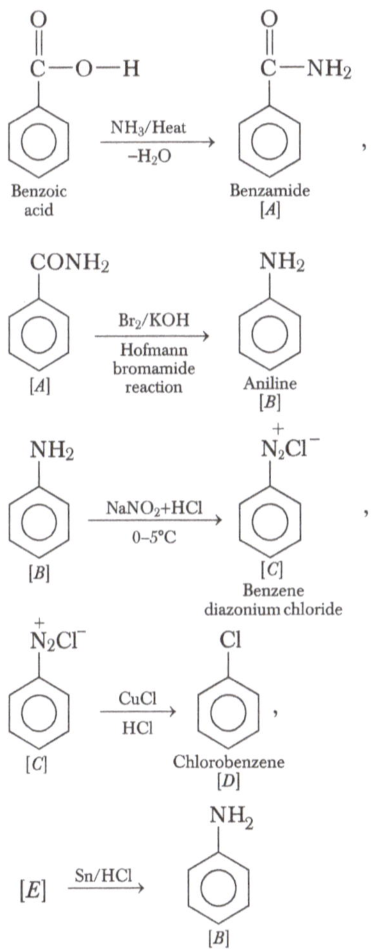

Since, E on reduction, gives aniline, hence it must be nitrobenzene, i.e. $C_6H_5NO_2$. $(5 \times 1 = 5)$

37. (i) $CH_3COOH \xrightarrow[\Delta]{NH_3} \underset{(A)}{CH_3CONH_2} \xrightarrow{Br_2 + KOH} CH_3NH_2 \xrightarrow{CHCl_3 + NaOH} CH_3NC$

(ii) $CH_3Br \xrightarrow{KCN} \underset{(A)}{CH_3CN} \xrightarrow{LiAlH_4} \underset{(B)}{CH_3CH_2NH_2} \xrightarrow[273\text{ K}]{HNO_2} \underset{(C)}{CH_3CH_2OH}$

38. (i) Ethyl bromide will react with alcoholic AgCN to give ethylisocyanide (C_2H_5—NC)

$$C_2H_5—Br + \xrightarrow{Aq.\ EtOH} C_2H_5—NC + AgBr$$

(ii) When aniline reacts with dil. HCl and *aq.* solution of sodium nitrite ($NaNO_2$) at 273-278 K, it will form benzene diazonium chloride called diazotisation reaction.

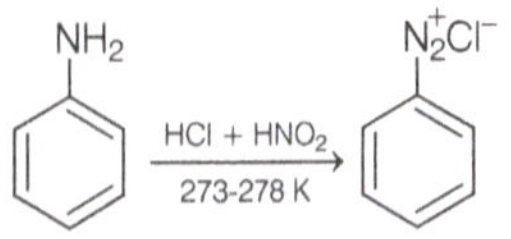

(iii) When diazonium salts are hydrolysed in the presence of dil. H_2SO_4, it give phenols.

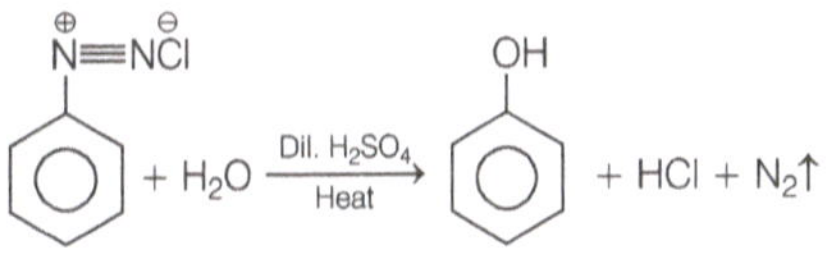

39. (i)

(a)

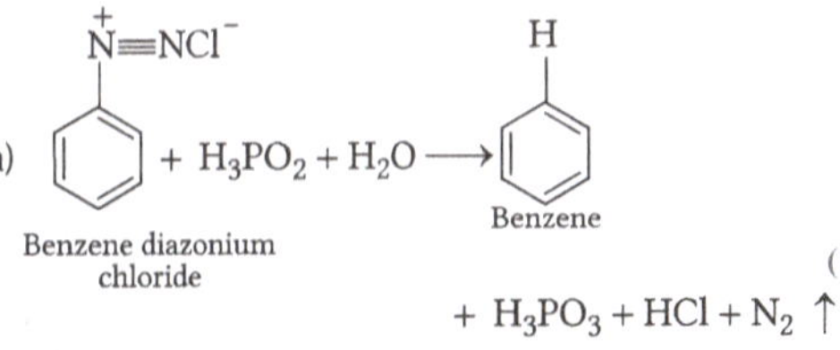

(1/2)

(b)

(1/2)

(c)

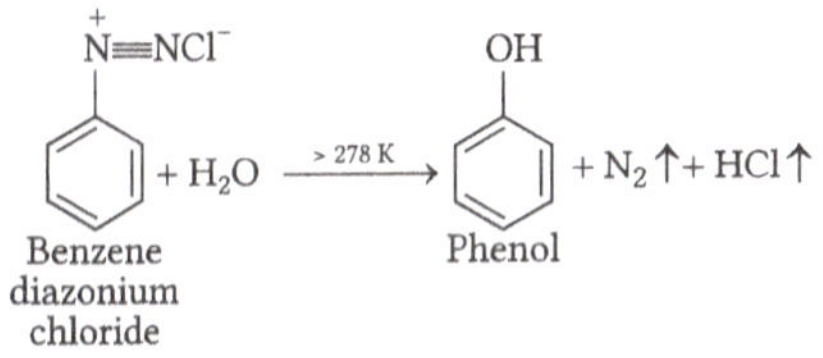

(1/2)

(ii) The relative basic strength of $C_2H_5NH_2$, $(C_2H_5)_2NH$ and $(C_2H_5)_3N$ depends upon the stabilisation of their corresponding conjugate acids formed as a result of accepting a proton from water by a number of factors such as H-bonding, steric hindrance created by the alkyl groups and + *I*-effect of the alkyl groups.

All these factors are favourable for 2° amines, therefore, $(C_2H_5)_2NH$ is a stronger base than $C_2H_5NH_2$ and $(C_2H_5)_3N$.

Since, $(C_2H_5)_3$ group is large, it exerts some steric hindrance to H-bond.

Thus, $(C_2H_5)_3N$ is more basic than $C_2H_5NH_2$. Hence, the overall basic strength of the three amines in aqueous medium increases in the order :

$C_2H_5NH_2 < (C_2H_5)_3N < (C_2H_5)_2NH$. (2)

(iii) The given amines are primary and secondary aromatic amines. In order to distinguish between primary and secondary amine, the amine is shaken with benzene sulphonyl chloride (Hinsberg's reagent) in the presence of excess of aqueous KOH solution. A primary amine gives a clear solution which on acidification gives an insoluble N-alkyl benzene sulphonamide.

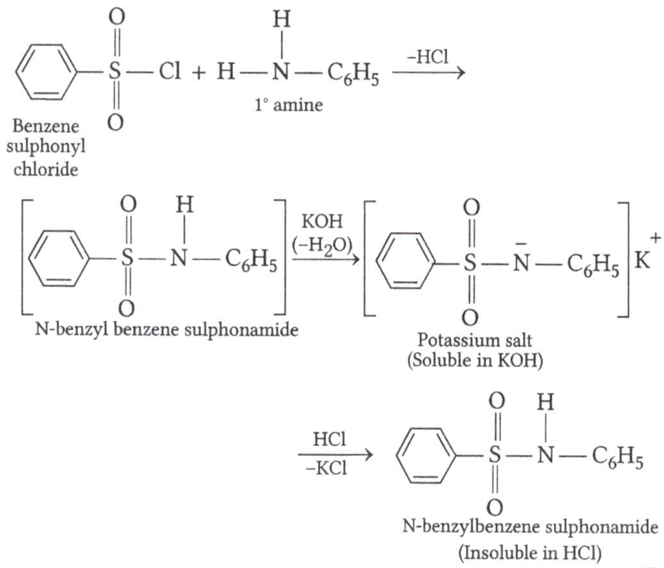

(1)

A secondary amine gives an insoluble N, N-dialkyl benzene sulphonamide which remains unaffected on addition of acid.

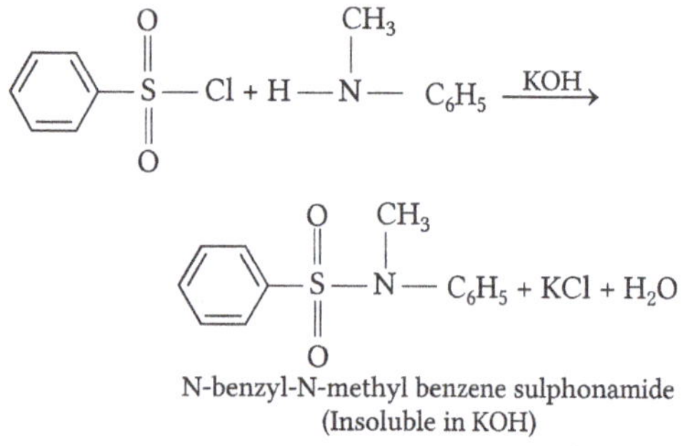

(1/2)

40.

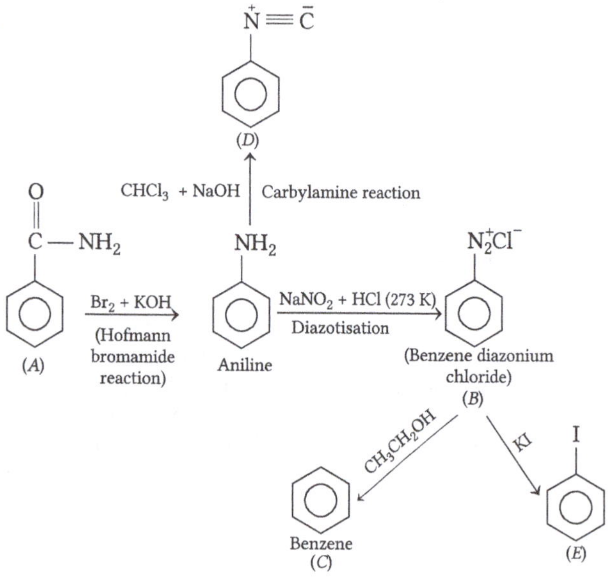

(5 × 1 = 5)

41. (i) Addition of HCl to compound '*A*' shows that compound '*A*' is alkene because compound '*B*' is C_4H_9Cl.

(ii) Compound '*B*' reacts with NH_3, to form amine '*C*'.

$$\underset{A}{C_4H_8} \xrightarrow{HCl} \underset{B}{C_4H_9Cl} \xrightarrow{NH_3} \underset{C}{C_4H_{11}N} \text{ or } C_4H_9NH_2$$

(iii) '*C*' gives diazonium salt with $NaNO_2$ / HCl, which yields an optically active alcohol. So, '*C*' is an aliphatic amine.

(iv) '*A*' on ozonolysis produces 2 moles of CH_3CHO. So, '*A*' is $CH_3—CH=CH—CH_3$ (but-2-ene). (1)

Therefore, overall reaction sequence looks like

(i) $\overset{4}{C}H_3—\overset{3}{C}H=\overset{2}{C}H—\overset{1}{C}H_3 \xrightarrow{HCl} \overset{4}{C}H_3—\overset{3}{C}H_2—\overset{2}{C}H(Cl)—\overset{1}{C}H_3$

But-2-ene (*A*) (C_4H_8) → 2-chlorobutane (*B*) (C_4H_9Cl) (1)

(ii) $CH_3—CH_2—CH(Cl)—CH_3 \xrightarrow{NH_3} CH_3—CH_2—CH(NH_2)—CH_3$

2- chlorobutane [*B*] → 2 - aminobutane (*C*) ($C_4H_{11}N$) (1)

(iii) $CH_3—CH_2—CH(NH_2)—CH_3 \xrightarrow[\text{(ii) } H_2O]{\text{(i) } NaNO_2 / HCl} CH_3—C(H)(CH_2CH_3)—OH$

2- aminobutane (*C*) ($C_4H_{11}N$) → Butan-2-ol (*D*) (Optically active) (1)

(iv) $CH_3—CH=CH—CH_3 + O_3 \longrightarrow$

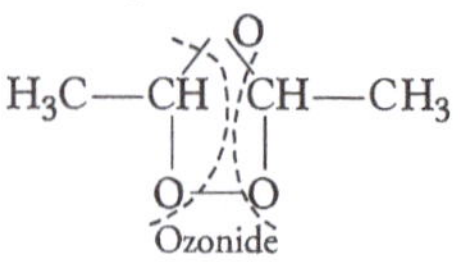

$\xrightarrow{Zn + CH_3COOH} CH_3CHO + CH_3CHO$

(1)

SUMMARY

- Amines are formed by the replacement of H-atom of ammonia by alkyl/aryl group.
- Amines are classified as : 1° amine (RNH_2), 2° amine (R_2NH) and 3° amine (R_3N)
- Methods of preparation of amines are:
  (i) Reduction of $—NO_2$, $—NO_2 \xrightarrow[\text{Metal + acid}]{\text{Raney Ni/Pt}} —NH_2$
  (ii) Reduction of $—CN$ or $—CONH_2$
  $—CN \xrightarrow{LiAlH_4} —CH_2NH_2$ or $—CONH_2$
  (iii) Hofmann bromamide reaction
  $—CONH_2 \xrightarrow[Br]{NaOH} —NH_2$
  (iv) Hofmann ammonolysis reaction
  $NH_3 \xrightarrow[-HX]{RX} RNH_2$ (1°) $\xrightarrow{RX}$ R_2NH (2°) $\xrightarrow{RX}$ R_3N (3°)
  (v) Gabriel-phthalimide reaction
  Phthalimide $\xrightarrow{KOH}$ Potassium salt of phthalimide $\xrightarrow{RX}$ N-alkyl phthalimide $\xrightarrow{NaOH}$ 1°amine (aliphatic)
- Solubility of amines decreases but boiling point increases with increase in molecular mass.
  - The order of boling point is 1° > 2° > 3° amines.
  - **Order of basicity**
    (i) In gaseous state is 3°amine > 2°amine > 1° amine.
    (ii) In aqueous solution is
    2°amine > 3°amine > 1°amine > NH_3. If $R = C_2H_5$ and 2° > 1° > 3° > NH_3, if $R = CH_3$.
- The chemical reactions of amines are :

(i) $R—NH_2$ (1°) $\xrightarrow[\text{Acylation}]{RCOCl}$ $R—N(H)—C(=O)—R'$ Substituted amide

$R—NH_2 \xrightarrow[\text{Carbylamine reaction}]{CHCl_3 + KOH} R—NC$

$R—NH_2 \xrightarrow[\text{Hinsberg's reagent}]{C_6H_5SO_2Cl}$ N-alkylbenzene sulphonamide (soluble in alkali)

(ii) R_2NH (2°) $\xrightarrow{\text{Hinsberg's reagent}}$ N,N-dialkylbenzene sulphonamide (insoluble in alkali)

(iii) R_3N (3°) $\xrightarrow{C_6H_5SO_2Cl}$ No reaction

(iv) RNH_2 $\xrightarrow[\text{(Here, } R = C_6H_5)]{\text{Electrophilic substitution}}$

$\xrightarrow[H_2O]{Br_2}$ 2,4,6-tribromoaniline

$\xrightarrow[Br_2]{(CH_3CO)_2O}$ p-bromoaniline

(Here, $R = C_6H_5$) $\xrightarrow[H_2SO_4]{HNO_3}$ $m + o + p$-nitroaniline (47%) (2%) (51%)

Diazonium salt

- The formula of diazonium salts is $C_6H_5N{=}N^+Cl^-$.
- It is prepared as follows :
  $C_6H_5—NH_2$ (1°amine (aromatic)) $\xrightarrow[\text{or } NaNO_2 + HCl,\ 0°C]{HNO_2}$ $C_6H_5\overset{+}{N_2}Cl^-$ (Diazonium salt)
- They are colourless, unstable, soluble in water and neutral to litmus.
  The chemical reactions of amines are:

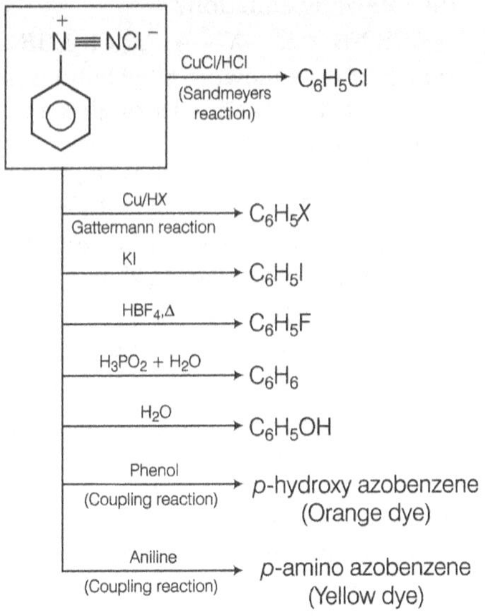

For Mind Map

Visit : https://goo.gl/19porm OR **Scan the Code**

Chapter Practice

Very Short Answer Type Questions

1 Mark

1 Fill in the Blanks

(i) Separation of primary, secondary and tertiary amines can be made with the help of reagent .... in Hinsberg method.

(ii) Carbylamine reaction is used for the test of ....

(iii) .... test is used to distinguish an aromatic amine from an aliphatic amine.

(iv) Ethyl isocyanide on hydrolysis with dilute sulphuric acid gives .... and ....

2 Objective Type Questions

(i) Amongst the following, the strongest base in aqueous medium is ....

(a) CH_3NH_2 (b) $NCCH_2NH_2$
(c) $(CH_3)_2NH$ (d) $C_6H_5NHCH_3$

(ii) Benzylamine may be alkylated as shown in the following equation?

$C_6H_5CH_2NH_2 + R—X \longrightarrow C_6H_5CH_2NHR$

Which of the following alkyl halides is best suited for this reaction through S_N1 mechanism?

(a) CH_3Br (b) C_6H_5Br
(c) $C_6H_5CH_2Br$ (d) C_2H_5Br

(iii) Amongst the given set of reactants, the most appropriate for preparing 2° amine is ....

(a) $2°R—Br + NH_3$

(b) $2°R—Br + NaCN$ followed by H_2 / Pt

(c) $1°R—NH_2 + CH_3OH$ followed by Al_2O_3 / 350°C

(d) $1°R—Br$(2 mole) + potassium phthalimide followed by H_3O^+/ heat

(iv) The best reagent for converting 2-phenylpropanamide into 2-phenylpropanamine is ....

(a) excess H_2
(b) Br_2 in aqueous NaOH
(c) iodine in the presence of red phosphorus
(d) $LiAlH_4$ in ether

(v) The best reagent for converting, 2-phenylpropanamide into 1-phenylethanamine is ....

(a) excess H_2/Pt (b) $NaOH/Br_2$
(c) $NaBH_4$/methanol (d) $LiAlH_4$/ether

(vi) Hofmann bromamide degradation reaction is shown by ....

(a) $ArNH_2$ (b) $ArCONH_2$
(c) $ArNO_2$ (d) $ArCH_2NH_2$

3 Matching Type Questions

(i) Match the following Columns and choose the correct option using the codes given below:

	Column I		Column II
A.	$CHCl_3$ + NaOH	(i)	Aniline
B.	Diazotisation	(ii)	Isocyanide test
C.	Hinsberg's reagent	(iii)	Hinsberg's reagent
D.	Aryl diazonium salts	(iv)	Conversion to alcohol
E.	Benzene sulphonyl chloride	(v)	Amines

Codes

	A	B	C	D	E
(a)	(ii)	(i)	(v)	(iv)	(iii)
(b)	(i)	(iv)	(v)	(ii)	(iii)
(c)	(ii)	(iii)	(v)	(iv)	(i)
(d)	(i)	(ii)	(iii)	(iv)	(v)

(ii) Match the following Columns and choose the correct option using the codes given below:

	Column I		Column II
A.	Primary amine + HNO_2	(i)	Soluble complex
B.	Nitroethane + $LiAlH_4$	(ii)	Insoluble compound
C.	Dimethylamine + Hinsberg's reagent +KOH	(iii)	Used to distinguiesh amines
D.	Silver chloride + Methylamine	(iv)	Methanamine
E.	Ethanamide $+Br_2$ + KOH	(v)	Ethanamine
F.	Hinsberg's reagent	(vi)	Primary alcohol

Codes

	A	B	C	D	E	F
(a)	(i)	(iii)	(ii)	(iv)	(vi)	(v)
(b)	(vi)	(v)	(ii)	(i)	(iv)	(iii)
(c)	(i)	(iii)	(iv)	(ii)	(vi)	(v)
(d)	(i)	(iv)	(iii)	(v)	(ii)	(vi)

4 Why does trimethylamine have an angle of 108°?

5 Draw the structure of N, N-*bis* (1-bromo ethyl) ethanamine.

6 Write the IUPAC nomenclature of the compound.

7 Write the structural formulae of *o*-toluidine Name the reagent that reacts with nitromethane to form methyl hydroxylamine.

8 Find out the incorrect names and correct them
(a) N-butylaminoethane
(b) 1-amino 2-ethanol
(c) methylaniline
(d) propanediamine
(e) 1-phenylaminoethane

9 Arrange the following in the decreasing order of basic strength in gaseous phase.
NH_3, $(C_2H_5)_2NH$, $(C_2H_5)_3N$, $C_2H_5\ NH_2$

10 Which is more acidic, aniline or ammonia?

11 Give the structure of *A* in the following reaction:

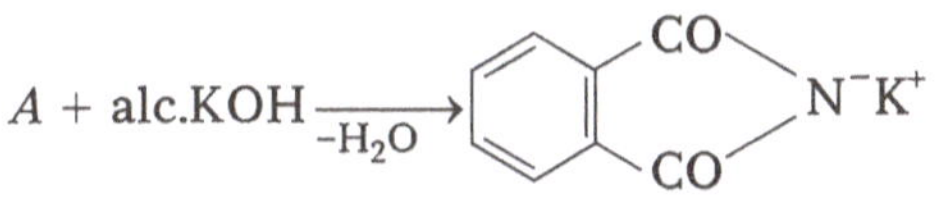

12 What is the number of 1° H-atoms present in an amine, obtained by reduction of benzamide?

13 Account for the following:
Ammonolysis of alkyl halide does not give a corresponding amine in pure state.

14 Reduction of nitrobenzene depends upon pH. Give reason.

15 How can you convert an amide into amine having one carbon atom less than the starting compound?

16 What happens, when nitroethane is treated with $LiAlH_4$?

17 Write *A* in the following sequence:

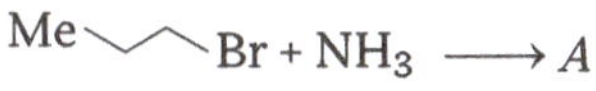

18 Complete the following chemical reaction.

$$R-\overset{\overset{\displaystyle O}{\|}}{C}-NH_2 \xrightarrow[H_2O]{LiAlH_4}$$

19 Explain the following reaction:
Gabriel phthalimide reaction

Assertion-Reason

■ **Directions** (Q. Nos. 25-35) In the following questions. an Assertion (A) is followed by a corresponding Reason (R) Use the following keys to choose the appropriate answer.

(a) Both (A) and (R) are correct, (R) is the correct explanation of (A).
(b) Both (A) and (R) are correct, (R) is not the correct explanation of (A).
(c) (A) is correct; (R) is incorrect.
(d) (A) is incorrect; (R) is correct.

20. **Assertion** (A) Aromatic primary amines cannot be prepared by Gabriel phthalimide synthesis.
Reason (R) Aryl halides do not undergo electrophilic substitution with anion formed by phthalimide.

21. **Assertion** (A) Only a small amount of HCl is required in the reduction of nitro compounds with iron scrap and HCl in the presence of steam.
Reason (R) $FeCl_2$ formed gets hydrolysed to release HCl during the reaction.

22. **Assertion** (A) In strongly acidic solutions, aniline becomes more reactive towards electrophilic reagents.
Reason (R) The amino group being completely protonated in strongly acidic solution, the lone pair of electrons on the nitrogen is no longer available for resonance.

23. **Assertion** (A) In acylation reaction of amines, equilibrium shifts to the right hand side in the presence of pyridine.
Reason (R) In the presence of strong base, HCl is removed and reaction shifts toward the right hand side.

24. **Assertion** (A) Acetanilide is less basic than aniline.
Reason (R) Acetylation of aniline results in decrease of electron density on nitrogen.

Case-Study

25. Amines are usually formed from nitro compounds, halides, amides, imides, etc. They exhibit hydrogen bonding which influences their physical properties. In alkyl amines, a combination of electron releasing, steric and hydrogen bonding factors influence the stability of the substituted ammonium cations

in protic polar solvents and thus affect the basic nature of amines.

In aromatic amines, electron releasing and withdrawing groups, respectively increase and decrease their basic character. Influence of the number of hydrogen atoms at nitrogen atom on the type of reactions and nature of products is responsible for identification and distinction between primary, secondary and tertiary amines.

Presence of amino group in aromatic ring enhances reactivity of the aromatic amines. Aryl diazonium salts provide advantageous methods for producing aryl halides, cyanides, phenols and arenes by reductive removal of the diazo group.

Answer the following questions

(i) Arrange the following in the increasing order of their pK_b values in aqueous solutions:

$C_2H_5NH_2$, $(C_2H_5)_2NH$, $(C_2H_5)_3N$

(ii) An aromatic compound '*A*' of molecular formula $C_7H_6O_2$ on treatment with aqueous ammonia and heating forms compound '*B*'. Compound '*B*' on heating with Br_2 and aqueous KOH gives a compound '*C*' of molecular formula C_6H_7N. Write the structures of *A*, *B* and *C*.

(iii) Complete the following reactions giving main products :

(a)

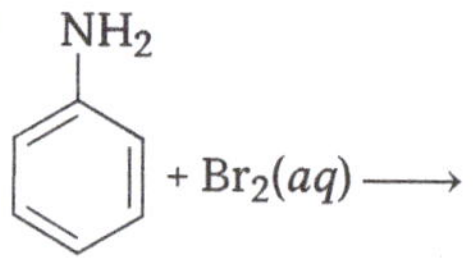

(b)

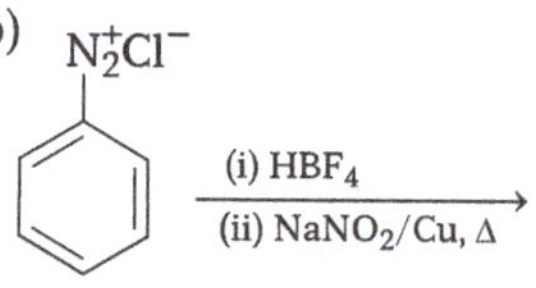

26. A student selected an amide '*A*' for producing 1° amine '*B*' (molar mass 59 g mol^{-1}) by using Br_2/KOH '*A*' could also be produced from isobutyric acid.

He was also able to prepare another 1° amine '*C*' from '*A*' by using reagent *Y*. The molar mass of '*C*' was determined to be 73 g mol^{-1}.

(i) What can be the structure of 1° amine '*B*'?

(ii) What is the molar mass of the amide '*A*' selected by the student?

(iii) The reagent *Y* used is ....

Short Answer Type I Questions

(2 Marks)

27 (i) *Tert*-butylamine cannot be prepared by the action of NH_3 on *tert*-butylbromide. Give reason.

(ii) How is aminomethane obtained from ethanal?

28 Account for the following :

(i) Amines are basic substances while amides are neutral.

(ii) Aromatic amines are weaker bases than aliphatic amines.

29 (i) Under what conditions, aniline gives *p*-nitro derivative as the major product?

(ii) Write the IUPAC name of the product formed when nitrobenzene is reduced using tin and concentrated hydrochloric acid.

30 Why the hydrogen atoms of the methyl group in *o*-and *p*-nitrotoluene are acidic in nature while those of toluene are not?

31 How will you convert cyclohexane carboxamide to N-methyl cyclohexylamine?

32 Which is the best method for preparing primary amines from alkyl halides, without changing the number of carbon atoms in the chain? Give mechanism.

33 How will you distinguish between the following pairs of compounds?

(i) Ethylamine and trimethylamine

(ii) Aniline and N-methylaniline

34 Give reasons for the following

(i) Acetylation of aniline reduces its activation effect.

(ii) Although —NH_2 is *o*/*p*-directing group, yet aniline on nitration gives a significant amount of *m*-nitroaniline.

35 Why does aliphatic amines are more reactive towards hydrochloric acid as comparison to arylamine?

36 What happens, when

(i) toluene is treated with conc. HNO_3 and conc. H_2SO_4 at 293 K?

(ii) nitrobenzene is treated with conc. HNO_3 and conc. H_2SO_4 at 363 K?

37 Write the structures of compounds A, B and C in the following reactions.

(i) $CH_3—COOH \xrightarrow{NH_3/\Delta} A \xrightarrow{Br_2/KOH\,(aq)} B \xrightarrow{CHCl_3 + alc.KOH} C$

(ii) $C_6H_5N_2^+ BF_4^- \xrightarrow[\Delta]{NaNO_2/Cu} A \xrightarrow{Fe/HCl} B \xrightarrow{CH_3COCl/\,pyridine} C$

38 (i) Why aniline does not undergo Friedel-Crafts reaction?

(ii) Why can primary aromatic amines be not prepared by Gabriel phthalimide synthesis?

39 Account for the following:
Diazonium salts of aromatic amines are more stable than those of aliphatic amines.

40 Identify A and B in each of the following processes

(i) $CH_3CH_2Cl \xrightarrow{NaCN} A \xrightarrow[Ni/H_2]{Reduction} B$

(ii) $C_6H_5NH_2 \xrightarrow{NaNO_2/HCl} A \xrightarrow[OH^-]{C_6H_5NH_2} B$

41 $\underset{(X)}{\underset{\text{(Optically active)}}{C_5H_{13}N}} \xrightarrow[HCl]{aq\ NaNO_2} \underset{3^\circ\text{-alcohol}}{Y}$ + Other products

(i) Identify X and Y.

(ii) Is Y optically active?

42 Identify the product of the following reaction:

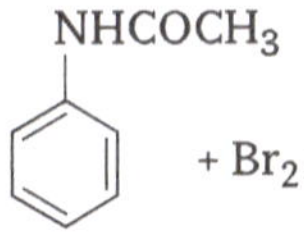

$+ Br_2/CH_3COOH \longrightarrow$

43 Usually, benzene diazonium salts are unstable but benzene diazonium fluoroborate is stable. Why?

44 Draw the resonating structures of benzene diazonium salt.

45 Aniline is diazotised in cold and then treated with dimethylaniline to give a coloured product. What is the structure of this product?

46 Identify A and B in the following reactions.

(i) $C_2H_5C \equiv N \xrightarrow{LiAlH_4} A \xrightarrow{HNO_2} B$

(ii) 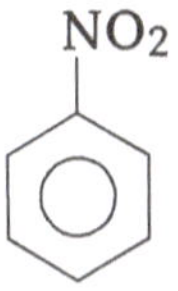 $\xrightarrow[273\ K]{NaNO_2/HCl} A \xrightarrow[H_2O]{CuCl} B$

47 Starting from toluene, outline a synthesis of each of the following compounds using diazonium salts as intermediates.

(i) p-fluorotoluene

(ii) p-cresol

Short Answer Type II Questions

3 Marks

48 Write structures of A, B and C in the following.

(i) $C_6H_5—CONH_2 \xrightarrow{Br_2/aq.KOH} A \xrightarrow{NaNO_2 + HCl} B \xrightarrow{KI} C$

(ii) $CH_3—Cl \xrightarrow{KCN} A \xrightarrow{LiAlH_4} B \xrightarrow{CHCl_3 + alc.KOH} C$

49 Explain the following observations.

(i) Electrophilic substitution in case of aromatic amines takes place more readily than benzene.

(ii) Aryl cyanides cannot be formed by the reaction of aryl halides and sodium cyanide.

(iii) Tertiary amines do not undergo acylation.

50 Describe the following giving the relevant chemical equation in each case

(i) Carbylamine reaction

(ii) Hofmann bromamide reaction.

51 Why does bromination of aniline, even under very mild conditions, give 2, 4, 6- tribromoaniline instantaneously?

52 Identify A and B in the following reactions.

(i) $CH_3—\underset{\underset{CH_3}{|}}{CH}—CONH_2 \xrightarrow{Br_2, NaOH} A \xrightarrow{HNO_2} B$

(ii) $C_6H_5NO_2 \xrightarrow{Br_2/Fe^{3+}} A \xrightarrow{HNO_2} B$

(iii) $CH_3CN \xrightarrow{H^+, H_2O} A \xrightarrow{LiAlH_4} B$

53 Accomplish the following conversions:

(i) Benzene to m-bromophenol

(ii) Aniline to 2, 4, 6-tribromofluorobenzene

54 Complete the following reactions:

(i) $CH_3CH_2NH_2 + CHCl_3 + (alc.)KOH \longrightarrow$

(ii) $C_6H_5N_2^+Cl^- \xrightarrow[\text{(Room temp.)}]{H_2O}$

(iii) 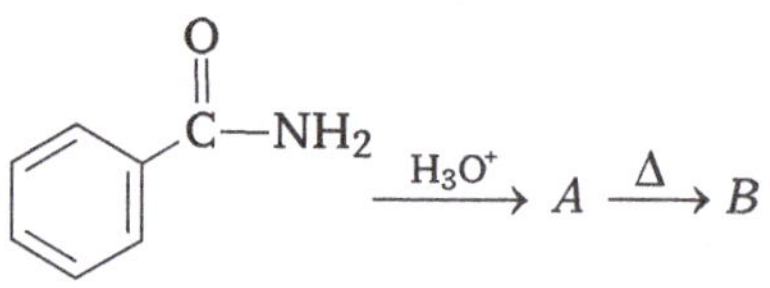

55 Write the main products of the following reactions:

(i) $C_6H_5N_2^+Cl^- \xrightarrow{H_3PO_2 + H_2O}$

(ii) 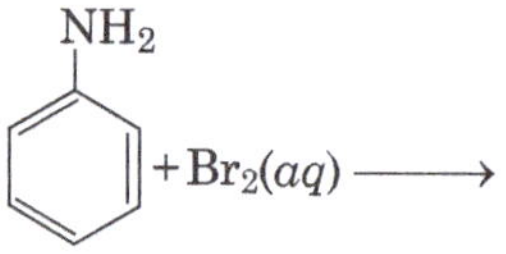

(iii) $CH_3-\overset{\overset{\displaystyle O}{\|}}{C}-NH_2 \xrightarrow{Br_2 + NaOH}$

56 (i) What are coupling reactions? How does the electrophilic substitution reaction take place during this reaction?

(ii) List some important applications of diazonium salts.

Answers

1. (i) Benzene sulphonyl chloride

(ii) Primary amines

(iii) Azodye

(iv) Ethylamine, formic acid

2. (i) c, (ii) c, (iii) c, (iv) d, (v) b, (vi) b

3. (i) (a) A → (iii), B → (i), C → (v), D → (iv), E → (iii)

(ii) (b) A → (vi), B → (v), C → (ii), D → (i), E → (iv), F → (iii)

4. Due to the presence of unshared pair of electrons, the angle C — N — C is less than 109.5°

5.

$$\begin{array}{l} Br \\ | \\ CH-CH_3 \\ | \\ N-CH_2CH_3 \\ | \\ CH-CH_3 \\ | \\ Br \end{array}$$

6. N-methylpropene

7. 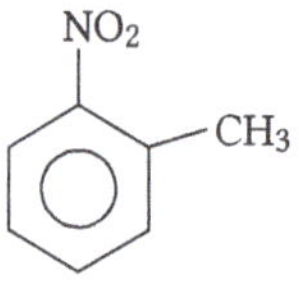

8. (a) N-ethylbutanamine

(b) 2-aminoethanol

(c) 2-aminotoluene

(e) 1-phenyl ethanamine

9. $(C_2H_5)_3N > (C_2H_5)_2NH > C_2H_5NH_2 > NH_3$

10. Aniline

11. 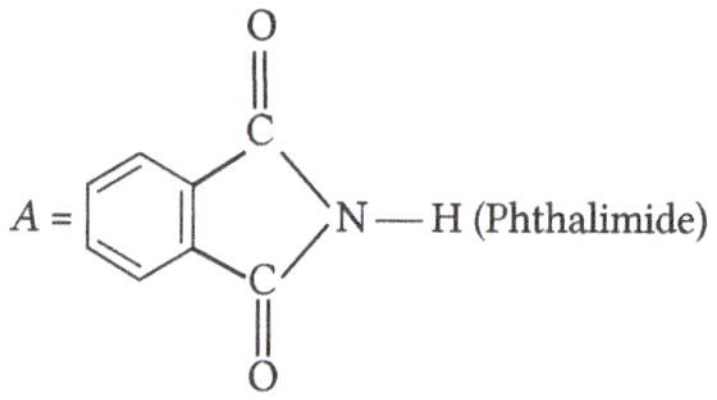

12. Two

13. **Hint** Formation of quaternary ammonium salt.
Refer to text on page 364 (Topic-1, Ammonolysis of alkyl halide).

14. Reduction of nitrobenzene is highly dependent on pH and give different products in different pH range.

$$C_6H_5NO_2 \xrightarrow{-O} C_6H_5NO \xrightarrow{2H} C_6H_5NHOH \xrightarrow{-O} C_6H_5NH_2$$

The nature of final product of reduction depends on the pH of the reducing medium.

15. **Hint** By Hofmann bromamide degradation.

16. $C_2H_5NO_2 \xrightarrow{LiAlH_4} C_2H_5NH_2$

17. 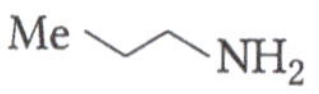

18. $R-\overset{\overset{\displaystyle O}{\|}}{C}-NH_2 \xrightarrow[H_2O]{LiAlH_4} R-CH_2-NH_2$

19. **Gabriel phthalimide reaction** Phthalimide on treatment with ethanolic KOH gives potassium phthalimide which on heating with a suitable alkyl halide gives N-substituted phthalimides, which upon subsequent hydrolysis with alkali gives primary amines.

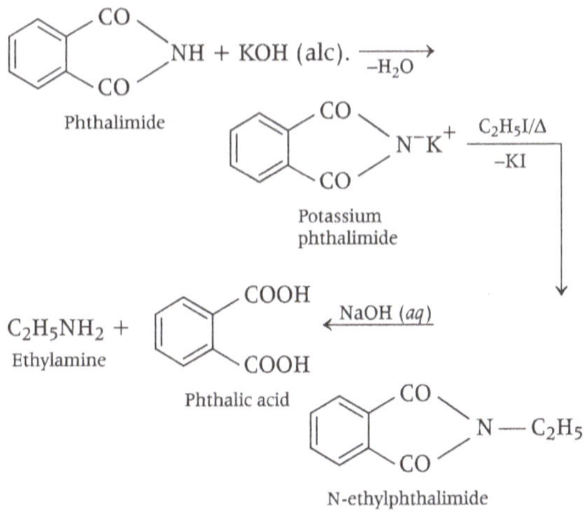

This reaction is called Gabriel phthalimide reaction.

20. (*c*) Aromatic primary amines cannot be prepared by the Gabriel phthalimide synthesis because aryl halides do not undergo nucleophilic substitution reaction with the anion formed by phthalimide. Thus, (A) is correct but (R) is incorrect.

21. (*a*) Only a small amount of HCl is required in the reduction of nitro compounds with iron scrap and HCl in the presence of steam, just to initiate the reaction as $FeCl_2$ formed gets hydrolysed to release HCl during the reaction.

22. (*d*) The amino group being completely protonated in acidic solution, the lone pair of electrons on the nitrogen atom is no longer available for resonance.

Hence, aniline becomes less reactive towards electrophilic reagents.

23. (*a*) In acylation reaction of amines, equilibrium shifts to the right side in the presence of pyridine because it is a stronger base than amine which removes HCl so formed in the reaction. Thus, both (A) and (R) are correct and (R) is the correct explanation of (A).

24. (*a*) Both (A) and (R) are correct and (R) is the correct explanation of (A).

Acetanilide is less basic than aniline as in amides the carbonyl group (C=O) is a stronger dipole than N—C dipole. Therefore, the ability of N—C group to act as H-bond acceptor (as a base) is restricted in the presence of a C=O dipole.

25. (i) $(C_2H_5)_2NH > (C_2H_5)_3N > C_2H_5NH_2$

(ii) $\underset{(A)}{C_7H_6O_2} \xrightarrow{NH_3/Heat} B \xrightarrow[\text{Hofmann bromamide degradation}]{Br_2+KOH} \underset{(C)}{C_6H_7N}$

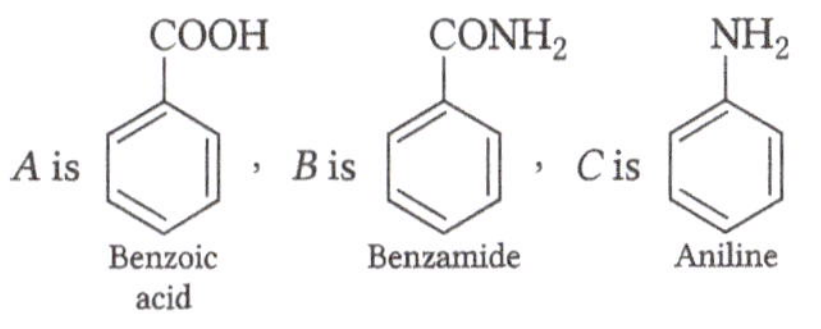

(iii)

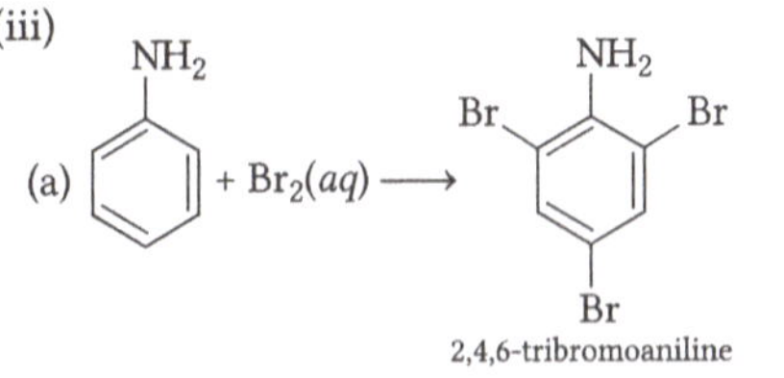

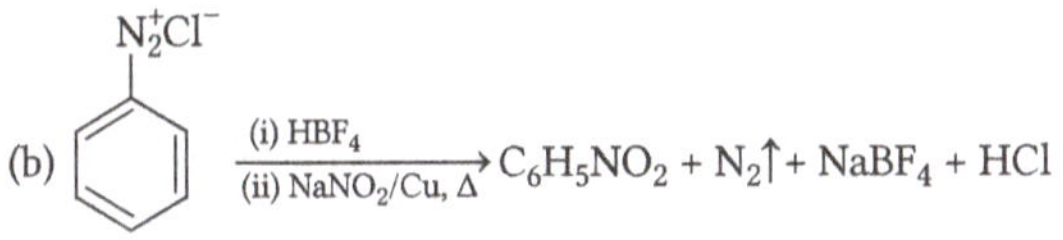

26. The complete sequence of reactions is as follows :

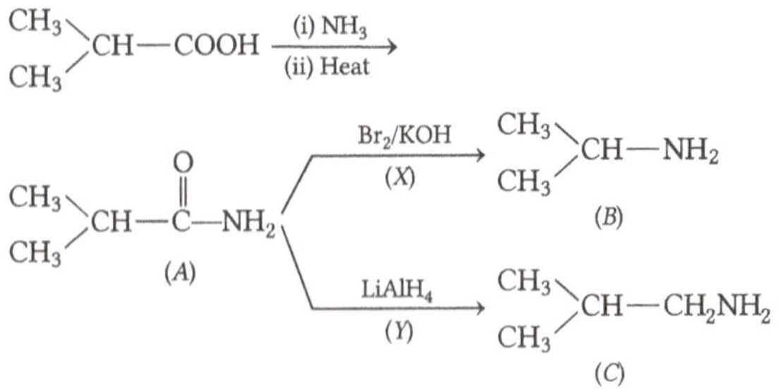

(i) The amine *B* is, 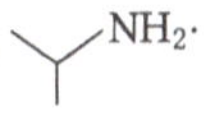

(ii) The molar mass of '*A*' is 87 g mol^{-1}.

(iii) *C* is a reduction product of *A*. The reducing agent can be $LiAlH_4$, Zn-Hg/alc, etc.

27. (i) *tert*-butyl bromide, being a 3° alkyl halide, on treatment with a base (i.e. NH_3) prefers to undergo elimination rather than substitution.

Therefore, the product is isobutylene rather than *tert*-butylamine.

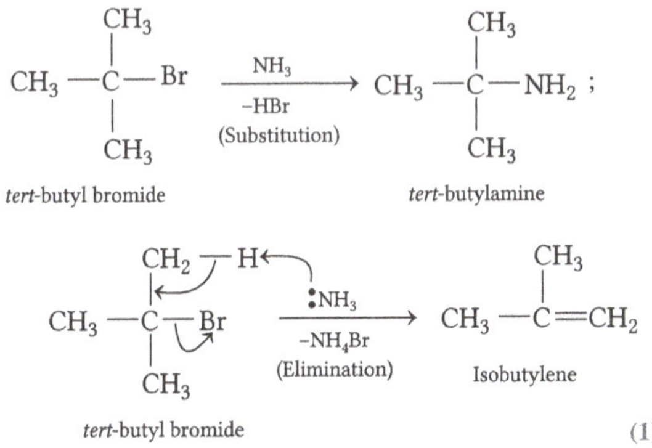

(1)

(ii)

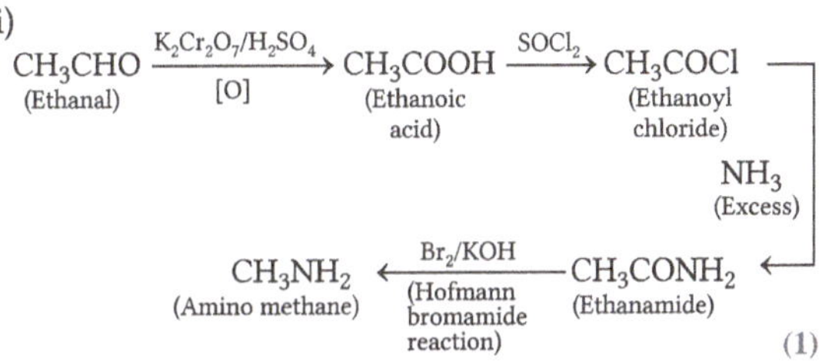

(1)

28. (i) Amines are basic because in amines lone pair of electrons on nitrogen is free to act as base.

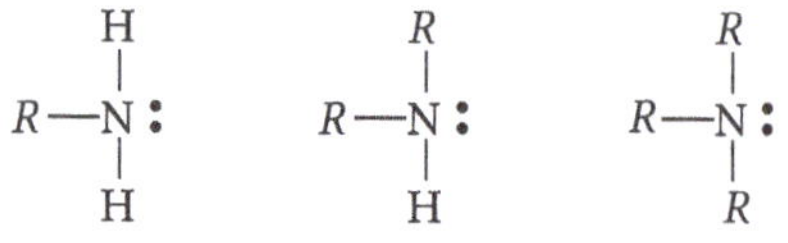

(1°) (2°) (3°)

But in amides, the lone pair on nitrogen is involved in conjugation with adjacent carbonyl group.

Now, it is no longer in condition to donate its lone pair of electrons to act as a base. This is the reason it is neutral. (1)

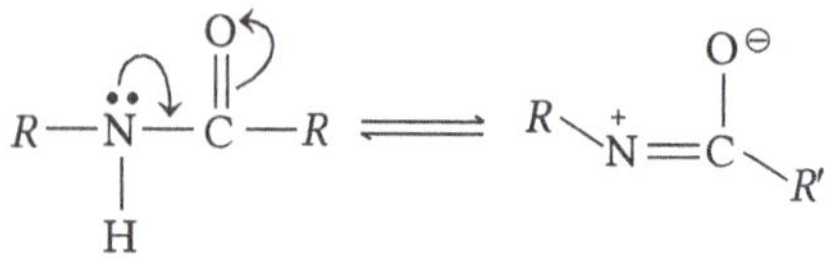

(ii) Refer to text on pages 370 and 371 (Topic-2, Basic character of amines). (1)

29. (i) Refer to text on pages 376 and 377 (Topic-2, Nitration).

(ii)

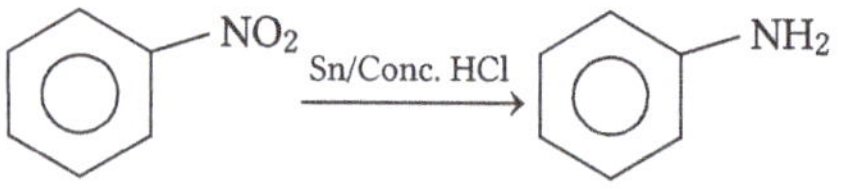

Aniline

30. Hint Due to the presence of electron withdrawing group in *o*-and *p*- nitrotoluene. (2)

31.

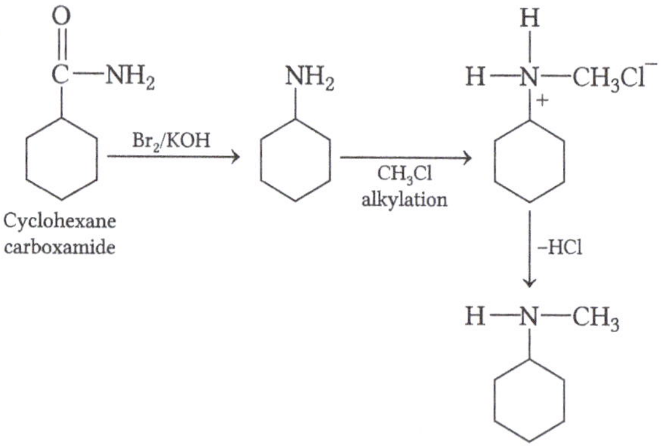

Cyclohexane carboxamide

N-methyl cyclohexylamine

(2)

32. Hint Gabriel phthalimide method. (2)

33. (i) **Hint** 1° and 3° amine.

(i) Refer to text on pages 372 and 373 (Topic-2, Carbylamine reaction) (1)

(ii) Refer to text on page 377 (Topic-2, Test for aniline). (1)

34. (i) Due to electron withdrawing effect of the acetyl group, the lone pair of electrons on N-atom is attracted by acetyl group.As a result, lone pair of electrons on N-atom is not exclusively available for donation to the benzene ring and hence, activating effect of the —NH_2 group is reduced. (1)

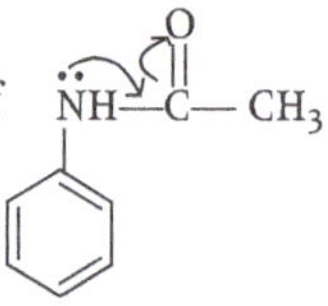

(ii) Nitration is usually carried out with a mixture of conc. HNO_3 and conc. H_2SO_4. So in the presence of these acids, aniline gets protonated to form anilinium ion.

Therefore, the reaction mixture consists of aniline and anilinium ion. — NH_2 group in aniline is *o, p*-directing and activating, whereas the $\overset{+}{N}H_3$ group in anilinium is *m*-directing and deactivating. Now, nitration of aniline mainly gives *p*-nitroaniline due to steric hindrance at *o*-position and the nitration of anilinium ion gives *m* -nitroaniline.

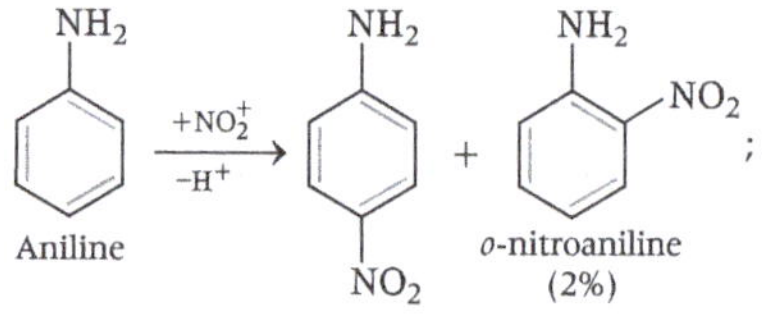

Aniline

o-nitroaniline (2%)

p-nitroaniline (51%)

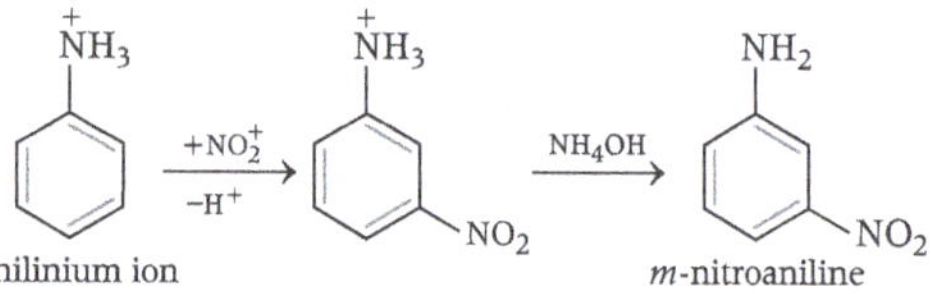

Anilinium ion

m-nitroaniline (47%) (1)

35. Hint $R—\ddot{N}H_2 + H—Cl \rightleftharpoons R—\overset{+}{N}H_3Cl^-$ (2)

36. (i)

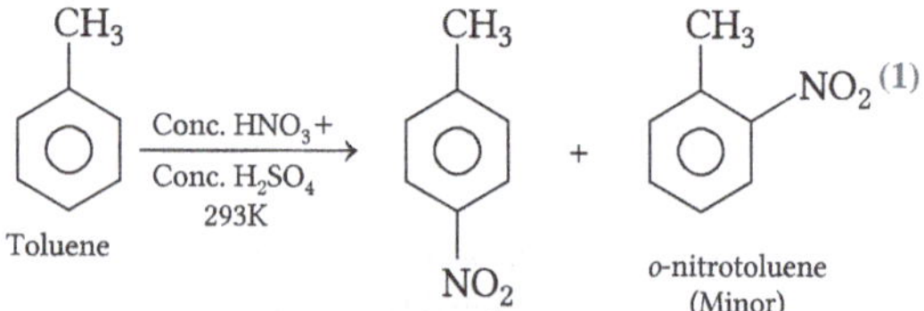

Toluene

p-nitrotoluene (Major)

o-nitrotoluene (Minor)

(ii)

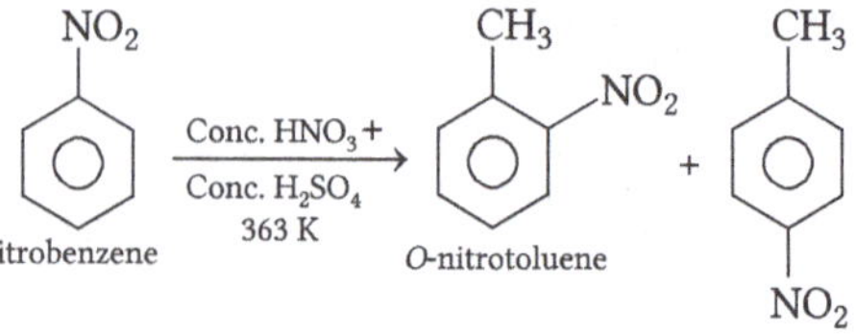

Nitrobenzene

O-nitrotoluene

p-nitrotoluene

37. (i) $CH_3COOH \xrightarrow[-H_2O]{NH_3/\Delta} CH_3CONH_2$
Acetic acid → Acetamide (*A*)

$\xrightarrow[\text{Hofmann bromamide degradation}]{Br_2/KOH\,(aq)}$

$CH_3NH_2 \xrightarrow[\text{Carbylamine reaction}]{CHCl_3 + \text{alc. } KOH} CH_3NC$
Methylamine (*B*) → Methyl isocyanide (*C*) (1)

(ii) $C_6H_5N_2^+BF_4^- \xrightarrow[-N_2, -NaBF_4]{NaNO_2/Cu, \Delta} C_6H_5NO_2$
Nitrobenzene (*A*)

$\xrightarrow[\text{Reduction}]{Fe/HCl} C_6H_5NH_2 \xrightarrow[-HCl]{CH_3COCl/\text{pyridine}} C_6H_5NHCOCH_3$
Aniline (*B*) → Acetanilide (*C*) (1)

38. (i) Aniline being a Lewis base reacts with Lewis acid ($AlCl_3$) to form a salt.

$$C_6H_5NH_2 + AlCl_3 \longrightarrow C_6H_5\overset{+}{N}H_2\,AlCl_3^-$$

As a result, N acquires a positive charge so, it acts as a strong deactivating group for electrophilic substitution reaction. Thus, aniline does not undergo Friedel-Crafts reaction. (1)

(ii) Primary aromatic amines cannot be prepared by Gabriel phthalimide synthesis because aryl halides do not undergo nucleophilic substitution with the anion formed by phthalimide. (1)

39. The diazonium salts of aromatic amines are more stable than those of aliphatic amines due to dispersal of the positive charge on the benzene ring as shown below.

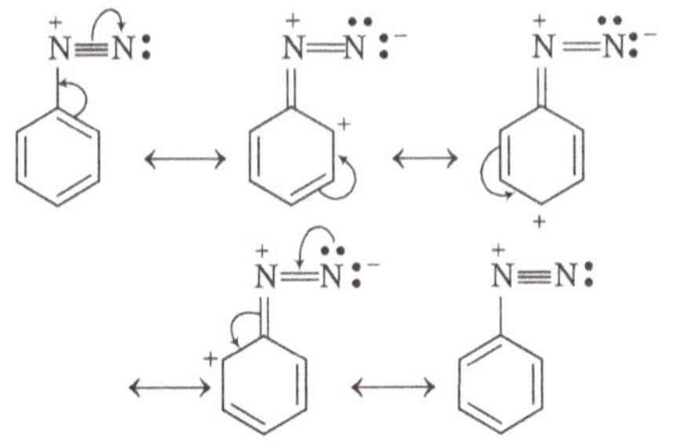

(2)

40. (i) $CH_3CH_2Cl \xrightarrow{NaCN} CH_3CH_2C\equiv N$
Chloroethane → Propane nitrile (*A*)

$\xrightarrow[Ni/H_2]{\text{Reduction}} CH_3CH_2CH_2NH_2$
1 - propanamine (*B*) (1)

(ii) $C_6H_5NH_2 \xrightarrow[0-5°C]{NaNO_2/HCl} C_6H_5N_2^+Cl^-$
Aniline → Benzene diazonium chloride (*A*)

$\xrightarrow[-KOH]{C_6H_5NH_2}$

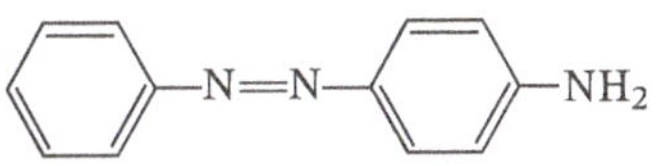

p-aminoazobenzene (*B*) (1)

41. Since, (*X*) gives N_2 gas on treatment with $NaNO_2/HCl$, therefore, it must be a primary amine.

Further, since *X* is optically active, therefore, it possess chiral structure.

Now, NH_2 group cannot be directly attached to the chiral carbon because such amines readily undergoes racemisation due to inversion at N-atom.

Therefore, the probable structure of *X* is

$$CH_3-CH_2-\underset{CH_3}{\underset{|}{CH}}-CH_2-NH_2$$

2-methyl butanamine (*X*) (optically active) (1)

To determine the structure of 3° alcohol (*Y*).

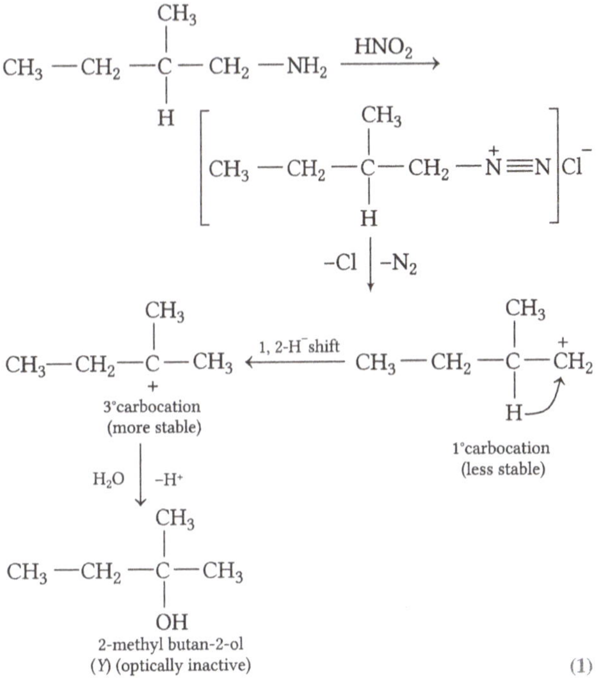

(1)

42. Refer to text on paged 376 and 377 (Topic-2, nitration). (2)

43. **Hint** On the basis of resonance structure. (2)

44. Refer to text on page 388 (Topic-3, Diazonium salts). (2)

45. **Hint**

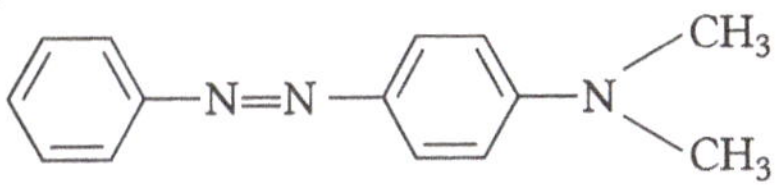

(2)

46. (i) $C_2H_5C\equiv N \xrightarrow{LiAlH_4} C_2H_5CH_2NH_2$
Propanamine (*A*)

$\xrightarrow{HNO_2} C_2H_5CH_2N_2^+Cl^-$
Propane diazonium chloride(*B*) (2)

47. (i)

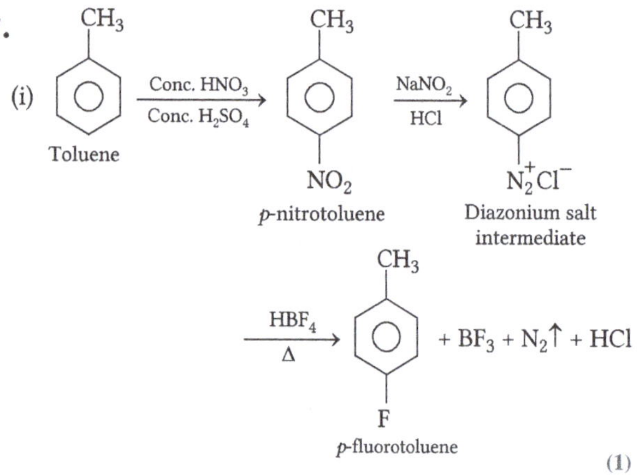

(1)

(ii)

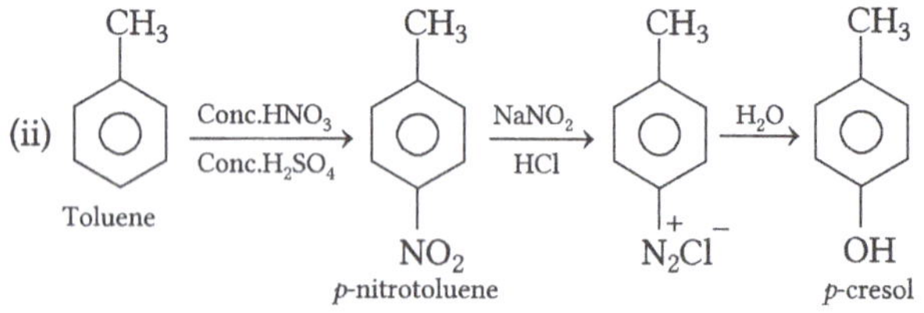

(1)

48. (i)

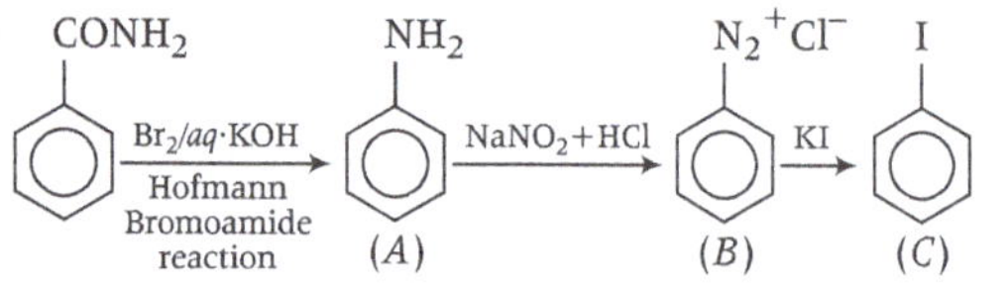

(1½)

(ii) $CH_3—Cl \xrightarrow[\text{Reduction}]{KCN} \underset{(A)}{CH_3 \cdot CN} \xrightarrow{LiAlH_4} \underset{(B)}{CH_3 \cdot CH_2 \cdot NH_2}$

$\xrightarrow[\text{Carbylamine reaction}]{CHCl_3 + KOH \text{ (alc.)}} \underset{(C)}{CH_3CH_2 \cdot NC}$

(1½)

49. (i) Due to strong electron donating effect of the NH_2 group, the electron density increases at the *o*-, *p* -positions.

Further, when aniline is treated with Br_2, the Br^+ attacks the benzene ring at *o*-, *p*-positions to form carbocation intermediates which are stabilised not only by the usual resonance of the benzene ring but also by the $—NH_2$ group. (1)

(ii) Refer to text on pages 372 and 373 (Topic-2, Carbylamine reaction). (1)

(iii) **Hint** Due to the absence of H-atom. Refer to text on page 373 (Topic-2, Distinction between primary, secondary and tertiary amines).

50. (i) **Carbylamine reaction** Aliphatic or aromatic primary amines on heating with chloroform and ethanolic potassium hydroxide form isocyanides or carbylamine which are foul smelling substances.

This reaction is known as carbylamine reaction.

$$\underset{\text{Aniline}}{C_6H_5NH_2} + CHCl_3 + 3KOH \xrightarrow{\Delta} C_6H_5NC + 3KCl + 3H_2O$$

This reaction is used as a test for primary aliphatic and aromatic amine. (1½)

(ii) **Hofmann bromamide degradation reaction** It is a method used for the preparation of primary amines by treating an amide with bromine in an aqueous or ethanolic solution of sodium hydroxide.

The amines so formed contain one carbon less than that present in the parent amide. (1½)

$$R—\overset{\overset{O}{\|}}{C}—NH_2 + Br_2 + 4NaOH \longrightarrow R—NH_2 + Na_2CO_3 + 2NaBr + 2H_2O$$

51. Refer to text on pages 376 and 377 (Topic-2, Electrophilic substitution reaction). (3)

52. (i) $A = CH_3CH(CH_3)NH_2$

$B = CH_3CH(CH_3)N_2^+Cl^-$ (1)

(ii)

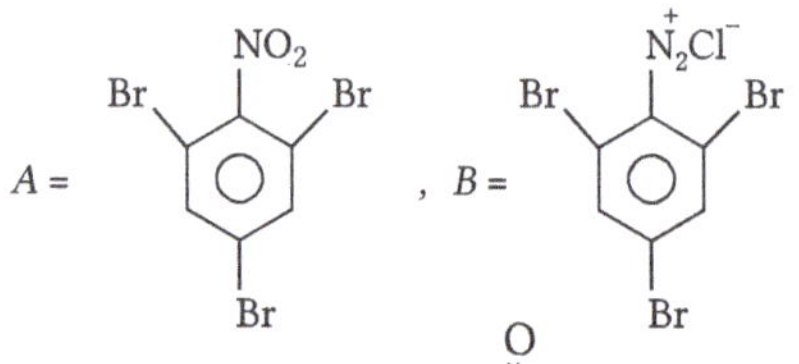

(1)

(iii) $A = CH_3COOH$, $B = CH_3\overset{\overset{O}{\|}}{C}—NH_2$ (1)

53. (i)

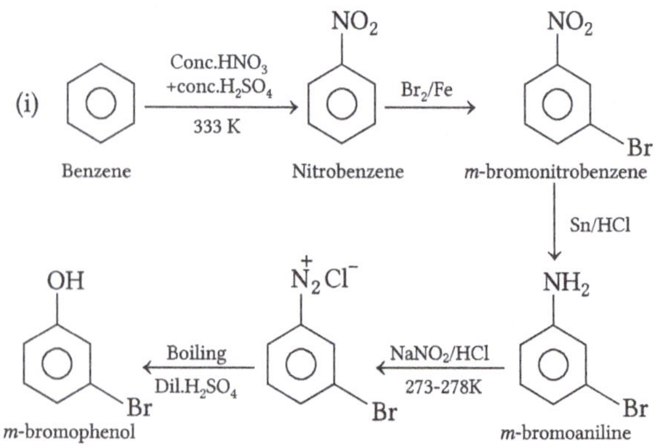

(1½)

(ii) 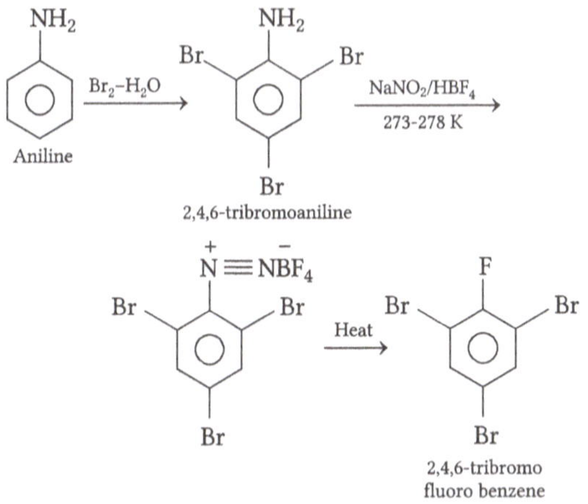

(1½)

54. (i) Refer to text on pages 372 and 373 (Topic-2, (Carbylamine reaction). (1)

(ii) Refer to text on pages 389 (Topic-3, Reactions involving displacenent of nitrogen). (1)

(iii) **Hint**

$A =$ 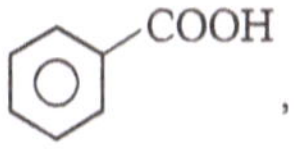

, $B =$ 

(1)

55. (i) $C_6H_5N_2^+Cl^- \xrightarrow{H_3PO_2 + H_2O} C_6H_6 + N_2\uparrow + H_3PO_3 + HCl$ (1)

(ii) 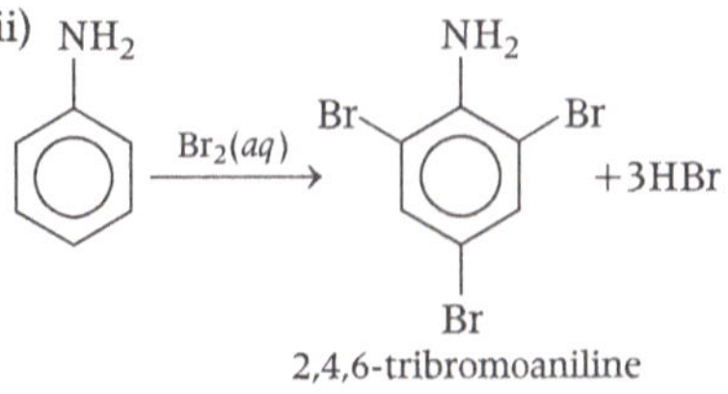

(1)

(iii) $CH_3-\underset{\underset{O}{\|}}{C}-NH_2 + Br_2 + 4NaOH \xrightarrow{\text{Hofmann bromamide reaction}}$

$\underset{\text{Methylamine}}{CH_3NH_2} + Na_2CO_3 + 2NaBr + 2H_2O$ **(1)**

56. (i) Refer to text on page 390 (Topic-3, Reactions involving retention of diazo group). (1½)

(ii) Refer to text on page 390 (Topic-3, Importance of diazonium salts in the synthesis of aromatic compounds). (1½)

RELATED ONLINE VIDEOS

Visit : https://youtu.be/JpS0fDg6vdg
OR **Scan the Code**

Visit : https://youtu.be/szlheSdr-xU
OR **Scan the Code**

Visit : https:/youtu.be/jaBy4oCjig4
OR **Scan the Code**

Visit : https://youtu.be/DjwpWJTG2O4
OR **Scan the Code**

CHAPTER

10

Biomolecules

Biomolecules are the organic molecules common to all living systems on earth. These molecules perform several physiological functions and act as building blocks of living body. These molecules include carbohydrates, proteins, enzymes, lipids, hormones, vitamins, nucleic acid, etc.

- Carbohydrates
- Proteins and Enzymes
- Vitamins, Nucleic Acids and Hormones

TOPIC 01 Carbohydrates

These are primarily produced by plants and form a very large group of naturally occurring organic compounds. Most of them have a general formula, $C_x(H_2O)_y$ and were considered as hydrates of carbon from where the name carbohydrate was derived, but all the compounds which fit into this formula may not be classified as carbohydrates, e.g. acetic acid (CH_3COOH).

Similarly, some carbohydrates do not fit into this formula but are carbohydrates, e.g. rhamnose ($C_6H_{12}O_5$).

A large number of chemical reactions have shown that carbohydrates contain specific functional groups. Thus, chemically, the carbohydrates may be defined as **optically active polyhydroxy aldehydes** or **polyhdroxy ketones** or large polymeric molecules which on hydrolysis yield polyhydroxy aldehydes and polyhydroxy ketones.

Some of the carbohydrates are sweet in taste which are also called sugars. These constitute an important class of compounds like glucose, fructose, sucrose, starch, cellulose, etc., which play a vital role in our daily life. Carbohydrates are also known as **saccharides.**

Classification of Carbohydrates

Carbohydrates can be classified into the following as shown in the flow chart.

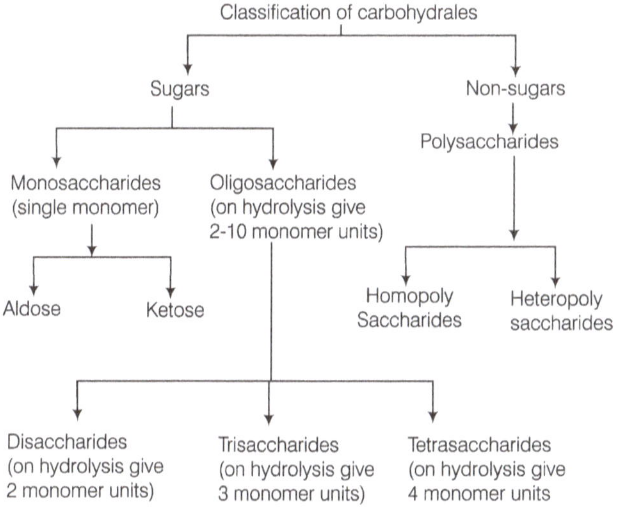

Carbohydrates can also be classified into reducing and non-reducing sugars on the basis of reducing behaviour.

Monosaccharides and disaccharides except sucrose are known as **reducing sugars** because they can reduce Fehling's solution or Tollen's reagents. These sugars have free aldehyde and ketonic groups. **Non-reducing sugars** have bounded aldehyde and ketone groups and hence, they cannot reduce Tollen's reagents or Fehling's solutions.

Monosaccharides

These are simplest form of saccharides and hence further cannot be hydrolysed. Their general formula is $(CH_2O)_n$. On the basis of number of carbon atoms and the functional group present in them, monosaccharides are further classified as :

(i) **Aldose** If aldehyde (—CHO) group is present in monosaccharides, then it is called aldose, e.g. sugar containing 3, 4, 5 carbon atoms are aldotriose, aldotetrose and aldopentose, respectively.

(ii) **Ketose** If monosaccharides contain keto ($\rangle C = O$) group, then it is called ketose, e.g. sugar containing 3, 4, 5 carbon atoms are ketotriose, ketotetrose and ketopentose, respectively.

Glucose

It is an aldohexose and occurs freely as well as in combined form in the nature. It is present in sweet fruits and honey. It is also present in large quantities in ripe grapes. It is also known as grape sugar or dextrose.

Preparation of Glucose

(i) **From Sucrose** (Cane Sugar) Glucose can be easily obtained in a laboratory by the hydrolysis of alcoholic solution of cane sugar, i.e. sucrose with dilute HCl or H_2SO_4 at 50°C to give glucose and fructose in equal amounts.

$$\underset{\text{Sucrose}}{C_{12}H_{22}O_{11}} + H_2O \xrightarrow{H^+} \underset{\text{Glucose}}{C_6H_{12}O_6} + \underset{\text{Fructose}}{C_6H_{12}O_6}$$

(ii) **From Starch** On large scale, glucose is obtained by the hydrolysis of starch by boiling it with hot dilute H_2SO_4 at 393 K, under 2-3 standard atmospheric pressure.

$$\underset{\text{Starch or Cellulose}}{(C_6H_{10}O_5)_n} + nH_2O \xrightarrow[393\,K;\ 2\text{-}3\ atm]{H^+} n\underset{\text{Glucose}}{C_6H_{12}O_6}$$

Structure of Glucose

As glucose is an aldohexose, it consists of six C-atoms and an aldehyde group. It is the monomer of many of the larger carbohydrates such as starch, cellulose, etc. It is the most abundant organic compound on the earth and used as an immediate source of energy for all metabolic reactions in the animals.

Structural Evidences for Open Chain Structure of Glucose

Glucose was assigned the following structure on the basis of the evidences mentioned below :

$$\begin{array}{ll} CHO & \longleftarrow \text{Aldehydic group} \\ | & \\ (CHOH)_4 & \longleftarrow \text{Four 2° alcoholic groups} \\ | & \\ CH_2OH & \longleftarrow \text{1° alcoholic group} \\ \text{Glucose} & \end{array}$$

(i) The molecular formula of glucose was found to be $C_6H_{12}O_6$.

(ii) **Reaction with HI** When heated with HI for a long time, it forms *n*-hexane which shows that all six carbon atoms are linked in a straight chain.

$$\begin{array}{c} CHO \\ | \\ (CHOH)_4 \\ | \\ CH_2OH \\ \text{Glucose} \end{array} \xrightarrow{HI,\ \Delta} \underset{n\text{-hexane}}{CH_3CH_2CH_2CH_2CH_2CH_3}$$

(iii) Glucose reacts with **hydroxylamine** to form an oxime and on adding a molecule of hydrogen cyanide to glucose, it give cyanohydrin.

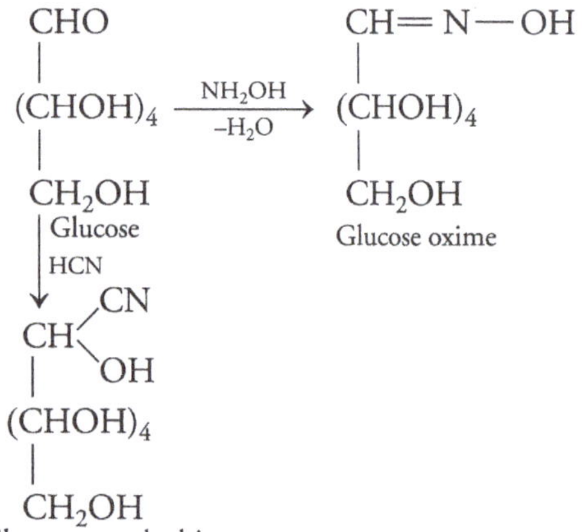

Glucose, Glucose oxime, Glucose cyanohydrin

(iv) **Oxidation** On reaction with a mild oxidising agent like **bromine water**, Tollen's reagent or Fehling's solution, glucose gets oxidised to six carbon carboxylic acid (gluconic acid).

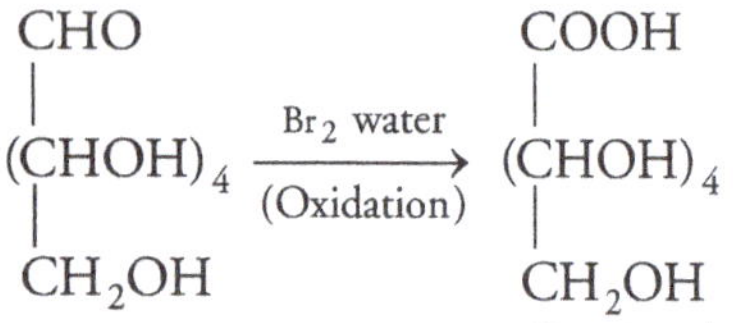

Gluconic acid

(v) Acetylation of glucose with acetic anhydride gives glucose pentaacetate which confirms the presence of five —OH groups.

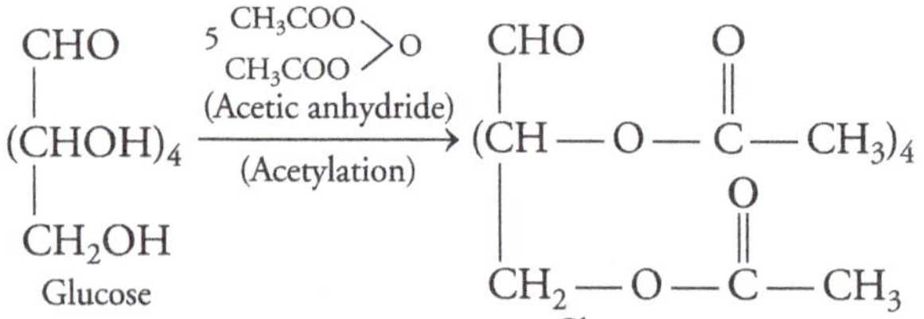

Glucose, Glucose pentaacetate (Stable compound)

Since, the presence of two or more OH groups on the same carbon atom makes the molecule unstable but as glucose exists as a stable compound, this suggests that five —OH groups should be attached to different carbon atoms.

(vi) On oxidation with nitric acid, glucose as well as gluconic acid both yield a dicarboxylic acid, called saccharic acid. This indicates the presence of one primary alcoholic (—OH) group in glucose.

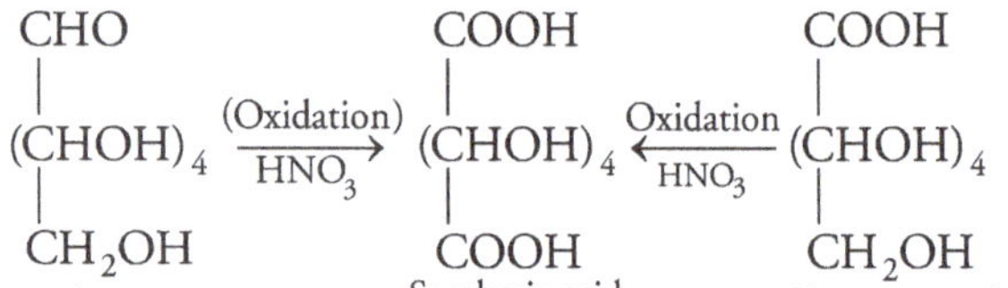

Glucose, Saccharic acid, Gluconic acid

(vii) It forms osazone with phenyl hydrazine ($PhNHNH_2$)

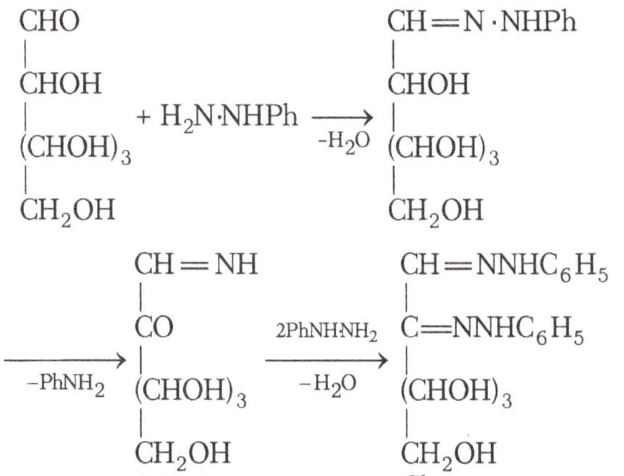

Imino ketone, Glucosazone

where, Ph is C_6H_5 (phenol).

Configuration of Glucose

Emil Fischer gave the exact spatial arrangement of different —OH groups in glucose after studying many other properties. Its configuration is correctly represented as I. So, gluconic acid is represented as II and saccharic acid as III.

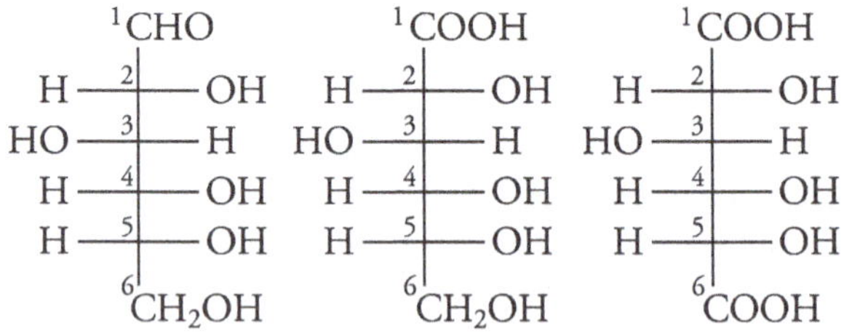

I D-(+)-glucose; II Gluconic acid; III Saccharic acid

Glucose is named as D-(+)-glucose in which 'D' represents the relative configuration whereas '(+)' represents the dextrorotatory nature of the molecule.

Note D and L has no relation with the optical activity of the compound.

D and L-Notations

(i) D and L before the name of any compound commonly indicate the relative configuration of a particular stereoisomer, e.g. glyceraldehyde contains one asymmetric carbon atom and exists in two enantiomeric forms as given below:

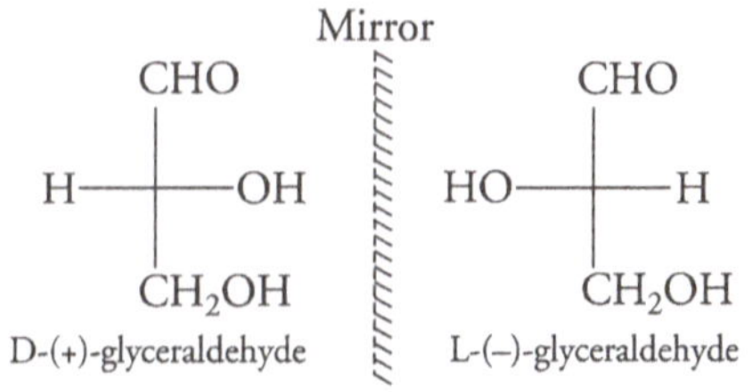

(ii) Compounds which can be chemically correlated to (+)-isomer of glyceraldehyde are said to have **D-configuration** whereas those which can be correlated to (–)-isomer of glyceraldehyde are said to have **L-configuration**.

(iii) For assigning the configuration of monosaccharides, it is the lowest asymmetric carbon atom (as shown below) which is compared, e.g. in (+)-glucose, —OH on the lowest asymmetric carbon is on the right side which is comparable to (+)-glyceraldehyde. Thus, it is assigned as D-configuration.

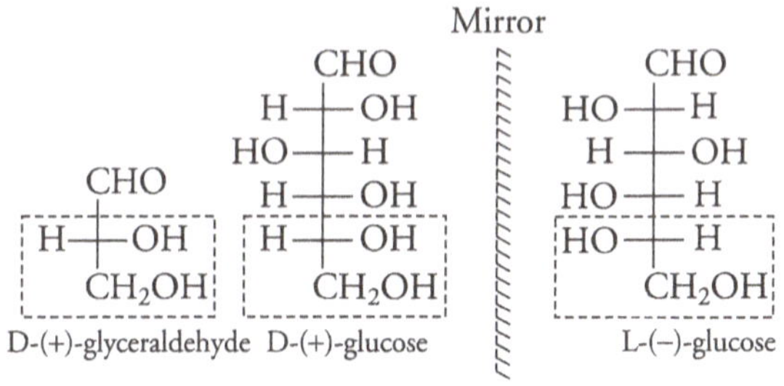

Cyclic Structure of Glucose

The linear open chain structure of glucose explained most of its properties but failed to explain the following facts and reactions:

(i) Even though an aldehyde group is present, the glucose does not react with NH_3, 2, 4-DNP and Grignard reagent.

(ii) Glucose do not restore the pink colour of Schiff's reagent, despite having an aldehydic group.

(iii) The pentaacetate of glucose does not react with hydroxylamine which shows the absence of free —CHO group.

(iv) Glucose exists in two different crystalline forms which are named as α and β. The α-form of glucose (mp 419 K) is obtained by crystallisation from concentrated solution of glucose at 303 K, while the β-form (mp 423 K) is obtained by crystallisation from hot and saturated aqueous solution at 371 K.

This behaviour could not be explained by the open chain structure of glucose. It was suggested that one of the —OH groups may add to the —CHO group and form a cyclic hemiacetal structure.

It was found that glucose forms a six membered ring in which —OH at C-5 is involved in the ring formation. This explains the absence of —CHO group and existence of glucose in two forms as shown below:

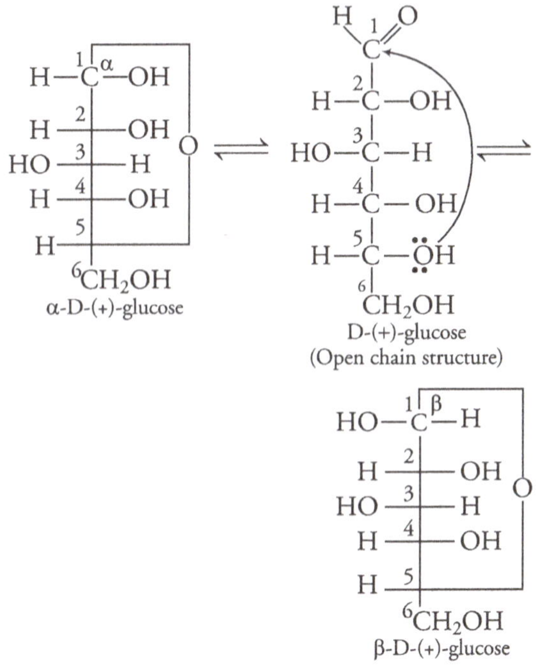

Fischer projection formulae

The two cyclic forms (α-and β-forms) exist in equilibrium with open chain structure.The above two cyclic hemiacetal forms of glucose differ only in the configuration of the hydroxyl group at C-1atom. This C-1atom is called **anomeric carbon.** α- form and β-form differ in configuration only around C_1 are called **anomers.**

Pyranose structure The six membered cyclic structure of glucose is known as pyranose structure (α- or β-). It is analogous to pyran which is a six membered cyclic organic compound with one oxygen atom and five carbon atoms in the ring.

The cyclic structure of glucose is more correctly represented by **Haworth structures** as given below :

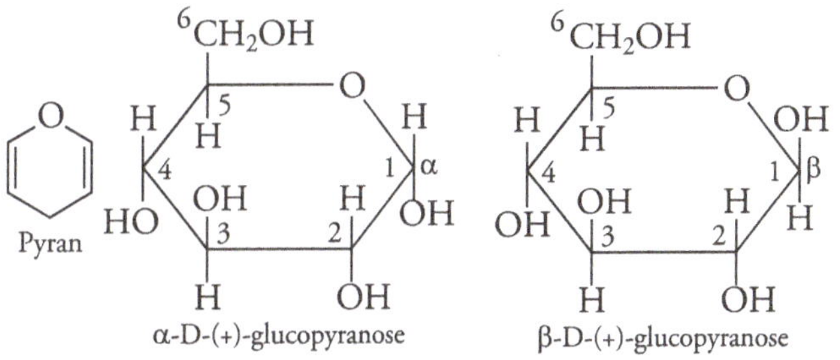

Haworth structures

Uses

(i) Sweetening agent in confectionery and syrups.
(ii) Reducing agent in silvering of mirrors.
(iii) Raw material for wine and alcohol manufacture.

Fructose

It is an important ketohexose which is obtained along with glucose by the hydrolysis of disaccharides like sucrose. It is also known as fruit sugar.

Structure of Fructose

Molecular formula of fructose is same as that of glucose, i.e. $C_6H_{12}O_6$.

On the basis of the reactions shown by fructose, it was found to have a ketonic functional group at C-2 and six carbon atoms in a straight chain as present in glucose. It is a laevorotatory compound and is appropriately written as D-(–)-fructose.

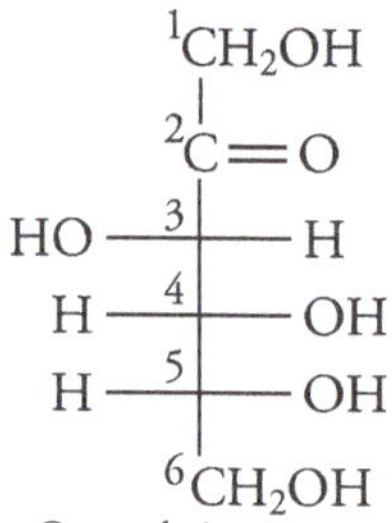
Open chain structure of D-(–)-fructose

It also exists in two cyclic forms which are obtained by the addition of —OH at C-5 to the (>C=O) group. The ring thus formed is a five membered ring named as furanose analogous to furan, which is a five membered cyclic compound with one oxygen and four carbon atoms.

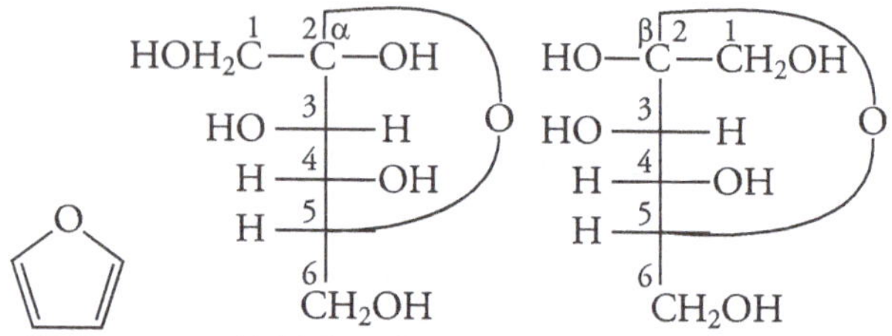
Furan α-D-(–)-fructofuranose β-D-(–)-fructofuranose

Fischer projection formulae

The cyclic structures of two anomers of fructose are represented by **Haworth structures** as given below:

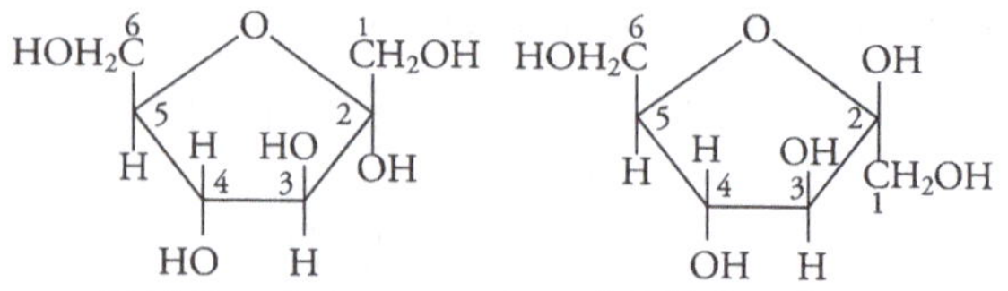
α-D-(–)-Fructofuranose β-D-(–)-Fructofuranose

Haworth structures

Uses

(i) Fructose is used as sweetening agent in confectionery.
(ii) It is also used as a substitute of cane sugar for diabetic patients.

Tests for Glucose and Fructose

Tests for glucose and fructose are as follows :

Test for Glucose

(i) **Bromine Water Test** When glucose is treated with bromine water, the red colour of bromine water disappears and the solution becomes colourless.
(ii) **Silver Mirror Test** On warming glucose with ammonical silver nitrate, silver mirror appear on the inner walls of test tube.
(iii) **Fehling's Solution Test** When it is warmed with Fehling's solution, a red precipitate of Cu_2O is formed.
(iv) **Osazone Formation Test** Glucose, when heated with excess of phenylhydrazine in acetic acid, gives a yellow crystalline compound.

Test for Fructose

(i) **Bromine Water Test** Fructose does not decolourise the red colour of bromine water (distinction from glucose).
(ii) **Selivanoff's Test** Fructose, when treated with resorcinol and HCl, a red or brown colouration or precipitate is obtained.
(iii) **Pinoff's Test** When fructose is heated with freshly prepared ammonium molybdate solution containing a few drops of acetic acid, a bluish green colouration is obtained.
(iv) **Furfural Test** On boiling fructose with alcoholic α-naphthol and conc. HCl a purple or violet colouration is obtained.

Oligosaccharides

These yield 2 to 10 monosaccharide units on hydrolysis. Further they can be classified as-di, tri and tetra saccharides etc. depending on the number of monosaccharides they produce on hydrolysis. These molecules may be either same or different monosaccharides. The two monosaccharide units are joined together through an oxide linkage which is formed by the loss of a water molecule. Such a linkage between two monosaccharide units through an oxygen atom is called **glycosidic linkage**.

Some important disaccharides are:

1. Sucrose

On hydrolysis with acids or enzyme, sucrose gives equimolar mixture of α-D-(+)-glucose and β-D-(–)-fructose.

$$\underset{\text{Sucrose}}{C_{12}H_{22}O_{11}} + H_2O \xrightarrow{HCl} \underset{\alpha\text{-D-(+)-glucose}}{C_6H_{12}O_6} + \underset{\alpha\text{-D-(–)-fructose}}{C_6H_{12}O_6}$$

These two monosaccharides are linked through a glycosidic linkage between C-1 of α-glucose and C-2 of β-fructose. Since, the reducing groups of glucose and fructose are involved in glycosidic bond formation, sucrose is a non-reducing sugar.

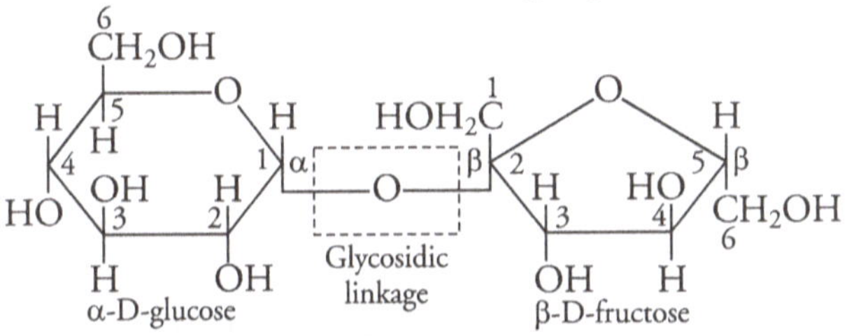

Haworth structure of sucrose

Although, sucrose is dextrorotatory but after hydrolysis, it gives dextrorotatory glucose and laevorotatory fructose. The mixture is laevorotatory because laevorotation of fructose (–92.4°) is more than dextrorotation of glucose (+52.5°). Therefore, hydrolysis of sucrose brings about a change in the sign of rotation, i.e. from dextro (+) to laevo (–) and hence, the product is known as **invert sugar.** This over all process is called **inversion of sugar.**

Sucrose is used as sweetening agent in food and syrups. It is also used as preservative for fruit products, e.g. jams, jellies.

2. Maltose

Hydrolysis of maltose yields two moles of α -D-glucose. Thus, it is composed of two α-D-glucose units in which C-1 of one glucose unit (I) is linked to C-4 of another glucose unit (II). The free aldehyde group can be produced at C-1 of second glucose in solution and it shows reducing properties. So, it is a reducing sugar.

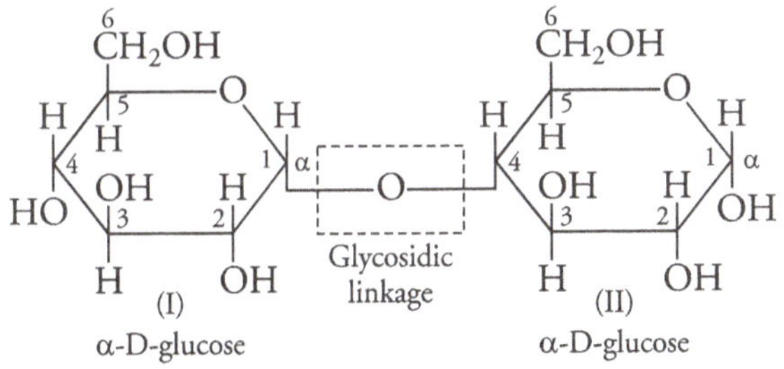

Haworth structure of maltose

3. Lactose

It is commonly known as milk sugar because it is found in milk. It is composed of β-D-galactose and β-D-glucose.

The linkage is between C-1 of galactose and C-4 of glucose. Since, it reduces Tollen's reagent or Fehling's solution, it is also called as **reducing sugar.**

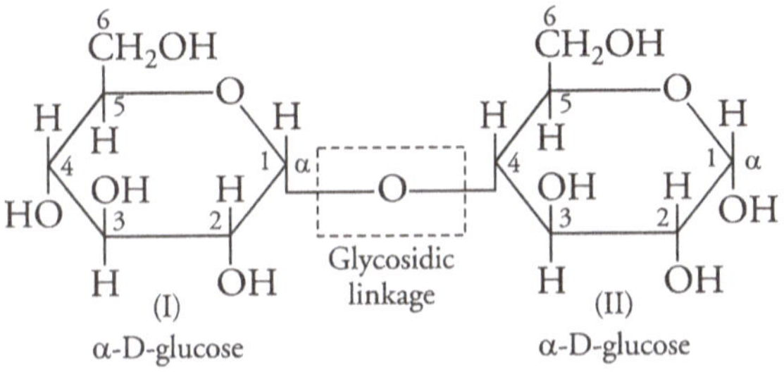

Haworth structure of maltose

Polysaccharides

These are the most commonly found carbohydrates in nature. They are composed of a large number of monosaccharide units joined together by glycosidic linkages. Their generalo formula is $(C_6H_{10}O_5)n$. These are colourless, tasteless, amorphous powders. They play a vital role in plant and animal life, by acting as the food storage material or structural materials.

Some important polysaccharides are :

1. Starch

It is important storage polysaccharide of plants and the most important dietary source of carbohydrate for human beings. High content of starch is found in cereals, roots, tubers and some vegetables.

It is a polymer of α-glucose and consists of two components, i.e. **amylose** and **amylopectin.** Amylose is soluble in water and constitutes 15-20% of starch while amylopectin is insoluble in water and constitutes about 80-85% of starch.

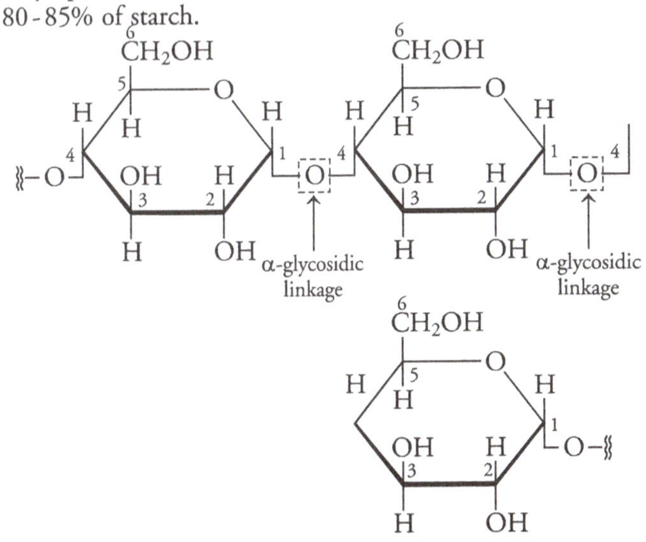

Structure of amylose

Chemically, amylose is a long unbranched chain with 200-1000 α-D(+)-glucose units that are held together by C_1-C_4 glycosidic linkage. On the other hand, amylopectin is a highly branched chain polymer of α-D-glucose units in which glycosidic linkage is present between C_1-C_4 atoms, whereas the branching occurs through C_1-C_6 glycosidic linkage.

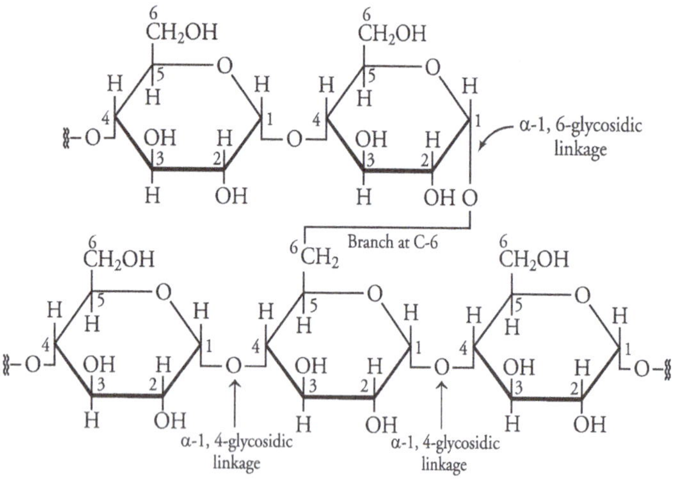

Structure of amylopectin

Uses

It is used :

(i) as cloth stiffener.
(ii) as source of glucose and alcohol.
(iii) as indicator for iodometric titrations.

2. Cellulose

It occurs exclusively in plants and it is the most abundant organic substance in plant kingdom. It is the main constituent of cell wall of plant cells. It is a straight chain polysaccharide composed only of β-D-glucose units that are linked together by β-glycosidic linkage between C-1 of one glucose unit and C-4 of the next glucose unit.

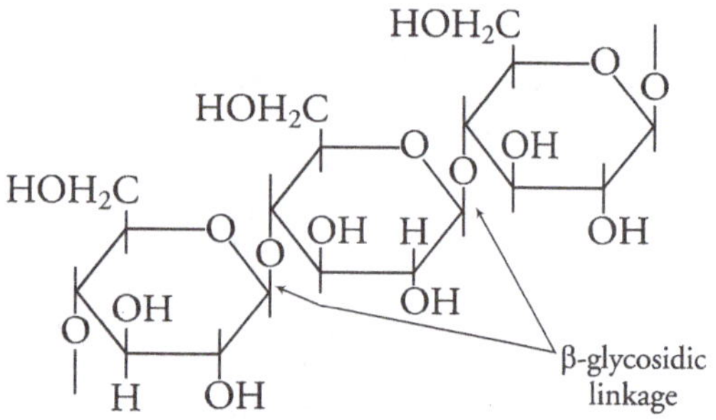

Structure of cellulose

Uses

It is used :

(i) in making of papers and cloths.
(ii) for manufacturing explosives, paints etc.

3. Glycogen

It is known to be the storage material of animals. Its structure is similar to amylopectin but it is highly branched that is why also known as animal starch. It is found in liver, muscles and brain.

When body requires energy, glycogen is broken down into glucose by the action of enzymes. It is also found in yeast and fungi.

Importance of Carbohydrates

Carbohydrates are very important and essential for life in both plants and animals.

Few important roles of carbohydrates are listed below:

(i) They form a major portion of our food.
(ii) They are used as storage materials like starch in plants and glycogen in animals.
(iii) Cellulose in the form of wood is used to build furniture and clothes in the form of cotton fibres.
(iv) They provide raw materials for many industries, like textiles, papers and lacquers.
(v) They act as a biofuel to provide energy for the functioning of living organisms.
(vi) They act as constituent of cell membranes of plants and bacteria.
(vii) In living systems, carbohydrates are also found in combination with many proteins and lipids such as glycoproteins and glycolipids.

Topic Practice 1

Very Short Answer Type Questions

1 Mark

1. **Fill in the Blanks**

(i) Sucrose is a .... and yields upon hydrolysis, a mixture of .... and fructose. **ISC 2017**

(ii) All monosaccharids are capable of reducing Fehling's solution or Tollen's reagent, therefore are called .... sugars.

(iii) When Glucose is heated with HI, it gives ....

(iv) Six membered cyclic structure of glucose is analogous to .... structure.

(v) Starch is a polymer of α-glucose and has two components .... and ....

2. Objective Type Questions

(i) The disaccharide present in milk is

(a) sucrose (b) maltose
(c) lactose (d) cellobiose

(ii) Which of the following compounds is found abundantly in nature?

(a) Fructose (b) Starch
(c) Glucose (d) Cellulose

(iii) Which of the following is an example of disaccharide? **ISC 2015**

(a) Glucose (b) Fructose
(c) Sucrose (d) Cellulose

(iv) D-glucose contains **ISC 2004**

(a) 50% each of α-D-glucose and β-D-glucose
(b) 64% of α-D-glucose and 36% of β-D-glucose
(c) 36% of α-D-glucose and 64% of β-D-glucose
(d) 33% of each α-D-glucose and β-D-glucose

(v) Glucose on treatment with NH_2OH undergoes. **ISC 2004**

(a) Condensation (b) Reduction
(c) Hydrolysis (d) Oxidation

(vi) On hydrolysis of starch we finally get

(a) glucose (b) fructose
(c) Both (a) and (b) (d) sucrose

(vii) The term invert sugar refers to an equimolar mixture of **ISC 2004**

(a) D-glucose and D-galactose
(b) D-glucose and D-fructose
(c) D-glucose and D-mannose
(d) D-glucose and D-ribose

(viii) The pair of sugars which give the same product with excess of phenylhydrazine are **ISC 2002**

(a) starch and cellulose
(b) cellulose and sucrose
(c) sucrose and glucose
(d) glucose and fructose

3. Match Column I with Column II and choose the correct option using the codes given below:

	Column I		Column II
A.	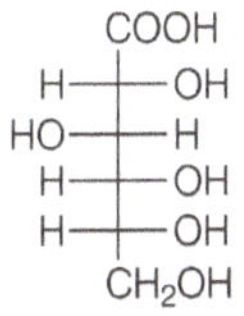	(i)	D-(+)-glucose
B.	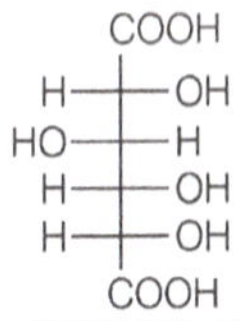	(ii)	Gluconic acid
C.	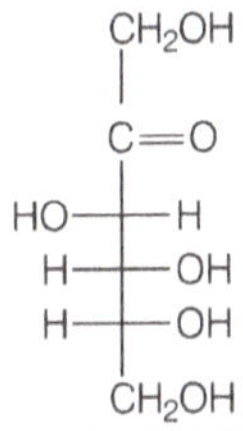	(iii)	D-(–)-fructose
D.	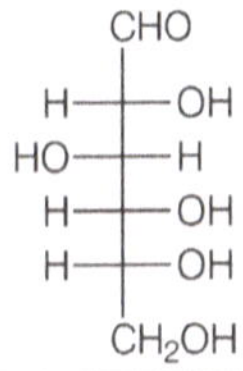	(iv)	Saccharic acid

Codes

	A	B	C	D
(a)	(i)	(ii)	(iii)	(iv)
(b)	(iv)	(iii)	(ii)	(i)
(c)	(ii)	(iv)	(iii)	(i)
(d)	(iv)	(ii)	(iii)	(i)

4. (i) What type of isomers glucose and fructose are?

(ii) Name the functional group common to both glucose and fructose. **ISC 2012**

5. Correct the following statement.
Oxidation of sucrose with concentrated nitric acid yields glycerol. **ISC 2006**

6. Give a test to distinguish between starch and cellulose. **ISC 2006**

7. How will you convert glucose to gluconic acid? **ISC 2003**

8. What do you observe when glucose solution is heated with Tollen's reagent? **ISC 2016**

9. Classify the following into monosaccharides and disaccharides. Ribose, 2-deoxyribose, maltose, galactose, fructose and lactose. **NCERT**

10. What are reducing sugars?

11. What do you understand by the term glycosidic linkage? **NCERT**

12. What are the products of hydrolysis of sucrose? **NCERT**

13. What are the expected products of hydrolysis of lactose? **NCERT Intext**

14. Write the two main functions of carbohydrate in plants. **NCERT**

Short Answer Type I Questions

(2 Marks)

15. Monosaccharides contain carbonyl group hence are classified, as aldose or ketose. The number of carbon atoms present in the monosaccharide molecule are also considered for classification. In which class of monosaccharide will you place fructose? **NCERT Exemplar**

16. Carbohydrates are essential for life in both plants and animals. Name the carbohydrates that are used as storage molecules in plants and animals. Also, name the carbohydrate which is present in wood or in the fibre of cotton cloth. **NCERT Exemplar**

Short Answer Type II Questions

(3 Marks)

17. How will you convert glucose to saccharic acid? **ISC 2009**

18. How will you chemically convert glucose to fructose?

19. What happens when D-glucose is treated with the following reagents? **NCERT**
    (i) HI (ii) Br_2 water (iii) HNO_3

20. How will you distinguish 1° and 2° hydroxyl groups present in glucose? Explain with reactions. **NCERT Exemplar**

21. What is glycogen? How is it different from starch? **NCERT**

22. What is the basic structural difference between starch and cellulose? **NCERT**

Hints & Solutions

1. (i) disaccharide; glucose (ii) reducing
   (iii) *n*-hexane (iv) pyran
   (v) amylose; amylopectin

2. (i) (c) In milk, lactose sugar is found which is a disaccharide.
   (ii) (d) Cellulose is probably the most abundant organic compound found in nature. About 50% of total organic matter found in the living world is cellulose.
   (iii) (c) Sucrose, as it gives glucose and fructose upon hydrolysis.
   (iv) (c) D-glucose contains 36% α-D-glucose and 64% of β-D-glucose.
   (v) (a) **Condensation.**
   Glucose condenses with hydroxylamine to form an oxime called D-glucose oxime.

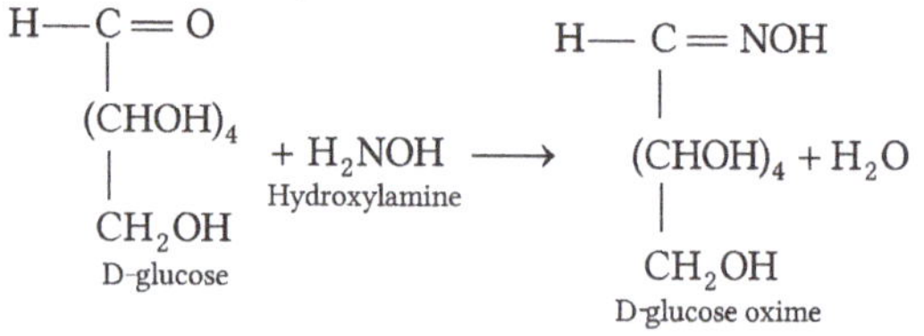

   Hence, option (a) is correct.
   (vi) (a) Starch is a poymer of D-glucose units, hence on hydrolysis it gives only glucose.
   (vii) (b) Sucrose (invert sugar is an equimolar mixture of D (+)-glucose and D(–)-fructose. It is called invert sugar due to the fact that on hydrolysis there is a change in the sign of rotation from positive to negative.
   (viii) (*d*) Glucose and fructose both form same product (osazone) with excess of phenylhydrazine.

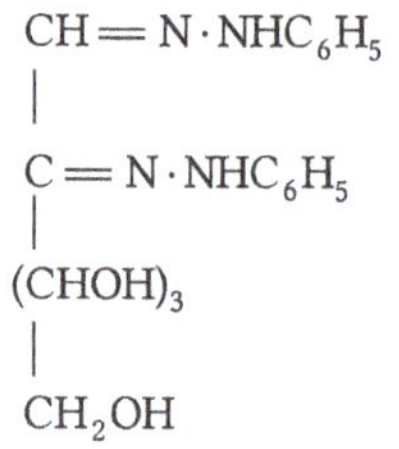

   Hence, option (d) is correct.

3. (c) (A)→(ii), (B)→(iv), (C)→(iii), (D)→(i)

4. (i) Glucose and fructose are functional isomers. (½)
   (ii) Alcoholic (—OH) group is common in both, glucose and fructose. (½)

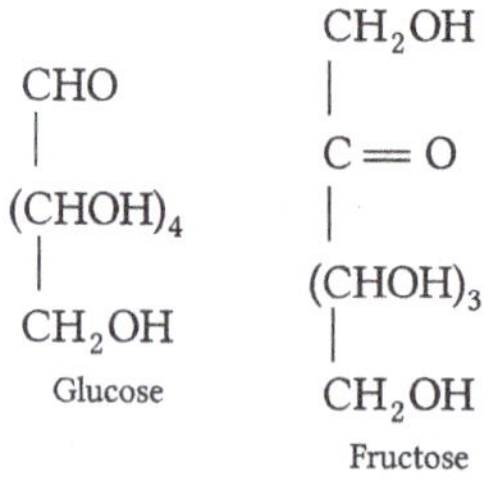

5. Oxidation of sucrose with concentrated nitric acid yields **oxalic acid.**

$$\underset{\text{Sucrose}}{C_{12}H_{22}O_{11}} + 9O_2 \xrightarrow[\text{Conc.}]{HNO_3} 6\underset{\text{Oxalic acid}}{(COOH)_2} + 5H_2O$$ (1)

6. Starch gives blue black colour with iodide whereas cellulose does not. (1)

7. Glucose with bromine water form gluconic acid.

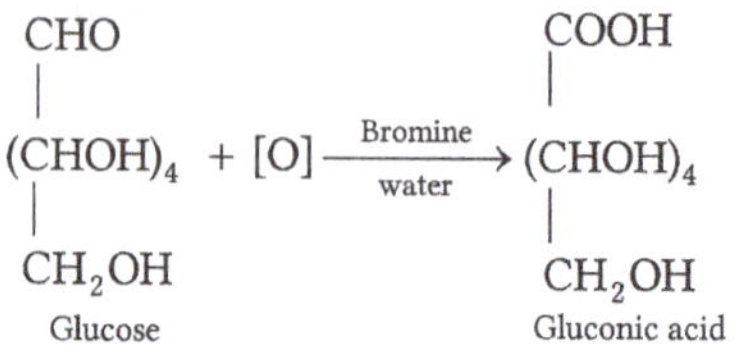

(1)

8. When glucose solution is heated with Tollen's reagent, silver mirror on the inner surface of the reaction vessel is observed. (1)

9. **Monosaccharides** are ribose, 2-deoxyribose, galactose, and fructose. **Disaccharides** are maltose and lactose. (1)

10. Carbohydrates in which ketonic or aldehydic groups are free and capable of reducing Fehling's solution or Tollen's reagent are known as reducing sugars. (1)

11. A linkage between two monosaccharide units through an oxygen atom is called glycosidic linkage. (1)

12. The products obtained on hydrolysis of sucrose are D-(+)-glucose and D-(−)-fructose. (1)

13. Lactose on hydrolysis gives β-D-glucose and β-D-galactose.

$$\underset{\text{Lactose}}{C_{12}H_{22}O_{11}} + H_2O \xrightarrow{H^+} \underset{\text{Glucose}}{C_6H_{12}O_6} + \underset{\text{Galactose}}{C_6H_{12}O_6}$$ (1)

14. (i) Carbohydrates are used as storage molecules as starch in plants. (½)
   (ii) Cell wall of bacteria and plants is made up of cellulose. (½)

15. Monosaccharides contain carbonyl group. Hence, are classified as aldose or ketose.When aldehyde group is present, the monosaccharides are known as aldose. When ketone group is present, the monosaccharides are known as ketose. Fructose has molecular formula $C_6H_{12}O_6$ containing six carbon and keto group. It is classified as ketohexose. (1)

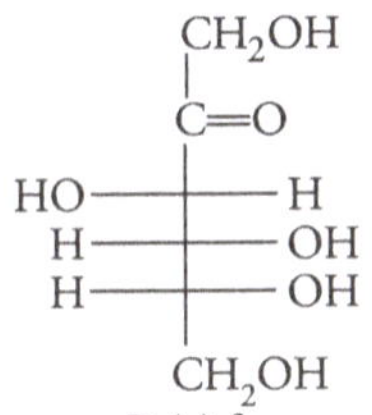

D-(−)-fructose (1)

16. In plants, carbohydrates are stored in the form of starch while in animals, these are stored in the form of glycogen. (1)
Cellulose, a carbohydrate is present in wood or in the fibre of cotton cloth. (1)

17. When glucose is oxidised with nitric acid, it yields a dicarboxylic acid known as saccharic acid.

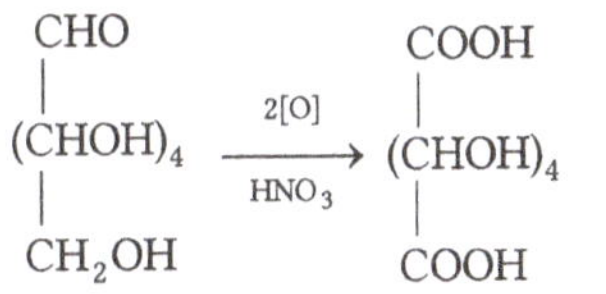

Glucose Saccharic acid (3)

18. **Key idea** Conversion of glucose into fructose can be carried in three steps:
   (i) Heating glucose with excess of phenylhydrazine to give glucosazone.
   (ii) Glucosazone on hydrolysis with hydrochloric acid yields glucosone and phenylhydrazine.
   (iii) Glucosone when reduced with zinc dust and acetic acid changes into fructose.

Therefore, write the reaction and convert the glucose into fructose.

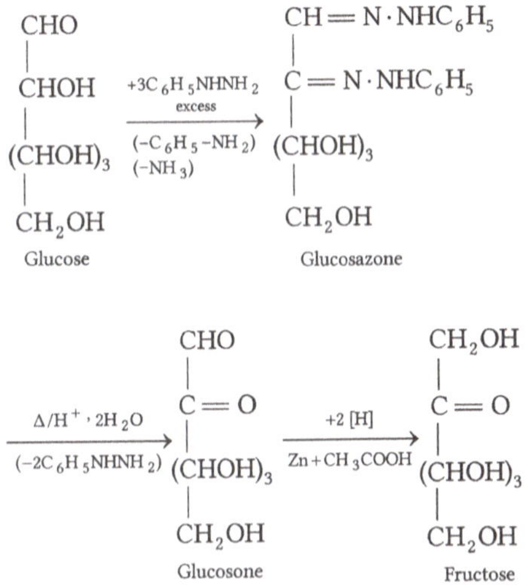

(3)

19. Refer to text on page 411 and 412 (Structure of glucose). (3)

20. Glucose consists of 5 —OH groups. Among these, the —OH group present on the terminal carbon atom (i.e. C-6 atom) is called 1° hydroxyl group while all the four remaining —OH groups present on C-2, C-3, C-4 and C-5 atoms are called 2° hydroxyl groups. 1° hydroxyl groups are easily oxidised to carboxylic acid group while 2° hydroxyl groups undergo oxidation only under drastic conditions. (1½)

e.g. On oxidation with nitric acid, glucose gives a dicarboxylic acid, saccharic acid (also called glycaric acid) having the same number of carbon atoms as glucose. This indicates that glucose contains one primary (1°) alcoholic or hydroxyl group.

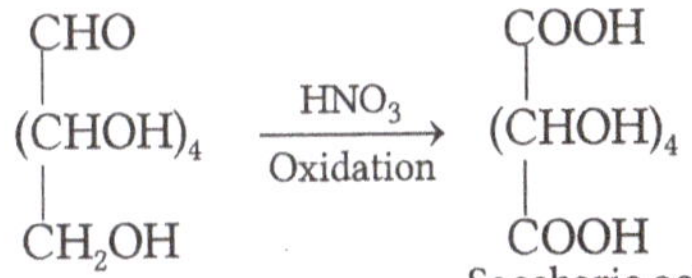

Glucose Saccharic acid (1½)

21. Glycogen is a highly branched condensed polymer of α-D-glucose. It is stored in the form of glucose in liver and muscles of human beings. In contrast, starch is a chief storage polysaccharide of plants and consists of a mixture of two components, amylose (water soluble component 15-20%) and amylopectin (water insoluble component 80-85%). Amylose is a linear polymer of α-D-glucose, while amylopectin is a highly branched polymer of α-D-glucose.
Thus, both glycogen and amylopectin are branched chain condensed polymer of α-D-glucose. The only difference is that amylopectin chain consists of 20-25 glucose units whereas glycogen chain consists of 10-14 glucose units.(3)

22. Refer to text on pages 415 and 416 (Polysaccharides) (3)

TOPIC 02 Proteins, Enzymes and Hormones

Another class of biomolecules which are essential for living systems, are proteins. Proteins are the most abundant biomolecules of the living system. The chief sources of proteins are milk, cheese, pulses, fish, meat, peanuts, etc.

They are found in every part of the body and form a fundamental basis of structure and functions of life. These are also required for growth and maintenance of body. The word protein is derived from Greek word, '*proteios*' meaning 'primary' or 'of prime importance'. Chemically, proteins are the polymers in which the monomeric units are the α-amino acids.

Amino Acids

Amino acids contain amino ($—NH_2$) and carboxyl ($—COOH$) functional groups. Depending upon the relative position of amino group with respect to carboxyl group, the amino acids can be classified as α, β, γ or δ.

$$\underset{\substack{|\\ NH_2 \longleftarrow \alpha\text{-amino group}}}{R—\overset{\alpha}{C}H}—COOH \longleftarrow \text{Carboxylic group}$$

α-amino acid
(R = side chain)

On hydrolysis of proteins, only α-amino acids are obtained.

$$\text{Proteins} \xrightarrow{\text{Hydrolysis}} \text{Peptides} \xrightarrow{\text{Hydrolysis}} \alpha\text{-amino acids}$$

Nomenclature of Amino Acids

Amino acids can be named according to the IUPAC system, but they are generally known by their trivial names depending upon the source from which they are obtained or the property of that compound etc.

e.g. Glycine is named due to its sweet taste (in Greek '*glykos*' means sweet).

Amino acids are represented by three letters symbol, which is first three letters of their respective common names.

The structures of some commonly occurring amino acids along with their symbols can be summarised as follows:

Natural Amino Acids

S.N.	Name of the amino acids	Characteristic feature of side chain, *R*	Three letters symbol	One letter code
1.	Glycine	$—H$	Gly	G
2.	Alanine	$—CH_3$	Ala	A
3.	Valine*	$(H_3C)_2CH—$	Val	V
4.	Leucine*	$(H_3C)_2CH—CH_2—$	Leu	L
5.	Isoleucine*	$H_3C—CH_2—(CH_3)—CH—$	Ile	I
6.	Arginine*	$HN{=}\underset{\substack{|\\ NH_2}}{C}—NH(CH_2)_3—$	Arg	R
7.	Lysine*	$H_2N—(CH_2)_4—$	Lys	K
8.	Glutamic acid	$HOOC—CH_2—CH_2—$	Glu	E
9.	Aspartic acid	$HOOC—CH_2—$	Asp	D
10.	Glutamine	$H_2N—CO—CH_2—CH_2—$	Gln	Q
11.	Asparagine	$H_2N—CO—CH_2—$	Asn	N
12.	Threonine*	$H_3C—CHOH—$	Thr	T
13.	Serine	$HO—CH_2—$	Ser	S
14.	Cysteine	$HS—CH_2—$	Cys	C
15.	Methionine*	$H_3C—S—CH_2—CH_2—$	Met	M
16.	Phenylalanine*	$C_6H_5—CH_2—$	Phe	F
17.	Tyrosine	$(p)\ HO—C_6H_4—CH_2—$	Tyr	Y
18.	Tryptophan*	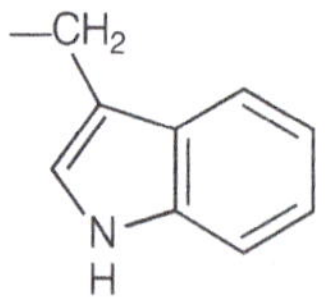	Trp	W
19.	Histidine*	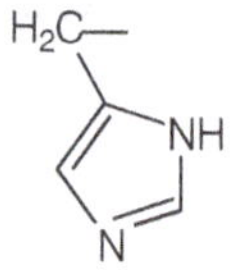	His	H
20.	Proline	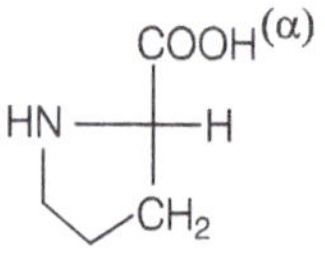	Pro	P

* Essential amino acids, α = complete structure

Classification of Amino Acids

Depending upon the relative number of amino and carboxyl groups present in their molecule, amino acids are classified as:

(i) **Acidic amino acids** These are the amino acids which contain more carboxyl group than amino groups, e.g. aspartic acid, glutamic acid, etc.

(ii) **Neutral amino acids** These are the amino acids which contain equal number of amino and carboxyl groups, e.g. glycine, alanine, etc.

(iii) **Basic amino acids** These are the amino acids which contain more number of amino groups than carboxyl groups, e.g. lycine, arginine, etc.

> **Essential and Non-Essential Amino Acids**
>
> Amino acids which are synthesised by the body, are called non-essential. On the other hand, those amino acids which cannot be synthesised in the human body and are supplied in the form of diet (because they are required for proper health and growth) are called essential amino acids. The ten essential amino acids are marked by asterisks * in the above table.

Properties of Amino Acids

Some of the important properties of amino acids are:

(i) Amino acids are usually colourless, crystalline solids. These are soluble in water and have high melting points.

(ii) Amino acids contain both acidic (carboxyl group) and basic (amino group) groups due to which they behave like salts rather than simple amines.

(iii) **Formation of Zwitter Ion** In aqueous solution, they neutralise each other involving transfer of a proton from the carboxyl group to the amino group, giving rise to a dipolar ion known as '**Zwitter ion**'. It is neutral but contains both positive and negative charges.

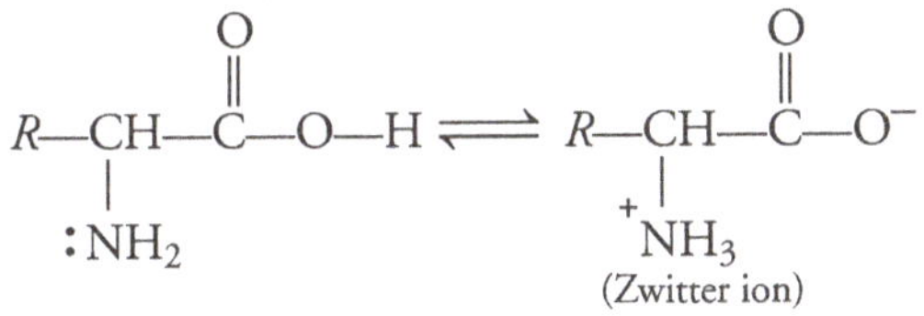

In Zwitter ionic form, amino acids show amphoteric behaviour as they can react with both acids and bases.

Isoelectric Point At a particular pH of the solution, amino acid molecule does not migrate towards any electrode and remains as a neutral dipolar ion, is known as **isoelectric point.**

(iv) Except glycine, all other α-amino acids are optically active as their α-carbon is asymmetric. These exist in both 'D' and 'L' forms. Most of the amino acids have L-configuration in which $—NH_2$ group is on left hand side.

Peptide Linkage and their Classification

Proteins are connected to each other by $—CO—NH—$ bond which is called the **peptide bond** or the peptide linkage. Chemically, peptide linkage is an amide ($—CO—NH—$) bond formed between carboxyl group ($—COOH$) and amino group ($—NH_2$).

The reaction between two molecules of similar or different amino acids, proceed through the combination of the amino group of one molecule with the carboxyl group of the other, resulting in the elimination of a water molecule and formation of a peptide bond ($—CONH—$). The product of the reaction is called **dipeptide** because it is made up of two amino acids. e.g. Glycylalanine is formed when carboxyl group of glycine combines with the amino group of alanine.

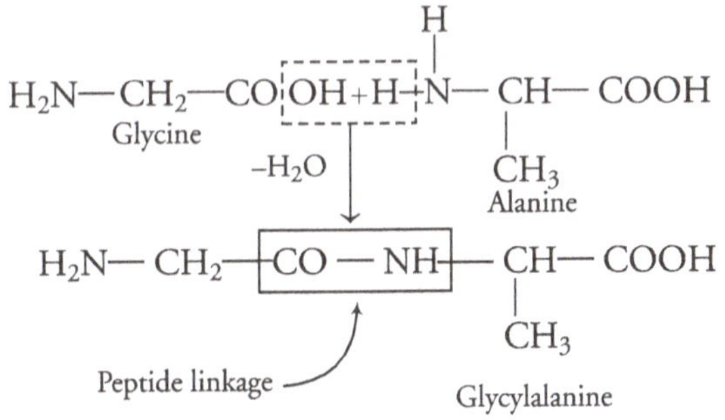

If a third amino acid combines to a dipeptide, the product is called a **tripeptide**. When the number of such amino acids is more than ten, then the products are called **polypeptides.** A polypeptide with more than hundred amino acid residues, having molecular mass higher than 10,000 u, is called a **protein**. However, the distinction between a polypeptide and a protein is not very sharp. Polypeptides with fewer amino acids are likely to be called proteins if they ordinarily have a well defined conformation of protein such as insulin which contains only 51 amino acids.

Classification of Proteins

On the basis of their molecular shape, proteins are of two types:

(i) Fibrous Proteins

They have thread or fibre like structures in which polypeptide chains run parallel and are held together by hydrogen and disulphide bonds. These proteins are insoluble in water, e.g. keratin (found in hair, skin, nails, wool, silk) and myosin (present in muscles).

(ii) Globular Proteins

They have spherical shape structure which results when the chains of polypeptides coil around. These are soluble in water, e.g. insulin and albumins.

S.No.	Fibrous proteins	Globular proteins
1.	These proteins possess thread like structures.	These proteins possess folded spheroidal structures.
2.	The polypeptide chains are held together by stronger intermolecular hydrogen bonds.	The intermolecular hydrogen bonding is comparatively weaker.
3.	These proteins are insoluble in water.	These proteins are soluble in water.
4.	They are stable to moderate changes in temperature and pH.	They are very sensitive to changes in temperature and pH.

Structure and Shape of Proteins

On the basis of structure and shape of proteins, four different levels are found:

(i) Primary Structure

Proteins may have one or more polypeptide chains. Each polypeptide chain has a large number of α-amino acids linked to one another in a specific sequence. The specific sequence in which various amino acids are linked with each other to form a polypeptide, is called its primary structure. So, the change of just one amino acid in the sequence can alter its biological activity and can create a different protein.

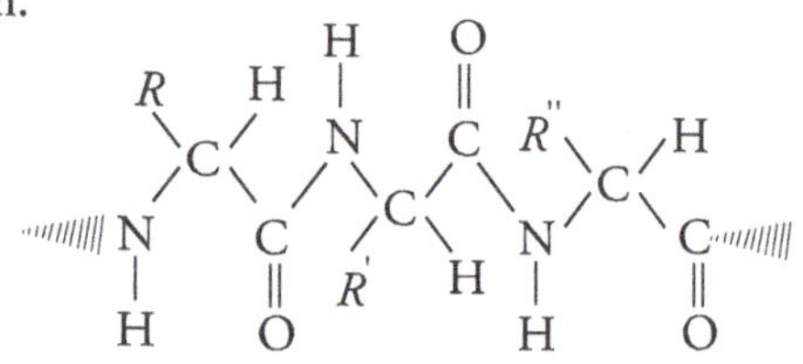

Primary structure of protein

(ii) Secondary Structure

The stabel conformation in which the polypeptide chains assume as a result of hydrogen bonding between $-\overset{\overset{\large O}{\|}}{C}-$ and —NH— groups of the peptide bond give rise secondary structure of proteins. Thus, the structure that describes, how a peptide chain is arranged or oriented is three dimensional spacs is called secondary structure of protein.

They exist in two different structures which are as follows :

(a) **α-helix Structure** It is one of the most common structure in which a polypeptide chain forms all possible hydrogen bonds by twisting into a right handed helix. In this structure, the —NH group of each amino acid unit is hydrogen bonded to the C=O of another amino acid unit present at an adjacent turn of the helix.

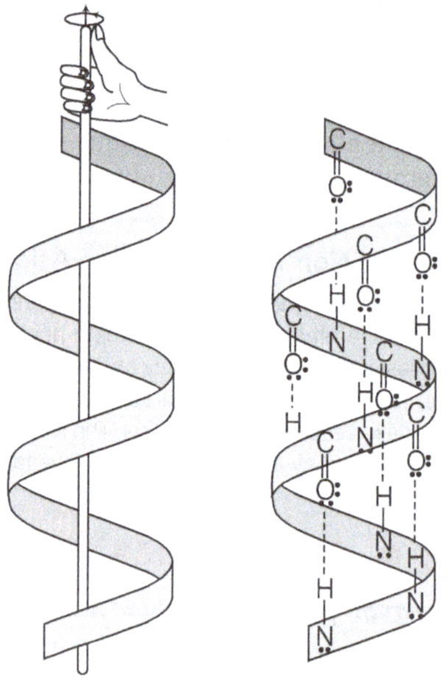

α-helix structure of proteins

(b) **β-pleated Sheet Structure** All peptide chains are stretched out to nearly maximum extension and then laid side by side which are held together by intermolecular hydrogen bonds.

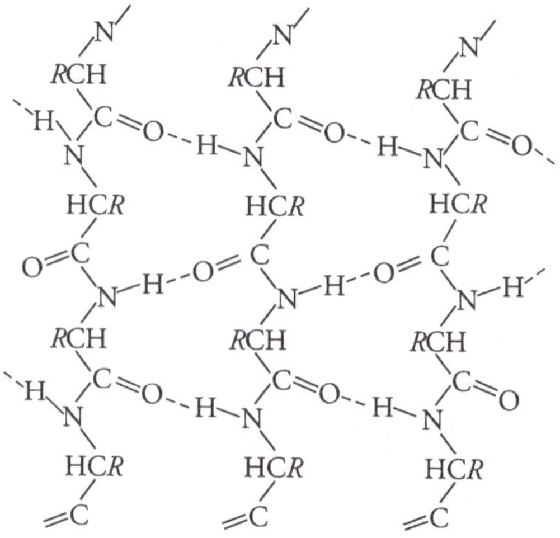

β-pleated sheet structure of proteins

The structure so formed resembles the pleated folds of drapery and thus, it is known as β-pleated sheet structure.

(iii) Tertiary Structure

The further folding of the secondary structure of proteins is known as tertiary structure. It gives rise to two major molecular shapes, fibrous and globular. The main forces that stabilise 2° and 3° structures of protein are hydrogen bonds, disulphide bonds, van der Waals' forces and electrostatic forces of attraction.

(iv) Quaternary Structure

Although many proteins exist as a single polypeptide chain, but some of the proteins are composed of two or more polypeptide chains called subunits.

The spatial arrangement of these subunits with respect to each other is known as quaternary structure.

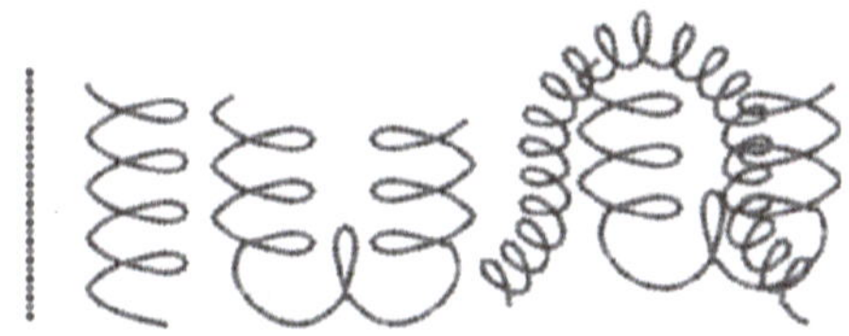

Diagrammatic representation of protein structures (two subunits of two types in quaternary structure)

Denaturation of Proteins

Protein found in a biological system with a unique three-dimensional structure and biological activity, is called native protein. When a native protein is subjected to physical change (like change in temperature) or chemical change (like change in pH), the hydrogen bonds are disturbed.

As a result, globules unfold and helix get uncoiled and protein loses its biological activity. This is known as denaturation of protein. During denaturation, 2° and 3° structures are destroyed but 1° structure remains intact, e.g. coagulation of an egg white on boiling and curding of milk caused due to the formation of lactic acid by the bacteria present in milk.

Enzymes

These are essential biological catalysts (or biocatalysts) which are needed to catalyse biochemical reactions. Almost all the enzymes are globular proteins. Enzymes are very specific for a particular reaction and for a particular substrate. They are generally named after the compound or class of compounds upon which they work, e.g. the enzyme that catalyses hydrolysis of maltose into glucose is named as maltase.

e.g. $\underset{\text{Maltose}}{C_{12}H_{22}O_{11}} \xrightarrow[H_2O]{\text{Maltase}} \underset{\text{Glucose}}{2C_6H_{12}O_6}$

Sometime enzymes are also named after the reaction, where they are used. The enzyme which catalyses the oxidation of one substrate with simultaneous reduction of another substrate are named as oxidoreductase enzymes.
The ending of the name of an enzyme is '-ase'.

In addition to the protein part most enzymes also have small non-protein parts called co-factor. The protein part is called apoenzyme and the combination of apoenzyme plus co-factor is called haloenzyme.

Mechanism of Enzyme Action

Enzymes are needed only in small quantities for the progress of a reaction. Like chemical catalysts, enzyme reduces the magnitude of activation energy by providing an alternate pathway, e.g. activation energy for acid hydrolysis of sucrose is 6.22 kJ mol^{-1}, while the activation energy is only 2.15 kJ mol^{-1}, when hydrolysed by the enzyme, sucrase. Thus, enzyme catalysed reaction occurs at much faster rate.

Note Mechanism for the enzyme action has been discussed in chapter 5.

Some Common Examples of Enzymes

Enzyme	Reaction Catalysed
Maltase	Maltose $\longrightarrow$ Glucose + Glucose
Lactase	Lactose $\longrightarrow$ Glucose + Galactose
Amylase	Starch $\longrightarrow n \times$ Glucose
Invertase	Surcose $\longrightarrow$ Glucose + Fructose
Urease	Urea $\longrightarrow CO_2 + NH_3$
Carbonic anhydrase	$H_2CO_3 \longrightarrow CO_2 + H_2O$
Pepsin	Proteins $\longrightarrow$ Amino acids
Trypsin	Proteins $\longrightarrow$ Amino acids

Hormones

These are the chemical substances, produced by endocrine glands in the body and are released directly in blood stream. From here, these are transported to the site of their action. These act as intercellular messengers and control various body functions. Different endocrine glands which produce hormones are thyroid, pituitary, pancreas, testes and ovaries.

Classification of Hormones

On the basis of chemical constitution, the hormones are mainly divided into two classes, i.e. steroid and non-steroid hormones.

(i) Steroid Hormones

The compounds which are the derivatives of four ring systems and consisting of three cyclopentane rings are called

steroids. Sex hormones, bile acids, etc., are steroid hormones. Steroid hormones can be further classified as sex hormones and adrenocortical hormones.

(a) **Sex Hormones** Sex hormones are mainly of three types, i.e. male sex hormone or androgen, female sex hormone or estrogen and pregnancy hormone or progesterone. Female sex hormone is responsible for the development of secondary female characteristics and participates in the control of menstrual cycle. Progesterone is responsible for preparing the uterus for the implantation of fertilized egg.

(b) **Adrenocortical Hormones or Corticosteroids** These hormones are involved in the regulation of large number of biological activities such as carbohydrates, proteins and lipid metabolism, etc.

(ii) Non-steroid Hormones

These hormones do not contain steroid ring. They are further classified as protein or peptide hormone, amino acid derivative or amine hormones. An example of this type of hormone is insulin, secreted by pancreas, its function is to lower the blood sugar level by increasing the rate of conversion of glucose into glycogen.

Functions of Hormones

(i) They help to maintain the balance of biological activities in the body.

(ii) Growth hormone and sex hormone play an important role in growth, development and reproduction.

(iii) Sex hormones are also responsible for the development of secondary sexual characters.

Topic Practice 2

Very Short Answer Type Questions

1 Mark

1. **Fill in the Blanks**

(i) Proteins are made up of .... units held together by .... linkages. **ISC 2004**

(ii) Proteins are .... polymers of .... **ISC 2001**

(iii) Correct the following statement.3 Glycine exists as a Zwitter ion at any pH. **ISC 2000**

(iv) On hydrolysis of proteins only .... are obtained

(v) When a native protein is subjected to a physical/chemical change, it loses its biological activity. This is known is ....

2. **Objective Type Questions**

(i) Which of the following set consists only of essential amino acids?

(a) Alanine, tyrosine, cystine
(b) Leucine, lysine, tryptophane
(c) Alanine, glutamine, lycine
(d) Leucine, proline, glycine

(ii) The amino acid which is not optically active is

(a) lactic acid (b) serine
(c) alanine (d) glycine

(iii) The secondary structure of a protein refers to

(a) α-helical backbone
(b) hydrophobic interaction
(c) sequence of α-amino acids
(d) fixed configuration of the polypeptide back bone

(iv) The enzymes which have control site in addition to active site are called

(a) holozymes (b) coenzymes
(c) aponenzymes (d) allosteric enzymes

(v) Which one is a fibrous protein?

(a) Globulin (b) Collagen
(c) Hordein (d) Glutin

(vi) The bond that determines the secondary structure of proteins is

(a) coordinate bond (b) covalent bond
(c) hydrogen bond (d) ionic bond

3. Match Column I Column with II and choose the correct option using the codes given below.

Column I (Amino acid)		Column II (One latter code)	
(A)	Alanine	(i)	A
(B)	Aspartic acid	(ii)	D
(C)	Tyrosine	(iii)	Y
(D)	Glutamine	(iv)	Q

Codes

	A	B	C	D		A	B	C	D
(a)	(i)	(ii)	(iii)	(iv)	(b)	(iv)	(iii)	(ii)	(i)
(c)	(i)	(ii)	(iv)	(iii)	(d)	(ii)	(i)	(iii)	(iv)

4. Amino acids can be classified as $\alpha, \beta, \gamma, \delta$ and so on depending upon the relative position of amino group with respect to carboxyl group. Which type of amino acids forms polypeptide chain in proteins? **NCERT Exemplar**

5. Structures of glycine and alanine are given below. Show the peptide linkage in glycylalanine.

$H_2N—CH_2—COOH$ (Glycine), $H_2N—CH(CH_3)—COOH$ (Alanine)

6. What type of bonding helps in stabilising the α-helix structure of proteins? **NCERT**

7. What are enzymes or biocatalysts? **NCERT**

Short answer Type I Questions

(2 Marks)

8. Write two differences between globular and fibrous proteins. **ISC 2017**

9. Give one example of fibrous protein. Name the final product of hydrolysis of proteins. What is denaturation of proteins? **ISC 2000, 2010**

10. Answer the following questions:
   (i) Give one example of an α-amino acid.
   (ii) Write the structure of the dipeptide using this example. **ISC 2000**

11. What are the essential and non-essential amino acids? Give one example of each type. **NCERT**

12. What are the common types of secondary structure of proteins? **NCERT**

13. Protein found in a biological system with a unique three-dimensional structure and biological activity is called a native protein.When a protein in its native form, is subjected to a physical change like change in temperature or a chemical change like, change in pH, denaturation of protein takes place. Explain the cause. **NCERT Exemplar**

Or

What is the effect of denaturation on the structure of proteins? **NCERT**

14. Activation energy for the acid catalysed hydrolysis of sucrose is 6.22 kJ mol^{-1} while the activation energy is only 2.15 kJ mol^{-1} when hydrolysis is catalysed by the enzyme sucrase. Explain. **NCERT Exemplar**

15. (i) Write the chemical equation for the reaction of glucose with bromine water. **ISC 2020**
   (ii) Write the Zwitter ion structure of glycine.

Short Answer Type II Questions

(3 Marks)

16. Define the following with an example of each:
   (i) Polysaccharides (ii) Denatured protein
   (iii) Essential amino acids

Or

   (i) Write the product when D-glucose reacts with conc. HNO_3.
   (ii) Amino acids show amphoteric behaviour. Why?
   (iii) Write one difference between α-helix and β-pleated structures of proteins.

17. The melting points and solubility of amino acids in water are generally higher than that of the corresponding halo acids. Explain. **NCERT Intext**

18. Write the function of the following enzymes.
   (i) Invertase (ii) Urease
   (iii) Maltase **NCERT Exemplar**

Hints & Solutions

1. (i) Proteins are made up of α-**amino acid** units held together by **peptide** linkage.
(ii) Proteins are **condensed** polymers of **monomer amino acids**.
(iii) Glycine exists as a Zwitter ion at a particular pH known as isoelectric point.
The pH at which concentration of cation and anion form of glycine becomes equal is called **isoelectric point**. The glycine will exist as Zwitter ion at this pH.
(iv) α-amino acids
(v) Denaturation of proteins.

2. (i) (b) Ten essential amino acids are as follows:

(i)	Arginine	(vi)	Methionine
(ii)	Histidine	(vii)	Phenylalanine
(iii)	Isoleucine	(viii)	Threonine
(iv)	Leucine	(ix)	Tryptophane
(v)	Lysine	(x)	Valine

Thus, the correct option is (b).
(ii) (d) Glycine is optically inactive amino acid due to absence of chiral carbon atom.

CH_2—COOH
|
NH_3
Glycine

(iii) (a) Primary structure involves sequence of α-amino acid in polypeptide chain. Secondary structure involves α-helical and β-pleated sheet like structures.
(iv) (d) Allosteric site is a control site in addition to the active site in enzymes.
(v) (a) Globulin is a fibrous protein. These are long and thread like molecules and insoluble in water.
(vi) (c) The secondary structure of protein refers to the shape in which long polypeptide chains are held together by means of hydrogen bonding.

3. (a) A → (i), B → (ii), C → (iii), D → (iv)

4. α-amino acids forms polypeptide chain in proteins.

5. 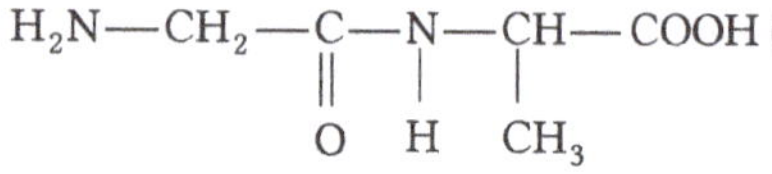

(1)

6. Hydrogen bonding. (1)

7. Enzyme or biocatalysts are proteins which catalyses the biochemical reactions. (1)

8. (i) **Fibrous proteins** They have thread or fibre like structures in which polypeptide chains run parallel. These proteins are insoluble in water, e.g. keratin (found in hair, skin, nails, wool, silk) and myosin (present in muscles). (1)

(ii) **Globular proteins** They have spherical shape in which chains of polypeptides coil around. These are soluble in water, e.g. insulin and albumins. (2)

9. Keratin is a fibrous protein. The final product of hydrolysis of a protein is a mixture of amino-acids. Change in physical and biological properties of a native protein without affecting its chemical composition is called **denaturation of proteins**. It may be caused by heating, reaction with alcohol, acid radiation etc. It changes only secondary and tertiary structures of proteins. (2)

10. (i) Alanine, 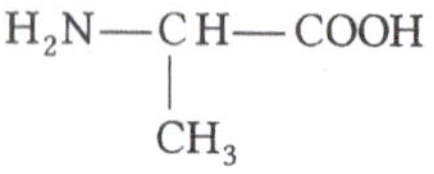
(1)

(ii) When two α-amino acids combine, a dipeptide is formed with the loss of a water molecule.

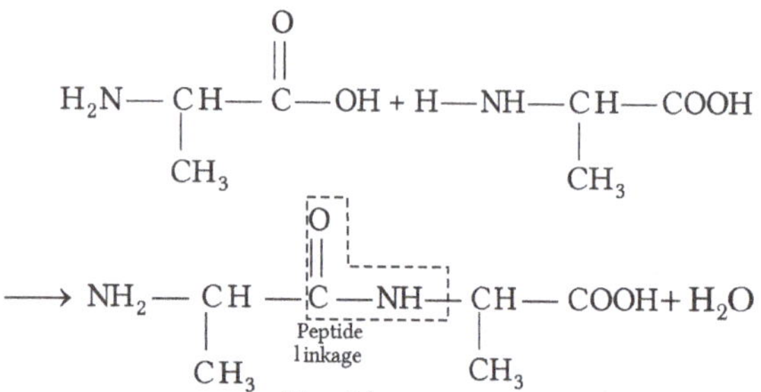

Dipeptide (1)

11. Refer to text on page 421 (Box matter). **(2)**

12. The stable conformation in which the polypeptide chain assume due to hydrogen bonding between $-\overset{O}{\overset{\|}{C}}-$ and NH group of the peptide bond is called **secondary structure of proteins.** (1)

These exist in two types of different structures:

(i) **α-helix** Refer to text on page 422.

(ii) **β-pleated sheet structure** Refer to text on page 528. (Structure and shape of protein) (2)

13. Refer to text on page 423 (Denaturation of protein). (2)

14. Enzymes are the essential biological catalysts which are needed to catalyse biochemical reactions. Enzymes are needed only in small quantities for the progress of a reaction. Like chemical catalysts, enzymes reduces the magnitude of activation energy by providing alternative pathway, e.g. hydrolysis of sucrose, the enzyme sucrase reduces the activation energy from 6.22 kJ mol^{-1} to 2.15 kJ mol^{-1}. Thus, enzyme catalysed reactions occur at a much faster rate. (2)

15. (i) Refer to page no. 412 (Oxidation).

(ii) Refer to page no. 421 (Formation of Zwitter ion).

16. (i) Carbohydrates which give a large number of monosaccharide units on hydrolysis are called polysaccharides, e.g. starch, cellulose, glycogen, etc. These are not sweet in taste, therefore they are also called non-sugars. (1)

(ii) Protein found in biological system with a unique three-dimensional structure and biological activity, as native proteins. When a native protein is subjected to a physical change (like change in temperature) or a chemical change (like change in pH), its hydrogen bonds are disturbed. As the result, globules unfold and helix get uncoiled and protein loses its biological activity.

This is known as denaturation of protein. During denaturation, 2° and 3° structures are destroyed but 1° structure remains intact, e.g. coagulation of an egg white on boiling and curding of milk caused due to the formation of lactic acid by the bacteria present in milk. (1)

(iii) Those amino acids which cannot be synthesised in the human body and are supplied through our diet (because they are required for proper health and growth) are called essential amino acids. e.g. Arginine lysine, etc. (1)

Or

(i) It is saccharic acid which is formed when D-glucose reacts with conc. HNO_3.

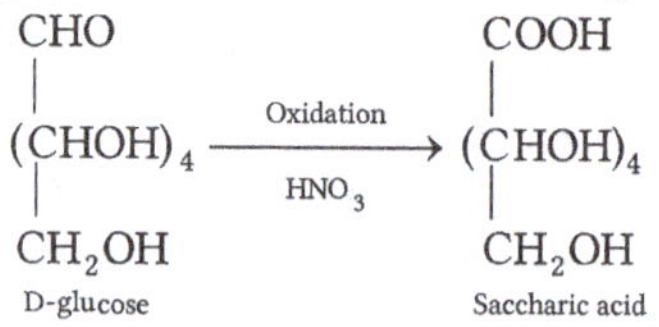

(1)

(ii) Refer to text on page 421 (Properties of amino acids, formation of Zwitter ion). (1)

(iii) Difference between α-helix and β-pleated structures

α-helix Structure	β-pleated Structure
If the size of *R*-group is large, intramolecular H-bonds are formed between C=O of molecule and NH of amino acid in polypeptide chain that gives right handed α-helix structure, i.e. it is formed by the folding of a single polypeptide chain due to hydrogen bonding.	If size of *R*-group is small intermolecular H-bonds forms between C=O of polypeptide chain with N—H of other, giving β-pleated sheet structure, i.e. it is formed by the folding in more than one polypeptide chain due to hydrogen bonding.

(1)

17. The amino acids exist as Zwitter ions ($H_3\overset{+}{N}$—CHR—COO^-) in aqueous solution. Due to this, dipolar salt like structure amino acids have strong dipole-dipole attractions.

Thus, their melting points are higher than corresponding halo acids which do not have salt like character.

Secondly, they interact strongly with H_2O due to their salt like character. As a result, polar amino acids dissolve in polar solvents like H_2O. Hence, the solubility of amino acids in water is higher than that of corresponding halo acids, which do not have any salt like character. (3)

18. (i) **Invertase** Hydrolysis of cane sugar. (1)

(ii) **Urease** Decomposition of urea into NH_3 and CO_2. (1)

(iii) **Maltase** Hydrolysis of maltose into glucose. (1)

TOPIC 03 Vitamins and Nucleic Acids

Vitamins

These are the organic compounds required in small amounts in our diet but their deficiency causes specific diseases. Most of the vitamins cannot be synthesised in our body but plants can synthesise almost all of them. Hence, vitamins are considered as essential food factors. All the vitamins are generally available in our diet. They are generally regarded as organic compounds which are required in the diet in small amounts to perform specific biological functions for normal maintenance of optimum growth and health of the organism.

Vitamins are designated by alphabets A, B, C, D, etc. Some of them are further named as subgroups which are designated by the number alphabet.
e.g. B_1, B_2, B_6, B_{12}, etc.

Classification of Vitamins

Vitamins are classified into two groups depending upon their solubility in water or fat.

These are as follows :

(i) **Fat Soluble Vitamins** These are the vitamins which are soluble in fat and oils but insoluble in water. These are vitamins A, D, E and K. These are stored in liver and adipose (fat storing) tissues.

(ii) **Water Soluble Vitamins** These are the vitamins which are soluble in water. B groups vitamins and vitamin C are soluble in water, so they are grouped together. Water soluble vitamins must be supplied regularly in diet, because they are readily excreted in urine and cannot be stored (except vitamin B_{12}) in our body.

Some Important Vitamins, their Sources and Deficiency Diseases

S. No.	Name of vitamins	Sources	Deficiency diseases
1.	Vitamin A (Retinol)	Fish liver oil, carrots, butter and milk	Xerophthalmia (hardening of cornea of eye) and night blindness.
2.	Vitamin B_1 (Thiamine)	Yeast, milk, green vegetables and cereals	Beri-beri (paralysis of legs, loss of appetite and retarded growth).
3.	Vitamin B_2 (Riboflavin)	Milk, egg white, liver, kidney	Cheilosis (fissuring at corners of mouth and lips), digestive disorders and burning sensation of the skin.
4.	Vitamin B_6 (Pyridoxine)	Yeast, milk, egg yolk, cereals and grams	Convulsions
5.	Vitamin B_{12} (Cyanocobalamin)	Meat, fish, egg and curd	Pernicious anaemia (RBC deficient in haemoglobin).
6.	Vitamin C (Ascorbic acid)	Citrus fruits, amla and green leafy vegetables	Scurvy (bleeding of gums).
7.	Vitamin D (Egrocalciferol)	Exposure to sunlight, fish and egg yolk.	Rickets (bone deformities in children) and osteomalacia (soft bones and joint pain in adults).
8.	Vitamin E (α- tocopherol)	Vegetable oils like wheat gram oil, sunflower oil, etc.	Increased fragility of RBCs and muscular weakness.
9.	Vitamin H (Biotin)	Yeast, liver, kidney and milk.	Dermatitis, skin disease, loss of hair and paralysis.
10.	Vitamin K (Phylloquinone)	Green leafy vegetables.	Increased blood clotting time.

Nucleic Acids

The nucleic acids are the chemical carriers of a cell's genetic information. The chemical composition of nucleic acids acts as coded information. This information when expressed determines the nature of the cell, controls cell growth and division and directs biosynthesis of proteins (including enzymes) required for cellular functions.

Nucleic acids are of two types :

(i) DNA-Deoxyribonucleic acid

(ii) RNA-Ribonucleic acid

Chemical Composition of Nucleic Acids

Nucleic acids are biopolymers made of **nucleotides** joined together to form a long chain. Hence, these are also called **polynucleotides.** Each nucleotide is composed of an aldopentose sugar linked to a heterocyclic nitrogenous base and further to a phosphate group.

Combined form of sugar and nitrogenous base is called **nucleoside** and that of nucleoside and phosphate group is called **nucleotide.**

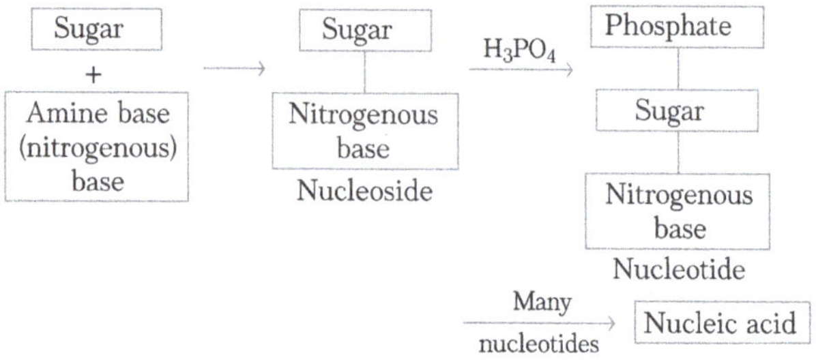

Thus, on complete hydrolysis of nucleic acid, three compounds (pentose sugar, phosphoric acid and nitrogenous base) are formed as discussed below.

(i) **Pentose Sugar** The sugar component in RNA is ribose, and the sugar component in DNA is 2′-deoxyribose.

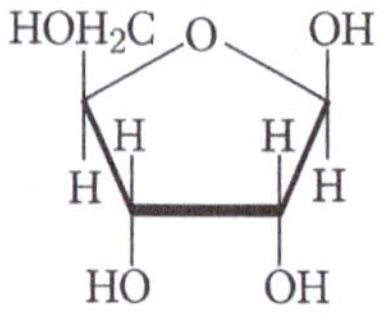

β-D-ribose used in RNA

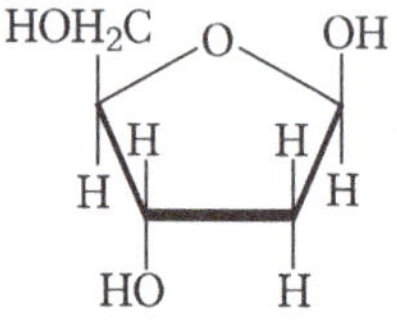

β-D-deoxyribose used in DNA

Note The prefix 2′-deoxy means that oxygen is missing from the 2′ position of ribose; numbers with a prime superscript refer to positions on the sugar component of a nucleotide and the numbers without a prime refer to positions on the heterocyclic amine base.

The nucleotides are abbreviated by three capital letters, preceded by *d* in case of deoxy series.

AMP — adenosine monophosphate

dAMP — deoxyadenosine monophosphate

ATP — adenosine triphosphate

UTP — uridine diphosphate

(ii) **Phosphoric Acid** It is present as a phosphate (PO_4^{3-}) group in the nucleotide. It plays an important role of linking two nucleotides. The linkage is called **phosphodiester linkage** (discussed later).

(iii) **Nitrogenous Bases** These are the heterocyclic compounds of nitrogen. These are further divided into two groups.

(a) **Purines** These are bicyclic groups containing N-atoms in each of the cycles.
Examples are adenine (A) and guanine (G)

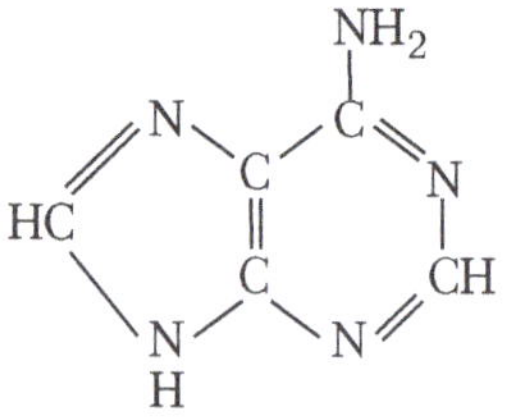

Adenine (A)

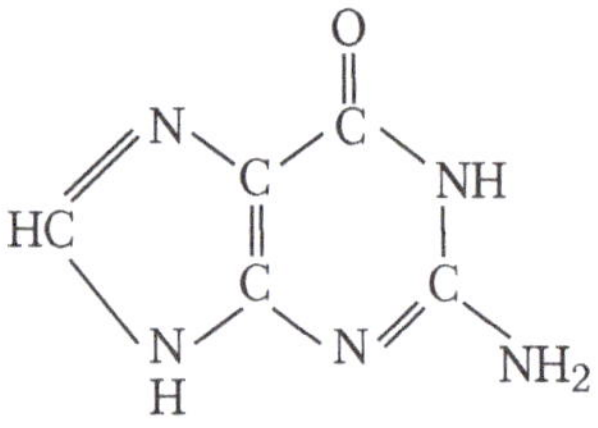

Guanine (G)

(b) **Pyrimidines** These are single cyclic bases. The examples are cytosine (C), thymine (T) and uracil (U).

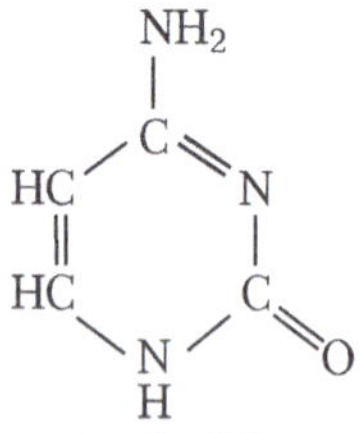

Cytosine (C)

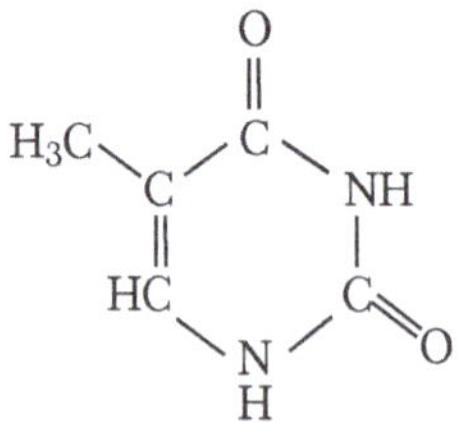

Thymine (T)

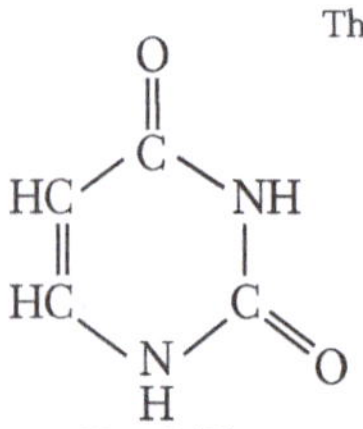

Uracil (U)

Note Three bases, A, G and C are common to both DNA and RNA. While the base 'T' is exclusive to DNA and the base 'U' is exclusive to RNA. So, there are four bases in each DNA and RNA. i.e. DNA = A, G, C, T and RNA = A, G, C, U

Thus, DNA differ from RNA in sugar as well as nitrogenous base.

Structure of Nucleic Acids

In both DNA and RNA, the heterocyclic amine base is bonded to C-1′ of the sugar, and the phosphoric acid is bonded by a phosphate ester linkage to C-5′ sugar position.

Thus, nucleosides and nucleotides have the general structure as shown below

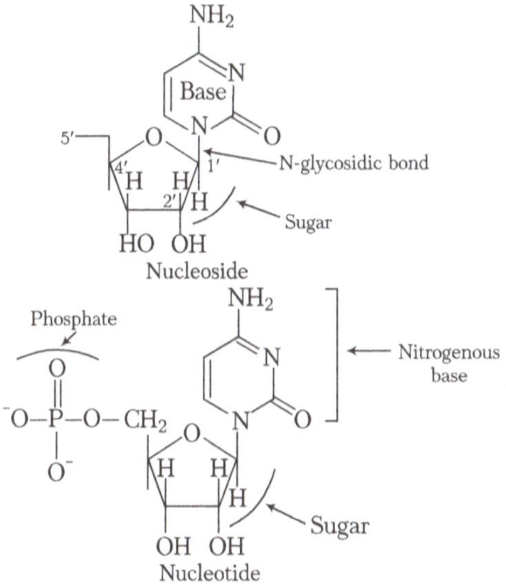

Structure of nucleic acid

The structure of nucleic acid can be divided into two following categories (with special reference to DNA).

(i) **Primary Structure** It gives information about the sequence of nucleotides in the chain of nucleic acid. This structure is formed or linkage of one nucleotide with other through the **phosphodiester linkage**.

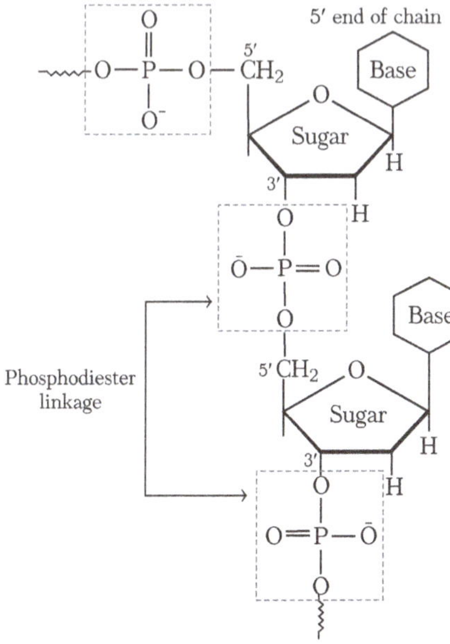

Primary structure of DNA

Phosphodiester linkage, connects a sugar base with other one. The phosphate group in this linkage is attached to C—5′ position of one sugar and the C—3′ position of the other one. One end of the nucleic acid polymer has a free hydroxyl group at C—3′ (the 3′ end and the other end) has a phosphate at C—5′ (the 5′ end)

(ii) **Secondary Structure** This structure explains the coiling of polynucleotide chains (primary structure). Watson and Crick proposed the secondary structure for DNA. This structure is called **double stranded helical structure.**

Here, two separate polynucleotide chains (or strands) are helically coiled with each other. These two strands are held together by H-bonds. The direction (with reference to sugar base) is opposite to each other (3′ or 5′).

The two strands are complementary to each other as adenine (A) of one strand is bonded to thymine (T) of the other one, (with 2 H-bonds), while guanine (G) is bonded to cytosine (C) of the other one (with 3 H-bonds) and *vice-versa.*

A ═ T ; C ≡ G
2 H-bonds ; 3 H-bond

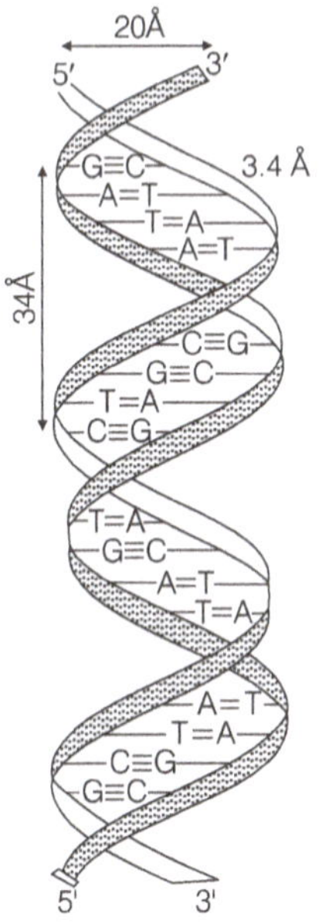

Double helix structure of DNA

In secondary structure of RNA, helixes are present which are single-stranded but sometimes they are folded back on themselves to form a double helix structure.

RNA molecules are of three types, i.e. **messenger RNA** (*m*RNA), **ribosomal RNA** (*r*RNA) and **transfer RNA** (*t*RNA). They all perform different functions.

Points of Differences between DNA and RNA

DNA	RNA
It has a double helix structure.	It exists as single chain structure.
Sugar is D-2-deoxyribose	Sugar is D-ribose.
Adenine (A) and guanine (G) as purine bases.	Adenine (A) and guanine (G) as purine bases.
Cytosine (C) and thymine (T) as pyrimidine bases.	Cytosine (C) and uracil (U) as pyrimidine bases.
It chiefly occurs in the nucleus.	It mainly occurs in the cytoplasm.
It has the unique property of replication.	It usually does not replicated.
It is responsible for inheritance of characters.	It is responsible for protein synthesis.

Biological Functions of Nucleic Acids

The important biological functions of nucleic acids are given below:

(i) **Heredity** DNA serves as the chemical basis of heredity and may be considered as reserve of genetic information.

DNA is mainly responsible for maintaining the identity of different species over millions of years.

(ii) **Replication** A DNA molecule is capable of self duplication (generally called replication) during cell division and identical DNA strands are transferred to daughter cells.

(iii) **Protein Synthesis** It is an important function of nucleic acids in the cell. Actually, the proteins are synthesised by various RNA molecules in the cell but the message for the synthesis of a particular protein is present in DNA. The synthesis of RNA by the DNA to conduct the message is called **transcription**, and synthesis of protein by these RNA is called **translation**.

The biological functions of nucleic acids can be concluded as **central dogma of the molecular biology** and can be represented as below.

Replication ⟲ DNA $\xrightarrow{\text{Transcription}}$ RNA $\xrightarrow{\text{Translation}}$ Protein

DNA Fingerprinting

Each and every individual has unique fingerprints which are present on the tips of the fingers and have been used for the identification purposes.

A sequence of bases on DNA is also unique for a person and information regarding this, is called DNA fingerprinting.

The sequence on DNA is same for each and every cell of a body and hence, these sequence cannot be altered.

Technique of DNA fingerprinting is used in the following ways:

(i) To determine the paternity of an individual.

(ii) To identify the racial groups to understand biological evolution better.

(iii) In forensic laboratories, for the identification of criminals.

(iv) To identify dead bodies in case of an accident by comparing the DNAs of parents and children.

Note Dr. Har Gobind Khurana shared the Nobel prize for medicine and physiology in 1968 with Marshall Nirenberg and Robert Holley for cracking the genetic code.

Topic Practice 3

Very Short Answer Type Questions

1 Mark

1. Fill in the Blanks

(i) Vitamin-B and C are .... soluble.

(ii) Vitamin-A, D, E and K are .... soluble.

(iii) Sun - light is the source of vitamin ....

(iv) Vitamin used to stop the bleeding is ....

(v) The disease caused by the dificiency of vitamin-B_{12} is known as ....

(vi) Nitrogen containing heterocyclic pyrimidine not present in structure of DNA is ....

(vii) Name of pentose sugar present in the structure of RNA is ....

2. Objective Type Questions

(i) A nucleotide consists of

(a) base and a sugar

(b) sugar and phosphate

(c) base, sugar and phosphate

(d) base and phosphate

(ii) Nucleic acids are polymers of

(a) nucleosides (b) globulins

(c) nucleons (d) nucleotides

(iii) If one strand of DNA has the sequence ATCGTATG, the sequence in the complementary strand would be

(a) TAGCTTAC (b) TCACATAC

(c) TAGCATAC (d) TACGATAC

(iv) Identify the vitamin whose deficiency in our blood decreases reproductive power?

(a) Vitamin-E (b) Vitamin-D

(c) Vitamin-A (d) Vitamin-C

(v) The pyrimidine bases present in DNA are

(a) cytosine and adenine

(b) cytosine and guanine

(c) cytosine and thymine

(d) cytosine and uracil

(vi) RNA and DNA are chiral molecules, their chirality is due to

(a) L-sugar component

(b) chiral bases

(c) D-sugar component

(d) chiral phosphate ester units

3. Match the vitamin in Column I with deficiency disease Column II and choose the correct option using the codes given below:

Column I		Column II	
A.	Vitamin-A	(i)	Scurvy
B.	Vitamin-B_{12}	(ii)	Pernicious anaemia
C.	Vitamin-C	(iii)	Sterility
D.	Vitamin-E	(iv)	Xerophthalmia

Codes

	A	B	C	D
(a)	(iii)	(iv)	(vi)	(ii)
(b)	(iii)	(vi)	(v)	(i)
(c)	(iv)	(ii)	(i)	(iii)
(d)	(iii)	(v)	(vi)	(ii)

4. Why cannot vitamin-C be stored in our body? **NCERT Intext**

Or

Why must vitamin-C be supplied regularly in the diet? **NCERT Exemplar**

5. Deficiency of which vitamin causes scurvy?
6. Deficiency of which vitamin causes rickets?

Or

Write the name of vitamin whose deficiency causes bone deformities in children.

7. Name the base that is present in RNA and not in DNA?
8. Why does vitamin-B must be supplied regularly in diet?
9. Why does nucleic acids are called polynucleotides?

Short Answer Type I Questions

(2 Marks)

10. Name two water soluble vitamins and the diseases caused by their deficiency in the diet of an individual. **ISC 2019**
11. Name the purine bases and pyrimidine bases present in RNA and DNA. **ISC 2018**
12. In nucleoside, a base is attached at 1′ position of sugar moiety. Nucleotide is formed by linking of phosphoric acid unit to the sugar unit of nucleoside. At which position of sugar unit is the phosphoric acid linked in a nucleoside to give a nucleotide? **NCERT Exemplar**
13. Name the bases present in RNA which one of these is not present in DNA?
14. What products would be formed when a nucleotide from DNA containing thymine is hydrolysed? **NCERT Intext**
15. What are the different types of RNA molecules which perform different functions?

Or

What are the different types of RNA found in the cell? **NCERT**

16. Mention the biological importance of insulin.
17. Why are vitamins-A and C essential to us? Give their important sources. **NCERT**
18. The two strands of DNA are not identical but are complementary. Explain. **NCERT**
19. Write the important structural and functional differences between DNA and RNA. **NCERT**

Short Answer Type II Questions

(3 Marks)

20. How are vitamins classified? Name the vitamin responsible for the coagulation of blood. **NCERT**
21. What are nucleic acids? Mention their two important functions. **NCERT**
22. What is the difference between a nucleoside and a nucleotide? **NCERT**
23. Give an example each of reducing sugar and non-reducing sugar.
    (i) Give an example each of reducing sugar and non-reducing sugar.
    (ii) What is denaturation of proteins ?
    (iii) Give an example each of water soluble vitamin and fat soluble vitamin. **ISC 2023**
24. (i) Aradhana visits a physician as she is suffering from rickets and joint pain. Which fat-soluble vitamin should the physician prescribe to her?
    (ii) Somesh put few drops of vinegar in milk. What change do you think he observed in the milk after some time? What is this phenomenon known as?
    (iii) Name the product of hydrolysis of sucrose. Is it a reducing sugar or a non-reducing sugar? **ISC 2024**

Hints & Solutions

1. (i) water (ii) fat
   (iii) D (iv) vitamin-K
   (v) pernicious anaemia (vi) uracil
   (vii) β - D - ribose sugar

2. (i) (c) A nucleotide consists of three chemical components : heterocyclic nitrogenous base (amine), A five carbon sugar, A phosphate group

(ii) (d) Nucleic acids are polymers of nucleotides. They play an important role in all living cells. There are two types of nucleic acids DNA and RNA.

(iii) (c) Because of size and geometries of the bases, the only possible pairing in DNA are between G (guanine) and C (cytosine through three H-bonds and between A (adenine) and T (thymine) through two H-bonds.

Hence, complementary stand of DNA will be

```
A T C G T A T G
| | | | | | | |
T A G C A T A C
```

(iv) (a) Deficiency of vitamin E in human being decreases reproductive power.

(v) (c) The pyrimidine bases present in DNA are cytosine and thymine while adenine and guanine are purine bases.

(vi) (c) RNA and DNA molecules have ribose and deoxyribose sugar respectively. Both are chiral, their chirality is due to D-ribose or deoxyribose sugar component.

3. (c)

Vitamin		Deficiency Disease	
A.	Vitamin A	1.	Xerophthalmia
B.	Vitamin B_{12}	2.	Pernicious anaemia
C.	Vitamin C	3.	Scurvy
D.	Vitamin E	4.	Sterility

4. Vitamin-C cannot be stored in our body because vitamin- C is soluble in water, it excreted readily in urine and hence, cannot be stored in the body. Thus, vitamin-C must be supplied regularly through diet. (1)

5. Deficiency of vitamin-C causes scurvy. (1)

6. Vitamin-D (1)

7. Uracil (1)

8. Because it is a water soluble vitamin and is excreted readily in urine and hence can't be stored in the body. (1)

9. They are made up of long chain polymers of nucleotides. (1)

10. Vitamin-B and vitamin-C are water soluble and by the deficiency of vitamin-B and C in the diet beri-beri and scurvy diseases occurs, resepectively.

11. Purine bases present in DNA and RNA are adenine (A) and guanine (G). Pyrimidine bases present in DNA and RNA are uracil (U), thymine (T) and cytosine (C). Uracil (U) is present only in RNA and thymine is present only in DNA. (2)

12. Phosphoric acid unit is linked at 5′ position of sugar moiety of a nucleoside to form nucleotide. (2)

13. Bases present in RNA are adenine (A), Guanine (G), uracil and cytosine (C). Uracil is not present in DNA. (2)

14. Complete hydrolysis of DNA containing thymine yields a pentose sugar (β-D-2-deoxyribose), phosphoric acid and nitrogeneous base thymine. (2)

15. Three different types of RNA molecules are as follows:
(i) Messenger RNA (*m*-RNA) (ii) Transfer RNA (*t*-RNA)
(iii) Ribosomal RNA (*r*-RNA) (2)

16. Controls the metabolism of glucose in the body and maintains glucose level in the blood.

17. Refer to table on page 427. (Vitamins) (2)

18. Refer to text on page 429. (Secondary structure) (2)

19. **Structural differences** The main structural differences between DNA and RNA are as follows :

(i) The sugar moiety present in DNA is β-D-2-deoxyribose, whereas in RNA molecule, it is β-D-ribose. (1/2)

(ii) DNA has a double stranded helical structure, while RNA has a single stranded helical structure. (1/2)

(iii) DNA contains cytosine and thymine as pyrimidine bases, whereas RNA has cytosine and uracil as pyrimidine bases. (1/2)

Functional difference DNA controls the transmission of hereditary effects while RNA controls the synthesis of proteins. (1/2)

20. **Classification of vitamins** Refer to text on page 427. (Vitamins). Vitamin-K is responsible for coagulation of blood. (3)

21. Refer to text on pages 428 and 430 (Nucleic acid and biological functions of nucleic acids). (3)

22. Refer to text on page 428 (Chemical composition nucleic acid). (3)

23. (i) Glucose, fructose and ribose are reducing sugars. Sucrose and raffinose are non-reducing sugars.

(ii) **Denaturation of proteins** A change in physical and biological properties of a protein without affecting its chemical composition is called denaturation of protein. It may be affected by the action of heat, alcohol, acid, radiation etc.

Denaturation changes only the secondary and tertiary structures of protein, the primary structure remains unchanged. This process is irreversible in most cases. However, in some cases, it may be reversed and is termed as renaturation. Coagulation of egg and curdling of milk are common examples of denaturation of proteins.

(iii) **Water soluble vitamins** Vitamins C and B group vitamins.

Fat soluble vitamins These are vitamins A, D, E and K.

24. (i) Vitamin D (fat soluble vitamin) should be prescribed to Aradhana by her physician.

(ii) When Somesh put few drops of vinegar in milk, small white chunks or curds become visible in the mixture. This phenomenon is known as denaturation of protein.

(iii) On hydrolysis with acids or enzyme, sucrose gives equimolar mixture of D-(+)-glucose and D-(−)-fructose. Sucrose is a non reducing sugar.

SUMMARY

- Carbohydrates are the polyhydroxy aldehyde or ketones. They are called hydrates of carbon and have general formula of $C_x(H_2O)_y$.
- **Monosaccharides** are the simplest carbohydrates whcih can't be further hydrolysed, e.g. glucose, fructose etc.
- **Oligosaccharides** are made up of 2-10 monomer monosaccharide units, e.g. sucrose, lactose etc.
- **Polysaccharides** are made up of more than 10 monomer units, e.g. glycogen, starch, cellulose etc.
- Carbohydrates having free functional group aldehyde or ketone reduce Fehling's solution and Tollen's reagent and thus are called reducing sugars.
- Glucose ($C_6H_{12}O_6$) is an aldohexose, as it has aldehydic group and six C-atoms, dextrorotatory in nature and is also called dextrose.
- It can be prepared by hydrolysis of cane sugar (sucrose) and starch.
- Cyclic structure of glucose resembles to pyran and hence it is also called glucopyranose.
- Glucose oxidises with Br_2 water to give gluconic acid and with HNO_3 to give glucaric acid.
- It reduces both Fehling's solution and Tollen's reagent also forms osazone upon reaction with phenyl hydrazine.
- Fructose ($C_6H_{12}O_6$) is a ketohexose and differs from glucose by having keto group instead of aldehyde group (as in glucose).
- Natural fructose (laevulose) is laevorotatory and can be prepared by hydrolysis of insulin or sucrose. Its cyclic structure resembles with furan, hence also called **fructofuranose**.
- Sucrose is disaccharide of glucose and fructose monomer.
- The two monomer units in a disaccharide (or in any polysaccharide) is joined by a linkage called **glycosidic linkage**.
- Solution of sucrose is dextrorotatory but that of its hydrolysed product (glucose + fructose) is laevorotatory. This observation is called **inversion of cane sugar**.
- **Proteins** are the polymers by α-amino acids.
- Amino acids are essentialy formed by two functional groups called amino ($—NH_2$) group and carboxyl ($—COOH$) group.
- Amino acid forms Zwitter ion, in which both positive and negative charges are present but molecules acts as a neutral one.
- Amino acid that cannot be synthesised in body and is required to be taken in our diet is called essential amino acid, e.g. val, leu, lys etc.
- The linkage that connects two amino acids is called peptide (or amide) bond.
- Amino acid through peptide linkage form polypeptide (upto 100 amino acids) which further link to form protein.
- **Primary structure** of protein is simply the formation of peptide bond between amino acids to form peptide.
- **Secondary** structure form three dimensional configuration of peptide chains involving H— bonds.
- **Tertiary structure** defines overall shape of a protein molecules. It involves H-bond, ionic bond, disulphide bond and hydrophobic bond.
- **Quaternary structure** involve assembling of two of more polypeptide chains. It involves H-bond, ionic bond and hydrophobic bond.
- **Fibrous proteins** are elongated and insoluble in water, e.g. keratin, collagen etc.
- **Globular proteins** are spherical and soluble in water, e.g. myoglobin, albumin etc.
- **Enzymes** are made up of proteins and act as a biocatalysts.
- The optimum temperature for working of enzymes is 37°(310 K) and optimum pH is 7.4.
- Vitamins are small organic molecules that are required for the proper functioning of the cell.
- Water soluble vitamins include vitamin B and vitamin C, vitamin A, D, E and K are fat soluble.
- **Nucleic acids** include DNA (deoxyribonucleic acid) and RNA (ribonucleic acid). These are composed of nitrogeneous base, sugar and phosphate group.
- Sugar and nitrogeneous base are combinely called **nucleoside**, where nucleoside and phosphate group is combinely called **nucleotide**. Therefore, nucleic acids are also called polynucleotides.
- Nitrogeneous bases are of two types : **Purine** – adenine (A) and guanine (G) **Pyrimidine**-cytosine (C), thymine (T) and uracil (U)
- The primary structure of nucleic acids is formed by nucleotides joined by the phosphodiester linkage.
- The secondary structure of nucleic acid is the coiled configuration of polynucleotidic chain, with the help of H-bonds.
- The two strands of DNA are complementary where adenine of one strand is connected to thymine (T) of the other one. While cytosine (C) of one strand is connected to guanine (G) of the other one.
- DNA and RNA replicate themselves to carry genetic information to next generation. DNA and RNA are also involved in protein synthesis.

Chapter Practice

Very Short Answer Type Questions

(1 Mark)

1 **Fill in the Blanks**

(i) ⟶ CO—NH ⟶ bond is known as .... bond

(ii) When glucose is treated with bromine-water, the red colour of bromine water becomes ....

(iii) In aqueous solution, amino acids exist as dipolar ion, which are called ...... ions

(iv) Two basic components of nucleosides are .... and ....

2 **Objective Type Questions**

(i) Which of the following statement about ribose is incorrect?

(a) It is a polyhydroxy compound
(b) It is an aldehyde sugar
(c) It has six carbon atoms
(d) It exhibits optical activity

(ii) On heating with conc. HNO_3 porteins give yellow colour. The test is called

(a) oxidising test (b) xanthoprteic test
(c) Hoppe's test (d) acid base test

(iii) The chemical name of vitamin B_1 is

(a) ascorbic acid (b) riboflavin
(c) pyridoxine (d) thiamine

(iv) Adenosine is an example of

(a) nucleotide (b) nucleoside
(c) purine base (d) pyrimidine base

3 Match Column I with column II and choose the correct option using the codes given below:

Column I		Column II	
A.	Cytosine	(i)	Amino acid
B.	Adenine	(ii)	Purine
C.	Pepsin	(iii)	Pyrimidine
D.	Valine	(iv)	Enzyme

Codes

	A	B	C	D
(a)	(i)	(iv)	(ii)	(iii)
(b)	(ii)	(iii)	(i)	(iv)
(c)	(iii)	(ii)	(iv)	(i)
(d)	(iii)	(i)	(iv)	(ii)

4 What is inversion of sugar?

5 Name two carbohydrates that are branched polymers of glucose.

6 In representation of D-(+)-glucose, what does 'D' represents?

7 What is the structural feature characterising reducing sugars?

8 Which type of carbohydrate is not digested by humans?

9 How do amino acids form proteins?

10 Name the protein and its type which is present in muscles.

11 What type of proteins acts as enzymes?

12 Which of the following biomolecule is soluble in water? collagen, myosin and albumin

13 What type of interactions stabilises β-pleated keratin structure?

14 What type of interactions stabilises the fibrous proteins?

15 Which enzyme converts glucose into ethylalcohol?

16 Deficiency of which vitamin causes osteomalacia?

Assertion-Reason

■ **Directions** (Q. Nos. 17-21) In the following questions. An Assertion (A) is followed by a corresponding Reason (R). Use the following keys to choose the appropriate answer.

(a) Both (A) and (R) are correct and (R) is the correct explanation of (A).
(b) Both (A) and (R) are correct but (R) is not the correct explanation of (A).
(c) (A) is correct but (R) is incorrect.
(d) (A) is incorrect but (R) is correct.

17. **Assertion** (A) D (+) – Glucose is dextrorotatory in nature.

Reason (R) 'D' represents its dextrorotatory nature.

18. **Assertion** (A) All naturally occurring α-amino acids except glycine are optically active.

Reason (R) Most naturally occurring amino acids have L-configuration.

19. **Assertion** (A) In the presence of enzyme, substrate molecule can be attacked by the reagent effectively.

Reason (R) Active sites of enzymes hold the substrate molecule in a suitable position.

20. **Assertion** (A) The two strands are complementary to each other.

Reason (R) The hydrogen bonds are formed between specific pairs of bases.

21. **Assertion** (A) In both DNA and RNA, heterocyclic base and phosphodiester linkages are at C-1′ and C-5′ respectively of the sugar molecule.

Reason (R) Nucleotides and nucleosides mainly differ from each other in presence of phosphate units.

Case Study

22. Carbohydrates are polyhydroxy aldehydes or ketones and are also called saccharides. Glucose is an example of monosaccharides. Glucose ($C_6H_{12}O_6$) is an aldohexose and its open chain structure was assigned on the basis of many reactions as evidences like presence of carbonyl group, presence of straight chain, presence of five –OH groups etc.

Glucose is correctly named as D-(+)-glucose. Glucose is found to exist in two different crystalline forms which are named as α and β. Despite having the aldehyde group, glucose does not give 2, 4-DNP test.

(i) What is the correct structure of D-(+)-glucose?

(ii) Glucose on oxidation with HNO_3 gives a dicarboxylic acid called saccharic acid. What does this result indicate?

(iii) The pentaacetate of glucose does not react with $H_2N—OH$. What does this result indicate?

23. Carbohydrates are optically active polyhydroxy aldehydes and ketones. They are also called saccharides. All those carbohydrates which reduce Fehling solution and Tollen's reagent are referred to as reducing sugars. Glucose, the most important sources of energy for mammals, is obtained by the hydrolysis of starch. Vitamins are accessory food factors required in the diet. Proteins are the polymers of α-amino acids and perform various structural and dynamic functions in the organisms. Deficiency of vitamins leads to many diseases.

Answer the following

(i) The penta-acetate of glucose does not react with hydroxylamine. What does it indicate?

(ii) Why cannot vitamin C be stored in our body?

(iii) Define the following as related to proteins:

(a) Peptide linkage

(b) Denaturation

Short Answer Type I Questions

2 Marks

24 Name and define the linkage connecting monosaccharide units in a polysaccharide.

25 Amylopectin and glycogen both have branched structures. How do they differ from one another?

26 Why do proteins form an indispensable part of our food?

27 Structures of valine and alanine are given below. Show the peptide linkage in valylalanine.

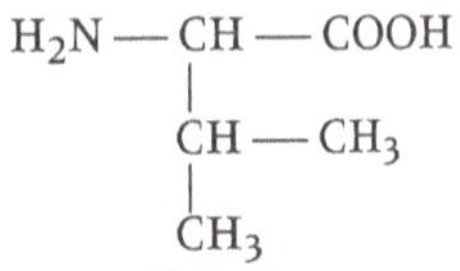
(Valine)

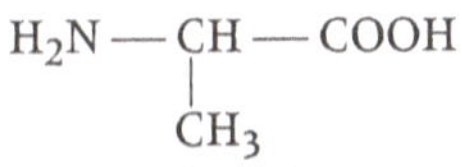
(Alanine)

28 Sulphanilic acid exists as a Zwitter ion, while *p*-aminobenzoic acid does not. Explain.

29 (i) Name an amino acid which is optically in active.

(ii) Draw the Zwitter ion of an essential amino acid which contains phenyl ring.

30 Mention the type of linkages responsible for the formation of the following:

(i) Primary structure of proteins

(ii) α-helix formation

(iii) β-pleated sheet structure

31 Why does a native protein loses its biological activity on heating?

32 What role do enzymes have in the functioning of our bodies?

33 Name the chemical components which constitute nucleotides. Write any two functions of nucleotides in a cell.

Short Answer Type II Questions

(3 Marks)

34 (i) What is the biological effect of proteins on denaturation?

(ii) Amylase present in the saliva becomes inactive in the stomach. Give reason.

35 Define the following as related to proteins.

(i) Peptide linkage

(ii) Primary structure

(iii) Denaturation

36 Write the four characteristic features of enzymes. Name a disease which is caused by the deficiency of a particular enzyme.

37 (i) Which vitamin is concerned with antisterility?

(ii) Write the chemical name of B_1 and name the disease caused by its deficiency.

38 (i) Explain the role of nucleic acids in replication.

(ii) Name the types of bases in nucleotides of RNA.

Long Answer Type Questions

(5 Marks)

39 A compound A $(C_6H_{12}O_6)$ is oxidised by bromine water into monbasic acid. It also reduces Tollen's reagent and reacts with HCN to give a compound B which on hydrolysis gives a compound C.

On treating C with HI/red P, n-heptanoic acid is obtained. Compound A on treatment with excess phenyl hydrazine gave D-glucoszone. Name the compound A and draw its cyclic from.

Answers

1 (i) peptide bond

(ii) colourless

(iii) Zwitter

(iv) Pentose sugar and nitrogeneous base.

2 (a) Ribose being a pentose sugar, has only five carbon atoms.

(b) Xanthoproteic test involves heating of a protein with conc HNO_3 then yellow colour is obtained.

(d) Vitamin-B_1 is also known as thiamine.

(b) Adenosine is a nucleoside while adenosine triphosphate is a nucleotide.

3 (c)

(A) → (iii) (B) → (ii)

(C) → (iv) (D) → (i)

4 Sucrose on hydrolysis brings about a change in the sign of rotation, i.e. from dextro (+) to laevo (−) and the product is known as invert sugar and the process is called as inversion of sugar. (1)

5 Glycogen and amylopectin. (1)

6 '*D*' represents the confingfuration. (1)

7 The structural feature characterising reducing sugar is the presence of a free aldehyde group (—CHO), e.g. glucose, galactose etc. (1)

8 Cellulose. (1)

9 More than 100 amino acid residues are joined together by peptide linkage to form a linear chain polymer (protein). (1)

10 Fibrous protein (myosin). (1)

11 Globular proteins (1)

12 Albumin (1)

13 Intermolecular hydrogen bonding stabilises β-pleated keratin structure. (1)

14 They are held together by hydrogen and disulphide bonds. (1)

15 Zymase enzyme. (1)

16 Deficiency of vitamin-D causes Osteomalacia. (1)

17. (*c*) (A) is correct but (R) is incorrect statement. D-(+)-glucose is dextrorotatory because it rotates the plane polarised light to right.

Here, D represents relative configuration of glucose with respect to glyceraldehyde.

18. (*b*) (A) and (R) both are correct and (R) is not the correct explanation of (A). All naturally occurring α-amino acids except glycine are optically active. Glycine is optically inactive because glycine does not have all four different substituents as shown below.

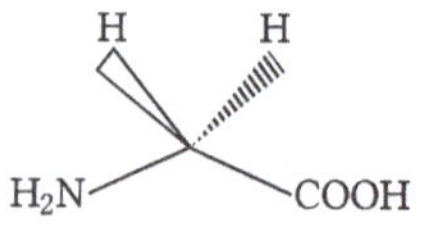

Glycine

19. (*a*) In the presence of an enzyme, substrate molecule can be attacked by the reagent effectively because active sites of enzymes hold the substrate molecule in a suitable position. Thus, both (A) and (R) are correct and (R) is the correct explanation of (A).

20. (*a*) The two strands of DNA are complementary to each other because the hydrogen bonds are formed between specific pairs of bases. Adenine of one strand is hydrogen bonded to thymine of the other through two

hydrogen bonds, whereas cytosine of one strand is hydrogen bonded with guanine of the other through 3 hydrogen bonds.

$A{=}T$ and $C{\equiv}G$

↓ 2 hydrogen bonds ↓ 3 hydrogen bonds

Hence, both (A) and (R) are correct and (R) is the correct explanation of (A).

21. (*b*)

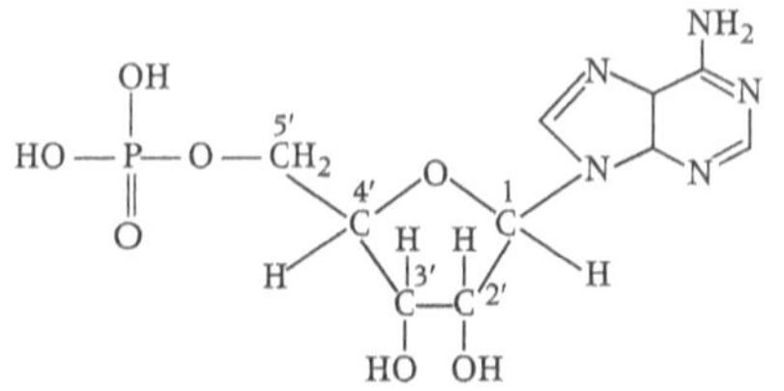

Nucleosides contain only sugar and a base, whereas nucleotides contain sugar, base and a phosphate group as well.

22. (i)

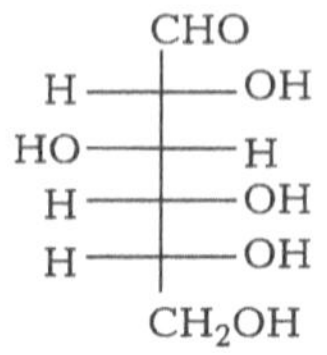

D-(+)-glucose

(ii) Glucose on oxidation with HNO_3 gives saccharic acid. This indicates the presence of a one primary alcoholic (—OH) group in glucose.

(iii) The pentaacetate of glucose does not react with hydroxylamine which shows the absence of **free aldehydic (—CHO) group**.

23. (i) The penta-acetate of glucose does not react with hydroxylamine. It indicates that the carbonyl group of glucose is not free as it is present in cyclic form.

(ii) Vitamin C is water soluble, that's why it cannot stored in our body.

(iii) (a) **Peptide linkage** Proteins are connected to each other by —CO—NH— bond which is called the peptide linkage.

(b) **Denaturation** When a native protein is subjected to physical change or chemical change, the hydrogen bonds are disturbed. As a result, globules unfold and helix gets uncoiled and protein loses its biological activity. This is known as denaturation of proteins.

24 Refer to text on pages 414 and 415 (Topic-1 Oligosaccharides) (2)

25 Glycogen consist of 10-15 glucose units while amylopectin consist of 20-25 glucose unit. (2)

26 **Hint** Providing strength to the cells and tissues.

27

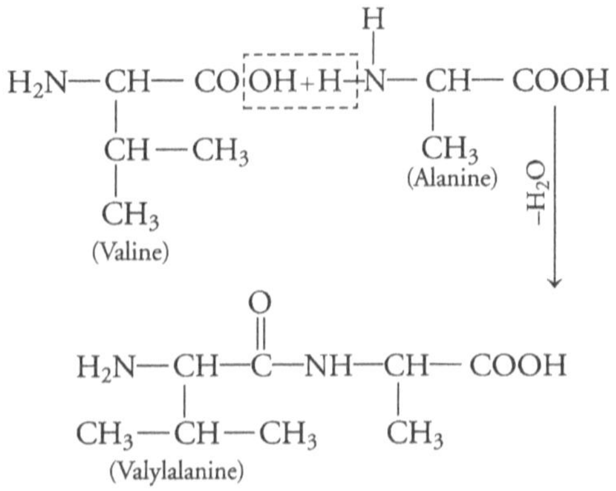

(2)

28 In *p*-aminobenzoic acid, electron withdrawing benzene ring is present due to which the lone pair of electrons present on NH_2 group is donated towards the ring and hence the acidic and basic character of —COOH and —NH_2 groups respectively decreases. (2)

29 (i) Glycine (1)

(ii) Refer to text on page 421 (Topic-2, Properties of amino acids). (1)

30 (i) Refer to text on pages 422 and 423 (Topic-2, Structure and shape of protein).

(ii) Refer to text on page 422 (Topic-2, α-helix structure)

(iii) Refer to text on page 422 (Topic-2, β-pleated sheet structure) (2)

31 Refer to text on page 423 (Topic-2, Denaturation of protein). (2)

32 **Hint** Aids indigestion and metabolism.

33 Refer to text on pages 428 and 429 (Topic-3, Chemical composition and structure nucleic acid). **(2)**

34 (i) Refer to text on page 423 (Topic-2, Denaturation of protein). (1½)

(ii) **Hint** Stomach has pH range 1-3. (1½)

35 (i) Refer to text on page 421 (Topic-2, Peptide linkage and their classification). (1)

(ii) Refer to text on pages 422 and 423 (Topic-2, Structure and shape of protein). (1)

(iii) Refer to text on page 423 (Topic-2, Denaturation of protein). (1)

36 (i) Refer to text on page 423 (Topic-2, Enzymes). (2)

(ii) Disease phenyl ketone urea (PKU) is caused by the deficiency of phenylalanine hydroxylose. (1)

37 (i) Vitamin-E (1)

(ii) Refer to table on page 427 (Topic-2, Vitamins). (2)

38 (i) Refer to text on page 430 (Topic-3, Biological functions of nucleic acids). (1½)

(ii) Refer to text on pages 428 (Topic-3, Chemical composition of nucleic acid, nitrogenous base). (1½)

39 Refer to text on pages 411 and 412 (Topic-1, Structure of glucose). (5)

Allinone®

COMPLETE STUDY | COMPLETE PRACTICE | COMPLETE ASSESSMENT

ISC Examination Question Paper 2025

Latest ISC Specimen Question Paper

3 Sample Question Paper

ISC EXAMINATION QUESTION PAPER 2025

CHEMISTRY (Fully Solved)

Time : 3 hours | Max. Marks : 70

GENERAL INSTRUCTIONS

- This paper is divided into four sections A, B , C and D. Answer all questions.
- **Section A** has **fourteen subparts.** Each question carries 1 mark.
- While attempting **Multiple Choice Questions** in Section A, you are required to **write only ONE option as the answer**.
- **Section B** has **ten questions.** Each question carries 2 marks.
- **Section C** has **seven questions.** Each question carries 3 marks.
- **Section D** has **three questions.** Each question carries 5 marks.
- Internal choices have been provided in **one question each in Section B, Section C & Section D.**
- All working, including rough work, should be done on the same sheet as, and adjacent to the rest of the answer.
- The intended marks for questions are given in brackets [].
- Balanced equations must be given wherever possible and diagrams where they are helpful.
- When solving numerical problems, all essential working must be shown.
- In working out problems, use the following data :
  Gas constant R = 1.987 cal deg^{-1} mol^{-1} = 8.314 J K^{-1} mol^{-1} = 0.0821 dm^3 atm K^{-1} mol^{-1} 1 L atm = 1 dm^3 atm = 101.3 J.
  1 Faraday = 96500 coulombs. **Avogadro's number** = 6.023 × 10^{23}.

FULLY SOLVED

Section-A [14 Marks]

1. (A) Fill in the blanks by choosing the appropriate word(s) from those given in the brackets: [4 × 1]

[+2, ethane, tetrahedral, square planar, zero, dry cell, nickel-cadmium cell, propane Wolff-Kishner, Stephen, completely filled, incompletely filled, paramagnetic, diamagnetic]

(i) .... is an example of a primary cell but ...... is an example of a secondary cell.

(ii) The complex compound [$Ni(CO_4)$] is .... in shape and nickel is in .... oxidation state in this complex compound.

(iii) When acetaldehyde is treated with hydrazine and KOH in a high boiling solvent glycol, ... is formed and the reaction is known as .... reduction.

(iv) The transition metal ions having .... *d*-orbitals are colourless and ....in nature.

(B) Select and write the correct alternative from the choices given below. [7×1]

(i) Which one of the following can produce the foul smelling compound methyl isocyanide in presence of alcoholic KOH?

(a) Chloroform and aniline

(b) Chloroform and methanol

(c) Chloroform and dimethyl amine

(d) Chloroform and methyl amine

(ii) The osmotic pressure of a solution:

(P) increases with an increase in number of moles of solute.

(Q) decreases with an increase in number of moles of solute.

(R) increases at a higher temperature.

(S) is dependent on the nature of solute.

Which one of the following is correct?

(a) Only (P) and (Q) are correct.

(b) Only (P) and (R) are correct.

(c) Only (P) and (S) are correct.

(d) Only (Q) and (S) are correct.

(iii) Which one of the following alcohols is the strongest acid?

(a) Phenol

(b) Methanol

(c) Ethanol

(d) *t*-butyl alcohol

(iv) Which one of the following does not form a silver mirror on heating with Tollen's reagent?

(a) Glucose (b) Fructose

(c) Sucrose (d) Lactose

(v) The coordination number and the oxidation state of the central metal '*D*' in the complex $[D(en)_2(H_2O)_2]Cl_3$ are respectively.

(a) 6 and 2 (b) 4 and 2

(c) 3 and 6 (d) 6 and 3

(vi) Given below are two statements marked Assertion and Reason. Read the two statements carefully and select the correct option.

Assertion (A) The process of halogenation of benzene takes place in the presence of anhydrous $FeCl_3$.

Reason (R) Anhydrous $FeCl_3$ prepares nucleophile to attack the benzene ring.

(a) Both Assertion and Reason are true and Reason is the correct explanation for Assertion.

(b) Both Assertion and Reason are true but Reason is not the correct explanation for Assertion.

(c) Assertion is true and Reason is false.

(d) Both Assertion and Reason are false.

(vii) Given below are two statements marked Assertion and Reason. Read the two statements carefully and select the correct option.

Assertion (A) The Zr-Hf pair of elements has the same value of atomic radii though Zr and Hf are placed in different periods in the periodic table.

Reason (R) The lanthanoid contraction prevents the expected increase in atomic radii of Hf.

(a) Both Assertion and Reason are true and Reason is the correct explanation for Assertion.

(b) Both Assertion and Reason are true, but Reason is not the correct explanation for Assertion.

(c) Assertion is true and Reason is false.

(d) Both Assertion and Reason are false.

(C) Read the passage carefully and answer the questions that follow. [3 × 1]

The rate of a reaction depends on the concentration of reactants. The rate law for a hypothetical reaction $aA + bB \longrightarrow cC + dD$ is rate $= k[A]^x[B]^y$ where x and y are calculated experimentally and known as order of reaction. In most cases, the mechanism of a reaction is not straight forward but broken down in simple elementary steps. These steps represent the progress of overall reaction at the molecular level.

(i) What will be the order of reaction if the unit of k is $mol^{-2}\ L^2\ s^{-1}$?

(ii) State any one difference between order of reaction and molecularity of reaction.

(iii) For the reaction $2A \longrightarrow B + C$, the rate law is rate $= k[A]^{3/2}$.

What is the order and molecularity of the reaction?

Section-B [20 Marks]

2. Calculate the number of coulombs required to electroplate 4.75 g of aluminium when electrode reaction is $Al^{3+} + 3e^- \rightarrow Al$.
(Given: Atomic weight of Al = 27 g mol^{-1}, 1 Faraday = 96,500 C)

FULLY SOLVED

3. An organic compound [A] has molecular formula $C_7H_6O_2$. When compound [A] is treated with $SOCl_2$, it yields compound [B]. On heating with NH_3, compound [B] forms compound [C]. Compound [C] forms compound [D] on reaction with Br_2/KOH. Compound [D] responds to carbylamine test. Identify compounds [A], [B], [C] and [D].

4. In the reaction $2NO + O_2 \longrightarrow 2NO_2$, the rate law is rate $= k[NO][O_2]^2$.

(i) How will the rate of reaction change if [NO] concentration is doubled and [O_2] concentration is halved at the same time?

(ii) Write the order of reaction if [NO] concentration is in large excess.

5. When an organic compound [A] having molecular formula C_4H_9Br is treated with aqueous KOH, the rate of reaction depends on concentration of compound [A] only. But when compound [B], with the same molecular formula, reacts with aqueous KOH, the rate of reaction depends on the concentration of compound [B] as well as of KOH. Compound (B) is a structural isomer of compound [A].
Identify compounds [A] and [B].

6. Write a balanced chemical equation for each of the following:

(i) Ethyl cyanide is reduced with $LiAlH_4$.

(ii) Aniline is treated with bromine water.

7. While conducting an experiment on coordination compounds, Shirin observed a white precipitate when $AgNO_3$, solution was added to the aqueous solution of the complex $[Co(NH_3)_3(en)SO_4]Cl$.
How can the ionisation isomer of this complex be detected by a chemical test? Write the structure and the IUPAC name of the ionisation isomer.

8. (i) Arrange the following in the increasing order of their acidic strength:

CH_3CH_2OH, CF_3CH_2OH, CCl_3CH_2OH

(ii) Arrange the following in the increasing order of their boiling points:

CH_3CH_2OH, $\underset{\displaystyle CH_2OH}{\underset{|}{C}H_2OH}$, CH_3CH_2Cl

9. (i) Identify the compounds [A], [B], [C] and [D] in the following reaction:

$$CH_3COOH + PCl_5 \longrightarrow [A] \xrightarrow[\text{Pd/BaSO}_4 \text{ Boiling xylene}]{H_2} [B] \xrightarrow[{[O]}]{K_2Cr_2O_7 + H_2SO_4} [C] \xrightarrow{Ca(OH)_2,\ \text{heat}} [D]$$

Or

(ii) Write chemical equations to convert the following:

(a) Benzaldehyde to benzene

(b) Benzoic acid to benzaldehyde

10. Calculate the E°_{cell} of the following if the cell potential (E_{cell}) is 0.59 V.
(Given: $Ni / Ni^{2+}(0.1\ M) \,||\, Cu^{2+}(0.01\ M / Cu)$)

11. Write the chemical test to distinguish between each of the following pairs of compounds.

(i) Ethanol and propan-1-al

(ii) Phenol and benzoic acid

Section-C [21 Marks]

12. Identify the compounds [A], [B] and [C] in each of the following reactions:

(i) $C_2H_5Br \xrightarrow{KCN} [A] \xrightarrow[{[4H]}]{LiAlH_4} [B] \xrightarrow[0°\text{–}5°C]{HNO_2} [C]$

(ii) $C_2H_5CONH_2 \xrightarrow{Br_2/KOH} [A] \xrightarrow{CHCl_3 + KOH} [B] \xrightarrow{Na/C_2H_5OH} [C]$

13. The scientist van't Hoff introduced a factor (i) to account for the extent of association or dissociation of solutes. It is mathematically expressed as:

$$i = \frac{\text{normal molecular mass}}{\text{experimental molecular mass}}$$

In case of association, $i < 1$ and in case of dissociation $i > 1$.

(i) In the calculation of molecular mass of $K_4[Fe(CN)_6]$ by using a colligative property, what will be the value of van't Hoff factor if the solute is 25% dissociated?

(ii) Find the value of van't Hoff factor for a dilute aqueous solution of benzoic acid in water when it is completely associated to form a dimer.

14. Write chemical equations to illustrate the following name reactions.

(i) Finkelstein reaction

(ii) Williamson's synthesis

(iii) Reimer-Tiemann reaction

15. According to Crystal-Field Theory, the electronic configuration of complex compound [A] is $t_{2g}^4 e_g^2$ and that of complex compound [B] is $t_{2g}^6 e_g^0$.

(i) Which of the two complex compounds, [A] or [B], is a low spin complex?

(ii) Write the number of unpaired electrons in complex compounds [A] and [B].

(iii) Does complex [A] have strong field ligands or weak field ligands? Give a reason.

16. (i) Answer the following questions.

(a) By referring to electrochemical series, how can anode and cathode half cells be identified in a galvanic cell?

(b) What is the role of salt bridge in a galvanic cell?

(c) Write an advantage and a disadvantage of a fuel cell.

Or

(ii) Answer the following questions.

(a) Specific conductance of a solution decreases upon dilution. Why?

(b) The emf of a cell should be positive for a spontaneous reaction. Give a reason.

(c) Name the type of cell in which reaction occurs only in one direction and cannot be reversed by an external energy source. Write any one disadvantage of this type of cell.

17. (i) The structure of amino acid exists in the following two forms:

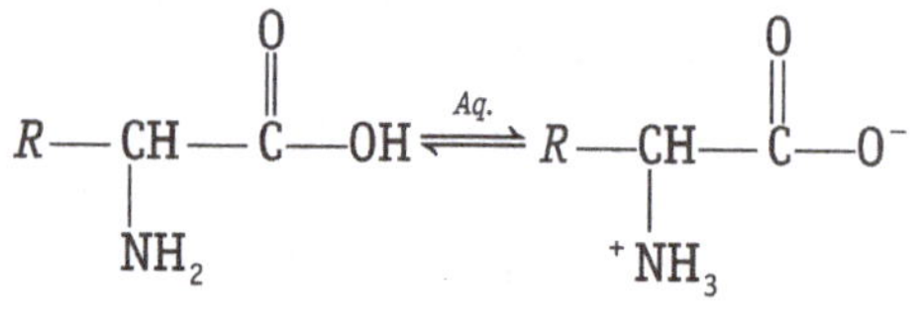

The above structure is an example of .... If the side chain R is replaced by hydrogen, the amino acid is known as ....

(ii) Janice notices that her gums bleed while brushing and eating food. Name the water soluble vitamin which she should consume to prevent bleeding of gums.

(iii) Which linkage holds two units of monosaccharides in a disaccharide?

18. The data given below is for the reaction between [NO] and [Cl_2] to form NOCl at 25°C.

S.No.	Conc. of [NO] mol L^{-1}	Conc. of [Cl_2] mol L^{-1}	Rate : mol L^{-1} sec^{-1}
1.	2.0	2.0	2.0×10^{-3}
2.	2.0	6.0	6.0×10^{-3}
3.	6.0	2.0	1.8×10^{-2}

Answer the following questions.

(i) What is the order of reaction with regard to NO and Cl_2?

(ii) Calculate the overall order of the reaction.

(iii) Find the value of rate constant (k).

Section-D [15 Marks]

19. Phenol is an aromatic alcohol that is used to prepare many important compounds such as picric acid. Phenol is widely used in household and industrial settings as a cleaner and disinfectant. It is also used as a primary chemical to make plastics. Phenol is less soluble in water as compared to aliphatic alcohol. Some aliphatic alcohols are toxic and can be addictive.

(i) How is the acid mentioned above prepared from phenol? Write the chemical reaction involved in this preparation.

(ii) 'Phenol is less soluble in water as compared to aliphatic alcohol'. Explain.

(iii) Write the chemical equation for the preparation of phenol from chlorobenzene.

(iv) An organic compound [A] having molecular formula $C_4H_{10}O$ gives positive Lucas test within five minutes at room temperature. Compound [A] upon oxidation with $K_2Cr_2O_7/H_2SO_4$ forms compound [B] which does not respond to Tollen's test.

Identify compounds [A] and [B].

(v) In the above reaction, compound [B] gets reduced with Zn/Hg and HCl and forms compound [C]. Identify compound [C] and write the balanced reaction for the conversion of compound [B] to compound (C).

20. (i) Give a reason for each of the following:

(a) Ti^{3+} salts are coloured whereas Ti^{4+} salts are colourless.

[Given: Atomic number of Ti = 22]

(b) Transition elements form alloys.

(c) The pink coloured $KMnO_4$ solution turns colourless when reacted with Mohr's salt (Fe^{2+}) in acidic medium.

(ii) Complete and balance the following reactions:

(a) $KMnO_4 + H_2SO_4 + H_2C_2O_4 \longrightarrow$ ...... + ... + ... + ...

(b) $K_2Cr_2O_7 + H_2SO_4 + H_2S \longrightarrow$ ...... + ... + ... + ...

21. (i) Osmotic pressure is the external pressure which should be applied to stop the flow of solvent into the solution when the two are separated by a semipermeable membrane. The osmotic pressure is a colligative property. Two solutions having the same osmotic pressure are called isotonic. If there are two solutions and one of them is of lower osmotic pressure, it is called hypotonic while the other is called hypertonic.

Answer the questions given below.

(a) What will happen if red blood corpuscles are placed in a 5% NaCl solution, which is a hypertonic solution?

(b) Show that osmotic pressure (π) is a colligative property.

(c) Calculate the amount of pressure required to stop osmosis of a solution, when 40 g of Na_2SO_4 is added to 1 L of water at 298 K.

(Given: Na = 23, O = 16, S = 32 and $R = 0.821$ L atm K^{-1} mol^{-1})

(d) Briefly discuss the process of reverse osmosis followed to desalinate sea water and convert it into drinking water.

Or

(ii) (a) An aqueous solution is made by dissolving 10 g of glucose ($C_6H_{12}O_6$) in 90 g of water at 300 K. If the vapour pressure of pure water at 300K is 32.8 mm Hg, what would be the vapour pressure of the solution?

(Given: C = 12, H = 1, and O = 16)

(b) A solution containing 12.5 g of a non-electrolyte solute in 175 g of water gave boiling point of 100.70°C. Calculate the molecular mass of the solute.

(Given: K_b for water = 0.52 K kg mol^{-1})

(c) Why are soda water bottles sealed under high pressure?

SOLUTIONS

1. (A) (i) Dry cell, nickel-cadmium cell

(ii) Tetrahedral, zero

(iii) Ethane, Wolff-kishner

(iv) Completely filled, diamagnetic

(B) (i) (d) Primary amines on heating with chloroform and alcoholic KOH form isocyanides or carbylamines which have foul smell.

$$\underset{\text{Amine}}{R\text{—}NH_2} + \underset{\text{Chloroform}}{CHCl_3} + 3KOH \xrightarrow{\Delta} \underset{\text{Alkyl or aryl isocyanide}}{R\text{—}NC} + 3KCl + 3H_2O$$

(ii) (b) Osmotic pressure of a solution increases with an increase in number of moles of solute and according to the Charles van't Hoff law it is directly proportional to the temperature, therefore, it increases at a higher temperature.

(iii) (a) Phenol is the strongest acid among the listed alcohols because, after losing a proton, the negative charge on the phenoxide ion is stabilised through resonance with the benzene ring.

(iv) (c) Sucrose does not form a silver mirror on heating with Tollen's reagent because sucrose is a non-reducing sugar, so it lacks a free aldehyde group which is necessary for the reaction, while the other three are reducing sugars and they give positive silver mirror test.

(v) (d) Since, *en* is a bidentate ligand, so two *en* in complex binds with the metal atom through four binding sites, and H_2O is a unidentate ligand, so two H_2O in the given complex binds to the metal atom through two binding sites. Therefore, the coordination number of the central metal '*D*' in the complex is 6.

Let the oxidation state of *D* in the complex is *x*.

$$\therefore \quad x + 2(0) + 2(0) = +3$$
$$x = +3$$

Thus, the oxidation state of the central metal '*D*' is 3.

(vi) (c) The process of halogenation of benzene takes place in the presence of anhydrous $FeCl_3$. The $FeCl_3$ reacts with the halogen to form a complex, which further dissociates to form the electrophile (Cl^+) which then attacks on the benzene ring to undergo electrophilic substitution reaction.

(vii) (a) Zr and Hf have nearly same value of atomic radii despite being in different periods due to the lanthanoid contraction. The ineffective shielding by 4*f* electrons in Hf increases the nuclear attraction, counteracting the expected increase in size and making their atomic radii almost same.

(C) (i) Unit of $k = (\text{mol L}^{-1})^{1-n}\text{s}^{-1}$.

For $n = 3$ (third order reaction)

Unit of $k = (\text{mol L}^{-1})^{1-3}\text{s}^{-1} = \text{L}^2\ \text{mol}^{-2}\ \text{s}^{-1}$.

Thus, for the given unit of k ($\text{mol}^{-2}\text{L}^2\text{s}^{-1}$) the order of reaction is three.

(ii) Refer to text on Pg. 102. (Difference between molecularity and order of reaction).

(iii) Since, the order of reaction is the sum of the exponents of the concentration term in the rate law, thus in the given rate law order of the reaction is $\frac{3}{2}$.

And from the given balanced equation, 2 molecules of *A* are reacting in a single step, hence the molecularity of reaction is 2.

2. Electrode reaction, $Al^{3+} + 3e^- \rightarrow Al$

For 27g (1 mol) of Al required $= 3 \times 96500$ C

$$\therefore \text{ 1g of Al required} = \frac{3 \times 96500\ \text{C}}{27}$$

$$\therefore \text{ 4.75 g of Al required} = \frac{3 \times 96500}{27} \times 4.75 = 50930.5\ \text{C}$$

Thus, the number of coulombs required to deposit 4.75 g of Al is 50930.5 C.

3.

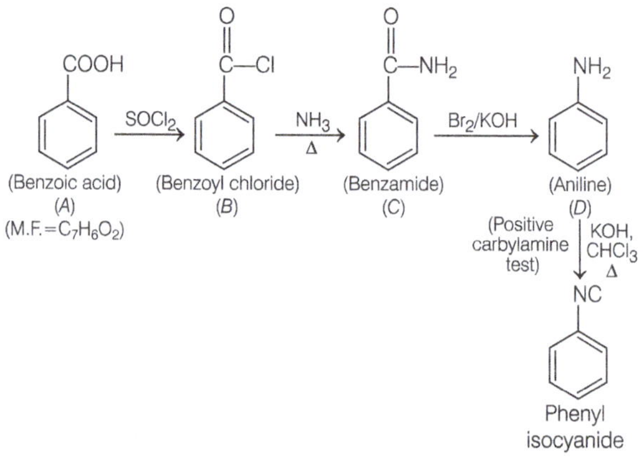

$\therefore$ *A* = Benzoic acid, *B* = Benzoyl chloride, *C* = Benzamide and *D* = Aniline.

4. (i) Rate $= r = k[NO][O_2]^2$

$$r' = k[2NO]\left[\frac{1}{2}O_2\right]^2$$
$$= k\ [2NO]\cdot\frac{1}{4}[O_2]^2 = \frac{1}{2}k\ [NO][O_2]^2$$
$$r' = \frac{1}{2}r$$

$\therefore$ rate of reaction will reduce to half, if [NO] concentration is doubled and $[O_2]$ concentration is halved.

(ii) If [NO] is in large excess then, $[NO] \approx 1$.

$\therefore$ rate equation becomes, rate $= k[O_2]^2$.

Thus, the reaction becomes second order.

5. Since, the nucleophilic substitution reaction of [*A*] depends only on concentration of compound [*A*], therefore, this is a S_N1 reaction (unimolecular substitution reaction).

FULLY SOLVED

So, [A] must be a tertiary alkyl halide, as S_N1 favours the formation of 3° carbocation.

Thus, [A] can be 2-bromobutane.

$$H_3C—\underset{\underset{}{}}{\overset{Br}{\overset{|}{C}H}}—CH_2—CH_3$$
[A]

While, the nucleophilic substitution reaction of [B] depends on both the concentration of [B] and nucleophile, thus, this is a S_N2 reaction (bimolecular substitution reaction). So, [B] must be a primary alkyl halide as S_N2 favours the primary halide due to less steric hindrance.

∴ [B] can be 1-bromobutane.

$$H_3C—CH_2—CH_2—CH_2—Br$$
[B]

6. (i) $CH_3CH_2CN + 4[H] \xrightarrow{LiAlH_4} CH_3CH_2CH_2NH_2$
(Ethyl cyanide) (Propan-1-amine)

(ii)
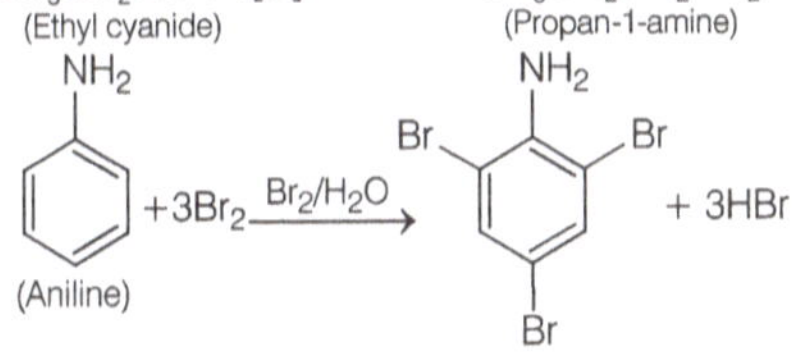

(2,4,6-tribromoaniline)

7. Shirin's observation of a white precipitate upon adding $AgNO_3$ solution to the complex, $[Co(NH_3)_3(en)(SO_4)]Cl$ indicates the presence of ionisable Cl^- ions outside the coordination sphere, leading to the formation of AgCl ppt.

The ionisation isomer of this complex, $[Co(NH_3)_3(en)(Cl)]SO_4$ would not produce a white ppt. with $AgNO_3$ as the Cl^- ion is inside the coordination sphere and is not ionisable. Thus, the ionisation isomer of the given complex can not be detected by $AgNO_3$ test. Therefore, we can perform $BaCl_2$ test to detect this ionisation isomers.

$$[Co(NH_3)_3(en)Cl]SO_4 + BaCl_2 \longrightarrow [Co(NH_3)_3(en)Cl]Cl_2 + \underset{\text{(white ppt.)}}{BaSO_4\downarrow}$$

Ionisation isomer = $[Co(NH_3)_3(en)(Cl)]SO_4$

Triamminechlorido (ethane-1, 2-diamine). cobalt (III) sulphate.

8. (i) The acidic character of alcohols is due to the polar nature of O—H bond. An electron withdrawing group decreases the electron density on oxygen, tending to decrease the polarity of O—H bond. Thus, this increases the acidic strength.

The order of electron withdrawing effect of substituents is :

$—CF_3 > —CCl_3 > —CH_3$. Therefore, the increasing order of acidic character is:

$$CH_3CH_2OH < CCl_3CH_2OH < CF_3CH_2OH$$

(ii) Boiling point of alcohols are usually higher than haloalkanes of comparable molecular masses. The —OH group in alcohols is involved in intermolecular H-bonding, which is absent in haloalkanes. Also, ethylene glycol with two —OH groups has a higher boiling point than ethanol due to presence of more extensive intermolecular H-bonding.

Therefore, the increasing order of the boiling points is

$$CH_3CH_2Cl < CH_3CH_2OH < \underset{\underset{CH_2OH}{|}}{CH_2}—OH$$

9. (i) $\underset{\text{(Acetic acid)}}{CH_3COOH} + PCl_5 \longrightarrow \underset{\text{(Acetyl chloride)}}{\underset{[A]}{CH_3COCl}} \xrightarrow[\text{Pd/BaSO}_4\text{, Boiling xylene}]{H_2} \underset{\text{(Acetaldehyde)}}{\underset{[B]}{CH_3CHO}}$

$$\underset{\text{(Acetaldehyde)}}{\underset{[B]}{CH_3CHO}} \xrightarrow{[O],\ K_2Cr_2O_7 + H_2SO_4} \underset{\text{(Acetic acid)}}{\underset{[C]}{CH_3COOH}} \xrightarrow{Ca(OH)_2,\ heat} \underset{\text{(Acetone)}}{\underset{[D]}{CH_3COCH_3}}$$

Or

(ii) (a)
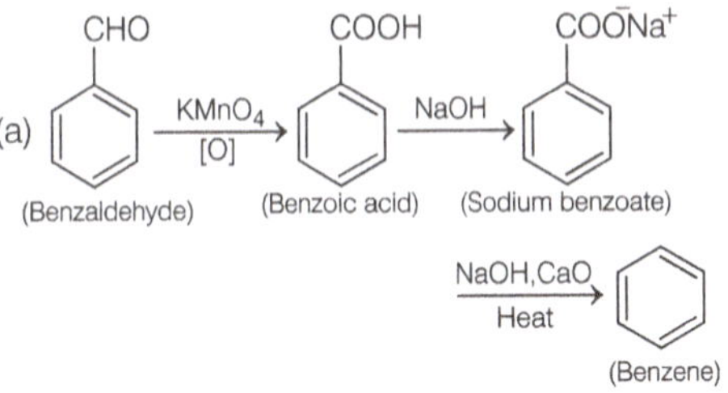

(b)
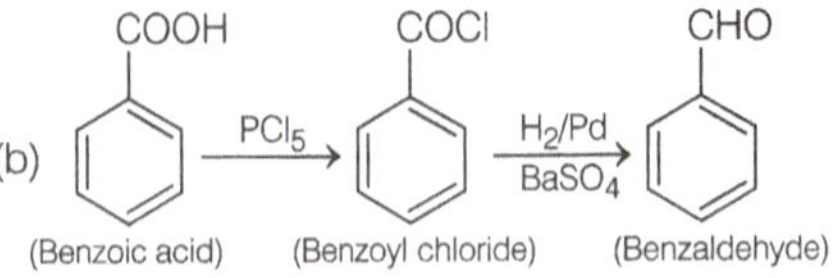

10. By applying Nernst equation,

$$E_{cell} = E^\circ_{cell} - \frac{0.0591}{n}\log\frac{[Ni^{2+}]}{[Cu^{2+}]}$$

$$\Rightarrow \quad 0.59 = E^\circ_{cell} - \frac{0.0591}{2}\log\frac{(0.1)}{(0.01)}$$

$$\Rightarrow \quad E^\circ_{cell} = 0.59 + \frac{0.0591}{2}\log(10) = 0.61955 \text{ V}$$

$$\Rightarrow \quad E^\circ_{cell} \approx 0.62\text{V}$$

11. (i) Ethanol and propan-1-al can be distinguished using the iodoform test. Ethanol gives a positive iodoform test, producing a yellow ppt. of iodoform (CHI_3). Propan-1-al does not give the iodoform test.

$$\underset{\text{(Ethanol)}}{CH_3CH_2OH} \xrightarrow[NaOH]{I_2} HCOO^-Na^+ + \underset{\text{(Yellow ppt.)}}{CHI_3\downarrow}$$

$$\underset{\text{(Propan-1-al)}}{CH_3CH_2CHO} \xrightarrow[NaOH]{I_2} \text{No reaction}$$

(ii) Phenol and benzoic acid can be distinguished by sodium bicarbonate test. Benzoic acid reacts with sodium bicarbonate to produce effervescence of carbon dioxide, whereas phenol does not.

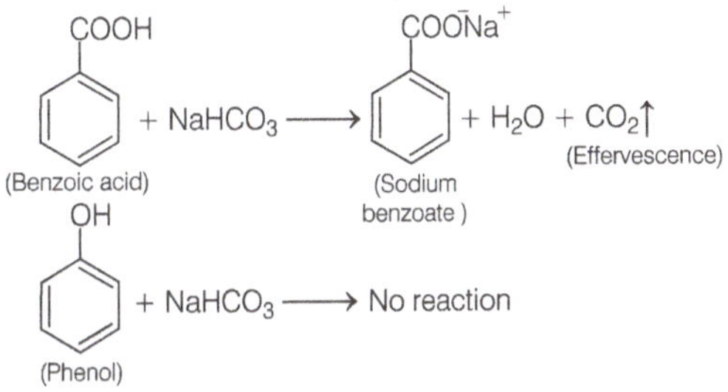

FULLY SOLVED

12. (i) $\underset{\text{Bromoethane}}{C_2H_5Br} \xrightarrow{KCN} \underset{\underset{(A)}{\text{Propanenitrile}}}{CH_3CH_2CN} \xrightarrow[\text{[4H]}]{LiAlH_4}$

$\underset{\underset{(B)}{\text{Propan-1-amine}}}{CH_3CH_2CH_2NH_2} \xrightarrow[0°-5°C]{HNO_2} \underset{\underset{(C)}{\text{Propan-1-ol}}}{CH_3CH_2CH_2OH}$

(ii) $\underset{\text{Propanamide}}{C_2H_5CONH_2} \xrightarrow{Br_2/KOH} \underset{\underset{(A)}{\text{Ethylamine}}}{CH_3CH_2NH_2}$

$\xrightarrow{CHCl_3+KOH} \underset{\underset{(B)}{\text{Ethyl isocyanide}}}{CH_3CH_2NC} \xrightarrow{Na/C_2H_5OH} \underset{\underset{(C)}{\text{N-methylethan-1-amine}}}{(CH_3CH_2NHCH_3)}$

13. (i) $K_4[Fe(CN)_6] \longrightarrow 4K^+ + [Fe(CN)_6]^-$

Here, $n = 5$ and $\alpha = 25\% = 0.25$.

$\therefore \quad \alpha = \frac{i-1}{n-1}$ [For dissociation]

$0.25 = \frac{i-1}{5-1} = \frac{i-1}{4}$

$1 = i - 1$

$\Rightarrow \quad i = 2$

(ii) $\underset{\text{(Benzoic acid)}}{2C_6H_5COOH} \rightleftharpoons \underset{\text{(Dimer)}}{(C_6H_5COOH)_2}$

van't Hoff factor (i)

$= \frac{\text{Total number of moles of particles after association}}{\text{Total number of moles of particles before association}}$

Since, two molecules of benzoic acid dimerises into one molecule,

Therefore, $i = \frac{1}{2}$.

14. (i) Refer to text on page -208.

(ii) Refer to text on page-282.

(iii) Refer to text on page-273.

15. (i) Complex compound [B] has 6 electrons in t_{2g} orbital, which are paired and there are no electrons in e_g. orbitals. Therefore, complex compound [B] is a low spin complex as it can form d^2sp^3 hybridistion (by involving inner d-orbital).

(ii) In complex compound [A], $t_{2g}^4 e_g^2$, there are 2 unpaired electrons in t_{2g} and 2 unpaired electrons in e_g orbitals, therefore, there are total four unpaired electrons in [A].

While, in complex compound [B], $t_{2g}^6 e_g^0$, there are zero unpaired electrons as all six electrons in t_{2g} are paired.

(iii) Complex [A] have high spin state, i.e., electrons are filled in t_{2g} and e_g first, before getting paired, therefore, complex [A] have weak field ligands (as they do not cause pairing).

16. (i) (a) By referring to electrochemical series, we can identify the anode and cathode half cells in a galvanic cell. The negative sign of standard reduction potential indicates that the electrode when joined with standard hydrogen electrode (SHE) behave as anode and oxidation occurs at that electrode.

Similarly, positive sign of standard reduction potential indicates that the electrode behaves as a cathode when joined with SHE and reduction occurs at this electrode.

(b) Refer to text on page-51 (Salt bridge).

(c) An advantage of a fuel cell is that it is highly efficient (70%).

Whereas, the disadvantage of a fuel cell is its high cost.

Or

(ii) (a) Specific conductance of a solution decreases upon dilution because the number of ions that carry current in a unit volume of solution always decreases with decrease in concentration.

(b) For a spontaneous reaction, $\Delta_r G°$ is negative, i.e., $\Delta_r G° < 0$. According to the equation, $\Delta_r G° = -nFE°_{cell}$.

For $\Delta_r G°$ to be negative, $E°_{cell}$ needs to be positive. Therefore, the emf of a cell should be positive for a spontaneous reactions.

(c) The type of cell in which reaction occurs only in one direction and cannot be reversed by an external energy source is primary cell. Its one disadvantage is that it is not reusable as it cannot be recharged.

17. (i) Zwitter ion, glycine

(ii) Janice should consume water soluble vitamin, vitamin C to prevent bleeding of gums.

(iii) Two units of monosaccharides are joined together through an oxide linkage, formed by the loss of water molecule. Such a linkage between two monosaccharide units to form a disaccharide is called a glycosidic linkage.

18. (i) Let the order w.r.t NO and Cl_2 be x and y.

Rate law expression can be written as;

Rate $= k[NO]^x[Cl_2]^y$

$\therefore \quad 2.0 \times 10^{-3} = k[2.0]^x[2.0]^y \quad \ldots(i)$

$6.0 \times 10^{-3} = [2.0]^x[6.0]^y \quad \ldots(ii)$

$1.8 \times 10^{-2} = [6.0]^x[2.0]^y \quad \ldots(iii)$

Dividing Equations (ii) by (i), we get

$\frac{6.0 \times 10^{-3}}{2.0 \times 10^{-3}} = \frac{[2.0]^x[6.0]^y}{[2.0]^x[2.0]^y}$

$(3)^1 = [3]^y$

$\therefore \quad y = 1$

Dividing (iii) by (i), we get

$\frac{1.8 \times 10^{-2}}{2.0 \times 10^{-3}} = \frac{[6.0]^x[2.0]^y}{[2.0]^x[2.0]^y}$

$9 = [3]^x \Rightarrow (3)^2 = [3]^x$

$\therefore \quad x = 2$

Hence, the order of reaction with regard to NO and Cl_2 is 2 and 1, respectively.

(ii) Overall order of reaction $= x + y = 2 + 1 = 3$

(iii) Rate $= k[NO]^2[Cl_2]$

FULLY SOLVED

From expression (1), rate constant can be calculated as :

$$2.0 \times 10^{-3} = k[2.0]^2[2.0]$$

$$k = \frac{2 \times 10^{-3} \text{mol L}^{-1}\text{s}^{-1}}{(4 \text{ mol}^2\text{L}^{-2})(2 \text{ mol L}^{-1})}$$

$$= 0.25 \times 10^{-3} \text{ L}^2\text{mol}^{-2} \text{ s}^{-1}$$

$$\Rightarrow \quad k = 2.5 \times 10^{-4} \text{L}^2\text{mol}^{-2} \text{ s}^{-1}.$$

19. (i) Picric acid can be prepared from phenol by reacting phenol with conc. HNO_3, in the presence of conc. H_2SO_4.

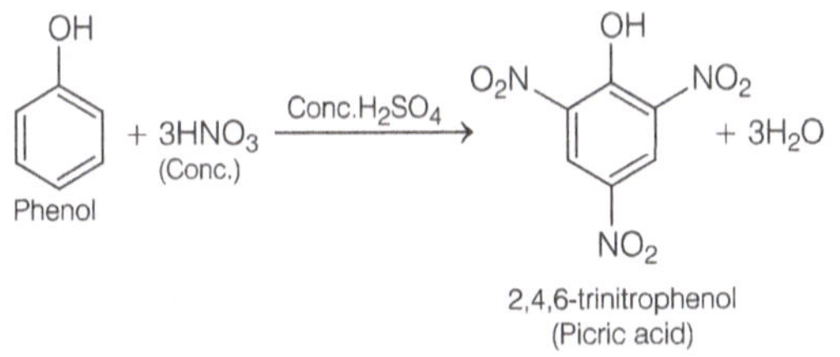

(ii) Phenol is less soluble in water as compared to aliphatic alcohols because phenol has a bulky phenyl ring, (hydrophophic group) which decreases its solubility.

(iii)

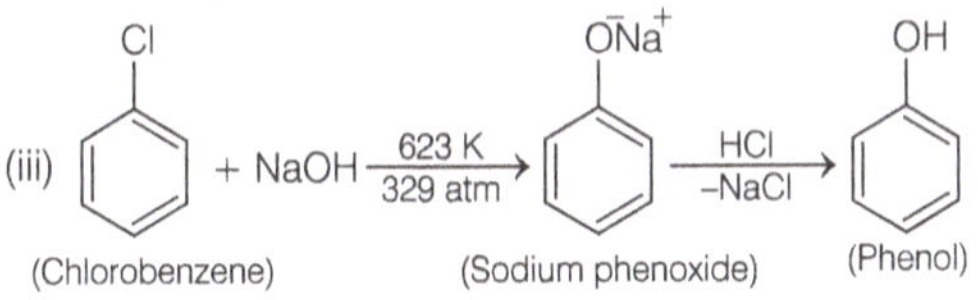

(iv) Since, compound [A] gives positive Lucas test within five minutes at room temperature, thus it is a secondary alcohol. Also, [A] on oxidation with $K_2Cr_2O_7$ /H_2SO_4 give [B], which does not respond to Tollen's test, thus, [B] is a ketone.

$$\underset{\text{(Butan-2-ol) [A]}}{CH_3-CH(OH)-CH_2-CH_3} \xrightarrow[H_2SO_4]{K_2Cr_2O_7} \underset{\text{(Butan-2-one) [B]}}{CH_3-\overset{O}{\overset{\|}{C}}-CH_2-CH_3}$$

Thus, [A] = Butan-2-ol and [B] = butan-2-one.

(v) Compound [B] i.e., butan-2-one undergoes Clemmensen reduction to form butane (Compound [C]).

$$\underset{\text{(Butan-2-one) [B]}}{CH_3-\overset{O}{\overset{\|}{C}}-CH_2-CH_3} + 4[H] \xrightarrow[\text{Conc. HCl}]{\text{Zn–Hg}} \underset{\text{(Butane) [C]}}{CH_3-CH_2-CH_2-CH_3} + H_2O$$

Thus, [C] = Butane.

20. (i) (a) Ti has an electronic configuration of $3d^2 4s^2$.

$Ti^{2+} = 3d^2 4s^0$

$Ti^{4+} = 3d^0$

Since, there are two unpaired electrons in Ti^{2+}, therefore Ti^{2+} salts are coloured due to *d-d* transition. Whereas, Ti^{4+} has no unpaired electrons, therefore, Ti^{4+} salts are colourless.

(b) Refer to text on page-139 (Alloy formation).

(c) Mohr's salt contains Fe^{2+} ions, which are oxidised to Fe^{3+} ions by $KMnO_4$ solution in acidic medium. Thus, $KMnO_4$ is reduced to Mn^{2+} during this reaction and pink colour of $KMnO_4$ decolourises.

(ii) (a) $2KMnO_4 + 3H_2SO_4 + 5H_2C_2O_4 \longrightarrow 2MnSO_4 + 10CO_2 + K_2SO_4 + 8H_2O$

(b) $K_2Cr_2O_7 + 4H_2SO_4 + 3H_2S \longrightarrow K_2SO_4 + Cr_2(SO_4)_3 + 7H_2O + 3S$

21. (i) (a) If red blood corpuscles are placed in 5% NaCl solution (a hypertonic solution), then the cells will shrink as the water will move out of the cells from area of higher water concentration to lower water concentration *via* osmosis.

(b) Colligative properties are those which depends on the number of solute particles rather than the nature of solute particles.

$$\text{Osmotic pressure } (\pi) = CRT = \frac{n}{V}RT \left[\because c = \frac{n}{V}\right]$$

Since, osmotic pressure depends on the number of moles of solute (*n*), therefore, it is a colligative property.

(c) osmotic pressure,

$$(\pi) = iCRT$$

Now, $Na_2SO_4 \longrightarrow 2Na^+ + SO_4^{2-}$

$\therefore \quad i = 3$

$$\pi = i\frac{n}{V}RT = \frac{i.W.R.T}{M \times V}$$

For Na_2SO_4, molecular weight

$(M) = 2(23) + 32 + 4(16) = 142 \text{ g mol}^{-1}$

Given, $W = 40$ g, $V = 1$ L, $R = 0.0821$ L atm K^{-1} mol^{-1} and $T = 298$ K.

$$\Rightarrow \pi = \frac{3 \times 40 \text{ g} \times 0.0821 \text{ Latm K}^{-1}\text{mol}^{-1} \times 298\text{K}}{142\text{g mol}^{-1} \times 1\text{L}}$$

$\therefore \quad \pi = 20.675$ atm

(d) Refer to text on page-27 (Reverse osmosis and water purification).

Or

(ii) (a) According to relative lowering of vapour pressure,

$$\frac{p_1^\circ - p_1}{p_1^\circ} = x_2 = \frac{n_2}{n_1 + n_2}$$

[Here, 1 represents solvent and 2 represents solute]

where, p_1° = vapour pressure of pure solvent

p_1 = vapour pressure of solution

x_2 = mole fraction of solute.

Given, $W_2 = 10$ g, $M_2 = 180 \text{ g mol}^{-1}$, $W_1 = 90$ g, $M_1 = 18$ g and $p_1^\circ = 32.8$ mm Hg.

$$\Rightarrow \quad n_1 = \frac{W_1}{M_1} = \frac{90 \text{ g}}{18 \text{ g mol}^{-1}} = 5 \text{ mol}$$

$$\Rightarrow \quad n_2 = \frac{W_2}{M_2} = \frac{10\text{g}}{180 \text{ g mol}^{-1}} = 0.0556 \text{ mol}$$

FULLY SOLVED

$$\therefore \frac{32.8 - p_1}{32.8} = \frac{0.0556}{0.0556 + 5} = \frac{0.0556}{5.0556}$$

$$\Rightarrow \frac{32.8 - p_1}{32.8} = 0.011$$

$$\Rightarrow 32.8 - p_1 = 0.3608$$

$$p_1 = 32.4392 \text{ mm Hg}$$

$$\Rightarrow p_1 \approx 32.44 \text{ mm Hg}$$

(b) Elevation in boiling point $(\Delta T_b) = K_b\, m$

(where, m = molality)

$$\Delta T_b = K_b \times \frac{\text{moles of solute}(n_2) \times 1000}{\text{weight of solvent } (W_1)(\text{in g})}$$

$$\Delta T_b = \frac{K_b \times W_2 \times 1000}{M_2 \times W_1} \quad \left[\because n_2 = \frac{W_2}{M_2}\right]$$

Also, $\Delta T_b = T_b - T_b^\circ$

[where, T_b = boiling point of solution, ΔT_b° = boiling point of water]

Given,

$T_b = 100.70°\text{C} = (100.70 + 273)\text{K} = 373.70$ K,

$T_b^\circ = 373$ K, $W_2 = 12.5$ g, $W_1 = 175$ g and

$K_b = 0.52$ K kg mol^{-1}

Now, $\Delta T_b = T_b - T_b^\circ = (373.70 - 373)\text{K} = 0.70$ K

$$\Delta T_b = 0.70 \text{ K}$$

$$= \frac{0.52 \text{ K kg mol}^{-1} \times 12.5 \text{ g} \times 1000}{M_2 \times 175 \text{ kg}}$$

$$\Rightarrow M_2 = \frac{0.52 \text{ K kg mol}^{-1} \times 12.5\text{g} \times 1000}{0.70 \text{ K} \times 175 \text{ kg}}$$

$$= 53.061 \text{ g mol}^{-1}$$

$$\therefore M_2 \approx 53.06 \text{ g mol}^{-1}$$

(c) Soda water bottles are sealed under high pressure to increase the solubility of carbon dioxide (CO_2) in the drink, which is essential for maintaining its characteristic fizz and flavours.

FULLY SOLVED

Latest

ISC Specimen Question Paper

Chemistry (Fully Solved)

Issued by Council for the Indian School Certificate Examinations

Time : 3 hours | Max. Marks : 70

GENERAL INSTRUCTIONS

- This paper is divided into four sections-A, B, C and D. Answer all questions.
- **Section A** consists of **one** question **having sub-parts** of one mark each. **Section B** consists of **ten** questions of **two** marks each. **Section C** consists of **seven** questions of three marks each and **Section D** consists of **three** questions of **five** marks each.
- Internal choices have been provided in one question each in Section B, Section C and Section D.
- All working, including rough work, should be done on the same sheet as, and adjacent to the rest of the answer.
- The intended marks for questions or parts of questions are given in brackets [].
- Balanced equations must be given, wherever possible and diagrams where they are helpful. When solving numerical problems, all essential working must be shown.
- In working out problems, use the following data:
  Gas constant (R)= 1.987 cal deg^{-1} mol^{-1} = 8.314 JK^{-1} mol^{-1} = 0.0821 dm^3 atm K^{-1} mol^{-1} 1 L atm = 1 dm^3 atm = 101.3 J,
  1 Faraday = 96500 Coulombs. **Avogadro's number** (N_A) = 6.023×10^{23}.

FULLY SOLVED

Section-A [14 Marks]

1. (A) Fill in the blanks by choosing the appropriate word(s) from those given in the brackets: [4 × 1]
[four, three, remains same, propane, ns^{1-2}, increases, six, propan-2-ol, $(n-1)\,d^{1-10}$, two, decreases, Clemmensen's, Wolff-Kishner]

(i) The molar conductance of a solution .... on dilution but the specific conductance of a solution .... on dilution. • *Understanding*

(ii) In the complex ion $[\mathrm{CoCl(en)_2ONO}]^+$, the coordination number and the oxidation number of the central metal ion are .... and .... • *Understanding*

(iii) Propanone on reaction with zinc amalgam in the presence of concentrated HCl gives .... and the reaction is called ...... reduction. • *Recall*

(iv) The variation and magnitude of oxidation state in coordination complexes is due to the participation of inner .... electrons in addition to outer .... electrons. • *Understanding*

(B) Select and write the correct alternative from the choices given below. [7 × 1]

(i) The correct order of the increasing basic nature of ammonia, methylamine and aniline is • *Analysis*

(a) Methylamine < aniline < ammonia
(b) Aniline < methylamine < ammonia
(c) Ammonia < aniline < methylamine
(d) Aniline < ammonia < methylamine

(ii) Colligative properties of a solution are • *Understanding*

(P) Independent of the nature of solute
(Q) Proportional to molecular mass of solute
(R) Proportional to concentration of solute

(*S*) Independent of the amount of solvent
(a) Only *P* and *Q* are correct
(b) Only *P* and *R* are correct
(c) Only *P* and *S* are correct
(d) Only *Q* and *S* are correct

(iii) According to Markownikoff's rule, "The negative part of the halogen acid attaches itself with that C-atom of an unsymmetrical alkene which has least number of H-atom."
Anti-Markownikoff's addition of HBr is not observed in • *Analysis*
(a) propene (b) but-2-ene
(c) but-1-ene (d) pent-2-ene

(iv) Most of the naturally occurring α-amino acids are optically active and have *L*-configuration. Which of the following amino acids is not asymmetric? • *Recall*
(a) Valine (b) Alanine
(c) Glycine (d) Leucine

(v) Which one of the following complex ions has geometrical isomers? • *Understanding*
(a) $[Ni(NH_3)_5Br]^+$ (b) $[Cr(NH_3)_4en]^{3+}$
(c) $[Co(NH_3)_2(en)_2]^{3+}$ (d) $[Co(NH_3)_6]^{3+}$

(vi) Given below are two statements marked Assertion and Reason. Read the two statements carefully and select the correct option.
Assertion (A) Tertiary butyl bromide undergoes Wurtz reaction to give 2,2,3,3 tetramethyl butane.
Reason (R) In Wurtz reaction, when same alkyl halides react with sodium in dry ether to give hydrocarbon; the hydrocarbon formed contains double the number of carbon atoms present in the alkyl halide. • *Analysis*
(a) Both Assertion and Reason are true and Reason is the correct explanation of Assertion.
(b) Both Assertion and Reason are true but Reason is not the correct explanation for Assertion.
(c) Assertion is true but Reason is false.
(d) Both Assertion and Reason are false.

(vii) Given below are two statements marked Assertion and Reason. Read the two statements carefully and select the correct option.
Assertion (A) There is a continuous increase in size among lanthanoids with an increase in atomic number.
Reason (R) Lanthanoids do not show lanthanoid contraction. • *Analysis*
(a) Both Assertion and Reason are true and Reason is the correct explanation of Assertion.
(b) Both Assertion and Reason are true but Reason is not the correct explanation for assertion.
(c) Assertion is true but Reason is false.
(d) Both Assertion and Reason are false.

(C) Read the passage carefully and answer the questions that follow. [3 × 1]

A plant or any other living being maintains a reasonable balance of C-14 (radioactive carbon) in its tissue during its lifetime. C-14 is used to determine the age of fossils. In the upper atmosphere, neutrons present in the cosmic rays are captured to produce the following nuclear reaction.

$$_{7}N^{14} + _{0}n^{1} \longrightarrow _{6}C^{14} + _{1}H^{1}$$

C-14 isotope is circulated in the atmosphere and gets absorbed by living organism during photosynthesis. The ratio of C-14 to C-12 in living being is $1:10^{12}$.

Once the living being dies, the level of C-14 in the dead being decreases due to the following reaction.

$$_{6}C^{14} \longrightarrow _{7}N^{14} + _{-1}e^{0} + \gamma \text{ rays}$$

The death of the plant brings an end to its tendency to take up C-14. The half-life period of C-14 is 5770 years. By knowing the concentration of C-14 in the living plant and the piece of dead material at a particular time, the age of the material (fossil) can be determined.

(i) Write the relation between the decay constant and half-life period. • *Recall*

(ii) In a piece of dead wood, the activity or concentration of C-14 is found to be one third of its initial activity. Calculate the age of the old wood. • *Application*

(iii) The half-life period ($t_{1/2}$) for a first order reaction is 30 minutes. Calculate the time taken to complete 87.5% of the reaction. • *Application*

Section-B [20 Marks]

2. The solution of two electrolytes *A* and *B* are diluted. Λ_m of *B* increases 1.5 times while that of *A* increases 25 times. Which of the two is a strong electrolyte? Give a reason. • *Understanding* [2]

3. An organic compound [*A*] which has characteristic odour, reacts with conc. NaOH to give two compounds [*B*] and [*C*]. Compound [*B*] has molecular formula C_7H_8O which upon oxidation gives back compound [*A*]. Compound [*C*] is the sodium salt of the acid and upon treatment with sodalime yields an aromatic hydrocarbon [*D*]. Identify the compounds [*A*], [*B*], [*C*] and [*D*]. [2] • *Understanding*

4. Devise a scheme for the synthesis of *n*-butane using CH_3I as the only source of carbon. Is it possible to obtain propane in pure state by applying this scheme? Give a reason for your answer. • *Evaluate* [2]

5. It is generally observed that the rate of a chemical reaction becomes double with every 10°C rise in temperature. If the generalisation holds true for a reaction in the temperature range of 298 K to 308 K, what would be the value of activation energy (E_a) for the reaction? • *Application* [2]

6. An organic compound [*X*] of molecular formula C_3H_5N, in one reaction produced a primary amine with $LiAlH_4$. In another case, the organic compound [*Y*] of same molecular formula C_3H_5N produced a secondary amine with $LiAlH_4$. Identify both the compounds [*X*] and [*Y*]. Why do these compounds form two different products? • *Understanding* [2]

7. During chemistry class, a teacher wrote $[Ni(CN)_4]^{2-}$ as a coordination complex ion on the board. The students were asked to find out the magnetic behaviour and shape of the complex. Pari, a student, wrote the answer paramagnetic and tetrahedral whereas another student Suhail wrote diamagnetic and square planer. • *Evaluate* [2]
Evaluate Pari's and Suhail's responses.

8. An organic compound '*X*' with molecular formula $C_4H_{10}O$ is found to be soluble in conc. H_2SO_4 and does not react with sodium metal or $KMnO_4$. Compound '*X*' when heated with excess of HI gives a single alkyl halide. Deduce the structure of the compound '*X*'. Explain all the reactions involved. [2] • *Understanding*

9. (i) Identify the compounds [*A*] and [*B*] in the following reactions. [2] • *Understanding*

(a) $C_6H_5CHO \xrightarrow[(2)\ SOCl_2]{(1)\ K_2Cr_2O_7/H_2SO_4} [A] \xrightarrow{C_6H_6\ (\text{anhy. } AlCl_3)} [B]$

(b) $CH_3{-}C{\equiv}CH \xrightarrow[(2)\ \text{Vigorous oxidation, conc. } HNO_3]{(1)\ H_2SO_4/HgSO_4} [A] \xrightarrow[\text{[Conc. } H_2SO_4]]{C_2H_5OH} [B]$

Or (ii) Three organic compounds *A*, *B* and *C* are non-cyclic functional isomers of carbonyl compounds with molecular formula C_4H_8O. Isomers *A* and *C* give positive Tollen's test while compound *B* does not give positive Tollen's test but gives positive iodoform test. Compounds *A* and *B* on reduction with Zn amalgam and conc. HCl give the same product.

(a) Write the structures of the compounds *A*, *B* and *C*. • *Understanding*

(b) Out of the compounds *A*, *B* and *C*, which one will be the least reactive towards addition of HCN. • *Understanding*

10. Calculate the value of E°_{cell}, E_{cell} and ΔG that can be obtained from the following cell at 298 K.
$Al/Al^{3+}_{(0.01\ M)}\ //\ Sn^{2+}_{(0.015\ M)}/Sn$ • *Application* [2]
Given, $E^\circ_{Al^{3+}/Al} = -1.66$ V, $E^\circ_{Sn^{2+}/Sn} = -0.14$ V

11. Write the chemical test to distinguish between the following pairs of compounds. [2]
(i) Propan-1-ol and propan-2-ol
(ii) Phenol and ethanol • *Understanding*

Section-C [21 Marks]

12. Identify the compounds [A], [B] and [C] in the following reactions. [3]

(i) $C_6H_5NO_2 \xrightarrow[Sn/HCl]{6[H]} [A] \xrightarrow[273\ K-278\ K]{HNO_2 + HCl} [B] \xrightarrow{C_6H_5NH_2} [C]$ • *Understanding*

(ii) $CH_3CH_2NH_2 \xrightarrow[(2)\ P/Cl_2]{(1)\ HNO_2} [A] \xrightarrow[(2)\ H_2O/H^+]{(1)\ KCN} [B] \xrightarrow[(2)\ Br_2/KOH]{(1)\ NH_3/heat} [C]$ • *Understanding*

13. The molar mass calculated through colligative properties is sometimes different from that of experimentally determined molecular mass and is known as abnormal molecular mass. This difference is due to the solute particles that undergo association or dissociation. [3]
Consider the two cases given below and answer the questions that follow.

(A) The freezing point of a solution containing 5.85 of NaCl in 100 g of water is −3.348°C. (K_f of water = 1.86 K kg mol^{-1}, molecular mass of NaCl = 58.5)

(B) The freezing point of benzene solution decreases by 0.45°C when 0.2 g of acetic acid is added to 20 g of benzene. (K_f of benzene = 5.12 K kg mol^{-1}, molecular mass of acetic acid = 60)

Answer the following questions.

(i) Calculate the abnormal molecular mass of solute in both the cases. • *Application*

(ii) Inferring the value of van't Hoff factor in both the cases, find out which solution undergoes association and which solution undergoes dissociation. • *Analysis*

(iii) Given below is the increasing order of depression in freezing point of water observed for equimolar concentrations of the compounds,
acetic acid < trichloro acetic acid < trifluoro acetic acid
Provide a reason to explain if the above ordered arrangement is correct or not. • *Understanding*

14. Write chemical equations to illustrate the following name reactions. • *Recall* [3]
(i) Rosenmund's reaction
(ii) Benzoin condensation
(iii) Perkin's reaction

15. (i) Assuming that cyanide is a strong ligand, write the formula of two coordination complex ions with cyanide and iron having coordination number six. Name the complex ions. • *Application* [3]

(ii) On the basis of Crystal Field Theory, write the electronic configuration of d^4 ion if: • *Application*
(a) $\Delta_o > P$ (b) $\Delta_o < P$

16. (i) Dry cells are commonly used in clocks, torches, calculators etc. They are the most familiar type of commercial cells. [3]
(a) What acts as anode and cathode in dry cell? • *Understanding*
(b) Which chemical compounds are filled between anode and cathode of this cell? • *Understanding*
(c) Why do dry cells not have a long life? • *Understanding*

Or (ii) Answer the following:
(a) What happens to the voltage when the salt bridge is removed from the two half cells and why? • *Understanding*
(b) Copper sulphate solution cannot be stored in a zinc pot. Why? • *Understanding*
(c) Why does the density of H_2SO_4 in a lead storage battery decrease as it is discharged? • *Understanding*

17. (i) The structures of glycine and alanine are given below. [3]
Show the peptide bond linkage in glycylalanine. • *Understanding* [3]

$H_2N—CH_2—COOH$ (Glycine) $H_2N—CH(CH_3)—COOH$ (Alanine)

(ii) What products would be formed when a nucleotide from DNA containing thymine is hydrolysed? • *Understanding*

(iii) What are reducing sugars? Give an example. • *Recall*

18. Consider the data given below for the reaction
$A + B \longrightarrow$ Product [3]

S.No.	conc. of [A] mol L^{-1}	conc. of [B] mol L^{-1}	Rate; mol L^{-1} sec^{-1}
1.	0.1	0.1	4.0×10^{-4}
2.	0.2	0.2	1.6×10^{-3}
3.	0.5	0.1	1.0×10^{-2}
4.	0.5	0.5	1.0×10^{-2}

Answer the following questions.

(i) What is the order of reaction with respect to *A* and *B* ? • *Application*

(ii) Calculate the rate constant. • *Application*

(iii) Determine the reaction rate when the concentration of *A* and *B* are 0.2 mol L^{-1} sec^{-1} and 0.35 mol L^{-1} sec^{-1} respectively. • *Evaluate*

Section-D [15 Marks]

19. Phenol, one of the deadliest acids, contains a hydroxyl group directly attached to the aromatic ring. A hydroxyl group attached to an aromatic ring is also referred to as a phenolic group. Due to the presence of —OH group, phenols show many reactions similar to those of alcohols.

The direct attachment of —OH group to the aromatic ring makes its behaviour very different from that of alcohols. That is why phenol behaves differently from alcohols in many reactions. The chemical reactions of phenol can be categorised as follows:

- Reactions involving —OH group
- Reactions involving benzene ring [5]

(i) Write the chemical equation for the preparation of phenol from benzene using H_2SO_4 and NaOH. • *Understanding*

(ii) What happens when phenol reacts with Br_2/CS_2 at low temperature? • *Recall*

(iii) What is observed when phenol is treated with neutral ferric chloride solution? • *Recall*

(iv) Write the reaction when phenol is treated with conc. HNO_3 in the presence of conc. H_2SO_4. • *Understanding*

(v) Write the reaction when phenol is treated with chloroform in the presence of aqueous NaOH at 340 K. • *Understanding*

20. (i) Give a reason for each of the following. [5]

(a) The purple colour of $KMnO_4$ disappears in the presence of acidified solution of oxalic acid. • *Understanding*

(b) Some transition metals and their compounds get attracted towards the magnetic field. • *Understanding*

(c) Why are Mn^{2+} compounds more stable than Fe^{2+} towards oxidation to the +3 state?
(Atomic no. of Mn = 25 and Fe = 26) • *Understanding*

(ii) Complete and balance the following reactions. • *Recall*

(a) $KMnO_4 + H_2SO_4 + FeSO_4 \longrightarrow$
.... + ... + ...

(b) $K_2Cr_2O_7 + H_2SO_4 + KI \longrightarrow$
.... + ... + ...

21. Osmosis and osmotic pressure play a very significant role in biological processes. The osmotic pressure of human blood is 8.21 atm at 27°C. It is interesting to know that a 0.91% (mass/volume) solution of NaCl, known as saline water is isotonic with fluids inside the human red blood cells. In this solution, the blood corpuscles neither swell nor shrink. Therefore, medicines are mixed with saline water before being injected into the veins. [5]
Answer the following questions.

(i) What is an isotonic solution? • *Recall*

(ii) How much glucose should be used per 100 ml (aqueous solution) for intravenous injection that is isotonic with blood at 27°C? • *Application*

(iii) What would be the osmotic pressure of blood if the temperature is 37°C? • *Application*

(iv) A pure NaCl solution with salt concentration less than 0.91% (mass/volume) is hypertonic solution to human blood. Is this statement true or false? Give a reason. • *Understanding*

(v) Name the disease caused by taking a lot of salt or salty food, which results in water retention in tissue cells causing puffiness or swelling. • *Recall*

Or

(i) Calculate the boiling point of urea solution when 8.0 g of urea is dissolved in 250 g of water. Boiling point of pure water is 373 K. (K_b of water = 0.52 K kg mol^{-1}, molecular mass of urea = 60 g mol^{-1}) • *Application*

(ii) Ethylene glycol is used as an antifreeze agent. Calculate the amount of ethylene glycol to be added to four kilogram of water to prevent it from freezing at −6°C.
(K_f of water = 1.86 K kg mol^{-1}) Assume that ethylene glycol ($CH_2OH \cdot CH_2OH$) does not dissociate or associate in aqueous solution. • *Application*

(iii) What will be the effect on the value of molality and molarity of a solution with change in temperature? • *Understanding*

SOLUTIONS

1. (A) (i) increases, decreases

(ii) six, three

(iii) propane, Clemmensen's

(iv) $(n-1)d^{1-10}, ns^{1-2}$

(B) (i) (d) Methylamine is a stronger base than ammonia due to +*I*-effect (electron-donating power) of alkyl group. On the other hand, aniline is a weaker base than ammonia due to electron withdrawing nature of aryl group. Thus, the correct order of the increasing basic nature is

Aniline < Ammonia < Methylamine

(ii) (b) Colligative properties of a solution depends only on the number of solute particles irrespective of their nature to the total number of particles present in the solution. Further, it is proportional to concentration of solute.

Thus, only statements (*P*) and (*R*) are correct.

(iii) (b) Anti-Markownikoff's addition of HBr is not observed in case of but-2-ene. This is because it a symmetrical alkene.

(iv) (c) The general formula of amino acid is

$$R-\underset{\displaystyle NH_2}{\underset{|}{CH}}-COOH,$$

where, *R* represents side chain. The characteristic feature of *R* of given amino acids are follows

Glycine-H

Alanine- $-CH_3$

Valine- $-HC(CH_3)_2$

Leucine - $-(H_3C)_2CH-CH_2-$

Thus, glycine is not an asymmetric amino acid.

(v) (c) Geometrical isomerism is shown by $[Co(NH_3)(en_2)]^{3+}$ due to different possible geometric arrangements of the ligands. The structures of isomers are as follows

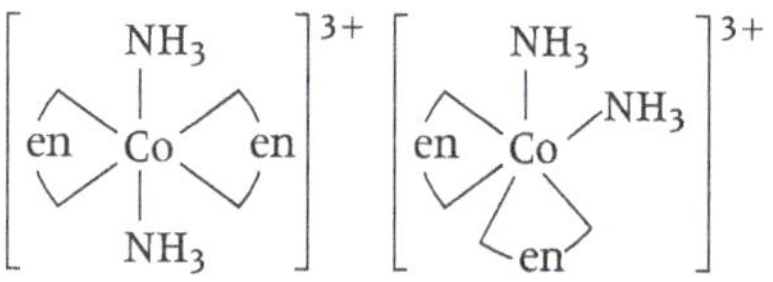

trans-isomer *cis*-isomer

(vi) (a) Tertiary butyl bromide undergoes Wurtz reaction to give 2, 2, 3, 3-tetramethyl butane. The reaction is as follows

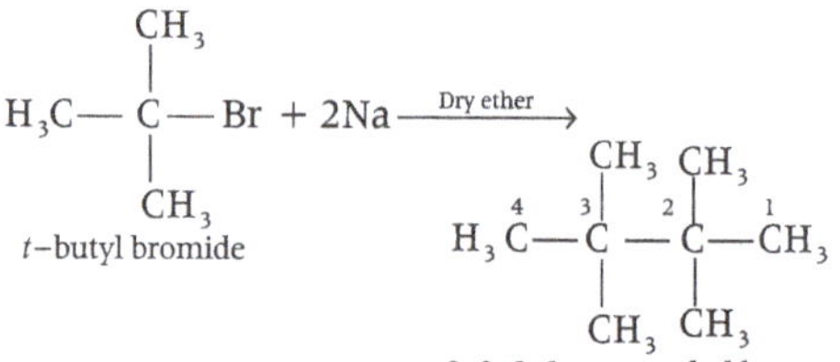

Here, the hydrocarbon formed contain double the number of carbon atoms present in the alkyl halide. Thus, both Assertion and Reason are true and Reason is the correct explanation of Assertion.

(vii) (d) There is a gradual decrease in size among lanthanoids with an increase in atomic number. This is due to lanthanoid contraction. Thus, both Assertion and Reason are false.

(C) (i) The radioactive decay of C-14 takes place by first order kinetics. Therefore, the relation between the decay constant (k) and half-life period is given as

$$t_{\frac{1}{2}} = \frac{0.693}{k}$$

or $$k = \frac{0.693}{t_{\frac{1}{2}}}$$

(ii) Given, $t_{1/2} = 5770$ years

$$(a-x) = \frac{a}{3}$$

As we know that, for first order reaction

$$t = \frac{2.303}{k}\log\frac{a}{(a-x)}$$

and, $$k = \frac{0.693}{t_{\frac{1}{2}}}$$

$$\therefore \quad t = \frac{2.303 \times 5770}{0.693}\log\frac{a}{a/3}$$

$$\Rightarrow \quad t = \frac{2.303 \times 5770 \times \log 3}{0.693}$$

$$t = \frac{2.303 \times 5770 \times 0.4771}{0.693}$$

$$[\because \log 3 = 0.4771]$$

$$\therefore \quad t = 9148.4 \text{ years}$$

(iii) Given, $t_{1/2} = 30$ minutes

If $a = 100$, $(a - x) = (100 - 87.5) = 12.5$

As we know that, for first order reaction,

$$t = \frac{2.303}{k}\log\frac{a}{a-x} \quad \left[\because k = \frac{0.693}{t_{1/2}}\right]$$

$$\therefore \quad t = \frac{2.303 \times 30}{0.693} \times \log\frac{100}{12.5}$$

$$\Rightarrow \quad t = \frac{2.303 \times 30}{0.693}(\log 100 - \log 12.5)$$

$$\text{or } t = \frac{2.303 \times 30}{0.693}(2 - 1.097) \quad \left[\begin{array}{l}\because \log 100 = 2 \\ \log 12.5 = 1.097\end{array}\right]$$

$$\therefore \quad t = 99.70 \times 0.903 \text{ mins}$$
$$= 90.03 \text{ mins}$$

2. B is a strong electrolyte as on dilution, Λ_m increases to a little extent. This is because in case of strong electrolyte, on dilution, number of ions remains almost the same and only inter ionic attraction decreases.

3. Compound $[A]$ has characteristic odour which means it can be benzaldehyde. It undergoes Cannizzaro reaction with NaOH to give alcohol and sodium salt of acid.

Compound $[B]$ can be benzyl alcohol as it contains only one oxygen atom, which on oxidation gives back compound $[A]$.

The reaction involved is

$$\underset{(B)}{C_6H_5CH_2OH} \xrightarrow{CrO_3} \underset{(A)}{C_6H_5CHO}$$

Compound 'C' can be sodium salt of benzoic acid which on heating with sodalime yields an aromatic compound 'D' which may be benzene.

Thus, $[A] = C_6H_5CHO$ (Benzaldehyde),

$[B] = C_6H_5CH_2OH$ (Benzyl alcohol)

$[C] = C_6H_5COONa$ (Sodium salt of benzoic acid)

$[D] = C_6H_6$ (Benzene)

4. The scheme/sequence of reactions for the synthesis of n-butane using CH_3I as the only source of carbon is as follows

$$\underset{\text{Methyl iodide}}{2CH_3I} \xrightarrow[\text{Wurtz reaction}]{\text{Na, dry ether}} \underset{\text{Ethane}}{CH_3-CH_3} \xrightarrow{Cl_2/h\nu} \underset{\text{Ethyl chloride}}{CH_3CH_2Cl}$$

$$2CH_3CH_2Cl \xrightarrow[\text{Wurtz reaction}]{\text{Na, dry ether}} \underset{\text{n-butane}}{CH_3CH_2CH_2CH_3}$$

Propane cannot be obtained in pure state by the above scheme. This is because, Wurtz reaction between CH_3I and C_2H_5I will give three products, i.e., ethane, propane and butane.

5. Given, $T_1 = 298$ K and $T_2 = 308$ K

$$\frac{k_2}{k_1} = 2,\ R = 8.314 \text{ J K}^{-1}\text{ mol}^{-1}$$

According to Arrhenius equation,

$$\log\frac{k_2}{k_1} = \frac{E_a}{2.303\,R}\left[\frac{1}{T_1} - \frac{1}{T_2}\right]$$

$$\log 2 = \frac{E_a}{2.303 \times 8.314 \text{ J/K/mol}}\left[\frac{-1}{298} - \frac{1}{308}\right]$$

$$0.3010 = \frac{E_a}{2.303 \times 8.314} \times \frac{10}{298 \times 308}$$

$$E_a = \frac{0.3010 \times 2.303 \times 8.314 \times 298 \times 308}{10} (\text{J mol}^{-1})$$

$$E_a = 52897.78 \text{ J/mol or } 52.898 \text{ kJ/mol}$$

6. Since, compound $[X]$ having molecular formula C_3H_5N produces primary amine on reaction with $LiAlH_4$. Therefore, it must be propanenitrile or ethyl cyanide (C_2H_5CN).

However, compound $[Y]$ of same formula (C_3H_5N) produces secondary amine on reaction with $LiAlH_4$. Therefore, it must be ethyl isocyanide (C_2H_5NC). The reactions are as follows :

$$\underset{\substack{\text{Ethyl cyanide} \\ [A]}}{CH_3CH_2C{\equiv}N} + LiAlH_4 \longrightarrow \underset{\substack{\text{Propanamine} \\ \text{(Primary amines)}}}{CH_3CH_2CH_2NH_2}$$

$$\underset{\substack{\text{Ethyl isocyanide} \\ [B]}}{CH_3CH_2-\overset{\oplus}{N}{\equiv}\overset{\ominus}{C}} \xrightarrow{LiAlH_4} \underset{\substack{\text{N-methyl ethanamine} \\ \text{(Secondary amines)}}}{CH_3CH_2NHCH_3}$$

7. In the complex $[Ni(CN)_4]^{2-}$, the oxidation state of Ni is +2.

Ni (atom $(Z = 28)$)

$= [Ar]3d^8 4s^2 =$ 3d: ⥮ ⥮ ⥮ 1 1 | 4s: ⥮ | 4p: _ _ _

$Ni^{2+} = [Ar]3d^8 =$ 3d: ⥮ ⥮ ⥮ ⥮ _ | 4s: _ | 4p: _ _ _

Since, CN^- is a strong field ligand, so pairing of electrons will take place.

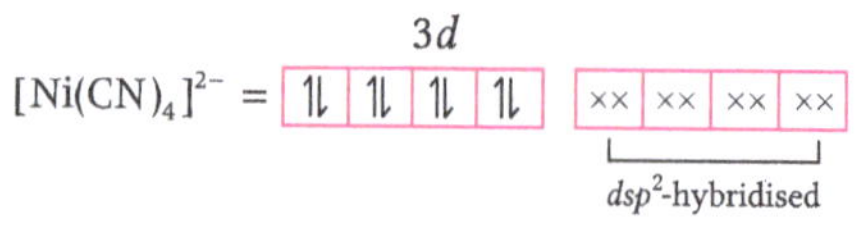

Thus, $[Ni(CN)_4]^{2-}$ is diamagnetic and the shape of the complex is square planar.

Therefore, out of Pari and Suhail's responses, Suhail's response was correct.

8. (i) As compound 'X' does not react with sodium metal or potassium permanganate, it cannot be an alcohol.

(ii) As compound 'X' dissolves in conc. H_2SO_4, it may be an ether.

(iii) As compound 'X' on heating with excess of HI, gives a single alkyl halide, therefore compound 'X' must be a symmetrical ether.

(iv) The only symmetrical ether having molecular formula $C_4H_{10}O$ is diethyl ether.

Thus, compound 'X' is diethyl ether, $CH_3—CH_2—O—CH_2—CH_3$.

$$CH_3CH_2—O—CH_2CH_3 \xrightarrow{\text{Conc. } H_2SO_4} \left[CH_3—CH_2—\overset{+}{\underset{|}{O}}—CH_2—CH_3\right]HSO_4^-$$
(with H on O) Soluble oxonium salt

$$\underset{\substack{(X)\\ \text{Diethyl ether}}}{CH_3CH_2OCH_2CH_3} \xrightarrow[\Delta]{HI} \underset{\text{Ethyl iodide}}{2CH_3CH_2—I}$$

9. (i) (a) $\underset{\text{Benzladehyde}}{C_6H_5CHO} \xrightarrow[(2)\ SOCl_2]{(1)\ K_2Cr_2O_7/H_2SO_4} \underset{\substack{\text{Benzoyl chloride}\\(A)}}{C_6H_5COCl} \xrightarrow{C_6H_6\ (\text{Anhy. } AlCl_3)} \underset{\substack{\text{Benzophenone}\\(B)}}{C_6H_5COC_6H_5}$

(b) $\underset{\text{Propyne}}{CH_3—C\equiv CH} \xrightarrow[\substack{(2)\ \text{Vigorous oxidation,}\\ \text{conc. } HNO_3}]{(1)\ H_2SO_4/HgSO_4} \underset{\substack{\text{Acetic acid}\\(A)}}{CH_3COOH} \xrightarrow[\text{conc. } H_2SO_4]{C_2H_5OH} \underset{\substack{\text{Ethyl ethanoate}\\(B)}}{CH_3COOC_2H_5}$

Or

(ii) (a) The possible functional isomers of carbonyl compound with molecular formula, C_4H_8O are

$CH_3—\underset{}{CH}(CH_3)—CHO$, $CH_3CH_2CH_2CHO$, $CH_3CH_2—\overset{O}{\overset{||}{C}}—CH_3$

- Isomers (A) and (C) give positive Tollen's test, thus they must be aldehydes.

$$\underset{\text{Aldehyde}}{RCHO} + \underset{\text{Tollen's reagent}}{2[Ag(NH_3)_2]^+} + 3OH^- \xrightarrow{\Delta} RCOO^- + \underset{\text{Silver mirror}}{2Ag\downarrow} + 2H_2O + 4NH_3\uparrow$$

$CH_3—CH(CH_3)—CHO$ and $CH_3CH_2CH_2CHO$

- Isomer (B) does not give Tollen's test, but gives positive Iodoform test, thus it must be a ketone with $CH_3—\overset{O}{\overset{||}{C}}—$ group.

$$RCOCH_3 \xrightarrow{NaOX} RCOONa + CHX_3\ [X = Cl, Br, I]$$

Isomers (A) and (B) on reduction with Zn(Hg) / conc. HCl give same product.

$$CH_3—CH(CH_3)—CHO + 4[H] \xrightarrow{\text{Zn-Hg/conc. HCl}} CH_3CH(CH_3)—CH_3 + H_2O$$

$$CH_3—CH_2—CH_2—CHO + 4[H] \xrightarrow{\text{Zn-Hg/conc. HCl}} CH_3—CH_2—CH_2—CH_3 + H_2O$$

$$CH_3CH_2COCH_3 + 4[H] \xrightarrow{\text{Zn-Hg/conc. HCl}} CH_3CH_2CH_2CH_3 + H_2O$$

So, the structures of (A), (B) and (C) are $\underset{(A)}{CH_3CH_2CH_2CHO}$, $\underset{(B)}{CH_3CH_2COCH_3}$, $\underset{(C)}{CH_3CH(CH_3)—CHO}$,

(b) The isomer (B) is least reactive towards addition of HCN.

Since, aldehydes are more reactive towards nucleophilic addition reactions than ketones due to inductive and steric effects.

10. Given, $E^\circ_{Al^{3+}/Al} = -1.66$ V

$E^\circ_{Sn^{2+}/Sn} = -0.14$ V

For the given cell,

Al/Al^{3+} (0.01 M) || Sn^{2+} (0.015 M)/Sn

$$E^\circ_{cell} = E^\circ_{cathode} - E^\circ_{anode}$$
$$= -0.14\text{ V} - (-1.66)\text{ V}$$
$$= 1.52\text{ V}$$

The half-cell reactions are as follows

At anode

$$Al(s) \longrightarrow Al^{3+}(aq) + 3e^-] \times 2$$

At cathode

$$Sn^{2+}(aq) + 2e^- \longrightarrow Sn(s)] \times 3$$

Overall reaction

$$2Al(s) + 3Sn^{2+}(aq) \longrightarrow 2Al^{3+}(aq) + 3Sn(s)$$

$$E_{cell} = E^{\circ}_{cell} - \frac{0.0591}{n}\log\frac{[Al^{3+}]^2}{[Sn^{2+}]^3}$$

Here, n = number of electrons transferred, i.e., 6

$$\therefore \quad E_{cell} = 1.52 - \frac{0.0591}{6}\log\frac{[0.01]^2}{[0.015]^3}$$

$$E_{cell} = 1.52 - \frac{0.0591}{6}(\log(10)^5 - \log(15)^3)$$

$$\Rightarrow \quad E_{cell} = 1.52 - \frac{0.0591}{6} \times (5 - 3.528)$$

$$\therefore \quad E_{cell} = 1.5056\ V$$

Now, $\Delta G = -nFE^{\circ}_{cell}$

$$\therefore \quad \Delta G = (-6\ mol) \times (96500\ C\ mol^{-1}) \times (1.5056\ V)$$

$$= -871742\ J$$

11. (i) **Propan-1-ol and propan-2-ol**

Propan-1-ol and propan-2-ol can be distinguished by Lucas test.

$$\underset{\substack{\text{Propan-1-ol}\\\text{(Primary alcohol)}}}{CH_3CH_2CH_2OH} + HCl \xrightarrow[ZnCl_2]{\text{Anhydrous}} \underset{\substack{n\text{-propyl chloride}\\\text{(Do not produce turbidity}\\\text{at room temperature)}}}{CH_3CH_2CH_2Cl} + H_2O$$

$$\underset{\substack{\text{Propan-2-ol}\\\text{(Secondary alcohol)}}}{CH_3-\underset{OH}{\underset{|}{CH}}-CH_3} + HCl \xrightarrow{\text{Anhydrous } ZnCl_2} \underset{\substack{\text{2-chloropropane}\\\text{(Produces turbidity after 5}\\\text{mins at room temperature)}}}{CH_3-\underset{Cl}{\underset{|}{CH}}-CH_3} + H_2O$$

(ii) **Ethanol and phenol**

Phenol gives violet colouration complex with $FeCl_3$ solution but ethanol does not

$$\underset{\text{Phenol}}{6C_6H_5OH} + FeCl_3 \longrightarrow \underset{\text{Violet colour complex}}{[Fe(OC_6H_5)_6]^{3-}} + 3H^+ + 3HCl$$

12. (i)

$$\underset{\text{Nitrobenzene}}{C_6H_5NO_2} \xrightarrow[Sn/HCl]{6[H]} \underset{\substack{\text{Aniline}\\(A)}}{C_6H_5NH_2} \xrightarrow[273-278\ K]{HNO_2 + HCl}$$

$$\underset{\substack{\text{Benzene diazonium}\\\text{chloride}\\(B)}}{C_6H_5N_2^+Cl^-} \xrightarrow[\text{(Coupling reaction)}]{C_6H_5NH_2} \underset{\substack{p\text{-aminoazobenzene}\\(C)}}{C_6H_5N=NC_6H_4NH_2}$$

(ii)

$$\underset{\text{Ethanamine}}{CH_3CH_2NH_2} \xrightarrow[\text{(2) Red P}/Cl_2]{\text{(1) }HNO_2} \underset{\substack{\text{Ethyl chloride}\\(A)}}{CH_3CH_2Cl} \xrightarrow[\text{(2) }H_2O/H^+]{\text{(1) KCN}}$$

$$\underset{\substack{\text{Propanoic acid}\\(B)}}{CH_3CH_2COOH} \xrightarrow[\text{(2) }Br_2/KOH]{\text{(1) }NH_3/\text{heat}} \underset{\substack{\text{Ehanamine}\\(C)}}{CH_3CH_2NH_2}$$

13. (i) For case A,

Given, $W_2 = 5.85$ g

$W_1 = 100$ g

$T_f = -3.348°C = 269.652$ K

$K_f = 1.86$ K Kg mol^{-1}

Molecular mass = 58.5 g/mol

As we know that,

$$\Delta T_f = T_f^{\circ} - T_f$$

$$\therefore \quad \Delta T_f = 273 - 269.652 = 3.348\ K$$

$\because$ Observed molecular mass

$$M_2 = \frac{K_f \times W_2 \times 1000}{\Delta T_f \times W_1}$$

$$\therefore \quad M_2 = \frac{1.86 \times 5.85 \times 1000}{3.348 \times 100} = 32.5\ g/mol$$

Now, For case B,

Given, $W_2 = 0.2$ g

$W_1 = 20$ g

$\Delta T_f = 0.45°C = 0.45$ K

$K_f = 5.12$ Kg mol^{-1}

Molecular mass = 60 g/mol

$\because$ Observed Molecular mass

$$M_2 = \frac{K_f \times W_2 \times 1000}{\Delta T_f \times W_1}$$

$$\therefore \quad M_2 = \frac{5.12 \times 0.2 \times 1000}{0.45 \times 20} = 113.78\ g/mol$$

(ii) As we know that,

$$\text{van't Hoff factor} = \frac{\text{Normal molecular mass}}{\text{Observed molecular mass}}$$

Therefore, $[A]$ will undergo dissociation as its van't Hoff factor (i) value is 18. Whereas, $[B]$ will undergo association as its van't Hoff factor (i) value is 0.53.

(iii) The given order of depression in freezing point is correct. This is because ΔT_f depends on the number of moles of solute molecules.

14. (i) **Rosenmund's reaction** Acyl chloride or acid chloride is hydrogenated in the presence of palladium catalyst supported over and partially poisoned by the addition of sulphur or barium sulphate.

$$\underset{\text{Acetyl chloride}}{CH_3-\overset{}{\underset{O}{\underset{\|}{C}}}-Cl} \xrightarrow[Pd/BaSO_4,\ S]{H_2} \underset{\text{Acetaldehyde}}{CH_3-\overset{O}{\overset{\|}{C}}-H}$$

(ii) **Benzoin condensation** The addition reaction between two kinds of aromatic aldehydes especially benzaldehyde in presence of cyanide ions as a catalyst to form, α-hydroxy ketone.

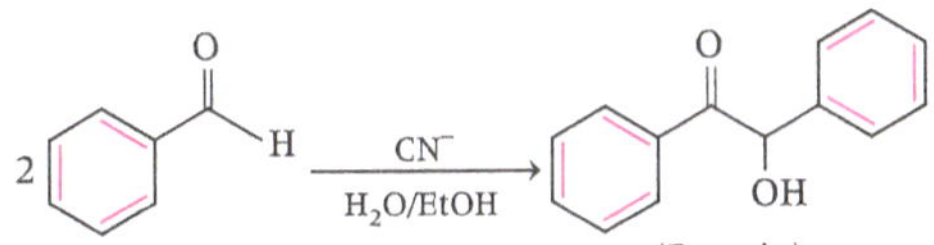

Benzaldehyde (Benzoin)

(iii) **Perkin's reaction** This reaction gives an α, β-unsaturated aromatic acid *via* Aldol condensation of aromatic aldehyde and an acid anhydride. It occurs in the presence of alkali, which acts as a base catalyst in the reaction.

FULLY SOLVED

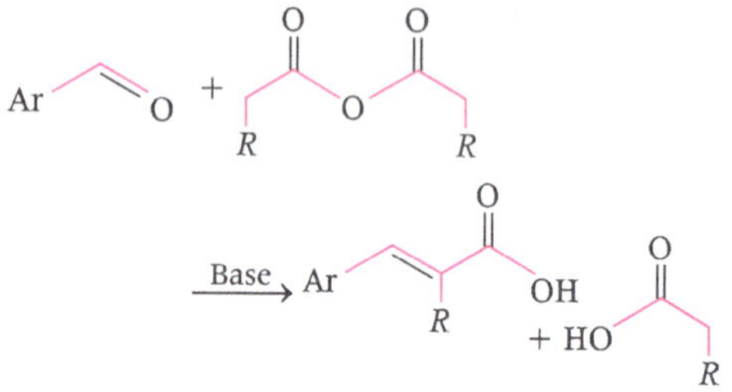

15. (i) The formula and IUPAC name of two coordination complex ions (C.N = 6) with cyanide ligand and iron as central metal atom is as follows

- $[Fe(CN)_6]^{4-}$
  IUPAC name — Hexacyanidoferrate (II) ion
- $[Fe(CN)_6]^{3-}$
  IUPAC name — Hexacyanidoferrate (III) ion

(ii) (a) If $\Delta_o > P$, then ligand will be a strong ligand. Therefore, it will become more energetically favourable for the fourth electron to occupy t_{2g} orbital with configuration $t_{2g}^4 e_g^0$.

If $\Delta_o < P$, then ligand will be a weak field ligand. Therefore, the fourth electron will enter one of the e_g orbitals giving the configuration $t_{2g}^3 e_g^1$.

16. (i) (a) • Dry cell consists of a zinc container which acts as the anode.

• The cathode is a carbon (graphite) rod surrounded by a mixture of powdered manganese dioxide and carbon.

(b) The space between anode and cathode is filled with moist paste of ammonium chloride and zinc chloride.

(c) Dry cell do not have a long life because the acidic NH_4Cl corrodes the zinc container.

Or

(ii) (a) If salt bridge is removed from the two half-cells, then cell will not function. This is because, electricity flow will stop after sometime as positive charge will accumulate at oxidation half-cell and negative at reduction half-cell which balance the redox free energy and thus, will stop the redox reaction.

(b) Copper sulphate solution cannot be stored in a zinc pot because zinc being more reactive than copper, displaces copper from its salt solution.

(c) The density of H_2SO_4 in a lead storage battery decreases as it is discharged. This is because sulphate is consumed from the electrolyte due to the formation of lead sulphate.

17. (i) The peptide bond linkage in glycylalanine is shown below.

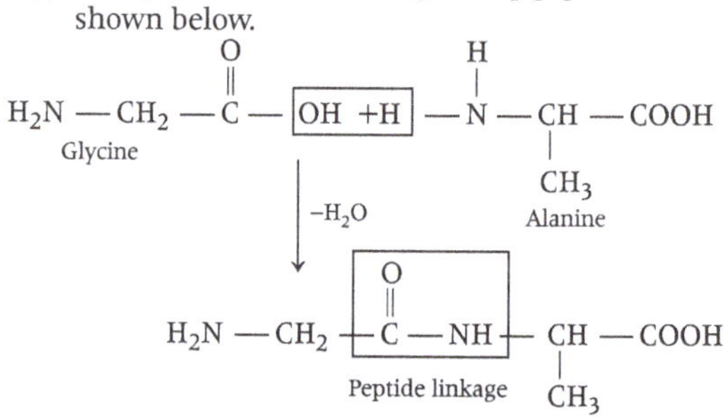

(ii) When a nucleotide from DNA containing thymine is hydrolysed, then β-D-2-deoxyribose (pentose sugar), phosphoric acid and thymine (nitrogenous base) are obtained as products.

(iii) Reducing sugars are the carbohydrates in which ketonic or aldehydic groups are free and are capable of reducing Fehling's solution or Tollen's reagent.
e.g. Glucose, fructose, ribose etc.

18. (i) Rate law for the given reaction
$A + B \rightarrow$ Product may be expressed as

$$\text{Rate} = k[A]^x[B]^y$$

$$(\text{Rate})_1 = 4.0 \times 10^{-4} = k(0.1)^x(0.1)^y \quad \ldots(\text{i})$$

$$(\text{Rate})_2 = 1.6 \times 10^{-3} = k(0.2)^x(0.2)^y \quad \ldots(\text{ii})$$

$$(\text{Rate})_3 = 1.0 \times 10^{-2} = k(0.5)^x(0.1)^y \quad \ldots(\text{iii})$$

$$(\text{Rate})_4 = 1.0 \times 10^{-2} = k(0.5)^x(0.5)^y \quad \ldots(\text{iv})$$

On dividing Eq^n (iii) by Eq^n (ii), we get

$$\frac{(\text{Rate})_3}{(\text{Rate})_1} = \frac{1.0 \times 10^{-2}}{4.0 \times 10^{-4}} = \frac{k(0.5)^x(0.1)^y}{k(0.1)^x(0.1)^y}$$

$$\Rightarrow (5)^2 = (5)^x \quad \therefore \quad x = 2$$

On dividing Eq^n (iv) by Eq^n (iii), we get

$$\frac{(\text{Rate})_4}{(\text{Rate})_3} = \frac{1.0 \times 10^{-2}}{1.0 \times 10^{-2}} = \frac{k(0.5)^x(0.5)^y}{k(0.5)^x(0.1)^y}$$

$$(1)^0 = (5)^y$$

$$\therefore \quad y = 0$$

Thus, order with respect A is 2 and with respect to B is 0.

(ii) Now, Rate $= k[A]^2[B]^0$
Putting values in Eq. (i), we get

$$4.0 \times 10^{-4} = k[0.1]^2$$

$$\therefore \quad k = \frac{4.0 \times 10^{-4}}{0.1 \times 0.1}$$

$$= 4 \times 10^{-2} \text{ mol}^{-1} \text{ L sec}^{-1}$$

(iii) If $[A] = 0.2$ mol $L^{-1}sec^{-1}$ and $[B] = 0.35$ mol $L^{-1}sec^{-1}$
Then, reaction rate can be calculated as

$$\text{Rate} = k[A]^2[B]^0$$

$$\therefore \quad \text{Rate} = 4 \times 10^{-2}[0.2]^2[0.35]^0$$

$$\Rightarrow \text{Rate} = 4 \times 10^{-2} \times 4 \times 10^{-2}$$

$$= 1.6 \times 10^{-3} \text{ mol L}^{-1}\text{sec}^{-1}$$

19. (i)

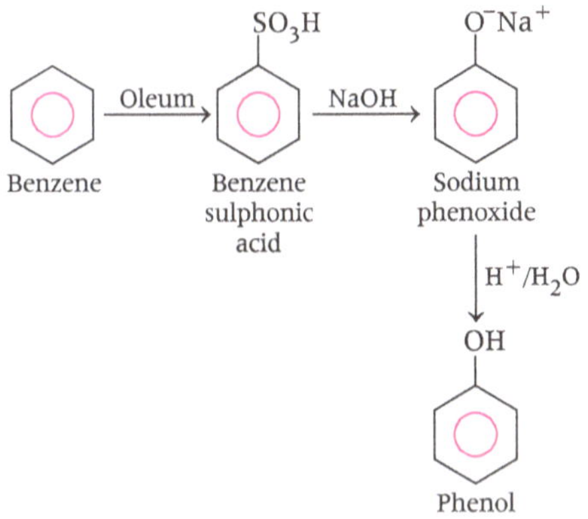

(ii) When phenol reacts with Br_2/CS_2 at low temperature, then monobromophenols are formed. The reaction is as follows

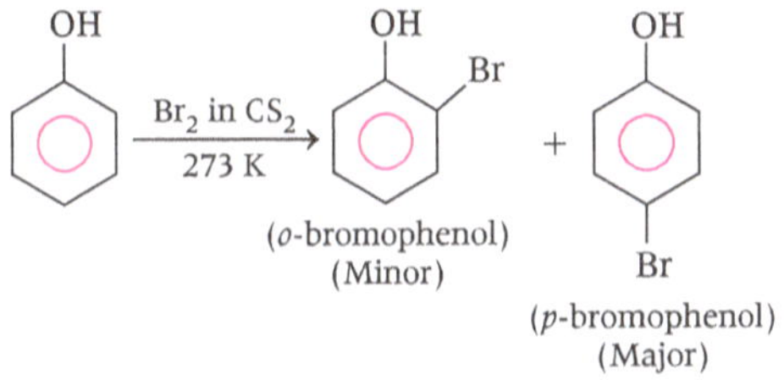

(iii) When phenol reacts with neutral $FeCl_3$ solution, then ferric phenoxide complex is formed. Following reaction takes place

$$6C_6H_5OH + FeCl_3 \longrightarrow \underset{\text{Violet colour complex}}{[Fe(OC_6H_5)_6]^{3-}} + 3H^+ + 3HCl$$

(iv) Picric acid is prepared by first treating phenol with conc. H_2SO_4 at 373 K and then with HNO_3.

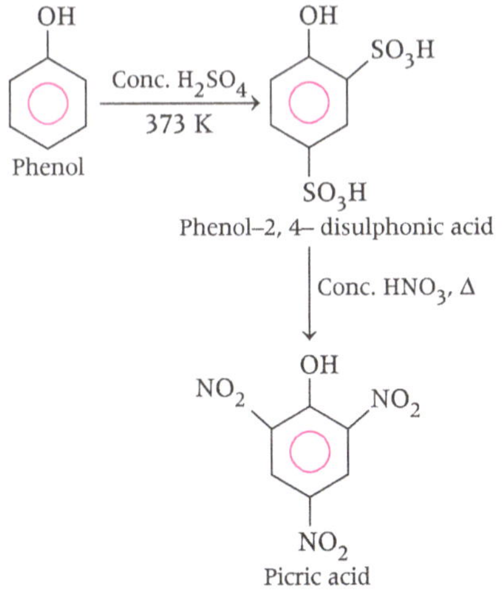

(v) On treating phenol with chloroform in the presence of sodium hydroxide, —CHO group is introduced at *ortho*-position of benzene ring.

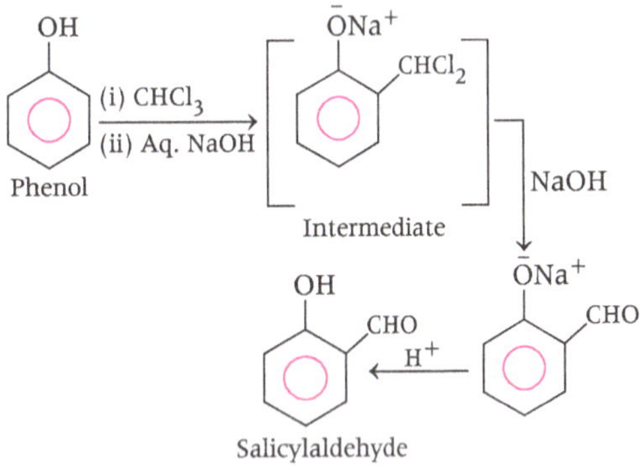

20. (i) (a) When oxalic acid is added to acidic solution of $KMnO_4$, its colour disappear due to the reduction of MnO_4^- ion to Mn^{2+}. Following chemical reaction takes place.

$$5C_2O_4^{2-} + 2MnO_4^- + 16H^+ \longrightarrow \underset{\text{(Colourless)}}{2Mn^{2+}} + 8H_2O + 10CO_2$$

(b) Some transition metals and their compounds are attracted towards magnetic field due to presence of unpaired electrons in *d*-orbitals.

(c) Mn^{2+} compounds (E.C, $[Ar]3d^5$) are more stable towards (+3) oxidation state due to half-filled *d*-orbitals.

On the other hand, Fe^{2+} compounds (E.C, $[Ar]3d^6$) are comparatively less stable as they have six electrons in their orbitals. So, they tend to lose one electron from Fe^{3+} and get stable $3d^5$ configuration.

(ii) (a) $2KMnO_4 + 8H_2SO_4 + 10FeSO_4 \longrightarrow K_2SO_4 + 2MnSO_4 + 5Fe_2(SO_4)_3 + 8H_2O$

(b) $K_2Cr_2O_7 + 7H_2SO_4 + 6KI \longrightarrow 4K_2SO_4 + Cr_2(SO_4)_3 + 3I_2 + 7H_2O$

21. (i) Two solutions having same osmotic pressure at a given temperature are called isotonic solutions.

(ii) Given, $\pi = 8.21$ atm

$$T = 273 + 27 = 300 \text{ K}$$

$$V = 100 \text{ mL} = 0.1 \text{ L}$$

As we know that, $\pi = \dfrac{n}{V} RT$

$$\therefore 8.21 = \frac{W_2 \times 0.0821 \times 300}{180 \times 0.1}$$

$$\Rightarrow W_2 = \frac{8.21 \times 180 \times 0.1}{0.0821 \times 300} = 6 \text{ g}$$

(iii) Given, $\pi = 8.21$ atm

$$T = 273 + 37 = 310 \text{ K}$$

$$V = 0.1 \text{ L}$$

As we know that,

$$\pi = \frac{n}{V} RT$$

$$\therefore \quad \pi = \frac{6 \times 0.0821 \times 310}{180 \times 0.1}$$

$$\pi = 8.48 \text{ atm}$$

(iv) The given statement is false. As solution having less osmotic pressure than the other solution is called hypotonic solution. Thus, a pure NaCl solution with salt concentration less than 0.91% (mass/volume) is hypotonic with human blood.

(v) Edema is caused by taking a lot of salt or salty food. This happens because people experience water retention in tissue, cells and intercellular spaces because of osmosis.

Or

(i) Mass of urea, $W_2 = 8.0$ g

Mass of water, $W_1 = 250$ g

$$T_b^{\circ} = 373 \text{ K}$$

$$K_b = 0.52 \text{ K kg mol}^{-1}$$

Molecular mass of urea, $M_2 = 60$ g/mol

As we know that,

$$\Delta T_b = \frac{K_b \times W_2 \times 1000}{M_2 \times W_1}$$

$$\therefore \quad \Delta T_b = \frac{0.52 \times 8 \times 1000}{250 \times 60}$$

$$\Delta T_b = 0.277 \text{ K}$$

Now, $\Delta T_b = T_b - T_b^{\circ}$

$\because$ Freezing point of urea solution,

$$T_b = (0.277 + 373) \text{ K}$$
$$= 373.277 \text{ K}$$

(ii) Mass of water, $W_1 = 4$ kg or 4000 g

$$T_f = -6°\text{C}$$

$$K_f = 1.86 \text{ K kg mol}^{-1}$$

As we know that,

$$\Delta T_f = T_f^{\circ} - T_f$$
$$= 0 - (-6°\text{C})$$
$$= 6°\text{C or } 6 \text{ K}$$

Now, $\Delta T_f = \dfrac{K_f \times W_2 \times 1000}{W_1 \times M_2}$

$$W_2 = \frac{6 \times 4000 \times 62.07}{1000 \times 1.86}$$

Amount of urea, $W_2 = 800.9$ g

(iii) Molality does not change with change in temperature. While, molarity of a solution decrease with rise in temperature due to increase in volume.

SAMPLE QUESTION PAPER 1

A Highly Simulated Sample Question Paper for ISC Class XII

CHEMISTRY (Fully Solved)

Time : 3 hours

Max. Marks : 70

GENERAL INSTRUCTIONS

- This paper is divided into four sections A, B , C and D. Answer all questions.
- **Section A** has **fourteen subparts**. Each question carries 1 mark.
- While attempting **Multiple Choice Questions** in Section A, you are required to **write only ONE option as the answer.**
- **Section B** has **ten questions.** Each question carries 2 marks.
- **Section C** has **seven questions.** Each question carries 3 marks.
- **Section D** has **three questions.** Each question carries 5 marks.
- Internal choices have been provided in **one question each in Section B, Section C & Section D.**
- All working, including rough work, should be done on the same sheet as, and adjacent to the rest of the answer.
- The intended marks for questions are given in brackets [].
- Balanced equations must be given wherever possible and diagrams where they are helpful.
- When solving numerical problems, all essential working must be shown.
- In working out problems, use the following data :

  Gas constant R = 1.987 cal deg^{-1} mol^{-1} = 8.314 J K^{-1} mol^{-1} = 0.0821 dm^3 atm K^{-1} mol^{-1} 1 L atm = 1 dm^3 atm = 101.3 J.

  1 Faraday = 96500 coulombs. **Avogadro's number** = 6.023×10^{23}.

FULLY SOLVED

Section A (14 Marks)

1. (A) Fill in the blanks by choosing the appropriate word(s) from those given in brackets.

[oxidation, *p*-benzoquinone, reduction, benzoic acid, mol $L^{-1}s^{-1}$, mol $^{-1}$L s^{-1}, s^{-1}, red, black, white, paramagnetic, diamagnetic, octahedral, tetrahedral] **[4 × 1]**

(i) For a first order reaction, the unit of rate is ...... and that of rate constant is .... • *Recall*

(ii) When formic acid reacts with Tollen's reagent and Fehling solution it gives ...... and ...... ppt. respectively. • *Recall*

(iii) The complex $[Mn(H_2O)_6]^{2+}$ ion has ...... geometry and is ...... magnetic in nature. • *Understanding*

(iv) Phenol on ...... with chromic acid gives .... • *Recall*

(B) Select and write the correct alternative from the choices given below. **[7 × 1]**

(i) Which of the following is resistant to nucleophilic attack by hydroxyl ions? • *Analysis*

(a) Methyl acetate (b) Acetonitrile
(c) Acetamide (d) Diethyl ether

(ii) At pH = 4, glycine exists as • *Understanding*

(a) $H_3N^+—CH_2—COO^-$ (b) $H_3N^+—CH_2—COOH$
(c) $H_2N—CH_2—COOH$ (d) $H_2N—CH_2COO^-$

(iii) For strong electrolytes, the plot of molar conductance *versus* $\sqrt{C}$ is • *Recall*

(a) parabolic (b) linear
(c) sinusoidal (d) circular

(iv) During a chemical reaction with increase in temperature, rate of a reaction • *Understanding*

(a) decreases
(b) increases
(c) remains constant
(d) show irregular trends

(v) Which of the following statements are correct, when a mixture of NaCl and $K_2Cr_2O_7$ is gently warmed with conc. H_2SO_4? • *Analysis*

I. A deep red vapours is evolved.

II. The vapours when passed into NaOH solution gives a yellow solution of Na_2CrO_4.

III. Chlorine gas is evolved.

IV. Chromyl chloride is formed.

Choose the correct option.

(a) Both I and II (b) I, II and III
(c) I, II and IV (d) Both III and IV

(vi) **Assertion** (A) On increasing dilution, specific conductance increases.

Reason (R) Degree of ionisation of weak electrolyte increases and mobility of ions also increases. • *Analysis*

(a) Both (A) and (R) are true and (R) is the correct explanation of (A).
(b) Both (A) and (R) are true but (R) is not the correct explanation of (A).
(c) (A) is true and (R) is false.
(d) (A) is false and (R) is true.

(vii) **Assertion** (A) Nitration of chlorobenzene leads to the formation of *ortho* and *para*-nitrochlorobenzene.

Reason (R) —NO_2 group is a *o*, *p*-directing group. • *Analysis*

(a) Both (A) and (R) are true and (R) is the correct explanation of (A).
(b) Both (A) and (R) are true but (R) is not the correct explanation of (A).
(c) (A) is true and (R) is false.
(d) (A) is false and (R) is true.

(C) Read the passage given below and answer the questions that follows. **[3 × 1]**

There are nuclear reactions constantly occuring in our body, but there are very few of them compared to the chemical reactions, and they do not affect our bodies much. Nuclear reactions occuring in our bodies is radioactive decay.

The most common natural radioactive isotopes in human are carbon-14 and potassium 40. The natural occurrence of carbon-14 decay in the body is the core principle behind carbon dating.

(i) Radioactive decay follows which order kinetics. Write the unit of rate constant for the reaction. • *Analysis*

(ii) Draw the plot of $t_{1/2}$ *vs* $[A]_o$ for first order reaction. • *Evaluate*

(iii) Approximately how old is a fossil with 12 g of carbon-14, if it initially possessed 32 g of carbon-14? (Given $\log 2.667 = 0.4260$, $t_{1/2} = 6000$) • *Application*

Section B (20 Marks)

2. The vapour pressure of water is 15.6 kPa at 300 K. Calculate the vapour pressure of a one molal solution of a non-volatile, non-ionic solute in water. • *Evaluate* **[2]**

3. Complete the following equations. • *Recall* **[2]**

(i) $2CrO_4^{2-} + 2H^+ \longrightarrow$ (ii) $KMnO_4 \xrightarrow{\text{Heat}}$

4. Calculate the mass of compound (molar mass = 256 g mol^{-1}) to be dissolved in 75 g of benzene to lower its freezing point by 0.48 K. ($K_f = 5.12$ K kg mol^{-1}) • *Application* **[2]**

5. Write equations involved in following reactions. • *Recall* **[2]**

(i) Williamson's ether synthesis (ii) Kolbe's reaction

6. Give reason for the following. **[2]**

(i) Zn^{2+} salts are white while Ni^{2+} salts are blue. • *Understanding*

(ii) Why Mn^{3+} acts as strong oxidising agent? • *Understanding*

7. Deficiency of which vitamin causes the following diseases. • *Recall* **[2]**

(i) Bleeding gums (ii) Weak eyesight

8. (i) During working of a mercury cell, write the reaction taking place at • *Understanding*

(a) anode (b) cathode

(ii) Given that the standard reduction potential for $Cr^{3+}/Cr = -0.72$ V and $Fe^{2+}/Fe = -0.42$ V. What will be the standard potential of the cell? • *Evaluate* **[2]**

9. Identify compounds [*A*] and [*B*] in the following reactions. **[2]**

(i) 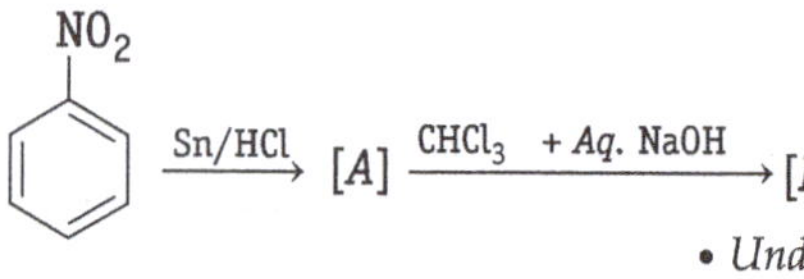

• *Understanding*

(ii) 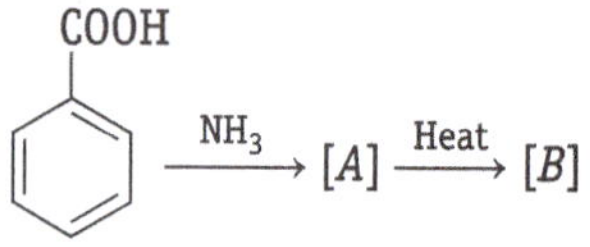

• *Understanding*

Or

An aromatic compound [*A*] on heating with Br_2 and KOH forms a compound [*B*] of molecular formula C_6H_7N which on reaction with $CHCl_3$ and alc. KOH produces a foul smelling compound *C*. Identify the compounds [*A*], [*B*], [*C*] and give the IUPAC name of [*C*]. • *Understanding*

10. A reactant has a half-life of 10 min. **[2]**

(i) Calculate the rate constant for the first order reaction. • *Application*

(ii) What fraction of the reactant will be left after an hour of the reaction has occurred? • *Application*

11. Write chemical equations when **[2]**

(i) ethyl chloride is treated with aqueous KOH. • *Understanding*

(ii) CH_3Br is treated with KCN. • *Understanding*

Section C (21 Marks)

12. In a reaction between *A* and *B*, the initial rate of reaction (r_0) was measured for different initial concentrations of *A* and *B* as given below:

$A/\text{mol L}^{-1}$	0.20	0.20	0.40
$B/\text{mol L}^{-1}$	0.30	0.10	0.05
$r_0/\text{mol L}^{-1}\text{ s}^{-1}$	5.07×10^{-5}	5.07×10^{-5}	1.43×10^{-4}

What is the order of the reaction with respect to *A* and *B*? • *Application* **[3]**

13. Give reasons for the following. • *Understanding*

(i) Ethyl iodide undergoes S_N2 reaction faster than ethyl bromide.

(ii) (±) 2-butanol is optically inactive.

(iii) C—*X* bond length in halobenzene is smaller than C—*X* bond length in CH_3—*X*. **[3]**

14. Arrange the following compounds in the increasing order of their property as indicated. • *Analysis*

$CH_3CH_2CH(Br)COOH$, $CH_3CH(Br)CH_2COOH$, $(CH_3)_2CHCOOH$, $CH_3CH_2CH_2COOH$. **[3]**

(i) in the increasing order of their acidic strength.

(ii) in the increasing order of their pK_a values.

15. Henry's law constant for the molality of methane in benzene at 298 K is 4.27×10^5 mm of Hg. Calculate the solubility of methane in benzene at 298 K under 760 mm of Hg. • *Application*

Or The solubility of $Ba(OH)_2 \cdot 8H_2O$ in water is 5.6 g per 100 g of water at 288 K. Calculate the molality of hydroxide ion in saturated solution of $Ba(OH)_2 \cdot 8H_2O$ at that temperature. • *Evaluate* **[3]**

16. Give reason for the following. • *Understanding*

(i) *d*-block elements exhibit a large number of oxidation states than *f*-block elements.

(ii) Sc^{3+} ion does not show paramagnetism.

(iii) Transition metal exhibit high enthalpy of atomisation. **[3]**

17. Identify the structures of *A*, *B* and *C* in the following reactions. • *Understanding* **[3]**

(i) $C_6H_5N_2Cl \xrightarrow{CuCN} [A] \xrightarrow[\Delta]{H_2O/H^+} [B] \xrightarrow[\Delta]{NH_3} [C]$

(ii) $CH_3CH_2I \xrightarrow{NaCN} [A] \xrightarrow[\text{Partial hydrolysis}]{OH^-} [B] \xrightarrow{NaOH+Br_2} [C]$

Or

How will the following be converted? (Give chemical equations) • *Understanding*

(i) Nitrobenzene to aniline

(ii) Acetamide to ethylamine

(iii) Benzene to acetanilide

18. Predict the major product of acid catalysed dehydration of • *Understanding* **[3]**

(i) 1-methyl cyclohexanol. (ii) Butan-1-ol.

Section D (15 Marks)

19. (i) A steady current of 2 amperes was passed through two electrolytic cells *X* and *Y* connected in series containing electrolytes $FeSO_4$ and $ZnSO_4$ until 2.8 g of Fe deposited at the cathode of cell *X*. How long did the current flow? Calculate the mass of Zn deposited at the cathode of cell *Y*. (Molar mass : Fe = 56 g mol^{-1} Zn = 65.3 g mol^{-1}, 1F = 96500 C mol^{-1}) • *Application*

(ii) In the plot of molar conductivity (Λ_m) *vs* square root of concentration ($C^{1/2}$), following curves are obtained for two electrolytes *A* and *B*.

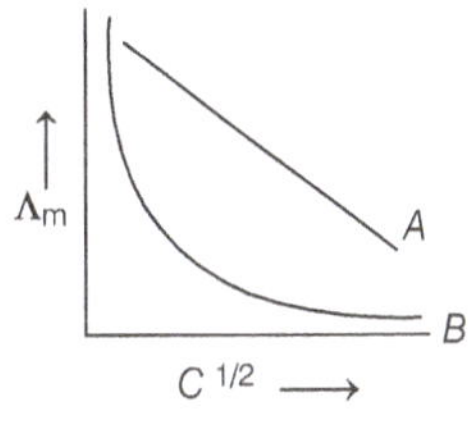

Predict the nature of electrolytes *A* and *B*. Justify your answer. • *Analysis*

Or

(i) Calculate E°_{cell} for the following reaction at 298 K:

$$2Al(s) + 3Cu^{2+}(0.01\text{ M}) \longrightarrow 2Al^{3+}(0.01\text{ M}) + 3Cu(s)$$

Given, $E_{cell} = 1.98$ V • *Evaluate*

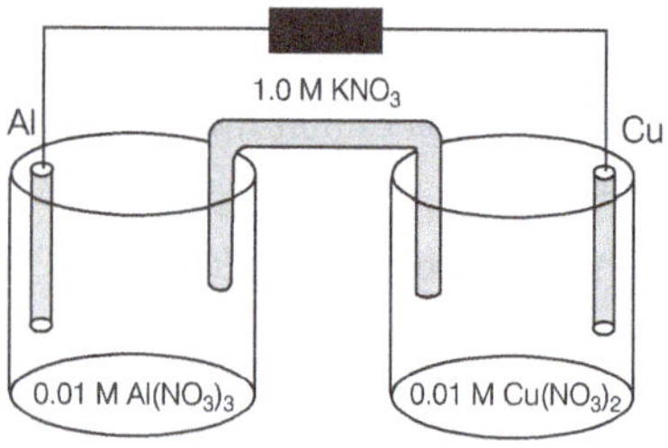

(ii) Calculate the potential of hydrogen electrode in contact with a solution whose pH is 10. • *Application* **[5]**

20. (i) Write the chemical equation to illustrate the following name reactions. • *Recall*

(a) Clemmensen reduction

(b) Rosenmund reduction

(c) HVZ reaction

(ii) Give one chemical test to distinguish between the pair of compounds. • *Understanding*

(a) Formaldehyde and acetaldehyde

(b) Acetone and acetic acid **[5]**

21. (i) Name the type of isomerism shown by the following pairs of coordination compounds. • *Understanding*

(a) $[Cu(NH_3)_4][PtCl_4]$ and $[Pt(NH_3)_4][CuCl_4]$

(b) $[Cr(SCN)(H_2O)_5]^{2+}$ and $[Cr(NCS)(H_2O)_5]^{2+}$

(c) $[Cr(H_2O)_6]Cl_3$ and $[CrCl(H_2O)_5]Cl_2 \cdot H_2O$

(ii) Find the hybridisation and magnetic nature of the complex $[Fe(H_2O)_6]^{2+}$. • *Understanding* **[5]**

SOLUTIONS

1. (A) (i) mol $L^{-1}s^{-1}$, s^{-1} (ii) black, red

(iii) octahedral, paramagnetic

(iv) oxidation, *p*-benzoquinone

(B) (i) (d) Diethyl ether is resistant to nucleophilic attack by hydroxyl ions because it is a Lewis base and is not easily attacked by nucleophile (OH^-).

(ii) (b) At pH = 4, glycine exist as

$$H_3N^+—CH_2—COOH.$$

In the acidic medium (pH = 4), COO^- group gets protonated.

(iii) (b) The plot of molar conductance (Λ_m) *versus* $\sqrt{C}$ it linear,

(iv) (b) Rate of a reaction increases with increase in temperature.

(v) (c) Statements I, II and IV are correct, while the statement III is incorrect. It's correct form is as follows

On warming the mixture of NaCl and $K_2Cr_2O_7$ gently with conc. H_2SO_4 deep red vapours of chromyl chloride is evolved. When it is passed into NaOH solution it gives a yellow solution of Na_2CrO_4.

(vi) (d) (A) is false and (R) is true. On dilution, conductance (*G*) decreases, so specific conductance (κ) also decreases because according to relation, $\kappa = G\sigma$ and $\kappa \propto G$.

(vii) (c) (A) is true and (R) is false, presence of —Cl in chlorobenzene activates the ring at *ortho* and *para*-positions and therefore, nitration of chlorobenzene leads to formation of *o*, *p*-nitrochlorobenezne. While $—NO_2$ group is a *meta*-directing group.

(C) (i) Radioactive decay follows first- order kinetics because the rate of decay is directly proportional to the number of radioactive nuclei present and not on any other factor. The unit of rate constant for first order kinetics is s^{-1}.

(ii) For first order reaction, $t_{1/2}$ is independent of $[A]_0$ (initial concentration). The graph between the concentration and $t_{1/2}$ for the reaction is as follows.

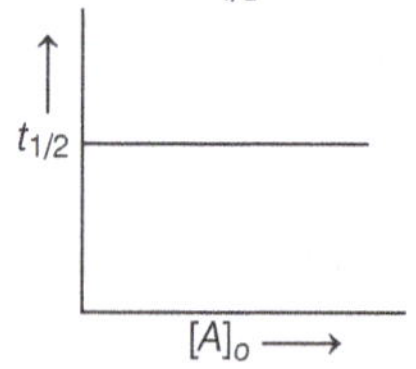

(iii) Given, initial amount of C-14 present in fossil $C_0 = 32$ g

Final amount of C -14, i.e., $C_t = 12$ g .

Time $(t) = ?$

For 1st order reaction, $k = \frac{0.693}{6000}$

[half-life, i.e. 6000, is given]

For 1st order reactions

$$t = \frac{2.303}{k}\log\left(\frac{C_0}{C_t}\right) \quad \ldots(i)$$

Substituting the given value in Eqn. (i), we get

$$t = \frac{2.303}{0.693} \times 6000 \times \log\frac{32}{12}$$

$$= 19939.4 \times \log 2.667$$

$$= 19939.4 \times 0.426 = 8494 \text{ years}$$

2. As solution is 1 molal, it means that 1 mole of solute is dissolved in 1000 g of solvent (water).

Moles of solute = 1 mol

Moles of water $= \frac{1000}{18} = 55.55$ mol

∴ Total moles = 56.55

Mole fraction of water $= \frac{55.55}{56.55}$

$$\left[\because \text{Mole fraction of solvent } (\chi) = \frac{\text{Moles of solvent}}{\text{Total moles}}\right]$$

Now, according to Raoult's law,

$$p_{solution} = p_{solvent} \times \chi_{solvent\,(H_2O)}$$

$$p_{solution} = 15.6 \times \frac{55.55}{56.55} = 15.32 \text{ kPa}$$

3. (i) $2CrO_4^{2-} + 2H^+ \longrightarrow Cr_2O_7^{2-} + H_2O$

(ii) $2KMnO_4 \xrightarrow{\text{Heat}} K_2MnO_4 + MnO_2 + O_2$

4. Given that, $K_f = 5.12$ K kg mol^{-1}

Mass of benzene, $W_1 = 75$ g

Depression in freezing point,

$$\Delta T_f = 0.48 \text{ K}, M_2 = 256 \text{ g mol}^{-1}$$

If w_2 is the mass of compound.

Then, $$\Delta T_f = \frac{K_f \times w_2 \times 1000}{W_1 \times M_2}$$

(where, M_2 is molar mass of compound)

or $$0.48 = \frac{5.12 \times w_2 \times 1000}{75 \times 256}$$

∴ $$w_2 = \frac{0.489 \times 75 \times 256}{5.12 \times 1000} = 1.8 \text{ g}$$

5. (i) When alkyl halide reacts with sodium alkoxide, ether is formed. This reaction is known as **Williamson's ether synthesis.**

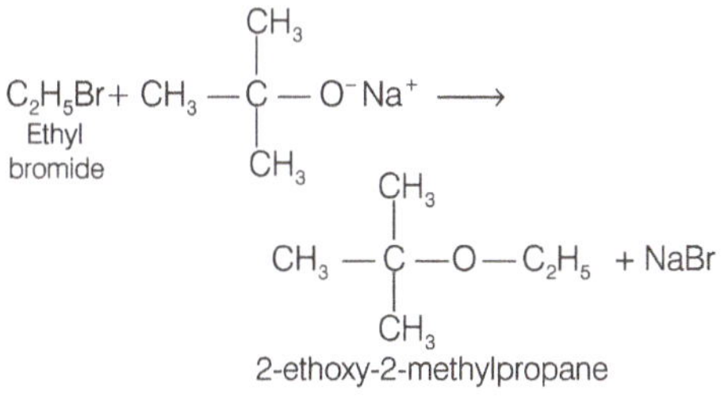

(ii) **Kolbe's reaction** When sodium phenoxide (generated by treating phenol with NaOH) is heated with CO_2 at about 400 K and under 4 to 7 atmospheric pressure, sodium salicylate is formed as major product, which on acidification gives salicylic acid.

e.g.

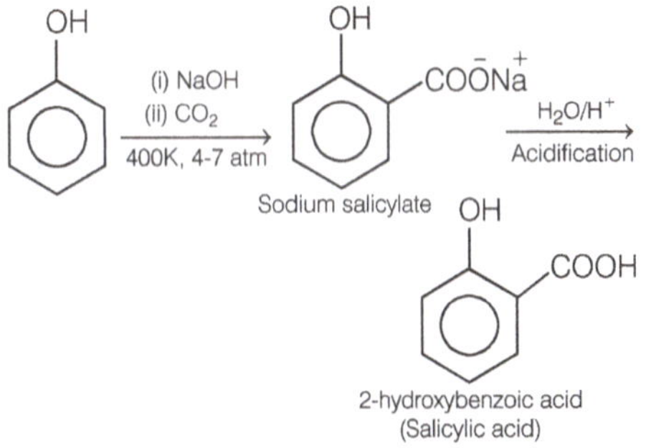

6. (i) Electronic configuration of $Zn^{2+} = 3d^{10}4s^0$

= | ⥮ | ⥮ | ⥮ | ⥮ | ⥮ |

Electronic configuration of $Ni^{2+} = 3d^8 4s^0$

= | ⥮ | ⥮ | ⥮ | ↿ | ↿ |

Salts that contains unpaired electrons are coloured due to presence of d-d transition thus, Zn^{2+} salts are white while Ni^{2+} salts are blue.

(ii) In the +3 oxidation state, Mn is a strong oxidising agent electronic configuration is $3d^4$ which is less stable and it can reduce to Mn^{+2} giving a more stable $3d^5$-configuration. Hence, it acts as a strong oxidising agent.

7. (i) Vitamin C

(ii) Vitamin A

8. (i) In mercury cell, anode is made up of zinc mercury amalgam and cathode is of paste of HgO and carbon powder.

Electrode reactions are as follows.

(a) At anode

$$Zn(Hg) + 2\bar{O}H \longrightarrow ZnO(s) + H_2O + 2e^-$$

(b) At cathode

$$HgO + H_2O + 2e^- \longrightarrow Hg(l) + 2OH^-$$

(ii) $$E^\circ_{cell} = E^\circ_{cathode} - E^\circ_{anode}$$

$$= -0.42 - (-0.72)$$

$$= 0.3 \text{ V}$$

9. (i)

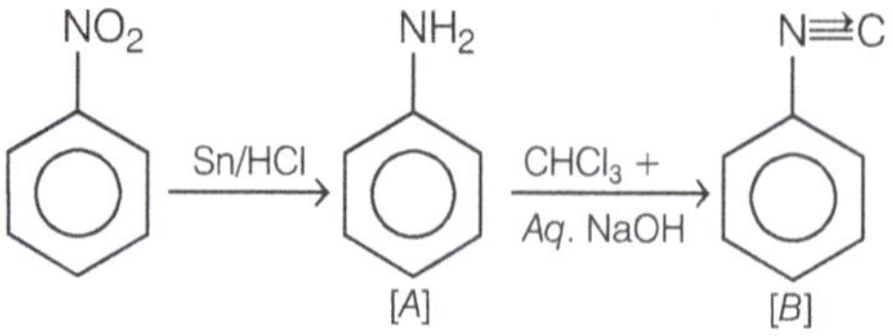

(ii)

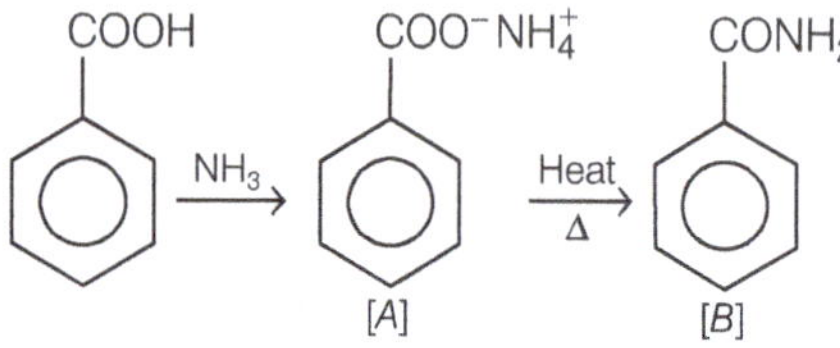

Or

Since, compound '*A*' on heating with Br_2 and KOH forms a compound '*B*' which further reacts with $CHCl_3$ and alc. KOH producing a foul smelling compound '*C*'.

Thus, compound '*C*' is an aromatic isocyanide and compound *B* is aniline with formula $C_6H_5NH_2$ and compound *A* must be benzamide. Reaction involved are as follows

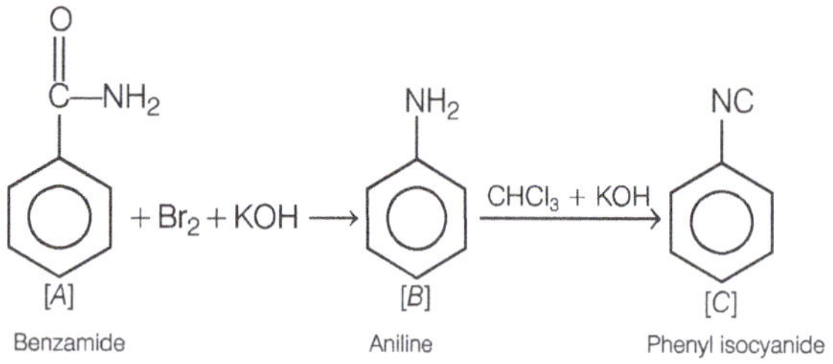

10. (i) $k = \frac{0.693}{t_{1/2}} = \frac{0.693}{10} = 0.0693\ \text{min}^{-1}$

(ii) $N = N_0\left(\frac{1}{2}\right)^n$

where, $n = \frac{\text{Total time}}{t_{1/2}} = \frac{60}{10} = 6$

$$\frac{N}{N_0} = \left(\frac{1}{2}\right)^6 = \frac{1}{64}$$

[where, N_0 = initial amount of reactant and N = amount of reactant left after time t]

11. (i) Ethyl chloride undergo hydrolysis when treated with aqueous KOH to form ethyl alcohol. (Through S_N2 nucleophilic substitution)

$$\underset{\text{Ethyl chloride}}{C_2H_5Cl} + KOH(aq) \longrightarrow \underset{\text{Ethyl alcohol}}{C_2H_5OH} + KCl$$

(ii) When CH_3Br is treated with KCN, methyl cyande is obtained.

$$\underset{\text{Bromomethane}}{CH_3 - Br} + \underset{\text{(alc.)}}{K{-}CN} \longrightarrow \underset{\text{Methyl cyanide}}{CH_3 - CN} + KBr$$

12. Rate law states that rate $= k\,[A]^x[B]^y$

$(\text{Rate})_1 = k\,[0.20]^x[0.30]^y = 5.07\times 10^{-5}$ ...(i)

$(\text{Rate})_2 = k\,[0.20]^x\,[0.10]^y = 5.07\times 10^{-5}$ ...(ii)

$(\text{Rate})_3 = k[0.40]^x[0.05]^y = 1.43\times 10^{-4}$ ...(iii)

On dividing Eq. (i) by Eq. (ii), we get

$$\frac{(\text{Rate})_1}{(\text{Rate})_2} = \frac{k[0.20]^x[0.30]^y}{k[0.20]^x[0.10]^y} = \frac{5.07\times10^{-5}}{5.07\times10^{-5}} = 1$$

$$[3]^y = [3]^0$$

$$y = 0$$

Now, on dividing Eq. (iii) by Eq. (ii), we get

$$\frac{(\text{Rate})_3}{(\text{Rate})_2} = \frac{k\,(0.40)^x(0.05)^0}{k\,(0.20)^x(0.10)^0} = \frac{1.43\times 10^{-4}}{5.07\times 10^{-5}}$$

$$2.8205 = 2^x\left(\frac{1}{2}\right)^0 = 2^x$$

$$\log 2.8205 = x \log 2$$

$$x = \frac{0.4503}{0.3010} = 1.5$$

Thus, order of the reaction with respect to *A* and *B* are 1.5 and 0, respectively.

13. (i) Iodide is a better leaving group because of its larger size than bromide, therefore, ethyl iodide undergoes S_N2 reaction faster than ethyl bromide.

(ii) (±) 2-butanol is a racemic mixture. It is a mixture which contains two enantiomers in equal proportion and thus, have zero optical rotation due to internal compensation. Therefore, it is optically inactive.

(iii) In halobenzenes (like chlorobenzene), the lone pair of electrons on halogen atom is delocalised on the benzene ring. As a result, C—*X* bond (C—Cl bond in case of chlorobenzene) acquires some double bond character while in CH_3—*X*, C—*X* bond is a pure single bond. Therefore, C—*X* bond in halobenzene is shorter than in CH_3—*X*.

14. (i) As +*I* - effect of isopropyl group is more than that of *n*-propyl group, therefore, $(CH_3)_2CHCOOH$ is a weaker acid than $CH_3CH_2CH_2COOH$. Since, –*I*- effect decreases with distance, therefore, $CH_3CH_2CH(Br)COOH$ is a stronger acid than $CH_3CH_2CH(Br)CH_2COOH$.

Hence, increasing order of acidic strength is:

$(CH_3)_2CHCOOH < CH_3CH_2CH_2COOH < CH_3CH(Br)CH_2COOH < CH_3CH_2CH(Br)COOH$

(ii) The pK_a values indicates the strength of an acid. Lower pK_a value means stronger acid. So, the correct order of their pK_a values is

$CH_3CH_2CH(Br)COOH < CH_3CH(Br)CH_2COOH < CH_3CH_2CH_2COOH < (CH_3)_2CHCOOH$

15. According to Henry's law, $p = K_H \cdot \chi$

So, $\chi = \frac{p}{K_H} = \frac{760}{4.27\times 10^5} = 1.78\times 10^{-3}$

or the mole fraction of methane in benzene is 1.78×10^{-3}.

FULLY SOLVED

Or Molar mass of $Ba(OH)_2 \cdot 8H_2O$

$$= 137 + 2 \times 17 + 8 \times 18$$
$$= 315 \text{ g mol}^{-1}$$

$\therefore$ 100 g water has 5.6 g of $Ba(OH)_2 \cdot 8H_2O$

$\therefore$ 1000 g water will have $Ba(OH)_2 \cdot 8H_2O = 56$ g

Number of moles of

$$Ba(OH)_2 \cdot 8H_2O = \frac{56}{315} = 0.178 \text{ mol}$$

Thus, molality of $Ba(OH)_2 = 0.178$ m

$$Ba(OH)_2 \longrightarrow Ba^{2+} + 2OH^-$$

Molality of OH^- ions = 2 × Molality of $Ba(OH)_2$

$$= 2 \times 0.178 = 0.356 \text{ m}$$

16. (i) This is because the difference of energy between $(n-1)d$ and ns-orbitals is very small. Hence, electrons from both the energy levels can be removed to exhibit variable oxidation states. In f-block elements, there is large gap in energy of $4f$ and $5d$-subshells, thus the number of oxidatioin states of f-block is limited.

(ii) E.C. of Sc = $[Ar]4s^2 3d^1$

E.C. of Sc^{3+} = [Ar]

Sc^{3+} ion does not show paramagnetism because it achieve noble gas configuration of Ar (argon), so it's d-orbitals are empty, hence no unpaired electron is present.

(iii) The transition element exhibit higher enthalpies of atomisation because of strong interatomic interaction due to large number of unpaired electrons in d-orbitals and hence the bond becomes stronger.

17. (i) $C_6H_5N_2Cl \xrightarrow{CuCN} \underset{\text{Benzonitrile (A)}}{C_6H_5CN}$

$$\xrightarrow[\Delta]{H_2O/H^+} \underset{\text{Benzoic acid (B)}}{C_6H_5COOH} \xrightarrow[\Delta]{NH_3} \underset{\text{Benzamide (C)}}{C_6H_5CONH_2}$$

(ii) $CH_3CH_2I \xrightarrow{NaCN} \underset{\text{Ethyl cyanide (A)}}{CH_3CH_2CN} \xrightarrow{OH^-}$

$$\underset{\text{Propanamide (B)}}{CH_3CH_2CONH_2} \xrightarrow{NaOH + Br_2} \underset{\text{Ethylamine (C)}}{CH_3CH_2NH_2}$$

Or

(i) $\underset{\text{Nitrobenzene}}{C_6H_5NO_2} + 3H_2 \xrightarrow[\text{Fe + HCl}]{\text{Sn + HCl Or}} \underset{\text{Aniline}}{C_6H_5NH_2} + 2H_2O$

(ii) $\underset{\text{Acetamide}}{CH_3-\overset{\overset{O}{\|}}{C}-NH_2} \xrightarrow[P_2O_5]{\Delta} \underset{\text{Methyl cyanide}}{CH_3C{\equiv}N} + H_2O$

$$\xrightarrow[LiAlH_4]{4[H]} \underset{\text{Ethylamine}}{CH_3CH_2NH_2}$$

(iii) $\underset{\text{Benzene}}{C_6H_6} \xrightarrow[-H_2O]{HNO_3/H_2SO_4} \underset{\text{Nitrobenzene}}{C_6H_5NO_2} \xrightarrow[-2H_2O]{4[H]\ (Sn + HCl)}$

$$\underset{\text{Aniline}}{C_6H_5NH_2} \xrightarrow[-HCl]{CH_3COCl} \underset{\text{Acetanilide}}{C_6H_5NHCOCH_3}$$

18. (i)

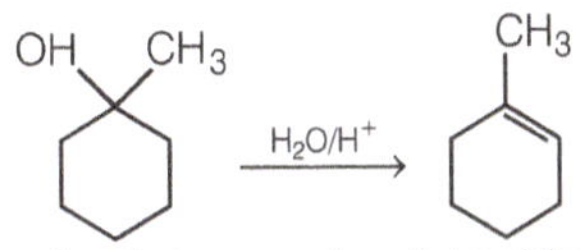

1-methyl cyclohexanol → 1-methyl cyclohex-1-ene

(ii) $\underset{\text{Butan-1-ol}}{CH_3CH_2CH_2CH_2-\ddot{O}H} \xrightarrow{+H^+}$

$$\underset{\text{Protonated alcohol}}{CH_3CH_2CH_2CH_2-\overset{+}{O}H_2} \xrightarrow{-H_2O} \underset{\text{1° carbocation}}{CH_3CH_2-\underset{H}{CH}-\overset{+}{C}H_2}$$

$$\xrightarrow{\text{1, 2-hydride shift}} \underset{\text{2° carbocation (II) (More stable)}}{CH_3-CH_2-\overset{\oplus}{C}H-CH_3} \xrightarrow{-H^+}$$

$$\underset{\text{But-1-ene (Minor)}}{CH_3CH_2CH{=}CH_2} + \underset{\text{But-2-ene (Major)}}{CH_3-CH{=}CH-CH_3}$$

19. (i) $Fe^{2+} + \underset{2F}{2e^-} \longrightarrow \underset{56g}{Fe}$

$\because$ 56 g of Fe is deposited by 2F or 2 × 96500 C charge

$\therefore$ 2.8 g of Fe will be deposited by

$$\frac{96500 \times 2 \times 2.8}{56} \text{ C charge} = 9650 \text{ C}$$

Now, $Q = It$

$\therefore$ Time, $t = \dfrac{9650}{2} = 4825$ s

$$Zn^{2+} + 2e^- \rightarrow Zn$$

$\because$ 2 × 96500 C charge deposits Zn = 65.3 g

$\therefore$ 9650 C charge will deposit

$$Zn = \frac{65.3 \times 9650}{96500 \times 2} = 3.27 \text{ g}$$

(ii) '*A*' is a strong electrolyte since there is a small increase in Λ_m with dilution while '*B*' is a weak electrolyte since Λ_m increases sharply near high dilution.

Or

(i) $2Al(s) + 3Cu^{2+}\ (0.01\text{ M}) \longrightarrow$

$2Al^{3+}\ (0.01\text{ M}) + 3\ Cu(s);\ E_{cell} = 1.98$ V

Applying Nernst equation for the given cell reaction,

$$E_{cell} = E^\circ_{cell} - \frac{0.0591}{n}\log\frac{[Al^{3+}]^2}{[Cu^{2+}]^3}$$

$$E^\circ_{cell} = E_{cell} - \frac{0.0591}{n}\log\frac{[Al^{3+}]^2}{[Cu^{2+}]^3}$$

FULLY SOLVED

Here, $n = 6$ (n = number of electrons transferred)

$$= 1.98 + \frac{0.0591}{6}\log\frac{(0.01)^2}{(0.01)^3}$$

$$= 1.98 + \frac{0.0591}{6}\log 100$$

$$= 1.98 + \frac{0.0591}{6}\times 2$$

[$\because \log 100 = \log 10^2 = 2\log 10 = 2$ as $\log 10 = 1$]

$$E^\circ_{cell} = 1.9997\ V \approx 2.0\ V$$

(ii) For hydrogen electrode,

$$H^+ + e^- \longrightarrow \frac{1}{2}H_2$$

Applying Nernst equation,

$$E_{(H^+/1/2H_2)} = E^\circ_{(H^+/1/2H_2)} - \frac{0.0591}{n}\log\frac{1}{[H^+]}$$

$$= 0 - \frac{0.0591}{1}\log\frac{1}{(10^{-10})}$$

($\because$ pH = 10, $[H^+] = 10^{-10}M$)

$$= 0 - \frac{0.0591}{1}\times(10\log 10) = -0.591\ V$$

Thus, $E_{(H^+/1/2H_2)} = -0.591\ V$

20. (i) (a) $CH_3-\underset{\underset{O}{\|}}{C}-CH_3 \xrightarrow[\text{Conc. HCl (Clemmensen reduction)}]{\text{Zn-Hg}} CH_3CH_2CH_3 + H_2O$

Acetone → Propane

(b) $CH_3-\underset{\underset{O}{\|}}{C}-Cl + H_2 \xrightarrow[\text{(Rosenmund reduction)}]{\text{Pd-BaSO}_4} CH_3-\underset{\underset{O}{\|}}{C}-Cl + HCl$

Acetyl chloride → Acetaldehyde

(c) $CH_3-CH_2-COOH \xrightarrow[\text{(II) } H_2O]{\text{(I) } Br_2,\ P} CH_3-\underset{\underset{Br}{|}}{CH}-COOH$

Carboxylic acid → α-bromocarboxylic acid

(ii) (a) **Iodoform test** When formaldehyde and acetaldehyde are treated with iodine in the presence of alkali, acetaldehyde gives yellow precipitate of iodoform, but formaldehyde does not give such precipitate.

$$\underset{\text{Acetaldehyde}}{CH_3CHO} + 4NaOH + 3I_2 \longrightarrow \underset{\text{Yellow ppt.}}{CHI_3\downarrow} + HCO\overset{-}{O}\overset{+}{Na} + 3NaI + 3H_2O$$

$$\underset{\text{Formaldehyde}}{HCHO} + 4NaOH + 3I_2 \longrightarrow \text{No iodoform test}$$

(b) Acetic acid when heated with ethyl alcohol in the presence of conc. H_2SO_4 it gives a fruity smell of an ester, (ethyl ethanoate) while acetone does not give this test.

$$\underset{\text{Acetic acid}}{CH_3COOH} + \underset{\text{Ethyl alcohol}}{C_2H_5OH} \xrightarrow[\text{Conc. } H_2SO_4]{\Delta} \underset{\text{Ethyl ethanoate}}{CH_3COOC_2H_5} + H_2O$$

$$\underset{\text{Acetone}}{CH_3-\overset{\overset{O}{\|}}{C}-CH_3} + \underset{\text{Ethyl alcohol}}{C_2H_5OH} \xrightarrow[\text{Conc. } H_2SO_4]{\Delta} \text{No reaction}$$

21. (i) (a) In both the given compounds, interchange of ligands (NH_3 and Cl) between cationic and anionic entities of different metal ion (Cu and Pt) takes place. Hence, they show **coordination isomerism**.

(b) In both compounds ambidentate ligand SCN is present. In $[Cr(SCN)(H_2O)_5]^{2+}$ complex, SCN is attached through S with Cr while in $[Cr(NCS)(H_2O)_5]^{2+}$ complex, NCS is attached through N with Cr. Hence, they show **linkage isomerism**.

(c) In both the compounds, number of solvent ligand molecules and counter ions differ in the crystal lattice. So, they show **hydrate isomerism**.

(ii) Let oxidation number of Fe in the complex ion $[Fe(H_2O)_6]^{2+}$ is x, then

$$x + 6\times 0 = +2$$

$$\Rightarrow \quad x = +2$$

Electronic configuration of Fe is $[Ar]3d^6 4s^2$.

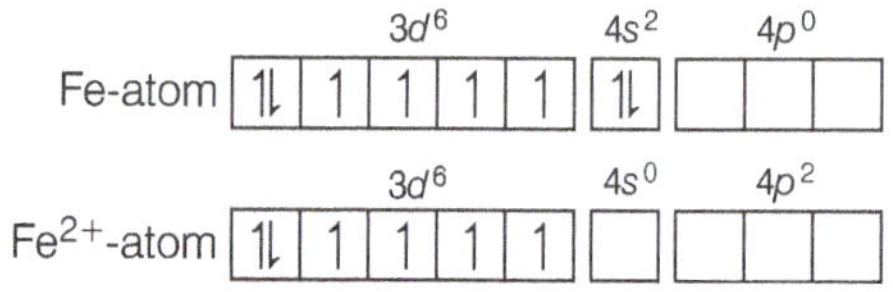

H_2O is a weak field ligand, so it will not pair up $3d^6$ electrons. Thus,

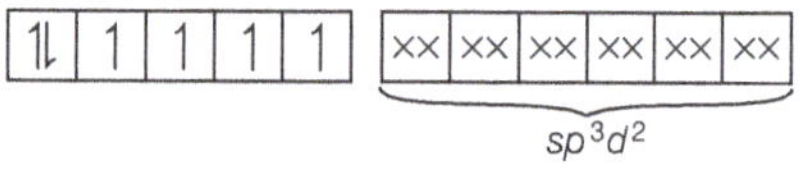

Coordination number of complex is 6. Hence, hybridisation is sp^3d^2.

It contains four unpaired electrons. So, it is paramagnetic.

SAMPLE QUESTION PAPER 2

A Highly Simulated Sample Question Paper for ISC Class XII

CHEMISTRY (Unsolved)

Time : 3 hours | Max. Marks : 70

GENERAL INSTRUCTIONS

- This paper is divided into four sections A, B , C and D. Answer all questions.
- **Section A** has **fourteen subparts**. Each question carries 1 mark.
- While attempting **Multiple Choice Questions** in Section A, you are required to **write only ONE option as the answer**.
- **Section B** has **ten questions**. Each question carries 2 marks.
- **Section C** has **seven questions**. Each question carries 3 marks.
- **Section D** has **three questions**. Each question carries 5 marks.
- Internal choices have been provided in **one question each in Section B, Section C & Section D.**
- All working, including rough work, should be done on the same sheet as, and adjacent to the rest of the answer.
- The intended marks for questions are given in brackets [].
- Balanced equations must be given wherever possible and diagrams where they are helpful.
- When solving numerical problems, all essential working must be shown.
- In working out problems, use the following data :
  Gas constant R = 1.987 cal deg^{-1} mol^{-1} = 8.314 J K^{-1} mol^{-1} = 0.0821 dm^3 atm K^{-1} mol^{-1} 1 L atm = 1 dm^3 atm = 101.3 J.
  1 Faraday = 96500 coulombs. **Avogadro's number** = 6.023×10^{23}.

UNSOLVED

Section A (14 Marks)

1. (A) Fill in the blanks by choosing the appropriate word(s) from those given in the brackets.

[mol $L^{-1}s^{-1}$, Co, second order, mol Ls^{-1}, nucleophilic, resonance stabilisation, CO_2, H_2O, first order, dihydric, explosive, trihydric] [4×1]

(i) The unit of the rate of a reaction is ...... and all radioactive disintegration reactions follow ...... kinetics. • *Recall*

(ii) The acidity of phenol is due to the .... of its anion and formation of phenol from chlorobenzene is an example of ...... aromatic substitution. • *Recall*

(iii) Formic acid when heated with conc. H_2SO_4 produces ...... and .... • *Recall*

(iv) Glycerol is a ...... alcohol and is used in making .... • *Understanding*

(B) Select and write the correct alternative from the choices given below. [7×1]

(i) Which of the following is/are rechargeable batteries? • *Recall*

(a) Nickel-cadmium
(b) Lead storage
(c) Both (a) and (b)
(d) None of these

(ii) Expression for the half-life of zero order reaction is given as • *Understanding*

(a) $t_{1/2} = \frac{[R]}{2k}$ (b) $t_{1/2} = \frac{[R]_0}{2k}$

(c) $t_{1/2} = \frac{0.693}{k}$ (d) $t_{1/2} = \frac{0.301}{k}$

(iii) The electrophile used in Reimer-Tiemann reaction is • *Understanding*

(a) $CCl_3^{\oplus}$ (b) $:CCl_2$

(c) $Cl^{\oplus}$ (d) H_2O

(iv) The spatial arrangement of the two or more polypeptide chains with respect to each other is known as ...*A*... of protein. Here, '*A*' is • *Analysis*

(a) primary structure
(b) secondary structure
(c) tertiary structure
(d) quaternary structure

(v) Which of the following statements are true about osmotic pressure? • *Analysis*

I. Flow of solvent from solution across a semipermeable membrane can be stopped, if some extra pressure is applied on solution.

II. It is the pressure that stops the flow of solvent towards solution.

III. It is the pressure that allows flow of solvent across the semipermeable membrane.

Choose the correct option.

(a) Both I and II
(b) Both II and III
(c) Both I and III
(d) I, II and III

(vi) **Assertion** (A) $H_2—O_2$ fuel cell gives a constant voltage throughout its life. • *Analysis*

Reason (R) In this fuel cell, H_2 reacts with OH^- ions yet the overall concentration of OH^- ions does not change. **[2 × 1]**

(a) Both (A) and (R) are true and (R) is the correct explanation of (A).
(b) Both (A) and (R) are true but (R) is not the correct explanation of (A).
(c) (A) is true and (R) is false.
(d) (A) is false and (R) is true.

(vii) **Assertion** (A) S_N1 mechanism is ruled out in case of haloarene.

Reason (R) Phenyl cation is formed as a result of self ionisation which is not stabilised by resonance. • *Analysis*

(a) Both (A) and (R) are true and (R) is the correct explanation of (A).
(b) Both (A) and (R) are true but (R) is not the correct explanation of (A).
(c) (A) is true and (R) is false.
(d) (A) is false and (R) is true.

UNSOLVED

(C) Read the passage given below and answer the questions that follows. **[3 × 1]**

In phenol, OH-group directly attached to sp^2-hybridised carbon of benzene ring acts as a electron withdrawing group and is responsible for the acidic nature of phenol. Due to this, the lone pair of electrons of O—H are involved in resonance with C-atoms of benzene ring. As a result of resonance, the oxygen atom acquires a partial positive charge. This weakens the O—H bond and, thus facilitates the release of a proton.

As a result, phenols behave as Bronsted acids. The reaction of phenol with aqueous NaOH indicates that phenols are stronger acids than alcohols. The reactions of phenol with metals such as Na, Al and NaOH indicate its acidic nature.

(i) Give the equation for the reaction of phenol with chloroform in presence of aqueous NaOH. • *Recall*

(ii) Which one is stronger acid, phenol or ethanol? • *Understanding*

(iii) Give one reaction showing the acidic nature of phenol. • *Recall*

Section B (20 Marks)

2. Calculate the molality of K_2CO_3 solution which is formed by dissolving 2.5 g of it in 1L of solution. Density of solution is 0.85 g mL^{-1}.
[**Ans.** 0.02 m] • *Evaluate* **[2]**

3. (i) A first order reaction has rate constant of $k = 1.15 \times 10^{-3} s^{-1}$. How long will it take for 6g of reactant to reduce to 3g.
[**Ans.** t = 602.8 s] • *Evaluate*

(ii) Express the rate of following reaction **[2]**
$N_2(g) + 3H_2(g) \longrightarrow 2NH_3(g)$ • *Understanding*

4. (i) Arrange the following solutions in order of increasing boiling point. • *Analysis*
1 M glucose, 2 M glucose and 3 M glucose.

(ii) What happens when the external pressure applied becomes more than osmotic pressure of the solutions. • *Understanding* **[2]**

5. Complete the following chemical equation.

(i) $Cr_2O_7^{2-} + 6Fe^{2+} + 14H^+ \longrightarrow$ • *Recall*

(ii) $2Cr_2O_4^{2-} + 2H^+ \longrightarrow$ **[2]**

6. Write the formula of the following compounds. • *Understanding* [2]
   (i) Triamminetriaquachromium(III) chloride
   (ii) Potassiumhexacyanoferrate(III)

7. (i) Give the reaction for the formation of phosgene gas. • *Understanding*
   (ii) What happens when phosgene gas reacts with ethanol? • *Understanding* [2]

8. How will you convert • *Recall* [2]
   (i) ethanoic acid into methanamine?
   (ii) hexane nitrile into 1-aminopentane?

Or An unknown aldehyde (A) reacts with an alkali to form β-hydroxy aldehyde which on heating produce but-2-en-1-ol (B). Compound (B) on reaction with conc. alkali produces two compounds (C) and (D). D is an alcohol with molecular formula C_7H_7O. Identify the compounds (A), (B), (C) and (D). • *Understanding*

9. Write IUPAC name of the following compound. • *Understanding* [2]

(i) 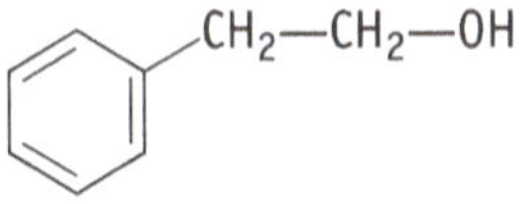

(ii) $H_3C—\underset{CH_3}{\underset{|}{C}}=\underset{Br}{\underset{|}{C}}—CH_2—OH$

10. Give a reason for each of the following. • *Understanding* [2]
    (i) Amino acids show amphoteric behaviour.
    (ii) Vitamin-C cannot be stored in our body.

11. Predict the product of electrolysis in each of the following. [2]
    (a) An aqueous solution of $AgNO_3$ with platinum electrodes. • *Understanding*
    (b) An aqueous solution of H_2SO_4 with platinum electrode. • *Understanding*

Section C (21 Marks)

12. Give reasons. • *Understanding*
    (i) *n*-butyl bromide has higher boiling point than *t*-butyl bromide.
    (ii) Racemic mixture is optically inactive.
    (iii) The presence of nitro group ($—NO_2$) at *o*/*p*-positions, increases the reactivity of haloarenes towards nucleophilic substitution reactions. [3]

13. (i) What is lanthanoid contraction? What are the consequences of lanthanoid contraction? • *Recall*
    (ii) Name the element which show only + 3 oxidation state. • *Recall* [3]

Or How would you account for following?
   (i) Transition metal shows variable oxidation state. • *Understanding*
   (ii) Orange colour of $Cr_2O_7^{2-}$ ion changes to yellow when treated with alkali. • *Understanding*
   (iii) Mn^{3+} is paramagnetic in nature. • *Understanding* [3]

14. At some temperature, the vapour pressure of pure C_6H_6 is 0.256 bar and that of pure $C_6H_5CH_3$ (toluene) is 0.0925 bar. If the mole fraction of toluene in solution is 0.6. Then, [3]
    (i) what will be the total pressure of the solution? • *Application*
    (ii) what will be the mole fraction of each component in vapour phase? • *Application*

15. Identify the compounds [A], [B] and [C] • *Understanding* [3]

(i) $C_6H_5Br \xrightarrow{\text{Mg/dry ether}} [A] \xrightarrow[\text{(b) } H_3O^+]{\text{(a) } CO_2(g)} [B] \xrightarrow{PCl_5} [C]$

(ii) $CH_3CN \xrightarrow[\text{(ii) } H_3O^+]{\text{(i) } SnCl_2/HCl} [A] \xrightarrow{\text{Dil. NaOH}} [B] \xrightarrow{\Delta} [C]$

16. The following results have been obtained during kinetic studies of the reaction: [3]

$$2A + B \longrightarrow C + D$$

Exp. No.	[A]	[B]	Initial rate of formation of D
1.	0.1 M	0.1 M	6.0×10^{-3} M min^{-1}
2.	0.3 M	0.2 M	7.2×10^{-3} M min^{-1}
3.	0.3 M	0.4 M	2.88×10^{-2} M min^{-1}
4.	0.4 M	0.1 M	2.40×10^{-2} M min^{-1}

Determine rate law and the rate constant for the reaction. • *Application*

17. Synthesize the following. • *Understanding* [3]
    (i) Butene to butanol
    (ii) 1-chloropropane to propan-1-ol
    (iii) Benzoic acid to benzyl alcohol

18. Arrange the following compounds. [3]
    $(CH_3)_3N$, $C_2H_5NH_2$, C_2H_5OH • *Analysis*
    (i) In the increasing order of their basic strength.
    (ii) In the decreasing order of their boiling point.

Section D (15 Marks)

19. (i) For the reaction,

$$2AgCl(s) + H_2(g)(1\ atm) \longrightarrow 2Ag(s) + 2H^+(0.1\ M) + 2Cl^-(0.1\ M),$$

$\Delta G° = -43600$ J at 25° C.

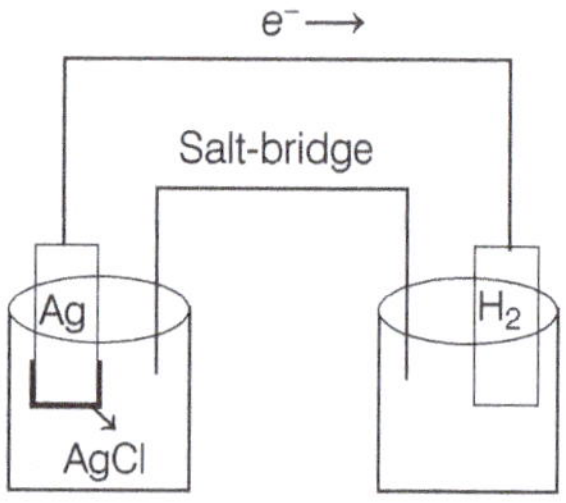

• *Application*

Calculate the emf of the cell.
[$\log 10^{-n} = -n$]

(ii) Define fuel cell and write its two advantages. • *Understanding* **[5]**

Or (i) The molar conductivity (Λ_m) of KCl solutions, at different concentration at 298 K, is plotted as shown in the figure given below.

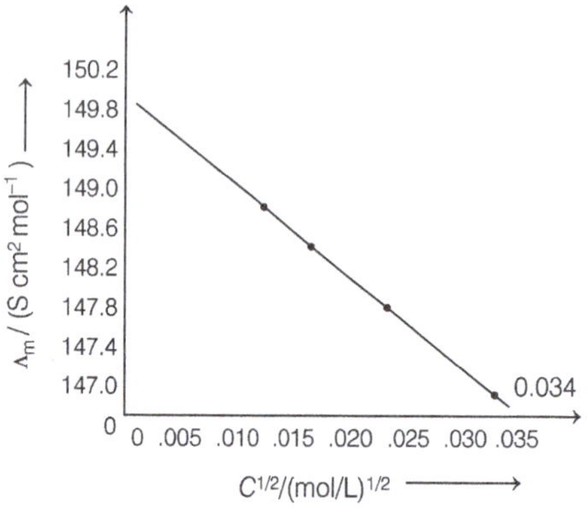

Determine the value of Λ_m° and A for KCl.
• *Application*

(ii) Calculate the emf of the following cell at 298 K.

$Mg(s)\,|Mg^{2+}(0.1\ M)\,||Cu^{2+}(1.0 \times 10^{-2}\ M)\,|Cu(s)$
[Given : $E^\circ_{cell} = 2.71$ V] [**Ans.** 2.6215 V]

• *Evaluate* **[5]**

20. (i) Write the hybridisation and magnetic character of the following complexes.

(a) $[Fe(H_2O)_6]^{2-}$ • *Understanding*
(b) $[Ni(CN)_4]^{2-}$
(c) $[Cr(NH_3)_3Cl_3]$

(Atomic number : Fe = 26, Ni = 28, Cr = 24]

(ii) Discuss the nature of bonding in the following coordiantion entities on the basis of valence bond theory. • *Understanding* **[5]**

(a) $[Fe(CN)_6]^{4-}$
(b) $[Co[C_2O_4)_3]^{3-}$

21. (i) Write the products formed when CH_3CHO reacts with the following reagents.

(a) HCN • *Understanding*
(b) $H_2N—OH$
(c) CH_3CHO in the presence of dilute NaOH.

(ii) Complete the following reaction. • *Recall*

(a) $2H—\underset{\underset{O}{||}}{C}—H \xrightarrow{\text{Conc. KOH}}$ **[5]**

(b) 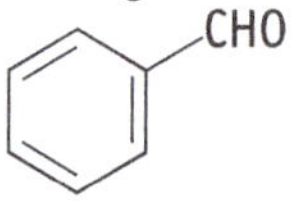 $\xrightarrow[273\text{-}283\ K]{HNO_3/H_2SO_4}$

Answers

(i) (c) (ii) (b) (iii) (b) (iv) (d)
(v) a (vi) (a) (vii) (a)

UNSOLVED

SAMPLE QUESTION PAPER 3

A Highly Simulated Sample Question Paper for ISC Class XII

CHEMISTRY (Unsolved)

Time : 3 hours | Max. Marks : 70

GENERAL INSTRUCTIONS

- This paper is divided into four sections A, B , C and D. Answer all questions.
- **Section A** has **fourteen subparts**. Each question carries 1 mark.
- While attempting **Multiple Choice Questions** in Section A, you are required to **write only ONE option as the answer.**
- **Section B** has **ten questions.** Each question carries 2 marks.
- **Section C** has **seven questions.** Each question carries 3 marks.
- **Section D** has **three questions.** Each question carries 5 marks.
- Internal choices have been provided in **one question each in Section B, Section C & Section D.**
- All working, including rough work, should be done on the same sheet as, and adjacent to the rest of the answer.
- The intended marks for questions are given in brackets [].
- Balanced equations must be given wherever possible and diagrams where they are helpful.
- When solving numerical problems, all essential working must be shown.
- In working out problems, use the following data :
  Gas constant R = 1.987 cal deg^{-1} mol^{-1} = 8.314 J K^{-1} mol^{-1} = 0.0821 dm^3 atm K^{-1} mol^{-1} 1 L atm = 1 dm^3 atm = 101.3 J.
  1 Faraday = 96500 coulombs. **Avogadro's number** = 6.023×10^{23}.

UNSOLVED

Section A (14 Marks)

1. (A) Fill in the blanks by choosing the appropriate word(s) from those given in brackets.

[log R, $\frac{1}{T}$, ln k, T, deoxyribose, ribose, HCl, H_2SO_4, anhydrous $ZnCl_2$, anhydrous $AlCl_3$, 1°, 2°, 3°] **[4 × 1]**

(i) The plot of ...... *versus* ...... has slopes equal to E_a/R. • *Recall*

(ii) In RNA, the sugar is ... but in DNA, it is .... • *Recall*

(iii) Lucas reagent is a mixture of conc. ... and ... . • *Recall*

(iv) Aldehyde gives ...... alcohol whereas ketones gives ...... alcohol on reduction. • *Understanding*

(B) Select and write the correct alternative from the choices given below. **[7 × 1]**

(i) Ionic mobility of Ag^+ is ($\lambda_{Ag^+} = 5 \times 10^{-4}$ ohm^{-1} cm^2 eq^{-1}) • *Evaluate*

(a) 5.2×10^{-9} (b) 2.4×10^{-9}
(c) 8.25×10^{-9} (d) 1.52×10^{-9}

(ii) Which of the following is most acidic? • *Understanding*

(a) Phenol
(b) Benzyl alcohol
(c) *m*-chlorophenol
(d) Cyclohexanol

(iii) 75% of first order reaction was completed in 32 min so, 50% of the reaction was completed in • *Application*

(a) 24 min (b) 8 min
(c) 16 min (d) 4 min

(iv) The pyrimidine bases present in DNA are • *Recall*
(a) cytosine and adenine
(b) cytosine and thymine
(c) cytosine and guanine
(d) cytosine and uracil

(v) Some of the following gases are soluble in water due to formation of their ions. • *Analysis*

I. CO_2 II. H_2 III. HCl IV. CH_4

Choose the water insoluble gases among them and mark the correct option.
(a) Only I and II
(b) Only II and IV
(c) Only II and III
(d) Only I and II

(vi) **Assertion** (A) Anhyd. HCl is a bad conductor of electricity while *aq*. HCl is a good conductor. • *Analysis*

Reason (R) Aqueous HCl is not fully ionised but anhyd. HCl is ionised to produce H^+ and Cl^- ions. **[2×1]**
(a) Both (A) and (R) are true and (R) is the correct explanation of (A).
(b) Both (A) and (R) are true but (R) is not the correct explanation of (A).
(c) (A) is true and (R) is false.
(d) (A) is false and (R) is true.

(vii) **Assertion** (A) CH_4 does not react with Cl_2 in dark.

Reason (R) Chlorination of CH_4 takes place in sunlight. • *Analysis*
(a) Both (A) and (R) are true and (R) is the correct explanation of (A).
(b) Both (A) and (R) are true but (R) is not the correct explanation of (A).
(c) (A) is true and (R) is false.
(d) (A) is false and (R) is true.

(C) Read the passage given below and answer the questions that follows **[3×1]**

Electrolysis is a process by which electric current passes through a substance to produce a chemical change. During electrolysis, the reactions occurring at the electrodes are the oxidation and reduction reactions.

Therefore, the products of electrolysis can be predicted on the basis of electrode potentials of different reactions.

The products of electrolysis depend on the nature of material being electrolysed and the types of electrodes being used.

If the electrode is inert such as gold or platinum, it does not take part in the chemical reaction and acts only as a source or sink for electrons. On the other hand, if the electrode is reactive, it takes part in the electrode reaction. Thus, the products of electrolysis may be different for inert and reactive electrodes.

The products of electrolysis mainly depend upon different oxidising and reducing species present in the electrolytic cell and their standard electrode potentials. It may be noted that some electrochemical processes, though feasible, are so slow kinetically that at lower voltages, these do not seem to occur.

(i) Why sugar cannot conduct electricity in aqueous solution ? • *Understanding*
(ii) At which electrode do oxidation and reduction takes place in electrolysis ? • *Understanding*
(iii) A solution of $Ni(NO_3)_2$ is electrolysed between platinum electrodes using a current of 5.0 A for 20 min. What mass nickel will be deposited at the cathode? • *Evaluate*

(Given : Atomic mass of Ni = 58.7 g mol^{-1}, 1 F = 96500 C mol^{-1})

Section B (20 Marks)

2. (i) Arrange the following equimolar solutions in order of decreasing order of osmotic pressure.

NaCl, $BaCl_2$, $AlCl_3$ and Glucose. • *Analysis*

(ii) Elevation of boiling point of 1 M KCl solution is nearly double than that of 1 M sugar solution. Justify the statement. • *Analysis* **[2]**

3. (i) On the basis of crystal field energy, write the electronic configuration of d^4 in terms of t_{2g} and e_g in an octahedral field when • *Application*
(a) $\Delta_o > P$
(b) $\Delta_o < P$

(ii) Find the number of unpaired electrons in complex $[Fe(H_2O)_6]^{3+}$ having magnetic moment value of 5.92 BM. • *Evaluate* **[2]**

4. On mixing liquid *X* and liquid *Y*, volume of the resulting solution decreases. What type of deviation from Raoult's law is shown by the resulting solution? What change in temperature would you observe after mixing liquids *X* and *Y*? • *Application* **[2]**

UNSOLVED

5. Balance and complete the following equations. [2]

(i) $(CH_3)_3—C—O—CH_3 + HI \longrightarrow$ • *Recall*

(ii) $CH_3—CH{=}CH_2 \xrightarrow[\text{(b) } 3H_2O_2/\overline{O}H]{\text{(a) } B_2H_6}$

6. Give reason for the following. [2]

(i) Lanthanoids do not form their carbonyl compound. • *Understanding*

(ii) The paramagnetic character in 3*d*-transition series elements increases upto Mn and then decreases. • *Understanding*

7. (i) What is the biological effect of denaturation of proteins? • *Understanding*

(ii) The two strands of DNA are not identical but are complementary. Explain. • *Understanding* [2]

8. The conductivity of 0.001 M acetic acid is 4×10^{-5} S/cm. Calculate the dissociation constant of acetic acid, if molar conductivity at infinite dilution for acetic acid is 390 S cm^2/mol.

[**Ans.** $K_a = 1.18 \times 10^{-5}$] • *Evaluate* [2]

9. Write equation for the following reactions. [2]

(i) Alkylation of anisole. • *Understanding*

(ii) *tert*-butylmethyl ether react with HBr at 373 K. • *Understanding*

Or

Compound *A* having molecular formula $C_4H_{10}O$, is found to be soluble in conc. H_2SO_4, but does not react with sodium metal or potassium permanganate. On heating with excess of HI it gives product *B*. Deduce *A* and *B*. • *Understanding*

10. Consider the reaction $R \rightarrow P$ for which the change in concentration of *R* with time is shown below. [2]

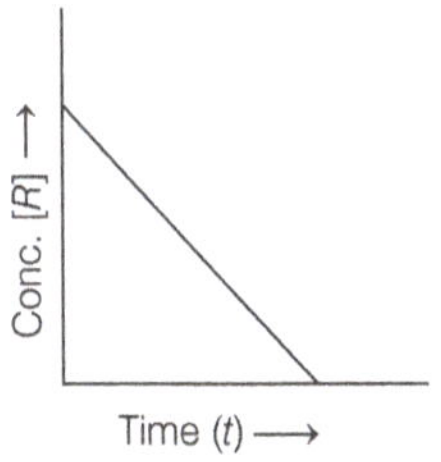

(i) Predict the order of reaction. • *Analysis*

(ii) What does the slope of the curve indicate ? • *Understanding*

11. Write equation for • *Recall* [2]

(i) Gabriel phthalimide reaction.

(ii) Hoffmann bromamide reaction.

Section C (21 Marks)

12. The following data were obtained during the first order thermal decomposition of SO_2Cl_2 at a constant volume: [3]

$$SO_2Cl_2(g) \longrightarrow SO_2(g) + Cl_2(g)$$

Experiment	Time	Total pressure/atm
1	0	0.4
2	100	0.7

Calculate the rate constant. • *Application*

(Given, log 4 = 0.6021, log 2 = 0.3010)

13. How can the following conversions be carried out? • *Understanding* [3]

(i) Ethyl chloride to propanoic acid

(ii) Ethanol to propane nitrile

(iii) 1-bromopropane to 2-bromopropane

14. Account for the following. [3]

(i) CH_3CHO is more reactive than CH_3COCH_3 towards reaction with HCN. • *Understanding*

(ii) Carboxylic acid is a stronger acid than phenol. • *Understanding*

(iii) $Cl—CH_2COOH$ is a stronger acid than CH_3COOH. • *Understanding*

15. 45 g of ethylene glycol ($C_2H_6O_2$) is mixed with 600 g of water. Calculate • *Application* [3]

(i) the freezing point depression and

(ii) the freezing point of the solution.

16. Arrange the following complexes, • *Analysis* [3]

$[CrCl_6]^{3-}$, $[Cr(CN)_6]^{3-}$ and $[Cr(NH_3)_6]^{3+}$

(i) in the increasing order of crystal field splitting energy.

(ii) in the increasing order of absorption of wavelength of light in visible region.

17. Identify the structures of *A*, *B* and *C* in the following reaction. • *Understanding* [3]

(a) $C_6H_5NO_2 \xrightarrow{\text{Sn + HCl}} [A] \xrightarrow[\text{273 K}]{NaNO_2 + HCl} [B] \xrightarrow[\Delta]{H_2O/H^+} [C]$

(b) $CH_3CN \xrightarrow{H_2O/H^+} [A] \xrightarrow[\Delta]{NH_3} [B] \xrightarrow{Br_2 + KOH} [C]$

Or

State reason for the following. • *Understanding*

(i) Fe scrap and HCl is preferred over other metals for the reduction of nitro compounds.

(ii) pK_b for aniline is more than that of methylamine.

(iii) Secondary amines is more basic than tertiary amine in an aqueous solution.

18. How will the following be obtained? **[3]**

(i) Toluene from phenol • *Understanding*

(ii) Aniline to phenol

(iii) Salicylic acid to aspirin

Section D (15 Marks)

19. (i) Calculate the value of E_{cell} at 298 K for the following cell: **[5]**

$Al \mid Al^{3+}(0.01\,M) \parallel Sn^{2+}(0.015\,M) \mid Sn$

Given, $E^{\circ}_{(Al^{3+}/Al)} = -1.66$ V and $E^{\circ}_{(Sn^{2+}/Sn)} = -0.14$ V

[**Ans.** $E_{cell} = 1.5055$ V] • *Application*

(ii) State Kohlrausch's law of independent migration of ions and why does the conductivity of solution decreases with dilution? • *Understanding*

Or

(i) How many molecules of chlorine should be deposited from molten sodium chloride in one minute by a current of 300 mA?

[**Ans.** 5.616×10^{19} molecules] • *Application*

(ii) What is the difference between primary and secondary cells? Differentiate using their applications also. • *Recall*

20. (i) Compute the following reactions. • *Recall* **[5]**

(a) 

(b) 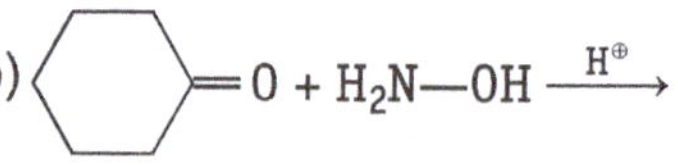

(c) 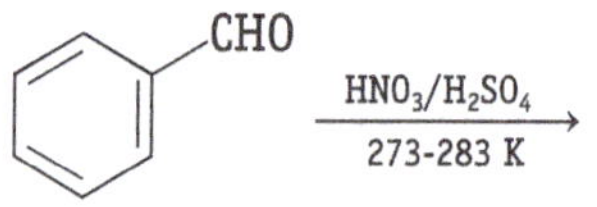

(ii) An aldehyde $A(C_{11}H_8O)$, which does not undergo self aldol condensation, gives benzaldehyde and 2 moles of B on ozonolysis. Compound B on oxidation with silver ion gives oxalic acid. Identify the compounds A and B. • *Understanding*

21. (i) On the bases of figure given below, answer the following question. **[5]**

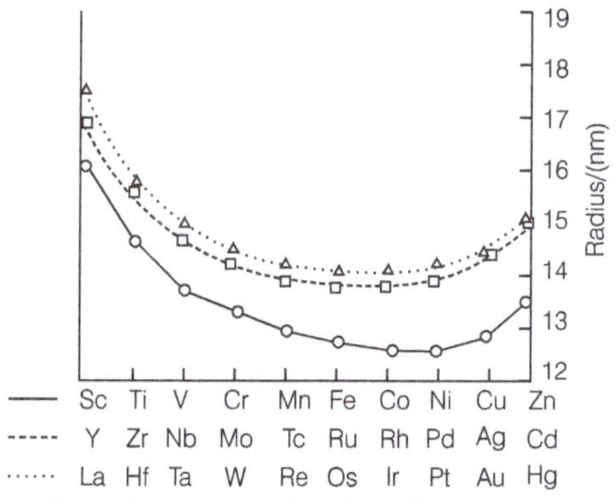

Trends in atomic radii of transition elements

Why atomic and ionic radii decreases and density increases along the period? Also write two elements have similar radii. • *Analysis*

(ii) Although Zr belongs to 4*d* and Hf belongs to 5*d* transition series but it is quite difficult to separate them. Why? • *Understanding*

Answers

(i) (a)	(ii) (c)	(iii) (c)	(iv) (b)
(v) (b)	(vi) (c)	(vii) (a)	